WEBSTER'S SPANISH-ENGLISH DICTIONARY

Created in Cooperation with the
Editors of MERRIAM-WEBSTER

FALL RIVER PRESS

© 2006 by Merriam-Webster, Incorporated

This 2009 edition published by Fall River Press, by arrangement with Federal Street Press, a division of Merriam-Webster, Incorporated.

Fall River Press
122 Fifth Avenue
New York, NY 10011

ISBN: 978-1-4351-1646-7

Printed and bound in the United States of America

10 9 8 7 6 5 4 3 2 1

Contents

Preface	iv
Conjugation of Spanish Verbs	v
Irregular English Verbs	xii
Abbreviations in this Work	xvi
Spanish-English Dictionary	**1**
English-Spanish Dictionary	**177**
Common Spanish Abbreviations	361
Spanish Numbers	365
English Numbers	366

Preface

This Spanish-English Dictionary is a concise reference to the core vocabulary of Spanish and English. Its 40,000 entries and over 50,000 translations provide up-to-date coverage of the basic vocabulary and idioms in both languages. In addition, the book includes many specifically Latin-American words and phrases.

This book shares many details of presentation with larger Spanish-English dictionaries, but for reasons of conciseness it also has a number of features uniquely its own. Users need to be familiar with the following major features of this dictionary.

Main entries follow one another in strict alphabetical order, without regard to intervening spaces or hyphens. The Spanish letter combinations *ch* and *ll* are alphabetized within the letters *C* and *L;* however, the Spanish letter *ñ* is alphabetized separately between *N* and *O*.

Homographs (words spelled the same but having different meanings or parts of speech) are run on at a single main entry if they are closely related. Run-on homograph entries are replaced in the text by a boldfaced swung dash (as **haber** . . . *v aux* . . . — ～ *nm* . . .). Homographs of distinctly different origin (as **date**[1] and **date**[2]) are given separate entries.

Run-on entries for related words that are not homographs may also follow the main entry. Thus we have the main entry **calcular** *vt* followed by run-on entries for — **calculador, -dora** *adj* . . . — **calculadora** *nf* . . . and — **cálculo** *nm*. However, if a related word falls later in the alphabet than a following unrelated main entry, it will be entered at its own place; **ear** and its run-on — **eardrum** precede the main entry **earl** which is followed by the main entry **earlobe**.

Variant spellings appear at the main entry separated by *or* (as **judgment** *or* **judgement, paralyze** *or Brit* **paralyse,** or **cacahuate** *or* **cacahuete**).

Inflected forms of English verbs, adjectives, adverbs, and nouns are shown when they are irregular (as **wage** . . . **waged, waging; ride** . . . **rode, ridden; good** . . . **better, best;** or **fly** . . . *n, pl* **flies**) or when there might be doubt about their spelling (as **ego** . . . *n, pl* **egos**). Inflected forms of Spanish irregular verbs are shown in the section Conjugation of Spanish Verbs on page v; numerical references to this table are included at the main entry (as **poseer** {20} *vt*). Irregular plurals of Spanish nouns or adjectives are shown at the main entry (as **ladrón, -drona** *n, mpl* **-drones**).

Cross-references are provided to lead the user to the appropriate main entry (as **mice** → **mouse** or **sobrestimar** → **sobreestimar**).

The grammatical function of entry words is indicated by an italic **functional label** (as *vt, adj, or nm*). Italic **usage labels** may be added at the entry or sense as well (as **timbre** *nm* . . . **4** *Lat* : postage stamp, **center** *or Brit* **centre** . . . *n* . . ., or **garra** *nf* . . . **2** *fam* : hand, paw). These labels are also included in the translations (**bag** *n* . . . **2** HANDBAG : bolso *m*, cartera *f Lat*).

Usage notes are occasionally placed before a translation to clarify meaning or use (as **que** *conj* . . . **2** (*in comparisons*) : than).

Synonyms may appear before the translation word(s) in order to provide context for the meaning of an entry word or sense (as **sitio** *nm* . . . **2** ESPACIO : room, space; or **meet** . . . *vt* . . . **2** SATISFY : satisfacer).

Bold notes are sometimes used before a translation to introduce a plural sense or a common phrase using the main entry word (as **mueble** *nm* . . . **2** ～s *nmpl* : furniture, furnishings, or **call** . . . *vt* . . . **2** ～ **off** : cancelar). Note that when an entry word is repeated in a bold note, it is replaced by a swung dash.

Conjugation of Spanish Verbs

Simple Tenses

-AR Verbs (hablar)		-ER Verbs (comer)		-IR Verbs (vivir)	
PRESENT INDICATIVE TENSE					
hablo	hablamos	como	comemos	vivo	vivimos
hablas	habláis	comes	coméis	vives	vivís
habla	hablan	come	comen	vive	viven
PRESENT SUBJUNCTIVE TENSE					
hable	hablemos	coma	comamos	viva	vivamos
hables	habléis	comas	comáis	vivas	viváis
hable	hablen	coma	coman	viva	vivan
PRETERIT INDICATIVE TENSE					
hablé	hablamos	comí	comimos	viví	vivimos
hablaste	hablasteis	comiste	comisteis	viviste	vivisteis
habló	hablaron	comió	comieron	vivió	vivieron
IMPERFECT INDICATIVE TENSE					
hablaba	hablábamos	comía	comíamos	vivía	vivíamos
hablabas	hablabais	comías	comíais	vivías	vivíais
hablaba	hablaban	comía	comían	vivía	vivían
IMPERFECT SUBJUNCTIVE TENSE					
hablara	habláramos	comiera	comiéramos	viviera	viviéramos
hablaras	hablarais	comieras	comierais	vivieras	vivierais
hablara	hablaran	comiera	comieran	viviera	vivieran
or		*or*		*or*	
hablase	hablásemos	comiese	comiésemos	viviese	viviésemos
hablases	hablaseis	comieses	comieseis	vivieses	vivieseis
hablase	hablasen	comiese	comiesen	viviese	viviesen
FUTURE INDICATIVE TENSE					
hablaré	hablaremos	comeré	comeremos	viviré	viviremos
hablarás	hablaréis	comerás	comeréis	vivirás	viviréis
hablará	hablarán	comerá	comerán	vivirá	vivirán
FUTURE SUBJUNCTIVE TENSE					
hablare	habláremos	comiere	comiéremos	viviere	viviéremos
hablares	hablareis	comieres	comiereis	vivieres	viviereis
hablare	hablaren	comiere	comieren	viviere	vivieren
CONDITIONAL TENSE					
hablaría	hablaríamos	comería	comeríamos	viviría	viviríamos
hablarías	hablaríais	comerías	comeríais	vivirías	viviríais
hablaría	hablarían	comería	comerían	viviría	vivirían
IMPERATIVE TENSE					
	hablemos		comamos		vivamos
habla	hablad	come	comed	vive	vivid
hable	hablen	coma	coman	viva	vivan
PRESENT PARTICIPLE (GERUND) TENSE					
hablando		comiendo		viviendo	
PAST PARTICIPLE TENSE					
hablado		comido		vivido	

Compound Tenses

1. Perfect Tenses

The perfect tenses are formed with *haber* and the past participle:

PRESENT PERFECT
> he hablado, etc. (*indicative*);
> haya hablado, etc. (*subjunctive*)

PAST PERFECT
> había hablado, etc. (*indicative*);
> hubiera hablado, etc. (*subjunctive*)
> *or*
> hubiese hablado, etc. (*subjunctive*)

PRETERIT PERFECT
> hube hablado, etc. (*indicative*)

FUTURE PERFECT
> habré hablado, etc. (*indicative*)

CONDITIONAL PERFECT
> habría hablado, etc. (*indicative*)

2. Progressive Tenses

The progressive tenses are formed with *estar* and the present participle:

PRESENT PROGRESSIVE
> estoy llamando, etc. (*indicative*);
> esté llamando, etc. (*subjunctive*)

IMPERFECT PROGRESSIVE
> estaba llamando, etc. (*indicative*);
> estuviera llamando, etc. (*subjunctive*)
> *or*
> estuviese llamando, etc. (*subjunctive*)

PRETERIT PROGRESSIVE
> estuve llamando, etc. (*indicative*)

FUTURE PROGRESSIVE
> estaré llamando, etc. (*indicative*)

CONDITIONAL PROGRESSIVE
> estaría llamando, etc. (*indicative*)

PRESENT PERFECT PROGRESSIVE
> he estado llamando, etc. (*indicative*);
> haya estado llamando, etc. (*subjunctive*)

PAST PERFECT PROGRESSIVE
> había estado llamando, etc. (*indicative*);
> hubiera estado llamando, etc. (*subjunctive*)
> *or*
> hubiese estado llamando, etc. (*subjunctive*)

Irregular Verbs

The *imperfect subjunctive*, the *future subjunctive*, the *conditional*, and most forms of the *imperative* are not included in the model conjugations, but can be derived as follows:

The *imperfect subjunctive* and the *future subjunctive* are formed from the third person plural form of the preterit tense by removing the last syllable (*-ron*) and adding the appropriate suffix:

PRETERIT INDICATIVE, THIRD PERSON PLURAL (querer)	quisieron
IMPERFECT SUBJUNCTIVE (querer)	quisiera, quisieras, etc. *or* quisiese, quisieses, etc.
FUTURE SUBJUNCTIVE (querer)	quisiere, quisieres, etc.

The conditional uses the same stem as the future indicative:

FUTURE INDICATIVE (poner)	pondré, pondrás, etc.
CONDITIONAL (poner)	pondría, pondrías, etc.

The third person singular, first person plural, and third person plural forms of the *imperative* are the same as the corresponding forms of the present subjunctive.

The second person singular form of the *imperative* is generally the same as the third person singular of the present indicative. Exceptions are noted in the model conjugations list.

The second person plural *(vosotros)* form of the *imperative* is formed by removing the final *-r* of the infinitive form and adding a *-d* (ex.: oír → oíd).

Model Conjugations of Irregular Verbs

The model conjugations below include the following simple tenses: the *present indicative* (*IND*), the *present subjunctive* (*SUBJ*), the *preterit indicative* (*PRET*), the *imperfect indicative* (*IMPF*), the *future indicative* (*FUT*), the second person singular form of the *imperative* (*IMPER*) when it differs from the third person singular of the present indicative, the *gerund* or *present participle* (*PRP*), and the *past participle* (*PP*). Each set of conjugations is preceded by the corresponding infinitive form of the verb, shown in bold type. Only tenses containing irregularities are listed, and the irregular verb forms within each tense are displayed in bold type.

Each irregular verb entry in the Spanish-English section of this dictionary is cross-referenced by number to one of the following model conjugations. These cross-reference numbers are shown in curly braces { } immediately following the entry's functional label.

1 **abolir** *(defective verb)* : *IND* abolimos, abolís *(other forms not used); SUBJ (not used); IMPER (only second person plural is used)*

2 **abrir** : *PP* abierto

3 **actuar** : *IND* **actúo, actúas, actúa,** actuamos, actuáis, **actúan;** *SUBJ* **actúe, actúes, actúe,** actuemos, actuéis, **actúen;** *IMPER* **actúa**

4 **adquirir** : *IND* **adquiero, adquieres, adquiere,** adquirimos, adquirís, **adquieren;** *SUBJ* **adquiera, adquieras, adquiera,** adquiramos, adquiráis, **adquieran;** *IMPER* **adquiere**

5 **airar** : *IND* **aíro, aíras, aíra,** airamos, airáis, **aíran;** *SUBJ* **aíre, aíres, aíre,** airemos, airéis, **aíren;** *IMPER* **aíra**

6 **andar** : *PRET* **anduve, anduviste, anduvo, anduvimos, anduvisteis, anduvieron**

7 **asir** : *IND* **asgo,** ases, ase, asimos, asís, asen; *SUBJ* **asga, asgas, asga, asgamos, asgáis, asgan**

8 **aunar** : *IND* **aúno, aúnas, aúna,** aunamos, aunáis, **aúnan;** *SUBJ* **aúne, aúnes, aúne,** aunemos, aunéis, **aúnen;** *IMPER* **aúna**

9 **avergonzar** : *IND* **avergüenzo, avergüenzas, avergüenza,** avergonzamos, avergonzáis, **avergüenzan;** *SUBJ* **avergüence, avergüences, avergüence,** avergoncemos, avergoncéis, **avergüencen;** *PRET* **avergoncé;** *IMPER* **avergüenza**

Conjugation of Spanish Verbs

10 **averiguar** : *SUBJ* **averigüe, averigües, averigüe, averigüemos, averigüéis, averigüen;** *PRET* **averigüé,** averiguaste, averiguó, averiguamos, averiguasteis, averiguaron

11 **bendecir** : *IND* **bendigo, bendices, bendice,** bendecimos, bendecís, **bendicen;** *SUBJ* **bendiga, bendigas, bendiga, bendigamos, bendigáis, bendigan;** *PRET* **bendije, bendijiste, bendijo, bendijimos, bendijisteis, bendijeron;** *IMPER* **bendice**

12 **caber** : *IND* **quepo,** cabes, cabe, cabemos, cabéis, caben; *SUBJ* **quepa, quepas, quepa, quepamos, quepáis, quepan;** *PRET* **cupe, cupiste, cupo, cupimos, cupisteis, cupieron;** *FUT* **cabré, cabrás, cabrá, cabremos, cabréis, cabrán**

13 **caer** : *IND* **caigo,** caes, cae, caemos, caéis, caen; *SUBJ* **caiga, caigas, caiga, caigamos, caigáis, caigan;** *PRET* caí, **caíste, cayó,** caímos, caísteis, **cayeron;** *PRP* **cayendo;** *PP* **caído**

14 **cocer** : *IND* **cuezo, cueces, cuece,** cocemos, cocéis, **cuecen;** *SUBJ* **cueza, cuezas, cueza,** cozamos, cozáis, **cuezan;** *IMPER* **cuece**

15 **coger** : *IND* **cojo,** coges, coge, cogemos, cogéis, cogen; *SUBJ* **coja, cojas, coja, cojamos, cojáis, cojan**

16 **colgar** : *IND* **cuelgo, cuelgas, cuelga,** colgamos, colgáis, **cuelgan;** *SUBJ* **cuelgue, cuelgues, cuelgue, colguemos, colguéis, cuelguen;** *PRET* **colgué,** colgaste, colgó, colgamos, colgasteis, colgaron; *IMPER* **cuelga**

17 **concernir** *(defective verb; used only in the third person singular and plural of the present indicative, present subjunctive, and imperfect subjunctive) see* 25 **discernir**

18 **conocer** : *IND* **conozco,** conoces, conoce, conocemos, conocéis, conocen; *SUBJ* **conozca, conozcas, conozca, conozcamos, conozcáis, conozcan**

19 **contar** : *IND* **cuento, cuentas, cuenta,** contamos, contáis, **cuentan;** *SUBJ* **cuente, cuentes, cuente,** contemos, contéis, **cuenten;** *IMPER* **cuenta**

20 **creer** : *PRET* creí, **creíste, creyó,** creímos, creísteis, **creyeron;** *PRP* **creyendo;** *PP* **creído**

21 **cruzar** : *SUBJ* **cruce, cruces, cruce, crucemos, crucéis, crucen;** *PRET* **crucé,** cruzaste, cruzó, cruzamos, cruzasteis, cruzaron

22 **dar** : *IND* **doy,** das, da, damos, **dais,** dan; *SUBJ* **dé,** des, **dé,** demos, **deis,** den; *PRET* **di, diste, dio, dimos, disteis, dieron**

23 **decir** : *IND* **digo, dices, dice,** decimos, decís, **dicen;** *SUBJ* **diga, digas, diga, digamos, digáis, digan;** *PRET* **dije, dijiste, dijo, dijimos, dijisteis, dijeron;** *FUT* **diré, dirás, dirá, diremos, diréis, dirán;** *IMPER* **di;** *PRP* **diciendo;** *PP* **dicho**

24 **delinquir** : *IND* **delinco,** delinques, delinque, delinquimos, delinquís, delinquen; *SUBJ* **delinca, delincas, delinca, delincamos, delincáis, delincan**

25 **discernir** : *IND* **discierno, disciernes, discierne,** discernimos, discernís, **disciernen;** *SUBJ* **discierna, disciernas, discierna,** discernamos, discernáis, **disciernan;** *IMPER* **discierne**

26 **distinguir** : *IND* **distingo,** distingues, distingue, distinguimos, distinguís, distinguen; *SUBJ* **distinga, distingas, distinga, distingamos, distingáis, distingan**

27 **dormir** : *IND* **duermo, duermes, duerme,** dormimos, dormís, **duermen;** *SUBJ* **duerma, duermas, duerma, durmamos, durmáis, duerman;** *PRET* dormí, dormiste, **durmió,** dormimos, dormisteis, **durmieron;** *IMPER* **duerme;** *PRP* **durmiendo**

28 **elegir** : *IND* **elijo, eliges, elige,** elegimos, elegís, **eligen;** *SUBJ* **elija, elijas, elija, elijamos, elijáis, elijan;** *PRET* elegí, elegiste, **eligió,** elegimos, elegisteis, **eligieron;** *IMPER* **elige;** *PRP* **eligiendo**

29 **empezar** : *IND* **empiezo, empiezas, empieza,** empezamos, empezáis, **empiezan;** *SUBJ* **empiece, empieces, empiece,** empecemos, empecéis, **empiecen;** *PRET* **empecé,** empezaste, empezó, empezamos, empezasteis, empezaron; *IMPER* **empieza**

30 **enraizar** : *IND* **enraízo, enraízas, enraíza,** enraizamos, enraizáis, **enraízan;** *SUBJ* **enraíce, enraíces, enraíce,** enraicemos, enraicéis, **enraícen;** *PRET* **enraicé,** enraizaste, enraizó, enraizamos, enraizasteis, enraizaron; *IMPER* **enraíza**

31 **erguir** : *IND* **irgo** *or* **yergo, irgues** *or* **yergues, irgue** *or* **yergue,** erguimos, erguís, **irguen** *or* **yerguen;** *SUBJ* **irga** *or* **yerga, irgas** *or* **yergas, irga** *or* **yerga, irgamos, irgáis, irgan** *or* **yergan;** *PRET* erguí, erguiste, **irguió,** erguimos, erguisteis, **irguieron;** *IMPER* **irgue** *or* **yergue;** *PRP* **irguiendo**

32 **errar** : *IND* **yerro, yerras, yerra,** erramos, erráis, **yerran;** *SUBJ* **yerre, yerres, yerre,** erremos, erréis, **yerren;** *IMPER* **yerra**

33 **escribir** : *PP* **escrito**

34 **estar** : *IND* **estoy, estás, está,** estamos, estáis, **están;** *SUBJ* **esté, estés, esté,** estemos, estéis, **estén;** *PRET* **estuve, estuviste, estuvo, estuvimos, estuvisteis, estuvieron;** *IMPER* **está**

35 **exigir** : *IND* **exijo,** exiges, exige, exigimos, exigís, exigen; *SUBJ* **exija, exijas, exija, exijamos, exijáis, exijan**

36 **forzar** : *IND* **fuerzo, fuerzas, fuerza,** forzamos, forzáis, **fuerzan;** *SUBJ* **fuerce, fuerces, fuerce,** forcemos, forcéis, **fuercen;** *PRET* **forcé,** forzaste, forzó, forzamos, forzasteis, forzaron; *IMPER* **fuerza**

37 **freír** : *IND* **frío, fríes, fríe,** freímos, freís, **fríen;** *SUBJ* **fría, frías, fría, friamos, friáis, frían;** *PRET* freí, **freíste, frió,** freímos, freísteis, frieron; *IMPER* **fríe;** *PRP* **friendo;** *PP* **frito**

38 **gruñir** : *PRET* gruñí, gruñiste, **gruñó,** gruñimos, gruñisteis, **gruñeron;** *PRP* **gruñendo**

39 **haber** : *IND* **he, has, ha, hemos,** habéis, **han;** *SUBJ* **haya, hayas, haya, hayamos, hayáis, hayan;** *PRET* **hube, hubiste, hubo, hubimos, hubisteis, hubieron;** *FUT* **habré, habrás, habrá, habremos, habréis, habrán;** *IMPER* **he**

40 **hacer** : *IND* **hago,** haces, hace, hacemos, hacéis, hacen; *SUBJ* **haga, hagas, haga, hagamos, hagáis, hagan;** *PRET* **hice, hiciste, hizo, hicimos, hicisteis, hicieron;** *FUT* **haré, harás, hará, haremos, haréis, harán;** *IMPER* **haz;** *PP* **hecho**

41 **huir** : *IND* **huyo, huyes, huye,** huimos, huís, **huyen;** *SUBJ* **huya, huyas, huya, huyamos, huyáis, huyan;** *PRET* huí, huiste, **huyó,** huimos, huisteis, **huyeron;** *IMPER* **huye;** *PRP* **huyendo**

42 **imprimir** : *PP* **impreso**

43 **ir** : *IND* **voy, vas, va, vamos, vais, van;** *SUBJ* **vaya, vayas, vaya, vayamos, vayáis, vayan;** *PRET* **fui, fuiste, fue, fuimos, fuisteis, fueron;** *IMPF* **iba, ibas, iba, íbamos, ibais, iban;** *IMPER* **ve;** *PRP* **yendo;** *PP* **ido**

44 **jugar** : *IND* **juego, juegas, juega,** jugamos, jugáis, **juegan;** *SUBJ* **juegue, juegues, juegue, juguemos, juguéis, jueguen;** *PRET* **jugué,** jugaste, jugó, jugamos, jugasteis, jugaron; *IMPER* **juega**

45 **lucir** : *IND* **luzco,** luces, luce, lucimos, lucís, lucen; *SUBJ* **luzca, luzcas, luzca, luzcamos, luzcáis, luzcan**

46 **morir** : *IND* **muero, mueres, muere,** morimos, morís, **mueren;** *SUBJ* **muera, mueras, muera, muramos, muráis, mueran;** *PRET* morí, moriste, **murió,** morimos, moristeis, **murieron;** *IMPER* **muere;** *PRP* **muriendo;** *PP* **muerto**

47 **mover** : *IND* **muevo, mueves, mueve,** movemos, movéis, **mueven;** *SUBJ* **mueva, muevas, mueva,** movamos, mováis, **muevan;** *IMPER* **mueve**

48 **nacer** : *IND* **nazco,** naces, nace, nacemos, nacéis, nacen; *SUBJ* **nazca, nazcas, nazca, nazcamos, nazcáis, nazcan**

49 **negar** : *IND* **niego, niegas, niega,** negamos, negáis, **niegan;** *SUBJ* **niegue, niegues, niegue,** neguemos, neguéis, **nieguen;** *PRET* **negué,** negaste, negó, negamos, negasteis, negaron; *IMPER* **niega**

50 **oír** : *IND* **oigo, oyes, oye, oímos,** oís, **oyen;** *SUBJ* **oiga, oigas, oiga, oigamos, oigáis, oigan;** *PRET* oí, **oíste, oyó, oímos,** oísteis, **oyeron;** *IMPER* **oye;** *PRP* **oyendo;** *PP* **oído**

51 **oler** : *IND* **huelo, hueles, huele,** olemos, oléis, **huelen;** *SUBJ* **huela, huelas, huela,** olamos, oláis, **huelan;** *IMPER* **huele**

Conjugation of Spanish Verbs

52 **pagar** : *SUBJ* **pague, pagues, pague, paguemos, paguéis, paguen;** *PRET* **pagué,** pagaste, pagó, pagamos, pagasteis, pagaron

53 **parecer** : *IND* **parezco,** pareces, parece, parecemos, parecéis, parecen; *SUBJ* **parezca, parezcas, parezca, parezcamos, parezcáis, parezcan**

54 **pedir** : *IND* **pido, pides, pide,** pedimos, pedís, **piden;** *SUBJ* **pida, pidas, pida, pidamos, pidáis, pidan;** *PRET* pedí, pediste, **pidió,** pedimos, pedisteis, **pidieron;** *IMPER* **pide;** *PRP* **pidiendo**

55 **pensar** : *IND* **pienso, piensas, piensa,** pensamos, pensáis, **piensan;** *SUBJ* **piense, pienses, piense,** pensemos, penséis, **piensen;** *IMPER* **piensa**

56 **perder** : *IND* **pierdo, pierdes, pierde,** perdemos, perdéis, **pierden;** *SUBJ* **pierda, pierdas, pierda,** perdamos, perdáis, **pierdan;** *IMPER* **pierde**

57 **placer** : *IND* **plazco,** places, place, placemos, placéis, placen; *SUBJ* **plazca, plazcas, plazca, plazcamos, plazcáis, plazcan;** *PRET* plací, placiste, plació *or* **plugo,** placimos, placisteis, placieron *or* **pluguieron**

58 **poder** : *IND* **puedo, puedes, puede,** podemos, podéis, **pueden;** *SUBJ* **pueda, puedas, pueda,** podamos, podáis, **puedan;** *PRET* **pude, pudiste, pudo, pudimos, pudisteis, pudieron;** *FUT* **podré, podrás, podrá, podremos, podréis, podrán;** *IMPER* **puede;** *PRP* **pudiendo**

59 **podrir** *or* **pudrir** : *PP* **podrido** *(all other forms based on* pudrir*)*

60 **poner** : *IND* **pongo,** pones, pone, ponemos, ponéis, ponen; *SUBJ* **ponga, pongas, ponga, pongamos, pongáis, pongan;** *PRET* **puse, pusiste, puso, pusimos, pusisteis, pusieron;** *FUT* **pondré, pondrás, pondrá, pondremos, pondréis, pondrán;** *IMPER* **pon;** *PP* **puesto**

61 **producir** : *IND* **produzco,** produces, produce, producimos, producís, producen; *SUBJ* **produzca, produzcas, produzca, produzcamos, produzcáis, produzcan;** *PRET* **produje, produjiste, produjo, produjimos, produjisteis, produjeron**

62 **prohibir** : *IND* **prohíbo, prohíbes, prohíbe,** prohibimos, prohibís, **prohíben;** *SUBJ* **prohíba, prohíbas, prohíba,** prohibamos, prohibáis, **prohíban;** *IMPER* **prohíbe**

63 **proveer** : *PRET* proveí, **proveíste, proveyó, proveímos, proveísteis, proveyeron;** *PRP* **proveyendo;** *PP* **provisto**

64 **querer** : *IND* **quiero, quieres, quiere,** queremos, queréis, **quieren;** *SUBJ* **quiera, quieras, quiera,** queramos, queráis, **quieran;** *PRET* **quise, quisiste, quiso, quisimos, quisisteis, quisieron;** *FUT* **querré, querrás, querrá, querremos, querréis, querrán;** *IMPER* **quiere**

65 **raer** : *IND* **rao** *or* **raigo** *or* **rayo,** raes, rae, raemos, raéis, raen; *SUBJ* **raiga** *or* **raya, raigas** *or* **rayas, raiga** *or* **raya, raigamos** *or* **rayamos, raigáis** *or* **rayáis, raigan** *or* **rayan;** *PRET* raí, **raíste, rayó, raímos, raísteis, rayeron;** *PRP* **rayendo;** *PP* **raído**

66 **reír** : *IND* **río, ríes, ríe, reímos,** reís, **ríen;** *SUBJ* **ría, rías, ría, riamos, riáis, rían;** *PRET* reí, **reíste, rió, reímos, reísteis, rieron;** *IMPER* **ríe;** *PRP* **riendo;** *PP* **reído**

67 **reñir** : *IND* **riño, riñes, riñe,** reñimos, reñís, **riñen;** *SUBJ* **riña, riñas, riña, riñamos, riñáis, riñan;** *PRET* reñí, reñiste, **riñó,** reñimos, reñisteis, **riñeron;** *PRP* **riñendo**

68 **reunir** : *IND* **reúno, reúnes, reúne,** reunimos, reunís, **reúnen;** *SUBJ* **reúna, reúnas, reúna,** reunamos, reunáis, **reúnan;** *IMPER* **reúne**

69 **roer** : *IND* **roo** *or* **roigo** *or* **royo,** roes, roe, roemos, roéis, roen; *SUBJ* **roa** *or* **roiga** *or* **roya,** roas *or* **roigas** *or* **royas,** roa *or* **roiga** *or* **roya,** roamos *or* **roigamos** *or* **royamos,** roáis *or* **roigáis** *or* **royáis,** roan *or* **roigan** *or* **royan;** *PRET* roí, **roíste, royó, roímos, roísteis, royeron;** *PRP* **royendo;** *PP* **roído**

70 **romper** : *PP* **roto**

71 **saber** : *IND* **sé,** sabes, sabe, sabemos, sabéis, saben; *SUBJ* **sepa, sepas, sepa, sepamos, sepáis, sepan;** *PRET* **supe, supiste, supo, supimos, supisteis, supieron;** *FUT* **sabré, sabrás, sabrá, sabremos, sabréis, sabrán**

72 **sacar** : *SUBJ* **saque, saques, saque, saquemos, saquéis, saquen;** *PRET* **saqué,** sacaste, sacó, sacamos, sacasteis, sacaron

73 **salir** : *IND* **salgo,** sales, sale, salimos, salís, salen; *SUBJ* **salga, salgas, salga, salgamos, salgáis, salgan;** *FUT* **saldré, saldrás, saldrá, saldremos, saldréis, saldrán;** *IMPER* **sal**

74 **satisfacer** : *IND* **satisfago,** satisfaces, satisface, satisfacemos, satisfacéis, satisfacen; *SUBJ* **satisfaga, satisfagas, satisfaga, satisfagamos, satisfagáis, satisfagan;** *PRET* **satisfice, satisficiste, satisfizo, satisficimos, satificisteis, satisficieron;** *FUT* **satisfaré, satisfarás, satisfará, satisfaremos, satisfaréis, satisfarán;** *IMPER* **satisfaz** or **satisface;** *PP* **satisfecho**

75 **seguir** : *IND* **sigo, sigues, sigue,** seguimos, seguís, **siguen;** *SUBJ* **siga, sigas, siga, sigamos, sigáis, sigan;** *PRET* seguí, seguiste, **siguió,** seguimos, seguisteis, **siguieron;** *IMPER* **sigue;** *PRP* **siguiendo**

76 **sentir** : *IND* **siento, sientes, siente,** sentimos, sentís, **sienten;** *SUBJ* **sienta, sientas, sienta, sintamos, sintáis, sientan;** *PRET* sentí, sentiste, **sintió,** sentimos, sentisteis, **sintieron;** *IMPER* **siente;** *PRP* **sintiendo**

77 **ser** : *IND* **soy, eres, es, somos, sois, son;** *SUBJ* **sea, seas, sea, seamos, seáis, sean;** *PRET* **fui, fuiste, fue, fuimos, fuisteis, fueron;** *IMPF* **era, eras, era, éramos, erais, eran;** *IMPER* **sé;** *PRP* **siendo;** *PP* **sido**

78 **soler** (*defective verb; used only in the present, preterit, and imperfect indicative, and the present and imperfect subjunctive*) *see* 47 **mover**

79 **tañer** : *PRET* tañí, tañiste, **tañó,** tañimos, tañisteis, **tañeron;** *PRP* **tañendo**

80 **tener** : *IND* **tengo, tienes, tiene,** tenemos, tenéis, **tienen;** *SUBJ* **tenga, tengas, tenga, tengamos, tengáis, tengan;** *PRET* **tuve, tuviste, tuvo, tuvimos, tuvisteis, tuvieron;** *FUT* **tendré, tendrás, tendrá, tendremos, tendréis, tendrán;** *IMPER* **ten**

81 **traer** : *IND* **traigo,** traes, trae, traemos, traéis, traen; *SUBJ* **traiga, traigas, traiga, traigamos, traigáis, traigan;** *PRET* **traje, trajiste, trajo, trajimos, trajisteis, trajeron;** *PRP* **trayendo;** *PP* **traído**

82 **trocar** : *IND* **trueco, truecas, trueca,** trocamos, trocáis, **truecan;** *SUBJ* **trueque, trueques, trueque, troquemos, troquéis, truequen;** *PRET* **troqué,** trocaste, trocó, trocamos, trocasteis, trocaron; *IMPER* **trueca**

83 **uncir** : *IND* **unzo,** unces, unce, uncimos, uncís, uncen; *SUBJ* **unza, unzas, unza, unzamos, unzáis, unzan**

84 **valer** : *IND* **valgo,** vales, vale, valemos, valéis, valen; *SUBJ* **valga, valgas, valga, valgamos, valgáis, valgan;** *FUT* **valdré, valdrás, valdrá, valdremos, valdréis, valdrán**

85 **variar** : *IND* **varío, varías, varía,** variamos, variáis, **varían;** *SUBJ* **varíe, varíes, varíe,** variemos, variéis, **varíen;** *IMPER* **varía**

86 **vencer** : *IND* **venzo,** vences, vence, vencemos, vencéis, vencen; *SUBJ* **venza, venzas, venza, venzamos, venzáis, venzan**

87 **venir** : *IND* **vengo, vienes, viene,** venimos, venís, **vienen;** *SUBJ* **venga, vengas, venga, vengamos, vengáis, vengan;** *PRET* **vine, viniste, vino, vinimos, vinisteis, vinieron;** *FUT* **vendré, vendrás, vendrá, vendremos, vendréis, vendrán;** *IMPER* **ven;** *PRP* **viniendo**

88 **ver** : *IND* **veo, ves, ve, vemos, veis, ven;** *PRET* **vi,** viste, **vio,** vimos, visteis, vieron; *IMPER* **ve;** *PRP* **viendo;** *PP* **visto**

89 **volver** : *IND* **vuelvo, vuelves, vuelve,** volvemos, volvéis, **vuelven;** *SUBJ* **vuelva, vuelvas, vuelva,** volvamos, volváis, **vuelvan;** *IMPER* **vuelve;** *PP* **vuelto**

90 **yacer** : *IND* **yazco** or **yazgo** or **yago,** yaces, yace, yacemos, yacéis, yacen; *SUBJ* **yazca** or **yazga** or **yaga, yazcas** or **yazgas** or **yagas, yazca** or **yazga** or **yaga, yazcamos** or **yazgamos** or **yagamos, yazcáis** or **yazgáis** or **yagáis, yazcan** or **yazgan** or **yagan;** *IMPER* **yace** or **yaz**

Irregular English Verbs

INFINITIVE	PAST	PAST PARTICIPLE
arise	arose	arisen
awake	awoke	awoken *or* awaked
be	was, were	been
bear	bore	borne
beat	beat	beaten *or* beat
become	became	become
befall	befell	befallen
begin	began	begun
behold	beheld	beheld
bend	bent	bent
beseech	beseeched *or* besought	beseeched *or* besought
beset	beset	beset
bet	bet	bet
bid	bade *or* bid	bidden *or* bid
bind	bound	bound
bite	bit	bitten
bleed	bled	bled
blow	blew	blown
break	broke	broken
breed	bred	bred
bring	brought	brought
build	built	built
burn	burned *or* burnt	burned *or* burnt
burst	burst	burst
buy	bought	bought
can	could	—
cast	cast	cast
catch	caught	caught
choose	chose	chosen
cling	clung	clung
come	came	come
cost	cost	cost
creep	crept	crept
cut	cut	cut
deal	dealt	dealt
dig	dug	dug
do	did	done
draw	drew	drawn
dream	dreamed *or* dreamt	dreamed *or* dreamt
drink	drank	drunk *or* drank
drive	drove	driven
dwell	dwelled *or* dwelt	dwelled *or* dwelt
eat	ate	eaten
fall	fell	fallen
feed	fed	fed
feel	felt	felt
fight	fought	fought
find	found	found
flee	fled	fled
fling	flung	flung
fly	flew	flown

INFINITIVE	PAST	PAST PARTICIPLE
forbid	forbade	forbidden
forecast	forecast	forecast
forego	forewent	foregone
foresee	foresaw	foreseen
foretell	foretold	foretold
forget	forgot	forgotten *or* forgot
forgive	forgave	forgiven
forsake	forsook	forsaken
freeze	froze	frozen
get	got	got *or* gotten
give	gave	given
go	went	gone
grind	ground	ground
grow	grew	grown
hang	hung	hung
have	had	had
hear	heard	heard
hide	hid	hidden *or* hid
hit	hit	hit
hold	held	held
hurt	hurt	hurt
keep	kept	kept
kneel	knelt *or* kneeled	knelt *or* kneeled
know	knew	known
lay	laid	laid
lead	led	led
lean	leaned	leaned
leap	leaped *or* leapt	leaped *or* leapt
learn	learned	learned
leave	left	left
lend	lent	lent
let	let	let
lie	lay	lain
light	lit *or* lighted	lit *or* lighted
lose	lost	lost
make	made	made
may	might	—
mean	meant	meant
meet	met	met
mow	mowed	mowed *or* mown
pay	paid	paid
put	put	put
quit	quit	quit
read	read	read
rend	rent	rent
rid	rid	rid
ride	rode	ridden
ring	rang	rung
rise	rose	risen
run	ran	run
saw	sawed	sawed *or* sawn
say	said	said
see	saw	seen
seek	sought	sought
sell	sold	sold

INFINITIVE	PAST	PAST PARTICIPLE
send	sent	sent
set	set	set
shake	shook	shaken
shall	should	—
shear	sheared	sheared *or* shorn
shed	shed	shed
shine	shone *or* shined	shone *or* shined
shoot	shot	shot
show	showed	shown *or* showed
shrink	shrank *or* shrunk	shrunk *or* shrunken
shut	shut	shut
sing	sang *or* sung	sung
sink	sank *or* sunk	sunk
sit	sat	sat
slay	slew	slain
sleep	slept	slept
slide	slid	slid
sling	slung	slung
smell	smelled *or* smelt	smelled *or* smelt
sow	sowed	sown *or* sowed
speak	spoke	spoken
speed	sped *or* speeded	sped *or* speeded
spell	spelled	spelled
spend	spent	spent
spill	spilled	spilled
spin	spun	spun
spit	spit *or* spat	spit *or* spat
split	split	split
spoil	spoiled	spoiled
spread	spread	spread
spring	sprang *or* sprung	sprung
stand	stood	stood
steal	stole	stolen
stick	stuck	stuck
sting	stung	stung
stink	stank *or* stunk	stunk
stride	strode	stridden
strike	struck	struck
swear	swore	sworn
sweep	swept	swept
swell	swelled	swelled *or* swollen
swim	swam	swum
swing	swung	swung
take	took	taken
teach	taught	taught
tear	tore	torn
tell	told	told
think	thought	thought
throw	threw	thrown
thrust	thrust	thrust
tread	trod	trodden *or* trod
wake	woke	woken *or* waked
waylay	waylaid	waylaid
wear	wore	worn
weave	wove *or* weaved	woven *or* weaved

Irregular English Verbs

INFINITIVE	PAST	PAST PARTICIPLE
wed	wedded	wedded
weep	wept	wept
will	would	—
win	won	won
wind	wound	wound
withdraw	withdrew	withdrawn
withhold	withheld	withheld
withstand	withstood	withstood
wring	wrung	wrung
write	wrote	written

Abbreviations in this Work

adj	adjective
adv	adverb
adv	adverbial phrase
algn	alguien (someone)
art	article
Brit	Great Britain
conj	conjunction
conj phr	conjunctive phrase
esp	especially
etc	et cetera
f	feminine
fam	familiar or colloquial
fpl	feminine plural
interj	interjection
Lat	Latin America
m	masculine
mf	masculine or feminine
mpl	masculine plural
n	noun
nf	feminine noun
nfpl	feminine plural noun
nfs & pl	invariable singular or plural feminine noun
nm	masculine noun

nmf	masculine or feminine noun
nmfpl	plural noun invariable for gender
nmfs & pl	noun invariable for both gender and number
nmpl	masculine plural noun
nms & pl	invariable singular or plural masculine noun
npl	plural noun
ns & pl	noun invariable for plural
pl	plural
pp	past participle
prep	preposition
prep phr	prepositional phrase
pron	pronoun
s.o.	someone
sth	something
usu	usually
v	verb
v aux	auxiliary verb
vi	intransitive verb
v impers	impersonal verb
vr	reflexive verb
vt	transitive verb

Spanish-English Dictionary

A

a¹ *nf* : a, first letter of the Spanish alphabet
a² *prep* **1** : to **2 ~ las dos** : at two o'clock **3 al día siguiente** : (on) the following day **4 ~ pied** : on foot **5 de lunes ~ viernes** : from Monday until Friday **6 tres veces ~ la semana** : three times per week **7 ~ la** : in the manner of, like
abadía *nf* : abbey
abajo *adv* **1** : down, below, downstairs **2 ~ de** *Lat* : under, beneath **3 de ~** : (at the) bottom **4 hacia ~** : downwards
abalanzarse {21} *vr* : hurl oneself, rush
abandonar *vt* **1** : abandon, leave **2** RENUNCIAR A : give up — **abandonarse** *vr* **1** : neglect oneself **2 ~ a** : give oneself over to — **abandonado, -da** *adj* **1** : abandoned, deserted **2** DESCUIDADO : neglected **3** DESALIÑADO : slovenly — **abandono** *nm* **1** : abandonment, neglect **2 por ~** : by default
abanico *nm* : fan — **abanicar** {72} *vt* : fan
abaratar *vt* : lower the price of — **abaratarse** *vr* : become cheaper
abarcar {72} *vt* **1** : cover, embrace **2** *Lat* : monopolize
abarrotar *vt* : pack, cram — **abarrotes** *nmpl* *Lat* **1** : groceries **2 tienda de ~** : grocery store
abastecer {53} *vt* : supply, stock — **abastecimiento** *nm* : supply, provisions — **abasto** *nm* **1** : supply **2 no dar ~ a** : be unable to cope with
abatir *vt* **1** : knock down, shoot down **2** DEPRIMIR : depress — **abatirse** *vr* **1** : get depressed **2 ~ sobre** : swoop down on — **abatido, -da** *adj* : dejected, depressed — **abatimiento** *nm* : depression, dejection
abdicar {72} *v* : abdicate — **abdicación** *nf, pl* **-ciones** : abdication
abdomen *nm, pl* **-dómenes** : abdomen — **abdominal** *adj* : abdominal
abecé *nm* : ABC — **abecedario** *nm* : alphabet
abedul *nm* : birch
abeja *nf* : bee — **abejorro** *nm* : bumblebee
aberración *nf, pl* **-ciones** : aberration
abertura *nf* : opening
abeto *nm* : fir (tree)
abierto, -ta *adj* : open
abigarrado, -da *adj* : multicolored
abismo *nm* : abyss, chasm — **abismal** *adj* : vast, enormous
abjurar *vi* **~ de** : abjure

ablandar *vt* : soften (up) — **ablandarse** *vr* : soften
abnegarse {49} *vr* : deny oneself — **abnegado, -da** *adj* : self-sacrificing — **abnegación** *nf, pl* **-ciones** : self-denial
abochornar *vt* : embarrass — **abochornarse** *vr* : get embarrassed
abofetear *vt* : slap
abogado, -da *n* : lawyer — **abogacía** *nf* : legal profession — **abogar** {52} *vi* **~ por** : plead for, defend
abolengo *nm* : lineage
abolir {1} *vt* : abolish — **abolición** *nf, pl* **-ciones** : abolition
abollar *vt* : dent — **abolladura** *nf* : dent
abominar *vt* : abominate — **abominable** *adj* : abominable — **abominación** *nf, pl* **-ciones** : abomination
abonar *vt* **1** : pay (a bill, etc.) **2** : fertilize (the soil) — **abonarse** *vr* : subscribe — **abonado, -da** *n* : subscriber — **abono** *nm* **1** : payment, installment **2** FERTILIZANTE : fertilizer **3** : season ticket (to the theater, etc.)
abordar *vt* **1** : tackle (a problem) **2** : accost, approach (a person) **3** *Lat* : board — **abordaje** *nm* : boarding
aborigen *nmf, pl* **-rígenes** : aborigine — **~** *adj* : aboriginal, native
aborrecer {53} *vt* : abhor, detest — **aborrecible** *adj* : hateful — **aborrecimiento** *nm* : loathing
abortar *vi* : have a miscarriage — *vt* : abort — **aborto** *nm* : abortion, miscarriage
abotonar *vt* : button — **abotonarse** *vr* : button up
abovedado, -da *adj* : vaulted
abrasar *vt* : burn, scorch — **abrasarse** *vr* : burn up — **abrasador, -dora** *adj* : burning
abrasivo, -va *adj* : abrasive — **abrasivo** *nm* : abrasive
abrazar {21} *vt* : hug, embrace — **abrazarse** *vr* : embrace — **abrazadera** *nf* : clamp — **abrazo** *nm* : hug, embrace
abrebotellas *nms & pl* : bottle opener — **abrelatas** *nms & pl* : can opener
abrevadero *nm* : watering trough
abreviar *vt* **1** : shorten, abridge **2** : abbreviate (a word) — **abreviación** *nf, pl* **-ciones** : shortening — **abreviatura** *nf* : abbreviation
abridor *nm* : bottle opener, can opener
abrigar {52} *vt* **1** : wrap up (in clothing) **2** ALBERGAR : cherish, harbor — **abrigarse** *vr*

: dress warmly — **abrigado, -da** *adj* **1** : sheltered **2** : warm, wrapped up (of persons) — **abrigo** *nm* **1** : coat, overcoat **2** REFUGIO : shelter, refuge

abril *nm* : April

abrillantar *vt* : polish, shine

abrir {2} *vt* **1** : open **2** : unlock, undo — *vi* : open up — **abrirse** *vr* **1** : open up **2** : clear up (of weather)

abrochar *vt* : button, fasten — **abrocharse** *vr* : fasten, do up

abrogar {52} *vt* : annul, repeal

abrumar *vt* : overwhelm — **abrumador, -dora** *adj* : overwhelming, oppressive

abrupto, -ta *adj* **1** ESCARPADO : steep **2** ÁSPERO : rugged, harsh **3** REPENTINO : abrupt

absceso *nm* : abscess

absolución *nf, pl* **-ciones 1** : absolution **2** : acquittal (in law)

absoluto, -ta *adj* **1** : absolute, unconditional **2 en absoluto** : not at all — **absolutamente** *adv* : absolutely

absolver {89} *vt* **1** : absolve **2** : acquit (in law)

absorber *vt* **1** : absorb **2** : take up (time, energy, etc.) — **absorbente** *adj* **1** : absorbent **2** INTERESANTE : absorbing — **absorción** *nf, pl* **-ciones** : absorption — **absorto, -ta** *adj* : absorbed, engrossed

abstemio, -mia *adj* : abstemious — **~** *n* : teetotaler

abstenerse {80} *vr* : abstain, refrain — **abstención** *nf, pl* **-ciones** : abstention — **abstinencia** *nf* : abstinence

abstracción *nf, pl* **-ciones** : abstraction — **abstracto, -ta** *adj* : abstract — **abstraer** {81} *vt* : abstract — **abstraerse** *vr* : lose oneself in thought — **abstraído, -da** *adj* : preoccupied

absurdo, -da *adj* : absurd, ridiculous — **absurdo** *nm* : absurdity

abuchear *vt* : boo, jeer — **abucheo** *nm* : booing

abuelo, -la *n* **1** : grandfather, grandmother **2 abuelos** *nmpl* : grandparents

abulia *nf* : apathy, lethargy

abultar *vi* : bulge, be bulky — *vt* : enlarge, expand — **abultado, -da** *adj* : bulky

abundar *vi* : abound, be plentiful — **abundancia** *nf* : abundance — **abundante** *adj* : abundant

aburrir *vt* : bore — **aburrirse** *vr* : get bored — **aburrido, -da** *adj* **1** : bored **2** TEDIOSO : boring — **aburrimiento** *nm* : boredom

abusar *vi* **1** : go too far **2 ~ de** : abuse — **abusivo, -va** *adj* : outrageous, excessive — **abuso** *nm* : abuse

abyecto, -ta *adj* : abject, wretched

acá *adv* : here, over here

acabar *vi* **1** : finish, end **2 ~ de** : have just (done something) **3 ~ con** : put an end to **4 ~ por** : end up (doing sth) — *vt* : finish — **acabarse** *vr* : come to an end — **acabado, -da** *adj* **1** : finished, perfect **2** AGOTADO : old, worn-out — **acabado** *nm* : finish

academia *nf* : academy — **académico, -ca** *adj* : academic

acaecer {53} *vi* : happen, occur

acallar *vt* : quiet, silence

acalorar *vt* : stir up, excite — **acalorarse** *vr* : get worked up — **acalorado, -da** *adj* : emotional, heated

acampar *vi* : camp — **acampada** *nf* **ir de ~** : go camping

acanalado, -da *adj* **1** : grooved **2** : corrugated (of iron, etc.)

acantilado *nm* : cliff

acaparar *vt* **1** : hoard **2** MONOPOLIZAR : monopolize

acápite *nm Lat* : paragraph

acariciar *vt* **1** : caress **2** : cherish (hopes, ideas, etc.)

ácaro *nm* : mite

acarrear *vt* **1** : haul, carry **2** OCASIONAR : give rise to — **acarreo** *nm* : transport

acaso *adv* **1** : perhaps, maybe **2 por si ~** : just in case

acatar *vt* : comply with, respect — **acatamiento** *nm* : compliance, respect

acatarrarse *vr* : catch a cold

acaudalado, -da *adj* : wealthy, rich

acaudillar *vt* : lead

acceder *vi* **1** : agree **2 ~ a** : gain access to, enter

acceso *nm* **1** : access **2** ENTRADA : entrance **3** : attack, bout (of an illness) — **accesible** *adj* : accessible

accesorio *nm* : accessory — **accesorio, -ria** *adj* : incidental

accidentado, -da *adj* **1** : eventful, turbulent **2** : rough, uneven (of land, etc.) **3** HERIDO : injured — **~** *n* : accident victim

accidental *adj* : accidental — **accidentarse** *vr* : have an accident — **accidente** *nm* **1** : accident **2** : unevenness (of land)

acción *nf, pl* **-ciones 1** : action **2** ACTO : act, deed **3** : share, stock (in finance) — **accionar** *vt* : activate — *vi* : gesticulate — **accionista** *nmf* : stockholder

acebo *nm* : holly

acechar *vt* : watch, stalk — **acecho** *nm* **estar al ~ por** : be on the lookout for

aceite *nm* : oil — **aceitar** *vt* : oil — **aceitera** *nf* **1** : oilcan **2** : cruet (in cookery) **3** *Lat* : oil refinery — **aceitoso, -sa** *adj* : oily

aceituna *nf* : olive

acelerar *v* : accelerate — **acelerarse** *vr*

: hurry up — **aceleración** *nf, pl* -**ciones** : acceleration — **acelerador** *nm* : accelerator

acelga *nf* : (Swiss) chard

acentuar {3} *vt* **1** : accent **2** ENFATIZAR : emphasize, stress — **acentuarse** *vr* : stand out — **acento** *nm* **1** : accent **2** ÉNFASIS : stress, emphasis

acepción *nf, pl* -**ciones** : sense, meaning

aceptar *vt* : accept — **aceptable** *adj* : acceptable — **aceptación** *nf, pl* -**ciones** **1** : acceptance **2** ÉXITO : success

acequia *nf* : irrigation ditch

acera *nf* : sidewalk

acerbo, -ba *adj* : harsh, caustic

acerca *prep* ~ **de** : about, concerning

acercar {72} *vt* : bring near or closer — **acercarse** *vr* : approach, draw near

acero *nm* **1** : steel **2** ~ **inoxidable** : stainless steel

acérrimo, -ma *adj* **1** : staunch, steadfast **2** : bitter (of an enemy)

acertar {55} *vt* : guess correctly — *vi* **1** ATINAR : be accurate **2** ~ **a** : manage to — **acertado, -da** *adj* : correct, accurate

acertijo *nm* : riddle

acervo *nm* : heritage

acetona *nf* : acetone, nail-polish remover

achacar {72} *vt* : attribute, impute

achacoso, -sa *adj* : sickly

achaparrado, -da *adj* : squat, stocky

achaque *nm* : aches and pains

achatar *vt* : flatten

achicar {72} *vt* **1** : make smaller **2** ACOBARDAR : intimidate **3** : bail out (water) — **achicarse** *vr* : become intimidated

achicharrar *vt* : scorch, burn to a crisp

achicoria *nf* : chicory

aciago, -ga *adj* : fateful, unlucky

acicalar *vt* : dress up, adorn — **acicalarse** *vr* : get dressed up

acicate *nm* **1** : spur **2** INCENTIVO : incentive

ácido, -da *adj* : acid, sour — **acidez** *nf, pl* -**deces** : acidity — **ácido** *nm* : acid

acierto *nm* **1** : correct answer **2** HABILIDAD : skill, sound judgment

aclamar *vt* : acclaim — **aclamación** *nf, pl* -**ciones** : acclaim, applause

aclarar *vt* **1** CLARIFICAR : clarify, explain **2** : rinse (clothing) **3** ~ **la voz** : clear one's throat — *vi* : clear up — **aclararse** *vr* : become clear — **aclaración** *nf, pl* -**ciones** : explanation — **aclaratorio, -ria** *adj* : explanatory

aclimatar *vt* : acclimatize — **aclimatarse** *vr* ~ **a** : get used to — **aclimatación** *nf, pl* -**ciones** : acclimatization

acné *nm* : acne

acobardar *vt* : intimidate — **acobardarse** *vr* : become frightened

acodarse *vr* ~ **en** : lean (one's elbows) on

acoger {15} *vt* **1** REFUGIAR : shelter **2** RECIBIR : receive, welcome — **acogerse** *vr* **1** : take refuge **2** ~ **a** : resort to — **acogedor, -dora** *adj* : cozy, welcoming — **acogida** *nf* **1** : welcome **2** REFUGIO : refuge

acolchar *vt* : pad

acólito *nm* MONAGUILLO : altar boy

acometer *vt* **1** : attack **2** EMPRENDER : undertake — *vi* ~ **contra** : rush against — **acometida** *nf* : attack, assault

acomodar *vt* **1** ADAPTAR : adjust **2** COLOCAR : put, make a place for — **acomodarse** *vr* **1** : settle in **2** ~ **a** : adapt to — **acomodado, -da** *adj* : well-to-do — **acomodaticio, -cia** *adj* : accommodating, obliging — **acomodo** *nm* : job, position

acompañar *vt* **1** : accompany **2** ADJUNTAR : enclose — **acompañamiento** *nm* : accompaniment — **acompañante** *nmf* **1** COMPAÑERO : companion **2** : accompanist (in music)

acompasado, -da *adj* : rhythmic, measured

acondicionar *vt* : fit out, equip — **acondicionado, -da** *adj* : equipped

acongojar *vt* : distress, upset — **acongojarse** *vr* : get upset

aconsejar *vt* : advise — **aconsejable** *adj* : advisable

acontecer {53} *vi* : occur, happen — **acontecimiento** *nm* : event

acopiar *vt* : gather, collect — **acopio** *nm* : collection, stock

acoplar *vt* : couple, connect — **acoplarse** *vr* : fit together — **acoplamiento** *nm* : connection, coupling

acorazado, -da *adj* : armored — **acorazado** *nm* : battleship

acordar {19} *vt* **1** : agree (on) **2** *Lat* : award — **acordarse** *vr* : remember

acorde *adj* **1** : in agreement **2** ~ **con** : in keeping with — ~ *nm* : chord (in music)

acordeón *nm, pl* -**deones** : accordion

acordonar *vt* **1** : cordon off **2** : lace up (shoes)

acorralar *vt* : corner, corral

acortar *vt* : shorten, cut short — **acortarse** *vr* : get shorter

acosar *vt* : hound, harass — **acoso** *nm* : harassment

acostar {19} *vt* : put to bed — **acostarse** *vr* **1** : go to bed **2** TUMBARSE : lie down

acostumbrar *vt* : accustom — *vi* ~ **a** : be in the habit of — **acostumbrarse** *vr* ~ **a** : get used to — **acostumbrado, -da** *adj* **1** HABITUADO : accustomed **2** HABITUAL : usual

acotar *vt* **1** ANOTAR : annotate **2** DELIMITAR : mark off (land) — **acotación** *nf, pl*

-ciones : marginal note — **acotado, -da** *adj* : enclosed

acre *adj* **1** : pungent **2** MORDAZ : harsh, biting

acrecentar {55} *vt* : increase — **acrecentamiento** *nm* : growth, increase

acreditar *vt* **1** : accredit, authorize **2** PROBAR : prove — **acreditarse** *vr* : prove oneself — **acreditado, -da** *adj* **1** : reputable **2** : accredited (in politics, etc.)

acreedor, -dora *adj* : worthy — ~ *n* : creditor

acribillar *vt* **1** : riddle, pepper **2** ~ **a** : harass with

acrílico *nm* : acrylic

acrimonia *nf or* **acritud** *nf* **1** : pungency **2** RESENTIMIENTO : bitterness, acrimony

acrobacia *nf* : acrobatics — **acróbata** *nmf* : acrobat — **acrobático, -ca** *adj* : acrobatic

acta *nf* **1** : certificate **2** : minutes *pl* (of a meeting)

actitud *nf* **1** : attitude **2** POSTURA : posture, position

activar *vt* **1** : activate **2** ESTIMULAR : stimulate, speed up — **actividad** *nf* : activity — **activo, -va** *adj* : active — **activo** *nm* : assets *pl*

acto *nm* **1** ACCIÓN : act, deed **2** : act (in theater) **3 en el** ~ : right away

actor *nm* : actor — **actriz** *nf, pl* **-trices** : actress

actual *adj* : present, current — **actualidad** *nf* **1** : present time **2** ~**es** *nfpl* : current affairs — **actualizar** {21} *vt* : modernize — **actualización** *nf, pl* **-ciones** : modernization — **actualmente** *adv* : at present, nowadays

actuar {3} *vi* **1** : act, perform **2** ~ **de** : act as

acuarela *nf* : watercolor

acuario *nm* : aquarium

acuartelar *vt* : quarter (troops)

acuático, -ca *adj* : aquatic, water

acuchillar *vt* : knife, stab

acudir *vi* **1** : go, come **2** ~ **a** : be present at, attend **3** ~ **a** : turn to

acueducto *nm* : aqueduct

acuerdo *nm* **1** : agreement **2 de** ~ : OK, all right **3 de** ~ **con** : in accordance with **4 estar de** ~ : agree

acumular *vt* : accumulate — **acumularse** *vr* : pile up — **acumulación** *nf, pl* **-ciones** : accumulation — **acumulador** *nm* : storage battery — **acumulativo, -va** *adj* : cumulative

acunar *vt* : rock

acuñar *vt* **1** : mint (money) **2** : coin (a word)

acuoso, -sa *adj* : watery

acupuntura *nf* : acupuncture

acurrucarse {72} *vr* : curl up, nestle

acusar *vt* **1** : accuse **2** MOSTRAR : reveal, show — **acusación** *nf, pl* **-ciones** : accusation, charge — **acusado, -da** *adj* : prominent, marked — ~ *n* : defendant

acuse *nm* ~ **de recibo** : acknowledgment of receipt

acústica *nf* : acoustics — **acústico, -ca** *adj* : acoustic

adagio *nm* **1** REFRÁN : adage, proverb **2** : adagio (in music)

adaptar *vt* **1** : adapt **2** AJUSTAR : adjust, fit — **adaptarse** *vr* ~ **a** : adapt to — **adaptable** *adj* : adaptable — **adaptación** *nf, pl* **-ciones** : adaptation — **adaptador** *nm* : adapter (in electricity)

adecuar {8} *vt* : adapt, make suitable — **adecuarse** *vr* ~ **a** : be appropriate for — **adecuado, -da** *adj* : suitable, appropriate

adelantar *vt* **1** : advance, move forward **2** PASAR : overtake **3** : pay in advance — **adelantarse** *vr* **1** : move forward, get ahead **2** : be fast (of a clock) — **adelantado, -da** *adj* **1** : advanced, ahead **2** : fast (of a clock) **3 por** ~ : in advance — **adelante** *adv* **1** : ahead, forward **2 ¡**~**!** : come in! **3 más** ~ : later on, further on — **adelanto** *nm* **1** : advance **2** *or* ~ **de dinero** : advance payment

adelgazar {21} *vt* : make thin — *vi* : lose weight

ademán *nm, pl* **-manes 1** GESTO : gesture **2** ~**es** *nmpl* : manners **3 en** ~ **de** : as if to

además *adv* **1** : besides, furthermore **2** ~ **de** : in addition to, as well as

adentro *adv* : inside, within — **adentrarse** *vr* ~ **en** : go into, get inside of

adepto, -ta *n* : follower, supporter

aderezar {21} *vt* : season, dress — **aderezo** *nm* : dressing, seasoning

adeudar *vt* **1** : debit **2** DEBER : owe — **adeudo** *nm* **1** DÉBITO : debit **2** *Lat* : debt

adherirse {76} *vr* : adhere, stick — **adherencia** *nf* : adherence — **adhesión** *nf, pl* **-siones 1** : adhesion **2** APOYO : support — **adhesivo, -va** *adj* : adhesive — **adhesivo** *nm* : adhesive

adición *nf, pl* **-ciones** : addition — **adicional** *adj* : additional

adicto, -ta *adj* : addicted — ~ *n* : addict

adiestrar *vt* : train

adinerado, -da *adj* : wealthy

adiós *nm, pl* **adioses 1** : farewell **2 ¡**~**!** : good-bye!

aditamento *nm* : attachment, accessory

aditivo *nm* : additive

adivinar *vt* **1** : guess **2** PREDECIR : foretell — **adivinación** *nf, pl* **-ciones** : guessing, prediction — **adivinanza** *nf* : riddle — **adivino, -na** *n* : fortune-teller

adjetivo *nm* : adjective

adjudicar {72} *vt* : award — **adjudicarse** *vr* : appropriate — **adjudicación** *nf, pl* **-ciones** : awarding

adjuntar *vt* : enclose (with a letter, etc.) — **adjunto, -ta** *adj* : enclosed, attached — ~ *n* : assistant

administración *nf, pl* **-ciones 1** : administration **2** : administering (of a drug, etc.) **3** DIRECCIÓN : management — **administrador, -dora** *n* : administrator, manager — **administrar** *vt* **1** : manage, run **2** : administer (a drug, etc.) — **administrativo, -va** *adj* : administrative

admirar *vt* : admire — **admirarse** *vr* : be amazed — **admirable** *adj* : admirable — **admiración** *nf, pl* **-ciones 1** : admiration **2** ASOMBRO : amazement — **admirador, -dora** *n* : admirer

admitir *vt* **1** : admit **2** ACEPTAR : accept — **admisible** *adj* : admissible, acceptable — **admisión** *nf, pl* **-siones 1** : admission **2** ACEPTACIÓN : acceptance

ADN *nm* : DNA

adobe *nm* : adobe

adobo *nm* : marinade

adoctrinar *vt* : indoctrinate — **adoctrinamiento** *nm* : indoctrination

adolecer {53} *vi* ~ **de** : suffer from

adolescente *adj & nmf* : adolescent — **adolescencia** *nf* : adolescence

adonde *conj* : where

adónde *adv* : where

adoptar *vt* : adopt (a child), take (a decision) — **adopción** *nf, pl* **-ciones** : adoption — **adoptivo, -va** *adj* : adopted, adoptive

adoquín *nm, pl* **-quines** : cobblestone

adorar *vt* : adore, worship — **adorable** *adj* : adorable — **adoración** *nf, pl* **-ciones** : adoration, worship

adormecer {53} *vt* **1** : make sleepy **2** ENTUMECER : numb — **adormecerse** *vr* : doze off — **adormecimiento** *nm* : drowsiness — **adormilarse** *vr* : doze

adornar *vt* : decorate, adorn — **adorno** *nm* : ornament, decoration

adquirir {4} *vt* **1** : acquire **2** COMPRAR : purchase — **adquisición** *nf, pl* **-ciones 1** : acquisition **2** COMPRA : purchase

adrede *adv* : intentionally, on purpose

adscribir {33} *vt* : assign, appoint

aduana *nf* : customs (office) — **aduanero, -ra** *adj* : customs — ~ *n* : customs officer

aducir {61} *vt* : cite, put forward

adueñarse *vr* ~ **de** : take possession of

adular *vt* : flatter — **adulación** *nf, pl* **-ciones** : adulation, flattery — **adulador, -dora** *adj* : flattering — ~ *n* : flatterer

adulterar *vt* : adulterate

adulterio *nm* : adultery — **adúltero, -ra** *n* : adulterer

adulto, -ta *adj & n* : adult

adusto, -ta *adj* : stern, severe

advenedizo, -za *n* : upstart

advenimiento *nm* : advent, arrival

adverbio *nm* : adverb — **adverbial** *adj* : adverbial

adversario, -ria *n* : adversary, opponent — **adverso, -sa** *adj* : adverse — **adversidad** *nf* : adversity

advertir {76} *vt* **1** AVISAR : warn **2** NOTAR : notice — **advertencia** *nf* : warning

adviento *nm* : Advent

adyacente *adj* : adjacent

aéreo, -rea *adj* : aerial, air

aerobic *nm* : aerobics *pl*

aerodinámico, -ca *adj* : aerodynamic

aeródromo *nm* : airfield

aerolínea *nf* : airline

aeromozo, -za *n* : flight attendant, steward *m*, stewardess *f*

aeronave *nf* : aircraft

aeropuerto *nm* : airport

aerosol *nm* : aerosol, spray

afable *adj* : affable — **afabilidad** *nf* : affability

afán *nm, pl* **afanes 1** ANHELO : eagerness **2** EMPEÑO : effort, hard work — **afanarse** *vr* : toil — **afanosamente** *adv* : industriously, busily — **afanoso, -sa** *adj* **1** : eager **2** TRABAJOSO : arduous

afear *vt* : make ugly, disfigure

afección *nf, pl* **-ciones** : ailment, complaint

afectar *vt* : affect — **afectación** *nf, pl* **-ciones** : affectation — **afectado, -da** *adj* : affected

afectivo, -va *adj* : emotional

afecto *nm* : affection — **afecto, -ta** *adj* ~ **a** : fond of — **afectuoso, -sa** *adj* : affectionate, caring

afeitar *vt* : shave — **afeitarse** *vr* : shave — **afeitada** *nf* : shave

afeminado, -da *adj* : effeminate

aferrarse {55} *vr* : cling, hold on

afianzar {21} *vt* : secure, strengthen — **afianzarse** *vr* : become established

afiche *nm Lat* : poster

afición *nf, pl* **-ciones 1** : penchant, fondness **2** PASATIEMPO : hobby — **aficionado, -da** *n* **1** ENTUSIASTA : enthusiast, fan **2** AMATEUR : amateur — **aficionarse** *vr* ~ **a** : become interested in

afilar *vt* : sharpen — **afilado, -da** *adj* : sharp — **afilador** *nm* : sharpener

afiliarse *vr* ~ **a** : join, become a member of

— **afiliación** *nf, pl* **-ciones** : affiliation — **afiliado, -da** *adj* : affiliated

afín *adj, pl* **afines** : related, similar — **afinidad** *nf* : affinity, similarity

afinar *vt* **1** : tune **2** PULIR : perfect, refine

afirmar *vt* **1** : state, affirm **2** REFORZAR : strengthen — **afirmación** *nf, pl* **-ciones** : statement, affirmation — **afirmativo, -va** *adj* : affirmative

afligir {35} *vt* **1** : afflict **2** APENAR : distress — **afligirse** *vr* : grieve — **aflicción** *nf, pl* **-ciones** : grief, sorrow — **afligido -da** *adj* : sorrowful, distressed

aflojar *vt* : loosen, slacken — *vi* : ease up — **aflojarse** *vr* : become loose, slacken

aflorar *vi* : come to the surface, emerge — **afloramiento** *nm* : outcrop

afluencia *nf* : influx — **afluente** *nm* : tributary

afortunado, -da *adj* : fortunate, lucky — **afortunadamente** *adv* : fortunately

afrentar *vt* : insult — **afrenta** *nf* : affront, insult

africano, -na *adj* : African

afrontar *vt* : confront, face

afuera *adv* **1** : out **2** : outside, outdoors — **afueras** *nfpl* : outskirts

agachar *vt* : lower — **agacharse** *vr* : crouch, stoop

agalla *nf* **1** BRANQUIA : gill **2 tener ∼s** *fam* : have guts

agarrar *vt* **1** ASIR : grasp **2** *Lat* : catch — **agarrarse** *vr* : hold on, cling — **agarradera** *nf Lat* : handle — **agarrado, -da** *adj fam* : stingy — **agarre** *nm* : grip, grasp — **agarrón** *nm, pl* **-rones** : tug, pull

agasajar *vt* : fête, wine and dine — **agasajo** *nm* : lavish attention

agave *nm* : agave

agazaparse *vr* : crouch down

agencia *nf* : agency, office — **agente** *nmf* : agent, officer

agenda *nf* **1** : agenda **2** LIBRETA : notebook

ágil *adj* : agile — **agilidad** *nf* : agility

agitar *vt* **1** : agitate, shake **2** : wave, flap (wings, etc.) **3** PERTURBAR : stir up — **agitarse** *vr* **1** : toss about **2** INQUIETARSE : get upset — **agitación** *nf, pl* **-ciones** **1** : agitation, shaking **2** INTRANQUILIDAD : restlessness — **agitado, -da** *adj* **1** : agitated, excited **2** : choppy, rough (of the sea)

aglomerar *vt* : amass — **aglomerarse** *vr* : crowd together

agnóstico, -ca *adj & n* : agnostic

agobiar *vt* **1** : oppress **2** ABRUMAR : overwhelm — **agobiado, -da** *adj* : weary, weighed down — **agobiante** *adj* : oppressing, oppressive

agonizar {21} *vi* : be dying — **agonía** *nf* **1** : death throes **2** PENA : agony — **agonizante** *adj* : dying

agorero, -ra *adj* : ominous

agostar *vt* : wither

agosto *nm* : August

agotar *vt* **1** : deplete, use up **2** CANSAR : exhaust, weary — **agotarse** *vr* **1** : run out, give out **2** CANSARSE : get tired — **agotado, -da** *adj* **1** CANSADO : exhausted **2** : sold out — **agotador, -dora** *adj* : exhausting — **agotamiento** *nm* : exhaustion

agraciado, -da *adj* **1** : attractive **2** AFORTUNADO : fortunate

agradar *vi* : be pleasing — **agradable** *adj* : pleasant, agreeable — **agrado** *nm* **1** : taste, liking **2 con ∼** : with pleasure

agradecer {53} *vt* : be grateful for, thank — **agradecido, -da** *adj* : grateful — **agradecimiento** *nm* : gratitude

agrandar *vt* : enlarge — **agrandarse** *vr* : grow larger

agrario, -ria *adj* : agrarian, agricultural

agravar *vt* **1** : make heavier **2** EMPEORAR : aggravate, worsen — **agravarse** *vr* : get worse

agraviar *vt* : insult — **agravio** *nm* : insult

agredir {1} *vt* : attack

agregar {52} *vt* : add, attach — **agregado, -da** *n* : attaché — **agregado** *nm* : aggregate

agresión *nf, pl* **-siones** : aggression, attack — **agresividad** *nf* : aggressiveness — **agresivo, -va** *adj* : aggressive — **agresor, -sora** *n* : aggressor, attacker

agreste *adj* : rugged, wild

agriar *vt* : sour — **agriarse** *vr* **1** : turn sour (of milk, etc.) **2** : become embittered

agrícola *adj* : agricultural — **agricultura** *nf* : agriculture, farming — **agricultor, -tora** *n* : farmer

agridulce *adj* **1** : bittersweet **2** : sweet-and-sour (in cooking)

agrietar *vt* : crack — **agrietarse** *vr* **1** : crack **2** : chap

agrimensor, -sora *n* : surveyor

agrio, agria *adj* : sour

agrupar *vt* : group together — **agruparse** *vr* : form a group — **agrupación** *nf, pl* **-ciones** : group, association — **agrupamiento** *nm* : grouping

agua *nf* **1** : water **2 ∼ oxigenada** : hydrogen peroxide **3 ∼s negras** *or* **∼s residuales** : sewage

aguacate *nm* : avocado

aguacero *nm* : downpour

aguado, -da *adj* **1** : watery **2** *Lat fam* : soft, flabby — **aguar** {10} *vt* **1** : water down, dilute **2 ∼ la fiesta** *fam* : spoil the party

aguafuerte *nm* : etching

aguanieve *nf* : sleet

aguantar *vt* **1** SOPORTAR : bear, withstand **2** SOSTENER : hold — *vi* : hold out, last — **aguantarse** *vr* **1** : resign oneself **2** CONTENERSE : restrain oneself — **aguante** *nm* **1** : patience **2** RESISTENCIA : endurance

aguardar *vt* : await

aguardiente *nm* : clear brandy

aguarrás *nm* : turpentine

agudo, -da *adj* **1** : acute, sharp **2** : shrill, high-pitched (in music) — **agudeza** *nf* **1** : sharpness **2** : witticism

agüero *nm* : augury, omen

aguijón *nm, pl* **-jones 1** : stinger (of an insect) **2** ESTÍMULO : goad, stimulus — **aguijonear** *vt* : goad

águila *nf* : eagle

aguja *nf* **1** : needle **2** : hand (of a clock) **3** : spire (of a church)

agujero *nm* : hole

agujeta *nf* **1** *Lat* : shoelace **2** ～s *nfpl* : (muscular) stiffness

aguzar {21} *vt* **1** : sharpen **2** ～ **el oído** : prick up one's ears

ahí *adv* **1** : there **2 por** ～ : somewhere, thereabouts

ahijado, -da *n* : godchild, godson *m*, goddaughter *f*

ahínco *nm* : eagerness, zeal

ahogar {52} *vt* **1** : drown **2** ASFIXIAR : smother — **ahogarse** *vr* : drown — **ahogo** *nm* : breathlessness

ahondar *vt* : deepen — *vi* : elaborate, go into detail

ahora *adv* **1** : now **2** ～ **mismo** : right now

ahorcar {72} *vt* : hang, kill by hanging — **ahorcarse** *vr* : hang oneself

ahorita *adv Lat fam* : right now

ahorrar *vt* : save, spare — *vi* : save up — **ahorrarse** *vr* : spare oneself — **ahorro** *nm* : saving

ahuecar {72} *vt* **1** : hollow out **2** : cup (one's hands)

ahumar {8} *vt* : smoke, cure — **ahumado, -da** *adj* : smoked

ahuyentar *vt* : scare away, chase away

airado, -da *adj* : irate, angry

aire *nm* **1** : air **2** ～ **acondicionado** : air-conditioning **3 al** ～ **libre** : in the open air, outdoors — **airear** *vt* : air, air out

aislar {5} *vt* **1** : isolate **2** : insulate (in electricity) — **aislamiento** *nm* **1** : isolation **2** : (electrical) insulation

ajar *vt* **1** : crumple, wrinkle **2** ESTROPEAR : spoil

ajedrez *nm* : chess

ajeno, -na *adj* **1** : someone else's **2** EXTRAÑO : alien **3** ～ **a** : foreign to

ajetreado, -da *adj* : hectic, busy — **aje-**

trearse *vr* : bustle about — **ajetreo** *nm* : hustle and bustle

ají *nm, pl* **ajíes** *Lat* : chili pepper

ajo *nm* : garlic

ajustar *vt* **1** : adjust, adapt **2** ACORDAR : agree on **3** SALDAR : settle — **ajustarse** *vr* : fit, conform — **ajustable** *adj* : adjustable — **ajustado, -da** *adj* **1** : close, tight **2** CEÑIDO : tight-fitting — **ajuste** *nm* : adjustment

ajusticiar *vt* : execute, put to death

al (*contraction of* **a** *and* **el**) → **a²**

ala *nf* **1** : wing **2** : brim (of a hat)

alabanza *nf* : praise — **alabar** *vt* : praise

alacena *nf* : cupboard, larder

alacrán *nm, pl* **-cranes** : scorpion

alado, -da *adj* : winged

alambre *nm* : wire

alameda *nf* **1** : poplar grove **2** : tree-lined avenue — **álamo** *nm* : poplar

alarde *nm* : show, display — **alardear** *vi* : boast

alargar {52} *vt* **1** : extend, lengthen **2** PROLONGAR : prolong — **alargarse** *vr* : become longer — **alargador** *nm* : extension cord

alarido *nm* : howl, shriek

alarmar *vt* : alarm — **alarma** *nf* : alarm — **alarmante** *adj* : alarming

alba *nf* : dawn

albahaca *nf* : basil

albañil *nm* : bricklayer, mason

albaricoque *nm* : apricot

albedrío *nm* **libre** ～ : free will

alberca *nf* **1** : reservoir, tank **2** *Lat* : swimming pool

albergar {52} *vt* : house, lodge — **albergue** *nm* **1** : lodging **2** REFUGIO : shelter **3** ～ **juvenil** : youth hostel

albóndiga *nf* : meatball

alborear *v impers* : dawn — **albor** *nm* : dawning — **alborada** *nf* : dawn

alborotar *vt* : excite, stir up — *vi* : make a racket — **alborotarse** *vr* : get excited — **alborotado, -da** *adj* : excited, agitated — **alborotador, -dora** *n* : agitator, rioter — **alboroto** *nm* : ruckus

alborozar {21} *vt* : gladden — **alborozo** *nm* : joy

álbum *nm* : album

alcachofa *nf* : artichoke

alcalde, -desa *n* : mayor

alcance *nm* **1** : reach **2** ÁMBITO : range, scope

alcancía *nf* : money box

alcantarilla *nf* : sewer, drain

alcanzar {21} *vt* **1** : reach **2** LLEGAR A : catch up with **3** LOGRAR : achieve, attain — *vi* **1** : suffice, be enough **2** ～ **a** : manage to

alcaparra *nf* : caper
alcázar *nm* : fortress, castle
alce *nm* : moose, European elk
alcoba *nf* : bedroom
alcohol *nm* : alcohol — **alcohólico, -ca** *adj* & *n* : alcoholic — **alcoholismo** *nm* : alcoholism
aldaba *nf* : door knocker
aldea *nf* : village — **aldeano, -na** *n* : villager
aleación *nf, pl* **-ciones** : alloy
aleatorio, -ria *adj* : random
aleccionar *vt* : instruct, teach
aledaño, -ña *adj* : bordering — **aledaños** *nmpl* : outskirts
alegar {52} *vt* : assert, allege — *vi Lat* : argue — **alegato** *nm* **1** : allegation (in law) **2** *Lat* : argument
alegoría *nf* : allegory — **alegórico, -ca** *adj* : allegorical
alegrar *vt* : make happy, cheer up — **alegrarse** *vr* : be glad — **alegre** *adj* **1** CONTENTO : glad, happy **2** : colorful, bright — **alegremente** *adv* : happily — **alegría** *nf* : joy, cheer
alejar *vt* **1** : remove, move away **2** ENAJENAR : estrange — **alejarse** *vr* : move away, drift apart — **alejado, -da** *adj* : remote — **alejamiento** *nm* **1** : removal **2** : estrangement (of persons)
alemán, -mana *adj, mpl* **-manes** : German — **alemán** *nm* : German (language)
alentar {55} *vt* : encourage — **alentador, -dora** *adj* : encouraging
alergia *nf* : allergy — **alérgico, -ca** *adj* : allergic
alero *nm* : eaves *pl*
alertar *vt* : alert — **alerta** *adv* : on the alert — **alerta** *adj* & *nf* : alert
aleta *nf* **1** : fin, flipper **2** : small wing
alevosía *nf* : treachery — **alevoso, -sa** *adj* : treacherous
alfabeto *nm* : alphabet — **alfabético, -ca** *adj* : alphabetical — **alfabetismo** *nm* : literacy — **alfabetizar** {21} *vt* **1** : teach literacy **2** : alphabetize
alfalfa *nf* : alfalfa
alfarería *nf* : pottery
alféizar *nm* : sill, windowsill
alfil *nm* : bishop (in chess)
alfiler *nm* **1** : pin **2** BROCHE : brooch — **alfiletero** *nm* : pincushion
alfombra *nf* : carpet, rug — **alfombrilla** *nf* : small rug, mat
alga *nf* : seaweed
álgebra *nf* : algebra
algo *pron* **1** : something **2** ~ **de** : some, a little — ~ *adv* : somewhat, rather
algodón *nm, pl* **-dones** : cotton
alguacil *nm* : constable, bailiff

alguien *pron* : somebody, someone
alguno, -na *adj* (**algún** *before masculine singular nouns*) **1** : some, any **2** (*in negative constructions*) : not any, not at all **3 algunas veces** : sometimes — ~ *pron* **1** : one, someone, somebody **2 algunos, -nas** *pron pl* : some, a few
alhaja *nf* : jewel
alharaca *nf* : fuss
aliado, -da *n* : ally — ~ *adj* : allied — **alianza** *nf* : alliance — **aliarse** {85} *vr* : form an alliance
alias *adv* & *nm* : alias
alicaído, -da *adj* : depressed
alicates *nmpl* : pliers
aliciente *nm* **1** : incentive **2** : attraction (to a place)
alienar *vt* : alienate — **alienación** *nf, pl* **-ciones** : alienation
aliento *nm* **1** : breath **2** ÁNIMO : encouragement, strength
aligerar *vt* **1** : lighten **2** APRESURAR : hasten, quicken
alimaña *nf* : pest, vermin
alimentar *vt* : feed, nourish — **alimentarse** *vr* ~ **con** : live on — **alimentación** *nf, pl* **-ciones 1** : feeding **2** NUTRICIÓN : nourishment — **alimenticio, -cia** *adj* : nourishing — **alimento** *nm* : food, nourishment
alinear *vt* : align, line up — **alinearse** *vr* ~ **con** : align oneself with — **alineación** *nf, pl* **-ciones 1** : alignment **2** : lineup (in sports)
aliño *nm* : dressing, seasoning — **aliñar** *vt* : season, dress
alisar *vt* : smooth
alistarse *vr* : join up, enlist — **alistamiento** *nm* : enlistment
aliviar *vt* : relieve, soothe — **aliviarse** *vr* : recover, get better — **alivio** *nm* : relief
aljibe *nm* : cistern, tank
allá *adv* **1** : there, over there **2 más** ~ : farther away **3 más** ~ **de** : beyond
allanar *vt* **1** : smooth, level out **2** *Spain* : break into (a house) **3** *Lat* : raid — **allanamiento** *nm* **1** *Spain* : breaking and entering **2** *Lat* : raid
allegado, -da *n* : close friend, relation
allí *adv* : there, over there
alma *nf* : soul
almacén *nm, pl* **-cenes 1** : warehouse **2** *Lat* : shop, store **3 grandes almacenes** : department store — **almacenamiento** *or* **almacenaje** *nm* : storage — **almacenar** *vt* : store
almádena *nf* : sledgehammer
almanaque *nm* : almanac
almeja *nf* : clam
almendra *nf* **1** : almond **2** : kernel (of nuts, fruit, etc.)

almiar *nm* : haystack

almíbar *nm* : syrup

almidón *nm, pl* **-dones** : starch — **almidonar** *vt* : starch

almirante *nm* : admiral

almohada *nf* : pillow — **almohadilla** *nf* : small pillow, pad — **almohadón** *nm, pl* **-dones** : bolster, large cushion

almorranas *nfpl* : hemorrhoids, piles

almorzar {36} *vi* : have lunch — *vt* : have for lunch — **almuerzo** *nm* : lunch

alocado, -da *adj* : crazy, wild

áloe *or* **aloe** *nm* : aloe

alojar *vt* : house, lodge — **alojarse** *vr* : lodge, room — **alojamiento** *nm* : lodging, accommodations *pl*

alondra *nf* : lark

alpaca *nf* : alpaca

alpinismo *nm* : mountain climbing — **alpinista** *nmf* : mountain climber

alpiste *nm* : birdseed

alquilar *vt* : rent, lease — **alquilarse** *vr* : be for rent — **alquiler** *nm* : rent, rental

alquitrán *nm, pl* **-tranes** : tar

alrededor *adv* **1** : around, about **2 ~ de** : approximately — **alrededor de** *prep phr* : around — **alrededores** *nmpl* : outskirts

alta *nf* : discharge (of a patient)

altanería *nf* : haughtiness — **altanero, -ra** *adj* : haughty

altar *nm* : altar

altavoz *nm, pl* **-voces** : loudspeaker

alterar *vt* **1** : alter, modify **2** PERTURBAR : disturb — **alterarse** *vr* : get upset — **alteración** *nf, pl* **-ciones 1** : alteration **2** ALBOROTO : disturbance — **altera- do, -da** *adj* : upset

altercado *nm* : altercation, argument

alternar *vi* **1** : alternate **2 ~ con** : socialize with — *vt* : alternate — **alternarse** *vr* : take turns — **alternativa** *nf* : alternative — **alternativo, -va** *adj* : alternating, alternative — **alterno, -na** *adj* : alternate

Alteza *nf* : Highness

altiplano *nm* : high plateau

altitud *nf* : altitude

altivez *nf, pl* **-veces** : haughtiness — **altivo, -va** *adj* : haughty

alto, -ta *adj* **1** : tall, high **2** RUIDOSO : loud — **alto** *adv* **1** ARRIBA : high **2** : loud, loudly — **~** *nm* : height, elevation **2** : stop, halt — **~** *interj* : halt!, stop! — **altoparlante** *nm Lat* : loudspeaker

altruista *adj* : altruistic — **altruismo** *nm* : altruism

altura *nf* **1** : height **2** ALTITUD : altitude **3 a la ~ de** : near, up by

alubia *nf* : kidney bean

alucinar *vi* : hallucinate — **alucinación** *nf, pl* **-ciones** : hallucination

alud *nm* : avalanche

aludir *vi* : allude, refer — **aludido, -da** *adj* **darse por ~** : take it personally

alumbrar *vt* **1** : light, illuminate **2** PARIR : give birth to — **alumbrado** *nm* : (electric) lighting — **alumbramiento** *nm* : childbirth

aluminio *nm* : aluminum

alumno, -na *n* : pupil, student

alusión *nf, pl* **-siones** : allusion

aluvión *nm, pl* **-viones** : flood, barrage

alzar {21} *vt* : lift, raise — **alzarse** *vr* : rise (up) — **alza** *nf* : rise — **alzamiento** *nm* : uprising

ama → amo

amabilidad *nf* : kindness — **amable** *adj* : kind, nice

amaestrar *vt* : train

amagar {52} *vt* **1** : show signs of **2** AMENAZAR : threaten — *vi* : be imminent — **amago** *nm* **1** INDICIO : sign **2** AMENAZA : threat

amainar *vi* : abate

amamantar *v* : breast-feed, nurse

amanecer {53} *v impers* : dawn — *vi* : wake up — **~** *nm* : dawn, daybreak

amanerado *adj* : affected, mannered

amansar *vt* **1** : tame **2** APACIGUAR : soothe — **amansarse** *vr* : calm down

amante *adj* **~ de** : fond of — **~** *nmf* : lover

amañar *vt* : rig, tamper with

amapola *nf* : poppy

amar *vt* : love

amargar {52} *vt* : make bitter — **amargado, -da** *adj* : embittered — **amargo, -ga** *adj* : bitter — **amargo** *nm* : bitterness — **amargura** *nf* : bitterness, grief

amarillo, -lla *adj* : yellow — **amarillo** *nm* : yellow

amarrar *vt* **1** : moor **2** ATAR : tie up

amasar *vt* **1** : knead **2** : amass (a fortune, etc.)

amateur *adj & nmf* : amateur

amatista *nf* : amethyst

ambages *nmpl* **sin ~** : without hesitation, straight to the point

ámbar *nm* : amber

ambición *nf, pl* **-ciones** : ambition — **ambicionar** *vt* : aspire to — **ambicioso, -sa** *adj* : ambitious

ambiente *nm* **1** AIRE : atmosphere **2** MEDIO : environment, surroundings *pl* — **ambiental** *adj* : environmental

ambigüedad *nf* : ambiguity — **ambiguo, -gua** *adj* : ambiguous

ámbito *nm* : domain, sphere

ambos, -bas *adj & pron* : both

ambulancia *nf* : ambulance

ambulante *adj* : traveling, itinerant
ameba *nf* : amoeba
amedrentar *vt* : intimidate
amén *nm* **1** : amen **2 ~ de** : in addition to
amenazar {21} *vt* : threaten — **amenaza** *nf* : threat, menace
amenizar {21} *vt* : make pleasant, enliven — **ameno, -na** *adj* : pleasant
americano, -na *adj* : American
ameritar *vt Lat* : deserve
ametralladora *nf* : machine gun
amianto *nm* : asbestos
amiba → **ameba**
amígdala *nf* : tonsil — **amigdalitis** *nf* : tonsilitis
amigo, -ga *adj* : friendly, close — **~** *n* : friend — **amigable** *adj* : friendly
amilanar *vt* : daunt — **amilanarse** *vr* : lose heart
aminorar *vt* : diminish
amistad *nf* : friendship — **amistoso, -sa** *adj* : friendly
amnesia *nf* : amnesia
amnistía *nf* : amnesty
amo, ama *n* **1** : master *m*, mistress *f* **2 ama de casa** : homemaker, housewife **3 ama de llaves** : housekeeper
amodorrado, -da *adj* : drowsy
amolar {19} *vt* **1** : grind, sharpen **2** MOLESTAR : annoy
amoldar *vt* : adapt, adjust — **amoldarse** *vr* **~ a** : adapt to
amonestar *vt* : admonish, warn — **amonestación** *nf, pl* **-ciones** : admonition, warning
amoníaco *or* **amoniaco** *nm* : ammonia
amontonar *vt* : pile up — **amontonarse** *vr* : pile up (of things), form a crowd (of persons)
amor *nm* : love
amordazar {21} *vt* : gag
amorío *nm* : love affair — **amoroso, -sa** *adj* **1** : loving **2** *Lat* : sweet, lovable
amortado, -da *adj* : black-and-blue
amortiguar {10} *vt* : muffle, soften, tone down — **amortiguador** *nm* : shock absorber
amortizar {21} *vt* : pay off — **amortización** *nf* : repayment
amotinar *vt* : incite (to riot) — **amotinarse** *vr* : riot, rebel
amparar *vt* : shelter, protect — **ampararse** *vr* **1 ~ de** : take shelter from **2 ~ en** : have recourse to — **amparo** *nm* : refuge, protection
ampliar {85} *vt* **1** : expand **2** : enlarge (a photograph) — **ampliación** *nf, pl* **-ciones** **1** : expansion, enlargement **2** : extension (of a building)

amplificar {72} *vt* : amplify — **amplificador** *nm* : amplifier
amplio, -plia *adj* : broad, wide, ample — **amplitud** *nf* **1** : breadth, extent **2** ESPACIOSIDAD : spaciousness
ampolla *nf* **1** : blister **2** : vial, ampoule — **ampollarse** *vr* : blister
ampuloso, -sa *adj* : pompous
amputar *vt* : amputate — **amputación** *nf, pl* **-ciones** : amputation
amueblar *vt* : furnish (a house, etc.)
amurallar *vt* : wall in
anacardo *nm* : cashew nut
anaconda *nf* : anaconda
anacrónico, -ca *adj* : anachronistic — **anacronismo** *nm* : anachronism
ánade *nmf* : duck
anagrama *nm* : anagram
anales *nmpl* : annals
analfabeto, -ta *adj & n* : illiterate — **analfabetismo** *nm* : illiteracy
analgésico *nm* : painkiller, analgesic
analizar {21} *vt* : analyze — **análisis** *nm* : analysis — **analítico, -ca** *adj* : analytical, analytic
analogía *nf* : analogy — **análogo, -ga** *adj* : analogous
ananá *or* **ananás** *nm, pl* **-nás** : pineapple
anaquel *nm* : shelf
anaranjado, -da *adj* : orange-colored
anarquía *nf* : anarchy — **anarquista** *adj & nmf* : anarchist
anatomía *nf* : anatomy — **anatómico, -ca** *adj* : anatomic, anatomical
anca *nf* **1** : haunch **2 ~s de rana** : frogs' legs
ancestral *adj* : ancestral
ancho, -cha *adj* : wide, broad, ample — **ancho** *nm* : width
anchoa *nf* : anchovy
anchura *nf* : width, breadth
anciano, -na *adj* : aged, elderly — **~** *n* : elderly person
ancla *nf* : anchor — **anclar** *v* : anchor
andadas *nfpl* **1** : tracks **2 volver a las ~** : go back to one's old ways
andadura *nf* : walking, journey
andaluz, -luza *adj & n, mpl* **-luces** : Andalusian
andamio *nm* : scaffold
andanada *nf* **1** : volley **2 soltar una ~** : reprimand
andanzas *nfpl* : adventures
andar {6} *vi* **1** CAMINAR : walk **2** IR : go, travel **3** FUNCIONAR : run, work **4 ~ en** : rummage around in **5 ~ por** : be approximately — *vt* : cover, travel — **~** *nm* : gait, walk

andén *nm, pl* **-denes 1** : (train) platform **2** *Lat* : sidewalk

andino, -na *adj* : Andean

andorrano, -na *adj* : Andorran

andrajos *nmpl* : tatters — **andrajoso, -sa** *adj* : ragged

anécdota *nf* : anecdote

anegar {52} *vt* : flood — **anegarse** *vr* **1** : be flooded **2** AHOGARSE : drown

anemia *nf* : anemia — **anémico, -ca** *adj* : anemic

anestesia *nf* : anesthesia — **anestésico, -ca** *adj* : anesthetic — **anestésico** *nm* : anesthetic

anexar *vt* : annex, attach — **anexo, -xa** *adj* : attached — **anexo** *nm* : annex

anfibio, -bia *adj* : amphibious — **anfibio** *nm* : amphibian

anfiteatro *nm* : amphitheater

anfitrión, -triona *n, mpl* **-triones** : host, hostess *f*

ángel *nm* : angel — **angelical** *adj* : angelic, angelical

angloparlante *adj* : English-speaking

anglosajón, -jona *adj, mpl* **-jones** : Anglo-Saxon

angosto, -ta *adj* : narrow

anguila *nf* : eel

ángulo *nm* **1** : angle **2** ESQUINA : corner — **angular** *adj* : angular — **anguloso, -sa** *adj* : angular

angustiar *vt* **1** : anguish, distress **2** INQUIETAR : worry — **angustiarse** *vr* : get upset — **angustia** *nf* **1** : anguish **2** INQUIETUD : worry — **angustioso, -sa** *adj* **1** : anguished **2** INQUIETANTE : distressing

anhelar *vt* : yearn for, crave — **anhelante** *adj* : yearning, longing — **anhelo** *nm* : longing

anidar *vi* : nest

anillo *nm* : ring

ánima *nf* : soul

animación *nf, pl* **-ciones 1** VIVEZA : liveliness **2** BULLICIO : hustle and bustle — **animado, -da** *adj* : cheerful, animated — **animador, -dora** *n* **1** : (television) host **2** : cheerleader

animadversión *nf, pl* **-siones** : animosity

animal *nm* : animal — ～ *nmf* : brute, beast — ～ *adj* : brutish

animar *vt* **1** ALENTAR : encourage **2** ALEGAR : cheer up — **animarse** *vr* **1** : liven up **2** ～ **a** : get up the nerve to

ánimo *nm* **1** : spirit, soul **2** HUMOR : mood, spirits *pl* **3** ALIENTO : encouragement

animosidad *nf* : animosity, ill will

animoso, -sa *adj* : spirited, brave

aniquilar *vt* : annihilate — **aniquilación** *n, pl* **-ciones** : annihilation

anís *nm* : anise

aniversario *nm* : anniversary

ano *nm* : anus

anoche *adv* : last night

anochecer {53} *vi* : get dark — ～ *nm* : dusk, nightfall

anodino, -na *adj* : insipid, dull

anomalía *nf* : anomaly

anonadado, -da *adj* : dumbfounded

anónimo, -ma *adj* : anonymous — **anonimato** *nm* : anonymity

anorexia *nf* : anorexia

anormal *adj* : abnormal — **anormalidad** *nf* : abnormality

anotar *vt* **1** : annotate **2** APUNTAR : jot down — **anotación** *nf, pl* **-ciones** : annotation, note

anquilosarse *vr* **1** : become paralyzed **2** ESTANCARSE : stagnate — **anquilosamiento** *nm* **1** : paralysis **2** ESTANCAMIENTO : stagnation

ansiar {85} *vt* : long for — **ansia** *nf* **1** INQUIETUD : uneasiness **2** ANGUSTIA : anguish **3** ANHELO : longing — **ansiedad** *nf* : anxiety — **ansioso, -sa** *adj* **1** : anxious **2** DESEOSO : eager

antagónico, -ca *adj* : antagonistic — **antagonismo** *nm* : antagonism — **antagonista** *nmf* : antagonist

antaño *adv* : yesteryear, long ago

antártico, -ca *adj* : antarctic

ante¹ *nm* **1** : elk, moose **2** GAMUZA : suede

ante² *prep* **1** : before, in front of **2** : in view of **3** ～ **todo** : above all

anteanoche *adv* : the night before last

anteayer *adv* : the day before yesterday

antebrazo *nm* : forearm

anteceder *vt* : precede — **antecedente** *adj* : previous, prior — ～ *nm* : precedent — **antecesor, -sora** *n* **1** : ancestor **2** PREDECESOR : predecessor

antedicho, -cha *adj* : aforesaid

antelación *nf, pl* **-ciones 1** : advance notice **2 con** ～ : in advance

antemano *adv* **de** ～ : beforehand

antena *nf* : antenna

antenoche → **anteanoche**

anteojos *nmpl* **1** : glasses, eyeglasses **2** ～ **bifocales** : bifocals

antepasado, -da *n* : ancestor

antepecho *nm* : ledge

antepenúltimo, -ma *adj* : third from last

anteponer {60} *vt* **1** : place before **2** PREFERIR : prefer

anterior *adj* **1** : previous, earlier **2** DELANTERO : front — **anterioridad** *nf* **con** ～ : beforehand, in advance — **anteriormente** *adv* : previously

antes *adv* **1** : before, earlier **2** ANTERIOR-

MENTE : previously **3** PRIMERO : first **4** MEJOR : rather **5 ~ de** : before, previous to **6 ~ que** : before

antesala *nf* : waiting room

antiaéreo, -rea *adj* : antiaircraft

antibiótico *nm* : antibiotic

anticipar *vt* **1** : move up (a date, etc.) **2** : pay in advance — **anticiparse** *vr* **1** : be early **2** ADELANTARSE : get ahead — **anticipación** *nf, pl* **-ciones 1** : anticipation **2 con ~** : in advance — **anticipado, -da** *adj* **1** : advance, early **2 por ~** : in advance — **anticipo** *nm* **1** : advance (payment) **2** : foretaste

anticoncepción *nf, pl* **-ciones** : contraception — **anticonceptivo, -va** *adj* : contraceptive — **anticonceptivo** *nm* : contraceptive

anticongelante *nm* : antifreeze

anticuado, -da *adj* : antiquated, outdated

anticuario, -ria *n* : antique dealer — **anticuario** *nm* : antique shop

anticuerpo *nm* : antibody

antídoto *nm* : antidote

antier → anteayer

antiestético, -ca *adj* : unsightly

antifaz *nm, pl* **-faces** : mask

antífona *nf* : anthem

antigualla *nf* : relic, old thing

antiguo, -gua *adj* **1** : ancient, old **2** ANTERIOR : former **3** ANTICUADO : old-fashioned **4 muebles antiguos** : antique furniture — **antiguamente** *adv* **1** : long ago **2** ANTES : formerly — **antigüedad** *nf* **1** : antiquity **2** : seniority (in the workplace) **3 ~es** *nfpl* : antiques

antihigiénico, -ca *adj* : unsanitary

antihistamínico *nm* : antihistamine

antiinflamatorio, -ria *adj* : anti-inflammatory

antílope *nm* : antelope

antinatural *adj* : unnatural

antipatía *nf* : aversion, dislike — **antipático, -ca** *adj* : unpleasant

antirreglamentario, -ria *adj* : unlawful

antirrobo, -ba *adj* : antitheft

antisemita *adj* : anti-Semitic — **antisemitismo** *nm* : anti-Semitism

antiséptico, -ca *adj* : antiseptic — **antiséptico** *nm* : antiseptic

antisocial *adj* : antisocial

antítesis *nf* : antithesis

antojarse *vr* **1** APETECER : crave **2** PARECER : seem, appear — **antojadizo, -za** *adj* : capricious — **antojo** *nm* : whim, craving

antología *nf* : anthology

antorcha *nf* : torch

antro *nm* : dive, den

antropófago, -ga *nmf* : cannibal

antropología *nf* : anthropology

anual *adj* : annual, yearly — **anualidad** *nf* : annuity — **anuario** *nm* : yearbook, annual

anudar *vt* : knot — **anudarse** *vr* : tie, knot

anular *vt* : annul, cancel — **anulación** *nf, pl* **-ciones** : annulment, cancellation

anunciar *vt* **1** : announce **2** : advertise (products) — **anunciante** *nmf* : advertiser — **anuncio** *nm* **1** : announcement **2 or ~ publicitario** : advertisement

anzuelo *nm* **1** : fishhook **2 morder el ~** : take the bait

añadir *vt* : add — **añadidura** *nf* **1** : additive, addition **2 por ~** : in addition, furthermore

añejo, -ja *adj* : aged, vintage

añicos *nmpl* **hacer(se) ~** : smash to pieces

añil *adj & nm* : indigo (color)

año *nm* **1** : year **2 Año Nuevo** : New Year

añorar *vt* : long for, miss — **añoranza** *nf* : nostalgia

añoso, -sa *adj* : aged, old

aorta *nf* : aorta

apabullar *vt* : overwhelm

apacentar {55} *vt* : pasture, graze

apachurrar *vt Lat* : crush

apacible *adj* : gentle, mild

apaciguar {10} *vt* : appease, pacify — **apaciguarse** *vr* : calm down

apadrinar *vt* **1** : be a godparent to **2** : sponsor (an artist, etc.)

apagar {52} *vt* **1** : turn or switch off **2** EXTINGUIR : extinguish, put out — **apagarse** *vr* **1** EXTINGUIRSE : go out **2** : die down — **apagado, -da** *adj* **1** : off, out **2** : dull, subdued (of colors, sounds, etc.) — **apagador** *nm Lat* : (light) switch — **apagón** *nm, pl* **-gones** : blackout

apalancar {72} *vt* **1** LEVANTAR : jack up **2** ABRIR : pry open — **apalancamiento** *nm* : leverage

apalear *vt* : beat up, thrash

aparador *nm* **1** : sideboard **2 Lat** : shop window

aparato *nm* **1** : machine, appliance, apparatus **2** : system (in anatomy) **3** OSTENTACIÓN : ostentation — **aparatoso, -sa** *adj* **1** : ostentatious **2** ESPECTACULAR : spectacular

aparcar {72} *v Spain* : park — **aparcamiento** *nm Spain* **1** : parking **2** : parking lot

aparcero, -ra *n* : sharecropper

aparear *vt* : mate, pair up — **aparearse** *vr* : mate

aparecer {53} *vi* **1** : appear **2** PRESENTARSE : show up — **aparecerse** *vr* : appear

aparejar *vt* **1** : rig (a ship) **2** : harness (an animal) — **aparejado, -da** *adj* **llevar ~** : entail — **aparejo** *nm* **1** : equipment, gear

2 : harness (for an animal) **3** : rigging (for a ship)

aparentar *vt* **1** : seem **2** FINGIR : feign — **aparente** *adj* : apparent, seeming

aparición *nf, pl* **-ciones 1** : appearance **2** FANTASMA : apparition — **apariencia** *nf* **1** : appearance, look **2 en ~** : apparently

apartado *nm* **1** : section, paragraph **2 ~ postal** : post office box

apartamento *nm* : apartment

apartar *vt* **1** ALEJAR : move away **2** SE-PARAR : set aside, separate — **apartarse** *vr* **1** : move away **2** DESVIARSE : stray — **aparte** *adv* **1** : apart, separately **2** ADEMÁS : besides

apasionar *vt* : excite, fascinate — **apasionarse** *vr* : get excited — **apasionado, -da** *adj* : passionate, excited — **apasionante** *adj* : exciting

apatía *nf* : apathy — **apático, -ca** *adj* : apathetic

apearse *vr* **1** : dismount **2** : get out of or off (a vehicle)

apedrear *vt* : stone

apegarse {52} *vr* **~ a** : become attached to, grow fond of — **apegado, -da** *adj* : devoted — **apego** *nm* : fondness

apelar *vi* **1** : appeal **2 ~ a** : resort to — **apelación** *nf, pl* **-ciones** : appeal

apellido *nm* : last name, surname — **apellidarse** *vr* : have for a last name

apenar *vt* : sadden — **apenarse** *vr* **1** : grieve **2** *Lat* : become embarrassed

apenas *adv* : hardly, scarcely — **~** *conj* : as soon as

apéndice *nm* : appendix — **apendicitis** *nf* : appendicitis

apercibir *vt* **1** : warn **2** *Lat* : notice — **apercibirse** *vr* **~ de** : notice — **apercibimiento** *nm* : warning

aperitivo *nm* **1** : appetizer **2** : aperitif

apero *nm* : tool, implement

apertura *nf* : opening

apesadumbrar *vt* : sadden — **apesadumbrarse** *vr* : be weighed down

apestar *vi* : stink — **apestoso, -sa** *adj* : stinking, foul

apetecer {53} *vt* : crave, long for — **apetecible** *adj* : appealing

apetito *nm* : appetite — **apetitoso, -sa** *adj* : appetizing

ápice *nm* **1** : apex, summit **2** PIZCA : bit, smidgen

apilar *vt* : pile up — **apilarse** *vr* : pile up

apiñar *vt* : pack, cram — **apiñarse** *vr* : crowd together

apio *nm* : celery

apisonadora *nf* : steamroller

aplacar {72} *vt* : appease, placate — **aplacarse** *vr* : calm down

aplanar *vt* : flatten, level

aplastar *vt* : crush — **aplastante** *adj* : overwhelming

aplaudir *v* : applaud — **aplauso** *nm* **1** : applause **2** : acclaim

aplazar {21} *vt* : postpone, defer — **aplazamiento** *nm* : postponement

aplicar {72} *vt* : apply — **aplicarse** *vr* : apply oneself — **aplicable** *adj* : applicable — **aplicación** *nf, pl* **-ciones** : application — **aplicado, -da** *adj* : diligent

aplomo *nm* : aplomb

apocarse {72} *vr* : belittle oneself — **apocado, -da** *adj* : timid — **apocamiento** *nm* : timidity

apodar *vt* : nickname

apoderar *vt* : empower — **apoderarse** *vr* **~ de** : seize — **apoderado, -da** *n* : agent, proxy

apodo *nm* : nickname

apogeo *nm* : peak, height

apología *nf* : defense, apology

apoplegía *nf* : stroke, apoplexy

aporrear *vt* : bang on, beat

aportar *vt* : contribute — **aportación** *nf, pl* **-ciones** : contribution

apostar[1] {19} *v* : bet, wager

apostar[2] *vt* : station, post

apostillar *vt* : annotate — **apostilla** *nf* : note

apóstol *nm* : apostle

apóstrofo *nm* : apostrophe

apostura *nf* : elegance, grace

apoyar *vt* **1** : support **2** INCLINAR : lean, rest — **apoyarse** *vr* **~ en** : lean on, rest on — **apoyo** *nm* : support

apreciar *vt* **1** ESTIMAR : appreciate **2** EVAL-UAR : appraise — **apreciable** *adj* : considerable — **apreciación** *nf, pl* **-ciones 1** : appreciation **2** VALORACIÓN : appraisal — **aprecio** *nm* **1** : appraisal **2** ESTIMA : esteem

aprehender *vt* : apprehend — **aprehensión** *nf, pl* **-siones** : apprehension, capture

apremiar *vt* : urge — *vi* : be urgent — **apremiante** *adj* : pressing, urgent — **apremio** *nm* : urgency

aprender *v* : learn — **aprenderse** *vr* : memorize

aprendiz, -diza *n, mpl* **-dices** : apprentice, trainee — **aprendizaje** *nm* : apprenticeship

aprensión *nf, pl* **-siones** : apprehension, dread — **aprensivo, -va** *adj* : apprehensive

apresar *vt* : capture, seize — **apresamiento** *nm* : seizure, capture

aprestar *vt* : make ready — **aprestarse** *vr* : get ready

apresurar *vt* : speed up — **apresurarse** *vr* : hurry — **apresuradamente** *adv* : hurriedly, hastily — **apresurado, -da** *adj* : in a rush

apretar {55} *vt* **1** : press, push (a button) **2** : tighten (a knot, etc.) **3** ESTRECHAR : squeeze — *vi* **1** : press (down) **2** : fit too tightly — **apretón** *nm, pl* **-tones 1** : squeeze **2** ~ **de manos** : handshake — **apretado, -da** *adj* **1** : tight **2** *fam* : tight-fisted

aprieto *nm* : predicament, jam

aprisa *adv* : quickly

aprisionar *vt* : imprison

aprobar {19} *vt* **1** : approve of **2** : pass (an exam, etc.) — *vi* : pass — **aprobación** *nf, pl* **-ciones** : approval

apropiarse *vr* ~ **de** : take possession of, appropriate — **apropiación** *nf, pl* **-ciones** : appropriation — **apropiado, -da** *adj* : appropriate

aprovechar *vt* : take advantage of, make good use of — *vi* : be of use — **aprovecharse** *vr* ~ **de** : take advantage of — **aprovechado, -da** *adj* **1** : diligent **2** OPORTUNISTA : opportunistic

aproximar *vt* : bring closer — **aproximarse** *vr* : approach — **aproximación** *nf, pl* **-ciones** : approximation — **aproximadamente** *adv* : approximately — **aproximado, -da** *adj* : approximate

apto, -ta *adj* **1** : suitable **2** CAPAZ : capable — **aptitud** *nf* : aptitude, capability

apuesta *nf* : bet, wager

apuesto, -ta *adj* : elegant, good-looking

apuntalar *vt* : prop up, shore up

apuntar *vt* **1** : aim, point **2** ANOTAR : jot down **3** SEÑALAR : point at **4** : prompt (in theater) — **apuntarse** *vr* **1** : sign up **2** : score, chalk up (a victory, etc.) — **apunte** *nm* : note

apuñalar *vt* : stab

apurar *vt* **1** : hurry, rush **2** AGOTAR : use up **3** PREOCUPAR : trouble — **apurarse** *vr* **1** : worry **2** *Lat* : hurry up — **apuradamente** *adv* : with difficulty — **apurado, -da** *adj* **1** : needy **2** DIFÍCIL : difficult **3** *Lat* : rushed — **apuro** *nm* **1** : predicament, jam **2** *Lat* : hurry

aquejar *vt* : afflict

aquel, aquella *adj, mpl* **aquellos** : that, those

aquél, aquélla *pron, mpl* **aquéllos 1** : that (one), those (ones) **2** : the former

aquello *pron* : that, that matter

aquí *adv* **1** : here **2** AHORA : now **3** por ~ : hereabouts

aquietar *vt* : calm — **aquietarse** *vr* : calm down

ara *nf* **1** : altar **2** en ~s de : for the sake of

árabe *adj* : Arab, Arabic — ~ *nm* : Arabic (language)

arado *nm* : plow

arancel *nm* : tariff

arándano *nm* : blueberry

araña *nf* **1** : spider **2** LÁMPARA : chandelier

arañar *v* : scratch, claw — **arañazo** *nm* : scratch

arar *v* : plow

arbitrar *v* **1** : arbitrate **2** : referee, umpire (in sports) — **arbitraje** *nm* : arbitration — **arbitrario, -ria** *adj* : arbitrary — **arbitrio** *nm* **1** : (free) will **2** JUICIO : judgment — **árbitro, -tra** *n* **1** : arbitrator **2** : referee, umpire (in sports)

árbol *nm* : tree — **arboleda** *nf* : grove

arbusto *nm* : shrub, bush

arca *nf* **1** : ark **2** COFRE : chest

arcada *nf* **1** : arcade **2** ~s *nfpl* : retching

arcaico, -ca *adj* : archaic

arcano, -na *adj* : arcane, secret

arce *nm* : maple tree

archipiélago *nm* : archipelago

archivar *vt* : file — **archivador** *nm* : filing cabinet — **archivo** *nm* **1** : file **2** : archives *pl*

arcilla *nf* : clay

arco *nm* **1** : arch **2** : bow (in sports, music, etc.) **3** : arc (in geometry) **4** ~ **iris** : rainbow

arder *vi* : burn

ardid *nm* : scheme, ruse

ardiente *adj* **1** : burning **2** FOGOSO : ardent

ardilla *nf* **1** : squirrel **2** ~ **listada** : chipmunk

ardor *nm* **1** : burning **2** ENTUSIASMO : passion, ardor

arduo, -dua *adj* : arduous

área *nf* : area

arena *nf* **1** : sand **2** PALESTRA : arena — **arenoso, -sa** *adj* : sandy, gritty

arenque *nm* : herring

arete *nm Lat* : earring

argamasa *nf* : mortar

argentino, -na *adj* : Argentinian, Argentine

argolla *nf* : hoop, ring

argot *nm* : slang

argüir {41} *vt* **1** : argue **2** DEMOSTRAR : prove, show — *vi* : argue

argumentar *vt* : argue, contend — **argumentación** *nf, pl* **-ciones** : (line of) argument — **argumento** *nm* **1** : argument, reasoning **2** TRAMA : plot, story line

árido, -da *adj* : dry, arid — **aridez** *nf, pl* **-deces** : aridity

arisco, -ca *adj* : surly

aristocracia *nf* : aristocracy — **aristócrata**

nmf : aristocrat — **aristocrático, -ca** *adj* : aristocratic

aritmética *nf* : arithmetic — **aritmético, -ca** *adj* : arithmetic, arithmetical

armar *vt* **1** : arm **2** MONTAR : assemble — **arma** *nf* **1** : arm, weapon **2** ~ **de fuego** : firearm — **armada** *nf* : navy — **armado, -da** *adj* : armed — **armadura** *nf* **1** : armor **2** ARMAZÓN : framework — **armamento** *nm* : armament, arms *pl*

armario *nm* **1** : (clothes) closet **2** : cupboard, cabinet

armazón *nmf, pl* **-zones** : frame, framework

armisticio *nm* : armistice

armonizar {21} *vt* **1** : harmonize **2** : reconcile (differences, etc.) — *vi* : harmonize, go together — **armonía** *nf* : harmony — **armónica** *nf* : harmonica — **armónico, -ca** *adj* : harmonic — **armonioso, -sa** *adj* : harmonious

arnés *nm, pl* **-neses** : harness

aro *nm* **1** : hoop, ring **2** *Lat* : earring

aroma *nm* : aroma, scent — **aromático, -ca** *adj* : aromatic

arpa *nf* : harp

arpón *nm, pl* **-pones** : harpoon

arquear *vt* : arch, bend — **arquearse** *vr* : bend, bow

arqueología *nf* : archaeology — **arqueológico, -ca** *adj* : archaeological — **arqueólogo, -ga** *n* : archaeologist

arquero, -ra *n* **1** : archer **2** PORTERO : goalkeeper, goalie

arquetipo *nm* : archetype

arquitectura *nf* : architecture — **arquitecto, -ta** *n* : architect — **arquitectónico, -ca** *adj* : architectural

arrabal *nm* **1** : slum **2** ~**es** *nmpl* : outskirts

arracimarse *vr* : cluster together

arraigar {52} *vi* : take root, become established — **arraigarse** *vr* : settle down — **arraigado, -da** *adj* : deeply rooted, well established — **arraigo** *nm* : roots *pl*

arrancar {72} *vt* **1** : pull out, tear off **2** : start (an engine), boot (a computer) — *vi* **1** : start an engine **2** : get going — **arranque** *nm* **1** : starter (of a car) **2** ARREBATO : outburst **3 punto de** ~ : starting point

arrasar *vt* **1** : destroy, devastate **2** LLENAR : fill to the brim

arrastrar *vt* **1** : drag **2** ATRAER : draw, attract — *vi* : hang down, trail — **arrastrarse** *vr* **1** : crawl, creep **2** HUMILLARSE : grovel — **arrastre** *nm* **1** : dragging **2** : trawling (for fish)

arrear *vt* : urge on

arrebatar *vt* **1** : snatch, seize **2** CAUTIVAR : captivate — **arrebatarse** *vr* : get carried away — **arrebatado, -da** *adj* : hotheaded, rash — **arrebato** *nm* : outburst

arreciar *vi* : intensify, worsen

arrecife *nm* : reef

arreglar *vt* **1** COMPONER : fix **2** ORDENAR : tidy up **3** SOLUCIONAR : solve, work out — **arreglárselas** *vr* **1** : get dressed (up) **2 arreglárselas** *fam* : get by, manage — **arreglado, -da** *adj* **1** : fixed, repaired **2** ORDENADO : tidy **3** SOLUCIONADO : settled, sorted out **4** ATAVIADO : smart, dressed-up — **arreglo** *nm* **1** : arrangement **2** REPARACIÓN : repair **3** ACUERDO : agreement

arremangarse {52} *vr* : roll up one's sleeves

arremeter *vi* : attack, charge — **arremetida** *nf* : attack, onslaught

arremolinarse *vr* **1** : crowd around, mill about **2** : swirl (about)

arrendar {55} *vt* : rent, lease — **arrendador, -dora** *n* : landlord, landlady *f* — **arrendamiento** *nm* : rent, rental — **arrendatario, -ria** *n* : tenant, renter

arrepentirse {76} *vr* **1** : regret, be sorry **2** : repent (for one's sins) — **arrepentido, -da** *adj* : repentant — **arrepentimiento** *nm* : regret, repentance

arrestar *vt* : arrest, detain — **arresto** *nm* : arrest

arriar *vt* : lower

arriba *adv* **1** (*indicating position*) : above, overhead **2** (*indicating direction*) : up, upwards **3** : upstairs (of a house) **4** ~ **de** : more than **5 de** ~ **abajo** : from top to bottom

arribar *vi* **1** : arrive **2** : dock, put into port — **arribista** *nmf* : parvenu, upstart — **arribo** *nm* : arrival

arriendo → **arrendimiento**

arriesgar {52} *vt* : risk, venture — **arriesgarse** *vr* : take a chance — **arriesgado, -da** *adj* : risky

arrimar *vt* : bring closer, draw near — **arrimarse** *vr* : approach

arrinconar *vt* **1** : corner, box in **2** ABANDONAR : push aside

arrobar *vt* : entrance — **arrobarse** *vr* : be enraptured — **arrobamiento** *nm* : rapture, ecstasy

arrodillarse *vr* : kneel (down)

arrogancia *nf* : arrogance — **arrogante** *adj* : arrogant

arrojar *vt* **1** : hurl, cast **2** EMITIR : give off, spew out **3** PRODUCIR : yield — **arrojarse** *vr* : throw oneself — **arrojado, -da** *adj* : daring — **arrojo** *nm* : boldness, courage

arrollar *vt* **1** : sweep away **2** DERROTAR : crush, overwhelm **3** : run over (with a vehicle) — **arrollador, -dora** *adj* : overwhelming

arropar *vt* : clothe, cover (up) — **arroparse** *vr* : wrap oneself up

arroyo *nm* **1** RIACHUELO : stream **2** : gutter (in a street)

arroz *nm, pl* **arroces** : rice

arrugar {52} *vt* : wrinkle, crease — **arrugarse** *vr* : get wrinkled — **arruga** *nf* : wrinkle, crease

arruinar *vt* : ruin, wreck — **arruinarse** *vr* **1** : be ruined **2** EMPOBRECERSE : go bankrupt

arrullar *vt* : lull to sleep — *vi* : coo — **arrullo** *nm* **1** : lullaby **2** : cooing (of doves)

arrumbar *vt* : lay aside

arsenal *nm* : arsenal

arsénico *nm* : arsenic

arte *nmf* (*usually m in singular, f in plural*) **1** : art **2** HABILIDAD : skill **3** ASTUCIA : cunning, cleverness **4** → **bello**

artefacto *nm* : artifact, device

arteria *nf* : artery

artesanía *nm* **1** : craftsmanship **2** : handicrafts *pl* — **artesanal** *adj* : handmade — **artesano, -na** *n* : artisan, craftsman

ártico, -ca *adj* : arctic

articular *vt* : articulate — **articulación** *nf, pl* **-ciones** **1** : articulation, pronunciation **2** COYUNTURA : joint

artículo *nm* **1** : article **2** ~s de primera necesidad : essentials **3** ~s de tocador : toiletries

artifice *nmf* : artisan, craftsman

artificial *adj* : artificial

artificio *nm* **1** HABILIDAD : skill **2** APARATO : device **3** ARDID : artifice, ruse — **artificioso, -sa** *adj* : cunning, deceptive

artillería *nf* : artillery

artilugio *nm* : gadget

artimaña *nf* : ruse, trick

artista *nmf* **1** : artist **2** ACTOR : actor, actress *f* — **artístico, -ca** *adj* : artistic

artritis *nms & pl* : arthritis — **artrítico, -ca** *adj* : arthritic

arveja *nf Lat* : pea

arzobispo *nm* : archbishop

as *nm* : ace

asa *nf* : handle

asado, -da *adj* : roasted, grilled — **asado** *nm* : roast — **asador** *nm* : spit — **asaduras** *nfpl* : offal, entrails

asalariado, -da *n* : wage earner — ~ *adj* : salaried

asaltar *vt* **1** : assault **2** ROBAR : mug, rob — **asaltante** *nmf* **1** : assailant **2** ATRACADOR : mugger, robber — **asalto** *nm* **1** : assault **2** ROBO : mugging, robbery

asamblea *nf* : assembly, meeting

asar *vt* : roast, grill — **asarse** *vr fam* : roast, feel the heat

asbesto *nm* : asbestos

ascender {56} *vi* **1** : ascend, rise up **2** : be promoted (in a job) **3** ~ **a** : amount to — *vt* : promote — **ascendencia** *nf* : ancestry, descent — **ascendiente** *nmf* : ancestor — ~ *nm* : influence — **ascensión** *nf, pl* **-siones** : ascent — **ascenso** *nm* **1** : ascent, rise **2** : promotion (in a job) — **ascensor** *nm* : elevator

asco *nm* **1** : disgust **2 hacer** ~s **de** : turn up one's nose at **3 me da** ~ : it makes me sick

ascua *nf* **1** : ember **2 estar en** ~s *fam* : be on edge

asear *vt* : clean, tidy up — **asearse** *vr* : get cleaned up — **aseado, -da** *adj* : clean, tidy

asediar *vt* **1** : besiege **2** ACOSAR : harass — **asedio** *nm* **1** : siege **2** ACOSO : harassment

asegurar *vt* **1** : assure **2** FIJAR : secure **3** : insure (a car, house, etc.) — **asegurarse** *vr* : make sure

asemejarse *vr* **1** : be similar **2** ~ **a** : look like, resemble

asentar {55} *vt* **1** : set down **2** INSTALAR : set up, establish **3** *Lat* : state — **asentarse** *vr* **1** : settle **2** ESTABLECERSE : settle down — **asentado, -da** *adj* : settled, established

asentir {76} *vi* : assent, agree — **asentimiento** *nm* : assent

aseo *nm* : cleanliness

asequible *adj* : accessible, attainable

aserrar {55} *vt* : saw — **aserradero** *nm* : sawmill — **aserrín** *nm, pl* **-rrines** : sawdust

asesinar *vt* **1** : murder **2** : assassinate — **asesinato** *nm* **1** : murder **2** : assassination — **asesino, -na** *n* **1** : murderer, killer **2** : assassin

asesorar *vt* : advise, counsel — **asesorarse** *vr* ~ **de** : consult — **asesor, -sora** *n* : advisor, consultant — **asesoramiento** *nm* : advice, counsel

asestar {55} *vt* **1** : aim (a weapon) **2** : deal (a blow)

aseverar *vt* : assert — **aseveración** *nf, pl* **-ciones** : assertion

asfalto *nm* : asphalt

asfixiar *vt* : asphyxiate, suffocate — **asfixiarse** *vr* : suffocate — **asfixia** *nf* : asphyxiation, suffocation

así *adv* **1** : like this, like that, thus **2** ~ **de** : so, that (much) **3** ~ **que** : so, therefore **4** ~ **que** : as soon as **5** ~ **como** : as well as — ~ *adj* : such, like that — ~ *conj* AUNQUE : even though

asiático, -ca *adj* : Asian, Asiatic

asidero *nm* : handle

asiduo, -dua *adj* : frequent, regular

asiento *nm* : seat

asignar *vt* **1** : assign, allocate **2** DESTINAR

: appoint — **asignación** *nf, pl* **-ciones 1** : assignment **2** SUELDO : salary, pay — **asignatura** *nf* : subject, course

asilo *nm* **1** : asylum, home **2** REFUGIO : refuge, shelter — **asilado, -da** *n* : inmate

asimilar *vt* : assimilate — **asimilarse** *vr* ~ **a** : resemble

asimismo *adv* **1** : similarly, likewise **2** TAMBIÉN : as well, also

asir {7} *vt* : seize, grasp — **asirse** *vr* ~ **a** : cling to

asistir *vi* ~ **a** : attend, be present at — *vt* : assist — **asistencia** *nf* **1** : attendance **2** AYUDA : assistance — **asistente** *nmf* **1** : assistant **2 los ~s** : those present

asma *nf* : asthma — **asmático, -ca** *adj* : asthmatic

asno *nm* : ass, donkey

asociar *vt* : associate — **asociarse** *vr* **1** : form a partnership **2** ~ **a** : join, become a member of — **asociación** *nf, pl* **-ciones** : association — **asociado, -da** *adj* : associate, associated — ~ *n* : associate, partner

asolar {19} *vt* : devastate

asomar *vt* : show, stick out — *vi* : appear, show — **asomarse** *vr* **1** : appear **2** : stick one's head out (of a window)

asombrar *vt* : amaze, astonish — **asombrarse** *vr* : be amazed — **asombro** *nm* : amazement, astonishment — **asombroso, -sa** *adj* : amazing, astonishing

asomo *nm* **1** : hint, trace **2 ni por ~** : by no means

aspaviento *nm* : exaggerated gestures, fuss

aspecto *nm* **1** : aspect **2** APARIENCIA : appearance, look

áspero, -ra *adj* : rough, harsh — **aspereza** *nf* : roughness, harshness

aspersión *nf, pl* **-siones** : sprinkling — **aspersor** *nm* : sprinkler

aspiración *nf, pl* **-ciones 1** : breathing in **2** ANHELO : aspiration

aspiradora *nf* : vacuum cleaner

aspirar *vi* ~ **a** : aspire to — *vt* : inhale, breathe in — **aspirante** *nmf* : applicant, candidate

aspirina *nf* : aspirin

asquear *vt* : sicken, disgust

asquerosidad *nf* : filth, foulness — **asqueroso, -sa** *adj* : disgusting, sickening

asta *nf* **1** : flagpole **2** CUERNO : antler, horn **3** : shaft (of a spear) — **astado, -da** *adj* : horned

asterisco *nm* : asterisk

asteroide *nm* : asteroid

astigmatismo *nm* : astigmatism

astillar *vt* : splinter — **astilla** *nf* : splinter, chip

astillero *nm* : shipyard

astral *adj* : astral

astringente *adj & nm* : astringent

astro *nm* **1** : heavenly body **2** : star (of movies, etc.)

astrología *nf* : astrology

astronauta *nmf* : astronaut — **astronáutica** *nf* : astronautics

astronave *nf* : spaceship

astronomía *nf* : astronomy — **astronómico, -ca** *adj* : astronomical — **astrónomo, -ma** *n* : astronomer

astucia *nf* **1** : astuteness **2** ARDID : cunning, guile — **astuto, -ta** *adj* **1** : astute **2** TAIMADO : crafty

asueto *nm* : time off, break

asumir *vt* : assume — **asunción** *nf, pl* **-ciones** : assumption

asunto *nm* **1** : matter, affair **2** NEGOCIO : business

asustar *vt* : scare, frighten — **asustarse** *vr* ~ **de** : be frightened of — **asustadizo, -za** *adj* : jumpy, skittish — **asustado, -da** *adj* : frightened, afraid

atacar {72} *v* : attack — **atacante** *nmf* : attacker

atado *nm* : bundle

atadura *nf* : tie, bond

atajar *vt* : block, cut off — *vi* ~ **por** : take a shortcut through — **atajo** *nm* : shortcut

atañer {79} *vi* ~ **a** : concern, have to do with

ataque *nm* **1** : attack, assault **2** ACCESO : fit **3** ~ **de nervios** : nervous breakdown

atar *vt* : tie up, tie down — **atarse** *vr* : tie (up)

atardecer {53} *v impers* : get dark — ~ *nm* : late afternoon, dusk

atareado, -da *adj* : busy

atascar {72} *vt* **1** : block, clog **2** ESTORBAR : hinder — **atascarse** *vr* **1** OBSTRUIRSE : become obstructed **2** : get bogged down — **atasco** *nm* **1** : blockage **2** EMBOTELLAMIENTO : traffic jam

ataúd *nm* : coffin

ataviar {85} *vt* : dress (up) — **ataviarse** *vr* : dress up — **atavío** *nm* : attire

atemorizar {21} *vt* : frighten — **atemorizarse** *vr* : get scared

atención *nf, pl* **-ciones 1** : attention **2 prestar ~** : pay attention **3 llamar la ~** : attract attention — ~ *interj* : attention!, watch out!

atender {56} *vt* **1** : attend to **2** CUIDAR : look after **3** : heed (advice, etc.) — *vi* : pay attention

atenerse {80} *vr* ~ **a** : abide by

atentamente *adv* **1** : attentively **2 le saluda ~** : sincerely yours

atentar {55} *vi* ~ **contra** : make an attempt on — **atentado** *nm* : attack

atento, -ta *adj* **1** : attentive, mindful **2** CORTÉS : courteous

atenuar {3} *vt* **1** : dim (lights), tone down (colors, etc.) **2** DISMINUIR : lessen — **atenuante** *nmf* : extenuating circumstances

ateo, atea *adj* : atheistic — ~ *n* : atheist

aterciopelado, -da *adj* : velvety, downy

aterido, -da *adj* : frozen stiff

aterrar {55} *vt* : terrify — **aterrador, -dora** *adj* : terrifying

aterrizar {21} *vi* : land — **aterrizaje** *nm* : landing

aterrorizar {21} *vt* : terrify

atesorar *vt* : hoard, amass

atestar {55} *vt* **1** : crowd, pack **2** : testify to (in law) — **atestado, -da** *adj* : stuffed, packed

atestiguar {10} *vt* : testify to

atiborrar *vt* : stuff, cram — **atiborrarse** *vr* : stuff oneself

ático *nm* **1** : penthouse **2** DESVÁN : attic

atildado, -da *adj* : smart, neat

atinar *vi* : be on target

atípico, -ca *adj* : atypical

atirantar *vt* : tighten

atisbar *vt* **1** : spy on **2** VISLUMBRAR : catch a glimpse of — **atisbo** *nm* : sign, hint

atizar {21} *vt* **1** : poke (a fire) **2** : rouse, stir up (passions, etc.) — **atizador** *nm* : poker

atlántico, -ca *adj* : Atlantic

atlas *nm* : atlas

atleta *nmf* : athlete — **atlético, -ca** *adj* : athletic — **atletismo** *nm* : athletics

atmósfera *nf* : atmosphere — **atmosférico, -ca** *adj* : atmospheric

atolondrado, -da *adj* **1** : scatterbrained **2** ATURDIDO : bewildered, dazed

átomo *nm* : atom — **atómico, -ca** *adj* : atomic — **atomizador** *nm* : atomizer

atónito, -ta *adj* : astonished, amazed

atontar *vt* : stun, daze

atorar *vt* : block — **atorarse** *vr* : get stuck

atormentar *vt* : torment, torture — **atormentarse** *vr* : torment oneself, agonize — **atormentador, -dora** *n* : tormenter

atornillar *vt* : screw

atorrante *nmf Lat* : bum, loafer

atosigar {52} *vt* : harass, annoy

atracar {72} *vi* : dock, land — *vt* : hold up, mug — **atracarse** *vr fam* ~ **de** : gorge oneself with — **atracadero** *nm* : dock, pier — **atracador, -dora** *n* : robber, mugger

atracción *nf, pl* **-ciones** : attraction

atraco *nm* : holdup, robbery

atractivo, -va *adj* : attractive — **atractivo** *nm* : attraction, appeal

atraer {81} *vt* : attract

atragantarse *vr* : choke

atrancar {72} *vt* : block, bar — **atrancarse** *vr* : get blocked, get stuck

atrapar *vt* : trap, capture

atrás *adv* **1** DETRÁS : back, behind **2** ANTES : before, earlier **3 para** ~ *or* **hacia** ~ : backwards

atrasar *vt* **1** : put back (a clock) **2** DEMORAR : delay — *vi* : lose time — **atrasarse** *vr* : fall behind — **atrasado, -da** *adj* **1** : late, overdue **2** : backward (of countries, etc.) **3** : slow (of a clock) — **atraso** *nm* **1** RETRASO : delay **2** : backwardness **3** ~**s** *nmpl* : arrears

atravesar {55} *vt* **1** CRUZAR : cross **2** TRASPASAR : pierce **3** : lay across (a road, etc.) **4** : go through (a situation) — **atravesarse** *vr* : be in the way

atrayente *adj* : attractive

atreverse *vr* : dare — **atrevido, -da** *adj* **1** : bold **2** INSOLENTE : insolent — **atrevimiento** *nm* **1** : boldness **2** DESCARO : insolence

atribuir {41} *vt* **1** : attribute **2** : confer (powers, etc.) — **atribuirse** *vr* : take credit for

atribular *vt* : afflict, trouble

atributo *nm* : attribute

atrincherar *vt* : entrench — **atrincherarse** *vr* : dig oneself in

atrocidad *nf* : atrocity

atronador, -dora *adj* : thunderous

atropellar *vt* **1** : run over **2** : violate, abuse (a person) — **atropellarse** *vr* : rush — **atropellado, -da** *adj* : hasty — **atropello** *nm* : abuse, outrage

atroz *adj, pl* **atroces** : atrocious

atuendo *nm* : attire

atufar *vt* : vex — **atufarse** *vr* : get angry

atún *nm, pl* **atunes** : tuna

aturdir *vt* **1** : stun, shock **2** CONFUNDIR : bewilder — **aturdido, -da** *adj* : dazed, bewildered

audaz *adj, pl* **-daces** : bold, daring — **audacia** *nf* : boldness, audacity

audible *adj* : audible

audición *nf, pl* **-ciones** **1** : hearing **2** : audition (in theater, etc.)

audiencia *nf* : audience

audífono *nm* **1** : hearing aid **2** ~**s** *nmpl Lat* : headphones, earphones

audiovisual *adj* : audiovisual

auditar *vt* : audit — **auditor, -tora** *n* : auditor

auditorio *nm* **1** : auditorium **2** PÚBLICO : audience

auge *nm* **1** : peak **2** : (economic) boom

augurar *vt* : predict, foretell — **augurio** *nm* : omen

augusto, -ta *adj* : august

aula *nf* : classroom
aullar {8} *vi* : howl — **aullido** *nm* : howl
aumentar *vt* : increase, raise — *vi* : increase, grow — **aumento** *nm* : increase, rise
aun *adv* **1** : even **2 ～ así** : even so
aún *adv* **1** : still, yet **2 más ～** : furthermore
aunar {8} *vt* : join, combine — **aunarse** *vr* : unite
aunque *conj* **1** : though, although, even if **2 ～ sea** : at least
aureola *nf* **1** : halo **2** FAMA : aura
auricular *nm* **1** : telephone receiver **2 ～es** *nmpl* : headphones
aurora *nf* : dawn
ausentarse *vr* : leave, go away — **ausencia** *nf* : absence — **ausente** *adj* : absent — **～** *nmf* **1** : absentee **2** : missing person (in law)
auspicios *nmpl* : sponsorship, auspices
austero, -ra *adj* : austere — **austeridad** *nf* : austerity
austral *adj* : southern
australiano, -na *adj* : Australian
austriaco *or* **austríaco, -ca** *adj* : Austrian
auténtico, -ca *adj* : authentic, genuine — **autenticidad** *nf* : authenticity
auto *nm* : auto, car
autoayuda *nf* : self-help
autobiografía *nf* : autobiography — **autobiográfico, -ca** *adj* : autobiographical
autobús *nm, pl* **-buses** : bus
autocompasión *nf* : self-pity
autocontrol *nm* : self-control
autocracia *nf* : autocracy
autóctono, -na *adj* : indigenous, native
autodefensa *nf* : self-defense
autodidacta *adj* : self-taught
autodisciplina *nf* : self-discipline
autoestop → **autostop**
autografiar *vt* : autograph — **autógrafo** *nm* : autograph
autómata *nm* : automaton
automático, -ca *adj* : automatic — **automatización** *nf, pl* **-ciones** : automation — **automatizar** {21} *vt* : automate
automotor, -triz *adj, fpl* **-trices** : self-propelled
automóvil *nm* : automobile — **automovilista** *nmf* : motorist — **automovilístico, -ca** *adj* : automobile, car
autonomía *nf* : autonomy — **autónomo, -ma** *adj* : autonomous
autopista *nf* : expressway, highway
autopropulsado, -da *adj* : self-propelled
autopsia *nf* : autopsy
autor, -tora *n* **1** : author **2** : perpetrator (of a crime)
autoridad *nf* : authority — **autoritario, -ria** *adj* : authoritarian

autorizar {21} *vt* : authorize, approve — **autorización** *nf, pl* **-ciones** : authorization — **autorizado, -da** *adj* **1** PERMITIDO : authorized **2** : authoritative
autorretrato *nm* : self-portrait
autoservicio *nm* **1** : self-service restaurant **2** SUPERMERCADO : supermarket
autostop *nm* **1** : hitchhiking **2 hacer ～** : hitchhike — **autostopista** *nmf* : hitchhiker
autosuficiente *adj* : self-sufficient
auxiliar *vt* : aid, assist — **～** *adj* : auxiliary — **～** *nmf* **1** : assistant, helper **2 ～ de vuelo** : flight attendant — **auxilio** *nm* **1** : aid, assistance **2 primeros ～s** : first aid
avalancha *nf* : avalanche
avalar *vt* : guarantee, endorse — **aval** *nm* : guarantee, endorsement
avanzar {21} *v* : advance, move forward — **avance** *nm* : advance — **avanzado, -da** *adj* : advanced
avaricia *nf* : greed, avarice — **avaricioso, -sa** *adj* : avaricious, greedy — **avaro, -ra** *adj* : miserly — **～** *n* : miser
avasallar *vt* : overpower, subjugate — **avasallador, -dora** *adj* : overwhelming
ave *nf* : bird
avecinarse *vr* : approach
avecindarse *vr* : settle, take up residence
avellana *nf* : hazelnut
avena *nf* **1** : oats *pl* **2** *or* **harina de ～** : oatmeal
avenida *nf* : avenue
avenir {87} *vt* : reconcile, harmonize — **avenirse** *vr* : agree, come to terms
aventajar *vt* : be ahead of, surpass
aventar {55} *vt* **1** : fan **2** : winnow (grain) **3** *Lat* : throw, toss
aventurar *vt* : venture, risk — **aventurarse** *vr* : take a risk — **aventura** *nf* **1** : adventure **2** RIESGO : risk **3** AMORÍO : love affair — **aventurado, -da** *adj* : risky — **aventurero, -ra** *adj* : adventurous — **～** *n* : adventurer
avergonzar {9} *vt* : shame, embarrass — **avergonzarse** *vr* : be ashamed, be embarrassed
averiar {85} *vt* : damage — **averiarse** *vr* : break down — **avería** *nf* **1** : damage **2** : breakdown (of an automobile) — **averiado, -da** *adj* **1** : damaged, faulty **2** : broken down (of an automobile)
averiguar {10} *vt* **1** : find out **2** INVESTIGAR : investigate — **averiguación** *nf, pl* **-ciones** : investigation, inquiry
aversión *nf, pl* **-siones** : aversion, dislike
avestruz *nm, pl* **-truces** : ostrich
aviación *nf, pl* **-ciones** : aviation — **aviador, -dora** *n* : aviator
aviar {85} *vt* : prepare, make ready

ávido, -da *adj* : eager, avid — **avidez** *nf, pl*
-deces : eagerness

avío *nm* **1** : preparation, provision **2 ~s**
nmpl : gear, equipment

avión *nm, pl* **aviones** : airplane — **avioneta**
nf : light airplane

avisar *vt* **1** : notify **2** ADVERTIR : warn —
aviso *nm* **1** : notice **2** ADVERTENCIA
: warning **3** *Lat* : advertisement, ad **4 estar**
sobre ~ : be on the alert

avispa *nf* : wasp — **avispón** *nm, pl* **-pones**
: hornet

avispado, -da *adj fam* : clever, sharp

avistar *vt* : catch sight of

avivar *vt* **1** : enliven, brighten **2** : arouse
(desire, etc.) **3** : intensify (pain)

axila *nf* : underarm, armpit

axioma *nm* : axiom

ay *interj* **1** : oh! **2** : ouch!, ow!

ayer *adv* : yesterday — **~** *nm* : yesteryear,
days gone by

ayote *nm Lat* : pumpkin

ayudar *vt* : help, assist — **ayudarse** *vr* **~**
de : make use of — **ayuda** *nf* : help, assistance — **ayudante** *nmf* : helper, assistant

ayunar *vi* : fast — **ayunas** *nfpl* **en ~** : fast-
ing — **ayuno** *nm* : fast

ayuntamiento *nm* **1** : town hall, city hall
(building) **2** : town or city council

azabache *nm* : jet

azada *nf* : hoe — **azadonar** *vt* : hoe

azafata *nf* : stewardess *f*

azafrán *nm, pl* **-franes** : saffron

azalea *nf* : azalea

azar *nm* **1** : chance **2 al ~** : at random —
azaroso, -sa *adj* : hazardous (of a journey,
etc.), eventful (of a life)

azorar *vt* **1** : alarm **2** DESCONCERTAR : embarrass — **azorarse** *vr* : get embarrassed

azotar *vt* : beat, whip — **azote** *nm* **1** LÁTIGO
: whip, lash **2** CALAMIDAD : scourge

azotea *nf* : flat or terraced roof

azteca *adj* : Aztec

azúcar *nmf* : sugar — **azucarado, -da** *adj*
: sugary — **azucarera** *nf* : sugar bowl —
azucarero, -ra *adj* : sugar

azufre *nm* : sulphur

azul *adj & nm* : blue — **azulado, -da** *adj*
: bluish

azulejo *nm* **1** : ceramic tile **2** *Lat* : bluebird

azur *n* : azure, sky blue

azuzar {21} *vt* : incite, urge on

B

b *nf* : b, second letter of the Spanish alphabet

babear *vi* : drool, slobber — **baba** *nf* : saliva,
drool

babel *nmf* : bedlam

babero *nm* : bib

babor *nm* : port (side)

babosa *nf* : slug — **baboso, -sa** *adj* **1**
: slimy **2** *Lat fam* : silly

babucha *nf* : slipper

babuino *nm* : baboon

bacalao *nm* : cod

bache *nm* **1** : pothole, rut **2** DIFICULTADES
: bad time

bachiller *nmf* : high school graduate —
bachillerato *nm* : high school diploma

bacon *nm Spain* : bacon

bacteria *nf* : bacterium

bagaje *nm* : baggage, luggage

bagatela *nf* : trinket

bagre *nm* : catfish

bahía *nf* : bay

bailar *v* : dance — **bailarín, -rina** *n, mpl*
-rines : dancer — **baile** *nm* **1** : dance **2** FI-
ESTA : dance party, ball

bajar *vt* **1** : bring down, lower **2** DESCENDER
: go down, come down — *vi* : descend, drop
— **bajarse** *vr* **~ de** : get out of, get off —
baja *nf* **1** : fall, drop **2** CESE : dismissal **3**
PERMISO : sick leave **4** : (military) casualty
— **bajada** *nf* **1** : descent, drop **2** PENDIENTE
: slope

bajeza *nf* : lowness, meanness

bajío *nm* : sandbank, shoal

bajo, -ja *adj* **1** : low, lower **2** : short (in
stature) **3** : soft, faint (of sounds) **4** VIL
: base, vile — **bajo** *adv* **1** : low **2 habla**
más ~ : speak more softly — **~** *nm* **1**
: ground floor **2** DOBLADILLO : hem **3**
: bass (in music) — **~** *prep* : under, below
— **bajón** *nm, pl* **-jones** : sharp drop, slump

bala *nf* **1** : bullet **2** : bale (of cotton, etc.)

balada *nf* : ballad

balancear *vt* **1** : balance **2** : swing (one's
arms, etc.), rock (a boat) — **balancearse** *vr*
: swing, sway — **balance** *nm* **1** : balance **2**

: balance sheet — **balanceo** *nm* : swaying, rocking

balancín *nm, pl* **-cines 1** : seesaw **2** MECE-DORA : rocking chair

balanza *nf* : scales *pl*, balance

balar *vi* : bleat

balaustrada *nf* : balustrade, banister

balazo *nm* **1** DISPARO : shot **2** : bullet wound

balbucear *vi* **1** : stammer, stutter **2** : babble (of a baby) — **balbuceo** *nm* : stammering, muttering, babbling

balcón *nm, pl* **-cones** : balcony

balde *nm* **1** : bucket, pail **2 en ~** : in vain

baldío, -día *adj* **1** : uncultivated **2** INÚTIL : useless — **baldío** *nm* : wasteland

baldosa *nf* : floor tile

balear *vt Lat* : shoot (at) — **baleo** *nm Lat* : shot, shooting

balido *nm* : bleat

balín *nm, pl* **-lines** : pellet

balística *nf* : ballistics — **balístico, -ca** *adj* : ballistic

baliza *nf* **1** : buoy **2** : beacon (for aircraft)

ballena *nf* : whale

ballesta *nf* **1** : crossbow **2** : spring (of an automobile)

ballet *nm* : ballet

balneario *nm* : spa

balompié *nm* : soccer

balón *nm, pl* **-lones** : ball — **baloncesto** *nm* : basketball — **balonvolea** *nm* : volleyball

balsa *nf* **1** : raft **2** ESTANQUE : pond, pool

bálsamo *nm* : balsam, balm — **balsámico, -ca** *adj* : soothing

baluarte *nm* : bulwark, bastion

bambolear *vi* : sway, swing — **bambolearse** *vr* : sway, rock

bambú *nm, pl* **-búes** *or* **-bús** : bamboo

banal *adj* : banal

banana *nf Lat* : banana — **banano** *nm Lat* : banana

banca *nf* **1** : banking **2** BANCO : bench — **bancario, -ria** *adj* : bank, banking — **bancarrota** *nf* : bankruptcy — **banco** *nm* **1** : bank **2** BANCA : stool, bench, pew **3** : school (of fish)

banda *nf* **1** : band, strip **2** : band (in music) **3** PANDILLA : gang **4** : flock (of birds) **5 ~ sonora** : sound track — **bandada** *nf* : flock (of birds), school (of fish)

bandazo *nm* : lurch

bandeja *nf* : tray, platter

bandera *nf* : flag, banner

banderilla *nf* : banderilla

banderín *nm, pl* **-rines** : pennant, small flag

bandido, -da *n* : bandit

bando *nm* **1** : proclamation, edict **2** PAR-TIDO : faction, side

bandolero, -ra *n* : bandit

banjo *nm* : banjo

banquero, -ra *n* : banker

banqueta *nf* **1** : stool, footstool **2** *Lat* : sidewalk

banquete *nm* : banquet

bañar *vt* **1** : bathe, wash **2** SUMERGIR : immerse **3** CUBRIR : coat, cover — **bañarse** *vr* **1** : take a bath **2** : go swimming — **bañera** *nf* : bathtub — **bañista** *nmf* : bather — **baño** *nm* **1** : bath, swim **2** BAÑERA : bathtub **3** ¿**donde está el ~?** : where is the bathroom? **4 ~ María** : double boiler

baqueta *nf* **1** : ramrod **2 ~s** *nfpl* : drumsticks

bar *nm* : bar, tavern

barajar *vt* **1** : shuffle (cards) **2** CONSIDERAR : consider — **baraja** *nf* : deck of cards

baranda *nf* : rail, railing — **barandal** *nm* : handrail, banister

barato, -ta *adj* : cheap — **barato** *adv* : cheap, cheaply — **barata** *nf Lat* : sale, bargain — **baratija** *nf* : trinket — **baratillo** *nm* : secondhand store, flea market

barba *nf* **1** : beard, stubble **2** BARBILLA : chin

barbacoa *nf* : barbecue

barbaridad *nf* **1** : barbarity, cruelty **2 ¡qué ~!** : that's outrageous! — **barbarie** *nf* : barbarism, savagery — **bárbaro, -ra** *adj* : barbaric

barbecho *nm* : fallow land

barbero, -ra *n* : barber — **barbería** *nf* : barbershop

barbilla *nf* : chin

barbudo, -da *adj* : bearded

barca *nf* **1** : boat **2 ~ de pasaje** : ferryboat — **barcaza** *nf* : barge — **barco** *nm* : boat, ship

barítono *nm* : baritone

barman *nm* : bartender

barnizar {21} *vt* **1** : varnish **2** : glaze (ceramics) — **barniz** *nm, pl* **-nices 1** : varnish **2** : glaze (on ceramics)

barómetro *nm* : barometer

barón *nm, pl* **-rones** : baron — **baronesa** *nf* : baroness

barquero *nm* : boatman

barquillo *nm* : wafer, cone

barra *nf* **1** : bar, rod, stick **2** : counter (of a bar, etc.)

barraca *nf* **1** : hut, cabin **2** CASETA : booth, stall

barranco *nm or* **barranca** *nf* : ravine, gorge, gully

barredera *nf* : street-sweeping machine

barrenar *vt* : drill — **barrena** *nf* : drill, auger

barrer *v* : sweep

barrera *nf* : barrier

barreta *nf* : crowbar
barriada *nf* : district, quarter
barrica *nf* : cask, keg
barricada *nf* : barricade
barrido *nm* : sweep, sweeping
barriga *nf* : belly
barril *nm* **1** : barrel, keg **2 de ~** : draft
barrio *nm* **1** : neighborhood **2 ~ bajo** : slums *pl*
barro *nm* **1** : mud **2** ARCILLA : clay **3** GRANO : pimple, blackhead — **barroso, -sa** *adj* : muddy
barrote *nm* : bar (on a window)
barrunto *nm* **1** : suspicion **2** INDICIO : sign, indication
bártulos *nmpl* : things, belongings
barullo *nm* : racket, ruckus
basa *nf* : base, pedestal — **basar** *vt* : base — **basarse** *vr* **~ en** : be based on
báscula *nf* : scales *pl*
base *nf* **1** : base **2** FUNDAMENTO : basis, foundation **3 ~ de datos** : database — **básico, -ca** *adj* : basic
basquetbol *or* **básquetbol** *nm Lat* : basketball
bastar *vi* : be enough, suffice — **bastante** *adv* **1** : fairly, rather **2** SUFICIENTE : enough — **~** *adj* : enough, sufficient — **~** *pron* : enough
bastardo, -da *adj & n* : bastard
bastidor *nm* **1** : frame **2** : wing (in theater) **3 entre ~es** : behind the scenes, backstage
bastilla *nf* : hem
bastión *nf, pl* **-tiones** : bastion, stronghold
basto, -ta *adj* : coarse, rough
bastón *nm, pl* **-tones 1** : cane, walking stick **2** : baton (in parades)
basura *nf* : garbage, rubbish — **basurero, -ra** *n* : garbage collector
bata *nf* **1** : bathrobe, housecoat **2** : smock (of a doctor, laboratory worker, etc.)
batallar *vi* : battle, fight — **batalla** *nf* **1** : battle, fight, struggle **2 de ~** : ordinary, everyday — **batallón** *nm, pl* **-llones** : battalion
batata *nf* : yam, sweet potato
batear *v* : bat, hit — **bate** *nm* : baseball bat — **bateador, -dora** *n* : batter, hitter
batería *nf* **1** : battery **2** : drums *pl* **3 ~ de cocina** : kitchen utensils *pl*
batir *vt* **1** : beat, whip **2** DERRIBAR : knock down — **batirse** *vr* : fight — **batido** *nm* : milk shake — **batidor** *nm* : eggbeater, whisk — **batidora** *nf* : electric mixer
batuta *nf* : baton
baúl *nm* : trunk, chest
bautismo *nm* : baptism — **bautismal** *adj* : baptismal — **bautizar** {21} *vt* : baptize — **bautizo** *nm* : baptism, christening

baya *nf* : berry
bayeta *nf* : cleaning cloth
bayoneta *nf* : bayonet
bazar *nm* : bazaar
bazo *nm* : spleen
bazofia *nf fam* : rubbish, hogwash
beato, -ta *adj* : blessed
bebé *nm* : baby
beber *v* : drink — **bebedero** *nm* : watering trough — **bebedor, -dora** *n* : (heavy) drinker — **bebida** *nf* : drink, beverage — **bebido, -da** *adj* : drunk
beca *nf* : grant, scholarship
becerro, -rra *n* : calf
befa *nf* : jeer, taunt
beige *adj & nm* : beige
beisbol *or* **béisbol** *nm* : baseball — **beisbolista** *nmf* : baseball player
beldad *nf* : beauty
belén *nf, pl* **-lenes** : Nativity scene
belga *adj* : Belgian
beliceño, -ña *adj* : Belizean
bélico, -ca *adj* : military, war — **belicoso, -sa** *adj* : warlike
beligerancia *nf* : belligerence — **beligerante** *adj & nmf* : belligerent
belleza *nf* : beauty — **bello, -lla** *adj* **1** : beautiful **2 bellas artes** : fine arts
bellota *nf* : acorn
bemol *adj & nm* : flat (in music)
bendecir {11} *vt* **1** : bless **2 ~ la mesa** : say grace — **bendición** *nf, pl* **-ciones** : benediction, blessing — **bendito, -ta** *adj* **1** : blessed, holy **2** DICHOSO : fortunate **3 ¡bendito sea Dios!** : thank goodness!
benefactor, -tora *n* : benefactor
beneficiar *vt* : benefit, assist — **beneficiarse** *vr* : benefit, profit — **beneficiario, -ria** *n* : beneficiary — **beneficio** *nm* **1** : gain, profit **2** BIEN : benefit — **beneficioso, -sa** *adj* : beneficial — **benéfico, -ca** *adj* : charitable
benemérito, -ta *adj* : worthy
beneplácito *nm* : approval, consent
benévolo, -la *adj* : benevolent, kind — **benevolencia** *nf* : benevolence, kindness
bengala *nf or* **luz de ~** : flare
benigno, -na *adj* **1** : mild **2** : benign (in medicine) — **benignidad** *nf* : mildness, kindness
benjamín, -mina *n, mpl* **-mines** : youngest child
beodo, -da *adj & n* : drunk
berenjena *nf* : eggplant
berrear *vi* **1** : bellow, low **2** : bawl, howl (of a person) — **berrido** *nm* **1** : bellowing **2** : howl, scream (of a person)
berro *nm* : watercress
berza *nf* : cabbage

besar *vt* : kiss — **besarse** *vr* : kiss (each other) — **beso** *nm* : kiss

bestia *nf* : beast, animal — **bestial** *adj* : bestial, brutal — **bestialidad** *nf* : brutality

betabel *nm Lat* : beet

betún *nm, pl* **-tunes** : shoe polish

bianual *adj* : biannual

biberón *nm, pl* **-rones** : baby's bottle

Biblia *nf* : Bible — **bíblico, -ca** *adj* : biblical

bibliografía *nf* : bibliography — **bibliográfico, -ca** *adj* : bibliographic, bibliographical

biblioteca *nf* : library — **bibliotecario, -ria** *n* : librarian

bicarbonato *nm* ∼ **de soda** : baking soda

bicentenario *nm* : bicentennial

bíceps *nms & pl* : biceps

bicho *nm* : small animal, bug

bicicleta *nf* : bicycle — **bici** *nf fam* : bike

bicolor *adj* : two-tone

bidón *nm, pl* **-dones** : large can, drum

bien *adv* **1** : well, good **2** CORRECTAMENTE : correctly, right **3** MUY : very, quite **4** DE BUENA GANA : willingly **5** ∼ **que** : although **6 más** ∼ : rather — **bien** *adj* **1** : all right, well **2** AGRADABLE : pleasant, nice **3** SATISFACTORIO : satisfactory **4** CORRECTO : correct, right — **bien** *nm* **1** : good **2** ∼ **es** *nmpl* : property, goods

bienal *adj & nf* : biennial

bienaventurado, -da *adj* : blessed, fortunate

bienestar *nm* : welfare, well-being

bienhechor, -chora *n* : benefactor

bienintencionado, -da *adj* : well-meaning

bienvenido, -da *adj* : welcome — **bienvenida** *nf* **1** : welcome **2 dar la** ∼ **a** : welcome (s.o.)

bife *nm Lat* : steak

bifocales *nmpl* : bifocals

bifurcarse {72} *vr* : fork — **bifurcación** *nf, pl* **-ciones** : fork, branch

bigamia *nf* : bigamy

bigote *nm* **1** : mustache **2** ∼ **s** *nmpl* : whiskers (of an animal)

bikini *nm* : bikini

bilingüe *adj* : bilingual

bilis *nf* : bile

billar *nm* : pool, billiards

billete *nm* **1** : bill, banknote **2** BOLETO : ticket — **billetera** *nf* : billfold, wallet

billón *nm, pl* **-llones** : trillion

bimensual, -suale *adj* : twice a month — **bimestral** *adj* : bimonthly

binario, -ria *adj* : binary

bingo *nm* : bingo

binoculares *nmpl* : binoculars

biodegradable *adj* : biodegradable

biofísica *nf* : biophysics

biografía *nf* : biography — **biográfico, -ca** *adj* : biographical — **biógrafo, -fa** *n* : biographer

biología *nf* : biology — **biológico, -ca** *adj* : biological, biologic — **biólogo, -ga** *n* : biologist

biombo *nm* : folding screen

biomecánica *nf* : biomechanics

biopsia *nf* : biopsy

bioquímica *nf* : biochemistry — **bioquímico, -ca** *adj* : biochemical

biotecnología *nf* : biotechnology

bipartidista *adj* : bipartisan

bípedo *nm* : biped

biquini → **bikini**

birlar *vt fam* : swipe, pinch

bis *adv* **1** : twice (in music) **2** : A (in an address) — ∼ *nm* : encore

bisabuelo, -la *n* : great-grandfather *m*, great-grandmother *f*

bisagra *nf* : hinge

bisecar {72} *vt* : bisect

biselar *vt* : bevel

bisexual *adj* : bisexual

bisiesto *adj* **año** ∼ : leap year

bisnieto, -ta *n* : great-grandson *m*, great-granddaughter *f*

bisonte *nm* : bison, buffalo

bisoño, -ña *n* : novice

bistec *nm* : steak

bisturí *nm* : scalpel

bisutería *nf* : costume jewelry

bit *nm* : bit (unit of information)

bizco, -ca *adj* : cross-eyed

bizcocho *nm* : sponge cake

bizquear *vi* : squint — **bizquera** *nf* : squint

blanco, -ca *adj* : white — **blanco, -ca** *n* : white person — **blanco** *nm* **1** : white **2** DIANA : target, bull's-eye **3** : blank (space) — **blancura** *nf* : whiteness

blandir {1} *vt* : wave, brandish

blando, -da *adj* **1** : soft, tender **2** DÉBIL : weak-willed **3** INDULGENTE : lenient — **blandura** *nf* **1** : softness, tenderness **2** DEBILIDAD : weakness **3** INDULGENCIA : leniency

blanquear *vt* **1** : whiten, bleach **2** : launder (money) — *vi* : turn white — **blanqueador** *nm Lat* : bleach

blasfemar *vi* : blaspheme — **blasfemia** *nf* : blasphemy — **blasfemo, -ma** *adj* : blasphemous

bledo *nm* **no me importa un** ∼ *fam* : I couldn't care less

blindaje *nm* : armor, armor plating — **blindado, -da** *adj* : armored

bloc *nm, pl* **blocs** : (writing) pad

bloquear *vt* **1** OBSTRUIR : block, obstruct **2** : blockade — **bloque** *nm* **1** : block **2** : bloc (in politics) — **bloqueo** *nm* **1** OBSTRUC-CIÓN : blockage **2** : blockade

blusa *nf* : blouse — **blusón** *nm, pl* **-sones** : smock

boato *nm* : showiness

bobina *nf* : bobbin, reel

bobo, -ba *adj* : silly, stupid — ~ *n* : fool, simpleton

boca *nf* **1** : mouth **2** ENTRADA : entrance **3** ~ **arriba** : faceup **4** ~ **abajo** : facedown, prone **5** ~ **de riego** : hydrant

bocacalle *nf* : entrance (to a street)

bocado *nm* **1** : bite, mouthful **2** : bit (of a bridle) — **bocadillo** *nm Spain* : sandwich

bocajarro *nm* **a** ~ : point-blank

bocallave *nf* : keyhole

bocanada *nf* **1** : swallow, swig **2** : puff, gust (of smoke, wind, etc.)

boceto *nm* : sketch, outline

bochorno *nm* **1** VERGÜENZA : embarrass-ment **2** : muggy weather — **bochornoso, -sa** *adj* **1** VERGONZOSO : embarrassing **2** : muggy, sultry

bocina *nf* **1** : horn **2** : mouthpiece (of a tele-phone) — **bocinazo** *nm* : honk, toot

boda *nf* : wedding

bodega *nf* **1** : wine cellar **2** : warehouse **3** : hold (of a ship or airplane) **4** *Lat* : grocery store

bofetear *vt* : slap — **bofetada** *nf or* **bofetón** *nm* : slap (in the face)

boga *nf* : fashion, vogue

bohemio, -mia *adj & n* : bohemian

boicotear *vt* : boycott — **boicot** *nm, pl* **-cots** : boycott

boina *nf* : beret

bola *nf* **1** : ball **2** *fam* : fib

bolera *nf* : bowling alley

boleta *nf Lat* : ticket — **boletería** *nf Lat* : ticket office

boletín *nm, pl* **-tines** **1** : bulletin **2** ~ **de noticias** : news release

boleto *nm* : ticket

boliche *nm* **1** : bowling **2** BOLERA : bowling alley

bolígrafo *nm* : ballpoint pen

bolillo *nm* : bobbin

boliviano, -na *adj* : Bolivian

bollo *nm* : bun, sweet roll

bolo *nm* **1** : bowling pin **2** ~**s** *nmpl* : bowl-ing

bolsa *nf* **1** : bag **2** *Lat* : pocketbook, purse **3 la Bolsa** : the stock market — **bolsillo** *nm* : pocket — **bolso** *nm Spain* : pocketbook, handbag

bomba *nf* **1** : bomb **2** ~ **de gasolina** : gas pump

bombachos *nmpl* : baggy trousers

bombardear *vt* : bomb, bombard — **bom-** **bardeo** *nm* : bombing, bombardment — **bombardero** *nm* : bomber (airplane)

bombear *vt* : pump — **bombero, -ra** *n* : fire-fighter

bombilla *nf* : lightbulb — **bombillo** *nm Lat* : lightbulb

bombo *nm* **1** : bass drum **2 a** ~**s y platillos** : with a great fanfare

bombón *nm, pl* **-bones** : candy, chocolate

bonachón, -chona *adj, mpl* **-chones** *fam* : good-natured

bonanza *nf* **1** : fair weather (at sea) **2** PROS-PERIDAD : prosperity

bondad *nf* : goodness, kindness — **bonda-doso, -sa** *adj* : kind, good

boniato *nm* : sweet potato

bonificación *nf, pl* **-ciones** **1** : bonus, extra **2** DESCUENTO : discount

bonito, -ta *adj* : pretty, lovely

bono *nm* **1** : bond **2** VALE : voucher

boquear *vi* : gasp — **boqueada** *nf* : gasp

boquerón *nm, pl* **-rones** : anchovy

boquete *nm* : gap, opening

boquiabierto, -ta *adj* : open-mouthed, speechless

boquilla *nf* : mouthpiece (of a musical in-strument)

borbollar *vi* : bubble

borbotar *or* **borbotear** *vi* : boil, bubble, gur-gle — **borbotón** *nm, pl* **-tones** **1** : spurt **2 salir a borbotones** : gush out

bordar *v* : embroider — **bordado** *nm* : em-broidery, needlework

borde *nm* **1** : border, edge **2 al** ~ **de** : on the verge of — **bordear** *vt* : border — **bor-dillo** *nm* : curb

bordo *nm* **a** ~ : aboard, on board

borla *nf* **1** : pom-pom, tassel **2** : powder puff

borracho, -cha *adj & n* : drunk — **bor-rachera** *nf* : drunkenness

borrar *vt* : erase, blot out — **borrador** *nm* **1** : rough draft **2** : eraser (for a blackboard)

borrascoso, -sa *adj* : stormy

borrego, -ga *n* : lamb, sheep — **borrego** *nm Lat* : false rumor, hoax

borrón *nm, pl* **-rrones** **1** : smudge, blot **2** ~ **y cuenta nueva** : let's forget about it — **borroso, -sa** *adj* **1** : blurry, smudgy **2** IN-DISTINTO : vague, hazy

bosque *nm* : woods, forest — **boscoso, -sa** *adj* : wooded

bosquejar *vt* : sketch (out) — **bosquejo** *nm* : outline, sketch

bostezar {21} *vi* : yawn — **bostezo** *nm* : yawn

bota *nf* : boot

botánica *nf* : botany — **botánico, -ca** *adj* : botanical

botar *vt* **1** : throw, hurl **2** *Lat* : throw away **3** : launch (a ship) — *vi* : bounce

bote *nm* **1** : small boat **2** *Spain* : can **3** TARRO : jar **4** SALTO : bounce, jump

botella *nf* : bottle

botín *nm, pl* **-tines 1** : ankle boot **2** DESPOJOS : booty, plunder

botiquín *nm, pl* **-quines 1** : medicine cabinet **2** : first-aid kit

botón *nm, pl* **-tones 1** : button **2** YEMA : bud — **botones** *nmfs & pl* : bellhop

botulismo *nm* : botulism

boutique *nf* : boutique

bóveda *nf* : vault

boxear *vi* : box — **boxeador, -dora** *n* : boxer — **boxeo** *nm* : boxing

boya *nf* : buoy — **boyante** *adj* **1** : buoyant **2** PRÓSPERO : prosperous, thriving

bozal *nm* **1** : muzzle **2** : halter (for a horse)

bracear *vi* **1** : wave one's arms **2** NADAR : swim, crawl

bracero, -ra *n* : day laborer

bragas *nf Spain* : panties

bragueta *nf* : fly, pants zipper

braille *adj & nm* : braille

bramante *nm* : twine, string

bramar *vi* **1** : bellow, roar **2** : howl (of the wind) — **bramido** *nm* : bellow, roar

brandy *nm* : brandy

branquia *nf* : gill

brasa *nf* : ember

brasier *nm Lat* : brassiere

brasileño, -ña *adj* : Brazilian

bravata *nf* **1** : boast, bravado **2** AMENAZO : threat

bravo, -va *adj* **1** : fierce, savage **2** : rough (of the sea) **3** *Lat* : angry — **~** *interj* : bravo!, well done! — **bravura** *nf* **1** FEROCIDAD : fierceness **2** VALENTÍA : bravery

braza *nf* **1** : breaststroke **2** : fathom (measurement) — **brazada** *nf* : stroke (in swimming)

brazalete *nm* **1** : bracelet **2** : (cloth) armband

brazo *nm* **1** : arm **2** : branch (of a river, etc.) **3 ~ derecho** : right-hand man **4 ~s** *nmpl* : hands, laborers

brea *nf* : tar

brebaje *nm* : concoction

brecha *nf* : breach, gap

brécol *nm* : broccoli

bregar {52} *vi* **1** LUCHAR : struggle **2** TRABAJAR : work hard — **brega** *nf* **andar a la ~** : struggle

breña *nf or* **breñal** *nm* : scrubland, brush

breve *adj* **1** : brief, short **2 en ~** : shortly, in short — **brevedad** *nf* : brevity, shortness — **brevemente** *adv* : briefly

brezal *nm* : moor, heath — **brezo** *nm* : heather

bricolaje *or* **bricolage** *nm* : do-it-yourself

brida *nf* : bridle

brigada *nf* **1** : brigade **2** EQUIPO : gang, team, squad

brillar *vi* : shine, sparkle — **brillante** *adj* : brilliant, shiny — **~** *nm* : diamond — **brillantez** *nf* : brilliance — **brillo** *nm* **1** : luster, shine **2** ESPLENDOR : splendor — **brilloso, -sa** *adj* : shiny

brincar {72} *vi* : jump about, frolic — **brinco** *nm* : jump, skip

brindar *vi* : drink a toast — *vt* : offer, provide — **brindarse** *vr* : offer one's assistance — **brindis** *nm* : drink, toast

brío *nm* **1** : force, determination **2** ÁNIMO : spirit, verve — **brioso, -sa** *adj* : spirited, lively

brisa *nf* : breeze

británico, -ca *adj* : British

brizna *nf* **1** : strand, thread **2** : blade (of grass)

brocado *nm* : brocade

brocha *nf* : paintbrush

broche *nm* **1** : fastener, clasp **2** ALFILER : brooch

brocheta *nf* : skewer

brócoli *nm* : broccoli

bromear *vi* : joke, fool around — **broma** *nf* : joke, prank — **bromista** *adj* : fun-loving, joking — **~** *nmf* : joker, prankster

bronca *nf fam* : fight, row

bronce *nm* : bronze — **bronceado, -da** *adj* : suntanned — **bronceado** *nm* : tan — **broncearse** *vr* : get a suntan

bronco, -ca *adj* **1** : harsh, rough **2** : untamed, wild (of a horse)

bronquitis *nf* : bronchitis

broqueta *nf* : skewer

brotar *vi* **1** : bud, sprout **2** : stream, gush (of a river, tears, etc.) **3** : arise (of feelings, etc.) **4** : break out (in medicine) — **brote** *nm* **1** : outbreak **2** : sprout, bud, shoot (of plants)

brujería *nf* : witchcraft — **bruja** *nf* **1** : witch **2** *fam* : old hag — **brujo** *nm* : warlock, sorcerer — **brujo, -ja** *adj* : bewitching

brújula *nf* : compass

bruma *nf* : haze, mist — **brumoso, -sa** *adj* : hazy, misty

bruñir {38} *vt* : burnish, polish

brusco, -ca *adj* **1** SÚBITO : sudden, abrupt **2** TOSCO : brusque, rough — **brusquedad** *nf* : abruptness, brusqueness

brutal *adj* : brutal — **brutalidad** *nf* : brutality

bruto, -ta *adj* **1** : brutish, stupid **2** : crude (of petroleum, etc.), uncut (of diamonds) **3 peso ~** : gross weight — **~** *n* : brute

bucal *adj* : oral
bucear *vi* **1** : dive, swim underwater **2** ~ **en** : delve into — **buceo** *nm* : (underwater) diving
bucle *nm* : curl
budín *nm, pl* **-dines** : pudding
budismo *nm* : Buddhism — **budista** *adj & nmf* : Buddhist
buenamente *adv* **1** : easily **2** VOLUNTARIA-MENTE : willingly
buenaventura *nf* **1** : good luck **2 decir la** ~ **a uno** : tell s.o.'s fortune
bueno, -na *adj* (**buen** *before masculine singular nouns*) **1** : good **2** AMABLE : kind **3** APROPIADO : appropriate **4** SALUDABLE : well, healthy **5** : nice, fine (of weather) **6 buenos días** : hello, good day **7 buenas noches** : good night **8 buenas tardes** : good afternoon, good evening — **bueno** *interj* : OK!, all right!
buey *nm* : ox, steer
búfalo *nm* : buffalo
bufanda *nf* : scarf
bufar *vi* : snort — **bufido** *nm* : snort
bufet *or* **bufé** *nm* : buffet-style meal
bufete *nm* **1** : law practice **2** MESA : writing desk
bufo, -fa *adj* : comic — **bufón, -fona** *n, mpl* **-fones** : buffoon, jester — **bufonada** *nf* : wisecrack
buhardilla *nf* : attic, garret
búho *nm* : owl
buitre *nm* : vulture
bujía *nf* : spark plug
bulbo *nm* : bulb (of a plant)
bulevar *nm* : boulevard
búlgaro, -ra *adj* : Bulgarian
bulla *nf* : uproar, racket

bulldozer *nm* : bulldozer
bullicio *nm* **1** : uproar **2** AJETREO : hustle and bustle — **bullicioso, -sa** *adj* : noisy, boisterous
bullir {38} *vi* **1** : boil **2** AJETREARSE : bustle, stir
bulto *nm* **1** : package, bundle **2** VOLUMEN : bulk, size **3** FORMA : form, shape **4** PRO-TUBERANCIA : lump, swelling
bumerán *nm, pl* **-ranes** : boomerang
buñuelo *nm* : fried pastry
buque *nm* : ship
burbujear *vi* : bubble — **burbuja** *nf* : bubble
burdel *nm* : brothel
burdo, -da *adj* : coarse, rough
burgués, -guesa *adj & n, mpl* **-gueses** : bourgeois — **burguesía** *nf* : bourgeoisie
burlar *vt* : trick, deceive — **burlarse** *vr* ~ **de** : make fun of — **burla** *nf* **1** MOFA : mockery, ridicule **2** BROMA : joke, trick
burlesco, -ca *adj* : comic, funny
burlón, -lona *adj, mpl* **-lones** : mocking
burocracia *nf* : bureaucracy — **burócrata** *nmf* : bureaucrat — **burocrático, -ca** *adj* : bureaucratic
burro, -rra *n* **1** : donkey **2** *fam* : dunce — ~ *adj* : stupid — **burro** *nm* **1** : sawhorse **2** *Lat* : stepladder
bus *nm* : bus
buscar {72} *vt* **1** : look for, seek **2 ir a** ~ **a uno** : fetch s.o. — *vi* : search — **busca** *nf* : search — **búsqueda** *nf* : search
busto *nm* : bust (in sculpture)
butaca *nf* **1** : armchair **2** : seat (in a theatre)
butano *nm* : butane
buzo *nm* : diver
buzón *nm, pl* **-zones** : mailbox
byte *nm* : byte

C

c *nf* : c, third letter of the Spanish alphabet
cabal *adj* **1** : exact **2** COMPLETO : complete — **cabales** *nmpl* **no estar en sus** ~ : not be in one's right mind
cabalgar {52} *vi* : ride — **cabalgata** *nf* : cavalcade
caballa *nf* : mackerel
caballería *nf* **1** : cavalry **2** CABALLO : horse, mount — **caballeriza** *nf* : stable
caballero *nm* **1** : gentleman **2** : knight (rank) — **caballerosidad** *nf* : chivalry — **caballeroso, -sa** *adj* : chivalrous

caballete *nm* **1** : ridge (of a roof) **2** : easel (for a canvas) **3** : bridge (of the nose)
caballito *nm* **1** : rocking horse **2** ~**s** *nmpl* : merry-go-round
caballo *nm* **1** : horse **2** : knight (in chess) **3** ~ **de fuerza** : horsepower
cabaña *nf* : cabin, hut
cabaret *nm, pl* **-rets** : nightclub, cabaret
cabecear *vi* **1** : shake one's head, nod **2** : pitch, lurch (of a boat)
cabecera *nf* **1** : head (of a bed, etc.) **2**

: heading (in a text) **3 médico de ~** : family doctor

cabecilla *nmf* : ringleader

cabello *nm* : hair — **cabelludo, -da** *adj* : hairy

caber {12} *vi* **1** : fit, go (into) **2 no cabe duda** : there's no doubt

cabestro *nm* : halter

cabeza *nf* **1** : head **2 de ~** : head first — **cabezada** *nf* **1** : butt (of the head) **2 dar ~s** : nod off

cabezal *nm* : bolster, headrest

cabida *nf* **1** : room, capacity **2 dar ~ a** : accomodate, find room for

cabina *nf* **1** : booth **2** : cab (of a truck, etc.) **3** : cabin, cockpit (of an airplane)

cabizbajo, -ja *adj* : downcast

cable *nm* : cable

cabo *nm* **1** : end, stub **2** TROZO : bit **3** : corporal (in the military) **4** : cape (in geography) **5 al fin y al ~** : after all **6 llevar a ~** : carry out, do

cabra *nf* : goat

cabriola *nf* **1** : leap, skip **2 hacer ~s** : prance around

cabrito *nm* : kid (goat)

cacahuate *or* **cacahuete** *nm* : peanut

cacao *nm* **1** : cacao (tree) **2** : cocoa (drink)

cacarear *vi* : crow, cackle — *vt fam* : boast about

cacería *nf* : hunt

cacerola *nf* : pan, saucepan

cacharro *nm* **1** *fam* : thing, piece of junk **2** *fam* : jalopy **3 ~s** *nmpl* : pots and pans

cachear *vt* : search, frisk

cachemir *nm or* **cachemira** *nf* : cashmere

cachete *nm Lat* : cheek — **cachetada** *nf Lat* : slap

cacho *nm* **1** *fam* : piece, bit **2** *Lat* : horn

cachorro, -rra *n* **1** : cub **2** PERRITO : puppy

cactus *or* **cacto** *nm* : cactus

cada *adj* : each, every

cadalso *nm* : scaffold

cadáver *nm* : corpse

cadena *nf* **1** : chain **2** : (television) channel **3 ~ de montaje** : assembly line

cadencia *nf* : cadence

cadera *nf* : hip

cadete *nm* : cadet

caducar {72} *vi* : expire — **caducidad** *nf* : expiration

caer {13} *vi* **1** : fall, drop **2 ~ bien a uno** : be to one's liking **3 dejar ~** : drop **4 me cae bien** : I like her, I like him — **caerse** *vr* : drop, fall (down)

café *nm* **1** : coffee **2** : café — **~** *adj Lat* : brown — **cafetera** *nf* : coffeepot — **cafetería** *nf* : coffee shop, cafeteria — **cafeína** *nf* : caffeine

caída *nf* **1** : fall, drop **2** PENDIENTE : slope

caimán *nm, pl* **-manes** : alligator

caja *nf* **1** : box, case **2** : checkout counter, cashier's desk (in a store) **3 ~ fuerte** : safe **4 ~ registradora** : cash register — **cajero, -ra** *n* **1** : cashier **2** : (bank) teller — **cajetilla** *nf* : pack (of cigarettes) — **cajón** *nm, pl* **-jones 1** : drawer (in furniture) **2** : large box, crate

cajuela *nf Lat* : trunk (of a car)

cal *nf* : lime

cala *nf* : cove

calabaza *nf* **1** : pumpkin, squash, gourd **2 dar ~s a** *fam* : give the brush-off to — **calabacín** *nm, pl* **-cines** *or* **calabacita** *nf Lat* : zucchini

calabozo *nm* **1** : prison **2** CELDA : cell

calamar *nm* : squid

calambre *nm* **1** ESPASMO : cramp **2** : (electric) shock

calamidad *nf* : calamity

calar *vt* **1** : soak (through) **2** PERFORAR : pierce — **calarse** *vr* : get drenched

calavera *nf* : skull

calcar {72} *vt* **1** : trace **2** IMITAR : copy, imitate

calcetín *nm, pl* **-tines** : sock

calcinar *vt* : char

calcio *nm* : calcium

calcomanía *nf* : decal

calcular *vt* : calculate, estimate — **calculador, -dora** *adj* : calculating — **calculadora** *nf* : calculator — **cálculo** *nm* **1** : calculation **2** : calculus (in mathematics and medicine) **3 ~ biliar** : gallstone

caldera *nf* **1** : cauldron **2** : boiler (for heating, etc.) — **caldo** *nm* : broth, stock

calefacción *nf, pl* **-ciones** : heating, heat

calendario *nm* : calendar

calentar {55} *vt* : heat (up), warm (up) — **calentarse** *vr* : get warm, heat up — **calentador** *nm* : heater — **calentura** *nf* : temperature, fever

calibre *nm* **1** : caliber **2** DIÁMETRO : bore, diameter — **calibrar** *vt* : calibrate

calidad *nf* **1** : quality **2 en ~ de** : as, in the capacity of

cálido, -da *adj* : hot, warm

calidoscopio *nm* : kaleidoscope

caliente *adj* **1** : hot **2** ACALORADO : heated, fiery

calificar {72} *vt* **1** : qualify **2** EVALUAR : rate **3** : grade (an exam, etc.) — **calificación** *nf, pl* **-ciones 1** : qualification **2** EVALUACIÓN : rating **3** NOTA : grade — **calificativo, -va** *adj* : qualifying — **calificativo** *nm* : qualifier, epithet

caligrafía *nf* : penmanship

calistenia *nf* : calisthenics

cáliz

cáliz *nm, pl* **-lices** : chalice
caliza *nf* : limestone
callar *vi* : keep quiet, be silent — *vt* **1** : silence, hush **2** OCULTAR : keep secret — **callarse** *vr* : remain silent — **callado, -da** *adj* : quiet, silent
calle *nf* : street, road — **callejear** *vi* : wander about the streets — **callejero, -ra** *adj* **1** : street **2 perro callejero** : stray dog — **callejón** *nm, pl* **-jones 1** : alley **2 ~ sin salida** : dead-end street
callo *nm* : callus, corn
calma *nf* : calm, quiet — **calmante** *adj* : soothing — **~** *nm* : tranquilizer — **calmar** *vt* : calm, soothe — **calmarse** *vr* : calm down — **calmo, -ma** *adj Lat* : calm — **calmoso, -sa** *adj* **1** : calm **2** LENTO : slow
calor *nm* **1** : heat, warmth **2 tener ~** : be hot — **caloría** *nf* : calorie
calumnia *nf* : slander, libel — **calumniar** *vt* : slander, libel
caluroso, -sa *adj* **1** : hot **2** : warm, enthusiastic (of applause, etc.)
calvo, -va *adj* : bald — **calvicie** *nf* : baldness
calza *nf* : wedge
calzada *nf* : roadway
calzado *nm* : footwear — **calzar** {21} *vt* **1** : wear (shoes) **2** : put shoes on (s.o.)
calzones *nmpl Lat* : panties — **calzoncillos** *nmpl* : underpants, briefs
cama *nf* : bed
camada *nf* : litter, brood
camafeo *nm* : cameo
cámara *nf* **1** : chamber **2** *or* **~ fotográfica** : camera **3** : house (in government)
camarada *nmf* : comrade — **camaradería** *nf* : camaraderie
camarero, -ra *n* **1** : waiter, waitress *f* **2** : steward *m*, stewardess *f* (on a ship, etc.) — **camarera** *nf* : chambermaid *f*
camarón *nm, pl* **-rones** : shrimp
camarote *nm* : cabin, stateroom
cambiar *vt* **1** : change **2** CANJEAR : exchange — *vi* **1** : change **2** : shift gears (of an automobile) — **cambiarse** *vr* **1** : change (clothing) **2** : move (to a new address) — **cambiable** *adj* : changeable — **cambio** *nm* **1** : change **2** CANJE : exchange **3 en ~** : on the other hand
camello *nm* : camel
camilla *nf* : stretcher — **camillero** *nm* : orderly (in a hospital)
caminar *vi* : walk — *vt* : cover (a distance) — **caminata** *nf* : hike
camino *nm* **1** : road, path **2** RUTA : way **3 a medio ~** : halfway (there) **4 ponerse en ~** : set out
camión *nm, pl* **-miones 1** : truck **2** *Lat* : bus — **camionero, -ra** *n* **1** : truck driver **2** *Lat* : bus driver — **camioneta** *nm* : light truck, van
camisa *nf* **1** : shirt **2 ~ de fuerza** : straitjacket — **camiseta** *nf* : T-shirt, undershirt — **camisón** *nm, pl* **-sones** : nightshirt, nightgown
camorra *nf fam* : fight, trouble
camote *nm Lat* : sweet potato
campamento *nm* : camp
campana *nf* : bell — **campanada** *nf* : stroke (of a bell), peal — **campanario** *nm* : bell tower — **campanilla** *nf* : (small) bell
campaña *nf* **1** : countryside **2** : (military or political) campaign
campeón, -peona *n, mpl* **-peones** : champion — **campeonato** *nm* : championship
campesino, -na *n* : peasant, farm laborer — **campestre** *adj* : rural, rustic
camping *nm* **1** : campsite **2 hacer ~** : go camping
campiña *nf* : countryside
campo *nm* **1** : field **2** CAMPIÑA : countryside, country **3** CAMPAMENTO : camp
camuflaje *nm* : camouflage — **camuflar** *vt* : camouflage
cana *nf* : gray hair
canadiense *adj* : Canadian
canal *nm* **1** : canal **2** MEDIO : channel **3** : (radio or television) channel — **canalizar** {21} *vt* : channel
canalete *nm* : paddle (of a canoe)
canalla *nf* : rabble — **~** *nmf fam* : swine, bastard
canapé *nm* **1** : canapé **2** SOFÁ : sofa, couch
canario *nm* : canary
canasta *nf* : basket — **canasto** *nm* : large basket
cancelar *vt* **1** : cancel **2** : pay off, settle (a debt) — **cancelación** *nf, pl* **-ciones 1** : cancellation **2** : payment in full (of a debt)
cáncer *nm* : cancer — **canceroso, -sa** *adj* : cancerous
cancha *nf* : court, field (for sports)
canciller *nm* : chancellor
canción *nf, pl* **-ciones 1** : song **2 ~ de cuna** : lullaby — **cancionero** *nm* : songbook
candado *nm* : padlock
candela *nf* : candle — **candelabro** *nm* : candelabra — **candelero** *nm* **1** : candlestick **2 estar en el ~** : be in the limelight
candente *adj* : red-hot
candidato, -ta *n* : candidate — **candidatura** *nf* : candidacy
cándido, -da *adj* : naïve — **candidez** *nf* **1** : simplicity **2** INGENUIDAD : naïveté
candil *nm* : oil lamp — **candilejas** *nfpl* : footlights
candor *nm* : naïveté, innocence

canela *nf* : cinnamon
cangrejo *nm* : crab
canguro *nm* : kangaroo
caníbal *nmf* : cannibal — **canibalismo** *nm* : cannibalism
canicas *nfpl* : (game of) marbles
canino, -na *adj* : canine — **canino** *nm* : canine (tooth)
canjear *vt* : exchange — **canje** *nm* : exchange, trade
cano, -na *adj* : gray, gray-haired
canoa *nf* : canoe
canon *nm, pl* **cánones** : canon
canonizar {21} *vt* : canonize
canoso, -sa *adj* : gray, gray-haired
cansar *vt* : tire (out) — *vi* : be tiring — **cansarse** *vr* : get tired — **cansado, -da** *adj* **1** : tired **2** PESADO : tiresome — **cansancio** *nm* : fatigue, weariness
cantalupo *nm* : cantaloupe
cantar *v* : sing — ~ *nm* : song — **cantante** *nmf* : singer
cántaro *nm* **1** : pitcher, jug **2 llover a** ~**s** *fam* : rain cats and dogs
cantera *nf* : quarry (excavation)
cantidad *nf* **1** : quantity, amount **2 una** ~ **de** : lots of
cantimplora *nf* : canteen, water bottle
cantina *nf* **1** : canteen, cafeteria **2** *Lat* : tavern, bar
canto *nm* **1** : singing, song **2** BORDE, LADO : edge **3 de** ~ : on end, sideways **4** ~ **rodado** : boulder — **cantor, -tora** *adj* **1** : singing **2 pájaro** ~ : songbird — ~ *n* : singer
caña *nf* **1** : cane, reed **2** ~ **de pescar** : fishing pole
cáñamo *nm* : hemp
cañería *nf* : pipes, piping — **caño** *nm* **1** : pipe **2** : spout (of a fountain) — **cañón** *nm, pl* **-ñones 1** : cannon **2** : barrel (of a gun) **3** : canyon (in geography)
caoba *nf* : mahogany
caos *nm* : chaos — **caótico, -ca** *adj* : chaotic
capa *nf* **1** : cape, cloak **2** : coat (of paint, etc.), coating (in cooking) **3** ESTRATO : layer, stratum **4** : (social) class
capacidad *nf* **1** : capacity **2** APTITUD : ability
capacitar *vt* : train, qualify — **capacitación** *nf, pl* **-ciones** : training
caparazón *nm, pl* **-zones** : shell
capataz *nmf, pl* **-taces** : foreman
capaz *adj, pl* **-paces 1** : capable, able **2** ESPACIOSO : spacious
capellán *nm, pl* **-llanes** : chaplain
capilla *nf* : chapel
capital *adj* **1** : capital **2** PRINCIPAL : chief, principal — ~ *nm* : capital (assets) — ~

nf : capital (city) — **capitalismo** *nm* : capitalism — **capitalista** *adj & nmf* : capitalist, capitalistic — **capitalizar** {21} *vt* : capitalize
capitán, -tana *n, mpl* **-tanes** : captain
capitolio *nm* : capitol
capitular *vi* : capitulate, surrender — **capitulación** *nf, pl* **-ciones** : surrender
capítulo *nm* : chapter
capó *nm* : hood (of a car)
capote *nm* : cloak, cape
capricho *nm* : whim, caprice — **caprichoso, -sa** *adj* : whimsical, capricious
cápsula *nf* : capsule
captar *vt* **1** : grasp **2** ATRAER : gain, attract (interest, etc.) **3** : harness (waters)
capturar *vt* : capture, seize — **captura** *nf* : capture, seizure
capucha *nf* : hood (of clothing)
capullo *nm* **1** : cocoon **2** : (flower) bud
caqui *adj & nm* : khaki
cara *nf* **1** : face **2** ASPECTO : appearance **3** *fam* : nerve, gall **4** ~ **a** *or* **de** ~ **a** : facing
carabina *nf* : carbine
caracol *nm* **1** : snail **2** *Lat* : conch **3** RIZO : curl
carácter *nm, pl* **-racteres 1** : character **2** ÍNDOLE : nature — **característica** *nf* : characteristic — **característico, -ca** *adj* : characteristic — **caracterizar** {21} *vt* : characterize
caramba *interj* : oh my!, good grief!
carámbano *nm* : icicle
caramelo *nm* **1** : caramel **2** DULCE : candy
carátula *nf* **1** CARETA : mask **2** : jacket (of a record, etc.) **3** *Lat* : face (of a watch)
caravana *nf* **1** : caravan **2** REMOLQUE : trailer
caray → **caramba**
carbohidrato *nm* : carbohydrate
carbón *nm, pl* **-bones 1** : coal **2** : charcoal (for drawing) — **carboncillo** *nm* : charcoal — **carbonero, -ra** *adj* : coal — **carbonizar** {21} *vt* : char — **carbono** *nm* : carbon —
carburador *nm* : carburetor — **carburante** *nm* : fuel
carcajada *nf* : loud laugh, guffaw
cárcel *nf* : jail, prison — **carcelero, -ra** *n* : jailer
carcinógeno *nm* : carcinogen
carcomer *vt* : eat away at — **carcomido, -da** *adj* : worm-eaten
cardenal *nm* **1** : cardinal **2** CONTUSIÓN : bruise
cardíaco *or* **cardiaco, -ca** *adj* : cardiac, heart
cárdigan *nm, pl* **-gans** : cardigan
cardinal *adj* : cardinal
cardiólogo, -ga *n* : cardiologist

cardo *nm* : thistle

carear *vt* : bring face-to-face

carecer {53} *vi* ~ **de** : lack — **carencia** *nf* : lack, want — **carente** *adj* ~ **de** : lacking (in)

carestía *nf* 1 : high cost 2 ESCASEZ : dearth, scarcity

careta *nf* : mask

cargar {52} *vt* 1 : load 2 : charge (a battery, a purchase, etc.) 3 LLEVAR : carry 4 ~ **de** : burden with — *vi* 1 : load 2 ~ **con** : pick up, carry away — **carga** *nf* 1 : load 2 CARGAMENTO : freight, cargo 3 RESPONSABILIDAD : burden 4 : charge (in electricity, etc.) — **cargado, -da** *adj* 1 : loaded, burdened 2 PESADO : heavy, stuffy 3 : charged (of a battery) 4 FUERTE : strong, concentrated — **cargamento** *nm* : cargo, load — **cargo** *nm* 1 : charge 2 PUESTO : position, office

cariarse *vr* : decay (of teeth)

caribe *adj* : Caribbean

caricatura *nf* 1 : caricature 2 : (political) cartoon — **caricaturizar** *vt* : caricature

caricia *nf* : caress

caridad *nf* 1 : charity 2 LIMOSNA : alms *pl*

caries *nfs & pl* : cavity (in a tooth)

cariño *nm* : affection, love — **cariñoso, -sa** *adj* : affectionate, loving

carisma *nf* : charisma — **carismático, -ca** *adj* : charismatic

caritativo, -va *adj* : charitable

cariz *nm, pl* **-rices** : appearance, aspect

carmesí *adj & nm* : crimson

carmín *nm, pl* **-mines** *or* ~ **de labios** : lipstick

carnada *nf* : bait

carnal *adj* 1 : carnal 2 **primo** ~ : first cousin

carnaval *nm* : carnival

carne *nf* 1 : meat 2 : flesh (of persons or fruits) 3 ~ **de cerdo** : pork 4 ~ **de gallina** : goose bumps 5 ~ **de ternera** : veal

carné *nm* → **carnet**

carnero *nm* 1 : ram, sheep 2 : mutton (in cooking)

carnet *nm* 1 ~ **de conducir** : driver's license 2 ~ **de identidad** : identification card, ID

carnicería *nf* 1 : butcher shop 2 MATANZA : slaughter — **carnicero, -ra** *n* : butcher

carnívoro, -ra *adj* : carnivorous — **carnívoro** *nm* : carnivore

carnoso, -sa *adj* : fleshy

caro, -ra *adj* 1 : expensive 2 QUERIDO : dear — **caro** *adv* : dearly

carpa *nf* 1 : carp 2 TIENDA : tent

carpeta *nf* : folder

carpintería *nf* : carpentry — **carpintero, -ra** *n* : carpenter

carraspear *vi* : clear one's throat — **carraspera** *nf* 1 : hoarseness 2 **tener** ~ : have a frog in one's throat

carrera *nf* 1 : running, run 2 COMPETICIÓN : race 3 : course (of studies) 4 PROFESIÓN : career, profession

carreta *nf* : cart, wagon

carrete *nm* : reel, spool

carretera *nf* : highway, road

carretilla *nf* : wheelbarrow

carril *nm* 1 : lane (of a road) 2 : rail (for a railroad)

carrillo *nm* : cheek

carrito *nm* : cart, trolley

carrizo *nm* : reed

carro *nm* 1 : wagon, cart 2 *Lat* : automobile, car — **carrocería** *nf* : body (of an automobile)

carroña *nf* : carrion

carroza *nf* 1 : carriage 2 : float (in a parade)

carruaje *nm* : carriage

carrusel *nm* : merry-go-round, carousel

carta *nf* 1 : letter 2 NAIPE : playing card 3 : charter (of an organization, etc.) 4 MENÚ : menu 5 MAPA : map, chart

cartel *nm* : poster, bill — **cartelera** *nf* : billboard

cartera *nf* 1 : briefcase 2 BILLETERA : wallet 3 *Lat* : pocketbook, handbag — **carterista** *nmf* : pickpocket

cartero, -ra *nm* : mail carrier, mailman *m*

cartílago *nm* : cartilage

cartilla *nf* 1 : primer, reader 2 : booklet, record (of a savings account, etc.)

cartón *nm, pl* **-tones** 1 : cardboard 2 : carton (of cigarettes, etc.)

cartucho *nm* : cartridge

casa *nf* 1 : house 2 HOGAR : home 3 EMPRESA : company, firm 4 ~ **flotante** : houseboat

casar *vt* : marry — *vi* : go together, match up — **casarse** *vr* 1 : get married 2 ~ **con** : marry — **casado, -da** *adj* : married — **casamiento** *nm* 1 : marriage 2 BODA : wedding

cascabel *nm* : small bell

cascada *nf* : waterfall

cascanueces *nms & pl* : nutcracker

cascar {72} *vt* : crack (a shell, etc.) — **cascarse** *vr* : crack, chip — **cáscara** *nf* : skin, peel, shell — **cascarón** *nm, pl* **-rones** : eggshell

casco *nm* 1 : helmet 2 : hull (of a boat) 3 : hoof (of a horse) 4 : fragment (of ceramics, etc.) 5 : center (of a town) 6 ENVASE : empty bottle

caserío *nm* **1** *Spain* : country house **2** POBLADO : hamlet

casero, -ra *adj* **1** : homemade **2** DOMÉS- TICO : domestic, household — **~** *n* : land- lord, landlady *f*

caseta *nf* : booth, stall

casete → **cassette**

casi *adv* **1** : almost, nearly **2** (*in negative phrases*) : hardly

casilla *nf* **1** : compartment, pigeonhole **2** CASETA : booth **3** : box (on a form)

casino *nm* **1** : casino **2** : (social) club

caso *nm* **1** : case **2 en ~ de** : in the event of **3 hacer ~** : pay attention **4 no venir al ~** : be beside the point

caspa *nf* : dandruff

cassette *nmf* : cassette

casta *nf* **1** : lineage, descent **2** : breed (of animals) **3** : caste (in India)

castaña *nf* : chestnut

castañetear *vi* : chatter (of teeth)

castaño, -ña *adj* : chestnut (color)

castañuela *nf* : castanet

castellano *nm* : Spanish, Castilian (lan- guage)

castidad *nf* : chastity

castigar {52} *vt* **1** : punish **2** : penalize (in sports) — **castigo** *nm* **1** : punishment **2** : penalty (in sports)

castillo *nm* : castle

casto, -ta *adj* : chaste, pure — **castizo, -za** *adj* : pure, traditional (in style)

castor *nm* : beaver

castrar *vt* : castrate

castrense *adj* : military

casual *adj* : chance, accidental — **casuali- dad** *nf* **1** : coincidence **2 por ~** *or* **de ~** : by chance — **casualmente** *adv* : by chance

cataclismo *nm* : cataclysm

catalán, -lana *adj, mpl* **-lanes** : Catalan — **catalán** *nm* : Catalan (language)

catalizador *nm* : catalyst

catalogar {52} *vt* : catalog, classify — **catálogo** *nm* : catalog

catapulta *nf* : catapult

catar *vt* : taste, sample

catarata *nf* **1** : waterfall **2** : cataract (in medicine)

catarro *nm* RESFRIADO : cold

catástrofe *nf* : catastrophe, disaster — **cata- strófico, -ca** *adj* : catastrophic, disastrous

catecismo *nm* : catechism

cátedra *nf* : chair (at a university)

catedral *nf* : cathedral

catedrático, -ca *n* : professor

categoría *nf* **1** : category **2** RANGO : rank **3 de ~** : first-rate — **categórico, -ca** *adj* : categorical

católico, -ca *adj & n* : Catholic — **catoli- cismo** *nm* : Catholicism

catorce *adj & nm* : fourteen — **catorceavo** *nm* : fourteenth

catre *nm* : cot

cauce *nm* **1** : riverbed **2** VÍA : channel, means *pl*

caucho *nm* : rubber

caución *nf, pl* **-ciones** : security, guarantee

caudal *nm* **1** : volume of water, flow **2** RIQUEZA : wealth

caudillo *nm* : leader, commander

causar *vt* : cause, provoke — **causa** *nf* **1** : cause **2** RAZÓN : reason **3** : case (in law) **4 a ~ de** : because of

cáustico, -ca *adj* : caustic

cautela *nf* : caution — **cauteloso, -sa** *adj* : cautious — **cautelosamente** *adv* : cau- tiously, warily

cautivar *vt* **1** : capture **2** ENCANTAR : capti- vate — **cautiverio** *nm* : captivity — **cau- tivo, -va** *adj & n* : captive

cauto, -ta *adj* : cautious

cavar *v* : dig

caverna *nf* : cavern, cave

cavidad *nf* : cavity

cavilar *vi* : ponder

cayado *nm* : crook, staff

cazar {21} *vt* **1** : hunt **2** ATRAPAR : catch, bag — *vi* : go hunting — **caza** *nf* **1** : hunt, hunting **2** : game (animals) — **cazador, -dora** *n* : hunter

cazo *nm* **1** : saucepan **2** CUCHARÓN : ladle — **cazuela** *nf* : casserole

CD *nm* : CD, compact disc

cebada *nf* : barley

cebar *vt* **1** : bait **2** : feed, fatten (animals) **3** : prime (a firearm, etc.) — **cebo** *nm* **1** CAR- NADA : bait **2** : charge (of a firearm)

cebolla *nf* : onion — **cebolleta** *nf* : scallion, green onion — **cebollino** *nm* : chive

cebra *nf* : zebra

cecear *vi* : lisp — **ceceo** *nm* : lisp

cedazo *nm* : sieve

ceder *vi* **1** : yield, give way **2** DISMINUIR : diminish, abate — *vt* : cede, hand over

cedro *nm* : cedar

cédula *nf* : document, certificate

cegar {49} *vt* **1** : blind **2** TAPAR : block, stop up — *vi* : be blinded, go blind — **ceguera** *nf* : blindness

ceja *nf* : eyebrow

cejar *vi* : give in, back down

celada *nf* : trap, ambush

celador, -dora *n* : guard, warden

celda *nf* : cell (of a jail)

celebrar *vt* **1** : celebrate **2** : hold (a meet- ing), say (Mass) **3** ALEGRARSE DE : be happy about — **celebrarse** *vr* : take place

— **celebración** *nf, pl* **-ciones** : celebration
— **célebre** *adj* : famous, celebrated —
celebridad *nf* : celebrity
celeridad *nf* : swiftness, speed
celeste *adj* **1** : celestial, heavenly **2** *or* **azul**
~ : sky blue — **celestial** *adj* : celestial,
heavenly
celibato *nm* : celibacy — **célibe** *adj* : celibate
celo *nm* **1** : zeal **2 en ~** : in heat **3 ~s**
nmpl : jealousy **4 tener ~s** : be jealous
celofán *nm, pl* **-fanes** : cellophane
celoso, -sa *adj* **1** : jealous **2** DILIGENTE
: zealous
célula *nf* : cell — **celular** *adj* : cellular
celulosa *nf* : cellulose
cementerio *nm* : cemetery
cemento *nm* **1** : cement **2 ~ armado** : reinforced concrete
cena *nf* : supper, dinner
cenagal *nm* : bog, quagmire — **cenagoso**
adj : swampy
cenar *vi* : have dinner, have supper — *vt*
: have for dinner or supper
cenicero *nm* : ashtray
cenit *nm* : zenith
ceniza *nf* : ash
censo *nm* : census
censurar *vt* **1** : censor **2** REPROBAR : censure, criticize — **censura** *nf* **1** : censorship
2 REPROBACIÓN : censure, criticism
centavo *nm* **1** : cent **2** : centavo (unit of currency)
centellear *vi* : sparkle, twinkle — **centella**
nf **1** : flash **2** CHISPA : spark — **centelleo**
nm : twinkling, sparkle
centenar *nm* : hundred — **centenario** *nm*
: centennial
centeno *nm* : rye
centésimo, -ma *adj* : hundredth
centígrado *adj* : centigrade, Celsius
centigramo *nm* : centigram
centímetro *nm* : centimeter
centinela *nmf* : sentinel, sentry
central *adj* : central — **~** *nf* : main office,
headquarters — **centralita** *nf* : switchboard
— **centralizar** {21} *vt* : centralize
centrar *vt* : center — **centrarse** *vr* **~ en**
: focus on — **céntrico, -ca** *adj* : central —
centro *nm* **1** : center **2** : downtown (of a
city) **3 ~ de mesa** : centerpiece
centroamericano, -na *adj* : Central American
ceñir {67} *vt* **1** : encircle **2** : fit (s.o.) tightly
— **ceñirse** *vr* **~ a** : limit oneself to —
ceñido, -da *adj* : tight
ceño *nm* **1** : frown **2 fruncir el ~** : knit
one's brow, frown
cepillo *nm* **1** : brush **2** : (carpenter's) plane

3 ~ de dientes : toothbrush — **cepillar** *vt*
1 : brush **2** : plane (wood)
cera *nf* **1** : wax, beeswax **2** : floor wax, furniture wax
cerámica *nf* **1** : ceramics *pl* **2** : (piece of)
pottery
cerca¹ *nf* : fence — **cercado** *nm* : enclosure
cerca² *adv* **1** : close, near **2 ~ de** : near,
close to **3 ~ de** : nearly, almost — **cercano, -na** *adj* : near, close — **cercanía** *nf* **1**
: proximity **2 ~s** *nfpl* : outskirts
cercar {72} *vt* **1** : fence in **2** RODEAR : surround
cerciorarse *vr* **~ de** : make sure of
cerco *nm* **1** : circle, ring **2** ASEDIO : siege **3**
Lat : fence
cerda *nf* : bristle
cerdo *nm* **1** : pig, hog **2 ~ macho** : boar
cereal *adj & nm* : cereal
cerebro *nm* : brain — **cerebral** *adj* : cerebral
ceremonia *nf* : ceremony — **ceremonial** *adj*
: ceremonial — **ceremonioso, -sa** *adj* : ceremonious
cereza *nf* : cherry
cerilla *nf* : match — **cerillo** *nm* *Lat* : match
cerner {56} *or* **cernir** *vt* : sift — **cernerse** *vr*
1 : hover **2 ~ sobre** : loom over — **cernidor** *nm* : sieve
cero *nm* : zero
cerrar {55} *vt* **1** : close, shut **2** : turn off (a
faucet, etc.) **3** : bring to an end — *vi* **1**
: close up, lock up **2** : close down (a business, etc.) — **cerrarse** *vr* **1** : close, shut **2**
TERMINAR : come to a close, end — **cerrado, -da** *adj* **1** : closed, shut, locked **2**
: overcast (of weather) **3** : sharp (of a
curve) **4** : thick, broad (of an accent) — **cerradura** *nf* : lock — **cerrajero, -ra** *n* : locksmith
cerro *nm* : hill
cerrojo *nm* : bolt, latch
certamen *nm, pl* **-támenes** : competition,
contest
certero, -ra *adj* : accurate, precise
certeza *nf* : certainty — **certidumbre** *nf*
: certainty
certificar {72} *vt* **1** : certify **2** : register
(mail) — **certificado, -da** *adj* : certified,
registered — **certificado** *nm* : certificate
cervato *nm* : fawn
cerveza *nf* **1** : beer **2 ~ de barril** : draft
beer — **cervecería** *nf* **1** : brewery **2** BAR
: beer hall, bar
cesar *vi* : cease, stop — *vt* : dismiss, lay off
— **cesación** *nf, pl* **-ciones** : cessation, suspension — **cesante** *adj* **1** : laid off **2** *Lat*
: unemployed — **cesantía** *nf Lat* : unemployment
cesárea *nf* : cesarean (section)

cese *nm* **1** : cessation, stop **2** DESTITUCIÓN : dismissal

césped *nm* : lawn, grass

cesta *nf* : basket — **cesto** *nm* **1** : (large) basket **2** ~ **de basura** : wastebasket

cetro *nm* : scepter

chabacano *nm Lat* : apricot

chabola *nf Spain* : shack, shanty

chacal *nm* : jackal

cháchara *nf fam* : gabbing, chatter

chacra *nf Lat* : (small) farm

chafar *vt fam* : flatten, crush

chal *nm* : shawl

chaleco *nm* : vest

chalet *nm Spain* : house

chalupa *nf* **1** : small boat **2** *Lat* : small stuffed tortilla

chamarra *nf* : jacket

chamba *nf Lat fam* : job

champaña *or* **champán** *nm* : champagne

champiñón *nm, pl* **-ñones** : mushroom

champú *nm, pl* **-pús** *or* **-púes** : shampoo

chamuscar {72} *vt* : scorch

chance *nm Lat* : chance, opportunity

chancho *nm Lat* : pig

chanclos *nmpl* : galoshes

chantaje *nm* : blackmail — **chantajear** *vt* : blackmail

chanza *nf* : joke, jest

chapa *nf* **1** : sheet, plate **2** INSIGNIA : badge — **chapado, -da** *adj* **1** : plated **2 chapado a la antigua** : old-fashioned

chaparrón *nm, pl* **-rrones** : downpour

chapotear *vi* : splash

chapucero, -ra *adj* : shoddy, sloppy — **chapuza** *nf* : botched job

chapuzón *nm, pl* **-zones** : dip, short swim

chaqueta *nf* : jacket

charca *nf* : pond — **charco** *nm* : puddle

charlar *vi* : chat — **charla** *nf* : chat, talk — **charlatán, -tana** *adj, mpl* **-tanes** : talkative — ~ *n* **1** : chatterbox **2** FARSANTE : charlatan

charol *nm* **1** : patent leather **2** BARNIZ : varnish

chasco *nm* **1** : trick, joke **2** DECEPCIÓN : disappointment

chasis *nms & pl* : chassis

chasquear *vt* **1** : click (the tongue), snap (one's fingers) **2** : crack (a whip) — **chasquido** *nm* **1** : click, snap **2** : crack (of a whip)

chatarra *nf* : scrap (metal)

chato, -ta *adj* **1** : pug-nosed **2** APLANADO : flat

chauvinismo *nm* : chauvinism — **chauvinista** *adj* : chauvinist, chauvinistic

chaval, -vala *n fam* : kid, boy *m*, girl *f*

checo, -ca *adj* : Czech — **checo** *nm* : Czech (language)

chef *nm* : chef

cheque *nm* : check — **chequera** *nf* : checkbook

chequear *vt Lat* **1** : check, inspect, verify **2** : check in (baggage) — **chequeo** *nm* **1** : (medical) checkup **2** *Lat* : check, inspection

chica → **chico**

chicano, -na *adj* : Chicano, Mexican-American

chícharo *nm Lat* : pea

chicharrón *nm, pl* **-rrones** : pork rind

chichón *nm, pl* **-chones** : bump

chicle *nm* : chewing gum

chico, -ca *adj* : little, small — ~ *n* : child, boy *m*, girl *f*

chiflar *vt* : whistle at, boo — *vi Lat* : whistle — **chiflado, -da** *adj fam* : crazy, nuts — **chiflido** *nm* : whistling

chile *nm* : chili pepper

chileno, -na *adj* : Chilean

chillar *vi* **1** : shriek, scream **2** CHIRRIAR : screech, squeal — **chillido** *nm* **1** : scream **2** CHIRRIDO : screech, squeal — **chillón, -llona** *adj, mpl* **-llones** : shrill, loud

chimenea *nf* **1** : chimney **2** HOGAR : fireplace

chimpancé *nm* : chimpanzee

chinche *nf* : bedbug

chino, -na *adj* : Chinese — **chino** *nm* : Chinese (language)

chiquillo, -lla *n* : kid, child

chiquito, -ta *adj* : tiny — ~ *n* : little child, tot

chiribita *nf* : spark

chiripa *nf* **1** : fluke **2 de** ~ : by sheer luck

chirivia *nf* : parsnip

chirriar {85} *vi* **1** : squeak, creak **2** : screech (of brakes, etc.) — **chirrido** *nm* **1** : squeak, creak **2** : screech (of brakes)

chisme *nm* : (piece of) gossip — **chismear** *vi* : gossip — **chismoso, -sa** *adj* : gossipy — ~ *n* : gossip

chispear *vi* : spark — **chispa** *nf* : spark

chisporrotear *vi* : crackle, sizzle — **chisporroteo** *nm* : crackle

chiste *nm* : joke, funny story — **chistoso, -sa** *adj* : funny, witty

chivo, -va *n* : kid, young goat

chocar {72} *vi* **1** : crash, collide **2** ENFRENTARSE : clash — **chocante** *adj* **1** : striking, shocking **2** *Lat* : unpleasant, rude

choclo *nm Lat* : ear of corn, corncob

chocolate *nm* : chocolate

chofer *or* **chófer** *nm* **1** : chauffeur **2** CONDUCTOR : driver

choque *nm* **1** : shock **2** : crash, collision (of vehicles) **3** CONFLICTO : clash

chorizo *nm* : chorizo, sausage

chorrear *vi* **1** : drip **2** BROTAR : pour out, gush — **chorro** *nm* **1** : stream, jet **2** HILO : trickle

chovinismo → **chauvinismo**

choza *nf* : hut, shack

chubasco *nm* : downpour, squall

chuchería *nf* **1** : knickknack, trinket **2** DULCE : sweet

chueco, -ca *adj Lat* : crooked

chuleta *nf* : cutlet, chop

chulo, -la *adj fam* : cute, pretty

chupar *vt* **1** : suck **2** ABSORBER : absorb *fam* : guzzle — *vi* : suckle — **chupada** *nf* : suck, sucking — **chupete** *nm* **1** : pacifier **2** *Lat* : lollipop

churro *nm* **1** : fried dough **2** *fam* : botch, mess

chusco, -ca *adj* : funny

chusma *nf* : riffraff, rabble

chutar *vi* : shoot (in soccer)

cianuro *nm* : cyanide

cicatriz *nf, pl* **-trices** : scar — **cicatrizar** {21} *vi* : form a scar, heal

cíclico, -ca *adj* : cyclical

ciclismo *nm* : cycling — **ciclista** *nmf* : cyclist

ciclo *nm* : cycle

ciclón *nm, pl* **-clones** : cyclone

ciego, -ga *adj* : blind — **ciegamente** *adv* : blindly

cielo *nm* **1** : sky **2** : heaven (in religion)

ciempiés *nms & pl* : centipede

cien *adj* : a hundred, hundred — **~** *nm* : one hundred

ciénaga *nf* : swamp, bog

ciencia *nf* **1** : science **2 a ~ cierta** : for a fact

cieno *nm* : mire, mud, silt

científico, -ca *adj* : scientific — **~** *n* : scientist

ciento *adj* (*used in compound numbers*) : one hundred — **~** *nm* **1** : hundred, group of a hundred **2 por ~** : percent

cierre *nm* **1** : closing, closure **2** BROCHE : fastener, clasp

cierto, -ta *adj* **1** : true **2** SEGURO : certain **3 por ~** : as a matter of fact

ciervo, -va *n* : deer, stag *m*, hind *f*

cifra *nf* **1** : number, figure **2** : sum (of money, etc.) **3** CLAVE : code, cipher — **cifrar** *vt* **1** : write in code **2 ~ la esperanza en** : pin all one's hopes on

cigarrillo *nm* : cigarrette — **cigarro** *nm* **1** : cigarette **2** PURO : cigar

cigüeña *nf* : stork

cilantro *nm* : cilantro, coriander

cilindro *nm* : cylinder — **cilíndrico, -ca** *adj* : cylindrical

cima *nf* : peak, summit

címbalo *nm* : cymbal

cimbrar *or* **cimbrear** *vt* : shake, rock — **cimbrarse** *or* **cimbrearse** *vr* : sway

cimentar {55} *vt* **1** : lay the foundation of **2** : cement, strengthen (relations, etc.) — **cimientos** *nmpl* : base, foundation(s)

cinc *nm* : zinc

cincel *nm* : chisel — **cincelar** *vt* : chisel

cinco *adj & nm* : five

cincuenta *adj & nm* : fifty — **cincuentavo, -va** *adj* : fiftieth — **cincuentavo** *nm* : fiftieth

cine *nm* **1** : cinema, movies *pl* — **cinematográfico, -ca** *adj* : movie, film

cínico, -ca *adj* : cynical — **~** *n* : cynic — **cinismo** *nm* : cynicism

cinta *nf* **1** : ribbon, band **2 ~ adhesiva** : adhesive tape **3 ~ métrica** : tape measure **4 ~ magnetofónica** : magnetic tape

cinto *nm* : belt, girdle — **cintura** *nf* : waist — **cinturón** *nm, pl* **-rones 1** : belt **2 ~ de seguridad** : seat belt

ciprés *nm, pl* **-preses** : cypress

circo *nm* : circus

circuito *nm* : circuit

circulación *nf, pl* **-ciones 1** : circulation **2** TRÁFICO : traffic — **circular** *vi* **1** : circulate **2** : drive (a vehicle) — **~** *adj* : circular

círculo *nm* : circle

circuncidar *vt* : circumcise — **circuncisión** *nf, pl* **-siones** : circumcision

circundar *vt* : surround

circunferencia *nf* : circumference

circunscribir {33} *vt* : confine, limit — **circunscribirse** *vr* **~ a** : limit oneself to — **circunscripción** *nf, pl* **-ciones** : district, constituency

circunspecto, -ta *adj* : circumspect, cautious

circunstancia *nf* : circumstance — **circunstancial** *adj* : chance — **circunstante** *nmf* **1** : bystander **2 los ~s** : those present

circunvalación *nf, pl* **-ciones 1** : encircling **2 carretera de ~** : bypass

cirio *nm* : candle

ciruela *nf* **1** : plum **2 ~ pasa** : prune

cirugía *nf* : surgery — **cirujano, -na** *n* : surgeon

cisma *nf* : schism

cisne *nm* : swan

cisterna *nf* : cistern

cita *nf* **1** : appointment, date **2** REFERENCIA : quote, quotation — **citación** *nf, pl* **-ciones** : summons — **citar** *vt* **1** : quote, cite **2** CONVOCAR : make an appointment with **3** : summon (in law) — **citarse** *vr* **~ con** : arrange to meet

cítrico *nm* : citrus (fruit)

ciudad *nf* : city, town — **ciudadano, -na** *n* 1 : citizen 2 HABITANTE : resident — **ciudadanía** *nf* : citizenship

cívico, -ca *adj* : civic

civil *adj* : civil — **~** *nmf* : civilian — **civilidad** *nf* : civility — **civilización** *nf, pl* **-ciones** : civilization — **civilizar** {21} *vt* : civilize

cizaña *nf* : discord, rift

clamar *vi* : clamor, cry out — **clamor** *nm* : clamor, outcry — **clamoroso, -sa** *adj* : clamorous, loud

clan *nm* : clan

clandestino, -na *adj* : clandestine, secret

clara *nf* : egg white

claraboya *nf* : skylight

claramente *adv* : clearly

clarear *v impers* 1 : dawn 2 ACLARAR : clear up — *vi* : be transparent

claridad *nf* 1 : clarity, clearness 2 LUZ : light

clarificar {72} *vt* : clarify — **clarificación** *nf, pl* **-ciones** : clarification

clarín *nm, pl* **-rines** : bugle

clarinete *nm* : clarinet

clarividente *adj* 1 : clairvoyant 2 PERSPICAZ : perspicacious — **clarividencia** *nf* 1 : clairvoyance 2 PERSPICACIA : farsightedness

claro *adv* 1 : clearly 2 POR SUPUESTO : of course, surely — **~** *nm* 1 : clearing, glade 2 **~ de luna** : moonlight — **claro, -ra** *adj* 1 : clear, bright 2 : light (of colors) 3 EVIDENTE : clear, evident

clase *nf* 1 : class 2 TIPO : sort, kind

clásico, -ca *adj* : classic, classical — **clásico** *nm* : classic

clasificar {72} *vt* 1 : classify, sort out 2 : rate, rank (a hotel, a team, etc.) — **clasificarse** *vr* : qualify (in competitions) — **clasificación** *nf, pl* **-ciones** 1 : classification 2 : league (in sports)

claudicar {72} *vi* : back down

claustro *nm* : cloister

claustrofobia *nf* : claustrophobia — **claustrofóbico, -ca** *adj* : claustrophobic

cláusula *nf* : clause

clausurar *vt* : close (down) — **clausura** *nf* : closure, closing

clavado *nm Lat* : dive

clavar *vt* 1 : nail, hammer 2 HINCAR : drive in, plunge

clave *nf* 1 CIFRA : code 2 SOLUCIÓN : key 3 : clef (in music) — **~** *adj* : key

clavel *nm* : carnation

clavicémbalo *nm* : harpsichord

clavícula *nf* : collarbone

clavija *nf* 1 : peg, pin 2 : (electric) plug

clavo *nm* 1 : nail 2 : clove (spice)

claxon *nm, pl* **cláxones** : horn (of an automobile)

clemencia *nf* : clemency, mercy — **clemente** *adj* : merciful

clerical *adj* : clerical — **clérigo, -ga** *n* : clergyman, cleric — **clero** *nm* : clergy

cliché *nm* 1 : cliché 2 : negative (of a photograph)

cliente, -ta *n* : customer, client — **clientela** *nf* : clientele, customers *pl*

clima *nm* 1 : climate 2 AMBIENTE : atmosphere — **climático, -ca** *adj* : climatic

climatizar {21} *vt* : air-condition — **climatizado, -da** *adj* : air-conditioned

clímax *nm* : climax

clínica *nf* : clinic — **clínico, -ca** *adj* : clinical

clip *nm, pl* **clips** : (paper) clip

cloaca *nf* : sewer

cloquear *vi* : cluck — **cloqueo** *nm* : cluck, clucking

cloro *nm* : chlorine

clóset *nm Lat, pl* **clósets** : (built-in) closet, cupboard

club *nm* : club

coacción *nf, pl* **-ciones** : coercion — **coaccionar** *vt* : coerce

coagular *v* : clot, coagulate — **coagularse** *vr* : coagulate — **coágulo** *nm* : clot

coalición *nf, pl* **-ciones** : coalition

coartada *nf* : alibi

coartar *vt* : restrict, limit

cobarde *nmf* : coward — **~** *adj* : cowardly — **cobardía** *nf* : cowardice

cobaya *nf* : guinea pig

cobertizo *nm* : shelter, shed

cobertor *nm* : bedspread

cobertura *nf* 1 : cover 2 : coverage (of news, etc.)

cobijar *vt* : shelter — **cobijarse** *vr* : take shelter — **cobija** *nf Lat* : blanket — **cobijo** *nm* : shelter

cobra *nf* : cobra

cobrar *vt* 1 : charge, collect 2 : earn (a salary, etc.) 3 ADQUERIR : acquire, gain 4 : cash (a check) — *vi* : be paid — **cobrador, -dora** *n* 1 : collector 2 : conductor (of a bus, etc.)

cobre *nm* : copper

cobro *nm* : collection (of money), cashing (of a check)

cocaína *nf* : cocaine

cocción *nf, pl* **-ciones** : cooking

cocear *vi* : kick

cocer {14} *vt* 1 : cook 2 HERVIR : boil

coche *nm* 1 : car, automobile 2 : coach (of a train) 3 *or* **~ de caballos** : carriage 4 **~ fúnebre** : hearse — **cochecito** *nm* : baby carriage, stroller — **cochera** *nf* : garage, carport

cochino, -na *n* : pig, hog — **~** *adj fam* : dirty, filthy — **cochinada** *nf fam* : dirty thing — **cochinillo** *nm* : piglet

cocido, -da *adj* **1** : boiled, cooked **2 bien ~** : well-done — **cocido** *nm* : stew

cociente *nm* : quotient

cocina *nf* **1** : kitchen **2** : (kitchen) stove **3** : (art of) cooking, cuisine — **cocinar** *v* : cook — **cocinero, -ra** *n* : cook, chef

coco *nm* : coconut

cocodrilo *nm* : crocodile

coctel *or* **cóctel** *nm* **1** : cocktail **2** FIESTA : cocktail party

codazo *nm* **1** : nudge **2 dar un ~ a** : elbow, nudge

codicia *nf* : greed — **codiciar** *vt* : covet — **codicioso, -sa** *adj* : covetous, greedy

código *nm* **1** : code **2 ~ postal** : zip code **3 ~ morse** : Morse code

codo *nm* : elbow

codorniz *nf, pl* **-nices** : quail

coexistir *vi* : coexist

cofre *nm* : chest, coffer

coger {15} *vt* **1** : take (hold of) **2** ATRAPAR : catch **3** : pick up (from the ground) **4** : pick (fruit, etc.) — **cogerse** *vr* : hold on

cohechar *vt* : bribe — **cohecho** *nm* : bribe, bribery

coherencia *nf* : coherence — **coherente** *adj* : coherent — **cohesión** *nf, pl* **-siones** : cohesion

cohete *nm* : rocket

cohibir {62} *vt* **1** : restrict **2** : inhibit (a person) — **cohibirse** *vr* : feel inhibited — **cohibido, -da** *adj* : inhibited, shy

coincidir *vi* **1** : coincide **2 ~ con** : agree with — **coincidencia** *nf* : coincidence

cojear *vi* **1** : limp **2** : wobble (of furniture, etc.) — **cojera** *nf* : limp

cojín *nm, pl* **-jines** : cushion — **cojinete** *nm* **1** : pad, cushion **2** : bearing (of a machine)

cojo, -ja *adj* **1** : lame **2** : wobbly (of furniture) — **~** *n* **1** : lame person

col *nf* **1** : cabbage **2 ~ de Bruselas** : Brussels sprout

cola *nf* **1** : tail **2** FILA : line (of people) **3** : end (of a line) **4** PEGAMENTO : glue **5 ~ de caballo** : ponytail

colaborar *vi* : collaborate — **colaboración** *nf, pl* **-nes** : collaboration — **colaborador, -dora** *n* **1** : collaborator **2** : contributor (to a periodical)

colada *nf Spain* **1** : laundry **2 hacer la ~** : do the washing

colador *nm* : colander, strainer

colapso *nm* : collapse

colar {19} *vt* : strain, filter — **colarse** *vr* : sneak in, gate-crash

colcha *nf* : bedspread, quilt — **colchón** *nm, pl* **-chones** : mattress — **colchoneta** *nf* : mat

colear *vi* : wag its tail

colección *nf, pl* **-ciones** : collection — **coleccionar** *vt* : collect — **coleccionista** *nmf* : collector — **colecta** *nf* : collection (of donations)

colectividad *nf* : community — **colectivo, -va** *adj* : collective — **colectivo** *nm* **1** : collective **2** *Lat* : city bus

colector *nm* : sewer

colega *nmf* : colleague

colegio *nm* **1** : school **2** : (professional) college — **colegial, -giala** *n* : schoolboy *m*, schoolgirl *f*

colegir {28} *vt* : gather

cólera *nm* : cholera — **~** *nf* : anger, rage — **colérico, -ca** *adj* **1** : bad-tempered **2** FURIOSO : angry

colesterol *nm* : cholesterol

coleta *nf* : pigtail

colgar {16} *vt* **1** : hang **2** : hang up (a telephone) **3** : hang out (laundry) — *vi* : hang up — **colgante** *adj* : hanging — **~** *nm* : pendant

colibrí *nm* : hummingbird

cólico *nm* : colic

coliflor *nf* : cauliflower

colilla *nf* : (cigarette) butt

colina *nf* : hill

colindar *vi* **~ con** : be adjacent to — **colindante** *adj* : adjacent

coliseo *nm* : coliseum

colisión *nf, pl* **-siones** : collision — **colisionar** *vi* **~ contra** : collide with

collar *nm* **1** : necklace **2** : collar (for pets)

colmar *vt* **1** : fill to the brim **2** : fulfill (a wish, etc.) **3 ~ de** : shower with — **colmado, -da** *adj* : heaping

colmena *nf* : beehive

colmillo *nm* **1** : canine (tooth) **2** : fang (of a dog, etc.), tusk (of an elephant)

colmo *nm* **1** : height, limit **2 ¡eso es el ~ !** : that's the last straw!

colocar {72} *vt* **1** PONER : place, put **2** : find a job for — **colocarse** *vr* **1** SITUARSE : position oneself **2** : get a job — **colocación** *nf, pl* **-ciones** **1** : placement, placing **2** EMPLEO : position, job

colombiano, -na *adj* : Colombian

colon *nm* : (intestinal) colon

colonia *nf* **1** : colony **2** PERFUME : cologne **3** *Lat* : residential area — **colonial** *adj* : colonial — **colonizar** {21} *vt* : colonize — **colonización** *nf, pl* **-ciones** : colonization — **colono, -na** *n* : settler, colonist

coloquial *adj* : colloquial — **coloquio** *nm* **1** : talk, discussion **2** CONGRESO : conference

color *nm* : color — **colorado, -da** *adj* : red — **colorear** *vt* : color — **colorete** *nm* : rouge — **colorido** *nm* : colors *pl*, coloring

colosal *adj* : colossal

columna *nf* **1** : column **2** ~ **vertebral** : spine, backbone — **columnista** *nmf* : columnist

columpiar *vt* : push (on a swing) — **columpiarse** *vr* : swing — **columpio** *nm* : swing

coma¹ *nm* : coma

coma² *nf* : comma

comadre *nf* **1** : godmother of one's child, mother of one's godchild **2** *fam* : (female) friend — **comadrear** *vi fam* : gossip

comadreja *nf* : weasel

comadrona *nf* : midwife

comandancia *nf* : command headquarters, command — **comandante** *nmf* **1** : commander **2** : major (in the military) — **comando** *nm* **1** : commando **2** *Lat* : command

comarca *nf* : region, area

combar *vt* : bend, curve

combatir *vt* : combat, fight against — *vi* : fight — **combate** *nm* **1** : combat **2** : fight (in boxing) — **combatiente** *nmf* : combatant, fighter

combinar *vt* **1** : combine **2** : put together, match (colors, etc.) — **combinarse** *vr* : get together — **combinación** *nf, pl* **-ciones 1** : combination **2** : connection (in travel)

combustible *nm* : fuel — ~ *adj* : combustible — **combustión** *nf, pl* **-tiones** : combustion

comedia *nf* : comedy

comedido, -da *adj* : moderate

comedor *nm* : dining room

comensal *nmf* : diner, dinner guest

comentar *vt* **1** : comment on, discuss **2** MENCIONAR : mention — **comentario** *nm* **1** : comment, remark **2** ANÁLISIS : commentary — **comentarista** *nmf* : commentator

comenzar {29} *v* : begin, start

comer *vt* **1** : eat **2** *fam* : eat up, eat into — *vi* **1** : eat **2** CENAR : have a meal **3 dar de** ~ : feed — **comerse** *vr* : eat up

comercio *nm* **1** : commerce, trade **2** NEGOCIO : business — **comercial** *adj* : commercial — **comercializar** {21} *vt* : market — **comerciante** *nmf* : merchant, dealer — **comerciar** *vi* : do business, trade

comestible *adj* : edible — **comestibles** *nmpl* : groceries, food

cometa *nm* : comet — ~ *nf* : kite

cometer *vt* **1** : commit **2** ~ **un error** : make a mistake — **cometido** *nm* : assignment, task

comezón *nf, pl* **-zones** : itchiness, itching

comicios *nmpl* : elections

cómico, -ca *adj* : comic, comical — ~ *n* : comic, comedian

comida *nf* **1** ALIMENTO : food **2** *Spain* : lunch **3** *Lat* : dinner **4 tres** ~**s al día** : three meals a day

comienzo *nm* : beginning

comillas *nfpl* : quotation marks

comino *nm* : cumin

comisario, -ria *n* : commissioner — **comisaría** *nf* : police station

comisión *nf, pl* **-siones 1** : commission **2** COMITÉ : committee

comité *nm* : committee

como *conj* **1** : as, since **2 sí** : if — ~ *prep* **1** : like, as **2 así** ~ : as well as — ~ *adv* **1** : as **2** APROXIMADAMENTE : around, about

cómo *adv* **1** : how **2** ~ **no** : by all means **3** ¿~ **te llamas?** : what's your name?

cómoda *nf* : chest of drawers

comodidad *nf* : comfort, convenience

comodín *nm, pl* **-dines** : joker (in playing cards)

cómodo, -da *adj* **1** : comfortable **2** ÚTIL : handy, convenient

comoquiera *adv* **1** : in any way **2** ~ **que** : however

compacto, -ta *adj* : compact

compadecer {53} *vt* : feel sorry for — **compadecerse** *vr* ~ **de** : take pity on

compadre *nm* **1** : godfather of one's child, father of one's godchild **2** *fam* : buddy

compañero, -ra *n* : companion, partner — **compañerismo** *nm* : companionship

compañía *nf* : company

comparar *vt* : compare — **comparable** *adj* : comparable — **comparación** *nf, pl* **-ciones** : comparison — **comparativo, -va** *adj* : comparative

comparecer *vt* : appear (before a court, etc.)

compartimiento *or* **compartimento** *nm* : compartment

compartir *vt* : share

compás *nm, pl* **-pases 1** : compass **2** : rhythm, time (in music)

compasión *nf, pl* **-siones** : compassion, pity — **compasivo, -va** *adj* : compassionate

compatible *adj* : compatible — **compatibilidad** *nf* : compatibility

compatriota *nmf* : compatriot, fellow countryman

compeler *vt* : compel

compendiar *vt* : summarize — **compendio** *nm* : summary

compensar *vt* : compensate for — **compensación** *nf, pl* **-ciones** : compensation

competir {54} *vi* : compete — **competencia** *nf* **1** : competition, rivalry **2** CAPACI-

DAD : competence — **competente** *adj* : competent — **competición** *nf, pl* **-ciones** : competition — **competidor, -dora** *n* : competitor

compilar *vt* : compile

compinche *nmf fam* : friend, chum

complacer {57} *vt* : please — **complacerse** *vr* ~ **en** : take pleasure in — **complaciente** *adj* : obliging, helpful

complejidad *nf* : complexity — **complejo, -ja** *adj* : complex — **complejo** *nm* : complex

complementar *vt* : complement — **complementario, -ria** *adj* : complementary — **complemento** *nm* **1** : complement **2** : object (in grammar)

completar *vt* : complete — **completo, -ta** *adj* **1** : complete **2** PERFECTO : perfect **3** LLENO : full — **completamente** *adv* : completely

complexión *nf, pl* **-xiones** : constitution, build

complicar {72} *vt* **1** : complicate **2** IMPLICAR : involve — **complicación** *nf, pl* **-ciones** : complication — **complicado, -da** *adj* : complicated, complex

cómplice *nmf* : accomplice — ~ *adj* : conspiratorial, knowing

complot *nm, pl* **-plots** : conspiracy, plot

componer {60} *vt* **1** : make up, compose **2** : compose, write (a song) **3** ARREGLAR : fix, repair — **componerse** *vr* ~ **de** : consist of — **componente** *adj & nm* : component, constituent

comportarse *vr* : behave — **comportamiento** *nm* : behavior

composición *nf, pl* **-ciones** : composition — **compositor, -tora** *n* : composer, songwriter

compostura *nf* **1** : composure **2** REPARACIÓN : repair

comprar *vt* : buy, purchase — **compra** *nf* **1** : purchase **2 ir de** ~**s** : go shopping — **comprador, -dora** *n* : buyer, shopper

comprender *vt* **1** : comprehend, understand **2** ABARCAR : cover, include — **comprensible** *adj* : understandable — **comprensión** *nf, pl* **-siones** : understanding — **comprensivo, -va** *adj* : understanding

compresa *nf* **1** : compress **2** *or* ~ **higiénica** : sanitary napkin

compresión *nf, pl* **-siones** : compression — **comprimido** *nm* : pill, tablet — **comprimir** *vt* : compress

comprobar {19} *vt* **1** VERIFICAR : check **2** DEMOSTRAR : prove — **comprobación** *nf, pl* **-ciones** : verification, check — **comprobante** *nm* **1** : proof **2** RECIBO : receipt, voucher

comprometer *vt* **1** : compromise **2** ARRIESGAR : jeopardize **3** OBLIGAR : commit, put under obligation — **comprometerse** *vr* **1** : commit oneself **2** ~ **con** : get engaged to — **comprometedor, -dora** *adj* : compromising — **comprometido, -da** *adj* **1** : compromising, awkward **2** : engaged (to be married) — **compromiso** *nm* **1** : obligation, commitment **2** : (marriage) engagement **3** ACUERDO : agreement **4** APURO : awkward situation

compuesto, -ta *adj* **1** : compound **2** ~ **de** : made up of, consisting of — **compuesto** *nm* : compound

compulsivo, -va *adj* : compelling, urgent

computar *vt* : compute, calculate — **computadora** *nf or* **computador** *nm* **1** : computer **2** ~ **portátil** : laptop computer — **cómputo** *nm* : calculation

comulgar {52} *vi* : receive Communion

común *adj, pl* **-munes 1** : common **2** ~ **y corriente** : ordinary **3 por lo** ~ : generally

comuna *nf* : commune — **comunal** *adj* : communal

comunicar {72} *vt* : communicate — **comunicarse** *vr* **1** : communicate **2** ~ **con** : get in touch with — **comunicación** *nf, pl* **-ciones** : communication — **comunicado** *nm* : communiqué — **comunicativo, -va** *adj* : communicative

comunidad *nf* : community

comunión *nf, pl* **-niones** : communion, Communion

comunismo *nm* : Communism — **comunista** *adj & nmf* : Communist

con *prep* **1** : with **2** A PESAR DE : in spite of **3** (*before an infinitive*) : by **4** ~ **(tal) que** : so long as

cóncavo, -va *adj* : concave

concebir {54} *v* : conceive — **concebible** *adj* : conceivable

conceder *vt* **1** : grant, bestow **2** ADMITIR : concede

concejal, -jala *n* : councilman, alderman

concentrar *vt* : concentrate — **concentrarse** *vr* : concentrate — **concentración** *nf, pl* **-ciones** : concentration

concepción *nf, pl* **-ciones** : conception — **concepto** *nm* **1** : concept **2** OPINIÓN : opinion

concernir {17} *vi* ~ **a** : concern — **concerniente** *adj* ~ **a** : concerning

concertar {55} *vt* **1** : arrange, coordinate **2** (*used before an infinitive*) : agree **3** : harmonize (in music) — *vi* : be in harmony

concesión *nf, pl* **-siones 1** : concession **2** : awarding (of prizes, etc.)

concha *nf* : shell

conciencia *nf* **1** : conscience **2** CONO-CIMIENTO : consciousness, awareness —
concientizar {21} *vt Lat* : make aware —
concientizarse *vr Lat* ∼ **de** : realize
concienzudo, -da *adj* : conscientious
concierto *nm* **1** : concert **2** : concerto (musical composition)
conciliar *vt* : reconcile — **conciliación** *nf, pl* **-ciones** : reconciliation
concilio *nm* : council
conciso, -sa *adj* : concise
conciudadano, -na *n* : fellow citizen
concluir {41} *vt* : conclude — *vi* : come to an end — **conclusión** *nf, pl* **-siones** : conclusion — **concluyente** *adj* : conclusive
concordar {19} *vi* : agree — *vt* : reconcile — **concordancia** *nf* : agreement — **concordia** *nf* : harmony, concord
concretar *vt* : make concrete, specify — **concretarse** *vr* : become definite, take shape — **concreto, -ta** *adj* **1** : concrete **2** DETERMINADO : specific **3 en** ∼ : specifically — **concreto** *nm Lat* : concrete
concurrir *vi* **1** : come together, meet **2** ∼ **a** : take part in — **concurrencia** *nf* : audience, turnout — **concurrido, -da** *adj* : busy, crowded
concursar *vi* : compete, participate — **concursante** *nmf* : competitor — **concurso** *nm* **1** : competition **2** CONCURRENCIA : gathering **3** AYUDA : help, cooperation
condado *nm* : county
conde, -desa *n* : count *m*, countess *f*
condenar *vt* **1** : condemn, damn **2** : sentence (a criminal) — **condena** *nf* **1** : condemnation **2** SENTENCIA : sentence — **condenación** *nf, pl* **-ciones** : condemnation, damnation
condensar *vt* : condense — **condensación** *nf, pl* **-ciones** : condensation
condesa *nf* → **conde**
condescender {56} *vi* **1** : acquiesce, agree **2** ∼ **a** : condescend to — **condescendiente** *adj* : condescending
condición *nf, pl* **-ciones 1** : condition, state **2** CALIDAD : capacity, position — **condicional** *adj* : conditional
condimento *nm* : condiment, seasoning
condolerse {47} *vr* : sympathize — **condolencia** *nf* : condolence
condominio *nm* **1** : joint ownership **2** *Lat* : condominium
condón *nm, pl* **-dones** : condom
conducir {61} *vt* **1** DIRIGIR : direct, lead **2** MANEJAR : drive — *vi* **1** : drive **2** ∼ **a** : lead to — **conducirse** *vr* : behave
conducta *nf* : behavior, conduct
conducto *nm* : conduit, duct
conductor, -tora *n* : driver

conectar *vt* **1** : connect **2** ENCHUFAR : plug in — *vi* : connect
conejo, -ja *n* : rabbit — **conejera** *nf* : (rabbit) hutch
conexión *nf, pl* **-xiones** : connection — **conexo, -xa** *adj* : connected
confabularse *vr* : conspire, plot
confeccionar *vt* : make (up), prepare — **confección** *nf, pl* **-ciones 1** : making, preparation **2** : tailoring, dressmaking
confederación *nf, pl* **-ciones** : confederation
conferencia *nf* **1** : lecture **2** REUNIÓN : conference
conferir {76} *vt* : confer, bestow
confesar {55} *v* : confess — **confesarse** *vr* : go to confession — **confesión** *nf, pl* **-siones 1** : confession **2** CREDO : religion, creed
confeti *nm* : confetti
confiar {85} *vi* : trust — *vt* : entrust — **confiable** *adj* : trustworthy, reliable — **confiado, -da** *adj* **1** : confident **2** CRÉDULO : trusting — **confianza** *nf* **1** : trust **2** : confidence (in oneself)
confidencia *nf* : confidence, secret — **confidencial** *adj* : confidential — **confidencialidad** *nf* : confidentiality — **confidente** *nmf* **1** : confidant, confidante *f* **2** : (police) informer
configuración *nf, pl* **-ciones** : configuration, shape
confín *nm, pl* **-fines** : boundary, limit — **confinar** *vt* **1** : confine **2** DESTERRER : exile
confirmar *vt* : confirm — **confirmación** *nf, pl* **-ciones** : confirmation
confiscar {72} *vt* : confiscate
confitería *nm* : candy store
confitura *nf* : jam
conflagración *nf, pl* **-ciones 1** : war, conflict **2** INCENDIO : fire
conflicto *nm* : conflict
confluencia *nf* : junction, confluence
conformar *vt* : shape, make up — **conformarse** *vr* **1** RESIGNARSE : resign oneself **2** ∼ **con** : content oneself with — **conforme** *adj* **1** : content, satisfied **2** ∼ **a** : in accordance with — ∼ *conj* : as — **conformidad** *nf* **1** : agreement **2** RESIGNACIÓN : resignation
confortar *vt* : comfort — **confortable** *adj* : comfortable
confrontar *vt* **1** : confront **2** COMPARAR : compare — *vi* : border — **confrontarse** *vr* ∼ **con** : face up to — **confrontación** *nf, pl* **-ciones** : confrontation
confundir *vt* : confuse, mix up — **confundirse** *vr* : make a mistake, be confused

— **confusión** *nf, pl* **-siones** : confusion — **confuso, -sa** *adj* **1** : confused **2** INDISTINTO : hazy, indistinct — **congelar** *vt* : freeze — **congelarse** *vr* : freeze — **congelación** *nf, pl* **-ciones** : freezing — **congelado, -da** *adj* : frozen — **congelador** *nm* : freezer

congeniar *vi* : get along

congestión *nf, pl* **-tiones** : congestion — **congestionado, -da** *adj* : congested

congoja *nf* : anguish, grief

congraciarse *vr* : ingratiate oneself

congratular *vt* : congratulate

congregar {52} *vt* : bring together — **congregarse** *vr* : congregate — **congregación** *nf, pl* **-ciones** : congregation, gathering

congreso *nm* : congress — **congresista** *nmf* : member of congress

conjeturar *vt* : guess, conjecture — **conjetura** *nf* : guess, conjecture

conjugar {52} *vt* : conjugate — **conjugación** *nf, pl* **-ciones** : conjugation

conjunción *nf, pl* **-ciones** : conjunction

conjunto, -ta *adj* : joint — **conjunto** *nm* **1** : collection **2** : outfit (of clothing) **3** GRUPO : band **4** en ~ : as a whole

conjurar *vt* : ward off — *vi* : conspire, plot

conllevar *vt* : entail

conmemorar *vt* : commemorate — **conmemoración** *nf, pl* **-ciones** : commemoration — **conmemorativo, -va** *adj* : commemorative

conmigo *pron* : with me

conminar *vt* : threaten

conmiseración *nf, pl* **-ciones** : pity, commiseration

conmocionar *vt* : shock — **conmoción** *nf, pl* **-ciones** **1** : shock, upheaval **2** *or* ~ **cerebral** : concussion

conmover {47} *vt* **1** : move, touch **2** SACUDIR : shake (up) — **conmoverse** *vr* : be moved — **conmovedor, -dora** *adj* : moving, touching

conmutador *nm* **1** : (electric) switch **2** *Lat* : switchboard

cono *nm* : cone

conocer {18} *vt* **1** : know **2** : meet (a person), get to know (a city, etc.) **3** RECONOCER : recognize — **conocerse** *vr* **1** : meet, get to know each other **2** : know oneself — **conocedor, -dora** *adj & n* : expert — **conocido, -da** *adj* : well-known — ~ *n* : acquaintance — **conocimiento** *nm* **1** : knowledge **2** SENTIDO : consciousness

conque *conj* : so

conquistar *vt* : conquer — **conquista** *nf* : conquest — **conquistador, -dora** *adj* : conquering — **conquistador** *nm* : conqueror

consabido, -da *adj* **1** : well-known **2** HABITUEL : usual

consagrar *vt* **1** : consecrate **2** DEDICAR : devote — **consagración** *nf, pl* **-ciones** : consecration

consciencia *nf* → **conciencia** — **consciente** *adj* : conscious, aware

consecución *nf, pl* **-ciones** : attainment

consecuencia *nf* **1** : consequence **2** en ~ : accordingly — **consecuente** *adj* : consistent

consecutivo, -va *adj* : consecutive

conseguir {75} *vt* **1** : get, obtain **2** ~ **hacer algo** : manage to do sth

consejo *nm* **1** : advice, counsel **2** : council (assembly) — **consejero, -ra** *n* : adviser, counselor

consenso *nm* : consensus

consentir {76} *vt* **1** : allow, permit **2** MIMAR : pamper, spoil — *vi* : consent — **consentimiento** *nm* : consent, permission

conserje *nmf* : caretaker, janitor

conservar *vt* **1** : preserve **2** GUARDAR : keep, conserve — **conservarse** *vr* : keep — **conserva** *nf* **1** : preserve(s) **2** ~**s** *nfpl* : canned goods — **conservación** *nf, pl* **-ciones** : conservation, preservation — **conservador, -dora** *adj & n* : conservative — **conservatorio** *nm* : conservatory

considerar *vt* **1** : consider **2** RESPETAR : respect — **considerable** *adj* : considerable — **consideración** *nf, pl* **-ciones** **1** : consideration **2** RESPETO : respect — **considerado, -da** *adj* **1** : considerate **2** RESPETADO : respected

consigna *nf* **1** ESLOGAN : slogan **2** ORDEN : orders **3** : checkroom (for baggage)

consigo *pron* : with her, with him, with you, with oneself

consiguiente *adj* **1** : consequent **2** por ~ : consequently

consistir *vi* ~ **en 1** : consist of **2** : lie in, consist in — **consistencia** *nf* : consistency — **consistente** *adj* **1** : firm, solid **2** ~ **en** : consisting of

consolar {19} *vt* : console, comfort — **consolarse** *vr* : console oneself — **consolación** *nf, pl* **-ciones** : consolation

consolidar *vt* : consolidate — **consolidación** *nf, pl* **-ciones** : consolidation

consomé *nm* : consommé

consonante *adj* : consonant, harmonious — ~ *nf* : consonant

consorcio *nm* : consortium

conspirar *vi* : conspire, plot — **conspiración** *nf, pl* **-ciones** : conspiracy — **conspirador, -dora** *n* : conspirator

constancia *nf* **1** : record, evidence **2** PERSEVERANCIA : perseverance — **constante**

adj : constant — **constantemente** *adv* : constantly, continually

constar *vi* **1** : be evident, be clear **2** ~ **de** : consist of

constatar *vt* **1** : verify **2** AFIRMAR : state, affirm

constelación *nf, pl* **-ciones** : constellation

consternación *nf, pl* **-ciones** : consternation

constipado, -da *adj* estar ~ : have a cold — **constipado** *nm* : cold — **constiparse** *vr* : catch a cold

constituir {41} *vt* **1** FORMAR : constitute, form **2** FUNDAR : establish, set up — **constituirse** *vr* ~ **en** : set oneself up as — **constitución** *nf, pl* **-ciones** : constitution — **constitucional** *adj* : constitutional — **constitutivo, -va** *adj* : constituent — **constituyente** *adj & nm* : constituent

constreñir {67} *vt* **1** : force, compel **2** RESTRINGIR : restrict, limit

construir {41} *vt* : build, construct — **construcción** *nf, pl* **-ciones** : construction, building — **constructivo, -va** *adj* : constructive — **constructor, -tora** *n* : builder

consuelo *nm* : consolation, comfort

consuetudinario, -ria *adj* : customary

cónsul *nmf* : consul — **consulado** *nm* : consulate

consultar *vt* : consult — **consulta** *nf* : consultation — **consultor, -tora** *n* : consultant — **consultorio** *nm* : office (of a doctor or dentist)

consumar *vt* **1** : consummate, complete **2** : commit (a crime)

consumir *vt* : consume — **consumirse** *vr* : waste away — **consumición** *nf, pl* **-ciones** **1** : consumption **2** : drink (in a restaurant) — **consumido, -da** *adj* : thin, emaciated — **consumidor, -dora** *n* : consumer — **consumo** *nm* : consumption

contabilidad *nf* **1** : accounting, bookkeeping **2** : accountancy (profession) — **contable** *nmf Spain* : accountant, bookkeeper

contactar *vi* ~ **con** : get in touch with, contact — **contacto** *nm* : contact

contado, -da *adj* : numbered, few — **contado** *nm* al ~ : (in) cash

contador, -dora *n Lat* : accountant — **contador** *nm* : meter

contagiar *vt* **1** : infect **2** : transmit (a disease) — **contagiarse** *vr* **1** : be contagious **2** : become infected (with a disease) — **contagio** *nm* : contagion, infection — **contagioso, -sa** *adj* : contagious, infectious

contaminar *vt* : contaminate, pollute — **contaminación** *nf, pl* **-ciones** : contamination, pollution

contar {19} *vt* **1** : count **2** NARRAR : tell — *vi* **1** : count **2** ~ **con** : rely on, count on

contemplar *vt* **1** MIRAR : look at, behold **2** CONSIDERAR : contemplate — **contemplación** *nf, pl* **-ciones** : contemplation

contemporáneo, -nea *adj & n* : contemporary

contender {56} *vi* : contend, compete — **contendiente** *nmf* : competitor

contener {80} *vt* **1** : contain **2** RESTRINGIR : restrain, hold back — **contenerse** *vr* : restrain oneself — **contenedor** *nm* : container — **contenido, -da** *adj* : restrained — **contenido** *nm* : contents *pl*

contentar *vt* : please, make happy — **contentarse** *vr* ~ **con** : be satisfied with — **contento, -ta** *adj* : glad, happy, contented

contestar *vt* : answer — *vi* : reply, answer back — **contestación** *nf, pl* **-ciones** : answer, reply

contexto *nm* : context

contienda *nf* **1** COMBATE : dispute, fight **2** COMPETICIÓN : contest

contigo *pron* : with you

contiguo, -gua *adj* : adjacent

continente *nm* : continent — **continental** *adj* : continental

contingencia *nf* : contingency — **contingente** *adj & nm* : contingent

continuar {3} *v* : continue — **continuación** *nf, pl* **-ciones** **1** : continuation **2** a ~ : next, then — **continuidad** *nf* : continuity — **continuo, -nua** *adj* **1** : continuous, steady **2** FRECUENTE : continual

contorno *nm* **1** : outline **2** ~s *nmpl* : surrounding area

contorsión *nf, pl* **-siones** : contortion

contra *prep* **1** : against **2** en ~ : against — ~ *nm* los pros y los ~s : the pros and cons

contraatacar {72} *v* : counterattack — **contraataque** *nm* : counterattack

contrabajo *nm* : double bass

contrabalancear *vt* : counterbalance

contrabandista *nmf* : smuggler — **contrabando** *nm* **1** : smuggling **2** : contraband (goods)

contracción *nf, pl* **-ciones** : contraction

contrachapado *nm* : plywood

contradecir {11} *vt* : contradict — **contradicción** *nf, pl* **-ciones** : contradiction — **contradictorio, -ria** *adj* : contradictory

contraer {81} *vt* **1** : contract **2** ~ **matrimonio** : get married — **contraerse** *vr* : contract, tighten up

contrafuerte *nm* : buttress

contragolpe *nm* : backlash

contralto *nmf* : contralto

contrapartida *nf* : compensation

contrapelo: **a ~** *adv phr* : the wrong way
contrapeso *nm* : counterbalance
contraponer {60} *vt* **1** : counter, oppose **2** COMPARAR : compare
contraproducente *adj* : counterproductive
contrariar {85} *vt* **1** : oppose **2** MOLESTAR : vex, annoy — **contrariedad** *nf* **1** : obstacle **2** DISGUSTO : annoyance — **contrario, -ria** *adj* **1** OPUESTO : opposite **2 al contrario** : on the contrary **3 ser ~ a** : be opposed to
contrarrestar *vt* : counteract
contrasentido *nm* : contradiction (in terms)
contraseña *nf* : password
contrastar *vt* **1** : check, verify **2** RESISTIR : resist — *vi* : contrast — **contraste** *nm* : contrast
contratar *vt* **1** : contract for **2** : hire, engage (workers)
contratiempo *nm* **1** : mishap **2** DIFICULTAD : setback
contrato *nm* : contract — **contratista** *nmf* : contractor
contraventana *nf* : shutter
contribuir {41} *vi* **1** : contribute **2** : pay taxes — **contribución** *nf, pl* **-ciones 1** : contribution **2** IMPUESTO : tax — **contribuyente** *nmf* **1** : contributor **2** : taxpayer
contrincante *nmf* : opponent
contrito, -ta *adj* : contrite
controlar *vt* **1** : control **2** COMPROBAR : monitor, check — **control** *nm* **1** : control **2** VERIFICACIÓN : inspection, check — **controlador, -dora** *n* : controller
controversia *nf* : controversy
contundente *adj* **1** : blunt **2** : forceful, convincing (of arguments, etc.)
contusión *nf, pl* **-siones** : bruise
convalecencia *nf* : convalescence — **convaleciente** *adj & nmf* : convalescent
convencer {86} *vt* : convince, persuade — **convencerse** *vr* : be convinced — **convencimiento** *nm* : conviction, belief
convención *nf, pl* **-ciones** : convention — **convencional** *adj* : conventional
convenir {87} *vi* **1** : be suitable, be advisable **2 ~ en** : agree on — **conveniencia** *nf* **1** : convenience **2** : suitability (of an action, etc.) — **conveniente** *adj* **1** : convenient **2** ACONSEJABLE : suitable, advisable **3** PROVECHOSO : useful — **convenio** *nm* : agreement, pact
convento *nm* : convent, monastery
converger {15} *or* **convergir** *vi* : converge
conversar *vi* : converse, talk — **conversación** *nf, pl* **-ciones** : conversation
conversión *nf, pl* **-siones** : conversion — **converso, -sa** *n* : convert
convertir {76} *vt* : convert — **convertirse**

vr **~ en** : turn into — **convertible** *adj & nm* : convertible
convexo, -xa *adj* : convex
convicción *nf, pl* **-ciones** : conviction — **convicto, -ta** *adj* : convicted
convidar *vt* : invite — **convidado, -da** *n* : guest
convincente *adj* : convincing
convite *nm* **1** : invitation **2** : banquet
convivir *vi* : live together — **convivencia** *nf* : coexistence, living together
convocar {72} *vt* : convoke, call together
convulsión *nf, pl* **-siones 1** : convulsion **2** TRASTORNO : upheaval — **convulsivo, -va** *adj* : convulsive
conyugal *adj* : conjugal — **cónyuge** *nmf* : spouse, partner
coñac *nm* : cognac, brandy
cooperar *vi* : cooperate — **cooperación** *nf, pl* **-ciones** : cooperation — **cooperativa** *nf* : cooperative, co-op — **cooperativo, -va** *adj* : cooperative
coordenada *nf* : coordinate
coordinar *vt* : coordinate — **coordinación** *nf, pl* **-ciones** : coordination — **coordinador, -dora** *n* : coordinator
copa *nf* **1** : glass, goblet **2** : cup (in sports) **3 tomar una ~** : have a drink
copia *nf* : copy — **copiar** *vt* : copy
copioso, -sa *adj* : copious, abundant
copla *nf* **1** : (popular) song **2** ESTROFA : verse, stanza
copo *nm* **1** : flake **2** *or* **~ de nieve** : snowflake
coquetear *vi* : flirt — **coqueteo** *nm* : flirting, flirtation — **coqueto, -ta** *adj* : flirtatious — **~** *n* : flirt
coraje *nm* **1** : valor, courage **2** IRA : anger
coral[1] *nm* : coral
coral[2] *adj* : choral — **~** *nf* : choir, chorale
Corán *nm* **el ~** : the Koran
coraza *nf* **1** : armor plating **2** : shell
corazón *nm, pl* **-zones 1** : heart **2** : core (of fruit) **3 mi ~** : my darling — **corazonada** *nf* **1** : hunch **2** IMPULSO : impulse
corbata *nf* : tie, necktie
corchete *nm* **1** : hook and eye, clasp **2** : square bracket (punctuation mark)
corcho *nm* : cork
cordel *nm* : cord, string
cordero *nm* : lamb
cordial *adj* : cordial — **cordialidad** *nf* : cordiality
cordillera *nf* : mountain range
córdoba *nf* : córdoba (Nicaraguan unit of currency)
cordón *nm, pl* **-dones 1** : cord **2 ~ policial** : (police) cordon **3 cordones** *nmpl* : shoelaces

cordura *nf* : sanity
corear *vt* : chant
coreografía *nf* : choreography
cornamenta *nf* : antlers *pl*
corneta *nf* : bugle
coro *nm* **1** : chorus **2** : (church) choir
corona *nf* **1** : crown **2** : wreath, garland (of flowers) — **coronación** *nf, pl* **-ciones** : coronation — **coronar** *vt* : crown
coronel *nm* : colonel
coronilla *nf* **1** : crown (of the head) **2 estar hasta la ~** : be fed up
corporación *nf, pl* **-ciones** : corporation
corporal *adj* : corporal, bodily
corporativo, -va *adj* : corporate
corpulento, -ta *adj* : stout
corral *nm* **1** : farmyard **2** : pen, corral (for animals) **3** *or* **corralito** : playpen
correa *nf* **1** : strap, belt **2** : leash (for a dog, etc.)
corrección *nf, pl* **-ciones 1** : correction **2** : correctness, propriety (of manners) — **correccional** *nm* : reformatory — **correctivo, -va** *adj* : corrective — **correcto, -ta** *adj* **1** : correct, right **2** CORTÉS : polite
corredizo, -za *adj* : sliding
corredor, -dora *n* **1** : runner, racer **2** AGENTE : agent, broker — **corredor** *nm* : corridor, hallway
corregir {28} *vt* : correct — **corregirse** *vr* : mend one's ways
correlación *nf, pl* **-ciones** : correlation
correo *nm* **1** : mail **2 ~ aéreo** : airmail
correr *vi* **1** : run, race **2** : flow (of a river, etc.) **3** : pass (of time) — *vt* **1** : run **2** RECORRER : travel over, cover **3** : draw (curtains) — **correrse** *vr* **1** : move along **2** : run (of colors)
corresponder *vi* **1** : correspond **2** PERTENECER : belong **3** ENCAJAR : fit **4 ~ a** : reciprocate, repay — **corresponderse** *vr* : write to each other — **correspondencia** *nf* **1** : correspondence **2** : connection (of a train, etc.) — **correspondiente** *adj* : corresponding, respective — **corresponsal** *nmf* : correspondent
corretear *vi* : run about, scamper
corrida *nf* **1** : run **2** *or* **~ de toros** : bullfight — **corrido, -da** *adj* **1** : straight, continuous **2** *fam* : worldly
corriente *adj* **1** : current **2** NORMAL : common, ordinary **3** : running (of water, etc.) — **~** *nf* **1** : current (of water, electricity, etc.), draft (of air) **2** TENDENCIA : tendency, trend — **~** *nm* **al ~ 1** : up-to-date **2** ENTERADO : aware, informed
corrillo *nm* : clique, circle — **corro** *nm* : ring, circle (of people)
corroborar *vt* : corroborate

corroer {69} *vt* **1** : corrode (of metals) **2** : erode, wear away — **corroerse** *vr* : corrode
corromper *vt* **1** : corrupt **2** PUDRIR : rot — **corrompido, -da** *adj* : corrupt
corrosión *nf, pl* **-siones** : corrosion — **corrosivo, -va** *adj* : corrosive
corrupción *nf, pl* **-ciones 1** : corruption **2** DESCOMPOSICIÓN : decay, rot — **corrupto, -ta** *adj* : corrupt
corsé *nm* : corset
cortar *vt* **1** : cut **2** RECORTAR : cut out **3** QUITAR : cut off — *vi* : cut — **cortarse** *vr* **1** : cut oneself **2** : be cut off (on the telephone) **3** : curdle (of milk) **4 ~ el pelo** : have one's hair cut — **cortada** *nf Lat* : cut — **cortante** *adj* : cutting, sharp
cortaúñas *nms & pl* : nail clippers
corte[1] *nm* **1** : cutting **2** ESTILO : cut, style **3 ~ de pelo** : haircut
corte[2] *nf* **1** : court **2 hacer la ~ a** : court, woo — **cortejar** *vt* : court, woo
cortejo *nm* **1** : entourage **2** NOVIAZGO : courtship **3 ~ fúnebre** : funeral procession
cortés *adj* : courteous, polite — **cortesía** *nf* : courtesy, politeness
corteza *nf* **1** : bark **2** : crust (of bread) **3** : rind, peel (of fruit)
cortina *nm* : curtain
corto, -ta *adj* **1** : short **2** ESCASO : scarce **3** *fam* : timid, shy **4 ~ de vista** : nearsighted — **cortocircuito** *nm* : short circuit
corvo, -va *adj* : curved, bent
cosa *nf* **1** : thing **2** ASUNTO : matter, affair **3 ~ de** : about **4 poca ~** : nothing much
cosechar *v* : harvest, reap — **cosecha** *nf* **1** : harvest, crop **2** : vintage (of wine)
coser *v* : sew
cosmético, -ca *adj* : cosmetic — **cosmético** *nm* : cosmetic
cósmico, -ca *adj* : cosmic
cosmopolita *adj* : cosmopolitan
cosmos *nm* : cosmos
cosquillas *nfpl* **1** : tickling **2 hacer ~** : tickle — **cosquilleo** *nm* : tickling sensation, tingle
costa *nf* **1** : coast, shore **2 a toda ~** : at any cost
costado *nm* **1** : side **2 al ~** : alongside
costar {19} *v* : cost
costarricense *or* **costarriqueño, -ña** *adj* : Costa Rican
coste *nm* → **costo** — **costear** *vt* : pay for
costero, -ra *adj* : coastal
costilla *nf* **1** : rib **2** CHULETA : chop, cutlet
costo *nm* : cost, price — **costoso, -sa** *adj* : costly
costra *nf* : scab

costumbre *nf* **1** : custom, habit **2 de ~** : usual

costura *nf* **1** : sewing, dressmaking **2** PUNTADAS : seam — **costurera** *nf* : dressmaker

cotejar *vt* : compare

cotidiano, -na *adj* : daily

cotizar {21} *vt* : quote, set a price on — **cotización** *nf, pl* **-ciones** : quotation, price — **cotizado, -da** *adj* : in demand

coto *nm* : enclosure, reserve

cotorra *nf* **1** : small parrot **2** *fam* : chatterbox — **cotorrear** *vi fam* : chatter, gab

coyote *nm* : coyote

coyuntura *nf* **1** : joint **2** SITUACIÓN : situation, moment

coz *nm, pl* **coces** : kick (of an animal)

cráneo *nf* : cranium, skull

cráter *nm* : crater

crear *vt* : create — **creación** *nf, pl* **-ciones** : creation — **creativo, -va** *adj* : creative — **creador, -dora** *n* : creator

crecer {53} *vi* **1** : grow **2** AUMENTAR : increase — **crecido, -da** *adj* **1** : full-grown **2** : large (of numbers) — **creciente** *adj* **1** : growing, increasing **2** : crescent (of the moon) — **crecimiento** *nm* **1** : growth **2** AUMENTO : increase

credenciales *nfpl* : credentials

credibilidad *nf* : credibility

crédito *nm* : credit

credo *nm* : creed

crédulo, -la *adj* : credulous, gullible

creer {20} *v* **1** : believe **2** SUPONER : suppose, think — **creerse** *vr* : regard oneself as — **creencia** *nf* : belief — **creíble** *adj* : believable, credible — **creído, -da** *adj fam* : conceited

crema *nf* : cream

cremación *nf, pl* **-ciones** : cremation

cremallera *nf* : zipper

cremoso, -sa *adj* : creamy

crepe *nmf* : crepe, pancake

crepitar *vi* : crackle

crepúsculo *nm* : twilight, dusk

crespo, -pa *adj* : curly, frizzy

crespón *nm, pl* **-pones** : crepe (fabric)

cresta *nf* **1** : crest **2** : comb (of a rooster)

cretino, -na *n* : cretin

creyente *nmf* : believer

criar {85} *vt* **1** : nurse (a baby) **2** EDUCAR : bring up, rear **3** : raise, breed (animals) — **cría** *nf* **1** : breeding, rearing **2** : young animal — **criadero** *nm* : farm, hatchery — **criado, -da** *n* : servant, maid *f* — **criador, -dora** *n* : breeder — **crianza** *nf* : upbringing, rearing

criatura *nf* **1** : creature **2** NIÑO : baby, child

crimen *nm, pl* **crímenes** : crime — **criminal** *adj & nmf* : criminal

críquet *nm* : cricket (game)

crin *nf* : mane

criollo, -lla *adj & n* : Creole

cripta *nf* : crypt

crisantemo *nm* : chrysanthemum

crisis *nf* **1** : crisis **2 ~ nerviosa** : nervous breakdown

crispar *vt* **1** : tense (muscles), clench (one's fist) **2** IRRITAR : irritate, set on edge — **crisparse** *vr* : tense up

cristal *nm* **1** : crystal **2** VIDRIO : glass, piece of glass — **cristalería** *nf* : glassware — **cristalino, -na** *adj* : crystalline — **cristalino** *nm* : lens (of the eye) — **cristalizar** {21} *vi* : crystallize

cristiano, -na *adj & n* : Christian — **cristianismo** *nm* : Christianity — **Cristo** *nm* : Christ

criterio *nm* **1** : criterion **2** JUICIO : judgment, opinion

criticar {72} *vt* : criticize — **crítica** *nf* **1** : criticism **2** RESEÑA : review, critique — **crítico, -ca** *adj* : critical — **~** *n* : critic, reviewer

croar *vi* : croak

cromo *nm* : chromium, chrome

cromosoma *nm* : chromosome

crónica *nf* **1** : chronicle **2** : (news) report

crónico, -ca *adj* : chronic

cronista *nmf* : reporter, newscaster

cronología *nf* : chronology — **cronológico, -ca** *adj* : chronological

cronometrar *vt* : time, clock — **cronómetro** *nm* : chronometer, stopwatch

croqueta *nf* : croquette

croquis *nms & pl* : (rough) sketch

cruce *nm* **1** : crossing **2** : crossroads, intersection **3 ~ peatonal** : crosswalk

crucero *nm* **1** : cruise **2** : cruiser (ship)

crucial *adj* : crucial

crucificar {72} *vt* : crucify — **crucifijo** *nm* : crucifix — **crucifixión** *nf, pl* **-fixiones** : crucifixion

crucigrama *nm* : crossword puzzle

crudo, -da *adj* **1** : harsh, crude **2** : raw (of food) — **crudo** *nm* : crude oil

cruel *adj* : cruel — **crueldad** *nf* : cruelty

crujir *vi* : rustle, creak, crackle, crunch — **crujido** *nm* : rustle, creak, crackle, crunch — **crujiente** *adj* : crunchy, crisp

cruzar {21} *vt* **1** : cross **2** : exchange (words) — **cruzarse** *vr* **1** : intersect **2** : pass each other — **cruz** *nf, pl* **cruces** : cross — **cruzada** *nf* : crusade — **cruzado, -da** *adj* : crossed — **cruzado** *nm* : crusader

cuaderno *nm* : notebook

cuadra *nf* **1** : stable **2** *Lat* : (city) block

cuadrado, -da *adj* : square — **cuadrado** *nm* : square

cuadragésimo, -ma *adj* : fortieth, forty- — **∼** *n* : fortieth, forty- (in a series)

cuadrar *vi* **1** : conform, agree **2** : add up, tally (numbers) — *vt* : square — **cuadrarse** *vr* : stand at attention

cuadrilátero *nm* **1** : quadrilateral **2** : ring (in sports)

cuadrilla *nf* : gang, group

cuadro *nm* **1** : square **2** PINTURA : painting **3** DESCRIPCIÓN : picture, description **4** : staff, management (of an organization) **5** CUADRADO : check, square **6** : (baseball) diamond

cuadrúpedo *nm* : quadruped

cuádruple *adj* : quadruple — **cuadruplicar** {72} *vt* : quadruple

cuajar *vi* **1** : curdle **2** COAGULAR : clot, coagulate **3** : set (of pudding, etc.) **4** AFIANZARSE : catch on — *vt* **1** : curdle **2** **∼ de** : fill with

cual *pron* **1 el ∼, la ∼, los ∼es, las ∼es** : who, whom, which **2 lo ∼** : which **3 cada ∼** : everyone, everybody — **∼** *prep* : like, as

cuál *pron* : which (one), what (one) — **∼** *adj* : which, what

cualidad *nf* : quality, trait

cualquiera (**cualquier** *before nouns*) *adj, pl* **cualesquiera** : any, whatever — **∼** *pron, pl* **cualesquiera** : anyone, whatever

cuán *adv* : how

cuando *conj* **1** : when **2** SI : since, if **3 ∼ más** : at the most **4 de vez en ∼** : from time to time — **∼** *prep* : during, at the time of

cuándo *adv* **1** : when **2 ¿desde ∼?** : since when?

cuantía *nf* **1** : quantity, extent **2** IMPORTANCIA : importance — **cuantioso, -sa** *adj* : abundant, considerable

cuanto *adv* **1** : as much as **2 ∼ antes** : as soon as possible **3 en ∼** : as soon as **4 en ∼ a** : as for, as regards — **cuanto, -ta** *adj* : as many, whatever — **∼** *pron* **1** : as much as, all that, everything **2 unos cuantos, unas cuantas** : a few

cuánto *adv* : how much, how many — **cuánto, -ta** *adj* : how much, how many — **∼** *pron* : how much, how many

cuarenta *adj & nm* : forty — **cuarentavo, -va** *adj* : fortieth — **cuarentavo** *nm* : fortieth

cuarentena *nf* : quarantine

Cuaresma *nf* : Lent

cuartear *vt* : quarter, divide up — **cuartearse** *vr* : crack, split

cuartel *nm* **1** : barracks *pl* **2 ∼ general** : headquarters **3 no dar ∼** : show no mercy

cuarteto *nm* : quartet

cuarto, -ta *adj* : fourth — **∼** *n* : fourth (in a series) — **cuarto** *nm* **1** : quarter, fourth **2** HABITACIÓN : room

cuarzo *nm* : quartz

cuatro *adj & nm* : four — **cuatrocientos, -tas** *adj* : four hundred — **cuatrocientos** *nms & pl* : four hundred

cuba *nf* : cask, barrel

cubano, -na *adj* : Cuban

cubeta *nf* **1** : keg, cask **2** *Lat* : pail, bucket

cúbico, -ca *adj* : cubic, cubed — **cubículo** *nm* : cubicle

cubierta *nf* **1** : cover, covering **2** : (automobile) tire **3** : deck (of a ship) — **cubierto** *nm* **1** : cutlery, place setting **2 a ∼** : under cover

cubo *nm* **1** : cube **2** *Spain* : pail, bucket **3** : hub (of a wheel)

cubrecama *nm* : bedspread

cubrir {2} *vt* : cover — **cubrirse** *vr* **1** : cover oneself **2** : cloud over

cucaracha *nf* : cockroach

cuchara *nf* : spoon — **cucharada** *nf* : spoonful — **cucharilla** *or* **cucharita** *nf* : teaspoon — **cucharón** *nm, pl* **-rones** : ladle

cuchichear *vi* : whisper — **cuchicheo** *nm* : whisper

cuchilla *nf* **1** : (kitchen) knife **2 ∼ de afeitar** : razor blade — **cuchillada** *nf* : stab, knife wound — **cuchillo** *nm* : knife

cuclillas *nfpl* **en ∼** : squatting, crouching

cuco *nm* : cuckoo — **cuco, -ca** *adj fam* : pretty, cute

cucurucho *nm* : ice-cream cone

cuello *nm* **1** : neck **2** : collar (of clothing)

cuenca *nf* **1** : river basin **2** : (eye) socket — **cuenco** *nm* **1** : bowl **2** CONCAVIDAD : hollow

cuenta *nf* **1** : calculation, count **2** : (bank) account **3** FACTURA : check, bill **4** : bead (for a necklace, etc.) **5 darse ∼** : realize **6 tener en ∼** : bear in mind

cuento *nm* **1** : story, tale **2 ∼ de hadas** : fairy tale

cuerda *nf* **1** : cord, rope, string **2 ∼s vocales** : vocal cords **3 dar ∼ a** : wind up

cuerdo, -da *adj* : sane, sensible

cuerno *nm* **1** : horn **2** : antlers *pl* (of a deer)

cuero *nm* **1** : leather, hide **2 ∼ cabelludo** : scalp

cuerpo *nm* **1** : body **2** : corps (in the military, etc.)

cuervo *nm* : crow

cuesta *nf* **1** : slope **2 a ∼s** : on one's back **3 ∼ abajo** : downhill **4 ∼ arriba** : uphill

cuestión *nf, pl* **-tiones** : matter, affair — **cuestionar** *vt* : question — **cuestionario** *nm* **1** : questionnaire **2** : quiz (in school)

cueva *nf* : cave

cuidar *vt* **1** : take care of, look after **2** : pay attention to (details, etc.) — *vi* **1** ~ **de** : look after **2** ~ **de que** : make sure that — **cuidarse** *vr* : take care of oneself — **cuidado** *nm* **1** : care **2** PREOCUPACIÓN : worry, concern **3 tener** ~ : be careful **4** ¡**cuidado!** : watch out!, careful! — **cuidadoso, -sa** *adj* : careful — **cuidadosamente** *adv* : carefully

culata *nf* : butt (of a gun) — **culatazo** *nf* : kick, recoil

culebra *nf* : snake

culinario, -ria *adj* : culinary

culminar *vi* : culminate — **culminación** *nf, pl* **-ciones** : culmination

culo *nm fam* : backside, bottom

culpa *nf* **1** : fault, blame **2** PECADO : sin **3 echar la** ~ **a** : blame **4 tener la** ~ : be at fault — **culpabilidad** *nf* : guilt — **culpable** *adj* : guilty — ~ *nmf* : culprit, guilty party — **culpar** *vt* : blame

cultivar *vt* : cultivate — **cultivo** *nm* **1** : farming, cultivation **2** ~**s** : crops

culto, -ta *adj* : cultured, educated — **culto** *nm* **1** : worship **2** : (religious) cult — **cultura** *nf* : culture — **cultural** *adj* : cultural

cumbre *nf* : summit, top

cumpleaños *nms & pl* : birthday

cumplido, -da *adj* **1** : complete, full **2** CORTÉS : courteous — **cumplido** *nm* : compliment, courtesy

cumplimentar *vt* **1** : congratulate **2** CUMPLIR : carry out — **cumplimiento** *nm* : carrying out, performance

cumplir *vt* **1** : accomplish, carry out **2** : keep (a promise), observe (a law, etc.) **3** : reach (a given age) — *vi* **1** : expire, fall due **2** ~ **con el deber** : do one's duty — **cumplirse** *vr* **1** : expire **2** REALIZARSE : come true

cúmulo *nm* **1** : heap, pile **2** : cumulus (cloud)

cuna *nf* **1** : cradle **2** ORIGEN : birthplace

cundir *vi* **1** PROPAGARSE : spread, propagate **2** : go a long way

cuneta *nf* : ditch (in a road), gutter (in a street)

cuña *nf* : wedge

cuñado, -da *n* : brother-in-law *m*, sister-in-law *f*

cuota *nf* **1** : fee, dues **2** CUPO : quota **3** *Lat* : installment, payment

cupo *nm* **1** : quota, share **2** *Lat* : capacity, room

cupón *nm, pl* **-pones** : coupon

cúpula *nf* : dome, cupola

cura *nf* : cure, treatment — ~ *nm* : priest — **curación** *nf, pl* **-ciones** : healing — **curar** *vt* **1** : cure **2** : dress (a wound) **3** CURTIR : tan (hides) — **curarse** *vr* : get well

curiosear *vi* **1** : snoop, pry **2** : browse (in a store) — *vt* : look over — **curiosidad** *nf* : curiosity — **curioso, -sa** *adj* **1** : curious, inquisitive **2** RARO : unusual, strange

currículum *nm, pl* **-lums** *or* **currículo** *nm* : résumé, curriculum vitae

cursar *vt* **1** : take (a course), study **2** ENVIAR : send, pass on

cursi *adj fam* : affected, pretentious

cursiva *nf* : italics *pl*

curso *nm* **1** : course **2** : (school) year **3 en** ~ : under way **4 en** ~ : current

curtir *vt* **1** : tan **2** : harden (skin, features, etc.) — **curtiduría** *nf* : tannery

curva *nf* **1** : curve, bend **2** ~ **de nivel** : contour — **curvo, -va** *adj* : curved, bent

cúspide *nf* : apex, peak

custodia *nf* : custody — **custodiar** *vt* : guard, look after — **custodio, -dia** *n* : guardian

cutáneo, -nea *adj* : skin

cutícula *nf* : cuticle

cutis *nms & pl* : skin, complexion

cuyo, -ya *adj* **1** : whose, of whom, of which **2 en cuyo caso** : in which case

D

d *nf* : d, fourth letter of the Spanish alphabet

dádiva *nf* : gift, handout — **dadivoso, -sa** *adj* : generous

dado, -da *adj* **1** : given **2 dado que** : provided that, since — **dados** *nmpl* : dice

daga *nf* : dagger

daltónico, -ca *adj* : color-blind

dama *nf* **1** : lady **2 ～s** *nfpl* : checkers

damnificar {72} *vt* : damage, injure

danés, -nesa *adj* : Danish — **danés** *nm* : Danish (language)

danzar {21} *v* : dance — **danza** *nf* : dance, dancing

dañar *vt* : damage, harm — **dañarse** *vr* **1** : be damaged **2** : hurt oneself — **dañino, -na** *adj* : harmful — **daño** *nm* **1** : damage, harm **2 ～s y perjuicios** : damages

dar {22} *vt* **1** : give **2** PRODUCIR : yield, produce **3** : strike (the hour) **4** MOSTRAR : show — *vi* **1 ～ como** : consider, regard as **2 ～ con** : run into, meet **3 ～ contra** : knock against **4 ～ para** : be enough for — **darse** *vr* **1** : happen **2 ～ contra** : bump into **3 ～ por** : consider oneself **4 dárselas de** : pose as

dardo *nm* : dart

dársena *nf* : dock

datar *vt* : date — *vi ～ de* : date from

dátil *nm* : date (fruit)

dato *nm* **1** : fact **2 ～s** *nmpl* : data

de *prep* **1** : of **2 ～ Managua** : from Managua **3 ～ niño** : as a child **4 ～ noche** : at night **5 las tres ～ la mañana** : three o'clock in the morning **6 más ～ 10** : more than 10

deambular *vi* : wander about, stroll

debajo *adv* **1** : underneath **2 ～ de** : under, underneath **3 por ～** : below, beneath

debatir *vt* : debate — **debatirse** *vr* : struggle — **debate** *nm* : debate

deber *vt* : owe — *v aux* **1** : have to, should **2** (*expressing probability*) : must — **deberse** *vr ～ a* : be due to — ～ *nm* **1** : duty **2 ～es** *nmpl* : homework — **debido, -da** *adj ～ a* : due to, owing to

débil *adj* : weak, feeble — **debilidad** *nf* : weakness — **debilitar** *vt* : weaken — **debilitarse** *vr* : get weak — **débilmente** *adv* : weakly, faintly

débito *nm* **1** : debit **2** DEUDA : debt

debutar *vi* : debut — **debut** *nm, pl ～s* : debut — **debutante** *nf* : debutante *f*

década *nf* : decade

decadencia *nf* : decadence — **decadente** *adj* : decadent

decaer {13} *vi* : decline, weaken

decano, -na *n* : dean

decapitar *vt* : behead

decena *nf* : ten, about ten

decencia *nf* : decency

decenio *nm* : decade

decente *adj* : decent

decepcionar *vt* : disappoint — **decepción** *nf, pl* **-ciones** : disappointment

decibelio *or* **decibel** *nm* : decibel

decidir *vt* : decide, determine — *vi* : decide — **decidirse** *vr* : make up one's mind — **decididamente** *adv* : definitely, decidedly — **decidido, -da** *adj* : determined, resolute

decimal *adj* : decimal

décimo, -ma *adj & n* : tenth

decimoctavo, -va *adj* : eighteenth — ～ *n* : eighteenth (in a series)

decimocuarto, -ta *adj* : fourteenth — ～ *n* : fourteenth (in a series)

decimonoveno, -na *or* **decimonono, -na** *adj* : nineteenth — ～ *n* : nineteenth (in a series)

decimoquinto, -ta *adj* : fifteenth — ～ *n* : fifteenth (in a series)

decimoséptimo, -ma *adj* : seventeenth — ～ *n* : seventeenth (in a series)

decimosexto, -ta *adj* : sixteenth — ～ *n* : sixteenth (in a series)

decimotercero, -ra *adj* : thirteenth — ～ *n* : thirteenth (in a series)

decir {23} *vt* **1** : say **2** CONTAR : tell **3 es ～** : that is to say **4 querer ～** : mean — **decirse** *vr* **1** : tell oneself **2 ¿cómo se dice...en español?** : how do you say...in Spanish? — ～ *nm* : saying, expression

decisión *nf, pl* **-siones** : decision — **decisivo, -va** *adj* : decisive

declarar *vt* : declare — *vi* : testify — **declararse** *vr* **1** : declare oneself **2** : break out (of a fire, an epidemic, etc.) — **declaración** *nf, pl* **-ciones** : statement

declinar *v* : decline

declive *nm* **1** : decline **2** PENDIENTE : slope

decolorar *vt* : bleach — **decolorarse** *vr* : fade

decoración *nf, pl* **-ciones** : decoration — **decorado** *nm* : stage set — **decorar** *vt* : decorate — **decorativo, -va** *adj* : decorative

decoro *nm* : decency, decorum — **decoroso, -sa** *adj* : decent, proper

decrecer {53} *vi* : decrease
decrépito, -ta *adj* : decrepit
decretar *vt* : decree — **decreto** *nm* : decree
dedal *nm* : thimble
dedicar {72} *vt* : dedicate — **dedicarse** *vr*
~ **a** : devote oneself to — **dedicación** *nf,*
pl **-ciones** : dedication — **dedicatoria** *nf*
: dedication, inscription
dedo *nm* **1** : finger **2** ~ **del pie** : toe
deducir {61} *vt* **1** INFERIR : deduce **2** DE-
SCONTAR : deduct — **deducción** *nf, pl*
-ciones : deduction
defecar {72} *vi* : defecate
defecto *nm* : defect — **defectuoso, -sa** *adj*
: defective, faulty
defender {56} *vt* : defend — **defenderse** *vr*
: defend oneself — **defensa** *nf* : defense —
defensiva *nf* : defensive — **defensivo, -va**
adj : defensive — **defensor, -sora** *n* **1** : defender **2** *or* **abogado defensor** : defense
counsel
deferencia *nf* : deference — **deferente** *adj*
: deferential
deficiencia *nf* : deficiency — **deficiente** *adj*
: deficient
déficit *nm, pl* **-cits** : deficit
definir *vt* : define — **definición** *nf, pl*
-ciones : definition — **definitivo, -va** *adj* **1**
: definitive **2 en definitiva** : in short
deformar *vt* **1** : deform **2** : distort (the truth,
etc.) — **deformación** *nf, pl* **-ciones** : distortion — **deforme** *adj* : deformed — **deformidad** *nf* : deformity
defraudar *vt* **1** : defraud **2** DECEPCIONAR
: disappoint
degenerar *vi* : degenerate — **degenerado,
-da** *adj* : degenerate
degradar *vt* **1** : degrade **2** : demote (in the
military)
degustar *vt* : taste
dehesa *nf* : pasture
deidad *nf* : deity
dejar *vt* **1** : leave **2** ABANDONAR : abandon
3 PERMITIR : allow — *vi* ~ **de** : quit — **de-
jado, -da** *adj* : slovenly, careless
dejo *nm* **1** : aftertaste **2** : (regional) accent
delantal *nm* : apron
delante *adv* **1** : ahead **2** ~ **de** : in front of
delantera *nf* **1** : front **2 tomar la** ~ : take
the lead — **delantero, -ra** *adj* : front, forward — ~ *n* : forward (in sports)
delatar *vt* : denounce, inform against
delegar {52} *vt* : delegate — **delegación** *nf,
pl* **-ciones** : delegation — **delegado, -da** *n*
: delegate, representative
deleitar *vt* : delight, please — **deleite** *nm*
: delight
deletrear *vi* : spell (out)
delfín *nm, pl* **-fines** : dolphin

delgado, -da *adj* : thin
deliberar *vi* : deliberate — **deliberación** *nf,
pl* **-ciones** : deliberation — **deliberado, -da**
adj : deliberate, intentional
delicadeza *nf* **1** : delicacy, daintiness **2**
SUAVIDAD : gentleness **3** TACTO : tact —
delicado, -da *adj* **1** : delicate **2** SENSIBLE
: sensible **3** DISCRETO : tactful
delicia *nf* : delight — **delicioso, -sa** *adj* **1**
: delightful **2** RICO : delicious
delictivo, -va *adj* : criminal
delimitar *vt* : define, set the boundaries of
delincuencia *nf* : delinquency, crime —
delincuente *adj & nmf* : delinquent, criminal — **delinquir** {24} *vi* : break the law
delirante *adj* : delirious — **delirar** *vi* **1** : be
delirious **2** ~ **por** *fam* : rave about —
delirio *nm* **1** : delirium **2** ~ **de grandeza**
: delusions of grandeur
delito *nm* : crime
delta *nm* : delta
demacrado, -da *adj* : emaciated
demandar *vt* **1** : sue **2** PEDIR : demand **3**
Lat : require — **demanda** *nf* **1** : lawsuit **2**
PETICIÓN : request **3 la oferta y la** ~ : supply and demand — **demandante** *nmf*
: plaintiff
demás *adj* : rest of the, other — ~ *pron* **1**
lo (la, los, las) ~ : the rest, others **2 por**
~ : extremely **3 por lo** ~ : otherwise **4 y**
~ : and so on
demasiado *adv* **1** : too **2** : too much — ~
adj : too much, too many
demencia *nf* : madness — **demente** *adj* : insane, mad
democracia *nf* : democracy — **demócrata**
nmf : democrat — **democrático, -ca** *adj*
: democratic
demoler {47} *vt* : demolish — **demolición**
nf, pl **-ciones** : demolition
demonio *nm* : devil, demon
demorar *v* : delay — **demorarse** *vr* : take a
long time — **demora** *nf* : delay
demostrar {19} *vt* **1** : demonstrate **2**
MOSTRAR : show — **demostración** *nf, pl*
-ciones : demonstration
demudar *vt* : change, alter
denegar {49} *vt* : deny, refuse — **denegación** *nf, pl* **-ciones** : denial, refusal
denigrar *vt* **1** : denigrate **2** INJURIAR : insult
denominador *nm* : denominator
denotar *vt* : denote, show
densidad *nf* : density — **denso, -sa** *adj*
: dense
dental *adj* : dental — **dentado, -da** *adj*
: toothed, notched — **dentadura** *nf* ~ **postiza** : dentures *pl* — **dentífrico** *nm* : toothpaste — **dentista** *nmf* : dentist

dentro *adv* **1** : in, inside **2** ~ **de poco** : soon, shortly **3 por** ~ : inside

denuedo *nm* : courage

denunciar *vt* **1** : denounce **2** : report (a crime) — **denuncia** *nf* **1** : accusation **2** : (police) report

departamento *nm* **1** : department **2** *Lat* : apartment

depender *vi* **1** : depend **2** ~ **de** : depend on — **dependencia** *nf* **1** : dependence, dependency **2** SUCURSAL : branch office — **dependiente** *adj* : dependent — **dependiente, -ta** *n* : clerk, salesperson

deplorar *vt* : deplore, regret

deponer {60} *vt* : remove from office, depose

deportar *vt* : deport — **deportación** *nf, pl* **-ciones** : deportation

deporte *nm* : sport, sports *pl* — **deportista** *nmf* : sportsman *m*, sportswoman *f* — **deportivo, -va** *adj* **1** : sporty **2 artículos deportivos** : sporting goods

depositar *vt* **1** : put, place **2** : deposit (in a bank, etc.) — **depósito** *nm* **1** : deposit **2** ALMACÉN : warehouse

depravado, -da *adj* : depraved

depreciarse *vr* : depreciate — **depreciación** *nf* : depreciation

depredador *nm* : predator

deprimir *vt* : depress — **deprimirse** *vr* : get depressed — **depresión** *nf, pl* **-siones** : depression

derecha *nf* **1** : right side **2** : right wing (in politics) — **derechista** *adj* : right-wing — **derecho** *nm* **1** : right **2** LEY : law — ~ *adv* : straight — **derecho, -cha** *adj* **1** : right, right-hand **2** VERTICAL : upright **3** RECTO : straight

deriva *nf* **1** : drift **2 a la** ~ : adrift — **derivación** *nf, pl* **-ciones** : derivation — **derivar** *vi* **1** : drift **2** ~ **de** : derive from

derramamiento *nm* ~ **de sangre** : bloodshed

derramar *vt* **1** : spill **2** : shed (tears, blood) — **derramarse** *vr* : overflow — **derrame** *nm* **1** : spilling **2** : discharge, hemorrhage

derrapar *vi* : skid — **derrape** *nm* : skid

derretir {54} *vt* : melt, thaw — **derretirse** *vr* **1** : melt, thaw **2** ~ **por** *fam* : be crazy about

derribar *vt* **1** : demolish **2** : bring down (a plane, a tree, etc.) **3** : overthrow (a government, etc.)

derrocar {72} *vt* : overthrow

derrochar *vt* : waste, squander — **derrochador, -dora** *n* : spendthrift — **derroche** *nm* : extravagance, waste

derrotar *vt* : defeat — **derrota** *nf* : defeat

derruir {41} *vt* : demolish, tear down

derrumbar *vt* : demolish, knock down — **derrumbarse** *vr* : collapse, break down — **derrumbamiento** *nm* : collapse — **derrumbe** *nm* : collapse

desabotonar *vt* : unbutton, undo

desabrido, -da *adj* : bland

desabrochar *vt* : unbutton, undo — **desabrocharse** *vr* : come undone

desacato *nm* **1** : disrespect **2** : contempt (of court) — **desacatar** *vt* : defy, disobey

desacertado, -da *adj* : mistaken, wrong — **desacertar** {55} *vi* : be mistaken — **desacierto** *nm* : mistake, error

desaconsejar *vt* : advise against — **desaconsejable** *adj* : inadvisable

desacreditar *vt* : discredit

desactivar *vt* : deactivate

desacuerdo *nm* : disagreement

desafiar {85} *vt* : defy, challenge — **desafiante** *adj* : defiant

desafilado, -da *adj* : blunt

desafinado, -da *adj* : out-of-tune, off-key

desafío *nm* : challenge, defiance

desafortunado, -da *adj* : unfortunate — **desafortunadamente** *adv* : unfortunately

desagradar *vt* : displease — **desagradable** *adj* : disagreeable, unpleasant

desagradecido, -da *adj* : ungrateful

desagrado *nm* **1** : displeasure **2 con** ~ : reluctantly

desagravio *nm* : amends, reparation

desagregarse {52} *vr* : disintegrate

desaguar {10} *vi* : drain, empty — **desagüe** *nm* **1** : drainage **2** : drain (of a sink, etc.)

desahogar {52} *vt* **1** : relieve **2** : give vent to (anger, etc.) — **desahogarse** *vr* : let off steam, unburden oneself — **desahogado, -da** *adj* **1** : roomy **2** ADINERADO : comfortable, well-off — **desahogo** *nm* **1** : relief **2 con** ~ : comfortably

desahuciar *vt* **1** : deprive of hope **2** DESALOJAR : evict — **desahucio** *nm* : eviction

desaire *nm* : snub, rebuff — **desairar** *vt* : snub, slight

desalentar {55} *vt* : discourage — **desaliento** *nm* : discouragement

desaliñado, -da *adj* : slovenly

desalmado, -da *adj* : heartless, cruel

desalojar *vt* **1** : evacuate **2** DESAHUCIAR : evict

desamparar *vt* : abandon — **desamparo** *nm* : abandonment, desertion

desamueblado, -da *adj* : unfurnished

desangrarse *vr* : lose blood, bleed to death

desanimar *vt* : discourage — **desanimarse** *vr* : get discouraged — **desanimado, -da** *adj* : downhearted, despondent — **desánimo** *nm* : discouragement

desanudar *vt* : untie

desaparecer {53} *vi* : disappear — **desaparecido, -da** *n* : missing person — **desaparición** *nf, pl* **-ciones** : disappearance

desapasionado, -da *adj* : dispassionate

desapego *nm* : indifference

desapercibido, -da *adj* : unnoticed

desaprobar {19} *vt* : disapprove of — **desaprobación** *nf, pl* **-ciones** : disapproval

desaprovechar *vt* : waste

desarmar *vt* **1** : disarm **2** DESMONTAR : dismantle, take apart — **desarme** *nm* : disarmament

desarraigar {52} *vt* : uproot, root out

desarreglar *vt* **1** : mess up **2** : disrupt (plans, etc.) — **desarreglado, -da** *adj* : disorganized — **desarreglo** *nm* : untidiness, disorder

desarrollar *vt* : develop — **desarrollarse** *vr* : take place — **desarrollo** *nm* : development

desarticular *vt* **1** : break up, dismantle **2** : dislocate (a bone)

desaseado, -da *adj* **1** : dirty **2** DESORDENADO : messy

desastre *nm* : disaster — **desastroso, -sa** *adj* : disastrous

desatar *vt* **1** : undo, untie **2** : unleash (passions) — **desatarse** *vr* **1** : come undone **2** DESENCADENARSE : break out, erupt

desatascar {72} *vt* : unclog

desatender {56} *vt* **1** : disregard **2** : neglect (an obligation, etc.) — **desatento, -ta** *adj* : inattentive

desatinado, -da *adj* : foolish, silly

desautorizado, -da *adj* : unauthorized

desavenencia *nf* : disagreement

desayunar *vi* : have breakfast — *vt* : have for breakfast — **desayuno** *nm* : breakfast

desbancar {72} *vt* : oust

desbarajuste *nm* : disorder, confusion

desbaratar *vt* : ruin, destroy — **desbaratarse** *vr* : fall apart

desbocarse {72} *vr* : run away, bolt

desbordar *vt* **1** : overflow **2** : exceed (limits) — **desbordarse** *vr* : overflow — **desbordamiento** *nm* : overflow

descabellado, -da *adj* : crazy

descafeinado, -da *adj* : decaffeinated

descalabrar *vt* : hit on the head — **descalabro** *nm* : misfortune, setback

descalificar {72} *vt* : disqualify — **descalificación** *nf, pl* **-ciones** : disqualification

descalzarse {21} *vr* : take off one's shoes — **descalzo, -za** *adj* : barefoot

descaminar *vt* : mislead, lead astray

descansar *v* : rest — **descanso** *nm* **1** : rest **2** : landing (of a staircase) **3** : intermission (in theater), halftime (in sports)

descapotable *adj & nm* : convertible

descarado, -da *adj* : insolent, shameless

descargar {52} *vt* **1** : unload **2** : discharge (a firearm, etc.) — **descarga** *nf* **1** : unloading **2** : discharge (of a firearm, of electricity, etc.) — **descargo** *nm* **1** : unloading **2** : discharge (of a duty, etc.) **3** : defense (in law)

descarnado, -da *adj* : scrawny, gaunt

descaro *nm* : insolence, nerve

descarrilar *vi* : derail — **descarrilarse** *vr* : be derailed

descartar *vt* : reject — **descartarse** *vr* : discard

descascarar *vt* : peel, shell, husk

descender {56} *vt* **1** : go down **2** BAJAR : lower — *vi* **1** : descend **2** ～ **de** : be descended from — **descendencia** *nf* **1** : descendants *pl* **2** LINAJE : lineage, descent — **descendiente** *nmf* : descendant — **descenso** *nm* **1** : descent **2** : drop, fall (in level, in temperature, etc.)

descifrar *vt* : decipher, decode

descolgar {16} *vt* **1** : take down **2** : pick up, answer (the telephone)

descolorarse *vr* : fade — **descolorido, -da** *adj* : faded, discolored

descomponer {60} *vt* : break down — **descomponerse** *vr* **1** : rot, decompose **2** *Lat* : break down — **descompuesto, -ta** *adj* *Lat* : out of order

descomunal *adj* : enormous

desconcertar {55} *vt* : disconcert, confuse — **desconcertante** *adj* : confusing — **desconcierto** *nm* : confusion, bewilderment

desconectar *vt* : disconnect

desconfiar {85} *vi* ～ **de** : distrust — **desconfiado, -da** *adj* : distrustful — **desconfianza** *nf* : distrust

descongelar *vt* **1** : thaw, defrost **2** : unfreeze (assets)

descongestionante *nm* : decongestant

desconocer {18} *vt* : not know, fail to recognize — **desconocido, -da** *adj* : unknown — ～ *n* : stranger

desconsiderado, -da *adj* : inconsiderate

desconsolar *vt* : distress — **desconsolado, -da** *adj* : heartbroken — **desconsuelo** *nm* : grief, sorrow

descontar {19} *vt* : discount

descontento, -ta *adj* : dissatisfied — **descontento** *nm* : discontent

descontinuar *vt* : discontinue

descorazonado, -da *adj* : discouraged

descorrer *vt* : draw back

descortés *adj, pl* **-teses** : rude — **descortesía** *nf* : discourtesy, rudeness

descoyuntar *vt* : dislocate

descrédito *nm* : discredit

descremado, -da *adj* : nonfat, skim
describir {33} *vt* : describe — **descripción** *nf, pl* **-ciones** : description — **descriptivo, -va** *adj* : descriptive
descubierto, -ta *adj* **1** : exposed, uncovered **2 al descubierto** : in the open — **descubierto** *nm* : deficit, overdraft
descubrir {2} *vt* **1** : discover **2** REVELAR : reveal — **descubrimiento** *nm* : discovery
descuento *nm* : discount
descuidar *vt* : neglect — **descuidarse** *vr* **1** : be careless **2** ABANDONARSE : let oneself go — **descuidado, -da** *adj* **1** : careless, sloppy **2** DESATENDIDO : neglected — **descuido** *nm* : neglect, carelessness
desde *prep* **1** : from (a place), since (a time) **2 ~ luego** : of course
desdén *nm* : scorn, disdain — **desdeñar** *vt* : scorn — **desdeñoso, -sa** *adj* : disdainful
desdicha *nf* **1** : misery **2** DESGRACIA : misfortune — **desdichado, -da** *adj* : unfortunate, unhappy
desear *vt* : wish, want — **deseable** *adj* : desirable
desecar *vt* : dry up
desechar *vt* **1** : throw away **2** RECHAZAR : reject — **desechable** *adj* : disposable — **desechos** *nmpl* : rubbish
desembarazarse {21} *vr* **~ de** : get rid of
desembarcar {72} *vi* : disembark — *vt* : unload — **desembarcadero** *nm* : jetty, landing pier — **desembarco** *nm* : landing
desembocar {72} *vi* **~ en 1** : flow into **2** : lead to (a result) — **desembocadura** *nf* **1** : mouth (of a river) **2** : opening, end (of a street)
desembolsar *vt* : pay out — **desembolso** *nm* : payment, outlay
desembragar *vi* : disengage the clutch
desempacar {72} *v Lat* : unpack
desempate *nm* : tiebreaker
desempeñar *vt* **1** : play (a role) **2** : redeem (from a pawnshop) — **desempeñarse** *vr* : get out of debt
desempleo *nm* : unemployment — **desempleado, -da** *adj* : unemployed
desempolvar *vt* : dust
desencadenar *vt* **1** : unchain **2** : trigger, unleash (protests, crises, etc.) — **desencadenarse** *vr* : break loose
desencajar *vt* **1** : dislocate **2** DESCONECTAR : disconnect
desencanto *nm* : disillusionment
desenchufar *vt* : disconnect, unplug
desenfadado, -da *adj* : carefree, confident — **desenfado** *nm* : confidence, ease
desenfrenado, -da *adj* : unrestrained — **desenfreno** *nm* : abandon, lack of restraint
desenganchar *vt* : unhook

desengañar *vt* : disillusion — **desengaño** *nm* : disappointment
desenlace *nm* : ending, outcome
desenmarañar *vt* : disentangle
desenmascarar *vt* : unmask
desenredar *vt* : untangle — **desenredarse** *vr* **~ de** : extricate oneself from
desenrollar *vt* : unroll, unwind
desentenderse {56} *vr* **~ de** : want nothing to do with
desenterrar {55} *vt* : dig up, disinter
desentonar *vi* **1** : be out of tune **2** : clash (of colors, etc.)
desenvoltura *nf* : confidence, ease
desenvolver {89} *vt* : unfold, unwrap — **desenvolverse** *vr* : unfold, develop
desenvuelto, -ta *adj* : confident, self-assured
deseo *nm* : desire — **deseoso, -sa** *adj* : eager, anxious
desequilibrar *vt* : throw off balance — **desequilibrado, -da** *adj* : unbalanced — **desequilibrio** *nm* : imbalance
desertar *vt* : desert — **deserción** *nf, pl* **-ciones** : desertion — **desertor, -tora** *n* : deserter
desesperar *vt* : exasperate — *vi* : despair — **desesperarse** *vr* : become exasperated — **desesperación** *nf, pl* **-ciones** : desperation, despair — **desesperado, -da** *adj* : desperate, hopeless
desestimar *vt* : reject
desfalcar {72} *vt* : embezzle — **desfalco** *nm* : embezzlement
desfallecer {53} *vi* **1** : weaken **2** DESMAYARSE : faint
desfavorable *adj* : unfavorable
desfigurar *vt* **1** : disfigure, mar **2** : distort (the truth)
desfiladero *nm* : mountain pass, gorge
desfilar *vi* : march, parade — **desfile** *nm* : parade, procession
desfogar {52} *vt* : vent — **desfogarse** *vr* : let off steam
desgajar *vt* : tear off, break apart — **desgajarse** *vr* : come off
desgana *nf* **1** : lack of appetite **2** : lack of enthusiasm, reluctance
desgarbado, -da *adj* : gawky, ungainly
desgarrar *vt* : tear, rip — **desgarrador, -dora** *adj* : heartbreaking — **desgarro** *nm* : tear
desgastar *vt* : wear away, wear down — **desgaste** *nm* : deterioration, wear and tear
desgracia *nf* **1** : misfortune **2 caer en ~** : fall into disgrace **3 por ~** : unfortunately — **desgraciadamente** *adv* : unfortunately — **desgraciado, -da** *adj* : unfortunate
deshabitado, -da *adj* : uninhabited

deshacer {40} *vt* **1** : undo **2** DESTRUIR : destroy, ruin **3** DISOLVER : dissolve **4** : break (an agreement), cancel (plans, etc.) — **deshacerse** *vr* **1** : come undone **2** ~ **de** : get rid of **3** ~ **en** : lavish, heap (praise, etc.) — **deshecho, -cha** *adj* **1** : undone **2** DESTROZADO : destroyed, ruined

desheredar *vt* : disinherit

deshidratar *vt* : dehydrate

deshielo *nm* : thaw

deshilachar *vt* : unravel — **deshilacharse** *vr* : fray

deshonesto, -ta *adj* : dishonest

deshonrar *vt* : dishonor, disgrace — **deshonra** *nf* : dishonor — **deshonroso, -sa** *adj* : dishonorable

deshuesar *vt* **1** : pit (a fruit) **2** : bone, debone (meat)

desidia *nf* **1** : indolence **2** DESASEO : sloppiness

desierto, -ta *adj* : deserted, uninhabited — **desierto** *nm* : desert

designar *vt* : designate — **designación** *nf, pl* **-ciones** : appointment (to an office, etc.)

designio *nm* : plan

desigual *adj* **1** : unequal **2** DISPAREJO : uneven — **desigualdad** *nf* : inequality

desilusionar *vt* : disappoint, disillusion — **desilusión** *nf, pl* **-siones** : disappointment, disillusionment

desinfectar *vt* : disinfect — **desinfectante** *adj & nm* : disinfectant

desinflar *vt* : deflate — **desinflarse** *vr* : deflate, go flat

desinhibido, -da *adj* : uninhibited

desintegrar *vt* : disintegrate — **desintegrarse** *vr* : disintegrate — **desintegración** *nf, pl* **-ciones** : disintegration

desinteresado, -da *adj* : unselfish, generous — **desinterés** *nm* : unselfishness

desistir *vi* ~ **de** : give up

desleal *adj* : disloyal — **deslealtad** *nf* : disloyalty

desleír {66} *vt* : dilute, dissolve

desligar {52} *vt* **1** : untie **2** SEPARAR : separate — **desligarse** *vr* : extricate oneself

desliz *nm, pl* **-lices** : slip, mistake — **deslizar** {21} *vt* : slide, slip — **deslizarse** *vr* : slide, glide

deslucido, -da *adj* : dingy, tarnished

deslumbrar *vt* : dazzle — **deslumbrante** *adj* : dazzling, blinding

deslustrar *vt* : tarnish, dull

desmán *nm, pl* **-manes** : outrage, excess

desmandarse *vr* : get out of hand

desmantelar *vt* : dismantle

desmañado, -da *adj* : clumsy

desmayar *vi* : lose heart — **desmayarse** *vr* : faint — **desmayo** *nm* : faint

desmedido, -da *adj* : excessive

desmejorar *vt* : impair — *vi* : deteriorate

desmemoriado, -da *adj* : forgetful

desmentir {76} *vt* : deny — **desmentido** *nm* : denial

desmenuzar {21} *vt* **1** : crumble **2** EXAMINAR : scrutinize — **desmenuzarse** *vr* : crumble

desmerecer {53} *vt* : be unworthy of — *vi* : decline in value

desmesurado, -da *adj* : excessive

desmigajar *vt* : crumble

desmontar *vt* **1** : dismantle, take apart **2** ALLANAR : level — *vi* : dismount

desmoralizar {21} *vt* : demoralize

desmoronarse *vr* : crumble

desnivel *nm* : unevenness

desnudar *vt* : undress, strip — **desnudarse** *vr* : get undressed — **desnudez** *nf, pl* **-deces** : nudity, nakedness — **desnudo, -da** *adj* : nude, naked — **desnudo** *nm* : nude

desnutrición *nf, pl* **-ciones** : malnutrition

desobedecer {53} *v* : disobey — **desobediencia** *nf* : disobedience — **desobediente** *adj* : disobedient

desocupar *vt* : empty, vacate — **desocupado, -da** *adj* **1** : vacant **2** DESEMPLEADO : unemployed

desodorante *adj & nm* : deodorant

desolado, -da *adj* **1** : desolate **2** DESCONSOLADO : devastated, distressed — **desolación** *nf, pl* **-ciones** : desolation

desorden *nm, pl* **desórdenes** : disorder, mess — **desordenado, -da** *adj* : untidy — **desordenadamente** *adv* : in a disorderly way

desorganizar {21} *vt* : disorganize — **desorganización** *nf, pl* **-ciones** : disorganization

desorientar *vt* : disorient, confuse — **desorientarse** *vr* : lose one's way

desovar *vi* : spawn

despachar *vt* **1** : deal with (a task, etc.) **2** ENVIAR : dispatch, send **3** : wait on, serve (customers) — **despacho** *nm* **1** : dispatch, shipment **2** OFICINA : office

despacio *adv* : slowly

desparramar *vt* : spill, scatter, spread

despavorido, -da *adj* : terrified

despecho *nm* **1** : spite **2 a** ~ **de** : despite, in spite of

despectivo, -va *adj* **1** : pejorative **2** DESPRECIATIVO : contemptuous

despedazar {21} *vt* : tear apart

despedir {54} *vt* **1** : see off **2** DESTITUIR : dismiss, fire **3** DESPRENDER : emit — **despedirse** *vr* : say good-bye — **despedida** *nf* : farewell, good-bye

despegar {52} *vt* : detach, unstick — *vi*

: take off — **despegado, -da** *adj* : cold, distant — **despegue** *nm* : takeoff

despeinar *vt* : ruffle (hair) — **despeinado, -da** *adj* : disheveled, unkempt

despejar *vt* : clear, free — *vi* : clear up — **despejado, -da** *adj* **1** : clear, fair **2** LÚCIDO : clear-headed

despellejar *vt* : skin (an animal)

despensa *nf* : pantry, larder

despeñadero *nm* : precipice

desperdiciar *vt* : waste — **desperdicio** *nm* **1** : waste **2 ~s** *nmpl* : scraps

desperfecto *nm* : flaw, defect

despertar {55} *vi* : awaken, wake up — *vt* : wake, rouse — **despertador** *nm* : alarm clock

despiadado, -da *adj* : pitiless, merciless

despido *nm* : dismissal, layoff

despierto, -ta *adj* : awake

despilfarrar *vt* : squander — **despilfarrador, -dora** *n* : spendthrift — **despilfarro** *nm* : extravagance, wastefulness

despistar *vt* : throw off the track, confuse — **despistarse** *vr* : lose one's way — **despistado, -da** *adj* **1** : absentminded **2** DESORIENTADO : confused — **despiste** *nm* **1** : absentmindedness **2** ERROR : mistake

desplazar {21} *vt* : displace — **desplazarse** *vr* : travel

desplegar {49} *vt* : unfold, spread out — **despliegue** *nm* : display

desplomarse *vr* : collapse

desplumar *vt* **1** : pluck **2** *fam* : fleece

despoblado, -da *adj* : uninhabited, deserted — **despoblado** *nm* : deserted area

despojar *vt* : strip, deprive — **despojos** *nmpl* **1** : plunder **2** RESTOS : remains, scraps

desportillar *vt* : chip — **desportillarse** *vr* : chip — **desportilladura** *nf* : chip, nick

despota *nmf* : despot

despotricar *vi* : rant (and rave)

despreciar *vt* : despise, scorn — **despreciable** *adj* **1** : despicable **2 una cantidad ~** : a negligible amount — **desprecio** *nm* : disdain, scorn

desprender *vt* **1** : detach, remove **2** EMITIR : give off — **desprenderse** *vr* **1** : come off **2** DEDUCIRSE : be inferred, follow — **desprendimiento** *nm* **~ de tierras** : landslide

despreocupado, -da *adj* : carefree, unconcerned

desprestigiar *vt* : discredit — **desprestigiarse** *vr* : lose face

desprevenido, -da *adj* : unprepared

desproporcionado, -da : out of proportion

despropósito *nm* : (piece of) nonsense, absurdity

desprovisto, -ta *adj* **~ de** : lacking in

después *adv* **1** : afterward **2** ENTONCES : then, next **3 ~ de** : after **4 después (de) que** : after **5 ~ de todo** : after all

despuntado, -da *adj* : blunt, dull

desquiciar *vt* : drive crazy

desquitarse *vr* **1** : retaliate **2 ~ con** : take it out on, get back at — **desquite** *nm* : revenge

destacar {72} *vt* : emphasize — *vi* : stand out — **destacado, -da** *adj* : outstanding

destapar *vt* : open, uncover — **destapador** *nm Lat* : bottle opener

destartalado, -da *adj* : dilapidated

destellar *vi* : flash, sparkle — **destello** *nm* : sparkle, twinkle, flash

destemplado, -da *adj* **1** : out of tune **2** MAL : out of sorts **3** : unpleasant (of weather)

desteñir {67} *vt* : fade, bleach — *vi* : run, fade — **desteñirse** *vr* : fade

desterrar {55} *vt* : banish, exile — **desterrado, -da** *n* : exile

destetar *vt* : wean

destiempo *adv* **a ~** : at the wrong time

destierro *nm* : exile

destilar *vt* : distill — **destilería** *nf* : distillery

destinar *vt* **1** : assign, allocate **2** NOMBRAR : appoint — **destinado, -da** *adj* : destined — **destinatario, -ria** *n* : addressee — **destino** *nm* **1** : destiny **2** RUMBO : destination

destituir {41} *vt* : dismiss — **destitución** *nf, pl* **-ciones** : dismissal

destornillar *vt* : unscrew — **destornillador** *nm* : screwdriver

destreza *nf* : skill, dexterity

destrozar {21} *vt* : destroy, wreck — **destrozos** *nmpl* : damage, destruction

destrucción *nf, pl* **-ciones** : destruction — **destructivo, -va** *adj* : destructive — **destruir** {41} *vt* : destroy

desunir *vt* : split, divide

desusado, -da *adj* **1** : obsolete **2** INSÓLITO : unusual — **desuso** *nm* **caer en ~** : fall into disuse

desvaído, -da *adj* **1** : pale, washed-out **2** BORROSO : vague, blurred

desvalido, -da *adj* : destitute, needy

desvalijar *vt* : rob

desván *nm, pl* **-vanes** : attic

desvanecer {53} *vt* : make disappear — **desvanecerse** *vr* **1** : vanish **2** DESMAYARSE : faint

desvariar {85} *vi* : be delirious — **desvarío** *nm* : delirium

desvelar *vt* : keep awake — **desvelarse** *vr* : stay awake — **desvelo** *nm* **1** : sleeplessness **2 ~s** *nmpl* : efforts

desvencijado, -da *adj* : dilapidated, rickety

desventaja *nf* : disadvantage

desventura *nf* : misfortune

desvergonzado, -da *adj* : shameless — **desvergüenza** *nf* : shamelessness

desvestir {54} *vt* : undress — **desvestirse** *vr* : get undressed

desviación *nf, pl* **-ciones** 1 : deviation 2 : detour (in a road) — **desviar** {85} *vt* : divert, deflect — **desviarse** *vr* 1 : branch off 2 APARTARSE : stray — **desvío** *nm* : diversion, detour

detallar *vt* : detail — **detallado, -da** *adj* : detailed, thorough — **detalle** *nm* 1 : detail 2 **al** ~ : retail — **detallista** *adj* : retail — ~ *nmf* : retailer

detectar *vt* : detect — **detective** *nmf* : detective

detener {80} *vt* 1 : arrest, detain 2 PARAR : stop 3 RETRASAR : delay — **detenerse** *vr* 1 : stop 2 DEMORARSE : linger — **detención** *nf, pl* **-ciones** : arrest, detention

detergente *nm* : detergent

deteriorar *vt* : damage — **deteriorarse** *vr* : wear out, deteriorate — **deteriorado, -da** *adj* : damaged, worn — **deterioro** *nm* : deterioration, damage

determinar *vt* 1 : determine 2 MOTIVAR : bring about 3 DECIDIR : decide — **determinarse** *vr* : decide — **determinación** *nf, pl* **-ciones** 1 : determination 2 **tomar una** ~ : make a decision — **determinado, -da** *adj* 1 : determined 2 ESPECÍFICO : specific

detestar *vt* : detest

detonar *vi* : explode, detonate — **detonación** *nf, pl* **-ciones** : detonation

detrás *adv* 1 : behind 2 ~ **de** : in back of 3 **por** ~ : from behind

detrimento *nm* **en** ~ **de** : to the detriment of

deuda *nf* : debt — **deudor, -dora** *n* : debtor

devaluar {3} *vt* : devalue — **devaluarse** *vr* : depreciate

devastar *vt* : devastate — **devastador, -dora** *adj* : devastating

devenir {87} *vi* 1 : come about 2 ~ **en** : become, turn into

devoción *nf, pl* **-ciones** : devotion

devolución *nf, pl* **-ciones** : return

devolver {89} *vt* 1 RESTITUIR : give back 2 : refund, pay back — *vi* : vomit — **devolverse** *vr Lat* : return, come back

devorar *vt* : devour

devoto, -ta *adj* : devout — ~ *n* : devotee

día *nm* 1 : day 2 : daytime 3 **al** ~ : up-to-date 4 **en pleno** ~ : in broad daylight

diabetes *nf* : diabetes — **diabético, -ca** *adj* & *n* : diabetic

diablo *nm* : devil — **diablillo** *nm* : imp, rascal — **diablura** *nf* : prank — **diabólico, -ca** *adj* : diabolic, diabolical

diafragma *nm* : diaphragm

diagnosticar {72} *vt* : diagnose — **diagnóstico, -ca** *adj* : diagnostic — **diagnóstico** *nm* : diagnosis

diagonal *adj* & *nf* : diagonal

diagrama *nm* : diagram

dial *nm* : dial (of a radio, etc.)

dialecto *nm* : dialect

dialogar {52} *vi* : have a talk — **diálogo** *nm* : dialogue

diamante *nm* : diamond

diámetro *nm* : diameter

diana *nf* 1 : reveille 2 BLANCO : target, bull's-eye

diario, -ria *adj* : daily — **diario** *nm* 1 : diary 2 PERIÓDICO : newspaper — **diariamente** *adv* : daily

diarrea *nf* : diarrhea

dibujar *vt* 1 : draw 2 DESCRIBIR : portray — **dibujante** *nmf* : draftsman *m*, draftswoman *f* — **dibujo** *nm* 1 : drawing 2 ~**s animados** : (animated) cartoons

diccionario *nm* : dictionary

dicha *nf* 1 ALEGRÍA : happiness 2 SUERTE : good luck — **dicho** *nm* : saying, proverb — **dichoso, -sa** *adj* 1 : happy 2 AFORTUNADO : lucky

diciembre *nm* : December

dictar *vt* 1 : dictate 2 : pronounce (a sentence), deliver (a speech) — **dictado** *nm* : dictation — **dictador, -dora** *n* : dictator — **dictadura** *nf* : dictatorship

diecinueve *adj* & *nm* : nineteen — **diecinueveavo, -va** *adj* : nineteenth

dieciocho *adj* & *nm* : eighteen — **dieciochoavo, -va** *or* **dieciochavo, -va** *adj* : eighteenth

dieciséis *adj* & *nm* : sixteen — **dieciseisavo, -va** *adj* : sixteenth

diecisiete *adj* & *nm* : seventeen — **diecisieteavo, -va** *adj* : seventeenth

diente *nm* 1 : tooth 2 : prong, tine (of a fork, etc.) 3 ~ **de ajo** : clove of garlic 4 ~ **de león** : dandelion

diesel *adj* & *nm* : diesel

diestra *nf* : right hand — **diestro, -tra** *adj* 1 : right 2 HÁBIL : skillful

dieta *nf* : diet — **dietético, -ca** *adj* : dietetic, dietary

diez *adj* & *nm, pl* **dieces** : ten

difamar *vt* : slander, libel — **difamación** *nf, pl* **-ciones** : slander, libel

diferencia *nf* : difference — **diferenciar** *vt* : distinguish between — **diferenciarse** *vr* : differ — **diferente** *adj* : different

diferir {76} *vt* : postpone — *vi* : differ

difícil *adj* : difficult — **dificultad** *nf* : difficulty — **dificultar** *vt* : hinder, obstruct

difteria *nf* : diphtheria

difundir *vt* **1** : spread (out) **2** : broadcast (television, etc.)

difunto, -ta *adj & n* : deceased

difusión *nf, pl* **-siones** : spreading

digerir {76} *vt* : digest — **digerible** *adj* : digestible — **digestión** *nf, pl* **-tiones** : digestion — **digestivo, -va** *adj* : digestive

dígito *nm* : digit — **digital** *adj* : digital

dignarse *vr* ~ **a** : deign to

dignatario, -ria *n* : dignitary — **dignidad** *nf* : dignity — **digno, -na** *adj* : worthy

digresión *nf, pl* **-ciones** : digression

dilapidar *vt* : waste, squander

dilatar *vt* **1** : expand, dilate **2** PROLONGAR : prolong **3** POSPONER : postpone

dilema *nm* : dilemma

diligencia *nf* **1** : diligence **2** TRÁMITE : procedure, task — **diligente** *adj* : diligent

diluir {41} *vt* : dilute

diluvio *nm* **1** : flood **2** LLUVIA : downpour

dimensión *nf, pl* **-siones** : dimension

diminuto, -ta *adj* : minute, tiny

dimitir *vi* : resign — **dimisión** *nf, pl* **-siones** : resignation

dinámico, -ca *adj* : dynamic

dinamita *nf* : dynamite

dínamo *or* **dinamo** *nmf* : dynamo

dinastía *nf* : dynasty

dineral *nm* : large sum, fortune

dinero *nm* : money

dinosaurio *nm* : dinosaur

diócesis *nfs & pl* : diocese

dios, diosa *n* : god, goddess *f* — **Dios** *nm* : God

diploma *nm* : diploma — **diplomado, -da** *adj* : qualified, trained

diplomacia *nf* : diplomacy — **diplomático, -ca** *adj* : diplomatic — ~ *n* : diplomat

diputación *nf, pl* **-ciones** : delegation — **diputado, -da** *n* : delegate

dique *nm* : dike

dirección *nf, pl* **-ciones** **1** : address **2** SENTIDO : direction **3** GESTIÓN : management **4** : steering (of an automobile) — **direccional** *nf Lat* : turn signal, blinker — **directa** *nf* : high gear — **directiva** *nf* : board of directors — **directivo, -va** *adj* : managerial — ~ *n* : manager, director — **directo, -ta** *adj* **1** : direct **2** DERECHO : straight — **director, -tora** *n* **1** : director, manager **2** : conductor (of an orchestra) — **directorio** *nm* : directory — **directriz** *nf, pl* **-trices** : guideline

dirigencia *nf* : leaders *pl,* leadership — **dirigente** *nmf* : director, leader

dirigible *nm* : dirigible, blimp

dirigir {35} *vt* **1** : direct, lead **2** : address (a letter, etc.) **3** ENCAMINAR : aim **4** : conduct (music) — **dirigirse** *vr* **1** ~ **a** : go towards **2** ~ **a algn** : speak to s.o., write to s.o.

discernir {25} *vt* : discern, distinguish — **discernimiento** *nm* : discernment

disciplinar *vt* : discipline — **disciplina** *nf* : discipline

discípulo, -la *n* : disciple, follower

disco *nm* **1** : disc, disk **2** : discus (in sports) **3** ~ **compacto** : compact disc

discordar *adj* : discordant — **discordia** *nf* : discord

discoteca *nf* : disco, discotheque

discreción *nf, pl* **-ciones** : discretion

discrepancia *nf* **1** : discrepancy **2** DESACUERDO : disagreement — **discrepar** *vi* : differ, disagree

discreto, -ta *adj* : discreet

discriminar *vt* **1** : discriminate against **2** DISTINGUIR : distinguish — **discriminación** *nf, pl* **-ciones** : discrimination

disculpar *vt* : excuse, pardon — **disculparse** *vr* : apologize — **disculpa** *nf* **1** : apology **2** EXCUSA : excuse

discurrir *vi* **1** : pass, go by **2** REFLEXIONAR : ponder, reflect

discurso *nm* : speech, discourse

discutir *vt* **1** : discuss **2** CUESTIONAR : dispute — *vi* : argue — **discusión** *nf, pl* **-siones** **1** : discussion **2** DISPUTA : argument — **discutible** *adj* : debatable

disecar {72} *vt* : dissect — **disección** *nf, pl* **-ciones** : dissection

diseminar *vt* : disseminate, spread

disentería *nf* : dysentery

disentir {76} *vi* ~ **de** : disagree with — **disentimiento** *nm* : disagreement, dissent

diseñar *vt* : design — **diseñador, -dora** *n* : designer — **diseño** *nm* : design

disertación *nf, pl* **-ciones** **1** : lecture **2** : (written) dissertation

disfrazar {21} *vt* : disguise — **disfrazarse** *vr* ~ **de** : disguise oneself as — **disfraz** *nm, pl* **-fraces** **1** : disguise **2** : costume (for a party, etc.)

disfrutar *vt* : enjoy — *vi* : enjoy oneself

disgustar *vt* : upset, annoy — **disgustarse** *vr* **1** : get annoyed **2** ENEMISTARSE : fall out (with s.o.) — **disgusto** *nm* **1** : annoyance, displeasure **2** RIÑA : quarrel

disidente *adj & nmf* : dissident

disimular *vt* : conceal, hide — *vi* : pretend — **disimulo** *nm* : pretense

disipar *vt* **1** : dispel **2** DERROCHAR : squander

diskette *nm* : floppy disk, diskette

dislexia *nf* : dyslexia — **disléxico, -ca** *adj* : dyslexic

dislocar {72} *vt* : dislocate — **dislocarse** *vr* : become dislocated

disminuir {41} *vt* : reduce — *vi* : decrease,

drop — **disminución** *nf, pl* **-ciones** : decrease

disociar *vt* : dissociate

disolver {89} *vt* : dissolve — **disolverse** *vr* : dissolve

disparar *vi* : shoot, fire — *vt* : shoot — **dispararse** *vr* : shoot up, skyrocket

disparatado, -da *adj* : absurd — **disparate** *nm* : nonsense, silly thing

disparejo, -ja *adj* : uneven — **disparidad** *nf* : difference, disparity

disparo *nm* : shot

dispensar *vt* **1** : dispense, distribute **2** DISCULPAR : excuse

dispersar *vt* : disperse, scatter — **dispersarse** *vr* : disperse — **dispersión** *nf, pl* **-siones** : scattering

disponer {60} *vt* **1** : arrange, lay out **2** ORDENAR : decide, stipulate — *vi* ~ **de** : have at one's disposal — **disponerse** *vr* ~ **a** : be ready to — **disponibilidad** *nf* : availability — **disponible** *adj* : available

disposición *nf, pl* **-ciones 1** : arrangement **2** APTITUD : aptitude **3** : order, provision (in law) **4 a** ~ **de** : at the disposal of

dispositivo *nm* : device, mechanism

dispuesto, -ta *adj* : prepared, ready

disputar *vi* **1** : argue **2** COMPETIR : compete — *vt* : dispute — **disputa** *nf* : dispute, argument

disquete → **diskette**

distanciar *vt* : space out — **distanciarse** *vr* : grow apart — **distancia** *nf* : distance — **distante** *adj* : distant

distinguir {26} *vt* **1** : distinguish — **distinguirse** *vr* : distinguish oneself, stand out — **distinción** *nf, pl* **-ciones** : distinction — **distintivo, -va** *adj* : distinctive — **distinto, -ta** *adj* **1** : different **2** CLARO : distinct, clear

distorsión *nf, pl* **-siones** : distortion

distraer {81} *vt* **1** : distract **2** DIVERTIR : entertain — **distraerse** *vr* **1** : get distracted **2** ENTRETENERSE : amuse oneself — **distracción** *nf, pl* **-ciones 1** : amusement **2** DESPISTE : absentmindedness — **distraído, -da** *adj* : distracted, absentminded

distribuir {41} *vt* : distribute — **distribución** *nf, pl* **-ciones** : distribution — **distribuidor, -dora** *n* : distributor

distrito *nm* : district

disturbio *nm* : disturbance

disuadir *vt* : dissuade, discourage — **disuasivo, -va** *adj* : deterrent

diurno, -na *adj* : day, daytime

divagar {52} *vi* : digress

diván *nm, pl* **-vanes** : divan, couch

divergir {35} *vi* **1** : diverge **2** ~ **en** : differ on

diversidad *nf* : diversity

diversificar {72} *vt* : diversify

diversión *nf, pl* **-siones** : fun, entertainment

diverso, -sa *adj* : diverse

divertir {76} *vt* : entertain — **divertirse** *vr* : enjoy oneself, have fun — **divertido, -da** *adj* : entertaining

dividendo *nm* : dividend

dividir *vt* **1** : divide **2** REPARTIR : distribute

divinidad *nf* : divinity — **divino, -na** *adj* : divine

divisa *nf* **1** : currency **2** EMBLEMA : emblem

divisar *vt* : discern, make out

división *nf, pl* **-siones** : division — **divisor** *nm* : denominator

divorciar *vt* : divorce — **divorciarse** *vr* : get a divorce — **divorciado, -da** *n* : divorcé *m*, divorcée *f* — **divorcio** *nm* : divorce

divulgar {52} *vt* **1** : divulge, reveal **2** PROPAGAR : spread, circulate

dizque *adv Lat* : supposedly, apparently

doblar *vt* **1** : double **2** PLEGAR : fold **3** : turn (a corner) **4** : dub (a film) — *vi* : turn — **doblarse** *vr* **1** : double over **2** ~ **a** : give in to — **dobladillo** *nm* : hem — **doble** *adj & nm* : double — ~ *nmf* : stand-in, double — **doblemente** *adv* : doubly — **doblegar** {52} *vt* : force to yield — **doblegarse** *vr* : give in — **doblez** *nm, pl* **-bleces** : fold, crease

doce *adj & nm* : twelve — **doceavo, -va** *adj* : twelfth — **docena** *nf* : dozen

docente *adj* : teaching

dócil *adj* : docile

doctor, -tora *n* : doctor — **doctorado** *nm* : doctorate

doctrina *nf* : doctrine

documentar *vt* : document — **documentación** *nf, pl* **-ciones** : documentation — **documental** *adj & nm* : documentary — **documento** *nm* : document

dogma *nm* : dogma — **dogmático, -ca** *adj* : dogmatic

dólar *nm* : dollar

doler {47} *vi* **1** : hurt **2 me duelen los pies** : my feet hurt — **dolerse** *vr* ~ **de** : complain about — **dolor** *nm* **1** : pain **2** PENA : grief **3** ~ **de cabeza** : headache **4** ~ **de estómago** : stomachache — **dolorido, -da 1** : sore **2** AFLIGIDO : hurt — **doloroso, -sa** *adj* : painful

domar *vt* : tame, break in

domesticar {72} *vt* : domesticate, tame — **doméstico, -ca** *adj* : domestic

domicilio *nm* : home, residence

dominar *vt* **1** : dominate, control **2** : master (a subject, a language, etc.) — **dominarse** *vr* : control oneself — **dominación** *nf, pl* **-ciones** : domination — **dominante** *adj* : dominant

domingo *nm* : Sunday — **dominical** *adj*
periódico ~ : Sunday newspaper
dominio *nm* **1** : authority **2** : mastery (of a subject) **3** TERRITORIO : domain
dominó *nm, pl* **-nós** : dominoes *pl* (game)
don[1] *nm* : courtesy title preceding a man's first name
don[2] *nm* **1** : gift **2** TALENTO : talent — **donación** *nf, pl* **-ciones** : donation — **donador, -dora** *n* : donor
donaire *nm* : grace, charm
donar *vt* : donate — **donante** *nmf* : donor — **donativo** *nm* : donation
donde *conj* : where — ~ *prep Lat* : over by
dónde *adv* **1** : where **2** ¿**de** ~ **eres?** : where are you from? **3** ¿**por** ~? : whereabouts?
dondequiera *adv* **1** : anywhere **2** ~ **que** : wherever, everywhere
doña *nf* : courtesy title preceding a woman's first name
doquier *adv* **por** ~ : everywhere
dorar *vt* **1** : gild **2** : brown (food) — **dorado, -da** *adj* : gold, golden
dormir {27} *vt* : put to sleep — *vi* : sleep — **dormirse** *vr* : fall asleep — **dormido, -da** *adj* **1** : asleep **2** ENTUMECIDO : numb — **dormilón, -lona** *n* : sleepyhead, late riser — **dormitar** *vi* : doze — **dormitorio** *nm* **1** : bedroom **2** : dormitory (in a college)
dorso *nm* : back
dos *adj & nm* : two — **doscientos, -tas** *adj* : two hundred — **doscientos** *nms & pl* : two hundred
dosel *nm* : canopy
dosis *nfs & pl* : dose, dosage
dotar *vt* **1** : provide, equip **2** ~ **de** : endow with — **dotación** *nf, pl* **-ciones 1** : endowment, funding **2** PERSONAL : personnel — **dote** *nf* **1** : dowry **2** ~**s** *nfpl* : gift, talent
dragar {52} *vt* : dredge — **draga** *nf* : dredge
dragón *nm, pl* **-gones** : dragon
drama *nm* : drama — **dramático, -ca** *adj*

: dramatic — **dramatizar** {21} *vt* : dramatize — **dramaturgo, -ga** *n* : dramatist, playwright
drástico, -ca *adj* : drastic
drenar *vt* : drain — **drenaje** *nm* : drainage
droga *nf* : drug — **drogadicto, -ta** *n* : drug addict — **drogar** {52} *vt* : drug — **drogarse** *vr* : take drugs — **droguería** *nf* : drugstore
dromedario *nm* : dromedary
dual *adj* : dual
ducha *nf* : shower — **ducharse** *vr* : take a shower
ducho, -cha *adj* : experienced, skilled
duda *nf* : doubt — **dudar** *vt* : doubt — *vi* ~ **en** : hesitate to — **dudoso, -sa** *adj* **1** : doubtful **2** SOSPECHOSO : questionable
duelo *nm* **1** : duel **2** LUTO : mourning
duende *nm* : elf, imp
dueño, -na *n* **1** : owner **2** : landlord, landlady *f*
dulce *adj* **1** : sweet **2** : fresh (of water) **3** SUAVE : mild, gentle — ~ *nm* : candy, sweet — **dulzura** *nf* : sweetness
duna *nf* : dune
dúo *nm* : duo, duet
duodécimo, -ma *adj* : twelfth — ~ *n* : twelfth (in a series)
dúplex *nms & pl* : duplex (apartment)
duplicar {72} *vt* **1** : double **2** : duplicate, copy (a document, etc.) — **duplicado, -da** *adj* : duplicate — **duplicado** *nm* : copy
duqe *nm* : duke — **duquesa** *nf* : duchess
durabilidad *nf* : durability
duración *nf, pl* **-ciones** : duration, length
duradero, -ra *adj* : durable, lasting
durante *prep* **1** : during **2** ~ **una hora** : for an hour
durar *vi* : endure, last
durazno *nm Lat* : peach
duro *adv* : hard — **duro, -ra** *adj* **1** : hard **2** SEVERO : harsh — **dureza** *nf* **1** : hardness **2** SEVERIDAD : harshness

E

e[1] *nf* : e, fifth letter of the Spanish alphabet
e[2] *conj (used instead of* **y** *before words beginning with* **i** *or* **hi***)* : and
ebanista *nmf* : cabinetmaker
ébano *nm* : ebony
ebrio, -bria *adj* : drunk
ebullición *nf, pl* **-ciones** : boiling
echar *vt* **1** : throw, cast **2** EXPULSAR : expel, dismiss **3** : give off, emit (smoke, sparks, etc.) **4** BROTAR : sprout **5** PONER : put (on) **6** ~ **a perder** : spoil, ruin **7** ~ **de menos** : miss — **echarse** *vr* **1** : throw oneself **2** ACOSTARSE : lie down **3** ~ **a** : start (to)
eclesiástico, -ca *adj* : ecclesiastic — ~ *nm* : clergyman
eclipse *nm* : eclipse — **eclipsar** *vi* : eclipse
eco *nm* : echo
ecología *nf* : ecology — **ecológico, -ca** *adj* : ecological — **ecologista** *nmf* : ecologist
economía *nf* **1** : economy **2** : economics (science) — **económico, -ca** *adj* **1** : economic, economical **2** BARATO : inexpensive — **economista** *nmf* : economist — **economizar** {21} *v* : save
ecosistema *nm* : ecosystem
ecuación *nf, pl* **-ciones** : equation
ecuador *nm* : equator
ecuánime *adj* **1** : even-tempered **2** : impartial (in law)
ecuatoriano, -na *adj* : Ecuadorian, Ecuadorean, Ecuadorian
ecuestre *adj* : equestrian
edad *nf* **1** : age **2 Edad Media** : Middle Ages *pl* **3 ¿qué** ~ **tienes?** : how old are you?
edición *nf, pl* **-ciones** **1** : publishing, publication **2** : edition (of a book, etc.)
edicto *nm* : edict
edificar {72} *vt* : build — **edificio** *nm* : building
editar *vt* **1** : publish **2** : edit (a film, a text, etc.) — **editor, -tora** *n* **1** : publisher **2** : editor — **editorial** *adj* : publishing — ~ *nm* : editorial — ~ *nf* : publishing house
edredón *nm, pl* **-dones** : (down) comforter, duvet
educar {72} *vt* **1** : educate **2** CRIAR : bring up, raise **3** : train (the body, the voice, etc.) — **educación** *nf, pl* **-ciones** **1** : education **2** MODALES : (good) manners *pl* — **educado, -da** *adj* : polite — **educador, -dora** *n* : educator — **educativo, -va** *adj* : educational
efectivo, -va *adj* **1** : effective **2** REAL : real

— **efectivo** *nm* : cash — **efectivamente** *adv* **1** : really **2** POR SUPUESTO : yes, indeed — **efecto** *nm* **1** : effect **2 en** ~ : in fact **3** ~**s** *nmpl* : goods, property — **efectuar** {3} *vt* : bring about, carry out
efervescente *adj* : effervescent — **efervescencia** *nf* : effervescence
eficaz *adj, pl* **-caces** **1** : effective **2** EFICIENTE : efficient — **eficacia** *nf* **1** : effectiveness **2** EFICIENCIA : efficiency
eficiente *adj* : efficient — **eficiencia** *nf* : efficiency
efímero, -ra *adj* : ephemeral
efusivo, -va *adj* : effusive
egipcio, -cia *adj* : Egyptian
ego *nm* : ego — **egocéntrico, -ca** *adj* : egocentric — **egoísmo** *nm* : egoism — **egoísta** *adj* : egoistic — ~ *nmf* : egoist
egresar *vi* : graduate — **egresado, -da** *n* : graduate — **egreso** *nm* : graduation, commencement
eje *nm* **1** : axis **2** : axle (of a wheel, etc.)
ejecutar *vt* **1** : execute, put to death **2** REALIZAR : carry out — **ejecución** *nf, pl* **-ciones** : execution
ejecutivo, -va *adj & n* : executive
ejemplar *adj* : exemplary — ~ *nm* **1** : copy, issue **2** EJEMPLO : example — **ejemplificar** {72} *vt* : exemplify — **ejemplo** *nm* **1** : example **2 por** ~ : for example
ejercer {86} *vt* **1** : practice (a profession) **2** : exercise (a right, etc.) — *vi* ~ **de** : practice as, work as — **ejercicio** *nm* **1** : exercise **2** : practice (of a profession, etc.)
ejército *nm* : army
el, la *art, pl* **los, las** : the — **el** *pron (referring to masculine nouns)* **1** : the one **2** ~ **que** : he who, whoever, the one that
él *pron* : he, him
elaborar *vt* **1** : manufacture, produce **2** : draw up (a plan, etc.)
elástico, -ca *adj* : elastic — **elástico** *nm* : elastic — **elasticidad** *nf* : elasticity
elección *nf, pl* **-ciones** **1** : election **2** SELECCIÓN : choice — **elector, -tora** *n* : voter — **electorado** *nm* : electorate — **electoral** *adj* : electoral
electricidad *nf* : electricity — **eléctrico, -ca** *adj* : electric, electrical — **electricista** *nmf* : electrician — **electrificar** {72} *vt* : electrify — **electrizar** {21} *vt* : electrify, thrill — **electrocutar** *vt* : electrocute
electrodo *nm* : electrode
electrodoméstico *nm* : electric appliance

electromagnético, -ca *adj* : electromagnetic

electrón *nm, pl* **-trones** : electron — **electrónico, -ca** *adj* : electronic — **electrónica** *nf* : electronics

elefante, -ta *n* : elephant

elegante *adj* : elegant — **elegancia** *nf* : elegance

elegía *nf* : elegy

elegir {28} *vt* **1** : elect **2** ESCOGER : choose, select — **elegible** *adj* : eligible

elemento *nm* : element — **elemental** *adj* **1** : elementary, basic **2** ESENCIAL : fundamental

elenco *nm* : cast (of actors)

elevar *vt* **1** : raise, lift **2** ASCENDER : elevate (in a hierarchy), promote — **elevarse** *vr* : rise — **elevación** *nf, pl* **-ciones** : elevation — **elevador** *nm* **1** : hoist **2** *Lat* : elevator

eliminar *vt* : eliminate — **eliminación** *nf, pl* **-ciones** : elimination

elipse *nf* : ellipse — **elíptico, -ca** *adj* : elliptical, elliptic

elite *or* **élite** *nf* : elite

elixir *or* **elíxir** *nm* : elixir

ella *pron* : she, her — **ello** *pron* : it — **ellos, ellas** *pron pl* **1** : they, them **2 de ellos, de ellas** : theirs

elocuente *adj* : eloquent — **elocuencia** *nf* : eloquence

elogiar *vt* : praise — **elogio** *nm* : praise

eludir *vt* : avoid, elude

emanar *vi* ∼ **de** : emanate from

emancipar *vt* : emancipate — **emanciparse** *vr* : free oneself — **emancipación** *nf, pl* **-ciones** : emancipation

embadurnar *vt* : smear, daub

embajada *nf* : embassy — **embajador, -dora** *n* : ambassador

embalar *vt* : wrap up, pack — **embalaje** *nm* : packing

embaldosar *vt* : pave with tiles

embalsamar *vt* : embalm

embalse *nm* : dam, reservoir

embarazar {21} *vt* **1** : make pregnant **2** IMPEDIR : restrict, hamper — **embarazada** *adj* : pregnant — **embarazo** *nm* **1** : pregnancy **2** IMPEDIMENTO : hindrance, obstacle — **embarazoso, -sa** *adj* : embarrassing

embarcar {72} *vt* : load — **embarcarse** *vr* : embark, board — **embarcación** *nf, pl* **-ciones** : boat, craft — **embarcadero** *nm* : pier, jetty — **embarco** *nm* : embarkation

embargar {52} *vt* **1** : seize, impound **2** : overwhelm (with emotion, etc.) — **embargo** *nm* **1** : embargo **2** : seizure (in law) **3 sin** ∼ : nevertheless

embarque *nm* : loading (of goods), boarding (of passengers)

embarrancar {72} *vi* : run aground

embarullarse *vr fam* : get mixed up

embaucar {72} *vt* : trick, swindle — **embaucador, -dora** *n* : swindler

embeber *vt* : absorb — *vi* : shrink — **embeberse** *vr* : become absorbed

embelesar *vt* : enchant, delight — **embelesado, -da** *adj* : spellbound

embellecer {53} *vt* : embellish, beautify

embestir {54} *vt* : attack, charge at — *vi* : charge, attack — **embestida** *nf* **1** : attack **2** : charge (of a bull)

emblema *nm* : emblem

embobar *vt* : amaze, fascinate

embocadura *nf* **1** : mouth (of a river, etc.) **2** : mouthpiece (of an instrument)

émbolo *nm* : piston

embolsarse *vr* : put in one's pocket

emborracharse *vr* : get drunk

emborronar *vt* **1** : smudge, blot **2** GARABATEAR : scribble

emboscar {72} *vt* : ambush — **emboscada** *nf* : ambush

embotar *vt* : dull, blunt

embotellar *vt* : bottle (up) — **embotellamiento** *nm* : traffic jam

embrague *nm* : clutch — **embragar** {52} *vi* : engage the clutch

embriagarse {52} *vr* : get drunk — **embriagado, -da** *adj* : intoxicated, drunk — **embriagador, -dora** *adj* : intoxicating — **embriaguez** *nf* : drunkenness

embrión *nm, pl* **-briones** : embryo

embrollo *nm* : tangle, confusion

embrujar *vt* : bewitch — **embrujo** *nm* : spell, curse

embrutecer *vt* : brutalize

embudo *nm* : funnel

embuste *nm* : lie — **embustero, -ra** *adj* : lying — ∼ *n* : liar, cheat

embutir *vt* : stuff — **embutido** *nm* : sausage, cold meat

emergencia *nf* : emergency

emerger {15} *vi* : emerge, appear

emigrar *vi* **1** : emigrate **2** : migrate (of animals) — **emigración** *nf, pl* **-ciones 1** : emigration **2** : migration (of animals) — **emigrante** *adj & nmf* : emigrant

eminente *adj* : eminent — **eminencia** *nf* : eminence

emitir *vt* **1** : emit **2** EXPRESAR : express (an opinion, etc.) **3** : broadcast (on radio or television) **4** : issue (money, stamps, etc.) — **emisión** *nf, pl* **-siones 1** : emission **2** : broadcast (on radio or television) **3** : issue (of money, etc.) — **emisora** *nf* : radio station

emoción *nf, pl* **-ciones** : emotion — **emocional** *adj* : emotional — **emocionante** *adj*

1 : moving, touching **2** APASIONANTE : exciting, thrilling — **emocionar** *vt* **1** : move, touch **2** APASIONAR : excite, thrill — **emocionarse** *vr* **1** : be moved **2** APASIONARSE : get excited — **emotivo, -va** *adj* **1** : emotional **2** CONMOVEDOR : moving

empacar {72} *vt Lat* : pack

empachar *vt* : give indigestion to — **empacharse** *vr* : get indigestion — **empacho** *nm* : indigestion

empadronarse *vr* : register to vote

empalagoso, -sa *adj* : excessively sweet, cloying

empalizada *nf* : palisade (fence)

empalmar *vt* : connect, link — *vi* : meet, converge — **empalme** *nm* **1** : connection, link **2** : junction (of a railroad, etc.)

empanada *nf* : pie, turnover — **empanadilla** *nf* : meat or seafood pie

empanar *vt* : bread (in cooking)

empantanar *vt* : flood — **empantanarse** *vr* **1** : become flooded **2** : get bogged down

empañar *vt* **1** : steam (up) **2** : tarnish (one's reputation, etc.) — **empañarse** *vr* : fog up

empapar *vt* : soak — **empaparse** *vr* : get soaking wet

empapelar *vt* : wallpaper

empaquetar *vt* : pack, package

emparedado, -da *adj* : walled in, confined — **emparedado** *nm* : sandwich

emparejar *vt* : match up, pair — **emparejarse** *vr* : pair off

emparentado, -da *adj* : related, kindred

empastar *vt* : fill (a tooth) — **empaste** *nm* : filling

empatar *vi* : result in a draw, be tied — **empate** *nm* : draw, tie

empedernido, -da *adj* : inveterate, hardened

empedrar {55} *vt* : pave (with stones) — **empedrado** *nm* : paving, pavement

empeine *nm* : instep

empeñar *vt* : pawn — **empeñarse** *vr* **1** : insist, persist **2** ENDEUDARSE : go into debt **3** ~ **en** : make an effort to — **empeñado, -da** *adj* **1** : determined, committed **2** ENDEUDADO : in debt — **empeño** *nm* **1** : determination, effort **2 casa de** ~**s** : pawnshop

empeorar *vi* : get worse — *vt* : make worse

empequeñecer {53} *vt* : diminish, make smaller

emperador *nm* : emperor — **emperatriz** *nf, pl* **-trices** : empress

empezar {29} *v* : start, begin

empinar *vt* : raise — **empinarse** *vr* : stand on tiptoe — **empinado, -da** *adj* : steep

empírico, -ca *adj* : empirical

emplasto *nm* : poultice

emplazar {21} *vt* **1** : summon, subpoena **2** SITUAR : place, locate — **emplazamiento**

nm **1** : location, site **2** CITACIÓN : summons, subpoena

emplear *vt* **1** : employ **2** USAR : use — **emplearse** *vr* **1** : get a job **2** USARSE : be used — **empleado, -da** *n* : employee — **empleador, -dora** *n* : employer — **empleo** *nm* **1** : occupation, job **2** USO : use

empobrecer {53} *vt* : impoverish — **empobrecerse** *vr* : become poor

empollar *vi* : brood (eggs) — *vt* : incubate

empolvarse *vr* : powder one's face

empotrar *vt* : fit, build into — **empotrado, -da** *adj* : built-in

emprender *vt* : undertake, begin — **emprendedor, -dora** *adj* : enterprising

empresa *nf* **1** COMPAÑIA : company, firm **2** TAREA : undertaking — **empresarial** *adj* : business, managerial — **empresario, -ria** *n* **1** : businessman *m*, businesswoman *f* **2** : impresario (in theater), promoter (in sports)

empujar *v* : push — **empuje** *nm* : impetus, drive — **empujón** *nm, pl* **-jones** : push, shove

empuñar *vt* : grasp, take hold of

emular *vt* : emulate

en *prep* **1** : in **2** DENTRO DE : into, inside (of) **3** SOBRE : on **4** ~ **avión** : by plane **5** ~ **casa** : at home

enajenar *vt* : alienate — **enajenación** *nf, pl* **-ciones** : alienation

enagua *nf* : slip, petticoat

enaltecer {53} *vt* : praise, extol

enamorar *vt* : win the love of — **enamorarse** *vr* : fall in love — **enamorado, -da** *adj* : in love — ~ *n* : lover, sweetheart

enano, -na *adj & n* : dwarf

enarbolar *vt* **1** : hoist, raise **2** : brandish (arms, etc.)

enardecer {53} *vt* : stir up, excite

encabezar {21} *vt* **1** : head, lead **2** : put a heading on (an article, a list, etc.) — **encabezamiento** *nm* **1** : heading **2** : headline (in a newspaper)

encabritarse *vr* : rear up

encadenar *vt* **1** : chain, tie (up) **2** ENLAZAR : connect, link

encajar *vt* : fit (together) — *vi* **1** : fit **2** CUADRAR : conform, tally — **encaje** *nm* : lace

encalar *vt* : whitewash

encallar *vi* : run aground

encaminar *vt* : direct, aim — **encaminarse** *vr* ~ **a** : head for — **encaminado, -da** *adj* ~ **a** : aimed at, designed to

encandilar *vt* : dazzle

encanecer {53} *vi* : turn gray

encantar *vt* : enchant, bewitch — *vi* **me encanta esta canción** : I love this song — **encantado, -da** *adj* **1** : delighted **2**

HECHIZADO : bewitched — **encantador, -dora** *adj* : charming, delightful — **encantamiento** *nm* : enchantment, spell — **encanto** *nm* **1** : charm, fascination **2** HECHIZO : spell

encapotarse *vr* : cloud over — **encapotado, -da** *adj* : overcast

encapricharse *vr* ~ **con** : be infatuated with

encapuchado, -da *adj* : hooded

encaramar *vt* : lift up — **encaramarse** *vr* ~ **a** : climb up on

encarar *vt* : face, confront

encarcelar *vt* : imprison — **encarcelamiento** *nm* : imprisonment

encarecer {53} *vt* : increase, raise (price, value, etc.) — **encarecerse** *vr* : become more expensive

encargar {52} *vt* **1** : put in charge of **2** PEDIR : order — **encargarse** *vr* ~ **de** : take charge of — **encargado, -da** *adj* : in charge — ~ *n* : manager, person in charge — **encargo** *nm* **1** : errand **2** TAREA : assignment, task **3** PEDIDO : order

encariñarse *vr* ~ **con** : become fond of

encarnar *vt* : embody — **encarnación** *nf, pl* **-ciones** : embodiment — **encarnado, -da** *adj* **1** : incarnate **2** ROJO : red

encarnizarse {21} *vr* ~ **con** : attack viciously — **encarnizado, -da** *adj* : bitter, bloody

encarrilar *vt* : put on the right track

encasillar *vt* : pigeonhole

encauzar {21} *vt* : channel

encender {56} *vt* **1** : light, set fire to **2** PRENDER : switch on, start **3** AVIVAR : arouse (passions, etc.) — **encenderse** *vr* **1** : get excited **2** RUBORIZARSE : blush — **encendedor** *nm* : lighter — **encendido, -da** *adj* : lit, on — **encendido** *nm* : ignition (switch)

encerar *vt* : wax, polish — **encerado, -da** *adj* : waxed — **encerado** *nm* : blackboard

encerrar {55} *vt* **1** : lock up, shut away **2** CONTENER : contain

encestar *vi* : score (in basketball)

enchilada *nf* : enchilada

enchufar *vt* : plug in, connect — **enchufe** *nm* : plug, socket

encía *nf* : gum (tissue)

encíclica *nf* : encyclical

enciclopedia *nf* : encyclopedia — **enciclopédico, -ca** *adj* : encyclopedic

encierro *nm* **1** : confinement **2** : sit-in (at a university, etc.)

encima *adv* **1** : on top **2** ADEMÁS : as well, besides **3** ~ **de** : on, over, on top of **4 por** ~ **de** : above, beyond

encinta *adj* : pregnant

enclenque *adj* : weak, sickly

encoger {15} *v* : shrink — **encogerse** *vr* **1** : shrink **2** : cower, cringe **3** ~ **de hombros** : shrug (one's shoulders) — **encogido, -da** *adj* **1** : shrunken **2** TÍMIDO : shy

encolar *vt* : glue, stick

encolerizar {21} *vt* : enrage, infuriate — **encolerizarse** *vr* : get angry

encomendar {55} *vt* : entrust

encomienda *nf* **1** : charge, mission **2** *Lat* : parcel

encono *nm* : rancor, animosity

encontrar {19} *vt* **1** : find **2** : meet, encounter (difficulties, etc.) — **encontrarse** *vr* **1** : meet **2** HALLARSE : find oneself, be — **encontrado, -da** *adj* : contrary, opposing

encorvar *vt* : bend, curve — **encorvarse** *vr* : bend over, stoop

encrespar *vt* **1** : curl **2** IRRITAR : irritate — **encresparse** *vr* **1** : curl one's hair **2** IRRITARSE : get annoyed **3** : become choppy (of the sea)

encrucijada *nf* : crossroads

encuadernar *vt* : bind (a book) — **encuadernación** *nf, pl* **-ciones** : bookbinding

encuadrar *vt* **1** : frame **2** ENCAJAR : fit **3** COMPRENDER : contain, include

encubrir {2} *vt* : conceal, cover (up) — **encubierto, -ta** *adj* : covert — **encubrimiento** *nm* : cover-up

encuentro *nm* : meeting, encounter

encuestar *vt* : poll, take a survey of — **encuesta** *nf* **1** : investigation, inquiry **2** SONDEO : survey — **encuestador, -dora** *n* : pollster

encumbrado, -da *adj* : eminent, distinguished

encurtir *vt* : pickle

endeble *adj* : weak, feeble — **endeblez** *nf* : weakness, frailty

endemoniado, -da *adj* : wicked

enderezar {21} *vt* **1** : straighten (out) **2** : put upright, stand on end

endeudarse *vr* : go into debt — **endeudado, -da** *adj* : indebted, in debt — **endeudamiento** *nm* : debt

endiablado, -da *adj* **1** : wicked, diabolical **2** : complicated, difficult

endibia *or* **endivia** *nf* : endive

endosar *vt* : endorse — **endoso** *nm* : endorsement

endulzar {21} *vt* **1** : sweeten **2** : soften, mellow (a tone, a response, etc.) — **endulzante** *nm* : sweetener

endurecer {53} *vt* : harden — **endurecerse** *vr* : become hardened

enema *nm* : enema

enemigo, -ga *adj* : hostile — ~ *n* : enemy — **enemistad** *nf* : enmity — **enemistar** *vt* : make enemies of — **enemistarse** *vr* ~ **con** : fall out with

energía *nf* : energy — **enérgico, -ca** *adj* : energetic, vigorous, forceful

enero *nm* : January

enervar *vt* **1** : enervate, weaken **2** *fam* : get on one's nerves

enésimo, -ma *adj* **por enésima vez** : for the umpteenth time

enfadar *vt* : annoy, make angry — **enfadarse** *vr* : get annoyed — **enfado** *nm* : anger, annoyance — **enfadoso, -sa** *adj* : annoying

enfatizar {21} *vt* : emphasize — **énfasis** *nms & pl* : emphasis — **enfático, -ca** *adj* : emphatic

enfermar *vt* : make sick — *vi* : get sick — **enfermedad** *nf* : sickness, disease — **enfermería** *nf* : infirmary — **enfermero, -ra** *n* : nurse — **enfermizo, -za** *adj* : sickly — **enfermo, -ma** *adj* : sick — ~ *n* : sick person, patient

enflaquecer {53} *vi* : lose weight

enfocar {72} *vt* **1** : focus (on) **2** : consider (a problem, etc.) — **enfoque** *nm* : focus

enfrascarse {72} *vr* ~ **en** : immerse oneself in, get caught up in

enfrentar *vt* **1** : confront, face **2** : bring face to face — **enfrentarse** *vr* ~ **con** : confront, clash with — **enfrente** *adv* **1** : opposite **2** ~ **de** : in front of

enfriar {85} *vt* : chill, cool — **enfriarse** *vr* **1** : get cold **2** RESFRIARSE : catch a cold — **enfriamiento** *nm* **1** : cooling off **2** CATARRO : cold

enfurecer {53} *vt* : infuriate — **enfurecerse** *vr* : fly into a rage

enfurruñarse *vr fam* : sulk

engalanar *vt* : decorate — **engalanarse** *vr* : dress up

enganchar *vt* : hook, snag, catch — **engancharse** *vr* **1** : get caught **2** ALISTARSE : enlist

engañar *vt* **1** EMBAUCAR : trick, deceive **2** : cheat on, be unfaithful to — **engañarse** *vr* **1** : deceive oneself **2** EQUIVOCARSE : be mistaken — **engaño** *nm* : deception, deceit — **engañoso, -sa** *adj* : deceptive, deceitful

engatusar *vt* : coax, cajole

engendrar *vt* **1** : beget **2** : engender, give rise to (suspicions, etc.)

englobar *vt* : include, embrace

engomar *vt* : glue

engordar *vt* : fatten — *vi* : gain weight

engorroso, -sa *adj* : bothersome

engranar *v* : mesh, engage — **engranaje** *nm* : gears *pl*

engrandecer {53} *vt* **1** : enlarge **2** ENALTECER : exalt

engrapar *vt Lat* : staple — **engrapadora** *nf Lat* : stapler

engrasar *vt* : lubricate, grease — **engrase** *nm* : lubrication

engreído, -da *adj* : conceited

engrosar {19} *vt* : swell — *vi* : gain weight

engrudo *nm* : paste

engullir {38} *vt* : gulp down, gobble up

enhebrar *vt* : thread

enhorabuena *nf* : congratulations *pl*

enigma *nm* : enigma — **enigmático, -ca** *adj* : enigmatic

enjabonar *vt* : soap (up), lather

enjaezar {21} *vt* : harness

enjalbegar {52} *vt* : whitewash

enjambrar *vi* : swarm — **enjambre** *nm* : swarm

enjaular *vt* **1** : cage **2** *fam* : jail

enjuagar {52} *vt* : rinse — **enjuague** *nm* **1** : rinse **2** ~ **bucal** : mouthwash

enjugar {52} *vt* **1** : wipe away (tears) **2** : wipe out (debt)

enjuiciar *vt* **1** : prosecute **2** JUZGAR : try

enjuto, -ta *adj* : gaunt, lean

enlace *nm* **1** : bond, link **2** : junction (of a highway, etc.)

enlatar *vt* : can

enlazar {21} *vt* : join, link — *vi* ~ **con** : link up with

enlistarse *vr Lat* : enlist

enlodar *vt* : cover with mud

enloquecer {53} *vt* : drive crazy — **enloquecerse** *vr* : go crazy

enlosar *vt* : pave, tile

enlutarse *vr* : go into mourning

enmarañar *vt* **1** : tangle **2** COMPLICAR : complicate **3** CONFUNDIR : confuse — **enmarañarse** *vr* **1** : get tangled up **2** CONFUNDIRSE : become confused

enmarcar {72} *vt* : frame

enmascarar *vt* : mask

enmendar {55} *vt* **1** : amend **2** CORREGIR : emend, correct — **enmendarse** *vr* : mend one's ways — **enmienda** *nf* **1** : amendment **2** CORRECCIÓN : correction

enmohecerse {53} *vr* **1** : become moldy **2** OXIDARSE : rust

enmudecer {53} *vt* : silence — *vi* : fall silent

ennegrecer {53} *vt* : blacken

ennoblecer {53} *vt* : ennoble, dignify

enojar *vt* **1** : anger **2** MOLESTAR : annoy — **enojarse** *vr* ~ **con** : get upset with — **enojo** *nm* **1** : anger **2** MOLESTIA : annoyance — **enojoso, -sa** *adj* : annoying

enorgullecer {53} *vt* : make proud — **enorgullecerse** *vr* ~ **de** : pride oneself on

enorme *adj* : enormous — **enormemente**

adv : enormously, extremely — **enormidad** *nf* : enormity

enraizar {30} *vi* : take root

enredadera *nf* : climbing plant, vine

enredar *vt* **1** : tangle up, entangle **2** CONFUNDIR : confuse **3** IMPLICAR : involve — **enredarse** *vr* **1** : become entangled **2** ~ **en** : get mixed up in — **enredo** *nm* **1** : tangle **2** EMBROLLO : confusion, mess — **enredoso, -sa** *adj* : tangled up, complicated

enrejado *nm* **1** : railing **2** REJILLA : grating, grille **3** : trellis (for plants)

enrevesado, -da *adj* : complicated

enriquecer {53} *vt* : enrich — **enriquecerse** *vr* : get rich

enrojecer {53} *vt* : redden — **enrojecerse** *vr* : blush

enrolar *vt* : enlist — **enrolarse** *vr* ~ **en** : enlist in

enrollar *vt* : roll up, coil

enroscar {72} *vt* **1** : roll up **2** ATORNILLAR : screw in

ensalada *nf* : salad

ensalzar {21} *vt* : praise

ensamblar *vt* : assemble, fit together

ensanchar *vt* **1** : widen **2** AMPLIAR : expand — **ensanche** *nm* **1** : widening **2** : (urban) expansion, development

ensangrentado, -da *adj* : bloody, bloodstained

ensañarse *vr* : act cruelly

ensartar *vt* : string, thread

ensayar *vi* : rehearse — *vt* : try out, test — **ensayo** *nm* **1** : essay **2** PRUEBA : trial, test **3** : rehearsal (in theater, etc.)

enseguida *adv* : right away, immediately

ensenada *nf* : inlet, cove

enseñar *vt* **1** : teach **2** MOSTRAR : show — **enseñanza** *nf* **1** EDUCACIÓN : education **2** INSTRUCCIÓN : teaching

enseres *nmpl* **1** : equipment **2** ~ **domésticos** : household goods

ensillar *vt* : saddle (up)

ensimismarse *vr* : lose oneself in thought

ensombrecer {53} *vt* : cast a shadow over, darken

ensoñación *nf, pl* **-ciones** : fantasy, daydream

ensordecer {53} *vt* : deafen — *vi* : go deaf — **ensordecedor, -dora** *adj* : deafening

ensortijar *vt* : curl

ensuciar *vt* : soil — **ensuciarse** *vr* : get dirty

ensueño *nm* : daydream, fantasy

entablar *vt* : initiate, start

entallar *vt* : tailor, fit (clothing) — *vi* : fit

entarimado *nm* : floorboards, flooring

ente *nm* **1** : being **2** ORGANISMO : body, organization

entender {56} *vt* **1** : understand **2** OPINAR : think, believe — *vi* **1** : understand **2** ~ **de** : know about, be good at — **entenderse** *vr* **1** : understand each other **2** LLEVARSE BIEN : get along well — ~ *nm* **a mi** ~ : in my opinion — **entendido, -da** *adj* **1** : understood **2 eso se da por** ~ : that goes without saying **3 tener** ~ : be under the impression — **entendimiento** *nm* **1** : understanding **2** INTELIGENCIA : intellect

enterar *vt* : inform — **enterarse** *vr* : find out, learn — **enterado, -da** *adj* : well-informed

entereza *nf* **1** HONRADEZ : integrity **2** FORTALEZA : fortitude **3** FIRMEZA : resolve

enternecer {53} *vt* : move, touch

entero, -ra *adj* **1** : whole **2** TOTAL : absolute, total **3** INTACTO : intact — **entero** *nm* : integer, whole number

enterrar {55} *vt* : bury

entibiar *vt* : cool (down) — **entibiarse** *vr* : become lukewarm

entidad *nf* **1** : entity **2** ORGANIZACIÓN : body, organization

entierro *nm* **1** : burial **2** : funeral (ceremony)

entomología *nf* : entomology — **entomólogo, -ga** *n* : entomologist

entonar *vt* : sing, intone — *vi* : be in tune

entonces *adv* **1** : then **2 desde** ~ : since then

entornado, -da *adj* : half-closed, ajar

entorno *nm* : surroundings *pl*, environment

entorpecer {53} *vt* **1** : hinder, obstruct **2** : numb, dull (wits, reactions, etc.)

entrada *nf* **1** : entrance, entry **2** BILLETE : ticket **3** COMIENZO : beginning **4** : inning (in baseball) **5** ~**s** *nfpl* : income **6 tener** ~**s** : have a receding hairline

entraña *nf* **1** : core, heart **2** ~**s** *nfpl* VÍSCERAS : entrails, innards — **entrañable** *adj* : close, intimate — **entrañar** *vt* : involve

entrar *vi* **1** : enter **2** EMPEZAR : begin — *vt* : introduce, bring in

entre *prep* **1** : between **2** : among

entreabrir {2} *vt* : leave ajar — **entreabierto, -ta** *adj* : half-open, ajar

entreacto *nm* : intermission

entrecejo *nm* **fruncir el** ~ : knit one's brows, frown

entrecortado, -da *adj* : faltering (of the voice), labored (of breathing)

entrecruzar {21} *vi* : intertwine

entredicho *nm* : doubt, question

entregar {52} *vt* : deliver, hand over — **entregarse** *vr* : surrender — **entrega** *nf* **1** : delivery **2** DEDICACIÓN : dedication, devotion **3** ~ **inicial** : down payment

entrelazar {21} *vt* : intertwine — **entrelazarse** *vr* : become intertwined
entremés *nm, pl* **-meses 1** : hors d'oeuvre **2** : short play (in theater)
entremeterse → **entrometerse**
entremezclar *vt* : mix (up)
entrenar *vt* : train, drill — **entrenarse** *vr* : train — **entrenador, -dora** *n* : trainer, coach — **entranamiento** *nm* : training
entrepierna *nf* : crotch
entresacar {72} *vt* : pick out, select
entresuelo *nm* : mezzanine
entretanto *adv* : meanwhile — ～ *nm* **en el** ～ : in the meantime
entretener {80} *vt* **1** : entertain **2** DESPISTAR : distract **3** RETRASAR : delay, hold up — **entretenerse** *vr* **1** : amuse oneself **2** DEMORARSE : dawdle — **entretenido, -da** *adj* : entertaining — **entretenimiento** *nm* **1** : entertainment, amusement **2** PASATIEMPO : pastime
entrever {88} *vt* : catch a glimpse of, make out
entrevistar *vt* : interview — **entrevista** *nf* : interview — **entrevistador, -dora** *n* : interviewer
entristecer {53} *vt* : sadden
entrometerse *vr* : interfere — **entrometido, -da** *adj* : meddling, nosy — *n* : meddler
entroncar {72} *vi* : be related, be connected
entumecer {53} *vt* : make numb — **entumecerse** *vr* : go numb — **entumecido, -da** *adj* **1** : numb **2** : stiff (of muscles, etc.)
enturbiar *vt* : cloud — **enturbiarse** *vr* : become cloudy
entusiasmar *vt* : fill with enthusiasm — **entusiasmarse** *vr* : get excited — **entusiasmo** *nm* : enthusiasm — **entusiasta** *adj* : enthusiastic — ～ *nmf* : enthusiast
enumerar *vt* : enumerate, list — **enumeración** *nf, pl* **-ciones** : enumeration, count
enunciar *vt* : enunciate — **enunciación** *nf, pl* **-ciones** : enunciation
envalentonar *vt* : make bold, encourage — **envalentonarse** *vr* : be brave
envanecerse {53} *vr* : become vain
envasar *vt* **1** : package **2** : bottle, can — **envase** *nm* **1** : packaging **2** RECIPIENTE : container **3** : jar, bottle, can
envejecer {53} *v* : age — **envejecido, -da** *adj* : aged, old — **envejecimiento** *nm* : aging
envenenar *vt* : poison — **envenenamiento** *nm* : poisoning
envergadura *nf* **1** ALCANCE : scope **2** : span (of wings, etc.)
envés *nm, pl* **-veses** : reverse side
enviar {85} *vt* : send — **enviado, -da** *n* : envoy, correspondent

envidiar *vt* : envy — **envidia** *nf* : envy, jealousy — **envidioso, -sa** *adj* : jealous, envious
envilecer {53} *vt* : degrade, debase — **envilecimiento** *nm* : degradation
envío *nm* **1** : sending, shipment **2** : remittance (of funds)
enviudar *vi* : be widowed
envolver {89} *vt* **1** : wrap **2** RODEAR : surround **3** IMPLICAR : involve — **envoltorio** *nm or* **envoltura** *nf* : wrapping, wrapper
enyesar *vt* **1** : plaster **2** ESCAYOLAR : put in a plaster cast
enzima *nf* : enzyme
épico, -ca *adj* : epic — **épica** *nf* : epic
epidemia *nf* : epidemic — **epidémico, -ca** *adj* : epidemic
epilepsia *nf* : epilepsy — **epiléptico, -ca** *adj & n* : epileptic
epílogo *nm* : epilogue
episodio *nm* : episode
epitafio *nm* : epitaph
epíteto *nm* : epithet
época *nf* **1** : epoch, period **2** ESTACIÓN : season
epopeya *nf* : epic poem
equidad *nf* : equity, justice
equilátero, -ra *adj* : equilateral
equilibrar *vt* : balance — **equilibrado, -da** *adj* : well-balanced — **equilibrio** *nm* **1** : balance, equilibrium **2** JUICIO : good sense
equinoccio *nm* : equinox
equipaje *nm* : baggage, luggage
equipar *vt* : equip
equiparar *vt* **1** IGUALAR : make equal **2** COMPARAR : compare — **equiparable** *adj* : comparable
equipo *nm* **1** : equipment **2** : team, crew (in sports, etc.)
equitación *nf, pl* **-ciones** : horseback riding
equitativo, -va *adj* : equitable, fair, just
equivaler {84} *vi* : be equivalent — **equivalencia** *nf* : equivalence — **equivalente** *adj & nm* : equivalent
equivocar {72} *vt* : mistake, confuse — **equivocarse** *vr* : make a mistake — **equivocación** *nf, pl* **-ciones** : error, mistake — **equivocado, -da** *adj* : mistaken, wrong
equívoco, -ca *adj* : ambiguous — **equívoco** *nm* : misunderstanding
era *nf* : era
erario *nm* : public treasury, funds *pl*
erección *nf, pl* **-ciones** : erection
erguir {31} *vt* : raise, lift — **erguirse** *vr* : rise (up) — **erguido, -da** *adj* : erect, upright
erigir {35} *vt* : build, erect — **erigirse** *vr* ～ **en** : set oneself up as

erizarse {21} *vr* : bristle, stand on end — **erizado, -da** *adj* : bristly

erizo *nm* **1** : hedgehog **2** ~ **de mar** : sea urchin

ermitaño, -ña *n* : hermit

erosionar *vt* : erode — **erosión** *nf, pl* **-siones** : erosion

erótico, -ca *adj* : erotic

erradicar {72} *vt* : eradicate

errar {32} *vt* : miss — *vi* **1** : be wrong, be mistaken **2** VAGAR : wander — **errado, -da** *adj Lat* : wrong, mistaken

errata *nf* : misprint

errático, -ca *adj* : erratic

error *nm* : error — **erróneo, -nea** *adj* : erroneous, mistaken

eructar *vi* : belch, burp — **eructo** *nm* : belch, burp

erudito, -ta *adj* : erudite, learned

erupción *nf, pl* **-ciones 1** : eruption **2** SARPULLIDO : rash

esa, ésa → **ese, ése**

esbelto, -ta *adj* : slender, slim

esbozar {21} *vt* : sketch, outline — **esbozo** *nm* : sketch, outline

escabechar *vt* : pickle — **escabeche** *nm* : brine (for pickling)

escabel *nm* : footstool

escabroso, -sa *adj* **1** : rugged, rough **2** ESPINOSO : thorny, difficult **3** ATREVIDO : shocking, risqué

escabullirse {38} *vr* : slip away, escape

escalar *vt* : climb, scale — *vi* : escalate — **escala** *nf* **1** : scale **2** ESCALERA : ladder **3** : stopover (of an airplane, etc.) — **escalada** *nf* : ascent, climb — **escalador, -dora** *n* ALPINISTA : mountain climber

escaldar *vt* : scald

escalera *nf* **1** : stairs *pl*, staircase **2** ESCALA : ladder **3** ~ **mecánica** : escalator

escalfar *vt* : poach

escalinata *nf* : flight of stairs

escalofrío *nm* : shiver, chill — **escalofriante** *adj* : chilling, horrifying

escalonar *vt* **1** : stagger, spread out **2** : terrace (land) — **escalón** *nm, pl* **-lones** : step, rung

escama *nf* **1** : scale (of fish or reptiles) **2** : flake (of skin) — **escamoso, -sa** *adj* : scaly

escamotear *vt* **1** : conceal **2** ~ **algo a algn** : rob s.o. of sth

escandalizar {21} *vt* : scandalize — **escandalizarse** *vr* : be shocked — **escándalo** *nm* **1** : scandal **2** ALBOROTO : scene, commotion — **escandaloso, -sa** *adj* **1** : shocking, scandalous **2** RUIDOSO : noisy

escandinavo, -va *adj* : Scandinavian

escáner *nm* : scanner

escaño *nm* **1** : seat (in a legislative body) **2** BANCO : bench

escapar *vi* : escape, run away — **escaparse** *vr* **1** : escape **2** : leak out (of gas, water, etc.) — **escapada** *nf* : escape

escaparate *nm* : store window

escapatoria *nf* : loophole, way out

escape *nm* **1** : leak (of gas, water, etc.) **2** : exhaust (from a vehicle)

escarabajo *nm* : beetle

escarbar *vt* **1** : dig, scratch, poke **2** ~ **en** : pry into

escarcha *nf* : frost (on a surface)

escarlata *adj & nf* : scarlet — **escarlatina** *nf* : scarlet fever

escarmentar {55} *vi* : learn one's lesson — **escarmiento** *nm* : lesson, punishment

escarnecer {53} *vt* : ridicule, mock — **escarnio** *nm* : ridicule, mockery

escarola *nf* : escarole, endive

escarpa *nf* : steep slope — **escarpado, -da** *adj* : steep

escasear *vi* : be scarce — **escasez** *nf, pl* **-seces** : shortage, scarcity — **escaso, -sa** *adj* **1** : scarce **2** ~ **de** : short of

escatimar *vt* : be sparing with, skimp on

escayolar *vt* : put in a plaster cast — **escayola** *nf* **1** : plaster (for casts) **2** : plaster cast

escena *nf* **1** : scene **2** ESCENARIO : stage — **escenario** *nm* **1** : setting, scene **2** ESCENA : stage — **escénico, -ca** *adj* : scenic

escepticismo *nm* : skepticism — **escéptico, -ca** *adj* : skeptical — ~ *n* : skeptic

esclarecer {53} *vt* : shed light on, clarify

esclavo, -va *n* : slave — **esclavitud** *nf* : slavery — **esclavizar** {21} *vt* : enslave

esclerosis *nf* ~ **múltiple** : multiple sclerosis

esclusa *nf* : floodgate, lock (of a canal)

escoba *nf* : broom

escocer {14} *vi* : sting

escocés, -cesa *adj, mpl* **-ceses 1** : Scottish **2** : tartan, plaid — **escocés** *nm, pl* **-ceses** : Scotch (whiskey)

escoger {15} *vt* : choose — **escogido, -da** *adj* : choice, select

escolar *adj* : school — ~ *nmf* : student, pupil

escolta *nmf* : escort — **escoltar** *vt* : escort, accompany

escombros *nmpl* : ruins, rubble

esconder *vt* : hide, conceal — **esconderse** *vr* : hide — **escondidas** *nfpl* **1** *Lat* : hide-and-seek **2 a** ~ : secretly, in secret — **escondite** *nm* **1** : hiding place **2** : hide-and-seek (game) — **escondrijo** *nm* : hiding place

escopeta *nf* : shotgun

escoplo *nm* : chisel

escoria *nf* **1** : slag **2** : dregs *pl* (of society, etc.)

escorpión *nm, pl* **-piones** : scorpion

escote *nm* **1** : (low) neckline **2 pagar a** ~ : go Dutch

escotilla *nf* : hatchway

escribir {33} *v* : write — **escribirse** *vr* **1** : write to one another, correspond **2** : be spelled — **escribiente** *nmf* : clerk — **escrito, -ta** *adj* : written — **escritos** *nmpl* : writings — **escritor, -tora** *n* : writer — **escritorio** *nm* : desk — **escritura** *nf* **1** : handwriting **2** : deed (in law)

escroto *nm* : scrotum

escrúpulo *nm* : scruple — **escrupuloso, -sa** *adj* : scrupulous

escrutar *vt* **1** : scrutinize **2** : count (votes) — **escrutinio** *nm* **1** : scrutiny **2** : count (of votes)

escuadra *nf* **1** : square (instrument) **2** : fleet (of ships), squad (in the military) — **escuadrón** *nm, pl* **-drones** : squadron

escuálido, -da *adj* **1** : skinny **2** SUCIO : squalid

escuchar *vt* **1** : listen to **2** *Lat* : hear — *vi* : listen

escudo *nm* **1** : shield **2** *or* ~ **de armas** : coat of arms

escudriñar *vt* : scrutinize, examine

escuela *nf* : school

escueto, -ta *adj* : plain, simple

esculpir *v* : sculpt — **escultor, -tora** *n* : sculptor — **escultura** *nf* : sculpture

escupir *v* : spit

escurrir *vt* **1** : drain **2** : wring out (clothes) — *vi* **1** : drain **2** : drip-dry (of clothes) — **escurrirse** *vr* **1** : drain **2** *fam* : slip away — **escurridizo, -da** *adj* : slippery, evasive — **escurridor** *nm* **1** : dish drainer **2** COLADOR : colander

ese, esa *adj, mpl* **esos** : that, those

ése, ésa *pron, mpl* **ésos** : that one, those ones *pl*

esencia *nf* : essence — **esencial** *adj* : essential

esfera *nf* **1** : sphere **2** : dial (of a watch) — **esférico, -ca** *adj* : spherical

esfinge *nf* : sphinx

esforzar {36} *vt* : strain — **esforzarse** *vr* : make an effort — **esfuerzo** *nm* : effort

esfumarse *vr* : fade away, vanish

esgrimir *vt* **1** : brandish, wield **2** : make use of (an argument, etc.) — **esgrima** *nf* **1** : fencing **2 hacer** ~ : fence

esguince *nm* : sprain, strain

eslabonar *vt* : link, connect — **eslabón** *nm, pl* **-bones** : link

eslavo, -va *adj* : Slavic

eslogan *nm, pl* **-lóganes** : slogan

esmaltar *vt* : enamel — **esmalte** *nm* **1** : enamel **2** ~ **de uñas** : nail polish

esmerado, -da *adj* : careful

esmeralda *nf* : emerald

esmerarse *vr* : take great care

esmeril *nm* : emery

esmoquin *nm, pl* **-móquines** : tuxedo

esnob *nmf, pl* **esnobs** : snob — ~ *adj* : snobbish

eso *pron (neuter)* **1** : that **2 ¡**~ **es!** : that's it!, that's right! **3 en** ~ : at that point, then

esófago *nm* : esophagus

esos, ésos → **ese, ése**

espabilarse *vr* **1** : wake up **2** DARSE PRISA : get moving — **espabilado, -da** *adj* **1** : awake **2** LISTO : bright, clever

espaciar *vt* : space out, spread out — **espacial** *adj* : space — **espacio** *nm* **1** : space **2** ~ **exterior** : outer space — **espacioso, -sa** *adj* : spacious

espada *nf* **1** : sword **2** ~**s** *nfpl* : spades (in playing cards)

espagueti *nm or* **espaguetis** *nmpl* : spaghetti

espalda *nf* **1** : back **2** ~**s** *nfpl* : shoulders, back

espantar *vt* : scare, frighten — **espantarse** *vr* : become frightened — **espantajo** *nm or* **espantapájaros** *nms & pl* : scarecrow — **espanto** *nm* : fright, fear — **espantoso, -sa** *adj* **1** : frightening, horrific **2** TERRIBLE : awful, terrible

español, -ñola *adj* : Spanish — **español** *nm* : Spanish (language)

esparadrapo *nm* : adhesive bandage

esparcir {83} *vt* : scatter, spread — **esparcirse** *vr* **1** : be scattered, spread out **2** DIVERTIRSE : enjoy oneself

espárrago *nm* : asparagus

espasmo *nm* : spasm — **espasmódico, -ca** *adj* : spasmodic

espátula *nf* : spatula

especia *nf* : spice

especial *adj & nm* : special — **especialidad** *nf* : specialty — **especialista** *nmf* : specialist — **especializarse** {21} *vr* ~ **en** : specialize in — **especialmente** *adv* : especially

especie *nf* **1** : species **2** CLASE : type, kind

especificar {72} *vt* : specify — **especificación** *nf, pl* **-ciones** : specification — **específico, -ca** *adj* : specific

espécimen *nm, pl* **especímenes** : specimen

espectáculo *nm* **1** : show, performance **2** VISIÓN : spectacle, view — **espectacular** *adj* : spectacular — **espectador, -dora** *n* : spectator

espectro *nm* **1** : spectrum **2** FANTASMA : ghost

especulación *nf, pl* **-ciones** : speculation
espejo *nm* : mirror — **espejismo** *nm* **1** : mirage **2** ILUSIÓN : illusion
espeluznante *adj* : terrifying, hair- raising
esperar *vt* **1** : wait for **2** CONTAR CON : expect **3** ~ **que** : hope (that) — *vi* : wait — **espera** *nf* : wait — **esperanza** *nf* : hope, expectation — **esperanzado, -da** *adj* : hopeful — **esperanzar** {21} *vt* : give hope to
esperma *nmf* **1** : sperm **2** ~ **de ballena** : blubber
esperpento *nm* : (grotesque) sight, fright
espesar *vt* : thicken — **espesarse** *vr* : thicken — **espeso, -sa** *adj* : thick, heavy — **espesor** *nm* : thickness, density — **espesura** *nf* **1** ESPESOR : thickness **2** : thicket
espetar *vt* : blurt (out)
espiar {85} *vt* : spy on — *vi* : spy — **espía** *nmf* : spy
espiga *nf* : ear (of wheat, etc.)
espina *nf* **1** : thorn **2** : (fish) bone **3** ~ **dorsal** : spine, backbone
espinaca *nf* **1** : spinach (plant) **2** ~**s** *nfpl* : spinach (food)
espinazo *nm* : spine, backbone
espinilla *nf* **1** : shin **2** GRANO : blackhead, pimple
espinoso, -sa *adj* **1** : prickly **2** : bony (of fish) **3** : difficult, thorny (of problems, etc.)
espionaje *nm* : espionage
espiral *adj & nf* : spiral
espirar *v* : breathe out, exhale
espíritu *nm* **1** : spirit **2 Espíritu Santo** : Holy Spirit — **espiritual** *adj* : spiritual — **espiritualidad** *nf* : spirituality
espita *nf* : spigot, faucet
espléndido, -da *adj* **1** : splendid **2** GENEROSO : lavish — **esplendor** *nm* : splendor
espliego *nm* : lavender
espolear *vt* : spur on
espoleta *nf* : fuse
espolvorear *vt* : sprinkle, dust
esponja *nf* **1** : sponge **2 tirar la** ~ : throw in the towel — **esponjoso, -sa** *adj* : spongy
espontaneidad *nf* : spontaneity — **espontáneo, -nea** *adj* : spontaneous
espora *nf* : spore
esporádico, -ca *adj* : sporadic
esposo, -sa *n* : spouse, wife *f*, husband *m* — **esposar** *vt* : handcuff — **esposas** *nfpl* : handcuffs
esprintar *vi* : sprint (in sports) — **esprint** *nm* : sprint
espuela *nf* : spur
espumar *vt* : skim — **espuma** *nf* **1** : foam, froth **2** : (soap) lather **3** : head (on beer) — **espumoso, -sa** *adj* **1** : foamy, frothy **2** : sparkling (of wine)

esqueleto *nm* : skeleton
esquema *nf* : outline, sketch
esquí *nm* **1** : ski **2** : skiing (sport) **3** ~ **acuático** : waterskiing — **esquiador, -dora** *n* : skier — **esquiar** {85} *vi* : ski
esquilar *vt* : shear
esquimal *adj* : Eskimo
esquina *nf* : corner
esquirol *nm* : strikebreaker, scab
esquivar *vt* **1** : evade, dodge (a blow) **2** EVITAR : avoid — **esquivo, -va** *adj* : shy, elusive
esquizofrenia *nf* : schizophrenia — **esquizofrénico, -ca** *adj & n* : schizophrenic
esta, ésta → **este**[1], **éste**
estable *adj* : stable — **estabilidad** *nf* : stability — **estabilizar** {21} *vt* : stabilize
establecer {53} *vt* : establish — **establecerse** *vr* : establish oneself, settle — **establecimiento** *nm* : establishment
establo *nm* : stable
estaca *nf* : stake — **estacada** *nf* **1** : (picket) fence **2 dejar en la** ~ : leave in a lurch
estación *nf, pl* **-ciones 1** : season **2** ~ **de servicio** : gas station — **estacionar** *v* : park — **estacionamiento** *nm* : parking — **estacionario, -ria** *adj* : stationary
estadía *nf Lat* : stay
estadio *nm* **1** : stadium **2** FASE : phase, stage
estadista *nmf* : statesman
estadística *nf* : statistics — **estadístico, -ca** *adj* : statistical
estado *nm* **1** : state **2** ~ **civil** : marital status
estadounidense *adj & nmf* : American (from the United States)
estafar *vt* : swindle, defraud — **estafa** *nf* : swindle, fraud — **estafador, -dora** *n* : cheat, swindler
estallar *vi* **1** : explode **2** : break out (of war, an epidemic, etc.) **3** ~ **en llamas** : burst into flames — **estallido** *nm* **1** : explosion **2** : report (of a gun) **3** : outbreak (of war, etc.)
estampar *vt* : stamp, print — **estampa** *nf* **1** : print, illustration **2** ASPECTO : appearance — **estampado, -da** *adj* : printed
estampida *nf* : stampede
estampilla *nf* : stamp
estancarse {72} *vr* **1** : stagnate **2** : come to a halt — **estancado, -da** *adj* : stagnant
estancia *nf* **1** : stay **2** HABITACIÓN : (large) room **3** *Lat* : (cattle) ranch
estanco, -ca *adj* : watertight
estándar *adj & nm* : standard — **estandarizar** {21} *vt* : standardize
estandarte *nm* : standard, banner
estanque *nm* **1** : pool, pond **2** : reservoir (for irrigation)

estante *nm* : shelf — **estantería** *nf* : shelves *pl*, bookcase

estaño *nm* : tin

estar {34} *v aux* : be — *vi* **1** : be **2** : be at home **3** QUEDARSE : stay, remain **4 ¿cómo estás?** : how are you? **5 ~ a** : cost **6 ~ bien (mal)** : be well (sick) **7 ~ para** : be in the mood for **8 ~ por** : be in favor of **9 ~ por** : be about to — **estarse** *vr* : stay, remain

estarcir {83} *vt* : stencil

estárter *nm* : choke (of an automobile)

estatal *adj* : state, national

estático, -ca *adj* **1** : static **2** INMÓVIL : unmoving, still — **estática** *nf* : static

estatua *nf* : statue

estatura *nf* : height

estatus *nm* : status, prestige

estatuto *nm* : statute — **estatutario, -ria** *adj* : statutory

este[1], **esta** *adj, mpl* **estos** : this, these

este[2] *adj* : eastern, east — **este** *nm* **1** : east **2** : east wind **3 el Este** : the Orient

éste, ésta *pron, mpl* **éstos 1** : this one, these ones *pl* **2** : the latter

estela *nf* **1** : wake (of a ship) **2** : trail (of smoke, etc.)

estera *nf* : mat

estéreo *adj & nm* : stereo — **estereofónico, -ca** *adj* : stereophonic

estereotipo *nm* : stereotype

estéril *adj* **1** : sterile **2** : infertile — **esterilidad** *nf* **1** : sterility **2** : infertility — **esterilizar** {21} *vt* : sterilize

estética *nf* : aesthetics — **estético, -ca** *adj* : aesthetic

estiércol *nm* : dung, manure

estigma *nm* : stigma — **estigmatizar** {21} *vt* : stigmatize

estilarse {21} *vr* : be in fashion

estilo *nm* **1** : style **2** MANERA : fashion, manner — **estilista** *nmf* : stylist

estima *nf* : esteem, regard — **estimación** *nf, pl* **-ciones 1** : esteem **2** VALORACIÓN : estimate — **estimado, -da** *adj* **Estimado señor** : Dear Sir — **estimar** *vt* **1** : esteem, respect **2** VALORAR : value, estimate **3** CONSIDERAR : consider

estimular *vt* **1** : stimulate **2** ALENTAR : encourage — **estimulante** *adj* : stimulating — **~** *nm* : stimulant — **estímulo** *nm* : stimulus

estío *nm* : summertime

estipular *vt* : stipulate

estirar *vt* : stretch (out), extend — **estirado, -da** *adj* **1** : stretched, extended **2** ALTANERO : stuck-up, haughty — **estiramiento** *nm* **~ facial** : face-lift — **estirón** *nm, pl* **-rones** : pull, tug

estirpe *nf* : lineage, stock

estival *adj* : summer

esto *pron (neuter)* **1** : this **2 en ~** : at this point **3 por ~** : for this reason

estofa *nf* **1** : class, quality **2 de baja ~** : low-class

estofar *vt* : stew — **estofado** *nm* : stew

estoicismo *nm* : stoicism — **estoico, -ca** *adj* : stoic, stoical — **~** *n* : stoic

estómago *nm* : stomach — **estomacal** *adj* : stomach

estorbar *vt* : obstruct — *vi* : get in the way — **estorbo** *nm* **1** : obstacle **2** MOLESTIA : nuisance

estornino *nm* : starling

estornudar *vi* : sneeze — **estornudo** *nm* : sneeze

estos, éstos → este, éste

estrabismo *nm* : squint

estrado *nm* : platform, stage

estrafalario, -ria *adj* : eccentric, bizarre

estragar {52} *vt* : devastate — **estragos** *nmpl* **1** : ravages **2 hacer ~ en** *or* **causar ~ entre** : wreak havoc with

estragón *nm* : tarragon

estrangular *vt* : strangle — **estrangulación** *nf* : strangulation

estratagema *nf* : stratagem

estrategia *nf* : strategy — **estratégico, -ca** *adj* : strategic

estrato *nm* : stratum

estratosfera *nf* : stratosphere

estrechar *vt* **1** : narrow **2** : strengthen (a bond) **3** ABRAZAR : embrace **4 ~ la mano a uno** : shake s.o.'s hand — **estrecharse** *vr* : narrow — **estrechez** *nf, pl* **-checes 1** : narrowness **2 estrecheces** *nfpl* : financial problems — **estrecho, -cha** *adj* **1** : tight, narrow **2** ÍNTIMO : close — **estrecho** *nm* : strait

estrella *nf* **1** : star **2** DESTINO : destiny **3 ~ de mar** : starfish — **estrellado, -da** *adj* **1** : starry **2** : star-shaped

estrellar *v* : crash — **estrellarse** *vr* **~ contre** : smash into

estremecer {53} *vt* : cause to shudder — *vi* : tremble, shake — **estremecerse** *vr* : shudder, shiver (with emotion) — **estremecimiento** *nm* : shaking, shivering

estrenar *vt* **1** : use for the first time **2** : premiere, open (a film, etc.) — **estrenarse** *vr* : make one's debut — **estreno** *nm* : debut, premiere

estreñirse {67} *vr* : be constipated — **estreñimiento** *nm* : constipation

estrépito *nm* : clamor, din — **estrepitoso, -sa** *adj* : noisy, clamorous

estrés *nm, pl* **estreses** : stress — **estresante** *adj* : stressful — **estresar** *vt* : stress (out)

estría *nf* : groove
estribaciones *nfpl* : foothills
estribar *vi* ~ **en** : stem from, lie in
estribillo *nm* : refrain, chorus
estribo *nm* **1** : stirrup **2** : running board (of a vehicle) **3** CONTRAFUERTE : buttress **4 perder los** ~**s** : lose one's temper
estribor *nm* : starboard
estricto, -ta *adj* : strict
estridente *adj* : strident, shrill
estrofa *nf* : stanza, verse
estropajo *nm* : scouring pad
estropear *vt* **1** : ruin, spoil **2** DAÑAR : damage — **estropearse** *vr* **1** : go bad **2** AVERIARSE : break down — **estropicio** *nm* : damage, havoc
estructura *nf* : structure — **estructural** *adj* : structural
estruendo *nm* : din, roar — **estruendoso, -sa** *adj* : thunderous
estrujar *vt* : squeeze
estuario *nm* : estuary
estuche *nm* : kit, case
estuco *nm* : stucco
estudiar *v* : study — **estudiante** *nmf* : student — **estudiantil** *adj* : student — **estudio** *nm* **1** : study **2** OFICINA : studio, office **3** ~**s** *nmpl* : studies, education — **estudioso, -sa** *adj* : studious
estufa *nf* : stove, heater
estupefaciente *adj & nm* : narcotic — **estupefacto, -ta** *adj* : astonished
estupendo, -da *adj* : stupendous, marvelous
estúpido, -da *adj* : stupid — **estupidez** *nf, pl* **-deces** : stupidity
estupor *nm* **1** : stupor **2** ASOMBRO : amazement
etapa *nf* : stage, phase
etcétera : et cetera, and so on
éter *nm* : ether
etéreo, -rea *adj* : ethereal
eterno, -na *adj* : eternal — **eternidad** *nf* : eternity — **eternizarse** {21} *vr* : take forever
ética *nf* : ethics — **ético, -ca** *adj* : ethical
etimología *nf* : etymology
etíope *adj* : Ethiopian
etiqueta *nf* **1** : tag, label **2** PROTOCOLO : etiquette **3 de** ~ : formal, dressy — **etiquetar** *vt* : label
étnico, -ca *adj* : ethnic
eucalipto *nm* : eucalyptus
Eucaristía *nf* : Eucharist, communion
eufemismo *nm* : euphemism — **eufemístico, -ca** *adj* : euphemistic
euforia *nf* : euphoria — **eufórico, -ca** *adj* : euphoric
europeo, -pea *adj* : European
eutanasia *nf* : euthanasia

evacuar *vt* : evacuate, vacate — *vi* : have a bowel movement — **evacuación** *nf, pl* **-ciones** : evacuation
evadir *vt* : evade, avoid — **evadirse** *vr* : escape
evaluar {3} *vt* : evaluate — **evaluación** *nf, pl* **-ciones** : evaluation
evangelio *nm* : gospel — **evangélico, -ca** *adj* : evangelical — **evangelismo** *nm* : evangelism
evaporar *vt* : evaporate — **evaporarse** *vr* : evaporate, disappear — **evaporación** *nf, pl* **-ciones** : evaporation
evasión *nf, pl* **-siones 1** : evasion **2** FUGA : escape — **evasiva** *nf* : excuse, pretext — **evasivo, -va** *adj* : evasive
evento *nm* : event
eventual *adj* **1** : temporary **2** POSIBLE : possible — **eventualidad** *nf* : possibility, eventuality
evidencia *nf* **1** : evidence, proof **2 poner en** ~ : demonstrate — **evidenciar** *vt* : demonstrate, show — **evidente** *adj* : evident — **evidentemente** *adj* : evidently, apparently
evitar *vt* **1** : avoid **2** IMPEDIR : prevent — **evitable** *adj* : avoidable
evocar {72} *vt* : evoke
evolución *nf, pl* **-ciones** : evolution — **evolucionar** *vi* : evolve
exacerbar *vt* **1** : exacerbate **2** IRRITAR : irritate
exacto, -ta *adj* : precise, exact — **exactamente** *adv* : exactly — **exactitud** *nf* : precision, accuracy
exagerar *v* : exaggerate — **exageración** *nf, pl* **-ciones** : exaggeration — **exagerado, -da** *adj* : exaggerated
exaltar *vt* **1** : exalt, extol **2** EXCITAR : excite, arouse — **exaltarse** *vr* : get worked-up — **exaltado, -da** *adj* : worked up, hotheaded
examen *nm, pl* **exámenes 1** : examination, test **2** ANÁLISIS : investigation — **examinar** *vt* **1** : examine **2** ESTUDIAR : study, inspect — **examinarse** *vr* : take an exam
exánime *adj* : lifeless
exasperar *vt* : exasperate, irritate — **exasperación** *nf, pl* **-ciones** : exasperation
excavar *v* : excavate — **excavación** *nf, pl* **-ciones** : excavation
exceder *vt* : exceed, surpass — **excederse** *vr* : go too far — **excedente** *adj & nm* : surplus, excess
excelente *adj* : excellent — **excelencia** *nf* **1** : excellence **2 Su Excelencia** : His/Her Excellency
excéntrico, -ca *adj & n* : eccentric — **excentricidad** *nf* : eccentricity

excepción *nf, pl* **-ciones** : exception — **excepcional** *adj* : exceptional

excepto *prep* : except (for) — **exceptuar** {3} *vt* : exclude, except

exceso *nm* **1** : excess **2 ~ de velocidad** : speeding — **excesivo, -va** *adj* : excessive

excitar *vt* : excite, arouse — **excitarse** *vr* : get excited — **excitable** *adj* : excitable — **excitación** *nf, pl* **-ciones** : excitement, agitation, arousal — **excitante** *adj* : exciting

exclamar *v* : exclaim — **exclamación** *nf, pl* **-ciones** : exclamation

excluir {41} *vt* : exclude — **exclusión** *nf, pl* **-siones** : exclusion — **exclusivo, -va** *adj* : exclusive

excomulgar {52} *vt* : excommunicate — **excomunión** *nf, pl* **-niones** : excommunication

excremento *nm* : excrement

exculpar *vt* : exonerate

excursión *nf, pl* **-siones** : excursion — **excursionista** *nmf* **1** : tourist, sightseer **2** : hiker

excusar *vt* **1** : excuse **2** EXIMIR : exempt — **excusarse** *vr* : apologize — **excusa** *nf* **1** : excuse **2** DISCULPA : apology

exento, -ta *adj* : exempt

exequias *nfpl* : funeral rites

exhalar *vt* **1** : exhale **2** : give off (an odor, etc.)

exhaustivo, -va *adj* : exhaustive — **exhausto, -ta** *adj* : exhausted, worn-out

exhibir *vt* : exhibit, show — **exhibición** *nf, pl* **-ciones** : exhibition

exhortar *vt* : exhort, admonish

exigir {35} *vt* : demand, require — **exigencia** *nf* : demand, requirement — **exigente** *adj* : demanding

exiguo, -gua *adj* : meager

exiliar *vt* : exile — **exiliarse** *vr* : go into exile — **exiliado, -da** *adj* : exiled, in exile — **~ n** : exile — **exilio** *nm* : exile

eximir *vt* : exempt

existir *vi* : exist — **existencia** *nf* **1** : existence **2 ~s** *nfpl* MERCANCÍA : goods, stock — **existente** *adj* : existing

éxito *nm* **1** : success, hit **2 tener ~** : be successful — **exitoso, -sa** *adj Lat* : successful

éxodo *nm* : exodus

exorbitante *adj* : exorbitant

exorcizar {21} *vt* : exorcize — **exorcismo** *nm* : exorcism

exótico, -ca *adj* : exotic

expandir *vt* : expand — **expandirse** *vr* : spread — **expansión** *nf, pl* **-siones** : expansion — **expansivo, -va** *adj* : expansive

expatriarse {85} *vr* **1** : emigrate **2** EXIL-IARSE : go into exile — **expatriado, -da** *adj & n* : expatriate

expectativa *nf* **1** : expectation, hope **2 ~s** *nfpl* : prospects

expedición *nf, pl* **-ciones** : expedition

expediente *nm* **1** : expedient **2** DOCUMENTOS : file, record **3** INVESTIGACIÓN : inquiry, proceedings

expedir {54} *vt* **1** : issue **2** ENVIAR : dispatch — **expedito, -ta** *adj* : free, clear

expeler *vt* : expel, eject

expendedor, -dora *n* : dealer, seller

expensas *nfpl* **1** : expenses **2 a ~ de** : at the expense of

experiencia *nf* : experience

experimentar *vi* : experiment — *vt* **1** : experiment with, test out **2** SENTIR : experience, feel — **experimentado, -da** *adj* : experienced — **experimental** *adj* : experimental — **experimento** *nm* : experiment

experto, -ta *adj & n* : expert

expiar {85} *vt* : atone for

expirar *vi* **1** : expire **2** MORIR : die

explayar *vt* : extend — **explayarse** *vr* **1** : spread out **2** HABLAR : speak at length

explicar {72} *vt* : explain — **explicarse** *vr* : understand — **explicación** *nf, pl* **-ciones** : explanation — **explicativo, -va** *adj* : explanatory

explícito, -ta *adj* : explicit

explorar *vt* : explore — **exploración** *nf, pl* **-ciones** : exploration — **explorador, -dora** *n* : explorer, scout — **exploratorio, -ria** *adj* : exploratory

explosión *nf, pl* **-siones** **1** : explosion **2** : outburst (of anger, laughter, etc.) — **explosivo, -va** *adj* : explosive — **explosivo** *nm* : explosive

explotar *vt* **1** : exploit **2** : operate, run (a factory, etc.), work (a mine) — *vi* : explode — **explotación** *nf, pl* **-ciones** **1** : exploitation **2** : running (of a business), working (of a mine)

exponer {60} *vt* **1** : expose **2** : explain, set out (ideas, theories, etc.) **3** EXHIBIR : exhibit, display — *vi* : exhibit — **exponerse** *vr* **~ a** : expose oneself to

exportar *vt* : export — **exportaciones** *nfpl* : exports — **exportador, -dora** *n* : exporter

exposición *nf, pl* **-ciones** **1** : exposure **2** : exhibition (of objects, art, etc.) **3** : exposition, setting out (of ideas, etc.) — **expositor, -tora** *n* **1** : exhibitor **2** : exponent (of a theory, etc.)

exprés *nms & pl* **1** : express (train) **2** *or* **café ~** : espresso

expresamente *adv* : expressly, on purpose

expresar *vt* : express — **expresarse** *vr* : express oneself — **expresión** *nf, pl* **-siones**

: expression — **expresivo, -va** *adj* **1** : expressive **2** CARIÑOSO : affectionate
expreso, -sa *adj* : express — **expreso** *nm* : express train, express
exprimir *vt* **1** : squeeze **2** EXPLOTAR : exploit — **exprimidor** *nm* : squeezer, juicer
expuesto, -ta *adj* **1** : exposed **2** PELIGROSO : risky, dangerous
expulsar *vt* : expel, eject — **expulsión** *nf, pl* **-siones** : expulsion
exquisito, -ta *adj* **1** : exquisite **2** RICO : delicious — **exquisitez** *nf* **1** : exquisiteness **2** : delicacy, special dish
éxtasis *nms & pl* : ecstasy — **extático, -ta** *adj* : ecstatic
extender {56} *vt* **1** : spread out **2** : draw up (a document), write out (a check) — **extenderse** *vr* **1** : extend, spread **2** DURAR : last — **extendido, -da** *adj* **1** : widespread **2** : outstretched (of arms, wings, etc.)
extensamente *adv* : extensively
extensión *nf, pl* **-siones 1** : extension **2** AMPLITUD : expanse **3** ALCANCE : range, extent — **extenso, -sa** *adj* : extensive
extenuar {3} *vt* : exhaust, tire out
exterior *adj* **1** : exterior, external **2** EXTRANJERO : foreign — **∼** *nm* **1** : outside **2 en el ∼** : abroad — **exteriorizar** {21} *vt* : show, reveal — **exteriormente** *adv* : outwardly, externally
exterminar *vt* : exterminate — **exterminación** *nf, pl* **-ciones** : extermination — **exterminio** *nm* : extermination
externo, -na *adj* : external
extinguir {26} *vt* **1** : extinguish (a fire) **2** : put an end to, wipe out — **extinguirse** *vr* **1** : go out (of fire, light, etc.) **2** : become extinct — **extinción** *nf, pl* **-ciones** : extinction — **extinguidor** *nm Lat* : fire extinguisher — **extinto, -ta** *adj* : extinct — **extintor** *nm* : fire extinguisher
extirpar *vt* : remove, eradicate

extorsión *nf, pl* **-siones 1** : extortion **2** MOLESTIA : trouble
extra *adv* : extra — **∼** *adj* **1** ADICIONAL : additional **2** : top-quality — **∼** *nmf* : extra (in movies) — **∼** *nm* : extra (expense)
extraditar *vt* : extradite
extraer {81} *vt* : extract — **extracción** *nf, pl* **-ciones** : extraction — **extracto** *nm* **1** : extract **2** RESUMEN : abstract, summary
extranjero, -ra *adj* : foreign — **∼** *n* : foreigner — **extranjero** *nm* : foreign countries *pl*
extrañar *vt* : miss (someone) — **extrañarse** *vr* : be surprised — **extrañeza** *nf* : surprise — **extraño, -ña** *adj* **1** : foreign **2** RARO : strange, odd — **∼** *n* : stranger
extraoficial *adj* : unofficial
extraordinario, -ria *adj* : extraordinary
extrasensorial *adj* : extrasensory
extraterrestre *adj & nmf* : extraterrestrial
extravagante *adj* : extravagant, outrageous — **extravagancia** *nf* : extravagance, outlandishness
extraviar {85} *vt* : lose, misplace — **extraviarse** *vr* : get lost — **extravío** *nm* : loss
extremar *vt* : carry to extremes — **extremarse** *vr* : do one's utmost — **extremadamente** *adv* : extremely — **extremado, -da** *adj* : extreme — **extremidad** *nf* **1** : tip, end **2 ∼es** *nfpl* : extremities — **extremista** *adj & nmf* : extremist — **extremo, -ma** *adj* **1** : extreme **2 en caso ∼** : as a last resort — **extremo** *nm* **1** : end **2 en ∼** : in the extreme, extremely **3 en ultimo ∼** : as a last resort
extrovertido -da *adj* : extroverted — **∼** *n* : extrovert
exuberante *adj* : exuberant — **exuberancia** *nf* : exuberance
exudar *vt* : exude
eyacular *vi* : ejaculate — **eyaculación** *nf, pl* **-ciones** : ejaculation

F

f *nf* : f, sixth letter of the Spanish alphabet

fabricar {72} *vt* **1** : manufacture **2** CONSTRUIR : build, construct **3** INVENTAR : fabricate — **fábrica** *nf* : factory — **fabricación** *nf, pl* **-ciones** : manufacture — **fabricante** *nmf* : manufacturer

fábula *nf* **1** : fable **2** MENTIRA : story, lie

fabuloso, -sa *adj* : fabulous

facción *nf, pl* **-ciones 1** : faction **2** ~es *nfpl* RASGOS : features

faceta *nf* : facet

facha *nf* : appearance, look

fachada *nf* : façade

facial *adj* : facial

fácil *adj* **1** : easy **2** PROBABLE : likely — **facilemente** *adv* : easily, readily — **facilidad** *nf* **1** : facility, ease **2** ~es *nfpl* : facilities, services — **facilitar** *vt* **1** : facilitate **2** PROPORCIONAR : provide, supply

facsímil *or* **facsímile** *nm* **1** COPIA : facsimile, copy **2** : fax

factible *adj* : feasible

factor *nm* : factor

factoría *nf* : factory

factura *nf* **1** : bill, invoice **2** HECHURA : making, manufacture — **facturar** *vt* **1** : bill for **2** : check in (baggage, etc.)

facultad *nf* **1** : faculty, ability **2** AUTORIDAD : authority **3** : school (of a university) — **facultativo, -va** *adj* : optional

faena *nf* **1** : task, job **2** ~s domésticas : housework

fagot *nm* : bassoon

faisán *nm, pl* **-sanes** : pheasant

faja *nf* **1** : sash **2** : girdle, corset **3** : strip (of land)

fajo *nm* : bundle, sheaf

falda *nf* **1** : skirt **2** : side, slope (of a mountain)

falible *adj* : fallible

fálico, -ca *adj* : phallic

fallar *vi* : fail, go wrong — *vt* **1** : pronounce judgment on **2** ERRAR : miss — **falla** *nf* **1** : flaw, defect **2** : (geological) fault

fallecer {53} *vi* : pass away, die — **fallecimiento** *nm* : demise, death

fallido, -da *adj* : failed, unsuccessful

fallo *nm* **1** : error **2** SENTENCIA : sentence, verdict

falo *nm* : phallus, penis

falsear *vt* : falsify, distort — **falsedad** *nf* **1** : falseness **2** MENTIRA : falsehood, lie — **falsificación** *nf, pl* **-ciones** : forgery, fake — **falsificador, -dora** *n* : forger — **falsi-**

ficar {72} *vt* **1** : counterfeit, forge **2** ALTERAR : falsify — **falso, -sa** *adj* **1** : false, untrue **2** FALSIFICADO : counterfeit, forged

falta *nf* **1** CARENCIA : lack **2** DEFECTO : defect, fault, error **3** AUSENCIA : absence **4** : offense, misdemeanor (in law) **5** : foul (in sports) **6** hacer ~ : be lacking, be needed **7** sin ~ : without fail — **faltar** *vi* **1** : be lacking, be needed **2** : be missing **3** QUEDAR : remain, be left **4** ¡no faltaba más! : don't mention it! — **falto, -ta** *adj* ~ **de** : lacking (in)

fama *nf* **1** : fame **2** REPUTACIÓN : reputation

famélico, -ca *adj* : starving

familia *nf* : family — **familiar** *adj* **1** : familial, family **2** CONOCIDO : familiar **3** : informal (of language, etc.) — ~ *nmf* : relation, relative — **familiaridad** *nf* : familiarity — **familiarizarse** {21} *vr* ~ **con** : familiarize oneself with

famoso, -sa *adj* : famous

fanático, -ca *adj* : fanatic, fanatical — ~ *n* : fanatic — **fanatismo** *nm* : fanaticism

fanfarria *nf* : fanfare

fanfarrón, -rrona *adj, mpl* **-rrones** *fam* : boastful — ~ *n fam* : braggart — **fanfarronear** *vi* : boast, brag

fango *nm* : mud, mire — **fangoso, -sa** *adj* : muddy

fantasear *vi* : fantasize, daydream — **fantasía** *nf* **1** : fantasy **2** IMAGINACIÓN : imagination

fantasma *nm* : ghost, phantom — **fantasmal** *adj* : ghostly

fantástico, -ca *adj* : fantastic

fardo *nm* : bundle

farfullar *v* : jabber, gabble

farmacéutico, -ca *adj* : pharmaceutical — ~ *n* : pharmacist — **farmacia** *nf* : drugstore, pharmacy

faro *nm* **1** : lighthouse **2** : headlight (of an automobile) — **farol** *nm* **1** LINTERNA : lantern **2** FAROLA : streetlight — **farola** *nf* **1** : lamppost **2** FAROL : streetlight

farsa *nf* : farce — **farsante** *nmf* : charlatan, fraud

fascículo *nm* : installment, part (of a publication)

fascinar *vt* : fascinate — **fascinación** *nf, pl* **-ciones** : fascination — **fascinante** *adj* : fascinating

fascismo *nm* : fascism — **fascista** *adj & nmf* : fascist

fase *nf* : phase

fiel

fastidiar *vt* : annoy, bother — *vi* : be annoying or bothersome — **fastidio** *nm* : annoyance — **fastidioso, -sa** *adj* : annoying, bothersome

fatal *adj* **1** : fateful **2** MORTAL : fatal **3** *fam* : awful, terrible — **fatalidad** *nf* **1** : fate, destiny **2** DESGRACIA : misfortune

fatídico, -ca *adj* : fateful, momentous

fatiga *nf* : fatigue — **fatigado, -da** *adj* : weary, tired — **fatigar** {52} *vt* : tire — **fatigarse** *vr* : get tired — **fatigoso, -sa** *adj* : fatiguing, tiring

fatuo, -tua *adj* **1** : fatuous **2** PRESUMIDO : conceited

fauna *nf* : fauna

favor *nm* **1** : favor **2 a ~ de** : in favor of **3 por ~** : please — **favorable** *adj* **1** : favorable **2 ser ~ a** : be in favor of — **favorecedor, -dora** *adj* : flattering — **favorecer** {53} *vt* **1** AYUDAR : favor **2** : look well on, suit — **favoritismo** *nm* : favoritism — **favorito, -ta** *adj* & *n* : favorite

fax *nm* : fax — **faxear** *vt* : fax

faz *nf, pl* **faces** : face, countenance

fe *nf* **1** : faith **2 dar ~ de** : bear witness to **3 de buena ~** : in good faith

fealdad *nf* : ugliness

febrero *nm* : February

febril *adj* : feverish

fecha *nf* **1** : date **2 ~ de caducidad** *or* **~ de vencimiento** : expiration date **3 ~ límite** : deadline — **fechar** *vt* : date, put a date on

fechoría *nf* : misdeed

fécula *nf* : starch (in food)

fecundar *vt* **1** : fertilize (an egg) **2** : make fertile — **fecundo, -da** *adj* : fertile

federación *nf, pl* **-ciones** : federation — **federal** *adj* : federal

felicidad *nf* **1** : happiness **2 ¡~es!** : best wishes!, congratulations!, happy birthday! — **felicitación** *nf, pl* **-ciones** : congratulation — **felicitar** *vt* : congratulate — **felicitarse** *vr* **~ de** : be glad about

feligrés, -gresa *n, mpl* **-greses** : parishioner

felino, -na *adj* & *n* : feline

feliz *adj, pl* **-lices** **1** : happy **2** AFORTUNADO : fortunate **3 Feliz Navidad** : Merry Christmas

felpa *nf* **1** : plush **2** : terry cloth (for towels, etc.)

felpudo *nm* : doormat

femenino, -na *adj* **1** : feminine **2** : female (in biology) — **femenino** *nm* : feminine (in grammar) — **femineidad** *nf* : femininity — **feminismo** *nm* : feminism — **feminista** *adj* & *nmf* : feminist

fenómeno *nm* : phenomenon — **fenomenal**

adj **1** : phenomenal **2** *fam* : fantastic, terrific

feo, fea *adj* **1** : ugly **2** DESAGRADABLE : unpleasant, nasty

féretro *nm* : coffin

feria *nf* **1** : fair, market **2** FIESTA : festival, holiday **3** *Lat fam* : small change — **feriado, -da** *adj* **día feriado** : public holiday

fermentar *v* : ferment — **fermentación** *nf, pl* **-ciones** : fermentation — **fermento** *nm* : ferment

feroz *adj, pl* **-roces** : ferocious, fierce — **ferocidad** *nf* : ferocity, fierceness

férreo, -rrea *adj* **1** : iron **2 vía férrea** : railroad track

ferretería *nf* : hardware store

ferrocarril *nm* : railroad, railway — **ferroviario, -ria** *adj* : rail, railroad

ferry *nm, pl* **ferrys** : ferry

fértil *adj* : fertile, fruitful — **fertilidad** *nf* : fertility — **fertilizante** *nm* : fertilizer — **fertilizar** *vt* : fertilize

fervor *nm* : fervor, zeal — **ferviente** *adj* : fervent

festejar *vt* **1** : celebrate **2** AGASAJAR : entertain, wine and dine — **festejo** *nm* : celebration, festivity

festín *nm, pl* **-tines** : banquet, feast

festival *nm* : festival — **festividad** *nf* : festivity — **festivo, -va** *adj* **1** : festive **2 día festivo** : holiday

fetiche *nm* : fetish

fétido, -da *adj* : foul-smelling, fetid

feto *nm* : fetus — **fetal** *adj* : fetal

feudal *adj* : feudal

fiable *adj* : reliable — **fiabilidad** *nf* : reliability

fiado, -da *adj* : on credit — **fiador, -dora** *n* : bondsman, guarantor

fiambres *nfpl* : cold cuts

fianza *nf* **1** : bail, bond **2 dar ~** : pay a deposit

fiar {85} *vt* **1** : guarantee **2** : sell on credit — *vi* **ser de ~** : be trustworthy — **fiarse** *vr* **~ de** : place trust in

fiasco *nm* : fiasco

fibra *nf* **1** : fiber **2 ~ de vidrio** : fiberglass

ficción *nf, pl* **-ciones** : fiction

ficha *nf* **1** : token **2** TARJETA : index card **3** : counter, chip (in games) — **fichar** *vt* : file, index — **fichero** *nm* **1** : card file **2** : filing cabinet

ficticio, -cia *adj* : fictitious

fidedigno, -na *adj* : reliable, trustworthy

fidelidad *nf* : fidelity, faithfulness

fideo *nm* : noodle

fiebre *nf* **1** : fever **2 ~ del heno** : hay fever **3 ~ palúdica** : malaria

fiel *adj* **1** : faithful, loyal **2** PRECISO : accurate, reliable — **~** *nm* **1** : pointer (of a scale) **2 los ~es** : the faithful — **fielmente** *adv* : faithfully

fieltro *nm* : felt

fiero, -ra *adj* : fierce, ferocious — **fiera** *nf* : wild animal, beast

fierro *nm Lat* : iron (bar)

fiesta *nf* **1** : party **2** DIA FESTIVO : holiday, feast day

figura *nf* **1** : figure **2** FORMA : shape, form — **figurar** *vi* **1** : figure (in), be included (among) **2** DESTACAR : stand out — *vt* : represent — **figurarse** *vr* : imagine

fijar *vt* **1** : fasten, affix **2** CONCRETAR : set, fix — **fijarse** *vr* **1** : settle **2 ~ en** : notice, pay attention to — **fijo, -ja** *adj* **1** : fixed, firm **2** PERMANENTE : permanent

fila *nf* **1** : line, file, row **2 ponerse en ~** : line up

filantropía *nf* : philanthropy — **filantrópico, -ca** *adj* : philanthropic — **filántropo, -pa** *n* : philanthropist

filatelia *nf* : philately, stamp collecting

filete *nm* : fillet

filial *adj* : filial — **~** *nf* : affiliate, subsidiary

filigrana *nf* **1** : filigree **2** : watermark (on paper)

filipino, -na *adj* : Filipino

filmar *vt* : film, shoot — **filme** *or* **film** *nm* : film, movie

filo *nm* **1** : edge **2 dar ~ a** : sharpen

filón *nm, pl* **-lones 1** : vein (of minerals) **2** *fam* : gold mine

filoso, -sa *adj Lat* : sharp

filosofía *nf* : philosophy — **filosófico, -ca** *adj* : philosophical — **filósofo, -fa** *n* : philosopher

filtrar *v* : filter — **filtrarse** *vr* : leak out, seep through — **filtro** *nm* : filter

fin *nm* **1** : end **2** OBJETIVO : purpose, aim **3 en ~** : well, in short **4 ~ de semana** : weekend **5 por ~** : finally, at last

final *adj* : final — **~** *nm* : end, conclusion — **~** *nf* : final (in sports) — **finalidad** *nf* : purpose, aim — **finalista** *nmf* : finalist — **finalizar** {21} *v* : finish, end — **finalmente** *adv* : finally

financiar *vt* : finance, fund — **financiero, -ra** *adj* : financial — **~** *n* : financier — **finanzas** *nfpl* : finance

finca *nf* **1** : farm, ranch **2** *Lat* : country house

fingir {35} *v* : feign, pretend — **fingido, -da** *adj* : false, feigned

finito, -ta *adj* : finite

finlandés, -desa *adj* : Finnish

fino, -na *adj* **1** : fine **2** DELGADO : slender **3** REFINADO : refined **4** AGUDO : sharp, keen

— finura *nf* **1** : fineness **2** REFINAMIENTO : refinement

firma *nf* **1** : signature **2** : (act of) signing **3** EMPRESA : firm, company

firmamento *nm* : firmament, sky

firmar *v* : sign

firme *adj* **1** : firm, resolute **2** ESTABLE : steady, stable — **firmeza** *nf* **1** : strength, resolve **2** ESTABILIDAD : firmness, stability

fiscal *adj* : fiscal — **~** *nmf* : district attorney — **fisco** *nm* : (national) treasury

fisgar {52} *vt* : pry into — *vi* : pry — **fisgón, -gona** *n, mpl* **-gones** : snoop, busybody

física *nf* : physics — **físico, -ca** *adj* : physical — **~** *n* : physicist — **físico** *nm* : physique

fisiología *nf* : physiology — **fisiológico, -ca** *adj* : physiological — **fisiólogo, -ga** *n* : physiologist

fisioterapia *nf* : physical therapy — **fisioterapeuta** *nmf* : physical therapist

fisonomía *nf* : features *pl,* appearance

fisura *nf* : fissure

fláccido, -da *or* **flácido, -da** *adj* : flaccid, flabby

flaco, -ca *adj* **1** : thin, skinny **2** DÉBIL : weak

flagrante *adj* : flagrant

flamante *adj* **1** : bright, brilliant **2** NUEVO : brand-new

flamenco, -ca *adj* **1** : flamenco (of music or dance) **2** : Flemish — **flamenco** *nm* **1** : flamingo **2** : flamenco (music or dance)

flaquear *vi* : weaken, flag — **flaqueza** *nf* **1** : thinness **2** DEBILIDAD : weakness

flash *nm* : flash

flatulencia *nf* : flatulence

flauta *nf* **1** : flute **2 ~ dulce** : recorder — **flautín** *nm, pl* **-tines** : piccolo — **flautista** *nmf* : flutist

flecha *nf* : arrow

fleco *nm* **1** : fringe **2** *Lat* : bangs *pl*

flema *nf* : phlegm — **flemático, -ca** *adj* : phlegmatic

flequillo *nm* : bangs *pl*

fletar *vt* **1** : charter, rent **2** *Lat* : transport — **flete** *nm* **1** : charter **2** : shipping (charges) **3** *Lat* : transport, freight

flexible *adj* : flexible — **flexibilidad** *nf* : flexibility

flirtear *vi* : flirt

flojo, -ja *adj* **1** SUELTO : loose, slack **2** DÉBIL : weak **3** PEREZOSO : lazy — **flojera** *nf fam* : lethargy

flor *nf* : flower — **flora** *nf* : flora — **floral** *adj* : floral — **floreado, -da** *adj* : flowered — **florear** *vi Lat* : flower, bloom — **florecer** {53} *vi* **1** : bloom, blossom **2** PROSPERAR : flourish — **floreciente** *adj* : flourishing — **florero** *nm* : vase — **florido, -da** *adj* : flow-

ery — **florista** *nmf* : florist — **floritura** *nf*
: frill, flourish
flota *nf* : fleet
flotar *vi* : float — **flotador** *nm* **1** : float **2**
: life preserver (for a swimmer) — **flotante**
adj : floating, buoyant — **flote: a ~** *adv
phr* : afloat
flotilla *nf* : flotilla, fleet
fluctuar {3} *vi* : fluctuate — **fluctuación** *nf,
pl* **-ciones** : fluctuation
fluir {41} *vi* : flow — **fluidez** *nf* **1** : fluidity
2 : fluency (of language, etc.) — **fluido, -da**
adj **1** : fluid **2** : fluent (of language) — **fluido** *nm* : fluid — **flujo** *nm* : flow
fluorescente *adj* : fluorescent
fluoruro *nm* : fluoride
fluvial *adj* : river
fobia *nf* : phobia
foca *nf* : seal (animal)
foco *nm* **1** : focus **2** : spotlight, floodlight
(in theater, etc.) **3** *Lat* : lightbulb
fofo, -fa *adj* : flabby
fogata *nf* : bonfire
fogón *nm, pl* **-gones** : burner
fogoso, -sa *adj* : ardent
folklore *nm* : folklore — **folklórico, -ca** *adj*
: folk, traditional
follaje *nm* : foliage
folleto *nm* : pamphlet, leaflet
fomentar *vt* : promote, encourage — **fomento** *nm* : promotion, encouragement
fonda *nf* : boarding house
fondear *vt* : sound out, examine — *vi* : anchor
fondillos *nmpl* : seat (of pants, etc.)
fondo *nm* **1** : bottom **2** : rear, back, end **3**
PROFUNDIDAD : depth **4** : background (of a
painting, etc.) **5** *Lat* : slip, petticoat **6 ~s**
nmpl : funds, resources **7 a ~** : thoroughly, in depth **8 en el ~** : deep down
fonético, -ca *adj* : phonetic — **fonética** *nf*
: phonetics
fontanería *nf Spain* : plumbing —
fontanero, -ra *n Spain* : plumber
footing *nm* **1** : jogging **2 hacer ~** : jog
forajido, -da *n* : bandit, outlaw
foráneo, -nea *adj* : foreign, strange
forastero, -ra *n* : stranger, outsider
forcejear *vi* : struggle — **forcejeo** *nm*
: struggle
forense *adj* : forensic
forja *nf* : forge — **forjar** *vt* **1** : forge **2**
CREAR, FORMAR : build up, create
forma *nf* **1** : form, shape **2** MANERA : manner, way **3 en ~** : fit, healthy **4 ~s** *nfpl*
: appearances, conventions — **formación**
nf, pl **-ciones 1** : formation **2** EDUCACIÓN
: training
formal *adj* **1** : formal **2** SERIO : serious **3** FI-

ABLE : dependable, reliable — **formalidad**
nf **1** : formality **2** SERIEDAD : seriousness
3 FIABILIDAD : reliability
formar *vt* **1** : form, shape **2** CONSTITUIR
: constitute **3** EDUCAR : train, educate —
formarse *vr* **1** DESARROLLARSE : develop,
take shape **2** EDUCARSE : be educated
formato *nm* : format
formidable *adj* **1** : tremendous **2** *fam* : fantastic, terrific
fórmula *nf* : formula
formular *vt* **1** : formulate, draw up **2**
: make, lodge (a complaint, etc.)
formulario *nm* : form
fornido, -da *adj* : well-built, burly
foro *nm* : forum
forraje *nm* : forage, fodder — **forrajear** *vi*
: forage
forrar *vt* **1** : line (a garment) **2** : cover (a
book) — **forro** *nm* **1** : lining **2** CUBIERTA
: book cover
fortalecer {53} *vt* : strengthen — **fortaleza**
nf **1** : fortress **2** FUERZA : strength **3**
: (moral) fortitude
fortificar {72} *vt* : fortify — **fortificación** *nf,
pl* **-ciones** : fortification
fortuito, -ta *adj* : fortuitous, chance
fortuna *nf* **1** SUERTE : fortune, luck **2**
RIQUEZA : wealth, fortune **3 por ~** : fortunately
forzar {36} *vt* **1** : force **2** : strain (one's
eyes) — **forzosamente** *adv* : necessarily —
forzoso, -sa *adj* : necessary, inevitable
fosa *nf* **1** : pit, ditch **2** TUMBA : grave **3 ~s
nasales** : nostrils
fósforo *nm* **1** : phosphorus **2** CERILLA
: match — **fosforescente** *adj* : phosphores-
cent
fósil *nm* : fossil
foso *nm* **1** : ditch **2** : pit (of a theater) **3**
: moat (of a castle)
foto *nf* : photo
fotocopia *nf* : photocopy — **fotocopiadora**
nf : photocopier — **fotocopiar** *vt* : photocopy
fotogénico, -ca *adj* : photogenic
fotografía *nf* **1** : photography **2** : photograph, picture — **fotografiar** {85} *vt* : photograph — **fotográfico, -ca** *adj* : photographic — **fotógrafo, -fa** *n* : photographer
fotosíntesis *nf* : photosynthesis
fracasar *vi* : fail — **fracaso** *nm* : failure
fracción *nf, pl* **-ciones 1** : fraction **2** : faction (in politics) — **fraccionamiento** *nm
Lat* : housing development
fractura *nf* : fracture — **fracturarse** *vr*
: fracture, break (a bone)
fragancia *nf* : fragrance, scent — **fragante**
adj : fragrant

fragata *nf* : frigate
frágil *adj* **1** : fragile **2** DÉBIL : frail, delicate
— **fragilidad** *nf* **1** : fragility **2** DEBILIDAD
: frailty
fragmento *nm* : fragment
fragor *nm* : clamor, din
fragoso, -sa *adj* : rough, rugged
fragua *nf* : forge — **fraguar** {10} *vt*
: forge **2** IDEAR : concoct — *vi* : harden, solidify
fraile *nm* : friar, monk
frambuesa *nf* : raspberry
francés, -cesa *adj, mpl* **-ceses** : French —
francés *nm* : French (language)
franco, -ca *adj* **1** : frank, candid **2** : free (in
commerce) — **franco** *nm* : franc
francotirador, -dora *n* : sniper
franela *nf* : flannel
franja *nf* **1** : stripe, band **2** FLECO : fringe
franquear *vt* **1** : clear (a path, etc.) **2** : cross
over (a doorstep, etc.) **3** : pay postage on
(mail) — **franqueo** *nm* : postage
franqueza *nf* : frankness
frasco *nm* : small bottle, vial, flask
frase *nf* **1** : phrase **2** ORACIÓN : sentence
fraternal *adj* : brotherly, fraternal — **fraternidad** *nf* : brotherhood, fraternity — **frater-
nizar** {21} *vi* : fraternize — **fraterno, -na**
adj : brotherly, fraternal
fraude *nm* : fraud — **fraudulento, -ta** *adj*
: fraudulent
fray *nm* (*used in titles*) : brother, friar
frazada *nf Lat* : blanket
frecuencia *nf* **1** : frequency **2 con ~**
: often, frequently — **frecuentar** *vt* : frequent, haunt — **frecuente** *adj* : frequent
fregadero *nm* : kitchen sink
fregar {49} *vt* **1** : scrub, wash **2** *Lat fam*
: annoy — *vi Lat fam* : be a pest
freír {37} *vt* : fry
fregona *nf Spain* : mop
frenar *vt* **1** : brake **2** RESTRINGIR : curb,
check
frenesí *nm* : frenzy — **frenético, -ca** *adj*
: frantic, frenzied
freno *nm* **1** : brake **2** : bit (of a bridle) **3**
CONTROL : check, restraint
frente *nm* **1** : front **2** : facade (of a building)
3 al ~ de : at the head of **4 ~ a** : opposite
5 de ~ : (facing) forward **6 hacer ~ a**
: face up to, brave — **~** *nf* : forehead
fresa *nf* : strawberry
fresco, -ca *adj* **1** : fresh **2** FRÍO : cool **3** *fam*
: insolent, nervy — **fresco** *nm* **1** : fresh air
2 FRESCOR : coolness **3** : fresco (art or
painting) — **frescor** *nm* : coolness, cool air
— **frescura** *nf* **1** : freshness **2** FRÍO : coolness **3** *fam* : nerve, insolence
fresno *nm* : ash (tree)

frialdad *nf* **1** : coldness **2** INDIFERENCIA
: indifference
fricción *nf, pl* **-ciones 1** : friction **2** MASAJE
: rubbing, massage — **friccionar** *vt* : rub
frigidez *nf* : frigidity
frigorífico *nm Spain* : refrigerator
frijol *nm Lat* : bean
frío, fría *adj* **1** : cold **2** INDIFERENTE : cool,
indifferent — **frío** *nm* **1** : cold **2** INDIFER-
ENCIA : coldness, indifference **3 hacer ~**
: be cold (outside) **4 tener ~** : be cold, feel
cold
frito, -ta *adj* **1** : fried **2** *fam* : fed up
frívolo, -la *adj* : frivolous — **frivolidad** *nf*
: frivolity
fronda *nf* **1** : frond **2** *or* **~s** *nfpl* : foliage
— **frondoso, -sa** *adj* : leafy
frontera *nf* : border, frontier — **fronterizo,
-za** *adj* : border, on the border — **frontero,
-ra** *adj* : facing, opposite
frotar *vt* : rub — **frotarse** *vr* **~ las manos**
: rub one's hands
fructífero, -ra *adj* : fruitful
frugal *adj* : frugal, thrifty — **frugalidad** *adj*
: frugality
fruncir {83} *vt* **1** : gather (in pleats) **2 ~ el
ceño** : frown **3 ~ la boca** : purse one's lips
frustrar *vt* : frustrate — **frustrarse** *vr* : fail
— **frustración** *nf, pl* **-ciones** : frustration
— **frustrado, -da** *adj* **1** : frustrated **2** FRA-
CASADO : failed, unsuccessful — **frustrante**
adj : frustrating
fruta *nf* : fruit — **frutilla** *nf Lat* : strawberry
— **fruto** *nm* **1** : fruit **2** RESULTADO : result,
consequence
fucsia *adj & nm* : fuchsia
fuego *nm* **1** : fire **2** : flame, burner (on a
stove) **3 ~s artificiales** *nmpl* : fireworks
4 ¿tienes fuego? : have you got a light?
fuelle *nm* : bellows
fuente *nf* **1** : fountain **2** MANANTIAL
: spring **3** ORIGEN : source **4** PLATO : platter, serving dish
fuera *adv* **1** : outside, out **2** : abroad, away
3 ~ de : outside of, beyond **4 ~ de**
: aside from, in addition to
fuerte *adj* **1** : strong **2** : bright (of colors),
loud (of sounds) **3** EXTREMO : intense **4**
DURO : hard — **~** *adv* **1** : strongly, hard **2**
: loudly **3** MUCHO : abundantly, a lot — **~**
nm **1** : fort **2** ESPECIALIDAD : strong point
fuerza *nf* **1** : strength **2** VIOLENCIA : force **3**
PODER : power, might **4 ~s armadas** *nfpl*
: armed forces **5 a ~ de** : by dint of **6 a la
~** : necessarily
fuga *nf* **1** : flight, escape **2** : fugue (in
music) **3** ESCAPE : leak — **fugarse** {52} *vr*
: flee, run away — **fugaz** *adj, pl* **-gaces**
: fleeting — **fugitivo, -va** *adj & n* : fugitive

fulano, -na *n* : so-and-so, what's-his-name, what's-her-name

fulgor *nm* : brilliance, splendor

fulminar *vt* **1** : strike with lightning **2** : strike down (with an illness, etc.) — **fulminante** *adj* : devastating

fumar *v* : smoke — **fumarse** *vr* **1** : smoke **2** *fam* : squander — **fumador, -dora** *n* : smoker

funámbulo, -la *n* : tightrope walker

función *nf, pl* **-ciones 1** : function **2** TRABAJOS : duties *pl* **3** : performance, show (in theater) — **funcional** *adj* : functional — **funcionamiento** *nm* **1** : functioning **2 en ~** : in operation — **funcionar** *vi* **1** : function, run, work **2 no funciona** : out of order — **funcionario, -ria** *n* : civil servant, official

funda *nf* **1** : cover, sheath **2** *or* **~ de almohada** : pillowcase

fundar *vt* **1** ESTABLECER : found, establish **2** BASAR : base — **fundarse** *vr* **~ en** : be based on — **fundación** *nf, pl* **-ciones** : foundation — **fundador, -dora** *n* : founder — **fundamental** *adj* : fundamental, basic — **fundamentalmente** *adv* : basically — **fundamentar** *vt* **1** : lay the foundations for **2** BASAR : base — **fundamento** *nm* **1** : foundation **2 ~s** *nmpl* : fundamentals

fundir *vt* **1** : melt down, smelt **2** FUSIONAR : fuse, merge — **fundirse** *vr* **1** : blend, merge **2** DERRETIRSE : melt **3** : burn out (of a lightbulb) — **fundición** *nf, pl* **-ciones 1** : smelting **2** : foundry

fúnebre *adj* **1** : funeral **2** LÚGUBRE : gloomy

funeral *adj* : funeral, funerary — **~** *nm* **1** : funeral **2 ~es** *nmpl* EXEQUIAS : funeral (rites) — **funeraria** *nf* : funeral home

funesto, ta *adj* : terrible, disastrous

fungir {35} *vi Lat* : act, function

furgón *nm, pl* **-gones 1** : van, truck **2** : freight car (of a train) **3 ~ de cola** : caboose — **furgoneta** *nf* : van

furia *nf* **1** CÓLERA : fury, rage **2** VIOLENCIA : violence — **furibundo, -da** *adj* : furious — **furioso, -sa** *adj* **1** : furious, irate **2** INTENSO : intense, violent — **furor** *nm* : fury

furtivo, -va *adj* : furtive

furúnculo *nm* : boil

fuselaje *nm* : fuselage

fusible *nm* : fuse

fusil *nm* : rifle — **fusilar** *vt* : shoot (by firing squad)

fusión *nf, pl* **-siones 1** : fusion **2** UNIÓN : union, merger — **fusionar** *vt* **1** : fuse **2** UNIR : merge — **fusionarse** *vr* : merge

futbol *or* **fútbol** *nm* **1** : soccer **2 ~ americano** : football — **futbolista** *nmf* : soccer player, football player

fútil *adj* : trifling, trivial

futuro, -ra *adj* : future — **futuro** *nm* : future

G

g *nf* : g, seventh letter of the Spanish alphabet

gabán *nm, pl* **-banes** : topcoat, overcoat

gabardina *nf* **1** : trench coat, raincoat **2** : gabardine (fabric)

gabinete *nm* **1** : cabinet (in government) **2** : (professional) office

gacela *nf* : gazelle

gaceta *nf* : gazette

gachas *nfpl* : porridge

gacho, -cha *adj* : drooping

gaélico, -ca *adj* : Gaelic

gafas *nfpl* **1** : eyeglasses **2 ~ de sol** : sunglasses

gaita *nf* : bagpipes *pl*

gajo *nm* : segment (of fruit)

gala *nf* **1** : gala **2 de ~** : formal **3 hacer ~ de** : display, show off **4 ~s** *nfpl* : finery

galáctico, -ca *adj* : galactic

galán *nm, pl* **-lanes 1** : leading man (in theater) **2** *fam* : boyfriend

galante *adj* : gallant — **galantear** *vt* : court, woo — **galantería** *nf* **1** : gallantry **2** CUMPLIDO : compliment

galápago *nm* : (aquatic) turtle

galardón *nm, pl* **-dones** : reward

galaxia *nf* : galaxy

galera *nf* : galley

galería *nf* **1** : corridor **2** : gallery, balcony (in a theater)

galés, -lesa *adj, mpl* **-leses** : Welsh

galgo *nm* : greyhound

galimatías *nms & pl* : gibberish

gallardía *nf* **1** : bravery **2** ELEGANCIA : elegance — **gallardo, -da** *adj* **1** : brave **2** APUESTO : elegant, good-looking

gallego, -ga *adj* : Galician

galleta *nf* **1** : (sweet) cookie **2** : (salted) cracker

gallina *nf* **1** : hen **2 ~ de Guinea** : guinea fowl — **gallinero** *nm* : henhouse, (chicken) coop — **gallo** *nm* : rooster, cock

galón *nm, pl* **-lones 1** : gallon **2** : stripe (military insignia)

galopar *vi* : gallop — **galope** *nm* : gallop

galvanizar {21} *vt* : galvanize

gama *nf* **1** : range, spectrum **2** : scale (in music)

gamba *nf* : large shrimp, prawn

gamuza *nf* **1** : chamois (animal) **2** : chamois (leather), suede

gana *nf* **1** : desire, wish **2** APETITO : appetite **3 de buena ~** : willingly, heartily **4 de mala ~** : unwillingly **5 no me da la ~** : I don't feel like it **6 tener ~s de** : feel like, be in the mood for

ganado *nm* **1** : cattle *pl,* livestock **2 ~ ovino** : sheep *pl* **3 ~ porcino** : swine *pl* — **ganadería** *nf* **1** : cattle raising **2** GANADO : livestock

ganador, -dora *adj* : winning — **~** *n* : winner

ganancia *nf* : profit

ganar *vt* **1** : earn **2** : win (in games, etc.) **3** CONSEGUIR : gain **4** ADQUERIR : get, obtain **5 ~ a algn** : win over s.o., beat s.o. — *vi* : win — **ganarse** *vr* **1** : win, gain **2 ~ la vida** : make a living

gancho *nm* **1** : hook **2** HORQUILLA : hairpin **3** *Lat* : (clothes) hanger

gandul, -dula *adj & n fam* : good-for-nothing — **gandul** *nm Lat* : pigeon pea

ganga *nf* : bargain

gangrena *nf* : gangrene

gángster *nmf* : gangster

ganso, -sa *n* : goose, gander *m* — **gansada** *nf* : silly thing, nonsense

gañir {38} *vi* : yelp — **gañido** *nm* : yelp

garabatear *v* : scribble — **garabato** *nm* : scribble

garaje *nm* : garage

garantizar {21} *vt* : guarantee — **garante** *nmf* : guarantor — **garantía** *nf* **1** : guarantee, warranty **2** FIANZA : surety

garapiñar *vt* : candy (fruits, etc.)

garbanzo *nm* : chickpea, garbanzo

garbo *nm* : grace, elegance — **garboso, -sa** *adj* : graceful, elegant

gardenia *nf* : gardenia

garfio *nm* : hook, gaff

garganta *nf* **1** : throat **2** CUELLO : neck **3** DESFILADERO : ravine, gorge — **gargantilla** *nf* : necklace

gárgara *nf* **1** : gargling, gargle **2 hacer ~s** : gargle

gárgola *nf* : gargoyle

garita *nf* **1** : sentry box **2** CABAÑA : cabin, hut

garito *nm* : gambling den

garra *nf* **1** : claw, talon **2** *fam* : hand, paw

garrafa *nf* : decanter, carafe — **garrafón** *nm, pl* **-fones** : large decanter or bottle

garrapata *nf* : tick

garrocha *nf* **1** : lance, pike **2** *Lat* : pole (in sports)

garrote *nm* : club, cudgel

garúa *nf Lat* : drizzle

garza *nf* : heron

gas *nm* **1** : gas **2 ~ lacrimógeno** : tear gas

gasa *nf* : gauze

gaseosa *nf* : soda, soft drink

gasolina *nf* : gasoline, gas — **gasoil** *or* **gasóleo** *nm* : diesel fuel — **gasolinera** *nf* : gas station, service station

gastar *vt* **1** : spend **2** CONSUMIR : consume, use up **3** DESPERDICIAR : squander, waste — **gastarse** *vr* **1** : spend **2** DETERIORARSE : wear out — **gastado, -da** *adj* **1** : spent **2** : worn-out (of clothing, etc.) — **gastador, -dora** *n* : spendthrift — **gasto** *nm* **1** : expense, expenditure **2 ~s generales** : overhead

gástrico, -ca *adj* : gastric

gastronomía *nf* : gastronomy — **gastrónomo, -ma** *n* : gourmet

gatas: a ~ *adv phr* : on all fours

gatear *vi* : crawl, creep

gatillo *nm* : trigger — **gatillero** *nm Mex* : gunman

gato, -ta *n* : cat — **gatito, -ta** *n* : kitten — **gato** *nm* : jack (for an automobile)

gaucho *nm* : gaucho

gaveta *nf* : drawer

gavilla *nf* **1** : sheaf **2** PANDILLA : gang

gaviota *nf* : gull, seagull

gay *adj* : gay (homosexual)

gaza *nf* : loop

gazpacho *nm* : gazpacho

géiser *nm* : geyser

gelatina *nf* : gelatin

gema *nf* : gem

gemelo, -la *adj & n* : twin — **gemelo** *nm* **1** : cuff link **2 ~s** *nmpl* : binoculars

gemir {54} *vi* : moan, groan, whine — **gemido** *nm* : moan, groan, whine

gen *or* **gene** *nm* : gene

genealogía *nf* : genealogy — **genealógico, -ca** *adj* : genealogical

generación *nf, pl* **-ciones** : generation

generador *nm* : generator

general *adj* **1** : general **2 en ~** *or* **por lo ~** : in general, generally — **~** *nmf* : general — **generalidad** *nf* **1** : generalization **2** MAYORÍA : majority — **generalizar** {21} *vi* : generalize — *vt* : spread (out) — **gener-**

alizarse *vr* : become widespread — **generalmente** *adv* : usually, generally

generar *vt* : generate

género *nm* **1** : kind, sort **2** : gender (in grammar) **3 ~ humano** : human race — **genérico, -ca** *adj* : generic

generoso, -sa *adj* **1** : generous, unselfish **2** : ample (in quantity) — **generosidad** *nf* : generosity

génesis *nfs & pl* : genesis

genética *nf* : genetics — **genético, -ca** *adj* : genetic

genial *adj* **1** : brilliant **2** ESTUPENDO : great, terrific

genio *nm* **1** : genius **2** CARÁCTER : temper, disposition **3** : genie (in mythology)

genital *adj* : genital — **genitales** *nmpl* : genitals

genocidio *nm* : genocide

gente *nf* **1** : people **2** *fam* : relatives *pl*, folks *pl* **3 ser buena ~** : be nice, be kind

gentil *adj* **1** AMABLE : kind **2** : gentile (in religion) — **gentileza** *nf* : kindness, courtesy

gentío *nm* : crowd, mob

gentuza *nf* : riffraff, rabble

genuflexión *nf, pl* **-xiones** : genuflection

genuino, -na *adj* : genuine

geografía *nf* : geography — **geográfico, -ca** *adj* : geographic, geographical

geología *nf* : geology — **geológico, -ca** *adj* : geologic, geological

geometría *nf* : geometry — **geométrico, -ca** *adj* : geometric, geometrical

geranio *nm* : geranium

gerencia *nf* : management — **gerente** *nmf* : manager

geriatría *nf* : geriatrics — **geriátrico, -ca** *adj* : geriatric

germen *nm, pl* **gérmenes** : germ

germinar *vi* : germinate, sprout

gestación *nf, pl* **-ciones** : gestation

gesticular *vi* : gesticulate, gesture — **gesticulación** *nf, pl* **-ciones** : gesticulation

gestión *nf, pl* **-tiones 1** : procedure, step **2** ADMINISTRACIÓN : management — **gestionar** *vt* **1** : negotiate, work towards **2** ADMINISTRAR : manage, handle

gesto *nm* **1** : gesture **2** : (facial) expression **3** MUECA : grimace

gigante *adj & nm* : giant — **gigantesco, -ca** *adj* : gigantic

gimnasia *nf* : gymnastics — **gimnasio** *nm* : gymnasium, gym — **gimnasta** *nmf* : gymnast

gimotear *vi* : whine, whimper

ginebra *nf* : gin

ginecología *nf* : gynecology — **ginecólogo, -ga** *n* : gynecologist

gira *nf* : tour

girar *vi* : turn (around), revolve — *vt* **1** : turn, twist, rotate **2** : draft (checks) **3** : transfer (funds)

girasol *nm* : sunflower

giratorio, -ria *adj* : revolving

giro *nm* **1** : turn, rotation **2** LOCUCIÓN : expression **3 ~ bancario** : bank draft **4 ~ postal** : money order

giroscopio *nm* : gyroscope

gis *nm Lat* : chalk

gitano, -na *adj & n* : Gypsy

glaciar *nm* : glacier — **glacial** *adj* : glacial, icy

gladiador *nm* : gladiator

glándula *nf* : gland

glasear *vt* : glaze, ice (cake, etc.) — **glaseado** *nm* : icing

glicerina *nf* : glycerin

globo *nm* **1** : globe **2** : balloon **3 ~ ocular** : eyeball — **global** *adj* **1** : global **2** TOTAL : total, overall

glóbulo *nm* : blood cell, corpuscle

gloria *nf* : glory

glorieta *nf* **1** : bower, arbor **2** *Spain* : rotary, traffic circle

glorificar {72} *vt* : glorify

glorioso, -sa *adj* : glorious

glosario *nm* : glossary

glotón, -tona *adj, mpl* **-tones** : gluttonous — **~** *n* : glutton — **glotonería** *nf* : gluttony

glucosa *nf* : glucose

gnomo *nm* : gnome

gobernar {55} *v* **1** : govern, rule **2** DIRIGIR : direct, manage **3** : steer (a boat, etc.) — **gobernación** *nf, pl* **-ciones** : governing, government — **gobernador, -dora** *n* : governor — **gobernante** *adj* : ruling, governing — **~** *n* : ruler, leader — **gobierno** *nm* : government

goce *nm* : enjoyment

gol *nm* : goal (in sports)

golf *nm* : golf — **golfista** *nmf* : golfer

golfo *nm* : gulf

golondrina *nf* **1** : swallow **2 ~ de mar** : tern

golosina *nf* : sweet, candy — **goloso, -sa** *adj* : fond of sweets

golpe *nm* **1** : blow **2** PUÑETAZO : punch **3** : knock (on a door, etc.) **4 de ~** : suddenly **5 de un ~** : all at once **6 ~ de estado** : coup d'etat — **golpear** *vt* **1** : hit, punch **2** : slam, bang (a door, etc.) — *vi* : knock (at a door)

goma *nf* **1** CAUCHO : rubber **2** PEGAMENTO : glue **3** *or* **~ elástica** : rubber band **4 ~ de mascar** : chewing gum **5 ~ de borrar** : eraser

gong *nm* : gong

gordo, -da *adj* **1 :** fat, plump **2** GRUESO
: thick **3 :** fatty (of meat) **4** *fam* **:** big, serious — ～ *n* **:** fat person — **gorda** *nf Lat*
: thick corn tortilla — **gordo** *nm* **1** GRASA
: fat **2 :** jackpot (in a lottery) — **gordura** *nf*
: fatness, flab
gorgotear *vi* **:** gurgle, bubble
gorila *nm* **:** gorilla
gorjear *vi* **1 :** chirp, tweet **2 :** gurgle (of a
baby) — **gorjeo** *nm* **:** chirping
gorra *nf* **1 :** cap, bonnet **2 de** ～ *fam* **:** for
free
gorrear *vt fam* **:** bum, scrounge
gorrión *nm, pl* **-rriones :** sparrow
gorro *nm* **1 :** cap, bonnet **2 de** ～ *fam* **:** for
free
gota *nf* **1 :** drop **2 :** gout (in medicine) —
gotear *vi* **:** drip, leak — **goteo** *nm* **:** drip,
dripping — **gotera** *nf* **:** leak
gótico, -ca *adj* **:** Gothic
gozar {21} *vi* **1 :** enjoy oneself **2** ～ **de**
algo : enjoy sth
gozne *nm* **:** hinge
gozo *nm* **1 :** joy **2** PLACER **:** enjoyment,
pleasure — **gozoso, -sa** *adj* **:** joyful, glad
grabar *vt* **1 :** engrave **2 :** record, tape —
grabación *nf, pl* **-ciones :** recording —
grabado *nm* **:** engraving — **grabadora** *nf*
: tape recorder
gracia *nf* **1 :** grace **2** FAVOR **:** favor, kindness
3 HUMOR **:** humor, wit **4** ～s *nfpl* **:** thanks
5 ¡(muchas) ～s! **:** thank you (very much)!
— **gracioso, -sa** *adj* **:** funny, amusing
grada *nf* **1 :** step, stair **2 :** row (in a theater,
etc.) **3** ～s *nfpl* **:** bleachers, grandstand —
gradación *nf, pl* **-ciones :** gradation, scale
— **gradería** *nf* **:** rows *pl*, stands *pl* — **grado**
nm **1 :** degree **2 :** grade (in school) **3 de**
buen ～ **:** willingly
graduar {3} *vt* **1 :** regulate, adjust **2** MAR-
CAR **:** calibrate **3 :** confer a degree on (in
education) — **graduarse** *vr* **:** graduate
(from a school) — **graduación** *nf, pl*
-ciones 1 : graduation **2 :** alcohol content,
proof — **graduado, -da** *n* **:** graduate —
gradual *adj* **:** gradual — **gradualmente** *adv*
: little by little, gradually
gráfico, -ca *adj* **:** graphic — **gráfica** *nf*
: graph — **gráfico** *nm* **1 :** graph **2 :** graphic
(in computers)
gragea *nf* **:** pill, tablet
grajo *nm* **:** rook (bird)
gramática *nf* **:** grammar — **gramatical** *adj*
: grammatical
gramo *nm* **:** gram
gran → **grande**
grana *nf* **:** scarlet
granada *nf* **1 :** pomegranate **2 :** grenade (in
the military)

granate *nm* **:** garnet
grande *adj* (**gran** *before singular nouns*) **1**
: large, big **2** ALTO **:** tall **3 :** great (in quality, intensity, etc.) **4** *Lat* **:** grown-up —
grandeza *nf* **1 :** greatness **2** NOBLEZA **:** nobility — **grandiosidad** *nf* **:** grandeur —
grandioso, -sa *adj* **:** grand, magnificent
granel: a ～ *adv phr* **1 :** in bulk **2 :** in abundance
granero *nm* **:** barn, granary
granito *nm* **:** granite
granizar {21} *v impers* **:** hail — **granizada** *nf*
: hailstorm — **granizado** *nm* **:** iced drink —
granizo *nm* **:** hail
granja *nf* **:** farm — **granjero, -ra** *n* **:** farmer
grano *nm* **1 :** grain **2** SEMILLA **:** seed **3**
: (coffee) bean **4** BARRO **:** pimple
granuja *nmf* **:** rascal
grapa *nf* **:** staple — **grapadora** *nf* **:** stapler —
grapar *vt* **:** staple
grasa *nf* **1 :** grease **2 :** fat (in cooking, etc.)
— **grasiento, -ta** *adj* **:** greasy, oily — **graso,**
-sa *adj* **:** fatty, greasy, oily — **grasoso, -sa**
adj Lat **:** greasy, oily
gratificar {72} *vt* **1 :** give a tip or bonus to **2**
SATISFACER **:** gratify, satisfy — **gratifi-**
cación *nf, pl* **-ciones 1 :** bonus, tip, reward
2 SATISFACCIÓN **:** gratification
gratis *adv & adj* **:** free
gratitud *nf* **:** gratitude
grato, -ta *adj* **:** pleasant, agreeable
gratuito, -ta *adj* **1 :** gratuitous, unwarranted
2 GRATIS **:** free
grava *nf* **:** gravel
gravar *vt* **1 :** tax **2** CARGAR **:** burden —
gravamen *nm, pl* **-vámenes 1 :** burden,
obligation **2** IMPUESTO **:** tax
grave *adj* **1 :** grave, serious **2 :** deep, low
(of a voice, etc.) — **gravedad** *nf* **:** gravity
gravilla *nf* **:** gravel
gravitar *vi* **1 :** gravitate **2** ～ **sobre :** weigh
on — **gravitación** *nf, pl* **-ciones :** gravita-
tion
gravoso, -sa *adj* **:** costly, burdensome
graznar *vi* **:** caw, quack, honk — **graznido**
nm **:** caw, quack, honk
gregario, -ria *adj* **:** gregarious
gremio *nm* **:** guild, (trade) union
greñas *nfpl* **:** shaggy hair, mop
griego, -ga *adj* **:** Greek — **griego** *nm*
: Greek (language)
grieta *nf* **:** crack, crevice
grifo *nm Spain* **:** faucet, tap
grillete *nm* **:** shackle
grillo *nm* **1 :** cricket **2** ～s *nmpl* **:** fetters,
shackles
grima *nf* **dar** ～ **:** annoy, irritate
gringo, -ga *adj & n Lat fam* **:** Yankee, gringo
gripe *nf or* **gripa** *nf Lat* **:** flu, influenza

gris *adj & nm* : gray
gritar *v* : shout, scream, cry — **grito** *nm* **1** : shout, scream, cry **2 dar ~s** : shout
grosella *nf* : currant
grosería *nf* **1** : vulgar remark **2** DES-CORTESÍA : rudeness — **grosero, -ra** *adj* **1** : coarse, vulgar **2** DESCORTÉS : rude
grosor *nm* : thickness
grotesco, -ca *adj* : grotesque, hideous
grúa *nf* : crane, derrick
grueso, -sa *adj* **1** : thick **2** CORPULENTO : stout, heavy — **gruesa** *nf* : gross — **grueso** *nm* **1** GROSOR : thickness **2** : main body, mass **3 en ~** : wholesale
grulla *nf* : crane (bird)
grumo *nm* : lump, clot — **grumoso, -sa** *adj* : lumpy
gruñir {38} *vi* **1** : growl, grunt **2** *fam* : grumble — **gruñido** *nm* **1** : growl, grunt **2** *fam* : grumble — **gruñón, -ñona** *adj, mpl* **-ñones** *fam* : grumpy, grouchy — **~** *n fam* : grouch
grupa *nf* : rump, hindquarters *pl*
grupo *nm* : group
gruta *nf* : grotto
guacamayo *nm or* **guacamaya** *nf Lat* : macaw
guacamole *nm* : guacamole
guadaña *nf* : scythe
guagua *nf Lat* **1** : baby **2** AUTOBÚS : bus
guajalote, -ta *or* **guajolote, -ta** *n Lat* : turkey
guante *nm* : glove
guapo, -pa *adj* : handsome, good-looking
guaraní *nm* : Guarani (language of Paraguay)
guarda *nmf* **1** : keeper, custodian **2** GUARDIÁN : security guard — **guardabarros** *nms & pl* : fender — **guardabosque** *nmf* : forest ranger — **guardacostas** *nmfs & pl* : coast guard vessel — **guardaespaldas** *nmfs & pl* : bodyguard — **guardameta** *nmf* : goalkeeper — **guardapolvo** *nm* : overalls *pl* — **guardar** *vt* **1** : keep **2** PROTEGER : guard, protect **3** RESERVAR : save — **guardarse** *vr* **~ de 1** : refrain from **2** : guard against — **guardarropa** *nm* **1** : cloakroom, checkroom **2** ARMARIO : wardrobe
guardería *nf* : nursery, day-care center
guardia *nf* **1** : guard, vigilence **2** TURNO : duty, watch — **~** *nmf* **1** : guard **2** *or* **~ municipal** : police officer — **guardián, -diana** *n, mpl* **-dianes 1** : guardian, keeper **2** GUARDA : security guard

guarecer {53} *vt* : shelter, protect — **guarecerse** *vr* : take shelter
guarida *nf* **1** : den, lair (of animals) **2** : hideout (of persons)
guarnecer {53} *vt* **1** : adorn, garnish **2** : garrison (an area) — **guarnición** *nf, pl* **-ciones 1** : garnish, trimming **2** : (military) garrison
guasa *nf fam* **1** : joke **2 de ~** : in jest — **guasón, -sona** *adj, mpl* **-sones** *fam* : joking, witty — **~** *n fam* : joker
guatemalteco, -ca *adj* : Guatemalan
guayaba *nf* : guava
gubernamental *or* **gubernativo, -va** *adj* : governmental
guepardo *nm* : cheetah
güero, -ra *adj Lat* : blond, fair
guerra *nf* **1** : war, warfare **2** LUCHA : conflict, struggle — **guerrear** *vi* : wage war — **guerrero, -ra** *adj* **1** : war, fighting **2** BELICOSO : warlike — **~** *n* : warrior — **guerrilla** *nf* : guerrilla warfare — **guerrillero, -ra** *adj & n* : guerrilla
gueto *nm* : ghetto
guiar {85} *vt* **1** : guide, lead **2** ACONSEJAR : advise — **guiarse** *vr* : be guided by, go by — **guía** *nf* **1** : guidebook **2** ORIENTACIÓN : guidance — **~** *nmf* : guide, leader
guijarro *nm* : pebble
guillotina *nf* : guillotine
guinda *nf* : morello (cherry)
guiñar *vi* : wink — **guiño** *nm* : wink
guión *nm, pl* **guiones 1** : script, screenplay **2** : hyphen, dash (in punctuation) — **guionista** *nmf* : scriptwriter, screenwriter
guirnalda *nf* : garland
guisa *nf* **1** : manner, fashion **2 a ~ de** : by way of **3 de tal ~** : in such a way
guisado *nm* : stew
guisante *nm* : pea
guisar *vt* : cook — **guiso** *nm* : stew, casserole
guitarra *nf* : guitar — **guitarrista** *nmf* : guitarist
gula *nf* : gluttony
gusano *nm* **1** : worm **2** : maggot (larva)
gustar *vt* **1** : taste **2** *Lat* : like — *vi* **1** : be pleasing **2 como guste** : as you like **3 me gustan los dulces** : I like sweets — **gusto** *nm* **1** : taste **2** PLACER : pleasure, liking **3 a ~** : comfortable, at ease **4 al ~** : to taste **5 mucho ~** : pleased to meet you — **gustoso, -sa** *adj* **1** : tasty **2** AGRADABLE : pleasant **3 hacer algo ~** : do sth willingly
gutural *adj* : guttural

H

h *nf* : h, eighth letter of the Spanish alphabet

haba *nf* : broad bean

habanero, -ra *adj* : Havanan — **habano** *nm* : Havana cigar

haber {39} *v aux* **1** : have, has **2** ~ **de** : must — *v impers* **1 hay** : there is, there are **2 hay que** : it is necessary (to) **3 ¿qué hay?** *or* **¿qué hubo?** : how's it going? — ~ *nm* **1** : assets *pl* **2** : credit side (in accounting) **3** ~**es** *nmpl* : income, earnings

habichuela *nf* **1** : bean **2** ~ **verde** : string bean

hábil *adj* **1** : able, skillful **2** LISTO : clever **3 horas** ~**es** : business hours — **habilidad** *nf* : ability, skill

habilitar *vt* **1** : equip, furnish **2** AUTORIZAR : authorize

habitar *vt* : inhabit — *vi* : reside, dwell — **habitable** *adj* : habitable, inhabitable — **habitación** *nf, pl* **-ciones 1** : room, bedroom **2** MORADA : dwelling, abode **3** : habitat (in biology) — **habitante** *nmf* : inhabitant, resident — **hábitat** *nm* : habitat

hábito *nm* : habit — **habitual** *adj* : habitual, usual — **habituar** {3} *vt* : accustom, habituate — **habituarse** *vr* ~ **a** : get used to

hablar *vi* **1** : speak, talk **2** ~ **de** : mention, talk about **3** ~ **con** : talk to, speak with — *vt* **1** : speak (a language) **2** DISCUTIR : discuss — **hablarse** *vr* **1** : speak to each other **2 se habla inglés** : English spoken — **habla** *nf* **1** : speech **2** IDIOMA : language, dialect **3 de** ~ **inglesa** : English-speaking — **hablador, -dora** *adj* : talkative — ~ *n* : chatterbox — **habladuría** *nf* **1** : rumor — ~**s** *nfpl* : gossip — **hablante** *nmf* : speaker

hacedor, -dora *n* : creator, maker

hacendado, -da *n* : landowner, rancher

hacer {40} *vt* **1** : do, perform **2** CONSTRUIR, CREAR : make **3** OBLIGAR : force, oblige — *vi* : act — *v impers* **1** ~ **calor/viento** : be hot/be windy **2** ~ **falta** : be necessary **3 hace mucho tiempo** : a long time ago **4 no lo hace** : it doesn't matter — **hacerse** *vr* **1** VOLVERSE : become **2** : pretend (to be) **3** ~ **a** : get used to **4 se hace tarde** : it's getting late

hacha *nf* **1** : hatchet, ax **2** ANTORCHA : torch

hachís *nm* : hashish

hacia *prep* **1** : toward, towards **2** CERCA DE : near, around, about **3** ~ **abajo** : downward **4** ~ **adelante** : forward

hacienda *nf* **1** : estate, ranch **2** BIENES : property **3** *Lat* : livestock **4 Hacienda** : department of revenue

hacinar *vt* : stack

hada *nf* : fairy

hado *nm* : fate

halagar {52} *vt* : flatter — **halagador, -dora** *adj* : flattering — **halago** *nm* : flattery — **halagüeño, -ña** *adj* **1** : flattering **2** PROMETEDOR : promising

halcón *nm, pl* **-cones** : hawk, falcon

halibut *nm, pl* **-buts** : halibut

hálito *nm* : breath

hallar *vt* **1** : find **2** DESCUBRIR : discover, find out — **hallarse** *vr* : be, find oneself — **hallazgo** *nm* : discovery, find

halo *nm* : halo

hamaca *nf* : hammock

hambre *nf* **1** : hunger **2** INANICIÓN : starvation, famine **3 tener** ~ : be hungry — **hambriento, -ta** *adj* : hungry, starving — **hambruna** *nf* : famine

hamburguesa *nf* : hamburger

hampa *nf* : underworld — **hampón, -pona** *n, mpl* **-pones** : criminal, thug

hámster *nm* : hamster

hándicap *nm* : handicap (in sports)

hangar *nm* : hangar

haragán, -gana *adj, mpl* **-ganes** : lazy, idle — ~ *n* : slacker, idler — **haraganear** : be lazy, loaf

harapiento, -ta *adj* : ragged, in rags — **harapos** *nmpl* : rags, tatters

harina *nf* : flour

hartar *vt* **1** : glut, satiate **2** FASTIDIAR : annoy — **hartarse** *vr* **1** : gorge oneself **2** CANSARSE : get fed up — **harto, -ta** *adj* **1** : full, satiated **2** CANSADO : tired, fed up — **harto** *adv* : extremely, very — **hartura** *nf* **1** : surfeit **2** ABUNDANCIA : abundance, plenty

hasta *prep* **1** : until, up until (in time) **2** : as far as, up to (in space) **3 ¡** ~ **luego!** : see you later! **4** ~ **que** : until — ~ *adv* : even

hastiar {85} *vt* **1** : make weary, bore **2** ASQUEAR : sicken — **hastiarse** *vr* ~ **de** : get tired of — **hastío** *nm* **1** : weariness, tedium **2** REPUGNANCIA : disgust

hato *nm* **1** : flock, herd **2** : bundle (of possessions)

haya *nf* : beech

haz *nm, pl* **haces 1** : bundle, sheaf **2** : beam (of light)

hazaña *nf* : feat, exploit

hazmerreír *nm fam* : laughingstock

he {39} *v impers* ~ **aquí** : here is, here are, behold

hebilla *nf* : buckle

hebra *nf* : strand, thread

hebreo, -brea *adj* : Hebrew — **hebreo** *nm* : Hebrew (language)

hecatombe *nm* : disaster

hechizo *nm* **1** : spell **2** ENCANTO : charm, fascination — **hechicería** *nf* : sorcery, witchcraft — **hechicero, -ra** *n* : sorcerer, sorceress *f* — **hechizar** {21} *vt* **1** : bewitch **2** CAUTIVAR : charm

hecho, -cha *adj* **1** : made, done **2** : ready-to-wear (of clothing) **3** ~ **y derecho** : full-fledged, mature — **hecho** *nm* **1** : fact **2** SUCESO : event **3** ACTO : act, deed **4 de** ~ : in fact — **hechura** *nf* **1** : making, creation **2** FORMA : shape, form **3** : build (of the body) **4** ARTESANÍA : workmanship

heder {56} *vi* : stink, reek — **hediondez** *nf*, *pl* **-deces** : stench — **hediondo, -da** *adj* : stinking — **hedor** *nm* : stench

helar {55} *v* : freeze — **helarse** *vr* : freeze up, freeze over — **helado, -da** *adj* **1** : freezing cold **2** CONGELADO : frozen — **helada** *nf* : frost — **heladería** *nf* : ice-cream parlor — **helado** *nm* : ice cream — **heladora** *nf* : freezer

helecho *nm* : fern

hélice *nf* **1** : propeller **2** ESPIRAL : spiral, helix

helicóptero *nm* : helicopter

helio *nm* : helium

hembra *nf* **1** : female **2** MUJER : woman

hemisferio *nm* : hemisphere

hemorragia *nf* **1** : hemorrhage **2** ~ **nasal** : nosebleed

hemorroides *nfpl* : hemorrhoids, piles

henchir {54} *vt* : stuff, fill

hender {56} *vt* : cleave, split — **hendidura** *nf* : crevice, fissure

henequén *nm*, *pl* **-quenes** : sisal

heno *nm* : hay

hepatitis *nf* : hepatitis

heraldo *nm* : herald

herbolario, -ria *n* : herbalist

heredar *vt* : inherit — **heredad** *nm* : rural property, estate — **heredero, -ra** *n* : heir, heiress *f* — **hereditario, -ria** *adj* : hereditary

hereje *nmf* : heretic — **herejía** *nf* : heresy

herencia *nf* **1** : inheritance **2** : heredity (in biology)

herir {76} *vt* **1** : injure, wound **2** : hurt (feelings, pride, etc.) — **herida** *nf* : injury, wound — **herido, -da** *adj* **1** : injured, wounded **2** : hurt (of feelings, pride, etc.) — ~ *n* : injured person, casualty

hermano, -na *n* : brother *m*, sister *f* — **hermanastro, -tra** *n* : half brother *m*, half sister *f* — **hermandad** *nf* : brotherhood

hermético, -ca *adj* : hermetic, watertight

hermoso, -sa *adj* : beautiful, lovely — **hermosura** *nf* : beauty

hernia *nf* : hernia

héroe *nm* : hero — **heroico, -ca** *adj* : heroic — **heroína** *nf* **1** : heroine **2** : heroin (narcotic) — **heroísmo** *nm* : heroism

herradura *nf* : horseshoe

herramienta *nf* : tool

herrero, -ra *n* : blacksmith

herrumbre *nf* : rust

hervir {76} *v* : boil — **hervidero** *nm* **1** : mass, swarm **2** : hotbed (of intrigue, etc.) — **hervidor** *nm* : kettle — **hervor** *nm* **1** : boiling **2** ENTUSIASMO : fervor, ardor

heterogéneo, -nea *adj* : heterogeneous

heterosexual *adj* & *nmf* : heterosexual

hexágono *nm* : hexagon — **hexagonal** *adj* : hexagonal

hez *nf*, *pl* **heces** : dregs *pl*, scum

hiato *nm* : hiatus

hibernar *vi* : hibernate — **hibernación** *nf*, *pl* **-ciones** : hibernation

híbrido, -da *adj* : hybrid — **híbrido** *nm* : hybrid

hidalgo, -ga *n* : nobleman *m*, noblewoman *f*

hidratante *adj* : moisturizing

hidrato *nm* ~ **de carbono** : carbohydrate

hidráulico, -ca *adj* : hydraulic

hidroavión *nm*, *pl* **-aviones** : seaplane

hidroeléctrico, -ca *adj* : hydroelectric

hidrofobia *nf* : rabies

hidrógeno *nm* : hydrogen

hidroplano *nm* : hydroplane

hiedra *nf* **1** : ivy **2** ~ **venenosa** : poison ivy

hiel *nm* **1** : bile **2** AMARGURA : bitterness

hielo *nm* **1** : ice **2** FRIALDAD : coldness **3 romper el** ~ : break the ice

hiena *nf* : hyena

hierba *nf* **1** : herb **2** CÉSPED : grass **3 mala** ~ : weed — **hierbabuena** *nf* : mint

hierro *nm* **1** : iron **2** ~ **fundido** : cast iron

hígado *nm* : liver

higiene *nf* : hygiene — **higiénico, -ca** *adj* : hygienic

higo *nm* : fig

hijo, -ja *n* **1** : son *m*, daughter *f* **2 hijos** *nmpl* : children, offspring — **hijastro, -tra** *n* : stepson *m*, stepdaughter *f*

hilar *v* **1** : spin **2** ~ **delgado** : split hairs — **hilado** *nm* : yarn, thread

hilaridad *nf* : hilarity

hilera *nf* : file, row

hilo *nm* **1** : thread **2** LINO : linen **3** ALAMBRE : wire **4** : trickle (of water, etc.) **5** ~ **dental** : dental floss

hilvanar *vt* **1** : baste, tack **2** : put together (ideas, etc.)

himno *nm* **1** : hymn **2** ~ **nacional** : national anthem

hincapié *nm* hacer ～ en : emphasize, stress
hincar {72} *vt* : drive in, plunge — **hincarse** *vr* ～ de rodillas : kneel (down)
hinchar *vt Spain* : inflate, blow up — **hincharse** *vr* 1 : swell (up) 2 *Spain fam* : stuff oneself — **hinchado, -da** *adj* 1 : swollen 2 POMPOSO : pompous — **hinchazón** *nf, pl* -zones : swelling
hindú *adj & nmf* : Hindu — **hinduismo** *nm* : Hinduism
hinojo *nm* : fennel
hiperactivo, -va *adj* : hyperactive
hipersensible *adj* : oversensitive
hipertensión *nf, pl* -siones : hypertension, high blood pressure
hípico, -ca *adj* : equestrian, horse
hipil → **huipil**
hipnosis *nfs & pl* : hypnosis — **hipnótico, -ca** *adj* : hypnotic — **hipnotismo** *nm* : hypnotism — **hipnotizador, -dora** *n* : hypnotist — **hipnotizar** {21} *vt* : hypnotize
hipo *nm* 1 : hiccup, hiccups *pl* 2 tener ～ : have hiccups
hipocondríaco, -ca *adj* : hypochondriacal — ～ *n* : hypochondriac
hipocresía *nf* : hypocrisy — **hipócrita** *adj* : hypocritical — ～ *nmf* : hypocrite
hipodérmico, -ca *adj* : hypodermic
hipódromo *nm* : racetrack
hipopótamo *nm* : hippopotamus
hipoteca *nf* : mortgage — **hipotecar** {72} *vt* : mortgage
hipótesis *nfs & pl* : hypothesis — **hipotético, -ca** *adj* : hypothetical
hiriente *adj* : hurtful, offensive
hirsuto, -ta *adj* 1 : hairy 2 : bristly, wiry (of hair)
hirviente *adj* : boiling
hispano, -na *or* **hispánico, -ca** *adj & n* : Hispanic — **hispanoamericano, -na** *adj* : Latin-American — ～ *n* : Latin American — **hispanohablante** *or* **hispanoparlante** *adj* : Spanish-speaking
histeria *nf* : hysteria — **histérico, -ca** *adj* : hysterical — **histerismo** *nm* : hysteria
historia *nf* 1 : history 2 CUENTO : story — **historiador, -dora** *n* : historian — **historial** *nm* : record, background — **histórico, -ca** *adj* 1 : historical 2 IMPORTANTE : historic, important — **historieta** *nf* : comic strip
hito *nm* : milestone, landmark
hocico *nm* : snout, muzzle
hockey *nm* : hockey
hogar *nm* 1 : home 2 CHIMENEA : hearth, fireplace — **hogareño, -ña** *adj* 1 : home-loving 2 DOMÉSTICO : home, domestic
hoguera *nf* : bonfire
hoja *nf* 1 : leaf 2 : sheet (of paper) 3 ～ de afeitar : razor blade — **hojalata** *nf* : tinplate

— **hojaldre** *nm* : puff pastry — **hojear** *vt* : leaf through — **hojuela** *nf Lat* : flake
hola *interj* : hello!, hi!
holandés, -desa *adj, mpl* -deses : Dutch
holgado, -da *adj* 1 : loose, baggy 2 : comfortable (of an economic situation, a victory, etc.) — **holgazán, -zana** *adj, mpl* -zanes : lazy — ～ *n* : slacker, idler — **holgazanear** *vi* : laze about, loaf — **holgura** *nf* 1 : looseness 2 BIENESTAR : comfort, ease
hollín *nm, pl* -llines : soot
holocausto *nm* : holocaust
hombre *nm* 1 : man 2 el ～ : mankind 3 ～ de estado : statesman 4 ～ de negocios : businessman
hombrera *nf* 1 : shoulder pad 2 : epaulet (of a uniform)
hombría *nf* : manliness
hombro *nm* : shoulder
hombruno, -na *adj* : mannish
homenaje *nm* 1 : homage 2 rendir ～ a : pay tribute to
homeopatía *nf* : homeopathy
homicidio *nm* : homicide, murder — **homicida** *adj* : homicidal, murderous — ～ *nmf* : murderer
homogéneo, -nea *adj* : homogeneous
homólogo, -ga *adj* : equivalent — ～ *n* : counterpart
homosexual *adj & nmf* : homosexual — **homosexualidad** *nf* : homosexuality
hondo, -da *adj* : deep — **hondo** *adv* : deeply — **hondonada** *nf* : hollow — **hondura** *nf* : depth
hondureño, -ña *adj* : Honduran
honesto, -ta *adj* : decent, honorable — **honestidad** *nf* : honesty, integrity
hongo *nm* 1 : mushroom 2 : fungus (in botany and medicine)
honor *nm* : honor — **honorable** *adj* : honorable — **honorario, -ria** *adj* : honorary — **honorarios** *nmpl* : payment, fee — **honra** *nf* : honor — **honradez** *nf, pl* -deces : honesty, integrity — **honrado, -da** *adj* : honest, upright — **honrar** *vt* : honor — **honrarse** *vr* : be honored — **honroso, -sa** *adj* : honorable
hora *nf* 1 : hour 2 : (specific) time 3 CITA : appointment 4 a la última ～ : at the last minute 5 ～ punta : rush hour 6 media ～ : half an hour 7 ¿qué ～ es? : what time is it? 8 ～s de oficina : office hours 9 ～s extraordinarias : overtime
horario *nm* : schedule, timetable
horca *nf* 1 : gallows *pl* 2 : pitchfork (in agriculture)
horcajadas: a ～ *adv phr* : astride
horda *nf* : horde
horizonte *nm* : horizon — **horizontal** *adj* : horizontal

85   huy

horma *nf* **1** : form, mold, last **2** : shoe tree

hormiga *nf* : ant

hormigón *nm, pl* **-gones** : concrete

hormigueo *nm* : tingling, pins and needles

hormiguero *nm* **1** : anthill **2** : swarm (of people)

hormona *nf* : hormone

horno *nm* **1** : oven (for cooking) **2** : small furnace, kiln — **hornada** *nf* : batch — **hornear** *vt* : bake — **hornillo** *nf* : portable stove

horóscopo *nm* : horoscope

horquilla *nf* **1** : hairpin, bobby pin **2** HORCA : pitchfork

horrendo, -da *adj* : horrendous, awful — **horrible** *adj* : horrible — **horripilante** *adj* : horrifying — **horror** *nm* **1** : horror, dread **2** ATROCIDAD : atrocity — **horrorizar** {21} *vt* : horrify, terrify — **horrorizarse** *vr* : be horrified — **horroroso, -sa** *adj* : horrifying, dreadful

hortaliza *nf* : (garden) vegetable — **hortelano, -na** *n* : truck farmer — **horticultura** *nf* : horticulture

hosco, -ca *adj* : sullen, gloomy

hospedar *vt* : put up, lodge — **hospedarse** *vr* : stay, lodge — **hospedaje** *nm* : lodging

hospital *nm* : hospital — **hospitalario, -ria** *adj* : hospitable — **hospitalidad** *nf* : hospitality — **hospitalizar** {21} *vt* : hospitalize

hostería *nf* : small hotel, inn

hostia *nf* : host (in religion)

hostigar {52} *vt* **1** : whip **2** ACOSAR : harass, pester

hostil *adj* : hostile — **hostilidad** *nf* : hostility

hotel *nm* : hotel — **hotelero, -ra** *adj* : hotel — **～** *n* : hotel manager, hotelier

hoy *adv* **1** : today **2 de ～ en adelante** : from now on **3 ～ (en) día** : nowadays **4 ～ mismo** : this very day

hoyo *nm* : hole — **hoyuelo** *nm* : dimple

hoz *nf, pl* **hoces** : sickle

huarache *nm* : huarache (sandal)

hueco, -ca *adj* **1** : hollow, empty **2** ESPONJOSO : soft, spongy **3** RESONANTE : resonant — **hueco** *nm* **1** : hollow, cavity **2** : recess (in a wall, etc.) **3 ～ de escalera** : stairwell

huelga *nf* **1** : strike **2 declararse en ～** : go on strike — **huelguista** *nmf* : striker

huella *nf* **1** : footprint **2** VESTIGIO : track, mark **3 ～ digital** *or* **～ dactilar** : fingerprint

huérfano, -na *n* : orphan — **～** *adj* : orphaned

huerta *nf* : truck farm — **huerto** *nm* **1** : vegetable garden **2** : (fruit) orchard

hueso *nm* **1** : bone **2** : pit, stone (of a fruit)

huésped, -peda *n* : guest — **huésped** *nm* : host (organism)

huesudo, -da *adj* : bony

huevo *nm* **1** : egg **2 ～s estrellados** : fried eggs **3 ～s revueltos** : scrambled eggs — **hueva** *nf* : roe

huida *nf* : flight, escape — **huidizo, -za** *adj* **1** : shy **2** FUGAZ : fleeting

huipil *nm Lat* : traditional embroidered blouse or dress

huir {41} *vi* **1** : escape, flee **2 ～ de** : shun, avoid

hule *nm* **1** : oilcloth **2** *Lat* : rubber

humano, -na *adj* **1** : human **2** COMPASIVO : humane — **humano** *nm* : human (being) — **humanidad** *nf* **1** : humanity, mankind **2** BENEVOLENCIA : humaneness **3 ～es** *nfpl* : humanities — **humanismo** *nm* : humanism — **humanista** *nmf* : humanist — **humanitario, -ria** *adj & n* : humanitarian

humear *vi* : smoke, steam — **humareda** *nf* : cloud of smoke

humedad *nf* **1** : dampness **2** : humidity (in meteorology) — **humedecer** {53} *vt* : moisten, dampen — **humedecerse** *vr* : become moist — **húmedo, -da** *adj* **1** : moist, damp **2** : humid (in meteorology)

humildad *nf* : humility — **humilde** *adj* : humble — **humillación** *nf, pl* **-ciones** : humiliation — **humillante** *adj* : humiliating — **humillar** *vt* : humiliate — **humillarse** *vr* : humble oneself

humo *nm* **1** : smoke, steam, fumes **2 ～s** *nmpl* : airs, conceit

humor *nm* **1** : mood, temper **2** GRACIA : humor **3 de buen ～** : in a good mood — **humorismo** *nm* : humor, wit — **humorista** *nmf* : humorist, comedian — **humorístico, -ca** *adj* : humorous

hundir *vt* **1** : sink **2** : destroy, ruin (a building, plans, etc.) — **hundirse** *vr* **1** : sink **2** DERRUMBARSE : collapse — **hundido, -da** *adj* : sunken — **hundimiento** *nm* **1** : sinking **2** DERRUMBE : collapse

húngaro, -ra *adj* : Hungarian

huracán *nm, pl* **-canes** : hurricane

huraño, -ña *adj* : unsociable

hurgar {52} *vi* **～ en** : rummage around in

hurón *nm, pl* **-rones** : ferret

hurra *interj* : hurrah!, hooray!

hurtadillas: a ～ *adv phr* : stealthily, on the sly

hurtar *vt* : steal — **hurto** *nm* **1** ROBO : theft **2** : stolen property

husmear *vt* : sniff out, pry into — *vi* : nose around

huy *interj* : ow!, ouch!

I

i *nf* : i, ninth letter of the Spanish alphabet
ibérico, -ca *adj* : Iberian — **ibero, -ra** *or* **íbero, -ra** *adj* : Iberian
iceberg *nm, pl* **-bergs** : iceberg
icono *nm* : icon
ictericia *nf* : jaundice
ida *nf* **1** : outward journey **2** ~ **y vuelta** : round-trip **3** ~**s y venidas** : comings and goings
idea *nf* **1** : idea **2** OPINIÓN : opinion
ideal *adj & nm* : ideal — **idealismo** *nm* : idealism — **idealista** *adj* : idealistic — ~ *nmf* : idealist — **idealizar** {21} *vt* : idealize
idear *vt* : devise, think up
ídem *nm* : the same, ditto
identidad *nf* : identity — **idéntico, -ca** *adj* : identical — **identificar** {72} *vt* : identify — **identificarse** *vr* **1** : identify oneself **2** ~ **con** : identify with — **identificación** *nf, pl* **-ciones** : identification
ideología *nf* : ideology — **ideológico, -ca** *adj* : ideological
idílico, -ca *adj* : idyllic
idioma *nm* : language — **idiomático, -ca** *adj* : idiomatic
idiosincrasia *nf* : idiosyncrasy — **idiosincrásico, -ca** *adj* : idiosyncratic
idiota *adj* : idiotic — ~ *nmf* : idiot — **idiotez** *nf* : idiocy
ídolo *nm* : idol — **idolatrar** *vt* : idolize — **idolatría** *nf* : idolatry
idóneo, -nea *adj* : suitable, fitting — **idoneidad** *nf* : fitness, suitability
iglesia *nf* : church
iglú *nm* : igloo
ignición *nf, pl* **-ciones** : ignition
ignífugo, -ga *adj* : fire-resistant, fireproof
ignorar *vt* **1** : ignore **2** DESCONOCER : be unaware of — **ignorancia** *nf* : ignorance — **ignorante** *adj* : ignorant — ~ *nmf* : ignorant person
igual *adv* **1** : in the same way **2 por** ~ : equally — ~ *adj* **1** : equal **2** IDÉNTICO : the same **3** LISO : smooth, even **4** SEMEJANTE : similar — ~ *nmf* : equal, peer — **igualar** *vt* **1** : make equal **2** : be equal to **3** NIVELAR : level (off) — **igualdad** *nf* **1** : equality **2** UNIFORMIDAD : uniformity — **igualmente** *adv* : likewise
iguana *nf* : iguana
ijada *nf* : flank
ilegal *adj* : illegal
ilegible *adj* : illegible

ilegítimo, -ma *adj* : illegitimate — **ilegitimidad** *nf* : illegitimacy
ileso, -sa *adj* : unharmed
ilícito, -ta *adj* : illicit
ilimitado, -da *adj* : unlimited
ilógico, -ca *adj* : illogical
iluminar *vt* : illuminate — **iluminarse** *vr* : light up — **iluminación** *nf, pl* **-ciones** **1** : illumination **2** ALUMBRADO : lighting
ilusionar *vt* : excite — **ilusionarse** *vr* : get one's hopes up — **ilusión** *nf, pl* **-siones** **1** : illusion **2** ESPERANZA : hope — **ilusionado, -da** *adj* : excited
iluso -sa *adj* : naïve, gullible — ~ *n* : dreamer, visionary — **ilusorio, -ria** *adj* : illusory
ilustrar *vt* **1** : illustrate **2** ACLARAR : explain — **ilustración** *nf, pl* **-ciones** **1** : illustration **2** SABER : learning **3 la Ilustración** : the Enlightenment — **ilustrado, -da** *adj* **1** : illustrated **2** ERUDITO : learned — **ilustrador, -dora** *n* : illustrator
ilustre *adj* : illustrious
imagen *nf, pl* **imágenes** : image, picture
imaginar *vt* : imagine — **imaginarse** *vr* : imagine — **imaginación** *nf, pl* **-ciones** : imagination — **imaginario, -ria** *adj* : imaginary — **imaginativo, -va** *adj* : imaginative
imán *nm, pl* **imanes** : magnet — **imantar** *vt* : magnetize
imbécil *adj* : stupid, idiotic — ~ *nmf* : idiot
imborrable *adj* : indelible
imbuir {41} *vt* ~ **de** : imbue with
imitar *vt* **1** COPIAR : imitate, copy **2** : impersonate — **imitación** *nf, pl* **-ciones** **1** COPIA : imitation, copy **2** : impersonation — **imitador, -dora** *n* : impersonator
impaciencia *nf* : impatience — **impacientar** *vt* : make impatient, exasperate —**impacientarse** *vr* : grow impatient — **impaciente** *adj* : impatient
impacto *nm* : impact
impar *adj* : odd — ~ *nm* : odd number
imparcial *adj* : impartial — **imparcialidad** *nf* : impartiality
impartir *vt* : impart, give
impasible *adj* : impassive
impasse *nm* : impasse
impávido, -da *adj* : fearless
impecable *adj* : impeccable, spotless
impedir {54} *vt* **1** : prevent **2** DIFICULTAR : impede, hinder — **impedido, -da** *adj* : dis-

abled — **impedimento** *nm* : obstacle, impediment

impeler *vt* : drive, propel

impenetrable *adj* : impenetrable

impenitente *adj* : unrepentant

impensable *adj* : unthinkable — **impensado, -da** *adj* : unexpected

imperar *vi* **1** : reign, rule **2** PREDOMINAR : prevail — **imperante** *adj* : prevailing

imperativo, -va *adj* : imperative — **imperativo** *nm* : imperative

imperceptible *adj* : imperceptible

imperdible *nm* : safety pin

imperdonable *adj* : unforgivable

imperfección *nf, pl* **-ciones** : imperfection — **imperfecto, -ta** *adj* : imperfect — **imperfecto** *nm* : imperfect (tense)

imperial *adj* : imperial — **imperialismo** *nm* : imperialism — **imperialista** *adj & nmf* : imperialist

impericia *nf* : lack of skill

imperio *nm* **1** : empire **2** DOMINIO : rule — **imperioso, -sa** *adj* **1** : imperious **2** URGENTE : pressing, urgent

impermeable *adj* **1** : waterproof **2** ~ **a** : impervious to — ~ *nm* : raincoat

impersonal *adj* : impersonal

impertinente *adj* : impertinent — **impertinencia** *nf* : impertinence

ímpetu *nm* **1** : impetus **2** ENERGÍA : energy, vigor **3** VIOLENCIA : force — **impetuoso, -sa** *adj* : impetuous — **impetuosidad** *nf* : impetuosity

impío, -pía *adj* : impious, ungodly

implacable *adj* : implacable

implantar *vt* **1** : implant **2** ESTABLECER : establish, introduce

implemento *nm Lat* : implement, tool

implicar {72} *vt* **1** : involve, implicate **2** SIGNIFICAR : imply — **implicación** *nf, pl* **-ciones** : implication

implícito, -ta *adj* : implicit

implorar *vt* : implore

imponer {60} *vt* **1** : impose **2** : command (respect, etc.) — *vi* : be imposing — **imponerse** *vr* **1** : assert oneself, command respect **2** PREVALECER : prevail — **imponente** *adj* : imposing, impressive — **imponible** *adj* : taxable

impopular *adj* : unpopular — **impopularidad** *nf* : unpopularity

importación *nf, pl* **-ciones 1** : importation **2 importaciones** *nfpl* : imports — **importado, -da** *adj* : imported — **importador, -dora** *adj* : importing — ~ *n* : importer

importancia *nf* : importance — **importante** *adj* : important — **importar** *vi* **1** : matter, be important **2 no me importa** : I don't care

— *vt* **1** : import **2** ASCENDER A : amount to, cost

importe *nm* **1** : price **2** CANTIDAD : sum, amount

importunar *vt* : bother — **importuno, -na** *adj* **1** : inopportune **2** MOLESTO : bothersome

imposible *adj* : impossible — **imposibilidad** *nf* : impossibility

imposición *nf, pl* **-ciones 1** : imposition **2** IMPUESTO : tax

impostor, -tora *n* : impostor

impotente *adj* : powerless, impotent — **impotencia** *nf* : impotence

impracticable *adj* **1** : impracticable **2** INTRANSITABLE : impassable

impreciso, -sa *adj* : vague, imprecise — **imprecisión** *nf, pl* **-siones 1** : vagueness **2** ERROR : inaccuracy

impredecible *adj* : unpredictable

impregnar *vt* : impregnate

imprenta *nf* **1** : printing **2** : printing shop, press

imprescindible *adj* : essential, indispensable

impresión *nf, pl* **-siones 1** : impression **2** IMPRENTA : printing — **impresionable** *adj* : impressionable — **impresionante** *adj* : impressive — **impresionar** *vt* **1** : impress **2** CONMOVER : affect, move — *vi* : make an impression — **impresionarse** *vr* **1** : be impressed **2** CONMOVERSE : be affected

impreso, -sa *adj* : printed — **impreso** *nm* **1** FORMULARIO : form **2** ~ **s** *nmpl* : printed matter — **impresor, -sora** *n* : printer — **impresora** *nf* : (computer) printer

imprevisible *adj* : unforeseeable — **imprevisto, -ta** *adj* : unexpected, unforeseen

imprimir {42} *vt* **1** : print **2** DAR : impart, give

improbable *adj* : improbable — **improbabilidad** *nf* : improbability

improcedente *adj* : inappropriate

improductivo, -va *adj* : unproductive

improperio *nm* : insult

impropio, -pia *adj* **1** : inappropriate **2** INCORRECTO : incorrect

improvisar *v* : improvise — **improvisado, -da** *adj* : improvised, impromptu — **improvisación** *nf, pl* **-ciones** : improvisation — **improviso: de** ~ *adv phr* : suddenly

imprudente *adj* : imprudent, rash — **imprudencia** *nf* : imprudence, carelessness

impúdico, -ca *adj* : shameless, indecent

impuesto *nm* **1** : tax **2** ~ **sobre la renta** : income tax

impugnar *vt* : challenge, contest

impulsar *vt* : propel, drive — **impulsividad**

nf : impulsiveness — **impulsivo, -va** *adj* : impulsive — **impulso** *nm* **1** : drive, thrust **2** MOTIVACIÓN : impulse

impune *adj* : unpunished — **impunidad** *nf* : impunity

impuro, -ra *adj* : impure — **impureza** *nf* : impurity

imputar *vt* : impute, attribute

inacabable *adj* : interminable, endless

inaccesible *adj* : inaccessible

inaceptable *adj* : unacceptable

inactivo, -va *adj* : inactive — **inactividad** *nf* : inactivity

inadaptado, -da *adj* : maladjusted — **~** *n* : misfit

inadecuado, -da *adj* **1** : inadequate **2** INAPROPIADO : inappropriate

inadmisible *adj* : inadmissible

inadvertido, -da *adj* **1** : unnoticed **2** DISTRAÍDO : distracted — **inadvertencia** *nf* : oversight

inagotable *adj* : inexhaustible

inaguantable *adj* : unbearable

inalámbrico, -ca *adj* : wireless, cordless

inalcanzable *adj* : unreachable, unattainable

inalterable *adj* **1** : unchangeable **2** : impassive (of character) **3** : fast (of colors)

inanición *nf, pl* **-ciones** : starvation, famine

inanimado, -da *adj* : inanimate

inaplicable *adj* : inapplicable

inapreciable *adj* : imperceptible

inapropiado, -da *adj* : inappropriate

inarticulado, -da *adj* : inarticulate

inasequible *adj* : unattainable

inaudito, -ta *adj* : unheard-of, unprecedented

inaugurar *vt* : inaugurate — **inauguración** *nf, pl* **-ciones** : inauguration — **inaugural** *adj* : inaugural

inca *adj* : Inca, Incan

incalculable *adj* : incalculable

incandescencia *nf* : incandescence — **incandescente** *adj* : incandescent

incansable *adj* : tireless

incapacitar *vt* : incapacitate, disable — **incapacidad** *nf* : incapacity, inability — **incapaz** *adj, pl* **-paces** : incapable

incautar *vt* : confiscate, seize

incendiar *vt* : set fire to, burn (down) — **incendiarse** *vr* : catch fire — **incendiario, -ria** *adj* : incendiary — **~** *n* : arsonist — **incendio** *nm* **1** : fire **2** **~** **premeditado** : arson

incentivo *nm* : incentive

incertidumbre *nf* : uncertainty

incesante *adj* : incessant

incesto *nm* : incest — **incestuoso, -sa** *adj* : incestuous

incidencia *nf* **1** : impact **2** SUCESO : inci-

dent — **incidental** *adj* : incidental — **incidente** *nm* : incident

incidir *vi* **~ en 1** : fall into (a habit, mistake, etc.) **2** INFLUIR EN : affect, influence

incienso *nm* : incense

incierto, -ta *adj* : uncertain

incinerar *vt* **1** : incinerate **2** : cremate (a corpse) — **incineración** *nf, pl* **-ciones 1** : incineration **2** : cremation (of a corpse) — **incinerador** *nm* : incinerator

incipiente *adj* : incipient

incisión *nf, pl* **-siones** : incision

incisivo, -va *adj* : incisive — **incisivo** *nm* : incisor

incitar *vt* : incite, rouse

incivilizado, -da *adj* : uncivilized

inclinar *vt* : tilt, lean — **inclinarse** *vr* **1** : lean (over) **2 ~ a** : be inclined to — **inclinación** *nf, pl* **-ciones 1** : inclination **2** LADEAR : incline, tilt

incluir {41} *vt* **1** : include **2** ADJUNTAR : enclose — **inclusión** *nf, pl* **-siones** : inclusion — **inclusive** *adv* : up to and including — **inclusivo, -va** *adj* : inclusive — **incluso** *adv* : even, in fact — **incluso, -sa** *adj* : enclosed

incógnito, -ta *adj* **1** : unknown **2 de ~** : incognito

incoherente *adj* : incoherent — **incoherencia** *nf* : incoherence

incoloro, -ra *adj* : colorless

incombustible *adj* : fireproof

incomible *adj* : inedible

incomodar *vt* **1** : inconvenience **2** ENFADAR : bother, annoy — **incomodarse** *vr* **1** : take the trouble **2** ENFADARSE : get annoyed — **incomodidad** *nf* : discomfort — **incómodo, -da** *adj* **1** : uncomfortable **2** INCONVENIENTE : inconvenient, awkward

incomparable *adj* : incomparable

incompatible *adj* : incompatible — **incompatibilidad** *nf* : incompatibility

incompetente *adj* : incompetent — **incompetencia** *nf* : incompetence

incompleto, -ta *adj* : incomplete

incomprendido, -da *adj* : misunderstood — **incomprensible** *adj* : incomprehensible — **incomprensión** *nf, pl* **-siones** : lack of understanding

incomunicado, -da *adj* **1** : isolated **2** : in solitary confinement

inconcebible *adj* : inconceivable

inconcluso, -sa *adj* : unfinished

incondicional *adj* : unconditional

inconformista *adj & nmf* : nonconformist

inconfundible *adj* : unmistakable

incongruente *adj* : incongruous

inconmensurable *adj* : vast, immeasurable

inconsciente *adj* **1** : unconscious, unaware **2** IRREFLEXIVO : reckless — **~** *nm* **el ~**

: the unconscious — **inconsciencia** *nf* **1** : unconsciousness **2** INSENSATEZ : thoughtlessness

inconsecuente *adj* : inconsistent — **inconsecuencia** *nf* : inconsistency

inconsiderado, -da *adj* : inconsiderate

inconsistente *adj* **1** : flimsy **2** : watery (of a sauce, etc.) **3** : inconsistent (of an argument) — **inconsistencia** *nf* : inconsistency

inconsolable *adj* : inconsolable

inconstante *adj* : changeable, unreliable — **inconstancia** *nf* : inconstancy

inconstitucional *adj* : unconstitutional

incontable *adj* : countless

incontenible *adj* : irrepressible

incontestable *adj* : indisputable

incontinente *adj* : incontinent — **incontinencia** *nf* : incontinence

inconveniente *adj* **1** : inconvenient **2** INAPROPIADO : inappropriate — **~** *nm* : obstacle, problem — **inconveniencia** *nf* **1** : inconvenience **2** : tactless remark

incorporar *vt* **1** AGREGAR : incorporate, add **2** : mix (in cooking) — **incorporarse** *vr* **1** : sit up **2 ~ a** : join — **incorporación** *nf, pl* **-ciones** : incorporation

incorrecto, -ta *adj* **1** : incorrect **2** DESCORTÉS : impolite

incorregible *adj* : incorrigible

incrédulo, -la *adj* : incredulous — **incredulidad** *nf* : incredulity, disbelief

increíble *adj* : incredible, unbelievable

incrementar *vt* : increase — **incremento** *nm* : increase

incriminar *vt* **1** : incriminate **2** ACUSAR : accuse

incrustar *vt* : set, inlay — **incrustarse** *vr* : become embedded

incubar *vt* : incubate — **incubadora** *nf* : incubator

incuestionable *adj* : unquestionable

inculcar {72} *vt* : instill

inculpar *vt* : accuse, charge

inculto, -ta *adj* **1** : uneducated **2** : uncultivated (of land)

incumplimiento *nm* **1** : noncompliance **2 ~ de contrato** : breach of contract

incurable *adj* : incurable

incurrir *vi* **~ en 1** : incur (expenses, etc.) **2** : fall into, commit (crimes)

incursión *nf, pl* **-siones** : raid

indagar {52} *vt* : investigate — **indagación** *nf, pl* **-ciones** : investigation

indebido, -da *adj* : undue

indecente *adj* : indecent, obscene — **indecencia** *nf* : indecency, obscenity

indecible *adj* : inexpressible

indecisión *nf, pl* **-siones** : indecision — **in-**deciso, -sa** *adj* **1** : undecided **2** IRRESOLUTO : indecisive

indefenso, -sa *adj* : defenseless, helpless

indefinido, -da *adj* : indefinite — **indefinidamente** *adv* : indefinitely

indeleble *adj* : indelible

indemnizar {21} *vt* : indemnify, compensate — **indemnización** *nf, pl* **-ciones** : compensation

independiente *adj* : independent — **independencia** *nf* : independence — **independizarse** {21} *vr* : become independent

indescifrable *adj* : indecipherable

indescriptible *adj* : indescribable

indeseable *adj* : undesirable

indestructible *adj* : indestructible

indeterminado, -da *adj* : indeterminate

indicar {72} *vt* **1** : indicate **2** MOSTRAR : show — **indicación** *nf, pl* **-ciones 1** : sign, indication **2 indicaciones** *nfpl* : directions — **indicador** *nm* **1** : sign, signal **2** : gauge, dial, meter — **indicativo, -va** *adj* : indicative — **indicativo** *nm* : indicative (mood)

índice *nm* **1** : indication **2** : index (of a book, etc.) **3** : index finger **4 ~ de natalidad** : birth rate

indicio *nm* : indication, sign

indiferente *adj* **1** : indifferent **2 me es ~** : it doesn't matter to me — **indiferencia** *nf* : indifference

indígena *adj* : indigenous, native — **~** *nmf* : native

indigente *adj & nmf* : indigent — **indigencia** *nf* : poverty

indigestión *nf, pl* **-tiones** : indigestion — **indigesto, -ta** *adj* : indigestible

indignar *vt* : outrage, infuriate — **indignarse** *vr* : become indignant — **indignación** *nf, pl* **-ciones** : indignation — **indignado, -da** *adj* : indignant — **indignidad** *nf* : indignity — **indigno, -na** *adj* : unworthy

indio, -dia *adj* **1** : American Indian **2** : Indian (from India)

indirecta *nf* **1** : hint **2 lanzar una ~** : drop a hint — **indirecto, -ta** *adj* : indirect

indisciplina *nf* : lack of discipline — **indisciplinado, -da** *adj* : undisciplined

indiscreto, -ta *adj* : indiscreet — **indiscreción** *nf, pl* **-ciones 1** : indiscretion **2** : tactless remark

indiscriminado, -da *adj* : indiscriminate

indiscutible *adj* : indisputable

indispensable *adj* : indispensable

indisponer {60} *vt* **1** : upset, make ill **2** ENEMISTAR : set against, set at odds — **indisponerse** *vr* **1** : become ill **2 ~ con** : fall out with — **indisposición** *nf, pl*

-ciones : indisposition, illness — **indispuesto, -ta** *adj* : unwell, indisposed
indistinto, -ta *adj* : indistinct
individual *adj* : individual — **individualidad** *nf* : individuality — **individualizar** {21} *vt* : individualize — **individuo** *nm* : individual
indivisible *adj* : indivisible
índole *nf* 1 : nature, character 2 TIPO : type, kind
indolente *adj* : indolent, lazy — **indolencia** *nf* : indolence, laziness
indoloro, -ra *adj* : painless
indómito, -ta *adj* : indomitable
indonesio, -sia *adj* : Indonesian
inducir {61} *vt* 1 : induce 2 DEDUCIR : infer
indudable *adj* : beyond doubt — **indudablemente** *adv* : undoubtedly
indulgente *adj* : indulgent — **indulgencia** *nf* : indulgence
indultar *vt* : pardon, reprieve — **indulto** *nm* : pardon, reprieve
industria *nf* : industry — **industrial** *adj* : industrial — **∼** *nmf* : industrialist, manufacturer — **industrialización** *nf, pl* **-ciones** : industrialization — **industrializar** {21} *vt* : industrialize — **industrioso, -sa** *adj* : industrious
inédito, -ta *adj* : unpublished
inefable *adj* : inexpressible
ineficaz *adj, pl* **-caces** 1 : ineffective 2 INEFICIENTE : inefficient
ineficiente *adj* : inefficient — **ineficiencia** *nf* : inefficiency
inelegible *adj* : ineligible
ineludible *adj* : unavoidable, inescapable
inepto, -ta *adj* : inept — **ineptitud** *nf* : ineptitude
inequívoco, -ca *adj* : unequivocal
inercia *nf* : inertia
inerme *adj* : unarmed, defenseless
inerte *adj* : inert
inesperado, -da *adj* : unexpected
inestable *adj* : unstable — **inestabilidad** *nf* : instability
inevitable *adj* : inevitable
inexacto, -ta *adj* 1 : inexact 2 INCORRECTO : incorrect, wrong
inexistente *adj* : nonexistent
inexorable *adj* : inexorable
inexperiencia *nf* : inexperience — **inexperto, -ta** *adj* : inexperienced, unskilled
inexplicable *adj* : inexplicable
infalible *adj* : infallible
infame *adj* 1 : infamous, vile 2 *fam* : horrible — **infamia** *nf* : infamy, disgrace
infancia *nf* : infancy — **infanta** *nf* : infanta, princess — **infante** *nm* 1 : infante, prince 2 : infantryman (in the military) — **infantería**

nf : infantry — **infantil** *adj* 1 : child's, children's 2 INMADURO : childish
infarto *nm* : heart attack
infatigable *adj* : tireless
infectar *vt* : infect — **infectarse** *vr* : become infected — **infección** *nf, pl* **-ciones** : infection — **infeccioso, -sa** *adj* : infectious — **infecto, -ta** *adj* 1 : infected 2 : foul, sickening
infecundo, -da *adj* : infertile
infeliz *adj, pl* **-lices** : unhappy — **infelicidad** *nf* : unhappiness
inferior *adj & nmf* : inferior — **inferioridad** *nf* : inferiority
inferir {76} *vt* 1 DEDUCIR : infer 2 : cause (harm or injury)
infernal *adj* : infernal, hellish
infestar *vt* : infest
infiel *adj* : unfaithful — **infidelidad** *nf* : infidelity
infierno *nm* 1 : hell 2 **el quinto ∼** *fam* : the middle of nowhere
infiltrar *vt* : infiltrate — **infiltrarse** *vr* : infiltrate
infinidad *nf* 1 : infinity 2 **una ∼ de** : countless — **infinitivo** *nm* : infinitive — **infinito, -ta** *adj* : infinite — **infinito** *nm* : infinity
inflación *nf, pl* **-ciones** : inflation — **inflacionario, -ria** *or* **inflacionista** *adj* : inflationary
inflamar *vt* : inflame — **inflamable** *adj* : flammable, inflammable — **inflamación** *nf, pl* **-ciones** : inflammation — **inflamatorio, -ria** *adj* : inflammatory
inflar *vt* 1 : inflate 2 EXAGERAR : exaggerate — **inflarse** *vr* **∼ de** : swell (up) with
inflexible *adj* : inflexible — **inflexión** *nf, pl* **-xiones** : inflection
infligir {35} *vt* : inflict
influencia *nf* : influence — **influenciar** → **influir**
influenza *nf* : influenza
influir {41} *vt* : influence — *vi* **∼ en** *or* **∼ sobre** : have an influence on — **influjo** *nm* : influence — **influyente** *adj* : influential
información *nf, pl* **-ciones** 1 : information 2 NOTICIAS : news 3 : directory assistance (on the telephone)
informal *adj* 1 : informal 2 IRRESPONSABLE : unreliable
informar *v* : inform — **informarse** *vr* : get information, find out — **informante** *nmf* : informant — **informática** *nf* : information technology — **informativo, -va** *adj* : informative — **informatizar** {21} *vt* : computerize
informe *adj* : shapeless — **∼** *nm* 1 : report 2 **∼s** *nmpl* : information, data 3 **∼s** *nmpl* : references (for employment)

infortunado, -da *adj* : unfortunate — **infortunio** *nm* : misfortune

infracción *nf, pl* **-ciones** : violation, infraction

infraestructura *nf* : infrastructure

infrahumano, -na *adj* : subhuman

infranqueable *adj* **1** : impassable **2** INSUPERABLE : insurmountable

infrarrojo, -ja *adj* : infrared

infrecuente *adj* : infrequent

infringir {35} *vt* : infringe

infructuoso, -sa *adj* : fruitless

infundado, -da *adj* : unfounded, baseless

infundir *vt* : instill, infuse — **infusión** *nf, pl* **-siones** : infusion

ingeniar *vt* : invent, think up

ingeniería *nf* : engineering — **ingeniero, -ra** *n* : engineer

ingenio *nm* **1** : ingenuity **2** AGUDEZA : wit **3** MÁQUINA : device, apparatus **4** ~ **azucarero** *Lat* : sugar refinery — **ingenioso, -sa** *adj* **1** : ingenious **2** AGUDO : clever, witty — **ingeniosamente** *adv* : cleverly

ingenuidad *nf* : naïveté, ingenuousness — **ingenuo, -nua** *adj* : naive

ingerir {76} *vt* : ingest, consume

ingle *nf* : groin

inglés, -glesa *adj, mpl* **-gleses** : English — **inglés** *nm* : English (language)

ingrato, -ta *adj* **1** : ungrateful **2 un trabajo ingrato** : a thankless task — **ingratitud** *nf* : ingratitude

ingrediente *nm* : ingredient

ingresar *vt* : deposit — *vi* ~ **en** : enter, be admitted into, join — **ingreso** *nm* **1** : entrance, entry **2** : admission (into a hospital, etc.) **3** ~**s** *nmpl* : income, earnings

inhábil *adj* **1** : unskillful, clumsy **2** ~ **para** : unsuited for — **inhabilidad** *nf* : unskillfulness

inhabitable *adj* : uninhabitable — **inhabitado, -da** *adj* : uninhabited

inhalar *vt* : inhale — **inhalación** *nf* : inhalation

inherente *adj* : inherent

inhibir *vt* : inhibit — **inhibición** *nf, pl* **-ciones** : inhibition

inhóspito, -ta *adj* : inhospitable

inhumano, -na *adj* : inhuman, inhumane — **inhumanidad** *nf* : inhumanity

iniciar *vt* : initiate, begin — **iniciación** *nf, pl* **-ciones** **1** : initiation **2** COMIENZO : beginning — **inicial** *adj & nf* : initial — **iniciativa** *nf* : initiative — **inicio** *nm* : start, beginning

inigualado, -da *adj* : unequaled

ininterrumpido, -da *adj* : uninterrupted

injerirse {76} *vr* : interfere — **injerencia** *nf* : interference

injertar *vt* : graft — **injerto** *nm* : graft

injuriar *vt* : insult — **injuria** *nf* : insult — **injurioso, -sa** *adj* : insulting, abusive

injusticia *nf* : injustice, unfairness — **injusto, -ta** *adj* : unfair, unjust

inmaculado, -da *adj* : immaculate

inmaduro, -ra *adj* **1** : immature **2** : unripe (of fruit) — **inmadurez** *nf* : immaturity

inmediaciones *nfpl* : surrounding area

inmediato, -ta *adj* **1** : immediate **2** CONTIGUO : adjoining **3 de** ~ : immediately, right away **4** ~ **a** : next to, close to — **inmediatamente** *adv* : immediately

inmejorable *adj* : excellent

inmenso, -sa *adj* : immense, vast — **inmensidad** *nf* : immensity

inmerecido, -da *adj* : undeserved

inmersión *nf, pl* **-siones** : immersion

inmigrar *vi* : immigrate — **inmigración** *nf, pl* **-ciones** : immigration — **inmigrante** *adj & nmf* : immigrant

inminente *adj* : imminent, impending — **inminencia** *nf* : imminence

inmiscuirse {41} *vr* : interfere

inmobiliario, -ria *adj* : real estate, property

inmodesto, -ta *adj* : immodest

inmoral *adj* : immoral — **inmoralidad** *nf* : immorality

inmortal *adj & nmf* : immortal — **inmortalidad** *nf* : immortality

inmóvil *adj* : motionless, still — **inmovilizar** {21} *vt* : immobilize

inmueble *nm* : building, property

inmundicia *nf* : filth, trash — **inmundo, -da** *adj* : dirty, filthy

inmunizar {21} *vt* : immunize — **inmune** *adj* : immune — **inmunidad** *nf* : immunity — **inmunización** *nf, pl* **-ciones** : immunization

inmutable *adj* : unchangeable

innato, -ta *adj* : innate

innecesario, -ria *adj* : unnecessary, needless

innegable *adj* : undeniable

innoble *adj* : ignoble

innovar *vt* : introduce — *vi* : innovate — **innovación** *nf, pl* **-ciones** : innovation — **innovador, -dora** *adj* : innovative — ~ *n* : innovator

innumerable *adj* : innumerable

inocencia *nf* : innocence — **inocente** *adj & nmf* : innocent — **inocentón, -tona** *adj, mpl* **-tones** : naive — ~ *n* : simpleton, dupe

inocular *vt* : inoculate — **inoculación** *nf, pl* **-ciones** : inoculation

inocuo, -cua *adj* : innocuous

inodoro, -ra *adj* : odorless — **inodoro** *nm* : toilet

inofensivo, -va *adj* : inoffensive, harmless

inolvidable *adj* : unforgettable

inoperable *adj* : inoperable

inoperante *adj* : ineffective

inopinado, -da *adj* : unexpected

inoportuno, -na *adj* : untimely, inopportune

inorgánico, -ca *adj* : inorganic

inoxidable *adj* **1** : rustproof **2 acero ~** : stainless steel

inquebrantable *adj* : unwavering

inquietar *vt* : disturb, worry — **inquietarse** *vr* : worry — **inquietante** *adj* : disturbing, worrisome — **inquieto, -ta** *adj* : anxious, worried — **inquietud** *nf* : anxiety, worry

inquilino, -na *n* : tenant

inquirir {4} *vi* : make inquiries — *vt* : investigate

insaciable *adj* : insatiable

insalubre *adj* : unhealthy

insatisfecho, -cha *adj* **1** : unsatisfied **2** DESCONTENTO : dissatisfied

inscribir {33} *vt* **1** : enroll, register **2** GRABAR : inscribe, engrave — **inscribirse** *vr* : register — **inscripción** *nf, pl* **-ciones** **1** : inscription **2** REGISTRO : registration

insecto *nm* : insect — **insecticida** *nm* : insecticide

inseguro, -ra *adj* **1** : insecure **2** PELIGROSO : unsafe **3** DUDOSO : uncertain — **inseguridad** *nf* **1** : insecurity **2** PELIGRO : lack of safety **3** DUDA : uncertainty

inseminar *vt* : inseminate — **inseminación** *nf, pl* **-ciones** : insemination

insensato, -ta *adj* : senseless, foolish — **insensatez** *nf* : foolishness, thoughtlessness

insensible *adj* **1** : insensitive, unfeeling **2** : numb (in medicine) **3** IMPERCEPTIBLE : imperceptible — **insensibilidad** *nf* : insensitivity

inseparable *adj* : inseparable

insertar *vt* : insert

insidia *nf* : snare, trap — **insidioso, -sa** *adj* : insidious

insigne *adj* : noted, famous

insignia *nf* **1** : insignia, badge **2** BANDERA : flag

insignificante *adj* : insignificant, negligible

insincero, -ra *adj* : insincere

insinuar {3} *vt* : insinuate — **insinuarse** *vr* **~ en** : worm one's way into — **insinuación** *nf, pl* **-ciones** : insinuation — **insinuante** *adj* : insinuating, suggestive

insípido, -da *adj* : insipid

insistir *v* : insist — **insistencia** *nf* : insistence — **insistente** *adj* : insistent

insociable *adj* : unsociable

insolación *nf, pl* **-ciones** : sunstroke

insolencia *nf* : insolence — **insolente** *adj* : insolent

insólito, -ta *adj* : rare, unusual

insoluble *adj* : insoluble

insolvencia *nf* : insolvency, bankruptcy — **insolvente** *adj* : insolvent, bankrupt

insomnio *nm* : insomnia — **insomne** *nmf* : insomniac

insondable *adj* : unfathomable

insonorizado, -da *adj* : soundproof

insoportable *adj* : unbearable

insospechado, -da *adj* : unexpected

insostenible *adj* : untenable

inspeccionar *vt* : inspect — **inspección** *nf, pl* **-ciones** : inspection — **inspector, -tora** *n* : inspector

inspirar *vt* : inspire — *vi* : inhale — **inspirarse** *vr* : be inspired — **inspiración** *nf, pl* **-ciones** **1** : inspiration **2** RESPIRACIÓN : inhalation — **inspirador, -dora** *adj* : inspirational

instalar *vt* : install — **instalarse** *vr* : settle — **instalación** *nf, pl* **-ciones** : installation

instancia *nf* **1** : request **2 en última ~** : ultimately, as a last resort

instantáneo, -nea *adj* : instantaneous, instant — **instantánea** *nf* : snapshot — **instante** *nm* **1** : instant **2 a cada ~** : frequently, all the time **3 al ~** : immediately

instar *vt* : urge, press

instaurar *vt* : establish — **instauración** *nf, pl* **-ciones** : establishment

instigar {52} *vt* : incite, instigate — **instigador, -dora** *n* : instigator

instinto *nm* : instinct — **instintivo, -va** *adj* : instinctive

institución *nf, pl* **-ciones** : institution — **institucional** *adj* : institutional — **institucionalizar** {21} *vt* : institutionalize — **instituir** {41} *vt* : institute, establish — **instituto** *nm* : institute — **institutriz** *nf, pl* **-trices** : governess

instruir {41} *vt* : instruct — **instrucción** *nf, pl* **-ciones** **1** : instruction **2 instrucciones** *nfpl* : instructions, directions — **instructivo, -va** *adj* : instructive — **instructor, -tora** *n* : instructor

instrumento *nm* : instrument — **instrumental** *adj* : instrumental

insubordinarse *vr* : rebel — **insubordinado, -da** *adj* : insubordinate — **insubordinación** *nf, pl* **-ciones** : insubordination

insuficiente *adj* : insufficient, inadequate — **insuficiencia** *nf* **1** : insufficiency, inadequacy **2 ~ cardíaca** : heart failure

insufrible *adj* : insufferable

insular *adj* : insular, island

insulina *nf* : insulin

insulso, -sa *adj* **1** : insipid, bland **2** SOSO : dull

insultar *vt* : insult — **insultante** *adj* : insulting — **insulto** *nm* : insult

insuperable *adj* : insurmountable

insurgente *adj & nmf* : insurgent

insurrección *nf, pl* **-ciones** : insurrection, uprising

intachable *adj* : irreproachable

intacto, -ta *adj* : intact

intangible *adj* : intangible

integrar *vt* : integrate — **integrarse** *vr* : become integrated — **integración** *nf, pl* **-ciones** : integration — **integral** *adj* **1** : integral **2 pan ~** : whole grain bread — **íntegro, -gra** *adj* **1** : honest, upright **2** ENTERO : whole, complete — **integridad** *nf* **1** RECTITUD : integrity **2** TOTALIDAD : wholeness

intelecto *nm* : intellect — **intelectual** *adj & nmf* : intellectual

inteligencia *nf* : intelligence — **inteligente** *adj* : intelligent — **inteligible** *adj* : intelligible

intemperie *nf* **a la ~** : in the open air, outside

intempestivo, -va *adj* : untimely, inopportune

intención *nf, pl* **-ciones** : intention, intent — **intencionado, -da** *adj* **1** : intended **2 bien ~** : well-meaning **3 mal ~** : malicious — **intencional** *adj* : intentional

intensidad *nf* : intensity — **intensificar** {72} *vt* : intensify — **intensificarse** *vr* : intensify — **intensivo, -va** *adj* : intensive — **intenso, -sa** *adj* : intense

intentar *vt* : attempt, try — **intento** *nm* **1** : intention **2** TENTATIVA : attempt

interactuar {3} *vi* : interact — **interacción** *nf, pl* **-ciones** : interaction — **interactivo, -va** *adj* : interactive

intercalar *vt* : insert, intersperse

intercambio *nm* : exchange — **intercambiable** *adj* : interchangeable — **intercambiar** *vt* : exchange, trade

interceder *vi* : intercede

interceptar *vt* : intercept — **intercepción** *nf, pl* **-ciones** : interception

intercesión *nf, pl* **-siones** : intercession

interés *nm, pl* **-reses** : interest — **interesado, -da** *adj* **1** : interested **2** EGOISTA : selfish — **interesante** *adj* : interesting — **interesar** *vt* : interest — *vi* : be of interest — **interesarse** *vr* : take an interest

interfaz *nf, pl* **-faces** : interface

interferir {76} *vi* : interfere — *vt* : interfere with — **interferencia** *nf* : interference

interino, -na *adj* : temporary, interim — **interiormente** *adv* : inwardly

interior *adj* : interior, inner — **~** *nm* : interior, inside — **interiormente** *adv* : inwardly

interjección *nf, pl* **-ciones** : interjection

interlocutor, -tora *n* : speaker

intermediario, -ria *adj & n* : intermediary

intermedio, -dia *adj* : intermediate — **intermedio** *nm* : intermission

interminable *adj* : interminable, endless

intermisión *nf, pl* **-siones** : intermission, pause

intermitente *adj* : intermittent — **~** *nm* : blinker, turn signal

internacional *adj* : international

internar *vt* : commit, confine — **internarse** *vr* : penetrate — **internado** *nm* : boarding school — **interno, -na** *adj* : internal — **~** *n* **1** : boarder **2** : inmate (in a jail, etc.)

interponer {60} *vt* : interpose — **interponerse** *vr* : intervene

interpretar *vt* **1** : interpret **2** : play, perform (in theater, etc.) — **interpretación** *nf, pl* **-ciones** : interpretation — **intérprete** *nmf* **1** TRADUCTOR : interpreter **2** : performer (of music)

interrogar {52} *vt* : interrogate, question — **interrogación** *nf, pl* **-ciones** **1** : interrogation **2 signo de ~** : question mark — **interrogativo, -va** *adj* : interrogative — **interrogatorio** *nm* : interrogation, questioning

interrumpir *v* : interrupt — **interrupción** *nf, pl* **-ciones** : interruption — **interruptor** *nm* : (electrical) switch

intersección *nf, pl* **-ciones** : intersection

intervalo *nm* : interval

intervenir {87} *vi* **1** : take part **2** MEDIAR : intervene — *vt* **1** : tap (a telephone) **2** INSPECCIONAR : audit **3** OPERAR : operate on — **intervención** *nf, pl* **-ciones** **1** : intervention **2** : audit (in business) **3 *or* ~ quirúrgica** : operation — **interventor, -tora** *n* : inspector, auditor

intestino *nm* : intestine — **intestinal** *adj* : intestinal

intimar *vi* **~ con** : become friendly with — **intimidad** *nf* **1** : private life **2** AMISTAD : intimacy

intimidar *vt* : intimidate

íntimo, -ma *adj* **1** : intimate, close **2** PRIVADO : private

intolerable *adj* : intolerable — **intolerancia** *nf* : intolerance — **intolerante** *adj* : intolerant

intoxicar {72} *vt* : poison — **intoxicación** *nf, pl* **-ciones** : poisoning

intranquilizar {21} *vt* : make uneasy — **intranquilizarse** *vr* : be anxious — **intranquilidad** *nf* : uneasiness, anxiety — **intranquilo, -la** *adj* : uneasy, worried

intransigente *adj* : unyielding, intransigent

intransitable *adj* : impassable

intransitivo, -va *adj* : intransitive

intrascendente *adj* : unimportant, insignificant

intravenoso, -sa *adj* : intravenous

intrépido

intrépido, -da *adj* : intrepid, fearless

intrigar {52} *v* : intrigue — **intriga** *nf* : intrigue — **intrigante** *adj* : intriguing

intrincado, -da *adj* : intricate, involved

intrínseco, -ca *adj* : intrinsic — **intrínsecament** *adv* : intrinsically, inherently

introducción *nf, pl* **-ciones** : introduction — **introducir** {61} *vt* **1** : introduce **2** METER : insert — **introducirse** *vr* ~ **en** : penetrate, get into — **introductorio, -ria** *adj* : introductory

intromisión *nf, pl* **-siones** : interference

introvertido, -da *adj* : introverted — ~ *n* : introvert

intrusión *nf, pl* **-siones** : intrusion — **intruso, -sa** *adj* : intrusive — ~ *n* : intruder

intuir {41} *vt* : sense — **intuición** *nf, pl* **-ciones** : intuition — **intuitivo, -va** *adj* : intuitive

inundar *vt* : flood — **inundarse** *vr* ~ **de** : be inundated with — **inundación** *nf, pl* **-ciones** : flood

inusitado, -da *adj* : unusual, uncommon

inútil *adj* **1** : useless **2** INVÁLIDO : disabled — **inutilidad** *nf* : uselessness — **inutilizar** {21} *vt* **1** : make useless **2** INCAPACITAR : disable

invadir *vt* : invade

invalidez *nf, pl* **-deces 1** : invalidity **2** : disability (in medicine) — **inválido, -da** *adj* & *n* : invalid

invalorable *adj Lat* : invaluable

invariable *adj* : invariable

invasión *nf, pl* **-siones** : invasion — **invasor, -sora** *adj* : invading — ~ *n* : invader

invencible *adj* : invincible

inventar *vt* **1** : invent **2** : fabricate, make up (a word, an excuse, etc.) — **invención** *nf, pl* **-ciones 1** : invention **2** MENTIRA : lie, fabrication

inventario *nm* : inventory

inventiva *nf* : inventiveness — **inventivo, -va** *adj* : inventive — **inventor, -tora** *n* : inventor

invernadero *nm* : greenhouse

invernal *adj* : winter

inverosímil *adj* : unlikely

inversión *nf, pl* **-siones 1** : inversion, reversal **2** : investment (of money, time, etc.)

inverso, -sa *adj* **1** : inverse **2** CONTRARIO : opposite **3 a la inversa** : the other way around, inversely

inversor, -sora *n* : investor

invertebrado, -da *adj* : invertebrate — **invertebrado** *nm* : invertebrate

invertir {76} *vt* **1** : invert, reverse **2** : invest (money, time, etc.) — *vi* : make an investment

investidura *nf* : investiture

investigar {52} *vt* **1** : investigate **2** ESTU-DIAR : research — *vi* ~ **sobre** : do research into — **investigación** *nf, pl* **-ciones 1** : investigation **2** ESTUDIO : research — **investigador, -dora** *n* : investigator, researcher

investir {54} *vt* : invest

inveterado, -da *adj* : deep-seated, inveterate

invicto, -ta *adj* : undefeated

invierno *nm* : winter

invisible *adj* : invisible — **invisibilidad** *nf* : invisibility

invitar *vt* : invite — **invitación** *nf, pl* **-ciones** : invitation — **invitado, -da** *n* : guest

invocar {72} *vt* : invoke — **invocación** *nf, pl* **-ciones** : invocation

involuntario, -ria *adj* : involuntary

invulnerable *adj* : invulnerable

inyectar *vt* : inject — **inyección** *nf, pl* **-ciones** : injection, shot — **inyectado, -da** *adj* **ojos inyectados** : bloodshot eyes

ion *nm* : ion — **ionizar** {21} *vt* : ionize

ir {43} *vi* **1** : go **2** FUNCIONAR : work, function **3** CONVENIR : suit **4 ¿cómo te va?** : how are you? **5** ~ **con prisa** : be in a hurry **6** ~ **por** : follow, go along **7 vamos** : let's go — *v aux* **1** ~ **a** : be going to, be about to **2** ~ **caminando** : take a walk **3 vamos a ver** : we shall see — **irse** *vr* : go away, be gone

ira *nf* : rage, anger — **iracundo, -da** *adj* : irate, angry

iraní *adj* : Iranian

iraquí *adj* : Iraqi

iris *nms & pl* **1** : iris (of the eye) **2 arco** ~ : rainbow

irlandés, -desa *adj, mpl* **-deses** : Irish

ironía *nf* : irony — **irónico, -ca** *adj* : ironic, ironical

irracional *adj* : irrational

irradiar *vt* : radiate, irradiate

irrazonable *adj* : unreasonable

irreal *adj* : unreal

irreconciliable *adj* : irreconcilable

irreconocible *adj* : unrecognizable

irrecuperable *adj* : irretrievable

irreductible *adj* : unyielding

irreemplazable *adj* : irreplaceable

irreflexivo, -va *adj* : rash, unthinking

irrefutable *adj* : irrefutable

irregular *adj* : irregular — **irregularidad** *nf* : irregularity

irrelevante *adj* : irrelevant

irreparable *adj* : irreparable

irreprimible *adj* : irrepressible

irreprochable *adj* : irreproachable

irresistible *adj* : irresistible

irresoluto, -ta *adj* : indecisive, irresolute

irrespetuoso, -sa *adj* : disrespectful

irresponsable *adj* : irresponsible — **irresponsabilidad** *nf* : irresponsibility

irreverente *adj* : irreverent
irreversible *adj* : irreversible
irrevocable *adj* : irrevocable
irrigar {52} *vt* : irrigate — **irrigación** *nf, pl* **-ciones** : irrigation
irrisorio, -ria *adj* : laughable, ridiculous
irritar *vt* : irritate — **irritarse** *vr* : get annoyed — **irritable** *adj* : irritable — **irritación** *nf, pl* **-ciones** : irritation — **irritante** *adj* : irritating
irrompible *adj* : unbreakable
irrumpir *vi* ~ **en** : burst into

isla *nf* : island
islámico, -ca *adj* : Islamic, Muslim
islandés, -desa *adj, mpl* **-deses** : Icelandic
isleño, -ña *n* : islander
israelí *adj* : Israeli
istmo *nm* : isthmus
italiano, -na *adj* : Italian — **italiano** *nm* : Italian (language)
itinerario *nm* : itinerary
izar {21} *vt* : hoist, raise
izquierda *nf* : left — **izquierdista** *adj & nmf* : leftist — **izquierdo, -da** *adj* : left

J

j *nf* : j, tenth letter of the Spanish alphabet
jabalí *nm, pl* **-líes** : wild boar
jabalina *nf* : javelin
jabón *nm, pl* **-bones** : soap — **jabonar** *vt* : soap (up) — **jabonera** *nf* : soap dish — **jabonoso, -sa** *adj* : soapy
jaca *nf* : pony
jacinto *nm* : hyacinth
jactarse *vr* : boast, brag — **jactancia** *nf* : boastfulness, bragging — **jactancioso, -sa** *adj* : boastful
jadear *vi* : pant, gasp — **jadeante** *adj* : panting, breathless — **jadeo** *nm* : gasp, panting
jaez *nm, pl* **jaeces** 1 : harness 2 **jaeces** *nmpl* : trappings
jaguar *nm* : jaguar
jaiba *nf Lat* : crab
jalapeño *nm Lat* : jalapeño pepper
jalar *v Lat* : pull, tug
jalea *nf* : jelly
jaleo *nm fam* 1 : uproar, racket 2 **armar un** ~ : raise a ruckus
jalón *nm, pl* **-lones** *Lat* : pull, tug
jamaicano, -na *or* **jamaiquino, -na** *adj* : Jamaican
jamás *adv* 1 : never 2 **para siempre** ~ : for ever and ever
jamelgo *nm* : nag (horse)
jamón *nm, pl* **-mones** 1 : ham 2 ~ **serrano** : cured ham
Januká *nmf* : Hanukkah
japonés, -nesa *adj, mpl* **-neses** : Japanese — **japonés** *nm* : Japanese (language)
jaque *nm* 1 : check (in chess) 2 ~ **mate** : checkmate
jaqueca *nf* : headache, migraine
jarabe *nm* : syrup
jardín *nm, pl* **-dines** 1 : garden 2 ~ **infan-**

til *or* ~ **de niños** *Lat* : kindergarten — **jardinería** *nf* : gardening — **jardinero, -ra** *n* : gardener
jarra *nf* : pitcher, jug — **jarro** *nm* : pitcher — **jarrón** *nm, pl* **-rones** : vase
jaula *nf* : cage
jauría *nf* : pack of hounds
jazmín *nm, pl* **-mines** : jasmine
jazz [cjas, cdʒas] *nm* : jazz
jeans [cjins, cdʒins] *nmpl* : jeans
jefe, -fa *n* 1 : chief, leader 2 PATRÓN : boss 3 ~ **de cocina** : chef — **jefatura** *nf* 1 : leadership 2 SEDE : headquarters
jengibre *nm* : ginger
jeque *nm* : sheikh, sheik
jerarquía *nf* 1 : hierarchy 2 RANGO : rank — **jerárquico, -ca** *adj* : hierarchical
jerez *nm, pl* **-reces** : sherry
jerga *nf* 1 : coarse cloth 2 ARGOT : jargon, slang
jerigonza *nf* 1 : jargon 2 GALIMATÍAS : gibberish
jeringa *or* **jeringuilla** *nf* : syringe — **jeringar** {52} *vt fam* : annoy, pester
jeroglífico *nm* : hieroglyphic
jersey *nm, pl* **-seys** : jersey
jesuita *adj & nm* : Jesuit
Jesús *nm* : Jesus
jilguero *nm* : goldfinch
jinete *nmf* : horseman, horsewoman *f*, rider
jirafa *nf* : giraffe
jirón *nm, pl* **-rones** : shred, tatter
jitomate *nm Lat* : tomato
jockey [cjɔki, cdʒɔ-] *nmf, pl* **-keys** : jockey
jocoso, -sa *adj* : humorous, jocular
jofaina *nf* : washbowl
jolgorio *nm* : merrymaking
jornada *nf* 1 : day's journey 2 : working

day — **jornal** *nm* : day's pay — **jornalero, -ra** *n* : day laborer

joroba *nf* : hump — **jorobado, -da** *adj* : hunchbacked, humpbacked — ~ *n* : hunchback — **jorobar** *vt fam* : annoy

jota *nf* **1** : iota, jot **2 no veo ni** ~ : I can't see a thing

joven *adj, pl* **jóvenes** : young — ~ *nmf* : young man *m,* young woman *f,* youth

jovial *adj* : jovial, cheerful

joya *nf* : jewel — **joyería** *nf* : jewelry store — **joyero, -ra** *n* : jeweler — **joyero** *nm* : jewelry box

juanete *nm* : bunion

jubilación *nf, pl* **-ciones** : retirement — **jubilado, -da** *adj* : retired — ~ *nmf* : retiree — **jubilar** *vt* : retire, pension off — **jubilarse** *vr* : retire — **jubileo** *nm* : jubilee

júbilo *nm* : joy, jubilation — **jubiloso, -sa** *adj* : joyous, jubilant

judaísmo *nm* : Judaism

judía *nf* **1** : bean **2** *or* ~ **verde** : green bean, string bean

judicial *adj* : judicial

judío, -día *adj* : Jewish — ~ *n* : Jew

judo *nm* : judo

juego *nm* **1** : game **2** : playing (of children, etc.) **3** *or* ~**s de azar** : gambling **4** CONJUNTO : set **5 estar en** ~ : be at stake **6 fuera de** ~ : offside (in sports) **7 hacer** ~ : go together, match **8** ~ **de manos** : conjuring trick **9 poner en** ~ : bring into play

juerga *nf fam* : spree, binge

jueves *nms & pl* : Thursday

juez *nmf, pl* **jueces 1** : judge **2** ÁRBITRO : umpire, referee

jugar {44} *vi* **1** : play **2** : gamble (in a casino, etc.) **3** APOSTAR : bet **4** ~ **(al) tenis** : play tennis — *vt* : play — **jugarse** *vr* : risk, gamble (away) — **jugada** *nf* **1** : play, move **2** TRETA : (dirty) trick — **jugador, -dora** *n* **1** : player **2** : gambler

juglar *nm* : minstrel

jugo *nm* **1** : juice **2** SUSTANCIA : substance, essence — **jugoso, -sa** *adj* **1** : juicy **2** SUSTANCIAL : substantial, important

juguete *nm* : toy — **juguetear** *vi* : play — **juguetería** *nf* : toy store — **juguetón, -tona** *adj, mpl* **-tones** : playful

juicio *nm* **1** : judgment **2** RAZÓN : reason, sense **3 a mi** ~ : in my opinion — **juicioso, -sa** *adj* : wise, sensible

julio *nm* : July

junco *nm* : reed, rush

jungla *nf* : jungle

junio *nm* : June

juntar *vt* **1** UNIR : join, unite **2** REUNIR : collect — **juntarse** *vr* **1** : join (together) **2** REUNIRSE : meet, get together — **junta** *nf* **1** : board, committee **2** REUNIÓN : meeting **3** : (political) junta **4** : joint, gasket — **junto, -ta** *adj* **1** : joined **2** PRÓXIMO : close, adjacent **3** (*used adverbially*) : together **4** ~ **a** : next to **5** ~ **con** : together with — **juntura** *nf* : joint

Júpiter *nm* : Jupiter

jurar *v* **1** : swear **2** ~ **en falso** : commit perjury — **jurado** *nm* **1** : jury **2** : juror, member of a jury — **juramento** *nm* : oath

jurídico, -ca *adj* : legal

jurisdicción *nf, pl* **-ciones** : jurisdiction

jurisprudencia *nf* : jurisprudence

justamente *adv* **1** : fairly, justly **2** PRECISAMENTE : precisely, exactly

justicia *nf* : justice, fairness

justificar {72} *vt* **1** : justify **2** DISCULPAR : excuse, vindicate — **justificación** *nf, pl* **-ciones** : justification

justo, -ta *adj* **1** : just, fair **2** EXACTO : exact **3** APRETADO : tight — **justo** *adv* **1** : just, exactly **2** ~ **a tiempo** : just in time

juvenil *adj* : youthful — **juventud** *nf* **1** : youth **2** JÓVENES : young people

juzgar {52} *vt* **1** : try (a case in court) **2** ESTIMAR : judge, consider **3 a** ~ **por** : judging by — **juzgado** *nm* : court, tribunal

K

k *nf* : k, eleventh letter of the Spanish alphabet

kaki → **caqui**

karate *or* **kárate** *nm* : karate

kilo *nm* : kilo — **kilogramo** *nm* : kilogram

kilómetro *nm* : kilometer — **kilometraje** *nm* : distance in kilometers, mileage — **kilométrico, -ca** *adj fam* : end- less

kilovatio *nm* : kilowatt

kiosco *nm* → **quiosco**

L

l *nf* : l, twelfth letter of the Spanish alphabet

la *pron* **1** : her, it **2** (*formal*) : you **3** ~ **que** : the one who — ~ *art* → **el**

laberinto *nm* : labyrinth, maze

labia *nf fam* : gift of gab

labio *nm* : lip

labor *nf* **1** : work, labor **2** TAREA : task **3** ~**es domésticas** : housework — **laborable** *adj* **día** ~ : business day — **laborar** *vi* : work — **laboratorio** *nm* : laboratory, lab — **laborioso, -sa** *adj* : laborious

labrar *vt* **1** : cultivate, till **2** : work (metals), carve (stone, wood) **3** CAUSAR : cause, bring about — **labrado, -da** *adj* **1** : cultivated, tilled **2** : carved, wrought — **labrador, -dora** *n* : farmer — **labranza** *nf* : farming

laca *nf* **1** : lacquer **2** : hair spray

lacayo *nm* : lackey

lacerar *vt* : lacerate

lacio, -cia *adj* **1** : limp **2** : straight (of hair)

lacónico, -ca *adj* : laconic

lacra *nf* : scar

lacrar *vt* : seal — **lacre** *nm* : sealing wax

lacrimógeno, -na *adj* **gas lacrimógeno** : tear gas — **lacrimoso, -sa** *adj* : tearful

lácteo, -tea *adj* **1** : dairy **2 Vía Láctea** : Milky Way

ladear *vt* : tilt — **ladearse** *vr* : lean

ladera *nf* : slope, hillside

ladino, -na *adj* : crafty

lado *nm* **1** : side **2 al** ~ : next door, nearby **3 al** ~ **de** : beside, next to **4 de** ~ : sideways **5 por otro** ~ : on the other hand — **por todos** ~**s** : everywhere, all around

ladrar *vi* : bark — **ladrido** *nm* : bark

ladrillo *nm* : brick

ladrón, -drona *n, mpl* **-drones** : thief

lagarto *nm* : lizard — **lagartija** *nf* : (small) lizard

lago *nm* : lake

lágrima *nf* : tear

laguna *nf* **1** : lagoon **2** VACÍO : gap

laico, -ca *adj* : lay, secular — ~ *n* : layman *m*, layperson

lamentar *vt* **1** : regret, be sorry about **2 lo lamento** : I'm sorry — **lamentarse** *vr* : lament — **lamentable** *adj* **1** : deplorable **2** TRISTE : sad, pitiful — **lamento** *nm* : lament, moan

lamer *vt* **1** : lick **2** : lap (against) — **lamida** *nf* : lick

lámina *nf* **1** PLANCHA : sheet **2** DIBUJO : plate, illustration — **laminar** *vt* : laminate

lámpara *nf* : lamp

lampiño, -ña *adj* : beardless, hairless

lana *nf* **1** : wool **2 de** ~ : woolen

lance *nm* **1** : event, incident **2** : throw (of dice, etc.) **3** RIÑA : quarrel

lanceta *nf* : lancet

lancha *nf* **1** : boat, launch **2** ~ **motora** : motorboat

langosta *nf* **1** : lobster **2** : locust (insect) — **langostino** *nm* : prawn, crayfish

languidecer {53} *vi* : languish — **languidez** *nf, pl* **-deces** : languor — **lánguido, -da** *adj* : languid, listless

lanilla *nf* : nap (of fabric)

lanudo, -da *adj* : woolly

lanza *nf* : spear, lance

lanzar {21} *vt* **1** : throw **2** : shoot (a glance), give (a sigh, etc.) **3** : launch (a missile, a project) — **lanzarse** *vr* : throw oneself — **lanzamiento** *nm* : throwing, launching

lapicero *nm* : (mechanical) pencil

lápida *nf* : tombstone

lapidar *vt* : stone

lápiz *nm, pl* **-pices 1** : pencil **2** ~ **de labios** : lipstick

lapso *nm* : lapse (of time) — **lapsus** *nms & pl* : lapse, slip (of the tongue)

largar {52} *vt* **1** AFLOJAR : loosen, slacken **2** *fam* : give — **largarse** *vr fam* : go away, beat it — **largo, -ga** *adj* **1** : long **2 a la larga** : in the long run **3 a lo largo** : lengthwise **4 a lo largo de** : along — **largo** *nm* : length — **largometraje** *nm* : feature film — **largueza** *nf* : generosity

laringe *nf* : larynx — **laringitis** *nfs & pl* : laryngitis

larva *nf* : larva

las → **el**

lascivo, -va *adj* : lascivious, lewd

láser *nm* : laser

lastimar *vt* : hurt — **lastimarse** *vr* : hurt oneself — **lástima** *nf* **1** : pity **2 dar** ~ : be pitiful **3 me dan** ~ : I feel sorry for them **4 ¡qué** ~**!** : what a shame! — **lastimero, -ra** *adj* : pitiful, wretched — **lastimoso, -sa** *adj* : pitiful, terrible

lastre *nm* : ballast

lata *nf* **1** : tinplate **2** : (tin) can **3** *fam* : nuisance, bore **4 dar (la) lata a** *fam* : bother, annoy

latente *adj* : latent

lateral *adj* : side, lateral

latido *nm* **1** : beat, throb **2** ~ **del corazón** : heartbeat

latifundio *nm* : large estate
látigo *nm* : whip — **latigazo** *nm* : lash
latín *nm* : Latin (language)
latino, -na *adj* **1** : Latin **2** : Latin-American — **∼** *n* : Latin American — **latinoamericano, -na** *adj* : Latin-American — **∼** *n* : Latin American
latir *vi* : beat, throb
latitud *nf* : latitude
latón *nm, pl* **-tones** : brass
latoso, -sa *adj fam* : annoying
laúd *nm* : lute
laudable *adj* : laudable
laureado, -da *adj* : prize-winning
laurel *nm* **1** : laurel **2** : bay leaf (in cooking)
lava *nf* : lava
lavar *vt* : wash — **lavarse** *vr* **1** : wash oneself **2** **∼ las manos** : wash one's hands — **lavable** *adj* : washable — **lavabo** *nm* **1** : sink **2** RETRETE : lavatory, toilet — **lavadero** *nm* : laundry room — **lavado** *nm* : wash, washing — **lavadora** *nf* : washing machine — **lavamanos** *nms & pl* : washbowl — **lavandería** *nf* : laundry (service) — **lavaplatos** *nms & pl* **1** : dishwasher **2** *Lat* : kitchen sink — **lavativa** *nf* : enema — **lavatorio** *nm* : lavatory, washroom — **lavavajillas** *nms & pl* : dishwasher
laxante *adj & nm* : laxative — **laxo, -xa** *adj* : loose
lazo *nm* **1** VÍNCULO : link, bond **2** LAZADA : bow **3** : lasso, lariat — **lazada** *nf* : bow, loop
le *pron* **1** : (to) her, (to) him, (to) it **2** (*formal*) : (to) you **3** (*as direct object*) : him, you
leal *adj* : loyal, faithful — **lealtad** *nf* : loyalty, allegiance
lebrel *nm* : hound
lección *nf, pl* **-ciones** **1** : lesson **2** : lecture (in a classroom)
leche *nf* **1** : milk **2** **∼ descremada** *or* **∼ desnatada** : skim milk **3** **∼ en polvo** : powdered milk — **lechera** *nf* : milk jug — **lechería** *nf* : dairy store — **lechero, -ra** *adj* : dairy — **∼** *n* : milkman *m*, milk dealer
lecho *nm* : bed
lechón, -chona *n, mpl* **-chones** : suckling pig
lechoso, -sa *adj* : milky
lechuga *nf* : lettuce
lechuza *nf* : owl
lector, -tora *n* : reader — **lectura** *nf* **1** : reading **2** ESCRITOS : reading matter
leer {20} *v* : read
legación *nf, pl* **-ciones** : legation
legado *nm* **1** : legacy **2** ENVIADO : legate, emissary
legajo *nm* : dossier, file

legal *adj* : legal — **legalidad** *nf* : legality — **legalizar** {21} *vt* : legalize — **legalización** *nf, pl* **-ciones** : legalization
legar {52} *vt* : bequeath
legendario, -ria *adj* : legendary
legible *adj* : legible
legión *nf, pl* **-giones** : legion — **legionario, -ria** *n* : legionnaire
legislar *vi* : legislate — **legislación** *nf, pl* **-ciones** : legislation — **legislador, -dora** *n* : legislator — **legislatura** *nf* : legislature
legítimo, -ma *adj* **1** : legitimate **2** GENUINO : authentic — **legitimidad** *nf* : legitimacy
lego, -ga *adj* **1** : secular, lay **2** IGNORANTE : ignorant — **∼** *n* : layman *m*, layperson
legua *nf* : league
legumbre *nf* : vegetable
leído, -da *adj* : well-read
lejano, -na *adj* : distant, far away — **lejanía** *nf* : distance
lejía *nf* : bleach
lejos *adv* **1** : far (away) **2 a lo ∼** : in the distance **3 de ∼** *or* **desde ∼** : from afar **4 ∼ de** : far from
lelo, -la *adj* : silly, stupid
lema *nm* : motto
lencería *nf* **1** : linen **2** : (women's) lingerie
lengua *nf* **1** : tongue **2** IDIOMA : language **3 morderse la ∼** : hold one's tongue
lenguado *nm* : sole, flounder
lenguaje *nm* : language
lengüeta *nf* **1** : tongue (of a shoe) **2** : reed (of a musical instrument)
lengüetada *nf* **beber a ∼s** : lap (up)
lente *nmf* **1** : lens **2 ∼s** *nmpl* : eyeglasses **3 ∼s de contacto** : contact lenses
lenteja *nf* : lentil — **lentejuela** *nf* : sequin
lento, -ta *adj* : slow — **lento** *adv* : slowly — **lentitud** *nf* : slowness
leña *nf* : firewood — **leñador, -dora** *n* : lumberjack, woodcutter — **leño** *nm* : log
león, -ona *n, mpl* **leones** : lion, lioness *f*
leopardo *nm* : leopard
leotardo *nm* : leotard, tights *pl*
lepra *nf* : leprosy — **leproso, -sa** *n* : leper
lerdo, -da *adj* **1** TORPE : clumsy **2** TONTO : slow-witted
les *pron* **1** : (to) them, (to) you **2** (*as direct object*) : them, you
lesbiano, -na *adj* : lesbian — **lesbiana** *nf* : lesbian — **lesbianismo** *nm* : lesbianism
lesión *nf, pl* **-siones** : lesion, wound — **lesionado, -da** *adj* : injured, wounded — **lesionar** *vt* **1** : injure, wound **2** DAÑAR : damage
letal *adj* : lethal
letanía *nf* : litany
letárgico, -ca *adj* : lethargic — **letargo** *nm* : lethargy

letra *nf* **1** : letter **2** ESCRITURA : handwriting **3** : lyrics *pl* (of a song) **4** ~ **de cambio** : bill of exchange **5** ~**s** *nfpl* : arts — **letrado, -da** *adj* : learned — **letrero** *nm* : sign, notice

letrina *nf* : latrine

leucemia *nf* : leukemia

levadizo, -za *adj* **puente levadizo** : drawbridge

levadura *nf* **1** : yeast **2** ~ **en polvo** : baking powder

levantar *vt* **1** : lift, raise **2** RECOGER : pick up **3** CONSTRUIR : erect, put up **4** ENCENDER : rouse, stir up **5** ~ **la mesa** *Lat* : clear the table — **levantarse** *vr* **1** : rise, stand up **2** : get out of bed **3** SUBLEVARSE : rise up — **levantamiento** *nm* **1** : raising, lifting **2** SUBLEVACIÓN : uprising

levante *nm* **1** : east **2** : east wind

levar *vt* ~ **anclas** : weigh anchor

leve *adj* **1** : light, slight **2** : minor, trivial (of wounds, sins, etc.) — **levedad** *nf* : lightness — **levemente** *adv* : lightly, slightly

léxico *nm* : vocabulary, lexicon

ley *nf* **1** : law **2 de (buena)** ~ : genuine, pure (of metals)

leyenda *nf* **1** : legend **2** : caption (of an illustration, etc.)

liar {85} *vt* **1** : bind, tie (up) **2** : roll (a cigarette) **3** CONFUNDIR : confuse, muddle — **liarse** *vr* : get mixed up

libanés, -nesa *adj, mpl* **-neses** : Lebanese

libelo *nm* **1** : libel **2** : petition (in court)

libélula *nf* : dragonfly

liberación *nf, pl* **-ciones** : liberation, deliverance

liberal *adj & nmf* : liberal — **liberalidad** *nf* : generosity, liberality

liberar *vt* : liberate, free — **libertad** *nf* **1** : freedom, liberty **2** ~ **bajo fianza** : bail **3** ~ **condicional** : parole **4 en** ~ : free — **libertar** *vt* : set free

libertinaje *nm* : licentiousness — **libertino, -na** *n* : libertine

libido *nf* : libido

libio, -bia *adj* : Libyan

libra *nf* **1** : pound **2** ~ **esterlina** : pound sterling

librar *vt* **1** : free, save **2** : wage, fight (a battle) **3** : draw, issue (a check, etc.) — **librarse** *vr* ~ **de** : free oneself from, get rid of

libre *adj* **1** : free **2** : unoccupied (of space), spare (of time) **3 al aire** ~ : in the open air **4** ~ **de impuestos** : tax-free

librea *nf* : livery

libro *nm* **1** : book **2** ~ **de bolsillo** : paperback — **librería** *nf* : bookstore — **librero, -ra** *n* : bookseller — **librero** *nm Lat* : bookcase — **libreta** *nf* : notebook

licencia *nf* **1** : license, permit **2** PERMISO : permission **3** : (military) leave — **licenciado, -da** *n* **1** : graduate **2** *Lat* : lawyer — **licenciar** *vt* : dismiss, discharge — **licenciarse** *vr* : graduate — **licenciatura** *nf* : degree

licencioso, -sa *adj* : licentious

liceo *nm* : high school

licitar *vt* : bid for

lícito, -ta *adj* **1** : lawful, legal **2** JUSTO : just, fair

licor *nm* **1** : liquor **2** : liqueur — **licorera** *nf* : decanter

licuadora *nf* : blender — **licuado** *nm* : milk shake — **licuar** {3} *vt* : liquefy

lid *nf* **1** : fight **2 en buena** ~ : fair and square

líder *adj* : leading — ~ *nmf* : leader — **liderato** *or* **liderazgo** *nm* : leadership

lidia *nf* : bullfight — **lidiar** *v* : fight

liebre *nf* : hare

lienzo *nm* **1** : cotton or linen cloth **2** : canvas (for a painting) **3** PARED : wall

liga *nf* **1** : league **2** *Lat* : rubber band **3** : garter (for stockings) — **ligadura** *nf* **1** ATADURA : tie, bond **2** : ligature (in medicine or music) — **ligamento** *nm* : ligament — **ligar** {52} *vt* : bind, tie (up)

ligero, -ra *adj* **1** : light, lightweight **2** LEVE : slight **3** ÁGIL : agile **4** FRÍVOLO : light-hearted, superficial — **ligeramente** *adv* : lightly, slightly — **ligereza** *nf* **1** : lightness **2** : flippancy (of character), thoughtlessness (of actions) **3** AGILIDAD : agility

lija *nf* : sandpaper — **lijar** *vt* : sand

lila *nf* : lilac

lima *nf* **1** : file **2** : lime (fruit) **3** ~ **para uñas** : nail file — **limar** *vt* : file

limbo *nm* : limbo

limitar *vt* : limit — *vi* ~ **con** : border on — **limitación** *nf, pl* **-ciones** : limitation, limit — **límite** *nm* **1** : limit **2** CONFÍN : boundary, border **3** ~ **de velocidad** : speed limit **4 fecha** ~ : deadline — **limítrofe** *adj* : bordering

limo *nm* : slime, mud

limón *nm, pl* **-mones 1** : lemon **2** ~ **verde** *Lat* : lime — **limonada** *nf* : lemonade

limosna *nf* **1** : alms **2 pedir** ~ : beg — **limosnero, -ra** *n* : beggar

limpiabotas *nmfs & pl* : bootblack

limpiaparabrisas *nms & pl* : windshield wiper

limpiar *vt* **1** : clean, wipe (away) **2** ~ **en seco** : dry-clean — **limpieza** *nf* **1** : cleanliness **2** : (act of) cleaning — **limpio** *adv* : cleanly, fairly — **limpio, -pia** *adj* **1** : clean, neat **2** HONRADO : honest **3** NETO : net, clear

limusina *nf* : limousine

linaje *nm* : lineage, ancestry
linaza *nf* : linseed
lince *nm* : lynx
linchar *vt* : lynch
lindar *vi* ∼ **con** : border on — **lindante** *adj* : bordering — **linde** *nmf or* **lindero** *nm* : boundary
lindo, -da *adj* **1** : pretty, lovely **2 de lo lindo** *fam* : a lot
línea *nf* **1** : line **2** ∼ **de conducta** : course of action **3 en** ∼ : on-line **4 guardar la** ∼ : watch one's figure — **lineal** *adj* : linear
lingote *nm* : ingot
lingüista *nmf* : linguist — **lingüística** *nf* : linguistics — **lingüístico, -ca** *adj* : linguistic
linimento *nm* : liniment
lino *nm* **1** : flax (plant) **2** : linen (fabric)
linóleo *nm* : linoleum
linterna *nf* **1** FAROL : lantern **2** : flashlight
lío *nm* **1** : bundle **2** *fam* : mess, trouble **3** *fam* : (love) affair
liofilizar {21} *vt* : freeze-dry
liquen *nm* : lichen
liquidar *vt* **1** : liquefy **2** : liquidate (merchandise, etc.) **3** : settle, pay off (a debt, etc.) — **liquidación** *nf, pl* **-ciones 1** : liquidation **2** REBAJA : clearance sale — **líquido, -da** *adj* **1** : liquid **2** NETO : net — **líquido** *nm* : liquid
lira *nf* : lyre
lírico, -ca *adj* : lyric, lyrical — **lírica** *nf* : lyric poetry
lirio *nm* : iris
lisiado, -da *adj* : disabled — ∼ *n* : disabled person — **lisiar** *vt* : disable, cripple
liso, -sa *adj* **1** : smooth **2** PLANO : flat **3** SENCILLO : plain **4 pelo** ∼ : straight hair
lisonjear *vt* : flatter — **lisonja** *nf* : flattery
lista *nf* **1** : stripe **2** ENUMERACIÓN : list **3** : menu (in a restaurant) — **listado, -da** *adj* : striped
listo, -ta *adj* **1** : clever, smart **2** PREPARADO : ready
listón *nm, pl* **-tones 1** : ribbon **2** : strip (of wood)
lisura *nf* : smoothness
litera *nf* : bunk bed, berth
literal *adj* : literal
literatura *nf* : literature — **literario, -ria** *adj* : literary
litigar {52} *vi* : litigate — **litigio** *nm* **1** : litigation **2 en** ∼ : in dispute
litografía *nf* **1** : lithography **2** : lithograph (picture)
litoral *adj* : coastal — ∼ *nm* : shore, seaboard
litro *nm* : liter

liturgia *nf* : liturgy — **litúrgico, -ca** *adj* : liturgical
liviano, -na *adj* **1** LIGERO : light **2** INCONSTANTE : fickle
lívido, -da *adj* : livid
llaga *nf* : sore, wound
llama *nf* **1** : flame **2** : llama (animal)
llamar *vt* **1** : call **2** : call up (on the telephone) — *vi* **1** : phone, call **2** : knock, ring (at the door) — **llamarse** *vr* **1** : be called **2 ¿cómo te llamas?** : what's your name? — **llamada** *nf* : call — **llamado, -da** *adj* : named, called — **llamamiento** *nm* : call, appeal
llamarada *nf* **1** : blaze **2** : flushing (of the face)
llamativo, -va *adj* : flashy, showy
llamear *vi* : flame, blaze
llano, -na *adj* **1** : flat **2** : straightforward (of a person, a message, etc.) **3** SENCILLO : plain, simple — **llano** *nm* : plain — **llaneza** *nf* : simplicity
llanta *nf* **1** : rim (of a wheel) **2** *Lat* : tire
llanto *nm* : crying, weeping
llanura *nf* : plain
llave *nf* **1** : key **2** *Lat* : faucet **3** INTERRUPTOR : switch **4 cerrar con** ∼ : lock **5** ∼ **inglesa** : monkey wrench — **llavero** *nm* : key chain
llegar {52} *vi* **1** : arrive, come **2** ALCANZAR : reach **3** BASTAR : be enough **4** ∼ **a** : manage to **5** ∼ **a ser** : become — **llegada** *nf* : arrival
llenar *vt* : fill (up), fill in — **lleno, -na** *adj* **1** : full **2 de lleno** : completely — **lleno** *nm* : full house
llevar *vt* **1** : take, carry **2** CONDUCIR : lead **3** : wear (clothing, etc.) **4** TENER : have **5 llevo una hora aquí** : I've been here for an hour — **llevarse** *vr* **1** : take (away) **2** ∼ **bien** : get along well — **llevadero, -ra** *adj* : bearable
llorar *vi* : cry, weep — **lloriquear** *vi* : whimper, whine — **lloro** *nm* : crying — **llorón, -rona** *n, mpl* **-rones** : crybaby, whiner — **lloroso, -sa** *adj* : tearful
llover {47} *v impers* : rain — **llovizna** *nf* : drizzle — **lloviznar** *v impers* : drizzle
lluvia *nf* : rain — **lluvioso, -sa** *adj* : rainy
lo *pron* **1** : him, it **2** *(formal, masculine)* : you **3** ∼ **que** : what, that which — ∼ *art* **1** : the **2** ∼ **mejor** : the best (part) **3 sé** ∼ **bueno que eres** : I know how good you are
loa *nf* : praise — **loable** *adj* : praiseworthy — **loar** *vt* : praise
lobo, -ba *n* : wolf
lóbrego, -ga *adj* : gloomy
lóbulo *nm* : lobe

local *adj* : local — **~** *nm* : premises *pl* — **localidad** *nf* : town, locality — **localizar** {21} *vt* **1** : localize **2** ENCONTRAR : locate — **localizarse** *vr* : be located
loción *nf, pl* **-ciones** : lotion
loco, -ca *adj* **1** : crazy, insane **2 a lo loco** : wildly, recklessly **3 volverse ~** : go mad — **~** *n* **1** : crazy person, lunatic **2 hacerse el loco** : act the fool
locomoción *nf, pl* **-ciones** : locomotion — **locomotora** *nf* : engine, locomotive
locuaz *adj, pl* **-cuaces** : talkative, loquacious
locución *nf, pl* **-ciones** : expression, phrase
locura *nf* **1** : insanity, madness **2** INSENSATEZ : crazy act, folly
locutor, -tora *n* : announcer
locutorio *nm* : phone booth
lodo *nm* : mud — **lodazal** *nm* : quagmire
logaritmo *nm* : logarithm
lógica *nf* : logic — **lógico, -ca** *adj* : logical — **logística** *nf* : logistics *pl*
logotipo *nm* : logo
lograr *vt* **1** : achieve, attain **2** CONSEGUIR : get, obtain **3 ~ hacer** : manage to do — **logro** *nm* : achievement, success
loma *nf* : hill, hillock
lombriz *nf, pl* **-brices** : worm
lomo *nm* **1** : back (of an animal) **2** : spine (of a book) **3 ~ de cerdo** : pork loin
lona *nf* : canvas
loncha *nf* : slice (of bacon, etc.)
lonche *nm Lat* : lunch — **lonchería** *nf Lat* : luncheonette
longaniza *nf* : sausage
longevidad *nf* : longevity — **longevo, -va** *adj* : long-lived
longitud *nf* **1** : longitude **2** LARGO : length
lonja → **loncha**
loro *nm* : parrot
los, las *pron* **1** : them **2** : you **3 los que, las que** : those who, the ones who — **los** *art* → **el**
losa *nf* **1** : flagstone **2** *or* **~ sepulcral** : tombstone
lote *nm* **1** : batch, lot **2** *Lat* : plot of land
lotería *nf* : lottery
loto *nm* : lotus
loza *nf* : crockery, earthenware
lozano, -na *adj* **1** : healthy-looking, vigorous **2** : luxuriant (of plants) — **lozanía** *nf*

1 : (youthful) vigor **2** : luxuriance (of plants)
lubricar {72} *vt* : lubricate — **lubricante** *adj* : lubricating — **~** *nm* : lubricant
lucero *nm* : bright star
luchar *vi* **1** : fight, struggle **2** : wrestle (in sports) — **lucha** *nf* **1** : struggle, fight **2** : wrestling (sport) — **luchador, -dora** *n* : fighter, wrestler
lucidez *nf, pl* **-deces** : lucidity — **lúcido, -da** *adj* : lucid
lucido, -da *adj* : magnificent, splendid
luciérnaga *nf* : firefly, glowworm
lucir {45} *vi* **1** : shine **2** *Lat* : appear, seem — *vt* **1** : wear, sport **2** OSTENTAR : show off — **lucirse** *vr* **1** : shine, excel **2** PRESUMIR : show off — **lucimiento** *nm* **1** : brilliance **2** ÉXITO : brilliant performance, success
lucrativo, -va *adj* : lucrative — **lucro** *nm* : profit
luego *adv* **1** : then **2** : later (on) **3 desde ~** : of course **4 ¡hasta ~!** : see you later! **5 ~ que** : as soon as — **~** *conj* : therefore
lugar *nm* **1** : place **2** ESPACIO : space, room **3 dar ~ a** : give rise to **4 en ~ de** : instead of **5 tener ~** : take place
lugarteniente *nmf* : deputy
lúgubre *adj* : gloomy
lujo *nm* **1** : luxury **2 de ~** : deluxe — **lujoso, -sa** *adj* : luxurious
lujuria *nf* : lust
lumbre *nf* **1** : fire **2 poner en la ~** : put on the stove
luminoso, -sa *adj* : shining, luminous
luna *nf* **1** : moon **2** : (window) glass **3** ESPEJO : mirror **4 ~ de miel** : honeymoon — **lunar** *adj* : lunar — **~** *nm* : mole, beauty spot
lunes *nms & pl* : Monday
lupa *nf* : magnifying glass
lúpulo *nm* : hops
lustrar *vt* : shine, polish — **lustre** *nm* **1** BRILLO : luster, shine **2** ESPLENDOR : glory — **lustroso, -sa** *adj* : lustrous, shiny
luto *nm* **1** : mourning **2 estar de ~** : be in mourning
luxación *nf, pl* **-ciones** : dislocation
luz *nf, pl* **luces 1** : light **2** : lighting (in a room, etc.) **3** *fam* : electricity **4 a la ~ de** : in light of **5 dar a ~** : give birth **6 sacar a la ~** : bring to light

M

m *nf* : m, 13th letter of the Spanish alphabet
macabro, -bra *adj* : macabre
macarrón *nm, pl* **-rrones 1** : macaroon **2 macarrones** *nmpl* : macaroni
maceta *nf* : flowerpot
machacar {72} *vt* : crush, grind — *vi* ~ **sobre** : go on about — **machacón, -cona** *adj, mpl* **-cones** : tiresome, boring
machete *nm* : machete — **machetear** *vt* : hack with a machete
macho *adj* **1** : male **2** *fam* : macho — ~ *nm* **1** : male **2** *fam* : he-man — **machista** *nm* : male chauvinist
machucar {72} *vt* **1** : beat, crush **2** : bruise (fruit)
macizo, -za *adj* : solid — **macizo** *nm* ~ **de flores** : flower bed
mácula *nf* : stain
madeja *nf* : skein, hank
madera *nf* **1** : wood **2** : lumber (for construction) **3** ~ **dura** : hardwood — **madero** *nm* : piece of lumber, plank
madre *nf* **1** : mother **2** ~ **política** : mother-in-law — **madrastra** *nf* : stepmother
madreselva *nf* : honeysuckle
madriguera *nf* : burrow, den
madrileño, -ña *adj* : of or from Madrid
madrina *nf* **1** : godmother **2** : bridesmaid (at a wedding)
madrugada *nf* : dawn, daybreak — **madrugador, -dora** *n* : early riser
madurar *v* **1** : mature **2** : ripen (of fruit) — **madurez** *nf, pl* **-reces 1** : maturity **2** : ripeness (of fruit) — **maduro, -ra** *adj* **1** : mature **2** : ripe (of fruit)
maestría *nf* : mastery, skill — **maestro, -tra** *adj* : masterly, skilled — ~ *n* **1** : teacher (in grammar school) **2** EXPERTO : expert, master
Mafia *nf* : Mafia
magia *nf* : magic — **mágico, -ca** *adj* : magic, magical
magisterio *nm* : teachers *pl*, teaching profession
magistrado, -da *n* : magistrate, judge
magistral *adj* **1** : masterful **2** : magisterial (of an attitude, etc.)
magnánimo, -ma *adj* : magnanimous — **magnanimidad** *nf* : magnanimity
magnate *nmf* : magnate, tycoon
magnesia *nf* : magnesia — **magnesio** *nm* : magnesium
magnético, -ca *adj* : magnetic — **magnet-**

ismo *nm* : magnetism — **magnetizar** {21} *vt* : magnetize
magnetófono *nm* : tape recorder
magnificencia *nf* : magnificence — **magnífico, -ca** *adj* : magnificent
magnitud *nf* : magnitude
magnolia *nf* : magnolia
mago, -ga *n* **1** : magician **2 los Reyes Magos** : the Magi
magro, -gra *adj* **1** : lean **2** MEZQUINO : poor, meager
magullar *vt* : bruise — **magulladura** *nf* : bruise
mahometano, -na *adj* : Islamic, Muslim — ~ *n* : Muslim
maicena *nf* : cornstarch
maíz *nm* : corn
maja *nf* : pestle
majadero, -ra *adj* : foolish, silly — ~ *n* : fool
majar *vt* : crush
majestad *nf* **1** : majesty **2 Su Majestad** : His/Her Majesty — **majestuoso, -sa** *adj* : majestic
majo, -ja *adj* **1** : nice **2** GUAPO : good-looking
mal *adv* **1** : badly, poorly **2** INCORRECTAMENTE : incorrectly **3** DIFÍCILMENTE : with difficulty, hardly **4 de** ~ **en peor** : from bad to worse **5 menos** ~ : it's just as well — ~ *nm* **1** : evil **2** DAÑO : harm, damage **3** ENFERMEDAD : illness — ~ *adj* → **malo**
malabarismo *nm* : juggling — **malabarista** *nmf* : juggler
malacostumbrar *vt* : spoil, pamper — **malacostumbrado, -da** *adj* : spoiled
malaria *nf* : malaria
malasio, -sia *adj* : Malaysian
malaventura *nf* : misfortune — **malaventurado, -da** *adj* : unfortunate
malayo, -ya *adj* : Malay, Malayan
malcriado, -da *adj* : bad-mannered, spoiled
maldad *nf* **1** : evil **2** : evil deed
maldecir {11} *vt* : curse, damn — *vi* **1** : curse, swear **2** ~ **de** : speak ill of — **maldición** *nf, pl* **-ciones** : curse — **maldito, -ta** *adj fam* : damned
maleable *adj* : malleable
maleante *nmf* : crook
malecón *nm, pl* **-cones** : jetty
maleducado, -da *adj* : rude
maleficio *nm* : curse — **maléfico, -ca** *adj* : evil, harmful
malentendido *nm* : misunderstanding

malestar *nm* **1** : discomfort **2** INQUIETUD : uneasiness

maleta *nf* **1** : suitcase **2 hacer la ~** : pack one's bags — **maletero, -ra** *n* : porter — **maletero** *nm* : trunk (of an automobile) — **maletín** *nm, pl* **-tines 1** PORTAFOLIO : briefcase **2** : overnight bag

malévolo, -la *adj* : malevolent — **malevolencia** *nf* : malevolence

maleza *nf* **1** : underbrush **2** MALAS HIERBAS : weeds *pl*

malgastar *vt* : waste, squander

malhablado, -da *adj* : foul-mouthed

malhechor, -chora *n* : criminal, delinquent

malhumorado, -da *adj* : bad-tempered, cross

malicia *nf* : malice — **malicioso, -sa** *adj* : malicious

maligno, -na *adj* **1** : malignant **2** PERNICIOSO : harmful, evil

malla *nf* **1** : mesh **2 ~s** *nfpl* : tights

malo, -la *adj* (**mal** *before masculine singular nouns*) **1** : bad **2** : poor (in quality) **3** ENFERMO : unwell **4 estar de malas** : be in a bad mood — **~** *n* : villain, bad guy (in movies, etc.)

malograr *vt* : waste — **malograrse** *vr* **1** FRACASAR : fail **2** : die young — **malogro** *nm* : failure

maloliente *adj* : smelly

malpensado, -da *adj* : malicious, nasty

malsano, -na *adj* : unhealthy

malsonante *adj* : rude

malta *nf* : malt

maltratar *vt* : mistreat

maltrecho, -cha *adj* : battered

malvado, -da *adj* : evil, wicked

malvavisco *nm* : marshmallow

malversar *vt* : embezzle — **malversación** *nf, pl* **-ciones** : embezzlement

mama *nf* : teat (of an animal), breast (of a woman)

mamá *nf fam* : mom, mama

mamar *vi* **1** : suckle **2 dar de ~ a** : breastfeed — *vt* **1** : suckle, nurse **2** : learn from childhood, grow up with — **mamario, -ria** *adj* : mammary

mamarracho *nm fam* : mess, sight

mambo *nm* : mambo

mamífero, -ra *adj* : mammalian — **mamífero** *nm* : mammal

mamografía *nf* : mammogram

mampara *nf* : screen, room divider

mampostería *nf* : masonry

manada *nf* **1** : flock, herd, pack **2 en ~** : in droves

manar *vi* **1** : flow **2 ~ en** : be rich in — **manantial** *nm* **1** : spring **2** ORIGEN : source

manchar *vt* **1** : stain, spot, mark **2** : tarnish

(a reputation, etc.) — **mancharse** *vr* : get dirty — **mancha** *nf* : stain

mancillar *vt* : sully, stain

manco, -ca *adj* : one-armed, one-handed

mancomunar *vt* : combine, join — **mancomunarse** *vr* : unite — **mancomunidad** *nf* : union

mandar *vt* **1** : command, order **2** ENVIAR : send **3** *Lat* : hurl, throw — *vi* **1** : be in charge **2 ¿mande?** *Lat* : yes?, pardon? — **mandadero, -ra** *nm* : messenger — **mandado** *nm* : errand — **mandamiento** *nm* **1** : order, warrant **2** : commandment (in religion)

mandarina *nf* : mandarin orange, tangerine

mandato *nm* **1** : term of office **2** ORDEN : mandate — **mandatario, -ria** *n* **1** : leader (in politics) **2** : agent (in law)

mandíbula *nf* : jaw, jawbone

mandil *nm* : apron

mando *nm* **1** : command, leadership **2 al ~ de** : in charge of **3 ~ a distancia** : remote control

mandolina *nf* : mandolin

mandón, -dona *adj, mpl* **-dones** : bossy

manecilla *nf* : hand (of a clock), pointer

manejar *vt* **1** : handle, operate **2** : manage (a business, etc.) **3** : manipulate (a person) **4** *Lat* : drive (a car) — **manejarse** *vr* **1** : manage, get by **2** *Lat* : behave — **manejo** *nm* **1** : handling, use **2** : management (of a business, etc.)

manera *nf* **1** : way, manner **2 de ~ que** : so that **3 de ninguna ~** : by no means **4 de todas ~s** : anyway

manga *nf* **1** : sleeve **2** MANGUERA : hose

mango *nm* **1** : hilt, handle **2** : mango (fruit)

mangonear *vt fam* : boss around — *vi* **1** : be bossy **2** HOLGAZANEAR : loaf, fool around

manguera *nf* : hose

maní *nm, pl* **-níes** *Lat* : peanut

manía *nf* **1** : mania, obsession **2** MODA PASAJERA : craze, fad **3** ANTIPATÍA : dislike — **maníaco, -ca** *adj* : maniacal — **~** *n* : maniac

maniatar *vt* : tie the hands of

maniático, -ca *adj* : obsessive, fussy — **~** *n* : fussy person, fanatic

manicomio *nm* : insane asylum

manicura *nf* : manicure — **manicuro, -ra** *n* : manicurist

manido, -da *adj* : stale, hackneyed

manifestar {55} *vt* **1** : demonstrate, show **2** DECLARAR : express, declare — **manifestarse** *vr* **1** : become evident **2** : demonstrate (in politics) — **manifestación** *nf, pl* **-ciones 1** : manifestation, sign **2** : demonstration (in politics) — **manifestante** *nmf* : protester, demonstrator — **manifiesto, -ta**

adj : manifest, evident — **manifiesto** *nm* : manifesto

manija *nf* : handle

manillar *nm* : handlebars *pl*

maniobra *nf* : maneuver — **maniobrar** *v* : maneuver

manipular *vt* **1** : manipulate **2** MANEJAR : handle — **manipulación** *nf, pl* **-ciones** : manipulation

maniquí *nmf, pl* **-quíes** : mannequin, model — ～ *nm* : mannequin, dummy

manirroto, -ta *adj* : extravagant — ～ *n* : spendthrift

manivela *nf* : crank

manjar *nm* : delicacy, special dish

mano *nf* **1** : hand **2** : coat (of paint, etc.) **3** **a** ～ *or* **a la** ～ : at hand, nearby **4 dar la** ～ : shake hands **5 de segunda** ～ : secondhand **6** ～ **de obra** : labor, manpower

manojo *nm* : bunch

manopla *nf* : mitten

manosear *vt* **1** : handle excessively **2** : fondle (a person)

manotazo *nm* : slap

mansalva: **a** ～ *adv phr* : at close range, without risk

mansarda *nf* : attic

mansedumbre *nf* **1** : gentleness **2** : tameness (of an animal)

mansión *nf, pl* **-siones** : mansion

manso, -sa *adj* **1** : gentle **2** : tame (of an animal)

manta *nf* **1** : blanket **2** *Lat* : poncho

manteca *nf* : lard, fat — **mantecoso, -sa** *adj* : greasy

mantel *nm* : tablecloth — **mantelería** *nf* : table linen

mantener {80} *vt* **1** : support **2** CONSERVAR : preserve **3** : keep up, maintain (relations, correspondence, etc.) **4** AFIRMAR : affirm — **mantenerse** *vr* **1** : support oneself **2** ～ **firme** : hold one's ground — **mantenimiento** *nm* **1** : maintenance **2** SUSTENTO : sustenance

mantequilla *nf* : butter — **mantequera** *nf* : churn — **mantequería** *nf* : dairy

mantilla *nf* : mantilla

manto *nm* : cloak

mantón *nm, pl* **-tones** : shawl

manual *adj* : manual — ～ *nm* : manual, handbook

manubrio *nm* **1** : handle, crank **2** *Lat* : handlebars *pl*

manufactura *nf* **1** : manufacture **2** FÁBRICA : factory

manuscrito *nm* : manuscript — **manuscrito, -ta** *adj* : handwritten

manutención *nf, pl* **-ciones** : maintenance

manzana *nf* **1** : apple **2** : (city) block —

manzanar *nm* : apple orchard — **manzano** *nm* : apple tree

maña *nf* **1** : skill **2** ASTUCIA : cunning, guile

mañana *adv* : tomorrow — ～ *nm* **el** ～ : the future — ～ *nf* : morning

mañoso, -sa *adj* **1** : skillful **2** *Lat* : finicky

mapa *nm* : map — **mapamundi** *nm* : map of the world

mapache *nm* : raccoon

maqueta *nf* : model, mock-up

maquillaje *nm* : makeup — **maquillarse** *vr* : put on makeup

máquina *nf* **1** : machine **2** LOCOMOTORA : locomotive **3 a toda** ～ : at full speed **4** ～ **de escribir** : typewriter — **maquinación** *nf, pl* **-ciones** : machination — **maquinal** *adj* : mechanical — **maquinaria** *nf* **1** : machinery **2** : mechanism, works *pl* (of a watch, etc.) — **maquinilla** *nf* : small machine — **maquinista** *nmf* **1** : machinist **2** : (railroad) engineer

mar *nmf* **1** : sea **2 alta** ～ : high seas *pl*

maraca *nf* : maraca

maraña *nf* **1** : thicket **2** ENREDO : tangle, mess

maratón *nm, pl* **-tones** : marathon

maravilla *nf* **1** : wonder, marvel **2** : marigold (flower) — **maravillar** *vt* : astonish — **maravillarse** *vr* : be amazed — **maravilloso, -sa** *adj* : marvelous

marca *nf* **1** : mark **2** : brand (on livestock) **3** *or* ～ **de fábrica** : trademark **4** : record (in sports) — **marcado, -da** *adj* : marked — **marcador** *nm* **1** : scoreboard **2** *Lat* : marker, felt-tipped pen

marcapasos *nms & pl* : pacemaker

marcar {72} *vt* **1** : mark **2** : brand (livestock) **3** INDICAR : indicate, show **4** : dial (a telephone, etc.) **5** : score (in sports) — *vi* **1** : score **2** : dial (on the telephone, etc.)

marchar *vi* **1** : go **2** CAMINAR : walk **3** FUNCIONAR : work, run — **marcharse** *vr* : leave, go — **marcha** *nf* **1** : march **2** PASO : pace, speed **3** : gear (of an automobile) **4 poner en** ～ : put in motion

marchitarse *vr* : wither, wilt — **marchito, -ta** *adj* : withered

marcial *adj* : martial, military

marco *nm* **1** : frame **2** : goalposts *pl* (in sports) **3** ENTORNO : setting, framework

marea *nf* : tide — **marear** *vt* **1** : make nauseous or dizzy **2** CONFUNDIR : confuse — **marearse** *vr* **1** : become nauseated or dizzy **2** CONFUNDIRSE : get confused — **mareado, -da** *adj* **1** : sick, nauseous **2** ATURDIDO : dazed, dizzy

maremoto *nm* : tidal wave

mareo *nm* **1** : nausea, seasickness **2** VÉRTIGO : dizziness

marfil *nm* : ivory

margarina *nf* : margarine

margarita *nf* : daisy

margen *nm, pl* **márgenes 1** : edge, border **2** : margin (of a page, etc.) — **marginado, -da** *adj* **1** : alienated **2 clases marginadas** : underclass — **~** *n* : outcast — **marginal** *adj* : marginal — **marginar** *vt* : ostracize, exclude

mariachi *nm* : mariachi musician or band

maridaje *nm* : marriage, union — **marido** *nm* : husband

marihuana *or* **mariguana** *or* **marijuana** *nf* : marijuana

marimba *nf* : marimba

marina *nf* **1** : coast **2** *or* **~ de guerra** : navy, fleet

marinada *nf* : marinade — **marinar** *vt* : marinate

marinero, -ra *adj* **1** : sea, marine **2** : seaworthy (of a ship) — **marinero** *nm* : sailor — **marino, -na** *adj* : marine — **marino** *nm* : seaman, sailor

marioneta *nf* : puppet, marionette

mariposa *nf* **1** : butterfly **2 ~ nocturna** : moth

mariquita *nf* : ladybug

marisco *nm* **1** : shellfish **2 ~s** *nmpl* : seafood

marisma *nf* : salt marsh

marítimo, -ma *adj* : maritime, shipping

mármol *nm* : marble

marmota *nf* **~ de América** : groundhog

marquesina *nf* : marquee, (glass) canopy

marrano, -na *n* **1** : pig, hog **2** *fam* : slob

marrar *vt* : miss (a target) — *vi* : fail

marrón *adj* & *nm, pl* **-rrones** : brown

marroquí *adj* : Moroccan

marsopa *nf* : porpoise

marsupial *nm* : marsupial

Marte *nm* : Mars

martes *nms* & *pl* : Tuesday

martillo *nm* **1** : hammer **2 ~ neumático** : jackhammer — **martillar** *or* **martillear** *v* : hammer

mártir *nmf* : martyr — **martirio** *nm* : martyrdom — **martirizar** {21} *vt* **1** : martyr **2** ATORMENTAR : torment

marxismo *nm* : Marxism — **marxista** *adj* & *nmf* : Marxist

marzo *nm* : March

mas *conj* : but

más *adv* **1** : more **2 el/la/lo ~** : (the) most **3** (*in negative constructions*) : (any) longer **4 ¡qué día ~ bonito!** what a beautiful day! — **~** *adj* **1** : more **2** : most **3 ¿quién ~?** : who else? — **~** *prep* : plus — **~** *pron* **1 a lo ~** : at most **2 de ~** : extra, spare **3**

~ o menos : more or less **4 ¿tienes ~?** : do you have more?

masa *nf* **1** : mass, volume **2** : dough (in cooking) **3 ~s** *nfpl* : people, masses

masacre *nf* : massacre

masaje *nm* : massage — **masajear** *vt* : massage

mascar {72} *v* : chew

máscara *nf* : mask — **mascarada** *nf* : masquerade — **mascarilla** *nf* : mask (in medecine, etc.)

mascota *nf* : mascot

masculino, -na *adj* **1** : masculine, male **2** VARONIL : manly **3** : masculine (in grammar) — **masculinidad** *nf* : masculinity

mascullar *v* : mumble

masilla *nf* : putty

masivo, -va *adj* : mass, large-scale

masón *nm, pl* **-sones** : Mason, Freemason — **masónico, -ca** *adj* : Masonic

masoquismo *nm* : masochism — **masoquista** *adj* : masochistic — **~** *nmf* : masochist

masticar {72} *v* : chew

mástil *nm* **1** : mast **2** ASTA : flagpole **3** : neck (of a stringed instrument)

mastín *nm, pl* **-tines** : mastiff

masturbarse *vr* : masturbate — **masturbación** *nf, pl* **-ciones** : masturbation

mata *nf* : bush, shrub

matadero *nm* : slaughterhouse

matador *nm* : matador, bullfighter

matamoscas *nms* & *pl* : flyswatter

matar *vt* **1** : kill **2** : slaughter (animals) — **matarse** *vr* **1** : be killed **2** SUICIDARSE : commit suicide — **matanza** *nf* : slaughter, killing

matasanos *nms* & *pl fam* : quack

matasellos *nms* & *pl* : postmark

mate *adj* : matte, dull — **~** *nm* **1** : maté **2 jaque ~** : checkmate

matemáticas *nfpl* : mathematics — **matemático, -ca** *adj* : mathematical — **~** *n* : mathematician

materia *nf* **1** ASUNTO : matter **2** MATERIAL : material — **material** *adj* **1** : material **2 daños ~es** : property damage — **~** *nm* **1** : material **2** EQUIPO : equipment, gear — **materialismo** *nm* : materialism — **materialista** *adj* : materialistic — **materializar** {21} *vt* : bring to fruition — **materializarse** *vr* : materialize — **materialmente** *adv* : absolutely

maternal *adj* : maternal — **maternidad** *nf* **1** : motherhood **2** : maternity hospital — **materno, -na** *adj* **1** : maternal **2 lengua materna** : mother tongue

matinal *adj* : morning

matinée *or* **matiné** *nf* : matinee

matiz *nm, pl* **-tices 1** : nuance **2** : hue, shade (of colors) — **matizar** {21} *vt* **1** : blend (colors) **2** : qualify (a statement, etc.) **3 ~ de** : tinge with

matón *nm, pl* **-tones 1** : bully **2** CRIMINAL : gangster, hoodlum

matorral *nm* : thicket

matraca *nf* **1** : rattle, noisemaker **2 dar la ~ a** : pester

matriarcado *nm* : matriarchy

matrícula *nf* **1** : list, roll, register **2** INSCRIPCIÓN : registration **3** : license plate (of an automobile) — **matricular** *vt* : register — **matricularse** *vr* : register, matriculate

matrimonio *nm* **1** : marriage **2** PAREJA : (married) couple — **matrimonial** *adj* : marital

matriz *nf, pl* **-trices 1** : matrix **2** : uterus, womb (in anatomy)

matrona *nf* : matron

matutino, -na *adj* : morning

maullar {8} *vi* : meow — **maullido** *nm* : meow

maxilar *nm* : jaw, jawbone

máxima *nf* : maxim

máxime *adv* : especially

máximo, -ma *adj* : maximum, highest — **máximo** *nm* **1** : maximum **2 al ~** : to the full

maya *adj* : Mayan

mayo *nm* : May

mayonesa *nf* : mayonnaise

mayor *adj* **1** (*comparative of* **grande**) : bigger, larger, greater, older **2** (*superlative of* **grande**) : biggest, largest, greatest, oldest **3 al por ~** : wholesale **4 ~ de edad** : of (legal) age — **~** *nmf* **1** : major (in the military) **2** ADULTO : adult **3 ~es** *nmfpl* : grown-ups — **mayoral** *nm* : foreman

mayordomo *nm* : butler

mayoreo *nm Lat* : wholesale

mayoría *nf* : majority

mayorista *adj* : wholesale — **~** *nmf* : wholesaler

mayormente *adv* : primarily

mayúscula *nf* : capital letter — **mayúsculo, -la** *adj* **1** : capital, uppercase **2 un fallo mayúsculo** : a terrible mistake

maza *nf* : mace (weapon)

mazapán *nm, pl* **-panes** : marzipan

mazmorra *nf* : dungeon

mazo *nm* **1** : mallet **2** MAJA : pestle

mazorca *nf* **~ de maíz** : corncob

me *pron* **1** (*direct object*) : me **2** (*indirect object*) : to me, for me, from me **3** (*reflexive*) : myself, to myself, for myself, from myself

mecánica *nf* : mechanics — **mecánico, -ca** *adj* : mechanical — **~** *n* : mechanic

mecanismo *nm* : mechanism — **mecanización** *nf, pl* **-ciones** : mechanization — **mecanizar** {21} *vt* : mechanize

mecanografiar {85} *vt* : type — **mecanografía** *nf* : typing — **mecanógrafo, -fa** *n* : typist

mecate *nm Lat* : rope

mecedora *nf* : rocking chair

mecenas *nmfs & pl* : patron, sponsor — **mecenazgo** *nm* : patronage, sponsorship

mecer {86} *vt* **1** : rock **2** : push (on a swing) — **mecerse** *vr* : rock, swing

mecha *nf* **1** : fuse (of a bomb, etc.) **2** : wick (of a candle)

mechero *nm* **1** : burner **2** *Spain* : cigarette lighter

mechón *nm, pl* **-chones** : lock (of hair)

medalla *nf* : medal — **medallón** *nm, pl* **-llones 1** : medallion **2** : locket (jewelry)

media *nf* **1** : average **2 ~s** *nfpl* : stockings **3 a ~s** : by halves, halfway

mediación *nf, pl* **-ciones** : mediation

mediado, -da *adj* **1** : half full, half empty, half over **2** : halfway through — **mediados** *nmpl* **a ~ de** : halfway through, in the middle of

mediador, -dora *n* : mediator

medialuna *nf* **1** : crescent **2** : croissant (pastry)

medianamente *adv* : fairly

medianero, -ra *adj* **pared medianera** : dividing wall

mediano, -na *adj* **1** : medium, average **2** MEDIOCRE : mediocre

medianoche *nf* : midnight

mediante *prep* : through, by means of

mediar *vi* **1** : be in the middle **2** INTERVENIR : mediate **3 ~ entre** : be between

medicación *nf, pl* **-ciones** : medication — **medicamento** *nm* : medicine — **medicar** {72} *vt* : medicate — **medicarse** *vr* : take medicine — **medicina** *nf* : medicine — **medicinal** *adj* : medicinal

medición *nf, pl* **-ciones** : measurement

médico, -ca *adj* : medical — **~** *n* : doctor, physician

medida *nf* **1** : measurement, measure **2** MODERACIÓN : moderation **3** GRADO : extent, degree **4 tomar ~s** : take steps — **medidor** *nm Lat* : meter, gauge

medieval *adj* : medieval

medio, -dia *adj* **1** : half **2** MEDIANO : average **3 una media hora** : half an hour **4 la clase media** : the middle class — **medio** *adv* : half — **~** *nm* **1** : half **2** MANERA : means *pl,* uso **3 en ~ de** : in the middle of **4 ~ ambiente** : environment **5 ~s** *nmpl* : means, resources

mediocre *adj* : mediocre, average — **mediocridad** *nf* : mediocrity
mediodía *nm* : noon, midday
medioevo *nm* : Middle Ages
medir {54} *vt* **1** : measure **2** CONSIDERAR : weigh, consider — **medirse** *vr* : be moderate
meditar *vi* : meditate, contemplate — *vt* **1** : think over, consider **2** PLANEAR : plan, work out — **meditación** *nf, pl* **-ciones** : meditation
mediterráneo, -nea *adj* : Mediterranean
medrar *vt* : flourish, thrive
medroso, -sa *adj* : fearful
médula *nf* **1** : marrow **2** ~ **espinal** : spinal cord
medusa *nf* : jellyfish
megabyte *nm* : megabyte
megáfono *nm* : megaphone
mejicano → **mexicano**
mejilla *nf* : cheek
mejillón *nm, pl* **-llones** : mussel
mejor *adv* **1** (*comparative*) : better **2** (*superlative*) : best **3 a lo** ~ : maybe, perhaps — ~ *adj* **1** (*comparative of* **bueno** *or* **bien**) : better **2** (*superlative of* **bueno** *or* **bien**) : best **3 lo** ~ : the best thing **4 tanto** ~ : so much the better — **mejora** *nf* : improvement
mejorana *nf* : marjoram
mejorar *vt* : improve — *vi* : improve, get better
mejunje *nm* : concoction, brew
melancolía *nf* : melancholy — **melancólico, -ca** *adj* : melancholic, melancholy
melaza *nf* : molasses
melena *nf* **1** : long hair **2** : mane (of a lion)
melindroso, -sa *adj* **1** : affected **2** *Lat* : finicky
mella *nf* : chip, nick — **mellado, -da** *adj* : chipped, jagged
mellizo, -za *adj* & *n* : twin
melocotón *nm, pl* **-tones** : peach
melodía *nf* : melody — **melódico, -ca** *adj* : melodic
melodrama *nm* : melodrama — **melodramático, -ca** *adj* : melodramatic
melón *nm, pl* **-lones** : melon
meloso, -sa *adj* **1** : sweet, honeyed **2** EMPALAGOSO : cloying
membrana *nf* : membrane
membrete *nm* : letterhead, heading
membrillo *nm* : quince
membrudo, -da *adj* : muscular, burly
memorable *adj* : memorable
memorándum *or* **memorando** *nm, pl* **-dums** *or* **-dos** **1** : memorandum **2** AGENDA : notebook
memoria *nf* **1** : memory **2** RECUERDO : remembrance **3** INFORME : report **4 de** ~ : by heart **5** ~**s** *nfpl* : memoirs — **memorizar** {21} *vt* : memorize
mena *nf* : ore
menaje *nm* : household goods *pl,* furnishings *pl*
mencionar *vt* : mention, refer to — **mención** *nf, pl* **-ciones** : mention
mendaz *adj, pl* **-daces** : lying
mendigar {52} *vi* : beg — *vt* : beg for — **mendicidad** *nf* : begging — **mendigo, -ga** *n* : beggar
mendrugo *nm* : crust (of bread)
menear *vt* **1** : move, shake **2** : sway (one's hips) **3** : wag (a tail) — **menearse** *vr* **1** : sway, shake, move **2** *fam* : hurry up
menester *nm* **ser** ~ : be necessary — **menesteroso, -sa** *adj* : needy
menguar *vt* : diminish, lessen — *vi* **1** : decline, decrease **2** : wane (of the moon) — **mengua** *nf* : decrease, decline
menopausia *nf* : menopause
menor *adj* **1** (*comparative of* **pequeño**) : smaller, lesser, younger **2** (*superlative of* **pequeño**) : smallest, least, youngest **3** : minor (in music) **4 al por** ~ : retail — ~ *nmf* : minor, juvenile
menos *adv* **1** (*comparative*) : less **2** (*superlative*) : least **3** ~ **de** : fewer than — ~ *adj* **1** (*comparative*) : less, fewer **2** (*superlative*) : least, fewest — ~ *prep* **1** : minus **2** EXCEPTO : except — ~ *pron* **1** : less, fewer **2 al** ~ *or* **por lo** ~ : at least **3 a** ~ **que** : unless — **menoscabar** *vt* **1** : lessen **2** ESTROPEAR : harm, damage — **menospreciar** *vt* **1** DESPRECIAR : scorn **2** SUBESTIMAR : undervalue — **menosprecio** *nm* : contempt
mensaje *nm* : message — **mensajero, -ra** *n* : messenger
menso, -sa *adj Lat fam* : foolish, stupid
menstruar {3} *vi* : menstruate — **menstruación** *nf* : menstruation
mensual *adj* : monthly — **mensualidad** *nf* **1** : monthly payment **2** : monthly salary
mensurable *adj* : measurable
menta *nf* **1** : mint, peppermint **2** ~ **verde** : spearmint
mental *adj* : mental — **mentalidad** *nf* : mentality
mentar {55} *vt* : mention, name
mente *nf* : mind
mentir {76} *vi* : lie — **mentira** *nf* : lie — **mentirilla** *nf* : fib — **mentiroso, -sa** *adj* : lying — ~ *n* : liar
mentís *nms & pl* : denial
mentol *nm* : menthol
mentón *nm, pl* **-tones** : chin
menú *nm, pl* **-nús** : menu

menudear *vi* : occur frequently — **menudeo** *nm Lat* : retail, retailing

menudillos *nmpl* : giblets

menudo, -da *adj* **1** : small, insignificant **2 a ~** : often

meñique *nm or* **dedo ~** : little finger, pinkie

meollo *nm* **1** : marrow **2** ESENCIA : essence, core

mercado *nm* **1** : market **2 ~ de valores** : stock market — **mercadería** *nf* : merchandise, goods *pl*

mercancía *nf* : merchandise, goods *pl* — **mercante** *nmf* : merchant, dealer — **mercantil** *adj* : commercial

mercenario, -ria *adj & n* : mercenary

mercería *nf* : notions store

mercurio *nm* : mercury

Mercurio *nm* : Mercury (planet)

merecer {53} *vt* : deserve — *vi* : be worthy — **merecedor, -dora** *adj* : deserving, worthy — **merecido** *nm* **recibir su ~** : get one's just deserts

merendar {55} *vi* : have an afternoon snack — *vt* : have as an afternoon snack — **merendero** *nm* **1** : snack bar **2** : picnic area

merengue *nm* **1** : meringue **2** : merengue (dance)

meridiano, -na *adj* **1** : midday **2** CLARO : crystal-clear — **meridiano** *nm* : meridian — **meridional** *adj* : southern

merienda *nf* : afternoon snack, tea

mérito *nm* : merit, worth — **meritorio, -ria** *adj* : deserving — **~** *n* : intern, trainee

mermar *vi* : decrease — *vt* : reduce, cut down — **merma** *nf* : decrease

mermelada *nf* : marmalade, jam

mero, -ra *adj* **1** : mere, simple **2** *Lat fam* (*used as an intensifier*) : very, real — **mero** *adv Lat fam* **1** : nearly, almost **2 aquí ~** : right here

merodear *vi* **1** : maraud **2 ~ por** : prowl about (a place)

mes *nm* : month

mesa *nf* **1** : table **2** COMITÉ : committee, board

mesarse *vr* **~ los cabellos** : tear one's hair

meseta *nf* : plateau

Mesías *nm* : Messiah

mesilla *nf* : small table

mesón *nm, pl* **-sones** : inn — **mesonero, -ra** *nm* : innkeeper

mestizo, -za *adj* **1** : of mixed ancestry **2** HÍBRIDO : hybrid — **~** *n* : person of mixed ancestry

mesura *nf* : moderation — **mesurado, -da** *adj* : moderate, restrained

meta *nf* : goal, objective

metabolismo *nm* : metabolism

metafísica *nf* : metaphysics — **metafísico, -ca** *adj* : metaphysical

metáfora *nf* : metaphor — **metafórico, -ca** *adj* : metaphoric, metaphorical

metal *nm* **1** : metal **2** : brass section (in an orchestra) — **metálico, -ca** *adj* : metallic, metal — **metalurgia** *nf* : metallurgy

metamorfosis *nfs & pl* : metamorphosis

metano *nm* : methane

metedura *nf* **~ de pata** *fam* : blunder

meteoro *nm* : meteor — **meteórico, -ca** *adj* : meteoric — **meteorito** *nm* : meteorite — **meteorología** *nf* : meteorology — **meteorólogo, -ga** *adj* : meteorological, meteorologic — **~** *n* : meteorologist

meter *vt* **1** : put (in) **2** : place (in a job, etc.) **3** ENREDAR : involve **4** CAUSAR : make, cause **5** : spread (a rumor) **6** *Lat* : strike (a blow) — **meterse** *vr* **1** : get in, enter **2 ~ en** : get involved in, meddle in **3 ~ con** *fam* : pick a fight with

meticuloso, -sa *adj* : meticulous

método *nm* : method — **metódico, -ca** *adj* : methodical — **metodología** *nf* : methodology

metomentodo *nmf fam* : busybody

metralla *nf* : shrapnel — **metralleta** *nf* : submachine gun

métrico, -ca *adj* : metric, metrical

metro *nm* **1** : meter **2** : subway (train)

metrópoli *nf or* **metrópolis** *nfs & pl* : metropolis — **metropolitano, -na** *adj* : metropolitan

mexicano, -na *adj* : Mexican — **mexicoamericano, -na** *adj* : Mexican-American

mezcla *nf* **1** : mixture **2** ARGAMASA : mortar — **mezclar** *vt* **1** : mix, blend **2** CONFUNDIR : mix up, muddle **3** INVOLUCRAR : involve — **mezclarse** *vr* **1** : get mixed up **2** : mingle (socially) — **mezcolanza** *nf* : mixture

mezclilla *nf Lat* : denim

mezquino, -na *adj* **1** : mean, petty **2** ESCASO : meager — **mezquindad** *nf* : meanness, stinginess

mezquita *nf* : mosque

mezquite *nm* : mesquite

mi *adj* : my

mí *pron* **1** : me **2 or ~ mismo, ~ misma** : myself **3 a ~ no me importa** : it doesn't matter to me

miajas → **migajas**

miau *nm* : meow

mica *nf* : mica

mico *nm* : (long-tailed) monkey

microbio *nm* : microbe, germ — **microbiología** *nf* : microbiology

microbús *nm, pl* **-buses** : minibus

microcosmos *nms & pl* : microcosm

microfilm *nm, pl* **-films** : microfilm
micrófono *nm* : microphone
microondas *nms & pl* : microwave (oven)
microorganismo *nm* : microorganism
microscopio *nm* : microscope — **microscópico, -ca** *adj* : microscopic
miedo *nm* **1** : fear **2 dar ~** : be frightening — **miedoso, -sa** *adj* : fearful
miel *nf* : honey
miembro *nm* **1** : member **2** EXTREMIDAD : limb, extremity
mientras *adv or* **~ tanto** : meanwhile, in the meantime — **~** *conj* **1** : while, as **2 ~ que** : while, whereas **3 ~ viva** : as long as I live
miércoles *nms & pl* : Wednesday
mies *nf* : (ripe) corn, grain
miga *nf* : crumb — **migajas** *nfpl* **1** : breadcrumbs **2** SOBRAS : leftovers
migración *nf, pl* **-ciones** : migration
migraña *nf* : migraine
migrar *vi* : migrate
mijo *nm* : millet
mil *adj & nm* : thousand
milagro *nm* : miracle — **milagroso, -sa** *adj* : miraculous
milenio *nm* : millennium
milésimo, -ma *adj* : thousandth
milicia *nf* **1** : militia **2** : military (service)
miligramo *nm* : milligram
mililitro *nm* : milliliter
milímetro *nm* : millimeter
militante *adj & nmf* : militant
militar *adj* : military — **~** *nmf* : soldier — **militarizar** {21} *vt* : militarize
milla *nf* : mile
millar *nm* : thousand
millón *nm, pl* **-llones 1** : million **2 mil millones** : billion — **millonario, -ria** *n* : millionaire — **millonésimo, -ma** *adj* : millionth
mimar *vt* : pamper, spoil
mimbre *nm* : wicker
mímica *nf* **1** : mime, sign language **2** IMITACIÓN : mimicry
mimo *nm* : pampering — **~** *nmf* : mime
mina *nf* **1** : mine **2** : lead (for pencils) — **minar** *vt* **1** : mine **2** DEBILITAR : undermine
mineral *adj* : mineral — **~** *nm* **1** : mineral **2** : ore (of a metal)
minería *nf* : mining — **minero, -ra** *adj* : mining — **~** *n* : miner
miniatura *nf* : miniature
minifalda *nf* : miniskirt
minifundio *nm* : small farm
minimizar {21} *vt* : minimize
mínimo, -ma *adj* **1** : minimum **2** MINÚSCULO : minute **3 en lo más ~** : in the slightest — **mínimo** *nm* : minimum

minino, -na *n fam* : pussycat
ministerio *nm* : ministry — **ministro, -tra** *n* **1** : minister, secretary **2 primer ministro** : prime minister
minoría *nf* : minority
minorista *adj* : retail — **~** *nmf* : retailer
minoritario, -ria *adj* : minority
minucia *nf* : trifle, small detail — **minucioso, -sa** *adj* **1** : detailed **2** METICULOSO : thorough
minué *nm* : minuet
minúsculo, -la *adj* : minuscule, tiny
minusvalía *nf* : handicap, disability — **minusválido, -da** *adj* : disabled
minuta *nf* **1** : bill, fee **2** BORRADOR : rough draft
minuto *nm* : minute — **minutero** *nm* : minute hand
mío, mía *adj* **1** : mine **2 una amiga mía** : a friend of mine — **~** *pron* **el mío, la mía** : mine, my own
miope *adj* : nearsighted
mirar *vt* **1** : look at **2** OBSERVAR : watch **3** CONSIDERAR : consider — *vi* **1** : look **2 ~ a** : face, overlook **3 ~ por** : look after — **mirarse** *vr* **1** : look at oneself **2** : look at each other — **mira** *nf* **1** : sight (of a firearm or instrument) **2** INTENCIÓN : aim, objective — **mirada** *nf* : look — **mirado, -da** *adj* **1** : careful **2** CONSIDERADO : considerate **3 bien ~** : well thought of — **mirador** *nm* **1** BALCÓN : balcony **2** : lookout, vantage point — **miramiento** *nm* : consideration
mirlo *nm* : blackbird
misa *nf* : Mass
miscelánea *nf* : miscellany
miserable *adj* **1** : poor **2** LASTIMOSO : miserable, wretched — **miseria** *nf* **1** : poverty **2** DESGRACIA : misfortune, misery
misericordia *nf* : mercy — **misericordioso, -sa** *adj* : merciful
mísero, -ra *adj* : wretched, miserable
misil *nm* : missile
misión *nf, pl* **-siones** : mission — **misionero, -ra** *adj & n* : missionary
mismo *adv* (*used for emphasis*) : right, exactly — **mismo, -ma** *adj* **1** : same **2** (*used for emphasis*) : very **3** : -self **4 por lo ~** : for that reason
misoginia *nf* : misogyny — **misógino** *nm* : misogynist
misterio *nm* : mystery — **misterioso, -sa** *adj* : mysterious
mística *nf* : mysticism — **místico, -ca** *adj* : mystic, mystical — **~** *n* : mystic
mitad *nf* **1** : half **2** MEDIO : middle
mítico, -ca *adj* : mythical, mythic
mitigar {52} *vt* : mitigate
mitin *nm, pl* **mítines** : (political) meeting

mito *nm* : myth — **mitología** *nm* : mythology — **mitológico, -ca** *adj* : mythological

mixto, -ta *adj* **1** : mixed, joint **2** : coeducational (of a school)

mnemónico, -ca *adj* : mnemonic

mobiliario *nm* : furniture

mocasín *nm, pl* **-sines** : moccasin

mochila *nf* : backpack, knapsack

moción *nf, pl* **-ciones** : motion

moco *nm* **1** : mucus **2 limpiarse los ~s** : wipe one's nose — **mocoso, -sa** *n fam* : kid, brat

moda *nf* **1** : fashion, style **2 a la ~** *or* **de ~** : in style, fashionable **3 ~ pasajera** : fad — **modal** *adj* : modal — **modales** *nmpl* : manners — **modalidad** *nf* : type, kind

modelar *vt* : model, mold — **modelo** *adj* : model — **~** *nm* : model, pattern — **~** *nmf* : model, mannequin

módem *or* **modem** [cmoðem] *nm* : modem

moderar *vt* **1** : moderate **2** : reduce (speed, etc.) **3** PRESIDIR : chair (a meeting) — **moderarse** *vr* : restrain oneself — **moderación** *nf, pl* **-ciones** : moderation — **moderado, -da** *adj* & *n* : moderate — **moderador, -dora** *n* : moderator, chairperson

moderno, -na *adj* : modern — **modernismo** *nm* : modernism — **modernizar** {21} *vt* : modernize

modesto, -ta *adj* : modest — **modestia** *nf* : modesty

modificar {72} *vt* : modify, alter — **modificación** *nf, pl* **-ciones** : alteration

modismo *nm* : idiom

modista *nmf* **1** : dressmaker **2** : (fashion) designer

modo *nm* **1** : way, manner **2** : mood (in grammar) **3** : mode (in music) **4 a ~ de** : by way of **5 de ~ que** : so (that) **6 de todos ~s** : in any case, anyway

modorra *nf* : drowsiness

modular *vt* : modulate — **modulación** *nf, pl* **-ciones** : modulation

módulo *nm* : module, unit

mofa *nf* : ridicule, mockery — **mofarse** *vr* **~ de** : make fun of

mofeta *nf* : skunk

moflete *nm fam* : fat cheek — **mofletudo, -da** *adj fam* : fat-cheeked, chubby

mohín *nm, pl* **-hines** : grimace — **mohino, -na** *adj* : sulky

moho *nm* **1** : mold, mildew **2** ÓXIDO : rust — **mohoso, -sa** *adj* **1** : moldy **2** OXIDADO : rusty

moisés *nm, pl* **-seses** : bassinet, cradle

mojar *vt* **1** : wet, moisten **2** : dunk (food) — **mojarse** *vr* : get wet — **mojado, -da** *adj* : wet, damp

mojigato, -ta *adj* : prudish — **~** *n* : prude

mojón *nm, pl* **-jones** : boundary stone, marker

molar *nm* : molar

moldear *vt* : mold, shape — **molde** *nm* : mold, form — **moldura** *nf* : molding

mole¹ *nf* : mass, bulk

mole² *nm* **1** : Mexican chili sauce **2** : meat served with mole

molécula *nf* : molecule — **molecular** *adj* : molecular

moler {47} *vt* : grind, crush

molestar *vt* **1** : annoy, bother **2 no ~** : do not disturb — *vi* : be a nuisance — **molestarse** *vr* **1** : bother **2** OFENDERSE : take offense — **molestia** *nf* **1** : annoyance, nuisance **2** MALESTAR : discomfort — **molesto, -ta** *adj* **1** : annoyed **2** FASTIDIOSO : annoying **3** INCÓMODO : in discomfort — **molestoso, -sa** *adj* : bothersome, annoying

molido, -da *adj* **1** : ground (of meat, etc.) **2** *fam* : worn out, exhausted

molino *nm* **1** : mill **2 ~ de viento** : windmill — **molinero, -ra** *n* : miller — **molinillo** *nm* : grinder, mill

mollera *nf* **1** : crown (of the head) **2** *fam* : brains *pl*

molusco *nm* : mollusk

momento *nm* **1** : moment, instant **2** : (period of) time **3** : momentum (in physics) **4 de ~** : for the moment **5 de un ~ a otro** : any time now — **momentáneamente** *adv* : momentarily — **momentáneo, -nea** *adj* **1** : momentary **2** PASAJERO : temporary

momia *nf* : mummy

monaguillo *nm* : altar boy

monarca *nmf* : monarch — **monarquía** *nf* : monarchy

monasterio *nm* : monastery — **monástico, -ca** *adj* : monastic

mondadientes *nms & pl* : toothpick

mondar *vt* : peel

mondongo *nm* : innards *pl*, guts *pl*

moneda *nf* **1** : coin **2** : currency (of a country) — **monedero** *nm* : change purse

monetario, -ria *adj* : monetary

monitor *nm* : monitor

monja *nf* : nun — **monje** *nm* : monk

mono, -na *n* : monkey — **~** *adj fam* : lovely, cute

monogamia *nf* : monogamy — **monógamo -ma** *adj* : monogamous

monografía *nf* : monograph

monograma *nm* : monogram

monolingüe *adj* : monolingual

monólogo *nm* : monologue

monopatín *nm, pl* **-tines** : scooter, skateboard

monopolio *nm* : monopoly — **monopolizar** {21} *vt* : monopolize

monosílabo *nm* : monosyllable — **monosilábico, -ca** *adj* : monosyllabic

monoteísmo *nm* : monotheism — **monoteísta** *adj* : monotheistic

monotonía *nf* : monotony — **monótono, -na** *adj* : monotonous

monóxido *nm* ~ **de carbono** : carbon monoxide

monstruo *nm* : monster — **monstruosidad** *nf* : monstrosity — **monstruoso, -sa** *adj* : monstrous

monta *nf* : importance, value

montaje *nm* **1** : assembly **2** : staging (in theater), editing (of films)

montaña *nf* **1** : mountain **2** ~ **rusa** : roller coaster — **montañero, -ra** *n* : mountain climber — **montañoso, -sa** *adj* : mountainous

montar *vt* **1** : mount **2** ESTABLECER : establish **3** ENSAMBLAR : assemble, put together **4** : stage (a performance) **5** : cock (a gun) — *vi* **1** ~ **a caballo** : ride horseback **2** ~ **en bicicleta** : get on a bicycle

monte *nm* **1** : mountain **2** BOSQUE : woodland **3** *or* ~ **bajo** : scrubland **4** ~ **de piedad** : pawnshop

montés *adj, pl* **-teses** : wild (of animals or plants)

montículo *nm* : mound, hillock

montón *nm, pl* **-tones 1** : heap, pile **2 un** ~ **de** *fam* : lots of

montura *nf* **1** : mount (horse) **2** SILLA : saddle **3** : frame (of glasses)

monumento *nm* : monument — **monumental** *adj fam* : monumental, huge

monzón *nm, pl* **-zones** : monsoon

moño *nm* **1** : bun (of hair) **2** *Lat* : bow (knot)

mora *nf* **1** : mulberry **2** ZARZAMORA : blackberry

morada *nf* : residence, dwelling

morado, -da *adj* : purple — **morado** *nm* : purple

moral *adj* : moral — ~ *nf* **1** : ethics, morals *pl* **2** ÁNIMO : morale — **moraleja** *nf* : moral (of a story) — **moralidad** *nf* : morality — **moralista** *adj* : moralistic — ~ *nmf* : moralist

morar *vi* : live, reside

morboso, -sa *adj* : morbid

mordaz *adj* : caustic, scathing — **mordacidad** *nf* : bite, sharpness

mordaza *nf* : gag

morder {47} *v* : bite — **mordedura** *nf* : bite (of an animal)

mordisquear *vt* : nibble (on) — **mordisco** *nm* : nibble, bite

moreno, -na *adj* **1** : dark-haired, brunette **2** : dark-skinned — ~ *n* **1** : brunette **2** : dark-skinned person

moretón *nm, pl* **-tones** : bruise

morfina *nf* : morphine

morir {46} *vi* **1** : die **2** APAGARSE : die out, go out — **morirse** *vr* **1** ~ **de** : die of **2** ~ **por** : be dying for — **moribundo, -da** *adj* : dying

moro, -ra *adj* : Moorish — ~ *n* : Moor

moroso, -sa *adj* : delinquent, in arrears — **morosidad** *nf* : delinquency (in payment)

morral *nm* : backpack

morriña *nf* : homesickness

morro *nm* : snout

morsa *nf* : walrus

morse *nm* : Morse code

mortaja *nf* : shroud

mortal *adj* **1** : mortal **2** : deadly (of a wound, an enemy, etc.) — ~ *nmf* : mortal — **mortalidad** *nf* : mortality — **mortandad** *nf* : death toll

mortero *nm* : mortar

mortífero, -ra *adj* : deadly, lethal

mortificar {72} *vt* **1** : mortify **2** ATORMENTAR : torment — **mortificarse** *vr* : be distressed

mosaico *nm* : mosaic

mosca *nf* : fly

moscada *adj* → **nuez**

mosquearse *vr fam* **1** : become suspicious **2** ENFADARSE : get annoyed

mosquito *nm* : mosquito — **mosquitero** *nm* **1** : (window) screen **2** : mosquito net

mostachón *nm, pl* **-chones** : macaroon

mostaza *nf* : mustard

mostrador *nm* : counter (in a store)

mostrar {19} *vt* : show — **mostrarse** *vr* : show oneself, appear

mota *nf* **1** : spot, speck — **moteado, -da** *adj* : speckled, spotted

mote *nm* : nickname

motel *nm* : motel

motín *nm, pl* **-tines 1** : riot, uprising **2** : mutiny (of troops)

motivo *nm* **1** : motive, cause **2** : motif (in art, music, etc.) — **motivación** *nf, pl* **-ciones** : motivation — **motivar** *vt* **1** : cause **2** IMPULSAR : motivate

moto *nf* : motorcycle, motorbike — **motocicleta** *nf* : motorcycle — **motociclista** *nmf* : motorcyclist

motor, -triz *or* **-tora** *adj* : motor — **motor** *nm* : motor, engine — **motorista** *nmf* **1** : motorcyclist **2** *Lat* : motorist

mover {47} *vt* **1** : move, shift **2** : shake (the head) **3** PROVOCAR : provoke — **moverse** *vr* **1** : move (over) **2** APRESURARSE : get a move on — **movedizo, -za** adj : movable, shifting — **movible** adj : movable

móvil adj : mobile — **~** nm **1** MOTIVO : motive **2** : mobile — **movilidad** nf : mobility — **movilizar** {21} vt : mobilize

movimiento nm **1** : movement, motion **2** **~ sindicalista** : labor movement

mozo, -za adj : young — **~** n **1** : young man m, young woman f **2** Lat : waiter m, waitress f

muchacho, -cha n : kid, boy m, girl f

muchedumbre nf : crowd

mucho adv **1** : very much, a lot **2** : long, a long time — **mucho, -cha** adj **1** : a lot of, many, much **2 muchas veces** : often — **~** pron : a lot, many, much

mucosidad nf : mucus

muda nf **1** : molting (of animals) **2** : change (of clothing) — **mudanza** nf **1** : change **2** TRASLADO : move, change of residence — **mudar** v **1** : molt, shed **2** CAMBIAR : change — **mudarse** vr **1** : change (one's clothes) **2** TRASLADARSE : move (one's residence)

mudo, -da adj **1** : mute **2** SILENCIOSO : silent

mueble nm **1** : piece of furniture **2** **~s** nmpl : furniture, furnishings

mueca nf **1** : grimace, face **2 hacer ~s** : makes faces

muela nf **1** : tooth, molar **2 ~ de juicio** : wisdom tooth

muelle adj : soft — **~** nm **1** : wharf, jetty **2** RESORTE : spring

muérdago nm : mistletoe

muerte nf : death — **muerto, -ta** adj **1** : dead **2** : dull (of colors, etc.) — **~** nm : dead person, deceased

muesca nf : nick, notch

muestra nf **1** : sample **2** SEÑAL : sign, show

mugir {35} vi : moo, bellow — **mugido** nm : mooing, bellowing

mugre nf : grime, filth — **mugriento, -ta** adj : filthy, grimy

muguete nm : lily of the valley

mujer nf **1** : woman **2** ESPOSA : wife **3 ~ de negocios** : businesswoman

mulato, -ta adj & n : mulatto

muleta nf **1** : crutch **2** APOYO : prop, support

mullido, -da adj : soft, spongy

mulo, -la n : mule

multa nf : fine — **multar** vt : fine

multicolor adj : multicolored

multicultural adj : multicultural

multimedia adj : multimedia

multinacional adj : multinational

multiplicar {72} v : multiply — **multiplicarse** vr : multiply, reproduce — **múltiple** adj : multiple — **multiplicación** nf, pl **-ciones** : multiplication — **múltiplo** nm : multiple

multitud nf : crowd, multitude

mundo nm **1** : world **2 todo el ~** : everyone, everybody — **mundanal** adj : worldly — **mundano, -na** adj **1** : worldly, earthly **2 la vida mundana** : high society — **mundial** adj : world, worldwide

municiones nfpl : ammunition

municipal adj : municipal — **municipio** nm **1** : municipality **2** AYUNTAMIENTO : town council

muñeca nf **1** : doll **2** : wrist (in anatomy) — **muñeco** nm **1** : boy doll **2** MANIQUÍ : dummy, puppet

muñon nm, pl **-ñones** : stump (of an arm or leg)

mural adj & nm : mural — **muralla** nf : wall, rampart

murciélago nm : bat (animal)

murmullo nm **1** : murmur, murmuring **2** : rustling (of leaves, etc.)

murmurar vi **1** : murmur, whisper **2** CRITICAR : gossip

muro nm : wall

musa nf : muse

musaraña nf : shrew

músculo nm : muscle — **muscular** adj : muscular — **musculatura** nf : muscles pl — **musculoso, -sa** adj : muscular

muselina nf : muslin

museo nm : museum

musgo nm : moss — **musgoso, -sa** adj : mossy

música nf : music — **musical** adj : musical — **músico, -ca** adj : musical — **~** n : musician

musitar vt : mumble

muslo nm : thigh

musulmán, -mana adj & n, mpl **-manes** : Muslim

mutar v : mutate — **mutación** nf, pl **-ciones** : mutation — **mutante** adj & nmf : mutant

mutilar vt : mutilate — **mutilación** nf, pl **-ciones** : mutilation

mutuo, -tua adj : mutual

muy adv **1** : very, quite **2** DEMASIADO : too

N

n *nf* : n, 14th letter of the Spanish alphabet

nabo *nm* : turnip

nácar *nm* : mother-of-pearl

nacer {48} *vi* **1** : be born **2** : hatch (of an egg), sprout (of a plant) **3** SURGIR : arise, spring up — **nacido, -da** *adj & n* **recién ~** : newborn — **naciente** *adj* **1** : new, growing **2** : rising (of the sun) — **nacimiento** *nm* **1** : birth **2** : source (of a river) **3** ORIGEN : beginning **4** BELÉN : Nativity scene

nación *nf, pl* **-ciones** : nation, country — **nacional** *adj* : national — **~** *nmf* : national, citizen — **nacionalidad** *nf* : nationality — **nacionalismo** *nm* : nationalism — **nacionalista** *adj & nmf* : nationalist — **nacionalizar** {21} *vt* **1** : nationalize **2** : naturalize (as a citizen) — **nacionalizarse** *vr* : become naturalized

nada *pron* **1** : nothing **2 de ~** : you're welcome **3 ~ más** : nothing else, nothing more — **~** *adv* : not at all — **~** *nf* **la ~** : nothingness

nadar *v* : swim — **nadador, -dora** *n* : swimmer

nadería *nf* : small thing, trifle

nadie *pron* : nobody, no one

nado: a ~ *adv phr* : swimming

nafta *nf Lat* : gasoline

naipe *nm* : playing card

nalgas *nfpl* : buttocks, bottom

nana *nf* : lullaby

naranja *adj & nm* : orange (color) — **~** *nf* : orange (fruit) — **naranjal** *nm* : orange grove — **naranjo** *nm* : orange tree

narciso *nm* : narcissus, daffodil

narcótico, -ca *adj* : narcotic — **narcótico** *nm* : narcotic — **narcotizar** {21} *vt* : drug — **narcotraficante** *nmf* : drug trafficker — **narcotráfico** *nm* : drug trafficking

nariz *nf, pl* **-rices** **1** : nose **2** OLFATO : sense of smell **3 narices** *nfpl* : nostrils

narrar *vt* : narrate, tell — **narración** *nf, pl* **-ciones** : narration — **narrador, -dora** *n* : narrator — **narrativa** *nf* : narrative, storytelling

nasal *adj* : nasal

nata *nf Spain* : cream

natación *nf, pl* **-ciones** : swimming

natal *adj* : native, birth — **natalicio** *nm* : birthday — **natalidad** *nf* : birthrate

natillas *nfpl* : custard

natividad *nf* : birth, nativity

nativo, -va *adj & n* : native

natural *adj* **1** : natural **2** NORMAL : normal **3 ~ de** : native of, from — **~** *nm* **1** : temperament **2** NATIVO : native — **naturaleza** *nf* : nature — **naturalidad** *nf* : naturalness — **naturalista** *adj* : naturalistic — **naturalización** *nf, pl* **-ciones** : naturalization — **naturalizar** {21} *vt* : naturalize — **naturalizarse** *vr* : become naturalized — **naturalmente** *adv* **1** : naturally **2** POR SUPUESTO : of course

naufragar {52} *vi* **1** : be shipwrecked **2** FRACASAR : fail — **naufragio** *nm* : shipwreck — **náufrago, -ga** *adj* : shipwrecked — **~** *n* : castaway

náusea *nf* **1** : nausea **2 dar ~s** : nauseate **3 ~s matutinas** : morning sickness — **nauseabundo, -da** *adj* : nauseating

náutico, -ca *adj* : nautical

navaja *nf* : pocketknife, penknife

naval *adj* : naval

nave *nf* **1** : ship **2** : nave (of a church) **3 ~ espacial** : spaceship

navegar {52} *v* : navigate, sail — **navegable** *adj* : navigable — **navegación** *nf, pl* **-ciones** : navigation — **navegante** *adj* : sailing, seafaring — **~** *nmf* : navigator

Navidad *nf* **1** : Christmas **2 feliz ~** : Merry Christmas — **navideño, -ña** *adj* : Christmas

naviero, -ra *adj* : shipping

nazi *adj & nmf* : Nazi — **nazismo** *nm* : Nazism

neblina *nf* : mist

nebuloso, -sa *adj* **1** : hazy, misty, foggy **2** VAGO : vague, nebulous

necedad *nf* **1** : stupidity **2 decir ~es** : talk nonsense

necesario, -ria *adj* : necessary — **necesariamente** *adv* : necessarily — **necesidad** *nf* **1** : need, necessity **2** POBREZA : poverty **3 ~es** *nfpl* : hardships — **necesitado, -da** *adj* : needy — **necesitar** *vt* : need — *vi* **~ de** : have need of

necio, -cia *adj* : silly, dumb

necrología *nf* : obituary

néctar *nm* : nectar

nectarina *nf* : nectarine

neerlandés, -desa *adj, mpl* **-deses** : Dutch — **neerlandés** *nm* : Dutch (language)

nefasto, -ta *adj* **1** : ill-fated **2** *fam* : terrible, awful

negar {49} *vt* **1** : deny **2** REHUSAR : refuse **3** : disown (a person) — **negarse** *vr* : refuse — **negación** *nf, pl* **-ciones** **1** : denial **2** : negative (in grammar) — **negativa** *nf* **1** : denial **2** RECHAZO : refusal — **negativo,**

-va *adj* : negative — **negativo** *nm* : negative (of a photograph)

negligente *adj* : negligent — **negligencia** *nf* : negligence

negociar *vt* : negotiate — *vi* : deal, do business — **negociable** *adj* : negotiable — **negociación** *nf, pl* **-ciones** : negotiation — **negociante** *nmf* : businessman *m*, businesswoman *f* — **negocio** *nm* **1** : business **2** TRANSACCIÓN : deal **3 ~s** : business, commerce

negro, -gra *adj* : black, dark — **~** *n* : dark-skinned person — **negro** *nm* : black (color) — **negrura** *nf* : blackness — **negruzco, -ca** *adj* : blackish

nene, -na *n fam* : baby, small child

nenúfar *nm* : water lily

neón *nm* : neon

neoyorquino, -na *adj* : of or from New York

nepotismo *nm* : nepotism

Neptuno *nm* : Neptune

nervio *nm* **1** : nerve **2** : sinew (in meat) **3** VIGOR : vigor, energy **4 tener ~s** : be nervous — **nerviosismo** *nf* : nervousness — **nervioso, -sa** *adj* **1** : nervous, anxious **2 sistema nervioso** : nervous system

nervudo, -da *adj* : sinewy

neto, -ta *adj* **1** : clear, distinct **2** : net (of weight, salaries, etc.)

neumático *nm* : tire

neumonía *nf* : pneumonia

neurología *nf* : neurology — **neurológico, -ca** *adj* : neurological, neurologic — **neurólogo, -ga** *n* : neurologist

neurosis *nfs & pl* : neurosis — **neurótico, -ca** *adj & n* : neurotic

neutral *adj* : neutral — **neutralidad** *nf* : neutrality — **neutralizar** {21} *vt* : neutralize — **neutro, -tra** *adj* **1** : neutral **2** : neuter (in biology and grammar)

neutrón *nm, pl* **-trones** : neutron

nevar {55} *v impers* : snow — **nevada** *nf* : snowfall — **nevado, -da** *adj* **1** : snow-covered, snowy **2** : snow-white — **nevasca** *nf* : snowstorm

nevera *nf* : refrigerator

nevisca *nf* : light snowfall, flurry

nexo *nm* : link, connection

ni *conj* **1** : neither, nor **2 ~ que** : as if **3 ~ siquiera** : not even

nicaragüense *adj* : Nicaraguan

nicho *nm* : niche

nicotina *nf* : nicotine

nidada *nf* : brood (of chicks, etc.)

nido *nm* **1** : nest **2** GUARIDA : hiding place, den

niebla *nf* : fog, mist

nieto, -ta *n* **1** : grandson *m*, granddaughter *f* **2 nietos** *nmpl* : grandchildren

nieve *nf* : snow

nigeriano, -na *adj* : Nigerian

nilón or **nilon** *nm, pl* **-lones** : nylon

nimio, -mia *adj* : insignificant, trivial — **nimiedad** *nf* **1** : trifle **2** INSIGNIFICANCIA : triviality

ninfa *nf* : nymph

ninguno, -na (**ningún** *before masculine singular nouns*) *adj* : no, not any — **~** *pron* **1** : neither, none **2** : no one, nobody

niña *nf* **1** : pupil (of the eye) **2 la ~ de los ojos** : the apple of one's eye

niño, -ña *n* : child, boy *m*, girl *f* — **~** *adj* **1** : young **2** INFANTIL : immature, childish — **niñero, -ra** *n* : baby-sitter, nanny — **niñez** *nf, pl* **-ñeces** : childhood

nipón, -pona *adj* : Japanese

níquel *nm* : nickel

nítido, -da *adj* : clear, sharp — **nitidez** *nf, pl* **-deces** : clarity, sharpness

nitrato *nm* : nitrate

nitrógeno *nm* : nitrogen

nivel *nm* **1** : level, height **2 ~ de vida** : standard of living — **nivelar** *vt* : level (out)

no *adv* **1** : not **2** (*in answer to a question*) : no **3 ¡como ~!** : of course! **4 ~ bien** : as soon as **5 ~ fumador** : non-smoker — **~** *nm* : no

noble *adj & nmf* : noble — **nobleza** *nf* : nobility

noche *nf* **1** : night, evening **2 buenas ~s** : good evening, good night **3 de ~** *or* **por la ~** : at night **4 hacerse de ~** : get dark — **Nochebuena** *nf* : Christmas Eve — **nochecita** *nf* : dusk — **Nochevieja** *nf* : New Year's Eve

noción *nf, pl* **-ciones 1** : notion, concept **2 nociones** *nfpl* : rudiments

nocivo, -va *adj* : harmful, noxious

nocturno, -na *adj* **1** : night **2** : nocturnal (of animals, etc.) — **nocturno** *nm* : nocturne

nogal *nm* **1** : walnut tree **2 ~ americano** : hickory

nómada *nmf* : nomad — **~** *adj* : nomadic

nomás *adv Lat* : only, just

nombrar *vt* **1** : appoint **2** CITAR : mention — **nombrado, -da** *adj* : famous, well-known — **nombramiento** *nm* : appointment, nomination — **nombre** *nm* **1** : name **2** SUSTANTIVO : noun **3** FAMA : fame, renown **4 ~ de pila** : first name

nómina *nf* : payroll

nominal *adj* : nominal

nominar *vt* : nominate — **nominación** *nf, pl* **-ciones** : nomination

nomo *nm* : gnome

non *adj* : odd, not even — **~** *nm* : odd number

nonagésimo, -ma *adj & n* : ninetieth

nopal *nm* : nopal, prickly pear

nordeste *or* **noreste** *adj* **1** : northeastern **2** : northeasterly (of wind, etc.) — **~** *nm* : northeast

nórdico, -ca *adj* : Scandinavian

noreste → **nordeste**

noria *nf* **1** : waterwheel **2** : Ferris wheel (at a fair, etc.)

norma *nf* : rule, norm, standard — **normal** *adj* **1** : normal **2 escuela ~** : teacher-training college — **normalidad** *nf* : normality — **normalizar** {21} *vt* **1** : normalize **2** ESTANDARIZAR : standardize — **normalizarse** *vr* : return to normal — **normalmente** *adv* : ordinarily, generally

noroeste *adj* **1** : northwestern **2** : northwesterly (of wind, etc.) — **~** *nm* : northwest

norte *adj* : north, northern — **~** *nm* **1** : north **2** : north wind

norteamericano, -na *adj* : North American

norteño, -ña *adj* : northern

noruego, -ga *adj* : Norwegian — **noruego** *nm* : Norwegian (language)

nos *pron* **1** (*direct object*) : us **2** (*indirect object*) : to us, for us, from us **3** (*reflexive*) : ourselves **4** : each other, one another

nosotros, -tras *pron* **1** (*subject*) : we **2** (*object*) : us **3** *or* **~ mismos** : ourselves

nostalgia *nf* **1** : nostalgia **2 sentir ~ por** : be homesick for — **nostálgico, -ca** *adj* : nostalgic

nota *nf* **1** : note **2** : grade, mark (in school) **3** CUENTA : bill, check — **notable** *adj* : noteworthy, notable — **notar** *vt* : notice — **notarse** *vr* : be evident, seem

notario, -ria *n* : notary (public)

noticia *nf* **1** : news item, piece of news **2 ~s** *nfpl* : news — **noticiario** *nm* : newscast — **noticiero** *nm Lat* : newscast

notificar {72} *vt* : notify — **notificación** *nf, pl* **-ciones** : notification

notorio, -ria *adj* **1** : obvious **2** CONOCIDO : well-known — **notoriedad** *nf* : fame, notoriety

novato, -ta *adj* : inexperienced — **~** *n* : beginner, novice

novecientos, -tas *adj* : nine hundred — **novecientos** *nms & pl* : nine hundred

novedad *nf* **1** : newness, innovation **2** NOTICIAS : news **3 ~es** : novelties, latest news — **novedoso, -sa** *adj* : original, novel

novela *nf* **1** : novel **2** : soap opera (on television) — **novelesco, -ca** *adj* : fictional **2** FANTÁSTICO : fabulous — **novelista** *nmf* : novelist

noveno, -na *adj* : ninth — **noveno** *nm* : ninth

noventa *adj & nm* : ninety — **noventavo,**

-va *adj* : ninetieth — **noventavo** *nm* : ninetieth

novia → **novio**

noviazgo *nm* : engagement

novicio, -cia *n* : novice

noviembre *nm* : November

novillo, -lla *n* : young bull *m*, heifer *f*

novio, -via *n* **1** : boyfriend *m*, girlfriend *f* **2** PROMETIDO : fiancé *m*, fiancée *f* **3** : bridegroom *m*, bride *f* (at a wedding)

novocaína *nf* : novocaine

nube *nf* : cloud — **nubarrón** *nm, pl* **-rrones** : storm cloud — **nublado, -da** *adj* **1** : cloudy **2** ENTURBIADO : clouded, dim — **nublado** *nm* : storm cloud — **nublar** *vt* **1** : cloud **2** OSCURECER : obscure — **nublarse** *vr* : get cloudy — **nuboso, -sa** *adj* : cloudy

nuca *nf* : nape, back of the neck

núcleo *nm* **1** : nucleus **2** CENTRO : center, core — **nuclear** *adj* : nuclear

nudillo *nm* : knuckle

nudismo *nm* : nudism — **nudista** *adj & nmf* : nudist

nudo *nm* **1** : knot **2** : crux, heart (of a problem, etc.) — **nudoso, -sa** *adj* : knotty, gnarled

nuera *nf* : daughter-in-law

nuestro, -tra *adj* : our — **~** *pron* (*with definite article*) : ours, our own

nuevamente *adv* : again, anew

nueve *adj & nm* : nine

nuevo, -va *adj* **1** : new **2 de nuevo** : again, once more

nuez *nf, pl* **nueces 1** : nut **2** *or* **~ de nogal** : walnut **3 ~ de Adán** : Adam's apple **4 ~ moscada** : nutmeg

nulo, -la *adj* **1** *or* **~ y sin efecto** : null and void **2** INCAPAZ : useless, inept — **nulidad** *nf* **1** : nullity **2 es una ~** *fam* : he's a total loss

numerar *vt* : number — **numeración** *nf, pl* **-ciones 1** : numbering **2** NÚMEROS : numbers *pl*, numerals *pl* — **numeral** *adj* : numeral — **número** *nm* **1** : number, numeral **2** : issue (of a publication) **3 sin ~** : countless — **numérico, -ca** *adj* : numerical — **numeroso, -sa** *adj* : numerous

nunca *adv* **1** : never, ever **2 ~ más** : never again **3 ~ jamás** : never ever

nupcial *adj* : nuptial, wedding — **nupcias** *nfpl* : nuptials, wedding

nutria *nf* : otter

nutrir *vt* **1** ALIMENTAR : feed, nourish **2** FOMENTAR : fuel, foster — **nutrición** *nf, pl* **-ciones** : nutrition — **nutrido, -da** *adj* **1** : nourished **2** ABUNDANTE : considerable, abundant — **nutriente** *nm* : nutrient — **nutritivo, -va** *adj* : nourishing, nutritious

O

o¹ *nf* : o, 16th letter of the Spanish alphabet

o² *conj* (**u** *before words beginning with o- or ho-*) **1** : or, either **2 ~ sea** : in other words

oasis *nms & pl* : oasis

obcecar {72} *vt* : blind (by emotions) — **obcecarse** *vr* : become stubborn

obedecer {53} *vt* : obey — *vi* **1** : obey **2 ~ a** : respond to **3 ~ a** : be due to — **obediencia** *nf* : obedience — **obediente** *adj* : obedient

obertura *nf* : overture

obeso, -sa *adj* : obese — **obesidad** *nf* : obesity

obispo *nm* : bishop

objetar *v* : object — **objeción** *nf, pl* **-ciones** : objection

objeto *nm* : object — **objetivo, -va** *adj* : objective — **objetivo** *nm* **1** : objective, goal **2** : lens (in photography, etc.)

objetor, -tora *n* **~ de conciencia** : conscientious objector

oblicuo, -cua *adj* : oblique

obligar {52} *vt* : require, oblige — **obligarse** *vr* : commit oneself (to do something) — **obligación** *nf, pl* **-ciones** : obligation — **obligado, -da** *adj* **1** : obliged **2** FORZOSO : obligatory — **obligatorio, -ria** *adj* : mandatory

oblongo, -ga *adj* : oblong

oboe *nm* : oboe — **~** *nmf* : oboist

obra *nf* **1** : work, deed **2** : work (of art, literature, etc.) **3** CONSTRUCCIÓN : construction work **4 ~ maestra** : masterpiece **5 ~s públicas** : public works — **obrar** *vt* : work, produce — *vi* : act, behave — **obrero, -ra** *adj* **la clase obrera** : the working class — **~** *n* : worker, laborer

obsceno, -na *adj* : obscene — **obscenidad** *nf* : obscenity

obsequiar *vt* : give, present — **obsequio** *nm* : gift, present

observar *vt* **1** : observe, watch **2** ADVERTIR : notice **3** ACATAR : observe, obey **4** COMENTAR : remark — **observación** *nf, pl* **-ciones** : observation — **observador, -dora** *adj* : observant — **~** *n* : observer — **observancia** *nf* : observance — **observatorio** *nm* : observatory

obsesionar *vt* : obsess — **obsesionarse** *vr* : be obsessed — **obsesión** *nf, pl* **-siones** : obsession — **obsesivo, -va** *adj* : obsessive — **obseso, -sa** *adj* : obsessed

obsoleto, -ta *adj* : obsolete

obstaculizar {21} *vt* : hinder — **obstáculo** *nm* : obstacle

obstante: **no ~** *conj phr* : nevertheless, however — **~** *prep phr* : in spite of, despite

obstar {21} *vi* **~ a** *or* **~ para** : stop, prevent

obstetricia *nf* : obstetrics — **obstetra** *nmf* : obstetrician

obstinarse *vr* : be stubborn — **obstinado, -da** *adj* **1** : obstinate, stubborn **2** TENAZ : persistent

obstruir {41} *vt* : obstruct — **obstrucción** *nf, pl* **-ciones** : obstruction

obtener {80} *vt* : obtain, get

obtuso, -sa *adj* : obtuse

obviar *vt* : get around, avoid

obvio, -via *adj* : obvious — **obviamente** *adv* : obviously, clearly

oca *nf* : goose

ocasión *nf, pl* **-siones** **1** : occasion **2** OPORTUNIDAD : opportunity **3** GANGA : bargain — **ocasional** *adj* **1** : occasional **2** ACCIDENTAL : accidental, chance — **ocasionar** *vt* : cause

ocaso *nm* **1** : sunset **2** DECADENCIA : decline

occidente *nm* **1** : west **2 el Occidente** : the West — **occidental** *adj* : western, Western

océano *nm* : ocean — **oceanografía** *nf* : oceanography

ochenta *adj & nm* : eighty

ocho *adj & nm* : eight — **ochocientos, -tas** *adj* : eight hundred — **ochocientos** *nms & pl* : eight hundred

ocio *nm* **1** : free time, leisure **2** INACTIVIDAD : idleness — **ociosidad** *nf* : idleness, inactivity — **ocioso, -sa** *adj* **1** : idle, inactive **2** INÚTIL : useless

ocre *adj & nm* : ocher

octágono *nm* : octagon — **octagonal** *adj* : octagonal

octava *nf* : octave

octavo, -va *adj & n* : eighth

octeto *nm* : byte

octogésimo, -ma *adj & n* : eightieth

octubre *nm* : October

ocular *adj* : ocular, eye — **oculista** *nmf* : ophthalmologist

ocultar *vt* : conceal, hide — **ocultarse** *vr* : hide — **oculto, -ta** *adj* : hidden, occult

ocupar *vt* **1** : occupy **2** : hold (a position, etc.) **3** : provide work for — **ocuparse** *vr* **1 ~ de** : concern oneself with **2 ~ de** : take care of (children, etc.) — **ocupación** *nf, pl*

-ciones 1 : occupation **2** EMPLEO : job — **ocupado, -da** *adj* **1 :** busy **2 :** occupied (of a place) **3 señal de occupado :** busy signal — **ocupante** *nmf* : occupant

ocurrir *vi* : occur, happen — **ocurrirse** *vr* ~ **a :** occur to — **ocurrencia** *nf* **1 :** occurrence, event **2** SALIDA : witty remark, quip

oda *nf* : ode

odiar *vt* : hate — **odio** *nm* : hatred — **odioso, -sa** *adj* : hateful

odisea *nf* : odyssey

odontología *nf* : dentistry, dental surgery — **odontólogo, -ga** *n* : dentist, dental surgeon

oeste *adj* : west, western — ~ *nm* **1 :** west **2 el Oeste :** the West

ofender *v* : offend — **ofenderse** *vr* : take offense — **ofensa** *nf* : offense, insult — **ofensiva** *nf* : offensive — **ofensivo, -va** *adj* : offensive

oferta *nf* **1 :** offer **2 de** ~ **:** on sale **3** ~ **y demanda :** supply and demand

oficial *adj* : official — ~ *nmf* **1 :** skilled worker **2 :** officer (in the military)

oficina *nf* : office — **oficinista** *nmf* : office worker

oficio *nm* : trade, profession — **oficioso, -sa** *adj* : unofficial

ofrecer {53} *vt* **1 :** offer **2 :** provide, present (an opportunity, etc.) — **ofrecerse** *vr* : volunteer — **ofrecimiento** *nm* : offer

ofrenda *nf* : offering

oftalmología *nf* : ophthalmology — **oftalmólogo, -ga** *n* : ophthalmologist

ofuscar {72} *vt* **1 :** blind, dazzle **2** CONFUNDIR : confuse — **ofuscarse** *vr* ~ **con** : be blinded by — **ofuscación** *nf, pl* **-ciones 1 :** blindness **2** CONFUSIÓN : confusion

ogro *nm* : ogre

oír {50} *vi* : hear — *vt* **1 :** hear **2** ESCUCHAR : listen to **3 ¡oiga!** *or* **¡oye! :** excuse me!, listen! — **oídas : de** ~ *adv phr* : by hearsay — **oído** *nm* **1 :** ear **2 :** (sense of) hearing **3 duro de** ~ **:** hard of hearing

ojal *nm* : buttonhole

ojalá *interj* : I hope so!, if only!

ojear *vt* : eye, look at — **ojeada** *nf* : glimpse, glance

ojeriza *nf* **1 :** ill will **2 tener** ~ **a :** have a grudge against

ojo *nm* **1 :** eye **2** PERSPICACIA : shrewdness **3 :** span (of a bridge) **4 ¡**~**! :** look out!, pay attention!

ola *nf* : wave — **oleada** *nf* : wave, surge — **oleaje** *nm* : swell (of the sea)

olé *interj* : bravo!

oleada *nf* : wave, swell — **oleaje** *nm* : waves *pl*, surf

óleo *nm* **1 :** oil **2** CUADRO : oil painting — **oleoducto** *nm* : oil pipeline

oler {51} *vt* : smell — *vi* **1 :** smell **2** ~ **a** : smell of — **olerse** *vr fam* : have a hunch about

olfatear *vt* **1 :** sniff **2** OLER : sense, sniff out — **olfato** *nm* **1 :** sense of smell **2** PERSPICACIA : nose, instinct

Olimpiada *or* **Olimpíada** *nf* : Olympics *pl*, Olympic Games *pl* — **olímpico, -ca** *adj* : Olympic

oliva *nf* : olive — **olivo** *nm* : olive tree

olla *nf* **1 :** pot **2** ~ **podrida :** (Spanish) stew

olmo *nm* : elm

olor *nm* : smell — **oloroso, -sa** *adj* : fragrant

olvidar *vt* **1 :** forget **2** DEJAR : leave (behind) — **olvidarse** *vr* : forget — **olvidadizo, -za** *adj* : forgetful — **olvido** *nm* **1 :** forgetfulness **2** DESCUIDO : oversight

ombligo *nm* : navel

omelette *nmf Lat* : omelet

ominoso, -sa *adj* : ominous

omitir *vt* : omit — **omisión** *nf, pl* **-siones** : omission

ómnibus *nm, pl* **-bus** *or* **-buses** : bus

omnipotente *adj* : omnipotent

omóplato *or* **omoplato** *nm* : shoulder blade

once *adj & nm* : eleven — **onceavo, -va** *adj & n* : eleventh

onda *nf* : wave — **ondear** *vi* : ripple — **ondulación** *nf, pl* **-ciones** : undulation — **ondulado, -da** *adj* : wavy — **ondular** *vt* : wave (hair) — *vi* : undulate, ripple

ónice *nmf or* **ónix** *nm* : onyx

onza *nf* : ounce

opaco, -ca *adj* **1 :** opaque **2** DESLUSTRADO : dull

ópalo *nm* : opal

opción *nf, pl* **-ciones** : option — **opcional** *adj* : optional

ópera *nf* : opera

operar *vt* **1 :** operate on **2** *Lat* : operate, run (a machine) — *vi* **1 :** operate **2** NEGOCIAR : deal, do business — **operarse** *vr* **1 :** have an operation **2** OCURRIR : take place — **operación** *nf, pl* **-ciones 1 :** operation **2** TRANSACCIÓN : transaction, deal — **operacional** *adj* : operational — **operador, -dora** *n* **1 :** operator **2 :** cameraman (for television, etc.)

opereta *nf* : operetta

opinar *vt* : think — *vi* : express an opinion — **opinión** *nf, pl* **-niones** : opinion

opio *nm* : opium

oponer {60} *vt* **1 :** raise, put forward (arguments, etc.) **2** ~ **resistencia :** put up a fight — **oponerse** *vr* ~ **a** : oppose, be against — **oponente** *nmf* : opponent

oporto *nm* : port (wine)
oportunidad *nf* : opportunity — **oportunista** *nmf* : opportunist — **oportuno, -na** *adj* **1** : opportune, timely **2** APROPIADO : suitable
opositor, -tora *n* **1** : opponent **2** : candidate (for a position) — **oposición** *nf, pl* **-ciones** : opposition
oprimir *vt* **1** : press, squeeze **2** TIRANIZAR : oppress — **opresión** *nf, pl* **-siones 1** : oppression **2** ~ **de pecho** : tightness in the chest — **opresivo, -va** *adj* : oppressive — **opresor, -sora** *n* : oppressor
optar *vi* **1** ~ **a** : apply for **2** ~ **por** : choose, opt for
óptica *nf* **1** : optics **2** : optician's (shop) — **óptico, -ca** *adj* : optical — ~ *n* : optician
optimismo *nm* : optimism — **optimista** *adj* : optimistic — ~ *nmf* : optimist
optometría *nf* : optometry — **optometrista** *nmf* : optometrist
opuesto *adj* **1** : opposite **2** CONTRADICTORIO : opposed, conflicting
opulencia *nf* : opulence — **opulento, -ta** *adj* : opulent
oración *nf, pl* **-ciones 1** : prayer **2** FRASE : sentence, clause
oráculo *nm* : oracle
orador, -dora *n* : speaker
oral *adj* : oral
orar *vi* : pray
órbita *nf* **1** : orbit (in astronomy) **2** : eye socket — **orbitar** *vi* : orbit
orden *nm, pl* **órdenes 1** : order **2** ~ **del día** : agenda (at a meeting) **3** ~ **público** : law and order — ~ *nf, pl* **órdenes 1** : order (of food) **2** ~ **religiosa** : religious order **3** ~ **de compra** : purchase order
ordenador *nm Spain* : computer
ordenar *vt* **1** : order, command **2** ARREGLAR : put in order **3** : ordain (a priest) — **ordenanza** *nm* : orderly (in the armed forces) — ~ *nf* : ordinance, regulation
ordeñar *vt* : milk
ordinal *adj & nm* : ordinal
ordinario, -ria *adj* **1** : ordinary **2** GROSERO : common, vulgar
orear *vt* : air
orégano *nm* : oregano
oreja *nf* : ear
orfanato *or* **orfelinato** *nm* : orphanage
orfebre *nmf* : goldsmith, silversmith
orgánico, -ca *adj* : organic
organigrama *nm* : flowchart
organismo *nm* **1** : organism **2** ORGANIZACIÓN : agency, organization
organista *nmf* : organist
organizar {21} *vt* : organize — **organizarse** *vr* : get organized — **organización** *nf, pl*

-ciones : organization — **organizador, -dora** *n* : organizer
órgano *nm* : organ
orgasmo *nm* : orgasm
orgía *nf* : orgy
orgullo *nm* : pride — **orgulloso, -sa** *adj* : proud
orientación *nf, pl* **-ciones 1** : orientation **2** DIRECCIÓN : direction **3** CONSEJO : guidance
oriental *adj* **1** : eastern **2** : oriental — ~ *nmf* : Oriental
orientar *vt* **1** : orient, position **2** GUIAR : guide, direct — **orientarse** *vr* **1** : orient oneself **2** ~ **hacia** : turn towards
oriente *nm* **1** : east, East **2 el Oriente** : the Orient
orificio *nm* : orifice, opening
origen *nm, pl* **orígenes** : origin — **original** *adj & nm* : original — **originalidad** *nf* : originality — **originar** *vt* : give rise to — **originarse** *vr* : originate, arise — **originario, -ria** *adj* ~ **de** : native of
orilla *nf* **1** : border, edge **2** : bank (of a river), shore (of the sea)
orinar *vi* : urinate — **orina** *nf* : urine
oriol *nm* : oriole
oriundo, -da *adj* ~ **de** : native of
orla *nf* : border
ornamental *adj* : ornamental — **ornamento** *nm* : ornament
ornar *vt* : adorn
ornitología *nf* : ornithology
oro *nm* : gold
orquesta *nf* : orchestra — **orquestar** *vt* : orchestrate
orquídea *nf* : orchid
ortiga *nf* : nettle
ortodoxia *nf* : orthodoxy — **ortodoxo, -xa** *adj* : orthodox
ortografía *nf* : spelling
ortopedia *nf* : orthopedics — **ortopédico, -ca** *adj* : orthopedic
oruga *nf* : caterpillar
orzuelo *nm* : sty (in the eye)
os *pron pl Spain* **1** (*direct or indirect object*) : you, to you **2** (*reflexive*) : yourselves, to yourselves **3** : each other, to each other
osado, -da *adj* : bold, daring — **osadía** *nf* **1** : boldness, daring **2** DESCARO : audacity, nerve
osamenta *nf* : skeleton
osar *vi* : dare
oscilar *vi* **1** : swing, sway **2** FLUCTUAR : fluctuate — **oscilación** *nf, pl* **-ciones 1** : swinging **2** FLUCTUACIÓN : fluctuation
oscuro, -ra *adj* **1** : dark **2** : obscure (of ideas, persons, etc.) **3 a oscuras** : in the dark — **oscurecer** {53} *vt* **1** : darken **2** : confuse,

cloud (the mind) **3 al ~** : at nightfall — *v impers* : get dark — **oscurecerse** *vr* : grow dark — **oscuridad** *nf* **1** : darkness **2** : obscurity (of ideas, persons, etc.)

óseo, ósea *adj* : skeletal, bony

oso, osa *n* **1** : bear **2 ~ de peluche** *or* **~ de felpa** : teddy bear

ostensible *adj* : evident, obvious

ostentar *vt* **1** : flaunt, display **2** POSEER : have, hold — **ostentación** *nf, pl* **-ciones** : ostentation — **ostentoso, -sa** *adj* : ostentatious, showy

osteopatía *n* : osteopathy — **osteópata** *nmf* : osteopath

osteoporosis *nf* : osteoporosis

ostra *nf* : oyster

ostracismo *nm* : ostracism

otear *vt* : scan, survey

otoño *nm* : autumn, fall — **otoñal** *adj* : autumn, fall

otorgar {52} *vt* **1** : grant, award **2** : draw up (a legal document)

otro, otra *adj* **1** : another, other **2 otra vez** : again — **~** *pron* **1** : another (one), other (one) **2 los otros, las otras** : the others, the rest

ovación *nf, pl* **-ciones** : ovation

óvalo *nm* : oval — **oval** *or* **ovalado, -da** *adj* : oval

ovario *nm* : ovary

oveja *nf* **1** : sheep, ewe **2 ~ negra** : black sheep

overol *nm Lat* : overalls *pl*

ovillo *nm* **1** : ball (of yarn) **2 hacerse un ~** : curl up (into a ball)

ovni *or* **OVNI** *nm* (*objeto volador no identificado*) : UFO

ovular *vi* : ovulate — **ovulación** *nf, pl* **-ciones** : ovulation

oxidar *vi* : rust — **oxidarse** *vr* : get rusty — **oxidación** *nf, pl* **-ciones** : rusting — **oxidado, -da** *adj* : rusty — **óxido** *nm* : rust

oxígeno *nm* : oxygen

oye → oír

oyente *nmf* **1** : listener **2** : auditor (student)

ozono *nm* : ozone

P

p *nf* : p, 17th letter of the Spanish alphabet

pabellón *nm, pl* **-llones 1** : pavilion **2** : block, building (in a hospital complex, etc.) **3** : summerhouse (in a garden, etc.) **4** BANDERA : flag

pabilo *nm* : wick

pacer {48} *v* : graze

paces → paz

paciencia *nf* : patience — **paciente** *adj & nmf* : patient

pacificar {72} *vt* : pacify, calm — **pacificarse** *vr* : calm down — **pacífico, -ca** *adj* : peaceful, pacific — **pacifismo** *nm* : pacifism — **pacifista** *adj & nmf* : pacifist

pacotilla *nf* **de ~** : second-rate, trashy

pacto *nm* : pact, agreement — **pactar** *vt* : agree on — *vi* : come to an agreement

padecer {53} *vt* : suffer, endure — *vi* **~ de** : suffer from — **padecimiento** *nm* : suffering

padre *nm* **1** : father **2 ~s** *nmpl* : parents — **~** *adj Lat fam* : great, fantastic — **padrastro** *nm* : stepfather — **padrino** *nm* **1** : godfather **2** : best man (at a wedding)

padrón *nm, pl* **-drones** : register, roll

paella *nf* : paella

paga *nf* : pay, wages *pl* — **pagadero, -ra** *adj* : payable

pagano, -na *adj & n* : pagan, heathen

pagar {52} *vt* : pay, pay for — *vi* : pay — **pagaré** *nm* : IOU

página *nf* : page

pago *nm* : payment

país *nm* **1** : country, nation **2** REGIÓN : region, land — **paisaje** *nm* : scenery, landscape — **paisano, -na** *n* : compatriot

paja *nf* **1** : straw **2** *fam* : nonsense

pájaro *nm* **1** : bird **2 ~ carpintero** : woodpecker — **pajarera** *nf* : aviary

pajita *nf* : (drinking) straw

pala *nf* **1** : shovel, spade **2** : blade (of an oar or a rotor) **3** : paddle, racket (in sports)

palabra *nf* **1** : word **2** HABLA : speech **3 tener la ~** : have the floor — **palabrota** *nf* : swearword

palacio *nm* **1** : palace, mansion **2 ~ de justicia** : courthouse

paladar *nm* : palate — **paladear** *vt* : savor

palanca *nf* **1** : lever, crowbar **2** *fam* : leverage, influence **3 ~ de cambio** *or* **~ de velocidades** : gearshift

palangana *nf* : washbowl

palco *nm* : box (in a theater)
palestino, -na *adj* : Palestinian
paleta *nf* 1 : small shovel, trowel 2 : palette (in art) 3 : paddle (in sports, etc.)
paletilla *nf* : shoulder blade
paliar *vt* : alleviate, ease — **paliativo, -va** *adj* : palliative
pálido, -da *adj* : pale — **palidecer** {53} *vi* : turn pale — **palidez** *nf, pl* **-deces** : paleness, pallor
palillo *nm* 1 : small stick 2 *or* ~ **de dientes** : toothpick
paliza *nf* : beating
palma *nf* 1 : palm (of the hand) 2 : palm (tree or leaf) 3 **batir** ~**s** : clap, applaud — **palmada** *nf* 1 : pat, slap 2 ~**s** *nfpl* : clapping
palmera *nf* : palm tree
palmo *nm* 1 : span, small amount 2 ~ **a** ~ : bit by bit
palmotear *vi* : applaud — **palmoteo** *nm* : clapping, applause
palo *nm* 1 : stick 2 MANGO : shaft, handle 3 MÁSTIL : mast 4 POSTE : pole 5 GOLPE : blow 6 : suit (of cards)
paloma *nf* : pigeon, dove — **palomilla** *nf* : moth — **palomitas** *nfpl* : popcorn
palpar *vt* : feel, touch — **palpable** *adj* : palpable
palpitar *vi* : palpitate, throb — **palpitación** *nf, pl* **-ciones** : palpitation
palta *nf Lat* : avocado
paludismo *nm* : malaria
pampa *nf* : pampa
pan *nm* 1 : bread 2 : loaf (of bread, etc.) 3 ~ **tostado** : toast
pana *nf* : corduroy
panacea *nf* : panacea
panadería *nf* : bakery, bread shop — **panadero, -ra** *n* : baker
panal *nm* : honeycomb
panameño, -ña *adj* : Panamanian
pancarta *nf* : placard, banner
pancito *nm Lat* : (bread) roll
páncreas *nms & pl* : pancreas
panda *nmf* : panda
pandemonio *nm* : pandemonium
pandero *nm* : tambourine — **pandereta** *nf* : (small) tambourine
pandilla *nf* : gang
panecillo *nm Spain* : (bread) roll
panel *nm* : panel
panfleto *nm* : pamphlet
pánico *nm* : panic
panorama *nm* : panorama — **panorámico, -ca** *adj* : panoramic
panqueque *nm Lat* : pancake
pantaletas *nfpl Lat* : panties
pantalla *nf* 1 : screen 2 : lampshade

pantalón *nm, pl* **-lones** 1 *or* **pantalones** *nmpl* : pants *pl*, trousers *pl* 2 **pantalones vaqueros** : jeans
pantano *nm* 1 : swamp, marsh 2 EMBALSE : reservoir — **pantanoso, -sa** *adj* : marshy, swampy
pantera *nf* : panther
pantimedias *nfpl Lat* : panty hose
pantomima *nf* : pantomime
pantorrilla *nf* : calf (of the leg)
pantufla *nf* : slipper
panza *nf* : belly, paunch — **panzón, -zona** *adj, mpl* **-zones** : potbellied
pañal *nm* : diaper
paño *nm* 1 : cloth 2 TRAPO : rag, dust cloth 3 ~ **de cocina** : dishcloth 4 ~ **higiénico** : sanitary napkin 5 ~**s menores** : underwear
pañuelo *nm* 1 : handkerchief 2 : scarf, kerchief
papa[1] *nm* : pope
papa[2] *nf Lat* 1 : potato 2 ~**s fritas** : potato chips, french fries
papá *nm fam* 1 : dad, pop 2 ~**s** *nmpl* : parents, folks
papada *nf* : double chin
papagayo *nm* : parrot
papal *adj* : papal
papalote *nm Lat* : kite
papanatas *nmfs & pl fam* : simpleton
papaya *nf* : papaya
papel *nm* 1 : paper, sheet of paper 2 : role, part (in theater, etc.) 3 ~ **de aluminio** : aluminum foil 4 ~ **higiénico** *or* ~ **de baño** : toilet paper 5 ~ **de lija** : sandpaper 6 ~ **pintado** : wallpaper — **papeleo** *nm* : paperwork, red tape — **papelera** *nf* : wastebasket — **papelería** *nf* : stationery store — **papeleta** *nf* 1 : ticket, slip 2 : ballot (paper)
paperas *nfpl* : mumps
papilla *nf* 1 : baby food, pap 2 **hacer** ~ : smash to bits
paquete *nm* 1 : package, parcel 2 : pack (of cigarettes, etc.)
paquistaní *adj* : Pakistani
par *nm* 1 : pair, couple 2 : par (in golf) 3 NOBLE : peer 4 **abierto de** ~ **en** ~ : wide open 5 **sin** ~ : without equal — ~ *adj* : even (in number) — ~ *nf* 1 : par 2 **a la** ~ **que** : at the same time as
para *prep* 1 : for 2 HACIA : towards 3 : (in order) to 4 : around, by (a time) 5 ~ **adelante** : forwards 6 ~ **atrás** : backwards 7 ~ **que** : so (that), in order that
parabienes *nmpl* : congratulations
parábola *nf* : parable
parabrisas *nms & pl* : windshield
paracaídas *nms & pl* : parachute — **para-**

caidista *nmf* **1** : parachutist **2** : paratrooper (in the military)

parachoques *nms & pl* : bumper

parada *nf* **1** : stop **2** : (act of) stopping **3** DESFILE : parade — **paradero** *nm* **1** : whereabouts **2** *Lat* : bus stop — **parado, -da** *adj* **1** : idle, stopped **2** *Lat* : standing (up) **3 bien (mal) parado** : in good (bad) shape

paradoja *nf* : paradox

parafernalia *nf* : paraphernalia

parafina *nf* : paraffin

parafrasear *vt* : paraphrase — **paráfrasis** *nfs & pl* : paraphrase

paraguas *nms & pl* : umbrella

paraguayo, -ya *adj* : Paraguayan

paraíso *nm* : paradise

paralelo, -la *adj* : parallel — **paralelo** *nm* : parallel — **paralelismo** *nm* : similarity

parálisis *nfs & pl* : paralysis — **paralítico, -ca** *adj* : paralytic — **paralizar** {21} *vt* : paralyze

parámetro *nm* : parameter

páramo *nm* : barren plateau

parangón *nm, pl* **-gones 1** : comparison **2 sin ~** : matchless

paraninfo *nm* : auditorium, hall

paranoia *nf* : paranoia — **paranoico, -ca** *adj & n* : paranoid

parapeto *nm* : parapet, rampart

parapléjico, -ca *adj & n* : paraplegic

parar *vt* **1** : stop **2** *Lat* : stand, prop — *vi* **1** : stop **2 ir a ~** : end up, wind up — **pararse** *vr* **1** : stop **2** *Lat* : stand up

pararrayos *nms & pl* : lightning rod

parásito, -ta *adj* : parasitic — **parásito** *nm* : parasite

parasol *nm* : parasol

parcela *nf* : parcel, tract (of land) — **parcelar** *vt* : parcel (up)

parche *nm* : patch

parcial *adj* **1** : partial **2 a tiempo ~** : part-time — **parcialidad** *nf* : partiality, bias

parco, -ca *adj* : sparing, frugal

pardo, -da *adj* : brownish grey

parear *vt* : pair (up)

parecer {53} *vi* **1** : seem, look **2** ASEMEJARSE A : look like, seem like **3 me parece que** : I think that, in my opinion **4 ¿qué te parece?** : what do you think? **5 según parece** : apparently — **parecerse** *vr* **~ a** : resemble — **~** *nm* **1** : opinion **2** ASPECTO : appearance **3 al ~** : apparently — **parecido, -da** *adj* **1** : similar **2 bien parecido** : good-looking — **parecido** *nm* : resemblance, similarity

pared *nf* : wall

parejo, -ja *adj* **1** : even, smooth **2** SEMEJANTE : similar — **pareja** *nf* **1** : couple, pair **2** : partner (person)

parentela *nf* : relatives *pl*, kin — **parentesco** *nm* : relationship, kinship

paréntesis *nms & pl* **1** : parenthesis **2** DIGRESIÓN : digression **3 entre ~** : by the way

paria *nmf* : outcast

paridad *nf* : equality

pariente *nmf* : relative, relation

parir *vi* : give birth, have a baby — *vt* : give birth to

parking *nm* : parking lot

parlamentar *vi* : discuss — **parlamentario, -ria** *adj* : parliamentary — **~** *n* : member of parliament — **parlamento** *nm* : parliament

parlanchín, -china *adj, mpl* **-chines** : talkative, chatty — **~** *n* : chatterbox

parlotear *vi fam* : chatter — **parloteo** *nm fam* : chatter

paro *nm* **1** : stoppage, shutdown **2** DESEMPLEO : unemployment **3** *Lat* : strike **4 ~ cardíaco** : cardiac arrest

parodia *nf* : parody — **parodiar** *vt* : parody

párpado *nm* : eyelid — **parpadear** *vi* **1** : blink **2** : flicker (of light), twinkle (of stars) — **parpadeo** *nm* **1** : blink **2** : flicker (of light), twinkling (of stars)

parque *nm* **1** : park **2 ~ de atracciones** : amusement park

parqué *nm* : parquet

parquear *vt Lat* : park

parquedad *nf* : frugality, moderation

parquímetro *nm* : parking meter

parra *nf* : grapevine

párrafo *nm* : paragraph

parranda *nf fam* : party, spree

parrilla *nf* **1** : broiler, grill **2** : grate (of a chimney, etc.) — **parrillada** *nf* : barbecue

párroco *nm* : parish priest — **parroquia** *nf* **1** : parish **2** : parish church — **parroquial** *adj* : parochial — **parroquiano, -na** *nm* **1** : parishioner **2** CLIENTE : customer

parsimonia *nf* **1** : calm **2** FRUGALIDAD : thrift — **parsimonioso, -sa** *adj* **1** : calm, unhurried **2** FRUGAL : thrifty

parte *nf* **1** : part **2** PORCIÓN : share **3** LADO : side **4** : party (in negotiations, etc.) **5 de ~ de** : on behalf of **6 ¿de ~ de quién?** : who is speaking? **7 en alguna ~** : somewhere **8 en todas ~s** : everywhere **9 tomar ~** : take part — **~** *nm* **1** : report **2 ~ meteorológico** : weather forecast

partero, -ra *n* : midwife

partición *nf, pl* **-ciones** : division, sharing

participar *vi* **1** : participate, take part **2 ~ en** : have a share in — *vt* : notify — **participación** *nf, pl* **-ciones 1** : participation **2** : share, interest (in a fund, etc.) **3** NOTICIA : notice — **participante** *adj* : participating

— ~ *nmf* : participant — **partícipe** *nmf* : participant

participio *nm* : participle

partícula *nf* : particle

particular *adj* **1** : particular **2** PRIVADO : private — ~ *nm* **1** : matter **2** PERSONA : individual — **particularidad** *nf* : peculiarity — **particularizar** {21} *vt* : distinguish, characterize — *vi* : go into details

partir *vt* **1** : split, divide **2** ROMPER : break, crack **3** REPARTIR : share (out) — *vi* **1** : depart **2** ~ **de** : start from **3 a** ~ **de** : as of, from — **partirse** *vr* **1** : split (open) **2** RAJARSE : crack — **partida** *nf* **1** : departure **2** : entry, item (in a register, etc.) **3** JUEGO : game **4** : group (of persons) **5 mala** ~ : dirty trick **6** ~ **de nacimiento** : birth certificate — **partidario, -ria** *n* : follower, supporter — **partido** *nm* **1** : (political) party **2** : game, match (in sports) **3** PARTIDARIOS : following **4 sacar** ~ **de** : make the most of

partitura *nf* : (musical) score

parto *nm* **1** : childbirth **2 estar de** ~ : be in labor

parvulario *nm* : nursery school

pasa *nf* **1** : raisin **2** ~ **de Corinto** : currant

pasable *adj* : passable

pasada *nf* **1** : pass, wipe, coat (of paint, etc.) **2 de** ~ : in passing **3 mala** ~ : dirty trick — **pasadizo** *nm* : corridor — **pasado, -da** *adj* **1** : past **2** PODRIDO : bad, spoiled **3** ANTICUADO : out-of-date **4 el año pasado** : last year — **pasado** *nm* : past

pasador *nm* **1** CERROJO : bolt **2** : barrette (for the hair)

pasaje *nm* **1** : passage **2** BILLETE : ticket, fare **3** PASILLO : passageway **4** PASAJEROS : passengers *pl* — **pasajero, -ra** *adj* : passing — ~ *n* : passenger

pasamanos *nms & pl* : handrail, banister

pasaporte *nm* : passport

pasar *vi* **1** : pass, go (by) **2** ENTRAR : come in **3** SUCEDER : happen **4** TERMINARSE : be over, end **5** ~ **de** : exceed **6 ¿qué pasa?** : what's the matter? — *vt* **1** : pass **2** : spend (time) **3** CRUZAR : cross **4** TOLERAR : tolerate **5** SUFRIR : go through, suffer **6** : show (a movie, etc.) **7 pasarlo bien** : have a good time **8** ~ **por alto** : overlook, omit — **pasarse** *vr* **1** : pass, go away **2** ESTROPEARSE : spoil, go bad **3** OLVIDARSE : slip one's mind **4** EXCEDERSE : go too far

pasarela *nf* **1** : footbridge **2** : gangway (on a ship)

pasatiempo *nm* : pastime, hobby

Pascua *nf* **1** : Easter (Christian feast) **2** : Passover (Jewish feast) **3** NAVIDAD : Christmas

pase *nm* : pass

pasear *vi* : take a walk, go for a ride — *vt* **1** : take for a walk **2** EXHIBIR : parade, show off — **pasearse** *vr* : go for a walk, go for a ride — **paseo** *nm* **1** : walk, ride **2** *Lat* : outing

pasillo *nm* : passage, corridor

pasión *nf, pl* **-siones** : passion

pasivo, -va *adj* : passive — **pasivo** *nm* : liabilities *pl*

pasmar *vt* : astonish, amaze — **pasmarse** *vr* : be astonished — **pasmado, -da** *adj* : stunned, flabbergasted — **pasmo** *nm* : astonishment — **pasmoso, -sa** *adj* : astonishing

paso¹, -sa *adj* : dried (of fruit)

paso² *nm* **1** : step **2** HUELLA : footprint **3** RITMO : pace **4** CRUCE : crossing **5** PASAJE : passage, way through **6** : (mountain) pass **7 de** ~ : in passing

pasta *nf* **1** : paste **2** MASA : dough **3** *or* ~**s** : pasta **4** ~ **de dientes** *or* ~ **dentífrica** : toothpaste

pastar *v* : graze

pastel *nm* **1** : cake **2** EMPANADA : pie **3** : pastel (crayon) — **pastelería** *nf* : pastry shop

pasteurizar {21} *vt* : pasteurize

pastilla *nf* **1** : pill, tablet **2** : bar (of chocolate, soap, etc.) **3** ~ **para la tos** : lozenge, cough drop

pasto *nm* **1** : pasture **2** *Lat* : grass, lawn — **pastor, -tora** *n* **1** : shepherd **2** : pastor (in religion) — **pastoral** *adj* : pastoral

pata *nf* **1** : paw, leg (of an animal) **2** : foot, leg (of furniture) **3 meter la** ~ *fam* : put one's foot in it — **patada** *nf* **1** : kick **2** : stamp (of the foot) — **patalear** *vi* **1** : kick **2** : stamp (one's feet)

patata *nf Spain* : potato

patear *vt* : kick — *vi* **1** : kick **2** : stamp (one's feet)

patentar *vt* : patent — **patente** *adj* : obvious, patent — ~ *nf* : patent

paternal *adj* : fatherly, paternal — **paternidad** *nf* **1** : fatherhood **2** : paternity (in law) — **paterno, -na** *adj* : paternal

patético, -ca *adj* : pathetic, moving

patillas *nfpl* : sideburns

patinar *vi* **1** : skate **2** RESBALAR : slip, slide — **patín** *nm, pl* **-tines** : skate — **patinador, -dora** *n* : skater — **patinaje** *nm* : skating — **patinazo** *nm* **1** : skid **2** *fam* : blunder — **patinete** *nm* : scooter

patio *nm* **1** : courtyard, patio **2** *or* ~ **de recreo** : playground

pato, -ta *n* **1** : duck **2 pagar el pato** *fam*
: take the blame — **patito, -ta** *n* : duckling
patología *nf* : pathology — **patológico, -ca**
adj : pathological
patraña *nf* : hoax
patria *nf* : native land
patriarca *nm* : patriarch
patrimonio *nm* **1** : inheritance **2** : (historical or cultural) heritage
patriota *adj* : patriotic — ~ *nmf* : patriot —
patriótico, -ca *adj* : patriotic — **patrio-
tismo** *nm* : patriotism
patrocinador, -dora *n* : sponsor — **patrocinar** *vt* : sponsor — **patrocinio** *nm* : sponsorship
patrón, -trona *n, mpl* **-trones 1** : patron **2**
JEFE : boss **3** : landlord, landlady *f* (of a
boarding house, etc.) — **patrón** *nm, mpl*
-trones : pattern (in sewing) — **patronato**
nm **1** : patronage **2** FUNDACIÓN : foundation, trust
patrulla *nf* **1** : patrol **2** : (police) cruiser —
patrullar *v* : patrol
paulatino, -na *adj* : gradual
pausa *nf* : pause, break — **pausado, -da** *adj*
: slow, deliberate
pauta *nf* : guideline
pavimento *nm* : pavement — **pavimentar** *vt*
: pave
pavo, -va *n* **1** : turkey **2 pavo real** : peacock
pavonearse *vr* : strut, swagger
pavor *nm* : dread, terror — **pavoroso, -sa**
adj : terrifying
payaso, -sa *n* : clown — **payasada** *nf*
: antic, buffoonery — **payasear** *vi Lat fam*
: clown (around)
paz *nf, pl* **paces 1** : peace **2 dejar en** ~
: leave alone **3 hacer las paces** : make up,
reconcile
peaje *nm* : toll
peatón *nm, pl* **-tones** : pedestrian
peca *nf* : freckle
pecado *nm* : sin — **pecador, -dora** *adj* : sinful — ~ *n* : sinner — **pecaminoso, -sa** *adj*
: sinful — **pecar** {72} *vi* : sin
pecera *nf* : fishbowl, fish tank
pecho *nm* **1** : chest **2** MAMA : breast **3**
CORAZÓN : heart, courage **4 dar el** ~
: breast-feed **5 tomar a** ~ : take to heart —
pechuga *nf* : breast (of fowl)
pecoso, -sa *adj* : freckled
pectoral *adj* : pectoral
peculiar *adj* **1** : particular **2** RARO : peculiar,
odd — **peculiaridad** *nf* : peculiarity
pedagogía *nf* : education, pedagogy — **ped-
agogo, -ga** *n* : educator, teacher
pedal *nm* : pedal — **pedalear** *vi* : pedal
pedante *adj* : pedantic, pompous

pedazo *nm* **1** : piece, bit **2 hacerse** ~**s**
: fall to pieces
pedernal *nm* : flint
pedestal *nm* : pedestal
pediatra *nmf* : pediatrician
pedigrí *nm* : pedigree
pedir {54} *vt* **1** : ask for, request **2** : order
(food, merchandise, etc.) — *vi* **1** : ask **2** ~
prestado : borrow — **pedido** *nm* **1** : order
2 hacer un ~ : place an order
pedregoso, -sa *adj* : rocky, stony
pedrería *nf* : precious stones *pl*
pegar {52} *vt* **1** : stick, glue, paste **2** : sew
on (a button, etc.) **3** JUNTAR : bring together
4 GOLPEAR : hit, strike **5** PROPINAR : deal (a
blow, etc.) **6** : transmit (an illness) **7** ~ **un
grito** : let out a scream — *vi* **1** : adhere, stick
2 GOLPEAR : hit — **pegarse** *vr* **1** : hit oneself, hit each other **2** ADHERIRSE : stick, adhere **3** CONTAGIARSE : be transmitted —
pegadizo, -za *adj* **1** : catchy **2** CONTA-
GIOSO : contagious — **pegajoso, -sa** *adj* **1**
: sticky **2** *Lat* : catchy — **pegamento** *nm*
: glue
peinar *vt* : comb — **peinarse** *vr* : comb
one's hair — **peinado** *nm* : hairstyle, hairdo
— **peine** *nm* : comb — **peineta** *nf* : ornamental comb
pelado, -da *adj* **1** : shorn, hairless **2**
: peeled (of fruit, etc.) **3** *fam* : bare **4** *fam*
: broke, penniless
pelaje *nm* : coat (of an animal), fur
pelar *vt* **1** : cut the hair of (a person) **2** MON-
DAR : peel (fruit) **3** : pluck (a chicken, etc.),
skin (an animal) — **pelarse** *vr* **1** : peel **2**
fam : get a haircut
peldaño *nm* **1** : step (of stairs) **2** : rung (of
a ladder)
pelear *vi* **1** : fight **2** DISCUTIR : quarrel —
pelearse *vr* : have a fight — **pelea** *nf* **1**
: fight **2** DISCUSIÓN : quarrel
peletería *nf* : fur shop
peliagudo, -da *adj* : tricky, difficult
pelícano *nm* : pelican
película *nf* : movie, film
peligro *nm* **1** : danger **2** RIESGO : risk —
peligroso, -sa *adj* : dangerous
pelirrojo, -ja *adj* : red-haired — ~ *n* : redhead
pellejo *nm* : skin, hide
pellizcar {72} *vt* : pinch — **pellizco** *nm*
: pinch
pelo *nm* **1** : hair **2** : coat, fur (of an animal)
3 : pile, nap (of fabric) **4 con** ~**s y
señales** : in great detail **5 no tener** ~ **en
la lengua** *fam* : not to mince words **6 tomar
el** ~ **a algn** *fam* : pull someone's leg —
pelón, -lona *adj fam, mpl* **-lones** : bald
pelota *nf* : ball

pelotón *nm, pl* **-tones** : squad, detachment

peltre *nm* : pewter

peluca *nf* : wig

peluche *nm* **1** : plush **2 oso de ~** : teddy bear

peludo, -da *adj* : hairy, furry

peluquería *nf* : hairdresser's, barber shop — **peluquero, -ra** *n* : barber, hairdresser

pelusa *nf* : fuzz, lint

pelvis *nfs & pl* : pelvis

pena *nf* **1** : penalty **2** TRISTEZA : sorrow **3** DOLOR : suffering, pain **4** *Lat* : embarrassment **5 a duras ~s** : with great difficulty **6 ¡qué ~!** : what a shame! **7 valer la ~** : be worthwhile

penacho *nm* **1** : crest, tuft **2** : plume (ornament)

penal *adj* : penal — **~** *nm* : prison, penitentiary — **penalidad** *nf* **1** : hardship **2** : penalty (in law) — **penalizar** {21} *vt* : penalize

penalty *nm* : penalty (in sports)

penar *vt* : punish — *vi* : suffer

pendenciero, -ra *adj* : quarrelsome

pender *vi* : hang — **pendiente** *adj* **1** : pending **2 estar ~ de** : be watching out for — **~** *nf* : slope — **~** *nm Spain* : earring

pendón *nm, pl* **-dones** : banner

péndulo *nm* : pendulum

pene *nm* : penis

penetrar *vi* **1** : penetrate **2 ~ en** : go into — *vt* **1** : penetrate **2** : pierce (one's heart, etc.) **3** ENTENDER : fathom, grasp — **penetración** *nf, pl* **-ciones** **1** : penetration **2** PERSPICACIA : insight — **penetrante** *adj* **1** : penetrating **2** : sharp (of odors, etc.), piercing (of sounds) **3** : deep (of a wound, etc.)

penicilina *nf* : penicillin

península *nf* : peninsula — **peninsular** *adj* : peninsular

penitencia *nf* **1** : penitence **2** CASTIGO : penance — **penitenciaría** *nf* : penitentiary — **penitente** *adj & nmf* : penitent

penoso, -sa *adj* **1** : painful, distressing **2** TRABAJOSO : difficult **3** *Lat* : shy

pensar {55} *vi* **1** : think **2 ~ en** : think about — *vt* **1** : think **2** CONSIDERAR : think about **3 ~ hacer algo** : intend to do sth — **pensador, -dora** *n* : thinker — **pensamiento** *nm* **1** : thought **2** : pansy (flower) — **pensativo, -va** *adj* : pensive, thoughtful

pensión *nf, pl* **-siones** **1** : boarding house **2** : (retirement) pension **3 ~ alimenticia** : alimony — **pensionista** *nmf* **1** : lodger **2** JUBILADO : retiree

pentágono *nm* : pentagon

pentagrama *nm* : staff (in music)

penúltimo, -ma *adj* : next to last, penultimate

penumbra *nf* : half-light

penuria *nf* : dearth, shortage

peña *nf* : rock, crag — **peñasco** *nm* : crag, large rock — **peñón** *nm, pl* **-ñones** : craggy rock

peón *nm, pl* **peones** **1** : laborer, peon **2** : pawn (in chess)

peonía *nf* : peony

peor *adv* **1** (*comparative of* **mal**) : worse **2** (*superlative of* **mal**) : worst — **~** *adj* **1** (*comparative of* **malo**) : worse **2** (*superlative of* **malo**) : worst

pepino *nm* : cucumber — **pepinillo** *nm* : pickle, gherkin

pepita *nf* **1** : seed, pip **2** : nugget (of gold, etc.)

pequeño, -ña *adj* : small, little — **pequeñez** *nf, pl* **-ñeces** **1** : smallness **2** NIMIEDAD : trifle

pera *nf* : pear — **peral** *nm* : pear tree

percance *nm* : mishap, setback

percatarse *vr* **~ de** : notice

percepción *nf, pl* **-ciones** : perception — **perceptible** *adj* : perceptible

percha *nf* **1** : perch (for birds) **2** : (coat) hanger **3** : coatrack (on a wall)

percibir *vt* **1** : perceive **2** : receive (a salary, etc.)

percusión *nf, pl* **-siones** : percussion

perder {56} *vt* **1** : lose **2** : miss (an opportunity, etc.) **3** DESPERDICIAR : waste (time) — *vi* : lose — **perderse** *vr* **1** : get lost **2** DESAPARECER : disappear **3** DESPERDICIARSE : be wasted — **perdedor, -dora** *n* : loser — **pérdida** *nf* **1** : loss **2** ESCAPE : leak **3 ~ de tiempo** : waste of time — **perdido, -da** *adj* **1** : lost **2 un caso perdido** *fam* : a hopeless case

perdigón *nm, pl* **-gones** : shot, pellet

perdiz *nf, pl* **-dices** : partridge

perdón *nm, pl* **-dones** : forgiveness, pardon — **perdón** *interj* : sorry! — **perdonar** *vt* **1** DISCULPAR : forgive **2** : pardon (in law)

perdurar *vi* : last, endure — **perdurable** *adj* : lasting

perecer {53} *vi* : perish, die — **perecedero, -ra** *adj* : perishable

peregrinación *nf, pl* **-ciones** *or* **peregrinaje** *nm* : pilgrimage — **peregrino, -na** *adj* **1** : migratory **2** RARO : unusual, odd — **~** *n* : pilgrim

perejil *nm* : parsley

perenne *adj & nm* : perennial

pereza *nf* : laziness — **perezoso, -sa** *adj* : lazy

perfección *nf, pl* **-ciones** : perfection — **perfeccionar** *vt* **1** : perfect **2** MEJORAR

: improve — **perfeccionista** *nmf* : perfectionist — **perfecto, -ta** *adj* : perfect

perfidia *nf* : treachery — **pérfido, -da** *adj* : treacherous

perfil *nm* **1** : profile **2** CONTORNO : outline **3** ~es *nmpl* RASGOS : features — **perfilar** *vt* : outline — **perfilarse** *vr* **1** : be outlined **2** CONCRETARSE : take shape

perforar *vt* **1** : perforate **2** : drill, bore (a hole) — **perforación** *nf, pl* **-ciones** : perforation — **perforadora** *nf* : (paper) punch

perfume *nm* : perfume, scent — **perfumar** *vt* : perfume — **perfumarse** *vr* : put perfume on

pergamino *nm* : parchment

pericia *nf* : skill

periferia *nf* : periphery, outskirts (of a city, etc.) — **periférico, -ca** *adj* : peripheral

perilla *nf* **1** : goatee **2** *Lat* : knob **3 venir de** ~s *fam* : come in handy

perímetro *nm* : perimeter

periódico, -ca *adj* : periodic — **periódico** *nm* : newspaper — **periodismo** *nm* : journalism — **periodista** *nmf* : journalist

período *or* **periodo** *nm* : period

periquito *nm* : parakeet

periscopio *nm* : periscope

perito, -ta *adj & n* : expert

perjudicar {72} *vt* : harm, damage — **perjudicial** *adj* : harmful — **perjuicio** *nm* **1** : harm, damage **2 en** ~ **de** : to the detriment of

perjurar *vi* : perjure oneself — **perjurio** *nm* : perjury

perla *nf* **1** : pearl **2 de** ~s *fam* : great, just fine

permanecer {53} *vi* : remain — **permanencia** *nf* **1** : permanence **2** : stay, staying (in a place) — **permanente** *adj* : permanent — ~ *nf* : permanent (wave)

permeable *adj* : permeable

permitir *vt* **1** : permit, allow **2 ¿me permite?** : may I? — **permitirse** *vr* : allow oneself — **permisible** *adj* : permissible, allowable — **permisivo, -va** *adj* : permissive — **permiso** *nm* **1** : permission **2** : permit, license (document) **3** : leave (in the military) **4 con** ~ : excuse me

permuta *nf* : exchange

pernicioso, -sa *adj* : pernicious, destructive

pero *conj* : but — ~ *nm* **1** : fault **2** REPARO : objection

perorar *vi* : make a speech — **perorata** *nf* : (long-winded) speech

perpendicular *adj & nf* : perpendicular

perpetrar *vt* : perpetrate

perpetuar {3} *vt* : perpetuate — **perpetuo, -tua** *adj* : perpetual

perplejo, -ja *adj* : perplexed — **perplejidad** *nf* : perplexity

perro, -rra *n* **1** : dog, bitch *f* **2 perro caliente** : hot dog — **perrera** *nf* : kennel

perseguir {75} *vt* **1** : pursue, chase **2** ACOSAR : persecute — **persecución** *nf, pl* **-ciones 1** : pursuit, chase **2** ACOSO : persecution

perseverar *vi* : persevere — **perseverancia** *nf* : perseverance

persiana *nf* : (venetian) blind

persistir *vi* : persist — **persistencia** *nf* : persistence — **persistente** *adj* : persistent

persona *nf* : person — **personaje** *nm* **1** : character (in literature, etc.) **2** : important person, celebrity — **personal** *adj* : personal — ~ *nm* : personnel, staff — **personalidad** *nf* : personality — **personificar** {72} *vt* : personify

perspectiva *nf* **1** : perspective **2** VISTA : view **3** POSIBILIDAD : prospect, outlook

perspicacia *nf* : shrewdness, insight — **perspicaz** *adj, pl* **-caces** : shrewd, discerning

persuadir *vt* : persuade — **persuadirse** *vr* : become convinced — **persuasión** *nf, pl* **-siones** : persuasion — **persuasivo, -va** *adj* : persuasive

pertenecer {53} *vi* ~ **a** : belong to — **perteneciente** *adj* ~ **a** : belonging to — **pertenencia** *nf* **1** : ownership **2** ~s *nfpl* : belongings

pertinaz *adj, pl* **-naces 1** OBSTINADO : obstinate **2** PERSISTENTE : persistent

pertinente *adj* : pertinent, relevant — **pertinencia** *nf* : relevance

perturbar *vt* : disturb — **perturbación** *nf, pl* **-ciones** : disturbance

peruano, -na *adj* : Peruvian

pervertir {76} *vt* : pervert — **perversión** *nf, pl* **-siones** : perversion — **perverso, -sa** *adj* : perverse — **pervertido, -da** *adj* : perverted, depraved — ~ *n* : pervert

pesa *nf* **1** : weight **2** ~s : weights (in sports) — **pesadez** *nf, pl* **-deces 1** : heaviness **2** *fam* : tediousness, drag

pesadilla *nf* : nightmare

pesado, -da *adj* **1** : heavy **2** LENTO : sluggish **3** MOLESTO : annoying **4** ABURRIDO : tedious **5** DURO : tough, difficult — ~ *n fam* : bore, pest — **pesadumbre** *nf* : grief, sorrow

pésame *nm* : condolences *pl*

pesar *vt* : weigh — *vi* **1** : weigh, be heavy **2** INFLUIR : carry weight **3 pese a** : despite — ~ *nm* **1** : sorrow, grief **2** REMORDIMIENTO : remorse **3 a** ~ **de** : in spite of

pescado *nm* : fish — **pesca** *nf* **1** : fishing **2** PECES : fish *pl*, catch **3 ir de** ~ : go fishing

— **pescadería** *nf* : fish market — **pesca-dor, -dora** *n, mpl* **-dores** : fisherman — **pescar** {72} *vt* **1** : fish for **2** *fam* : catch (a cold, etc.) **3** *fam* : catch hold of, nab — *vi* : fish

pescuezo *nm* : neck (of an animal)

pese a → **pesar**

pesebre *nm* : manger

pesero *nm Lat* : minibus

peseta *nf* : peseta

pesimismo *nm* : pessimism — **pesimista** *adj* : pessimistic — ~ *nmf* : pessimist

pésimo, -ma *adj* : awful

peso *nm* **1** : weight **2** CARGA : burden **3** : peso (currency) **4** ~ **pesado** : heavyweight

pesquero, -ra *adj* : fishing

pesquisa *nf* : inquiry

pestaña *nf* : eyelash — **pestañear** *vi* : blink — **pestañeo** *nm* : blink

peste *nm* **1** : plague **2** *fam* : stench, stink **3** *Lat fam* : cold, bug — **pesticida** *nm* : pesticide — **pestilencia** *nf* **1** : stench **2** PLAGA : pestilence

pestillo *nm* : bolt, latch

petaca *nf Lat* : suitcase

pétalo *nm* : petal

petardo *nm* : firecracker

petición *nf, pl* **-ciones** : petition, request

petirrojo *nm* : robin

petrificar {72} *vt* : petrify

petróleo *nm* : oil, petroleum — **petrolero, -ra** *adj* : oil — **petrolero** *nm* : oil tanker

petulante *adj* : insolent, arrogant

peyorativo, -va *adj* : pejorative

pez *nm, pl* **peces** **1** : fish **2** ~ **de colores** : goldfish **3** ~ **espada** : swordfish **4** ~ **gordo** *fam* : big shot

pezón *nm, pl* **-zones** : nipple

pezuña *nf* : hoof

piadoso, -sa *adj* **1** : compassionate **2** DEVOTO : pious, devout

piano *nm* : piano — **pianista** *nmf* : pianist, piano player

piar {85} *vi* : chirp, tweet

pibe, -ba *n Lat fam* : kid, child

pica *nf* **1** : pike, lance **2** : spade (in playing cards)

picado, -da *adj* **1** : perforated **2** : minced, chopped (of meat, etc.) **3** : decayed (of teeth) **4** : choppy (of the sea) **5** *fam* : annoyed — **picada** *nf* **1** : bite, sting **2** *Lat* : sharp descent — **picadillo** *nm* : minced meat — **picadura** *nf* **1** : sting, bite **2** : (moth) hole

picante *adj* : hot, spicy

picaporte *nm* **1** : door handle **2** ALDABA : door knocker **3** PESTILLO : latch

picar {72} *vt* **1** : sting, bite **2** : peck at, nib-

ble on (food) **3** PERFORAR : prick, puncture **4** TRITURAR : chop, mince — *vi* **1** : bite, take the bait **2** ESCOCER : sting, itch **3** COMER : nibble **4** : be spicy (of food) — **picarse** *vr* **1** : get a cavity **2** ENFADARSE : take offense

picardía *nf* **1** : craftiness **2** TRAVESURA : prank — **picaresco, -ca** *adj* **1** : picaresque **2** TRAVIESO : roguish — **pícaro, -ra** *adj* **1** : mischievous **2** MALICIOSO : villainous — ~ *n* : rascal, scoundrel

picazón *nf, pl* **-zones** : itch

pichón, -chona *n, mpl* **-chones** : (young) pigeon

picnic *nm, pl* **-nics** : picnic

pico *nm* **1** : beak **2** CIMA : peak **3** PUNTA : (sharp) point **4** : pick, pickax (tool) **5 las siete y** ~ : a little after seven — **picotazo** *nm* : peck — **picotear** *vt* : peck — *vi fam* : nibble, pick — **picudo, -da** *adj* : pointy

pie *nm* **1** : foot (in anatomy) **2** : base, bottom, stem **3 al** ~ **de la letra** : word for word **4 dar** ~ **a** : give rise to **5 de** ~ : standing (up) **6 de** ~**s a cabeza** : from top to bottom

piedad *nf* **1** : pity, mercy **2** DEVOCIÓN : piety

piedra *nf* **1** : stone **2** : flint (of a lighter) **3** GRANIZO : hailstone **4** ~ **angular** : cornerstone **5** → **pómez**

piel *nf* **1** : skin **2** CUERO : leather **3** PELO : fur, pelt

pienso *nm* : feed, fodder

pierna *nf* : leg

pieza *nf* **1** : piece, part **2** *or* ~ **de teatro** : play **3** HABITACIÓN : room

pigmento *nm* : pigment — **pigmentación** *nf, pl* **-ciones** : pigmentation

pigmeo, -mea *adj* : pygmy

pijama *nm* : pajamas *pl*

pila *nf* **1** : battery **2** MONTÓN : pile **3** FREGADERO : sink **4** : basin (of a fountain, etc.)

pilar *nm* : pillar

píldora *nf* : pill

pillar *vt* **1** : catch **2** : get (a joke, etc.) — **pillaje** *nm* : pillage — **pillo, -lla** *adj* : crafty — ~ *n* : rascal, scoundrel

piloto *nmf* : pilot — **pilotar** *vt* : pilot

pimienta *nf* : pepper (condiment) — **pimiento** *nm* : pepper (fruit) — **pimentero** *nm* : pepper shaker — **pimentón** *nm, pl* **-tones** **1** : paprika **2** : cayenne pepper

pináculo *nm* : pinnacle

pincel *nm* : paintbrush

pinchar *vt* **1** : pierce, prick **2** : puncture (a tire, etc.) **3** INCITAR : goad — **pinchazo** *nm* **1** : prick **2** : puncture (of a tire, etc.)

pingüino *nm* : penguin

pino *nm* : pine (tree)

plátano

pintar *v* : paint — **pintarse** *vr* : put on makeup — **pinta** *nf* **1** : spot **2** : pint (measure) **3** *fam* : appearance — **pintada** *nf* : graffiti — **pinto, -ta** *adj* : speckled, spotted — **pintor, -tora** *n*, *mpl* **-tores** : painter — **pintoresco, -ca** *adj* : picturesque, quaint — **pintura** *nf* **1** : paint **2** CUADRO : painting

pinza *nf* **1** : clothespin **2** : claw, pincer (of a crab, etc.) **3** ~s *nfpl* : tweezers

pinzón *nm*, *pl* **-zones** : finch

piña *nf* **1** : pine cone **2** ANANÁS : pineapple

piñata *nf* : piñata

piñón *nm*, *pl* **-ñones** : pine nut

pío¹, pía *adj* **1** : pious **2** : piebald (of a horse)

pío² *nm* : peep, chirp

piojo *nm* : louse

pionero, -ra *n* : pioneer

pipa *nf* **1** : pipe (for smoking) **2** *Spain* : seed, pip

pique *nm* **1** : grudge **2** RIVALIDAD : rivalry **3** irse a ~ : sink, founder

piqueta *nf* : pickax

piquete *nm* : picket (line) — **piquetear** *v* : picket

piragua *nf* : canoe

pirámide *nf* : pyramid

piraña *nf* : piranha

pirata *adj* : bootleg, pirated — ~ *nmf* : pirate — **piratear** *vt* **1** : bootleg, pirate **2** : hack into (a computer)

piropo *nm* : (flirtatious) compliment

pirueta *nf* : pirouette

pirulí *nm* : (cone-shaped) lollipop

pisada *nf* **1** : footstep **2** HUELLA : footprint

pisapapeles *nms & pl* : paperweight

pisar *vt* **1** : step on **2** HUMILLAR : walk all over, abuse — *vi* : step, tread

piscina *nf* **1** : swimming pool **2** : (fish) pond

piso *nm* **1** : floor, story **2** *Lat* : floor (of a room) **3** *Spain* : apartment

pisotear *vt* : trample (on)

pista *nf* **1** : trail, track **2** INDICIO : clue **3** ~ de aterrizaje : runway, airstrip **4** ~ de baile : dance floor **5** ~ de hielo : ice-skating rink

pistacho *nm* : pistachio

pistola *nf* **1** : pistol, gun **2** PULVERIZADOR : spray gun — **pistolera** *nf* : holster — **pistolero** *nm* : gunman

pistón *nm*, *pl* **-tones** : piston

pito *nm* **1** SILBATO : whistle **2** CLAXON : horn — **pitar** *vi* **1** : blow a whistle **2** : beep, honk (of a horn) — *vt* : whistle at — **pitido** *nm* **1** : whistle, whistling **2** : beep (of a horn) — **pitillo** *nm fam* : cigarette

pitón *nm*, *pl* **-tones** *nm* : python

pitorro *nm* : spout

pivote *nm* : pivot

piyama *nmf Lat* : pajamas *pl*

pizarra *nf* **1** : slate **2** ENCERADO : blackboard — **pizarrón** *nm*, *pl* **-rrones** *Lat* : blackboard

pizca *nf* **1** : pinch (of salt) **2** ÁPICE : speck, tiny bit **3** *Lat* : harvest

pizza *nf* : pizza — **pizzería** *nf* : pizzeria

placa *nf* **1** : sheet, plate **2** INSCRIPCIÓN : plaque **3** : (police) badge

placenta *nf* : placenta

placer {57} *vt* : please — ~ *nm* : pleasure — **placentero, -ra** *adj* : pleasant, agreeable

plácido, -da *adj* : placid, calm

plaga *nf* **1** : plague **2** CALAMIDAD : disaster — **plagar** {52} *vt* : plague, infest

plagiar *vt* : plagiarize — **plagio** *nm* : plagiarism

plan *nm* **1** : plan **2** en ~ de : as **3** no te pongas en ese ~ *fam* : don't be that way

plana *nf* **1** : page **2** en primera ~ : on the front page

plancha *nf* **1** : iron (for ironing) **2** : grill (for cooking) **3** LÁMINA : sheet, plate — **planchar** *v* : iron — **planchado** *nm* : ironing

planear *vt* : plan — *vi* : glide — **planeador** *nm* : glider

planeta *nm* : planet

planicie *nf* : plain

planificar {72} *vt* : plan — **planificación** *nf*, *pl* **-ciones** : planning

planilla *nf Lat* : list, roster

plano, -na *adj* : flat — **plano** *nm* **1** : map, plan **2** : plane (surface) **3** NIVEL : level **4** de ~ : flatly, outright **5** primer ~ : foreground, close-up (in photography)

planta *nf* **1** : plant **2** PISO : floor, story **3** : sole (of the foot) — **plantación** *nf*, *pl* **-ciones** **1** : plantation **2** : (action of) planting — **plantar** *vt* **1** : plant **2** *fam* : deal, land — **plantarse** *vr* : stand firm

plantear *vt* **1** : expound, set forth **2** : raise (a question) **3** CAUSAR : create, pose (a problem) — **plantearse** *vr* : think about, consider

plantel *nm* **1** : staff, team **2** *Lat* : educational institution

plantilla *nf* **1** : insole **2** PATRÓN : pattern, template **3** : staff (of a business, etc.)

plasma *nm* : plasma

plástico, -ca *adj* : plastic — **plástico** *nm* : plastic

plata *nf* **1** : silver **2** *Lat fam* : money **3** ~ de ley : sterling silver

plataforma *nf* **1** : platform **2** ~ petrolífera : oil rig **3** ~ de lanzamiento : launching pad

plátano *nm* **1** : banana **2** : plantain

platea *nf* : orchestra, pit (in a theater)

plateado, -da *adj* **1** : silver, silvery (color) **2** : silver-plated

platicar {72} *vi* : talk, chat — **plática** *nf* : chat, conversation

platija *nf* : flatfish, flounder

platillo *nm* **1** : saucer CÍMBALO : cymbal **3** *Lat* : dish, course

platino *nm* : platinum

plato *nm* **1** : plate, dish **2** : course (of a meal) **3** ~ **principal** : entrée

platónico, -ca *adj* : platonic

playa *nf* **1** : beach, seashore **2** ~ **de estacionamiento** *Lat* : parking lot

plaza *nf* **1** : square, plaza **2** : seat (in transportation) **3** PUESTO : post, position **4** MERCADO : market, marketplace **5** ~ **de toros** : bullring

plazo *nm* **1** : period, term **2** PAGO : installment **3 a largo** ~ : long-term

plazoleta *or* **plazuela** *nf* : small square

pleamar *nf* : high tide

plebe *nf* : common people — **plebeyo, -ya** *adj & nm* : plebeian

plegar {49} *vt* : fold, bend — **plegarse** *vr* **1** : give in, yield **2** : jackknife (of a truck) — **plegable** *or* **plegadizo, -za** *adj* : folding, collapsible

plegaria *nf* : prayer

pleito *nm* **1** : lawsuit **2** *Lat* : dispute, fight

plenilunio *nm* : full moon

pleno, -na *adj* **1** : full, complete **2 en plena forma** : in top form **3 en pleno día** : in broad daylight — **plenitud** *nf* : fullness, abundance

pleuresía *nf* : pleurisy

pliego *nm* : sheet (of paper) — **pliegue** *nm* **1** : crease, fold **2** : pleat (in fabric)

plisar *vt* : pleat

plomería *nf Lat* : plumbing — **plomero, -ra** *n Lat* : plumber

plomo *nm* **1** : lead **2** FUSIBLE : fuse

pluma *nf* **1** : feather **2** : (fountain) pen — **plumaje** *nm* : plumage — **plumero** *nm* : feather duster — **plumilla** *nf* : nib — **plumón** *nm, pl* **-mones** : down

plural *adj & nm* : plural — **pluralidad** *nf* : plurality

pluriempleo *nm* **hacer** ~ : have more than one job

plus *nm* : bonus

plusvalía *nf* : appreciation, capital gain

plutocracia *nf* : plutocracy

Plutón *nm* : Pluto

plutonio *nm* : plutonium

pluvial *adj* : rain

poblar {19} *vt* **1** : settle, colonize **2** HABITAR : inhabit — **poblarse** *vr* : become crowded — **población** *nf, pl* **-ciones 1**

: city, town, village **2** HABITANTES : population — **poblado, -da** *adj* **1** : populated **2** : thick, bushy (of a beard, eyebrows, etc.) — **poblado** *nm* : village

pobre *adj* **1** : poor **2 ¡~ de mí!** : poor me! — ~ *nmf* **1** : poor person **2 los** ~**s** : the poor **3 ¡pobre!** : poor thing! — **pobreza** *nf* : poverty

pocilga *nf* : pigsty

poción *nf, pl* **-ciones** *or* **pócima** *nf* : potion

poco, -ca *adj* **1** : little, not much, (a) few **2 pocas veces** : rarely — ~ *pron* **1** : little, few **2 hace poco** : not long ago **3 poco a poco** : bit by bit, gradually **4 por poco** : nearly, just about **5 un poco** : a little, a bit — **poco** *adv* : little, not much

podar *vt* : prune

poder {58} *v aux* **1** : be able to, can **2** (*expressing possibility*) : might, may **3** (*expressing permission*) : can, may **4 ¿cómo puede ser?** : how can it be? **5 ¿puedo pasar?** : may I come in? — *vi* **1** : be possible **2** ~ **con** : cope with, manage **3 no puedo más** : I've had enough — ~ *nm* **1** : power **2** POSESIÓN : possession — **poderío** *nm* : power — **poderoso, -sa** *adj* : powerful

podólogo, -ga *n* : chiropodist

podrido, -da *adj* : rotten

poema *nm* : poem — **poesía** *nf* **1** : poetry **2** POEMA : poem — **poeta** *nmf* : poet — **poético, -ca** *adj* : poetic

póker *nm* → **póquer**

polaco, -ca *adj* : Polish

polar *adj* : polar — **polarizar** {21} *vt* : polarize

polea *nf* : pulley

polémica *nf* : controversy — **polémico, -ca** *adj* : controversial — **polemizar** *vt* : argue

polen *nm, pl* **pólenes** : pollen

policía *nf* : police — ~ *nmf* : police officer, policeman *m*, policewoman *f* — **policíaco, -ca** *adj* **1** : police **2 novela policíaca** : detective story

poliéster *nm* : polyester

poligamia *nf* : polygamy — **polígamo, -ma** *n* : polygamist

polígono *nm* : polygon

polilla *nf* : moth

polio *or* **poliomielitis** *nf* : polio, poliomyelitis

politécnico, -ca *adj* : polytechnic

política *nf* **1** : politics **2** POSTURA : policy — **político, -ca** *adj* **1** : political **2 hermano político** : brother-in-law — ~ *n* : politician

póliza *nf or* ~ **de seguros** : insurance policy

polizón *nm, pl* **-zones** : stowaway

pollo, -lla *n* **1** : chicken, chick **2** : chicken

(for cooking) — **pollera** *nf Lat* : skirt — **pollería** *nf* : poultry shop — **pollito, -ta** *n* : chick

polo *nm* **1** : pole **2** : polo (sport) **3** ~ **norte** : North Pole

poltrona *nf* : easy chair

polución *nf, pl* **-ciones** : pollution

polvo *nm* **1** : powder **2** SUCIEDAD : dust **3** ~s *nmpl* : face powder **4 hacer** ~ *fam* : crush, shatter — **polvareda** *nf* : cloud of dust — **polvera** *nf* : compact (for powder) — **pólvora** *nf* : gunpowder — **polvoriento, -ta** *adj* : dusty

pomada *nf* : ointment

pomelo *nm* : grapefruit

pómez *nm or* **piedra** ~ *nf* : pumice

pomo *nm* : knob, doorknob

pompa *nf* **1** : (soap) bubble **2** ESPLENDOR : pomp **3** ~s **fúnebres** : funeral — **pomposo, -sa** *adj* **1** : pompous **2** ESPLÉNDIDO : splendid

pómulo *nm* : cheekbone

ponchar *vt Lat* : puncture — **ponchadura** *nf Lat* : puncture

ponche *nm* : punch (drink)

poncho *nm* : poncho

ponderar *vt* **1** : consider **2** ALABAR : speak highly of

poner {60} *vt* **1** : put **2** AGREGAR : add **3** CONTRIBUIR : contribute **4** SUPONER : suppose **5** DISPONER : arrange, set out **6** : give (a name), call **7** ENCENDER : turn on **8** ESTABLECER : set up, establish **9** : lay (eggs) — *vi* : lay eggs — **ponerse** *vr* **1** : move (into a position) **2** : put on (clothing, etc.) **3** : set (of the sun) **4** ~ **furioso** : become angry

poniente *nm* **1** OCCIDENTE : west **2** : west wind

pontífice *nm* : pontiff

pontón *nm, pl* **-tones** : pontoon

ponzoña *nf* : poison, venom

popa *nf* **1** : stern **2 a** ~ : astern

popelín *nm, pl* **-lines** : poplin

popote *nm Lat* : (drinking) straw

populacho *nm* : rabble, masses *pl*

popular *adj* **1** : popular **2** : colloquial (of language) — **popularidad** *nf* : popularity — **popularizar** {21} *vt* : popularize — **populoso, -sa** *adj* : populous

póquer *nm* : poker (card game)

por *prep* **1** : for **2** (*indicating an approximate time*) : around, during **3** (*indicating an approximate place*) : around, about **4** A TRAVÉS DE : through, along **5** A CAUSA DE : because of **6** (*indicating rate or ratio*) : per **7** *or* ~ **medio de** : by means of **8** : times (in mathematics) **9** SEGÚN : as for, according to **10 estar** ~ : be about to **11**

~ **ciento** : percent **12** ~ **favor** : please **13** ~ **lo tanto** : therefore **14 ¿por qué?** : why?

porcelana *nf* : porcelain, china

porcentaje *nm* : percentage

porción *nf, pl* **-ciones** : portion, piece

pordiosero, -ra *n* : beggar

porfiar {85} *vi* : insist — **porfiado, -da** *adj* : obstinate, persistent

pormenor *nm* : detail

pornografía *nf* : pornography — **pornográfico, -ca** *adj* : pornographic

poro *nm* : pore — **poroso, -sa** *adj* : porous

poroto *nm Lat* : bean

porque *conj* **1** : because **2** *or* **por que** : in order that — **porqué** *nm* : reason

porquería *nf* **1** SUCIEDAD : filth **2** : shoddy thing, junk

porra *nf* : nightstick, club — **porrazo** *nm* : blow, whack

portaaviones *nms & pl* : aircraft carrier

portada *nf* **1** : facade **2** : title page (of a book), cover (of a magazine)

portador, -dora *n* : bearer

portaequipajes *nms & pl* : luggage rack

portafolio *or* **portafolios** *nm, pl* **-lios 1** : portfolio **2** MALETÍN : briefcase

portal *nm* **1** : doorway **2** VESTÍBULO : hall, vestibule

portamonedas *nms & pl* : purse

portar *vt* : carry, bear — **portarse** *vr* : behave

portátil *adj* : portable

portaviones *nm* → **portaaviones**

portavoz *nmf, pl* **-voces** : spokesperson, spokesman *m*, spokeswoman *f*

portazo *nm* **dar un** ~ : slam the door

porte *nm* **1** : transport, freight **2** ASPECTO : bearing, appearance **3** ~ **pagado** : postage paid

portento *nm* : marvel, wonder — **portentoso, -sa** *adj* : marvelous

porteño, -ña *adj* : of or from Buenos Aires

portería *nf* **1** : superintendent's office **2** : goal, goalposts *pl* (in sports) — **portero, -ra** *n* **1** : goalkeeper, goalie **2** CONSERJE : janitor, superintendent

portezuela *nf* : door (of an automobile)

pórtico *nm* : portico

portilla *nf* : porthole

portugués, -guesa *adj, mpl* **-gueses** : Portuguese — **portugués** *nm* : Portuguese (language)

porvenir *nm* : future

pos: en ~ **de** *adv phr* : in pursuit of

posada *nf* : inn

posaderas *nfpl fam* : backside, bottom

posar *vi* : pose — *vt* : place, lay — **posarse** *vr* : settle, rest

posavasos *nms & pl* : coaster
posdata *nf* : postscript
pose *nf* : pose
poseer {20} *vt* : possess, own — **poseedor, -dora** *n* : possessor, owner — **poseído, -da** *adj* : possessed — **posesión** *nf, pl* **-siones** : possession — **posesionarse** *vr* ~ **de** : take possession of, take over — **posesivo, -va** *adj* : possessive
posguerra *nf* : postwar period
posibilidad *nf* : possibility — **posibilitar** *vt* : make possible — **posible** *adj* **1** : possible **2 de ser** ~ : if possible
posición *nf, pl* **-ciones** : position — **posicionar** *vt* : position — **posicionarse** *vr* : take a stand
positivo, -va *adj* : positive
poso *nm* : sediment, (coffee) grounds
posponer {60} *vt* **1** : postpone **2** RELEGAR : put behind, subordinate
postal *adj* : postal — ~ *nf* : postcard
postdata → **posdata**
poste *nm* : post, pole
póster *nm, pl* **-ters** : poster
postergar {52} *vt* **1** : pass over **2** APLAZAR : postpone
posteridad *nf* : posterity — **posterior** *adj* **1** : later, subsequent **2** TRASERO : back, rear — **posteriormente** *adv* : subsequently, later
postigo *nm* **1** : small door **2** CONTRAVENTANA : shutter
postizo, -za *adj* : artificial, false
postrarse *vr* : prostrate oneself — **postrado, -da** *adj* : prostrate
postre *nm* : dessert
postular *vt* **1** : advance, propose **2** *Lat* : nominate — **postulado** *nm* : postulate
póstumo, -ma *adj* : posthumous
postura *nf* : position, stance
potable *adj* : drinkable, potable
potaje *nm* : thick vegetable soup
potasio *nm* : potassium
pote *nm* : jar
potencia *nf* : power — **potencial** *adj & nm* : potential — **potente** *adj* : powerful
potro, -tra *n* : colt *m*, filly *f* — **potro** *nm* : horse (in gymnastics)
pozo *nm* **1** : well **2** : shaft (in a mine)
práctica *nf* **1** : practice **2 en la** ~ : in practice — **practicable** *adj* : practicable, feasible — **practicante** *adj* : practicing — ~ *nmf* : practitioner — **practicar** {72} *vt* **1** : practice **2** REALIZAR : perform, carry out — *vi* : practice — **práctico, -ca** *adj* : practical
pradera *nf* : grassland, prairie — **prado** *nm* : meadow
pragmático, -ca *adj* : pragmatic

preámbulo *nm* : preamble
precario, -ria *adj* : precarious
precaución *nf, pl* **-ciones 1** : precaution **2** PRUDENCIA : caution, care **3 con** ~ : cautiously
precaver *vt* : guard against — **precavido, -da** *adj* : prudent, cautious
preceder *v* : precede — **precedencia** *nf* : precedence, priority — **precedente** *adj* : preceding, previous — ~ *nm* : precedent
precepto *nm* : precept
preciado, -da *adj* : prized, valuable — **preciarse** *vr* ~ **de** : pride oneself on, boast about
precinto *nm* : seal
precio *nm* : price, cost — **preciosidad** *nf* **1** VALOR : value **2** : beautiful thing — **precioso, -sa** *adj* **1** HERMOSO : beautiful **2** VALIOSO : precious
precipicio *nm* : precipice
precipitar *vt* **1** : hasten, speed up **2** ARROJAR : hurl — **precipitarse** *vr* **1** APRESURARSE : rush **2** : act rashly **3** ARROJARSE : throw oneself — **precipitación** *nf, pl* **-ciones 1** : precipitation **2** PRISA : haste — **precipitadamente** *adv* : in a rush, hastily — **precipitado, -da** *adj* : hasty
preciso, -sa *adj* **1** : precise **2** NECESARIO : necessary — **precisamente** *adv* : precisely, exactly — **precisar** *vt* **1** : specify, determine **2** NECESITAR : require — **precisión** *nf, pl* **-siones 1** : precision **2** NECESIDAD : necessity
preconcebido *adj* : preconceived
precoz *adj, pl* **-coces 1** : early **2** : precocious (of children)
precursor, -sora *n* : forerunner
predecesor, -sora *n* : predecessor
predecir {11} *vt* : foretell, predict
predestinado, -da *adj* : predestined
predeterminar *vt* : predetermine
prédica *nf* : sermon
predicado *nm* : predicate
predicar {72} *v* : preach — **predicador, -dora** *n* : preacher
predicción *nf, pl* **-ciones 1** : prediction **2** PRONÓSTICO : forecast
predilección *nf, pl* **-ciones** : preference — **predilecto, -ta** *adj* : favorite
predisponer {60} *vt* : predispose — **predisposición** *nf, pl* **-ciones** : predisposition
predominar *vi* : predominate — **predominante** *adj* : predominant, prevailing — **predominio** *nm* : predominance
preeminente *adj* : preeminent
prefabricado, -da *adj* : prefabricated
prefacio *nm* : preface
preferir {76} *vt* : prefer — **preferencia** *nf* **1** : preference **2 de** ~ : preferably — **prefer-**

ente *adj* : preferential — **preferible** *adj* : preferable — **preferido, -da** *adj* : favorite

prefijo *nm* **1** : prefix **2** *Spain* : area code

pregonar *vt* : proclaim, announce

pregunta *nf* **1** : question **2 hacer ~s** : ask questions — **preguntar** *v* : ask — **preguntarse** *vr* : wonder

prehistórico, -ca *adj* : prehistoric

prejuicio *nm* : prejudice

preliminar *adj & nm* : preliminary

preludio *nm* : prelude

prematrimonial *adj* : premarital

prematuro, -ra *adj* : premature

premeditar *vt* : premeditate — **premeditación** *nf, pl* **-ciones** : premeditation

premenstrual *adj* : premenstrual

premio *nm* **1** : prize **2** RECOMPENSA : reward **3 ~ gordo** : jackpot — **premiado, -da** *adj* : prizewinning — **premiar** *vt* **1** : award a prize to **2** RECOMPENSAR : reward

premisa *nf* : premise

premonición *nf, pl* **-ciones** : premonition

premura *nf* : haste, urgency

prenatal *adj* : prenatal

prenda *nf* **1** : piece of clothing **2** GARANTÍA : pledge **3** : forfeit (in a game) — **prendar** *vt* : captivate — **prendarse** *vr* **~ de** : fall in love with

prender *vt* **1** SUJETAR : pin, fasten **2** APRESAR : capture **3** : light (a match, etc.) **4** *Lat* : turn on (a light, etc.) — *vi* **1** : take root **2** ARDER : catch, burn (of fire) — **prenderse** *vr* : catch fire — **prendedor** *nm* *Lat* : brooch, pin

prensa *nf* : press — **prensar** *vt* : press

preñado, -da *adj* **1** : pregnant **2 ~ de** : filled with

preocupar *vt* : worry — **preocuparse** *vr* **1** : worry **2 ~ de** : take care of — **preocupación** *nf, pl* **-ciones** : worry

preparar *vt* : prepare — **prepararse** *vr* : get ready — **preparación** *nf, pl* **-ciones** : preparation — **preparado, -da** *adj* : prepared, ready — **preparado** *nm* : preparation — **preparativo, -va** *adj* : preparatory, preliminary — **preparativos** *nmpl* : preparations —**preparatorio, -ria** *adj* : preparatory

preposición *nf, pl* **-ciones** : preposition

prepotente *adj* : arrogant, domineering

prerrogativa *nf* : prerogative

presa *nf* **1** : catch, prey **2** DIQUE : dam **3 hacer ~ en** : seize

presagiar *vt* : presage, forebode — **presagio** *nm* **1** : omen **2** PREMONICIÓN : premonition

presbítero *nm* : presbyter, priest

prescindir *vi* **~ de 1** : do without **2** OMITIR : dispense with

prescribir {33} *vt* : prescribe — **prescripción** *nf, pl* **-ciones** : prescription

presencia *nf* **1** : presence **2** ASPECTO : appearance — **presenciar** *vt* : be present at, witness

presentar *vt* **1** : present **2** OFRECER : offer, give **3** MOSTRAR : show **4** : introduce (persons) — **presentarse** *vr* **1** : show up **2** : arise, come up (of a problem, etc.) **3** : introduce oneself — **presentación** *nf, pl* **-ciones 1** : presentation **2** : introduction (of persons) **3** ASPECTO : appearance — **presentador, -dora** *n* : presenter, host (of a television program, etc.)

presente *adj* **1** : present **2 tener ~** : keep in mind — **~** *nm* **1** : present **2 entre los ~s** : among those present

presentir {76} *vt* : have a presentiment of — **presentimiento** *nm* : premonition

preservar *vt* : preserve, protect — **preservación** *nf, pl* **-ciones** : preservation — **preservativo** *nm* : condom

presidente, -ta *n* **1** : president **2** : chair, chairperson (of a meeting) — **presidencia** *nf* **1** : presidency **2** : chairmanship (of a meeting) — **presidencial** *adj* : presidential

presidio *nm* : prison — **presidiario, -ria** *n* : convict

presidir *vt* **1** : preside over, chair **2** PREDOMINAR : dominate

presión *nf, pl* **-siones 1** : pressure **2 ~ arterial** : blood pressure **3 hacer ~** : press — **presionar** *vt* **1** : press **2** COACCIONAR : put pressure on

preso, -sa *adj* : imprisoned — **~** *n* : prisoner

prestar *vt* **1** : lend, loan **2** : give (aid) **3 ~ atención** : pay attention — **prestado, -da** *adj* **1** : borrowed, on loan **2 pedir ~** : borrow — **prestamista** *nmf* : moneylender — **préstamo** *nm* : loan

prestidigitación *nf, pl* **-ciones** : sleight of hand — **prestidigitador, -dora** *n* : magician

prestigio *nm* : prestige — **prestigioso, -sa** *adj* : prestigious

presto, -ta *adj* : prompt, ready — **presto** *adv* : promptly, right away

presumir *vt* : presume — *vi* : boast, show off — **presumido, -da** *adj* : conceited, vain — **presunción** *nf, pl* **-ciones 1** : presumption **2** VANIDAD : vanity — **presunto, -ta** *adj* : presumed, alleged — **presuntuoso, -sa** *adj* : conceited

presuponer {60} *vt* : presuppose — **presupuesto** *nm* **1** : budget, estimate **2** SUPUESTO : assumption

presuroso, -sa *adj* : hasty, quick

pretender *vt* **1** : try to **2** AFIRMAR : claim **3** CORTEJAR : court, woo **4 ~ que** : expect

— **pretencioso, -sa** *adj* : pretentious — **pretendido** *adj* : supposed — **pretendiente** *nmf* **1** : candidate **2** : pretender (to a throne) — **~** *nm* : suitor — **pretensión** *nf, pl* **-siones 1** INTENCIÓN : intention, aspiration **2** : claim (to a throne, etc.) **3 pretensiones** *nfpl* : pretensions

pretérito *nm* : past (in grammar)

pretexto *nm* : pretext, excuse

prevalecer {53} *vi* : prevail — **prevaleciente** *adj* : prevailing, prevalent

prevenir {87} *vt* **1** : prevent **2** AVISAR : warn — **prevenirse** {87} *vr* **~ contra** *or* **~ de** : take precautions against — **prevención** *nf, pl* **-ciones 1** : prevention **2** PRECAUCIÓN : precaution **3** PREJUICIO : prejudice — **prevenido, -da** *adj* **1** : prepared, ready **2** PRECAVIDO : cautious — **preventivo, -va** *adj* : preventive

prever {88} *vt* **1** : foresee **2** PLANEAR : plan

previo, -via *adj* : previous, prior

previsible *adj* : foreseeable — **previsión** *nf, pl* **-siones 1** : foresight **2** PREDICCIÓN : prediction, forecast — **previsor, -sora** *adj* : farsighted, prudent

prieto, -ta *adj* **1** CEÑIDO : tight **2** *Lat fam* : dark-skinned

prima *nf* **1** : bonus **2** : (insurance) premium **3** → **primo**

primario, -ria *adj* **1** : primary **2 escuela primaria** : elementary school

primate *nm* : primate

primavera *nf* **1** : spring (season) **2** : primrose (flower) — **primaveral** *adj* : spring

primero, -ra *adj* (**primer** before masculine singular nouns) **1** : first **2** MEJOR : top, leading **3** PRINCIPAL : main, basic **4 de primera** : first-rate — **~** *n* : first (person or thing) — **primero** *adv* **1** : first **2** MÁS BIEN : rather, sooner

primitivo, -va *adj* : primitive

primo, -ma *n* : cousin

primogénito, -ta *adj & n* : firstborn

primor *nm* : beautiful thing

primordial *adj* : basic, fundamental

primoroso, -sa *adj* **1** : exquisite, fine **2** HÁBIL : skillful

princesa *nf* : princess

principado *nm* : principality

principal *adj* : main, principal

príncipe *nm* : prince

principio *nm* **1** : principle **2** COMIENZO : beginning, start **3** ORIGEN : origin **4 al ~** : at first **5 a ~s de** : at the beginning of — **principiante** *nmf* : beginner

pringar {52} *vt* : spatter (with grease) — **pringoso, -sa** *adj* : greasy

prioridad *nf* : priority

prisa *nf* **1** : hurry, rush **2 a ~** *or* **de ~**

: quickly **3 a toda ~** : as fast as possible **4 darse ~** : hurry **5 tener ~** : be in a hurry

prisión *nf, pl* **-siones 1** : prison **2** ENCARCELAMIENTO : imprisonment — **prisionero, -ra** *n* : prisoner

prisma *nm* : prism — **prismáticos** *nmpl* : binoculars

privar *vt* **1** : deprive **2** PROHIBIR : forbid **3** *Lat* : knock out — **privarse** *vr* : deprive oneself — **privación** *nf, pl* **-ciones** : deprivation — **privado, -da** *adj* : private — **privativo, -va** *adj* : exclusive

privilegio *nm* : privilege — **privilegiado, -da** *adj* : privileged

pro *prep* : for, in favor of — **~** *nm* **1** : pro, advantage **2 en ~ de** : for, in support of **3 los pros y los contras** : the pros and cons

proa *nf* : bow, prow

probabilidad *nf* : probability — **probable** *adj* : probable, likely — **probablemente** *adv* : probably

probar {19} *vt* **1** : try, test **2** : try on (clothing) **3** DEMOSTRAR : prove **4** DEGUSTAR : taste — *vi* : try — **probarse** *vr* : try on (clothing) — **probeta** *nf* : test tube

problema *nm* : problem — **problemático, -ca** *adj* : problematic

proceder *vi* **1** : proceed, act **2** : be appropriate **3 ~ de** : come from — **procedencia** *nf* : origin — **procedente** *adj* **~ de** : coming from, originating in — **procedimiento** *nm* **1** : procedure, method **2** : proceedings *pl* (in law)

procesar *vt* **1** : prosecute **2** : process (data) — **procesador** *nm* **~ de textos** : word processor — **procesamiento** *nm* : processing — **procesión** *nf, pl* **-siones** : procession — **proceso** *nm* **1** : process **2** : trial, proceedings *pl* (in law)

proclamar *vt* : proclaim — **proclama** *nf* : proclamation — **proclamación** *nf, pl* **-ciones** : proclamation

procrear *vi* : procreate — **procreación** *nf, pl* **-ciones** : procreation

procurar *vt* **1** : try, endeavor **2** CONSEGUIR : obtain, procure — **procurador, -dora** *n* : attorney

prodigar {52} *vt* : lavish — **prodigio** *nm* : wonder, prodigy — **prodigioso, -sa** *adj* : prodigious

pródigo, -ga *adj* : extravagant, prodigal

producir {61} *vt* **1** : produce **2** CAUSAR : cause **3** : yield, bear (interest, fruit, etc.) — **producirse** *vr* : take place — **producción** *nf, pl* **-ciones** : production — **productividad** *nf* : productivity — **productivo, -va** *adj* : productive — **producto** *nm* : product — **productor, -tora** *n* : producer

proeza *nf* : exploit

profanar *vt* : profane, desecrate — **profanación** *nf, pl* **-ciones** : desecration — **profano, -na** *adj* : profane

profecía *nf* : prophecy

proferir {76} *vt* **1** : utter **2** : hurl (insults)

profesar *vt* **1** : profess **2** : practice (a profession, etc.) — **profesión** *nf, pl* **-siones** : profession — **profesional** *adj* & *nmf* : professional — **profesor, -sora** *n* **1** : teacher **2** : professor (at a university, etc.) — **profesorado** *nm* **1** : teaching profession **2** PROFESORES : faculty

profeta *nm* : prophet — **profético, -ca** *adj* : prophetic — **profetista** *nf* : (female) prophet — **profetizar** {21} *vt* : prophesy

prófugo, -ga *adj* & *n* : fugitive

profundo, -da *adj* **1** HONDO : deep **2** : profound (of thoughts, etc.) — **profundamente** *adv* : deeply, profoundly — **profundidad** *nf* : depth — **profundizar** {21} *vt* : study in depth

profuso, -sa *adj* : profuse — **profusión** *nf, pl* **-siones** : profusion

progenie *nf* : progeny, offspring

programa *nm* **1** : program **2** : curriculum (in education) — **programación** *nf, pl* **-ciones** : programming — **programador, -dora** *n* : programmer — **programar** *vt* **1** : schedule **2** : program (a computer, etc.)

progreso *nm* : progress — **progresar** *vi* : (make) progress — **progresión** *nf, pl* **-ciones** : progression — **progresista** *adj* & *nmf* : progressive — **progresivo, -va** *adj* : progressive, gradual

prohibir {62} *vt* : prohibit, forbid — **prohibición** *nf, pl* **-ciones** : ban, prohibition — **prohibido, -da** *adj* : forbidden — **prohibitivo, -va** *adj* : prohibitive

prójimo *nm* : neighbor, fellow man

prole *nf* : offspring

proletariado *nm* : proletariat — **proletario, -ria** *adj* & *n* : proletarian

proliferar *vi* : proliferate — **proliferación** *nf, pl* **-ciones** : proliferation — **prolífico, -ca** *adj* : prolific

prolijo, -ja *adj* : wordy, long-winded

prólogo *nm* : prologue, foreword

prolongar {52} *vt* **1** : prolong **2** ALARGAR : lengthen — **prolongarse** *vr* : last, continue — **prolongación** *nf, pl* **-ciones** : extension

promedio *nm* : average

promesa *nf* : promise — **prometedor, -dora** *adj* : promising, hopeful — **prometer** *vt* : promise — *vi* : show promise — **prometerse** *vr* : get engaged — **prometido, -da** *adj* : engaged — *~ n* : fiancé *m*, fiancée *f*

prominente *adj* : prominent — **prominencia** *nf* : prominence

promiscuo, -cua *adj* : promiscuous — **promiscuidad** *nf* : promiscuity

promocionar *vt* : promote — **promoción** *nf, pl* **-ciones** : promotion

promontorio *nm* : promontory

promover {47} *vt* **1** : promote **2** CAUSAR : cause — **promotor, -tora** *n* : promoter

promulgar {52} *vt* **1** : proclaim **2** : enact (a law)

pronombre *nm* : pronoun

pronosticar {72} *vt* : predict, forecast — **pronóstico** *nm* **1** : prediction, forecast **2** : (medical) prognosis

pronto, -ta *adj* **1** : quick, prompt **2** PREPARADO : ready — **pronto** *adv* **1** : soon **2** RAPIDAMENTE : quickly, promptly **3** de *~* : suddenly **4** por lo *~* : for the time being **5** tan *~* como : as soon as

pronunciar *vt* **1** : pronounce **2** : give, deliver (a speech) — **pronunciarse** *vr* **1** : declare oneself **2** SUBLEVARSE : revolt — **pronunciación** *nf, pl* **-ciones** : pronunciation

propagación *nf, pl* **-ciones** : propagation

propaganda *nf* **1** : propaganda **2** PUBLICIDAD : advertising

propagar {52} *vt* : propagate, spread — **propagarse** *vr* : propagate

propano *nm* : propane

propasarse *vr* : go too far

propensión *nf, pl* **-siones** : inclination, propensity — **propenso, -sa** *adj* : prone, inclined

propiamente *adv* : exactly

propicio, -cia *adj* : favorable, propitious

propiedad *nf* **1** : property **2** PERTINENCIA : ownership, possession — **propietario, -ria** *n* : owner, proprietor

propina *nf* : tip

propinar *vt* : give, deal (a blow, etc.)

propio, -pia *adj* **1** : own **2** APROPIADO : proper, appropriate **3** CARACTERÍSTICO : characteristic, typical **4** MISMO : himself, herself, oneself

proponer {60} *vt* **1** : propose **2** : nominate (a person) — **proponerse** *vr* : propose, intend

proporción *nf, pl* **-ciones** : proportion — **proporcionado, -da** *adj* : proportionate — **proporcional** *adj* : proportional — **proporcionar** *vt* **1** : provide **2** AJUSTAR : adapt, proportion

proposición *nf, pl* **-ciones** : proposal, proposition

propósito *nm* **1** : purpose, intention **2** a *~* : incidentally, by the way **3** a *~* : on purpose, intentionally

propuesta *nf* **1** : proposal **2** : offer (of employment, etc.)

propulsar *vt* **1** : propel, drive **2** PROMOVER

: promote — **propulsión** *nf*, *pl* **-siones** : propulsion

prorrogar {52} *vt* **1** : extend **2** APLAZAR : postpone — **prórroga** *nf* **1** : extension, deferment **2** : overtime (in sports)

prorrumpir *vi* : burst forth, break out

prosa *nf* : prose

proscribir {33} *vt* **1** : prohibit, ban **2** DESTERRAR : exile — **proscripción** *nf*, *pl* **-ciones 1** : ban **2** DESTIERRO : banishment — **proscrito, -ta** *adj* : banned — ~ *n* : exile, outlaw

proseguir {75} *v* : continue — **prosecución** *nf*, *pl* **-ciones** : continuation

prospección *nf*, *pl* **-ciones** : prospecting, exploration

prospecto *nm* : prospectus

prosperar *vi* : prosper, thrive — **prosperidad** *nf* : prosperity — **próspero, -ra** *adj* : prosperous, flourishing

prostituir {41} *vt* : prostitute — **prostitución** *nf*, *pl* **-ciones** : prostitution — **prostituta** *nf* : prostitute

protagonista *nmf* : protagonist — **protagonizar** *vt* : star in

proteger {15} *vt* : protect — **protegerse** *vr* : protect oneself — **protección** *nf*, *pl* **-ciones** : protection — **protector, -tora** *adj* : protective — ~ *n* : protector — **protegido, -da** *n* : protégé

proteína *nf* : protein

protestar *v* : protest — **protesta** *nf* : protest — **protestante** *adj* & *nmf* : Protestant

protocolo *nm* : protocol

prototipo *nm* : prototype

protuberancia *nf* : protuberance — **protuberante** *adj* : protuberant

provecho *nm* **1** : benefit, advantage **2** ¡buen ~! : enjoy your meal! — **provechoso, -sa** *adj* : profitable, beneficial

proveer {63} *vt* : provide, supply — **proveedor, -dora** *n* : supplier

provenir {87} *vi* ~ **de** : come from

proverbio *nm* : proverb — **proverbial** *adj* : proverbial

providencia *nf* **1** : providence **2** PRECAUCIÓN : precaution — **providencial** *adj* : providential

provincia *nf* : province — **provincial** *adj* : provincial — **provinciano, -na** *adj* : provincial, parochial

provisión *nf*, *pl* **-siones** : provision — **provisional** *adj* : provisional

provocar {72} *vt* **1** : provoke, cause **2** IRRITAR : irritate — **provocación** *nf*, *pl* **-ciones** : provocation — **provocativo, -va** *adj* : provocative

próximo, -ma *adj* **1** CERCANO : near **2** SIGUIENTE : next — **próximamente** *adv*

: shortly, soon — **proximidad** *nf* **1** : proximity **2** ~**es** *nfpl* : vicinity

proyectar *vt* **1** : plan **2** LANZAR : throw, hurl **3** : cast (light) **4** : show (a film) — **proyección** *nf*, *pl* **-ciones** : projection — **proyectil** *nm* : missile — **proyecto** *nm* : plan, project — **proyector** *nm* : projector

prudencia *nf* : prudence, care — **prudente** *adj* : prudent, sensible

prueba *nf* **1** : proof, evidence **2** : test (in education, medicine, etc.) **3** : event (in sports) **4 a ~ de agua** : waterproof

psicoanálisis *nm* : psychoanalysis — **psicoanalista** *nmf* : psychoanalyst — **psicoanalizar** {21} *vt* : psychoanalyze

psicología *nf* : psychology — **psicológico, -ca** *adj* : psychological — **psicólogo, -ga** *n* : psychologist

psicópata *nmf* : psychopath

psicosis *nfs* & *pl* : psychosis

psicoterapia *nf* : psychotherapy — **psicoterapeuta** *nmf* : psychotherapist

psicótico, -ca *adj* & *n* : psychotic

psiquiatría *nf* : psychiatry — **psiquiatra** *nmf* : psychiatrist — **psiquiátrico, -ca** *adj* : psychiatric

psíquico, -ca *adj* : psychic

púa *nf* **1** : sharp point **2** : tooth (of a comb) **3** : thorn (of a plant), quill (of a porcupine, etc.) **4** : (guitar) pick

pubertad *nf* : puberty

publicar {72} *vt* **1** : publish **2** DIVULGAR : divulge, disclose — **publicación** *nf*, *pl* **-ciones** : publication

publicidad *nf* **1** : publicity **2** : advertising (in marketing) — **publicista** *nmf* : publicist — **publicitar** *vt* **1** : publicize **2** : advertise (a product, etc.) — **publicitario, -ria** *adj* : advertising

público, -ca *adj* : public — **público** *nm* **1** : public **2** : audience (of theater, etc.), spectators *pl* (of sports)

puchero *nm* **1** : (cooking) pot **2** GUISADO : stew **3 hacer ~s** : pout

púdico, -ca *adj* : modest

pudiente *adj* : wealthy

pudín *nm*, *pl* **-dines** : pudding

pudor *nm* : modesty — **pudoroso, -sa** *adj* : modest

pudrir {59} *vt* **1** : rot **2** *fam* : annoy — **pudrirse** *vr* : rot

pueblo *nm* **1** : town, village **2** NACIÓN : people, nation

puente *nm* **1** : bridge **2 hacer ~** : have a long weekend **3 ~ levadizo** : drawbridge

puerco, -ca *n* **1** : pig **2 puerco espín** : porcupine — ~ *adj* : dirty, filthy

pueril *adj* : childish

puerro *nm* : leek

puerta *nf* **1** : door, gate **2 a ~ cerrada** : behind closed doors

puerto *nm* **1** : port **2** : (mountain) pass **3** REFUGIO : haven

puertorriqueño, -ña *adj* : Puerto Rican

pues *conj* **1** : since, because **2** POR LO TANTO : so, therefore **3** (*used interjectionally*) : well, then

puesta *nf* **1 ~ a punto** : tune-up **2 ~ de sol** : sunset **3 ~ en marcha** : starting up — **puesto, -ta** *adj* **1** : put, set **2** VESTIDO : dressed — **puesto** *nm* **1** : place **2** EMPLEO : position, job **3** : stand, stall (in a market) **4 ~ avanzado** : outpost — **~ que** *conj* : since, given that

púgil *nm* : boxer

pugnar *vi* : fight — **pugna** *nf* : fight, battle

pulcro, -cra *adj* : tidy, neat

pulga *nf* **1** : flea **2 tener malas ~s** : have a bad temper

pulgada *nf* : inch — **pulgar** *nm* **1** : thumb **2** : big toe

pulir *vt* **1** : polish **2** REFINAR : touch up, perfect

pulla *nf* : cutting remark, gibe

pulmón *nm, pl* **-mones** : lung — **pulmonar** *adj* : pulmonary — **pulmonía** *nf* : pneumonia

pulpa *nf* : pulp

pulpería *nf Lat* : grocery store

púlpito *nm* : pulpit

pulpo *nm* : octopus

pulsar *vt* **1** : press (a button), strike (a key) **2** : play (music) — **pulsación** *nf, pl* **-ciones 1** : beat, throb **2** : keystroke (on a typewriter, etc.)

pulsera *nf* : bracelet

pulso *nm* **1** : pulse **2** : steadiness (of hand)

pulular *vi* : swarm

pulverizar {21} *vt* **1** : pulverize, crush **2** : spray (a liquid) — **pulverizador** *nm* : atomizer, spray

puma *nf* : puma

punitivo, -va *adj* : punitive

punta *nf* **1** : tip, end **2** : point (of a needle, etc.) **3 ~ del dedo** : fingertip **4 sacar ~ a** : sharpen

puntada *nf* **1** : stitch **2 ~s** *nfpl* : seam

puntal *nm* : prop, support

puntapié *nm* : kick

puntear *vt* : pluck (a guitar)

puntería *nf* : aim, marksmanship

puntiagudo, -da *adj* : sharp, pointed

puntilla *nf* **1** : lace edging **2 de ~s** : on tiptoe

punto *nm* **1** : dot, point **2** : period (in punctuation) **3** ASUNTO : item, question **4** LUGAR : spot, place **5** MOMENTO : moment **6** : point (in a score) **7** PUNTADA : stitch **8 a las dos en ~** : at two o'clock sharp **9 dos ~s** : colon **10 hasta cierto ~** : up to a point **11 ~ de partida** : starting point **12 ~ muerto** : deadlock **13 ~ y coma** : semicolon

puntuación *nf, pl* **-ciones 1** : punctuation **2** : scoring, score (in sports)

puntual *adj* **1** : prompt, punctual **2** EXACTO : accurate, detailed — **puntualidad** *nf* **1** : punctuality **2** EXACTITUD : accuracy

puntuar {3} *vt* : punctuate — *vi* : score (in sports)

punzar {21} *vt* : prick, puncture — **punzada** *nf* **1** PINCHAZO : prick **2** : sharp pain — **punzante** *adj* **1** : sharp **2** MORDAZ : biting, caustic

puñado *nm* **1** : handful **2 a ~s** : by the handful

puñal *nm* : dagger — **puñalada** *nf* : stab

puño *nm* **1** : fist **2** : cuff (of a shirt) **3** : handle, hilt (of a sword, etc.) — **puñetazo** *nm* : punch (with the fist)

pupila *nf* : pupil (of the eye)

pupitre *nm* : desk

puré *nm* **1** : purée **2 ~ de papas** *or* **~ de patatas** *Spain* : mashed potatoes

pureza *nf* : purity

purga *nf* : purge — **purgar** {52} *vt* : purge — **purgatorio** *nm* : purgatory

purificar {72} *vt* : purify — **purificación** *nf, pl* **-ciones** : purification

puritano, -na *adj* : puritanical — **~** *n* : puritan

puro, -ra *adj* **1** : pure **2** SIMPLE : plain, simple **3** *Lat fam* : only, just — **puro** *nm* : cigar

púrpura *nf* : purple — **purpúreo, -rea** *adj* : purple

pus *nm* : pus

pusilánime *adj* : cowardly

puta *nf* : whore

putrefacción *nf, pl* **-ciones** : putrefaction, rot — **pútrido, -da** *adj* : putrid, rotten

Q

q *nf* : q, 18th letter of the Spanish alphabet
que *conj* **1** : that **2** (*in comparisons*) : than **3** (*introducing a reason or cause*) : so that, or else **4 es ~** : the thing is that **5 yo ~ tú** : if I were you — **~ pron 1** (*referring to persons*) : who, whom **2** (*referring to things*) : that, which **3 el (la, lo, las, los) ~** : he (she, it, they) who, whoever, the one(s) that
qué *adv* **1** : how, what **2 ¡~ lindo!** : how lovely! — **~ adj** : what, which — **~ pron 1** : what **2 ¿~ crees?** : what do you think?
quebrar {55} *vt* : break — *vi* : go bankrupt — **quebrarse** *vr* : break — **quebrada** *nf* : ravine, gorge — **quebradizo, -za** *adj* : breakable, fragile — **quebrado, -da** *adj* **1** : bankrupt **2** : rough, uneven (of land, etc.) **3** ROTO : broken — **quebrado** *nm* : fraction — **quebradura** *nf* : crack, fissure — **quebrantar** *vt* **1** : break **2** DEBILITAR : weaken — **quebranto** *nm* **1** : harm, damage **2** AFLICCIÓN : grief, pain
queda *nf* → **toque**
quedar *vi* **1** PERMANECER : remain, stay **2** ESTAR : be **3** FALTAR : be left **4** : fit, look (of clothing, etc.) **5 no queda lejos** : it's not far **6 ~ en** : agree to, agree on — **quedarse** *vr* **1** : stay **2 ~ con** : keep
quedo, -da *adj* : quiet, still — **quedo** *adv* : softly, quietly
quehacer *nm* **1** : task **2 ~es** *nmpl* : chores
queja *nf* : complaint — **quejarse** *vr* **1** : complain **2** GEMIR : moan, groan — **quejido** *nm* : moan, whimper — **quejoso, -sa** *adj* : complaining, whining
quemar *vt* **1** : burn **2** MALGASTAR : squander — *vi* : burn — **quemarse** *vr* **1** : burn oneself **2** : burn (up) **3** : get sunburned — **quemado, -da** *adj* **1** : burned **2** AGOTADO : burned-out **3 estar ~** : be fed up — **quemador** *nm* : burner — **quemadura** *nf* : burn — **quemarropa: a ~** *adj & adv phr* : point-blank
querella *nf* **1** : dispute, quarrel **2** : charge (in law)
querer {64} *vt* **1** : want **2** AMAR : love **3 ~ decir** : mean **4 ¿quieres pasarme la leche?** : please pass the milk **5 sin ~** : unintentionally — **~** *nm* : love — **querido, -da** *adj* : dear, beloved — **~** *n* **1** : darling **2** AMANTE : lover
queroseno *nm* : kerosene

querubín *nm, pl* **-bines** : cherub
queso *nm* : cheese — **quesadilla** *nf Lat* : quesadilla
quicio *nm* **1 estar fuera de ~** : be beside oneself **2 sacar de ~** : drive crazy
quiebra *nf* **1** : break **2** BANCARROTA : bankruptcy
quien *pron, pl* **quienes 1** (*subject*) : who **2** (*object*) : whom **3** (*indefinite*) : whoever, anyone, some people
quién *pron, pl* **quiénes 1** (*subject*) : who **2** (*object*) : whom **3 ¿de ~ es este lápiz?** : whose pencil is this?
quienquiera *pron, pl* **quienesquiera** : whoever, whomever
quieto, -ta *adj* **1** : calm, quiet **2** INMÓVIL : still — **quietud** *nf* : stillness
quijada *nf* : jaw, jawbone (of an animal)
quilate *nm* : carat, karat
quilla *nf* : keel
quimera *nf* : illusion — **quimérico, -ca** *adj* : fanciful
química *nf* : chemistry — **químico, -ca** *adj* : chemical — **~** *n* : chemist
quince *adj & nm* : fifteen — **quinceañero, -ra** *n* : fifteen-year-old, teenager — **quincena** *nf* : two-week period, fortnight — **quincenal** *adj* : semimonthly, twice a month
quincuagésimo, -ma *adj & n* : fiftieth
quinientos, -tas *adj* : five hundred — **quinientos** *nms & pl* : five hundred
quinina *nf* : quinine
quinqué *nm* : oil lamp
quinta *nf* : country house, villa
quintaesencia *nf* : quintessence
quinteto *nm* : quintet
quinto, -ta *adj & n* : fifth — **quinto** *nm* : fifth
quiosco *nm* : kiosk, newsstand
quiropráctico, -ca *n* : chiropractor
quirúrgico, -ca *adj* : surgical
quisquilloso, -sa *adj* : fastidious, fussy
quiste *nm* : cyst
quitar *vt* **1** : remove, take away **2** : take off (clothes) **3** : get rid of, relieve (pain, etc.) — **quitarse** *vr* **1** : withdraw, leave **2** : take off (one's clothes) **3 ~ de** : give up (a habit) **4 ~ de encima** : get rid of — **quitaesmalte** *nm* : nail-polish remover — **quitamanchas** *nms & pl* : stain remover — **quitanieves** *nm* : snowplow — **quitasol** *nm* : parasol
quizá *or* **quizás** *adv* : maybe, perhaps

R

r *nf* : r, 19th letter of the Spanish alphabet

rábano *nm* **1** : radish **2 ~ picante** : horse-radish

rabí *nmf, pl* **-bíes** : rabbi

rabia *nf* **1** : rage, anger **2** : rabies (disease) — **rabiar** *vi* **1** : be furious **2** : be in great pain **3 ~ por** : be dying for — **rabioso, -sa** *adj* **1** : enraged, furious **2** : rabid, having rabies

rabino, -na *n* : rabbi

rabo *nm* **1** : tail **2 el ~ del ojo** : the corner of one's eye

racha *nf* **1** : gust of wind **2** SERIE : series, string — **racheado, -da** *adj* : gusty

racial *adj* : racial

racimo *nm* : bunch, cluster

raciocinio *nm* : reason, reasoning

ración *nf, pl* **-ciones 1** : share, ration **2** : helping (of food)

racional *adj* : rational — **racionalizar** {21} *vt* : rationalize

racionar *vt* : ration — **racionamiento** *nm* : rationing

racismo *nm* : racism — **racista** *adj & nmf* : racist

radar *nm* : radar

radiación *nf, pl* **-ciones** : radiation

radiactivo, -va *adj* : radioactive — **radiactividad** *nf* : radioactivity

radiador *nm* : radiator

radiante *adj* : radiant

radical *adj & nmf* : radical

radicar {72} *vi* **~ en** : lie in, be rooted in

radio *nm* **1** : radius **2** : spoke (of a wheel) **3** : radium (element) — **~** *nmf* : radio

radioactivo, -va *adj* : radioactive — **radioactividad** *nf* : radioactivity

radiodifusión *nf, pl* **-siones** : broadcasting — **radioemisora** *nf* : radio station — **radioescucha** *nmf* : listener — **radiofónico, -ca** *adj* : radio

radiografía *nf* : X ray — **radiografiar** {85} *vt* : x-ray

radiología *nf* : radiology — **radiólogo, -ga** *n* : radiologist

raer {65} *vt* : scrape off

ráfaga *nf* **1** : gust (of wind) **2** : flash (of light)

raído, -da *adj* : worn, shabby

raíz *nf, pl* **raíces 1** : root **2** ORIGEN : origin, source **3 echar raíces** : take root

raja *nf* **1** : crack, slit **2** RODAJA : slice — **rajar** *vt* : crack, split — **rajarse** *vr* **1** : crack, split open **2** *fam* : back out

rajatabla: a ~ *adv phr* : strictly, to the letter

ralea *nf* : sort, kind

ralentí *nm* : neutral (gear)

rallar *vt* : grate — **rallador** *nm* : grater

rama *nf* : branch — **ramaje** *nm* : branches *pl* — **ramal** *nm* : branch (of a railroad, etc.) — **ramificarse** {72} *vr* : branch (off) — **ramillete** *nm* **1** : bouquet **2** GRUPO : cluster, bunch — **ramo** *nm* **1** : branch **2** RAMILLETE : bouquet

rampa *nf* : ramp, incline

rana *nf* **1** : frog **2 ~ toro** : bullfrog

rancho *nm* : ranch, farm — **ranchero, -ra** *n* : rancher, farmer

rancio, -cia *adj* **1** : rancid **2** : aged (of wine)

rango *nm* **1** : rank **2** : (social) standing

ranúnculo *nm* : buttercup

ranura *nf* : groove, slot

rapar *vt* **1** : shave **2** : crop (hair)

rapaz *adj, pl* **-paces** : rapacious, predatory

rápido, -da *adj* : rapid, quick — **rápidamente** *adv* : rapidly, fast — **rapidez** *nf* : speed — **rápido** *adv* : quickly, fast — **~** *nm* **1** : express train **2 ~s** *nmpl* : rapids

rapiña *nf* **1** : plunder **2 ave de ~** : bird of prey

rapsodia *nf* : rhapsody

raptar *vt* : kidnap — **rapto** *nm* : kidnapping — **raptor, -tora** *n* : kidnapper

raqueta *nf* : racket (in sports)

raro, -ra *adj* **1** : rare **2** EXTRAÑO : odd, strange — **raramente** *adv* : rarely, infrequently — **rareza** *nf* : rarity

ras *nm* **a ~ de** : level with

rascacielos *nms & pl* : skyscraper

rascar {72} *vt* **1** : scratch **2** RASPAR : scrape — **rascarse** *vr* : scratch oneself

rasgar {52} *vt* : rip, tear — **rasgarse** *vr* : rip

rasgo *nm* **1** : stroke (of a pen) **2** CARACTERÍSTICA : trait, characteristic **3 ~s** *nmpl* FACCIONES : features

rasguear *vt* : strum

rasguñar *vt* : scratch — **rasguño** *nm* : scratch

raso, -sa *adj* **1** : level, flat **2** : low (of a flight) **3 soldado raso** : private (in the army) — **raso** *nm* : satin

raspar *vt* **1** : scrape **2** LIMAR : file down, smooth — *vi* : be rough — **raspadura** *nf* **1** : scratch **2 ~s** *nfpl* : scrapings

rastra *nf* **1** : rake **2 a ~s** : unwillingly — **rastrear** *vt* : track, trace — **rastrero, -ra** *adj* **1** : creeping **2** DESPRECIABLE : despicable

— **rastrillar** *vt* : rake — **rastrillo** *nm* : rake — **rastro** *nm* **1** : trail, track **2** SEÑAL : sign

rasurar *vt Lat* : shave — **rasurarse** *vr Lat* : shave

rata *nf* : rat

ratear *vt* : steal — **ratero, -ra** *n* : thief

ratificar {72} *vt* : ratify — **ratificación** *nf, pl* **-ciones** : ratification

rato *nm* **1** : while **2 al poco ∼** : shortly after **3 pasar el ∼** : pass the time

ratón *nm, pl* **-tones** : mouse — **ratonera** *nf* : mousetrap

raudal *nm* **1** : torrent **2 a ∼es** : in abundance — **raudo, -da** *adj* : swift

raya *nf* **1** : line LISTA : stripe **3** : part (in the hair) — **rayar** *vt* : scratch — *vi* **1 al ∼ el día** : at daybreak **2 ∼ en** : border on — **rayarse** *vr* : get scratched

rayo *nm* **1** : ray, beam **2** : bolt of lightning **3 ∼s X** : X rays

rayón *nm* : rayon

raza *nf* **1** : (human) race **2** : breed (of animals) **3 de ∼** : thoroughbred, pedigreed

razón *nf, pl* **-zones** **1** : reason **2 dar ∼** : inform **3 en ∼ de** : because of **4 tener ∼** : be right — **razonable** *adj* : reasonable — **razonamiento** *nm* : reasoning — **razonar** *v* : reason, think

reacción *nf, pl* **-ciones** : reaction — **reaccionar** *vi* : react — **reaccionario, -ria** *adj & n* : reactionary

reacio, -cia *adj* : resistant, stubborn

reactivar *vt* : reactivate, revive

reactor *nm* **1** : jet (airplane) **2 ∼ nuclear** : nuclear reactor

reajustar *vt* : readjust — **reajuste** *nm* : readjustment

real *adj* **1** : royal **2** VERDADERO : real, true

realce *nm* **1** : relief **2 dar ∼** : highlight

realeza *nf* : royalty

realidad *nf* **1** : reality **2 en ∼** : actually, in fact

realismo *nm* : realism — **realista** *adj* : realistic — **∼** *nmf* : realist

realizar {21} *vt* **1** : carry out **2** : achieve (a goal) **3** : produce (a film or play) **4** : realize (a profit) — **realizarse** *vr* **1** : fulfill oneself **2** : come true (of a dream, etc.) — **realización** *nf, pl* **-ciones** : execution, realization

realmente *adv* : really, actually

realzar {21} *vt* : highlight, enhance

reanimar *vt* : revive

reanudar *vt* : resume, renew — **reanudarse** *vr* : resume

reaparecer {53} *vi* : reappear — **reaparición** *nf, pl* **-ciones** : reappearance

reavivar *vt* : revive

rebajar *vt* **1** : lower, reduce **2** HUMILLAR : humiliate — **rebajarse** *vr* **1** : humble oneself **2 ∼ a** : stoop to — **rebaja** *nf* **1** : reduction **2** DESCUENTO : discount **3 ∼s** *nfpl* : sales

rebanada *nf* : slice

rebaño *nm* **1** : herd **2** : flock (of sheep)

rebasar *vt* : surpass, exceed

rebatir *vt* : refute

rebelarse *vr* : rebel — **rebelde** *adj* : rebellious — **∼** *nmf* : rebel — **rebeldía** *nf* : rebelliousness — **rebelión** *nf, pl* **-liones** : rebellion

reblandecer *vt* : soften

rebobinar *vt* : rewind

rebosar *vi* **1** : overflow **2 ∼ de** : be bursting with — *vt* : overflow with

rebotar *vi* : bounce, rebound — **rebote** *nm* **1** : bounce **2 de ∼** : on the rebound

rebozar {21} *vt* : coat in batter

rebuscado, -da *adj* : pretentious

rebuznar *vi* : bray

recabar *vt* **1** : obtain, collect **2 ∼ fondos** : raise money

recado *nm* **1** MENSAJE : message **2** *Spain* : errand

recaer {13} *vi* **1** : relapse **2 ∼ sobre** : fall on — **recaída** *nf* : relapse

recalcar {72} *vt* : emphasize, stress

recalcitrante *adj* : recalcitrant

recalentar {55} *vt* **1** : overheat **2** : reheat, warm up (food) — **recalentarse** *vr* : overheat

recámara *nf* **1** : chamber (of a firearm) **2** *Lat* : bedroom

recambio *nm* **1** : spare part **2** : refill (for a pen, etc.)

recapitular *vt* : recapitulate, sum up — **recapitulación** *nf, pl* **-ciones** : recapitulation

recargar {52} *vt* **1** : overload **2** : recharge (a battery), reload (a firearm, etc.) — **recargado, -da** *adj* : overly elaborate — **recargo** *nm* : surcharge

recato *nm* : modesty — **recatado, -da** *adj* : modest, demure

recaudar *vt* : collect — **recaudación** *nf, pl* **-ciones** : collection — **recaudador, -dora** *n* **∼ de impuestos** : tax collector

recelar *vt* : distrust, fear — **recelo** *nm* : distrust, suspicion — **receloso, -sa** *adj* : distrustful, suspicious

recepción *nf, pl* **-ciones** : reception — **recepcionista** *nmf* : receptionist

receptáculo *nm* : receptacle

receptivo, -va *adj* : receptive — **receptor, -tora** *n* : recipient — **receptor** *nm* : receiver (of a radio, etc.)

recesión *nf, pl* **-siones** : recession

receso *nm Lat* : recess, adjournment

receta *nf* **1** : recipe **2** : prescription (in medicine)

rechazar {21} *vt* **1** : reject, refuse **2** REPELER : repel **3** : reflect (light) — **rechazo** *nm* : rejection

rechinar *vi* **1** : squeak, creak **2** : grind, gnash (one's teeth)

rechoncho, -cha *adj fam* : chubby

recibir *vt* **1** : receive **2** ACOGER : welcome — *vi* : receive visitors — **recibidor** *nm* : vestibule, entrance hall — **recibimiento** *nm* : reception, welcome — **recibo** *nm* : receipt

reciclar *vt* **1** : recycle **2** : retrain (workers) — **reciclaje** *nm* : recycling

recién *adv* **1** : newly, recently **2** ~ **casados** : newlyweds — **reciente** *adj* : recent — **recientemente** *adv* : recently

recinto *nm* **1** : enclosure **2** ÁREA : area, site

recio, -cia *adj* : tough, strong

recipiente *nm* : container, receptacle — ~ *nmf* : recipient

recíproco, -ca *adj* : reciprocal, mutual

recitar *vt* : recite — **recital** *nm* : recital

reclamar *vt* : demand, ask for — *vi* : complain — **reclamación** *nf, pl* **-ciones 1** : claim, demand **2** QUEJA : complaint — **reclamo** *nm* **1** : lure (in hunting) **2** *Lat* : inducement, attraction

reclinar *vt* : rest, lean — **reclinarse** *vr* : recline, lean back

recluir {41} *vt* : confine, lock up — **recluirse** *vr* : shut oneself away — **reclusión** *nf, pl* **-siones** : imprisonment — **recluso, -sa** *n* : prisoner

recluta *nmf* : recruit — **reclutamiento** *nm* : recruitment — **reclutar** *vt* : recruit, enlist

recobrar *vt* : recover, regain — **recobrarse** *vr* ~ **de** : recover from

recodo *nm* : bend

recoger {15} *vt* **1** : collect, gather **2** COGER : pick up **3** LIMPIAR, ORDENAR : clean up, tidy (up) — **recogerse** *vr* : retire, withdraw — **recogedor** *nm* : dustpan — **recogido, -da** *adj* : quiet, secluded

recolección *nf, pl* **-ciones 1** : collection **2** COSECHA : harvest

recomendar {55} *vt* : recommend — **recomendación** *nf, pl* **-ciones** : recommendation

recompensar *vt* : reward — **recompensa** *nf* : reward

reconciliar *vt* : reconcile — **reconciliarse** *vr* : be reconciled — **reconciliación** *nf, pl* **-ciones** : reconciliation

recóndito, -ta *adj* : hidden

reconfortar *vt* : comfort

reconocer {18} *vt* **1** : recognize **2** ADMITIR : admit **3** EXAMINAR : examine — **reconocible** *adj* : recognizable — **reconocido, -da** *adj* **1** : recognized, accepted **2** AGRADECIDO : grateful — **reconocimiento** *nm* **1** : recognition **2** AGRADECIMIENTO : gratitude **3** : (medical) examination

reconsiderar *vt* : reconsider

reconstruir {41} *vt* : reconstruct — **reconstrucción** *nf, pl* **-ciones** : reconstruction

recopilar *vt* **1** RECOGER : collect, gather **2** : compile — **recopilación** *nf, pl* **-ciones** : collection, compilation

récord *nm, pl* **-cords** : record

recordar {19} *vt* **1** ACORDARSE DE : remember **2** : remind — *vi* : remember — **recordatorio** *nm* : reminder

recorrer *vt* **1** : travel through **2** : cover (a distance) — **recorrido** *nm* **1** : journey, trip **2** TRAYECTO : route, course

recortar *vt* **1** : reduce **2** CORTAR : cut (out) **3** : trim (hair) — **recortarse** *vr* : stand out — **recorte** *nm* **1** : cut, cutting **2** ~**s de periódicos** : newspaper clippings

recostar {19} *vt* : lean, rest — **recostarse** *vr* : lie down

recoveco *nm* **1** : bend **2** RINCÓN : nook, corner

recrear *vt* **1** : recreate **2** ENTRETENER : entertain — **recrearse** *vr* : to enjoy oneself — **recreativo, -va** *adj* : recreational — **recreo** *nm* **1** : recreation, amusement **2** : recess, break (at school)

recriminar *vt* : reproach

recrudecer {53} *vi* : worsen — **recrudecerse** *vr* : intensify, get worse

rectángulo *nm* : rectangle — **rectangular** *adj* : rectangular

rectificar {72} *vt* **1** : rectify, correct **2** AJUSTAR : straighten (out) — **rectitud** *nf* **1** : straightness **2** : (moral) rectitude — **recto, -ta** *adj* **1** : straight **2** ÍNTEGRO : upright, honorable — **recto** *nm* : rectum

rector, -tora *adj* : governing, managing — ~ *n* : rector — **rectoría** *nf* : rectory

recubrir {2} *vt* : cover, coat

recuento *nm* : count, recount

recuerdo *nm* **1** : memory **2** : souvenir, remembrance (of a journey, etc.) **3** ~**s** *nmpl* SALUDOS : regards

recuperar *vt* **1** : recover, retrieve **2** ~ **el tiempo perdido** : make up for lost time — **recuperarse** *vr* ~ **de** : recover from — **recuperación** *nf, pl* **-ciones 1** : recovery **2** ~ **de datos** : data retrieval

recurrir *vi* ~ **a** : turn to (a person), resort to (force, etc.) — **recurso** *nm* **1** : recourse, resort **2** : appeal (in law) **3** ~**s** *nmpl* : resources

red *nf* **1** : net **2** SISTEMA : network, system **3 la Red** : the Internet

redactar *vt* : write (up), draft — **redacción** *nf, pl* **-ciones 1** : writing, drafting **2** : editing (of a newspaper, etc.) — **redactor, -tora** *n* : editor

redada *nf* **1** : (police) raid **2** : catch (in fishing)

redescubrir {2} *vt* : rediscover

redención *nf, pl* **-ciones** : redemption — **redentor, -tora** *adj* : redeeming

redil *nm* : fold, pen

rédito *nm* : interest, yield

redoblar *vt* : redouble

redomado, -da *adj* : out-and-out

redondear *vt* **1** : make round **2** : round off (a number, etc.) — **redonda** *nf* **1** : whole note (in music) **2 a la ~** : in the surrounding area — **redondel** *nm* **1** : ring, circle **2** : bullring — **redondo, -da** *adj* **1** : round **2** PERFECTO : excellent

reducir {61} *vt* : reduce — **reducirse** *vr* **~ a** : come down to, amount to — **reducción** *nf, pl* **-ciones** : reduction — **reducido, -da** *adj* **1** : reduced, limited **2** PEQUEÑO : small

redundante *adj* : redundant — **redundancia** *nf* : redundancy

reedición *nf, pl* **-ciones** : reprint

reembolsar *vt* : refund, reimburse, repay — **reembolso** *nm* : refund, reimbursement

reemplazar {21} *vt* : replace — **reemplazo** *nm* : replacement

reencarnación *nf, pl* **-ciones** : reincarnation

reencuentro *nm* : reunion

reestructurar *vt* : restructure

refaccionar *vt Lat* : repair, renovate — **refacciones** *nfpl Lat* : repairs, renovations

referir {76} *vt* **1** : tell **2** REMITIR : refer — **referirse** *vr* **~ a** : refer to — **referencia** *nf* **1** : reference **2 hacer ~ a** : refer to — **referéndum** *nm, pl* **-dums** : referendum — **referente** *adj* **~ a** : concerning

refinar *vt* : refine — **refinado, -da** *adj* : refined — **refinamiento** *nm* : refinement — **refinería** *nf* : refinery

reflector *nm* **1** : reflector **2** : spotlight, searchlight, floodlight

reflejar *vt* : reflect — **reflejarse** *vr* : be reflected — **reflejo** *nm* **1** : reflection **2** : (physical) reflex **3 ~s** *nmpl* : highlights (in hair)

reflexionar *vi* : reflect, think — **reflexión** *nf, pl* **-xiones** : reflection, thought — **reflexivo, -va** *adj* **1** : reflective, thoughtful **2** : reflexive (in grammar)

reflujo *nm* : ebb (tide)

reforma *nf* **1** : reform **2 ~s** *nfpl* : renovations — **reformador, -dora** *n* : reformer — **reformar** *vt* **1** : reform **2** : renovate, repair (a house, etc.) — **reformarse** *vr* : mend one's ways — **reformatorio** *nm* : reformatory

reforzar {36} *vt* : reinforce

refrán *nm, pl* **-franes** : proverb, saying

refregar {49} *vt* : scrub

refrenar *vt* **1** : rein in (a horse) **2** CONTENER : restrain — **refrenarse** *vr* : restrain oneself

refrendar *vt* : approve, endorse

refrescar {72} *vt* **1** : refresh, cool **2** : brush up on (knowledge) — *vi* : turn cooler — **refrescante** *adj* : refreshing — **refresco** *nm* : soft drink

refriega *nf* : scuffle, skirmish

refrigerar *vt* **1** : refrigerate **2** CLIMATIZAR : air-condition — **refrigeración** *nf, pl* **-ciones 1** : refrigeration **2** AIRE ACONDICIONADO : air-conditioning — **refrigerador** *nmf Lat* : refrigerator — **refrigerio** *nm* : refreshments *pl*

refrito, -ta *adj* : refried — **refrito** *nm* : rehash

refuerzo *nm* : reinforcement

refugiar *vt* : shelter — **refugiarse** *vr* : take refuge — **refugiado, -da** *n* : refugee — **refugio** *nm* : refuge, shelter

refulgir {35} *vi* : shine brightly

refunfuñar *vi* : grumble, groan

refutar *vt* : refute

regadera *nf* **1** : watering can **2** *Lat* : shower head, shower

regalar *vt* : give (as a gift) — **regalarse** *vr* **~ con** : treat oneself to

regaliz *nm, pl* **-lices** : licorice

regalo *nm* **1** : gift, present **2** PLACER : pleasure, delight

regañadientes: **a ~** *adv phr* : reluctantly, unwillingly

regañar *vt* : scold — *vi* **1** QUEJARSE : grumble **2** *Spain* : quarrel — **regañón, -ñona** *adj, mpl* **-ñones** *fam* : grumpy, irritable

regar {49} *vt* **1** : irrigate, water **2** ESPARCIR : scatter

regatear *vt* **1** : haggle over **2** ESCATIMAR : skimp on — *vi* : bargain, haggle

regazo *nm* : lap (of a person)

regenerar *vt* : regenerate

regentar *vt* : run, manage

régimen *nm, pl* **regímenes 1** : regime **2** DIETA : diet **3 ~ de vida** : lifestyle

regimiento *nm* : regiment

regio, -gia *adj* : royal, regal

región *nf, pl* **-giones** : region, area — **regional** *adj* : regional

regir {28} *vt* **1** : rule **2** ADMINISTRAR : manage, run **3** DETERMINAR : govern, determine — *vi* : apply, be in force — **regirse** *vr* **~ por** : be guided by

registrar *vt* **1** : register **2** GRABAR : record, tape **3** : search (a house, etc.), frisk (a person) — **registrarse** *vr* **1** : register **2** : be recorded (of temperatures, etc.) — **registrador, -dora** *adj* **caja registradora** : cash register — **~** *n* : registrar — **registro** *nm* **1** : registration **2** : register (book) **3** : registry (office) **4** : range (of a voice, etc.) **5** INSPECCIÓN : search

regla *nf* **1** : rule, regulation **2** : ruler (for measuring) **3** MENSTRUACIÓN : period — **reglamentación** *nf, pl* **-ciones 1** : regulation **2** REGLAS : rules *pl* — **reglamentar** *vt* : regulate — **reglamentario, -ria** *adj* : regulation, official — **reglamento** *nm* : regulations *pl*, rules *pl*

regocijar *vt* : gladden, delight — **regocijarse** *vr* : rejoice — **regocijo** *nm* : delight, rejoicing

regodearse *vr* : be delighted — **regodeo** *nm* : delight

regordete *adj fam* : chubby

regresar *vi* : return, come back, go back — *vt Lat* : give back — **regresión** *nf, pl* **-siones** : regression — **regresivo, -va** *adj* : regressive — **regreso** *nm* **1** : return **2 estar de ~** : be back, be home again

reguero *nm* **1** : irrigation ditch **2** SEÑAL : trail, trace **3 correr como un ~ de pólvora** : spread like wildfire

regular *adj* **1** : regular **2** MEDIANO : medium, average **3 por lo ~** : in general — **~** *vt* : regulate, control — **regulación** *nf, pl* **-ciones** : regulation, control — **regularidad** *nf* : regularity — **regularizar** {21} *vt* : normalize, make regular

rehabilitar *vt* **1** : rehabilitate **2** : reinstate (s.o. in a position) **3** : renovate (a building, etc.) — **rehabilitación** *nf* **1** : rehabilitation **2** : reinstatement (in a position) **3** : renovation (of a building, etc.)

rehacer {40} *vt* **1** : redo **2** REPARAR : repair — **rehacerse** *vr* **1** : recover **2 ~ de** : get over

rehén *nm, pl* **-henes** : hostage

rehuir {41} *vt* : avoid, shun

rehusar {8} *v* : refuse

reimprimir *vt* : reprint — **reimpresión** *nf, pl* **-siones** : reprinting, reprint

reina *nf* : queen — **reinado** *nm* : reign — **reinante** *adj* : reigning — **reinar** *vi* **1** : reign **2** PREVALECER : prevail

reincidir *vi* : backslide, relapse

reino *nm* : kingdom, realm

reintegrar *vt* **1** : reinstate **2** : refund (money), reimburse (expenses, etc.) — **reintegrarse** *vr* **~ a** : return to — **reintegro** *nm* : reimbursement

reír {66} *vi* : laugh — *vt* : laugh at — **reírse** *vr* : laugh

reiterar *vt* : repeat, reiterate

reivindicar {72} *vt* **1** : claim **2** RESTAURAR : restore

reja *nf* : grille, grating — **rejilla** *nf* : grille, grate, screen

rejuvenecer {53} *vt* : rejuvenate — **rejuvenecerse** *vr* : be rejuvenated

relación *nf, pl* **-ciones 1** : relation, connection **2** COMUNICACIÓN : relationship, relations *pl* **3** RELATO : account **4** LISTA : list **5 con ~ a** *or* **en ~ a** : in relation to — **relacionar** *vt* : relate, connect — **relacionarse** *vr* **~ con** : be connected to, interact with

relajar *vt* : relax — **relajarse** *vr* : relax — **relajación** *nf, pl* **-ciones** : relaxation — **relajado, -da** *adj* **1** : relaxed **2** : dissolute, lax (in behavior)

relamerse *vr* : smack one's lips, lick its chops

relámpago *nm* : flash of lightning — **relampaguear** *vi* : flash

relatar *vt* : relate, tell

relativo, -va *adj* **1** : relative **2 en lo relativo a** : with regard to — **relatividad** *nf* : relativity

relato *nm* **1** : account, report **2** CUENTO : story, tale

releer {20} *vt* : reread

relegar {52} *vt* : relegate

relevante *adj* : outstanding, important

relevar *vt* **1** : relieve, take over from **2 ~ de** : exempt from — **relevo** *nm* **1** : relief, replacement **2 carrera de ~s** : relay race

relieve *nm* **1** : relief (in art, etc.) **2** IMPORTANCIA : prominence, importance **3 poner en ~** : emphasize

religión *nf, pl* **-giones** : religion — **religioso, -sa** *adj* : religious — **~** *n* : monk *m*, nun *f*

relinchar *vi* : neigh, whinny — **relincho** *nm* : neigh, whinny

reliquia *nf* **1** : relic **2 ~ de familia** : family heirloom

rellenar *vt* **1** : refill **2** : stuff, fill (in cooking) — **relleno, -na** *adj* : stuffed, filled — **relleno** *nm* : stuffing, filling

reloj *nm* **1** : clock **2** *or* **~ de pulsera** : wristwatch **3 ~ de arena** : hourglass **4 como un ~** : like clockwork

relucir {45} *vi* **1** : glitter, shine **2 sacar a ~** : bring up, mention — **reluciente** *adj* : brilliant, shining

relumbrar *vi* : shine brightly

remachar *vt* **1** : rivet **2** RECALAR : stress, drive home — **remache** *nm* : rivet

remanente *nm* : remainder, surplus

remanso *nm* : pool

remar *vi* : row

rematar *vt* **1** : conclude, finish up **2** MATAR : finish off **3** LIQUIDAR : sell off cheaply **4**

Lat : auction — *vi* **1** : shoot (in sports) **2** TERMINAR : end — **rematado, -da** *adj* : utter, complete — **remate** *nm* **1** : shot (in sports) **2** FIN : end

remedar *vt* : imitate, mimic

remediar *vt* **1** : remedy, repair **2** : solve (a problem) **3** EVITAR : avoid — **remedio** *nm* **1** : remedy, cure SOLUCIÓN : solution **3** **sin** ∼ : hopeless

rememorar *vi* : recall

remendar {55} *vt* : mend

remesa *nf* **1** : remittance **2** : shipment (of merchandise)

remezón *nm*, *pl* **-zones** *Lat* : mild earthquake, tremor

remiendo *nm* : mend, patch

remilgado, -da *adj* **1** : prudish **2** AFECTADO : affected — **remilgo** *nm* : primness, affectation

reminiscencia *nf* : reminiscence

remisión *nf*, *pl* **-siones** : remission

remiso, -sa *adj* **1** : reluctant **2** NEGLIGENTE : remiss

remitir *vt* **1** : send, remit **2** ∼ **a** : refer to, direct to — *vi* : subside, let up — **remite** *nm* : return address — **remitente** *nmf* : sender (of a letter, etc.)

remo *nm* : paddle, oar

remodelar *vt* **1** : remodel **2** : restructure (an organization)

remojar *vt* : soak, steep — **remojo** *nm* **poner en** ∼ : soak

remolacha *nf* : beet

remolcar {72} *vt* : tow, tug — **remolcador** *nm* : tugboat

remolino *nm* **1** : whirlwind, whirlpool **2** : crowd (of people) **3** : cowlick (of hair)

remolque *nm* **1** : towing, tow **2** : trailer (vehicle)

remontar *vt* **1** : overcome **2** SUBIR : go up — **remontarse** *vr* **1** : soar **2** ∼ **a** : date from, go back to

rémora *nf* : hindrance

remorder {47} *vt* : trouble, worry — **remordimiento** *nm* : remorse

remoto, -ta *adj* : remote — **remotamente** *adv* : remotely, slightly

remover {47} *vt* **1** : stir **2** : move around, turn over (earth, embers, etc.) **3** REAVIVAR : bring up again **4** DESPEDIR : fire, dismiss

remunerar *vt* : remunerate

renacer {48} *vi* : be reborn, revive — **renacimiento** *nm* **1** : rebirth, revival **2 el Renacimiento** : the Renaissance

renacuajo *nm* : tadpole, pollywog

rencilla *nf* : quarrel

renco, -ca *adj Lat* : lame

rencor *nm* **1** : rancor, hostility **2 guardar**

∼ : hold a grudge — **rencoroso, -sa** *adj* : resentful

rendición *nf*, *pl* **-ciones** : surrender — **rendido, -da** *adj* **1** : submissive **2** AGOTADO : exhausted

rendija *nf* : crack, split

rendir {54} *vt* **1** : render, give **2** PRODUCIR : yield, produce **3** CANSAR : exhaust — *vi* : make progress, go a long way — **rendirse** *vr* : surrender, give up — **rendimiento** *nm* **1** : performance **2** : yield, return (in finance, etc.)

renegar {49} *vt* : deny — *vi* **1** QUEJARSE : grumble **2** ∼ **de** ABJURAR : renounce, disown — **renegado, -da** *n* : renegade

renglón *nm*, *pl* **-glones 1** : line (of writing) **2** *Lat* : line (of products)

reno *nm* : reindeer

renombre *nm* : renown — **renombrado, -da** *adj* : famous, renowned

renovar {19} *vt* **1** : renew, restore **2** : renovate (a building, etc.) — **renovación** *nf*, *pl* **-ciones 1** : renewal **2** : renovation (of a building, etc.)

renquear *vi* : limp, hobble

rentar *vt* **1** : produce, yield **2** *Lat* : rent — **renta** *nf* **1** : income **2** ALQUILER : rent **3 impuesto sobre la** ∼ : income tax — **rentable** *adj* : profitable

renunciar *vi* **1** : resign **2** ∼ **a** : renounce, relinquish — **renuncia** *nf* **1** : renunciation **2** DIMISIÓN : resignation

reñir {67} *vi* ∼ **con** : argue with, fall out with — *vt* **1** : scold **2** DISPUTAR : fight — **reñido, -da** *adj* **1** : hard-fought **2** ∼ **con** : on bad terms with

reo, rea *n* **1** : accused, defendant **2** CULPABLE : culprit

reojo *nm* **de** ∼ : out of the corner of one's eye

reorganizar {21} *vt* : reorganize

repantigarse {52} *vr* : sprawl out

reparar *vt* **1** : repair, fix **2** : make amends for (an offense, etc.) — *vi* **1** ∼ **en** ADVERTIR : take notice of **2** ∼ **en** CONSIDERAR : consider — **reparación** *nf*, *pl* **-ciones 1** : reparation, amends **2** ARREGLO : repair — **reparo** *nm* **1** : reservation, objection **2 poner** ∼**s a** : object to

repartir *vt* **1** : allocate **2** DISTRIBUIR : distribute **3** ESPARCIR : spread — **repartición** *nf*, *pl* **-ciones** : distribution — **repartidor, -dora** *n* : delivery person, distributor — **reparto** *nm* **1** : allocation **2** DISTRIBUCIÓN : delivery **3** : cast (of characters)

repasar *vt* **1** : review, go over **2** ZURCIR : mend — **repaso** *nm* **1** : review **2** : mending (of clothes)

repeler *vt* **1** : repel **2** REPUGNAR : disgust — **repelente** *adj* : repellent, repulsive

repente *nm* **1** : fit, outburst **2 de ~** : suddenly — **repentino, -na** *adj* : sudden

repercutir *vi* **1** : reverberate **2 ~ en** : have repercussions on — **repercusión** *nf, pl* **-siones** : repercussion

repertorio *nm* : repertoire

repetir {54} *vt* **1** : repeat **2** : have a second helping of (food) — **repetirse** *vr* **1** : repeat oneself **2** : recur (of an event, etc.) — **repetición** *nf, pl* **-ciones** **1** : repetition **2** : rerun, repeat (of a program, etc.) — **repetido, -da** *adj* **1** : repeated **2 repetidas veces** : repeatedly, time and again — **repetitivo, -va** *adj* : repetitive, repetitious

repicar {72} *vt* : ring — *vi* : ring out, peal — **repique** *nm* : ringing, pealing

repisa *nf* **1** : shelf, ledge **2 ~ de ventana** : windowsill

replegar {49} *vt* : fold — **replegarse** *vr* : retreat, withdraw

repleto, -ta *adj* **1** : replete, full **2 ~ de** : packed with

replicar {72} *vt* : reply, retort — *vi* : answer back — **réplica** *nf* **1** RESPUESTA : reply **2** COPIA : replica, reproduction

repliegue *nm* **1** : fold **2** : (military) withdrawal

repollo *nm* : cabbage

reponer {60} *vt* **1** : replace **2** REPLICAR : reply — **reponerse** *vr* : recover

reportar *vt* **1** : yield, bring **2** *Lat* : report — **reportaje** *nm* : article, (news) report — **reporte** *nm* *Lat* : report — **reportero, -ra** *n* : reporter

reposar *vi* **1** DESCANSAR : rest **2** : stand, settle (of liquids, dough, etc.) — **reposado, -da** *adj* : calm, relaxed — **reposición** *nf, pl* **-ciones** **1** : replacement **2** : rerun, repeat (of a program, etc.) — **reposo** *nm* : rest

repostar *vi* **1** : stock up on **2** : refuel (an airplane, etc.) — *vi* : fill up, refuel

reprender *vt* : reprimand, scold — **reprensible** *adj* : reprehensible

represalia *nf* **1** : reprisal **2 tomar ~s** : retaliate

represar *vt* : dam

representar *vt* **1** : represent **2** : perform (a play, etc.) **3** APARENTAR : look, appear as — **representación** *nf, pl* **-ciones** **1** : representation **2** : performance (of a play, etc.) **3 en ~ de** : on behalf of — **representante** *nmf* **1** : representative **2** ACTOR : performer — **representativo, -va** *adj* : representative

represión *nf, pl* **-siones** : repression

reprimenda *nf* : reprimand

reprimir *vt* **1** : repress **2** : suppress (a rebellion, etc.)

reprobar {19} *vt* **1** : reprove, condemn **2** *Lat* : fail (an exam, etc.)

reprochar *vt* : reproach — **reprocharse** *vr* : reproach oneself — **reproche** *nm* : reproach

reproducir {61} *vt* : reproduce — **reproducirse** *vr* **1** : breed, reproduce **2** : recur (of an event, etc.) — **reproducción** *nf, pl* **-ciones** : reproduction — **reproductor, -tora** *adj* : reproductive

reptil *nm* : reptile

república *nf* : republic — **republicano, -na** *adj & n* : republican

repudiar *vt* : repudiate

repuesto *nm* : spare (auto) part

repugnar *vt* : disgust — **repugnancia** *nf* : disgust — **repugnante** *adj* : disgusting

repujar *vt* : emboss

repulsivo, -va *adj* : repulsive

reputar *vt* : consider, deem — **reputación** *nf, pl* **-ciones** : reputation

requerir {76} *vt* **1** : require **2** : summon, send for (a person)

requesón *nm, pl* **-sones** : cottage cheese

réquiem *nm* : requiem

requisito *nm* **1** : requirement **2 ~ previo** : prerequisite

res *nf* **1** : beast, animal **2** *Lat or* **carne de ~** : beef

resabio *nm* **1** VICIO : bad habit, vice **2** DEJO : aftertaste

resaca *nf* **1** : undertow **2 tener ~** : have a hangover

resaltar *vi* **1** : stand out **2 hacer ~** : bring out, highlight — *vt* : emphasize

resarcir {83} *vt* : compensate, repay — **resarcirse** *vr* **~ de** : make up for

resbalar *vi* **1** : slip, slide **2** : skid (of an automobile) — **resbalarse** *vr* : slip, skid — **resbaladizo, -za** *adj* : slippery — **resbalón** *nm, pl* **-lones** : slip — **resbaloso, -sa** *adj* *Lat* : slippery

rescatar *vt* **1** : rescue, ransom **2** RECUPERAR : recover, get back — **rescate** *nm* **1** : rescue **2** : ransom (money) **3** RECUPERACIÓN : recovery

rescindir *vt* : cancel — **rescisión** *nf, pl* **-siones** : cancellation

rescoldo *nm* : embers *pl*

resecar {72} *vt* : dry (out) — **resecarse** *vr* : dry up — **reseco, -ca** *adj* : dry, dried-up

resentirse {76} *vr* **1** : suffer, be weakened **2** OFENDERSE : be offended **3 ~ de** : feel the effects of — **resentido, -da** *adj* : resentful — **resentimiento** *nm* : resentment

reseñar *vt* **1** : review **2** DESCRIBIR : describe — **reseña** *nf* **1** : review, report **2** DESCRIPCIÓN : description

reservar *vt* **1** : reserve **2** GUARDAR : keep,

save — **reservarse** vr 1 : save oneself 2 : keep for oneself — **reserva** nf 1 : reservation 2 PROVISIÓN : reserve 3 **de ~** : spare, in reserve — **reservación** nf, pl **-ciones** : reservation — **reservado, -da** adj 1 : reserved 2 : confidential (of a document, etc.)

resfriar {85} vt : cool — **resfriarse** vr 1 : cool off 2 CONSTIPARSE : catch a cold — **resfriado** nm CATARRO : cold — **resfrío** nm Lat : cold

resguardar vt : protect — **resguardarse** vr : protect oneself — **resguardo** nm 1 : protection 2 RECIBO : receipt

residir vi 1 : reside, live 2 **~ en** : lie in — **residencia** nf 1 : residence 2 or **~ universitaria** : dormitory — **residencial** adj : residential — **residente** adj & nmf : resident

residuo nm 1 : residue 2 **~s** nmpl : waste — **residual** adj : residual

resignar vt : resign — **resignarse** vr **~ a** : resign oneself to — **resignación** nf, pl **-ciones** : resignation

resina nf 1 : resin 2 **~ epoxídica** : epoxy

resistir vt 1 AGUANTAR : stand, bear 2 : withstand (temptation, etc.) — vi : resist — **resistirse** vr **~ a** : be resistant to — **resistencia** nf 1 : resistance 2 AGUANTE : endurance, stamina — **resistente** adj : resistant, strong, tough

resma nf : ream

resollar {19} vi : breathe heavily, pant

resolver {89} vt 1 : resolve 2 DECIDIR : decide — **resolverse** vr : make up one's mind — **resolución** nf, pl **-ciones** 1 : resolution 2 DECISIÓN : decision 3 FIRMEZA : determination, resolve

resonar {19} vi : resound — **resonancia** nf 1 : resonance 2 CONSECUENCIAS : impact, repercussions pl — **resonante** adj : resonant, resounding

resoplar vi 1 : puff, pant 2 : snort (with annoyance)

resorte nm 1 MUELLE : spring 2 **tocar ~s** : pull strings

respaldar vt : back, endorse — **respaldarse** vr : lean back — **respaldo** nm 1 : back (of a chair, etc.) 2 APOYO : support, backing

respectar vt : concern, relate to — **respectivo, -va** adj : respective — **respecto** nm 1 **al ~** : in this respect 2 **~ a** : in regard to, concerning

respetar vt : respect — **respetable** adj : respectable — **respeto** nm 1 : respect 2 **presentar sus ~s** : pay one's respects — **respetuoso, -sa** adj : respectful

respingo nm : start, jump

respirar v : breathe — **respiración** nf, pl **-ciones** : respiration, breathing — **respiratorio, -ria** adj : respiratory — **respiro** nm 1 : breath 2 DESCANSO : respite, break

resplandecer {53} vi : shine — **resplandeciente** adj : shining, gleaming — **resplandor** nm 1 : brilliance, gleam 2 : flash (of lightning, etc.)

responder vt : answer, reply — vi 1 : answer 2 REPLICAR : answer back 3 **~ a** : respond to 4 **~ de** : answer for (something)

responsable adj : responsible — **responsabilidad** nf : responsibility

respuesta nf 1 : answer, reply 2 REACCIÓN : response

resquebrajar vt : split, crack — **resquebrajarse** vr : crack

resquicio nm 1 : crack, crevice 2 VESTIGIO : trace, glimmer

resta nf : subtraction

restablecer {53} vt : reestablish, restore — **restablecerse** vr : recover — **restablecimiento** nm : restoration, recovery

restallar vi : crack, crackle

restar vt 1 : deduct, subtract 2 DISMINUIR : minimize — vi : be left — **restante** adj 1 : remaining 2 **lo ~** : the rest

restauración nf, pl **-ciones** : restoration

restaurante nm : restaurant

restaurar vt : restore

restituir {41} vt : return, restore — **restitución** nf, pl **-ciones** : restitution

resto nm 1 : rest, remainder 2 **~s** nmpl : leftovers 3 or **~s mortales** : mortal remains

restregar {49} vt : rub, scrub — **restregarse** vr : rub

restringir {35} vt : restrict, limit — **restricción** nf, pl **-ciones** : restriction, limitation — **restrictivo, -va** adj : restrictive

resucitar vt : resuscitate, revive — vi : come back to life

resuelto, -ta adj : determined, resolved

resuello nm : heavy breathing, panting

resultar vi 1 : succeed, work out 2 SALIR : turn out (to be) 3 **~ de** : be the result of 4 **~ en** : result in — **resultado** nm : result, outcome

resumir v : summarize, sum up — **resumen** nm, pl **-súmenes** 1 : summary 2 **en ~** : in short

resurgir {35} vi : reappear, revive — **resurgimiento** nm : resurgence — **resurrección** nf, pl **-ciones** : resurrection

retahíla nf : string, series

retal nm : remnant

retardar vt 1 RETRASAR : delay 2 POSPONER : postpone

retazo nm 1 : remnant, scrap 2 : fragment (of a text, etc.)

retener {80} *vt* **1** : retain, keep **2** : withhold (funds, etc.) **3** DETENER : detain — **retención** *nf, pl* **-ciones 1** : retention **2** : deduction, withholding (of funds)

reticente *adj* : reluctant — **reticencia** *nf* : reluctance

retina *nf* : retina

retintín *nm, pl* **-tines 1** : tinkling, jingle **2 con ~** : sarcastically

retirar *vt* **1** : remove, take away **2** : withdraw (funds, statements, etc.) — **retirarse** *vr* **1** : retreat, withdraw **2** JUBILARSE : retire — **retirada** *nf* **1** : withdrawal **2 batirse en ~** : beat a retreat — **retirado, -da** *adj* **1** : remote, secluded **2** JUBILADO : retired — **retiro** *nm* **1** : retreat **2** JUBILACIÓN : retirement **3** *Lat* : withdrawal

reto *nm* : challenge, dare

retocar {72} *vt* : touch up

retoño *nm* : sprout, shoot

retoque *nm* **1** : retouching **2 el último ~** : the finishing touch

retorcer {14} *vt* **1** : twist, contort **2** : wring out (clothes, etc.) — **retorcerse** *vr* **1** : get twisted up **2** : squirm, writhe (in pain) — **retorcijón** *nm, pl* **-jones** : cramp, spasm — **retorcimiento** *nm* : twisting, wringing out

retórica *nf* : rhetoric — **retórico, -ca** *adj* : rhetorical

retornar *v* : return — **retorno** *nm* : return

retozar {21} *vi* : frolic, romp — **retozón, -zona** *adj* : playful, frisky

retractarse *vr* **1** : withdraw, back down **2 ~ de** : take back, retract

retraer {81} *vt* : retract — **retraerse** *vr* : withdraw — **retraído, -da** *adj* : withdrawn, shy

retrasar *vt* **1** : delay, hold up **2** APLAZAR : postpone **3** : set back (a clock) — **retrasarse** *vr* **1** : be late **2** : fall behind (in work, etc.) — **retrasado, -da** *adj* **1** : retarded **2** : in arrears (of payments) **3** : backward (of a country) **4** : slow (of a clock) — **retraso** *nm* **1** : delay **2** SUBDESARROLLO : backwardness **3 ~ mental** : mental retardation

retratar *vt* **1** : portray **2** FOTOGRAFIAR : photograph **3** DIBUJAR : paint a portrait of — **retrato** *nm* **1** : portrayal **2** DIBUJO : portrait **3** FOTOGRAFÍA : photograph

retrete *nm* : restroom, toilet

retribuir {41} *vt* **1** : pay **2** RECOMPENSAR : reward — **retribución** *nf, pl* **-ciones 1** : payment **2** RECOMPENSA : reward

retroactivo, -va *adj* : retroactive

retroceder *vi* **1** : go back, turn back **2** CEDER : back down — **retroceso** *nm* **1** : backward movement **2** : backing down

retrógrado, -da *adj & nmf* : reactionary

retrospectiva *nf* : hindsight — **retrospectivo, -va** *adj* : retrospective

retrovisor *nm* : rearview mirror

retumbar *vi* : resound, reverberate, rumble

reumatismo *nm* : rheumatism

reunir {68} *vt* **1** : unite, join **2** TENER : have, possess **3** RECOGER : gather, collect — **reunirse** *vr* : meet, gather — **reunión** *nf, pl* **-niones 1** : meeting **2** : (social) gathering, reunion

revalidar *vt* : confirm, ratify

revancha *nf* **1** : revenge **2** : rematch (in sports)

revelar *vt* **1** : reveal, disclose **2** : develop (film) — **revelación** *nf, pl* **-ciones** : revelation — **revelado** *nm* : developing (of film) — **revelador, -dora** *adj* : revealing

reventar {55} *v* : burst, blow up — **reventarse** *vr* : burst — **reventón** *nm, pl* **-tones** : blowout, flat tire

reverberar *vi* : reverberate — **reverberación** *nf, pl* **-ciones** : reverberation

reverenciar *vt* : revere — **reverencia** *nf* **1** : bow, curtsy **2** VENERACIÓN : reverence — **reverendo, -da** *adj & nmf* : reverend — **reverente** *adj* : reverent

reversa *nf Lat* : reverse (gear)

reverso *nm* **1** : back, reverse **2 el ~ de la medalla** : the complete opposite — **reversible** *adj* : reversible

revertir {76} *vi* **1** : revert **2 ~ en** : result in

revés *nm, pl* **-veses 1** : back, wrong side **2** CONTRATIEMPO : setback **3** BOFETADA : slap **4** : backhand (in sports) **5 al ~** : the other way around, upside down, inside out

revestir {54} *vt* **1** : coat, cover **2** ASUMIR : take on, assume — **revestimiento** *nm* : covering, coating

revisar *vt* **1** : examine, inspect **2** : check over, overhaul (machinery, etc.) **3** MODIFICAR : revise — **revisión** *nf, pl* **-siones 1** : revision **2** INSPECCIÓN : inspection, check — **revisor, -sora** *n* : inspector

revistar *vt* : review, inspect (troops, etc.) — **revista** *nf* **1** : magazine, journal **2** : revue (in theater) **3 pasar ~** : review, inspect

revivir *vi* : revive, come alive again — *vt* : relive

revocar {72} *vt* : revoke

revolcar {82} *vt* : knock over, knock down — **revolcarse** *vr* : roll around

revolotear *vi* : flutter, flit — **revoloteo** *nm* : fluttering, flitting

revoltijo *nm* : mess, jumble

revoltoso, -sa *adj* : rebellious

revolución *nf, pl* **-ciones** : revolution — **revolucionar** *vt* : revolutionize — **revolucionario, -ria** *adj & n* : revolutionary

revolver {89} *vt* **1** : mix, stir **2** : upset (one's stomach) **3** DESORGANIZAR : mess up — **re-volverse** *vr* **1** : toss and turn **2** VOLVERSE : turn around

revólver *nm* : revolver

revuelo *nm* : commotion

revuelta *nf* : uprising, revolt — **revuelto, -ta** *adj* **1** : choppy, rough **2** DESORDENADO : messed up **3 huevos revueltos** : scrambled eggs

rey *nm* : king

reyerta *nf* : brawl, fight

rezagarse {52} *vr* : fall behind, lag

rezar {21} *vi* **1** : pray **2** DECIR : say — *vt* : say, recite — **rezo** *nm* : prayer

rezongar {52} *vi* : gripe, grumble

rezumar *v* : ooze

ría *nf* : estuary

riachuelo *nm* : brook, stream

riada *nf* : flood

ribera *nf* : bank, shore

ribetear *vt* : border, trim — **ribete** *nm* **1** : border, trim **2** : embellishment

rico, -ca *adj* **1** : rich, wealthy **2** ABUNDANTE : abundant **3** SABROSO : rich, tasty — ~ *n* : rich person

ridiculizar {21} *vt* : ridicule — **ridículo, -la** *adj* : ridiculous — **ridículo** *nm* **1 hacer el** ~ : make a fool of oneself **2 poner en** ~ : ridicule

riego *nm* : irrigation

riel *nm* : rail

rienda *nf* **1** : rein **2 dar** ~ **suelta a** : give free rein to

riesgo *nm* : risk

rifa *nf* : raffle — **rifar** *vt* : raffle (off) — **rifarse** *vr fam* : fight over

rifle *nm* : rifle

rígido, -da *adj* **1** : rigid, stiff **2** SEVERO : harsh, strict — **rigidez** *nf, pl* **-deces 1** : rigidity, stiffness **2** SEVERIDAD : harshness, strictness

rigor *nm* **1** : rigor, harshness **2** EXACTITUD : precision **3 de** ~ : essential, obligatory — **riguroso, -sa** *adj* : rigorous

rima *nf* **1** : rhyme **2** ~**s** *nfpl* : verse, poetry — **rimar** *vi* : rhyme

rimbombante *adj* : showy, pompous

rímel *nm* : mascara

rincón *nm, pl* **-cones** : corner, nook

rinoceronte *nm* : rhinoceros

riña *nf* **1** : fight, brawl **2** DISPUTA : dispute, quarrel

riñón *nm, pl* **-ñones** : kidney

río *nm* **1** : river **2** TORRENTE : torrent, stream

riqueza *nf* **1** : wealth **2** ABUNDANCIA : richness **3** ~**s naturales** : natural resources

risa *nf* **1** : laughter, laugh **2 dar** ~ **a algn** : make s.o. laugh **3 morirse de la** ~ *fam* : die laughing

risco *nm* : crag, cliff

risible *adj* : laughable

ristra *nf* : string, series

risueño, -ña *adj* : cheerful, smiling

ritmo *nm* **1** : rhythm **2** VELOCIDAD : pace, speed — **rítmico, -ca** *adj* : rhythmical

rito *nm* : rite, ritual — **ritual** *adj & nm* : ritual

rival *adj & nmf* : rival — **rivalidad** *nf* : rivalry, competition — **rivalizar** {21} *vi* ~ **con** : rival, compete with

rizar {21} *vt* **1** : curl **2** : ripple (a surface) — **rizarse** *vr* : curl — **rizado, -da** *adj* **1** : curly **2** : choppy (of water) — **rizo** *nm* **1** : curl **2** : ripple (in water) **3** : loop (in aviation)

róbalo *nm* : bass (fish)

robar *vt* **1** : steal **2** : burglarize (a house, etc.) **3** SECUESTRAR : kidnap — **robo** *nm* : robbery, theft

roble *nm* : oak

robot *nm, pl* **-bots** : robot — **robótica** *nf* : robotics

robustecer {53} *vt* : make stronger, strengthen — **robusto, -ta** *adj* : robust, sturdy

roca *nf* : rock, boulder

roce *nm* **1** : rubbing, chafing **2** RASGUÑO : graze, scratch **3 tener un** ~ **con** : have a brush with

rociar {85} *vt* : spray, sprinkle — **rocío** *nm* : dew

rocoso, -sa *adj* : rocky

rodaja *nf* : slice

rodar {19} *vi* **1** : roll, roll down, roll along **2** GIRAR : turn, go around **3** : travel (of a vehicle) **4** : film (of movies, etc.) — *vt* **1** : film, shoot **2** : break in (a vehicle) — **rodaje** *nm* **1** : filming, shooting **2** : breaking in (of a vehicle)

rodear *vt* **1** : surround, encircle **2** *Lat* : round up (cattle) — **rodearse** *vr* ~ **de** : surround oneself with — **rodeo** *nm* **1** : rodeo, roundup **2** DESVÍO : detour **3 andar con** ~**s** : beat around the bush

rodilla *nf* : knee

rodillo *nm* **1** : roller **2** : rolling pin (for pastry)

roer {69} *vt* **1** : gnaw **2** ATORMENTAR : eat away at, torment — **roedor** *nm* : rodent

rogar {16} *vt* : beg, request — *vi* : pray

rojo, -ja *adj* **1** : red **2 ponerse** ~ : blush — **rojo** *nm* : red — **rojez** *nf* : redness — **rojizo, -za** *adj* : reddish

rollizo, -za *adj* : plump, chubby

rollo *nm* **1** : roll, coil **2** *fam* : boring speech, lecture

romance *nm* **1** : romance **2** : Romance (language)

romano, -na *adj & n* : Roman

romántico, -ca *adj* : romantic — **romanticismo** *nm* : romanticism
romería *nf* : pilgrimage, procession
romero *nm* : rosemary
romo, -ma *adj* : blunt, dull
rompecabezas *nms & pl* : puzzle
romper {70} *vt* **1** : break **2** RASGAR : rip, tear **3** : break off (relations), break (a contract) — *vi* **1** : break (of the day, waves, etc.) **2** ~ **a** : begin to, burst out with **3** ~ **con** : break off with — **romperse** *vr* : break
ron *nm* : rum
roncar {72} *vi* : snore — **ronco, -ca** *adj* : hoarse
ronda *nf* **1** : rounds *pl*, patrol **2** : round (of drinks, etc.) — **rondar** *vt* **1** : patrol **2** : hang around (a place) **3** : be approximately (an age, a number, etc.) — *vi* **1** : be on patrol **2** MERODEAR : prowl about
ronquera *nf* : hoarseness
ronquido *nm* : snore
ronronear *vi* : purr — **ronroneo** *nm* : purr, purring
ronzar {21} *vt* : munch, crunch
roña *nf* **1** : mange **2** SUCIEDAD : dirt, filth — **roñoso, -sa** *adj* **1** : mangy **2** SUCIO : dirty **3** *fam* : stingy
ropa *nf* **1** : clothes *pl*, clothing **2** ~ **interior** : underwear — **ropaje** *nm* : robes *pl*, regalia — **ropero** *nm* : wardrobe, closet
rosa *nf* : rose (flower) — ~ *adj* : rose-colored — ~ *nm* : rose (color) — **rosado, -da** *adj* **1** : pink **2 vino rosado** : rosé — **rosado** *nm* : pink (color) — **rosal** *nm* : rose-bush
rosario *nm* : rosary
rosbif *nm* : roast beef
rosca *nf* **1** : thread (of a screw) **2** ESPIRAL : ring, coil
roseta *nf* : rosette
rosquilla *nf* : doughnut
rostro *nm* : face
rotación *nf, pl* **-ciones** : rotation — **rotativo, -va** *adj* : rotary, revolving
roto, -ta *adj* : broken, torn
rotonda *nf* : traffic circle, rotary
rótula *nf* : kneecap
rótulo *nm* **1** : heading, title **2** ETIQUETA : label, sign
rotundo, -da *adj* : categorical, absolute
rotura *nf* : break, tear, fracture
rozar {21} *vt* **1** : graze, touch lightly **2** APROXIMARSE DE : touch on, border on — *vi*

: scrape, rub — **rozarse** *vr* **1** : rub, chafe **2** ~ **con** *fam* : rub elbows with — **rozadura** *nf* : scratch
rubí *nm, pl* **rubíes** : ruby
rubicundo, -da *adj* : ruddy
rubio, -bia *adj & n* : blond
rubor *nm* : flush, blush — **ruborizarse** {21} *vr* : blush
rúbrica *nf* **1** : flourish (in writing) **2** TÍTULO : title, heading
rudeza *nf* : roughness, coarseness
rudimentos *nmpl* : rudiments, basics — **rudimentario, -ria** *adj* : rudimentary
rudo, -da *adj* **1** : rough, harsh **2** GROSERO : coarse, unpolished
rueda *nf* **1** : wheel **2** CORRO : circle, ring **3** RODAJA : (round) slice **4 ir sobre** ~**s** : go smoothly — **ruedo** *nm* : bullring
ruego *nm* : request
rugir {35} *vi* : roar — **rugido** *nm* : roar
rugoso, -sa *adj* **1** : rough **2** ARRUGADO : wrinkled
ruibarbo *nm* : rhubarb
ruido *nm* : noise — **ruidoso, -sa** *adj* : loud, noisy
ruina *nf* **1** : ruin, destruction **2** COLAPSO : collapse **3** ~**s** *nfpl* : ruins, remains — **ruinoso, -sa** *adj* : run-down, dilapidated
ruiseñor *nm* : nightingale
ruleta *nf* : roulette
rulo *nm* : curler, roller
rumano, -na *adj* : Romanian, Rumanian
rumba *nf* : rumba
rumbo *nm* **1** : direction, course **2** ESPLENDIDEZ : lavishness **3 con** ~ **a** : bound for, heading for **4 perder el** ~ : go off course
rumiar *vt* : mull over — *vi* : chew the cud — **rumiante** *adj & nm* : ruminant
rumor *nm* **1** : rumor **2** MURMULLO : murmur — **rumorearse** *or* **rumorarse** *vr* : be rumored — **rumoroso, -sa** *adj* : murmuring, babbling
ruptura *nf* **1** : break, rupture **2** : breach (of a contract) **3** : breaking off (of relations)
rural *adj* : rural
ruso, -sa *adj* : Russian — **ruso** *nm* : Russian (language)
rústico, -ca *adj* **1** : rural, rustic **2 en rústica** : in paperback
ruta *nf* : route
rutina *nf* : routine — **rutinario, -ria** *adj* : routine

S

s *nf* : s, 20th letter of the Spanish alphabet
sábado *nm* : Saturday
sábana *nf* : sheet
sabandija *nf* : bug
saber {71} *vt* **1** : know **2** SER CAPAZ DE : know how to, be able to **3** ENTERARSE : learn, find out **4 a ~** : namely — *vi* **1** : taste **2 ~ de** : know about — **~** *nm* : knowledge — **sabelotodo** *nmf fam* : know-it-all — **sabido, -da** *adj* : well-known — **sabiduría** *nf* **1** : wisdom **2** CONOCIMIENTO : learning, knowledge — **sabiendas: a ~** *adv phr* : knowingly — **sabio, -bia** *adj* **1** : learned **2** PRUDENTE : wise, sensible
sabor *nm* : flavor, taste — **saborear** *vt* : savor
sabotaje *nm* : sabotage — **saboteador, -dora** *n* : saboteur — **sabotear** *vt* : sabotage
sabroso, -sa *adj* : delicious, tasty
sabueso *nm* **1** : bloodhound **2** *fam* : sleuth
sacacorchos *nms & pl* : corkscrew
sacapuntas *nms & pl* : pencil sharpener
sacar {72} *vt* **1** : take out **2** OBTENER : get, obtain **3** EXTRAER : extract, withdraw **4** : bring out (a book, a product, etc.) **5** : take (photos), make (copies) **6** QUITAR : remove **7 ~ adelante** : bring up (children), carry out (a project, etc.) **8 ~ la lengua** : stick out one's tongue — *vi* : serve (in sports)
sacarina *nf* : saccharin
sacerdote, -tisa *n* : priest *m*, priestess *f* — **sacerdocio** *nm* : priesthood — **sacerdotal** *adj* : priestly
saciar *vt* : satisfy
saco *nm* **1** : bag, sack **2** : sac (in anatomy) **3** *Lat* : jacket
sacramento *nm* : sacrament — **sacramental** *adj* : sacramental
sacrificar {72} *vt* : sacrifice — **sacrificarse** *vr* : sacrifice oneself — **sacrificio** *nm* : sacrifice
sacrilegio *nm* : sacrilege — **sacrílego, -ga** *adj* : sacrilegious
sacro, -cra *adj* : sacred — **sacrosanto, -ta** *adj* : sacrosanct
sacudir *vt* **1** : shake **2** GOLPEAR : beat **3** CONMOVER : shake up, shock — **sacudirse** *vr* : shake off — **sacudida** *nf* **1** : shaking **2** : jolt (of a train, etc.), tremor (of an earthquake) **3** : (emotional) shock
sádico, -ca *adj* : sadistic — **~** *n* : sadist — **sadismo** *nm* : sadism
saeta *nf* : arrow

safari *nm* : safari
sagaz *adj, pl* **-gaces** : shrewd, sagacious — **sagacidad** *nf* : shrewdness
sagrado, -da *adj* : sacred, holy
sal *nf* : salt
sala *nf* **1** : room, hall **2** : living room (of a house) **3 ~ de espera** : waiting room
salar *vt* : salt — **salado, -da** *adj* **1** : salty **2** GRACIOSO : witty **3 agua salada** : salt water
salario *nm* : salary, wage
salchicha *nf* : sausage — **salchichón** *nf, pl* **-chones** : salami-like cold cut
saldar *vt* **1** : settle, pay off **2** VENDER : sell off — **saldo** *nm* **1** : balance (of an account) **2 ~s** *nmpl* : remainders, sale items
salero *nm* : saltshaker
salir {73} *vi* **1** : go out, come out **2** PARTIR : leave **3** APARECER : appear **4** RESULTAR : turn out **5** : rise (of the sun) **6 ~ adelante** : get by **7 ~ con** : go out with, date **8 ~ de** : come from — **salirse** *vr* **1** : leave **2** ESCAPARSE : leak out, escape **3** SOLTARSE : come off **4 ~ con la suya** : get one's own way — **salida** *nf* **1** : exit **2** : (action of) leaving, departure **3** SOLUCIÓN : way out **4** : leak (of gas, liquid, etc.) **5** OCURRENCIA : witty remark **6 ~ de emergencia** : emergency exit **7 ~ del sol** : sunrise — **saliente** *adj* **1** : departing, outgoing **2** DESTACADO : outstanding
saliva *nf* : saliva
salmo *nm* : psalm
salmón *nm, pl* **-mones** : salmon
salmuera *nf* : brine
salón *nm, pl* **-lones** **1** : lounge, sitting room **2 ~ de belleza** : beauty salon **3 ~ de clase** : classroom
salpicar {72} *vt* **1** : splash, spatter **2 ~ de** : pepper with — **salpicadera** *nf Lat* : fender — **salpicadura** *nf* : splash
salsa *nf* **1** : sauce **2** : (meat) gravy **3** : salsa (music)
saltamontes *nms & pl* : grasshopper
saltar *vi* **1** : jump, leap **2** REBOTAR : bounce **3** : come off (of a button, etc.) **4** ROMPERSE : shatter **5** ESTALLAR : explode, blow up — *vt* **1** : jump (over) **2** OMITIR : skip, miss — **saltarse** *vr* **1** : come off **2** OMITIR : skip, miss
saltear *vt* : sauté
saltimbanqui *nmf* : acrobat
salto *nm* **1** : jump, leap **2** : dive (into water) **3 ~ de agua** : waterfall — **saltón, -tona** *adj, mpl* **-tones** : bulging, protruding

salud *nf* **1** : health **2 ¡salud! :** here's to your health! **3 ¡salud!** *Lat* : bless you! (when someone sneezes) — **saludable** *adj* : healthy

saludar *vt* **1** : greet, say hello to **2** : salute (in the military) — **saludo** *nm* **1** : greeting **2** : (military) salute **3 ~s** : best wishes, regards

salva *nf* **~ de aplausos** : round of applause

salvación *nf, pl* **-ciones** : salvation

salvado *nm* : bran

salvador, -dora *n* : savior, rescuer

salvadoreño, -ña *adj* : (El) Salvadoran

salvaguardar *vt* : safeguard

salvaje *adj* **1** : wild **2** PRIMITIVO : savage, primitive — **~** *nmf* : savage

salvar *vt* **1** : save, rescue **2** RECORRER : cover, travel **3** SUPERAR : overcome — **salvarse** *vr* : save oneself — **salvavidas** *nms & pl* **1** : life preserver **2 bote ~** : lifeboat

salvia *nf* : sage (plant)

salvo, -va *adj* : safe — **salvo** *prep* **1** : except (for), save **2 ~ que** : unless

samba *nf* : samba

San → santo

sanar *vt* : heal, cure — *vi* : recover — **sanatorio** *nm* **1** : sanatorium **2** HOSPITAL : clinic, hospital

sanción *nf, pl* **-ciones** : sanction — **sancionar** *vt* : sanction

sandalia *nf* : sandal

sándalo *nm* : sandalwood

sandía *nf* : watermelon

sandwich [ˈsandwitʃ, ˈsaŋgwitʃ] *nm, pl* **-wiches** [-dwitʃes, -gwi-] : sandwich

saneamiento *nm* : sanitation

sangrar *vt* **1** : bleed **2** : indent (a paragraph) — *vi* : bleed — **sangrante** *adj* : bleeding — **sangre** *nf* **1** : blood **2 a ~ fría** : in cold blood — **sangriento, -ta** *adj* : bloody

sanguijuela *nf* : leech

sanguinario, -ria *adj* : bloodthirsty — **sanguíneo, -nea** *adj* : blood

sano, -na *adj* **1** : healthy **2** : (morally) wholesome **3** ENTERO : intact **4 sano y salvo** : safe and sound — **sanidad** *nf* **1** : health **2** : public health, sanitation — **sanitario, -ria** *adj* : sanitary, health — **sanitario** *nm Lat* : toilet

santiamén *nm* **en un ~** : in no time at all

santo, -ta *adj* **1** : holy **2 Santo, Santa** (**San** *before masculine names except those beginning with D or T*) : Saint — **~** *n* : saint — **santo** *nm* **1** : saint's day **2** *Lat* : birthday — **santidad** *nf* : holiness, sanctity — **santiguarse** {10} *vr* : cross oneself — **santuario** *nm* : sanctuary

saña *nf* **1** : fury **2** BRUTALIDAD : viciousness

sapo *nm* : toad

saque *nm* : serve (in tennis, etc.), throw-in (in soccer)

saquear *vt* : sack, loot — **saqueador, -dora** *n* : looter — **saqueo** *nm* : sacking, looting

sarampión *nm* : measles *pl*

sarape *nm Lat* : serape

sarcasmo *nm* : sarcasm — **sarcástico, -ca** *adj* : sarcastic

sardina *nf* : sardine

sardónico, -ca *adj* : sardonic

sargento *nmf* : sergeant

sarpullido *nm* : rash

sartén *nmf, pl* **-tenes** : frying pan

sastre, -tra *n* : tailor — **sastrería** *nf* **1** : tailoring **2** : tailor's shop

Satanás *nm* : Satan — **satánico, -ca** *adj* : satanic

satélite *nm* : satellite

sátira *nf* : satire — **satírico, -ca** *adj* : satirical

satisfacer {74} *vt* **1** : satisfy **2** CUMPLIR : fulfill, meet **3** PAGAR : pay — **satisfacerse** *vr* **1** : be satisfied **2** VENGARSE : take revenge — **satisfacción** *nf, pl* **-ciones** : satisfaction — **satisfactorio, -ria** *adj* : satisfactory — **satisfecho, -cha** *adj* : satisfied

saturar *vt* : saturate — **saturación** *nf, pl* **-ciones** : saturation

Saturno *nm* : Saturn

sauce *nm* : willow

sauna *nmf* : sauna

savia *nf* : sap

saxofón *nm, pl* **-fones** : saxophone

sazón *nf, pl* **-zones** **1** : seasoning **2** MADUREZ : ripeness **3 a la ~** : at that time, then **4 en ~** : ripe, in season — **sazonar** *vt* : season

se *pron* **1** (*reflexive*) : himself, herself, itself, oneself, yourself, yourselves, themselves **2** (*indirect object*) : (to) him, (to) her, (to) you, (to) them **3** : each other, one another **4 ~ dice que** : it is said that **5 ~ habla inglés** : English spoken

sebo *nm* **1** : fat **2** : tallow (for candles, etc.) **3** : suet (for cooking)

secar {72} *v* : dry — **secarse** *vr* : dry (up) — **secador** *nm* : hair dryer — **secadora** *nf* : (clothes) dryer

sección *nf, pl* **-ciones** : section

seco, -ca *adj* **1** : dry **2** : dried (of fruits, etc.) **3** TAJANTE : sharp, brusque **4** *fam* : thin, skinny **5 a secas** : simply, just **6 en seco** : suddenly

secretar *vt* : secrete — **secreción** *nf, pl* **-ciones** : secretion

secretario, -ria *n* : secretary — **secretaría** *nf* : secretariat

secreto, -ta *adj* : secret — **secreto** *nm* **1** : secret **2 en ~** : in confidence

secta *nf* : sect

sector *nm* : sector

secuaz *nmf, pl* **-cuaces** : follower, henchman

secuela *nf* : consequence

secuencia *nf* : sequence

secuestrar *vt* **1** : kidnap **2** : hijack (an airplane, etc.) **3** EMBARGAR : confiscate, seize — **secuestrador, -dora** *n* **1** : kidnapper **2** : hijacker (of an airplane, etc.) — **secuestro** *nm* **1** : kidnapping **2** : hijacking (of an airplane, etc.) **3** : seizure (of goods)

secular *adj* : secular

secundar *vt* : support, second — **secundario, -ria** *adj* : secondary

sed *nf* **1** : thirst **2 tener ~** : be thirsty

seda *nf* : silk

sedal *nm* : fishing line

sedar *vt* : sedate — **sedante** *adj & nm* : sedative

sede *nf* **1** : seat, headquarters **2 Santa Sede** : Holy See

sedentario, -ria *adj* : sedentary

sedición *nf, pl* **-ciones** : sedition — **sedicioso, -sa** *adj* : seditious

sediento, -ta *adj* : thirsty

sedimento *nm* : sediment

sedoso, -sa *adj* : silky, silken

seducir {61} *vt* **1** : seduce **2** ATRAER : captivate, charm — **seducción** *nf, pl* **-ciones** : seduction — **seductor, -tora** *adj* **1** : seductive **2** ENCANTADOR : charming — **~** *n* : seducer

segar {49} *vt* : reap — **segador, -dora** *n* : reaper, harvester

seglar *adj* : lay, secular — **~** *nm* : layperson, layman *m*, laywoman *f*

segmento *nm* : segment

segregar {52} *vt* : segregate — **segregación** *nf, pl* **-ciones** : segregation

seguir {75} *vt* : follow — *vi* : go on, continue — **seguida: en ~** *adv phr* : right away — **seguido** *adv* **1** : straight (ahead) **2** *Lat* : often — **seguido, -da** *adj* **1** : continuous **2** CONSECUTIVO : consecutive — **seguidor, -dora** *n* : follower

según *prep* : according to — **~** *adv* : it depends — **~** *conj* : as, just as

segundo, -da *adj* : second — **~** *n* : second (one) — **segundo** *nm* : second (unit of time)

seguro, -ra *adj* **1** : safe **2** FIRME : secure **3** CIERTO : sure, certain **4** FIABLE : reliable — **seguramente** *adv* : for sure, surely — **seguridad** *nf* **1** : safety **2** GARANTÍA : security **3** CERTEZA : certainty **4** CONFIANZA : confidence — **seguro** *adv* : certainly — **~** *nm* **1** : insurance **2** : safety (device)

seis *adj & nm* : six — **seiscientos, -tas** *adj* : six hundred — **seiscientos** *nms & pl* : six hundred

seísmo *nm* : earthquake

selección *nf, pl* **-ciones** : selection — **seleccionar** *vt* : select, choose — **selectivo, -va** *adj* : selective — **selecto, -ta** *adj* : choice, select

sellar *vt* **1** : seal **2** TIMBRAR : stamp — **sello** *nm* **1** : seal **2** TIMBRE : stamp **3** *or* **~ distintivo** : hallmark

selva *nf* **1** : jungle **2** BOSQUE : forest

semáforo *nm* : traffic light

semana *nf* : week — **semanal** *adj* : weekly — **semanario** *nm* : weekly

semántica *nf* : semantics — **semántico, -ca** *adj* : semantic

semblante *nm* **1** : countenance, face **2** APARIENCIA : look

sembrar {55} *vt* **1** : sow **2 ~ de** : strew with

semejar *vi* : resemble — **semejarse** *vr* : look alike — **semejante** *adj* **1** : similar **2** TAL : such — **~** *nm* : fellowman — **semejanza** *nf* : similarity

semen *nm* : semen — **semental** *nm* **1** : stud **2 caballo ~** : stallion

semestre *nm* : semester

semiconductor *nm* : semiconductor

semifinal *nf* : semifinal

semilla *nf* : seed — **semillero** *nm* **1** : nursery (for plants) **2** HERVIDERO : hotbed, breeding ground

seminario *nm* **1** : seminary **2** CURSO : seminar, course

sémola *nf* : semolina

senado *nm* : senate — **senador, -dora** *n* : senator

sencillo, -lla *adj* **1** : simple **2** ÚNICO : single — **sencillez** *nf* : simplicity

senda *nf or* **sendero** *nm* : path, way

sendos, -das *adj pl* : each, both

senil *adj* : senile

seno *nm* **1** : breast, bosom **2** : sinus (in anatomy) **3 ~ materno** : womb

sensación *nf, pl* **-ciones** : feeling, sensation — **sensacional** *adj* : sensational — **sensacionalista** *adj* : sensationalistic, lurid

sensato, -ta *adj* : sensible — **sensatez** *nf* : good sense

sensible *adj* **1** : sensitive **2** APRECIABLE : considerable, significant — **sensibilidad** *nf* : sensitivity — **sensitivo, -va** *or* **sensorial** *adj* : sense, sensory

sensual *adj* : sensual, sensuous — **sensualidad** *nf* : sensuality

sentar {55} *vt* **1** : seat, sit **2** ESTABLECER : establish, set — *vi* **1** : suit **2 ~ bien a** : agree with (of food or drink) — **sentarse**

vr : sit (down) — **sentado, -da** *adj* **1** : sitting, seated **2 dar por sentado** : take for granted

sentencia *nf* **1** FALLO : sentence, judgment **2** MÁXIMA : saying — **sentenciar** *vt* : sentence

sentido, -da *adj* **1** : heartfelt, sincere **2** SENSIBLE : touchy, sensitive — **sentido** *nm* **1** : sense **2** CONOCIMIENTO : consciousness **3** DIRECCIÓN : direction **4 doble ~** : double entendre **5 ~ común** : common sense **6 ~ del humor** : sense of humor **7 ~ único** : one-way

sentimiento *nm* **1** : feeling, emotion **2** PESAR : regret — **sentimental** *adj* : sentimental — **sentimentalismo** *nm* : sentimentality

sentir {76} *vt* **1** : feel **2** OÍR : hear **3** LAMENTAR : be sorry for **4 lo siento** : I'm sorry — *vi* : feel — **sentirse** *vr* : feel

seña *nf* **1** : sign **2 ~s** *nfpl* DIRECCIÓN : address **3 ~s particulares** : distinguishing marks

señal *nf* **1** : signal **2** AVISO, INDICIO : sign **3** DEPÓSITO : deposit **4 dar ~es de** : show signs of **5 en ~ de** : as a token of — **señalado, -da** *adj* : notable — **señalar** *vt* **1** INDICAR : indicate, point out **2** MARCAR : mark **3** FIJAR : fix, set — **señalarse** *vr* : distinguish oneself

señor, -ñora *n* **1** : gentleman *m*, man *m*, lady *f*, woman *f* **2** : Sir *m*, Madam *f* **3** : Mr. *m*, Mrs. *f* **4 señora** : wife *f* **5 el Señor** : the Lord — **señorial** *adj* : stately — **señorita** *nf* **1** : young lady, young woman **2** : Miss

señuelo *nm* **1** : decoy **2** TRAMPA : bait, lure

separar *vt* **1** : separate **2** QUITAR : detach, remove **3** APARTAR : move away **4** DESTITUIR : dismiss — **separarse** *vr* **1** APARTARSE : separate **2** : part company — **separación** *nf, pl* **-ciones** : separation — **separado, -da** *adj* **1** : separate **2** : separated (of persons) **3 por separado** : separately

septentrional *adj* : northern

séptico, -ca *adj* : septic

septiembre *nm* : September

séptimo, -ma *adj* : seventh — **~** *n* : seventh

sepulcro *nm* : tomb, sepulchre — **sepultar** *vt* : bury — **sepultura** *nf* **1** : burial **2** TUMBA : grave

sequedad *nf* : dryness — **sequía** *nf* : drought

séquito *nm* : retinue, entourage

ser {77} *vi* **1** : be **2 a no ~ que** : unless **3 ¿cuánto es?** : how much is it? **4 es más** : what's more **5 ~ de** : belong to **6 ~ de** : come from **7 son las diez** : it's ten o'clock — **~** *nm* **1** ENTE : being **2 ~ humano** : human being

serbio, -bia *adj* : Serb, Serbian

serenar *vt* : calm — **serenarse** *vr* : calm down — **serenata** *nf* : serenade — **serenidad** *nf* : serenity — **sereno, -na** *adj* **1** : serene, calm **2** : fair, clear (of weather) — **sereno** *nm* : night watchman

serie *nf* **1** : series **2 fabricación en ~** : mass production **3 fuera de ~** : extraordinary — **serial** *nm* : serial

serio, -ria *adj* **1** : serious **2** RESPONSABLE : reliable **3 en serio** : seriously — **seriedad** *nf* : seriousness

sermón *nm, pl* **-mones** : sermon — **sermonear** *vt* : lecture, reprimand

serpentear *vi* : twist, wind — **serpiente** *nf* **1** : serpent, snake **2 ~ de cascabel** : rattlesnake

serrado, -da *adj* : serrated

serrano, -na *adj* **1** : mountain **2 jamón serrano** : cured ham

serrar {55} *vt* : saw — **serrín** *nm, pl* **-rrines** : sawdust — **serrucho** *nm* : saw, handsaw

servicio *nm* **1** : service **2 ~s** *nmpl* : restroom — **servicial** *adj* : obliging, helpful — **servidor, -dora** *n* **1** : servant **2 su seguro servidor** : yours truly — **servidumbre** *nf* **1** : servitude **2** CRIADOS : help, servants *pl* — **servil** *adj* : servile

servilleta *nf* : napkin

servir {54} *vt* : serve — *vi* **1** : work, function **2** VALER : be of use — **servirse** *vr* **1** : help oneself **2 sírvase sentarse** : please have a seat

sesenta *adj & nm* : sixty

sesgo *nm* : bias, slant

sesión *nf, pl* **-siones** **1** : session **2** : showing (of a film), performance (of a play)

seso *nm* : brain — **sesudo, -da** *adj* **1** : sensible **2** *fam* : brainy

seta *nf* : mushroom

setecientos, -tas *adj* : seven hundred — **setecientos** *nms & pl* : seven hundred

setenta *adj & nm* : seventy

setiembre *nm* → **septiembre**

seto *nm* **1** : fence **2 ~ vivo** : hedge

seudónimo *nm* : pseudonym

severo, -ra *adj* **1** : harsh, severe **2** : strict (of a teacher, etc.) — **severidad** *nf* : severity

sexagésimo, -ma *adj & n* : sixtieth

sexo *nm* : sex — **sexismo** *nm* : sexism — **sexista** *adj & nmf* : sexist

sexteto *nm* : sextet

sexto, -ta *adj & n* : sixth

sexual *adj* : sexual — **sexualidad** *nf* : sexuality

sexy *adj, pl* **sexy** *or* **sexys** : sexy

si *conj* **1** : if **2** (*in indirect questions*) : whether **3 ~ bien** : although **4 ~ no** : otherwise, or else

sí¹ *adv* **1** : yes **2 creo que ~** : I think so **3 porque ~** *fam* : (just) because — **~** *nm* : consent

sí² *pron* **1 de por ~** *or* **en ~** : by itself, in itself, per se **2 fuera de ~** : beside oneself **3 para ~ (mismo)** : to himself, to herself, for himself, for herself **4 entre ~** : among themselves

sico- → **psico-**

SIDA *or* **sida** *nm* : AIDS

siderurgia *nf* : iron and steel industry

sidra *nf* : (hard) cider

siega *nf* **1** : harvesting **2** : harvest (time)

siembra *nf* **1** : sowing **2** : sowing season

siempre *adv* **1** : always **2** *Lat* : still **3 para ~** : forever, for good **4 ~ que** : whenever, every time **5 ~ que** *or* **~ y cuando** : provided that

sien *nf* : temple

sierra *nf* **1** : saw **2** CORDILLERA : mountain range **3 la ~** : the mountains *pl*

siervo, -va *n* : slave

siesta *nf* : nap, siesta

siete *adj & nm* : seven

sífilis *nf* : syphilis

sifón *nm, pl* **-fones** : siphon

sigilo *nm* : secrecy

sigla *nf* : acronym, abbreviation

siglo *nm* **1** : century **2 hace ~s** : for ages

significar {72} *vt* **1** : mean, signify **2** EXPRESAR : express — **significación** *nf, pl* **-ciones** **1** : significance, importance **2** : meaning (of a word, etc.) — **significado, -da** *adj* : well-known — **significado** *nm* : meaning — **significativo, -va** *adj* : significant

signo *nm* **1** : sign **2 ~ de admiración** : exclamation point **3 ~ de interrogación** : question mark

siguiente *adj* : next, following

sílaba *nf* : syllable

silbar *v* **1** : whistle **2** ABUCHEAR : hiss, boo — **silbato** *nm* : whistle — **silbido** *nm* **1** : whistle, whistling **2** ABUCHEO : hiss, booing

silenciar *vt* : silence — **silenciador** *nm* : muffler — **silencio** *nm* : silence — **silencioso, -sa** *adj* : silent, quiet

silicio *nm* : silicon

silla *nf* **1** : chair **2** *or* **~ de montar** : saddle **3 ~ de ruedas** : wheelchair — **sillón** *nm, pl* **-llones** : armchair, easy chair

silo *nm* : silo

silueta *nf* **1** : silhouette **2** CONTORNO : outline, shape

silvestre *adj* : wild

silvicultura *nf* : forestry

símbolo *nm* : symbol — **simbólico, -ca** *adj* : symbolic — **simbolismo** *nm* : symbolism — **simbolizar** {21} *vt* : symbolize

simetría *nf* : symmetry — **simétrico, -ca** *adj* : symmetrical, symmetric

simiente *nf* : seed

símil *nm* : simile **2** COMPARACIÓN : comparison — **similar** *adj* : similar, alike

simio *nm* : ape

simpatía *nf* **1** : liking, affection **2** AMABILIDAD : friendliness — **simpático, -ca** *adj* **1** : nice, likeable **2** AMABLE : pleasant, kind — **simpatizante** *nmf* : sympathizer — **simpatizar** {21} *vi* **1** : get along, hit it off **2 ~ con** : sympathize with

simple *adj* **1** SENCILLO : simple **2** MERO : pure, sheer **3** TONTO : simpleminded — **~** *n* : fool, simpleton — **simpleza** *nf* **1** : simpleness **2** TONTERÍA : silly thing — **simplicidad** *nf* : simplicity — **simplificar** {72} *vt* : simplify

simposio *or* **simposium** *nm* : symposium

simular *vt* **1** : simulate **2** FINGIR : feign — **simulacro** *nm* : simulation, drill

simultáneo, -nea *adj* : simultaneous

sin *prep* **1** : without **2 ~ que** : without

sinagoga *nf* : synagogue

sincero, -ra *adj* : sincere — **sinceramente** *adv* : sincerely — **sinceridad** *nf* : sincerity

síncopa *nf* : syncopation

sincronizar {21} *vt* : synchronize

sindicato *nm* : (labor) union — **sindical** *adj* : union, labor

síndrome *nm* : syndrome

sinfín *nm* **1** : endless number **2 un ~ de** : no end of

sinfonía *nf* : symphony — **sinfónico, -ca** *adj* : symphonic

singular *adj* **1** : exceptional, outstanding **2** PECULIAR : peculiar **3** : singular (in grammar) — **~** *nm* : singular — **singularizar** {21} *vt* : single out — **singularizarse** *vr* : stand out

siniestro, -tra *adj* **1** : sinister **2** IZQUIERDO : left — **siniestro** *nm* : disaster

sinnúmero *nm* → **sinfín**

sino *conj* **1** : but, rather **2** EXCEPTO : except, save

sinónimo, -ma *adj* : synonymous — **sinónimo** *nm* : synonym

sinopsis *nfs & pl* : synopsis

sinrazón *nf, pl* **-zones** : wrong

sintaxis *nfs & pl* : syntax

síntesis *nfs & pl* : synthesis — **sintético, -ca** *adj* : synthetic — **sintetizar** {21} *vt* **1** : synthesize **2** RESUMIR : summarize

síntoma *nm* : symptom — **sintomático, -ca** *adj* : symptomatic

sintonía *nf* **1** : tuning in (of a radio) **2 en ∼ con** : in tune with — **sintonizar** {21} *vt* : tune (in) to

sinuoso, -sa *adj* : winding

sinvergüenza *nmf* : scoundrel

sionismo *nm* : Zionism

siquiera *adv* **1** : at least **2 ni ∼** : not even — **∼** *conj* : even if

sirena *nf* **1** : mermaid **2** : siren (of an ambulance, etc.)

sirio, -ria *adj* : Syrian

sirviente, -ta *n* : servant, maid *f*

sisear *vi* : hiss — **siseo** *nm* : hiss

sismo *nm* : earthquake — **sísmico, -ca** *adj* : seismic

sistema *nm* **1** : system **2 por ∼** : systematically — **sistemático, -ca** *adj* : systematic

sitiar *vt* : besiege

sitio *nm* **1** : place, site **2** ESPACIO : room, space **3** CERCO : siege **4 en cualquier ∼** : anywhere

situar {3} *vt* : situate, place — **situarse** *vr* **1** : be located **2** ESTABLECERSE : get oneself established — **situación** *nf, pl* **-ciones** : situation, position — **situado, -da** *adj* : situated, placed

slip *nm* : briefs *pl*, underpants *pl*

smoking *nm* : tuxedo

so *prep* : under

sobaco *nm* : armpit

sobar *vt* **1** : finger, handle **2** : knead (dough) — **sobado, -da** *adj* : worn, shabby

soberanía *nf* : sovereignty — **soberano, -na** *adj & n* : sovereign

soberbia *nf* : pride, arrogance — **soberbio, -bia** *adj* : proud, arrogant

sobornar *vt* : bribe — **soborno** *nm* **1** : bribe **2** : (action of) bribery

sobrar *vi* **1** : be more than enough **2** RESTAR : be left over — **sobra** *nf* **1** : surplus **2 de ∼** : to spare **3 ∼s** *nfpl* : leftovers — **sobrado, -da** *adj* : more than enough — **sobrante** *adj* : remaining

sobre[1] *nm* : envelope

sobre[2] *prep* **1** : on, on top of **2** POR ENCIMA DE : over, above **3** ACERCA DE : about **4 ∼ todo** : especially, above all

sobrecama *nmf Lat* : bedspread

sobrecargar {52} *vt* : overload, overburden

sobrecoger {15} *vt* : startle — **sobrecogerse** *vr* : be startled

sobrecubierta *nf* : dust jacket

sobredosis *nfs & pl* : overdose

sobreentender {56} *vt* : infer, understand — **sobreentenderse** *vr* : be understood

sobreestimar *vt* : overestimate

sobregiro *nm* : overdraft

sobrellevar *vt* : endure, bear

sobremesa *nf* **de ∼** : after-dinner

sobrenatural *adj* : supernatural

sobrenombre *nm* : nickname

sobrentender → **sobreentender**

sobrepasar *vt* : exceed

sobreponer {60} *vt* **1** : superimpose **2** ANTEPONER : put before — **sobreponerse** *vr* **∼ a** : overcome

sobresalir {73} *vi* **1** : protrude **2** DESTACARSE : stand out — **sobresaliente** *adj* : outstanding

sobresaltar *vt* : startle — **sobresaltarse** *vr* : start, jump up — **sobresalto** *nm* : fright

sobrestimar → **sobreestimar**

sobretodo *nm* : overcoat

sobrevenir {87} *vi* : happen, ensue

sobrevivencia *nf* → **supervivencia**

sobreviviente *adj & nmf* → **superviviente**

sobrevivir *vi* : survive — *vt* : outlive

sobrevolar {19} *vt* : fly over

sobriedad *nf* **1** : sobriety **2** MODERACIÓN : restraint

sobrino, -na *n* : nephew *m,* niece *f*

sobrio, -bria *adj* : sober

socarrón, -rrona *adj, mpl* **-rrones** : sarcastic

socavar *vt* : undermine

sociable *adj* : sociable — **social** *adj* : social — **socialismo** *nm* : socialism — **socialista** *adj & nmf* : socialist — **sociedad** *nf* **1** : society **2** EMPRESA : company **3 ∼ anónima** : incorporated company — **socio, -cia** *n* **1** : partner **2** MIEMBRO : member — **sociología** *nf* : sociology — **sociólogo, -ga** *n* : sociologist

socorrer *vt* : help — **socorrista** *nmf* : lifeguard — **socorro** *nm* : help

soda *nf* : soda (water)

sodio *nf* : sodium

sofá *nm* : couch, sofa

sofisticación *nf, pl* **-ciones** : sophistication — **sofisticado, -da** *adj* : sophisticated

sofocar {72} *vt* **1** : suffocate, smother **2** : put out (a fire), stifle (a rebellion, etc.) — **sofocarse** *vr* **1** : suffocate **2** *fam* : get upset — **sofocante** *adj* : suffocating, stifling

sofreír {66} *vt* : sauté

soga *nf* : rope

soja *nf* → **soya**

sojuzgar *vt* : subdue, subjugate

sol *nm* **1** : sun **2 hacer ∼** : be sunny

solamente *adv* : only, just

solapa *nf* **1** : lapel (of a jacket) **2** : flap (of an envelope) — **solapado, -da** *adj* : secret, underhanded

solar[1] *adj* : solar, sun

solar[2] *nm* : lot, site

solariego, -ga *adj* : ancestral

solaz *nm, pl* **-laces** : solace **2** DESCANSO : relaxation — **solazarse** {21} *vr* : relax

soldado *nm* **1** : soldier **2 ～ raso** : private
soldar {19} *vt* : weld, solder — **soldador**
nm : soldering iron — **soldador, -dora** *n*
: welder
soleado, -da *adj* : sunny
soledad *nf* : loneliness, solitude
solemne *adj* : solemn — **solemnidad** *nf*
: solemnity
soler {78} *vi* **1** : be in the habit of **2 suele**
llegar tarde : he usually arrives late
solicitar *vt* **1** : request, solicit **2** : apply for
(a job, etc.) — **solicitante** *nmf* : applicant
— **solícito, -ta** *adj* : solicitous, obliging —
solicitud *nf* **1** : concern **2** PETICIÓN : request **3** : application (for a job, etc.)
solidaridad *nf* : solidarity
sólido, -da *adj* **1** : solid **2** : sound (of an argument, etc.) — **sólido** *nm* : solid —
solidez *nf* : solidity — **solidificar** {72} *vt*
: solidify — **solidificarse** *vr* : solidify,
harden
soliloquio *nm* : soliloquy
solista *nmf* : soloist
solitario, -ria *adj* **1** : solitary **2** AISLADO
: lonely, deserted — **～** *n* : recluse — **soli-**
taria *nf* : tapeworm — **solitario** *nm* : soli-
taire
sollozar {21} *vi* : sob — **sollozo** *nm* : sob
solo, -la *adj* **1** : alone **2** AISLADO : lonely **3**
a solas : alone, by oneself — **solo** *nm* : solo
sólo *adv* : just, only
solomillo *nm* : sirloin
solsticio *nm* : solstice
soltar {19} *vt* **1** : release **2** DEJAR CAER : let
go of, drop **3** DESATAR : unfasten, undo —
soltarse *vr* **1** : break free **2** DESATARSE
: come undone
soltero, -ra *adj* : single, unmarried — **～** *n*
1 : bachelor *m*, single woman *f* **2 apellido**
de soltera : maiden name
soltura *nf* **1** : looseness **2** : fluency (in language) **3** AGILIDAD : agility, ease
soluble *adj* : soluble
solución *nf*, *pl* **-ciones** : solution — **solu-**
cionar *vt* : solve, resolve
solventar *vt* **1** : settle, pay **2** RESOLVER : resolve — **solvente** *adj* & *nm* : solvent
sombra *nf* **1** : shadow **2** : shade (of a tree,
etc.) **3 ～s** *nfpl* : darkness, shadows —
sombreado, -da *adj* : shady
sombrero *nm* : hat
sombrilla *nf* : parasol, umbrella
sombrío, -bría *adj* : dark, somber, gloomy
somero, -ra *adj* : superficial
someter *vt* **1** : subjugate **2** SUBORDINAR
: subordinate **3** : subject (to treatment, etc.)
4 PRESENTAR : submit, present — **some-**
terse *vr* **1** : submit, yield **2 ～ a** : undergo
somnífero, -ra *adj* : soporific — **somnífero**

nm : sleeping pill — **somnoliento, -ta** *adj*
: drowsy, sleepy
somos → **ser**
son¹ → **ser**
son² *nm* **1** : sound **2 en ～ de** : as, in the
manner of
sonajero *nm* : (baby's) rattle
sonámbulo, -la *n* : sleepwalker
sonar {19} *vi* **1** : sound **2** : ring (as a bell)
3 : look or sound familiar **4 ～ a** : sound
like — **sonarse** *vr or* **～ las narices** : blow
one's nose
sonata *nf* : sonata
sondear *vt* **1** : sound, probe **2** : survey,
sound out (opinions, etc.) — **sondeo** *nm* **1**
: sounding, probing **2** ENCUESTA : survey,
poll
soneto *nm* : sonnet
sónico, -ca *adj* : sonic
sonido *nm* : sound
sonoro, -ra *adj* **1** : resonant, sonorous **2**
RUIDOSO : loud
sonreír {66} *vi* : smile — **sonreírse** *vr*
: smile — **sonriente** *adj* : smiling — **son-**
risa *nf* : smile
sonrojar *vt* : cause to blush — **sonrojarse** *vr*
: blush — **sonrojo** *nm* : blush
sonrosado, -da *adj* : rosy, pink
sonsacar {72} *vt* : wheedle (out)
soñar {19} *v* **1** : dream **2 ～ con** : dream
about **3 ～ despierto** : daydream —
soñador, -dora *adj* : dreamy — **～** *n*
: dreamer — **soñoliento, -ta** *adj* : sleepy,
drowsy
sopa *nf* : soup
sopesar *vt* : weigh, consider
soplar *vi* : blow — *vt* : blow out, blow off,
blow up — **soplete** *nm* : blowtorch —
soplo *nm* : puff, gust
soplón, -plona *n*, *pl* **-plones** *fam* : sneak
sopor *nm* : drowsiness — **soporífero, -ra**
adj : soporific
soportar *vt* **1** SOSTENER : support **2** AGUAN-
TAR : bear — **soporte** *nm* : support
soprano *nmf* : soprano
sor *nf* : Sister (in religion)
sorber *vt* **1** : sip **2** ABSORBER : absorb **3**
CHUPAR : suck up — **sorbete** *nm* : sherbet
— **sorbo** *nm* **1** : sip, swallow **2 beber a**
～s : sip
sordera *nf* : deafness
sórdido, -da *adj* : sordid, squalid
sordo, -da *adj* **1** : deaf **2** : muted (of a
sound) — **sordomudo, -da** *n* : deaf-mute
sorna *nf* : sarcasm
sorprender *vt* : surprise — **sorprenderse** *vr*
: be surprised — **sorprendente** *adj* : surprising — **sorpresa** *nf* : surprise
sortear *vt* **1** : raffle off, draw lots for **2**

ESQUIVAR : dodge — **sorteo** *nm* : drawing, raffle

sortija *nf* **1** : ring **2** : ringlet (of hair)

sortilegio *nm* **1** HECHIZO : spell **2** HECHI-CERÍA : sorcery

sosegar {49} *vt* : calm, pacify — **sosegarse** *vr* : calm down — **sosegado, -da** *adj* : calm, tranquil — **sosiego** *nm* : calm

soslayo: **de** ∼ *adv phr* : obliquely, sideways

soso, -sa *adj* **1** : insipid, tasteless **2** ABURRIDO : dull

sospechar *vt* : suspect — **sospecha** *nf* : suspicion — **sospechoso, -sa** *adj* : suspicious — ∼ *n* : suspect

sostener {80} *vt* **1** : support **2** SUJETAR : hold **3** MANTENER : sustain, maintain — **sostenerse** *vr* **1** : stand (up) **2** CONTINUAR : remain **3** SUSTENTARSE : support oneself — **sostén** *nm, pl* **-tenes 1** APOYO : support **2** SUSTENTO : sustenance **3** : brassiere, bra — **sostenido, -da** *adj* **1** : sustained **2** : sharp (in music) — **sostenido** *nm* : sharp

sótano *nm* : basement

soterrar {55} *vt* **1** : bury **2** ESCONDER : hide

soto *nm* : grove

soviético, -ca *adj* : Soviet

soy → **ser**

soya *nf* : soy

Sr. *nm* : Mr. — **Sra.** *nf* : Mrs., Ms. — **Srta.** *or* **Srita.** *nf* : Miss, Ms.

su *adj* **1** : his, her, its, their, one's **2** (*formal*) : your

suave *adj* **1** : soft **2** LISO : smooth **3** APACIBLE : gentle, mild — **suavidad** *nf* **1** : softness, smoothness **2** APACIBILIDAD : mildness, gentleness — **suavizar** {21} *vt* : soften, smooth

subalimentado, -da *adj* : undernourished, underfed

subalterno, -na *adj* **1** SUBORDINADO : subordinate **2** SECUNDARIO : secondary — ∼ *n* : subordinate

subarrendar {55} *vt* : sublet

subasta *nf* : auction — **subastar** *vt* : auction (off)

subcampeón, -peona *n, mpl* **-peones** : runner-up

subcomité *nm* : subcommittee

subconsciente *adj & nm* : subconscious

subdesarrollado, -da *adj* : underdeveloped

subdirector, -tora *n* : assistant manager

súbdito, -ta *n* : subject

subdividir *vt* : subdivide — **subdivisión** *nf, pl* **-siones** : subdivision

subestimar *vt* : underestimate

subir *vt* **1** : climb, go up **2** LLEVAR : bring up, take up **3** AUMENTAR : raise — *vi* **1** : go up, come up **2** ∼ **a** : get in (a car), get

on (a bus, etc.) — **subirse** *vr* **1** : climb (up) **2** ∼ **a** : get in (a car), get on (a bus, etc.) **3** ∼ **a la cabeza** : go to one's head — **subida** *nf* **1** : ascent, climb **2** AUMENTO : rise **3** PENDIENTE : slope — **subido, -da** *adj* **1** : bright, strong **2** ∼ **de tono** : risqué

súbito, -ta *adj* **1** : sudden **2 de súbito** : all of a sudden, suddenly

subjetivo, -va *adj* : subjective

subjuntivo, -va *adj* : subjunctive — **subjuntivo** *nm* : subjunctive (case)

sublevar *vt* : stir up, incite to rebellion — **sublevarse** *vr* : rebel — **sublevación** *nf, pl* **-ciones** : uprising, rebellion

sublime *adj* : sublime

submarino, -na *adj* : underwater — **submarino** *nm* : submarine — **submarinismo** *nm* : scuba diving

subordinar *vt* : subordinate — **subordinado, -da** *adj & n* : subordinate

subproducto *nm* : by-product

subrayar *vt* **1** : underline **2** ENFATIZAR : emphasize, stress

subrepticio, -cia *adj* : surreptitious

subsanar *vt* **1** : rectify, correct **2** : make up for (a deficiency), overcome (an obstacle)

subscribir → **suscribir**

subsidio *nm* : subsidy, benefit

subsiguiente *adj* : subsequent

subsistir *vi* **1** : live, subsist **2** SOBREVIVIR : survive — **subsistencia** *nf* : subsistence

substancia *nf* → **sustancia**

subterfugio *nm* : subterfuge

subterráneo, -nea *adj* : underground, subterranean — **subterráneo** *nm* : underground passage

subtítulo *nm* : subtitle

suburbio *nm* **1** : suburb **2** : slum (outside a city) — **suburbano, -na** *adj* : suburban

subvencionar *vt* : subsidize — **subvención** *nf, pl* **-ciones** : subsidy, grant

subvertir {76} *vt* : subvert — **subversión** *nf, pl* **-siones** : subversion — **subversivo, -va** *adj & n* : subversive

subyacente *adj* : underlying

subyugar {52} *vt* : subjugate, subdue

succión *nf, pl* **-ciones** : suction — **succionar** *vt* : suck up, draw in

sucedáneo *nm* : substitute

suceder *vi* **1** : happen, occur **2** ∼ **a** : follow **3 suceda lo que suceda** : come what may — **sucesión** *nf, pl* **-siones** : succession — **sucesivo, -va** *adj* : successive — **suceso** *nm* **1** : event **2** INCIDENTE : incident — **sucesor, -sora** *n* : successor

suciedad *nf* **1** : dirtiness **2** MUGRE : dirt, filth

sucinto, -ta *adj* : succinct, concise

sucio, -cia *adj* : dirty, filthy

suculento, -ta *adj* : succulent
sucumbir *vi* : succumb
sucursal *nf* : branch (of a business)
sudadera *nf* : sweatshirt — **sudado, -da** *adj*
: sweaty
sudafricano, -na *adj* : South African
sudamericano, -na *adj* : South American
sudar *vi* : sweat
sudeste → **sureste**
sudoeste → **suroeste**
sudor *nm* : sweat — **sudoroso, -sa** *adj*
: sweaty
sueco, -ca *adj* : Swedish — **sueco** *nm*
: Swedish (language)
suegro, -gra *n* 1 : father-in-law *m*, mother-in-law *f* 2 **suegros** *nmpl* : in-laws
suela *nf* : sole (of a shoe)
sueldo *nm* : salary, wage
suelo *nm* 1 : ground 2 : floor (in a house) 3
TIERRA : soil, land
suelto, -ta *adj* : loose, free — **suelto** *nm*
: loose change
sueño *nm* 1 : dream 2 **coger el ～** : get to
sleep 3 **tener ～** : be sleepy
suero *nm* 1 : whey 2 : serum (in medicine)
suerte *nf* 1 : luck, fortune 2 AZAR : chance
3 DESTINO : fate 4 CLASE : sort, kind 5 **por**
～ : luckily 6 **tener ～** : be lucky
suéter *nm* : sweater
suficiencia *nf* 1 CAPACIDAD : competence,
proficiency 2 PRESUNCIÓN : smugness —
suficiente *adj* 1 : enough, sufficient 2
PRESUNTUOSO : smug — **suficientemente**
adv : enough
sufijo *nm* : suffix
sufragio *nm* : suffrage, vote
sufrir *vt* 1 : suffer 2 SOPORTAR : bear, stand
— *vi* : suffer — **sufrido, -da** *adj* 1 : long-suffering 2 : sturdy, serviceable (of clothing) — **sufrimiento** *nm* : suffering
sugerir {76} *vt* : suggest — **sugerencia** *nf*
: suggestion — **sugestión** *nf, pl* **-tiones**
: suggestion — **sugestionable** *adj* : impressionable — **sugestionar** *vt* : influence
— **sugestivo, -va** *adj* 1 : suggestive 2 ES-
TIMULANTE : interesting, stimulating
suicidio *nm* : suicide — **suicida** *adj* : suicidal — **～** *nmf* : suicide (victim) — **suicidarse** *vr* : commit suicide
suite *nf* : suite
suizo, -za *adj* : Swiss
sujetar *vt* 1 : hold (on to) 2 FIJAR : fasten 3
DOMINAR : subdue — **sujetarse** *vr* 1 **～ a**
: hold on to, cling to 2 **～ a** : abide by —
sujeción *nf, pl* **-ciones** 1 : fastening 2
DOMINACIÓN : subjection — **sujetador** *nm*
Spain : brassiere, bra — **sujetapapeles**
nms & pl : paper clip — **sujeto, -ta** *adj* 1

: fastened 2 **～ a** : subject to — **sujeto** *nm*
1 : individual 2 : subject (in grammar)
sulfuro *nm* : sulfur — **sulfúrico, -ca** *adj*
: sulfuric
sultán *nm, pl* **-tanes** : sultan
suma *nf* 1 : sum, total 2 : addition (in mathematics) 3 **en ～** : in short — **sumamente**
adv : extremely — **sumar** *vt* 1 : add (up) 2
TOTALIZAR : add up to, total — *vi* : add up —
sumarse *vr* **～ a** : join
sumario, -ria *adj* : concise — **sumario** *nm* 1
: summary 2 : indictment (in law)
sumergir {35} *vt* : submerge, plunge —
sumergirse *vr* : be submerged — **sumergible** *adj* : waterproof (of a watch, etc.)
sumidero *nm* : drain
suministrar *vt* : supply, provide — **suministro** *nm* : supply, provision
sumir *vt* : plunge, immerse — **sumirse** *vr*
～ en : sink into
sumisión *nf, pl* **-siones** : submission —
sumiso, -sa *adj* : submissive
sumo, -ma *adj* 1 : highest, supreme 2 **de**
suma importancia : of great importance
suntuoso, -sa *adj* : sumptuous, lavish
super *or* **súper** *nm fam* : supermarket
superabundancia *nf* : overabundance
superar *vt* 1 : surpass, outdo 2 VENCER
: overcome — **superarse** *vr* : improve oneself
superávit *nm* : surplus
superestructura *nf* : superstructure
superficie *nf* 1 : surface 2 ÁREA : area —
superficial *adj* : superficial
superfluo, -flua *adj* : superfluous
superintendente *nmf* : supervisor, superintendent
superior *adj* 1 : superior 2 : upper (of a
floor, etc.) 3 **～ a** : above, higher than —
～ *nm* : superior — **superioridad** *nf* : superiority
superlativo, -va *adj* : superlative — **superlativo** *nm* : superlative
supermercado *nm* : supermarket
superpoblado, -da *adj* : overpopulated
supersónico, -ca *adj* : supersonic
superstición *nf, pl* **-ciones** : superstition —
supersticioso, -sa *adj* : superstitious
supervisar *vt* : supervise, oversee — **supervisión** *nf, pl* **-siones** : supervision — **supervisor, -sora** *n* : supervisor
supervivencia *nf* : survival — **superviviente** *adj* : surviving — **～** *nmf* : survivor
suplantar *vt* : supplant, replace
suplemento *nm* : supplement — **suplementario, -ria** *adj* : supplementary
suplente *adj & nmf* : substitute

suplicar {72} *vt* : beg, entreat — **súplica** *nf*
: plea, entreaty

suplicio *nm* : ordeal, torture

suplir *vt* **1** : make up for **2** REEMPLAZAR
: replace

supo, etc. → **saber**

suponer {60} *vt* **1** : suppose, assume **2** SIG-
NIFICAR : mean **3** IMPLICAR : involve, entail
— **suposición** *nf, pl* **-ciones** : supposition

supositorio *nm* : suppository

supremo, -ma *adj* : supreme — **supremacía** *nf* : supremacy

suprimir *vt* **1** : suppress, eliminate **2**
: delete (text) — **supresión** *nf, pl* **-siones**
1 : suppression, elimination **2** : deletion (of
text)

supuesto, -ta *adj* **1** : supposed, alleged **2**
por supuesto : of course — **supuesto** *nm*
: assumption — **supuestamente** *adv* : allegedly

sur *nm* **1** : south, South **2** : south wind **3**
del ∼ : south, southerly

surafricano, -na → **sudafricano**

suramericano, -na → **sudamericano**

surcar {72} *vt* **1** : plow (earth) **2** : cut
through (air, water, etc.) — **surco** *nm*
: groove, furrow, rut

sureño, -ña *adj* : southern, Southern — **∼** *n*
: Southerner

sureste *adj* **1** : southeast, southeastern **2**
: southeasterly (of wind, etc.) — **∼** *nm*
: southeast, Southeast

surf *or* **surfing** *nm* : surfing

surgir {35} *vi* **1** : arise **2** APARECER : appear
— **surgimiento** *nm* : rise, emergence

suroeste *adj* **1** : southwest, southwestern **2**
: southwesterly (of wind, etc.) — **∼** *nm*
: southwest, Southwest

surtir *vt* **1** : supply, provide **2 ∼ efecto**
: have an effect — **surtirse** *vr* **∼ de** : stock
up on — **surtido, -da** *adj* **1** : assorted, varied **2** : stocked (with merchandise) — **surtido** *nm* : assortment, selection — **surtidor**
nm : gas pump

susceptible *adj* **1** : susceptible, sensitive **2**
∼ de : capable of — **susceptibilidad** *nf*
: sensitivity

suscitar *vt* : provoke, arouse

suscribir {33} *vt* **1** : sign (a formal document) **2** RATIFICAR : endorse — **suscribirse** *vr* **∼ a** : subscribe to — **suscripción**
nf, pl **-ciones** : subscription — **suscriptor,
-tora** *n* : subscriber

susodicho, -cha *adj* : aforementioned

suspender *vt* **1** : suspend **2** COLGAR : hang
3 *Spain* : fail (an exam, etc.) — **suspensión** *nf, pl* **-siones** : suspension — **suspenso** *nm* **1** *Spain* : failure (in an exam,
etc.) **2** *Lat* : suspense

suspicaz *adj, pl* **-caces** : suspicious

suspirar *vi* : sigh — **suspiro** *nm* : sigh

sustancia *nf* **1** : substance **2 sin ∼** : shallow, lacking substance — **sustancial** *adj*
: substantial, significant — **sustancioso,
-sa** *adj* : substantial, solid

sustantivo *nm* : noun

sustentar *vt* **1** : support **2** ALIMENTAR : sustain, nourish **3** MANTENER : maintain —
sustentarse *vr* : support oneself — **sus-
tentación** *nf, pl* **-ciones** : support — **sustento** *nm* **1** : means of support, livelihood
2 ALIMENTO : sustenance

sustituir {41} *vt* : replace, substitute —
sustitución *nf, pl* **-ciones** : replacement,
substitution — **sustituto, -ta** *n* : substitute

susto *nm* : fright, scare

sustraer {81} *vt* **1** : remove, take away **2**
: subtract (in mathematics) — **sustraerse**
vr **∼ a** : avoid, evade — **sustracción** *nf, pl*
-ciones : subtraction

susurrar *vi* **1** : whisper **2** : murmur (of
water) **3** : rustle (of leaves, etc.) — *vt*
: whisper — **susurro** *nm* **1** : whisper **2**
: murmur (of water) **3** : rustle, rustling (of
leaves, etc.)

sutil *adj* **1** : delicate, fine **2** : subtle (of fra-
grances, differences, etc.) — **sutileza** *nf*
: subtlety

sutura *nf* : suture

suyo, -ya *adj* **1** : his, her, its, one's, theirs **2**
(*formal*) : yours **3 un primo suyo** : a cousin
of his/hers — **∼** *pron* **1** : his, hers, its
(own), one's own, theirs **2** (*formal*) : yours

switch *nm Lat* : switch

T

t *nf* : t, 21st letter of the Spanish alphabet
taba *nf* : anklebone
tabaco *nm* : tobacco — **tabacalero, -ra** *adj* : tobacco
tábano *nm* : horsefly
taberna *nf* : tavern
tabicar {72} *vt* : wall up — **tabique** *nm* : thin wall, partition
tabla *nf* **1** : board, plank **2** LISTA : table, list **3** ~ **de planchar** : ironing board **4** ~**s** *nfpl* : stage, boards *pl* — **tablado** *nm* **1** : flooring **2** PLATAFORMA : platform **3** : (theater) stage — **tablero** *nm* **1** : bulletin board **2** : board (in games) **3** PIZARRA : blackboard **4** ~ **de instrumentos** : dashboard, instrument panel
tableta *nf* **1** : tablet, pill **2** : bar (of chocolate)
tablilla *nf* : slat — **tablón** *nm, pl* **-lones 1** : plank, beam **2** ~ **de anuncios** : bulletin board
tabú *adj* : taboo — **tabú** *nm, pl* **-búes** or **-bús** : taboo
tabular *vt* : tabulate
taburete *nm* : stool
tacaño, -na *adj* : stingy, miserly
tacha *nf* **1** : flaw, defect **2 sin** ~ : flawless
tachar *vt* **1** : cross out, delete **2** ~ **de** : accuse of, label as
tachón *nm, pl* **-chones** : stud, hobnail — **tachuela** *nf* : tack, hobnail
tácito, -ta *adj* : tacit
taciturno, -na *adj* : taciturn
taco *nm* **1** : stopper, plug **2** *Lat* : heel (of a shoe) **3** : cue (in billiards) **4** : taco (in cooking)
tacón *nm, pl* **-cones 1** : heel (of a shoe) **2 de** ~ **alto** : high-heeled
táctica *nf* : tactic, tactics *pl* — **táctico, -ca** *adj* : tactical
tacto *nm* **1** : (sense of) touch, feel **2** DELICADEZA : tact
tafetán *nm, pl* **-tanes** : taffeta
tailandés, -desa *adj* : Thai
taimado, -da *adj* : crafty, sly
tajar *vt* : cut, slice — **tajada** *nf* **1** : slice **2 sacar** ~ *fam* : get one's share — **tajante** *adj* : categorical — **tajo** *nm* **1** : cut, gash **2** ESCARPA : steep cliff
tal *adv* **1** : so, in such a way **2 con** ~ **que** : provided that, as long as **3 ¿qué** ~**?** : how are you?, how's it going? — ~ *adj* **1** : such, such a **2** ~ **vez** : maybe, perhaps — ~ *pron* **1** : such a one, such a thing **2** ~ **para cual** : two of a kind

taladrar *vt* : drill — **taladro** *nm* : drill
talante *nm* **1** HUMOR : mood **2** VOLUNTAD : willingness
talar *vt* : cut down, fell
talco *nm* : talcum powder
talego *nm* : sack
talento *nm* : talent — **talentoso, -sa** *adj* : talented
talismán *nm, pl* **-manes** : talisman, charm
talla *nf* **1** : sculpture, carving **2** ESTATURA : height **3** : size (in clothing) — **tallar** *vt* **1** : sculpt, carve **2** : measure (someone's height)
tallarín *nf, pl* **-rines** : noodle
talle *nm* **1** : waist, waistline **2** FIGURA : figure **3** : measurements *pl* (of clothing)
taller *nm* **1** : workshop **2** : studio (of an artist)
tallo *nm* : stalk, stem
talón *nm, pl* **-lones 1** : heel (of the foot) **2** : stub (of a check) — **talonario** *nm* : checkbook
taltuza *nf* : gopher
tamal *nm* : tamale
tamaño, -ña *adj* : such a, such a big — **tamaño** *nm* **1** : size **2 de** ~ **natural** : lifesize
tambalearse *vr* **1** : teeter, wobble **2** : stagger, totter (of persons)
también *adv* : too, as well, also
tambor *nm* : drum — **tamborilear** *vi* : drum
tamiz *nm* : sieve — **tamizar** {21} *vt* : sift
tampoco *adv* : neither, not either
tampón *nm, pl* **-pones 1** : tampon **2** : ink pad (for stamping)
tan *adv* **1** : so, so very **2** ~ **pronto como** : as soon as **3** ~ **sólo** : only, merely
tanda *nf* **1** TURNO : turn, shift **2** GRUPO : batch, lot, series
tangente *nf* : tangent
tangible *adj* : tangible
tango *nm* : tango
tanque *nm* : tank
tantear *vt* **1** : feel, grope **2** SOPESAR : size up, weigh — *vi* : feel one's way — **tanteador** *nm* : scoreboard — **tanteo** *nm* **1** : weighing, sizing up **2** PUNTUACIÓN : scoring (in sports)
tanto *adv* **1** : so much **2** (*in expressions of time*) : so long — ~ *nm* **1** : certain amount **2** : goal, point (in sports) **3 un** ~ : somewhat, rather — **tanto, -ta** *adj* **1** : so much, so many **2** (*in comparisons*) : as much, as many **3** *fam* : however many — ~ *pron* **1**

: so much, so many **2 entre ~** : meanwhile **3 por lo ~** : therefore

tañer {79} *vt* **1** : ring (a bell) **2** : play (a musical instrument)

tapa *nf* **1** : cover, top, lid **2** *Spain* : snack

tapacubos *nms & pl* : hubcap

tapar *vt* **1** : cover, put a lid on **2** OCULTAR : block out **3** ENCUBRIR : cover up — **tapadera** *nf* **1** : cover, lid **2** : front (to hide a deception)

tapete *nm* **1** : small rug, mat **2** : cover (for a table)

tapia *nf* : (adobe) wall, garden wall — **tapiar** *vt* **1** : wall in **2** : block off (a door, etc.)

tapicería *nf* **1** : upholstery **2** TAPIZ : tapestry — **tapicero, -ra** *n* : upholsterer

tapioca *nf* : tapioca

tapiz *nm, pl* **-pices** : tapestry — **tapizar** {21} *vt* : upholster

tapón *nm, pl* **-pones** **1** : cork **2** : cap (for a bottle, etc.) **3** : plug, stopper (for a sink)

tapujo *nm* **sin ~s** : openly, outright

taquigrafía *nf* : stenography, shorthand — **taquígrafo, -fa** *n* : stenographer

taquilla *nf* **1** : box office **2** RECAUDACIÓN : earnings *pl*, take — **taquillero, -ra** *adj* **un éxito taquillero** : a box-office hit

tarántula *nf* : tarantula

tararear *vt* : hum

tardar *vi* **1** : take a long time, be late **2 a más ~** : at the latest — *vt* : take (time) — **tardanza** *nf* : lateness, delay — **tarde** *adv* **1** : late **2 ~ o temprano** : sooner or later — **~** *nf* **1** : afternoon, evening **2 ¡buenas ~s!** : good afternoon!, good evening! **3 en la ~** *or* **por la ~** : in the afternoon, in the evening — **tardío, -día** *adj* : late, tardy — **tardo, -da** *adj* : slow

tarea *nf* **1** : task, job **2** : homework (in education)

tarifa *nf* **1** : fare, rate **2** LISTA : price list **3** ARANCEL : duty, tariff

tarima *nf* : platform, stage

tarjeta *nf* **1** : card **2 ~ de crédito** : credit card **3 ~ postal** : postcard

tarro *nm* : jar, pot

tarta *nf* **1** : cake **2** TORTA : tart

tartamudear *vi* : stammer, stutter — **tartamudeo** *nm* : stutter, stammer

tartán *nm, pl* **-tanes** : tartan, plaid

tártaro *nm* : tartar

tarugo *nm* **1** : block (of wood) **2** *fam* : blockhead, dunce

tasa *nf* **1** : rate **2** IMPUESTO : tax **3** VALORACIÓN : appraisal — **tasación** *nf, pl* **-ciones** : appraisal — **tasar** *vt* **1** : set the price of **2** VALORAR : appraise, value

tasca *nf* : cheap bar, dive

tatuar {3} *vt* : tattoo — **tatuaje** *nm* : tattoo, tattooing

taurino, -na *adj* : bull, bullfighting — **tauromaquia** *nf* : (art of) bullfighting

taxi *nm, pl* **taxis** : taxi, taxicab — **taxista** *nmf* : taxi driver

taza *nf* **1** : cup **2** : (toilet) bowl — **tazón** *nm, pl* **-zones** : bowl

te *pron* **1** (*direct object*) : you **2** (*indirect object*) : for you, to you, from you **3** (*reflexive*) : yourself, for yourself, to yourself, from yourself

té *nm* : tea

teatro *nm* : theater — **teatral** *adj* : theatrical

techo *nm* **1** : roof **2** : ceiling (of a room) **3** LÍMITE : upper limit, ceiling — **techumbre** *nf* : roofing

tecla *nf* : key (of a musical instrument or a machine) — **teclado** *nm* : keyboard — **teclear** *vt* : type in, enter

técnica *nf* **1** : technique, skill **2** TECNOLOGÍA : technology — **técnico, -ca** *adj* : technical — **~** *n* : technician

tecnología *nf* : technology — **tecnológico, -ca** *adj* : technological

tecolote *nm* *Lat* : owl

tedio *nm* : boredom — **tedioso, -sa** *adj* : tedious, boring

teja *nf* : tile — **tejado** *nm* : roof

tejer *v* **1** : knit, crochet **2** : weave (on a loom)

tejido *nm* **1** : fabric, cloth **2** : tissue (of the body)

tejón *nm, pl* **-jones** : badger

tela *nf* **1** : fabric, material **2 ~ de araña** : spiderweb — **telar** *nm* : loom — **telaraña** *nf* : spiderweb, cobweb

tele *nf fam* : TV, television

telecomunicación *nf, pl* **-ciones** : telecommunication

teledifusión *nf, pl* **-siones** : television broadcasting

teledirigido, -da *adj* : remote-controlled

telefonear *v* : telephone, call — **telefónico, -ca** *adj* : telephone — **telefonista** *nmf* : telephone operator — **teléfono** *nm* **1** : telephone **2 llamar por ~** : make a phone call

telegrafiar {85} *v* : telegraph — **telegráfico, -ca** *adj* : telegraphic — **telégrafo** *nm* : telegraph

telegrama *nm* : telegram

telenovela *nf* : soap opera

telepatía *nf* : telepathy — **telepático, -ca** *adj* : telepathic

telescopio *nm* : telescope — **telescópico, -ca** *adj* : telescopic

telespectador, -dora *n* : (television) viewer

telesquí *nm, pl* **-squís** : ski lift

televidente *nmf* : (television) viewer
televisión *nf, pl* **-siones** : television, TV —
televisar *vt* : televise — **televisor** *nm* : television set
telón *nm, pl* **-lones** 1 : curtain (in theater) 2 ~ **de fondo** : backdrop, background
tema *nm* : theme
temblar {55} *vi* 1 : tremble, shiver 2 : shake (of a building, the ground, etc.) — **temblor** *nm* 1 : shaking, trembling 2 *or* ~ **de tierra** : tremor, earthquake — **tembloroso, -sa** *adj* : trembling, shaky
temer *vt* : fear, dread — *vi* : be afraid — **temerario, -ria** *adj* : reckless — **temeridad** *nf* 1 : recklessness 2 : rash act — **temeroso, -sa** *adj* : fearful — **temor** *nm* : fear, dread
temperamento *nm* : temperament — **temperamental** *adj* : temperamental
temperatura *nf* : temperature
tempestad *nf* : storm — **tempestuoso, -sa** *adj* : stormy
templar *vt* 1 : temper (steel) 2 : moderate (temperature) 3 : tune (a musical instrument) — **templarse** *vr* : warm up, cool down — **templado, -da** *adj* 1 : temperate, mild 2 TIBIO : lukewarm 3 VALIENTE : courageous — **templanza** *nf* 1 : moderation 2 : mildness (of weather)
templo *nm* : temple, synagogue
tempo *nm* : tempo
temporada *nf* 1 : season, time 2 PERÍODO : period, spell — **temporal** *adj* 1 : temporal 2 PROVISIONAL : temporary — ~ *nm* : storm — **temporero, -ra** *n* : temporary or seasonal worker
temporizador *nm* : timer
temprano, -na *adj* : early — **temprano** *adv* : early
tenaz *adj, pl* **-naces** : tenacious — **tenaza** *nf* *or* **tenazas** *nfpl* 1 : pliers 2 : tongs (for the fireplace, etc.) 3 : claw (of a crustacean)
tendedero *nm* : clothesline
tendencia *nf* : tendency, trend
tender {56} *vt* 1 : spread out, stretch out 2 : hang out (clothes) 3 : lay (cables, etc.) 4 : set (a trap) — *vi* ~ **a** : have a tendency towards — **tenderse** *vr* : stretch out, lie down
tendero, -ra *n* : shopkeeper
tendido *nm* 1 : laying (of cables, etc.) 2 : seats *pl*, stand (at a bullfight)
tendón *nm, pl* **-dones** : tendon
tenebroso, -sa *adj* 1 : gloomy, dark 2 SINIESTRO : sinister
tenedor, -dora *n* 1 : holder 2 ~ **de libros** : bookkeeper — **tenedor** *nm* : table fork — **teneduría** *nf* ~ **de libros** : bookkeeping
tener {80} *vt* 1 : have, possess 2 SUJETAR : hold 3 TOMAR : take 4 ~ **frío (hambre,**

etc.) : be cold (hungry, etc.) 5 ~ **... años** : be … years old 6 ~ **por** : think, consider — *v aux* 1 ~ **que** : have to, ought to 2 **tenía pensado escribirte** : I've been thinking of writing to you — **tenerse** *vr* 1 : stand up 2 ~ **por** : consider oneself
tenería *nf* : tannery
tengo → **tener**
tenia *nf* : tapeworm
teniente *nmf* : lieutenant
tenis *nms & pl* 1 : tennis 2 ~ *nmpl* : sneakers — **tenista** *nmf* : tennis player
tenor *nm* 1 : tenor 2 : tone, sense (in style)
tensar *vt* 1 : tense, make taut 2 : draw (a bow) — **tensarse** *vr* : become tense — **tensión** *nf, pl* **-siones** 1 : tension 2 ~ **arterial** : blood pressure — **tenso, -sa** *adj* : tense
tentación *nf, pl* **-ciones** : temptation
tentáculo *nm* : tentacle
tentar {55} *vt* 1 : feel, touch 2 ATRAER : tempt — **tentador, -dora** *adj* : tempting
tentativa *nf* : attempt
tentempié *nm fam* : snack
tenue *adj* 1 : tenuous 2 : faint, weak (of sounds) 3 : light, fine (of thread, rain, etc.)
teñir {67} *vt* 1 : dye 2 ~ **de** : tinge with
teología *nf* : theology — **teólogo, -ga** *n* : theologian
teorema *nm* : theorem
teoría *nf* : theory — **teórico, -ca** *adj* : theoretical
tequila *nm* : tequila
terapia *nf* 1 : therapy 2 ~ **ocupacional** : occupational therapy — **terapeuta** *nmf* : therapist — **terapéutico, -ca** *adj* : therapeutic
tercermundista *adj* : third-world
tercero, -ra *adj* (**tercer** *before masculine singular nouns*) 1 : third 2 **el Tercer Mundo** : the Third World — ~ *n* : third (in a series)
terciar *vt* : sling (sth over one's shoulders), tilt (a hat) — *vi* 1 : intervene 2 ~ **en** : take part in
tercio *nm* : third
terciopelo *nm* : velvet
terco, -ca *adj* : obstinate, stubborn
tergiversar *vt* : distort, twist
termal *adj* : thermal, hot — **termas** *nfpl* : hot springs
terminar *vt* : conclude, finish — *vi* 1 : finish 2 ACABARSE : come to an end — **terminarse** *vr* 1 : run out 2 ACABARSE : come to an end — **terminación** *nf, pl* **-ciones** : termination, conclusion — **terminal** *adj* : terminal, final — ~ *nm* (*in some regions f*) : (electric or electronic) terminal — ~ *nf* (*in some regions m*) : terminal, station —

término *nm* **1** : end **2** PLAZO : period, term **3** ~ **medio** : happy medium **4** ~**s** *nmpl* : terms — **terminología** *nf* : terminology

termita *nf* : termite

termo *nm* : thermos

termómetro *nm* : thermometer

termóstato *nm* : thermostat

ternero, -ra *n* : calf — **ternera** *nf* : veal

ternura *nf* : tenderness

terquedad *nf* : obstinacy, stubbornness

terracota *nf* : terra-cotta

terraplén *nm, pl* **-plenes** : embankment

terráqueo, -quea *adj* : earth, terrestrial

terrateniente *nmf* : landowner

terraza *nf* **1** : terrace **2** BALCÓN : balcony

terremoto *nm* : earthquake

terreno *nm* **1** : terrain **2** SUELO : earth, ground **3** SOLAR : plot, tract of land — **terreno, -na** *adj* : earthly — **terrestre** *adj* : terrestrial

terrible *adj* : terrible

terrier *nmf* : terrier

territorio *nm* : territory — **territorial** *adj* : territorial

terrón *nm, pl* **-rones** **1** : clod (of earth) **2** ~ **de azúcar** : lump of sugar

terror *nm* : terror — **terrorífico, -ca** *adj* : terrifying — **terrorismo** *nm* : terrorism — **terrorista** *adj & nmf* : terrorist

terroso, -sa *adj* : earthy

terso, -sa *adj* **1** : smooth **2** : polished, flowing (of a style) — **tersura** *nf* : smoothness

tertulia *nf* : gathering, group

tesis *nfs & pl* : thesis

tesón *nm* : persistence, tenacity

tesoro *nm* **1** : treasure **2** : thesaurus (book) **3 el Tesoro** : the Treasury — **tesorero, -ra** *n* : treasurer

testaferro *nm* : figurehead

testamento *nm* : testament, will — **testamentario, -ria** *n* : executor, executrix *f* — **testar** *vi* : draw up a will

testarudo, -da *adj* : stubborn

testículo *nm* : testicle

testificar {72} *v* : testify — **testigo** *nmf* **1** : witness **2** ~ **ocular** : eyewitness — **testimoniar** *vi* : testify — **testimonio** *nm* : testimony

tétano *or* **tétanos** *nm* : tetanus

tetera *nf* : teapot

tetilla *nf* **1** : teat, nipple (of a man) **2** : nipple (of a baby bottle) — **tetina** *nf* : nipple (of a baby bottle)

tétrico, -ca *adj* : somber, gloomy

textil *adj & nm* : textile

texto *nm* : text — **textual** *adj* **1** : textual **2** EXACTO : literal, exact

textura *nf* : texture

tez *nf, pl* **teces** : complexion

ti *pron* **1** : you **2** ~ **mismo,** ~ **misma** : yourself

tía → **tío**

tianguis *nms & pl Lat* : open-air market

tibio, -bia *adj* : lukewarm

tiburón *nm, pl* **-rones** : shark

tic *nm* : tic

tiempo *nm* **1** : time **2** ÉPOCA : age, period **3** : weather (in meteorology) **4** : halftime (in sports) **5** : tempo (in music) **6** : tense (in grammar)

tienda *nf* **1** : store, shop **2** *or* ~ **de campaña** : tent

tiene → **tener**

tienta *nf* **andar a** ~**s** : feel one's way, grope around

tierno, -na *adj* **1** : tender, fresh, young **2** CARIÑOSO : affectionate

tierra *nf* **1** : land **2** SUELO : ground, earth **3** *or* ~ **natal** : native land **4 la Tierra** : the Earth **5 por** ~ : overland **6** ~ **adentro** : inland

tieso, -sa *adj* **1** : stiff, rigid **2** ERGUIDO : erect **3** ENGREÍDO : haughty

tiesto *nm* : flowerpot

tifoideo, -dea *adj* **fiebre tifoidea** : typhoid fever

tifón *nm, pl* **-fones** : typhoon

tifus *nm* : typhus

tigre, -gresa *n* **1** : tiger, tigress *f* **2** *Lat* : jaguar

tijera *nf or* **tijeras** *nfpl* : scissors — **tijeretada** *nf* : cut, snip

tildar *vt* ~ **de** : brand as, call

tilde *nf* **1** : tilde **2** ACENTO : accent mark

tilo *nm* : linden (tree)

timar *vt* : swindle, cheat

timbre *nm* **1** : bell **2** : tone, timbre (of a voice, etc.) **3** SELLO : seal, stamp **4** *Lat* : postage stamp — **timbrar** *vt* : stamp

tímido, -da *adj* : timid, shy — **timidez** *nf* : timidity, shyness

timo *nm fam* : swindle, hoax

timón *nm, pl* **-mones** **1** : rudder **2 coger el** ~ : take the helm, take charge

tímpano *nm* **1** : eardrum **2** ~**s** *nmpl* : timpani, kettledrums

tina *nf* **1** : vat **2** BAÑERA : bathtub

tinieblas *nfpl* **1** : darkness **2 estar en** ~ **sobre** : be in the dark about

tino *nm* **1** : good judgment, sense **2** TACTO : tact

tinta *nf* **1** : ink **2 saberlo de buena** ~ : have it on good authority — **tinte** *nm* **1** : dye, coloring **2** MATIZ : overtone — **tintero** *nm* : inkwell

tintinear *vi* : jingle, tinkle, clink — **tintineo** *nm* : jingle, tinkle, clink

tinto, -ta *adj* **1** : dyed, stained **2** : red (of wine)

tintorería *nf* : dry cleaner (service)

tintura *nf* **1** : dye, tint **2 ~ de yodo** : tincture of iodine

tiña *nf* : ringworm

tío, tía *n* : uncle *m*, aunt *f*

tiovivo *nm* : merry-go-round

típico, -ca *adj* : typical

tiple *nm* : soprano

tipo *nm* **1** : type, kind **2** FIGURA : figure (of a woman), build (of a man) **3** : rate (of interest, etc.) **4** : (printing) type, typeface — **tipo, -pa** *n fam* : guy *m*, gal *f*

tipografía *nf* : typography, printing — **tipográfico, -ca** *adj* : typographical — **tipógrafo, -fa** *n* : printer

tique *or* **tíquet** *nm* : ticket — **tiquete** *nm Lat* : ticket

tira *nf* **1** : strip, strap **2 ~ cómica** : comic strip

tirabuzón *nf, pl* **-zones 1** : corkscrew **2** RIZO : curl, coil

tirada *nf* **1** : throw **2** DISTANCIA : distance **3** IMPRESIÓN : printing, issue — **tirador** *nm* : handle, knob — **tirador, -dora** *n* : marksman *m*, markswoman *f*

tiranía *nf* : tyranny — **tiránico, -ca** *adj* : tyrannical — **tiranizar** {21} *vt* : tyrannize — **tirano, -na** *adj* : tyrannical — **~** *n* : tyrant

tirante *adj* **1** : taut, tight **2** : tense (of a situation, etc.) — **~** *nm* **1** : (shoulder) strap **2 ~s** *nmpl* : suspenders

tirar *vt* **1** : throw **2** DESECHAR : throw away **3** DERRIBAR : knock down **4** DISPARAR : shoot, fire **5** IMPRIMIR : print — *vi* **1** : pull **2** DISPARAR : shoot **3** ATRAER : attract **4** *fam* : get by, manage **5 ~ a** : tend towards — **tirarse** *vr* **1** : throw oneself **2** *fam* : spend (time)

tiritar *vi* : shiver

tiro *nm* **1** : shot, gunshot **2** : shot, kick (in sports) **3** : team (of horses, etc.) **4 a ~** : within range

tiroides *nmf* : thyroid (gland)

tirón *nm, pl* **-rones 1** : pull, yank **2 de un ~** : in one go

tirotear *vt* : shoot at — **tiroteo** *nm* : shooting

tisis *nfs & pl* : tuberculosis

títere *nm* : puppet

titilar *vi* : flicker

titiritero, -ra *n* **1** : puppeteer **2** ACRÓBATA : acrobat

titubear *vi* **1** : hesitate **2** BALBUCEAR : stutter, stammer — **titubeante** *adj* : hesitant, faltering — **titubeo** *nm* : hesitation

titular *vt* : title, call — **titularse** *vr* **1** : be called, be titled **2** LICENCIARSE : receive a degree — **~** *adj* : titular, official — **~** *nm* : headline — **~** *nmf* : holder, incumbent — **título** *nm* **1** : title **2** : degree, qualification (in education)

tiza *nf* : chalk

tiznar *vt* : blacken (with soot, etc.) — **tizne** *nm* : soot

toalla *nf* : towel — **toallero** *nm* : towel rack

tobillo *nm* : ankle

tobogán *nm, pl* **-ganes 1** : toboggan, sled **2** : slide (in a playground, etc.)

tocadiscos *nms & pl* : record player

tocado, -da *adj fam* : touched, not all there — **tocado** *nm* : headgear, headdress

tocador *nm* : dressing table

tocar {72} *vt* **1** : touch, feel **2** MENCIONAR : touch on, refer to **3** : play (a musical instrument) — *vi* **1** : knock, ring **2 ~ en** : touch on, border on

tocayo, -ya *n* : namesake

tocino *nm* **1** : bacon **2** : salt pork (for cooking) — **tocineta** *nf Lat* : bacon

tocólogo, -ga *n* : obstetrician

tocón *nm, pl* **-cones** : stump (of a tree)

todavía *adv* **1** AÚN : still **2** (*in comparisons*) : even **3 ~ no** : not yet

todo, -da *adj* **1** : all **2** CADA, CUALQUIER : every, each **3 a toda velocidad** : at top speed **4 todo el mundo** : everyone, everybody — **~** *pron* **1** : everything, all **2 todos, -das** *pl* : everybody, everyone, all — **todo** *nm* : whole — **todopoderoso, -sa** *adj* : almighty, all-powerful

toga *nf* **1** : toga **2** : gown, robe (of a judge, etc.)

toldo *nm* : awning, canopy

tolerar *vt* : tolerate — **tolerancia** *nf* : tolerance — **tolerante** *adj* : tolerant

toma *nf* **1** : capture **2** DOSIS : dose **3** : take (in film) **4 ~ de corriente** : wall socket, outlet **5 ~ y daca** : give-and-take — **tomar** *vt* **1** : take **2** : have (food or drink) **3** CAPTURAR : capture, seize **4 ~ el sol** : sunbathe **5 ~ tierra** : land — *vi* : drink (alcohol) — **tomarse** *vr* **1** : take (time, etc.) **2** : drink, eat, have (food, drink)

tomate *nm* : tomato

tomillo *nm* : thyme

tomo *nm* : volume

ton *nm* **sin ~ ni son** : without rhyme or reason

tonada *nf* : tune

tonel *nm* : barrel, cask

tonelada *nf* : ton — **tonelaje** *nm* : tonnage

tónica *nf* **1** : tonic (water) **2** TENDENCIA : trend, tone — **tónico, -ca** *adj* : tonic — **tónico** *nm* : tonic (in medicine)

tono *nm* **1** : tone **2** : shade (of colors) **3** : key (in music)

tontería *nf* **1** : silly thing or remark **2** ESTU-PIDEZ : foolishness **3 decir ~s** : talk non-sense — **tonto, -ta** *adj* **1** : stupid, silly **2 a tontas y a locas** : haphazardly — **~** *n* : fool, idiot

topacio *nm* : topaz

toparse *vr* **~ con** : run into, come across

tope *nm* **1** : limit, end **2** *or* **~ de puerta** : doorstop **3** *Lat* : bump — **~** *adj* : maxi-mum

tópico, -ca *adj* **1** : topical, external **2** MANI-DO : trite — **tópico** *nm* : cliché

topo *nm* : mole (animal)

toque *nm* **1** : (light) touch **2** : ringing, peal (of a bell) **3 ~ de queda** : curfew **4 ~ de diana** : reveille — **toquetear** *vt* : finger, handle

tórax *nms & pl* : thorax

torbellino *nm* : whirlwind

torcer {14} *vt* **1** : twist, bend **2** : turn (a cor-ner) **3** : wring (out) — *vi* : turn — **torcerse** *vr* **1** : twist, sprain **2** FRUSTRARSE : go wrong **3** DESVIARSE : go astray — **torce-dura** *nf* **1** : twisting **2** ESGUINCE : sprain — **torcido, -da** *adj* : twisted, crooked

tordo, -da *adj* : dappled — **tordo** *nm* : thrush (bird)

torear *vt* **1** : fight (bulls) **2** ELUDIR : dodge, sidestep — *vi* : fight bulls — **toreo** *nm* : bullfighting — **torero, -ra** *n* : bullfighter

tormenta *nf* : storm — **tormento** *nm* **1** : tor-ture **2** ANGUSTIA : torment, anguish — **tor-mentoso, -sa** *adj* : stormy

tornado *nm* : tornado

tornar *vt* CONVERTIR : render, turn — *vi* : go back, return — **tornarse** *vr* : become, turn into

torneo *nm* : tournament

tornillo *nm* : screw

torniquete *nm* **1** : turnstile **2** : tourniquet (in medicine)

torno *nm* **1** : winch **2** : (carpenter's) lathe **3 ~ de alfarero** : (potter's) wheel **4 ~ de banco** : vise **5 en ~ a** : around, about

toro *nm* **1** : bull **2 ~s** *nmpl* : bullfight

toronja *nf* : grapefruit

torpe *adj* **1** : clumsy, awkward **2** ESTÚPIDO : stupid, dull

torpedear *vt* : torpedo — **torpedo** *nm* : tor-pedo

torpeza *nf* **1** : clumsiness, awkwardness **2** ESTUPIDEZ : slowness, stupidity

torre *nf* **1** : tower **2** : turret (on a ship, etc.) **3** : rook, castle (in chess)

torrente *nm* **1** : torrent **2 ~ sanguíneo** : bloodstream — **torrencial** *adj* : torrential

tórrido, -da *adj* : torrid

torsión *nf, pl* **-siones** : twisting

torta *nf* **1** : torte, cake **2** *Lat* : sandwich

tortazo *nm fam* : blow, wallop

tortícolis *nfs & pl* : stiff neck

tortilla *nf* **1** : tortilla **2** *or* **~ de huevo** : omelet

tórtola *nf* : turtledove

tortuga *nf* **1** : turtle, tortoise **2 ~ de agua dulce** : terrapin

tortuoso, -sa *adj* : tortuous, winding

tortura *nf* : torture — **torturar** *vt* : torture

tos *nf* **1** : cough **2 ~ ferina** : whooping cough

tosco, -ca *adj* : rough, coarse

toser *vi* : cough

tosquedad *nf* : coarseness

tostar {19} *vt* **1** : toast **2** BRONCEAR : tan — **tostarse** *vr* : get a tan — **tostada** *nf* **1** : piece of toast **2** *Lat* : tostada — **tostador** *nm* : toaster

tostón *nm, pl* **-tones** *Lat* : fried plantain chip

total *adj & nm* : total — **~** *adv* : so, after all — **totalidad** *nf* : whole — **totalitario, -ria** *adj & n* : totalitarian — **totalitarismo** *nm* : totalitarianism — **totalizar** {21} *vt* : total, add up to

tóxico, -ca *adj* : toxic, poisonous — **tóxico** *nm* : poison — **toxicomanía** *nf* : drug ad-diction — **toxicómano, -na** *n* : drug addict — **toxina** *nf* : toxin

tozudo, -da *adj* : stubborn

traba *nf* : obstacle, hindrance

trabajar *vi* **1** : work **2** : act, perform (in the-ater, etc.) — *vt* **1** : work (metal) **2** : knead (dough) **3** MEJORAR : work on, work at — **trabajador, -dora** *adj* : hard-working — **~** *n* : worker — **trabajo** *nm* **1** : work **2** EM-PLEO : job **3** TAREA : task **4** ESFUERZO : ef-fort **5 costar ~** : be difficult **6 ~ en equipo** : teamwork **7 ~s** *nmpl* : hard-ships, difficulties — **trabajoso, -sa** *adj* : hard, laborious

trabalenguas *nms & pl* : tongue twister

trabar *vt* **1** : join, connect **2** OBSTACULIZAR : impede **3** : strike up (a conversation, etc.) **4** : thicken (sauces) — **trabarse** *vr* **1** : jam **2** ENREDARSE : become entangled **3 se le traba la lengua** : he gets tongue-tied

trabucar {72} *vt* : mix up

tracción *nf* : traction

tractor *nm* : tractor

tradición *nf, pl* **-ciones** : tradition — **tradi-cional** *adj* : traditional

traducir {61} *vt* : translate — **traducción** *nf, pl* **-ciones** : translation — **traductor, -tora** *n* : translator

traer {81} *vt* **1** : bring **2** CAUSAR : cause, bring about **3** CONTENER : carry, have **4** LL-EVAR : wear — **traerse** *vr* **1** : bring along **2 traérselas** : be difficult

traficar {72} *vi* ~ **en** : traffic in — **traficante** *nmf* : dealer, trafficker — **tráfico** *nm* **1** : trade (of merchandise) **2** : traffic (of vehicles)

tragaluz *nf, pl* **-luces** : skylight

tragar {52} *vt* **1** : swallow **2** *fam* : put up with — *vi* : swallow — **tragarse** *vr* **1** : swallow **2** ABSORBER : absorb, swallow up

tragedia *nf* : tragedy — **trágico, -ca** *adj* : tragic

trago *nm* **1** : swallow, swig **2** *fam* : drink, liquor — **tragón, -gona** *adj fam* : greedy — ~ *nmf fam* : glutton

traicionar *vt* : betray — **traición** *nf, pl* **-ciones** **1** : betrayal **2** : treason (in law) — **traidor, -dora** *adj* : traitorous, treacherous — ~ *n* : traitor

trailer *nm* : trailer

traje *nm* **1** : dress, costume **2** : (man's) suit **3** ~ **de baño** : bathing suit

trajinar *vi fam* : rush around — **trajín** *nm, pl* **-jines** *fam* : hustle and bustle

trama *nf* **1** : plot **2** : weave, weft (of fabric) — **tramar** *vt* **1** : plot, plan **2** : weave (fabric)

tramitar *vt* : negotiate — **trámite** *nm* : procedure, step

tramo *nm* **1** : stretch, section **2** : flight (of stairs)

trampa *nf* **1** : trap **2 hacer** ~**s** : cheat — **trampear** *vt* : cheat

trampilla *nf* : trapdoor

trampolín *nm, pl* **-lines** **1** : diving board **2** : trampoline (in a gymnasium, etc.)

tramposo, -sa *adj* : crooked, cheating — ~ *n* : cheat, swindler

tranca *nf* **1** : cudgel, club **2** : bar (for a door or window)

trance *nm* **1** : critical juncture **2** : (hypnotic) trance **3 en** ~ **de** : in the process of

tranquilo, -la *adj* : calm, tranquil — **tranquilidad** *nf* : tranquility, peace — **tranquilizante** *nm* : tranquilizer — **tranquilizar** {21} *vt* : calm, soothe — **tranquilizarse** *vr* : calm down

trans- *see also* **tras-**

transacción *nf, pl* **-ciones** : transaction

transatlántico, -ca *adj* : transatlantic — **transatlántico** *nm* : ocean liner

transbordador *nm* **1** : ferry **2** ~ **espacial** : space shuttle — **transbordar** *vt* : transfer — *vi* : change (of trains, etc.) — **transbordo** *nm* **hacer** ~ : change (trains, etc.)

transcribir {33} *vt* : transcribe — **transcripción** *nf, pl* **-ciones** : transcription

transcurrir *vi* : elapse, pass — **transcurso** *nm* : course, progression

transeúnte *nmf* : passerby

transferir {76} *vt* : transfer — **transferencia** *nf* : transfer, transference

transformar *vt* **1** : transform, change **2** CONVERTIR : convert — **transformarse** *vr* : be transformed — **transformación** *nf, pl* **-ciones** : transformation — **transformador** *nm* : transformer

transfusión *nf, pl* **-siones** : transfusion

transgredir {1} *vt* : transgress — **transgresión** *nf* : transgression

transición *nf, pl* **-ciones** : transition

transido, -da *adj* : overcome, stricken

transigir {35} *vi* : give in, compromise

transistor *nm* : transistor

transitar *vi* : go, travel — **transitable** *adj* : passable

transitivo, -va *adj* : transitive

tránsito *nm* **1** : transit **2** TRÁFICO : traffic **3 hora de máximo** ~ : rush hour — **transitorio, -ria** *adj* : transitory

transmitir *vt* **1** : transmit **2** : broadcast (radio, TV, etc.) **3** CEDER : pass on — **transmisión** *nf, pl* **-siones** **1** : broadcast **2** TRANSFERENCIA : transfer **3** : transmission (of an automobile) — **transmisor** *nm* : transmitter

transparentarse *vr* : be transparent — **transparente** *adj* : transparent

transpirar *vi* : perspire, sweat — **transpiración** *nf, pl* **-ciones** : perspiration, sweat

transponer {60} *vt* : transpose, move — **transponerse** *vr* **1** : set (of the sun, etc.) **2** DORMITAR : doze off

transportar *vt* : transport, carry — **transportarse** *vr* : get carried away — **transporte** *nm* : transport, transportation

transversal *adj* **corte** ~ : cross section

tranvía *nm* : streetcar, trolley

trapear *vt Lat* : mop

trapecio *nm* : trapeze

trapisonda *nf* : scheme, plot

trapo *nm* **1** : cloth, rag **2** ~**s** *nmpl fam* : clothes

tráquea *nf* : trachea, windpipe

traquetear *vi* : rattle around, shake — **traqueteo** *nm* : rattling

tras *prep* **1** DESPUÉS DE : after **2** DÉTRAS DE : behind

tras- *see also* **trans-**

trascender {56} *vi* **1** : leak out, become known **2** EXTENDERSE : spread **3** ~ **de** : transcend — **trascendencia** *nf* : importance — **trascendental** *adj* **1** : transcendental **2** IMPORTANTE : important

trasegar *vt* : move around

trasero, -ra *adj* : rear, back — **trasero** *nm* : buttocks *pl*

trasfondo *nm* **1** : background **2** : undercurrent (of suspicion, etc.)

trasladar *vt* **1** : transfer, move **2** POSPONER : postpone — **trasladarse** *vr* : move, relocate — **traslado** *nm* **1** : transfer, move **2** COPIA : copy

traslapar *vt* : overlap — **traslaparse** *vr* : overlap

traslucirse {45} *vr* **1** : be translucent **2** REVELARSE : be revealed — **traslúcido, -da** : translucent

trasnochar *vi* : stay up all night

traspasar *vt* **1** : pierce, go through **2** EXCEDER : go beyond **3** ATRAVESAR : cross, go across **4** : transfer (a business, etc.) — **traspaso** *nm* : transfer, sale

traspié *nm* **1** : stumble, trip **2** ERROR : blunder

trasplantar *vt* : transplant — **trasplante** *nm* : transplant

trasquilar *vt* : shear

traste *nm* **1** : fret (on a guitar, etc.) **2** *Lat* : (kitchen) utensil **3 dar al ~ con** : ruin **4 irse al ~** : fall through

trastos *nmpl fam* : pieces of junk, stuff

trastornar *vt* **1** : disturb, disrupt **2** VOLVER LOCO : drive crazy — **trastornarse** *vr* : go crazy — **trastornado, -da** *adj* : disturbed, deranged — **trastorno** *nm* **1** : disturbance, disruption **2** : (medical or psychological) disorder

trastrocar *vt* : change, switch around

tratable *adj* : friendly, sociable

tratar *vi* **1 ~ con** : deal with **2 ~ de** : try to **3 ~ de** *or* **~ sobre** : be about, concern **4 ~ en** : deal in — *vt* **1** : treat **2** MANEJAR : deal with, handle — **tratarse** *vr* **~ de** : be about, concern — **tratado** *nm* **1** : treatise **2** CONVENIO : treaty — **tratamiento** *nm* : treatment — **trato** *nm* **1** : treatment **2** ACUERDO : deal, agreement **3 ~s** *nmpl* : dealings

trauma *nm* : trauma — **traumático, -ca** *adj* : traumatic

través *nm* **1 a ~ de** : across, through **2 de ~** : sideways

travesaño *nm* : crosspiece

travesía *nf* : voyage, crossing (of the sea)

travesura *nf* **1** : prank **2 ~s** *nfpl* : mischief — **travieso, -sa** *adj* : mischievous, naughty

trayecto *nm* **1** : trajectory, path **2** VIAJE : journey **3** RUTA : route — **trayectoria** *nf* : path, trajectory

traza *nf* **1** : design, plan **2** ASPECTO : appearance — **trazado** *nm* **1** : outline, sketch **2** DISEÑO : plan, layout — **trazar** {21} *vt* **1** : trace, outline **2** : draw up (a plan, etc.) — **trazo** *nm* : stroke, line

trébol *nm* **1** : clover, shamrock **2 ~es** *nmpl* : clubs (in playing cards)

trece *adj & nm* : thirteen — **treceavo, -va** *adj* : thirteenth — **treceavo** *nm* : thirteenth (fraction)

trecho *nm* **1** : stretch, period **2** DISTANCIA : distance **3 de ~ a ~** : at intervals

tregua *nf* **1** : truce **2 sin ~** : without respite

treinta *adj & nm* : thirty — **treintavo, -va** *adj* : thirtieth — **treintavo** *nm* : thirtieth (fraction)

tremendo, -da *adj* : tremendous, enormous

trementina *nf* : turpentine

trémulo, -la *adj* : trembling, flickering

tren *nm* **1** : train **2 ~ de aterrizaje** : landing gear

trenza *nf* : braid, pigtail — **trenzar** {21} *vt* : braid — **trenzarse** *vr Lat* : get involved

trepar *vi* **1** : climb **2** : creep, spread (of a plant) — **treparse** *vr* : climb (up) — **trepador, -dora** *adj* : climbing — **trepadora** *nf* **1** : climbing plant **2** *fam* : social climber

trepidar *vi* : shake, vibrate

tres *adj & nm* : three — **trescientos, -tas** *adj* : three hundred — **trescientos** *nms & pl* : three hundred

treta *nf* : trick

triángulo *nm* : triangle — **triangular** *adj* : triangular

tribu *nf* : tribe — **tribal** *adj* : tribal

tribulación *nf, pl* **-ciones** : tribulation

tribuna *nf* **1** : dais, platform **2** : grandstand, bleachers *pl* (in a stadium)

tribunal *nm* : court, tribunal

tributar *vt* : pay, render — *vi* : pay taxes — **tributo** *nm* **1** : tribute **2** IMPUESTO : tax

triciclo *nm* : tricycle

tricolor *adj* : tricolored

tridimensional *adj* : three-dimensional

trigésimo, -ma *adj & n* : thirtieth

trigo *nm* : wheat

trigonometría *nf* : trigonometry

trillado, -da *adj* : trite

trillar *vt* : thresh — **trilladora** *nf* : threshing machine

trillizo, -za *n* : triplet

trilogía *nf* : trilogy

trimestral *adj* : quarterly

trinar *vi* : warble

trinchar *vt* : carve

trinchera *nf* **1** : trench, ditch **2** IMPERMEABLE : trench coat

trineo *nm* : sled, sleigh

trinidad *nf* : trinity

trino *nm* : trill, warble

trío *nm* : trio

tripa *nf* **1** : gut, intestine **2 ~s** *nfpl fam* : belly, tummy

triple *adj & nm* : triple — **triplicar** {72} *vt* : triple

trípode *nm* : tripod

tripular *vt* : man — **tripulación** *nf, pl* **-ciones** : crew — **tripulante** *nmf* : crew member

tris *nm* **estar en un ~ de** : be within an inch of

triste *adj* **1** : sad **2** SOMBRÍO : dismal, gloomy **3** MISERABLE : sorry, miserable — **tristeza** *nf* : sadness, grief

tritón *nm, pl* **-tones** : newt

triturar *vt* : crush, grind

triunfar *vi* : triumph, win — **triunfal** *adj* : triumphal — **triunfante** *adj* : triumphant — **triunfo** *nm* : triumph, victory

trivial *adj* : trivial

triza *nf* **1** : shred, bit **2 hacer ~s** : smash to pieces

trocar {82} *vt* **1** CONVERTIR : change **2** INTERCAMBIAR : exchange

trocha *nf* : path, trail

trofeo *nm* : trophy

trombón *nm, pl* **-bones 1** : trombone **2** : trombonist (musician)

trombosis *nf* : thrombosis

trompa *nf* **1** : trunk (of an elephant), snout **2** : horn (musical instrument) **3** : tube (in anatomy)

trompeta *nf* : trumpet — **trompetista** *nmf* : trumpet player

trompo *nm* : top (toy)

tronada *nf* : thunderstorm — **tronar** {19} *vi* : thunder, rage — *vt Lat fam* : shoot — *v impers* : thunder

tronchar *vt* **1** : snap **2** TRUNCAR : cut short

tronco *nm* **1** : trunk (of a tree) **2** : torso (of a person) **3 dormir como un ~** : sleep like a log

trono *nm* : throne

tropa *nf* : troops *pl*, soldiers *pl*

tropel *nm* : mob

tropezar {29} *vi* **1** : trip, stumble **2 ~ con** : come up against, run into — **tropezón** *nm, pl* **-zones 1** : stumble **2** EQUIVOCACIÓN : mistake, slip

trópico *nm* : tropic — **tropical** *adj* : tropical

tropiezo *nm* **1** CONTRATIEMPO : snag, setback **2** EQUIVOCACIÓN : mistake, slip

trotar *vi* **1** : trot **2** *fam* : rush about — **trote** *nm* **1** : trot **2** *fam* : rush, bustle **3 al ~** : at a trot, quickly

trozo *nm* : piece, bit, chunk

trucha *nf* : trout

truco *nm* **1** : knack **2** ARDID : trick

trueno *nm* : thunder

trueque *nm* : barter, exchange

trufa *nf* : truffle

truncar {72} *vt* **1** : cut short **2** : thwart, spoil (plans, etc.)

tu *adj* : your

tú *pron* : you

tuba *nf* : tuba

tuberculosis *nf* : tuberculosis

tubo *nm* **1** : tube, pipe **2 ~ de escape** : exhaust pipe (of a vehicle) **3 ~ de desagüe** : drainpipe — **tubería** *nf* : pipes *pl*, tubing

tuerca *nf* : nut (for a screw)

tuerto, -ta *adj* : one-eyed, blind in one eye

tuétano *nm* : marrow

tufo *nm* **1** : vapor **2** *fam* : stench, stink

tugurio *nm* : hovel

tulipán *nm, pl* **-panes** : tulip

tullido, -da *adj* : crippled, paralyzed

tumba *nf* : tomb, grave

tumbar *vt* : knock down, knock over — **tumbarse** *vr* : lie down — **tumbo** *nm* **dar ~s** : jolt, bump around

tumor *nm* : tumor

tumulto *nm* **1** : commotion, tumult **2** MOTÍN : riot — **tumultuoso, -sa** *adj* : tumultuous

tuna *nf* : prickly pear

túnel *nm* : tunnel

túnica *nf* : tunic

tupé *nm* : toupee

tupido, -da *adj* : dense, thick

turba *nf* **1** : peat **2** MUCHEDUMBRE : mob, throng

turbación *nf, pl* **-ciones 1** : disturbance **2** CONFUSIÓN : confusion

turbante *nm* : turban

turbar *vt* **1** : disturb, upset **2** CONFUNDIR : confuse, bewilder

turbina *nf* : turbine

turbio, -bia *adj* **1** : cloudy, murky **2** : blurred (of vision, etc.) — **turbión** *nm, pl* **-biones** : squall

turbulencia *nf* : turbulence — **turbulento, -ta** *adj* : turbulent

turco, -ca *adj* : Turkish — **turco** *nm* : Turkish (language)

turista *nmf* : tourist — **turismo** *nm* : tourism, tourist industry — **turístico, -ca** *adj* : tourist, travel

turnarse *vr* : take turns, alternate — **turno** *nm* **1** : turn **2 ~ de noche** : night shift

turquesa *nf* : turquoise

turrón *nm, pl* **-rrones** : nougat

tutear *vt* : address as *tú*

tutela *nf* **1** : guardianship (in law) **2 bajo la ~ de** : under the protection of

tuteo *nm* : addressing as *tú*

tutor, -tora *n* **1** : guardian **2** : tutor (in education)

tuyo, -ya *adj* : yours, of yours — **~** *pron* **1 el tuyo, la tuya, lo tuyo, los tuyos, las tuyas** : yours **2 los tuyos** : your family, your friends

U

u¹ *nf* : u, 22d letter of the Spanish alphabet
u² *conj* (*used before words beginning with o- or ho-*) : or
uapití *nm* : American elk, wapiti
ubicar {72} *vt Lat* **1** COLOCAR : place, position **2** LOCALIZAR : find — **ubicarse** *vr* : be located
ubre *nf* : udder
Ud., Uds. → **usted**
ufanarse *vr* ~ **de** : boast about — **ufano, -na** *adj* **1** : proud **2** ENGREÍDO : self-satisfied
ujier *nm* : usher
úlcera *nf* : ulcer
ulterior *adj* : later, subsequent — **ulteriormente** *adv* : subsequently
últimamente *adv* : lately, recently
ultimar *vt* **1** : complete, finish **2** *Lat* : kill — **ultimátum** *nm, pl* **-tums** : ultimatum
último, -ma *adj* **1** : last **2** : latest, most recent (in time) **3** : farthest (in space) **4 por último** : finally
ultrajar *vt* : outrage, insult — **ultraje** *nm* : outrage, insult
ultramar *nm* **de** ~ *or* **en** ~ : overseas — **ultramarino, -na** *adj* : overseas — **ultramarinos** *nmpl* **tienda de** ~ : grocery store
ultranza: a ~ *adv phr* : to the extreme — **a** ~ *adj phr* : out-and-out, complete
ultrasonido *nm* : ultrasound
ultravioleta *adj* : ultraviolet
ulular *vi* **1** : hoot (of an owl) **2** : howl (of a wolf, the wind, etc.) — **ululato** *nm* : hoot (of an owl)
umbilical *adj* : umbilical
umbral *nm* : threshold
un, una *art, mpl* **unos 1** : a, an **2 unos** *or* **unas** *pl* : some, a few **3 unos** *or* **unas** *pl* : about, approximately — **un** *adj* → **uno**
unánime *adj* : unanimous — **unanimidad** *nf* : unanimity
uncir {83} *vt* : yoke
undécimo, -ma *adj & n* : eleventh
ungir {35} *vt* : anoint — **ungüento** *nm* : ointment
único, -ca *adj* **1** : only, sole **2** EXCEPCIONAL : unique — ~ *n* : only one — **únicamente** *adv* : only
unicornio *nm* : unicorn
unidad *nf* **1** : unit **2** ARMONÍA : unity — **unido, -da** *adj* **1** : united **2** : close (of friends, etc.)
unificar {72} *vt* : unify — **unificación** *nf, pl* **-ciones** : unification

uniformar *vt* **1** : standardize **2** : put into uniform — **uniformado, -da** *adj* : uniformed — **uniforme** *adj & nm* : uniform — **uniformidad** *nf* : uniformity
unilateral *adj* : unilateral
unir *vt* **1** : unite, join **2** COMBINAR : combine, mix together — **unirse** *vr* **1** : join together **2** ~ **a** : join — **unión** *nf, pl* **uniones 1** : union **2** JUNTURA : joint, coupling
unísono *nm* **al** ~ : in unison
unitario, -ria *adj* : unitary
universal *adj* : universal
universidad *nf* : university, college — **universitario, -ria** *adj* : university, college
universo *nm* : universe
uno, una (**un** *before masculine singular nouns*) *adj* : one — ~ *pron* **1** : one **2 unos, unas** *pl* : some **3 uno(s) a otro(s)** : one another, each other **4 uno y otro** : both — **uno** *nm* : one (number)
untar *vt* **1** : smear, grease **2** *fam* : bribe — **untuoso, -sa** *adj* : greasy, sticky
uña *nf* **1** : nail, fingernail **2** : claw (of a cat, etc.), hoof (of a horse, etc.)
uranio *nm* : uranium
Urano *nm* : Uranus
urbano, -na *adj* : urban, city — **urbanidad** *nf* : politeness, courtesy — **urbanización** *nf, pl* **-ciones** : housing development — **urbanizar** *vt* : develop, urbanize — **urbe** *nf* : large city
urdir *vt* **1** : warp **2** PLANEAR : plot — **urdimbre** *nf* : warp (of a fabric)
urgir {35} *v impers* : be urgent, be pressing — **urgencia** *nf* **1** : urgency **2** EMERGENCIA : emergency — **urgente** *adj* : urgent
urinario, -ria *adj* : urinary — **urinario** *nm* : urinal (place)
urna *nf* **1** : urn **2** : ballot box (for voting)
urraca *nf* : magpie
uruguayo, -ya *adj* : Uruguayan
usar *vt* **1** : use **2** LLEVAR : wear — **usarse 1** EMPLEARSE : be used **2** : be worn, be in fashion — **usado, -da** *adj* **1** : used **2** GASTADO : worn, worn-out — **usanza** *nf* : custom, usage — **uso** *nm* **1** : use **2** DESGASTE : wear and tear **3** USANZA : custom, usage
usted *pron* **1** (*used in formal address; often written as* **Ud.** *or* **Vd.**) : you **2** ~**es** *pl* (*often written as* **Uds.** *or* **Vds.**) : you (all)
usual *adj* : usual
usuario, -ria *n* : user
usura *nf* : usury — **usurero, -ra** *n* : usurer

usurpar *vt* : usurp
utensilio *nm* : utensil, tool
útero *nm* : uterus, womb
utilizar {21} *vt* : use, utilize — **útil** *adj* : useful — **útiles** *nmpl* : implements, tools —

utilidad *nf* : utility, usefulness — **utilitario, -ria** *adj* : utilitarian — **utilización** *nf, pl* **-ciones** : utilization, use
uva *nf* : grape

V

v *nf* : v, 23d letter of the Spanish alphabet
va → **ir**
vaca *nf* : cow
vacaciones *nfpl* **1** : vacation **2 estar de ~** : be on vacation **3 irse de ~** : go on vacation
vacante *adj* : vacant — **~** *nf* : vacancy
vaciar {85} *vt* **1** : empty (out) **2** AHUECAR : hollow out **3** : cast, mold (a statue, etc.)
vacilar *vi* **1** : hesitate, waver **2** : flicker (of light) **3** TAMBALEARSE : be unsteady, wobble **4** *fam* : joke, fool around — **vacilación** *nf, pl* **-ciones** : hesitation — **vacilante** *adj* **1** : hesitant **2** OSCILANTE : unsteady
vacío, -cía *adj* : empty — **vacío** *nm* **1** : void **2** : vacuum (in physics) **3** HUECO : space, gap
vacuna *nf* : vaccine — **vacunación** *nf, pl* **-ciones** : vaccination — **vacunar** *vt* : vaccinate
vacuno, -na *adj* : bovine
vadear *vt* : ford — **vado** *nm* : ford
vagabundear *vi* : wander — **vagabundo, -da** *adj* **1** : vagrant **2** : stray (of a dog, etc.) — **~** *n* : hobo, bum — **vagancia** *nf* **1** : vagrancy **2** PEREZA : laziness, idleness — **vagar** {52} *vi* : roam, wander
vagina *nf* : vagina
vago, -ga *adj* **1** : vague **2** PEREZOSO : lazy, idle — **~** *n* : idler, loafer
vagón *nm, pl* **-gones** : car (of a train)
vahído *nm* : dizzy spell
vaho *nm* **1** : breath **2** VAPOR : vapor, steam
vaina *nf* **1** : sheath, scabbard **2** : pod (in botany) **3** *Lat fam* : bother, pain
vainilla *nf* : vanilla
vaivén *nm, pl* **-venes 1** : swinging, swaying **2** : coming and going (of people, etc.) **3 vaivenes** *nmpl* : ups and downs
vajilla *nf* : dishes *pl*
vale *nm* **1** : voucher **2** PAGARÉ : IOU — **valedero, -ra** *adj* : valid
valentía *nf* : courage, bravery
valer {84} *vt* **1** : be worth **2** COSTAR : cost **3** GANAR : gain, earn **4** EQUIVALER A : be

equal to — *vi* **1** : have value, cost **2** SER VÁLIDO : be valid, count **3** SERVIR : be of use **4 hacerse ~** : assert oneself **5 más vale** : it's better — **valerse** *vr* **1 ~ de** : take advantage of **2 ~ solo** *or* **~ por sí mismo** : look after oneself
valeroso, -sa *adj* : courageous
valga, etc. → **valer**
valía *nf* : worth
validar *vt* : validate — **validez** *nf* : validity — **válido, -da** *adj* : valid
valiente *adj* **1** : brave **2** (*used ironically*) : fine, great
valija *nf* : case, valise
valioso, -sa *adj* : valuable
valla *nf* **1** : fence **2** : hurdle (in sports) — **vallar** *vt* : put a fence around
valle *nm* : valley
valor *nm* **1** : value, worth **2** VALENTÍA : courage, valor **3 objetos de ~** : valuables **4 sin ~** : worthless **5 ~es** *nmpl* : values, principles **6 ~es** *nmpl* : securities, bonds — **valoración** *nf, pl* **-ciones** : valuation — **valorar** *vt* : evaluate, assess
vals *nm* : waltz
válvula *nf* : valve
vamos → **ir**
vampiro *nm* : vampire
van → **ir**
vanagloriarse *vr* : boast, brag
vándalo *nm* : vandal — **vandalismo** : vandalism
vanguardia *nf* **1** : vanguard **2** : avant-garde (in art, music, etc.) **3 a la ~** : at/in the forefront
vanidad *nf* : vanity — **vanidoso, -sa** *adj* : vain, conceited
vano, -na *adj* **1** INÚTIL : vain, useless **2** SUPERFICIAL : empty, hollow **3 en vano** : in vain
vapor *nm* **1** : steam, vapor **2 al ~** : steamed — **vaporizador** *nm* : vaporizer — **vaporizar** {21} *vt* : vaporize
vaquero, -ra *n* : cowboy *m*, cowgirl *f* — **vaqueros** *nmpl* : jeans

vara *nf* **1** : stick, rod **2** : staff (of office)

varado, -da *adj* : stranded

variar {85} *vt* **1** : vary **2** CAMBIAR : change, alter — *vi* : vary, change — **variable** *adj & nf* : variable — **variación** *nf, pl* **-ciones** : variation — **variado, -da** *adj* : varied — **variante** *nf* : variant

varicela *nf* : chicken pox

varicoso, -sa *adj* : varicose

variedad *nf* : variety

varilla *nf* : rod, stick

vario, -ria *adj* **1** : varied **2 ~s** *pl* : several

varita *nf* : wand

variz *nf, pl* **-rices** *or* **várices** : varicose vein

varón *nm, pl* **-rones 1** : man, male **2** NIÑO : boy — **varonil** *adj* : manly

vas → **ir**

vasco, -ca *adj* : Basque — **vasco** *nm* : Basque (language)

vasija *nf* : container, vessel

vaso *nm* **1** : glass **2** : vessel (in anatomy)

vástago *nm* **1** : offspring, descendent **2** BROTE : shoot **3** VARILLA : rod

vasto, -ta *adj* : vast

vaticinar *vt* : prophesy, predict — **vaticinio** *nm* : prophecy

vatio *nm* : watt

vaya, etc. → **ir**

Vd., Vds. → **usted**

ve, etc. → **ir, ver**

vecinal *adj* : local

vecino, -na *n* **1** : neighbor **2** HABITANTE : resident, inhabitant — **~** *adj* : neighboring — **vecindad** *nf* : neighborhood, vicinity — **vecindario** *nm* **1** : neighborhood **2** VECINOS : community, residents *pl*

vedar *vt* : prohibit — **veda** *nf* **1** : prohibition, ban **2** : closed season (for hunting and fishing) — **vedado** *nm* : preserve (for game, etc.)

vega *nf* : fertile lowland

vegetal *nm* : vegetable, plant — **~** *adj* : vegetable — **vegetación** *nf, pl* **-ciones** : vegetation — **vegetar** *vi* : vegetate — **vegetariano, -na** *adj & n* : vegetarian

vehemente *adj* : vehement

vehículo *nm* : vehicle

veinte *adj & nm* : twenty — **veinteavo, -va** *adj* : twentieth — **veinteavo** *nm* : twentieth — **veintena** *nf* : group of twenty, score

vejar *vt* : mistreat, humiliate — **vejación** *nf, pl* **-ciones** : humiliation

vejez *nf* : old age

vejiga *nf* **1** : bladder **2** AMPOLLA : blister

vela *nf* **1** : candle **2** : sail (of a ship) **3** VIGILIA : vigil **4 pasar la noche en ~** : have a sleepless night

velada *nf* : evening (party)

velar *vt* **1** : hold a wake over **2** CUIDAR : watch over **3** : blur (a photograph) **4** OCULTAR : veil, mask — *vi* **1** : stay awake **2 ~ por** : watch over — **velado, -da** *adj* **1** : veiled, hidden **2** : blurred (of a photograph)

velero *nm* : sailing ship

veleta *nf* : weather vane

vello *nm* **1** : body hair **2** PELUSA : down, fuzz — **vellón** *nm, pl* **-llones** : fleece — **velloso, -sa** *adj* : downy, fluffy — **velludo, -da** *adj* : hairy

velo *nm* : veil

veloz *adj, pl* **-loces** : fast, quick — **velocidad** *nf* **1** : speed, velocity **2** MARCHA : gear (of an automobile) — **velocímetro** *nm* : speedometer

vena *nf* **1** : vein **2** : grain (of wood) **3** DISPOSICIÓN : mood **4 tener ~ de** : have a talent for

venado *nm* **1** : deer **2** : venison (in cooking)

vencer {86} *vt* **1** : beat, defeat **2** SUPERAR : overcome — *vi* **1** : win **2** CADUCAR : expire — **vencerse** *vr* : collapse, give way — **vencedor, -dora** *adj* : winning — **~** *n* : winner — **vencido, -da** *adj* **1** : beaten, defeated **2** CADUCADO : expired **3** : due, payable (in finance) **4 darse por ~** : give up — **vencimiento** *nm* **1** : expiration **2** : maturity (of a loan)

venda *nf* : bandage — **vendaje** *nm* : bandage, dressing — **vendar** *vt* **1** : bandage **2 ~ los ojos** : blindfold

vendaval *nm* : gale

vender *vt* : sell — **venderse** *vr* **1** : be sold **2 se vende** : for sale — **vendedor, -dora** *n* **1** : seller **2** : salesman *m*, saleswoman *f* (in a store)

vendimia *nf* : grape harvest

vendrá, etc. → **venir**

veneno *nm* **1** : poison **2** : venom (of a snake, etc.) — **venenoso, -sa** *adj* : poisonous

venerar *vt* : venerate, revere — **venerable** *adj* : venerable — **veneración** *nf, pl* **-ciones** : veneration, reverence

venéreo, -rea *adj* : venereal

venezolano, -na *adj* : Venezuelan

venga → **venir**

vengar {52} *vt* : avenge — **vengarse** *vr* : get even, take revenge — **venganza** *nf* : vengeance, revenge — **vengativo, -va** *adj* : vindictive, vengeful

venia *nf* **1** : permission **2** : pardon (in law)

venial *adj* : venial, petty

venir {87} *vi* **1** : come **2** LLEGAR : arrive **3** HALLARSE : be, appear **4** QUEDAR : fit **5 que viene** : coming, next **6 ~ a ser** : turn out to be **7 ~ bien** : be suitable — **venirse** *vr* **1** : come **2 ~ abajo** : fall apart, collapse — **venida** *nf* **1** : arrival, coming **2** REGRESO : return — **venidero, -ra** *adj* : coming

venta *nf* **1** : sale, selling **2 en ~** : for sale

ventaja *nf* : advantage — **ventajoso, -sa** *adj* : advantageous

ventana *nf* **1** : window **2 ~ de la nariz** : nostril — **ventanilla** *nf* **1** : window (of a vehicle or airplane) **2** : ticket window, box office (of a theater, etc.)

ventilar *vt* : ventilate, air (out) — **ventilación** *nf, pl* **-ciones** : ventilation — **ventilador** *nm* : fan, ventilator

ventisca *nf* : blizzard — **ventisquero** *nm* : snowdrift

ventoso, -sa *adj* : windy — **ventosidad** *nf* : wind, flatulence

ventrílocuo, -cua *n* : ventriloquist

ventura *nf* **1** : fortune, luck **2** SATISFACCIÓN : happiness **3 a la ~** : at random — **venturoso, -sa** *adj* : fortunate, happy

ver {88} *vt* **1** : see **2** : watch (television, etc.) — *vi* **1** : see **2 a ~** *or* **vamos a ~** : let's see **3 no tener nada que ~ con** : have nothing to do with **4 ya veremos** : we'll see — **verse** *vr* **1** : see oneself **2** HALLARSE : find oneself **3** ENCONTRARSE : see each other, meet

vera *nf* **1** : side, edge **2** : bank (of a river)

veracidad *nf* : truthfulness

verano *nm* : summer — **veraneante** *nmf* : summer vacationer — **veranear** *vi* : spend the summer — **veraniego, -ga** *adj* : summer

veras *nfpl* **de ~** : really

veraz *adj, pl* **-races** : truthful

verbal *adj* : verbal

verbena *nf* : festival, fair

verbo *nm* : verb — **verboso, -sa** *adj* : verbose

verdad *nf* **1** : truth **2 de ~** : really, truly **3 ¿verdad?** : right?, isn't that so? — **verdaderamente** *adv* : really, truly — **verdadero, -dera** *adj* : true, real

verde *adj* **1** : green **2** : dirty, risqué (of a joke, etc.) — **~** *nm* : green — **verdor** *nm* : greenness

verdugo *nm* **1** : executioner, hangman **2** : cruel person, tyrant

verdura *nf* : vegetable(s), green(s)

vereda *nf* **1** : path, trail **2** *Lat* : sidewalk

veredicto *nm* : verdict

vergüenza *nf* **1** : shame **2** TIMIDEZ : bashfulness, shyness — **vergonzoso, -sa** *adj* **1** : shameful **2** TÍMIDO : bashful, shy

verídico, -ca *adj* : true, truthful

verificar {72} *vt* **1** : verify, confirm **2** EXAMINAR : test, check out — **verificarse** *vr* **1** : take place **2** : come true (of a prophecy,

etc.) — **verificación** *nf, pl* **-ciones** : verification

verja *nf* **1** : (iron) gate **2** : rails *pl* (of a fence) **3** ENREJADO : grating, grille

vermut *nm, pl* **-muts** : vermouth

vernáculo, -la *adj* : vernacular

verosímil *adj* **1** : probable, likely **2** CREÍBLE : credible

verraco *nm* : boar

verruga *nf* : wart

versar *vi* **~ sobre** : deal with, be about — **versado, -da** *adj* **~ en** : versed in

versátil *adj* **1** : versatile **2** VOLUBLE : fickle

versión *nf, pl* **-siones** **1** : version **2** TRADUCCIÓN : translation

verso *nm* **1** : poem, verse **2** : line (of poetry)

vértebra *nf* : vertebra

verter {56} *vt* **1** : pour (out) **2** DERRAMAR : spill **3** TIRAR : dump — *vi* : flow — **vertedero** *nm* **1** : dump, landfill **2** DESAGÜE : drain, outlet

vertical *adj & nf* : vertical

vértice *nm* : vertex, apex

vertiente *nf* : slope

vértigo *nm* : vertigo, dizziness — **vertiginoso, -sa** *adj* : dizzy

vesícula *nf* **1** : blister **2 ~ biliar** : gallbladder

vestíbulo *nm* : vestibule, hall, foyer

vestido *nm* **1** : dress **2** ROPA : clothing, clothes *pl*

vestigio *nm* : vestige, trace

vestir {54} *vt* **1** : dress, clothe **2** LLEVAR : wear — *vi* : dress — **vestirse** *vr* : get dressed — **vestimenta** *nf* : clothing — **vestuario** *nm* **1** : wardrobe, clothes *pl* **2** : dressing room (in a theater), locker room (in sports)

veta *nf* **1** : vein, seam **2** : grain (of wood)

vetar *vt* : veto

veteado, -da *adj* : streaked, veined

veterano, -na *adj & n* : veteran

veterinaria *nf* : veterinary medicine — **veterinario, -ria** *adj* : veterinary — **~** *n* : veterinarian

veto *nm* : veto

vetusto, -ta *adj* : ancient

vez *nf, pl* **veces** **1** : time **2** TURNO : turn **3 a la ~** : at the same time **4 a veces** : sometimes **5 de una ~** : all at once **6 de una ~ para siempre** : once and for all **7 de ~ en cuando** : from time to time **8 dos veces** : twice **9 en ~ de** : instead of **10 una ~** : once

vía *nf* **1** : way, road, route **2** MEDIO : means **3** : track, line (of a railroad) **4** : (anatomical) tract **5 en ~ de** : in the process of — **~** *prep* : via

viable *adj* : viable, feasible — **viabilidad** *nf* : viability

viaducto *nm* : viaduct

viajar *vi* : travel — **viajante** *nmf* : traveling salesperson — **viaje** *nm* : trip, journey — **viajero, -ra** *adj* : traveling — ~ *n* **1** : traveler **2** PASAJERO : passenger

vial *adj* : road, traffic

víbora *nf* : viper

vibrar *vi* : vibrate — **vibración** *nf, pl* **-ciones** : vibration — **vibrante** *adj* : vibrant

vicario, -ria *n* : vicar

vicepresidente, -ta *n* : vice president

viceversa *adv* : vice versa

vicio *nm* **1** : vice **2** MALA COSTUMBRE : bad habit **3** DEFECTO : defect — **viciado, -da** *adj* **1** : corrupt **2** : stuffy, stale (of air, etc.) — **viciar** *vt* **1** : corrupt **2** ESTROPEAR : spoil, pollute — **vicioso, -sa** *adj* : depraved, corrupt

vicisitud *nf* : vicissitude

víctima *nf* : victim

victoria *nf* : victory — **victorioso, -sa** *adj* : victorious

vid *nf* : vine, grapevine

vida *nf* **1** : life **2** DURACIÓN : lifetime **3 de por** ~ : for life **4 estar con** ~ : be alive

video *or* **vídeo** *nm* **1** : video **2** : VCR, videocassette recorder

vidrio *nm* : glass — **vidriado** *nm* : glaze — **vidriar** *vt* : glaze — **vidriera** *nf* **1** : stained-glass window **2** : glass door **3** *Lat* : shopwindow — **vidrioso, -sa** *adj* **1** : delicate (of a subject, etc.) **2 ojos vidriosos** : glassy eyes

vieira *nf* : scallop

viejo, -ja *adj* : old — ~ *n* **1** : old man *m*, old woman *f* **2 hacerse** ~ : get old

viene, etc. → **venir**

viento *nm* : wind

vientre *nm* **1** : abdomen, belly **2** MATRIZ : womb **3** INTESTINO : bowels *pl*

viernes *nms & pl* **1** : Friday **2 Viernes Santo** : Good Friday

vietnamita *adj & nm* : Vietnamese

viga *nf* : beam, girder

vigencia *nf* **1** : validity **2 entrar en** ~ : go into effect — **vigente** *adj* : valid, in force

vigésimo, -ma *adj & n* : twentieth

vigía *nmf* : lookout

vigilar *vt* : look after, watch over — *vi* : keep watch — **vigilancia** *nf* **1** : vigilance **2 bajo** ~ : under surveillance — **vigilante** *adj* : vigilant — ~ *nmf* : watchman, guard — **vigilia** *nf* **1** : wakefulness **2** : vigil (in religion)

vigor *nm* **1** : vigor **2 entrar en** ~ : go into effect — **vigorizante** *adj* : invigorating — **vigoroso, -sa** *adj* : vigorous

VIH *nm* : HIV

vil *adj* : vile, despicable — **vileza** *nf* **1** : vileness **2** : despicable act — **vilipendiar** *vt* : revile

villa *nf* **1** : town, village **2** : villa (house)

villancico *nm* : (Christmas) carol

villano, -na *n* : villain

vilo *nm* **en** ~ : suspended, in the air

vinagre *nm* : vinegar — **vinagrera** *nf* : cruet — **vinagreta** *nf* : vinaigrette

vincular *vt* : tie, link — **vínculo** *nm* : link, tie, bond

vindicar *vt* **1** : vindicate **2** VENGAR : avenge

vino¹, etc. → **venir**

vino² *nm* : wine

viña *nf or* **viñedo** *nm* : vineyard

vio, etc. → **ver**

viola *nf* : viola

violar *vt* **1** : violate (a law, etc.) **2** : rape (a person) — **violación** *nf, pl* **-ciones 1** : violation, offense **2** : rape (of a person)

violencia *nf* : violence, force — **violentar** *vt* **1** : force **2** : break into (a house, etc.) — **violentarse** *vr* **1** : force oneself **2** AVERGONZARSE : be embarrassed — **violento, -ta** *adj* **1** : violent **2** INCÓMODO : awkward, embarrassing

violeta *adj & nm* : violet (color) — ~ *nf* : violet (flower)

violín *nm, pl* **-lines** : violin — **violinista** *nmf* : violinist — **violoncelista** *or* **violonchelista** *nmf* : cellist — **violoncelo** *or* **violonchelo** *nm* : cello, violoncello

virar *vi* : turn, change direction — **viraje** *nm* **1** : turn, swerve **2** CAMBIO : change

virgen *adj & nmf, pl* **vírgenes** : virgin — **virginal** *adj* : virginal — **virginidad** *nf* : virginity

viril *adj* : virile — **virilidad** *nf* : virility

virtual *adj* : virtual

virtud *nf* **1** : virtue **2 en** ~ **de** : by virtue of — **virtuoso, -sa** *adj* : virtuous — ~ *n* : virtuoso

viruela *nf* **1** : smallpox **2 picado de** ~**s** : pockmarked

virulento, -ta *adj* : virulent

virus *nms & pl* : virus

visa *nf Lat* : visa — **visado** *nm Spain* : visa

vísceras *nfpl* : entrails — **visceral** *adj* : visceral

viscoso, -sa *adj* : viscous — **viscosidad** *nf* : viscosity

visera *nf* : visor

visible *adj* : visible — **visibilidad** *nf* : visibility

visión *nf, pl* **-siones 1** : eyesight **2** APARICIÓN : vision, illusion **3** PUNTO DE VISTA : view, perspective — **visionario, -ria** *adj & n* : visionary

visitar *vt* : visit — **visita** *nf* **1** : visit **2 tener** ~ : have company — **visitante** *adj* : visiting — ~ *nmf* : visitor

vislumbrar *vt* : make out, discern — **vislumbre** *nf* **1** : glimpse, sign **2** RESPLANDOR : glimmer, gleam

viso *nm* **1** : sheen **2 tener** ~**s de** : seem, show signs of

visón *nm, pl* **-sones** : mink

víspera *nf* : eve, day before

vista *nf* **1** : vision, eyesight **2** MIRADA : look, gaze **3** PANORAMA : view, vista **4** : hearing (in court) **5 a primera** ~ *or* **a simple** ~ : at first sight **6 hacer la** ~ **gorda** : turn a blind eye **7 perder de** ~ : lose sight of — **vistazo** *nm* **1** : glance **2 echar un** ~ : have a look

visto, -ta *adj* **1** : clear, obvious **2** COMÚN : commonly seen **3 estar bien** ~ : be approved of **4 estar mal** ~ : be frowned upon **5 nunca** ~ : unheard-of **6 por lo visto** : apparently **7 visto que** : since, given that — **visto** *nm* ~ **bueno** : approval — ~ *pp* → **ver**

vistoso, -sa *adj* : colorful, bright

visual *adj* : visual — **visualizar** {21} *vt* : visualize

vital *adj* : vital — **vitalicio, -cia** *adj* : life, for life — **vitalidad** *nf* : vitality

vitamina *nf* : vitamin

viticultor, -tora *n* : winegrower — **viticultura** *nf* : wine growing

vitorear *vt* : cheer, acclaim

vítreo, -trea *adj* : glassy

vitrina *nf* **1** : showcase, display case **2** *Lat* : shopwindow

vituperar *vt* : censure — **vituperio** *nm* : censure

viudo, -da *n* : widower *m*, widow *f* — ~ *adj* : widowed — **viudez** *nf* : widowerhood, widowhood

viva *nm* **dar** ~**s** : cheer

vivacidad *nf* : vivacity, liveliness

vivamente *adv* **1** : vividly **2** PROFUNDAMENTE : deeply, acutely

vivaz *adj, pl* **-vaces 1** : lively, vivacious **2** AGUDO : vivid, sharp

víveres *nmpl* : provisions, supplies

vivero *nm* **1** : nursery (for plants) **2** : (fish) hatchery, (oyster) bed

viveza *nf* **1** : liveliness **2** : vividness (of colors, descriptions, etc.) **3** ASTUCIA : sharpness (of mind) — **vívido, -da** *adj* : vivid

vividor, -dora *n* : freeloader

vivienda *nf* **1** : housing **2** MORADA : dwelling

viviente *adj* : living

vivificar {72} *vt* : enliven

vivir *vi* **1** : live, be alive **2** ~ **de** : live on —

vt : experience, live (through) — ~ *nm* **1** : life, lifestyle **2 de mal** ~ : disreputable — **vivo, -va** *adj* **1** : alive **2** INTENSO : intense, bright **3** ANIMADO : lively **4** ASTUTO : sharp, quick **5 en vivo** : live

vocablo *nm* : word — **vocabulario** *nm* : vocabulary

vocación *nf, pl* **-ciones** : vocation — **vocacional** *adj* : vocational

vocal *adj* : vocal — ~ *nmf* : member (of a committee, etc.) — ~ *nf* : vowel — **vocalista** *nmf* : singer, vocalist

vocear *v* : shout — **vocerío** *nm* : shouting

vociferar *vi* : shout

vodka *nmf* : vodka

volar {19} *vi* **1** : fly **2** : blow away (of papers, etc.) **3** *fam* : disappear **4 irse volando** : rush off — *vt* : blow up — **volador, -dora** *adj* : flying — **volandas: en** ~ *adv phr* : in the air — **volante** *adj* : flying — ~ *nm* **1** : steering wheel **2** : shuttlecock (in badminton) **3** : flounce (of fabric) **4** *Lat* : flier, circular

volátil *adj* : volatile

volcán *nm, pl* **-canes** : volcano — **volcánico, -ca** *adj* : volcanic

volcar {82} *vt* **1** : upset, knock over **2** VACIAR : empty out — *vi* : overturn — **volcarse** *vr* **1** : overturn, tip over **2** ~ **en** : throw oneself into

voleibol *nm* : volleyball

voltaje *nm* : voltage

voltear *vt* : turn over, turn upside down — **voltearse** *vr Lat* : turn (around) — **voltereta** *nf* : somersault

voltio *nm* : volt

voluble *adj* : fickle

volumen *nm, pl* **-lúmenes** : volume — **voluminoso, -sa** *adj* : voluminous

voluntad *nf* **1** : will **2** DESEO : wish **3** INTENCIÓN : intention **4 a** ~ : at will **5 buena** ~ : goodwill **6 mala** ~ : ill will **7 fuerza de** ~ : willpower — **voluntario, -ria** *adj* : voluntary — ~ *n* : volunteer — **voluntarioso, -sa** *adj* **1** : willing **2** TERCO : stubborn, willful

voluptuoso, -sa *adj* : voluptuous

volver {89} *vi* **1** : return, come or go back **2** ~ **a** : return to, do again **3** ~ **en sí** : come to — *vt* **1** : turn, turn over, turn inside out **2** CONVERTIR EN : turn (into) **3** ~ **loco** : drive crazy — **volverse** *vr* **1** : turn (around) **2** HACERSE : become

vomitar *vi* : vomit — *vt* **1** : vomit **2** : spew (out) — **vómito** *nm* **1** : (action of) vomiting **2** : vomit

voraz *adj, pl* **-races** : voracious

vos *pron Lat* : you

vosotros, -tras *pron Spain* : you, yourselves

votar *vi* : vote — *vt* : vote for — **votación** *nf, pl* **-ciones** : vote, voting — **votante** *nmf* : voter — **voto** *nm* **1** : vote **2** : vow (in religion)

voy → **ir**

voz *nf, pl* **voces** **1** : voice **2** GRITO : shout, yell **3** VOCABLO : word, term **4** RUMOR : rumor **5 dar voces** : shout **6 en ~ alta** : loudly **7 en ~ baja** : softly

vuelco *nm* : upset, overturning

vuelo *nm* **1** : flight **2** : (action of) flying **3** : flare (of clothing) **4 al ~** : on the wing

vuelta *nf* **1** : turn **2** REVOLUCIÓN : circle, revolution **3** CURVA : bend, curve **4** REGRESO : return **5** : round, lap (in sports) **6** PASEO : walk, drive, ride **7** REVÉS : back, other side **8** *Spain* : change **9 dar ~s** : spin **10 estar de ~** : be back — **vuelto** *nm Lat* : change

vuestro, -tra *adj Spain* : your, of yours — **~** *pron Spain* (*with definite article*) : yours

vulgar *adj* **1** : vulgar **2** CORRIENTE : common — **vulgaridad** *nf* **1** : vulgarity **2** BANALIDAD : banality — **vulgo** *nm* **el ~** : the masses, common people

vulnerable *adj* : vulnerable — **vulnerabilidad** *nf* : vulnerability

WXYZ

w *nf* : w, 24th letter of the Spanish alphabet

wáter *nm Spain* : toilet

whisky *nm, pl* **-skys** *or* **-skies** : whiskey

x *nf* : x, 25th letter of the Spanish alphabet

xenofobia *nf* : xenophobia

xilófono *nm* : xylophone

y¹ *nf* : y, 26th letter of the Spanish alphabet

y² *conj* : and

ya *adv* **1** : already **2** AHORA : (right) now **3** MÁS TARDE : later, soon **4 ~ no** : no longer **5 ~ que** : now that, since, inasmuch as

yacer {90} *vi* : lie (on or in the ground) — **yacimiento** *nm* : bed, deposit

yanqui *adj & nmf* : Yankee

yate *nm* : yacht

yegua *nf* : mare

yelmo *nm* : helmet

yema *nf* **1** : bud, shoot **2** : yolk (of an egg) **3** *or* **~ del dedo** : fingertip

yerba *nf* **1** *or* **~ mate** : maté **2** → **hierba**

yermo, -ma *adj* : barren, deserted — **yermo** *nm* : wasteland

yerno *nm* : son-in-law

yerro *nm* : blunder, mistake

yerto, -ta *adj* : stiff

yesca *nf* : tinder

yeso *nm* **1** : gypsum **2** : plaster (for art, construction)

yo *pron* **1** (*subject*) : I **2** (*object*) : me **3 soy ~** : it is I, it's me — **~** *nm* : ego, self

yodo *nm* : iodine

yoga *nm* : yoga

yogurt *or* **yogur** *nm* : yogurt

yuca *nf* : yucca

yugo *nm* : yoke (of oxen)

yugoslavo, -va *adj* : Yugoslavian

yugular *adj* : jugular

yunque *nm* : anvil

yunta *nf* : yoke

yuxtaponer {60} *vt* : juxtapose — **yuxtaposición** *nf, pl* **-ciones** : juxtaposition

z *nf* : z, 27th letter of the Spanish alphabet

zacate *nm Lat* : grass

zafar *vt Lat* : loosen, untie — **zafarse** *vr* **1** : come undone **2** : get free of (an obligation, etc.)

zafio, -fia *adj* : coarse

zafiro *nm* : sapphire

zaga *nf* **a la ~** *or* **en ~** : behind, in the rear

zaguán *nm, pl* **-guanes** : (entrance) hall

zaherir {76} *vt* : hurt (s.o.'s feelings)

zaino, -na *adj* : chestnut (color)

zalamería *nf* : flattery — **zalamero, -ra** *adj* : flattering — **~** *n* : flatterer

zambullirse {38} *vr* : dive, plunge — **zambullida** *nf* : dive, plunge

zanahoria *nf* : carrot

zancada *nf* : stride, step — **zancadilla** *nf* **1** : trip, stumble **2 hacer una ~ a algn** : trip s.o. up

zancos *nmpl* : stilts

zancudo *nm Lat* : mosquito

zángano, -na *n fam* : lazy person, slacker — **zángano** *nm, pl* : drone (bee)

zanja *nf* : ditch, trench — **zanjar** *vt* : settle, resolve

zapallo *nm Lat* : pumpkin — **zapallito** *nm Lat* : zucchini

zapapico *nm* : pickax

zapato *nm* : shoe — **zapatería** *nf* : shoe store — **zapatero, -ra** *n* : shoemaker, cobbler — **zapatilla** *nf* **1** : slipper **2** : sneaker (for sports, etc.)

zar *nm* : czar

zarandear *vt* **1** : sift **2** SACUDIR : shake

zarcillo *nm* : earring

zarpa *nf* : paw

zarpar *vi* : set sail, raise anchor

zarza *nf* : bramble — **zarzamora** *nf* : blackberry

zigzag *nm, pl* **-zags** *or* **-zagues** : zigzag — **zigzaguear** *vi* : zigzag

zinc *nm* : zinc

zíper *nm Lat* : zipper

zircón *nm, pl* **-cones** : zircon

zócalo *nm* **1** : base (of a column, etc.) **2** : baseboard (of a wall) **3** *Lat* : main square, plaza

zodíaco *nm* : zodiac

zona *nf* : zone, area

zoo *nm* : zoo — **zoología** *nf* : zoology — **zoológico, -ca** *adj* : zoological — **zoológico** *nm* : zoo — **zoólogo, -ga** *n* : zoologist

zopilote *nm Lat* : buzzard

zoquete *nmf fam* : oaf, blockhead

zorrillo *nm Lat* : skunk

zorro, -rra *n* : fox, vixen *f* — ~ *adj* : foxy, sly

zozobra *nf* : anxiety, worry — **zozobrar** *vi* : capsize

zueco *nm* : clog (shoe)

zumbar *vi* : buzz — *vt fam* : hit, beat — **zumbido** *nm* : buzzing

zumo *nf* : juice

zurcir {83} *vt* : darn, mend

zurdo, -da *adj* : left-handed — ~ *n* : left-handed person — **zurda** *nf* : left hand

zutano, -na → **fulano**

English-Spanish
Dictionary

A

a¹ *n, pl* **a's** *or* **as** : a *f*, primera letra del alfabeto inglés

a² *art* (**an** *before vowel or silent h*) **1** : un *m*, una *f* **2** PER : por, a la, al

aback *adv* **be taken ~** : quedarse desconcertado

abacus *n, pl* **abaci** *or* **abacuses** : ábaco *m*

abandon *vt* **1** DESERT : abandonar **2** GIVE UP : renunciar a — **~** *n* : desenfreno *m* — **abandonment** *n* : abandono *m*

abashed *adj* : avergonzado

abate *vi* **abated; abating** : amainar, disminuir

abattoir *n* : matadero *m*

abbey *n, pl* **-beys** : abadía *f* — **abbot** *n* : abad *m*

abbreviate *vt* **-ated; -ating** : abreviar — **abbreviation** *n* : abreviatura *f*, abreviación *f*

abdicate *v* **-cated; -cating** : abdicar — **abdication** *n* : abdicación *f*

abdomen *n* : abdomen *m*, vientre *m* — **abdominal** *adj* : abdominal

abduct *vt* : secuestrar — **abduction** *n* : secuestro *m*

aberration *n* : aberración *f*

abet *vt* **abetted; abetting** *or* **aid and ~** : ser cómplice de

abeyance *n* : desuso *m*

abhor *vt* **-horred; -horring** : aborrecer

abide *v* **abode** *or* **abided; abiding** *vt* : soportar, tolerar — *vi* **1** DWELL : morar **2 ~ by** : atenerse a

ability *n, pl* **-ties** **1** CAPABILITY : aptitud *f*, capacidad *f* **2** SKILL : habilidad *f*

abject *adj* : miserable, desdichado

ablaze *adj* : en llamas

able *adj* **abler; ablest** **1** CAPABLE : capaz, hábil **2** COMPETENT : competente

abnormal *adj* : anormal — **abnormality** *n, pl* **-ties** : anormalidad *f*

aboard *adv* : a bordo — **~** *prep* : a bordo de

abode *n* : morada *f*, domicilio *m*

abolish *vt* : abolir, suprimir — **abolition** *n* : abolición *f*

abominable *adj* : abominable, aborrecible — **abomination** *n* : abominación *f*

aborigine *n* : aborigen *mf*

abort *vt* : abortar — **abortion** *n* : aborto *m* — **abortive** *adj* UNSUCCESSFUL : malogrado

abound *vi* **~ in** : abundar en

about *adv* **1** APPROXIMATELY : aproximadamente, más o menos **2** AROUND : alrededor **3 be ~ to** : estar a punto de **4 be up and ~** : estar levantado — **~** *prep* **1** AROUND : alrededor de **2** CONCERNING : acerca de, sobre

above *adv* : arriba — **~** *prep* **1** : encima de **2 ~ all** : sobre todo — **aboveboard** *adj* : honrado

abrasive *adj* **1** : abrasivo **2** BRUSQUE : brusco, mordaz

abreast *adv* **1** : al lado **2 keep ~ of** : mantenerse al corriente de

abridge *vt* **abridged; abridging** : abreviar

abroad *adv* **1** : en el extranjero **2** WIDELY : por todas partes **3 go ~** : ir al extranjero

abrupt *adj* **1** SUDDEN : repentino **2** BRUSQUE : brusco

abscess *n* : absceso *m*

absence *n* **1** : ausencia *f* **2** LACK : falta *f*, carencia *f* — **absent** *adj* : ausente — **absentee** *n* : ausente *mf* — **absentminded** *adj* : distraído, despistado

absolute *adj* : absoluto — **absolutely** *adv* : absolutamente

absolve *vt* **-solved; -solving** : absolver

absorb *vt* : absorber — **absorbent** *adj* : absorbente — **absorption** *n* : absorción *f*

abstain *vi* **~ from** : abstenerse de — **abstinence** *n* : abstinencia *f*

abstract *adj* : abstracto — **~** *vt* : extraer — **~** *n* : resumen *m* — **abstraction** *n* : abstracción *f*

absurd *adj* : absurdo — **absurdity** *n, pl* **-ties** : absurdo *m*

abundant *adj* : abundante — **abundance** *n* : abundancia *f*

abuse *vt* **abused; abusing** **1** MISUSE : abusar de **2** MISTREAT : maltratar **3** REVILE : insultar — **~** *n* **1** : abuso *m* **2** INSULTS : insultos *mpl* — **abusive** *adj* : injurioso

abut *vi* **abutted; abutting** **~ on** : colindar con

abyss *n* : abismo *m* — **abysmal** *adj* : atroz, pésimo

academy *n, pl* **-mies** : academia *f* — **academic** *adj* **1** : académico **2** THEORETICAL : teórico

accelerate *v* **-ated; -ating** : acelerar — **acceleration** *n* : aceleración *f*

accent *vt* : acentuar — **~** *n* : acento *m* — **accentuate** *vt* **-ated; -ating** : acentuar, subrayar

accept *vt* : aceptar — **acceptable** *adj* : aceptable — **acceptance** *n* **1** : aceptación *f* **2** APPROVAL : aprobación *f*

access n : acceso m — **accessible** adj : accesible, asequible

accessory n, pl **-ries 1** : accesorio m **2** ACCOMPLICE : cómplice mf

accident n **1** MISHAP : accidente m **2** CHANCE : casualidad f — **accidental** adj : accidental — **accidentally** adv **1** BY CHANCE : por casualidad **2** UNINTENTIONALLY : sin querer

acclaim vt : aclamar — ～ n : aclamación f

acclimatize vt **-tized; -tizing** : aclimatar

accommodate vt **-dated; -dating 1** ADAPT : acomodar, adaptar **2** SATISFY : complacer, satisfacer **3** HOLD : tener cabida para — **accomodation** n **1** : adaptación f **2** ～s npl LODGING : alojamiento m

accompany vt **-nied; -nying** : acompañar

accomplice n : cómplice mf

accomplish vt : realizar, llevar a cabo — **accomplishment** n **1** COMPLETION : realización f **2** ACHIEVEMENT : logro m, éxito m

accord n **1** AGREEMENT : acuerdo m **2** of one's own ～ : voluntariamente — **accordance** n **in** ～ **with** : conforme a, de acuerdo con — **accordingly** adv : en consecuencia — **according to** prep : según

accordion n : acordeón m

accost vt : abordar

account n **1** : cuenta f **2** REPORT : relato m, informe m **3** WORTH : importancia f **4** on ～ of : a causa de, debido a **5** on no ～ : de ninguna manera — ～ vi ～ for : dar cuenta de, explicar — **accountable** adj : responsable — **accountant** n : contador m, -dora f Lat; contable mf Spain — **accounting** n : contabilidad f

accrue vi **-crued; -cruing** : acumularse

accumulate v **-lated; -lating** vt : acumular — vi : acumularse — **accumulation** n : acumulación f

accurate adj : exacto, preciso — **accuracy** n : exactitud f, precisión f

accuse vt **-cused; -cusing** : acusar — **accusation** n : acusación f

accustomed adj **1** : acostumbrado **2** become ～ to : acostumbrarse a

ace n : as m

ache vi **ached; aching** : doler — ～ n : dolor m

achieve vt **achieved; achieving** : lograr, realizar — **achievement** n : logro m, éxito m

acid adj : ácido — ～ n : ácido m

acknowledge vt **-edged; -edging 1** ADMIT : admitir **2** RECOGNIZE : reconocer **3** ～ receipt of : acusar recibo de — **acknowledgment** n **1** : reconocimiento m **2** THANKS : agradecimiento m **3** ～ of receipt : acuse m de recibo

acne n : acné m

acorn n : bellota f

acoustic or **acoustical** adj : acústico — **acoustics** ns & pl : acústica f

acquaint vt **1** ～ s.o. with : poner a algn al corriente de **2** be ～ed with : conocer a (una persona), saber (un hecho) — **acquaintance** n **1** : conocimiento m **2** : conocido m, -da f (persona)

acquire vt **-quired; -quiring** : adquirir — **acquisition** n : adquisición f

acquit vt **-quitted; -quitting** : absolver

acre n : acre m — **acreage** n : superficie f en acres

acrid adj : acre

acrobat n : acróbata mf — **acrobatic** adj : acrobático

acronym n : siglas fpl

across adv **1** : de un lado a otro **2** CROSSWISE : a través **3** go ～ : atravesar — ～ prep **1** : a través de **2** ～ the street : al otro lado de la calle

acrylic n : acrílico m

act vi **1** : actuar **2** PRETEND : fingir **3** FUNCTION : funcionar **4** ～ as : servir de — vt : interpretar (un papel) — ～ n **1** ACTION : acto m, acción f **2** DECREE : ley f **3** : acto m (en una obra de teatro), número m (en un espectáculo) — **acting** adj : interino

action n **1** : acción f **2** LAWSUIT : demanda f **3** take ～ : tomar medidas

activate vt **-vated; -vating** : activar

active adj **1** : activo **2** LIVELY : enérgico **3** ～ volcano : volcán m en actividad — **activity** n, pl **-ties** : actividad f

actor n : actor m — **actress** n : actriz f

actual adj : real, verdadero — **actually** adv : realmente, en realidad

acupuncture n : acupuntura f

acute adj **acuter; acutest 1** : agudo **2** PERCEPTIVE : perspicaz

ad → advertisement

adamant adj : inflexible

adapt vt : adaptar — vi : adaptarse — **adaptable** adj : adaptable — **adaptation** n : adaptación f — **adapter** n : adaptador m

add vt **1** : añadir **2** or ～ up : sumar — vi : sumar

addict n **1** : adicto m, -ta f **2** or drug ～ : drogadicto m, -ta f; toxicómano m, -na f — **addiction** n : dependencia f

addition n **1** : suma f (en matemáticas) **2** ADDING : adición f **3** in ～ : además — **additional** adj : adicional — **additive** n : aditivo m

address vt **1** : dirigirse a (una persona) **2** : ponerle la dirección a (una carta) **3** : tratar (un asunto) — ～ n **1** : dirección f, domicilio m **2** SPEECH : discurso m

adept adj : experto, hábil

adequate *adj* : adecuado, suficiente

adhere *vi* **-hered; -hering 1** STICK : adherirse **2 ~ to** : observar — **adherence** *n* **1** : adhesión *f* **2** : observancia *f* (de una ley, etc.) — **adhesive** *adj* : adhesivo — **~** *n* : adhesivo *m*

adjacent *adj* : adyacente, contiguo

adjective *n* : adjetivo *m*

adjoining *adj* : contiguo, vecino

adjourn *vt* : aplazar, suspender — *vi* : suspenderse

adjust *vt* : ajustar, arreglar — *vi* : adaptarse — **adjustable** *adj* : ajustable — **adjustment** *n* : ajuste *m* (a una máquina, etc.), adaptación *f* (de una persona)

ad–lib *v* **-libbed; -libbing** : improvisar

administer *vt* : administrar — **administration** *n* : administración *f* — **administrative** *adj* : administrativo — **administrator** *n* : administrador *m*, -dora *f*

admirable *adj* : admirable

admiral *n* : almirante *m*

admire *vt* **-mired; -miring** : admirar — **admiration** *n* : admiración *f* — **admirer** *n* : admirador *m*, -dora *f*

admit *vt* **-mitted; -mitting 1** : admitir, dejar entrar **2** ACKNOWLEDGE : reconocer — **admission** *n* **1** ADMITTANCE : entrada *f*, admisión *f* **2** ACKNOWLEDGMENT : reconocimiento *m* — **admittance** *n* : admisión *f*, entrada *f*

admonish *vt* : amonestar, reprender

ado *n* **1** : alboroto *m*, bulla *f* **2 without further ~** : sin más (preámbulos)

adolescent *n* : adolescente *mf* — **adolescence** *n* : adolescencia *f*

adopt *vt* : adoptar — **adoption** *n* : adopción *f*

adore *vt* **adored; adoring 1** : adorar **2** LIKE, LOVE : encantarle (algo a uno) — **adorable** *adj* : adorable — **adoration** *n* : adoración *f*

adorn *vt* : adornar — **adornment** *n* : adorno *m*

adrift *adj & adv* : a la deriva

adroit *adj* : diestro, hábil

adult *adj* : adulto — **~** *n* : adulto *m*, -ta *f*

adultery *n, pl* **-teries** : adulterio *m*

advance *v* **-vanced; -vancing** *vt* : adelantar — *vi* : avanzar, adelantarse — **~** *n* **1** : avance *m* **2** PROGRESS : adelanto *m* **3 in ~** : por adelantado — **advancement** *n* : adelanto *m*, progreso *m*

advantage *n* **1** : ventaja *f* **2 take ~ of** : aprovecharse de — **advantageous** *adj* : ventajoso

advent *n* **1** ARRIVAL : llegada *f* **2 Advent** : Adviento *m*

adventure *n* : aventura *f* — **adventurous** *adj* **1** : intrépido **2** RISKY : arriesgado

adverb *n* : adverbio *m*

adversary *n, pl* **-saries** : adversario *m*, -ria *f*

adverse *adj* : adverso, desfavorable — **adversity** *n, pl* **-ties** : adversidad *f*

advertise *v* **-tised; -tising** *vt* : anunciar — *vi* : hacer publicidad — **advertisement** *n* : anuncio *m* — **advertiser** *n* : anunciante *mf* — **advertising** *n* : publicidad *f*

advice *n* : consejo *m*

advise *vt* **-vised; -vising 1** COUNSEL : aconsejar, asesorar **2** RECOMMEND : recomendar **3** INFORM : informar — **advisable** *adj* : aconsejable — **adviser** *n* : consejero *m*, -ra *f*; asesor *m*, -sora *f* — **advisory** *adj* : consultivo

advocate *vt* **-cated; -cating** : recomendar — **~** *n* : defensor *m*, -sora *f*

aerial *adj* : aéreo — **~** *n* : antena *f*

aerobics *ns & pl* : aeróbic *m*

aerodynamic *adj* : aerodinámico

aerosol *n* : aerosol *m*

aesthetic *adj* : estético

afar *adv* : lejos

affable *adj* : afable

affair *n* **1** : asunto *m*, cuestión *f* **2** *or* **love ~** : amorío *m*, aventura *f*

affect *vt* **1** : afectar **2** FEIGN : fingir — **affection** *n* : afecto *m*, cariño *m* — **affectionate** *adj* : afectuoso, cariñoso

affinity *n, pl* **-ties** : afinidad *f*

affirm *vt* : afirmar — **affirmative** *adj* : afirmativo

affix *vt* : fijar, pegar

afflict *vt* : afligir — **affliction** *n* : aflicción *f*

affluent *adj* : próspero, adinerado

afford *vt* **1** : tener los recursos para, permitirse (el lujo de) **2** PROVIDE : brindar

affront *n* : afrenta *f*

afloat *adv & adj* : a flote

afoot *adv* : en marcha

afraid *adj* **1 be ~** : tener miedo **2 I'm ~ not** : me temo que no

African *adj* : africano

after *adv* **1** AFTERWARD : después **2** BEHIND : detrás, atrás — **~** *conj* : después de (que) — **~** *prep* **1** : después de **2 ~ all** : después de todo **3 it's ten ~ five** : son las cinco y diez

aftereffect *n* : efecto *m* secundario

aftermath *n* : consecuencias *fpl*

afternoon *n* : tarde *f*

afterward *or* **afterwards** *adv* : después, más tarde

again *adv* **1** : otra vez, de nuevo **2 ~ and ~** : una y otra vez **3 then ~** : por otra parte

against *prep* : contra, en contra de

age *n* **1** : edad *f* **2** ERA : era *f*, época *f* **3 be of ~** : ser mayor de edad **4 for ~s** : hace agency

siglos **5 old ～** : vejez *f* — **～** *vi* **aged;
aging** : envejecer — **aged** *adj* **1** OLD : anciano, viejo **2 children ～ 10 to 17** : niños de 10 a 17 años
agency *n, pl* **-cies** : agencia *f*
agenda *n* : orden *m* del día
agent *n* : agente *mf*, representante *mf*
aggravate *vt* **-vated; -vating 1** WORSEN : agravar, empeorar **2** ANNOY : irritar
aggregate *adj* : total, global — **～** *n* : total *m*
aggression *n* : agresión *f* — **aggressive** *adj* : agresivo — **aggressor** *n* : agresor *m*, -sora *f*
aghast *adj* : horrorizado
agile *adj* : ágil — **agility** *n, pl* **-ties** : agilidad *f*
agitate *v* **-tated; -tating** *vt* **1** SHAKE : agitar **2** TROUBLE : inquietar — **agitation** *n* : agitación *f*, inquietud *f*
agnostic *n* : agnóstico *m*, -ca *f*
ago *adv* **1** : hace **2 long ～** : hace mucho tiempo
agony *n, pl* **-nies 1** PAIN : dolor *m* **2** ANGUISH : angustia *f* — **agonize** *vi* **-nized; -nizing** : atormentarse — **agonizing** *adj* : angustioso
agree *v* **agreed; agreeing** *vt* **1** : acordar **2 ～ that** : estar de acuerdo de que — *vi* **1** : estar de acuerdo **2** CORRESPOND : concordar **3 ～ to** : acceder a **4 this climate ～s with me** : este clima me sienta bien — **agreeable** *adj* **1** PLEASING : agradable **2** WILLING : dispuesto — **agreement** *n* : acuerdo *m*
agriculture *n* : agricultura *f* — **agricultural** *adj* : agrícola
aground *adv* **run ～** : encallar
ahead *adv* **1** IN FRONT : delante, adelante **2** BEFOREHAND : por adelantado **3** LEADING : a la delantera **4 get ～** : adelantar — **ahead of** *prep* **1** : delante de, antes de **2 get ～ of** : adelantarse a
aid *vt* : ayudar — **～** *n* : ayuda *f*, asistencia *f*
AIDS *n* : SIDA *m*, sida *m*
ail *vi* : estar enfermo — **ailment** *n* : enfermedad *f*
aim *vt* : apuntar (un arma), dirigir (una observación) — *vi* **1** : apuntar **2** ASPIRE : aspirar — **～** *n* **1** : puntería *f* **2** GOAL : propósito *m*, objetivo *m* — **aimless** *adj* : sin objetivo
air *vt or* **～ out** : airear **2** EXPRESS : expresar **3** BROADCAST : emitir — **～** *n* **1** : aire *m* **2 be on the ～** : estar en el aire — **air–conditioning** *n* : aire *m* acondicionado — **air conditioned** *n* : climatizado — **aircraft** *ns & pl* **1** : avión *m*, aeronave *f* **2 ～ carrier** : portaaviones *m* — **air force** *n*

: fuerza *f* aérea — **airline** *n* : aerolínea *f*, línea *f* aérea — **airliner** *n* : avión *m* de pasajeros — **airmail** *n* : correo *m* aéreo — **airplane** *n* : avión *m* — **airport** *n* : aeropuerto *m* — **airstrip** *n* : pista *f* de aterrizaje — **airtight** *adj* : hermético — **airy** *adj* **airier; -est** : aireado, bien ventilado
aisle *n* **1** : pasillo *m* **2** : nave *f* lateral (de una iglesia)
ajar *adj* : entreabierto
akin *adj* **～ to** : semejante a
alarm *n* **1** : alarma *f* **2** ANXIETY : inquietud *f* — *vt* : alarmar, asustar — **alarm clock** *n* : despertador *m*
alas *interj* : ¡ay!
album *n* : álbum *m*
alcohol *n* : alcohol *m* — **alcoholic** *adj* : alcohólico — **～** *n* : alcohólico *m*, -ca *f* — **alcoholism** *n* : alcoholismo *m*
alcove *n* : nicho *m*, hueco *m*
ale *n* : cerveza *f*
alert *adj* **1** WATCHFUL : alerta, atento **2** LIVELY : vivo — **～** *n* : alerta *f* — **～** *vt* : alertar, poner sobre aviso
alfalfa *n* : alfalfa *f*
alga *n, pl* **-gae** : alga *f*
algebra *n* : álgebra *f*
alias *adv* : alias — **～** *n* : alias *m*
alibi *n* : coartada *f*
alien *adj* : extranjero — **～** *n* **1** FOREIGNER : extranjero *m*, -ra *f* **2** EXTRATERRESTRIAL : extraterrestre *mf*
alienate *vt* **-ated; -ating** : enajenar — **alienation** *n* : enajenación *f*
alight *vi* **1** LAND : posarse **2 ～ from** : apearse de
align *vt* : alinear — **alignment** *n* : alineación *f*
alike *adv* : igual, del mismo modo — **～** *adj* : parecido
alimony *n, pl* **-nies** : pensión *f* alimenticia
alive *adj* **1** LIVING : vivo, viviente **2** LIVELY : animado, activo
all *adv* **1** COMPLETELY : todo, completamente **2 ～ the better** : tanto mejor **3 ～ the more** : aún más, todavía más — **～** *adj* : todo — **～** *pron* **1** : todo, -da **2 ～ in ～** : en general **3 not at ～** : de ninguna manera — **all–around** *adj* VERSATILE : completo
allay *vt* **1** ALLEVIATE : aliviar **2** CALM : aquietar
allege *vt* **-leged; -leging** : alegar — **allegation** *n* : alegato *m*, acusación *f* — **alleged** *adj* : presunto — **allegedly** *adv* : supuestamente
allegiance *n* : lealtad *f*
allegory *n, pl* **-ries** : alegoría *f* — **allegorical** *adj* : alegórico

allergy *n, pl* **-gies** : alergia *f* — **allergic** *adj*
: alérgico
alleviate *vt* **-ated; -ating** : aliviar
alley *n, pl* **-leys** : callejón *m*
alliance *n* : alianza *f*
alligator *n* : caimán *m*
allocate *vt* **-cated; -cating** : asignar — **allocation** *n* : asignación *f*, reparto *m*
allot *vt* **-lotted; -lotting** : asignar — **allot-
ment** *n* : reparto *m*, asignación *f*
allow *vt* **1** PERMIT : permitir **2** GRANT : dar,
conceder **3** ADMIT : admitir **4** CONCEDE
: reconocer — *vi* ~ **for** : tener en cuenta —
allowance *n* **1** : pensión *f*, subsidio *m* **2**
make ~**s for** : tener en cuenta, disculpar
alloy *n* : aleación *f*
all right *adv* **1** YES : sí, de acuerdo **2** WELL
: bien **3** DEFINITELY : bien, sin duda — ~
adj : bien, bueno
allude *vi* **-luded; -luding** : aludir
allure *vt* **-lured; -luring** : atraer — **alluring**
adj : atrayente, seductor
allusion *n* : alusión *f*
ally *vi* **-lied; -lying** ~ **oneself with** : aliarse
con — ~ *n* : aliado *m*, -da *f*
almanac *n* : almanaque *m*
almighty *adj* : omnipotente, todopoderoso
almond *n* : almendra *f*
almost *adv* : casi
alms *ns & pl* : limosna *f*
alone *adv* : sólo, solamente, únicamente —
~ *adj* : solo
along *adv* **1** FORWARD : adelante **2** ~ **with**
: con, junto con **3** all ~ : desde el principio
— ~ *prep* : por, a lo largo de — **alongside**
adv : al costado — ~ *or* ~ **of** *prep* : al
lado de
aloof *adj* : distante, reservado
aloud *adv* : en voz alta
alphabet *n* : alfabeto *m* — **alphabetical** *or*
alphabetic *adj* : alfabético
already *adv* : ya
also *adv* : también, además
altar *n* : altar *m*
alter *vt* : alterar, modificar — **alteration** *n*
: alteración *f*, modificación *f*
alternate *adj* : alterno — ~ *v* **-nated; -nat-
ing** : alternar — **alternating current** *n*
: corriente *f* alterna — **alternative** *adj* : alternativo — ~ *n* : alternativa *f*
although *conj* : aunque
altitude *n* : altitud *f*
altogether *adv* **1** COMPLETELY : completamente, del todo **2** ON THE WHOLE : en
suma, en general
aluminum *n* : aluminio *m*
always *adv* **1** : siempre **2** FOREVER : para
siempre
am → **be**

amass *vt* : amasar, acumular
amateur *adj* : amateur — ~ *n* : amateur *mf*;
aficionado *m*, -da *f*
amaze *vt* **amazed; amazing** : asombrar —
amazement *n* : asombro *m* — **amazing** *adj*
: asombroso
ambassador *n* : embajador *m*, -dora *f*
amber *n* : ámbar *m*
ambiguous *adj* : ambiguo — **ambiguity** *n*,
pl **-ties** : ambigüedad *f*
ambition *n* : ambición *f* — **ambitious** *adj*
: ambicioso
ambivalence *n* : ambivalencia *f* — **ambiva-
lent** *adj* : ambivalente
amble *vi or* ~ **along** : andar sin prisa
ambulance *n* : ambulancia *f*
ambush *vt* : emboscar — ~ *n* : emboscada *f*
amen *interj* : amén
amenable *adj* ~ **to** : receptivo a
amend *vt* : enmendar — **amendment** *n* : enmienda *f* — **amends** *ns & pl* **make** ~ **for**
: reparar
amenities *npl* : servicios *mpl*, comodidades
fpl
American *adj* : americano
amethyst *n* : amatista *f*
amiable *adj* : amable, agradable
amicable *adj* : amigable, amistoso
amid *or* **amidst** *prep* : en medio de, entre
amiss *adv* **1** : mal **2 take sth** ~ : tomar
algo a mal — ~ *adj* **1** WRONG : malo **2**
something is ~ : algo anda mal
ammonia *n* : amoníaco *m*
ammunition *n* : municiones *fpl*
amnesia *n* : amnesia *f*
amnesty *n, pl* **-ties** : amnistía *f*
among *prep* : entre
amorous *adj* : amoroso
amount *vi* **1** ~ **to** : equivaler a **2** ~ **to**
TOTAL : sumar, ascender a — ~ *n* : canti-
dad *f*
amphibian *n* : anfibio *m* — **amphibious** *adj*
: anfibio
amphitheater *n* : anfiteatro *m*
ample *adj* **-pler; -plest 1** SPACIOUS : amplio, extenso **2** ABUNDANT : abundante
amplify *vt* **-fied; -fying** : amplificar — **amplifier** *n* : amplificador *m*
amputate *vt* **-tated; -tating** : amputar —
amputation *n* : amputación *f*
amuse *vt* **amused; amusing 1** : hacer reír,
divertir **2** ENTERTAIN : entretener —
amusement *n* : diversión *f* — **amusing** *adj*
: divertido
an → **a²**
analogy *n, pl* **-gies** : analogía *f* — **analogous** *adj* : análogo
analysis *n, pl* **-yses** : análisis *m* — **analytic**

or **analytical** *adj* : analítico — **analyze** *vt*
-lyzed; -lyzing : analizar

anarchy *n* : anarquía *f*

anatomy *n, pl* **-mies** : anatomía *f* —
anatomic *or* **anatomical** *adj* : anatómico

ancestor *n* : antepasado *m*, -da *f* — **ancestral** *adj* : ancestral — **ancestry** *n* **1** DE-
SCENT : linaje *m*, abolengo *m* **2** ANCESTORS
: antepasados *mpl*, -das *fpl*

anchor *n* **1** : ancla *f* **2** : presentador *m*, -dora
f (en televisión) — **∼** *vt* **1** : anclar **2** FAS-
TEN : sujetar — *vi* : anclar

anchovy *n, pl* **-vies** *or* **-vy** : anchoa *f*

ancient *adj* : antiguo, viejo

and *conj* **1** : y (e *before words beginning
with i- or hi-*) **2 come ∼ see** : ven a ver **3
more ∼ more** : cada vez más **4 try ∼ finish it soon** : trata de terminarlo pronto

anecdote *n* : anécdota *f*

anemia *n* : anemia *f* — **anemic** *adj* : anémico

anesthesia *n* : anestesia *f* — **anesthetic** *adj*
: anestésico — **∼** *n* : anestésico *m*

anew *adv* : de nuevo, nuevamente

angel *n* : ángel *m* — **angelic** *or* **angelical**
adj : angélico

anger *vt* : enojar, enfadar — **∼** *n* : ira *f*,
enojo *m*, enfado *m*

angle *n* **1** : ángulo *m* **2** POINT OF VIEW : perspectiva *f*, punto *m* de vista — **angler** *n*
: pescador *m*, -dora *f*

Anglo–Saxon *adj* : anglosajón

angry *adj* **-grier; -est** : enojado, enfadado

anguish *n* : angustia *f*

angular *adj* **1** : angular **2 ∼ features** : rasgos *mpl* angulosos

animal *n* : animal *m*

animate *adj* : animado — **∼** *vt* **-mated;
-mating** : animar — **animated** *adj* **1** : animado **2 ∼ cartoon** : dibujos *mpl* animados — **animation** *n* : animación *f*

animosity *n, pl* **-ties** : animosidad *f*

anise *n* : anís *m*

ankle *n* : tobillo *m*

annals *npl* : anales *mpl*

annex *vt* : anexar — **∼** *n* : anexo *m*

annihilate *vt* **-lated; -lating** : aniquilar —
annihilation *n* : aniquilación *f*

anniversary *n, pl* **-ries** : aniversario *m*

annotate *vt* **-tated; -tating** : anotar — **annotation** *n* : anotación *f*

announce *vt* **-nounced; -nouncing** : anunciar — **announcement** *n* : anuncio *m* —
announcer *n* : locutor *m*, -tora *f*

annoy *vt* : fastidiar, molestar — **annoyance**
n : fastidio *m*, molestia *f* — **annoying** *adj*
: molesto, fastidioso

annual *adj* : anual — **∼** *n* : anuario *m*

annuity *n, pl* **-ties** : anualidad *f*

annul *vt* **annulled; annulling** : anular — **annulment** *n* : anulación *f*

anoint *vt* : ungir

anomaly *n, pl* **-lies** : anomalía *f*

anonymous *adj* : anónimo — **anonymity** *n*
: anonimato *m*

another *adj* **1** : otro **2 in ∼ minute** : en un
minuto más — **∼** *pron* : otro, otra

answer *n* **1** REPLY : respuesta *f*, contestación
f **2** SOLUTION : solución *f* — **∼** *vt* **1** : contestar a, responder a **2 ∼ the door** : abrir
la puerta — *vi* : contestar, responder

ant *n* : hormiga *f*

antagonize *vt* **-nized; -nizing** : provocar la
enemistad de — **antagonism** *n* : antagonismo *m*

antarctic *adj* : antártico

antelope *n, pl* **-lope** *or* **-lopes** : antílope *m*

antenna *n, pl* **-nae** *or* **-nas** : antena *f*

anthem *n* : himno *m*

anthology *n, pl* **-gies** : antología *f*

anthropology *n* : antropología *f*

antibiotic *adj* : antibiótico — **∼** *n* : antibiótico *m*

antibody *n, pl* **-bodies** : anticuerpo *m*

anticipate *vt* **-pated; -pating 1** FORESEE
: anticipar, prever **2** EXPECT : esperar — **anticipation** *n* : anticipación *f*, expectación *f*

antics *npl* : payasadas *fpl*

antidote *n* : antídoto *m*

antifreeze *n* : anticongelante *m*

antipathy *n, pl* **-thies** : antipatía *f*

antiquated *adj* : anticuado

antique *adj* : antiguo — **∼** *n* : antigüedad *f*
— **antiquity** *n, pl* **-ties** : antigüedad *f*

anti–Semitic *adj* : antisemita

antiseptic *adj* : antiséptico — **∼** *n* : antiséptico *m*

antisocial *adj* **1** : antisocial **2** UNSOCIABLE
: poco sociable

antithesis *n, pl* **-eses** : antítesis *f*

antlers *npl* : cornamenta *f*

antonym *n* : antónimo *m*

anus *n* : ano *m*

anvil *n* : yunque *m*

anxiety *n, pl* **-eties 1** APPREHENSION : inquietud *f*, ansiedad *f* **2** EAGERNESS : anhelo
m — **anxious** *adj* **1** WORRIED : inquieto,
preocupado **2** EAGER : ansioso — **anx-
iously** *adv* : con ansiedad

any *adv* **1** SOMEWHAT : algo, un poco **2 it's
not ∼ good** : no sirve para nada **3 we
can't wait ∼ longer** : no podemos esperar
más — **∼** *adj* **1** : alguno **2** (*in negative
constructions*) : ningún **3** WHATEVER
: cualquier **4 in ∼ case** : en todo caso —
∼ *pron* **1** : alguno, -na **2** : ninguno, -na **3
do you want ∼ more rice?** : ¿quieres más
arroz?

anybody → **anyone**

anyhow *adv* **1** : de todas formas **2** HAPHAZARDLY : de cualquier modo

anymore *adv* **not ~** : ya no

anyone *pron* **1** SOMEONE : alguien **2** WHOEVER : quienquiera **3 I don't see ~** : no veo a nadie

anyplace → **anywhere**

anything *pron* **1** SOMETHING : algo, alguna cosa **2** (*in negative constructions*) : nada **3** WHATEVER : cualquier cosa, lo que sea

anytime *adv* : en cualquier momento

anyway → **anyhow**

anywhere *adv* **1** : en cualquier parte, dondequiera **2** (*used in questions*) : en algún sitio **3 I can't find it ~** : no lo encuentro por ninguna parte

apart *adv* **1** : aparte **2 ~ from** : excepto, aparte de **3 fall ~** : deshacerse, hacerse pedazos **4 live ~** : vivir separados **5 take ~** : desmontar, desmantelar

apartment *n* : apartamento *m*

apathy *n* : apatía *f* — **apathetic** *adj* : apático, indiferente

ape *n* : simio *m*

aperture *n* : abertura *f*

apex *n, pl* **apexes** *or* **apices** : ápice *m,* cumbre *f*

apiece *adv* : cada uno

aplomb *n* : aplomo *m*

apology *n, pl* **-gies** : disculpa *f* — **apologetic** *adj* : lleno de disculpas — **apologize** *vi* **-gized; -gizing** : disculparse, pedir perdón

apostle *n* : apóstol *m*

apostrophe *n* : apóstrofo *m*

appall *vt* : horrorizar — **appalling** *adj* : horroroso

apparatus *n, pl* **-tuses** *or* **-tus** : aparato *m*

apparel *n* : ropa *f*

apparent *adj* **1** OBVIOUS : claro, evidente **2** SEEMING : aparente — **apparently** *adv* : al parecer, por lo visto

apparition *n* : aparición *f*

appeal *vi* **1 ~ for** : solicitar **2 ~ to** : apelar a (la bondad de algn, etc.) **3 ~ to** ATTRACT : atraer a — **~** *n* **1** : apelación *f* (en derecho) **2** REQUEST : llamamiento *m* **3** ATTRACTION : atractivo *m* — **appealing** *adj* : atractivo

appear *vi* **1** : aparecer **2** : comparecer (ante un tribunal), actuar (en el teatro) **3** SEEM : parecer — **appearance** *n* **1** : aparición *f* **2** LOOK : apariencia *f,* aspecto *m*

appease *vt* **-peased; -peasing** : apaciguar, aplacar

appendix *n, pl* **-dixes** *or* **-dices** : apéndice *m* — **appendicitis** *n* : apendicitis *f*

appetite *n* : apetito *m* — **appetizer** *n* : aperitivo *m* — **appetizing** *adj* : apetitoso

applaud *v* : aplaudir — **applause** *n* : aplauso *m*

apple *n* : manzana *f*

appliance *n* : aparato *m*

apply *v* **-plied; -plying** *vt* **1** : aplicar **2 ~ oneself** : aplicarse — *vi* **1** : aplicarse **2 ~ for** : solicitar, pedir — **applicable** *adj* : aplicable — **applicant** *n* : solicitante *mf;* candidato *m,* -ta *f* — **application** *n* **1** : aplicación *f* **2** : solicitud *f* (para un empleo, etc.)

appoint *vt* **1** NAME : nombrar **2** FIX, SET : fijar, señalar — **appointment** *n* **1** APPOINTING : nombramiento *m* **2** ENGAGEMENT : cita *f*

apportion *vt* : distribuir, repartir

appraise *vt* **-praised; -praising** : evaluar, valorar — **appraisal** *n* : evaluación *f*

appreciate *v* **-ated; -ating** *vt* **1** VALUE : apreciar **2** UNDERSTAND : darse cuenta de **3 I ~ your help** : te agradezco tu ayuda — *vi* : aumentar en valor — **appreciation** *n* **1** GRATITUDE : agradecimiento *m* **2** VALUING : apreciación *f,* valoración *f* — **appreciative** *adj* **1** : apreciativo **2** GRATEFUL : agradecido

apprehend *vt* **1** ARREST : aprehender, detener **2** DREAD : temer **3** COMPREHEND : comprender — **apprehension** *n* **1** ARREST : detención *f,* aprehensión *f* **2** ANXIETY : aprensión *f,* temor *m* — **apprehensive** *adj* : aprensivo, inquieto

apprentice *n* : aprendiz *m,* -diza *f*

approach *vt* **1** NEAR : acercarse a **2** : dirigirse a (algn), abordar (un problema, etc.) — *vi* : acercarse — **~** *n* **1** NEARING : acercamiento *m* **2** POSITION : enfoque *m* **3** ACCESS : acceso *m* — **approachable** *adj* : accesible, asequible

appropriate *vt* **-ated; -ating** : apropiarse de — **~** *adj* : apropiado

approve *vt* **-proved; -proving** : aprobar — **approval** *n* : aprobación *f*

approximate *adj* : aproximado — **~** *vt* **-mated; -mating** : aproximarse a — **approximately** *adv* : aproximadamente

apricot *n* : albaricoque *m,* chabacano *m Lat*

April *n* : abril *m*

apron *n* : delantal *m*

apropos *adv* : a propósito

apt *adj* **1** FITTING : apto, apropiado **2** LIABLE : propenso — **aptitude** *n* : aptitud *f*

aquarium *n, pl* **-iums** *or* **-ia** : acuario *m*

aquatic *adj* : acuático

aqueduct *n* : acueducto *m*

Arab *n* : árabe — **Arabic** *adj* : árabe — **~** *n* : árabe *m* (idioma)

arbitrary *adj* : arbitrario

arbitrate *v* **-trated; -trating** : arbitrar — **arbitration** *n* : arbitraje *m*

arc *n* : arco *m*

arcade *n* **1** : arcada *f* **2 shopping ~** : galería *f* comercial

arch *n* : arco *m* — **~** *vt* : arquear — *vi* : arquearse

archaeology *or* **archeology** *n* : arqueología *f* — **archaeological** *adj* : arque-ológico — **archaeologist** *n* : arqueólogo *m*, -ga *f*

archaic *adj* : arcaico

archbishop *n* : arzobispo *m*

archery *n* : tiro *m* al arco

archipelago *n, pl* **-goes** *or* **-gos** : archipiélago *m*

architecture *n* : arquitectura *f* — **architect** *n* : arquitecto *m*, -ta *f* — **architectural** *adj* : arquitectónico

archives *npl* : archivo *m*

archway *n* : arco *m* (de entrada)

arctic *adj* : ártico

ardent *adj* : ardiente, fervoroso — **ardor** *n* : ardor *m*, fervor *m*

arduous *adj* : arduo

are → **be**

area *n* **1** REGION : área *f*, zona *f* **2** FIELD : campo *m* **3 ~ code** : código *m* de la zona *Lat*, prefijo *m Spain*

arena *n* : arena *f*, ruedo *m*

aren't (*contraction of* **are not**) → **be**

Argentine *or* **Argentinean** *or* **Argentinian** *adj* : argentino

argue *v* **-gued; -guing** *vi* **1** QUARREL : discutir **2 ~ against** : argumentar contra — *vt* : argumentar, sostener — **argument** *n* **1** QUARREL : disputa *f*, discusión *f* **2** REASONING : argumentos *mpl*

arid *adj* : árido — **aridity** *n* : aridez *f*

arise *vi* **arose; arisen; arising 1** : levantarse **2 ~ from** : surgir de

aristocracy *n, pl* **-cies** : aristocracia *f* — **aristocrat** *n* : aristócrata *mf* — **aristocratic** *adj* : aristocrático

arithmetic *n* : aritmética *f*

ark *n* : arca *f*

arm *n* **1** : brazo *m* **2** WEAPON : arma *f* — **~** *vt* : armar — **armament** *n* : armamento *m* — **armchair** *n* : sillón *m* — **armed** *adj* **1 ~ forces** : fuerzas *fpl* armadas **2 ~ robbery** : robo *m* a mano armada

armistice *n* : armisticio *m*

armor *or Brit* **armour** *n* : armadura *f* — **armored** *or Brit* **armoured** *adj* : blindado, acorazado — **armory** *or Brit* **armoury** *n* : arsenal *m*

armpit *n* : axila *f*, sobaco *m*

army *n, pl* **-mies** : ejército *m*

aroma *n* : aroma *m* — **aromatic** *adj* : aromático

around *adv* **1** : de circunferencia **2** NEARBY : por ahí **3** APPROXIMATELY : más o menos, aproximadamente **4 all ~** : por todos lados, todo alrededor **5 turn ~** : voltearse — **~** *prep* **1** SURROUNDING : alrededor de **2** THROUGHOUT : por **3** NEAR : cerca de **4 ~ the corner** : a la vuelta de la esquina

arouse *vt* **aroused; arousing 1** AWAKE : despertar **2** EXCITE : excitar

arrange *vt* **-ranged; -ranging** : arreglar, poner en orden — **arrangement** *n* **1** ORDER : arreglo *m* **2 ~s** *npl* : preparativos *mpl*

array *n* : selección *f*, surtido *m*

arrears *npl* **1** : atrasos *mpl* **2 be in ~** : estar atrasado en pagos

arrest *vt* : detener — **~** *n* **1** : arresto *m*, detención *f* **2 under ~** : detenido

arrive *vi* **-rived; -riving** : llegar — **arrival** *n* : llegada *f*

arrogance *n* : arrogancia *f* — **arrogant** *adj* : arrogante

arrow *n* : flecha *f*

arsenal *n* : arsenal *m*

arsenic *n* : arsénico *m*

arson *n* : incendio *m* premeditado

art *n* **1** : arte *m* **2 ~s** *npl* : letras *fpl* (en educación) **3 fine ~s** : bellas artes *fpl*

artefact *Brit* → **artifact**

artery *n, pl* **-teries** : arteria *f*

artful *adj* : astuto, taimado

arthritis *n, pl* **-tides** : artritis *f* — **arthritic** *adj* : artrítico

artichoke *n* : alcachofa *f*

article *n* : artículo *m*

articulate *vt* **-lated; -lating** : articular — **~** *adj* **be ~** : expresarse bien

artifact *or Brit* **artefact** *n* : artefacto *m*

artificial *adj* : artificial

artillery *n, pl* **-leries** : artillería *f*

artisan *n* : artesano *m*, -na *f*

artist *n* : artista *mf* — **artistic** *adj* : artístico

as *adv* **1** : tan, tanto **2 ~ much** : tanto como **3 ~ tall ~** : tan alto como **4 ~ well** : también — **~** *conj* **1** WHILE : mientras **2** (*referring to manner*) : como **3** SINCE : ya que **4** THOUGH : por más que — **~** *prep* **1** : de **2** LIKE : como — **~** *pron* : que

asbestos *n* : asbesto *m*, amianto *m*

ascend *vi* : ascender, subir — *vt* : subir (a) — **ascent** *n* : ascensión *f*, subida *f*

ascertain *vt* : averiguar, determinar

ascribe *vt* **-cribed; -cribing** : atribuir

as for *prep* : en cuanto a

ash[1] *n* : ceniza *f*

ash[2] *n* : fresno *m* (árbol)

ashamed *adj* : avergonzado, apenado *Lat*

ashore *adv* **1** : en tierra **2 go ~** : desembarcar

ashtray *n* : cenicero *m*

Asian *adj* : asiático

aside *adv* **1** : a un lado **2** APART : aparte **3 set ~** : guardar — **aside from** *prep* **1** BESIDES : además de **2** EXCEPT : aparte de, menos

as if *conj* : como si

ask *vt* **1** : preguntar **2** REQUEST : pedir **3** INVITE : invitar — *vi* : preguntar

askance *adv* **look ~** : mirar de soslayo

askew *adj* : torcido, ladeado

asleep *adj* **1** : dormido **2 fall ~** : dormirse, quedarse dormido

as of *prep* : desde, a partir de

asparagus *n* : espárrago *m*

aspect *n* : aspecto *m*

asphalt *n* : asfalto *m*

asphyxiate *v* **-ated; -ating** *vt* : asfixiar — **asphyxiation** *n* : asfixia *f*

aspire *vi* **-pired; -piring** : aspirar — **aspiration** *n* : aspiración *f*

aspirin *n, pl* **aspirin** *or* **aspirins** : aspirina *f*

ass *n* **1** : asno *m* **2** IDIOT : imbécil *mf*, idiota *mf*

assail *vt* : atacar, asaltar — **assailant** *n* : asaltante *mf*, atacante *mf*

assassin *n* : asesino *m*, -na *f* — **assassinate** *vt* **-nated; -nating** : asesinar — **assassination** *n* : asesinato *m*

assault *n* **1** : ataque *m*, asalto *m* **2** : agresión *f* (contra algn) — **~** *vt* : atacar, asaltar

assemble *v* **-bled; -bling** *vt* **1** GATHER : reunir, juntar **2** CONSTRUCT : montar — *vi* : reunirse — **assembly** *n, pl* **-blies 1** MEETING : reunión *f*, asamblea *f* **2** CONSTRUCTING : montaje *m*

assent *vi* : asentir, consentir — **~** *n* : asentimiento *m*

assert *vt* **1** : afirmar **2 ~ oneself** : hacerse valer — **assertion** *n* : afirmación *f* — **assertive** *adj* : firme, enérgico

assess *vt* : evaluar, valorar — **assessment** *n* : evaluación *f*, valoración *f*

asset *n* **1** : ventaja *f*, recurso *m* **2 ~s** *npl* : bienes *mpl*, activo *m*

assiduous *adj* : asiduo

assign *vt* **1** APPOINT : designar, nombrar **2** ALLOT : asignar — **assignment** *n* **1** TASK : misión *f* **2** HOMEWORK : tarea *f* **3** ASSIGNING : asignación *f*

assimilate *vt* **-lated; -lating** : asimilar

assist *vt* : ayudar — **assistance** *n* : ayuda *f* — **assistant** *n* : ayudante *mf*

associate *v* **-ated; -ating** *vt* : asociar — *vi* : asociarse — **~** *n* : asociado *m*, -da *f*; socio *m*, -cia *f* — **association** *n* : asociación *f*

as soon as *conj* : tan pronto como

assorted *adj* : surtido — **assortment** *n* : surtido *m*, variedad *f*

assume *vt* **-sumed; -suming 1** SUPPOSE : suponer **2** UNDERTAKE : asumir **3** TAKE ON : adquirir, tomar — **assumption** *n* : suposición *f*

assure *vt* **-sured; -suring** : asegurar — **assurance** *n* **1** CERTAINTY : certeza *f*, garantía *f* **2** CONFIDENCE : confianza *f*, seguridad *f* (de sí mismo)

asterisk *n* : asterisco *m*

asthma *n* : asma *m*

as though → **as if**

as to *prep* : sobre, acerca de

astonish *vt* : asombrar — **astonishing** *adj* : asombroso — **astonishment** *n* : asombro *m*

astound *vt* : asombrar, pasmar — **astounding** *adj* : asombroso, pasmoso

astray *adv* **1 go ~** : extraviarse **2 lead ~** : llevar por mal camino

astrology *n* : astrología *f*

astronaut *n* : astronauta *mf*

astronomy *n, pl* **-mies** : astronomía *f* — **astronomer** *n* : astrónomo *m*, -ma *f* — **astronomical** *adj* : astronómico

astute *adj* : astuto, sagaz — **astuteness** *n* : astucia *f*

as well as *conj* : tanto como — **~** *prep* : además de, aparte de

asylum *n* **1** : asilo *m* **2 insane ~** : manicomio *m*

at *prep* **1** : a **2 ~ home** : en casa **3 ~ night** : en la noche, por la noche **4 ~ two o'clock** : a las dos **5 be angry ~** : estar enojado con **6 laugh ~** : reírse de — **at all** *adv* **not ~** : en absoluto, nada

ate → **eat**

atheist *n* : ateo *m*, atea *f* — **atheism** *n* : ateísmo *m*

athlete *n* : atleta *mf* — **athletic** *adj* : atlético — **athletics** *ns & pl* : atletismo *m*

atlas *n* : atlas *m*

atmosphere *n* **1** : atmósfera *f* **2** AMBIENCE : ambiente *m* — **atmospheric** *adj* : atmosférico

atom *n* : átomo *m* — **atomic** *adj* : atómico

atomizer *n* : atomizador *m*

atone *vt* **atoned; atoning ~ for** : expiar

atrocity *n, pl* **-ties** : atrocidad *f* — **atrocious** *adj* : atroz

atrophy *vi* **-phied; -phying** : atrofiarse

attach *vt* **1** : sujetar, atar **2** : adjuntar (un documento, etc.) **3 ~ importance to** : atribuir importancia a **4 become ~ed to s.o.** : encariñarse con algn — **attachment** *n* **1** ACCESSORY : accesorio *m* **2** FONDNESS : cariño *m*

attack *v* : atacar — **~** *n* : ataque *m* — **attacker** *n* : agresor *m*, -sora *f*

attain *vt* : lograr, alcanzar — **attainment** *n* : logro *m*

attempt *vt* : intentar — $\sim$ *n* : intento *m*

attend *vt* : asistir a — *vi* **1** : asistir **2** $\sim$ **to** : ocuparse de — **attendance** *n* **1** : asistencia *f* **2** TURNOUT : concurrencia *f* — **attendant** *n* : encargado *m*, -da *f*; asistente *mf*

attention *n* **1** : atención *f* **2 pay** $\sim$: prestar atención, hacer caso — **attentive** *adj* : atento

attest *vt* : atestiguar

attic *n* : desván *m*

attire *n* : atavío *m*

attitude *n* **1** : actitud *f* **2** POSTURE : postura *f*

attorney *n, pl* **-neys** : abogado *m*, -da *f*

attract *vt* : atraer — **attraction** *n* **1** : atracción *f* **2** APPEAL : atractivo *m* — **attractive** *adj* : atractivo, atrayente

attribute *n* : atributo *m* — $\sim$ *vt* **-tributed; -tributing** : atribuir, imputar

auburn *adj* : castaño rojizo

auction *n* : subasta *f* — $\sim$ *vt or* $\sim$ **off** : subastar

audacious *adj* : audaz — **audacity** *n, pl* **-ties** : audacia *f*, atrevimiento *m*

audible *adj* : audible

audience *n* **1** INTERVIEW : audiencia *f* **2** PUBLIC : público *m*

audiovisual *adj* : audiovisual

audition *n* : audición *f*

auditor *n* **1** : auditor *m*, -tora *f* (de finanzas) **2** STUDENT : oyente *mf*

auditorium *n, pl* **-riums** *or* **-ria** : auditorio *m*

augment *vt* : aumentar

augur *vi* $\sim$ **well** : ser de buen agüero

August *n* : agosto *m*

aunt *n* : tía *f*

aura *n* : aura *f*

auspices *npl* : auspicios *mpl*

auspicious *adj* : propicio, prometedor

austere *adj* : austero — **austerity** *n, pl* **-ties** : austeridad *f*

Australian *adj* : australiano

authentic *adj* : auténtico

author *n* : autor *m*, -tora *f*

authority *n, pl* **-ties** : autoridad *f* — **authoritarian** *adj* : autoritario — **authoritative** *adj* **1** RELIABLE : autorizado **2** DICTATORIAL : autoritario — **authorization** *n* : autorización *f* — **authorize** *vt* **-rized; -rizing** : autorizar

autobiography *n, pl* **-phies** : autobiografía *f* — **autobiographical** *adj* : autobiográfico

autograph *n* : autógrafo *m* — $\sim$ *vt* : autografiar

automatic *adj* : automático — **automate** *vt* **-mated; -mating** : automatizar — **automation** *n* : automatización *f*

automobile *n* : automóvil *m*

autonomy *n, pl* **-mies** : autonomía *f* — **autonomous** *adj* : autónomo

autopsy *n, pl* **-sies** : autopsia *f*

autumn *n* : otoño *m*

auxiliary *adj* : auxiliar — $\sim$ *n, pl* **-ries** : auxiliar *mf*

avail *vt* $\sim$ **oneself of** : aprovecharse de — $\sim$ *n* **to no** $\sim$: en vano — **available** *adj* : disponible — **availability** *n, pl* **-ties** : disponibilidad *f*

avalanche *n* : avalancha *f*

avarice *n* : avaricia *f*

avenge *vt* **avenged; avenging** : vengar

avenue *n* **1** : avenida *f* **2** MEANS : vía *f*

average *n* : promedio *m* — $\sim$ *adj* **1** MEAN : medio **2** ORDINARY : regular, ordinario — $\sim$ *vt* **-aged; -aging 1** : hacer un promedio de **2** *or* $\sim$ **out** : calcular el promedio de

averse *adj* **be** $\sim$ **to** : sentir aversión por — **aversion** *n* : aversión *f*

avert *vt* **1** AVOID : evitar, prevenir **2** $\sim$ **one's eyes** : apartar los ojos

aviation *n* : aviación *f* — **aviator** *n* : aviador *m*, -dora *f*

avid *adj* : ávido — **avidly** *adv* : con avidez

avocado *n, pl* **-dos** : aguacate *m*

avoid *vt* : evitar — **avoidable** *adj* : evitable

await *vt* : esperar

awake *v* **awoke; awoken** *or* **awaked; awaking** : despertar — $\sim$ *adj* : despierto — **awaken** *v* → **awake**

award *vt* **1** : otorgar, conceder (un premio, etc.) **2** : adjudicar (daños y perjuicios) — $\sim$ *n* **1** PRIZE : premio *m* **2** : adjudicación *f*

aware *adj* **be** $\sim$ **of** : estar consciente de — **awareness** *n* : conciencia *f*

away *adv* **1** (*referring to distance*) : de aquí, de distancia **2 far** $\sim$: lejos **3 give** $\sim$: regalar **4 go** $\sim$: irse **5 right** $\sim$: en seguida **6 take** $\sim$: quitar — $\sim$ *adj* **1** ABSENT : ausente **2** $\sim$ **game** : partido *m* fuera de casa

awe *n* : temor *m* reverencial — **awesome** *adj* : imponente, formidable

awful *adj* **1** : terrible, espantoso **2 an** $\sim$ **lot** : muchísimo — **awfully** *adv* : terriblemente

awhile *adv* : un rato

awkward *adj* **1** CLUMSY : torpe **2** EMBARRASSING : embarazoso, delicado **3** DIFFICULT : difícil — **awkwardly** *adv* **1** : con dificultad **2** CLUMSILY : de manera torpe

awning *n* : toldo *m*

awry *adj* **1** ASKEW : torcido **2 go** $\sim$: salir mal

ax *or* **axe** *n* : hacha *f*

axiom *n* : axioma *m*

axis *n, pl* **axes** : eje *m*

axle *n* : eje *m*

B

b *n, pl* **b's** *or* **bs** : b, segunda letra del alfabeto inglés

babble *vi* **-bled; -bling** 1 : balbucear 2 MURMUR : murmurar — **~** *n* : balbuceo *m* (de bebé), murmullo *m* (de voces, de un arroyo)

baboon *n* : babuino *m*

baby *n, pl* **-bies** : bebé *m*; niño *m*, -ña *f* — **baby** *vt* **-bied; -bying** : mimar, consentir — **babyish** *adj* : infantil — **baby–sit** *vi* **-sat; -sitting** : cuidar a los niños

bachelor *n* 1 : soltero *m* 2 GRADUATE : licenciado *m*, -da *f*

back *n* 1 : espalda *f* 2 REVERSE : reverso *m*, dorso *m*, revés *m* 3 REAR : fondo *m*, parte *f* trasera 4 : defensa *mf* (en deportes) — **~** *adv* 1 : atrás 2 **be ~** : estar de vuelta 3 **go ~** : volver 4 **two years ~** : hace dos años — **~** *adj* 1 REAR : de atrás, trasero 2 OVERDUE : atrasado — **~** *vt* 1 SUPPORT : apoyar 2 *or* **~ up** : darle marcha atrás a (un vehículo) — *vi* 1 **~ down** : volverse atrás 2 **~ up** : retroceder — **backache** *n* : dolor *m* de espalda — **backbone** *n* : columna *f* vertebral — **backfire** *vi* **-fired; -firing** : petardear — **background** *n* 1 : fondo *m* (de un cuadro, etc.), antecedentes *mpl* (de una situación) 2 EXPERIENCE : formación *f* — **backhand** *adv* : de revés, con el revés — **backhanded** *adj* : indirecto — **backing** *n* : apoyo *m*, respaldo *m* — **backlash** *n* : reacción *f* violenta — **backlog** *n* : atrasos *mpl* — **backpack** *n* : mochila *f* — **backstage** *adv & adj* : entre bastidores — **backtrack** *vi* : dar marcha atrás — **backup** *n* 1 SUPPORT : respaldo *m*, apoyo *m* 2 : copia *f* de seguridad (para computadoras) — **backward** *or* **backwards** *adv* 1 : hacia atrás 2 **do it ~** : hacerlo al revés 3 **fall ~** : caer de espaldas 4 **bend over ~s** : hacer todo lo posible — **backward** *adj* 1 : hacia atrás 2 RETARDED : retrasado 3 SHY : tímido 4 UNDERDEVELOPED : atrasado

bacon *n* : tocino *m*, tocineta *f Lat*, bacon *m Spain*

bacteria : bacterias *fpl*

bad *adj* **worse; worst** 1 : malo 2 ROTTEN : podrido 3 SEVERE : grave 4 **from ~ to worse** : de mal en peor 5 **too ~!** : ¡qué lástima! — **~** *adv* → **badly**

badge *n* : insignia *f*, chapa *f*

badger *n* : tejón *m* — **~** *vt* : acosar

badly *adv* 1 : mal 2 SEVERELY : gravemente 3 **want ~** : desear mucho

baffle *vi* **-fled; -fling** : desconcertar

bag *n* 1 : bolsa *f*, saco *m* 2 HANDBAG : bolso *m*, cartera *f Lat* 3 SUITCASE : maleta *f* — **~** *vt* **bagged; bagging** : ensacar, poner en una bolsa

baggage *n* : equipaje *m*

baggy *adj* **-gier; -est** : holgado

bail *n* : fianza *f* — **~** *vt* 1 : achicar (agua de un bote) 2 **~ out** RELEASE : poner en libertad bajo fianza 3 **~ out** EXTRICATE : sacar de apuros

bailiff *n* : alguacil *mf*

bait *vt* 1 : cebar 2 HARASS : acosar — **~** *n* : cebo *m*, carnada *f*

bake *v* **baked; baking** *vt* : cocer al horno — *vi* : cocerse (al horno) — **baker** *n* : panadero *m*, -ra *f* — **bakery** *n, pl* **-ries** : panadería *f*

balance *n* 1 SCALES : balanza *f* 2 COUNTERBALANCE : contrapeso *m* 3 EQUILIBRIUM : equilibrio *m* 4 REMAINDER : resto *m* 5 *or* **bank ~** : saldo *m* — **~** *v* **-anced; -ancing** *vt* 1 : hacer el balance de (una cuenta) 2 EQUALIZE : equilibrar 3 WEIGH : sopesar — *vi* 1 : sostenerse en equilibrio 2 : cuadrar (dícese de una cuenta)

balcony *n, pl* **-nies** 1 : balcón *m* 2 : galería *f* (de un teatro)

bald *adj* 1 : calvo 2 WORN : pelado 3 **the ~ truth** : la pura verdad

bale *n* : bala *f*, fardo *m*

baleful *adj* : siniestro

balk *vi* **~ at** : resistirse a

ball *n* 1 : pelota *f*, bola *f*, balón *m* 2 DANCE : baile *m* 3 **~ of string** : ovillo *m* de cuerda

ballad *n* : balada *f*

ballast *n* : lastre *m*

ball bearing *n* : cojinete *m* de bola

ballerina *n* : bailarina *f*

ballet *n* : ballet *m*

ballistic *adj* : balístico

balloon *n* : globo *m*

ballot *n* 1 : papeleta *f* (de voto) 2 VOTING : votación *f*

ballpoint pen *n* : bolígrafo *m*

ballroom *n* : sala *f* de baile

balm *n* : bálsamo *m* — **balmy** *adj* **balmier; -est** : templado, agradable

baloney *n* NONSENSE : tonterías *fpl*

bamboo *n* : bambú *m*

bamboozle *vt* **-zled; -zling** : engañar, embaucar

ban *vt* **banned; banning** : prohibir — **~** *n* : prohibición *f*

banal *adj* : banal

banana *n* : plátano *m*, banana *f Lat*, banano *m Lat*

band *n* **1** STRIP : banda *f* **2** GROUP : banda *f*, grupo *m*, conjunto *m* — **~** *vi* **~ together** : unirse, juntarse

bandage *n* : vendaje *m*, venda *f* — **~** *vt* **-daged; -daging** : vendar

bandit *n* : bandido *m*, **-da** *f*

bandy *vt* **-died; -dying ~ about** : circular, repetir

bang *vt* **1** STRIKE : golpear **2** SLAM : cerrar de un golpe — *vi* **1** SLAM : cerrarse de un golpe **2 ~ on** : golpear — **~** *n* **1** BLOW : golpe *m* **2** NOISE : estrépito *m* **3** SLAM : portazo *m*

bangle *n* : brazalete *m*, pulsera *f*

bangs *npl* : flequillo *m*

banish *vt* : desterrar

banister *n* : pasamanos *m*, barandal *m*

bank *n* **1** : banco *m* **2** : orilla *f*, ribera *f* (de un río) **3** EMBANKMENT : terraplén *m* — **~** *vt* : depositar — *vi* **1** : ladearse (dícese de un avión) **2** : tener una cuenta (en un banco) **3 ~ on** : contar con — **banker** *n* : banquero *m*, **-ra** *f* — **banking** *n* : banca *f*

bankrupt *adj* : en bancarrota, en quiebra — **bankruptcy** *n*, *pl* **-cies** : quiebra *f*, bancarrota *f*

banner *n* : bandera *f*, pancarta *f*

banquet *n* : banquete *m*

banter *n* : bromas *fpl* — **~** *vi* : hacer bromas

baptize *vt* **-tized; -tizing** : bautizar — **baptism** *n* : bautismo *m*

bar *n* **1** : barra *f* **2** BARRIER : barrera *f*, obstáculo *m* **3** COUNTER : mostrador *m*, barra *f* **4** TAVERN : bar *m* **5 behind ~s** : entre rejas **6 ~ of soap** : pastilla *f* de jabón — **~** *vt* **barred; barring 1** OBSTRUCT : obstruir, bloquear **2** EXCLUDE : excluir **3** PROHIBIT : prohibir — **~** *prep* **1** : excepto **2 ~ none** : sin excepción

barbarian *n* : bárbaro *m*, **-ra** *f*

barbecue *vt* **-cued; -cuing** : asar a la parrilla — **~** *n* : barbacoa *f*

barbed wire *n* : alambre *m* de púas

barber *n* : barbero *m*, **-ra** *f*

bare *adj* **1** : desnudo **2** EMPTY : vacío **3** MINIMUM : mero, esencial — **barefaced** *adj* : descarado — **barefoot** *or* **barefooted** *adv* & *adj* : descalzo — **barely** *adv* : apenas, por poco

bargain *n* **1** AGREEMENT : acuerdo *m* **2** BUY : ganga *f* — **~** *vi* **1** : regatear, negociar **2 ~ for** : contar con

barge *n* : barcaza *f* — **~** *vi* **barged; barging ~ in** : entrometerse, interrumpir

baritone *n* : barítono *m*

bark[1] *vi* : ladrar — **~** *n* : ladrido *m* (de un perro)

bark[2] *n* : corteza *f* (de un árbol)

barley *n* : cebada *f*

barn *n* : granero *m* — **barnyard** *n* : corral *m*

barometer *n* : barómetro *m*

baron *n* : barón *m* — **baroness** *n* : baronesa *f*

barracks *ns* & *pl* : cuartel *m*

barrage *n* **1** : descarga *f* (de artillería) **2** : aluvión *m* (de preguntas, etc.)

barrel *n* **1** : barril *m*, tonel *m* **2** : cañón *m* (de un arma de fuego)

barren *adj* : estéril

barricade *vt* **-caded; -cading** : cerrar con barricadas — **~** *n* : barricada *f*

barrier *n* : barrera *f*

barring *prep* : salvo

barrio *n* : barrio *m*

bartender *n* : camarero *m*, **-ra** *f*

barter *vt* : cambiar, trocar — **~** *n* : trueque *m*

base *n*, *pl* **bases** : base *f* — **~** *vt* **based; basing** : basar, fundamentar — **~** *adj* **baser; basest** : vil

baseball *n* : beisbol *m*, béisbol *m*

basement *n* : sótano *m*

bash *vt* : golpear violentamente — **~** *n* **1** BLOW : golpe *m* **2** PARTY : fiesta *f*

bashful *adj* : tímido, vergonzoso

basic *adj* : básico, fundamental — **basically** *adv* : fundamentalmente

basil *n* : albahaca *f*

basin *n* **1** WASHBOWL : palangana *f*, lavabo *m* **2** : cuenca *f* (de un río)

basis *n*, *pl* **bases** : base *f*

bask *vi* **~ in the sun** : tostarse al sol

basket *n* : cesta *f*, cesto *m* — **basketball** *n* : baloncesto *m*, basquetbol *m Lat*

bass[1] *n*, *pl* **bass** *or* **basses** : róbalo *m* (pesca)

bass[2] *n* : bajo *m* (tono, voz, instrumento)

bassoon *n* : fagot *m*

bastard *n* : bastardo *m*, **-da** *f*

baste *vt* **basted; basting 1** STITCH : hilvanar **2** : bañar (carne)

bat[1] *n* : murciélago *m* (animal)

bat[2] *n* : bate *m* — **~** *vt* **batted; batting** : batear

batch *n* : hornada *f* (de pasteles, etc.), lote *m* (de mercancías), montón *m* (de trabajo), grupo *m* (de personas)

bath *n*, *pl* **baths 1** : baño *m* **2** BATHROOM : baño *m*, cuarto *m* de baño **3 take a ~** : bañarse — **bathe** *v* **bathed; bathing** *vt* : bañar, lavar — *vi* : bañarse — **bathrobe** *n* : bata *f* (de baño) — **bathroom** *n* : baño *m*, cuarto *m* de baño — **bathtub** *n* : bañera *f*, tina *f* (de baño)

baton *n* : batuta *f*

battalion *n* : batallón *m*

batter *vt* **1** BEAT : golpear **2** MISTREAT : maltratar — ～ *n* **1** : masa *f* para rebozar **2** HITTER : bateador *m*, -dora *f*

battery *n*, *pl* **-teries** : batería *f*, pila *f* (de electricidad)

battle *n* **1** : batalla *f* **2** STRUGGLE : lucha *f* — ～ *vi* **-tled; -tling** : luchar — **battlefield** *n* : campo *m* de batalla — **battleship** *n* : acorazado *m*

bawl *vi* : llorar a gritos

bay[1] *n* INLET : bahía *f*

bay[2] *n or* ～ **leaf** : laurel *m*

bay[3] *vi* : aullar — ～ *n* : aullido *m*

bayonet *n* : bayoneta *f*

bay window *n* : ventana *f* en saliente

bazaar *n* **1** : bazar *m* **2** SALE : venta *f* benéfica

be *v* **was , were; been; being; am , is , are** *vi* **1** : ser **2** (*expressing location*) : estar **3** (*expressing existence*) : ser, existir **4** (*expressing a state of being*) : estar, tener — *v impers* **1** (*indicating time*) : ser **2** (*indicating a condition*) : hacer, estar — *v aux* **1** (*expressing occurrence*) : ser **2** (*expressing possibility*) : poderse **3** (*expressing obligation*) : deber **4** (*expressing progression*) : estar

beach *n* : playa *f*

beacon *n* : faro *m*

bead *n* **1** : cuenta *f* **2** DROP : gota *f* **3** ～**s** *npl* NECKLACE : collar *m*

beak *n* : pico *m*

beam *n* **1** : viga *f* (de madera, etc.) **2** RAY : rayo *m* — ～ *vi* SHINE : brillar — *vt* BROADCAST : transmitir, emitir

bean *n* **1** : habichuela *f*, frijol *m* **2 coffee** ～ : grano *m* **3 string** ～ : judía *f*

bear[1] *n*, *pl* **bears** *or* **bear** : oso *m*, osa *f*

bear[2] *v* **bore; borne; bearing** *vt* **1** CARRY : portar **2** ENDURE : soportar — *vi* ～ **right/left** : doble a la derecha/a la izquierda — **bearable** *adj* : soportable

beard *n* : barba *f*

bearer *n* : portador *m*, -dora *f*

bearing *n* **1** MANNER : comportamiento *m* **2** SIGNIFICANCE : relación *f*, importancia *f* **3 get one's** ～**s** : orientarse

beast *n* : bestia *f*

beat *v* **beat; beaten** *or* **beat; beating** *vt* **1** HIT : golpear **2** : batir (huevos, etc.) **3** DEFEAT : derrotar — *vi* : latir (dícese del corazón) — ～ *n* **1** : golpe *m* **2** : latido *m* (del corazón) **3** RHYTHM : ritmo *m*, tiempo *m* — **beating** *n* **1** : paliza *f* **2** DEFEAT : derrota *f*

beauty *n*, *pl* **-ties** : belleza *f* — **beautiful** *adj* : hermoso, lindo — **beautifully** *adv* WON-

DERFULLY : maravillosamente — **beautify** *vt* **-fied; -fying** : embellecer

beaver *n* : castor *m*

because *conj* : porque — **because of** *prep* : por, a causa de, debido a

beckon *vt* : llamar, hacer señas a — *vi* : hacer una seña

become *v* **-came; -come; -coming** *vi* : hacerse, ponerse — *vt* SUIT : favorecer — **becoming** *adj* **1** SUITABLE : apropiado **2** FLATTERING : favorecedor

bed *n* **1** : cama *f* **2** : cauce *m* (de un río), fondo *m* (del mar) **3** : macizo *m* (de flores) **4 go to** ～ : irse a la cama — **bedclothes** *npl* : ropa *f* de cama

bedlam *n* : confusión *f*, caos *m*

bedraggled *adj* : desaliñado, sucio

bedridden *adj* : postrado en cama

bedroom *n* : dormitorio *m*, recámara *f* *Lat*

bedspread *n* : colcha *f*

bedtime *n* : hora *f* de acostarse

bee *n* : abeja *f*

beech *n*, *pl* **beeches** *or* **beech** : haya *f*

beef *n* : carne *f* de vaca, carne *f* de res *Lat* — **beefsteak** *n* : bistec *m*

beehive *n* : colmena *f*

beeline *n* **make a** ～ **for** : irse derecho a

beep *n* : pitido *m* — ～ *v* : pitar

beer *n* : cerveza *f*

beet *n* : remolacha *f*

beetle *n* : escarabajo *m*

before *adv* **1** : antes **2 the month** ～ : el mes anterior — ～ *prep* **1** (*in space*) : delante de, ante **2** (*in time*) : antes de — ～ *conj* : antes de que — **beforehand** *adv* : antes

befriend *vt* : hacerse amigo de

beg *v* **begged; begging** *vt* **1** : pedir, mendigar **2** ENTREAT : suplicar — *vi* : mendigar, pedir limosna — **beggar** *n* : mendigo *m*, -ga *f*

begin *v* **-gan; -gun; -ginning** : empezar, comenzar — **beginner** *n* : principiante *mf* — **beginning** *n* : principio *m*, comienzo *m*

begrudge *vt* **-grudged; -grudging** **1** : dar de mala gana **2** ENVY : envidiar

behalf *n* **on** ～ **of** : de parte de, en nombre de

behave *vi* **-haved; -having** : comportarse, portarse — **behavior** *n* : comportamiento *m*, conducta *f*

behind *adv* **1** : detrás **2 fall** ～ : atrasarse — *prep* **1** : atrás de, detrás de **2 be** ～ **schedule** : ir retrasado **3 her friends are** ～ **her** : tiene el apoyo de sus amigos

behold *vt* **-held; -holding** : contemplar

beige *adj & nm* : beige

being *n* **1** : ser *m* **2 come into** ～ : nacer

belated *adj* : tardío

belch *vi* : eructar — **~** *n* : eructo *m*

Belgian *adj* : belga

belie *vt* **-lied; -lying** : contradecir, desmentir

belief *n* **1** TRUST : confianza *f* **2** CONVICTION : creencia *f*, convicción *f* **3** FAITH : fe *f* — **believable** *adj* : creíble — **believe** *v* **-lieved; -lieving** : creer — **believer** *n* : creyente *mf*

belittle *vt* **-littled; -littling** : menospreciar

Belizean *adj* : beliceño *m*, -ña *f*

bell *n* **1** : campana *f* **2** : timbre *m* (de teléfono, de la puerta, etc.)

belligerent *adj* : beligerante

bellow *vi* : bramar, mugir — *vt or* **~** **out** : gritar

bellows *ns & pl* : fuelle *m*

belly *n, pl* **-lies** : vientre *m*

belong *vi* **1** **~ to** : pertenecer a, ser propiedad de **2** **~ to** : ser miembro de (un club, etc.) **3** where does it **~** : ¿dónde va? — **belongings** *npl* : pertenencias *fpl*, efectos *mpl* personales

beloved *adj* : querido, amado — **~** *n* : querido *m*, -da *f*

below *adv* : abajo — **~** *prep* **1** : abajo de, debajo de **2** **~ average** : por debajo del promedio **3** **~ zero** : bajo cero

belt *n* **1** : cinturón *m* **2** BAND, STRAP : cinta *f*, correa *f* **3** AREA : frente *m*, zona *f* — **~** *vt* **1** : ceñir con un cinturón **2** THRASH : darle una paliza a

bench *n* **1** : banco *m* **2** WORKBENCH : mesa *f* de trabajo **3** COURT : tribunal *m*

bend *v* **bent; bending** *vt* : doblar, torcer — *vi* **1** : torcerse **2** **~ over** : inclinarse — **~** *n* : curva *f*, ángulo *m*

beneath *adv* : abajo, debajo — **~** *prep* : bajo, debajo de

benediction *n* : bendición *f*

benefactor *n* : benefactor *m*, -tora *f*

benefit *n* **1** ADVANTAGE : ventaja *f*, provecho *m* **2** AID : asistencia *f*, beneficio *m* — **~** *vt* : beneficiar — *vi* : beneficiarse — **beneficial** *adj* : beneficioso — **beneficiary** *n, pl* **-ries** : beneficiario *m*, -ria *f*

benevolent *adj* : benévolo

benign *adj* **1** KIND : benévolo, amable **2** : benigno (en medicina)

bent *adj* **1** : encorvado **2 be ~ on** : estar empeñado en — **~** *n* : aptitud *f*, inclinación *f*

bequeath *vt* : legar — **bequest** *n* : legado *m*

berate *vt* **-rated; -rating** : reprender, regañar

bereaved *adj* : desconsolado, a luto

beret *n* : boina *f*

berry *n, pl* **-ries** : baya *f*

berserk *adj* **1** : enloquecido **2 go ~** : volverse loco

berth *n* **1** MOORING : atracadero *m* **2** BUNK : litera *f*

beseech *vt* **-sought** *or* **-seeched; -seeching** : suplicar, implorar

beset *vt* **-set; -setting 1** HARASS : acosar **2** SURROUND : rodear

beside *prep* **1** : al lado de, junto a **2 be ~ oneself** : estar fuera de sí — **besides** *adv* : además — **~** *prep* **1** : además de **2** EXCEPT : excepto

besiege *vt* **-sieged; -sieging** : asediar

best *adj* (*superlative of* **good**) : mejor — **~** *adv* (*superlative of* **well**) : mejor — **~** *n* **1 at ~** : a lo más **2 do one's ~** : hacer todo lo posible **3 the ~** : lo mejor — **best man** *n* : padrino *m* (de boda)

bestow *vt* : otorgar, conceder

bet *n* : apuesta *f* — **~** *v* **bet; betting** *vt* : apostar — *vi* **~ on sth** : apostarle a algo

betray *vt* : traicionar — **betrayal** *n* : traición *f*

better *adj* (*comparative of* **good**) **1** : mejor **2 get ~** : mejorar — **~** *adv* (*comparative of* **well**) **1** : mejor **2 all the ~** : tanto mejor — **~** *n* **1 the ~** : el mejor, la mejor **2 get the ~ of** : vencer a — **~** *vt* **1** IMPROVE : mejorar **2** SURPASS : superar

between *prep* : entre — **~** *adv or* **in ~** : en medio

beverage *n* : bebida *f*

beware *vi* **~ of** : tener cuidado con

bewilder *vt* : desconcertar — **bewilderment** *n* : desconcierto *m*

bewitch *vt* : hechizar, encantar

beyond *adv* : más allá, más lejos (en el espacio), más adelante (en el tiempo) — **~** *prep* : más allá de

bias *n* **1** PREJUDICE : prejuicio *m* **2** TENDENCY : inclinación *f*, tendencia *f* — **biased** *adj* : parcial

bib *n* : babero *m* (para niños)

Bible *n* : Biblia *f* — **biblical** *adj* : bíblico

bibliography *n, pl* **-phies** : bibliografía *f*

bicarbonate of soda *n* : bicarbonato *m* de soda

biceps *ns & pl* : bíceps *m*

bicker *vi* : reñir

bicycle *n* : bicicleta *f* — **~** *vi* **-cled; -cling** : ir en bicicleta

bid *vt* **bade** *or* **bid; bidden** *or* **bid; bidding 1** OFFER : ofrecer **2 ~ farewell** : decir adiós — **~** *n* **1** OFFER : oferta *f* **2** ATTEMPT : intento *m*, tentativa *f*

bide *vt* **bode** *or* **bided; bided; biding ~ one's time** : esperar el momento oportuno

bifocals *npl* : anteojos *mpl* bifocales

big *adj* **bigger; biggest** : grande

bigamy *n* : bigamia *f*

bigot *n* : intolerante *mf* — **bigotry** *n, pl* **-tries** : intolerancia *f,* fanatismo *m*

bike *n* **1** BICYCLE : bici *f fam* **2** MOTORCY-CLE : moto *f*

bikini *n* : bikini *m*

bile *n* : bilis *f*

bilingual *adj* : bilingüe

bill *n* **1** BEAK : pico *m* **2** INVOICE : cuenta *f,* factura *f* **3** BANKNOTE : billete *m* **4** LAW : proyecto *m* de ley, ley *f* — ~ *vt* : pasarle la cuenta a — **billboard** *n* : cartelera *f* — **billfold** *n* : billetera *f,* cartera *f*

billiards *n* : billar *m*

billion *n, pl* **billions** *or* **billion** : mil millones *mpl*

billow *vi* : ondular, hincharse

billy goat *n* : macho *m* cabrío

bin *n* : cubo *m,* cajón *m*

binary *adj* : binario *m*

bind *vt* **bound; binding 1** TIE : atar **2** OBLI-GATE : obligar **3** UNITE : unir **4** BANDAGE : vendar **5** : encuadernar (un libro) — **binder** *n* FOLDER : carpeta *f* — **binding** *n* : encuadernación *f* (de libros)

binge *n* : juerga *f fam*

bingo *n, pl* **-gos** : bingo *m*

binoculars *npl* : binoculares *mpl,* gemelos *mpl*

biochemistry *n* : bioquímica *f*

biography *n, pl* **-phies** : biografía *f* — **biographer** *n* : biógrafo *m,* -fa *f* — **biographical** *adj* : biográfico

biology *n* : biología *f* — **biological** *adj* : biológico — **biologist** *n* : biólogo *m,* -ga *f*

birch *n* : abedul *m*

bird *n* : pájaro *m* (pequeño), ave *f* (grande)

birth *n* **1** : nacimiento *m,* parto *m* **2 give ~ to** : dar a luz a — **birthday** *n* : cumpleaños *m* — **birthmark** *n* : mancha *f* de nacimiento — **birthplace** *n* : lugar *m* de nacimiento — **birthrate** *n* : índice *m* de natalidad

biscuit *n* : bizcocho *m*

bisect *vt* : bisecar

bisexual *adj* : bisexual

bishop *n* : obispo *m*

bison *ns & pl* : bisonte *m*

bit[1] *n* : bocado *m* (de una brida)

bit[2] **1** : trozo *m,* pedazo *m* **2** : bit *m* (de información) **3 a ~** : un poco

bitch *n* : perra *f* — ~ *vi* COMPLAIN : quejarse, reclamar

bite *v* **bit; bitten; biting** *vt* **1** : morder **2** STING : picar — *vi* : morder — *n* **1** : picadura *f* (de un insecto), mordedura *f* (de un animal) **2** SNACK : bocado *m* — **biting** *adj* **1** PENETRATING : cortante, penetrante **2** CAUSTIC : mordaz

bitter *adj* **1** : amargo **2 it's ~ cold** : hace

un frío glacial **3 to the ~ end** : hasta el final — **bitterness** *n* : amargura *f*

bizarre *adj* : extraño

black *adj* : negro — ~ *n* **1** : negro *m* (color) **2** : negro *m,* -gra *f* (persona) — **black-and–blue** *adj* : amoratado — **blackberry** *n, pl* **-ries** : mora *f* — **blackbird** *n* : mirlo *m* — **blackboard** *n* : pizarra *f,* pizarrón *m Lat* — **blacken** *vt* : ennegrecer — **blackmail** *n* : chantaje *m* — ~ *vt* : chantajear — **black market** *n* : mercado *m* negro — **blackout** *n* **1** : apagón *m* (de poder eléctrico) **2** FAINT : desmayo *m* — **blacksmith** : herrero *m* — **blacktop** *n* : asfalto *m*

bladder *n* : vejiga *f*

blade *n* **1** : hoja *f* (de un cuchillo), cuchilla *f* (de un patín) **2** : pala *f* (de un remo, una hélice, etc.) **3 ~ of grass** : brizna *f* (de hierba)

blame *vt* **blamed; blaming** : culpar, echar la culpa a — ~ *n* : culpa *f* — **blameless** *adj* : inocente

bland *adj* : soso, insulso

blank *adj* **1** : en blanco (dícese de un papel), liso (dícese de una pared) **2** EMPTY : vacío — ~ *n* : espacio *m* en blanco

blanket *n* **1** : manta *f,* cobija *f Lat* **2 ~ of snow** : manto *m* de nieve — ~ *vt* : cubrir

blare *vi* **blared; blaring** : resonar

blasphemy *n, pl* **-mies** : blasfemia *f*

blast *n* **1** GUST : ráfaga *f* **2** EXPLOSION : explosión *f* **3** : toque *m* (de trompeta, etc.) — ~ *vt* BLOW UP : volar — **blast-off** *n* : despegue *m*

blatant *adj* : descarado

blaze *n* **1** FIRE : fuego *m* **2** BRIGHTNESS : resplandor *m,* brillantez *f* **3 ~ of anger** : arranque *m* de cólera — ~ *v* **blazed; blazing** *vi* : arder, brillar — *vt* ~ **a trail** : abrir un camino

blazer *n* : chaqueta *f* deportiva

bleach *vt* : blanquear, decolorar — ~ *n* : lejía *f,* blanqueador *m Lat*

bleachers *ns & pl* : gradas *fpl*

bleak *adj* **1** DESOLATE : desolado **2** GLOOMY : triste, sombrío

bleary–eyed *adj* : con los ojos nublados

bleat *vi* : balar — ~ *n* : balido *m*

bleed *v* **bled; bleeding** : sangrar

blemish *vt* : manchar, marcar — ~ *n* : mancha *f,* marca *f*

blend *vt* : mezclar, combinar — ~ *n* : mezcla *f,* combinación *f* — **blender** *n* : licuadora *f*

bless *vt* **blessed; blessing** : bendecir — **blessed** *or* **blest** *adj* : bendito — **blessing** *n* : bendición *f*

blew → blow

blind *adj* : ciego — ~ *vt* **1** : cegar, dejar

ciego **2** DAZZLE : deslumbrar — ~ *n* **1**
: persiana *f* (para una ventana) **2 the ~**
: los ciegos — **blindfold** *vt* : vendar los ojos
— ~ *n* : venda *f* (para los ojos) — **blindly**
adv : ciegamente — **blindness** *n* : ceguera *f*
blink *vi* **1** : parpadear **2** FLICKER : brillar in-
termitentemente — ~ *n* : parpadeo *m* —
blinker *n* : intermitente *m*, direccional *f Lat*
bliss *n* : dicha *f*, felicidad *f* (absoluta) —
blissful *adj* : feliz
blister *n* : ampolla *f* — ~ *vi* : ampollarse
blitz *n* : bombardeo *m* aéreo
blizzard *n* : ventisca *f* (de nieve)
bloated *adj* : hinchado
blob *n* **1** DROP : gota *f* **2** SPOT : mancha *f*
block *n* **1** : bloque *m* **2** OBSTRUCTION : obstrucción *f* **3** : manzana *f*, cuadra *f Lat* (de
edificios) **4** *or* **building ~** : cubo *m* de
construcción — ~ *vt* : obstruir, bloquear —
blockade *n* : bloqueo *m* — **blockage** *n*
: obstrucción *f*
blond *or* **blonde** *adj* : rubio — ~ *n* : rubio
m, -bia *f*
blood *n* : sangre *f* — **bloodhound** *n*
: sabueso *m* — **blood pressure** *n* : tensión *f*
(arterial) — **bloodshed** *n* : derramamiento
m de sangre — **bloodshot** *adj* : inyectado
de sangre — **bloodstained** *adj* : manchado
de sangre — **bloodstream** *n* : sangre *f*, torrente *m* sanguíneo — **bloody** *adj* **bloodier;**
-est : ensangrentado, sangriento
bloom *n* **1** : flor *f* **2 in full ~** : en plena flo-
ración — ~ *vi* : florecer
blossom *n* : flor *f* — ~ *vi* : florecer
blot *n* **1** : borrón *m* (de tinta, etc.) **2** BLEM-
ISH : mancha *f* — ~ *vt* **blotted; blotting 1**
: emborronar **2** DRY : secar
blotch *n* : mancha *f*, borrón *m* — **blotchy** *adj*
blotchier; -est : lleno de manchas
blouse *n* : blusa *f*
blow *v* **blew; blown; blowing** *vi* **1** : soplar
2 SOUND : sonar **3** *or* **~ out** : fundirse
(dícese de un fusible eléctrico), reventarse
(dícese de una llanta) — *vt* **1** : soplar **2**
SOUND : tocar, sonar **3** BUNGLE : echar a
perder — ~ *n* : golpe *m* — **blowout** *n*
: reventón *m* — **blow up 1** : estallar, hacer
explosión — *vt* **2** EXPLODE : volar **2** IN-
FLATE : inflar
blubber *n* : esperma *f* de ballena
bludgeon *vt* : aporrear
blue *adj* **bluer; bluest 1** : azul **2** MELAN-
CHOLY : triste — ~ *n* : azul *m* — **blueberry**
n, *pl* **-ries** : arándano *m* — **bluebird** *n*
: azulejo *m* — **blue cheese** *n* : queso *m* azul
— **blueprint** *n* PLAN : proyecto *m* — **blues**
npl **1** SADNESS : tristeza *f* **2** : blues *m* (en
música)
bluff *vi* : hacer un farol — ~ *n* : farol *m*

blunder *vi* : meter la pata *fam* — ~ *n* : metedura *f* de pata *fam*
blunt *adj* **1** DULL : desafilado **2** DIRECT : directo, franco
blur *n* : imágen *f* borrosa — ~ *vt* **blurred;**
blurring : hacer borroso
blurb *n* : nota *f* publicitaria
blurt *vt or* **~ out** : espetar
blush *n* : rubor *m* — ~ *vi* : ruborizarse
blustery *adj* : borrascoso, tempestuoso
boar *n* : cerdo *m* macho
board *n* **1** PLANK : tabla *f*, tablón *m* **2** COM-
MITTEE : junta *f*, consejo *m* **3** : tablero *m* (de
juegos) **4 room and ~** : comida y alojamiento — ~ *vt* **1** : subir a bordo de (una
nave, un avión, etc.), subir a (un tren) **2**
LODGE : hospedar **3 ~ up** : cerrar con
tablas — **boarder** *n* : huésped *mf*
boast *n* : jactancia *f* — ~ *vi* : alardear, jactarse — **boastful** *adj* : jactancioso
boat *n* : barco *m* (grande), barca *f* (pequeña)
bob *vi* **bobbed; bobbing** *or* **~ up and**
down : subir y bajar
bobbin *n* : bobina *f*, carrete *m*
bobby pin *n* : horquilla *f*
body *n*, *pl* **bodies 1** : cuerpo *m* **2** CORPSE
: cadáver *m* **3** : carrocería (de un automóvil, etc.) **4** COLLECTION : conjunto *m*
5 ~ of water : masa *f* de agua — **bodily**
adj : corporal — **bodyguard** *n* : guardaespaldas *mf*
bog *n* : ciénaga *f* — ~ *vt* **bogged; bogging**
or **~ down** : empantanarse
bogus *adj* : falso
boil *v* : hervir — **boiler** *n* : caldera *f*
bold *adj* **1** DARING : audaz **2** IMPUDENT
: descarado — **boldness** *n* : audacia *f*
Bolivian *adj* : boliviano *m*, -na *f*
bologna *n* : salchicha *f* ahumada
bolster *vt* **-stered; -stering** *or* **~ up** : reforzar
bolt *n* **1** LOCK : cerrojo *m* **2** SCREW : tornillo
m **3 ~ of lightning** : relámpago *m*, rayo *m*
— ~ *vt* **1** FASTEN : atornillar **2** LOCK
: echar el cerrojo a — *vi* FLEE : salir corriendo
bomb *n* : bomba *f* — ~ *vt* : bombardear —
bombard *vt* : bombardear — **bombard-**
ment *n* : bombardeo *m* — **bomber** *n* : bombardero *m*
bond *n* **1** TIE : vínculo *m*, lazo *m* **2** SURETY
: fianza *f* **3** : bono *m* (en finanzas) — ~ *vi*
STICK : adherirse
bondage *n* : esclavitud *f*
bone *n* : hueso *m* — ~ *vt* **boned; boning**
: deshuesar
bonfire *n* : hoguera *f*
bonus *n* **1** PAY : prima *f* **2** BENEFIT : beneficio *m* adicional

bony *adj* **bonier; -est 1** : huesudo **2** : lleno de espinas (dícese de pescados)

boo *n*, *pl* **boos** : abucheo *m* — **~** *vt* : abuchear

book *n* **1** : libro *m* **2** NOTEBOOK : libreta *f*, cuaderno *m* — **~** *vt* : reservar — **bookcase** *n* : estantería *f* — **bookkeeping** *n* : teneduría *f* de libros, contabilidad *f* — **booklet** *n* : folleto *m* — **bookmark** *n* : marcador *m* de libros — **bookseller** *n* : librero *m*, -ra *f* — **bookshelf** *n*, *pl* **-shelves** : estante *m* — **bookstore** *n* : librería *f*

boom *vi* **1** : tronar, resonar **2** PROSPER : estar en auge, prosperar — **~** *n* **1** : bramido *m*, estruendo *m* **2** : auge *m* (económico)

boon *n* : ayuda *f*, beneficio *m*

boost *vt* **1** LIFT : levantar **2** INCREASE : aumentar — **~** *n* **1** INCREASE : aumento *m* **2** ENCOURAGEMENT : estímulo *m*

boot *n* : bota *f*, botín *m* — **~** *vt* **1** : dar una patada a **2** *or* **~ up** : cargar (un ordenador)

booth *n*, *pl* **booths** : cabina *f* (de teléfono, de votar), caseta *f* (de información)

booty *n*, *pl* **-ties** : botín *m*

booze *n* : trago *m*, bebida *f* (alcohólica)

border *n* **1** EDGE : borde *m*, orilla *f* **2** TRIM : ribete *m* **3** FRONTIER : frontera *f*

bore¹ *vt* **bored; boring** DRILL : taladrar

bore² *vt* TIRE : aburrir — **~** *n* : pesado *m*, -da *fam f* (persona), lata *f fam* (cosa, situación) — **boredom** *n* : aburrimiento *m* — **boring** *adj* : aburrido, pesado

born *adj* **1** : nacido **2 be ~** : nacer

borough *n* : distrito *m* municipal

borrow *vt* : pedir prestado, tomar prestado

Bosnian *adj* : bosnio *m*, -nia *f*

bosom *n* BREAST : pecho *m*, seno *m* — **~** *adj* **~ friend** : amigo *m* íntimo

boss *n* : jefe *m*, -fa *f*; patrón *m*, -trona *f* — **~** *vt* SUPERVISE : dirigir — **bossy** *adj* **bossier; -est** : autoritario

botany *n* : botánica *f* — **botanical** *adj* : botánico

botch *vt* : hacer una chapuza de, estropear

both *adj* : ambos, los dos, las dos — **~** *pron* : ambos *m*, -bas *f*; los dos, las dos

bother *vt* **1** TROUBLE : preocupar **2** PESTER : molestar, fastidiar — *vi* **~ to** : molestarse en — **~** *n* : molestia *f*

bottle *n* **1** : botella *f*, frasco *m* **2** *or* **baby ~** : biberón *m* — **~** *vt* **bottled; bottling** : embotellar — **bottleneck** *n* : embotellamiento *m*

bottom *n* **1** : fondo *m* (de una caja, del mar, etc.), pie *m* (de una escalera, una montaña, etc.), final *m* (de una lista) **2** BUTTOCKS : nalgas *fpl*, trasero *m* — **~** *adj* : más bajo, inferior, de abajo — **bottomless** *adj* : sin fondo

bough *n* : rama *f*

bought → **buy**

bouillon *n* : caldo *m*

boulder *n* : canto *m* rodado

boulevard *n* : bulevar *m*

bounce *v* **bounced; bouncing** *vt* : hacer rebotar — *vi* : rebotar — **~** *n* : rebote *m*

bound¹ *adj* **be ~ for** : ir rumbo a

bound² *adj* **1** OBLIGED : obligado **2** DETERMINED : decidido **3 be ~ to** : tener que

bound³ *n* **out of ~s** : (en) zona prohibida — **boundary** *n*, *pl* **-aries** : límite *m* — **boundless** *adj* : sin límites

bouquet *n* : ramo *m*

bourgeois *adj* : burgués

bout *n* **1** : combate *m* (en deportes) **2** : ataque *m* (de una enfermedad) **3** : período *m* (de actividad)

bow¹ *vi* : inclinarse — *vt* **~ one's head** : inclinar la cabeza — **~** *n* : reverencia *f*, inclinación *f*

bow² *n* **1** : arco *m* **2 tie a ~** : hacer un lazo

bow³ *n* : proa *f* (de un barco)

bowels *npl* **1** : intestinos *mpl* **2** DEPTHS : entrañas *fpl*

bowl¹ *n* : tazón *m*, cuenco *m*

bowl² *vi* : jugar a los bolos — **bowling** *n* : bolos *mpl*

box¹ *vi* FIGHT : boxear — **boxer** *n* : boxeador *m*, -dora *f* — **boxing** *n* : boxeo *m*

box² *n* **1** : caja *f*, cajón *m* **2** : palco *m* (en el teatro) — **~** *vt* : empaquetar — **box office** *n* : taquilla *f*, boletería *f Lat*

boy *n* : niño *m*, chico *m*

boycott *vt* : boicotear — **~** *n* : boicot *m*

boyfriend *n* : novio *m*

bra → **brassiere**

brace *n* **1** SUPPORT : abrazadera *f* **2 ~s** *npl* : aparatos *mpl* (para dientes) — **~** *vi* **~ oneself for** : prepararse para

bracelet *n* : brazalete *m*

bracket *n* **1** SUPPORT : soporte *m* **2** : corchete *m* (marca de puntuación) **3** CATEGORY : categoría *f* — **~** *vt* **1** : poner entre corchetes **2** CATEGORIZE : catalogar

brag *vi* **bragged; bragging** : jactarse

braid *vt* : trenzar — **~** *n* : trenza *f*

braille *n* : braille *m*

brain *n* **1** : cerebro *m* **2 ~s** *npl* : inteligencia *f* — **brainstorm** *n* : idea *f* genial — **brainwash** *vt* : lavar el cerebro — **brainy** *adj* **brainier; -est** : inteligente, listo

brake *n* : freno *m* — **~** *v* **braked; braking** : frenar

bramble *n* : zarza *f*

bran *n* : salvado *m*

branch *n* **1** : rama *f* (de una planta) **2** DIVISION : ramal *m* (de un camino, etc.), sucursal *f* (de una empresa), agencia *f* (del gobierno) — ~ *vi or* ~ **off** : ramificarse, bifurcarse

brand *n* **1** : marca *f* (de ganado) **2** *or* ~ **name** : marca *f* de fábrica — ~ *vt* **1** : marcar (ganado) **2** LABEL : tachar, tildar

brandish *vt* : blandir

brand–new *adj* : flamante

brandy *n, pl* **-dies** : brandy *m*, coñac *m*

brass *n* **1** : latón *m* **2** : metales *mpl* (de una orquesta)

brassiere *n* : sostén *m*, brasier *m Lat*

brat *n* : mocoso *m*, -sa *f fam*

bravado *n, pl* **-does** *or* **-dos** : bravuconadas *fpl*

brave *adj* **braver; bravest** : valiente, valeroso — ~ *vt* **braved; braving** : afrontar, hacer frente a — ~ *n* : guerrero *m* indio — **bravery** *n* : valor *m*, valentía *f*

brawl *n* : pelea *f*, reyerta *f*

brawn *n* : músculos *mpl* — **brawny** *adj* **brawnier; -est** : musculoso

bray *vi* : rebuznar

brazen *adj* : descarado

Brazilian *adj* : brasileño *m*, -ña *f*

breach *n* **1** VIOLATION : infracción *f*, violación *f* **2** GAP : brecha *f*

bread *n* **1** : pan *m* **2** ~ **crumbs** : migajas *fpl*

breadth *n* : anchura *f*

break *v* **broke; broken; breaking** *vt* **1** : romper, quebrar **2** VIOLATE : infringir, violar **3** INTERRUPT : interrumpir **4** SURPASS : batir (un récord, etc.) **5** ~ **a habit** : quitarse una costumbre **6** ~ **the news** : dar la noticia — *vi* **1** : romperse, quebrarse **2** ~ **away** : escapar **3** ~ **down** : estropearse (dícese de una máquina), fallar (dícese de un sistema, etc.) **4** ~ **into** : entrar en **5** ~ **off** : interrumpirse **6** ~ **out of** : escaparse de **7** ~ **up** SEPARATE : separarse — ~ *n* **1** : ruptura *f*, fractura *f* **2** GAP : interrupción *f*, claro *m* (entre las nubes) **3** **lucky** ~ : golpe *m* de suerte **4 take a** ~ : tomar(se) un descanso — **breakable** *adj* : quebradizo, frágil — **breakdown** *n* **1** : avería *f* (de máquinas), interrupción *f* (de comunicaciones), fracaso *m* (de negociaciones) **2** *or* **nervous** ~ : crisis *f* nerviosa

breakfast *n* : desayuno *m*

breast *n* **1** : seno *m* (de una mujer) **2** CHEST : pecho *m* — **breast–feed** *vt* **-fed; -feeding** : amamantar

breath *n* : aliento *m*, respiración *f* — **breathe** *v* **breathed; breathing** : respirar — **breathless** *adj* : sin aliento, jadeante — **breathtaking** *adj* : impresionante

breed *v* **bred; breeding** *vt* **1** : criar (animales) **2** ENGENDER : engendrar, producir

— *vi* : reproducirse — ~ *n* **1** : raza *f* **2** CLASS : clase *f*, tipo *m*

breeze *n* : brisa *f* — **breezy** *adj* **breezier; -est 1** WINDY : ventoso **2** NONCHALANT : despreocupado

brevity *n, pl* **-ties** : brevedad *f*

brew *vt* : hacer (cerveza, etc.), preparar (té) — *vi* **1** : fabricar cerveza **2** : amenazar (dícese de una tormenta) — **brewery** *n, pl* **-eries** : cervecería *f*

bribe *n* : soborno *m* — ~ *vt* **bribed; bribing** : sobornar — **bribery** *n, pl* **-eries** : soborno *m*

brick *n* : ladrillo *m* — **bricklayer** *n* : albañil *mf*

bride *n* : novia *f* — **bridal** *adj* : nupcial, de novia — **bridegroom** *n* : novio *m* — **bridesmaid** *n* : dama *f* de honor

bridge *n* **1** : puente *m* **2** : caballete *m* (de la nariz) **3** : bridge *m* (juego de naipes) — ~ *vt* **bridged; bridging 1** : tender un puente sobre **2** ~ **the gap** : salvar las diferencias

bridle *n* : brida *f* — ~ *vt* **-dled; -dling** : embridar

brief *adj* : breve — ~ *n* **1** : resumen *m*, sumario *m* **2** ~**s** *npl* UNDERPANTS : calzoncillos *mpl* — ~ *vt* : dar órdenes a, instruir — **briefcase** *n* : portafolio *m*, maletín *m* — **briefly** *adv* : brevemente

bright *adj* **1** : brillante, claro **2** CHEERFUL : alegre, animado **3** INTELLIGENT : listo, inteligente — **brighten** *vi* **1** : hacerse más brillante **2** *or* ~ **up** : animarse, alegrarse — *vt* **1** ILLUMINATE : iluminar **2** ENLIVEN : alegrar, animar

brilliant *adj* : brillante — **brilliance** *n* **1** BRIGHTNESS : resplandor *m*, brillantez *f* **2** INTELLIGENCE : inteligencia *f*

brim *n* **1** : borde *m* (de una taza, etc.) **2** : ala *f* (de un sombrero) — ~ *vi* **brimmed; brimming** *or* ~ **over** : desbordarse, rebosar

brine *n* : salmuera *f*

bring *vt* **brought; bringing 1** : traer **2** ~ **about** : ocasionar **3** ~ **around** PERSUADE : convencer **4** ~ **back** : devolver **5** ~ **down** : derribar **6** ~ **on** CAUSE : provocar **7** ~ **out** : sacar **8** ~ **to an end** : terminar (con) **9** ~ **up** REAR : criar **10** ~ **up** MENTION : sacar

brink *n* : borde *m*

brisk *adj* **1** FAST : rápido **2** LIVELY : enérgico

bristle *n* : cerda *f* (de un animal), pelo *m* (de una planta) — ~ *vi* **-tled; -tling** : erizarse

British *adj* : británico

brittle *adj* **-tler; -tlest** : frágil, quebradizo

broach *vt* : abordar

broad *adj* **1** WIDE : ancho **2** GENERAL : general **3 in** ~ **daylight** : en pleno día

broadcast *vt* -cast; -casting : emitir — ~ *n* : emisión *f*

broaden *vt* : ampliar, ensanchar — *vi* : ensancharse — **broadly** *adv* : en general — **broad–minded** *adj* : de miras amplias, tolerante

broccoli *n* : brócoli *m*, brécol *m*

brochure *n* : folleto *m*

broil *vt* : asar a la parrilla

broke → **break** — ~ *adj* : pelado *fam* — **broken** *adj* : roto, quebrado — **brokenhearted** *adj* : desconsolado, con el corazón destrozado

broker *n* : corredor *m*, -dora *f*

bronchitis *n* : bronquitis *f*

bronze *n* : bronce *m*

brooch *n* : broche *m*

brood *n* : nidada *f* (de pájaros), camada *f* (de mamíferos) — ~ *vi* **1** INCUBATE : empollar **2** ~ **about** : dar vueltas a, pensar demasiado en

brook *n* : arroyo *m*

broom *n* : escoba *f* — **broomstick** *n* : palo *m* de escoba

broth *n, pl* **broths** : caldo *m*

brothel *n* : burdel *m*

brother *n* : hermano *m* — **brotherhood** *n* : fraternidad *f* — **brother–in–law** *n, pl* **brothers–in–law** : cuñado *m* — **brotherly** *adj* : fraternal

brought → **bring**

brow *n* **1** EYEBROW : ceja *f* **2** FOREHEAD : frente *f* **3** : cima *f* (de una colina)

brown *adj* : marrón, castaño (dícese del pelo), moreno (dícese de la piel) — ~ *n* : marrón *m* — ~ *vt* : dorar (en cocinar)

browse *vi* **browsed; browsing** : mirar, echar un vistazo

bruise *vt* **bruised; bruising** **1** : contusionar, magullar (a una persona) **2** : machucar (frutas) — ~ *n* : cardenal *m*, magulladura *f*

brunch *n* : brunch *m*

brunet *or* **brunette** *adj* : moreno — ~ *n* : moreno *m*, -na *f*

brunt *n* **bear the** ~ **of** : aguantar el mayor impacto de

brush *n* **1** : cepillo *m*, pincel *m* (de artista), brocha *f* (de pintor) **2** UNDERBRUSH : maleza *f* — ~ *vt* **1** : cepillar **2** GRAZE : rozar **3** ~ **aside** : rechazar **4** ~ **off** DISREGARD : hacer caso omiso de — *vi* ~ **up on** : repasar — **brush–off** *n* **give the** ~ **to** : dar calabazas a

brusque *adj* : brusco

brutal *adj* : brutal — **brutality** *n, pl* **-ties** : brutalidad *f*

brute *adj* : bruto — ~ *n* : bestia *f*; bruto *m*, -ta *f*

bubble *n* : burbuja *f* — ~ *vi* -bled; -bling : burbujear

buck *n, pl* **buck** *or* **bucks** **1** : animal *m* macho, ciervo *m* (macho) **2** DOLLAR : dólar *m* — ~ *vi* **1** : corcovear (dícese de un caballo) **2** ~ **up** : animarse, levantar el ánimo — *vt* OPPOSE : oponerse a, ir en contra de

bucket *n* : cubo *m*

buckle *n* : hebilla *f* — ~ *v* -led; -ling *vt* **1** FASTEN : abrochar **2** BEND : combar, torcer — *vi* **1** : combarse, torcerse **2** : doblarse (dícese de las rodillas)

bud *n* **1** : brote *m* **2** *or* **flower** ~ : capullo *m* — ~ *vi* **budded; budding** : brotar, hacer brotes

Buddhism *n* : budismo *m* — **Buddhist** *adj* : budista — ~ *n* : budista *mf*

buddy *n, pl* **-dies** : compañero *m*, -ra *f*

budge *vi* **budged; budging** **1** MOVE : moverse **2** YIELD : ceder

budget *n* : presupuesto *m* — ~ *vi* : presupuestar — **budgetary** *adj* : presupuestario

buff *n* **1** : beige *m*, color *m* de ante **2** ENTHUSIAST : aficionado *m*, -da *f* — ~ *adj* : beige — ~ *vt* POLISH : pulir

buffalo *n, pl* **-lo** *or* **-loes** : búfalo *m*

buffet *n* **1** : bufé *m* (comida) **2** SIDEBOARD : aparador *m*

bug *n* **1** INSECT : bicho *m*, insecto *m* **2** FLAW : defecto *m* **3** GERM : microbio *m* **4** MICROPHONE : micrófono *m* (oculto) — ~ *vt* **bugged; bugging 1** PESTER : fastidiar, molestar **2** : ocultar micrófonos en (una habitación, etc.)

buggy *n, pl* **-gies 1** CARRIAGE : calesa *f* **2** *or* **baby** ~ : cochecito *m* (para niños)

bugle *n* : clarín *m*, corneta *f*

build *v* **built; building** *vt* **1** : construir **2** DEVELOP : desarrollar — *vi* **1** *or* ~ **up** INTENSIFY : aumentar, intensificar **2** *or* ~ **up** ACCUMULATE : acumularse — ~ *n* PHYSIQUE : físico *m*, complexión *f* — **builder** *n* : constructor *m*, -tora *f* — **building** *n* **1** STRUCTURE : edificio *m* **2** CONSTRUCTION : construcción *f* — **built–in** *adj* : empotrado

bulb *n* **1** : bulbo *m* (de una planta) **2** LIGHTBULB : bombilla *f*

bulge *vi* **bulged; bulging** : sobresalir — ~ *n* : bulto *m*, protuberancia *f*

bulk *n* **1** VOLUME : volumen *m*, bulto *m* **2** **in** ~ : en grandes cantidades — **bulky** *adj* **bulkier; -est** : voluminoso

bull *n* **1** : toro *m* **2** MALE : macho *m*

bulldog *n* : buldog *m*

bulldozer *n* : bulldozer *m*

bullet *n* : bala *f*

bulletin *n* : boletín *m* — **bulletin board** *n* : tablón *m* de anuncios

bulletproof *adj* : a prueba de balas
bullfight *n* : corrida *f* (de toros) — **bullfighter** *n* : torero *m*, -ra *f*; matador *m*
bullion *n* : oro *m* en lingotes, plata *f* en lingotes
bull's-eye *n, pl* **bull's-eyes** : diana *f*
bully *n, pl* **-lies** : matón *m* — ~ *vt* **-lied; -lying** : intimidar
bum *n* : vagabundo *m*, -da *f*
bumblebee *n* : abejorro *m*
bump *n* **1** BULGE : bulto *m*, protuberancia *f* **2** IMPACT : golpe *m* **3** JOLT : sacudida *f* — ~ *vt* : chocar contra — *vi* ~ **into** MEET : encontrarse con — **bumper** *n* : parachoques *mpl* — ~ *adj* : extraordinario, récord — **bumpy** *adj* **bumpier; -est 1** : desigual, lleno de baches (dícese de un camino) **2 a** ~ **flight** : un vuelo agitado
bun *n* : bollo *m*
bunch *n* : grupo *m* (de personas), racimo *m* (de frutas, etc.), ramo *m* (de flores), manojo *m* (de llaves) — ~ *vi or* ~ **up** : amontonarse, agruparse
bundle *n* **1** : lío *m*, bulto *m*, atado *m*, haz *m* (de palos) **2** PARCEL : paquete *m* **3** ~ **of nerves** : manojo *m* de nervios — ~ *vt* **-dled; -dling** *or* ~ **up** : liar, atar
bungalow *n* : casa *f* de un solo piso
bungle *vt* **-gled; -gling** : echar a perder
bunion *n* : juanete *m*
bunk *n or* **bunk bed** : litera *f*
bunny *n, pl* **-nies** : conejo *m*, -ja *f*
buoy *n* : boya *f* — ~ *vt or* ~ **up** HEARTEN : animar, levantar el ánimo a — **buoyant** *adj* **1** : boyante, flotante **2** LIGHTHEARTED : alegre, optimista
burden *n* : carga *f* — ~ *vt* ~ **s.o. with** : cargar a algn con — **burdensome** *adj* : oneroso
bureau *n* **1** : cómoda *f* (mueble) **2** : departamento *m* (del gobierno) **3** AGENCY : agencia *f* — **bureaucracy** *n, pl* **-cies** : burocracia *f* — **bureaucrat** *n* : burócrata *mf* — **bureaucratic** *adj* : burocrático
burglar *n* : ladrón *m*, -drona *f* — **burglarize** *vt* **-ized; -izing** : robar — **burglary** *n, pl* **-glaries** : robo *m*
burgundy *n, pl* **-dies** : borgoña *m*, vino *m* de Borgoña
burial *n* : entierro *m*
burly *adj* **-lier; -liest** : fornido
burn *v* **burned** *or* **burnt; burning** *vt* **1** : quemar **2** *or* ~ **down** : incendiar **3** ~ **up** : consumir — *vi* **1** : arder (dícese de un fuego), quemarse (dícese de la comida, etc.) **2** : estar encendido (dícese de una luz) **3** ~ **out** : apagarse — ~ *n* : quemadura *f* — **burner** *n* : quemador *m*
burnish *vt* : pulir

burp *vi* : eructar — ~ *n* : eructo *m*
burro *n, pl* **-os** : burro *m*
burrow *n* : madriguera *f* — ~ *vi* **1** : cavar **2** ~ **into** : hurgar en
bursar *n* : tesorero *m*, -ra *f*
burst *v* **burst** *or* **bursted; bursting** *vi* : reventarse — *vt* : reventar — ~ *n* **1** EXPLOSION : estallido *m*, explosión *f* **2** OUTBURST : arranque *m*, arrebato *m* **3** ~ **of laughter** : carcajada *f*
bury *vt* **buried; burying 1** INTER : enterrar **2** HIDE : esconder
bus *n, pl* **buses** *or* **busses** : autobús *m*, bus *m* — ~ *v* **bused** *or* **bussed; busing** *or* **bussing** *vt* : transportar en autobús — *vi* : viajar en autobús
bush *n* SHRUB : arbusto *m*, mata *f*
bushel *n* : medida *f* de áridos igual a 35.24 litros
bushy *adj* **bushier; -est** : poblado, espeso
busily *adv* : afanosamente
business *n* **1** COMMERCE : negocios *mpl*, comercio *m* **2** COMPANY : empresa *f*, negocio *m* **3 it's none of your** ~ : no es asunto tuyo — **businessman** *n, pl* **-men** : empresario *m*, hombre *m* de negocios — **businesswoman** *n, pl* **-women** : empresaria *f*, mujer *f* de negocios
bust¹ *vt* BREAK : romper
bust² *n* **1** : busto *m* (en la escultura) **2** BREASTS : pecho *m*, senos *mpl*
bustle *vi* **-tled; -tling** *or* ~ **about** : ir y venir, ajetrearse — ~ *n or* **hustle and** ~ : bullicio *m*, ajetreo *m*
busy *adj* **busier; -est 1** : ocupado **2** BUSTLING : concurrido
but *conj* **1** : pero **2 not one** ~ **two** : no uno sino dos — ~ *prep* : excepto, menos
butcher *n* : carnicero *m*, -ra *f* — ~ *vt* **1** : matar **2** BOTCH : hacer una carnicería de
butler *n* : mayordomo *m*
butt *vt* : embestir (con los cuernos), darle un cabezazo a — *vi* ~ **in** : interrumpir — ~ *n* **1** BUTTING : embestida *f* (de cuernos) **2** TARGET : blanco *m* **3** : extremo *m*, culata *f* (de un rifle), colilla *f* (de un cigarrillo)
butter *n* : mantequilla *f* — ~ *vt* : untar con mantequilla
buttercup *n* : ranúnculo *m*
butterfly *n, pl* **-flies** : mariposa *f*
buttocks *npl* : nalgas *fpl*
button *n* : botón *m* — ~ *vt* : abotonar — *vi or* ~ **up** : abotonarse — **buttonhole** *n* : ojal *m* — ~ *vt* **-holed; -holing** : acorralar
buy *vt* **bought; buying** : comprar — ~ *n* : compra *f* — **buyer** *n* : comprador *m*, -dora *f*
buzz *vi* : zumbar — ~ *n* : zumbido *m*
buzzard *n* : buitre *m*

buzzer *n* : timbre *m*
by *prep* **1** NEAR : cerca de **2** VIA : por **3** PAST : por, por delante de **4** DURING : de, durante **5** (*in expressions of time*) : para **6** (*indicating cause or agent*) : por, de, a — $\sim$ *adv* **1** $\sim$ **and** $\sim$: poco después **2** $\sim$ **and large** : en general **3 go** $\sim$: pasar **4 stop** $\sim$: pasar por casa

bygone *adj* : pasado — $\sim$ *n* **let** $\sim$**s be** $\sim$**s** : lo pasado, pasado está
bypass *n* : carretera *f* de circunvalación — $\sim$ *vt* : evitar
by–product *n* : subproducto *m*
bystander *n* : espectador *m*, -dora *f*
byte *n* : byte *m*, octeto *m*
byword *n* **be a** $\sim$ **for** : estar sinónimo de

C

c *n, pl* **c's** *or* **cs** : c, tercera letra del alfabeto inglés
cab *n* **1** : taxi *m* **2** : cabina *f* (de un camión, etc.)
cabbage *n* : col *f*, repollo *m*
cabin *n* **1** : cabaña *f* **2** : cabina *f* (de un avión, etc.), camarote *m* (de un barco)
cabinet *n* **1** CUPBOARD : armario *m* **2** : gabinete *m* (del gobierno) **3** *or* **medicine** $\sim$: botiquín *m*
cable *n* **1** : cable *m* — **cable television** *n* : televisión *f* por cable
cackle *vi* **-led; -ling 1** CLUCK : cacarear **2** LAUGH : reírse a carcajadas
cactus *n, pl* **cacti** *or* **-tuses** : cactus *m*
cadence *n* : cadencia *f*, ritmo *m*
cadet *n* : cadete *mf*
café *n* : café *m*, cafetería *f* — **cafeteria** *n* : restaurante *m* autoservicio, cantina *f*
caffeine *n* : cafeína *f*
cage *n* : jaula *f* — $\sim$ *vt* **caged; caging** : enjaular
cajole *vt* **-joled; -joling** : engatusar
cake *n* **1** : pastel *m*, torta *f* **2** : pastilla *f* (de jabón) **3 take the** $\sim$: ser el colmo — **caked** *adj* $\sim$ **with** : cubierto de
calamity *n, pl* **-ties** : calamidad *f*
calcium *n* : calcio *m*
calculate *v* **-lated; -lating** : calcular — **calculating** *adj* : calculador — **calculation** *n* : cálculo *m* — **calculator** *n* : calculadora *f*
calendar *n* : calendario *m*
calf[1] *n, pl* **calves 1** : becerro *m*, -rra *f*; ternero *m*, -ra *f* (de vacunos) **2** : cría *f* (de otros mamíferos)
calf[2] *n, pl* **calves** : pantorrilla *f* (de la pierna)
caliber *or* **calibre** *n* : calibre *m*
call *vi* **1** : llamar **2** VISIT : pasar, hacer (una) visita **3** $\sim$ **for** : requerir — *vt* **1** : llamar **2** $\sim$ **off** : cancelar — $\sim$ *n* **1** : llamada *f* **2** SHOUT : grito *m* **3** VISIT : visita *f* **4** DEMAND : petición *f* — **calling** *n* : vocación *f*

callous *adj* : insensible, cruel
calm *n* : calma *f*, tranquilidad *f* — $\sim$ *vt* : calmar — *vi* *or* $\sim$ **down** : calmarse — $\sim$ *adj* : tranquilo, en calma — **calmly** *adv* : con calma
calorie *n* : caloría *f*
came → **come**
camel *n* : camello *m*
camera *n* : cámara *f*
camouflage *n* : camuflaje *m* — $\sim$ *vt* **-flaged; -flaging** : camuflar
camp *n* **1** : campamento *m* **2** FACTION : bando *m* — $\sim$ *vi* : acampar, ir de camping
campaign *n* : campaña *f* — $\sim$ *vi* : hacer (una) campaña
camping *n* : camping *m*
campus *n* : ciudad *f* universitaria
can[1] *v aux, past* **could**; *present s & pl* **can 1** (*expressing possibility or permission*) : poder **2** (*expressing knowledge or ability*) : saber **3 that cannot be!** : ¡no puede ser!
can[2] *n* : lata *f* — $\sim$ *vt* **canned; canning** : enlatar
Canadian *adj* : canadiense
canal *n* : canal *m*
canary *n, pl* **-naries** : canario *m*
cancel *vt* **-celed** *or* **-celled; -celing** *or* **-celling** : cancelar — **cancellation** *n* : cancelación *f*
cancer *n* : cáncer *m* — **cancerous** *adj* : canceroso
candelabra *n, pl* **-bra** *or* **-bras** : candelabro *m*
candid *adj* : franco
candidate *n* : candidato *m*, -ta *f* — **candidacy** *n, pl* **-cies** : candidatura *f*
candle *n* : vela *f* — **candlestick** *n* : candelero *m*
candor *or Brit* **candour** *n* : franqueza *f*
candy *n, pl* **-dies** : dulce *m*, caramelo *m*
cane *n* **1** : bastón *m* (para andar), vara *f* (para castigar) **2** REED : caña *f*, mimbre *m*

— ~ *vt* **caned; caning 1** : tapizar con mimbre **2** FLOG : azotar

canine *n or* ~ **tooth** : colmillo *m*, diente *m* canino — ~ *adj* : canino

canister *n* : lata *f*, bote *m Spain*

cannibal *n* : caníbal *mf*

cannon *n, pl* **-nons** *or* **-non** : cañón *m*

cannot (can not) → **can**[1]

canny *adj* **cannier; -est** : astuto

canoe *n* : canoa *f*, piragua *f* — ~ *vt* **-noed; -noeing** : ir en canoa

canon *n* : canon *m* — **canonize** *vt* **-ized; -izing** : canonizar

can opener *n* : abrelatas *m*

canopy *n, pl* **-pies** : dosel *m*

can't (*contraction of* **can not**) → **can**[1]

cantaloupe *n* : melón *m*, cantalupo *m*

cantankerous *adj* : irritable, irascible

canteen *n* **1** FLASK : cantimplora *f* **2** CAFETERIA : cantina *f*

canter *vi* : ir a medio galope — ~ *n* : medio galope *m*

canvas *n* **1** : lona *f* (tela) **2** : lienzo *m* (de pintar)

canvass *vt* **1** : solicitar votos de, hacer campaña entre **2** POLL : sondear — ~ *n* **1** : solicitación *f* (de votos) **2** POLL : sondeo *m*

canyon *n* : cañón *m*

cap *n* **1** : gorra *f*, gorro *m* **2** TOP : tapa *f*, tapón *m* (de botellas) **3** LIMIT : tope *m* — ~ *vt* **capped; capping 1** COVER : tapar, cubrir **2** OUTDO : superar

capable *adj* : capaz, competente — **capability** *n, pl* **-ties** : capacidad *f*

capacity *n, pl* **-ties 1** : capacidad *f* **2** ROLE : calidad *f*

cape[1] *n* : cabo *m* (en geografía)

cape[2] *n* CLOAK : capa *f*

caper[1] *n* : alcaparra *f*

caper[2] *n* PRANK : broma *f*, travesura *f*

capital *adj* **1** : capital **2** : mayúsculo (dícese de las letras) — ~ *n* **1** *or* ~ **city** : capital *f* **2** WEALTH : capital *m* **3** *or* ~ **letter** : mayúscula *f* — **capitalism** *n* : capitalismo *m* — **capitalist** *or* **capitalistic** *adj* : capitalista — **capitalize** *vt* **-ized; -izing 1** FINANCE : capitalizar **2** : escribir con mayúscula — *vi* ~ **on** : sacar partido de

capitol *n* : capitolio *m*

capitulate *vi* **-lated; -lating** : capitular

capsize *v* **-sized; -sizing** *vt* : hacer volcar — *vi* : zozobrar, volcar(se)

capsule *n* : cápsula *f*

captain *n* : capitán *m*, -tana *f*

caption *n* **1** : leyenda *f* (al pie de una ilustración) **2** SUBTITLE : subtítulo *m*

captivate *vt* **-vated; -vating** : cautivar, encantar

captive *adj* : cautivo — ~ *n* : cautivo *m*, -va *f* — **captivity** *n* : cautiverio *m*

capture *n* : captura *f*, apresamiento *m* — ~ *vt* **-tured; -turing 1** SEIZE : capturar, apresar **2** ~ **one's interest** : captar el interés de uno

car *n* **1** : automóvil *m*, coche *m*, carro *m Lat* **2** *or* **railroad** ~ : vagón *m*

carafe *n* : garrafa *f*

caramel *n* : caramelo *m*, azúcar *f* quemada

carat *n* : quilate *m*

caravan *n* : caravana *f*

carbohydrate *n* : carbohidrato *m*, hidrato *m* de carbono

carbon *n* : carbono *m* — **carbon copy** *n* : copia *f*, duplicado *m*

carburetor *n* : carburador *m*

carcass *n* : cuerpo *m* (de un animal muerto)

card *n* **1** : tarjeta *f* **2** *or* **playing** ~ : carta *f*, naipe *m* — **cardboard** *n* : cartón *m*

cardiac *adj* : cardíaco

cardigan *n* : cárdigan *m*

cardinal *n* : cardenal *m* — ~ *adj* : cardinal, fundamental

care *n* **1** : cuidado *m* **2** WORRY : preocupación *f* **3** **take** ~ **of** : cuidar (de) — ~ *vi* **cared; caring 1** : preocuparse, inquietarse **2** ~ **for** TEND : cuidar (de), atender **3** ~ **for** LIKE : querer **4 I don't** ~ : no me importa

career *n* : carrera *f* — ~ *vi* : ir a toda velocidad

carefree *adj* : despreocupado

careful *adj* : cuidadoso — **carefully** *adv* : con cuidado, cuidadosamente — **careless** *adj* : descuidado — **carelessness** *n* : descuido *m*

caress *n* : caricia *f* — ~ *vt* : acariciar

cargo *n, pl* **-goes** *or* **-gos** : cargamento *m*, carga *f*

caricature *n* : caricatura *f* — ~ *vt* **-tured; -turing** : caricaturizar

caring *adj* : solícito, afectuoso

carnage *n* : matanza *f*, carnicería *f*

carnal *adj* : carnal

carnation *n* : clavel *m*

carnival *n* : carnaval *m*

carol *n* : villancico *m*

carp *vi* ~ **at** : quejarse de

carpenter *n* : carpintero *m*, -ra *f* — **carpentry** *n* : carpintería *f*

carpet *n* : alfombra *f*

carriage *n* **1** : transporte *m* (de mercancías) **2** BEARING : porte *m* **3** *or* **baby** ~ : cochecito *m* **4** *or* **horse– drawn** ~ : carruaje *m*, coche *m*

carrier *n* **1** : transportista *mf*, empresa *f* de transportes **2** : portador *m*, -dora *f* (de una enfermedad)

carrot *n* : zanahoria *f*

carry *v* **-ried; -rying** *vt* **1** : llevar **2** TRANSPORT : transportar **3** STOCK : vender **4** ENTAIL : acarrear, implicar **5** ～ **oneself** : portarse — *vi* : oírse (dícese de sonidos) — **carry away** *vt* **get carried away** : exaltarse, entusiasmarse — **carry on** *vt* CONDUCT : realizar — *vi* **1** : portarse inapropiadamente **2** CONTINUE : seguir, continuar — **carry out** *vt* **1** PERFORM : llevar a cabo, realizar **2** FULFILL : cumplir

cart *n* : carreta *f*, carro *m* — ～ *vt or* ～ **around** : acarrear

cartilage *n* : cartílago *m*

carton *n* : caja *f* (de cartón)

cartoon *n* **1** : caricatura *f* **2** COMIC STRIP : historieta *f* **3** *or* **animated** ～ : dibujos *mpl* animados

cartridge *n* : cartucho *m*

carve *vt* **carved; carving** **1** : tallar, esculpir **2** : trinchar (carne)

case *n* **1** : caso *m* **2** BOX : caja *f* **3 in any** ～ : en todo caso **4 in** ～ **of** : en caso de **5 just in** ～ : por si acaso

cash *n* : efectivo *m*, dinero *m* en efectivo — ～ *vt* : convertir en efectivo, cobrar

cashew *n* : anacardo *m*

cashier *n* : cajero *m*, -ra *f*

cashmere *n* : cachemira *f*

cash register *n* : caja *f* registradora

casino *n, pl* **-nos** : casino *m*

cask *n* : barril *m*

casket *n* : ataúd *m*

casserole *n* **1** *or* ～ **dish** : cazuela *f* **2** : guiso *m* (comida)

cassette *n* : cassette *mf*

cast *vt* **cast; casting** **1** THROW : arrojar, lanzar **2** : depositar (un voto) **3** : repartir (papeles dramáticos) **4** MOLD : fundir — ～ *n* **1** : elenco *m*, reparto *m* (de actores) **2** *or* **plaster** ～ : molde *m* de yeso, escayola *f*

castanets *npl* : castañuelas *fpl*

castaway *n* : náufrago *m*, -ga *f*

cast iron *n* : hierro *m* fundido

castle *n* **1** : castillo *m* **2** : torre *f* (en ajedrez)

castrate *vt* **-trated; -trating** : castrar

casual *adj* **1** CHANCE : casual, fortuito **2** INDIFFERENT : despreocupado **3** INFORMAL : informal — **casually** *adv* **1** : de manera despreocupada **2** INFORMALLY : informalmente

casualty *n, pl* **-ties** **1** : accidente *m* **2** VICTIM : víctima *f;* herido *m*, -da *f* **3 casualties** *npl* : bajas *fpl* (militares)

cat *n* : gato *m*, -ta *f*

catalog *or* **catalogue** *n* : catálogo *m* — ～ *vt* **-loged** *or* **-logued; -loging** *or* **-loguing** : catalogar

catapult *n* : catapulta *f*

cataract *n* : catarata *f*

catastrophe *n* : catástrofe *f* — **catastrophic** *adj* : catastrófico

catch *v* **caught; catching** *vt* **1** CAPTURE, TRAP : capturar, atrapar **2** SURPRISE : sorprender **3** GRASP : agarrar, captar **4** SNAG : enganchar **5** : tomar (un tren, etc.) **6** ～ **a cold** : resfriarse — *vi* **1** SNAG : engancharse **2** ～ **fire** : prender fuego — **catching** *adj* : contagioso — **catchy** *adj* **catchier; -est** : pegadizo, pegajoso *Lat*

category *n, pl* **-ries** : categoría *f* — **categorical** *adj* : categórico

cater *vi* **1** : proveer comida **2** ～ **to** : atender a — **caterer** *n* : proveedor *m*, -dora *f* de comida

caterpillar *n* : oruga *f*

catfish *n* : bagre *m*

cathedral *n* : catedral *f*

catholic *adj* **1** : universal **2 Catholic** : católico — **catholicism** *n* : catolicismo *m*

cattle *npl* : ganado *m* (vacuno)

caught → **catch**

cauldron *n* : caldera *f*

cauliflower *n* : coliflor *f*

cause *n* **1** : causa *f* **2** REASON : motivo *m* — ～ *vt* **caused; causing** : causar

caustic *adj* : cáustico

caution *n* **1** WARNING : advertencia *f* **2** CARE : precaución *f,* cautela *f* — ～ *vt* : advertir — **cautious** *adj* : cauteloso, precavido — **cautiously** *adv* : con precaución

cavalier *adj* : arrogante, desdeñoso

cavalry *n, pl* **-ries** : caballería *f*

cave *n* : cueva *f* — ～ *vi* **caved; caving** *or* ～ **in** : hundirse

cavern *n* : caverna *f*

cavity *n, pl* **-ties** **1** : cavidad *f* **2** : caries *f* (dental)

cavort *vi* : brincar

CD *n* : CD *m*, disco *m* compacto

cease *v* **ceased; ceasing** *vt* : dejar de — *vi* : cesar — **cease-fire** *n* : alto *m* el fuego — **ceaseless** *adj* : incesante

cedar *n* : cedro *m*

ceiling *n* : techo *m*

celebrate *v* **-brated; -brating** *vt* : celebrar — *vi* : divertirse — **celebrated** *adj* : célebre — **celebration** *n* **1** : celebración *f* **2** FESTIVITY : fiesta *f* — **celebrity** *n, pl* **-ties** : celebridad *f*

celery *n, pl* **-eries** : apio *m*

cell *n* **1** : célula *f* **2** : celda *f* (en una cárcel, etc.)

cellar *n* **1** BASEMENT : sótano *m* **2** : bodega *f* (de vinos)

cello *n, pl* **-los** : violoncelo *m*

cellular *adj* : celular

cement *n* : cemento *m* — ～ *vt* : cementar

cemetery *n, pl* **-teries** : cementerio *m*

censor *vt* : censurar — **censorship** *n* : censura *f* — **censure** *n* : censura *f* — ~ *vt* **-sured; -suring** : censurar, criticar

census *n* : censo *m*

cent *n* : centavo *m*

centennial *n* : centenario *m*

center *or Brit* **centre** *n* : centro *m* — ~ *v* **centered** *or Brit* **centred; centering** *or Brit* **centring** *vt* : centrar — *vi* ~ **on** : centrarse en

centigrade *adj* : centígrado

centimeter *n* : centímetro *m*

centipede *n* : ciempiés *m*

central *adj* **1** : central **2 a** ~ **location** : un lugar céntrico — **centralize** *vt* **-ized; -izing** : centralizar

centre → **center**

century *n, pl* **-ries** : siglo *m*

ceramics *npl* : cerámica *f*

cereal *n* : cereal *m*

ceremony *n, pl* **-nies** : ceremonia *f* — **ceremonial** *adj* : ceremonial

certain *adj* **1** : cierto **2 be** ~ **of** : estar seguro de **3 for** ~ : seguro, con toda seguridad **4 make** ~ **of** : asegurarse de — **certainly** *adv* : desde luego, por supuesto — **certainty** *n, pl* **-ties** : certeza *f*, seguridad *f*

certify *vt* **-fied; -fying** : certificar — **certificate** *n* : certificado *m*, partida *f*, acta *f*

chafe *v* **chafed; chafing** *vi* : rozarse — *vt* : rozar

chain *n* **1** : cadena *f* **2** ~ **of events** : serie *f* de acontecimientos — ~ *vt* : encadenar

chair *n* **1** : silla *f* **2** : cátedra *f* (en una universidad) — ~ *vt* : presidir — **chairman** *n, pl* **-men** : presidente *m* — **chairperson** *n* : presidente *m*, -ta *f*

chalk *n* : tiza *f*, gis *m Lat*

challenge *vt* **-lenged; -lenging 1** DISPUTE : disputar, poner en duda **2** DARE : desafiar — ~ *n* : reto *m*, desafío *m* — **challenging** *adj* : estimulante

chamber *n* : cámara *f* — **chambermaid** *n* : camarera *f*

champagne *n* : champaña *m*, champán *m*

champion *n* : campeón *m*, -peona *f* — ~ *vt* : defender — **championship** *n* : campeonato *m*

chance *n* **1** LUCK : azar *m*, suerte *f* **2** OPPORTUNITY : oportunidad *f* **3** LIKELIHOOD : probabilidad *f* **4 by** ~ : por casualidad **5 take a** ~ : arriesgarse — ~ *vt* **chanced; chancing** RISK : arriesgar — ~ *adj* : fortuito

chandelier *n* : araña *f* (de luces)

change *v* **changed; changing** *vt* **1** : cambiar **2** SWITCH : cambiar de — *vi* **1** : cambiar **2** *or* ~ **clothes** : cambiarse (de ropa)

— ~ *n* : cambio *m* — **changeable** *adj* : cambiable

channel *n* **1** : canal *m* **2** : cauce *m* (de un río) **3** MEANS : vía *f*, medio *m*

chant *v* : cantar — ~ *n* : canto *m*

chaos *n* : caos *m* — **chaotic** *adj* : caótico

chap[1] *vi* **chapped; chapping** : agrietarse

chap[2] *n* : tipo *m fam*

chapel *n* : capilla *f*

chaperon *or* **chaperone** *n* : acompañante *mf*

chaplain *n* : capellán *m*

chapter *n* : capítulo *m*

char *vt* **charred; charring** : carbonizar

character *n* **1** : carácter *m* **2** : personaje *m* (en una novela, etc.) — **characteristic** *adj* : característico — ~ *n* : característica *f* — **characterize** *vt* **-ized; -izing** : caracterizar

charcoal *n* : carbón *m*

charge *n* **1** : carga *f* (eléctrica) **2** COST : precio *m* **3** BURDEN : carga *f*, peso *m* **4** ACCUSATION : cargo *m*, acusación *f* **5 in** ~ **of** : encargado de **6 take** ~ **of** : hacerse cargo de — ~ *v* **charged; charging** *vt* **1** : cargar **2** ENTRUST : encargar **3** COMMAND : ordenar, mandar **4** ACCUSE : acusar — *vi* **1** : cargar **2** ~ **too much** : cobrar demasiado

charisma *n* : carisma *m* — **charismatic** *adj* : carismático

charity *n, pl* **-ties 1** : organización *f* benéfica **2** GOODWILL : caridad *f*

charlatan *n* : charlatán *m*, -tana *f*

charm *n* **1** : encanto *m* **2** SPELL : hechizo *m* — ~ *vt* : encantar, cautivar — **charming** *adj* : encantador

chart *n* **1** MAP : carta *f* **2** DIAGRAM : gráfico *m*, tabla *f* — ~ *vt* : trazar un mapa de

charter *n* : carta *f* — ~ *vt* : alquilar, fletar

chase *n* : persecución *f* — ~ *vt* **chased; chasing 1** PURSUE : perseguir **2** *or* ~ **away** : ahuyentar

chasm *n* : abismo *m*

chaste *adj* **chaster; -est** : casto — **chastity** *n* : castidad *f*

chat *vi* **chatted; chatting** : charlar — ~ *n* : charla *f* — **chatter** *vi* **1** : parlotear *fam* **2** : castañetear (dícese de los dientes) — ~ *n* : parloteo *m*, cháchara *f* — **chatterbox** *n* : parlanchín *m*, -china *f* — **chatty** *adj* **chattier; chattiest 1** : parlanchín **2** INFORMAL : familiar

chauffeur *n* : chofer *mf*

chauvinist *or* **chauvinistic** *adj* : chauvinista, patriotero

cheap *adj* **1** INEXPENSIVE : barato **2** SHODDY : de baja calidad — ~ *adv* : barato — **cheapen** *vt* : rebajar — **cheaply** *adv* : barato, a precio bajo

cheat *vt* : defraudar, estafar — *vi* **1** : hacer

trampa(s) **2 ∼ on s.o.** : engañar a algn — **∼** *or* **cheater** *n* : tramposo *m*, -sa *f*
check *n* **1** RESTRAINT : freno *m* **2** INSPECTION : inspección *f*, comprobación *f* **3** DRAFT : cheque *m* **4** BILL : cuenta *f* **5** : jaque *m* (en ajedrez) **6** : tela *f* a cuadros — **∼** *vt* **1** RESTRAIN : frenar, contener **2** INSPECT : revisar **3** VERIFY : comprobar **4** : dar jaque (en ajedrez) **5 ∼ in** : enregistrarse (en un hotel) **6 ∼ out** : irse (de un hotel) **7 ∼ out** VERIFY : verificar, comprobar
checkers *n* : damas *fpl*
checkmate *n* : jaque *m* mate
checkpoint *n* : puesto de control
checkup *n* : chequeo *m*, examen *m* médico
cheek *n* : mejilla *f*
cheer *n* **1** CHEERFULNESS : alegría *f* **2** APPLAUSE : aclamación *f* **3 ∼s!** : ¡salud! — **∼** *vt* **1** GLADDEN : alegrar **2** APPLAUD, SHOUT : aclamar, aplaudir — **cheerful** *adj* : alegre
cheese *n* : queso *m*
cheetah *n* : guepardo *m*
chef *n* : chef *m*
chemical *adj* : químico — **∼** *n* : sustancia *f* química — **chemist** *n* : químico *m*, -ca *f* — **chemistry** *n*, *pl* **-tries** : química *f*
cheque *Brit* → **check**
cherish *vt* **1** : querer, apreciar **2** HARBOR : abrigar (un recuerdo, una esperanza, etc.)
cherry *n*, *pl* **-ries** : cereza *f*
chess *n* : ajedrez *m*
chest *n* **1** BOX : cofre *m* **2** : pecho *m* (del cuerpo) **3** *or* **∼ of drawers** : cómoda *f*
chestnut *n* : castaña *f*
chew *vt* : masticar, mascar — **chewing gum** *n* : chicle *m*
chic *adj* : elegante
chick *n* : polluelo *m*, -la *f* — **chicken** *n* : pollo *m* — **chicken pox** *n* : varicela *f*
chicory *n*, *pl* **-ries 1** : endivia *f* (para ensaladas) **2** : achicoria *f* (aditivo de café)
chief *adj* : principal — **∼** *n* : jefe *m*, -fa *f* — **chiefly** *adv* : principalmente
child *n*, *pl* **children 1** : niño *m*, -ña *f* **2** OFFSPRING : hijo *m*, -ja *f* — **childbirth** *n* : parto *m* — **childhood** *n* : infancia *f*, niñez *f* — **childish** *adj* : infantil — **childlike** *adj* : infantil, inocente — **childproof** *adj* : a prueba de niños
Chilean *adj* : chileno
chili *or* **chile** *or* **chilli** *n*, *pl* **chilies** *or* **chiles** *or* **chillies 1** *or* **∼ pepper** : chile *m* **2** : chile *m* con carne
chill *n* **1** CHILLINESS : frío *m* **2 catch a ∼** : resfriarse **3 there's a ∼ in the air** : hace fresco — **∼** *adj* : frío — **∼** *v* : enfriar — **chilly** *adj* **chillier; -est** : fresco, frío

chime *vi* **chimed; chiming** : repicar, sonar — **∼** *n* : carillón *m*
chimney *n*, *pl* **-neys** : chimenea *f*
chimpanzee *n* : chimpancé *m*
chin *n* : barbilla *f*
china *n* : porcelana *f*, loza *f*
Chinese *adj* : chino — **∼** *n* : chino *m* (idioma)
chink *n* : grieta *f*
chip *n* **1** : astilla *f* (de madera o vidrio), lasca *f* (de piedra) **2** : ficha *f* (de póker, etc.) **3** NICK : desportilladura *f* **4** *or* **computer ∼** : chip *m* **5** → **potato chips** — **∼** *v* **chipped; chipping** *vt* : desportillar — *vi* **1** : desportillarse **2 ∼ in** : contribuir
chipmunk *n* : ardilla *f* listada
chiropodist *n* : podólogo *m*, -ga *f*
chiropractor *n* : quiropráctico *m*, -ca *f*
chirp *vi* : piar, gorjear
chisel *n* : cincel *m* (para piedras, etc.), formón *m*, escoplo *m* (para madera) — **∼** *vt* **-eled** *or* **-elled; -eling** *or* **-elling** : cincelar, tallar
chit *n* : nota *f*
chitchat *n* : cháchara *f fam*
chivalrous *adj* : caballeroso — **chivalry** *n*, *pl* **-ries** : caballerosidad *f*
chive *n* : cebollino *m*
chlorine *n* : cloro *m*
chock–full *adj* : repleto, atestado
chocolate *n* : chocolate *m*
choice *n* **1** : elección *f*, selección *f* **2** PREFERENCE : preferencia *f* — **∼** *adj* **choicer; -est** : selecto
choir *n* : coro *m*
choke *v* **choked; choking** *vt* **1** : asfixiar, estrangular **2** BLOCK : atascar — *vi* : asfixiarse, atragantarse (con comida) — **∼** *n* : estárter *m* (de un motor)
choose *v* **chose; chosen; choosing** *vt* **1** SELECT : escoger, elegir **2** DECIDE : decidir — *vi* : escoger — **choosy** *or* **choosey** *adj* **choosier; -est** : exigente
chop *vt* **chopped; chopping 1** : cortar, picar (carne, etc.) **2 ∼ down** : talar — **∼** *n* : chuleta *f* (de cerdo, etc.) — **choppy** *adj* **-pier; -est** : picado, agitado
chopsticks *npl* : palillos *mpl*
chord *n* : acorde *m* (en música)
chore *n* **1** : tarea *f* **2 household ∼s** : faenas *fpl* domésticas
choreography *n*, *pl* **-phies** : coreografía *f*
chortle *vi* **-tled; -tling** : reírse (con satisfacción o júbilo)
chorus 1 : coro *m* (grupo de personas) **2** REFRAIN : estribillo *m*
chose, chosen → **choose**
christen *vt* : bautizar — **christening** *n* : bautizo *m*

Christian *n* : cristiano *m*, -na *f* — ~ *adj* : cristiano — **Christianity** *n* : cristianismo *m*

Christmas *n* : Navidad *f*

chrome *n* : cromo *m*

chronic *adj* : crónico

chronicle *n* : crónica *f*

chronology *n, pl* **-gies** : cronología *f* — **chronological** *adj* : cronológico

chrysanthemum *n* : crisantemo *m*

chubby *adj* **-bier; -est** : regordete *fam*, rechoncho *fam*

chuck *vt* : tirar, arrojar

chuckle *vi* **-led; -ling** : reírse (entre dientes) — ~ *n* : risa *f* ahogada

chum *n* : amigo *m*, -ga *f*; compinche *mf fam* — **chummy** *adj* **-mier; -est** : muy amigable

chunk *n* : trozo *m*, pedazo *m*

church *n* : iglesia *f*

churn *n* : mantequera *f* — ~ *vt* **1** : agitar **2** ~ **out** : producir en grandes cantidades

chute *n* **1** : vertedor *m* **2** SLIDE : tobogán *m*

cider *n* : sidra *f*

cigar *n* : puro *m* — **cigarette** *n* : cigarrillo *m*, cigarro *m*

cinch *n* **it's a** ~ : es pan comido

cinema *n* : cine *m*

cinnamon *n* : canela *f*

cipher *n* **1** ZERO : cero *m* **2** CODE : cifra *f*

circa *prep* : hacia

circle *n* : círculo *m* — ~ *v* **-cled; -cling** *vt* **1** : dar vueltas alrededor de **2** : trazar un círculo alrededor de (un número, etc.) — *vi* : dar vueltas

circuit *n* : circuito *m* — **circuitous** *adj* : tortuoso

circular *adj* : circular — ~ *n* LEAFLET : circular *f*

circulate *v* **-lated; -lating** *vt* : hacer circular — *vi* : circular — **circulation** *n* **1** : circulación *f* **2** : tirada *f* (de una publicación)

circumcise *vt* **-cised; -cising** : circuncidar — **circumcision** *n* : circuncisión *f*

circumference *n* : circunferencia *f*

circumspect *adj* : circunspecto, prudente

circumstance *n* **1** : circunstancia *f* **2 under no** ~**s** : bajo ningún concepto

circus *n* : circo *m*

cistern *n* : cisterna *f*

cite *vt* **cited; citing** : citar — **citation** *n* : citación *f*

citizen *n* : ciudadano *m*, -na *f* — **citizenship** *n* : ciudadanía *f*

citrus *n, pl* **-rus** *or* **-ruses** *or* ~ **fruit** : cítrico *m*

city *n, pl* **cities** : ciudad *f*

civic *adj* : cívico — **civics** *ns & pl* : civismo *m*

civil *adj* : civil — **civilian** *n* : civil *mf* — **civility** *n, pl* **-ties** : cortesía *f* — **civilization** *n* : civilización *f* — **civilize** *vt* **-lized; -lizing** : civilizar

clad *adj* ~ **in** : vestido de

claim *vt* **1** DEMAND : reclamar **2** MAINTAIN : afirmar, sostener **3** ~ **responsibility** : atribuirse la responsabilidad — ~ *n* **1** DEMAND : demanda *f*, reclamación *f* **2** ASSERTION : afirmación *f*

clam *n* : almeja *f*

clamber *vi* : trepar (con torpeza)

clammy *adj* **-mier; -est** : húmedo y algo frío

clamor *n* : clamor *m* — ~ *vi* : clamar

clamp *n* : abrazadera *f* — ~ *vt* : sujetar con abrazaderas — *vi* ~ **down on** : reprimir

clan *n* : clan *m*

clandestine *adj* : clandestino

clang *n* : ruido *m* metálico

clap *v* **clapped; clapping** *vt* **1** : aplaudir **2** ~ **one's hands** : dar palmadas — *vi* : aplaudir — ~ *n* : palmada *f*

clarify *vt* **-fied; -fying** : aclarar — **clarification** *n* : clarificación *f*

clarinet *n* : clarinete *m*

clarity *n* : claridad *f*

clash *vi* **1** : chocar, enfrentarse **2** CONFLICT : estar en conflicto — ~ *n* **1** CRASH : choque *m* **2** CONFLICT : conflicto *m*

clasp *n* : broche *m*, cierre *m* — ~ *vt* **1** : abrazar (a una persona), agarrar (una cosa) **2** FASTEN : abrochar

class *n* : clase *f*

classic *or* **classical** *adj* : clásico — **classic** *n* : clásico *m*

classify *vt* **-fied; -fying** : clasificar — **classification** *n* : clasificación *f* — **classified** *adj* RESTRICTED : secreto

classmate *n* : compañero *m*, -ra *f* de clase

classroom *n* : aula *f*, salón *m* de clase

clatter *vi* : hacer ruido — ~ *n* : estrépito *m*

clause *n* : cláusula *f*

claustrophobia *n* : claustrofobia *f*

claw *n* : garra *f*, uña *f* (de un gato), pinza *f* (de un crustáceo) — ~ *v* : arañar

clay *n* : arcilla *f*

clean *adj* **1** : limpio **2** UNADULTERATED : puro **3** SPOTLESS : impecable — ~ *vt* : limpiar — ~ *adv* : limpio — **cleaner** *n* **1** : limpiador *m*, -dora *f* **2** DRY CLEANER : tintorería *f* — **cleanliness** *n* : limpieza *f* — **cleanse** *vt* **cleansed; cleansing** : limpiar, purificar

clear *adj* **1** : claro **2** TRANSPARENT : transparente **3** UNOBSTRUCTED : despejado, libre — ~ *vt* **1** : despejar (una superficie), desatascar (un tubo, etc.) **2** EXONERATE : absolver **3** : saltar por encima de (un obstáculo) **4** ~ **the table** : levantar la mesa **5** ~ **up** RESOLVE : aclarar, resolver — *vi* **1** ~ **up** BRIGHTEN : despejarse (dícese del tiempo, etc.) **2 ~ up** VANISH : desaparecer (dícese de una infección, etc.) — **~** *adv* **1 make oneself ~** : explicarse **2 stand ~ !** : ¡aléjate! — **clearance** *n* **1** SPACE : espacio *m* (libre) **2** AUTHORIZATION : autorización *f* **3 ~ sale** : liquidación *f* — **clearing** *n* : claro *m* — **clearly** *adv* **1** DISTINCTLY : claramente **2** OBVIOUSLY : obviamente

cleaver *n* : cuchillo *m* de carnicero

clef *n* : clave *f*

cleft *n* : hendidura *f*, grieta *f*

clement *adj* : clemente — **clemency** *n* : clemencia *f*

clench *vt* : apretar

clergy *n*, *pl* **-gies** : clero *m* — **clergyman** *n*, *pl* **-men** : clérigo *m* — **clerical** *adj* **1** : clerical **2 ~ work** : trabajo *m* de oficina

clerk *n* **1** : oficinista *mf*; empleado *m*, -da *f* de oficina **2** SALESPERSON : dependiente *m*, -ta *f*

clever *adj* **1** SKILLFUL : ingenioso, hábil **2** SMART : listo, inteligente — **cleverly** *adv* : ingeniosamente — **cleverness** *n* **1** SKILL : ingenio *m* **2** INTELLIGENCE : inteligencia *f*

cliché *n* : cliché *m*

click *vt* : chasquear — *vi* **1** : chasquear **2** GET ALONG : llevarse bien — **~** *n* : chasquido *m*

client *n* : cliente *m*, -ta *f* — **clientele** *n* : clientela *f*

cliff *n* : acantilado *m*

climate *n* : clima *m*

climax *n* : clímax *m*, punto *m* culminante

climb *vt* : escalar, subir a, trepar a — *vi* **1** RISE : subir **2** *or* **~ up** : subirse, treparse — **~** *n* : subida *f*

clinch *vt* : cerrar (un acuerdo, etc.)

cling *vi* clung; **clinging** : adherirse, pegarse

clinic *n* : clínica *f* — **clinical** *adj* : clínico

clink *vi* : tintinear

clip *vt* **clipped; clipping 1** CUT : cortar, recortar **2** FASTEN : sujetar (con un clip) — **~** *n* **1** FASTENER : clip *m* **2 at a good ~** : a buen trote **3 ~ paper clip** — **clippers** *npl* **1** : maquinilla *f* para cortar el pelo **2** *or* **nail ~** : cortaúñas *m*

cloak *n* : capa *f*

clock 1 : reloj *m* (de pared) **2 around the ~** : las veinticuatro horas — **clockwise** *adv & adj* : en el sentido de las agujas del reloj — **clockwork** *n* **1** : mecanismo *m* de relojería **2 like ~** : con precisión

clog *n* : zueco *m* — **~** *v* **clogged; clogging** *vt* : atascar, obstruir — *vi or* **~ up** : atascarse

cloister *n* : claustro *m*

close[1] *v* **closed; closing** *vt* : cerrar — *vi* **1** : cerrarse **2** TERMINATE : terminar **3 ~ in** : acercarse — **~** *n* : final *m*

close[2] *adj* **closer; closest 1** NEAR : cercano, próximo **2** INTIMATE : íntimo **3** STRICT : estricto **4** STUFFY : sofocante **5 a ~ game** : un juego reñido — **~** *adv* : cerca, de cerca — **closely** *adv* : cerca, de cerca — **closeness** *n* **1** NEARNESS : cercanía *f* **2** INTIMACY : intimidad *f*

closet *n* : armario *m*, clóset *m Lat*

closure *n* : cierre *m*

clot *n* : coágulo *m* — **~** *v* **clotted; clotting** *vt* : coagular, cuajar — *vi* : coagularse

cloth *n*, *pl* **cloths 1** FABRIC : tela *f* **2** RAG : trapo *m*

clothe *vt* **clothed** *or* **clad; clothing** : vestir — **clothes** *npl* **1** : ropa *f* **2 put on one's ~** : vestirse — **clothespin** *n* : pinza *f* (para la ropa) — **clothing** *n* : ropa *f*

cloud *n* : nube *f* — **~** *vt* : nublar — *vi or* **~ over** : nublarse — **cloudy** *adj* **cloudier; -est** : nublado

clout *n* **1** BLOW : golpe *m*, tortazo *m fam* **2** INFLUENCE : influencia *f*

clove *n* **1** : clavo *m* **2** : diente *m* (de ajo)

clover *n* : trébol *m*

clown *n* : payaso *m*, -sa *f* — **~** *or* **~ around** *vi* : payasear

cloying *adj* : empalagoso

club *n* **1** : garrote *m*, porra *f* **2** ASSOCIATION : club *m* **3 ~s** *mpl* : tréboles *mpl* (en los naipes) — **~** *vt* **clubbed; clubbing** : aporrear

cluck *vi* : cloquear

clue *n* **1** : pista *f*, indicio *m* **2 I haven't got a ~** : no tengo la menor idea

clump *n* : grupo *m* (de arbustos)

clumsy *adj* **-sier; -est** : torpe — **clumsiness** *n* : torpeza *f*

cluster *n* : grupo *m*, racimo *m* (de uvas, etc.) — **~** *vi* : agruparse

clutch *vt* : agarrar, asir — *vi* **~ at** : tratar de agarrarse de — **~** *n* : embrague *m*, clutch *m Lat* (de un automóvil)

clutter *vt* : llenar desordenadamente — **~** *n* : desorden *m*, revoltijo *m*

coach *n* **1** CARRIAGE : carruaje *m*, carroza *f* **2** : vagón *m* de pasajeros (de un tren) **3** BUS : autobús *m* **4** : pasaje *m* aéreo de segunda clase **5** TRAINER : entrenador *m*, -dora *f* — *vt* : entrenar (un atleta), dar clases particulares a (un alumno)

coagulate *v* **-lated; -lating** *vt* : coagular — *vi* : coagularse

coal *n* : carbón *m*

coalition *n* : coalición *f*

coarse *adj* **coarser; -est 1** : tosco, basto **2** CRUDE, VULGAR : grosero, ordinario — **coarseness** *n* : aspereza *f*, tosquedad *f*

coast *n* : costa *f* — **~** *vi* : ir en punto muerto (dícese de un automóvil), deslizarse (dícese de una bicicleta) — **coastal** *adj* : costero

coaster *n* : posavasos *m*
coast guard *n* : guardacostas *mpl*
coastline *n* : litoral *m*
coat *n* **1** : abrigo *m* **2** : pelaje *m* (de un animal) **3** : mano *f* (de pintura) — ~ *vt* : cubrir, revestir — **coating** *n* : capa *f* —
coat of arms *n* : escudo *m* de armas
coax *vt* : engatusar
cob → **corncob**
cobblestone *n* : adoquín *m*
cobweb *n* : telaraña *f*
cocaine *n* : cocaína *f*
cock *n* **1** ROOSTER : gallo *m* **2** FAUCET : grifo *m* **3** : martillo *m* (de un arma de fuego) — ~ *vt* **1** : amartillar (un arma de fuego) **2** ~ **one's head** : ladear la cabeza — **cockeyed** *adj* **1** ASKEW : ladeado **2** ABSURD : absurdo
cockpit *n* : cabina *f*
cockroach *n* : cucaracha *f*
cocktail *n* : coctel *m*, cóctel *m*
cocky *adj* **cockier; -est** : engreído, arrogante
cocoa *n* **1** : cacao *m* **2** : chocolate *m* (bebida)
coconut *n* : coco *m*
cocoon *n* : capullo *m*
cod *ns & pl* : bacalao *m*
coddle *vt* **-dled; -dling** : mimar
code *n* : código *m*
coeducational *adj* : mixto
coerce *vt* **-erced; -ercing** : coaccionar, forzar — **coercion** *n* : coacción *f*
coffee *n* : café *m* — **coffeepot** *n* : cafetera *f*
coffer *n* : cofre *m*
coffin *n* : ataúd *m*, féretro *m*
cog *n* : diente *m* (de una rueda)
cogent *adj* : convincente, persuasivo
cognac *n* : coñac *m*
cogwheel *n* : rueda *f* dentada
coherent *adj* : coherente
coil *vt* : enrollar — *vi* : enrollarse — ~ *n* **1** ROLL : rollo *m* **2** : tirabuzón *m* (de pelo), espiral *f* (de humo)
coin *n* : moneda *f* — ~ *vt* : acuñar
coincide *vi* **-cided; -ciding** : coincidir — **coincidence** *n* : coincidencia *f*, casualidad *f* — **coincidental** *adj* : casual, fortuito
coke *n* : coque *m* (combustible)
colander *n* : colador *m*
cold *adj* **1** : frío **2 be** ~ : tener frío **3 it's** ~ **today** : hace frío hoy — ~ *n* **1** : frío *m* **2** : resfriado *m* (en medicina) **3 catch a** ~ : resfriarse
coleslaw *n* : ensalada *f* de col
colic *n* : cólico *m*
collaborate *vi* **-rated; -rating** : colaborar — **collaboration** *n* : colaboración *f* — **collaborator** *n* : colaborador *m*, -dora *f*

collapse *vi* **-lapsed; -lapsing 1** : derrumbarse, hundirse **2** : sufrir un colapso (físico o mental) — ~ *n* **1** FALL : derrumbamiento *m* **2** BREAKDOWN : colapso *m* — **collapsible** *adj* : plegable
collar *n* : cuello *m* (de camisa, etc.), collar *m* (para animales) — **collarbone** *n* : clavícula *f*
colleague *n* : colega *mf*
collect *vt* **1** GATHER : reunir **2** : coleccionar, juntar (timbres, etc.) **3** : recaudar (fondos, etc.) — *vi* **1** ACCUMULATE : acumularse, juntarse **2** CONGREGATE : congregarse, reunirse — ~ *adv* **call** ~ : llamar a cobro revertido, llamar por cobrar *Lat* — **collection** *n* **1** : colección *f* **2** : colecta *f* (de contribuciones) — **collective** *adj* : colectivo — **collector** *n* **1** : coleccionista *mf* **2** : cobrador *m*, -dora *f* (de deudas)
college *n* **1** : instituto *m* (a nivel universitario) **2** : colegio *m* (electoral, etc.)
collide *vi* **-lided; -liding** : chocar, colisionar — **collision** *n* : choque *m*, colisión *f*
colloquial *adj* : coloquial, familiar
cologne *n* : colonia *f*
Colombian *adj* : colombiano
colon¹ *n*, *pl* **colons** *or* **cola** : colon *m* (en anatomía)
colon² *n*, *pl* **colons** : dos puntos *mpl* (signo de puntuación)
colonel *n* : coronel *m*
colony *n*, *pl* **-nies** : colonia *f* — **colonial** *adj* : colonial — **colonize** *vt* **-nized; -nizing** : colonizar
color *or Brit* **colour** *n* : color *m* — ~ *vt* : colorear, pintar — *vi* BLUSH : sonrojarse — **color–blind** *or Brit* **colour-blind** *adj* : daltónico — **colored** *or Brit* **coloured** *adj* : de color — **colorful** *or Brit* **colourful** *adj* **1** : de vivos colores **2** PICTURESQUE : pintoresco — **colorless** *or Brit* **colourless** *adj* : incoloro
colossal *adj* : colosal
colt *n* : potro *m*
column *n* : columna *f* — **columnist** *n* : columnista *mf*
coma *n* : coma *m*
comb *n* **1** : peine *m* **2** : cresta *f* (de un gallo) — ~ *vt* : peinar
combat *n* : combate *m* — ~ *vt* **-bated** *or* **-batted; -bating** *or* **-batting** : combatir — **combatant** *n* : combatiente *mf*
combine *v* **-bined; -bining** *vt* : combinar — *vi* : combinarse — ~ *n* HARVESTER : cosechadora *f* — **combination** *n* : combinación *f*
combustion *n* : combustión *f*
come *vi* **came; come; coming 1** : venir **2** ARRIVE : llegar **3** ~ **about** : suceder **4** ~

back : regresar, volver **5 ～ from** : venir de, provenir de **6 ～ in** : entrar **7 ～ out** : salir **8 ～ to** REVIVE : volver en sí **9 ～ on!** : ¡ándale! **10 ～ up** OCCUR : surgir **11 how ～?** : ¿por qué? — **comeback** n **1** RETURN : retorno m **2** RETORT : réplica f
comedy n, pl **-dies** : comedia f — **comedian** n : cómico m, **-ca** f
comet n : cometa m
comfort vt : consolar — **～** n **1** : comodidad f **2** SOLACE : consuelo m — **comfortable** adj : cómodo
comic or **comical** adj : cómico — **～** n **1** COMEDIAN : cómico m, **-ca** f **2** or **～ book** : revista f de historietas, cómic m — **comic strip** n : tira f cómica, historieta f
coming adj : próximo, que viene
comma n : coma f
command vt **1** ORDER : ordenar, mandar **2** : estar al mando de (un barco, etc.) **3 ～ respect** : inspirar (el) respeto — vi : dar órdenes — **～** n **1** ORDER : orden f **2** LEADERSHIP : mando m **3** MASTERY : maestría f, dominio m — **commander** n : comandante mf — **commandment** n : mandamiento m
commemorate vt **-rated; -rating** : conmemorar — **commemoration** n : conmemoración f
commence v **-menced; -mencing** : comenzar, empezar — **commencement** n **1** BEGINNING : comienzo m **2** GRADUATION : ceremonia f de graduación
commend vt **1** ENTRUST : encomendar **2** PRAISE : alabar — **commendable** adj : loable
comment n : comentario m, observación f — **～** vi : hacer comentarios — **commentary** n, pl **-taries** : comentario m — **commentator** n : comentarista mf
commerce n : comercio m — **commercial** adj : comercial — **～** n : anuncio m, aviso m Lat — **commercialize** vt **-ized; -izing** : comercializar
commiserate vi **-ated; -ating** : compadecerse
commission n : comisión f — **～** vt : encargar (una obra de arte) — **commissioner** n : comisario m, **-ria** f
commit vt **-mitted; -mitting 1** ENTRUST : confiar **2** : cometer (un crimen) **3** : internar (a algn en un hospital) **4 ～ oneself** : comprometerse **5 ～ to memory** : aprender de memoria — **commitment** n : compromiso m
committee n : comité m, comisión f
commodity n, pl **-ties** : artículo m de comercio, producto m
common adj **1** : común **2** ORDINARY : ordinario, común y corriente — **～** n **in ～** : en

común — **commonly** adv : comúnmente — **commonplace** adj : común, banal — **common sense** n : sentido m común
commotion n : alboroto m, jaleo m
commune[1] n : comuna f — **communal** adj : comunal
commune[2] vi **-muned; -muning ～ with** : comunicarse con
communicate v **-cated; -cating** vt : comunicar — vi : comunicarse — **communicable** adj : transmisible — **communication** n : comunicación f — **communicative** adj : comunicativo
communion n : comunión f
Communism n : comunismo m — **Communist** adj : comunista — **～** n : comunista mf
community n, pl **-ties** : comunidad f
commute v **-muted; -muting** vt : conmutar, reducir (una sentencia) — vi : viajar de la residencia al trabajo
compact adj : compacto — **～** n **1** or **～ car** : auto m compacto **2** or **powder ～** : polvera f — **compact disc** n : disco m compacto
companion n : compañero m, **-ra** f — **companionship** n : compañerismo m
company n, pl **-nies 1** : compañía f **2** GUESTS : visita f
compare v **-pared; -paring** vt : comparar — vi **～ with** : poderse comparar con — **comparable** adj : comparable — **comparative** adj : comparativo, relativo — **comparison** n : comparación f
compartment n : compartimento m
compass n **1** : compás m **2 points of the ～** : puntos mpl cardinales
compassion n : compasión f — **compassionate** adj : compasivo
compatible adj : compatible, afín — **compatibility** n : compatibilidad f
compel vt **-pelled; -pelling** : obligar — **compelling** adj : convincente
compensate v **-sated; -sating** vi **～ for** : compensar — vt : indemnizar, compensar — **compensation** n : compensación f, indemnización f
compete vi **-peted; -peting** : competir — **competent** adj : competente — **competition** n **1** : competencia f **2** CONTEST : concurso m — **competitor** n : competidor m, **-dora** f
compile vt **-piled; -piling** : compilar, recopilar
complacency n : satisfacción f consigo mismo — **complacent** adj : satisfecho de sí mismo
complain vi : quejarse — **complaint** n **1** : queja f **2** AILMENT : enfermedad f
complement n : complemento m — **～** vt

: complementar — **complementary** adj : complementario

complete adj -pleter; -est 1 WHOLE : completo, entero 2 FINISHED : terminado 3 TOTAL : total — ～ vt -pleted; -pleting : completar — **completion** n : conclusión f

complex adj : complejo — ～ n : complejo m

complexion n : cutis m, tez f

complexity n, pl -ties : complejidad f

compliance n 1 : acatamiento m 2 in ～ with : conforme a — **compliant** adj : sumiso

complicate vt -cated; -cating : complicar — **complicated** adj : complicado — **complication** n : complicación f

compliment n 1 : cumplido m 2 ～s npl : saludos mpl — ～ vt : felicitar — **complimentary** adj 1 FLATTERING : halagador, halagueño 2 FREE : de cortesía, gratis

comply vi -plied; -plying ～ with : cumplir, obedecer

component n : componente m

compose vt -posed; -posing 1 : componer 2 ～ oneself : serenarse — **composer** n : compositor m, -tora f — **composition** n 1 : composición f 2 ESSAY : ensayo m — **composure** n : calma f

compound[1] vt 1 COMPOSE : componer 2 : agravar (un problema, etc.) — ～ adj : compuesto — ～ n : compuesto m

compound[2] n ENCLOSURE : recinto m

comprehend vt : comprender — **comprehension** n : comprensión f — **comprehensive** adj 1 INCLUSIVE : inclusivo 2 BROAD : amplio

compress vt : comprimir — **compression** n : compresión f

comprise vt -prised; -prising : comprender

compromise n : acuerdo m, arreglo m — ～ v -mised; -mising vi : llegar a un acuerdo — vt : comprometer

compulsion n 1 COERCION : coacción f 2 URGE : impulso m — **compulsive** adj : compulsivo — **compulsory** adj : obligatorio

compute vt -puted; -puting : computar — **computer** n : computadora f, computador m, ordenador m Spain — **computerize** vt -ized; -izing : informatizar

comrade n : camarada mf

con vt conned; conning : estafar — ～ n 1 SWINDLE : estafa f 2 the pros and ～s : los pros y los contras

concave adj : cóncavo

conceal vt : ocultar

concede vt -ceded; -ceding : conceder, admitir

conceit n : vanidad f — **conceited** adj : engreído

conceive v -ceived; -ceiving vt : concebir — vi ～ of : concebir — **conceivable** adj : concebible

concentrate v -trated; -trating vt : concentrar — vi : concentrarse — **concentration** n : concentración f

concept n : concepto m — **conception** n : concepción f

concern vt 1 : concernir 2 ～ oneself about : preocuparse por — ～ n 1 AFFAIR : asunto m 2 WORRY : preocupación f 3 BUSINESS : negocio m — **concerned** adj 1 ANXIOUS : ansioso 2 as far as I'm ～ : en cuanto a mí — **concerning** prep : con respecto a

concert n : concierto m — **concerted** adj : concertado

concession n : concesión f

concise adj : conciso

conclude v -cluded; -cluding : concluir — **conclusion** n : conclusión f — **conclusive** adj : concluyente

concoct vt 1 PREPARE : confeccionar 2 DEVISE : inventarse, tramar — **concoction** n : mezcla f, brebaje m

concourse n : vestíbulo m, salón m

concrete adj : concreto — ～ n : hormigón m, concreto m Lat

concur vi concurred; concurring AGREE : estar de acuerdo

concussion n : conmoción f cerebral

condemn vt : condenar — **condemnation** n : condenación f

condense v -densed; -densing vt : condensar — vi : condensarse — **condensation** n : condensación f

condescending adj : condescendiente

condiment n : condimento m

condition n 1 : condición f 2 in good ～ : en buen estado — **conditional** adj : condicional

condolences npl : pésame m

condom n : condón m

condominium n, pl -ums : condominio m Lat

condone vt -doned; -doning : aprobar

conducive adj : propicio, favorable

conduct n : conducta f — ～ vt 1 DIRECT, GUIDE : conducir, dirigir 2 CARRY OUT : llevar a cabo 3 ～ oneself : conducirse, comportarse — **conductor** n : revisor m, -sora f (en un tren); cobrador m, -dora f (en un autobús); director m, -tora f (de una orquesta)

cone n 1 : cono m 2 or ice– cream ～ : cucurucho m, barquillo m Lat

confection n : dulce m

confederation n : confederación f

confer v -ferred; -ferring vt : conferir, otorgar — *vi* ~ **with** : consultar — **conference** *n* : conferencia *f*

confess *vt* : confesar — *vi* **1** : confesarse **2** ~ **to** : confesar, admitir — **confession** *n* : confesión *f*

confetti *n* : confeti *m*

confide *v* **-fided; -fiding** : confiar — **confidence** *n* **1** TRUST : confianza *f* **2** SELF-ASSURANCE : confianza *f* en sí mismo **3** SECRET : confidencia *f* — **confident** *adj* **1** SURE : seguro **2** SELF-ASSURED : confiado, seguro de sí mismo — **confidential** *adj* : confidencial

confine *vt* **-fined; -fining 1** LIMIT : confinar, limitar **2** IMPRISON : encerrar — **confines** *npl* : confines *mpl*

confirm *vt* : confirmar — **confirmation** *n* : confirmación *f* — **confirmed** *adj* : inveterado

confiscate *vt* **-cated; -cating** : confiscar

conflict *n* : conflicto *m* — ~ *vi* : estar en conflicto, oponerse

conform *vi* **1** COMPLY : ajustarse **2** ~ **with** : corresponder a — **conformity** *n, pl* **-ties** : conformidad *f*

confound *vt* : confundir, desconcertar

confront *vt* : afrontar, encarar — **confrontation** *n* : confrontación *f*

confuse *vt* **-fused; -fusing** : confundir — **confusing** *adj* : confuso, desconcertante — **confusion** *n* : confusión *f,* desconcierto *m*

congeal *vi* : coagularse

congenial *adj* : agradable

congested *adj* : congestionado — **congestion** *n* : congestión *f*

congratulate *vt* **-lated; -lating** : felicitar — **congratulations** *npl* : felicitaciones *fpl*

congregate *vi* **-gated; -gating** : congregarse — **congregation** *n* : feligreses *mpl* (en religión)

congress *n* : congreso *m* — **congressional** *adj* : del congreso — **congressman** *n, pl* **-men** : congresista *mf*

conjecture *n* : conjetura *f,* presunción *f* — ~ *v* **-tured; -turing** *vt* : conjeturar — *vi* : hacer conjeturas

conjugal *adj* : conyugal

conjugate *vt* **-gated; -gating** : conjugar — **conjugation** *n* : conjugación *f*

conjunction *n* **1** : conjunción *f* **2 in** ~ **with** : en combinación con

conjure *v* **-jured; -juring** *vi* : hacer juegos de manos — ~ *vt or* ~ **up** : evocar

connect *vi* : conectarse — *vt* **1** JOIN : conectar, juntar **2** ASSOCIATE : asociar — **connection** *n* **1** : conexión *f* **2** : enlace *m* (con un tren, etc.) **3** ~**s** *npl* : relaciones *fpl* (personas)

connoisseur *n* : conocedor *m,* -dora *f*

connote *vt* **-noted; -noting** : connotar, implicar

conquer *vt* : conquistar — **conqueror** *n* : conquistador *m,* -dora *f* — **conquest** *n* : conquista *f*

conscience *n* : conciencia *f* — **conscientious** *adj* : concienzudo

conscious *adj* **1** AWARE : consciente **2** INTENTIONAL : intencional — **consciously** *adv* : deliberadamente — **consciousness** *n* **1** AWARENESS : consciencia *f* **2 lose** ~ : perder el conocimiento

consecrate *vt* **-crated; -crating** : consagrar — **consecration** *n* : consagración *f*

consecutive *adj* : consecutivo, sucesivo

consensus *n* : consenso *m*

consent *vi* : consentir — ~ *n* : consentimiento *m*

consequence *n* **1** : consecuencia *f* **2 of no** ~ : sin importancia — **consequent** *adj* : consiguiente — **consequently** *adv* : por consiguiente

conserve *vt* **-served; -serving** : conservar, preservar — **conservation** *n* : conservación *f* — **conservative** *adj* **1** : conservador **2** CAUTIOUS : moderado, prudente — ~ *n* : conservador *m,* -dora *f* — **conservatory** *n, pl* **-ries** : conservatorio *m*

consider *vt* **1** : considerar **2 all things considered** : teniéndolo todo en cuenta — **considerable** *adj* : considerable — **considerate** *adj* : considerado — **consideration** *n* **1** : consideración *f* **2 take into** ~ : tener en cuenta — **considering** *prep* : teniendo en cuenta

consign *vt* **1** : relegar **2** SEND : enviar — **consignment** *n* : envío *m*

consist *vi* **1** ~ **in** : consistir en **2** ~ **of** : constar de, componerse de — **consistency** *n, pl* **-cies 1** TEXTURE : consistencia *f* **2** COHERENCE : coherencia *f* **3** UNIFORMITY : regularidad *f* — **consistent** *adj* **1** UNCHANGING : constante, regular **2** ~ **with** : consecuente con

console *vt* **-soled; -soling** : consolar — **consolation** *n* **1** : consuelo *m* **2** ~ **prize** : premio *m* de consolación

consolidate *vt* **-dated; -dating** : consolidar — **consolidation** *n* : consolidación *f*

consonant *n* : consonante *f*

conspicuous *adj* **1** OBVIOUS : visible, evidente **2** STRIKING : llamativo — **conspicuously** *adv* : de manera llamativa

conspire *vi* **-spired; -spiring** : conspirar — **conspiracy** *n, pl* **-cies** : conspiración *f*

constant *adj* : constante — **constantly** *adv* : constantemente

constellation *n* : constelación *f*

constipated *adj* : estreñido — **constipation** *n* : estreñimiento *m*

constituent *n* **1** COMPONENT : componente *m* **2** VOTER : elector *m*, -tora *f;* votante *mf*

constitute *vt* **-tuted; -tuting** : constituir — **constitution** *n* : constitución *f* — **constitutional** *adj* : constitucional

constraint *n* : restricción *f,* limitación *f*

construct *vt* : construir — **construction** *n* : construcción *f* — **constructive** *adj* : constructivo

construe *vt* **-strued; -struing** : interpretar

consul *n* : cónsul *mf* — **consulate** *n* : consulado *m*

consult *v* : consultar — **consultant** *n* : asesor *m*, -sora *f;* consultor *m*, -tora *f* — **consultation** *n* : consulta *f*

consume *vt* **-sumed; -suming** : consumir — **consumer** *n* : consumidor *m*, -dora *f* — **consumption** *n* : consumo *m*

contact *n* : contacto *m* — ~ *vt* : ponerse en contacto con — **contact lens** *n* : lente *mf* (de contacto)

contagious *adj* : contagioso

contain *vt* **1** : contener **2** ~ **oneself** : contenerse — **container** *n* : recipiente *m*, envase *m*

contaminate *vt* **-nated; -nating** : contaminar — **contamination** *n* : contaminación *f*

contemplate *vt* **-plated; -plating** *vt* **1** : contemplar **2** CONSIDER : considerar, pensar en — *vi* : reflexionar — **contemplation** *n* : contemplación *f*

contemporary *adj* : contemporáneo — ~ *n, pl* **-raries** : contemporáneo *m*, -nea *f*

contempt *n* : desprecio *m* — **contemptible** *adj* : despreciable — **contemptuous** *adj* : desdeñoso

contend *vi* **1** COMPETE : contender, competir **2** ~ **with** : enfrentarse a — *vt* : sostener, afirmar — **contender** *n* : contendiente *mf*

content¹ *n* **1** : contenido *m* **2 table of** ~**s** : índice *m* de materias

content² *adj* : contento — ~ *vt* ~ **oneself with** : contentarse con — **contented** *adj* : satisfecho, contento

contention *n* **1** DISPUTE : disputa *f* **2** OPINION : argumento *m*, opinión *f*

contentment *n* : satisfacción *f*

contest *vt* : disputar — ~ *n* **1** STRUGGLE : contienda *f* **2** COMPETITION : concurso *m*, competencia *f* — **contestant** *n* : concursante *mf*, contendiente *mf*

context *n* : contexto *m*

continent *n* : continente *m* — **continental** *adj* : continental

contingency *n, pl* **-cies** : contingencia *f*

continue *v* **-tinued; -tinuing** : continuar — **continual** *adj* : continuo, constante — **continuation** *n* : continuación *f* — **continuity** *n, pl* **-ties** : continuidad *f* — **continuous** *adj* : continuo

contort *vt* : retorcer — **contortion** *n* : contorsión *f*

contour *n* **1** : contorno *m* **2** *or* ~ **line** : curva *f* de nivel

contraband *n* : contrabando *m*

contraception *n* : anticoncepción *f* — **contraceptive** *adj* : anticonceptivo — ~ *n* : anticonceptivo *m*

contract *n* : contrato *m* — ~ *vt* : contraer — *vi* : contraerse — **contraction** *n* : contracción *f* — **contractor** *n* : contratista *mf*

contradiction *n* : contradicción *f* — **contradict** *vt* : contradecir — **contradictory** *adj* : contradictorio

contraption *n* : artilugio *m*, artefacto *m*

contrary *n, pl* **-traries 1** : contrario **2 on the** ~ : al contrario — ~ *adj* **1** : contrario, opuesto **2** ~ **to** : en contra de

contrast *v* : contrastar — ~ *n* : contraste *m*

contribute *v* **-uted; -uting** : contribuir — **contribution** *n* : contribución *f* — **contributor** *n* **1** : contribuyente *mf* **2** : colaborador *m*, -dora *f* (en periodismo)

contrite *adj* : arrepentido

contrive *vt* **-trived; -triving 1** DEVISE : idear **2** ~ **to do sth** : lograr hacer algo

control *vt* **-trolled; -trolling** : controlar — ~ *n* **1** : control *m* **2** ~**s** *npl* : mandos *mpl*

controversy *n, pl* **-sies** : controversia *f* — **controversial** *adj* : polémico

convalescence *n* : convalecencia *f* — **convalescent** *adj* : convaleciente — ~ *n* : convaleciente *mf*

convene *v* **-vened; -vening** *vt* : convocar — *vi* : reunirse

convenience *n* : conveniencia *f,* comodidad *f* — **convenient** *adj* : conveniente

convent *n* : convento *m*

convention *n* : convención *f* — **conventional** *adj* : convencional

converge *vi* **-verged; -verging** : converger, convergir

converse¹ *vi* **-versed; -versing** : conversar — **conversation** *n* : conversación *f* — **conversational** *adj* : familiar

converse² *adj* : contrario, opuesto — **conversely** *adv* : a la inversa

conversion *n* : conversión *f* — **convert** *vt* : convertir — *vi* : convertirse — **convertible** *adj* : convertible — ~ *n* : descapotable *m*, convertible *m Lat*

convex *adj* : convexo

convey *vt* **1** TRANSPORT : llevar, transportar **2** TRANSMIT : comunicar

convict *vt* : declarar culpable a — ~ *n* : presidiario *m*, -ria *f* — **conviction** *n* **1** : condena *f* (de un acusado) **2** BELIEF : convicción *f*

convince *vt* **-vinced; -vincing** : convencer — **convincing** *adj* : convincente

convoke *vt* **-voked; -voking** : convocar

convoluted *adj* : complicado

convulsion *n* : convulsión *f* — **convulsive** *adj* : convulsivo

cook *n* : cocinero *m*, -ra *f* — ~ *vi* : cocinar, guisar — *vt* : preparar (comida) — **cookbook** *n* : libro *m* de cocina

cookie *or* **cooky** *n, pl* **-ies** : galleta *f* (dulce)

cooking *n* : cocina *f*

cool *adj* **1** : fresco **2** CALM : tranquilo **3** UNFRIENDLY : frío — ~ *vt* : enfriar — *vi* : enfriarse — ~ *n* **1** : fresco *m* **2** COMPOSURE : calma *f* — **cooler** *n* : nevera *f* portátil — **coolness** *n* : frescura *f*

coop *n* : gallinero *m* — ~ *vt or* ~ **up** : encerrar

cooperate *vi* **-ated; -ating** : cooperar — **cooperation** *n* : cooperación *f* — **cooperative** *adj* : cooperativo

coordinate *v* **-nated; -nating** *vt* : coordinar — **coordination** *n* : coordinación *f*

cop *n* **1** : poli *mf fam* **2 the ~s** : la poli *fam*

cope *vi* **coped; coping 1** : arreglárselas **2** ~ **with** : hacer frente a, poder con

copier *n* : fotocopiadora *f*

copious *adj* : copioso

copper *n* : cobre *m*

copy *n, pl* **copies 1** : copia *f* **2** : ejemplar *m* (de un libro), número *m* (de una revista) — ~ *vt* **copied; copying 1** DUPLICATE : hacer una copia de **2** IMITATE : copiar — **copyright** *n* : derechos *mpl* de autor

coral *n* : coral *m*

cord *n* **1** : cuerda *f* **2** *or* **electric ~** : cable *m* (eléctrico)

cordial *adj* : cordial

corduroy *n* : pana *f*

core *n* **1** : corazón *m* (de una fruta) **2** CENTER : núcleo *m*, centro *m*

cork *n* : corcho *m* — **corkscrew** *n* : sacacorchos *m*

corn *n* **1** : grano *m* **2** *or* **Indian ~** : maíz *m* **3** : callo *m* (del pie) — **corncob** *n* : mazorca *f*

corner *n* : ángulo *m*, rincón *m* (en una habitación), esquina *f* (de una intersección) — ~ *vt* **1** TRAP : acorralar **2** MONOPOLIZE : acaparar (un mercado) — **cornerstone** *n* : piedra *f* angular

cornmeal *n* : harina *f* de maíz — **cornstarch** *n* : maicena *f*

corny *adj* : cursi, sentimental

coronary *n, pl* **-naries** : trombosis *f* coronaria

coronation *n* : coronación *f*

corporal *n* : cabo *m*

corporation *n* : sociedad *f* anónima, compañía *f* — **corporate** *adj* : corporativo

corps *n, pl* **corps** : cuerpo *m*

corpse *n* : cadáver *m*

corpulent *adj* : obeso, gordo

corpuscle *n* : glóbulo *m*

corral *n* : corral *m* — ~ *vt* **-ralled; -ralling** : acorralar

correct *vt* : corregir — ~ *adj* : correcto — **correction** *n* : corrección *f*

correlation *n* : correlación *f*

correspond *vi* **1** WRITE : corresponderse **2** ~ **to** : corresponder a — **correspondence** *n* : correspondencia *f*

corridor *n* : pasillo *m*

corroborate *vt* **-rated; -rating** : corroborar

corrode *v* **-roded; -roding** *vt* : corroer — *vi* : corroerse — **corrosion** *n* : corrosión *f* — **corrosive** *adj* : corrosivo

corrugated *adj* : ondulado

corrupt *vt* : corromper — ~ *adj* : corrupto, corrompido — **corruption** *n* : corrupción *f*

corset *n* : corsé *m*

cosmetic *n* : cosmético *m* — ~ *adj* : cosmético

cosmic *adj* : cósmico

cosmopolitan *adj* : cosmopolita

cosmos *n* : cosmos *m*

cost *n* : costo *m*, coste *m* — ~ *vi* **cost; costing 1** : costar **2 how much does it ~?** : ¿cuánto cuesta?, ¿cuánto vale?

Costa Rican *adj* : costarricense

costly *adj* : costoso

costume *n* **1** OUTFIT : traje *m* **2** DISGUISE : disfraz *m*

cot *n* : catre *m*

cottage *n* : casita *f* (de campo) — **cottage cheese** *n* : requesón *m*

cotton *n* : algodón *m*

couch *n* : sofá *m*

cough *vi* : toser — ~ *n* : tos *f*

could → **can**[1]

council *n* **1** : concejo *m* **2** *or* **city ~** : ayuntamiento *m* — **councillor** *or* **councilor** *n* : concejal *m*, -jala *f*

counsel *n* **1** ADVICE : consejo *m* **2** LAWYER : abogado *m*, -da *f* — ~ *vt* **-seled** *or* **-selled; -seling** *or* **-selling** : aconsejar — **counselor** *or* **counsellor** *n* : consejero *m*, -ra *f*

count[1] *vt* : contar — *vi* **1** : contar **2** ~ **on** : contar con **3 that doesn't ~** : eso no vale — ~ *n* **1** : recuento *m* **2 keep ~ of** : llevar la cuenta de

count[2] *n* : conde *m* (noble)

counter[1] *n* **1** : mostrador *m* (de un negocio) **2** TOKEN : ficha *f* (de un juego)

counter[2] *vt* : oponerse a — *vi* : contraatacar

— ~ *adv* ~ **to** : contrario a — **counteract** *vt* : contrarrestar — **counterattack** *n* : contraataque *m* — **counterbalance** *n* : contrapeso *m* — **counterclockwise** *adv & adj* : en sentido opuesto a las agujas del reloj — **counterfeit** *vt* : falsificar — ~ *adj* : falsificado — ~ *n* : falsificación *f* — **counterpart** *n* : homólogo *m* (de una persona), equivalente *m* (de una cosa) — **counterproductive** *adj* : contraproducente

countess *n* : condesa *f*

countless *adj* : incontable, innumerable

country *n, pl* **-tries** **1** NATION : país *m* **2** COUNTRYSIDE : campo *m* — ~ *adj* : campestre, rural — **countryman** *n, pl* **-men** *or* **fellow** ~ : compatriota *mf* — **countryside** *n* : campo *m*, campiña *f*

county *n, pl* **-ties** : condado *m*

coup *n, pl* **coups** *or* ~ **d'etat** : golpe *m* (de estado)

couple *n* **1** : pareja *f* (de personas) **2 a** ~ **of** : un par de — ~ *vt* **-pled; -pling** : acoplar, unir

coupon *n* : cupón *m*

courage *n* : valor *m* — **courageous** *adj* : valiente

courier *n* : mensajero *m*, -ra *f*

course *n* **1** : curso *m* **2** : plato *m* (de una cena) **3** *or* **golf** ~ : campo *m* de golf **4 in the** ~ **of** : en el transcurso de **5 of** ~ : desde luego, por supuesto

court *n* **1** : corte *f* (de un rey, etc.) **2** : cancha *f*, pista *f* (en deportes) **3** TRIBUNAL : corte *f*, tribunal *m* — ~ *vt* : cortejar

courteous *adj* : cortés — **courtesy** *n, pl* **-sies** : cortesía *f*

courthouse *n* : palacio *m* de justicia, juzgado *m* — **courtroom** *n* : sala *f* (de un tribunal)

courtship *n* : cortejo *m*, noviazgo *m*

courtyard *n* : patio *m*

cousin *n* : primo *m*, -ma *f*

cove *n* : ensenada *f*, cala *f*

covenant *n* : pacto *m*, convenio *m*

cover *vt* **1** : cubrir **2** *or* ~ **up** : encubrir, ocultar **3** TREAT : tratar — ~ *n* **1** : cubierta *f* **2** SHELTER : abrigo *m*, refugio *m* **3** LID : tapa *f* **4** : cubierta *f* (de un libro), portada *f* (de una revista) **5** ~**s** *npl* BEDCLOTHES : mantas *fpl*, cobijas *fpl* *Lat* **6 take** ~ : ponerse a cubierto **7 under** ~ **of** : al amparo de — **coverage** *n* : cobertura *f* — **covert** *adj* : encubierto — **cover–up** *n* : encubrimiento *m*

covet *vt* : codiciar — **covetous** *adj* : codicioso

cow *n* : vaca *f* — ~ *vt* : intimidar, acobardar

coward *n* : cobarde *mf* — **cowardice** *n* : cobardía *f* — **cowardly** *adj* : cobarde

cowboy *n* : vaquero *m*

cower *vi* : encogerse (de miedo)

coy *adj* : tímido y coqueto

coyote *n, pl* **coyotes** *or* **coyote** : coyote *m*

cozy *adj* **-zier; -est** : acogedor

crab *n* : cangrejo *m*, jaiba *f Lat*

crack *vt* **1** SPLIT : rajar, partir **2** : cascar (nueces, huevos) **3** : chasquear (un látigo, etc.) **4** ~ **down on** : tomar medidas enérgicas contra — *vi* **1** SPLIT : rajarse, agrietarse **2** : chasquear (dícese de un látigo) **3** ~ **up** : sufrir una crisis nerviosa — ~ *n* **1** CRACKING : chasquido *m*, crujido *m* **2** CREVICE : raja *f*, grieta *f* **3 have a** ~ **at** : intentar

cracker *n* : galleta *f* (de soda, etc.)

crackle *vi* **-led; -ling** : crepitar, chisporrotear — ~ *n* : crujido *m*, chisporroteo *m*

cradle *n* : cuna *f* — ~ *vt* **-dled; -dling** : acunar

craft *n* **1** TRADE : oficio *m* **2** CUNNING : astucia *f* **3** → **craftsmanship** **4** *pl usually* **craft** BOAT : embarcación *f* — **craftsman** *n, pl* **-men** : artesano *m*, -na *f* — **craftsmanship** *n* : artesanía *f*, destreza *f* — **crafty** *adj* **craftier; -est** : astuto, taimado

crag *n* : peñasco *m*

cram *v* **crammed; cramming** *vt* **1** STUFF : embutir **2** ~ **with** : atiborrar de — *vi* : estudiar a última hora

cramp *n* **1** : calambre *m*, espasmo *m* (de los músculos) **2** ~**s** *npl* : retorcijones *mpl*

cranberry *n, pl* **-berries** : arándano *m* (rojo y agrio)

crane *n* **1** : grulla *f* (ave) **2** : grúa *f* (máquina) — ~ *vt* **craned; craning** : estirar (el cuello)

crank *n* **1** : manivela *f* **2** ECCENTRIC : excéntrico *m*, -ca *f* — **cranky** *adj* **crankier; -est** : malhumorado

crash *vi* **1** : caerse con estrépito **2** COLLIDE : estrellarse, chocar — *vt* : estrellar — ~ *n* **1** DIN : estrépito *m* **2** COLLISION : choque *m*

crass *adj* : burdo, grosero

crate *n* : cajón *m* (de madera)

crater *n* : cráter *m*

crave *vt* **craved; craving** : ansiar — **craving** *n* : ansia *f*

crawl *vi* : arrastrarse, gatear (dícese de un bebé) — ~ *n* **at a** ~ : a paso lento

crayon *n* : lápiz *m* de cera

craze *n* : moda *f* pasajera, manía *f*

crazy *adj* **-zier; -est** **1** : loco **2 go** ~ : volverse loco — **craziness** *n* : locura *f*

creak *vi* : chirriar, crujir — ~ *n* : chirrido *m*, crujido *m*

cream *n* : crema *f*, nata *f Spain* — **cream cheese** *n* : queso *m* crema — **creamy** *adj* **creamier; -est** : cremoso

crease n : pliegue m, raya f (del pantalón) — ∼ vt **creased; creasing** : plegar, poner una raya en (el pantalón)
create vt **-ated; -ating** : crear — **creation** n : creación f — **creative** adj : creativo — **creator** n : creador m, -dora f
creature n : criatura f, animal m
credence n **lend** ∼ **to** : dar crédito a
credentials npl : credenciales fpl
credible adj : creíble — **credibility** n : credibilidad f
credit n **1** : crédito m **2** RECOGNITION : reconocimiento m **3 be a** ∼ **to** : ser el orgullo de — ∼ vt **1** BELIEVE : creer **2** : abonar (en una cuenta) **3** ∼ **s.o. with sth** : atribuir algo a algn — **credit card** n : tarjeta f de crédito
credulous adj : crédulo
creed n : credo m
creek n : arroyo m, riachuelo m
creep vi **crept; creeping 1** CRAWL : arrastrarse **2** SLINK : ir a hurtadillas — ∼ n **1** CRAWL : paso m lento **2 the** ∼**s** : escalofríos mpl — **creeping** adj ∼ **plant** : planta f trepadora
cremate vt **-mated; -mating** : incinerar
crescent n : media luna f
cress n : berro m
crest n : cresta f — **crestfallen** adj : alicaído
crevice n : grieta f
crew n **1** : tripulación f (de una nave) **2** TEAM : equipo m
crib n : cuna f (de un bebé)
cricket n **1** : grillo m (insecto) **2** : críquet m (juego)
crime n : crimen m — **criminal** adj : criminal — ∼ n : criminal mf
crimp vt : rizar
crimson n : carmesí m
cringe vi **cringed; cringing** : encogerse
crinkle vt **-kled; -kling** : arrugar
cripple vt **-pled; -pling 1** DISABLE : lisiar, dejar inválido **2** INCAPACITATE : inutilizar, paralizar
crisis n, pl **crises** : crisis f
crisp adj **1** CRUNCHY : crujiente **2** : frío y vigorizante (dícese del aire) — **crispy** adj **crispier; -est** : crujiente
crisscross vt : entrecruzar
criterion n, pl **-ria** : criterio m
critic n : crítico m, -ca f — **critical** adj : crítico — **criticism** n : crítica f — **criticize** vt **-cized; -cizing** : criticar
croak vi : croar
crock n : vasija f de barro — **crockery** n : vajilla f, loza f
crocodile n : cocodrilo m
crony n, pl **-nies** : amigote m fam
crook n **1** STAFF : cayado m **2** THIEF : ratero

m, -ra f; ladrón m, -drona f **3** BEND : pliegue m — **crooked** adj **1** BENT : torcido, chueco Lat **2** DISHONEST : deshonesto
crop n **1** WHIP : fusta f **2** HARVEST : cosecha f **3** : cultivo m (de maíz, tabaco, etc.) — ∼ v **cropped; cropping** vt TRIM : recortar, cortar — vi ∼ **up** : surgir
cross n **1** : cruz f **2** HYBRID : cruce m — ∼ vt **1** : cruzar, atravesar **2** CROSSBREED : cruzar **3** or ∼ **out** : tachar — ∼ adj **1** : que atraviesa **2** ANGRY : enojado — **crossbreed** vt **-bred; -breeding** : cruzar — **cross–examine** vt : interrogar — **cross–eyed** adj : bizco — **cross fire** n : fuego m cruzado — **crossing** n **1** INTERSECTION : cruce m, paso m **2** VOYAGE : travesía f (del mar) — **cross–reference** n : referencia f — **crossroads** n : cruce m — **cross section** n **1** : corte m transversal **2** SAMPLE : muestra f representativa — **crosswalk** n : cruce m peatonal, paso m de peatones — **crossword puzzle** n : crucigrama m
crotch n : entrepierna f
crouch vi : agacharse
crouton n : crutón m
crow n : cuervo m — ∼ vi **crowed** or Brit **crew; crowing** : cacarear
crowbar n : palanca f
crowd vi : amontonarse — vt : atestar, llenar — ∼ n : multitud f, muchedumbre f
crown n **1** : corona f **2** : cima f (de una colina) — ∼ vt : coronar
crucial adj : crucial
crucify vt **-fied; -fying** : crucificar — **crucifix** n : crucifijo m — **crucifixion** n : crucifixión f
crude adj **cruder; -est 1** RAW : crudo **2** VULGAR : grosero **3** ROUGH : tosco, rudo
cruel adj **-eler** or **-eller; -elest** or **-ellest** : cruel — **cruelty** n, pl **-ties** : crueldad f
cruet n : vinagrera f
cruise vi **cruised; cruising 1** : hacer un crucero **2** : ir a velocidad de crucero — ∼ n : crucero m — **cruiser** n **1** WARSHIP : crucero m **2** : patrulla f (de policía)
crumb n : miga f, migaja f
crumble v **-bled; -bling** vt : desmenuzar — vi : desmenuzarse, desmoronarse
crumple vt **-pled; -pling** : arrugar
crunch vt : ronzar (con los dientes), hacer crujir (con los pies, etc.) — **crunchy** adj **crunchier; -est** : crujiente
crusade n : cruzada f
crush vt : aplastar, apachurrar Lat — ∼ n **have a** ∼ **on** : estar chiflado por
crust n : corteza f
crutch n : muleta f
crux n : quid m

cry *vi* **cried; crying 1** SHOUT : gritar **2** WEEP : llorar — ~ *n, pl* **cries** : grito *m*

crypt *n* : cripta *f*

crystal *n* : cristal *m*

cub *n* : cachorro *m*, -rra *f*

Cuban *adj* : cubano

cube *n* : cubo *m* — **cubic** *adj* : cúbico

cubicle *n* : cubículo *m*

cuckoo *n* : cuco *m*, cuclillo *m*

cucumber *n* : pepino *m*

cuddle *v* **-dled; -dling** *vi* : acurrucarse, abrazarse — *vt* : abrazar

cudgel *n* : porra *f* — ~ *vt* **-geled** *or* **-gelled; -geling** *or* **-gelling** : aporrear

cue¹ *n* SIGNAL : señal *f*

cue² *n* : taco *m* (de billar)

cuff¹ 1 : puño *m* (de una camisa) **2** ~s *npl* → **handcuffs**

cuff² *vt* : bofetear — ~ *n* SLAP : bofetada *f*

cuisine *n* : cocina *f*

culinary *adj* : culinario

cull *vt* : seleccionar, entresacar

culminate *vi* **-nated; -nating** : culminar — **culmination** *n* : culminación *f*

culprit *n* : culpable *mf*

cult *n* : culto *m*

cultivate *vt* **-vated; -vating** : cultivar — **cultivation** *n* : cultivo *m*

culture *n* **1** : cultura *f* **2** : cultivo *m* (en biología) — **cultural** *adj* : cultural — **cultured** *adj* : culto

cumbersome *adj* : torpe (y pesado), difícil de manejar

cumulative *adj* : acumulativo

cunning *adj* : astuto, taimado — ~ *n* : astucia *f*

cup *n* **1** : taza *f* **2** TROPHY : copa *f*

cupboard *n* : alacena *f*, armario *m*

curator *n* : conservador *m*, -dora *f*; director *m*, -tora *f*

curb *n* **1** RESTRAINT : freno *m* **2** : borde *m* de la acera — ~ *vt* : refrenar

curdle *v* **-dled; -dling** *vi* : cuajarse — *vt* : cuajar

cure *n* : cura *f*, remedio *m* — ~ *vt* **cured; curing** : curar

curfew *n* : toque *m* de queda

curious *adj* : curioso — **curio** *n, pl* **-rios** : curiosidad *f* — **curiosity** *n, pl* **-ties** : curiosidad *f*

curl *vt* **1** : rizar **2** COIL : enrollar, enroscar — *vi* **1** : rizarse **2** ~ **up** : acurrucarse — ~ *n* : rizo *m* — **curler** *n* : rulo *m* — **curly** *adj* **curlier; -est** : rizado

currant *n* **1** : grosella *f* (fruta) **2** RAISIN : pasa *f* de Corinto

currency *n, pl* **-cies 1** MONEY : moneda *f* **2** **gain** ~ : ganar aceptación

current *adj* **1** PRESENT : actual **2** PREVALENT : corriente — ~ *n* : corriente *f*

curriculum *n, pl* **-la** : plan *m* de estudios

curry *n, pl* **-ries** : curry *m*

curse *n* : maldición *f* — ~ *v* **cursed; cursing** : maldecir

cursor *n* : cursor *m*

cursory *adj* : superficial

curt *adj* : corto, seco

curtail *vt* : acortar

curtain *n* : cortina *f* (de una ventana), telón *m* (en un teatro)

curtsy *vi* **-sied** *or* **-seyed; -sying** *or* **-seying** : hacer una reverencia — ~ *n* : reverencia *f*

curve *v* **curved; curving** *vi* : hacer una curva — *vt* : encorvar — ~ *n* : curva *f*

cushion *n* : cojín *m* — ~ *vt* : amortiguar

custard *n* : natillas *fpl*

custody *n, pl* **-dies 1** : custodia *f* **2 be in** ~ : estar detenido — **custodian** *n* : custodio *m*, -dia *f*; guardián, -diana *f*

custom *n* : costumbre *f* — **customary** *adj* : habitual, acostumbrado — **customer** *n* : cliente *m*, -ta *f* — **customs** *npl* : aduana *f*

cut *v* **cut; cutting** *vt* **1** : cortar **2** REDUCE : reducir, rebajar **3** ~ **oneself** : cortarse **4** ~ **up** : cortar en pedazos — *vi* **1** : cortar **2** ~ **in** : interrumpir — ~ *n* **1** : corte *m* **2** REDUCTION : rebaja *f*, reducción *f*

cute *adj* **cuter; -est** : mono *fam*, lindo

cutlery *n* : cubiertos *mpl*

cutlet *n* : chuleta *f*

cutting *adj* : cortante, mordaz

cyanide *n* : cianuro *m*

cycle *n* **1** : ciclo *m* **2** BICYCLE : bicicleta *f* — ~ *vi* **-cled; -cling** : ir en bicicleta — **cyclic** *or* **cyclical** *adj* : cíclico — **cyclist** *n* : ciclista *mf*

cyclone *n* : ciclón *m*

cylinder *n* : cilindro *m* — **cylindrical** *adj* : cilíndrico

cymbal *n* : platillo *m*, címbalo *m*

cynic *n* : cínico *m*, -ca *f* — **cynical** *adj* : cínico — **cynicism** *n* : cinismo *m*

cypress *n* : ciprés *m*

cyst *n* : quiste *m*

czar *n* : zar *m*

Czech *adj* : checo — ~ *n* : checo *m* (idioma)

D

d *n*, *pl* **d's** *or* **ds** : d *f*, cuarta letra del alfabeto inglés

dab *n* : toque *m* — ∼ *vt* **dabbed; dabbing** : dar toques ligeros a, aplicar suavemente

dabble *vi* **-bled; -bling** ∼ **in** : interesarse superficialmente en — **dabbler** *n* : aficionado *m*, **-da** *f*

dad *n* : papá *m fam* — **daddy** *n*, *pl* **-dies** : papá *m fam*

daffodil *n* : narciso *m*

dagger *n* : daga *f*, puñal *m*

daily *adj* : diario — ∼ *adv* : diariamente

dainty *adj* **-tier; -est** : delicado

dairy *n*, *pl* **-ies** **1** : lechería *f* (tienda) **2** *or* ∼ **farm** : granja *f* lechera

daisy *n*, *pl* **-sies** : margarita *f*

dam *n* : presa *f* — ∼ *vt* **dammed; damming** : represar

damage *n* **1** : daño *m*, perjuicio *m* **2** ∼**s** *npl* : daños y perjuicios *mpl* — ∼ *vt* **-aged; -aging** : dañar

damn *vt* **1** CONDEMN : condenar **2** CURSE : maldecir — ∼ *n* **not give a** ∼ : no importarse un comino *fam* — ∼ *or* **damned** *adj* : maldito *fam*

damp *adj* : húmedo — **dampen** *vt* **1** MOISTEN : humedecer **2** DISCOURAGE : desalentar, desanimar — **dampness** *n* : humedad *f*

dance *v* **danced; dancing** : bailar — ∼ *n* : baile *m* — **dancer** *n* : bailarín *m*, **-rina** *f*

dandelion *n* : diente *m* de león

dandruff *n* : caspa *f*

dandy *adj* **-dier; -est** : de primera, excelente

danger *n* : peligro *m* — **dangerous** *adj* : peligroso

dangle *v* **-gled; -gling** *vi* HANG : colgar, pender — *vt* : hacer oscilar

Danish *adj* : danés — ∼ *n* : danés *m* (idioma)

dank *adj* : frío y húmedo

dare *v* **dared; daring** *vt* : desafiar — *vi* : osar — ∼ *n* : desafío *m* — **daredevil** *n* : persona *f* temeraria — **daring** *adj* : atrevido, audaz — ∼ *n* : audacia *f*

dark *adj* **1** : oscuro **2** : moreno (dícese del pelo o de la piel) **3** GLOOMY : sombrío **4** **get** ∼ : hacerse de noche — **darken** *vt* : oscurecer — *vi* : oscurecerse — **darkness** *n* : oscuridad *f*

darling *n* BELOVED : querido *m*, **-da** *f* — ∼ *adj* : querido

darn *vt* : zurcir — ∼ *adj* : maldito *fam*

dart *n* **1** : dardo *m* **2** ∼**s** *npl* : juego *m* de dardos — ∼ *vi* : precipitarse

dash *vt* **1** SMASH : romper **2** HURL : lanzar **3** ∼ **off** : hacer (algo) rápidamente — *vi* : lanzarse, irse corriendo — ∼ *n* **1** : guión *m* largo (signo de puntuación) **2** PINCH : poquito *m*, pizca *f* **3** RACE : carrera *f* — **dashboard** *n* : tablero *m* de instrumentos — **dashing** *adj* : gallardo, apuesto

data *ns & pl* : datos *mpl* — **database** *n* : base *f* de datos

date¹ *n* : dátil *m* (fruta)

date² *n* **1** : fecha *f* **2** APPOINTMENT : cita *f* — ∼ *v* **dated; dating** *vt* **1** : fechar (una carta, etc.) **2** : salir con (algn) — *vi* ∼ **from** : datar de — **dated** *adj* : pasado de moda

daub *vt* : embadurnar

daughter *n* : hija *f* — **daughter–in–law** *n*, *pl* **daughters–in–law** : nuera *f*

daunt *vt* : intimidar

dawdle *vi* **-dled; -dling** : entretenerse, perder tiempo

dawn *vi* **1** : amanecer **2** **it** ∼**ed on him that** : cayó en la cuenta de que — ∼ *n* : amanecer *m*

day *n* **1** : día *m* **2** *or* **working** ∼ : jornada *f* **3** **the** ∼ **before** : el día anterior **4** **the** ∼ **before yesterday** : anteayer **5** **the** ∼ **after** : el día siguiente **6** **the** ∼ **after tomorrow** : pasada mañana — **daybreak** *n* : amanecer *m* — **daydream** *n* : ensueño *m* — ∼ *vi* : soñar despierto — **daylight** *n* : luz *f* del día — **daytime** *n* : día *m*

daze *vt* **dazed; dazing** : aturdir — ∼ *n* **in a** ∼ : aturdido

dazzle *vt* **-zled; -zling** : deslumbrar

dead *adj* **1** LIFELESS : muerto **2** NUMB : entumecido — ∼ *n* **1** **in the** ∼ **of night** : en plena noche **2** **the** ∼ : los muertos — ∼ *adv* ABSOLUTELY : absolutamente — **deaden** *vt* **1** : atenuar (dolores) **2** MUFFLE : amortiguar — **dead end** *n* : callejón *m* sin salida — **deadline** *n* : fecha *f* límite — **deadlock** *n* : punto *m* muerto — **deadly** *adj* **-lier; -est** **1** : mortal, letal **2** ACCURATE : certero, preciso

deaf *adj* : sordo — **deafen** *vt* : ensordecer — **deafness** *n* : sordera *f*

deal *n* **1** TRANSACTION : trato *m*, transacción *f* **2** : reparto *m* (de naipes) **3** **a good** ∼ : mucho — ∼ *v* **dealt; dealing** *vt* **1** : dar **2** : repartir, dar (naipes) **3** ∼ **a blow** : asestar un golpe — *vi* **1** : dar, repartir (en juegos de naipes) **2** ∼ **in** : comerciar en **3** ∼ **with** CONCERN : tratar de **4** ∼ **with s.o.** : tratar con algn — **dealer** *n* : comerciante *mf* — **dealings** *npl* : trato *m*, relaciones *fpl*

dean *n* : decano *m*, -na *f*

dear *adj* : querido — ∼ *n* : querido *m*, -da *f* — **dearly** *adv* **1** : mucho **2 pay** ∼ : pagar caro

death *n* : muerte *f*

debar *vt* : excluir

debate *n* : debate *m*, discusión *f* — ∼ *vt* -bated; -bating : debatir, discutir

debit *vt* : adeudar, cargar — ∼ *n* : débito *m*, debe *m*

debris *n, pl* -bris : escombros *mpl*

debt *n* : deuda *f* — **debtor** *n* : deudor *m*, -dora *f*

debunk *vt* : desmentir

debut *n* : debut *m* — ∼ *vi* : debutar

decade *n* : década *f*

decadence *n* : decadencia *f* — **decadent** *adj* : decadente

decal *n* : calcomanía *f*

decanter *n* : licorera *f*

decapitate *vt* -tated; -tating : decapitar

decay *vi* **1** DECOMPOSE : descomponerse **2** DETERIORATE : deteriorarse **3** : cariarse (dícese de los dientes) — ∼ *n* **1** : descomposición *f* **2** : deterioro *m* (de un edificio, etc.) **3** : caries *f* (de los dientes)

deceased *adj* : difunto — ∼ *n* the ∼ : el difunto, la difunta

deceive *vt* -ceived; -ceiving : engañar — **deceit** *n* : engaño *m* — **deceitful** *adj* : engañoso

December *n* : diciembre *m*

decent *adj* **1** : decente **2** KIND : bueno, amable — **decency** *n, pl* -cies : decencia *f*

deception *n* : engaño *m* — **deceptive** *adj* : engañoso

decide *v* -cided; -ciding *vt* : decidir — *vi* : decidirse — **decided** *adj* **1** UNQUESTIONABLE : indudable **2** RESOLUTE : decidido — **decidedly** *adv* **1** DEFINITELY : decididamente **2** RESOLUTELY : con decisión

decimal *adj* : decimal — ∼ *n* : número *m* decimal — **decimal point** *n* : coma *f* decimal

decipher *vt* : descifrar

decision *n* : decisión *f* — **decisive** *adj* **1** RESOLUTE : decidido **2** CONCLUSIVE : decisivo

deck *n* **1** : cubierta *f* (de un barco) **2** *or* ∼ **of cards** : baraja *f* (de naipes) **3** TERRACE : entarimado *m*

declare *vt* -clared; -claring : declarar — **declaration** *n* : declaración *f*

decline *v* -clined; -clining *vt* REFUSE : declinar, rehusar — *vi* DECREASE : disminuir — ∼ *n* **1** DETERIORATION : decadencia *f*, deterioro *m* **2** DECREASE : disminución *f*

decode *vt* -coded; -coding : descodificar

decompose *vt* -posed; -posing : descomponer — *vi* : descomponerse

decongestant *n* : descongestionante *m*

decorate *vt* -rated; -rating : decorar — **decor** *or* **décor** *n* : decoración *f* — **decoration** *n* : decoración *f* — **decorator** *n* : decorador *m*, -dora *f*

decoy *n* : señuelo *m*

decrease *v* -creased; -creasing : disminuir — ∼ *n* : disminución *f*

decree *n* : decreto *m* — ∼ *vt* -creed; -creeing : decretar

decrepit *adj* **1** FEEBLE : decrépito **2** DILAPIDATED : ruinoso

dedicate *vt* -cated; -cating **1** : dedicar **2** ∼ **oneself to** : consagrarse a — **dedication** *n* **1** DEVOTION : dedicación *f* **2** INSCRIPTION : dedicatoria *f*

deduce *vt* -duced; -ducing : deducir — **deduct** *vt* : deducir — **deduction** *n* : deducción *f*

deed *n* **1** : acción *f*, hecho *m*

deem *vt* : considerar, juzgar

deep *adj* : hondo, profundo — ∼ *adv* **1** DEEPLY : profundamente **2** ∼ **down** : en el fondo **3 dig** ∼ : cavar hondo — **deepen** *vt* : ahondar — *vi* : hacerse más profundo — **deeply** *adv* : hondo, profundamente

deer *ns & pl* : ciervo *m*

deface *vt* -faced; -facing : desfigurar

default *n* **by** ∼ : en rebeldía — ∼ *vi* **1** ∼ **on** : no pagar (una deuda) **2** : no presentarse (en deportes)

defeat *vt* **1** BEAT : vencer, derrotar **2** FRUSTRATE : frustrar — ∼ *n* : derrota *f*

defect *n* : defecto *m* — ∼ *vi* : desertar — **defective** *adj* : defectuoso

defend *vt* : defender — **defendant** *n* : acusado *m*, -da *f* — **defense** *or Brit* **defence** *n* : defensa *f* — **defenseless** *or Brit* **defenceless** *adj* : indefenso — **defensive** *adj* : defensivo — ∼ *n* **on the** ∼ : a la defensiva

defer *v* -ferred; -ferring *vt* : diferir, aplazar — *vi* ∼ **to** : deferir a — **deference** *n* : deferencia *f* — **deferential** *adj* : deferente

defiance *n* **1** : desafío *m* **2 in** ∼ **of** : a despecho de — **defiant** *adj* : desafiante

deficiency *n, pl* -cies : deficiencia *f* — **deficient** *adj* : deficiente

deficit *n* : déficit *m*

defile *vt* -filed; -filing **1** DIRTY : ensuciar **2** DESECRATE : profanar

define *vt* -fined; -fining : definir — **definite** *adj* **1** : definido **2** CERTAIN : seguro, incuestionable — **definition** *n* : definición *f* — **definitive** *adj* : definitivo

deflate *v* -flated; -flating *vt* : desinflar (una llanta, etc.) — *vi* : desinflarse

deflect *vt* : desviar — *vi* : desviarse
deform *vt* : deformar — **deformity** *n, pl* **-ties** : deformidad *f*
defraud *vt* : defraudar
defrost *vt* : descongelar — *vi* : descongelarse
deft *adj* : hábil, diestro
defy *vt* **-fied; -fying 1** CHALLENGE : desafiar **2** RESIST : resistir
degenerate *vi* : degenerar — ~ *adj* : degenerado
degrade *vt* **-graded; -grading** : degradar — **degrading** *adj* : degradante
degree *n* **1** : grado *m* **2** *or* **academic** ~ : título *m*
dehydrate *vt* **-drated; -drating** : deshidratar
deign *vi* ~ **to** : dignarse (a)
deity *n, pl* **-ties** : deidad *f*
dejected *adj* : abatido — **dejection** *n* : abatimiento *m*
delay *n* : retraso *m* — ~ *vt* **1** POSTPONE : aplazar **2** HOLD UP : retrasar — *vi* : demorar
delectable *adj* : delicioso
delegate *n* : delegado *m*, -da *f* — ~ *v* **-gated; -gating** : delegar — **delegation** *n* : delegación *f*
delete *vt* **-leted; -leting** : borrar
deliberate *v* **-ated; -ating** *vt* : deliberar sobre — *vi* : deliberar — ~ *adj* : deliberado — **deliberately** *adv* INTENTIONALLY : a propósito — **deliberation** *n* : deliberación *f*
delicacy *n, pl* **-cies 1** : delicadeza *f* **2** FOOD : manjar *m*, exquisitez *f* — **delicate** *adj* : delicado
delicatessen *n* : charcutería *f*
delicious *adj* : delicioso
delight *n* : placer *m*, deleite *m* — ~ *vt* : deleitar, encantar — *vi* ~ **in** : deleitarse con — **delightful** *adj* : delicioso, encantador
delinquent *adj* : delincuente — ~ *n* : delincuente *mf*
delirious *adj* : delirante — **delirium** *n* : delirio *m*
deliver *vt* **1** DISTRIBUTE : entregar, repartir **2** FREE : liberar **3** : asistir en el parto de (un niño) **4** : pronunciar (un discurso, etc.) **5** DEAL : asestar (un golpe, etc.) — **delivery** *n, pl* **-eries 1** DISTRIBUTION : entrega *f*, reparto *m* **2** LIBERATION : liberación *f* **3** CHILDBIRTH : parto *m*, alumbramiento *m*
delude *vt* **-luded; -luding 1** : engañar **2** ~ **oneself** : engañarse
deluge *n* : diluvio *m*
delusion *n* : ilusión *f*
deluxe *adj* : de lujo
delve *vi* **delved; delving 1** : escarbar **2** ~ **into** PROBE : investigar
demand *n* **1** REQUEST : petición *f* **2** CLAIM

: reclamación *f*, exigencia *f* **3** → **supply** — ~ *vt* : exigir — **demanding** *adj* : exigente
demean *vt* ~ **oneself** : rebajarse
demeanor *n* : comportamiento *m*
demented *adj* : demente, loco
demise *n* : fallecimiento *m*
democracy *n, pl* **-cies** : democracia *f* — **democrat** *n* : demócrata *mf* — **democratic** *adj* : democrático
demolish *vt* : demoler — **demolition** *n* : demolición *f*
demon *n* : demonio *m*
demonstrate *v* **-strated; -strating** *vt* : demostrar — *vi* RALLY : manifestarse — **demonstration** *n* **1** : demostración *f* **2** RALLY : manifestación *f*
demoralize *vt* **-ized; -izing** : desmoralizar
demote *vt* **-moted; -moting** : bajar de categoría
demure *adj* : recatado
den *n* LAIR : guarida *f*
denial *n* **1** : negación *f*, rechazo *m* **2** REFUSAL : denegación *f*
denim *n* : tela *f* vaquera, mezclilla *f Lat*
denomination *n* **1** : confesión *f* (religiosa) **2** : valor *m* (de una moneda)
denounce *vt* **-nounced; -nouncing** : denunciar
dense *adj* **denser; -est 1** THICK : denso **2** STUPID : estúpido — **density** *n, pl* **-ties** : densidad *f*
dent *vt* : abollar — ~ *n* : abolladura *f*
dental *adj* : dental — **dental floss** *n* : hilo *m* dental — **dentist** *n* : dentista *mf* — **dentures** *npl* : dentadura *f* postiza
deny *vt* **-nied; -nying 1** : negar **2** REFUSE : denegar
deodorant *n* : desodorante *m*
depart *vi* **1** : salir **2** ~ **from** : apartarse de (la verdad, etc.)
department *n* : sección *f* (de una tienda, etc.), departamento *m* (de una empresa, etc.), ministerio *m* (del gobierno) — **department store** *n* : grandes almacenes *mpl*
departure *n* **1** : salida *f* **2** DEVIATION : desviación *f*
depend *vi* **1** ~ **on** : depender de **2** ~ **on s.o.** : contar con algn **3 that** ~**s** : eso depende — **dependable** *adj* : digno de confianza — **dependence** *n* : dependencia *f* — **dependent** *adj* : dependiente
depict *vt* **1** PORTRAY : representar **2** DESCRIBE : describir
deplete *vt* **-pleted; -pleting** : agotar, reducir
deplore *vt* **-plored; -ploring** : deplorar, lamentar — **deplorable** *adj* : lamentable
deploy *vt* : desplegar

deport *vt* : deportar, expulsar (de un país) — **deportation** *n* : deportación *f*

depose *vt* **-posed; -posing** : deponer

deposit *vt* **-ited; -iting** : depositar — **~** *n* **1** : depósito *m* **2** DOWN PAYMENT : entrega *f* inicial

depot *n* **1** WAREHOUSE : almacén *m*, depósito *m* **2** STATION : terminal *mf*

depreciate *vi* **-ated; -ating** : depreciarse — **depreciation** *n* : depreciación *f*

depress *vt* **1** : deprimir **2** PRESS : apretar — **depressed** *adj* : abatido, deprimido — **depressing** *adj* : deprimente — **depression** *n* : depresión *f*

deprive *vt* **-prived; -priving** : privar

depth *n, pl* **depths 1** : profundidad *f* **2 in the ~s of night** : en lo más profundo de la noche

deputy *n, pl* **-ties** : suplente *mf;* sustituto *m*, -ta *f*

derail *vt* : hacer descarrilar

deranged *adj* : trastornado

derelict *adj* : abandonado

deride *vt* **-rided; -riding** : burlarse de — **derision** *n* : mofa *f*

derive *vi* **-rived; -riving** : derivar — **derivation** *n* : derivación *f*

derogatory *adj* : despectivo

descend *v* **1** : descender, bajar — **descendant** *n* : descendiente *mf* —**descent** *n* **1** : descenso *m* **2** LINEAGE : descendencia *f*

describe *vt* **-scribed; -scribing** : describir — **description** *n* : descripción *f* — **descriptive** *adj* : descriptivo

desecrate *vt* **-crated; -crating** : profanar

desert *n* : desierto *m* — **~** *adj* **~ island** : isla *f* desierta — **~** *vt* : abandonar — *vi* : desertar — **deserter** *n* : desertor *m*, -tora *f*

deserve *vt* **-served; -serving** : merecer

design *vt* **1** DEVISE : diseñar **2** PLAN : proyectar — **~** *n* **1** : diseño *m* **2** PLAN : plan *m*, proyecto *m*

designate *vt* **-nated; -nating** : nombrar, designar

designer *n* : diseñador *m*, -dora *f*

desire *vt* **-sired; -siring** : desear — **~** *n* : deseo *m* — **desirable** *adj* : deseable

desk *n* : escritorio *m*, pupitre *m* (en la escuela)

desolate *adj* : desolado

despair *vi* : desesperar — **~** *n* : desesperación *f*

desperate *adj* : desesperado — **desperation** *n* : desesperación *f*

despise *vt* **-spised; -spising** : despreciar — **despicable** *adj* : despreciable

despite *prep* : a pesar de

despondent *adj* : desanimado

dessert *n* : postre *m*

destination *n* : destino *m* — **destined** *adj* **1** : destinado **2 ~ for** : con destino a — **destiny** *n, pl* **-nies** : destino *m*

destitute *adj* : indigente

destroy *vt* : destruir — **destruction** *n* : destrucción *f* — **destructive** *adj* : destructivo

detach *vt* : separar — **detached** *adj* **1** : separado **2** IMPARTIAL : imparcial

detail *n* **1** : detalle *m* **2 go into ~** : entrar en detalles — **~** *vt* : detallar — **detailed** *adj* : detallado

detain *vt* **1** : detener (un prisionero) **2** DELAY : entretener

detect *vt* : detectar — **detection** *n* : detección *f*, descubrimiento *m* — **detective** *n* : detective *mf*

detention *n* : detención *m*

deter *vt* **-terred; -terring** : disuadir

detergent *n* : detergente *m*

deteriorate *vi* **-rated; -rating** : deteriorarse — **deterioration** *n* : deterioro *m*

determine *vt* **-mined; -mining** : determinar — **determined** *adj* RESOLUTE : decidido — **determination** *n* : determinación *f*

deterrent *n* : medida *f* disuasiva

detest *vt* : detestar — **detestable** *adj* : odioso

detonate *v* **-nated; -nating** *vt* : hacer detonar — *vi* EXPLODE : detonar, estallar — **detonation** *n* : detonación *f*

detour *n* **1** : desviación *f* **2 make a ~** : dar un rodeo — **~** *vi* : desviarse

detract *vi* **~ from** : aminorar, restar importancia a

detrimental *adj* : perjudicial

devalue *vt* **-ued; -uing** : devaluar

devastate *vt* **-tated; -tating** : devastar — **devastating** *adj* : devastador — **devastation** *n* : devastación *f*

develop *vt* **1** : desarrollar **2 ~ an illness** : contraer una enfermedad — *vi* **1** GROW : desarrollarse **2** HAPPEN : aparecer — **development** *n* : desarrollo *m*

deviate *v* **-ated; -ating** *vi* : desviarse — **deviation** *n* : desviación *f*

device *n* : dispositivo *m*, mecanismo *m*

devil *n* : diablo *m*, demonio *m* — **devilish** *adj* : diabólico

devious *adj* **1** CRAFTY : taimado **2** WINDING : tortuoso

devise *vt* **-vised; -vising** : idear, concebir

devoid *adj* **~ of** : desprovisto de

devote *vt* **-voted; -voting** : consagrar, dedicar — **devoted** *adj* : leal — **devotee** *n* : devoto *m*, -ta *f* — **devotion** *n* **1** : devoción *f*, dedicación *f* **2** : oración *f* (en religión)

devour *vt* : devorar

devout *adj* : devoto

dew *n* : rocío *m*

dexterity *n, pl* **-ties** : destreza *f*
diabetes *n* : diabetes *f* — **diabetic** *adj* : diabético — ~ *n* : diabético *m*, -ca *f*
diabolic *or* **diabolical** *adj* : diabólico
diagnosis *n, pl* **-noses** : diagnóstico *m* — **diagnose** *vt* **-nosed; -nosing** : diagnosticar — **diagnostic** *adj* : diagnóstico
diagonal *adj* : diagonal, en diagonal — ~ *n* : diagonal *f*
diagram *n* : diagrama *m*
dial *n* : esfera *f* (de un reloj), dial *m* (de un radio, etc.) — ~ *v* **dialed** *or* **dialled; dialing** *or* **dialling** : marcar
dialect *n* : dialecto *m*
dialogue *n* : diálogo *m*
diameter *n* : diámetro *m*
diamond *n* **1** : diamante *m* **2** : rombo *m* (forma) **3** *or* **baseball** ~ : cuadro *m*, diamante *m*
diaper *n* : pañal *m*
diaphragm *n* : diafragma *m*
diarrhea *n* : diarrea *f*
diary *n, pl* **-ries** : diario *m*
dice *ns & pl* : dados *mpl* (juego)
dictate *vt* **-tated; -tating** : dictar — **dictation** *n* : dictado *m* — **dictator** *n* : dictador *m*, -dora *f* — **dictatorship** *n* : dictadura *f*
dictionary *n, pl* **-naries** : diccionario *m*
did → do
die¹ *vi* **died; dying 1** : morir **2** ~ **down** : amainar, disminuir **3** ~ **out** : extinguirse **4 be dying for** : morirse por
die² *n* **1** *pl* **dice** : dado *m* (para jugar) **2** *pl* **dies** MOLD : molde *m*
diesel *n* : diesel *m*
diet *n* **1** FOOD : alimentación *f* **2 go on a** ~ : ponerse a régimen — ~ *vi* : estar a régimen
differ *vi* **-ferred; -ferring 1** : diferir, ser distinto **2** DISAGREE : no estar de acuerdo — **difference** *n* : diferencia *f* — **different** *adj* : distinto, diferente — **differentiate** *v* **-ated; -ating** *vt* : diferenciar — *vi* : distinguir — **differently** *adv* : de otra manera
difficult *adj* : difícil — **difficulty** *n, pl* **-ties** : dificultad *f*
diffident *adj* : tímido, que falta confianza
dig *v* **dug; digging** *vt* **1** : cavar **2** ~ **up** : desenterrar — *vi* : cavar — ~ *n* **1** GIBE : pulla *f* **2** EXCAVATION : excavación *f*
digest *n* : resumen *m* — ~ *vt* **1** : digerir **2** SUMMARIZE : resumir — **digestible** *adj* : digerible — **digestion** *n* : digestión *f* — **digestive** *adj* : digestivo
digit *n* **1** NUMERAL : dígito *m*, número *m* **2** FINGER, TOE : dedo *m* — **digital** *adj* : digital
dignity *n, pl* **-ties** : dignidad *f* — **dignified** *adj* : digno, decoroso

digress *vi* : desviarse del tema, divagar — **digression** *n* : digresión *f*
dike *n* : dique *m*
dilapidated *adj* : ruinoso
dilate *v* **-lated; -lating** *vt* : dilatar — *vi* : dilatarse
dilemma *n* : dilema *m*
diligence *n* : diligencia *f* — **diligent** *adj* : diligente
dilute *vt* **-luted; -luting** : diluir
dim *v* **dimmed; dimming** *vt* : atenuar — *vi* : irse atenuando — ~ *adj* **dimmer; dimmest 1** DARK : oscuro **2** FAINT : débil, tenue
dime *n* : moneda *f* de diez centavos
dimension *n* : dimensión *f*
diminish *v* : disminuir
diminutive *adj* : diminuto
dimple *n* : hoyuelo *m*
din *n* : estrépito *m*
dine *vi* **dined; dining** : cenar — **diner** *n* **1** : comensal *mf* (persona) **2** : cafetería *f* (restaurante)
dingy *adj* **-gier; -est** : sucio, deslucido
dinner *n* : cena *f*, comida *f*
dinosaur *n* : dinosaurio *m*
dint *n* **by** ~ **of** : a fuerza de
dip *v* **dipped; dipping** *vt* : mojar — *vi* **1** : bajar, descender — ~ *n* **1** DROP : descenso *m*, caída *f* **2** SWIM : chapuzón *m* **3** SAUCE : salsa *f*
diploma *n, pl* **-mas** : diploma *m*
diplomacy *n* : diplomacia *f* — **diplomat** *n* : diplomático *m*, -ca *f* — **diplomatic** *adj* : diplomático
dire *adj* **direr; direst 1** : grave, terrible **2** EXTREME : extremo
direct *vt* **1** : dirigir **2** ORDER : mandar — ~ *adj* **1** STRAIGHT : directo **2** FRANK : franco — ~ *adv* : directamente — **direct current** *n* : corriente *f* continua — **direction** *n* **1** : dirección *f* **2 ask** ~**s** : pedir indicaciones — **directly** *adv* **1** STRAIGHT : directamente **2** IMMEDIATELY : en seguida — **director** *n* **1** : director *m*, -tora *f* **2 board of** ~**s** : directorio *m* — **directory** *n, pl* **-ries** : guía *f* (telefónica)
dirt *n* **1** : suciedad *f* **2** SOIL : tierra *f* — **dirty** *adj* **dirtier; -est 1** : sucio **2** INDECENT : obsceno, cochino *fam*
disability *n, pl* **-ties** : minusvalía *f*, invalidez *f* — **disable** *vt* **-abled; -abling** : incapacitar — **disabled** *adj* : minusválido
disadvantage *n* : desventaja *f*
disagree *vi* **1** : no estar de acuerdo (con algn) **2** CONFLICT : no coincidir — **disagreeable** *adj* : desagradable — **disagreement** *n* **1** : desacuerdo *m* **2** ARGUMENT : discusión *f*

disappear *vi* : desaparecer — **disappearance** *n* : desaparición *f*

disappoint *vt* : decepcionar, desilusionar — **disappointment** *n* : decepción *f*, desilusión *f*

disapprove *vi* **-proved; -proving** ~ **of** : desaprobar — **disapproval** *n* : desaprobación *f*

disarm *vt* : desarmar — **disarmament** *n* : desarme *m*

disarray *n* : desorden *m*

disaster *n* : desastre *m* — **disastrous** *adj* : desastroso

disbelief *n* : incredulidad *f*

disc → **disk**

discard *vt* : desechar, deshacerse de

discern *vt* : percibir, discernir — **discernible** *adj* : perceptible

discharge *vt* **-charged; -charging 1** UNLOAD : descargar **2** RELEASE : liberar, poner en libertad **3** DISMISS : despedir **4** CARRY OUT : cumplir con (una obligación) — ~ *n* **1** : descarga *f* (de electricidad), emisión *f* (de humo, etc.) **2** DISMISSAL : despido *m* **3** RELEASE : alta *f* (de un paciente), puesta *f* en libertad (de un preso) **4** : supuración *f* (en medicina)

disciple *n* : discípulo *m*, -la *f*

discipline *n* **1** : disciplina *f* **2** PUNISHMENT : castigo *m* — ~ *vt* **-plined; -plining 1** CONTROL : disciplinar **2** PUNISH : castigar

disclaim *vt* : negar

disclose *vt* **-closed; -closing** : revelar — **disclosure** *n* : revelación *f*

discomfort *n* **1** : incomodidad *f* **2** PAIN : malestar *m* **3** UNEASINESS : inquietud *f*

disconcert *vt* : desconcertar

disconnect *vt* : desconectar

disconsolate *adj* : desconsolado

discontented *adj* : descontento

discontinue *vt* **-ued; -uing** : suspender, descontinuar

discount *n* : descuento *m*, rebaja *f* — ~ *vt* **1** : descontar (precios) **2** DISREGARD : descartar

discourage *vt* **-aged; -aging** : desalentar, desanimar — **discouragement** *n* : desánimo *m*, desaliento *m*

discover *vt* : descubrir — **discovery** *n, pl* **-ries** : descubrimiento *m*

discredit *vt* : desacreditar — ~ *n* : descrédito *m*

discreet *adj* : discreto

discrepancy *n, pl* **-cies** : discrepancia *f*

discretion *n* : discreción *f*

discriminate *vi* **-nated; -nating 1** ~ **against** : discriminar **2** ~ **between** : distinguir entre — **discrimination** *n* **1** PREJUDICE : discriminación *f* **2** DISCERNMENT : discernimiento *m*

discuss *vt* : hablar de, discutir — **discussion** *n* : discusión *f*

disdain *n* : desdén *m* — ~ *vt* : desdeñar

disease *n* : enfermedad *f* — **diseased** *adj* : enfermo

disembark *vi* : desembarcar

disengage *vt* **-gaged; -gaging 1** RELEASE : soltar **2** ~ **the clutch** : desembragar

disentangle *vt* **-gled; -gling** : desenredar

disfavor *n* : desaprobación *f*

disfigure *vt* **-ured; -uring** : desfigurar

disgrace *vt* **-graced; -gracing** : deshonrar — ~ *n* **1** DISHONOR : deshonra *f* **2** SHAME : vergüenza *f* — **disgraceful** *adj* : vergonzoso, deshonroso

disgruntled *adj* : descontento

disguise *vt* **-guised; -guising** : disfrazar — ~ *n* : disfraz *m*

disgust *n* : asco *m*, repugnancia *f* — ~ *vt* : asquear — **disgusting** *adj* : asqueroso

dish *n* **1** : plato *m* **2** *or* serving ~ : fuente *f* **3** wash the ~es : lavar los platos — ~ *vt or* ~ **up** : servir — **dishcloth** *n* : paño *m* de cocina (para secar), trapo *m* de fregar (para lavar)

dishearten *vt* : desanimar

disheveled *or* **dishevelled** *adj* : desaliñado, despeinado (dícese del pelo)

dishonest *adj* : deshonesto — **dishonesty** *n, pl* **-ties** : falta *f* de honradez

dishonor *n* : deshonra *f* — ~ *vt* : deshonrar — **dishonorable** *adj* : deshonroso

dishwasher *n* : lavaplatos *m*, lavavajillas *m*

disillusion *vt* : desilusionar — **disillusionment** *n* : desilusión *f*

disinfect *vt* : desinfectar — **disinfectant** *n* : desinfectante *m*

disintegrate *vi* **-grated; -grating** : desintegrarse

disinterested *adj* : desinteresado

disk *or* **disc** *n* : disco *m*

dislike *n* : aversión *f*, antipatía *f* — ~ *vt* **-liked; -liking 1** : tener aversión a **2 I** ~ **dancing** : no me gusta bailar

dislocate *vt* **-cated; -cating** : dislocar

dislodge *vt* **-lodged; -lodging** : sacar, desalojar

disloyal *adj* : desleal — **disloyalty** *n, pl* **-ties** : deslealtad *f*

dismal *adj* : sombrío, deprimente

dismantle *vt* **-tled; -tling** : desmontar, desarmar

dismay *vt* : consternar — ~ *n* : consternación *f*

dismiss *vt* **1** DISCHARGE : despedir, destituir **2** REJECT : descartar, rechazar — **dismissal** *n* **1** : despido *m* (de un empleado), destitución *f* (de un funcionario) **2** REJECTION : rechazo *m*

dismount *vi* : desmontar
disobey *v* : desobedecer — **disobedience** *n* : desobediencia *f* — **disobedient** *adj* : desobediente
disorder *n* **1** : desorden *m* **2** AILMENT : afección *f*, problema *m* — **disorderly** *adj* : desordenado
disorganize *vt* **-nized; -nizing** : desorganizar
disown *vt* : renegar de
dispassionate *adj* : desapasionado
dispatch *vt* : despachar, enviar
dispel *vt* **-pelled; -pelling** : disipar
dispensation *n* EXEMPTION : exención *m*, dispensa *f*
dispense *v* **-pensed; -pensing** *vt* : repartir, distribuir — *vi* ~ **with** : prescindir de
disperse *v* **-persed; -persing** *vt* : dispersar — *vi* : dispersarse
displace *vt* **-placed; -placing** **1** : desplazar **2** REPLACE : reemplazar
display *vt* **1** EXHIBIT : exponer, exhibir **2** ~ **anger** : manifestar la ira — ~ *n* : muestra *f*, exposición *f*
displease *vt* **-pleased; -pleasing** : desagradar — **displeasure** *n* : desagrado *m*
dispose *v* **-posed; -posing** *vt* : disponer — *vi* ~ **of** : deshacerse de — **disposable** *adj* : desechable — **disposal** *n* **1** REMOVAL : eliminación *f* **2 have at one's** ~ : tener a su disposición — **disposition** *n* **1** ARRANGEMENT : disposición *f* **2** TEMPERAMENT : temperamento *m*, carácter *m*
disprove *vt* **-proved; -proving** : refutar
dispute *v* **-puted; -puting** *vt* QUESTION : cuestionar — *vi* ARGUE : discutir — ~ *n* : disputa *f*, conflicto *m*
disqualification *n* : descalificación *f* — **disqualify** *vt* **-fied; -fying** : descalificar
disregard *vt* : ignorar, hacer caso omiso de — ~ *n* : indiferencia *f*
disrepair *n* : mal estado *m*
disreputable *adj* : de mala fama
disrespect *n* : falta *f* de respeto — **disrespectful** *adj* : irrespetuoso
disrupt *vt* : trastornar, perturbar — **disruption** *n* : trastorno *m*
dissatisfaction *n* : descontento *m* — **dissatisfied** *adj* : descontento
dissect *vt* : disecar
disseminate *vt* **-nated; -nating** : diseminar, difundir
dissent *vi* : disentir — ~ *n* : disentimiento *m*
dissertation THESIS : tesis *f*
disservice *n* **do a** ~ **to** : no hacer justicia a
dissident *n* : disidente *mf*
dissimilar *adj* : distinto

dissipate *vt* **-pated; -pating** **1** DISPEL : disipar **2** SQUANDER : desperdiciar
dissolve *v* **-solved; -solving** *vt* : disolver — *vi* : disolverse
dissuade *vt* **-suaded; -suading** : disuadir
distance *n* **1** : distancia *f* **2 in the** ~ : a lo lejos — **distant** *adj* : distante
distaste *n* : desagrado *m* — **distasteful** *adj* : desagradable
distend *vt* : dilatar — *vi* : dilatarse
distill *or Brit* **distil** *vt* **-tilled; -tilling** : destilar
distinct *adj* **1** DIFFERENT : distinto **2** CLEAR : claro — **distinction** *n* : distinción *f* — **distinctive** *adj* : distintivo
distinguish *vt* : distinguir — **distinguished** *adj* : distinguido
distort *vt* : deformar, distorsionar — **distortion** *n* : deformación *f*
distract *vt* : distraer — **distraction** *n* : distracción *f*
distraught *adj* : muy afligido
distress *n* **1** : angustia *f*, aflicción *f* **2 in** ~ : en peligro — ~ *vt* : afligir — **distressing** *adj* : penoso
distribute *vt* **-uted; -uting** : distribuir, repartir — **distribution** *n* : distribución *f* — **distributor** *n* : distribuidor *m*, -dora *f*
district *n* **1** REGION : región *f*, zona *f*, barrio *m* (de una ciudad) **2** : distrito *m* (zona política)
distrust *n* : desconfianza *f* — ~ *vt* : desconfiar de
disturb *vt* **1** BOTHER : molestar, perturbar **2** WORRY : inquietar — **disturbance** *n* **1** COMMOTION : alboroto *m*, disturbio *m* **2** INTERRUPTION : interrupción *f*
disuse *n* **fall into** ~ : caer en desuso
ditch *n* : zanja *f*, cuneta *f* — ~ *vt* DISCARD : deshacerse de, botar
ditto *n*, *pl* **-tos** **1** : ídem *m* **2** ~ **marks** : comillas *fpl*
dive *vi* **dived** *or* **dove; dived; diving** **1** : zambullirse, tirarse al agua **2** DESCEND : bajar en picada (dícese de un avión, etc.) — ~ *n* **1** : zambullida *f*, clavado *m Lat* **2** DESCENT : descenso *m* en picada — **diver** *n* : saltador *m*, -dora *f*
diverge *vi* **-verged; -verging** : divergir
diverse *adj* : diverso — **diversify** *v* **-fied; -fying** *vt* : diversificar — *vi* : diversificarse
diversion *n* **1** : desviación *f* **2** AMUSEMENT : diversión *f*, distracción *f*
diversity *n*, *pl* **-ties** : diversidad *f*
divert *vt* **1** : desviar **2** DISTRACT : distraer **3** AMUSE : divertir
divide *v* **-vided; -viding** *vt* : dividir — *vi* : dividirse
dividend *n* : dividendo *m*

divine *adj* **-viner; -est** : divino — **divinity** *n,
pl* **-ties** : divinidad *f*
division *n* : división *f*
divorce *n* : divorcio *m* — ~ *v* **-vorced;
-vorcing** *vt* : divorciar — *vi* : divorciarse —
divorcée *n* : divorciada *f*
divulge *vt* **-vulged; -vulging** : revelar, divulgar
dizzy *adj* **dizzier; -est 1** : mareado **2 a ~
speed** : una velocidad vertiginosa — **dizziness** *n* : mareo *m*, vértigo *m*
DNA *n* : AND *m*
do *v* **did; done; doing; does** *vt* **1** : hacer **2**
PREPARE : preparar — *vi* **1** BEHAVE : hacer
2 FARE : estar, ir, andar **3** SUFFICE : ser suficiente **4 ~ away with** : abolir, eliminar **5
how are you doing?** : ¿cómo estás? — *v
aux* **1** (*used in interrogative sentences*) **do
you know her?** : ¿la conoces? **2** (*used in
negative statements*) **I don't know** : yo no
se **3** (*used as a substitute verb to avoid repetition*) **do you speak English? yes, I do**
: ¿habla inglés? sí
dock *n* : muelle *m* — ~ *vt* : descontar
dinero de (un sueldo) — *vi* ANCHOR
: fondear, atracar
doctor *n* **1** : doctor *m*, -tora *f* (en derecho,
etc.) **2** PHYSICIAN : médico *m*, -ca; doctor
m, -tora *f* — ~ *vt* ALTER : alterar, falsificar
doctrine *n* : doctrina *f*
document *n* : documento *m* — ~ *vt* : documentar — **documentary** *n, pl* **-ries** : documental *m*
dodge *n* : artimaña *f*, truco *m* — ~ *v*
dodged; dodging *vt* : esquivar, eludir — *vi*
: echarse a un lado
doe *n, pl* **does** *or* **doe** : gama *f*, cierva *f*
does → **do**
dog *n* : perro *m*, -rra *f* — ~ *vt* **dogged;
dogging** : perseguir — **dogged** *adj* : tenaz
dogma *n* : dogma *m* — **dogmatic** *adj* : dogmático
doily *n, pl* **-lies** : tapete *m*
doings *npl* : actividades *fpl*
doldrums *npl* **be in the ~** : estar abatido
dole *n* : subsidio *m* de desempleo — ~ *vt*
doled; doling *or* ~ **out** : repartir
doleful *adj* : triste, lúgubre
doll *n* : muñeco *m*, -ca *f*
dollar *n* : dólar *m*
dolphin *n* : delfín *m*
domain *n* **1** TERRITORY : dominio *m* **2**
FIELD : campo *m*, esfera *f*
dome *n* : cúpula *f*
domestic *adj* **1** : doméstico **2** INTERNAL
: nacional — ~ *n* SERVANT : empleado *m*
doméstico, empleada *f* doméstica — **domesticate** *vt* **-cated; -cating** : domesticar
domination *n* : dominación *f* — **dominant**

adj : dominante — **dominate** *v* **-nated;
-nating** : dominar — **domineer** *vi* : dominar, tiranizar
dominos *n* : dominó *m* (juego)
donate *vt* **-nated; -nating** : donar, hacer un
donativo de — **donation** *n* : donativo *m*
done → **do** — ~ *adj* **1** FINISHED : terminado, hecho **2** COOKED : cocido
donkey *n, pl* **-keys** : burro *m*
donor *n* : donante *mf*
don't (*contraction of* **do not**) → **do**
doodle *v* **-dled; -dling** : garabatear — ~ *n*
: garabato *m*
doom *n* : perdición *f*, fatalidad *f* — ~ *vt*
: condenar
door *n* **1** : puerta *f* **2** ENTRANCE : entrada *f*
— **doorbell** *n* : timbre *m* — **doorknob** *n*
: pomo *m* — **doorman** *n, pl* **-men** : portero
m — **doormat** *n* : felpudo *m* — **doorstep** *n*
: umbral *m* — **doorway** *n* : entrada *f*, portal
m
dope *n* **1** DRUG : droga *f* **2** IDIOT : idiota *mf*
— ~ *vt* **doped; doping** : drogar
dormant *adj* : inactivo, latente
dormitory *n, pl* **-ries** : dormitorio *m*
dose *n* : dosis *f* — **dosage** *n* : dosis *f*
dot *n* **1** : punto *m* **2 on the ~** : en punto
dote *vi* **doted; doting ~ on** : adorar
double *adj* : doble — ~ *v* **-bled; -bling** *vt*
: doblar — *vi* : doblarse — ~ *adv* : (el)
doble — ~ *n* : doble *mf* — **double bass** *n*
: contrabajo *m* — **double–cross** *vt*
: traicionar — **doubly** *adv* : doblemente
doubt *vt* **1** : dudar **2** DISTRUST : desconfiar
de, dudar de — ~ *n* : duda *f* — **doubtful**
adj : dudoso — **doubtless** *adv* : sin duda
dough *n* : masa *f* — **doughnut** *n* : rosquilla
f, dona *f Lat*
douse *vt* **doused; dousing 1** DRENCH : empapar, mojar **2** EXTINGUISH : apagar
dove[1] → **dive**
dove[2] *n* : paloma *f*
dowdy *adj* **dowdier; -est** : poco elegante
down *adv* **1** DOWNWARD : hacia abajo **2
come/go ~** : bajar **3 ~ here** : aquí abajo
4 fall ~ : caer **5 lie ~** : acostarse **6 sit ~**
: sentarse — ~ *prep* **1** ALONG : a lo largo
de **2** THROUGH : a través de **3 ~ the hill**
: cuesta abajo — ~ *adj* **1** DESCENDING : de
bajada **2** DOWNCAST : abatido — ~ *n*
: plumón *m* — **downcast** *adj* : triste,
abatido — **downfall** *n* : ruina *f* — **downhearted** *adj* : desanimado — **downhill** *adv*
& adj : cuesta abajo — **down payment** *n*
: entrega *f* inicial — **downpour** *n* : chaparrón *m* — **downright** *adv* : absolutamente —
~ *adj* : absoluto, categórico — **downstairs** *adv* : abajo — ~ *adj* : de abajo —
downstream *adv* : río abajo — **down–**

to–earth *adj* : realista — **downtown** *n* : centro *m* (de la ciudad) — ~ *adv* : al centro, en el centro — ~ *adj* : del centro — **downward** *or* **downwards** *adv* & *adj* : hacia abajo

dowry *n, pl* **-ries** : dote *f*

doze *vi* **dozed; dozing** : dormitar

dozen *n, pl* **dozens** *or* **dozen** : docena *f*

drab *adj* **drabber; drabbest** : monótono, apagado

draft *n* **1** : corriente *f* de aire **2** *or* **rough ~** : borrador *m* **3** : conscripción *f* (militar) **4** *or* ~ **beer** : cerveza *f* de barril — ~ *vt* **1** SKETCH : hacer el borrador de **2** CONSCRIPT : reclutar — **drafty** *adj* **draftier; -est** : con corrientes de aire

drag *v* **dragged; dragging** *vt* **1** : arrastrar **2** DREDGE : dragar — *vi* : arrastrar(se) — ~ *n* **1** RESISTANCE : resistencia *f* (aerodinámica) **2** BORE : pesadez *f*, plomo *m fam*

dragon *n* : dragón *m* — **dragonfly** *n, pl* **-flies** : libélula *f*

drain *vt* **1** EMPTY : vaciar, drenar **2** EXHAUST : agotar — *vi* **1** : escurrir(se) (se dice de los platos) **2** *or* ~ **away** : desaparecer poco a poco — ~ *n* **1** : desagüe *m* **2** SEWER : alcantarilla *f* **3** DEPLETION : agotamiento *m* — **drainage** *n* : drenaje *m* — **drainpipe** *n* : tubo *m* de desagüe

drama *n* : drama *m* — **dramatic** *adj* : dramático — **dramatist** *n* : dramaturgo *m*, -ga *f* — **dramatize** *vt* **-tized; -tizing** : dramatizar

drank → **drink**

drape *vt* **draped; draping 1** COVER : cubrir (con tela) **2** HANG : drapear — **drapes** *npl* CURTAINS : cortinas *fpl*

drastic *adj* : drástico

draught → **draft**

draw *v* **drew ; drawn ; drawing** *vt* **1** PULL : tirar de **2** ATTRACT : atraer **3** SKETCH : dibujar, trazar **4** : sacar (una espada, etc.) **5** ~ **a conclusion** : llegar a una conclusión **6** ~ **up** DRAFT : redactar — *vi* **1** SKETCH : dibujar **2** ~ **near** : acercarse — ~ *n* **1** DRAWING : sorteo *m* **2** TIE : empate *m* **3** ATTRACTION : atracción *f* — **drawback** *n* : desventaja *f* — **drawer** *n* : gaveta *f*, cajón *m* (en un mueble) — **drawing** *n* **1** LOTTERY : sorteo *m* **2** SKETCH : dibujo *m*

drawl *n* : habla *f* lenta y con vocales prolongadas

dread *vt* : temer — ~ *n* : pavor *m*, temor *m* — **dreadful** *adj* : espantoso, terrible

dream *n* : sueño *m* — ~ *v* **dreamed** *or* **dreamt; dreaming** *vi* : soñar — *vt* **1** : soñar **2** ~ **up** : idear — **dreamer** *n* : soñador *m*, -dora *f* — **dreamy** *adj* **dreamier; -est** : soñador

dreary *adj* **-rier; -est** : sombrío, deprimente

dredge *vt* **dredged; dredging** : dragar — ~ *n* : draga *f*

dregs *npl* : heces *fpl*

drench *vt* : empapar

dress *vt* **1** : vestir **2** : preparar (pollo o pescado), aliñar (ensalada) — *vi* **1** : vestirse **2** ~ **up** : ponerse elegante — ~ *n* **1** CLOTHING : ropa *f* **2** : vestido *m* (de mujer) — **dresser** *n* : cómoda *f* con espejo — **dressing** *n* **1** : aliño *m* (de ensalada), relleno *m* (de pollo) **2** BANDAGE : vendaje *m* — **dressmaker** *n* : modista *mf* — **dressy** *adj* **dressier; -est** : elegante

drew → **draw**

dribble *vi* **-bled; -bling 1** DRIP : gotear **2** DROOL : babear **3** : driblar (en basquetbol) — ~ *n* **1** TRICKLE : goteo *m*, hilo *m* **2** DROOL : baba *f*

drier, driest → **dry**

drift *n* **1** MOVEMENT : movimiento *m* **2** HEAP : montón *m* (de arena, etc.), ventisquero *m* (de nieve) **3** MEANING : sentido *m* — ~ *vi* **1** : ir a la deriva **2** ACCUMULATE : amontonarse

drill *n* **1** : taladro *m* **2** : ejercicio *m* (en educación), simulacro *m* (de incendio, etc.) — ~ *vt* **1** : perforar, taladrar **2** TRAIN : instruir por repetición — *vi* ~ **for** : perforar en busca de

drink *v* **drank; drunk** *or* **drank; drinking** : beber — ~ *n* : bebida *f*

drip *vi* **dripped; dripping** : gotear — ~ *n* **1** DROP : gota *f* **2** DRIPPING : goteo *m*

drive *v* **drove; driven; driving** *vt* **1** : manejar **2** IMPEL : impulsar **3** ~ **crazy** : volver loco **4** ~ **s.o. to (do sth)** : llevar a algn a (hacer algo) — *vi* : manejar, conducir — ~ *n* **1** : paseo *m* (en coche) **2** CAMPAIGN : campaña *f* **3** VIGOR : energía *f* **4** NEED : instinto *m*

drivel *n* : tonterías *fpl*

driver *n* : conductor *m*, -tora *f*; chofer *m*

driveway *n* : camino *m* de entrada

drizzle *n* : llovizna *f* — ~ *vi* **-zled; -zling** : lloviznar

drone *n* **1** BEE : zángano *m* **2** HUM : zumbido *m* — ~ *vi* **droned; droning 1** BUZZ : zumbar **2** *or* ~ **on** : hablar con monotonía

drool *vi* : babear — ~ *n* : baba *f*

droop *vi* : inclinarse (dícese de la cabeza), encorvarse (dícese de los escombros), marchitarse (dícese de las flores)

drop *n* **1** : gota *f* (de líquido) **2** DECLINE, FALL : caída *f* — ~ *v* **dropped; dropping** *vt* **1** : dejar caer **2** LOWER : bajar **3** ABANDON : abandonar, dejar **4** ~ **off** LEAVE

: dejar — *vi* **1** FALL : caer(se) **2** DECREASE : bajar, descender **3** ~ **by** *or* ~ **in** : pasar

drought *n* : sequía *f*

drove → **drive**

droves *n* **in** ~ : en manada

drown *vt* : ahogar — *vi* : ahogarse

drowsy *adj* **drowsier; -est** : somnoliento

drudgery *n, pl* **-eries** : trabajo *m* pesado

drug *n* **1** MEDICATION : medicamento *m* **2** NARCOTIC : droga *f*, estupefaciente *m* — ~ *vt* **drugged; drugging** : drogar — **drugstore** *n* : farmacia *f*

drum *n* **1** : tambor *m* **2** *or* **oil** ~ : bidón *m* (de petróleo) — ~ *v* **drummed; drumming** *vi* : tocar el tambor — *vt* : tamborilear con (los dedos, etc.) — **drumstick** *n* **1** : palillo *m* (de tambor) **2** : muslo *m* (de pollo)

drunk → **drink** — ~ *adj* : borracho — ~ *or* **drunkard** *n* : borracho *m*, -cha *f* — **drunken** *adj* : borracho, ebrio

dry *adj* **drier; driest** : seco — ~ *v* **dried; drying** *vt* : secar — *vi* : secarse — **dry-clean** *vt* : limpiar en seco — **dry cleaner** *n* : tintorería *f* (servicio) — **dry cleaning** *n* : limpieza *f* en seco — **dryer** *n* : secadora *f* — **dryness** *n* : sequedad *f*, aridez *f*

dual *adj* : doble

dub *vt* **dubbed; dubbing 1** CALL : apodar **2** : doblar (una película)

dubious *adj* **1** UNCERTAIN : dudoso **2** QUESTIONABLE : sospechoso

duchess *n* : duquesa *f*

duck *n, pl* **duck** *or* **ducks** : pato *m*, -ta *f* — ~ *vt* **1** LOWER : agachar, bajar **2** EVADE : eludir, esquivar — *vi* : agacharse — **duckling** *n* : patito *m*, -ta *f*

duct *n* : conducto *m*

due *adj* **1** PAYABLE : pagadero **2** APPROPRIATE : debido, apropiado **3** EXPECTED : esperado **4** ~ **to** : debido a — ~ *n* **1 give s.o. their** ~ : hacer justicia a algn **2** ~**s** *npl* : cuota *f* — ~ *adv* ~ **east** : justo al este

duel *n* : duelo *m*

duet *n* : dúo *m*

dug → **dig**

duke *n* : duque *m*

dull *adj* **1** STUPID : torpe **2** BLUNT : desafilado **3** BORING : aburrido **4** LACKLUSTER : apagado — ~ *vt* : entorpecer (los sentidos), aliviar (el dolor)

dumb *adj* **1** MUTE : mudo **2** STUPID : estúpido

dumbfound *or* **dumfound** *vt* : dejar sin habla

dummy *n, pl* **-mies 1** SHAM : imitación *f* **2** MANNEQUIN : maniquí *m* **3** IDIOT : tonto *m*, -ta *f*

dump *vt* : descargar, verter — ~ *n* **1** : vertedero *m*, tiradero *m Lat* **2 down in the** ~**s** : triste, deprimido

dumpling *n* : bola *f* de masa hervida

dumpy *adj* **dumpier; -est** : regordete

dunce *n* : burro *m*, -rra *f fam*

dune *n* : duna *f*

dung *n* **1** : excrementos *mpl* **2** MANURE : estiércol *m*

dungarees *npl* JEANS : vaqueros *mpl*, jeans *mpl*

dungeon *n* : calabozo *m*

dunk *vt* : mojar

duo *n, pl* **duos** : dúo *m*

dupe *vt* **duped; duping** : engañar — ~ *n* : inocentón *m*, -tona *f*

duplex *n* : casa *f* de dos viviendas, dúplex *m*

duplicate *adj* : duplicado — ~ *vt* **-cated; -cating** : duplicar, hacer copias de — ~ *n* : duplicado *m*, copia *f*

durable *adj* : duradero

duration *n* : duración *f*

duress *n* : coacción *f*

during *prep* : durante

dusk *n* : anochecer *m*, crepúsculo *m*

dust *n* : polvo *m* — ~ *vt* **1** : quitar el polvo a **2** SPRINKLE : espolvorear — **dustpan** *n* : recogedor *m* — **dusty** *adj* **dustier; -est** : polvoriento

Dutch *adj* : holandés — ~ *n* **1** : holandés *m* (idioma) **2 the** ~ : los holandeses

duty *n, pl* **-ties 1** OBLIGATION : deber *m* **2** TAX : impuesto *m* **3 on** ~ : de servicio — **dutiful** *adj* : obediente

dwarf *n, pl* **dwarfs** *or* **dwarves** : enano *m*, -na *f* — ~ *vt* : hacer parecer pequeño

dwell *vi* **dwelled** *or* **dwelt; dwelling 1** RESIDE : morar, vivir **2** ~ **on** : pensar demasiado en — **dweller** *n* : habitante *mf* — **dwelling** *n* : morada *f*, vivienda *f*

dwindle *vi* **-dled; -dling** : disminuir

dye *n* : tinte *m* — ~ *vt* **dyed; dyeing** : teñir

dying → **die**[1]

dynamic *adj* : dinámico

dynamite *n* : dinamita *f*

dynamo *n, pl* **-mos** : dínamo *m*

dynasty *n, pl* **-ties** : dinastía *f*

dysentery *n, pl* **-teries** : disentería *f*

E

e *n, pl* **e's** *or* **es** : e *f*, quinta letra del alfabeto inglés

each *adj* : cada — ~ *pron* **1** : cada uno *m*, cada una *f* **2** ~ **other** : el uno al otro **3 they hate** ~ **other** : se odian — ~ *adv* : cada uno, por persona

eager *adj* **1** ENTHUSIASTIC : entusiasta **2** IMPATIENT : impaciente — **eagerness** *n* : entusiasmo *m*, impaciencia *f*

eagle *n* : águila *f*

ear *n* **1** : oreja *f* **2** ~ **of corn** : mazorca *f*, choclo *m Lat* — **eardrum** *n* : tímpano *m*

earl *n* : conde *m*

earlobe *n* : lóbulo *m* de la oreja

early *adv* **earlier; -est 1** : temprano **2 as** ~ **as possible** : lo más pronto posible **3 ten minutes** ~ : diez minutos de adelanto — ~ *adj* **earlier; -est 1** FIRST : primero **2** ANCIENT : primitivo, antiguo **3 an** ~ **death** : una muerte prematura **4 be** ~ : llegar temprano **5 in the** ~ **spring** : a principios de la primavera

earmark *vt* : destinar

earn *vt* **1** : ganar **2** DESERVE : merecer

earnest *adj* : serio — ~ *n* **in** ~ : en serio

earnings *npl* **1** WAGES : ingresos *mpl* **2** PROFITS : ganancias *fpl*

earphone *n* : audífono *m*

earring *n* : pendiente *m*, arete *m Lat*

earshot *n* **within** ~ : al alcance del oído

earth *n* : tierra *f* — **earthenware** *n* : loza *f* — **earthly** *adj* : terrenal — **earthquake** *n* : terremoto *m* — **earthworm** *n* : lombriz *f* (de tierra) — **earthy** *adj* **earthier; -est 1** : terroso **2** COARSE, CRUDE : grosero

ease *n* **1** FACILITY : facilidad *f* **2** COMFORT : comodidad *f* **3 feel at** ~ : sentir cómodo — ~ *v* **eased; easing** *vt* **1** ALLEVIATE : aliviar, calmar **2** FACILITATE : facilitar — *vi* **1** : calmarse **2** ~ **up** : disminuir

easel *n* : caballete *m*

easily *adv* **1** : fácilmente, con facilidad **2** UNQUESTIONABLY : con mucho, de lejos *Lat*

east *adv* : al este — ~ *adj* : este, del este — ~ *n* **1** : este *m* **2 the East** : el Oriente

Easter *n* : Pascua *f*

easterly *adv & adj* : del este

eastern *adj* **1** : del este **2 Eastern** : oriental, del este

easy *adj* **easier; -est 1** : fácil **2** RELAXED : relajado — **easygoing** *adj* : tolerante, relajado

eat *v* **ate; eaten; eating** *vt* : comer — *vi* **1** : comer **2** ~ **into** CORRODE : corroer **3** ~ **into** DEPLETE : comerse — **eatable** *adj* : comestible

eaves *npl* : alero *m* — **eavesdrop** *vi* **-dropped; -dropping** : escuchar a escondidas

ebb *n* : reflujo *m* — ~ *vi* **1** : bajar (dícese de la marea) **2** DECLINE : decaer

ebony *n, pl* **-nies** : ébano *m*

eccentric *adj* : excéntrico — ~ *n* : excéntrico *m*, -ca *f* — **eccentricity** *n, pl* **-ties** : excentricidad *f*

echo *n, pl* **echoes** : eco *m* — ~ *v* **echoed; echoing** *vt* : repetir — *vi* : hacer eco, resonar

eclipse *n* : eclipse *m* — ~ *vt* **eclipsed; eclipsing** : eclipsar

ecology *n, pl* **-gies** : ecología *f* — **ecological** *adj* : ecológico

economy *n, pl* **-mies** : economía *f* — **economic** *or* **economical** *adj* : económico — **economics** *n* : economía *f* — **economist** *n* : economista *mf* — **economize** *v* **-mized; -mizing** : economizar

ecstasy *n, pl* **-sies** : éxtasis *m* — **ecstatic** *adj* : extático

Ecuadoran *or* **Ecuadorean** *or* **Ecuadorian** *adj* : ecuatoriano

edge *n* **1** BORDER : borde *m* **2** : filo *m* (de un cuchillo) **3** ADVANTAGE : ventaja *f* — ~ *v* **edged; edging** *vt* : bordear, ribetear — *vi* : avanzar poco a poco — **edgewise** *adv* : de lado — **edgy** *adj* **edgier; -est** : nervioso

edible *adj* : comestible

edit *vt* **1** : editar, redactar, corregir **2** ~ **out** : suprimir, cortar — **edition** *n* : edición *f* — **editor** *n* : director *m*, -tora *f* (de un periódico); redactor *m*, -tora *f* (de un libro) — **editorial** *n* : editorial *m*

educate *vt* **-cated; -cating 1** TEACH : educar, instruir **2** INFORM : informar — **education** *n* : educación *f* — **educational** *adj* **1** : educativo, instructivo **2** TEACHING : docente — **educator** *n* : educador *m*, -dora *f*

eel *n* : anguila *f*

eerie *adj* **-rier; -est** : extraño e inquietante, misterioso

effect *n* **1** : efecto *m* **2 go into** ~ : entrar en vigor — ~ *vt* : efectuar, llevar a cabo — **effective** *adj* **1** : eficaz **2** ACTUAL : efectivo, vigente — **effectiveness** *n* : eficacia *f*

effeminate *adj* : afeminado

effervescent *adj* : efervescente

efficient *adj* : eficiente — **efficiency** *n, pl* **-cies** : eficiencia *f*

effort n **1** : esfuerzo m **2 it's not worth the ～** : no vale la pena — **effortless** adj : fácil, sin esfuerzo

egg n : huevo m — **～** vt **～ on** : incitar — **eggplant** n : berenjena f — **eggshell** n : cascarón m

ego n, pl **egos 1** SELF : ego m, yo m **2** SELF-ESTEEM : amor m propio — **egotism** n : egotismo m — **egotist** n : egotista mf — **egotistic** or **egotistical** adj : egotista

eiderdown n **1** DOWN : plumón m **2** COMFORTER : edredón m

eight n : ocho m — **～** adj : ocho — **eight hundred** n : ochocientos m

eighteen n : dieciocho m — **～** adj : dieciocho — **eighteenth** adj : decimoctavo — **～** n **1** : decimoctavo m, -va f (en una serie) **2** : dieciochoavo m, dieciochoava parte f

eighth n **1** : octavo m, -va f (en una serie) **2** : octavo m, octava parte f — **～** adj : octavo

eighty n, pl **eighties** : ochenta m — **～** adj : ochenta

either adj **1** : cualquiera (de los dos) **2** (in negative constructions) : ninguno (de los dos) **3** EACH : cada — **～** pron **1** : cualquiera mf (de los dos) **2** (in negative constructions) : ninguno m, -na f (de los dos) **3** or **～ one** : algún m, alguna f — **～** conj **1** : o **2** (in negative constructions) : ni

eject vt : expulsar, expeler

eke vt **eked; eking** or **～ out** : ganar a duras penas

elaborate adj **1** DETAILED : detallado **2** COMPLEX : complicado — **～** v **-rated; -rating** vt : elaborar — vi : entrar en detalles

elapse vi **elapsed; elapsing** : transcurrir

elastic adj : elástico — **～** n **1** : elástico m **2** RUBBER BAND : goma f (elástica) — **elasticity** n, pl **-ties** : elasticidad f

elated adj : regocijado

elbow n : codo m

elder adj : mayor — **～** n **1** : mayor mf **2** : anciano m, -na f (de un tribu, etc.) — **elderly** adj : mayor, anciano

elect vt : elegir — **～** adj : electo — **election** n : elección f — **electoral** adj : electoral — **electorate** n : electorado m

electricity n, pl **-ties** : electricidad f — **electric** or **electrical** adj : eléctrico — **electrician** n : electricista mf — **electrify** vt **-fied; -fying** : electrificar — **electrocute** vt **-cuted; -cuting** : electrocutar

electron n : electrón m — **electronic** adj : electrónico — **electronic mail** n : correo m electrónico — **electronics** n : electrónica f

elegant adj : elegante — **elegance** n : elegancia f

element n **1** : elemento m **2 ～s** npl BASICS : elementos mpl, rudimentos mpl — **elementary** adj : elemental — **elementary school** n : escuela f primaria

elephant n : elefante m, -ta f

elevate vt **-vated; -vating** : elevar — **elevator** n : ascensor m

eleven n : once m — **～** adj : once — **eleventh** adj : undécimo — **～** n **1** : undécimo m, -ma f (en una serie) **2** : onceavo m, onceava parte f

elf n, pl **elves** : duende m

elicit vt : provocar

eligible adj : elegible

eliminate vt **-nated; -nating** : eliminar — **elimination** n : eliminación f

elite n : elite f

elk n : alce m (de Europa), uapití m (de América)

elliptical or **elliptic** adj : elíptico

elm n : olmo m

elongate vt **-gated; -gating** : alargar

elope vi **eloped; eloping** : fugarse — **elopement** n : fuga f

eloquence n : elocuencia f — **eloquent** adj : elocuente

else adv **1 how ～?** : ¿de qué otro modo? **2 where ～?** : ¿en qué otro sitio? **3 or ～** : si no, de lo contrario — **～** adj **1 everyone ～** : todos los demás **2 nobody ～** : ningún otro, nadie más **3 nothing ～** : nada más **4 what ～?** : ¿qué más? — **elsewhere** adv : en otra parte

elude vt **eluded; eluding** : eludir, esquivar — **elusive** adj : esquivo

elves → elf

emaciated adj : esquálido, demacrado

E–mail → electronic mail

emanate vi **-nated; -nating** : emanar

emancipate vt **-pated; -pating** : emancipar — **emancipation** n : emancipación f

embalm vt : embalsamar

embankment n : terraplén m, dique m (de un río)

embargo n, pl **-goes** : embargo m

embark vt : embarcar — vi **1** : embarcarse **2 ～ upon** : emprender — **embarkation** n : embarque m, embarco m

embarrass vt : avergonzar — **embarrassing** adj : embarazoso — **embarrassment** n : vergüenza f

embassy n, pl **-sies** : embajada f

embed vt **-bedded; -bedding** : incrustar, enterrar

embellish vt : adornar, embellecer — **embellishment** n : adorno m

embers npl : ascuas fpl

embezzle vt **-zled; -zling** : desfalcar, malversar — **embezzlement** n : desfalco m, malversación f

emblem n : emblema m

embody *vt* **-bodied; -bodying** : encarnar, personificar

emboss *vt* : repujar, grabar en relieve

embrace *v* **-braced; -bracing** *vt* : abrazar — *vi* : abrazarse — $\sim$ *n* : abrazo *m*

embroider *vt* : bordar — **embroidery** *n, pl* **-deries** : bordado *m*

embryo *n, pl* **embryos** : embrión *m*

emerald *n* : esmeralda *f*

emerge *vi* **emerged; emerging** : salir, aparecer — **emergence** *n* : aparición *f*

emergency *n, pl* **-cies** **1** : emergencia *f* **2** $\sim$ **exit** : salida *f* de emergencia **3** $\sim$ **room** : sala *f* de urgencias, sala *f* de guardia

emery *n, pl* **-eries** **1** : esmeril *m* **2** $\sim$ **board** : lima *f* de uñas

emigrant *n* : emigrante *mf* — **emigrate** *vi* **-grated; -grating** : emigrar — **emigration** *n* : emigración *f*

eminence *n* : eminencia *f* — **eminent** *adj* : eminente

emission *n* : emisión *f* — **emit** *vt* **emitted; emitting** : emitir

emotion *n* : emoción *f* — **emotional** *adj* **1** : emocional **2** MOVING : emotivo

emperor *n* : emperador *m*

emphasis *n, pl* **-phases** : énfasis *m* — **emphasize** *vt* **-sized; -sizing** : subrayar, hacer hincapié en — **emphatic** *adj* : enérgico, categórico

empire *n* : imperio *m*

employ *vt* : emplear — **employee** *n* : empleado *m*, -da *f* — **employer** *n* : patrón *m*, -trona *f*; empleador *m*, -dora *f* — **employment** *n* : trabajo *m*, empleo *m*

empower *vt* : autorizar

empress *n* : emperatriz *f*

empty *adj* **emptier; -est** **1** : vacío **2** MEANINGLESS : vano — $\sim$ *v* **-tied; -tying** *vt* : vaciar — *vi* : vaciarse — **emptiness** *n* : vacío *m*

emulate *vt* **-lated; -lating** : emular

enable *vt* **-abled; -abling** : hacer posible, permitar

enact *vt* **1** : promulgar (un ley o un decreto) **2** PERFORM : representar

enamel *n* : esmalte *m*

encampment *n* : campamento *m*

encase *vt* **-cased; -casing** : encerrar, revestir

enchant *vt* : encantar — **enchanting** *adj* : encantador — **enchantment** *n* : encanto *m*

encircle *vt* **-cled; -cling** : rodear

enclose *vt* **-closed; -closing** **1** SURROUND : encerrar, cercar **2** INCLUDE : adjuntar (a una carta) — **enclosure** *n* **1** AREA : recinto *m* **2** : anexo *m* (con una carta)

encompass *vt* **1** ENCIRCLE : cercar **2** INCLUDE : abarcar

encore *n* : bis *m*

encounter *vt* : encontrar — $\sim$ *n* : encuentro *m*

encourage *vt* **-aged; -aging** **1** : animar, alentar **2** FOSTER : promover, fomentar — **encouragement** *n* **1** : aliento *m* **2** PROMOTION : fomento *m*

encroach *vi* $\sim$ **on** : invadir, usurpar, quitar (el tiempo)

encyclopedia *n* : enciclopedia *f*

end *n* **1** : fin **2** EXTREMITY : extremo *m*, punta *f* **3 come to an** $\sim$: llegar a su fin **4 in the** $\sim$: por fin — $\sim$ *vt* : terminar, poner fin a — *vi* : terminar(se)

endanger *vt* : poner en peligro

endearing *adj* : simpático

endeavor *or Brit* **endeavour** *vt* $\sim$ **to** : esforzarse por — $\sim$ *n* : esfuerzo *m*

ending *n* : final *m*, desenlace *m*

endive *n* : endibia *f*, endivia *f*

endless *adj* **1** INTERMINABLE : interminable **2** INNUMERABLE : innumerable **3** $\sim$ **possibilities** : posibilidades *fpl* infinitas

endorse *vt* **-dorsed; -dorsing** **1** SIGN : endosar **2** APPROVE : aprobar — **endorsement** *n* APPROVAL : aprobación *f*

endow *vt* : dotar

endure *v* **-dured; -during** *vt* : soportar, aguantar — *vi* LAST : durar — **endurance** *n* : resistencia *f*

enemy *n, pl* **-mies** : enemigo *m*, -ga *f*

energy *n, pl* **-gies** : energía *f* — **energetic** *adj* : enérgico

enforce *vt* **-forced; -forcing** **1** : hacer cumplir (un ley, etc.) **2** IMPOSE : imponer — **enforced** *adj* : forzoso — **enforcement** *n* : imposición *f* del cumplimiento

engage *v* **-gaged; -gaging** *vt* **1** : captar, atraer (la atención, etc.) **2** $\sim$ **the clutch** : embragar — *vi* $\sim$ **in** : dedicarse a, entrar en — **engagement** *n* **1** APPOINTMENT : cita *f*, hora *f* **2** BETROTHAL : compromiso *m* — **engaging** *adj* : atractivo

engine *n* **1** : motor *m* **2** LOCOMOTIVE : locomotora *f* — **engineer** *n* **1** : ingeniero *m*, -ra *f* **2** : maquinista *mf* (de locomotoras) — $\sim$ *vt* **1** CONSTRUCT : construir **2** CONTRIVE : tramar — **engineering** *n* : ingeniería *f*

English *adj* : inglés — $\sim$ *n* : inglés *m* (idioma) — **Englishman** *n* : inglés *m* — **Englishwoman** *n* : inglesa *f*

engrave *vt* **-graved; -graving** : grabar — **engraving** *n* : grabado *m*

engross *vt* : absorber

engulf *vt* : envolver

enhance *vt* **-hanced; -hancing** : aumentar, mejorar

enjoy *vt* **1** : disfrutar, gozar de **2** $\sim$ **one-**

self : divertirse — **enjoyable** *adj* : agradable — **enjoyment** *n* : placer *m*

enlarge *v* **-larged; -larging** *vt* : agrandar, ampliar — *vi* **1** : agrandarse **2** ~ **upon** : extenderse sobre — **enlargement** *n* : ampliación *f*

enlighten *vt* : aclarar, iluminar

enlist *vt* **1** ENROLL : alistar **2** OBTAIN : conseguir — *vi* : alistarse

enliven *vt* : animar

enmity *n, pl* **-ties** : enemistad *f*

enormous *adj* : enorme

enough *adj* : bastante, suficiente — ~ *adv* : bastante — ~ *pron* **1** : (lo) suficiente, (lo) bastante **2 it's not** ~ : no basta **3 I've had** ~ **!** : ¡estoy harto!

enquire , **enquiry** → **inquire, inquiry**

enrage *vt* **-raged; -raging** : enfurecer

enrich *vt* : enriquecer

enroll *or* **enrol** *v* **-rolled; -rolling** *vt* : matricular, inscribir — *vi* : matricularse, inscribirse

ensemble *n* : conjunto *m*

ensign *n* **1** FLAG : enseña *f* **2** : alférez *mf* (de fragata)

enslave *vt* **-slaved; -slaving** : esclavizar

ensue *vi* **-sued; -suing** : seguir, resultar

ensure *vt* **-sured; -suring** : asegurar

entail *vt* : suponer, conllevar

entangle *vt* **-gled; -gling** : enredar — **entanglement** *n* : enredo *m*

enter *vt* **1** : entrar en **2** RECORD : inscribir — *vi* **1** : entrar **2** ~ **into** : firmar (un acuerdo), entablar (negociaciones, etc.)

enterprise *n* **1** : empresa *f* **2** INITIATIVE : iniciativa *f* — **enterprising** *adj* : emprendedor

entertain *vt* **1** AMUSE : entretener, divertir **2** CONSIDER : considerar **3** ~ **guests** : recibir invitados — **entertainment** *n* : entretenimiento *m*, diversión *f*

enthrall *or* **enthral** *vt* **-thralled; -thralling** : cautivar, embelesar

enthusiasm *n* : entusiasmo *m* — **enthusiast** *n* : entusiasta *mf* — **enthusiastic** *adj* : entusiasta

entice *vt* **-ticed; -ticing** : atraer, tentar

entire *adj* : entero, completo — **entirely** *adv* : completamente — **entirety** *n, pl* **-ties** : totalidad *f*

entitle *vt* **-tled; -tling** **1** NAME : titular **2** AUTHORIZE : dar derecho a — **entitlement** *n* : derecho *m*

entity *n, pl* **-ties** : entidad *f*

entrails *npl* : entrañas *fpl*, vísceras *fpl*

entrance¹ *vt* **-tranced; -trancing** : encantar, fascinar

entrance² *n* : entrada *f* — **entrant** *n* : participante *mf*

entreat *vt* : suplicar

entrée *or* **entree** *n* : plato *m* principal

entrepreneur *n* : empresario *m*, -ria *f*

entrust *vt* : confiar

entry *n, pl* **-tries** **1** ENTRANCE : entrada *f* **2** NOTATION : entrada *f*, anotación *f*

enumerate *vt* **-ated; -ating** : enumerar

enunciate *vt* **-ated; -ating** **1** STATE : enunciar **2** PRONOUNCE : articular

envelop *vt* : envolver — **envelope** *n* : sobre *m*

envious *adj* : envidioso — **enviously** *adv* : con envidia

environment *n* : medio *m* ambiente — **environmental** *adj* : ambiental — **environmentalist** *n* : ecologista *mf*

envision *vt* : prever, imaginar

envoy *n* : enviado *m*, -da *f*

envy *n, pl* **envies** : envidia *f* — ~ *vt* **-vied; -vying** : envidiar

enzyme *n* : enzima *f*

epic *adj* : épico — ~ *n* : epopeya *f*

epidemic *n* : epidemia *f* — ~ *adj* : epidémico

epilepsy *n, pl* **-sies** : epilepsia *f* — **epileptic** *adj* : epiléptico — ~ *n* : epiléptico *m*, -ca *f*

episode *n* : episodio *m*

epitaph *n* : epitafio *m*

epitome *n* : personificación *f* — **epitomize** *vt* **-mized; -mizing** : ser la personificación de, personificar

epoch *n* : época *f*

equal *adj* **1** SAME : igual **2 be** ~ **to** : estar a la altura de (una tarea, etc.) — ~ *n* : igual *mf* — ~ *vt* **equaled** *or* **equalled; equaling** *or* **equalling** **1** : igualar **2** : ser igual a (en matemáticas) — **equality** *n, pl* **-ties** : igualdad *f* — **equalize** *vt* **-ized; -izing** : igualar — **equally** *adv* **1** : igualmente **2** ~ **important** : igual de importante

equate *vt* **equated; equating** ~ **with** : equiparar con — **equation** *n* : ecuación *f*

equator *n* : ecuador *m*

equilibrium *n, pl* **-riums** *or* **-ria** : equilibrio *m*

equinox *n* : equinoccio *m*

equip *vt* **equipped; equipping** : equipar — **equipment** *n* : equipo *m*

equity *n, pl* **-ties** **1** FAIRNESS : equidad *f* **2 equities** *npl* STOCKS : acciones *fpl* ordinarias

equivalent *adj* : equivalente — ~ *n* : equivalente *m*

era *n* : era *f*, época *f*

eradicate *vt* **-cated; -cating** : erradicar

erase *vt* **erased; erasing** : borrar — **eraser** *n* : goma *f* de borrar, borrador *m*

erect *adj* : erguido — ~ *vt* : erigir, levantar

— **erection** n **1** BUILDING : construcción f **2** : erección f (en fisiología)

erode vt **eroded; eroding** : erosionar (el suelo), corroer (metales) — **erosion** n : erosión f, corrosión f

erotic adj : erótico

err vi : equivocarse, errar

errand n : mandado m, recado m Spain

erratic adj : errático, irregular

error n : error m — **erroneous** adj : erróneo

erupt vi **1** : hacer erupción (dícese de un volcán) **2** : estallar (dícese de la cólera, la violencia, etc.) — **eruption** n : erupción f

escalate vi **-lated; -lating** : intensificarse

escalator n : escalera f mecánica

escapade n : aventura f

escape v **-caped; -caping** vt : escapar a, evitar — vi : escaparse, fugarse — ~ n **1** : fuga f **2** ~ **from reality** : evasión f de la realidad — **escapee** n : fugitivo m, -va f

escort n **1** GUARD : escolta f **2** COMPANION : acompañante mf — ~ vt **1** : escoltar **2** ACCOMPANY : acompañar

Eskimo adj : esquimal

especially adv : especialmente

espionage n : espionaje m

espresso n, pl **-sos** : café m exprés

essay n : ensayo m (literario), composición f (académica)

essence n : esencia f — **essential** adj : esencial — ~ n **1** : elemento m esencial **2** the ~s : lo indispensable

establish vt : establecer — **establishment** n : establecimiento m

estate n **1** POSSESSIONS : bienes mpl **2** LAND, PROPERTY : finca f

esteem n : estima f — ~ vt : estimar

esthetic → **aesthetic**

estimate vt **-mated; -mating** : calcular, estimar — ~ n **1** : cálculo m (aproximado) **2** or ~ **of costs** : presupuesto m — **estimation** n **1** JUDGMENT : juicio m **2** ESTEEM : estima f

estuary n, pl **-aries** : estuario m, ría f

eternal adj : eterno — **eternity** n, pl **-ties** : eternidad f

ether n : éter m

ethical adj : ético — **ethics** ns & pl : ética f, moralidad f

ethnic adj : étnico

etiquette n : etiqueta f

Eucharist n : Eucaristía f

eulogy n, pl **-gies** : elogio m, panegírico m

euphemism n : eufemismo m

euphoria n : euforia f

European adj : europeo

evacuate vt **-ated; -ating** : evacuar — **evacuation** n : evacuación f

evade vt **evaded; evading** : evadir, eludir

evaluate vt **-ated; -ating** : evaluar

evaporate vi **-rated; -rating** : evaporarse

evasion n : evasión f — **evasive** adj : evasivo

eve n : víspera f

even adj **1** REGULAR, STEADY : regular, constante **2** LEVEL : plano, llano **3** SMOOTH : liso **4** EQUAL : igual **5** ~ **number** : número m par **6 get** ~ **with** : desquitarse con — ~ adv **1** : hasta, incluso **2** ~ **better** : aún mejor, todavía mejor **3** ~ **if** : aunque **4** ~ **so** : aun así — ~ vt : igualar — vi or **out** : nivelarse

evening n : tarde f, noche f

event n **1** : acontecimiento m, suceso m **2** : prueba f (en deportes) **3 in the** ~ **of** : en caso de — **eventful** adj : lleno de incidentes

eventual adj : final — **eventuality** n, pl **-ties** : eventualidad f — **eventually** adv : al fin, finalmente

ever adv **1** ALWAYS : siempre **2** ~ **since** : desde entonces **3 hardly** ~ : casi nunca **4 have you** ~ **done it?** : ¿lo has hecho alguna vez?

evergreen n : planta f de hoja perenne

everlasting adj : eterno

every adj **1** EACH : cada **2** ~ **month** : todos los meses **3** ~ **other day** : cada dos días — **everybody** pron : todos mpl, -das fpl; todo el mundo — **everyday** adj : cotidiano, de todos los días — **everyone** → **everybody** — **everything** pron : todo — **everywhere** adv : en todas partes, por todas partes

evict vt : desahuciar, desalojar — **eviction** n : desahucio m

evidence n **1** PROOF : pruebas fpl **2** TESTIMONY : testimonio m, declaración f — **evident** adj : evidente — **evidently** adv **1** OBVIOUSLY : obviamente **2** APPARENTLY : evidentemente, al parecer

evil adj **eviler** or **eviller; evilest** or **evillest** : malvado, malo — ~ n : mal m, maldad f

evoke vt **evoked; evoking** : evocar

evolution n : evolución f, desarrollo m — **evolve** vi **evolved; evolving** : evolucionar, desarrollarse

exact adj : exacto, preciso — ~ vt : exigir — **exacting** adj : exigente — **exactly** adv : exactamente

exaggerate v **-ated; -ating** : exagerar — **exaggeration** n : exageración f

examine vt **-ined; -ining** **1** : examinar **2** INSPECT : revisar **3** QUESTION : interrogar — **exam** n : examen m — **examination** n : examen m

example n : ejemplo m

exasperate vt **-ated; -ating** : exasperar — **exasperation** n : exasperación f

excavate *vt* **-vated; -vating** : excavar — **excavation** *n* : excavación *f*

exceed *vt* : exceder, sobrepasar — **exceedingly** *adv* : extremadamente

excel *v* **-celled; -celling** *vi* : sobresalir — *vt* SURPASS : superar — **excellence** *n* : excelencia *f* — **excellent** *adj* : excelente

except *prep or* ~ **for** : excepto, menos, salvo — ~ *vt* : exceptuar — **exception** *n* : excepción *f* — **exceptional** *adj* : excepcional

excerpt *n* : extracto *m*

excess *n* : exceso *m* — ~ *adj* : excesivo, de sobra — **excessive** *adj* : excesivo

exchange *n* **1** : intercambio *m* **2** : cambio *m* (en finanzas) — ~ *vt* **-changed; -changing** : cambiar, intercambiar

excise *n* ~ **tax** : impuesto *m* interno, impuesto *m* sobre el consumo

excite *vt* **-cited; -citing** : excitar, emocionar — **excited** *adj* : excitado, entusiasmado — **excitement** *n* : entusiasmo *m*, emoción *f*

exclaim *v* : exclamar — **exclamation** *n* : exclamación *f* — **exclamation point** *n* : signo *m* de admiración

exclude *vt* **-cluded; -cluding** : excluir — **excluding** *prep* : excepto, con excepción de — **exclusion** *n* : exclusión *f* — **exclusive** *adj* : exclusivo

excrement *n* : excremento *m*

excruciating *adj* : insoportable, atroz

excursion *n* : excursión *f*

excuse *vt* **-cused; -cusing 1** : perdonar **2** ~ **me** : perdóne, perdón — ~ *n* : excusa *f*

execute *vt* **-cuted; -cuting** : ejecutar — **execution** *n* : ejecución *f* — **executioner** *n* : verdugo *m*

executive *adj* : ejecutivo — ~ *n* **1** MANAGER : ejecutivo *m*, -va *f* **2** *or* ~ **branch** : poder *m* ejecutivo

exemplify *vt* **-fied; -fying** : ejemplificar — **exemplary** *adj* : ejemplar

exempt *adj* : exento — ~ *vt* : dispensar — **exemption** *n* : exención *f*

exercise *n* : ejercicio *m* — ~ *v* **-cised; -cising** *vt* USE : ejercer, hacer uso de — *vi* : hacer ejercicio

exert *vt* **1** : ejercer **2** ~ **oneself** : esforzarse — **exertion** *n* : esfuerzo *m*

exhale *v* **-haled; -haling** : exhalar

exhaust *vt* : agotar — ~ *n* **1** *or* ~ **fumes** : gases *mpl* de escape **2** *or* ~ **pipe** : tubo *m* de escape — **exhaustion** *n* : agotamiento *m* — **exhaustive** *adj* : exhaustivo

exhibit *vt* **1** DISPLAY : exponer **2** SHOW : mostrar — ~ *n* **1** : objeto *m* expuesto **2** EXHIBITION : exposición *f* — **exhibition** *n* : exposición *f*

exhilarate *vt* **-rated; -rating** : alegrar — **exhilaration** *n* : regocijo *m*

exile *n* **1** : exilio *m* **2** OUTCAST : exiliado *m*, -da *f* — ~ *vt* **exiled; exiling** : exiliar

exist *vi* : existir — **existence** *n* : existencia *f* — **existing** *adj* : existente

exit *n* : salida *f* — ~ *vi* : salir

exodus *n* : éxodo *m*

exonerate *vt* **-ated; -ating** : exonerar, disculpar

exorbitant *adj* : exorbitante, excesivo

exotic *adj* : exótico

expand *vt* **1** : ampliar, extender **2** : dilatar (metales, etc.) — *vi* **1** : ampliarse, extenderse **2** : dilatarse (dícese de metales, etc.) — **expanse** *n* : extensión *f* — **expansion** *n* : expansión *f*

expatriate *n* : expatriado *m*, -da *f* — ~ *adj* : expatriado

expect *vt* **1** : esperar **2** REQUIRE : contar con — *vi* **be expecting** : estar embarazada — **expectancy** *n*, *pl* **-cies** : esperanza *f* — **expectant** *adj* **1** : expectante **2** ~ **mother** : futura madre *f* — **expectation** *n* : esperanza *f*

expedient *adj* : conveniente — ~ *n* : expediente *m*, recurso *m*

expedition *n* : expedición *f*

expel *vt* **-pelled; -pelling** : expulsar (a una persona), expeler (humo, etc.)

expend *vt* : gastar — **expendable** *adj* : prescindible — **expenditure** *n* : gasto *m* — **expense** *n* **1** : gasto *m* **2** ~**s** *npl* : gastos *mpl*, expensas *fpl* **3** **at the** ~ **of** : a expensas de — **expensive** *adj* : caro

experience *n* : experiencia *f* — ~ *vt* **-enced; -encing** : experimentar — **experienced** *adj* : experimentado — **experiment** *n* : experimento *m* — ~ *vi* : experimentar — **experimental** *adj* : experimental

expert *adj* : experto — ~ *n* : experto *m*, -ta *f* — **expertise** *n* : pericia *f*, competencia *f*

expire *vi* **-pired; -piring 1** : caducar, vencer **2** DIE : expirar, morir — **expiration** *n* : vencimiento *m*, caducidad *f*

explain *vt* : explicar — **explanation** *n* : explicación *f* — **explanatory** *adj* : explicativo

explicit *adj* : explícito

explode *v* **-ploded; -ploding** *vt* : hacer explotar — *vi* : explotar, estallar

exploit *n* : hazaña *f*, proeza *f* — ~ *vt* : explotar — **exploitation** *n* : explotación *f*

exploration *n* : exploración *f* — **explore** *vt* **-plored; -ploring** : explorar — **explorer** *n* : explorador *m*, -dora *f*

explosion *n* : explosión *f* — **explosive** *adj* : explosivo — ~ *n* : explosivo *m*

export *vt* : exportar — ~ *n* : exportación *f*

expose *vt* **-posed; -posing 1** : exponer **2**

REVEAL : descubrir, revelar — **exposed** *adj* : expuesto, al descubierto — **exposure** *n* : exposición *f*

express *adj* **1** SPECIFIC : expreso, específico **2** FAST : expreso, rápido — ～ *adv* : por correo urgente — ～ *n or* ～ **train** : expreso *m* — ～ *vt* : expresar — **expression** *n* : expresión *f* — **expressive** *adj* : expresivo — **expressly** *adv* : expresamente — **expressway** *n* : autopista *f*

expulsion *n* : expulsión *f*

exquisite *adj* : exquisito

extend *vt* **1** STRETCH : extender **2** LENGTHEN : prolongar **3** ENLARGE : ampliar **4** ～ **one's hand** : tender la mano — *vi* : extenderse — **extension** *n* **1** : extensión *f* **2** LENGTHENING : prolongación *f* **3** ANNEX : ampliación *f*, anexo *m* **4** ～ **cord** : alargador *m* — **extensive** *adj* : extenso — **extent** *n* **1** SIZE : extensión *f* **2** DEGREE : alcance *m*, grado *m* **3 to a certain** ～ : hasta cierto punto

extenuating *adj* ～ **circumstances** : circunstancias *fpl* atenuantes

exterior *adj* : exterior — ～ *n* : exterior *m*

exterminate *vt* **-nated; -nating** : exterminar — **extermination** *n* : exterminación *f*

external *adj* : externo — **externally** *adv* : exteriormente

extinct *adj* : extinto — **extinction** *n* : extinción *f*

extinguish *vt* : extinguir, apagar — **extinguisher** *n* : extintor *m*

extol *vt* **-tolled; -tolling** : ensalzar, alabar

extort *vt* : arrancar (algo a algn) por la fuerza — **extortion** *n* : extorsión *f*

extra *adj* : suplementario, de más — ～ *n* : extra *m* — ～ *adv* **1** : extra, más **2** ～ **special** : super especial

extract *vt* : extraer, sacar — ～ *n* : extracto *m* — **extraction** *n* : extracción *f*

extracurricular *adj* : extracurricular

extradite *vt* **-dited; -diting** : extraditar

extraordinary *adj* : extraordinario

extraterrestrial *adj* : extraterrestre — ～ *n* : extraterrestre *mf*

extravagant *adj* **1** WASTEFUL : despilfarrador, derrochador **2** EXAGGERATED : extravagante, exagerado — **extravagance** *n* **1** WASTEFULNESS : derroche *m*, despilfarro *m* **2** LUXURY : lujo *m* **3** EXAGGERATION : extravagancia *f*

extreme *adj* : extremo — ～ *n* : extremo *m* — **extremely** *adv* : extremadamente — **extremity** *n, pl* **-ties** : extremidad *f*

extricate *vt* **-cated; -cating** : librar, (lograr) sacar

extrovert *n* : extrovertido *m*, -da *f* — **extroverted** *adj* : extrovertido

exuberant *adj* **1** JOYOUS : eufórico **2** LUSH : exuberante — **exuberance** *n* **1** JOYOUSNESS : euforia *f* **2** VIGOR : exuberancia *f*

exult *vi* : exultar

eye *n* **1** : ojo *m* **2** VISION : visión *f*, vista *f* **3** GLANCE : mirada *f* — ～ *vt* **eyed; eyeing** *or* **eying** : mirar — **eyeball** *n* : globo *m* ocular — **eyebrow** *n* : ceja *f* — **eyeglasses** *npl* : anteojos *mpl*, lentes *mpl* — **eyelash** *n* : pestaña *f* — **eyelid** *n* : párpado *m* — **eyesight** *n* : vista *f*, visión *f* — **eyesore** *n* : monstruosidad *f* — **eyewitness** *n* : testigo *mf* ocular

F

f *n, pl* **f's** *or* **fs** : f, sexta letra del alfabeto inglés

fable *n* : fábula *f*

fabric *n* : tela *f*, tejido *m*

fabulous *adj* : fabuloso

facade *n* : fachada *f*

face *n* **1** : cara *f*, rostro *m* (de una persona) **2** APPEARANCE : fisonomía *f*, aspecto *m* **3** : cara *f* (de una moneda), fachada *f* (de un edificio) **4** ～ **value** : valor *m* nominal **5 in the** ～ **of** : en medio de, ante **6 lose** ～ : desprestigiarse **7 make** ～**s** : hacer muecas — ～ **faced; facing** *vt* **1** : estar frente a **2** CONFRONT : enfrentarse a **3** OVERLOOK : dar a — *vi* ～ **to the north** : mirar hacia el norte — **facedown** *adv* : boca abajo — **faceless** *adj* : anónimo — **face–lift** *n* : estiramiento *m* facial

facet *n* : faceta *f*

face–to–face *adv & adj* : cara a cara

facial *adj* : de la cara, facial — ～ *n* : limpieza *f* de cutis

facetious *adj* : gracioso, burlón

facility *n, pl* **-ties** **1** EASE : facilidad *f* **2** CENTER : centro *m* **3 facilities** *npl* : comodidades *fpl*, servicios *mpl*

facsimile *n* : facsímile *m*, facsímil *m*

fact *n* **1** : hecho *m* **2 in ~** : en realidad, de hecho

faction *n* : facción *m*, bando *m*

factor *n* : factor *m*

factory *n*, *pl* **-ries** : fábrica *f*

factual *adj* : basado en hechos

faculty *n*, *pl* **-ties** : facultad *f*

fad *n* : moda *f* pasajera, manía *f*

fade *v* **faded; fading** *vi* **1** WITHER : marchitarse **2** DISCOLOR : desteñirse, decolorarse **3** DIM : apagarse **4** VANISH : desvanecerse — *vt* : desteñir

fail *vi* **1** : fracasar (dícese de una empresa, un matrimonio, etc.) **2** BREAK DOWN : fallar **3 ~ in** : faltar a, no cumplir con **4** FLUNK : suspender *Spain*, ser reprobado *Lat* **5 ~ to do sth** : no hacer algo — *vt* **1** DISAPPOINT : fallar **2** FLUNK : suspender *Spain*, reprobar *Lat* — **~** *n* **without ~** : sin falta — **failing** *n* : defecto *m* — **failure** *n* **1** : fracaso *m* **2** BREAKDOWN : falla *f*

faint *adj* **1** WEAK : débil **2** INDISTINCT : tenue, indistinto **3 feel ~** : estar mareado — **~** *vi* : desmayarse — **~** *n* : desmayo *m* — **fainthearted** *adj* : cobarde, pusilánime — **faintly** *adv* **1** WEAKLY : débilmente **2** SLIGHTLY : ligeramente, levemente

fair¹ *n* : feria *f*

fair² *adj* **1** BEAUTIFUL : bello, hermoso **2** : bueno (dícese del tiempo) **3** JUST : justo **4** : rubio (dícese del pelo), blanco (dícese de la tez) **5** ADEQUATE : adecuado — **~** *adv* **play ~** : jugar limpio — **fairly** *adv* **1** JUSTLY : justamente **2** QUITE : bastante — **fairness** *n* : justicia *f*

fairy *n*, *pl* **fairies 1** : hada *f* **2 ~ tale** : cuento *m* de hadas

faith *n*, *pl* **faiths** : fe *f* — **faithful** *adj* : fiel — **faithfully** *adv* : fielmente — **faithfulness** *n* : fidelidad *f*

fake *v* **faked; faking** *vt* **1** FALSIFY : falsificar, falsear **2** FEIGN : fingir — *vi* PRETEND : fingir — **~** *adj* : falso — **~** *n* **1** IMITATION : falsificación *f* **2** IMPOSTOR : impostor *m*, -tora *f*

falcon *n* : halcón *m*

fall *vi* **fell; fallen; falling 1** : caer, bajar (dícese de los precios), descender (dícese de la temperatura) **2 ~ asleep** : dormirse **3 ~ back** : retirarse **4 ~ back on** : recurrir a **5 ~ down** : caerse **6 ~ in love** : enamorarse **7 ~ out** QUARREL : pelearse **8 ~ through** : fracasar — **~** *n* **1** : caída *f*, bajada *f* (de precios), descenso *m* (de temperatura) **2** AUTUMN : otoño *m* **3 ~s** *npl* WATERFALL : cascada *f*, catarata *f*

fallacy *n*, *pl* **-cies** : concepto *m* erróneo

fallible *adj* : falible

fallow *adj* **lie ~** : estar en barbecho

false *adj* **falser; falsest 1** : falso **2 ~ alarm** : falsa alarma *f* **3 ~ teeth** : dentadura *f* postiza — **falsehood** *n* : mentira — **falseness** *n* : falsedad *f* — **falsify** *vt* **-fied; -fying** : falsificar, falsear

falter *vi* **-tered; -tering 1** STUMBLE : tambalearse **2** WAVER : vacilar

fame *n* : fama *f*

familiar *adj* **1** : familiar **2 be ~ with** : estar familiarizado con — **familiarity** *n*, *pl* **-ties** : familiaridad *f* — **familiarize** *vt* **-ized; -izing ~ oneself** : familiarizarse

family *n*, *pl* **-lies** : familia *f*

famine *n* : hambre *f*, hambruna *f*

famished *adj* : famélico

famous *adj* : famoso

fan *n* **1** : ventilador *m*, abanico *m* **2** : aficionado *m*, -da *f* (a un pasatiempo); admirador *m*, -dora *f* (de una persona) — **~** *vt* **fanned; fanning** : abanicar (a una persona), avivar (un fuego)

fanatic *or* **fanatical** *adj* : fanático — **~** *n* : fanático *m*, -ca *f* — **fanaticism** *n* : fanatismo *m*

fancy *vt* **-cied; -cying 1** IMAGINE : imaginarse **2** DESIRE : apetecerle (algo a uno) — **~** *adj* **-cier; -est 1** ELABORATE : elaborado **2** LUXURIOUS : lujoso, elegante — **~** *n*, *pl* **-cies 1** WHIM : capricho *m* **2** IMAGINATION : imaginación *f* **3 take a ~ to** : aficionarse a (una cosa), tomar cariño a (una persona) — **fanciful** *adj* **1** CAPRICIOUS : caprichoso **2** IMAGINATIVE : imaginativo

fanfare *n* : fanfarria *f*

fang *n* : colmillo *m* (de un animal), diente *m* (de una serpiente)

fantasy *n*, *pl* **-sies** : fantasía *f* — **fantasize** *vi* **-sized; -sizing** : fantasear — **fantastic** *adj* : fantástico

far *adv* **farther** *or* **further; farthest** *or* **furthest 1** : lejos **2** MUCH : muy, mucho **3 as ~ as** : hasta (un lugar), con respecto a (un tema) **4 by ~** : con mucho **5 ~ and wide** : por todas partes **6 ~ away** : a lo lejos **7 ~ from it!** : ¡todo lo contrario! **8 so ~** : hasta ahora, todavía — **~** *adj* **farther** *or* **further; farthest** *or* **furthest 1** REMOTE : lejano **2** EXTREME : extremo — **faraway** *adj* : remoto, lejano

farce *n* : farsa *f*

fare *vi* **fared; faring** : irle a uno — **~** *n* **1** : precio *m* del pasaje **2** FOOD : comida *f*

farewell *n* : despedida *f* — **~** *adj* : de despedida

far-fetched *adj* : improbable, exagerado

farm *n* : granja *f*, hacienda *f* — **~** *vt* : cultivar (la tierra), criar (animales) — *vi* : ser agricultor — **farmer** *n* : agricultor *m*, -tora *f*;

granjero *m*, -jera *f* — **farmhand** *n* : peón *m* — **farmhouse** *n* : granja *f*, casa *f* de hacienda — **farming** *n* : agricultura *f*, cultivo *m* (de plantas), crianza *f* (de animales) — **farmyard** *n* : corral *m*

far–off *adj* : lejano

far–reaching *adj* : de gran alcance

farsighted *adj* **1** : hipermétrope **2** PRUDENT : previsor

farther *adv* **1** : más lejos **2** MORE : más — *adj* : más lejano — **farthest** *adv* **1** : lo más lejos **2** MOST : más — *adj* : más lejano

fascinate *vt* **-nated; -nating** : fascinar — **fascination** *n* : fascinación *f*

fascism *n* : fascismo *m* — **fascist** *adj* : fascista — ~ *n* : fascista *mf*

fashion *n* **1** MANNER : manera *f* **2** STYLE : moda *f* **3 out of** ~ : pasada de moda — **fashionable** *adj* : de moda

fast[1] *vi* : ayunar — ~ *n* : ayuno *m*

fast[2] *adj* **1** SWIFT : rápido **2** SECURE : firme, seguro **3** : adelantado (dícese de un reloj) **4** ~ **friends** : amigos *mpl* leales — ~ *adv* **1** SECURELY : firmemente **2** SWIFTLY : rápidamente **3** ~ **asleep** : profundamente dormido

fasten *vt* : sujetar (papeles, etc.), abrochar (una blusa, etc.), cerrar (una maleta, etc.) — *vi* : abrocharse, cerrar — **fastener** *n* : cierre *m*

fat *adj* **fatter; fattest 1** : gordo **2** THICK : grueso — ~ *n* : grasa *f*

fatal *adj* **1** : mortal **2** FATEFUL : fatal, fatídico — **fatality** *n, pl* **-ties** : víctima *f* mortal

fate *n* **1** : destino *m* **2** LOT : suerte *f* — **fateful** *adj* : fatídico

father *n* : padre *m* — ~ *vt* : engendrar — **fatherhood** *n* : paternidad *f* — **father–in–law** *n, pl* **fathers–in–law** : suegro *m* — **fatherly** *adj* : paternal

fathom *vt* : comprender

fatigue *n* : fatiga *f* — ~ *vt* **-tigued; -tiguing** : fatigar

fatten *vt* : engordar — **fattening** *adj* : que engorda

fatty *adj* **fattier; -est** : graso

faucet *n* : llave *f* Lat, grifo *m* Spain

fault *n* **1** FLAW : defecto *m* **2** RESPONSIBILITY : culpa *f* **3** : falla *f* (geológica) — *vt* : encontrar defectos a — **faultless** *adj* : impecable — **faulty** *adj* **faultier; -est** : defectuoso

fauna *n* : fauna *f*

favor *or Brit* **favour** *n* **1** : favor *m* **2 in** ~ **of** : a favor de — ~ *vt* **1** : favorecer **2** SUPPORT : estar a favor de **3** PREFER : preferir — **favorable** *or Brit* **favourable** *adj* : favorable — **favorite** *or Brit* **favourite** *n* : favorito *m*,

-ta *f* — ~ *adj* : favorito — **favoritism** *or Brit* **favouritism** *n* : favoritismo *m*

fawn[1] *vi* ~ **over** : adular

fawn[2] *n* : cervato *m*

fax *n* : fax *m* — ~ *vt* : faxear, enviar por fax

fear *v* : temer — ~ *n* **1** : miedo *m*, temor *m* **2 for** ~ **of** : por temor a — **fearful** *adj* **1** FRIGHTENING : espantoso **2** AFRAID : temeroso

feasible *adj* : viable, factible

feast *n* **1** BANQUET : banquete *m*, festín *m* **2** FESTIVAL : fiesta *f* — ~ *vi* **1** : banquetear **2** ~ **upon** : darse un festín de

feat *n* : hazaña *f*

feather *n* : pluma *f*

feature *n* **1** : rasgo *m* (de la cara) **2** CHARACTERISTIC : característica *f* **3** : artículo *m* (en un periódico) **4** ~ **film** : largometraje *m* — *v* **-tured; -turing** *vt* **1** PRESENT : presentar **2** EMPHASIZE : destacar — *vi* : figurar

February *n* : febrero *m*

feces *npl* : excremento *mpl*

federal *adj* : federal — **federation** *n* : federación *f*

fed up *adj* : harto

fee *n* **1** : honorarios *mpl* **2 entrance** ~ : entrada *f*

feeble *adj* **-bler; -blest 1** : débil **2 a** ~ **excuse** : una pobre excusa

feed *v* **fed; feeding** *vt* **1** : dar de comer a, alimentar **2** SUPPLY : alimentar — *vi* : comer, alimentarse — ~ *n* : pienso *m*

feel *v* **felt; feeling** *vt* **1** : sentir (una sensación, etc.) **2** TOUCH : tocar, palpar **3** BELIEVE : creer — *vi* **1** : sentirse (bien, cansado, etc.) **2** SEEM : parecer **3** ~ **hot/thirsty** : tener calor/sed **4** ~ **like doing** : tener ganas de hacer — ~ *n* : tacto *m*, sensación *f* — **feeling** *n* **1** SENSATION : sensación *f* **2** EMOTION : sentimiento *m* **3** OPINION : opinión *f* **4 hurt s.o.'s** ~**s** : herir los sentimientos de algn

feet → **foot**

feign *vt* : fingir

feline *adj* : felino — ~ *n* : felino *m*, -na *f*

fell[1] → **fall**

fell[2] *vt* : talar (un árbol)

fellow *n* **1** COMPANION : compañero *m*, -ra *f* **2** MEMBER : socio *m*, -cia *f* **3** MAN : tipo *m* — **fellowship** *n* **1** : compañerismo *m* **2** ASSOCIATION : fraternidad *f* **3** GRANT : beca *f*

felon *n* : criminal *mf* — **felony** *n, pl* **-nies** : delito *m* grave

felt[1] → **feel**

felt[2] *n* : fieltro *m*

female *adj* : femenino — ~ *n* **1** : hembra *f* (animal) **2** WOMAN : mujer *f*

feminine *adj* : femenino — **femininity** *n* : femineidad *f* — **feminism** *n* : feminismo *m*

— **feminist** *adj* : feminista — ~ *n* : feminista *mf*

fence *n* : cerca *f*, valla *f*, cerco *m Lat* — ~ *v* **fenced; fencing** *vt or* ~ **in** : vallar, cercar — *vi* : hacer esgrima — **fencing** : esgrima *m* (deporte)

fend *vt* ~ **off** : rechazar (un enemigo), eludir (una pregunta) — *vi* ~ **for oneself** : valerse por sí mismo

fender *n* : guardabarros *mpl*

fennel *n* : hinojo *m*

ferment *v* : fermentar — **fermentation** *n* : fermentación *f*

fern *n* : helecho *m*

ferocious *adj* : feroz — **ferocity** *n* : ferocidad *f*

ferret *n* : hurón *m* — ~ *vt* ~ **out** : descubrir

Ferris wheel *n* : noria *f*

ferry *vt* **-ried; -rying** : transportar — ~ *n, pl* **-ries** : ferry *m*

fertile *adj* : fértil — **fertility** *n* : fertilidad *f* — **fertilize** *vt* **-ized; -izing** : fecundar (un huevo), abonar (el suelo) — **fertilizer** *n* : fertilizante *m*, abono *m*

fervent *adj* : ferviente — **fervor** *or Brit* **fervour** *n* : fervor *m*

fester *vi* : enconarse

festival *n* **1** : fiesta *f* **2 film** ~ : festival *m* de cine — **festive** *adj* : festivo — **festivity** *n, pl* **-ties** : festividad *f*

fetch *vt* **1** : ir a buscar **2** : venderse por (un precio)

fête *n* : fiesta *f*

fetid *adj* : fétido

fetish *n* : fetiche *m*

fetters *npl* : grillos *mpl* — **fetter** *vt* : encadenar

fetus *n* : feto *m*

feud *n* : enemistad *f* (entre familiares) — ~ *vi* : pelear

feudal *adj* : feudal — **feudalism** *n* : feudalismo *m*

fever *n* : fiebre *f* — **feverish** *adj* : febril

few *adj* **1** : pocos **2 a** ~ **times** : varias veces — ~ *pron* **1** : pocos **2 a** ~ : algunos, unos cuantos **3 quite a** ~ : muchos — **fewer** *adj & pron* : menos

fiancé, fiancée *n* : prometido *m*, -da *f*; novio *m*, -via *f*

fiasco *n, pl* **-coes** : fiasco *m*

fib *n* : mentirilla *f* — ~ *vi* **fibbed; fibbing** : decir mentirillas

fiber *or* **fibre** *n* : fibra *f* — **fiberglass** *n* : fibra *f* de vidrio — **fibrous** *adj* : fibroso

fickle *adj* : inconstante

fiction *n* : ficción *f* — **fictional** *or* **fictitious** *adj* : ficticio

fiddle *n* : violín *m* — ~ *vi* **-dled; -dling** **1** : tocar el violín **2** ~ **with** : juguetear con

fidelity *n, pl* **-ties** : fidelidad *f*

fidget *vi* **1** : estarse inquieto, moverse **2** ~ **with** : juguetear con — **fidgety** *adj* : inquieto, nervioso

field *n* : campo *m* — ~ *vt* : interceptar (una pelota), sortear (una pregunta) — **field glasses** *n* : binoculares *mpl*, gemelos *mpl* — **field trip** *n* : viaje *m* de estudio

fiend *n* **1** : demonio *m* **2** FANATIC : fanático *m*, -ca *f* — **fiendish** *adj* : diabólico

fierce *adj* **fiercer; -est 1** : feroz **2** INTENSE : fuerte (dícese del viento), acalorado (dícese de un debate) — **fierceness** *n* : ferocidad *f*

fiery *adj* **fierier; -est 1** BURNING : llameante **2** SPIRITED : ardiente, fogoso — **fieriness** *n* : pasión *f*, ardor *m*

fifteen *n* : quince *m* — ~ *adj* : quince — **fifteenth** *adj* : decimoquinto — ~ *n* **1** : decimoquinto *m*, -ta *f* (en una serie) **2** : quinceavo *m* (en matemáticas)

fifth *n* **1** : quinto *m*, -ta *f* (en una serie) **2** : quinto *m* (en matemáticas) — ~ *adj* : quinto

fiftieth *adj* : quincuagésimo — ~ *n* **1** : quincuagésimo *m*, -ma *f* (en una serie) **2** : cincuentavo *m* (en matemáticas)

fifty *n, pl* **-ties** : cincuenta *m* — ~ *adj* : cincuenta — **fifty–fifty** *adv* : a medias, mitad y mitad — ~ *adj* **a** ~ **chance** : un cincuenta por ciento de posibilidades

fig *n* : higo *m*

fight *v* **fought; fighting** *vi* **1** BATTLE : luchar **2** QUARREL : pelear **3** ~ **back** : defenderse — *vt* : luchar contra — ~ *n* **1** STRUGGLE : lucha *f* **2** QUARREL : pelea *f* — **fighter** *n* **1** : luchador *m*, -dora *f* **2** *or* ~ **plane** : avión *m* de caza

figment *n* ~ **of the imagination** : producto *m* de la imaginación

figurative *adj* : figurado

figure *n* **1** NUMBER : número *m*, cifra *f* **2** PERSON, SHAPE : figura *f* **3** ~ **of speech** : figura *f* retórica **4 watch one's** ~ : cuidar la línea — ~ *v* **-ured; -uring** *vt* : calcular — *vi* **1** : figurar **2 that** ~**s!** : ¡no me extraña! — **figurehead** *n* : testaferro *m* — **figure out** *vt* **1** UNDERSTAND : entender **2** RESOLVE : resolver

file¹ *n* : lima *f* (instrumento) — ~ *vt* **filed; filing** : limar

file² *vt* **filed; filing 1** : archivar (documentos) **2** ~ **charges** : presentar cargos — ~ *n* : archivo *m*

file³ *n* LINE : fila *f* — ~ *vi* ~ **in/out** : entrar/salir en fila

fill *vt* **1** : llenar, rellenar **2** : cumplir con (un requisito) **3** : tapar (un agujero), empastar (un diente) — *vi* **1** ~ **in for** : reemplazar **2**

or ~ **up** : llenarse — ~ *n* **1 eat one's** ~ : comer lo suficiente **2 have one's** ~ **of** : estar harto de

fillet *n* : filete *m*

filling *n* **1** : relleno *m* **2** : empaste *m* (de dientes) **3** ~ **station** → **service station**

filly *n*, *pl* **-lies** : potra *f*

film *n* : película *f* — ~ *vt* : filmar

filter *n* : filtro *m* — ~ *vt* : filtrar

filth *n* : mugre *f* — **filthy** *adj* **filthier; -est 1** : mugriento **2** OBSCENE : obsceno

fin *n* : aleta *f*

final *adj* **1** LAST : último **2** DEFINITIVE : definitivo **3** ULTIMATE : final — ~ *n* **1** : final *f* (en deportes) **2** ~**s** *npl* : exámenes *mpl* finales — **finalist** *n* : finalista *mf* — **finalize** *vt* **-ized; -izing** : finalizar — **finally** *adv* : finalmente

finance *n* **1** : finanzas *fpl* **2** ~**s** *npl* : recursos *mpl* financieros — ~ *vt* **-nanced; -nancing** : financiar — **financial** *adj* : financiero — **financially** *adv* : económicamente

find *vt* **found; finding 1** LOCATE : encontrar **2** REALIZE : darse cuenta de **3** ~ **guilty** : declarar culpable **4** *or* ~ **out** : descubrir — *vi* ~ **out** : enterarse — ~ *n* : hallazgo *m* — **finding** *n* **1** FIND : hallazgo *m* **2** ~**s** *npl* : conclusiones *fpl*

fine¹ *n* : multa *f* — ~ *vt* **fined; fining** : multar

fine² *adj* **finer; -est 1** DELICATE : fino **2** EXCELLENT : excelente **3** SUBTLE : sutil **4** : bueno (dícese del tiempo) **5** ~ **print** : letra *f* menuda **6 it's** ~ **with me** : me parece bien — ~ *adv* OK : bien — **fine arts** *npl* : bellas artes *fpl* — **finely** *adv* **1** EXCELLENTLY : excelentemente **2** PRECISELY : con precisión **3** MINUTELY : fino, menudo

finger *n* : dedo *m* — ~ *vt* : tocar, toquetear — **fingernail** *n* : uña *f* — **fingerprint** *n* : huella *f* digital — **fingertip** *n* : punta *f* del dedo

finicky *adj* : maniático, mañoso *Lat*

finish *v* : acabar, terminar — ~ *n* **1** END : fin *m*, final *m* **2** *or* ~ **line** : meta *f* **3** SURFACE : acabado *m*

finite *adj* : finito

fir *n* : abeto *m*

fire *n* **1** : fuego *m* **2** CONFLAGRATION : incendio *m* **3 catch** ~ : incendiarse (dícese de bosques, etc.), prenderse (dícese de fósforos, etc.) **4 on** ~ : en llamas **5 open** ~ **on** : abrir fuego sobre — ~ *vt* **fired; firing 1** DISMISS : despedir **2** SHOOT : disparar — *vi* : disparar — **fire alarm** *n* : alarma *f* contra incendios — **firearm** *n* : arma *f* de fuego — **firecracker** *n* : petardo *m* — **fire engine** *n* : carro *m* de bomberos *Lat*, coche *m* de

bomberos *Spain* — **fire escape** *n* : escalera *f* de incendios — **fire extinguisher** *n* : extintor *m* (de incendios) — **firefighter** *n* : bombero *m*, -ra *f* — **firefly** *n*, *pl* **-flies** : luciérnaga *f* — **firehouse** → **fire station** — **fireman** *n*, *pl* **-men** → **firefighter** — **fireplace** *n* : hogar *m*, chimenea *f* — **fireproof** *adj* : ignífugo — **fireside** *n* : hogar *m* — **fire station** *n* : estación *f* de bomberos *Lat*, parque *m* de bomberos *Spain* —— **firewood** *n* : leña *f* — **fireworks** *npl* : fuegos *mpl* artificiales

firm¹ *n* : empresa *f*

firm² *adj* : firme — **firmly** *adv* : firmemente — **firmness** *n* : firmeza *f*

first *adj* **1** : primero **2 at** ~ **sight** : a primera vista **3 for the** ~ **time** : por primera vez — ~ *adv* **1** : primero **2** ~ **and foremost** : ante todo **3** ~ **of all** : en primer lugar — ~ *n* **1** : primero *m*, -ra *f* **2 at** ~ : al principio — **first aid** *n* : primeros auxilios *mpl* — **first–class** *adv* : en primera — ~ *adj* : de primera *f* — **firsthand** *adv* : directamente — ~ *adj* : de primera mano — **firstly** *adv* : en primer lugar — **first name** *n* : nombre *m* de pila — **first–rate** *adj* → **first–class**

fiscal *adj* : fiscal

fish *n*, *pl* **fish** *or* **fishes** : pez *m* (vivo), pescado *m* (para comer) — ~ *vi* **1** : pescar **2** ~ **for** SEEK : buscar **3 go** ~**ing** : ir de pesca — **fisherman** *n*, *pl* **-men** : pescador *m*, -dora *f* — **fishhook** *n* : anzuelo *m* — **fishing** *n* : pesca *f* — **fishing pole** *n* : caña *f* de pescar — **fish market** *n* : pescadería *f* — **fishy** *adj* **fishier; -est 1** : a pescado (dícese de sabores, etc.) **2** SUSPICIOUS : sospechoso

fist *n* : puño *m*

fit¹ *n* **1** : ataque *m* **2 he had a** ~ : le dio un ataque

fit² *adj* **fitter; fittest 1** SUITABLE : apropiado **2** HEALTHY : en forma **3 be** ~ **for** : ser apto para — ~ *v* **fitted; fitting** *vt* **1** : encajar en (un hueco, etc.) **2** *(relating to clothing)* : quedar bien a **3** SUIT : ser apropiado para **4** MATCH : coincidir con **5** *or* ~ **out** : equipar — *vi* **1** : caber (en una caja, etc.), encajar (en un hueco, etc.) **2** *or* ~ **in** BELONG : encajar **3 this dress doesn't** ~ : este vestido no me queda bien — ~ *n* **it's a good fit** : me queda bien — **fitful** *adj* : irregular — **fitness** *n* **1** HEALTH : salud *f* **2** SUITABILITY : idoneidad *f* — **fitting** *adj* : apropiado

five *n* : cinco *m* — ~ *adj* : cinco — **five hundred** *n* : quinientos *m* — ~ *adj* : quinientos

fix *vt* **1** ATTACH : fijar, sujetar **2** REPAIR : arreglar **3** PREPARE : preparar — ~ *n* PREDICAMENT : aprieto *m*, apuro *m* — **fixed** *adj* : fijo — **fixture** *n* : instalación *f*

fizz *vi* : burbujear — ~ *n* : efervescencia *f*

fizzle *vi* **-zled; -zling** *or* ~ **out** : quedar en nada

flabbergasted *adj* : estupefacto, pasmado

flabby *adj* **-bier; -est** : fofo

flaccid *adj* : fláccido

flag¹ *vi* WEAKEN : flaquear

flag² *n* : bandera *f* — ~ *vt* **flagged; flagging** *or* ~ **down** : hacer señales de parada a — **flagpole** *n* : asta *f*

flagrant *adj* : flagrante

flair *n* : don *m*, facilidad *f*

flake *n* : copo *m* (de nieve), escama *f* (de pintura, de la piel) — ~ *vi* **flaked; flaking** : pelarse

flamboyant *adj* : extravagante

flame *n* **1** : llama *f* **2 burst into** ~**s** : estallar en llamas **3 go up in** ~**s** : incendiarse

flamingo *n, pl* **-gos** : flamenco *m*

flammable *adj* : inflamable

flank *n* : ijada *m* (de un animal), flanco *m* (militar) — ~ *vt* : flanquear

flannel *n* : franela *f*

flap *n* : solapa *f* (de un sobre, un libro, etc.), tapa *f* (de un recipiente) — ~ *v* **flapped; flapping** *vi* : agitarse — *vt* : batir, agitar

flapjack → **pancake**

flare *vi* **flared; flaring 1** ~ **up** BLAZE : llamear **2** ~ **up** EXPLODE, ERUPT : estallar, explotar — ~ *n* **1** BLAZE : llamarada *f* **2** SIGNAL : (luz *f* de) bengala *f*

flash *vi* **1** : brillar, destellar **2** ~ **past** : pasar como un rayo — *vt* **1** : dirigir (una luz) **2** SHOW : mostrar **3** ~ **a smile** : sonreír — ~ *n* **1** : destello *m* **2** ~ **of lightning** : relámpago *m* **3 in a** ~ : de repente — **flashlight** *n* : linterna *f* — **flashy** *adj* **flashier; -est** : ostentoso

flask *n* : frasco *m*

flat *adj* **flatter; flattest 1** LEVEL : plano, llano **2** DOWNRIGHT : categórico **3** FIXED : fijo **4** MONOTONOUS : monótono **5** : bemol (en la música) **6** ~ **tire** : neumático *m* desinflado — ~ *n* **1** : bemol *m* (en la música) **2** *Brit* APARTMENT : apartamento *m*, departamento *m* *Lat* **3** PUNCTURE : pinchazo *m* — ~ *adv* **1** ~ **broke** : pelado **2 in one hour** ~ : en una hora justa — **flatly** *adv* : categóricamente — **flat-out** *adj* **1** : frenético **2** DOWNRIGHT : categórico — **flatten** *vt* **1** LEVEL : aplanar, allanar **2** KNOCK DOWN : arrasar

flatter *vt* **1** : halagar **2** BECOME : favorecer — **flatterer** *n* : adulador *m*, -dora *f* — **flattering** *adj* **1** : halagador **2** BECOMING : favorecedor — **flattery** *n, pl* **-ries** : halagos *mpl*

flaunt *vt* : hacer alarde de

flavor *or Brit* **flavour** *n* : gusto *m*, sabor *m* — ~ *vt* : sazonar — **flavorful** *or Brit* **flavourful** *adj* : sabroso — **flavoring** *or Brit* **flavouring** *n* : condimento *m*, sazón *f*

flaw *n* : defecto *m* — **flawless** *adj* : perfecto

flax *n* : lino *m*

flea *n* : pulga *f*

fleck *n* **1** PARTICLE : mota *f* **2** SPOT : pinta *f*

flee *v* **fled; fleeing** *vi* : huir — *vt* : huir de

fleece *n* : vellón *m* — ~ *vt* **fleeced; fleecing 1** SHEAR : esquilar **2** DEFRAUD : desplumar

fleet *n* : flota *f*

fleeting *adj* : fugaz

Flemish *adj* : flamenco

flesh *n* **1** : carne *f* **2** PULP : pulpa *f* **3 in the** ~ : en persona — **fleshy** *adj* **fleshier; -est 1** : gordo **2** PULPY : carnoso

flew → **fly**

flex *vt* : flexionar — **flexibility** *n, pl* **-ties** : flexibilidad *f* — **flexible** *adj* : flexible

flick *n* : golpecito *m* — ~ *vt* : dar un golpecito a — *vi* ~ **through** : hojear

flicker *vi* : parpadear — ~ *n* **1** : parpadeo *m* **2 a** ~ **of hope** : un rayo de esperanza

flier *n* **1** AVIATOR : aviador *m*, -dora *f* **2** *or* **flyer** LEAFLET : folleto *m*, volante *m* *Lat*

flight¹ *n* **1** : vuelo *m* **2** TRAJECTORY : trayectoria *f* **3** ~ **of stairs** : tramo *m*

flight² *n* ESCAPE : huida *f*

flimsy *adj* **flimsier; -est 1** LIGHT : ligero **2** SHAKY : poco sólido **3 a** ~ **excuse** : una excusa floja

flinch *vi* ~ **from** : encogerse ante

fling *vt* **flung; flinging 1** : arrojar **2** ~ **open** : abrir de un golpe — ~ *n* **1** AFFAIR : aventura *f* **2 have a** ~ **at** : intentar

flint *n* : pedernal *m*

flip *v* **flipped; flipping** *vt* **1** *or* ~ **over** : dar la vuelta a **2** ~ **a coin** : echarlo a cara o cruz — *vi* **1** *or* ~ **over** : volcarse **2** ~ **through** : hojear — ~ *n* SOMERSAULT : voltereta *f*

flippant *adj* : ligero, frívolo

flipper *n* : aleta *f*

flirt *vi* : coquetear — ~ *n* : coqueto *m*, -ta *f* — **flirtatious** *adj* : coqueto

flit *vi* **flitted; flitting** : revolotear

float *n* **1** : flotador *m* **2** : carroza *f* (en un desfile) — ~ *vi* : flotar — *vt* : hacer flotar

flock *n* : rebaño *m* (de ovejas), bandada *f* (de pájaros) — ~ *vi* : congregarse

flog *vt* **flogged; flogging** : azotar

flood *n* **1** : inundación *f* **2** : torrente *m* (de palabras, de lágrimas, etc.) — ~ *vt* : inundar — **floodlight** *n* : foco *m*

floor *n* **1** : suelo *m*, piso *m* *Lat* **2** STORY : piso *m* **3 dance** ~ : pista *f* de baile **4**

ground ~ : planta *f* baja — **~** *vt* **1** KNOCK DOWN : derribar **2** NONPLUS : desconcertar — **floorboard** *n* : tabla *f* del suelo

flop *vi* **flopped; flopping 1** FLAP : agitarse **2** COLLAPSE : dejarse caer **3** FAIL : fracasar — **~** *n* FAILURE : fracaso *m* — **floppy** *adj* **-pier; -est** : flojo, flexible — **floppy disk** *n* : diskette *m*, disquete *m*

flora *n* : flora *f* — **floral** *adj* : floral — **florid** *adj* **1** FLOWERY : florido **2** RUDDY : rojizo — **florist** *n* : florista *mf*

floss *n* → **dental floss**

flounder¹ *n, pl* **flounder** *or* **flounders** : platija *f*

flounder² *vi* **1** *or* **~ about** : resbalarse, revolcarse **2** : titubear (en un discurso)

flour *n* : harina *f*

flourish *vi* : florecer — *vt* BRANDISH : blandir — **~** *n* : floritura *f* — **flourishing** *adj* : floreciente

flout *vt* : desacatar, burlarse de

flow *vi* : fluir, correr — **~** *n* **1** : flujo *m*, circulación *f* **2** : corriente *f* (de información, etc.)

flower *n* : flor *f* — **~** *vi* : florecer — **flowered** *adj* : floreado — **flowerpot** *n* : maceta *f* — **flowery** *adj* : florido

flown → **fly**

flu *n* : gripe *f*

fluctuate *vi* **-ated; -ating** : fluctuar — **fluctuation** *n* : fluctuación *f*

fluency *n* : fluidez *f* — **fluent** *adj* **1** : fluido **2 be ~ in** : hablar con fluidez — **fluently** *adv* : con fluidez

fluff *n* : pelusa *f* — **fluffy** *adj* **fluffier; -est** : de pelusa, velloso

fluid *adj* : fluido — **~** *n* : fluido *m*

flung → **fling**

flunk *vt* : reprobar *Lat*, suspender *Spain* — *vi* : ser reprobado *Lat*, suspender *Spain*

fluorescence *n* : fluorescencia *f* — **fluorescent** *adj* : fluorescente

flurry *n, pl* **-ries 1** GUST : ráfaga *f* **2** *or* **snow ~** : nevisca *f* **3 ~ of questions** : aluvión *m* de preguntas

flush *vi* BLUSH : ruborizarse, sonrojarse — *vt* **~ the toilet** : tirar de la cadena, jalarle a la cadena *Lat* — **~** *n* BLUSH : rubor *m*, sonrojo *m* — **~** *adj* **~ with** : a nivel con, a ras de — **~** *adv* : al mismo nivel, a ras

fluster *vt* : poner nervioso

flute *n* : flauta *f*

flutter *vi* **1** FLIT : revolotear **2** WAVE : ondear **3** *or* **~ about** : ir y venir — **~** *n* **1** : revoloteo *m* (de alas) **2** STIR : revuelo *m*

flux *n* **be in a state of ~** : cambiar continuamente

fly¹ *v* **flew; flown; flying** *vi* **1** : volar **2** TRAVEL : ir en avión **3** WAVE : ondear **4** RUSH : correr **5 ~ by** : pasar volando — *vt* **1** PILOT : pilotar **2** : hacer volar (una cometa), enarbolar (una bandera) — **~** *n, pl* **flies** : bragueta *f* (de un pantalón)

fly² *n, pl* **flies** : mosca *f* (insecto)

flyer → **flier**

flying saucer *n* : platillo *m* volador *Lat*, platillo *m* volante *Spain*

flyswatter *n* : matamoscas *m*

foal *n* : potro *m*, -tra *f*

foam *n* : espuma *f* — **~** *vi* : hacer espuma — **foamy** *adj* **foamier; -est** : espumoso

focus *n, pl* **-ci 1** : foco *m* **2 be in ~** : estar enfocado **3 ~ of attention** : centro *m* de atención — **~** *v* **-cused** *or* **-cussed; -cusing** *or* **-cussing** *vt* **1** : enfocar **2** : centrar (la atención, etc.) — *vi* **~ on** : enfocar (con los ojos), concentrarse en (con la mente)

fodder *n* : forraje *m*

foe *n* : enemigo *m*, -ga *f*

fog *n* : niebla *f* — **~** *v* **fogged; fogging** *vt* : empañar — *vi* *or* **~ up** : empañarse — **foggy** *adj* **foggier; -est** : nebuloso — **foghorn** *n* : sirena *f* de niebla

foil¹ *vt* : frustrar

foil² *n* *or* **aluminum ~** : papel *m* de aluminio

fold¹ *n* **1** : redil *m* (para ovejas) **2 return to the ~** : volver al redil

fold² *vt* **1** : doblar, plegar **2 ~ one's arms** : cruzar los brazos — *vi* **1** *or* **~ up** : doblarse, plegarse **2** FAIL : fracasar — **~** *n* : pliegue *m* — **folder** *n* : carpeta *f*

foliage *n* : follaje *m*

folk *n, pl* **folk** *or* **folks 1** : gente *f* **2 ~s** *npl* PARENTS : padres *mpl* — **~** *adj* **1** : popular **2 ~ dance** : danza *f* folklórica — **folklore** *n* : folklore *m*

follow *vt* **1** : seguir **2** UNDERSTAND : entender **3 ~ up** : seguir — *vi* **1** : seguir **2** UNDERSTAND : entender **3 ~ up on** : seguir con — **follower** *n* : seguidor *m*, -dora *f* — **following** *adj* : siguiente — **~** *n* : seguidores *mpl* — **~** *prep* : después de

folly *n, pl* **-lies** : locura *f*

fond *adj* **1** : cariñoso **2 be ~ of sth** : ser aficionado a algo **3 be ~ of s.o.** : tener cariño a algn

fondle *vt* **-dled; -dling** : acariciar

fondness *n* **1** LOVE : cariño *m* **2** LIKING : afición *f*

food *n* : comida *f*, alimento *m* — **foodstuffs** *npl* : comestibles *mpl*

fool *n* **1** : idiota *mf* **2** JESTER : bufón *m*, -fona *f* — **~** *vi* **1** JOKE : bromear **2 ~ around** : perder el tiempo — *vt* TRICK : engañar — **foolhardy** *adj* : temerario — **foolish** *adj* : tonto — **foolishness** *n* : tontería *f* — **foolproof** *adj* : infalible

foot n, pl **feet** : pie m — **footage** n : secuencias fpl (cinemáticas) — **football** n : fútbol m americano — **footbridge** n : pasarela f, puente m peatonal — **foothills** npl : estribaciones fpl — **foothold** n : punto m de apoyo — **footing** n **1** BALANCE : equilibrio m **2 on equal ~** : en igualdad — **footlights** npl : candilejas fpl — **footnote** n : nota f al pie de la página — **footpath** n : sendero m — **footprint** n : huella f — **footstep** n : paso m — **footstool** n : escabel m — **footwear** n : calzado m

for prep **1** (indicating purpose, etc.) : para **2** (indicating motivation, etc.) : por **3** (indicating duration) : durante **4 we walked ~ 3 miles** : andamos 3 millas **5** AS FOR : con respecto a — **~** conj : puesto que, porque

forage n : forraje m — **~** vi **-aged; -aging 1** : forrajear **2 ~ for** : buscar

foray n : incursión f

forbid vt **-bade** or **-bad; -bidden; -bidding** : prohibir — **forbidding** adj : intimidante, severo

force n **1** : fuerza f **2 by ~** : por la fuerza **3 in ~** : en vigor, en vigencia **4 armed ~s** : fuerzas fpl armadas — **~** vt **forced; forcing 1** : forzar **2** OBLIGATE : obligar — **forced** adj : forzado, forzoso — **forceful** adj : fuerte, energético

forceps ns & pl : fórceps m

forcibly adv : por la fuerza

ford n : vado m — **~** vt : vadear

fore n **come to the ~** : empezar a destacarse

forearm n : antebrazo m

foreboding n : premonición f, presentimiento m

forecast vt **-cast; -casting** : predecir, pronosticar — **~** n : predicción f, pronóstico m

forefathers n : antepasados mpl

forefinger n : índice m, dedo m índice

forefront n **at/in the ~** : a la vanguardia

forego → **forgo**

foregone adj **~ conclusion** : resultado m inevitable

foreground n : primer plano m

forehead n : frente f

foreign adj **1** : extranjero **2 ~ trade** : comercio m exterior — **foreigner** n : extranjero m, -ra f

foreman n, pl **-men** : capataz mf

foremost adj : principal — **~** adv **first and ~** : ante todo

forensic adj : forense

forerunner n : precursor m, -sora f

foresee vt **-saw; -seen; -seeing** : prever — **foreseeable** adj : previsible

foreshadow vt : presagiar

foresight n : previsión f

forest n : bosque m — **forestry** n : silvicultura f

foretaste n : anticipo m

foretell vt **-told; -telling** : predecir

forethought n : reflexión f previa

forever adv **1** ETERNALLY : para siempre **2** CONTINUALLY : siempre, constantemente

forewarn vt : advertir, prevenir

foreword n : prólogo m

forfeit n **1** PENALTY : pena f **2** : prenda f (en un juego) — **~** vt : perder

forge n : forja f — **~** v **forged; forging** vt **1** : forjar (metal, etc.) **2** COUNTERFEIT : falsificar — vi **~ ahead** : avanzar, seguir adelante — **forger** n : falsificador m, -dora f — **forgery** n, pl **-eries** : falsificación f

forget v **-got; -gotten** or **-got; -getting** vt : olvidar, olvidarse de — vi **1** : olvidarse **2 I forgot** : se me olvidó — **forgetful** adj : olvidadizo

forgive vt **-gave; -given; -giving** : perdonar — **forgiveness** n : perdón m

forgo or **forego** vt **-went; -gone; -going** : privarse de, renunciar a

fork n **1** : tenedor m **2** PITCHFORK : horca f **3** : bifurcación f (de un camino, etc.) — vi : ramificarse, bifurcarse — vt **~ over** : desembolsar

forlorn adj : triste

form n **1** : forma f **2** DOCUMENT : formulario m **3** KIND : tipo m — **~** vt **1** : formar **2 ~ a habit** : adquirir un hábito — vi : formarse

formal adj : formal — **~** n **1** BALL : baile m (formal) **2** or **~ dress** : traje m de etiqueta — **formality** n, pl **-ties** : formalidad f

format n : formato m — **~** vt **-matted; -matting** : formatear

formation n **1** : formación f **2** SHAPE : forma f

former adj **1** PREVIOUS : antiguo, anterior **2** : primero (de dos) — **formerly** adv : anteriormente, antes

formidable adj : formidable

formula n, pl **-las** or **-lae 1** : fórmula f **2** or **baby ~** : preparado m para biberón

forsake vt **-sook; -saken; -saking** : abandonar

fort n : fuerte m

forth adv **1 and so ~** : etcétera **2 back and ~** → **back 3 from this day ~** : de hoy en adelante — **forthcoming** adj **1** COMING : próximo **2** OPEN : comunicativo — **forthright** adj : directo, franco

fortieth adj : cuadragésimo — **~** n **1** : cuadragésimo m, -ma f (en una serie) **2** : cuarentavo m, cuarentava parte f

fortify *vt* **-fied; -fying** : fortificar — **fortification** *n* : fortificación *f*

fortitude *n* : fortaleza *f*

fortnight *n* : quince días *mpl*, quincena *f*

fortress *n* : fortaleza *f*

fortunate *adj* : afortunado — **fortunately** *adv* : afortunadamente — **fortune** *n* : fortuna *f* — **fortune–teller** *n* : adivino *m*, -na *f*

forty *n, pl* **forties** : cuarenta *m* — ~ *adj* : cuarenta

forum *n, pl* **-rums** : foro *m*

forward *adj* **1** : hacia adelante (en dirección), delantero (en posición) **2** BRASH : descarado — ~ *adv* **1** : (hacia) adelante **2 from this day ~** : de aquí en adelante — ~ *vt* : remitir, enviar — ~ *n* : delantero *m*, -ra *f* (en deportes) — **forwards** *adv* → **forward**

fossil *n* : fósil *m*

foster *adj* : adoptivo — ~ *vt* : promover, fomentar

fought → **fight**

foul *adj* **1** REPULSIVE : asqueroso **2 ~ language** : palabrotas *fpl* **3 ~ play** : actos *mpl* criminales **4 ~ weather** : mal tiempo *m* — ~ *n* : falta *f* (en deportes) — ~ *vi* : cometer faltas (en deportes) — *vt* : ensuciar

found¹ → **find**

found² *vt* : fundar, establecer — **foundation** *n* **1** : fundación *f* **2** BASIS : fundamento *m* **3** : cimientos *mpl* (de un edificio)

founder¹ *n* : fundador *m*, -dora *f*

founder² *vi* SINK : hundirse

fountain *n* : fuente *f*

four *n* : cuatro *m* — ~ *adj* : cuatro — **fourfold** *adj* : cuadruple — **four hundred** *adj* : cuatrocientos — ~ *n* : cuatrocientos *m*

fourteen *n* : catorce *m* — ~ *adj* : catorce — **fourteenth** *adj* : decimocuarto — ~ *n* **1** : decimocuarto *m*, -ta *f* (en una serie) **2** : catorceavo *m*, catorceava parte *f*

fourth *n* **1** : cuarto *m*, -ta *f* (en una serie) **2** : cuarto *m*, cuarta parte *f* — ~ *adj* : cuarto

fowl *n, pl* **fowl** *or* **fowls** : ave *f*

fox *n, pl* **foxes** : zorro *m*, -ra *f* — ~ *vt* TRICK : engañar — **foxy** *adj* **foxier; -est** SHREWD : astuto

foyer *n* : vestíbulo *m*

fraction *n* : fracción *f*

fracture *n* : fractura *f* — ~ *vt* **-tured; -turing** : fracturar

fragile *adj* : frágil

fragment *n* : fragmento *m*

fragrant *adj* : fragante — **fragrance** *n* : fragancia *f*, aroma *m*

frail *adj* : débil, delicado

frame *vt* **framed; framing 1** ENCLOSE : enmarcar **2** COMPOSE, DRAFT : formular **3** INCRIMINATE : incriminar — ~ *n* **1** : armazón *mf* (de un edificio, etc.) **2** : marco *m* (de un cuadro, una puerta, etc.) **3** *or* **~s** *npl* : montura *f* (para anteojos) **4 ~ of mind** : estado *m* de ánimo — **framework** *n* : armazón *f*

franc *n* : franco *m*

frank *adj* : franco — **frankly** *adv* : francamente — **frankness** *n* : franqueza *f*

frantic *adj* : frenético

fraternal *adj* : fraterno, fraternal — **fraternity** *n, pl* **-ties** : fraternidad *f* — **fraternize** *vi* **-nized; -nizing** : confraternizar

fraud *n* **1** DECEIT : fraude *m* **2** IMPOSTOR : impostor *m*, -tora *f* — **fraudulent** *adj* : fraudulento

fraught *adj* **~ with** : lleno de, cargado de

fray¹ *n* **1 join the ~** : salir a la palestra **2 return to the ~** : volver a la carga

fray² *vt* : crispar (los nervios) — *vi* : deshilacharse

freak *n* **1** ODDITY : fenómeno *m* **2** ENTHUSIAST : entusiasta *mf* — **freakish** *adj* : anormal

freckle *n* : peca *f*

free *adj* **freer; freest 1** : libre **2** *or* **~ of charge** : gratuito, gratis **3** LOOSE : suelto — ~ *vt* **freed; freeing 1** : liberar, poner en libertad **2** RELEASE, UNFASTEN : soltar, desatar — ~ *adv* *or* **for ~** : gratis — **freedom** *n* : libertad *f* — **freelance** *adj* : por cuenta propia — **freely** *adv* **1** : libremente **2** LAVISHLY : con generosidad — **freeway** *n* : autopista *f* — **free will** *n* **1** : libre albedrío *m* **2 of one's own ~** : por su propia voluntad

freeze *v* **froze; frozen; freezing** *vi* **1** : congelarse, helarse **2** STOP : quedarse inmóvil — *vt* : helar (agua, etc.), congelar (alimentos, precios, etc.) — **freeze–dry** *vt* **-dried; -drying** : liofilizar — **freezer** *n* : congelador *m* — **freezing** *adj* **1** CHILLY : helado **2 it's freezing!** : ¡hace un frío espantoso!

freight *n* **1** SHIPPING : porte *m*, flete *m* *Lat* **2** CARGO : carga *f*

French *adj* : francés — ~ *n* **1** : francés *m* (idioma) **2 the ~** *npl* : los franceses — **Frenchman** *n* : francés *m* — **Frenchwoman** *n* : francesa *f* — **french fries** *npl* : papas *fpl* fritas

frenetic *adj* : frenético

frenzy *n, pl* **-zies** : frenesí *m* — **frenzied** *adj* : frenético

frequent *vt* : frecuentar — ~ *adj* : frecuente — **frequency** *n, pl* **-cies** : frecuencia *f* — **frequently** *adv* : a menudo, frecuentemente

fresco *n, pl* **-coes** : fresco *m*

fresh *adj* **1** : fresco **2** IMPUDENT : descarado **3** CLEAN : limpio **4** NEW : nuevo **5 ~ water** : agua *m* dulce — **freshen** *vt* : refrescar — *vi* ~ **up** : arreglarse — **freshly** *adv* : recién — **freshman** *n, pl* **-men** : estudiante *mf* de primer año — **freshness** *n* : frescura *f*

fret *vi* **fretted; fretting** : preocuparse — **fretful** *adj* : nervioso, irritable

friar *n* : fraile *m*

friction *n* : fricción *f*

Friday *n* : viernes *m*

friend *n* : amigo *m*, -ga *f* — **friendliness** *n* : simpatía *f* — **friendly** *adj* **-lier; -est** : simpático, amable — **friendship** *n* : amistad *f*

frigate *n* : fragata *f*

fright *n* : miedo *m*, susto *m* — **frighten** *vt* : asustar, espantar — **frightened** *adj* **1** : asustado, temeroso **2 be ~ of** : tener miedo de — **frightening** *adj* : espantoso — **frightful** *adj* : espantoso, terrible

frigid *adj* : frío, glacial

frill *n* **1** RUFFLE : volante *m* **2** LUXURY : lujo *m*

fringe *n* **1** : fleco *m* **2** EDGE : periferia *f*, margen *m* **3 ~ benefits** : incentivos *mpl*, extras *mpl*

frisk *vt* SEARCH : cachear, registrar — **frisky** *adj* **friskier; -est** : retozón, juguetón

fritter *n* : buñuelo *m* — ~ *vt or* ~ **away** : malgastar (dinero), desperdiciar (tiempo)

frivolous *adj* : frívolo — **frivolity** *n, pl* **-ties** : frivolidad *f*

frizzy *adj* **frizzier; -est** : rizado, crespo

fro *adv* **to and** ~ → **to**

frock *n* : vestido *m*

frog *n* **1** : rana *f* **2 have a ~ in one's throat** : tener carraspera

frolic *vi* **-icked; -icking** : retozar

from *prep* **1** : de **2** (*indicating a starting point*) : desde **3** (*indicating a cause*) : de, por **4 ~ now on** : a partir de ahora

front *n* **1** : parte *f* delantera **2** : delantera *f* (de un vestido, etc.), fachada *f* (de un edificio), frente *m* (militar) **3 cold ~** : frente *m* frío **4 in ~ of** : delante de, adelante de *Lat* — ~ *vi or* ~ **on** : dar a, estar orientado a — ~ *adj* **1** : delantero, de adelante **2 the ~ row** : la primera fila

frontier *n* : frontera *f*

frost *n* **1** : helada *f* **2** : escarcha *f* (en una superficie) — ~ *vt* ICE : bañar (pasteles) — **frostbite** *n* : congelación *f* — **frosting** *n* ICING : baño *m* — **frosty** *adj* **frostier; -est** **1** : cubierto de escarcha **2** CHILLY : helado, frío

froth *n, pl* **froths** : espuma *f* — **frothy** *adj* **frothier; -est** : espumoso

frown *vi* **1** : fruncir el ceño, fruncir el entrecejo **2 ~ at** : mirar con ceño **3 ~ upon** : desaprobar — ~ *n* : ceño *m* (fruncido)

froze, frozen → **freeze**

frugal *adj* : frugal

fruit *n* **1** : fruta *f* **2** PRODUCT, RESULT : fruto *m* — **fruitcake** *n* : pastel *m* de frutas — **fruitful** *adj* : fructífero — **fruition** *n* **come to ~** : realizarse — **fruitless** *adj* : infructuoso — **fruity** *adj* **fruitier; -est** : (con sabor) a fruta

frustrate *vt* **-trated; -trating** : frustrar — **frustrating** *adj* : frustrante — **frustration** *n* : frustración *f*

fry *vt* **fried; frying** : freír — ~ *n, pl* **fries 1 small ~** : gente *f* de poca monta **2 fries** *npl* → **french fries** — **frying pan** *n* : sartén *mf*

fudge *n* : dulce *m* blando de chocolate y leche

fuel *n* : combustible *m* — ~ *vt* **-eled** *or* **-elled; -eling** *or* **-elling 1** : alimentar (un horno), abastecer de combustible (un avión) **2** STIMULATE : estimular

fugitive *n* : fugitivo *m*, -va *f*

fulfill *or* **fulfil** *vt* **-filled; -filling 1** : cumplir con (una obligación), desarrollar (potencial) **2** FILL, MEET : cumplir — **fulfillment** *n* **1** ACCOMPLISHMENT : cumplimiento *m* **2** SATISFACTION : satisfacción *f*

full *adj* **1** FILLED : lleno **2** COMPLETE : complete, detallado **3** : redondo (dícese de la cara), amplio (dícese de ropa) **4 at ~ speed** : a toda velocidad **5 in ~ bloom** : en plena flor — ~ *adv* **1** DIRECTLY : de lleno **2 know ~ well** : saber muy bien — ~ *n* **1 pay in ~** : pagar en su totalidad **2 to the ~** : al máximo — **full–fledged** *adj* : hecho y derecho — **fully** *adv* **1** COMPLETELY : completamente **2** AT LEAST : al menos, por lo menos

fumble *vi* **-bled; -bling 1** RUMMAGE : hurgar **2 ~ with** : manejar con torpeza

fume *vi* **fumed; fuming 1** SMOKE : echar humo, humear **2** RAGE : estar furioso — **fumes** *npl* : gases *mpl*

fumigate *vt* **-gated; -gating** : fumigar

fun *n* **1** AMUSEMENT : diversión *f* **2 have ~** : divertirse **3 make ~ of** : reírse de, burlarse de — ~ *adj* : divertido

function *n* **1** : función *f* **2** GATHERING : recepción *f*, reunión *f* social — ~ *vi* : funcionar — **functional** *adj* : funcional

fund *n* **1** : fondo *m* **2 ~s** *npl* RESOURCES : fondos *mpl* — ~ *vt* : financiar

fundamental *adj* : fundamental — **fundamentals** *npl* : fundamentos *mpl*

funeral *adj* : funeral, fúnebre — ~ *n* : funeral *m*, funerales *mpl* — **funeral home** *or* **funeral parlor** *n* : funeraria *f*

fungus *n, pl* **fungi** : hongo *m*

funnel *n* **1** : embudo *m* **2** SMOKESTACK : chimenea *f*

funny *adj* **funnier; -est 1** : divertido, gracioso **2** STRANGE : extraño, raro — **funnies** *npl* : tiras *fpl* cómicas

fur *n* **1** : pelaje *m*, pelo *m* (de un animal) **2** *or* ~ **coat** : (prenda *f* de) piel *f* — ~ *adj* : de piel

furious *adj* : furioso

furnace *n* : horno *m*

furnish *vt* **1** SUPPLY : proveer **2** : amueblar (una casa, etc.) — **furnishings** *npl* : muebles *mpl*, mobiliario *m* — **furniture** *n* : muebles *mpl*, mobiliario *m*

furrow *n* : surco *m*

furry *adj* **furrier; -est** : peludo (dícese de un animal), de peluche (dícese de un juguete, etc.)

further *adv* **1** FARTHER : más lejos **2** MOREOVER : además **3** MORE : más — ~ *vt* : promover, fomentar — ~ *adj* **1** FARTHER : más lejano **2** ADDITIONAL : adicional, más **3 until** ~ **notice** : hasta nuevo aviso — **furthermore** *adv* : además — **furthest** → **farthest**

fumble *vi* **-bled; -bling 1** RUMMAGE : hurgar **2** ~ **with** : manejar con torpeza

fume *vi* **fumed; fuming 1** SMOKE : echar humo, humear **2** RAGE : estar furioso — **fumes** *npl* : gases *mpl*

fumigate *vt* **-gated; -gating** : fumigar

fun *n* **1** AMUSEMENT : diversión *f* **2 have** ~ : divertirse **3 make** ~ **of** : reírse de, burlarse de — ~ *adj* : divertido

function *n* **1** : función *f* **2** GATHERING : recepción *f*, reunión *f* social — ~ *vi* : funcionar — **functional** *adj* : funcional

fund *n* **1** : fondo *m* **2** ~**s** *npl* RESOURCES : fondos *mpl* — ~ *vt* : financiar

fundamental *adj* : fundamental — **fundamentals** *npl* : fundamentos *mpl*

funeral *adj* : funeral, fúnebre — ~ *n* : funeral *m*, funerales *mpl* — **funeral home** *or* **funeral parlor** *n* : funeraria *f*

fungus *n, pl* **fungi** : hongo *m*

funnel *n* **1** : embudo *m* **2** SMOKESTACK : chimenea *f*

funny *adj* **funnier; -est 1** : divertido, gracioso **2** STRANGE : extraño, raro — **funnies** *npl* : tiras *fpl* cómicas

fur *n* **1** : pelaje *m*, pelo *m* (de un animal) **2** *or* ~ **coat** : (prenda *f* de) piel *f* — ~ *adj* : de piel

furious *adj* : furioso

furnace *n* : horno *m*

furnish *vt* **1** SUPPLY : proveer **2** : amueblar (una casa, etc.) — **furnishings** *npl* : muebles *mpl*, mobiliario *m* — **furniture** *n* : muebles *mpl*, mobiliario *m*

furrow *n* : surco *m*

furry *adj* **furrier; -est** : peludo (dícese de un animal), de peluche (dícese de un juguete, etc.)

further *adv* **1** FARTHER : más lejos **2** MOREOVER : además **3** MORE : más — ~ *vt* : promover, fomentar — ~ *adj* **1** FARTHER : más lejano **2** ADDITIONAL : adicional, más **3 until** ~ **notice** : hasta nuevo aviso — **furthermore** *adv* : además — **furthest** → **farthest**

furtive *adj* : furtivo

fury *n, pl* **-ries** : furia *f*

fuse[1] *or* **fuze** *n* : mecha *f* (de una bomba, etc.)

fuse[2] *v* **fused; fusing** *vt* **1** MELT : fundir **2** UNITE : fusionar — *vi* : fundirse, fusionarse — ~ *n* **1** : fusible *m* **2 blow a** ~ : fundir un fusible — **fusion** *n* : fusión *f*

fuss *n* **1** : jaleo *m*, alboroto *m* **2 make a** ~ : armar un escándalo — ~ *vi* **1** WORRY : preocuparse **2** COMPLAIN : quejarse — **fussy** *adj* **fussier; -est 1** IRRITABLE : irritable **2** ELABORATE : recargado **3** FINICKY : quisquilloso

futile *adj* : inútil, vano — **futility** *n, pl* **-ties** : inutilidad *f*

future *adj* : futuro — ~ *n* : futuro *m*

fuze → **fuse**[1]

fuzz *n* : pelusa *f* — **fuzzy** *adj* **fuzzier; -est 1** FURRY : con pelusa, peludo **2** BLURRY : borroso **3** VAGUE : confuso

G

g *n, pl* **g's** *or* **gs** : g *f*, séptima letra del alfabeto inglés

gab *vi* **gabbed; gabbing** : charlar, cotorrear *fam* — ~ *n* CHATTER : charla *f*

gable *n* : aguilón *m*

gadget *n* : artilugio *m*

gag *v* **gagged; gagging** *vt* : amordazar — *vi* CHOKE : atragantarse — ~ *n* **1** : mordaza *f* **2** JOKE : chiste *m*

gage → **gauge**

gaiety *n, pl* **-eties** : alegría *f* — **gaily** *adv* : alegremente

gain *n* **1** PROFIT : ganancia *f* **2** INCREASE : aumento *m* — ~ *vt* **1** OBTAIN : ganar, adquirir **2** ~ **weight** : aumentar de peso — *vi* **1** PROFIT : beneficiarse **2** : adelantar(se) (dícese de un reloj) — **gainful** *adj* : lucrativo

gait *n* : modo *m* de andar

gala *n* : fiesta *f*

galaxy *n, pl* **-axies** : galaxia *f*

gale *n* **1** : vendaval *f* **2** ~**s of laughter** : carcajadas *fpl*

gall *n* **have the** ~ **to** : tener el descaro de

gallant *adj* **1** BRAVE : valiente **2** CHIVALROUS : galante

gallbladder *n* : vesícula *f* biliar

gallery *n, pl* **-leries** : galería *f*

gallon *n* : galón *m*

gallop *vi* : galopar — ~ *n* : galope *m*

gallows *n, pl* **-lows** *or* **-lowses** : horca *f*

gallstone *n* : cálculo *m* biliar

galore *adj* : en abundancia

galoshes *n* : galochas *fpl*, chanclos *mpl*

galvanize *vt* **-nized; -nizing** : galvanizar

gamble *v* **-bled; -bling** *vi* : jugar — *vt* : jugarse — ~ *n* **1** BET : apuesta *f* **2** RISK : riesga *f* — **gambler** *n* : jugador *m*, -dora *f*

game *n* **1** : juego *m* **2** MATCH : partido *m* **3** *or* ~ **animals** : caza *f* — ~ *adj* READY : listo, dispuesto

gamut *n* : gama *f*

gang *n* : banda *f*, pandilla *f* — ~ *vi* ~ **up on** : unirse contra

gangplank *n* : pasarela *f*

gangrene *n* : gangrena *f*

gangster *n* : gángster *mf*

gangway *n* → **gangplank**

gap *n* **1** OPENING : espacio *m* **2** INTERVAL : intervalo *m* **3** DISPARITY : brecha *f*, distancia *f* **4** DEFICIENCY : laguna *f*

gape *vi* **gaped; gaping** **1** OPEN : estar abierto **2** STARE : mirar boquiabierto

garage *n* : garaje *m* — ~ *vt* **-raged; -raging** : dejar en un garaje

garb *n* : vestido *m*

garbage *n* : basura *f* — **garbage can** *n* : cubo *m* de la basura

garble *vt* **-bled; -bling** : tergiversar — **garbled** *adj* : confuso, incomprensible

garden *n* : jardín *m* — ~ *vi* : trabajar en el jardín — **gardener** *n* : jardinero *m*, -ra *f* — **gardening** *n* : jardinería *f*

gargle *vi* **-gled; -gling** : hacer gárgaras

garish *adj* : chillón

garland *n* : guirnalda *f*

garlic *n* : ajo *m*

garment *n* : prenda *f*

garnish *vt* : guarnecer — ~ *n* : adorno *m*, guarnición *f*

garret *n* : buhardilla *f*

garrison *n* : guarnición *f*

garrulous *adj* : charlatán, parlanchín

garter *n* : liga *f*

gas *n, pl* **gases** **1** : gas *m* **2** GASOLINE : gasolina *f* — ~ *v* **gassed; gassing** *vt* : asfixiar con gas — *vi* ~ **up** : llenar el tanque con gasolina

gash *n* : tajo *m* — ~ *vt* : hacer un tajo en, cortar

gasket *n* : junta *f*

gasoline *n* : gasolina *f*

gasp *vi* **1** : dar un grito ahogado **2** PANT : jadear — ~ *n* : grito *m* ahogado

gas station *n* : gasolinera *f*

gastric *adj* : gástrico

gastronomy *n* : gastronomía *f*

gate *n* **1** DOOR : puerta *f* **2** BARRIER : barrera *f* — **gateway** *n* : puerta *f*

gather *vt* **1** ASSEMBLE : reunir **2** COLLECT : recoger **3** CONCLUDE : deducir **4** : fruncir (una tela) **5** ~ **speed** : acelerar — *vi* : reunirse (dícese de personas), acumularse (dícese de cosas) — **gathering** *n* : reunión *f*

gaudy *adj* **gaudier; -est** : chillón, llamativo

gauge *n* **1** INDICATOR : indicador *m* **2** CALIBER : calibre *m* — ~ *vt* **gauged; gauging** **1** MEASURE : medir **2** ESTIMATE : calcular, evaluar

gaunt *adj* : demacrado, descarnado

gauze *n* : gasa *f*

gave → **give**

gawky *adj* **gawkier; -est** : desgarbado

gay *adj* **1** : alegre **2** HOMOSEXUAL : gay, homosexual

gaze *vi* **gazed; gazing** : mirar (fijamente) — ~ *n* : mirada *f*

gazelle *n* : gacela *f*

gazette *n* : gaceta *f*

gear *n* **1** EQUIPMENT : equipo *m* **2** POSSESSIONS : efectos *mpl* personales **3** : marcha *f* (de un vehículo) **4** *or* ~ **wheel** : rueda *f* dentada — ~ *vt* : orientar, adaptar — *vi* ~ **up** : prepararse — **gearshift** *n* : palanca *f* de cambio, palanca *f* de velocidades *Lat*

geese → **goose**

gelatin *n* : gelatina *f*

gem *n* : gema *f*, piedra *f* preciosa — **gemstone** *n* : piedra *f* preciosa

gender *n* **1** SEX : sexo *m* **2** : género *m* (en la gramática)

gene *n* : gen *m*, gene *m*

genealogy *n*, *pl* **-gies** : genealogía *f*

general *adj* : general — ~ *n* **1** : general *mf* (militar) **2 in** ~ : en general, por lo general — **generalize** *v* **-ized; -izing** : generalizar — **generally** *adv* : generalmente, en general — **general practitioner** *n* : médico *m*, -ca *f* de cabecera

generate *vt* **-ated; -ating** : generar — **generation** *n* : generación *f* — **generator** *n* : generador *m*

generous *adj* **1** : generoso **2** AMPLE : abundante — **generosity** *n*, *pl* **-ties** : generosidad *f*

genetic *adj* : genético — **genetics** *n* : genética *f*

genial *adj* : afable, simpático

genital *adj* : genital — **genitals** *npl* : genitales *mpl*

genius *n* : genio *m*

genocide *n* : genocidio *m*

genteel *adj* : refinado

gentle *adj* **-tler; -tlest 1** MILD : suave, dulce **2** LIGHT : ligero **3 a** ~ **hint** : una indirecta discreta — **gentleman** *n*, *pl* **-men 1** MAN : caballero *m*, señor *m* **2 a perfect** ~ : un perfecto caballero — **gentleness** *n* : delicadeza *f*, ternura *f*

genuine *adj* **1** AUTHENTIC : verdadero, auténtico **2** SINCERE : sincero

geography *n*, *pl* **-phies** : geografía *f* — **geographic** *or* **geographical** *adj* : geográfico

geology *n* : geología *f* — **geologic** *or* **geological** *adj* : geológico

geometry *n*, *pl* **-tries** : geometría *f* — **geometric** *or* **geometrical** *adj* : geométrico

geranium *n* : geranio *m*

geriatric *adj* : geriátrico — **geriatrics** *n* : geriatría *f*

germ *n* **1** : germen *m* **2** MICROBE : microbio *m*

German *adj* : alemán — ~ *n* : alemán *m* (idioma)

germinate *v* **-nated; -nating** *vi* : germinar — *vt* : hacer germinar

gestation *n* : gestación *f*

gesture *n* : gesto *m* — ~ *vi* **-tured; -turing 1** : hacer gestos **2** ~ **to** : hacer señas a

get *v* **got; got** *or* **gotten; getting** *vt* **1** OBTAIN : conseguir, obtener **2** RECEIVE : recibir **3** EARN : ganar **4** FETCH : traer **5** CATCH : coger, agarrar *Lat* **6** UNDERSTAND : entender **7** PREPARE : preparar **8** ~ **one's hair cut** : cortarse el pelo **9** ~ **s.o. to do sth** : lograr que uno haga algo **10 have got** : tener **11 have got to** : tener que — *vi* **1** BECOME : ponerse, hacerse **2** GO, MOVE : ir **3** PROGRESS : avanzar **4** ~ **ahead** : progresar **5** ~ **at** MEAN : querer decir **6** ~ **away** : escaparse **7** ~ **away with** : salir impune de **8** ~ **back at** : desquitarse con **9** ~ **by** : arreglárselas **10** ~ **home** : llegar a casa **11** ~ **out** : salir **12** ~ **over** : reponerse de, consolarse de **13** ~ **together** : reunirse **14** ~ **up** : levantarse — **getaway** *n* : fuga *f*, huida *f* — **get–together** *n* : reunión *f*

geyser *n* : géiser *m*

ghastly *adj* **-lier; -est** : horrible, espantoso

ghetto *n*, *pl* **-tos** *or* **-toes** : gueto *m*

ghost *n* : fantasma *f*, espectro *m* — **ghostly** *adv* : fantasmal

giant *n* : gigante *m*, -ta *f* — ~ *adj* : gigantesco

gibberish *n* : galimatías *m*, jerigonza *f*

gibe *vi* **gibed; gibing** ~ **at** : mofarse de — ~ *n* : pulla *f*, mofa *f*

giblets *npl* : menudillos *mpl*

giddy *adj* **-dier; -est** : mareado, vertiginoso — **giddiness** *n* : vértigo *m*

gift *n* **1** PRESENT : regalo *m* **2** TALENT : don *m* — **gifted** *adj* : talentoso, de talento

gigantic *adj* : gigantesco

giggle *vi* **-gled; -gling** : reírse tontamente — ~ *n* : risa *f* tonta

gild *vt* **gilded** *or* **gilt; gilding** : dorar

gill *n* : agalla *f*, branquia *f*

gilt *adj* : dorado

gimmick *n* : truco *m*, ardid *m*

gin *n* : ginebra *f*

ginger *n* : jengibre *m* — **ginger ale** *n* : refresco *m* de jengibre — **gingerbread** *n* : pan *m* de jengibre — **gingerly** *adv* : con cuidado, cautelosamente

giraffe *n* : jirafa *f*

girder *n* : viga *f*

girdle *n* CORSET : faja *f*

girl *n* **1** : niña *f*, muchacha *f*, chica *f* — **girlfriend** *n* : novia *f*, amiga *f*

girth *n* : circunferencia *f*

gist *n* **get the** ~ **of** : comprender lo esencial de

give *v* **gave; given; giving** *vt* **1** : dar **2** INDICATE : señalar **3** PRESENT : presentar **4** ~ **away** : regalar **5** ~ **back** : devolver **6**

~ out : repartir **7** ~ **up smoking** : dejar de fumar — *vi* **1** YIELD : ceder **2** COLLAPSE : romperse **3** ~ **out** : agotarse **4** ~ **up** : rendirse — ~ *n* : elasticidad *f* — **given** *adj* **1** SPECIFIED : determinado **2** INCLINED : dado, inclinado — **given name** *n* : nombre *m* de pila

glacier *n* : glaciar *m*

glad *adj* **gladder; gladdest 1** : alegre, contento **2 be** ~ : alegrarse **3** ~ **to meet you!** : ¡mucho gusto! — **gladden** *vt* : alegrar — **gladly** *adv* : con mucho gusto — **gladness** *n* : alegría *f*, gozo *m*

glade *n* : claro *m*

glamor *or* **glamour** *n* : atractivo *m*, encanto *m* — **glamorous** *adj* : atractivo

glance *vi* **glanced; glancing 1** ~ **at** : mirar, dar un vistazo a **2** ~ **off** : rebotar en — ~ *n* : mirada *f*, vistazo *m*

gland *n* : glándula *f*

glare *vi* **glared; glaring 1** : brillar, relumbrar **2** ~ **at** : lanzar una mirada feroz a — ~ *n* **1** : luz *f* deslumbrante **2** STARE : mirada *f* feroz — **glaring** *adj* **1** BRIGHT : deslumbrante **2** FLAGRANT : flagrante

glass *n* **1** : vidrio *m*, cristal *m* **2 a** ~ **of milk** : un vaso de leche **3** ~**es** *npl* SPECTACLES : anteojos *mpl*, lentes *fpl* — ~ *adj* : de vidrio — **glassware** *n* : cristalería *f* — **glassy** *adj* **glassier; -est 1** : vítreo **2** ~ **eyes** : ojos *mpl* vidriosos

glaze *vt* **glazed; glazing 1** : poner vidrios a (una ventana, etc.) **2** : vidriar (cerámica) **3** ICE : glasear — ~ *n* **1** : vidriado *m*, barniz *m* (de cerámica) **2** ICING : glaseado *m*

gleam *n* **1** : destello *m* **2 a** ~ **of hope** : un rayo de esperanza — ~ *vi* : destellar, relucir

glee *n* : alegría *f* — **gleeful** *adj* : lleno de alegría

glib *adj* **glibber; glibbest 1** : de mucha labia **2 a** ~ **reply** : una respuesta simplista — **glibly** *adv* : con mucha labia

glide *vi* **glided; gliding** : deslizarse (en una superficie), planear (en el aire) — **glider** *n* : planeador *m*

glimmer *vi* : brillar con luz trémula — ~ *n* : luz *f* trémula, luz *f* tenue

glimpse *vt* **glimpsed; glimpsing** : vislumbrar — ~ *n* : vislumbre

glint *vi* : destellar — ~ *n* : destello *m*

glisten *vi* : brillar

glitter *vi* : relucir, brillar

gloat *vi* ~ **over** : regodearse con

globe *n* : globo *m* — **global** *adj* : global, mundial

gloom *n* **1** DARKNESS : oscuridad *f* **2** SADNESS : tristeza *f* — **gloomy** *adj* **gloomier; -est 1** DARK : sombrío, tenebroso **2** DIS-

MAL : deprimente, lúgubre **3** PESSIMISTIC : pesimista

glory *n, pl* **-ries** : gloria *f* — **glorify** *vt* **-fied; -fying** : glorificar — **glorious** *adj* : glorioso, espléndido

gloss *n* : lustre *m*, brillo *m* — ~ *vt* ~ **over** : minimizar (la importancia de algo)

glossary *n, pl* **-ries** : glosario *m*

glossy *adj* **glossier; -est** : lustroso, brillante

glove *n* : guante *m*

glow *vi* **1** : brillar, resplandecer **2** ~ **with health** : rebosar de salud — ~ *n* : resplandor *m*, brillo *m*

glue *n* : pegamento *m*, cola *f* — ~ *vt* **glued; gluing** *or* **glueing** : pegar

glum *adj* **glummer; glummest** : sombrío, triste

glut *n* : superabundancia *f*, exceso *m*

glutton *n* : glotón *m*, -tona *f* — **gluttonous** *adj* : glotón — **gluttony** *n, pl* **-tonies** : glotonería *f*

gnarled *adj* : nudoso

gnash *vt* ~ **one's teeth** : hacer rechinar los dientes

gnat *n* : jején *m*

gnaw *vt* : roer

go *v* **went; gone; going; goes** *vi* **1** : ir **2** LEAVE : irse, salir **3** EXTEND : ir, extenderse **4** SELL : venderse **5** FUNCTION : funcionar, marchar **6** DISAPPEAR : desaparecer **7** ~ **back on one's word** : faltar a su palabra **8** ~ **crazy** : volverse loco **9** ~ **for** LIKE : gustar **10** ~ **off** EXPLODE : estallar **11** ~ **with** MATCH : armonizar con **12** ~ **without** : pasar sin — *v aux* **be going to** : ir a — ~ *n, pl* **goes 1 be on the** ~ : no parar **2 have a** ~ **at** : intentar

goad *vt* : aguijonear (un animal), incitar (a una persona)

goal *n* **1** AIM : meta *m*, objetivo *m* **2** : gol *m* (en deportes) — **goalkeeper** *or* **goalie** *n* : portero *m*, -ra *f*; arquero *m*, -ra *f*

goat *n* : cabra *f*

goatee *n* : barbita *f* de chivo

gobble *vt* **-bled; -bling** *or* ~ **up** : engullir

goblet *n* : copa *f*

goblin *n* : duende *m*

god *n* **1** : dios *m* **2 God** : Dios *m* — **goddess** *n* : diosa *f* — **godchild** *n, pl* **-children** : ahijado *m*, -da *f* — **godfather** *n* : padrino *m* — **godmother** *n* : madrina *f* — **godparents** *npl* : padrinos *mpl* — **godsend** *n* : bendición *f* (del cielo)

goes → **go**

goggles *npl* : gafas *fpl* (protectoras), anteojos *mpl*

goings-on *npl* : sucesos *mpl*

gold *n* : oro *m* — **golden** *adj* **1** : (hecho) de oro **2** : dorado, de color oro — **goldfish** *n*

: pez *m* de colores — **goldsmith** *n* : orfebre *mf*

golf *n* : golf *m* — ∼ *vi* : jugar (al) golf — **golf ball** *n* : pelota *f* de golf — **golf course** *n* : campo *m* de golf — **golfer** *n* : golfista *mf*

gone *adj* **1** : ido, pasado **2** DEAD : muerto **3** LOST : desaparecido

good *adj* **better; best 1** : bueno **2** KIND : amable **3** ∼ **afternoon (evening)** : buenas tardes **4 be** ∼ **at** : tener facilidad para **5 feel** ∼ : sentirse bien **6** ∼ **for a cold** : beneficioso para los resfriados **7 have a** ∼ **time** : divertirse **8** ∼ **morning** : buenos días **9** ∼ **night** : buenas noches — ∼ *n* **1** : bien *m* **2** GOODNESS : bondad *f* **3** ∼**s** *npl* PROPERTY : bienes *mpl* **4** ∼**s** *npl* WARES : mercancías *fpl*, mercaderías *fpl* **5 for** ∼ : para siempre — ∼ *adv* : bien — **good–bye** *or* **good–by** *n* : adiós *m* — **Good Friday** *n* : Viernes *m* Santo — **good–looking** *adj* : bello, guapo — **goodness** *n* **1** : bondad *f* **2 thank** ∼ **!** : ¡gracias a Dios!, ¡menos mal! — **goodwill** *n* : buena voluntad *f* — **goody** *n*, *pl* **goodies** : golosina *f*

gooey *adj* **gooier; gooiest** : pegajoso

goof *n* : pifia *f fam* — ∼ *vi* **1** *or* ∼ **up** : cometer un error **2** ∼ **around** : hacer tonterías

goose *n*, *pl* **geese** : ganso *m*, -sa *f*; oca *f* — **goose bumps** *or* **goose pimples** *npl* : carne *f* de gallina

gopher *n* : taltuza *f*

gore¹ *n* BLOOD : sangre *f*

gore² *vt* **gored; goring** : cornear

gorge *n* RAVINE : cañón *m* — ∼ *vt* **gorged; gorging** ∼ **oneself** : hartarse

gorgeous *adj* : magnífico, espléndido

gorilla *n* : gorila *m*

gory *adj* **gorier; -est** : sangriento

gospel *n* **1** : evangelio *m* **2 the Gospel** : el Evangelio

gossip *n* **1** : chismoso *m*, -sa *f* (persona) **2** RUMOR : chisme *m* — ∼ *vi* : chismear, contar chismes — **gossipy** *adj* : chismoso

got → **get**

Gothic *adj* : gótico

gotten → **get**

gourmet *n* : gastrónomo *m*, -ma *f*

gout *n* : gota *f*

govern *v* : gobernar — **governess** *n* : institutriz *f* — **government** *n* : gobierno *m* — **governor** *n* : gobernador *m*, -dora *f*

gown *n* **1** : vestido *m* **2** : toga *f* (de magistrados, etc.)

grab *v* **grabbed; grabbing** *vt* : agarrar, arrebatar

grace *n* **1** : gracia *f* **2 say** ∼ : bendecir la mesa — ∼ *vt* **graced; gracing 1** HONOR : honrar **2** ADORN : adornar — **graceful** *adj* : lleno de gracia, grácil — **gracious** *adj* : cortés, gentil

grade *n* **1** QUALITY : calidad *f* **2** RANK : grado *m*, rango *m* (militar) **3** YEAR : grado *m*, año *m* (a la escuela) **4** MARK : nota *f* **5** SLOPE : cuesta *f* — ∼ *vt* **graded; grading 1** CLASSIFY : clasificar **2** MARK : calificar (exámenes, etc.) — **grade school** → **elementary school**

gradual *adj* : gradual — **gradually** *adv* : gradualmente, poco a poco

graduate *n* : licenciado *m*, -da *f* (de la universidad), bachiller *mf* (de la escuela secundaria) — ∼ *v* **-ated; -ating** *vi* : graduarse, licenciarse — *vt* CALIBRATE : graduar — **graduation** *n* : graduación *f*

graffiti *npl* : graffiti *mpl*

graft *n* : injerto *m* — ∼ *vt* : injertar

grain *n* **1** : grano *m* **2** CEREALS : cereales *mpl* **3** : veta *f*, vena *f* (de madera)

gram *n* : gramo *m*

grammar *n* : gramática *f* — **grammar school** → **elementary school**

grand *adj* **1** : magnífico, espléndido **2** FABULOUS, GREAT : fabuloso, estupendo — **grandchild** *n*, *pl* **-children** : nieto *m*, -ta *f* — **granddaughter** *n* : nieta *f* — **grandeur** *n* : grandiosidad *f* — **grandfather** *n* : abuelo *m* — **grandiose** *adj* : grandioso — **grandmother** *n* : abuela *f* — **grandparents** *npl* : abuelos *mpl* — **grandson** *n* : nieto *m* — **grandstand** *n* : tribuna *f*

granite *n* : granito *m*

grant *vt* **1** : conceder, admitir **2** ADMIT : reconocer, admitir **3 take for granted** : dar (algo) por sentado — ∼ *n* **1** SUBSIDY : subvención *f* **2** SCHOLARSHIP : beca *f*

grape *n* : uva *f*

grapefruit *n* : toronja *f*, pomelo *m*

grapevine *n* **1** : vid *f*, parra *f* **2 I heard it through the** ∼ : me lo dijo un pajarito *fam*

graph *n* : gráfica *f*, gráfico *m* — **graphic** *adj* : gráfico

grapple *vi* **-pled; -pling** ∼ **with** : forcejear con (una persona), luchar con (un problema)

grasp *vt* **1** : agarrar **2** UNDERSTAND : comprender, captar — ∼ *n* **1** : agarre *m* **2** UNDERSTANDING : comprensión *f* **3** REACH : alcance *m*

grass *n* **1** : hierba *f* (planta) **2** LAWN : césped *m*, pasto *m* *Lat* — **grasshopper** *n* : saltamontes *m* — **grassy** *adj* **grassier; -est** : cubierto de hierba

grate¹ *v* **grated; -ing** *vt* **1** : rallar (en cocina) **2** ∼ **one's teeth** : hacer rechinar los dientes — *vi* RASP : chirriar

grate² *n* GRATING : reja *f*, rejilla *f*

grateful *adj* : agradecido — **gratefully** *adv*
: con agradecimiento — **gratefulness** *n*
: gratitud *f*, agradecimiento *m*
grater *n* : rallador *m*
gratify *vt* **-fied; -fying 1** PLEASE : complacer
2 SATISFY : satisfacer
grating *n* : reja *f*, rejilla *f*
gratitude *n* : gratitud *f*
gratuitous *adj* : gratuito
grave[1] *n* : tumba *f*, sepultura *f*
grave[2] *adj* **graver; -est** : grave
gravel *n* : grava *f*, gravilla *f*
gravestone *n* : lápida *f* — **graveyard** *n* : cementerio *m*
gravity *n, pl* **-ties** : gravedad *f*
gravy *n, pl* **-vies** : salsa *f* (preparada con
jugo de carne)
gray *adj* **1** : gris **2** ~ **hair** : pelo *m* canoso
— ~ *n* : gris *m* — ~ *vi or* **turn** ~ : encanecer, ponerse gris
graze[1] *vi* **grazed; grazing** : pastar, pacer
graze[2] *vt* **1** TOUCH : rozar **2** SCRATCH : ras-
guñarse
grease *n* : grasa *f* — ~ *vt* **greased; greas-
ing** : engrasar — **greasy** *adj* **greasier; -est**
1 : grasiento **2** OILY : graso, grasoso
great *adj* **1** : grande **2** FANTASTIC : estupendo, fabuloso — **great–grandchild** *n, pl*
-children : bisnieto *m*, -ta *f* —
great–grandfather *n* : bisabuelo *m* —
great–grandmother *n* : bisabuela *f* —
greatly *adv* **1** MUCH : mucho **2** VERY : muy
— **greatness** *n* : grandeza *f*
greed *n* **1** : codicia *f*, avaricia *f* **2** GLUTTONY
: glotonería *f* — **greedily** *adv* : con avaricia
— **greedy** *adj* **greedier; -est** **1** : codicioso,
avaro **2** GLUTTONOUS : glotón
Greek *adj* : griego — ~ *n* : griego *m* (idioma)
green *adj* **1** : verde **2** INEXPERIENCED : novato — ~ *n* **1** : verde *m* (color) **2** ~**s** *npl*
: verduras *fpl* — **greenery** *n, pl* **-eries** : vegetación *f* — **greenhouse** *n* : invernadero *m*
greet *vt* **1** : saludar **2** WELCOME : recibir —
greeting *n* **1** : saludo *m* **2** ~**s** *npl* RE-
GARDS : saludos *mpl*, recuerdos *mpl*
gregarious *adj* : sociable
grenade *n* : granada *f*
grew → **grow**
grey → **gray**
greyhound *n* : galgo *m*
grid *n* **1** GRATING : rejilla *f* **2** NETWORK : red
f **3** : cuadriculado *m* (de un mapa)
griddle *n* : plancha *f*
grief *n* : dolor *m*, pesar *m* — **grievance** *n*
: queja *f* — **grieve** *v* **grieved; grieving** *vt*
: entristecer — *vi* ~ **for** : llorar (a), lamentar — **grievous** *adj* : grave, doloroso
grill *vt* **1** : asar a la parrilla **2** INTERROGATE

: interrogar — ~ *n* : parrilla *f* (para cocinar) — **grille** *or* **grill** GRATING *n* : reja *f*, rejilla *f*
grim *adj* **grimmer; grimmest 1** STERN
: severo **2** GLOOMY : sombrío
grimace *n* : mueca *f* — ~ *vi* **-maced; -mac-
ing** : hacer muecas
grime *n* : mugre *f*, suciedad *f* — **grimy** *adj*
grimier; -est : mugriento, sucio
grin *vi* **grinned; grinning** : sonreír (abiertamente) — ~ *n* : sonrisa *f* (abierta)
grind *v* **ground; grinding** *vt* **1** : moler (el
café, etc.) **2** SHARPEN : afilar **3** ~ **one's
teeth** : rechinar los dientes — *vi* : rechinar
— ~ *n* **the daily** ~ : la rutina diaria —
grinder *n* : molinillo *m*
grip *vt* **gripped; gripping 1** : agarrar, asir **2**
INTEREST : captar el interés de — ~ *n* **1**
GRASP : agarre *m* **2** CONTROL : control *m*,
dominio *m* **3** HANDLE : empuñadura *f* **4**
come to ~**s with** : llegar a entender de
gripe *vi* **griped; griping** : quejarse — ~ *n*
: queja *f*
grisly *adj* **-lier; -est** : espeluznante, horrible
gristle *n* : cartílago *m*
grit *n* **1** : arena *f*, grava *f* **2** GUTS : agallas *fpl
fam* **3** ~**s** *npl* : sémola *f* de maíz — ~ *vt*
gritted; gritting ~ **one's teeth** : aco-
razarse
groan *vi* : gemir — ~ *n* : gemido *m*
grocery *n, pl* **-ceries 1** *or* ~ **store** : tienda
f de comestibles, tienda *f* de abarrotes *Lat* **2**
groceries *npl* : comestibles *mpl*, abarrotes
mpl Lat — **grocer** *n* : tendero *m*, -ra *f*
groggy *adj* **-gier; -est** : atontado, grogui *fam*
groin *n* : ingle *f*
groom *n* BRIDEGROOM : novio *m* — ~ *vt*
1 : almohazar (un animal) **2** PREPARE
: preparar
groove *n* : ranura *f*, surco *m*
grope *vi* **groped; groping 1** : andar a tientas
2 ~ **for**: buscar a tientas
gross *adj* **1** SERIOUS : grave **2** OBESE : obeso
3 TOTAL : bruto **4** VULGAR : grosero, basto
— ~ *n* **1** *or* ~ **income** : ingresos *mpl* bru-
tos **2** *pl* ~ : gruesa *f* (12 docenas) —
grossly *adv* **1** EXTREMELY : enormemente
2 CRUDELY : groseramente
grotesque *adj* : grotesco
grouch *n* : gruñón *m*, -ñona *f fam* —
grouchy *adj* **grouchier; -est** : gruñon *fam*
ground[1] → **grind**
ground[2] *n* **1** : suelo *m*, tierra *f* **2** *or* ~**s**
LAND : terreno *m* **3** ~**s** REASON : razón *f*,
motivos *mpl* **4** ~**s** DREGS : pozo *m* (de
café) — ~ *vt* **1** BASE : fundar, basar **2**
: conectar a tierra (un aparato eléctrico) **3**
: restringir (un avión o un piloto) a la tierra
— **groundhog** *n* : marmota *f* (de América)

— **groundless** *adj* : infundado — **ground-work** *n* : trabajo *m* preparatorio
group *n* : grupo *m* — ～ *vt* : agrupar — *vi or* ～ **together** : agruparse
grove *n* : arboleda *f*
grovel *vi* -**eled** *or* -**elled**; -**eling** *or* -**elling** : arrastrarse, humillarse
grow *v* **grew**; **grown**; **growing** *vi* **1** : crecer **2** INCREASE : aumentar **3** BECOME : volverse, ponerse **4** ～ **dark** : oscurecerse **5** ～ **up** : hacerse mayor — *vt* **1** CULTIVATE : cultivar **2** : dejarse crecer (el pelo, etc.) — **grower** *n* : cultivador *m*, -dora *f*
growl *vi* : gruñir — ～ *n* : gruñido *m*
grown–up *adj* : mayor — ～ *n* : persona *f* mayor
growth *n* **1** : crecimiento *m* **2** INCREASE : aumento *m* **3** DEVELOPMENT : desarrollo *m* **4** TUMOR : tumor *m*
grub *n* **1** LARVA : larva *f* **2** FOOD : comida *f*
grubby *adj* **grubbier**; -**est** : mugriento, sucio
grudge *vt* **grudged**; **grudging** : dar de mala gana — ～ *n* **hold a** ～ : guardar rencor
grueling *or* **gruelling** *adj* : extenuante, agotador
gruesome *adj* : horripilante
gruff *adj* **1** BRUSQUE : brusco **2** HOARSE : bronco
grumble *vi* -**bled**; -**bling** : refunfuñar, rezongar
grumpy *adj* **grumpier**; -**est** : malhumorado, gruñón *fam*
grunt *vi* : gruñir — ～ *n* : gruñido *m*
guarantee *n* : garantía *f* — ～ *vt* -**teed**; -**teeing** : garantizar
guard *n* **1** : guardia *f* **2** PRECAUTION : protección *f* — ～ *vt* : proteger, vigilar — *vi* ～ **against** : protegerse contra — **guardian** *n* **1** : tutor *m*, -tora *f* (de niños) **2** PROTECTOR : guardián *m*, -diana *f*
guava *n* : guayaba *f*
guerrilla *or* **guerilla** *n* **1** : guerrillero *m*, -ra *f* **2** ～ **warfare** : guerra *f* de guerrillas
guess *vt* **1** : adivinar **2** SUPPOSE : suponer, creer — *vi* ～ **at** : adivinar — ～ *n* : conjetura *f*, suposición *f*
guest *n* **1** : invitado *m*, -da *f* **2** : huésped *mf* (a un hotel)
guide *n* : guía *mf* (persona), guía *f* (libro, etc.) — ～ *vt* **guided**; **guiding** : guiar — **guidance** *n* : orientación *f* — **guidebook** *n* : guía *f* — **guideline** *n* : pauta *f*, directriz *f*
guild *n* : gremio *m*

guile *n* : astucia *f*
guilt *n* : culpa *f*, culpabilidad *f* — **guilty** *adj* **guiltier**; -**est** : culpable
guinea pig *n* : conejillo *m* de Indias, cobaya *f*
guise *n* : apariencia *f*
guitar *n* : guitarra *f*
gulf *n* **1** : golfo *m* **2** ABYSS : abismo *m*
gull *n* : gaviota *f*
gullet *n* **1** THROAT : garganta *f* **2** ESOPHAGUS : esófago *m*
gullible *adj* : crédulo
gully *n*, *pl* -**lies** : barranco *m*
gulp *vt or* ～ **down** : tragarse, engullir — *vi* : tragar saliva — ～ *n* : trago *m*
gum[1] *n* : encía *f* (de la boca)
gum[2] *n* **1** : resina *f* (de plantas) **2** CHEWING GUM : goma *f* de mascar, chicle *m*
gumption *n* : iniciativa *f*, agallas *fpl fam*
gun *n* **1** FIREARM : arma *f* de fuego **2** *or* **spray** ～ : pistola *f* **3** → **cannon, pistol, revolver, rifle** — ～ *vt* **gunned**; **gunning 1** *or* ～ **down** : matar a tiros, asesinar **2** ～ **the engine** : acelerar (el motor) — **gunboat** *n* : cañonero *m* — **gunfire** *n* : disparos *mpl* — **gunman** *n*, *pl* -**men** : pistolero *m*, gatillero *m Lat* — **gunpowder** *n* : pólvora *f* — **gunshot** *n* : disparo *m*, tiro *m*
gurgle *vi* -**gled**; -**gling 1** : borbotar, gorgotear **2** : gorjear (dícese de un niño)
gush *vi* **1** SPOUT : salir a chorros **2** ～ **with praise** : deshacerse en elogios
gust *n* : ráfaga *f*
gusto *n*, *pl* **gustoes** : entusiasmo *m*
gusty *adj* **gustier**; -**est** : racheado, ventoso
gut *n* **1** : intestino *m* **2** ～**s** *npl* INNARDS : tripas *fpl* **3** ～**s** *npl* COURAGE : agallas *fpl fam* — ～ *vt* **gutted**; **gutting 1** EVISCERATE : destripar (un pollo, etc.), limpiar (un pescado) **2** : destruir el interior de (un edificio)
gutter *n* : canaleta *f* (de un techo), cuneta *f* (de una calle)
guy *n* : tipo *m fam*
guzzle *vt* -**zled**; -**zling** : chupar *fam*, tragar
gym *or* **gymnasium** *n*, *pl* -**siums** *or* -**sia** : gimnasio *m* — **gymnast** *n* : gimnasta *mf* — **gymnastics** *ns & pl* : gimnasia *f*
gynecology *n* : ginecología *f* — **gynecologist** *n* : ginecólogo *m*, -ga *f*
gyp *vt* **gypped**; **gypping** : estafar, timar
Gypsy *n*, *pl* -**sies** : gitano *m*, -na *f*
gyrate *vi* -**rated**; -**rating** : girar

H

h *n, pl* **h's** *or* **hs** : h *f,* octava letra del alfabeto inglés

habit *n* **1** CUSTOM : hábito *m,* costumbre *f* **2** : hábito *m* (religioso)

habitat *n* : hábitat *m*

habitual *adj* **1** CUSTOMARY : habitual **2** INVETERATE : empedernido

hack¹ *n* **1** : caballo *m* de alquiler **2** *or* ~ **writer** : escritorzuelo *m,* -la *f*

hack² *vt* : cortar — *vi or* ~ **into** : piratear (un sistema informático)

hackneyed *adj* : manido, trillado

hacksaw *n* : sierra *f* para metales

had → **have**

haddock *ns & pl* : eglefino *m*

hadn't (*contraction of* **had not**) → **have**

hag *n* : bruja *f*

haggard *adj* : demacrado

haggle *vi* **-gled; -gling** : regatear

hail¹ *vt* **1** GREET : saludar **2** : llamar (un taxi)

hail² *n* : granizo *m* (en meteorología) — ~ *vi* : granizar — **hailstone** *n* : piedra *f* de granizo

hair *n* **1** : pelo *m,* cabello *m* **2** : vello *m* (en las piernas, etc.) — **hairbrush** *n* : cepillo *m* (para el pelo) — **haircut** *n* **1** : corte *m* de pelo **2 get a** ~ : cortarse el pelo — **hairdo** *n, pl* **-dos** : peinado *m* — **hairdresser** *n* : peluquero *m,* -ra *f* — **hairless** *adj* : sin pelo, calvo — **hairpin** *n* : horquilla *f* — **hair–raising** *adj* : espeluznante — **hairstyle** → **hairdo** — **hair spray** *n* : laca *f* (para el pelo) — **hairy** *adj* **hairier; -est** : peludo, velludo

hale *adj* : saludable, robusto

half *n, pl* **halves 1** : mitad *f* **2** *or* **halftime** : tiempo *m* (en deportes) **3 in** ~ : por la mitad — ~ *adj* **1** : medio **2** ~ **an hour** : una media hora — ~ *adv* : medio — **half brother** *n* : medio hermano *m,* hermanastro *m* — **halfhearted** *adj* : sin ánimo, poco entusiasta — **half sister** *n* : media hermana *f,* hermanastra *f* — **halfway** *adv* : a medio camino — ~ *adj* : medio

halibut *ns & pl* : halibut *m*

hall *n* **1** HALLWAY : corredor *m,* pasillo *m* **2** AUDITORIUM : sala *f* **3** LOBBY : vestíbulo *m* **4** DORMITORY : residencia *f* universitaria

hallmark *n* : sello *m* (distintivo)

Halloween *n* : víspera *f* de Todos los Santos

hallucination *n* : alucinación *f*

hallway *n* **1** ENTRANCE : entrada *f* **2** CORRIDOR : corredor *m,* pasillo *m*

halo *n, pl* **-los** *or* **-loes** : aureola *f,* halo *m*

halt *n* **1 call a** ~ **to** : poner fin a **2 come to a** ~ : pararse — ~ *vi* : pararse — *vt* : parar

halve *vt* **halved; halving 1** DIVIDE : partir por la mitad **2** REDUCE : reducir a la mitad — **halves** → **half**

ham *n* : jamón *m*

hamburger *or* **hamburg** *n* **1** : carne *f* molida **2** *or* ~ **patty** : hamburguesa *f*

hammer *n* : martillo *m* — ~ *v* : martillar, martillear

hammock *n* : hamaca *f*

hamper¹ *vt* : obstaculizar, dificultar

hamper² *n* : cesto *m,* canasta *f* (para ropa sucia)

hamster *n* : hámster *m*

hand *n* **1** : mano *f* **2** : manecilla *f,* aguja *f* (de un reloj, etc.) **3** HANDWRITING : letra *f,* escritura *f* **4** WORKER : obrero *m,* -ra *f* **5 by** ~ : a mano **6 lend a** ~ : echar una mano **7 on** ~ : a mano, disponible **8 on the other** ~ : por otro lado — ~ *vt* **1** : pasar, dar **2** ~ **out** : distribuir **3** ~ **over** : entregar — **handbag** *n* : cartera *f Lat,* bolso *m Spain* — **handbook** *n* : manual *m* — **handcuffs** *npl* : esposas *fpl* — **handful** *n* : puñado *m* — **handgun** *n* : pistola *f,* revólver *m*

handicap *n* **1** : minusvalía *f* (física) **2** : hándicap *m* (en deportes) — ~ *vt* **-capped; -capping 1** : asignar un handicap a (en deportes) **2** HAMPER : obstaculizar — **handicapped** *adj* : minusválido

handicrafts *npl* : artesanía(s) *f(pl)*

handiwork *n* : trabajo *m* (manual)

handkerchief *n, pl* **-chiefs** : pañuelo *m*

handle *n* : asa *m* (de una taza, etc.), mango *m* (de un utensilio), pomo *m* (de una puerta), tirador *m* (de un cajón) — ~ *vt* **-dled; -dling 1** TOUCH : tocar **2** MANAGE : tratar, manejar — **handlebars** *npl* : manillar *m,* manubrio *m Lat*

handmade *adj* : hecho a mano

handout *n* **1** ALMS : dádiva *f,* limosna *f* **2** LEAFLET : folleto *m*

handrail *n* : pasamanos *m*

handshake *n* : apretón *m* de manos

handsome *adj* **-somer; -est 1** ATTRACTIVE : apuesto, guapo **2** GENEROUS : generoso **3** SIZABLE : considerable

handwriting *n* : letra *f,* escritura *f* — **handwritten** *adj* : escrito a mano

handy *adj* **handier; -est 1** NEARBY : a mano **2** USEFUL : práctico, útil **3** DEFT : habilidoso — **handyman** *n, pl* **-men** : hombre *m* habilidoso

hang *v* **hung**; **hanging** *vt* **1** : colgar **2** (*past tense often* **hanged**) EXECUTE : ahorcar **3** ~ **one's head** : bajar la cabeza — *vi* **1** : colgar, pender **2** : caer (dícese de la ropa, etc.) **3** ~ **up on s.o.** : colgar a algn — ~ *n* **1** DRAPE : caída *f* **2 get the** ~ **of** : agarrar la onda de

hangar *n* : hangar *m*

hanger *n* : percha *f,* gancho *m* (para ropa) *Lat*

hangover *n* : resaca *f*

hanker *vi* ~ **for** : tener ansias de — **hankering** *n* : ansia *f,* anhelo *m*

haphazard *adj* : casual, fortuito

happen *vi* **1** : pasar, suceder, ocurrir **2** ~ **to do sth** : hacer algo por casualidad **3 it so happens that...** : da la casualidad de que... — **happening** *n* : suceso *m,* acontecimiento *m*

happy *adj* **-pier; -est 1** : feliz **2 be** ~ : alegrarse **3 be** ~ **with** : estar contento con **4 be** ~ **to do sth** : hacer algo con mucho gusto — **happily** *adv* : alegremente — **happiness** *n* : felicidad *f* — **happy–go–lucky** *adj* : despreocupado

harass *vt* : acosar — **harassment** *n* : acoso *m*

harbor *or Brit* **harbour** *n* : puerto *m* — *vt* **1** SHELTER : albergar **2** ~ **a grudge against** : guardar rencor a

hard *adj* **1** : duro **2** DIFFICULT : difícil **3 be a** ~ **worker** : ser muy trabajador **4** ~ **liquor** : bebidas *fpl* fuertes **5** ~ **water** : agua *f* dura — *adv* **1** FORCEFULLY : fuerte **2 work** ~ : trabajar duro **3 take sth** ~ : tomarse algo muy mal — **harden** *vt* : endurecer — **hardheaded** *adj* : testarudo, terco — **hard–hearted** *adj* : duro de corazón — **hardly** *adv* **1** : apenas **2** ~ **ever** : casi nunca — **hardness** *n* **1** : dureza *f* **2** DIFFICULTY : dificultad *f* — **hardship** *n* : dificultad *f* — **hardware** *n* **1** : ferretería *f* **2** : hardware *m* (en informática) — **hardworking** *adj* : trabajador

hardy *adj* **-dier; -est** : fuerte (dícese de personas), resistente (dícese de las plantas)

hare *n, pl* **hare** *or* **hares** : liebre *f*

harm *n* : daño *m* — ~ *vt* : hacer daño a (una persona), dañar (una cosa), perjudicar (la reputación de algn, etc.) — **harmful** *adj* : perjudicial — **harmless** *adj* : inofensivo

harmonica *n* : armónica *f*

harmony *n, pl* **-nies** : armonía *f* — **harmonious** *adj* : armonioso — **harmonize** *v* **-nized; -nizing** : armonizar

harness *n* : arnés *m* — ~ *vt* **1** : enjaezar **2** UTILIZE : utilizar

harp *n* : arpa *m* — ~ *vi* ~ **on** : insistir sobre

harpoon *n* : arpón *m*

harpsichord *n* : clavicémbalo *m*

harsh *adj* **1** ROUGH : áspero **2** SEVERE : duro, severo **3** : fuerte (dícese de una luz), discordante (dícese de sonidos) — **harshness** *n* : severidad *f*

harvest *n* : cosecha *f* — ~ *v* : cosechar

has → **have**

hash *vt* **1** CHOP : picar **2** ~ **over** DISCUSS : discutir — ~ *n* : picadillo *m* (comida)

hasn't (*contraction of* **has not**) → **has**

hassle *n* : problemas *mpl,* lío *m* — ~ *vt* **-sled; -sling** : fastidiar

haste *n* : prisa *f,* apuro *m Lat* **2 make** ~ : darse prisa, apurarse *Lat* — **hasten** *vt* : acelerar — *vi* : apresurarse, apurarse *Lat* — **hasty** *adj* **hastier; -est** : precipitado

hat *n* : sombrero *m*

hatch *n* : escotilla *f* — ~ *vt* **1** : empollar (huevos) **2** CONCOCT : tramar — *vi* : salir del cascarón

hatchet *n* : hacha *f*

hate *n* : odio *m* — ~ *vt* **hated; hating** : odiar, aborrecer — **hateful** *adj* : odioso, aborrecible — **hatred** *n* : odio *m*

haughty *adj* **-tier; -est** : altanero, altivo

haul *vt* : arrastrar, jalar *Lat* — ~ *n* **1** CATCH : redada *f* (de peces) **2** LOOT : botín *m* **3 a long** ~ : un trayecto largo

haunch *n* : cadera *f* (de una persona), anca *f* (de un animal)

haunt *vt* **1** : frecuentar, rondar **2** TROUBLE : inquietar — ~ *n* : sitio *m* predilecto — **haunted** *adj* : embrujado

have *v* **had**; **having**; **has** *vt* **1** : tener **2** CONSUME : comer, tomar **3** ALLOW : permitir **4** : dar (una fiesta, etc.), convocar (una reunión) **5** ~ **one's hair cut** : cortarse el pelo **6** ~ **sth done** : mandar hacer algo — *v aux* **1** : haber **2** ~ **just done sth** : acabar de hacer algo **4 you've finished, haven't you?** : has terminado, ¿no?

haven *n* : refugio *m*

havoc *n* : estragos *mpl*

hawk[1] *n* : halcón *m*

hawk[2] *vt* : pregonar (mercancías)

hay *n* : heno *m* — **hay fever** *n* : fiebre *f* del heno — **haystack** *n* : almiar *m* — **haywire** *adj* **go** ~ : estropearse

hazard *n* : peligro *m,* riesgo *m* — ~ *vt* : arriesgar, aventurar — **hazardous** *adj* : arriesgado, peligroso

haze *n* : bruma *f,* neblina *f*

hazel *n* : color *m* avellana — **hazelnut** *n* : avellana *f*

hazy *adj* **hazier; -est** : nebuloso

he *pron* : él

head *n* **1** : cabeza *f* **2** END, TOP : cabeza *f* (de un clavo, etc.), cabecera *f* (de una mesa) **3** LEADER : jefe *m*, -fa *f* **4 be out of one's ~** : estar loco **5 come to a ~** : llegar a un punto crítico **6 ~s or tails** : cara o cruz **7 per ~** : por cabeza — **~** *adj* MAIN : principal — **~** *vt* : encabezar — *vi* : dirigirse — **headache** *n* : dolor *m* de cabeza — **headband** *n* : cinta *f* del pelo — **headdress** *n* : tocado *m* — **headfirst** *adv* : de cabeza — **heading** *n* : encabezamiento *m*, título *m* — **headland** *n* : cabo *m* — **headlight** *n* : faro *m* — **headline** *n* : titular *m* — **headlong** *adv* **1** HEADFIRST : de cabeza **2** HASTILY : precipitadamente — **headmaster** *n* : director *m* — **headmistress** *n* : directora *f* — **head-on** *adv & adj* : de frente — **headphones** *npl* : auriculares *mpl*, audífonos *mpl Lat* — **headquarters** *ns & pl* : oficina *f* central (de una compañía), cuartel *m* general (de los militares) — **head start** *n* : ventaja *f* — **headstrong** *adj* : testarudo, obstinado — **headwaiter** *n* : jefe *m*, -fa *f* de comedor — **headway** *n* **1** : progreso *m* **2 make ~** : avanzar — **heady** *adj* **headier; -est** : embriagador

heal *vt* : curar — *vi* : cicatrizar

health *n* : salud *f* — **healthy** *adj* **healthier; -est** : sano, saludable

heap *n* : montón *m* — **~** *vt* : amontonar

hear *v* **heard; hearing** *vt* : oír — *vi* **1** : oír **2 ~ about** : enterarse de **3 ~ from** : tener noticias de — **hearing** *n* **1** : oído *m* **2** : vista *f* (en un tribunal) — **hearing aid** *n* : audífono *m* — **hearsay** *n* : rumores *mpl*

hearse *n* : coche *m* fúnebre

heart *n* **1** : corazón *m* **2 at ~** : en el fondo **3 by ~** : de memoria **4 lose ~** : descorazonarse **5 take ~** : animarse — **heartache** *n* : pena *f*, dolor *m* — **heart attack** *n* : infarto *m*, ataque *m* al corazón — **heartbeat** *n* : latido *m* (del corazón) — **heartbreak** *n* : congoja *f*, angustia *f* — **heartbroken** *adj* : desconsolado — **heartburn** *n* : acidez *f* estomacal

hearth *n* : hogar *m*

heartily *adv* : de buena gana

heartless *adj* : de mal corazón, cruel

hearty *adj* **heartier; -est 1** : cordial, caluroso **2** : abundante (dícese de una comida)

heat *vt* : calentar — *vi or* **~ up** : calentarse — **~** *n* **1** : calor *m* **2** HEATING : calefacción *f* — **heated** *adj* : acalorado — **heater** *n* : calentador *m*

heath *n* : brezal *m*

heathen *adj* : pagano — **~** *n, pl* **-thens or -then** : pagano *m*, -na *f*

heather *n* : brezo *m*

heave *v* **heaved** *or* **hove; heaving** *vt* **1** LIFT : levantar (con esfuerzo) **2** HURL : lanzar, tirar **3 ~ a sigh** : suspirar — **~** *vi or* **~ up** : levantarse

heaven *n* : cielo *m* — **heavenly** *adj* **1** : celestial **2 ~ body** : cuerpo *m* celeste

heavy *adj* **heavier; -est 1** : pesado **2** INTENSE : fuerte **3 ~ sigh** : suspiro *m* profundo **4 ~ traffic** : tráfico *m* denso — **heavily** *adv* **1** : pesadamente **2** EXCESSIVELY : mucho — **heaviness** *n* : peso *m*, pesadez *f* — **heavyweight** *n* : peso *m* pesado

Hebrew *adj* : hebreo — **~** *n* : hebreo *m* (idioma)

heckle *vt* **-led; -ling** : interrumpir (a un orador) con preguntas molestas

hectic *adj* : agitado, ajetreado

he'd (*contraction of* **he had** *or* **he would**) → **have, would**

hedge *n* : seto *m* vivo — **~** *v* **hedged; hedging** *vt* **~ one's bets** : cubrirse — *vi* : contestar con evasivas — **hedgehog** *n* : erizo *m*

heed *vt* : prestar atención a, hacer caso de — **~** *n* **take ~** : tener cuidado — **heedless** *adj* **be ~ of** : hacer caso omiso de

heel *n* : talón *m* (del pie), tacón *m* (de un zapato)

hefty *adj* **heftier; -est** : robusto y pesado

heifer *n* : novilla *f*

height *n* **1** : estatura *f* (de una persona), altura *f* (de un objeto) **2** PEAK : cumbre *f* **3 the ~ of folly** : el colmo de la locura **4 what is your ~?** : ¿cuánto mides? — **heighten** *vt* : aumentar, intensificar

heir *n* : heredero *m*, -ra *f* — **heiress** *n* : heredera *f* — **heirloom** *n* : reliquia *f* de familia

held → **hold**

helicopter *n* : helicóptero *m*

hell *n* : infierno *m* — **hellish** *adj* : infernal

he'll (*contraction of* **he shall** *or* **he will**) → **shall, will**

hello *interj* : ¡hola!

helm *n* : timón *m*

helmet *n* : casco *m*

help *vt* **1** : ayudar **2 ~ oneself** : servirse **3 I can't ~ it** : no lo puedo remediar — **~** *n* **1** : ayuda *f* **2** STAFF : personal *m* **3 help!** : ¡socorro!, ¡auxilio! — **helper** *n* : ayudante *mf* — **helpful** *adj* **1** OBLIGING : servicial, amable **2** USEFUL : útil — **helping** *n* : porción *f* — **helpless** *adj* **1** POWERLESS : incapaz **2** DEFENSELESS : indefenso

hem *n* : dobladillo *m* — **~** *vt* **hemmed; hemming ~ in** : encerrar

hemisphere *n* : hemisferio *m*

hemorrhage *n* : hemorragia *f*

hemorrhoids *npl* : hemorroides *fpl,* almorranas *fpl*
hemp *n* : cáñamo *m*
hen *n* : gallina *f*
hence *adv* **1** : de aquí, de ahí **2** THEREFORE : por lo tanto **3 ten years ~** : de aquí a 10 años — **henceforth** *adv* : de ahora en adelante
henpeck *vt* : dominar (al marido)
hepatitis *n, pl* **-titides** : hepatitis *f*
her *adj* : su, sus — **~** *pron* **1** (*used as direct object*) : la **2** (*used as indirect object*) : le, se **3** (*used as object of a preposition*) : ella
herald *vt* : anunciar
herb *n* : hierba *f*
herd *n* : manada *f* — **~** *vt* : conducir (en manada) — *vi or* **~ together** : reunir
here *adv* **1** : aquí, acá **2 ~ you are!** : ¡toma! — **hereabouts** *or* **hereabout** *adv* : por aquí (cerca) — **hereafter** *adv* : en el futuro — **hereby** *adv* : por este medio
hereditary *adj* : hereditario — **heredity** *n* : herencia *f*
heresy *n, pl* **-sies** : herejía *f*
herewith *adv* : adjunto
heritage *n* **1** : herencia *f* **2** : patrimonio *m* (nacional)
hermit *n* : ermitaño *m,* -ña *f*
hernia *n, pl* **-nias** *or* **-niae** : hernia *f*
hero *n, pl* **-roes** : héroe *m* — **heroic** *adj* : heroico — **heroine** *n* : heroína *f* — **heroism** *n* : heroísmo *m*
heron *n* : garza *f*
herring *n, pl* **-ring** *or* **-rings** : arenque *m*
hers *pron* **1** : (el) suyo, (la) suya, (los) suyos, (las) suyas **2 some friends of ~** : unos amigos suyos, unos amigos de ella — **herself** *pron* **1** (*used reflexively*) : se **2** (*used emphatically*) : ella misma
he's (*contraction of* **he is** *or* **he has**) → **be**, **have**
hesitant *adj* : titubeante, vacilante — **hesitate** *vi* **-tated; -tating** : vacilar, titubear — **hesitation** *n* : vacilación *f,* titubeo *m*
heterosexual *adj* : heterosexual — **~** *n* : heterosexual *mf*
hexagon *n* : hexágono *m*
hey *interj* : ¡eh!, ¡oye!
heyday *n* : auge *m,* apogeo *m*
hi *interj* : ¡hola!
hibernate *vi* **-nated; -nating** : hibernar
hiccup *n* **have the ~s** : tener hipo — **~** *vi* **-cuped; -cuping** : tener hipo
hide¹ *n* : piel *f,* cuero *m*
hide² *v* **hid; hidden** *or* **hid; hiding** *vt* **1** : esconder **2** : ocultar (motivos, etc.) — *vi* : esconderse — **hide–and–seek** *n* : escondite *m,* escondidas *fpl Lat*
hideous *adj* : horrible, espantoso

hideout *n* : escondite *m,* guarida *f*
hierarchy *n, pl* **-chies** : jerarquía *f* — **hierarchical** *adj* : jerárquico
high *adj* **1** : alto **2** INTOXICATED : borracho, drogado **3 a ~ voice** : una voz aguda **4 it's two feet ~** : tiene dos pies de alto **5 ~ winds** : fuertes vientos *mpl* — **~** *adv* : alto — **~** *n* : récord *m,* máximo *m* — **higher** *adj* **1** : superior **2 ~ education** : enseñanza *f* superior — **highlight** *n* : punto *m* culminante — **highly** *adv* **1** VERY : muy, sumamente **2 think ~ of** : tener en mucho a — **Highness** *n* **His/Her ~** : Su Alteza *f* — **high school** *n* : escuela *f* superior, escuela *f* secundaria — **high–strung** *adj* : nervioso, excitable — **highway** *n* : carretera *f*
hijack *vt* : secuestrar — **hijacker** *n* : secuestrador *m,* -dora *f* — **hijacking** *n* : secuestro *m*
hike *v* **hiked; hiking** *vi* : ir de caminata — *vt or* **~ up** RAISE : subir — **~** *n* : caminata *f,* excursión *f* — **hiker** *n* : excursionista *mf*
hilarious *adj* : muy divertido — **hilarity** *n* : hilaridad *f*
hill *n* **1** : colina *f,* cerro *m* **2** SLOPE : cuesta *f* — **hillside** *n* : ladera *f,* cuesta *f* — **hilly** *adj* **hillier; -est** : accidentado
hilt *n* : puño *m*
him *pron* **1** (*used as direct object*) : lo **2** (*used as indirect object*) : le, se **3** (*used as object of a preposition*) : él — **himself** *pron* **1** (*used reflexively*) : se **2** (*used emphatically*) : él mismo
hind *adj* : trasero, posterior
hinder *vt* : dificultar, estorbar — **hindrance** *n* : obstáculo *m*
hindsight *n* **in ~** : en retrospectiva
Hindu *adj* : hindú
hinge *n* : bisagra *f,* gozne *m* — **~** *vi* **hinged; hinging ~ on** : depender de
hint *n* **1** : indirecta *f* **2** TIP : consejo *m* **3** TRACE : asomo *m,* toque *m* — **~** *vt* : dar a entender — *vi* **~ at** : insinuar
hip *n* : cadera *f*
hippopotamus *n, pl* **-muses** *or* **-mi** : hipopótamo *m*
hire *n* **1** : alquiler *m* **2 for ~** : se alquila — **~** *vt* **hired; hiring 1** EMPLOY : contratar, emplear **2** RENT : alquilar
his *adj* : su, sus, de él — **~** *pron* **1** : (el) suyo, (la) suya, (los) suyos, (las) suyas **2 some friends of ~** : unos amigos suyos, unos amigos de él
Hispanic *adj* : hispano, hispánico
hiss *vi* : silbar — *n* : silbido *m*
history *n, pl* **-ries 1** : historia *f* **2** BACKGROUND : historial *m* — **historian** *n* : historiador *m,* -dora *f* — **historic** *or* **historical** *adj* : histórico

hit v **hit; hitting** vt **1** : golpear, pegar **2** : dar (con un proyectil) **3** AFFECT : afectar **4** REACH : alcanzar **5 the car ~ a tree** : el coche chocó contra un árbol — vi : pegar — **~** n **1** : golpe m **2** SUCCESS : éxito m

hitch vt **1** ATTACH : enganchar **2** or **~ up** RAISE : subirse **3 ~ a ride** : hacer autostop — **~** n PROBLEM : problema m — **hitchhike** vi **-hiked; -hiking** : hacer autostop — **hitchhiker** n : autostopista mf

hitherto adv : hasta ahora

HIV n : VIH m, virus m del sida

hive n : colmena f

hives ns & pl : urticaria f

hoard n : tesoro m (de dinero), reserva f (de provisiones) — **~** vt : acumular

hoarse adj **hoarser; -est** : ronco

hoax n : engaño m

hobble vi **-bled; -bling** : cojear

hobby n, pl **-bies** : pasatiempo m

hobo n, pl **-boes** : vagabundo m, -da f

hockey n : hockey m

hoe n : azada f — **~** vt **hoed; hoeing** : azadonar

hog n : cerdo m — **~** vt **hogged; hogging** MONOPOLIZE : acaparar

hoist vt **1** : izar (una vela, etc.) **2** LIFT : levantar — **~** n : grúa f

hold¹ n : bodega f (en un barco o un avión)

hold² v **held; holding** vt **1** GRIP : agarrar **2** POSSESS : tener **3** SUPPORT : sostener **4** : celebrar (una reunión, etc.), mantener (una conversación) **5** CONTAIN : contener **6** CONSIDER : considerar **7** or **~ back** : detener **8 ~ hands** : agarrarse de la mano **9 ~ up** ROB : atracar **10 ~ up** DELAY : retrasar — vi **1** LAST : durar, continuar **2** APPLY : ser válido — **~** n **1** GRIP : agarre m **2 get ~ of** : conseguir **3 get ~ of oneself** : controlarse — **holder** n : tenedor m, -dora f — **holdup** n **1** ROBBERY : atraco m **2** DELAY : retraso m, demora f

hole n : agujero m, hoyo m

holiday n **1** : día m feriado, fiesta f **2** Brit VACATION : vacaciones fpl

holiness n : santidad f

holler vi : gritar — **~** n : grito m

hollow n **1** : hueco m **2** VALLEY : hondonada f — **~** adj **-lower; -est 1** : hueco **2** FALSE : vacío, falso — **~** vt or **~ out** : ahuecar

holly n, pl **-lies** : acebo m

holocaust n : holocausto m

holster n : pistolera f

holy adj **-lier; -est** : santo, sagrado

homage n : homenaje m

home n **1** : casa f **2** FAMILY : hogar m **3** INSTITUTION : residencia f, asilo m **4 at ~ and abroad** : dentro y fuera del país — **~** adv **go ~** : ir a casa — **homeland** n : patria f — **homeless** adj : sin hogar — **homely** adj **-lier; -est 1** DOMESTIC : casero **2** UGLY : feo — **homemade** adj : casero, hecho en casa — **homemaker** n : ama f de casa — **home run** n : jonrón m — **homesick** adj **be ~** : echar de menos a la familia — **homeward** adj : de vuelta, de regreso — **homework** n : tarea f, deberes mpl — **homey** adj **homier; -est** : hogareño, acogedor

homicide n : homicidio m

homogeneous adj : homogéneo

homosexual adj : homosexual — **~** n : homosexual mf — **homosexuality** n : homosexualidad f

honest adj **1** : honrado **2** FRANK : sincero — **honestly** adv : sinceramente — **honesty** n, pl **-ties** : honradez f

honey n, pl **-eys** : miel f — **honeycomb** n : panal m — **honeymoon** n : luna f de miel

honk vi : tocar la bocina — **~** n : bocinazo m

honor or Brit **honour** n : honor m — **~** vt **1** : honrar **2** : aceptar (un cheque, etc.), cumplir con (una promesa) — **honorable** or Brit **honourable** adj : honorable, honroso — **honorary** adj : honorario

hood n **1** : capucha f (de un abrigo, etc.) **2** : capó m (de un automóvil)

hoodlum n : matón m

hoodwink vt : engañar

hoof n, pl **hooves** or **hoofs** : pezuña f (de una vaca, etc.), casco m (de un caballo)

hook n **1** : gancho m **2** or **~ and eye** : corchete m **3** → **fishhook 4 off the ~** : descolgado — **~** vt : enganchar — vi : engancharse

hoop n : aro m

hooray → **hurrah**

hoot vi **1** : ulular (dícese de un búho) **2 ~ with laughter** : reírse a carcajadas — **~** n **1** : ululato m (de un búho) **2 I don't give a ~** : me importa un comino

hop¹ vi **hopped; hopping** : saltar a la pata coja — **~** n : salto m a la pata coja

hop² n **~s** : lúpulo m (planta)

hope v **hoped; hoping** vi : esperar — vt : esperar que — **~** n : esperanza f — **hopeful** adj : esperanzado — **hopefully** adv **1** : con esperanza **2 ~ it will help** : se espera que ayude — **hopeless** adj : desesperado — **hopelessly** adv : desesperadamente

horde n : horda f

horizon n : horizonte m — **horizontal** adj : horizontal

hormone n : hormona f

horn n **1** : cuerno m (de un animal) **2** : trompa f (instrumento musical) **3** : bocina f, claxon m (de un vehículo)

hornet n : avispón m

horoscope *n* : horóscopo *m*

horror *n* : horror *m* — **horrendous** *adj* : horrendo — **horrible** *adj* : horrible — **horrid** *adj* : horroroso, horrible — **horrify** *vt* **-fied; -fying** : horrorizar

hors d'oeuvre *n, pl* **hors d'oeuvres** : entremés *m*

horse *n* : caballo *m* — **horseback** *n* **on ~** : a caballo — **horsefly** *n, pl* **-flies** : tábano *m* — **horseman** *n, pl* **-men** : jinete *m* — **horseplay** *n* : payasadas *fpl* — **horsepower** *n* : caballo *m* de fuerza — **horseradish** *n* : rábano *m* picante — **horseshoe** *n* : herradura *f* — **horsewoman** *n, pl* **-women** : jinete *f*

horticulture *n* : horticultura *f*

hose *n* **1** *pl* **hoses** : manguera *f*, manga *f* **2** **hose** *pl* STOCKINGS : medias *fpl* — **~** *vt* **hosed; hosing** : regar (con manguera) — **hosiery** *n* : calcetería *f*

hospice *n* : hospicio *m*

hospital *n* : hospital *m* — **hospitable** *adj* : hospitalario — **hospitality** *n, pl* **-ties** : hospitalidad *f* — **hospitalize** *vt* **-ized; -izing** : hospitalizar

host¹ *n* **a ~ of** : toda una serie de

host² *n* **1** : anfitrión *m*, -triona *f* **2** : presentador *m*, -dora *f* (de televisión, etc.) — **~** *vt* : presentar (un programa de televisión, etc.)

host³ *n* EUCHARIST : hostia *f*, Eucaristía *f*

hostage *n* : rehén *m*

hostel *n or* **youth ~** : albergue *m* juvenil

hostess *n* : anfitriona *f*

hostile *adj* : hostil — **hostility** *n, pl* **-ties** : hostilidad *f*

hot *adj* **hotter; hottest** **1** : caliente, caluroso (dícese del tiempo), cálido (dícese del clima) **2** SPICY : picante **3 feel ~** : tener calor **4 have a ~ temper** : tener mal genio **5 ~ news** : noticias *fpl* de última hora **6 it's ~ today** : hace calor

hot dog *n* : perro *m* caliente

hotel *n* : hotel *m*

hotheaded *adj* : exaltado

hound *n* : perro *m* (de caza) — **~** *vt* : acosar, perseguir

hour *n* : hora *f* — **hourglass** *n* : reloj *m* de arena — **hourly** *adv & adj* : cada hora, por hora

house *n, pl* **houses** **1** : casa *f* **2** : cámara *f* (del gobierno) **3 publishing ~** : editorial *f* — **~** *vt* **housed; housing** : albergar — **houseboat** *n* : casa *f* flotante — **housefly** *n, pl* **-flies** : mosca *f* común — **household** *adj* **1** : doméstico **2 ~ name** : nombre *m* muy conocido — **~** *n* : casa *f* — **housekeeper** *n* : ama *f* de llaves — **housekeeping** *n* : gobierno *m* de la casa — **housewarming** *n* : fiesta *f* de estreno de una casa

— housewife *n, pl* **-wives** : ama *f* de casa

— housework *n* : faenas *fpl* domésticas —

housing *n* **1** : viviendas *fpl* **2** CASE : caja *f* protectora

hove → **heave**

hovel *n* : casucha *f*, tugurio *m*

hover *vi* **1** : cernerse **2 ~ about** : rondar

how *adv* **1** : cómo **2** (*used in exclamations*) : qué **3 ~ are you?** : ¿cómo está Ud.? **4 ~ come** : por qué **5 ~ much** : cuánto **6 ~ do you do?** : mucho gusto **7 ~ old are you?** : ¿cuántos años tienes? — **~** *conj* : como

however *conj* **1** : de cualquier manera que **2 ~ you like** : como quieras — **~** *adv* **1** NEVERTHELESS : sin embargo, no obstante **2 ~ difficult it is** : por difícil que sea **3 ~ hard I try** : por más que me esfuerce

howl *vi* : aullar — **~** *n* : aullido *m*

hub *n* **1** CENTER : centro *m* **2** : cubo *m* (de una rueda)

hubbub *n* : alboroto *m*, jaleo *m*

hubcap *n* : tapacubos *m*

huddle *vi* **-dled; -dling** *or* **~ together** : apiñarse

hue *n* : color *m*, tono *m*

huff *n* **be in a ~** : estar enojado

hug *vt* **hugged; hugging** : abrazar — **~** *n* : abrazo *m*

huge *adj* **huger; hugest** : inmenso, enorme

hull *n* : casco *m* (de un barco, etc.)

hum *v* **hummed; humming** *vi* **1** : tararear **2** BUZZ : zumbar — *vt* : tararear (una melodía) — **~** *n* : zumbido *m*

human *adj* : humano — **~** *n* : (ser *m*) humano *m* — **humane** *adj* : humano, humanitario — **humanitarian** *adj* : humanitario — **humanity** *n, pl* **-ties** : humanidad *f*

humble *vt* **-bled; -bling** **1** : humillar **2 ~ oneself** : humillarse — **~** *adj* **-bler; -blest** : humilde

humdrum *adj* : monótono, rutinario

humid *adj* : húmedo — **humidity** *n, pl* **-ties** : humedad *f*

humiliate *vt* **-ated; -ating** : humillar — **humiliating** *adj* : humillante — **humiliation** *n* : humillación *f* — **humility** *n* : humildad *f*

humor *or Brit* **humour** *n* : humor *m* — **~** *vt* : seguir la corriente a, complacer — **humorous** *adj* : humorístico, cómico

hump *n* : joroba *f*

hunch *vi or* **~ over** : encorvarse — **~** *n* : presentimiento *m*

hundred *adj* : cien, ciento — **~** *n, pl* **-dreds** *or* **-dred** : ciento *m* — **hundredth** *adj* : centésimo — **~** *n* **1** : centésimo *m*, -ma *f* (en una serie) **2** : centésimo *m* (en matemáticas)

hung → **hang**

Hungarian *adj* : húngaro — **~** *n* : húngaro *m* (idioma)

hunger *n* : hambre *m* — **~** *vi* **1** : tener hambre **2 ~ for** : ansiar, anhelar — **hungry** *adj* **-grier; -est 1** : hambriento **2 be ~** : tener hambre

hunk *n* : pedazo *m* (grande)

hunt *vt* **1** : cazar **2 ~ for** : buscar — **~** *n* **1** : caza *f*, cacería *f* **2** SEARCH : búsqueda *f*, busca *f* — **hunter** *n* : cazador *m*, -dora *f* — **hunting** *n* **1** : caza *f* **2 go ~** : ir de caza

hurdle *n* **1** : valla *f* (en deportes) **2** OBSTACLE : obstáculo *m*

hurl *vt* : lanzar, arrojar

hurrah *interj* : ¡hurra!

hurricane *n* : huracán *m*

hurry *n* : prisa *f*, apuro *f Lat* — *v* **-ried; -rying** *vi* : darse prisa, apurarse *Lat* — *vt* : apurar, dar prisa a — **hurried** *adj* : apresurado — **hurriedly** *adv* : apresuradamente, de prisa

hurt *v* **hurt; hurting** *vt* **1** INJURE : hacer daño a, lastimar **2** OFFEND : ofender, herir — *vi* **1** : doler **2 my foot ~s** : me duele el pie — **~** *n* **1** INJURY : herida *f* **2** DISTRESS : dolor *m*, pena *f* — **hurtful** *adj* : hiriente, doloroso

hurtle *vi* **-tled; -tling** : lanzarse, precipitarse

husband *n* : esposo *m*, marido *m*

hush *vt* : hacer callar, acallar — **~** *n* : silencio *m*

husk *n* : cáscara *f*

husky¹ *adj* **-kier; -est** HOARSE : ronco

husky² *n, pl* **-kies** : perro *m*, -rra *f* esquimal

husky³ *adj* BURLY : fornido

hustle *v* **-tled; -tling** *vt* : dar prisa a, apurar *Lat* — *vi* : darse prisa, apurarse *Lat* — **~** *n* **~ and bustle** : ajetreo *m*, bullicio *m*

hut *n* : cabaña *f*

hutch *n or* **rabbit ~** : conejera *f*

hyacinth *n* : jacinto *m*

hybrid *n* : híbrido *m* — **~** *adj* : híbrido

hydrant *n or* **fire ~** : boca *f* de incendios

hydraulic *adj* : hidráulico

hydroelectric *adj* : hidroeléctrico

hydrogen *n* : hidrógeno *m*

hyena *n* : hiena *f*

hygiene *n* : higiene *f* — **hygienic** *adj* : higiénico

hymn *n* : himno *m*

hyperactive *adj* : hiperactivo

hyphen *n* : guión *m*

hypnosis *n, pl* **-noses** : hipnosis *f* — **hypnotic** *adj* : hipnótico — **hypnotism** *n* : hipnotismo *m* — **hypnotize** *vt* **-tized; -tizing** : hipnotizar

hypochondriac *n* : hipocondríaco *m*, -ca *f*

hypocrisy *n, pl* **-sies** : hipocresía *f* — **hypocrite** *n* : hipócrita *mf* — **hypocritical** *adj* : hipócrita

hypothesis *n, pl* **-eses** : hipótesis *f* — **hypothetical** *adj* : hipotético

hysteria *n* : histeria *f*, histerismo *m* — **hysterical** *adj* : histérico

I

i *n, pl* **i's** *or* **is** : i *f*, novena letra del alfabeto inglés

I *pron* : yo

ice *n* : hielo *m* — **~** *v* **iced; icing** *vt* **1** FREEZE : congelar **2** CHILL : enfriar **3** : bañar (pasteles, etc.) — **~** *vi or* **~ up** : helarse, congelarse — **iceberg** *n* : iceberg *m* — **icebox** → **refrigerator** — **ice-cold** *adj* : helado — **ice cream** *n* : helado *m* — **ice cube** *n* : cubito *m* de hielo — **ice-skate** *vi* **-skated; -skating** : patinar — **ice skate** *n* : patín *m* de cuchilla — **icicle** *n* : carámbano *m* — **icing** *n* : baño *m*

icon *n* : icono *m*

icy *adj* **icier; -est 1** : cubierto de hielo (dícese de pavimento, etc.) **2** FREEZING : helado

I'd (*contraction of* **I should** *or* **I would**) → **should, would**

idea *n* : idea *f*

ideal *adj* : ideal — **~** *n* : ideal *m* — **idealist** *n* : idealista *mf* — **idealistic** *adj* : idealista — **idealize** *vt* **-ized; -izing** : idealizar

identity *n, pl* **-ties** : identidad *f* — **identical** *adj* : idéntico — **identify** *v* **-fied; -fying** *vt* : identificar — *vi* **~ with** : identificarse con — **identification** *n* **1** : identificación *f* **2 ~ card** : carnet *m*, carné *m*

ideology *n, pl* **-gies** : ideología *f* — **ideological** *adj* : ideológico

idiocy *n, pl* **-cies** : idiotez *f*

idiom *n* EXPRESSION : modismo *m* — **idiomatic** *adj* : idiomático

idiosyncrasy *n, pl* **-sies** : idiosincrasia *f*

idiot *n* : idiota *mf* — **idiotic** *adj* : idiota

idle *adj* **idler; idlest 1** LAZY : haragán, holgazán **2** INACTIVE : parado (dícese de una máquina) **3** UNEMPLOYED : desocupado **4** VAIN : frívolo, vano **5 out of ~ curiosity** : por pura curiosidad — **~** *v* **idled; idling** *vi* : andar al ralentí (dícese de un motor) — *vt* **~ away the hours** : pasar el rato — **idleness** *n* : ociosidad *f*

idol *n* : ídolo *m* — **idolize** *vt* **-ized; -izing** : idolatrar

idyllic *adj* : idílico

if *conj* **1** : si **2** THOUGH : aunque, si bien **3** **~ so** : si es así

igloo *n, pl* **-loos** : iglú *m*

ignite *v* **-nited; -niting** *vt* : encender — *vi* : encenderse — **ignition** *n* **1** : ignición *f* **2** *or* **~ switch** : encendido *m*

ignore *vt* **-nored; -noring** : ignorar, no hacer caso de — **ignorance** *n* : ignorancia *f* — **ignorant** *adj* **1** : ignorante **2 be ~ of** : desconocer, ignorar

ilk *n* : tipo *m*, clase *f*

ill *adj* **worse; worst 1** SICK : enfermo **2** BAD : malo — *adv* **worse; worst** : mal — **ill–advised** *adj* : imprudente — **ill at ease** *adj* : incómodo

I'll (*contraction of* **I shall** *or* **I will**) → **shall, will**

illegal *adj* : ilegal

illegible *adj* : ilegible

illegitimate *adj* : ilegítimo — **illegitimacy** *n* : ilegitimidad *f*

illicit *adj* : ilícito

illiterate *adj* : analfabeto — **illiteracy** *n, pl* **-cies** : analfabetismo *m*

ill–mannered *adj* : descortés, maleducado

ill–natured *adj* : de mal genio

illness *n* : enfermedad *f*

illogical *adj* : ilógico

ill–treat *vt* : maltratar

illuminate *vt* **-nated; -nating** : iluminar — **illumination** *n* : iluminación *f*

illusion *n* : ilusión *f* — **illusory** *adj* : ilusorio

illustrate *v* **-trated; -trating** : ilustrar — **illustration** *n* **1** : ilustración *f* **2** EXAMPLE : ejemplo *m* — **illustrative** *adj* : ilustrativo

illustrious *adj* : ilustre, glorioso

ill will *n* : animadversión *f*, mala voluntad *f*

I'm (*contraction of* **I am**) → **be**

image *n* : imagen *f* — **imaginary** *adj* : imaginario — **imagination** *n* : imaginación *f* — **imaginative** *adj* : imaginativo — **imagine** *vt* **-ined; -ining** : imaginar(se)

imbalance *n* : desequilibrio *m*

imbecile *n* : imbécil *mf*

imbue *vt* **-bued; -buing** : imbuir

imitation *n* : imitación *f* — **~** *adj* : de imitación, artificial — **imitate** *vt* **-tated; -tat-**ing : imitar, remedar — **imitator** *n* : imitador *m*, -dora *f*

immaculate *adj* : inmaculado

immaterial *adj* : irrelevante, sin importancia

immature *adj* : inmaduro — **immaturity** *n, pl* **-ties** : inmadurez *f*

immediate *adj* : inmediato — **immediately** *adv* : inmediatamente

immense *adj* : inmenso — **immensity** *n, pl* **-ties** : inmensidad *f*

immerse *vt* **-mersed; -mersing** : sumergir — **immersion** *n* : inmersión *f*

immigrate *vi* **-grated; -grating** : inmigrar — **immigrant** *n* : inmigrante *mf* — **immigration** *n* : inmigración *f*

imminent *adj* : inminente — **imminence** *n* : inminencia *f*

immobile *adj* : inmóvil — **immobilize** *vt* **-lized; -lizing** : inmovilizar

immoral *adj* : inmoral — **immorality** *n, pl* **-ties** : inmoralidad *f*

immortal *adj* : inmortal — **~** *n* : inmortal *mf* — **immortality** *n* : inmortalidad *f*

immune *adj* : inmune — **immunity** *n, pl* **-ties** : inmunidad *f* — **immunization** *n* : inmunización *f* — **immunize** *vt* **-nized; -niz-**ing : inmunizar

imp *n* RASCAL : diablillo *m*

impact *n* : impacto *m*

impair *vt* : dañar, perjudicar

impart *vt* : impartir (información), conferir (una calidad, etc.)

impartial *adj* : imparcial — **impartiality** *n, pl* **-ties** : imparcialidad *f*

impassable *adj* : intransitable

impasse *n* : impasse *m*

impassioned *adj* : apasionado

impassive *adj* : impasible

impatience *n* : impaciencia *f* — **impatient** *adj* : impaciente — **impatiently** *adv* : con impaciencia

impeccable *adj* : impecable

impede *vt* **-peded; -peding** : dificultar — **impediment** *n* : impedimento *m*, obstáculo *m*

impel *vt* **-pelled; -pelling** : impeler

impending *adj* : inminente

impenetrable *adj* : impenetrable

imperative *adj* **1** COMMANDING : imperativo **2** NECESSARY : imprescindible — **~** *n* : imperativo *m*

imperceptible *adj* : imperceptible

imperfection *n* : imperfección *f* — **imperfect** *adj* : imperfecto — **~** *n or* **~ tense** : imperfecto *m*

imperial *adj* : imperial — **imperialism** *n* : imperialismo *m* — **imperious** *adj* : imperioso

impersonal *adj* : impersonal

impersonate *vt* **-ated; -ating** : hacerse pasar por, imitar — **impersonation** *n* : imitación *f* — **impersonator** *n* : imitador *m*, **-dora** *f*

impertinent *adj* : impertinente — **impertinence** *n* : impertinencia *f*

impervious *adj* ~ **to** : impermeable a

impetuous *adj* : impetuoso, impulsivo

impetus *n* : ímpetu *m*, impulso *m*

impinge *vi* **-pinged; -pinging** ~ **on** : afectara, incidir en

impish *adj* : pícaro, travieso

implant *vt* : implantar

implausible *adj* : inverosímil

implement *n* : instrumento *m*, implemento *m* *Lat* — ~ *vt* : poner en práctica

implicate *vt* **-cated; -cating** : implicar — **implication** *n* **1** INVOLVEMENT : implicación *f* **2** CONSEQUENCE : consecuencia *f* **3 by** ~ : de forma indirecta

implicit *adj* **1** : implícito **2** UNQUESTIONING : absoluto, incondicional

implore *vt* **-plored; -ploring** : implorar, suplicar

imply *vt* **-plied; -plying 1** HINT : insinuar **2** ENTAIL : implicar

impolite *adj* : descortés, maleducado

import *vt* : importar (mercancías) — **important** *adj* : importante — **importance** *n* : importancia *f* — **importation** *n* : importación *f* — **importer** *n* : importador *m*, **-dora** *f*

impose *v* **-posed; -posing** *vt* : imponer — *vi* ~ **on** : importunar, molestar — **imposing** *adj* : imponente — **imposition** *n* **1** ENFORCEMENT : imposición *f* **2 be an** ~ **on** : molestar

impossible *adj* : imposible — **impossibility** *n*, *pl* **-ties** : imposibilidad *f*

impostor *or* **imposter** *n* : impostor *m*, **-tora** *f*

impotent *adj* : impotente — **impotence** *n* : impotencia *f*

impound *vt* : incautar, embargar

impoverished *adj* : empobrecido

impracticable *adj* : impracticable

impractical *adj* : poco práctico

imprecise *adj* : impreciso — **imprecision** *n* : imprecisión *f*

impregnable *adj* : impenetrable

impregnate *vt* **-nated; -nating 1** : impregnar **2** FERTILIZE : fecundar

impress *vt* **1** : causar una buena impresión a **2** AFFECT : impresionar **3** ~ **sth on s.o.** : recalcar algo a algn — *vi* : impresionar — **impression** *n* : impresión *f* — **impressionable** *adj* : impresionable — **impressive** *adj* : impresionante

imprint *vt* : imprimir — ~ *n* MARK : impresión *f*, huella *f*

imprison *vt* : encarcelar — **imprisonment** *n* : encarcelamiento *m*

improbable *adj* : improbable — **improbability** *n*, *pl* **-ties** : improbabilidad *f*

impromptu *adj* : improvisado

improper *adj* **1** UNSEEMLY : indecoroso **2** INCORRECT : impropio — **impropriety** *n*, *pl* **-eties** : inconveniencia *f*

improve *v* **-proved; -proving** : mejorar — **improvement** *n* : mejora *f*

improvise *v* **-vised; -vising** : improvisar — **improvisation** *n* : improvisación *f*

impudent *adj* : insolente — **impudence** *n* : insolencia *f*

impulse *n* **1** : impulso *m* **2 on** ~ : sin reflexionar — **impulsive** *adj* : impulsivo — **impulsiveness** *n* : impulsividad *f*

impunity *n* **1** : impunidad *f* **2 with** ~ : impunemente

impure *adj* : impuro — **impurity** *n*, *pl* **-ties** : impureza *f*

in *prep* **1** : en **2** DURING : por, en *Lat* **3** WITHIN : dentro de **4 dressed** ~ **red** : vestido de rojo **5** ~ **the rain** : bajo la lluvia **6** ~ **the sun** : al sol **7** ~ **this way** : de esta manera **8 the best** ~ **the world** : el mejor del mundo **9 written** ~ **ink/French** : escrito con tinta/en francés — *adv* **1** INSIDE : dentro, adentro **2 be** ~ : estar (en casa) **3 be** ~ **on** : participar en **4 come in!** : ¡entre!, ¡pase! **5 he's** ~ **for a shock** : se va a llevar un shock — ~ *adj* : de moda

inability *n*, *pl* **-ties** : incapacidad *f*

inaccessible *adj* : inaccesible

inaccurate *n* : inexacto

inactive *n* : inactivo — **inactivity** *n*, *pl* **-ties** : inactividad *f*

inadequate *adj* : insuficiente

inadvertently *adv* : sin querer

inadvisable *adj* : desaconsejable

inane *adj* **inaner; -est** : estúpido, tonto

inanimate *adj* : inanimado

inapplicable *adj* : inaplicable

inappropriate *adj* : impropio, inoportuno

inarticulate *adj* : incapaz de expresarse

inasmuch as *conj* : ya que, puesto que

inattentive *adj* : poco atento

inaudible *adj* : inaudible

inaugural *adj* **1** : inaugural **2** ~ **address** : discurso *m* de investidura — **inaugurate** *vt* **-rated; -rating 1** : investir (a un presidente, etc.) **2** BEGIN : inaugurar — **inauguration** *n* : investidura *f* (de una persona), inauguración *f* (de un edificio, etc.)

inborn *adj* : innato

inbred *adj* INNATE : innato

incalculable *adj* : incalculable

incapable *adj* : incapaz — **incapacitate** *vt* **-tated; -tating** : incapacitar — **incapacity** *n*, *pl* **-ties** : incapacidad *f*

incarcerate *vt* **-ated; -ating** : encarcelar

incarnate *adj* : encarnado — **incarnation** *n* : encarnación *f*

incendiary *adj* : incendiario

incense¹ *n* : incienso *m*

incense² *vt* **-censed; -censing** : indignar, enfurecer

incentive *n* : incentivo *m*

inception *n* : comienzo *m*, principio *m*

incessant *adj* : incesante

incest *n* : incesto *m* — **incestuous** *adj* : incestuoso

inch *n* : pulgada *f* — ～ *v* : avanzar poco a poco

incident *n* : incidente *m* — **incidence** *n* : índice *m* (de crímenes, etc.) — **incidental** *adj* **1** MINOR : incidental **2** CHANCE : casual — **incidentally** *adv* : a propósito

incinerate *vt* **-ated; -ating** : incinerar — **incinerator** *n* : incinerador *m*

incision *n* : incisión *f*

incite *vt* **-cited; -citing** : incitar, instigar

incline *v* **-clined; -clining** *vt* **1** BEND : inclinar **2 be ～ed to** : inclinarse a, tender a — ～ *vi* : inclinarse — ～ *n* : pendiente *f* — **inclination** *n* **1** : inclinación *f* **2** DESIRE : deseo *m*, ganas *fpl*

include *vt* **-cluded; -cluding** : incluir — **inclusion** *n* : inclusión *f* — **inclusive** *adj* : inclusivo

incognito *adv & adj* : de incógnito

incoherent *adj* : incoherente — **incoherence** *n* : incoherencia *f*

income *n* : ingresos *mpl* — **income tax** *n* : impuesto *m* sobre la renta

incomparable *adj* : incomparable

incompatible *adj* : incompatible

incompetent *adj* : incompetente — **incompetence** *n* : incompetencia *f*

incomplete *adj* : incompleto

incomprehensible *adj* : incomprensible

inconceivable *adj* : inconcebible

inconclusive *adj* : no concluyente

incongruous *adj* : incongruente

inconsiderate *adj* : desconsiderado

inconsistent *adj* **1** : inconsecuente **2 be ～ with** : no concordar con — **inconsistency** *n, pl* **-cies** : inconsecuencia *f*

inconspicuous *adj* : que no llama la atención

inconvenient *adj* : incómodo, inconveniente — **inconvenience** *n* **1** BOTHER : incomodidad *f*, molestia *f* **2** DRAWBACK : inconveniente *m* — ～ *vt* **-nienced; -niencing** *vt* : importunar, molestar

incorporate *vt* **-rated; -rating** : incorporar

incorrect *adj* : incorrecto

increase *n* : aumento *m* — ～ *v* **-creased; -creasing** : aumentar — **increasingly** *adv* : cada vez más

incredible *adj* : increíble

incredulous *adj* : incrédulo

incriminate *vt* **-nated; -nating** : incriminar

incubator *n* : incubadora *f*

incumbent *n* : titular *mf*

incur *vt* **incurred; incurring** : provocar (al enojo, etc.), incurrir en (gastos)

incurable *adj* : incurable

indebted *adj* **1** : endeudado **2 be ～ to s.o.** : estar en deuda con algn

indecent *adj* : indecente — **indecency** *n, pl* **-cies** : indecencia *f*

indecisive *adj* : indeciso

indeed *adv* **1** TRULY : verdaderamente, sin duda **2** IN FACT : en efecto **3 ～?** : ¿de veras?

indefinite *adj* **1** : indefinido **2** VAGUE : impreciso — **indefinitely** *adv* : indefinidamente

indelible *adj* : indeleble

indent *vt* : sangrar (un párrafo) — **indentation** *n* DENT, NOTCH : mella *f*

independent *adj* : independiente — **independence** *n* : independencia *f*

indescribable *adj* : indescriptible

indestructible *adj* : indestructible

index *n, pl* **-dexes** *or* **-dices** : índice *m* — ～ *vt* : incluir en un índice — **index finger** *n* : dedo *m* índice

Indian *adj* : indio *m*, -dia *f*

indication *n* : indicio *m*, señal *f* — **indicate** *vt* **-cated; -cating** : indicar — **indicative** *adj* : indicativo — **indicator** *n* : indicador *m*

indict *vt* : acusar (de un crimen) — **indictment** *n* : acusación *f*

indifferent *adj* **1** : indiferente **2** MEDIOCRE : mediocre — **indifference** *n* : indiferencia *f*

indigenous *adj* : indígena

indigestion *n* : indigestión *f* — **indigestible** *adj* : indigesto

indignation *n* : indignación *f* — **indignant** *adj* : indignado — **indignity** *n, pl* **-ties** : indignidad *f*

indigo *n, pl* **-gos** *or* **-goes** : añil *m*

indirect *adj* : indirecto

indiscreet *adj* : indiscreto — **indiscretion** *n* : indiscreción *f*

indiscriminate *adj* : indiscriminado

indispensable *adj* : indispensable, imprescindible

indisputable *adj* : indiscutible

indistinct *adj* : indistinto

individual *adj* **1** : individual **2** PARTICULAR : particular — ～ *n* : individuo *m* — **individuality** *n, pl* **-ties** : individualidad *f* — **individually** *adv* : individualmente

indoctrinate *vt* **-nated; -nating** : adoctrinar — **indoctrination** *n* : adoctrinamiento *m*

indoor *adj* **1** : (de) interior **2 ~ plant** : planta *f* de interior **3 ~ pool** : piscina *f* cubierta **4 ~ sports** : deportes *mpl* bajo techo — **indoors** *adv* : adentro, dentro

induce *vt* **-duced; -ducing 1** : inducir **2** CAUSE : provocar — **inducement** *n* : incentivo *m*

indulge *v* **-dulged; -dulging** *vt* **1** GRATIFY : satisfacer **2** PAMPER : consentir — *vi* **~ in** : permitirse — **indulgence** *n* **1** : indulgencia *f* **2** SATISFYING : satisfacción *f* — **indulgent** *adj* : indulgente

industry *n, pl* **-tries 1** : industria *f* **2** DILIGENCE : diligencia *f* — **industrial** *adj* : industrial — **industrialize** *vt* **-ized; -izing** : industrializar — **industrious** *adj* : diligente, trabajador

inebriated *adj* : ebrio, embriagado

inedible *adj* : no comestible

ineffective *adj* **1** : ineficaz **2** INCOMPETENT : incompetente — **ineffectual** *adj* : inútil, ineficaz

inefficient *adj* **1** : ineficiente **2** INCOMPETENT : incompetente — **inefficiency** *n, pl* **-cies** : ineficiencia *f*

ineligible *adj* : ineligible

inept *adj* **1** : inepto **2 ~ at** : incapaz para

inequality *n, pl* **-ties** : desigualdad *f*

inert *adj* : inerte — **inertia** *n* : inercia *f*

inescapable *adj* : ineludible

inevitable *adj* : inevitable — **inevitably** *adv* : inevitablemente

inexcusable *adj* : inexcusable

inexpensive *adj* : barato, económico

inexperienced *adj* : inexperto

inexplicable *adj* : inexplicable

infallible *adj* : infalible

infamous *adj* : infame

infancy *n, pl* **-cies** : infancia *f* — **infant** *n* : bebé *m;* niño *m,* -ña *f* — **infantile** *adj* : infantil

infantry *n, pl* **-tries** : infantería *f*

infatuated *adj* be **~ with** : estar encaprichado con — **infatuation** *n* : encaprichamiento *m*

infect *vt* : infectar — **infection** *n* : infección *f* — **infectious** *adj* : contagioso

infer *vt* **inferred; inferring** : deducir, inferir — **inference** *n* : deducción *f*

inferior *adj* : inferior — **~** *n* : inferior *mf* — **inferiority** *n, pl* **-ties** : inferioridad *f*

infernal *adj* : infernal — **inferno** *n, pl* **-nos** : infierno *m*

infertile *adj* : estéril — **infertility** *n* : esterilidad *f*

infest *vt* : infestar

infidelity *n, pl* **-ties** : infidelidad *f*

infiltrate *v* **-trated; -trating** *vt* : infiltrar — *vi* : infiltrarse

infinite *adj* : infinito

infinitive *n* : infinitivo *m*

infinity *n, pl* **-ties 1** : infinito *m* **2 an ~ of** : una infinidad de

infirm *adj* : enfermizo, endeble — **infirmary** *n, pl* **-ries** : enfermería *f* — **infirmity** *n, pl* **-ties 1** FRAILTY : endeblez *f* **2** AILMENT : enfermedad *f*

inflame *vt* **-flamed; -flaming** : inflamar — **inflammable** *adj* : inflamable — **inflammation** *n* : inflamación *f* — **inflammatory** *adj* : inflamatorio

inflate *vt* **-flated; -flating** : inflar — **inflation** *n* : inflación *f* — **inflationary** *adj* : inflacionario, inflacionista

inflexible *adj* : inflexible

inflict *vt* : infligir

influence *n* **1** : influencia *f* **2 under the ~** : embriagado — **~** *vt* **-enced; -encing** : influir en, influenciar — **influential** *adj* : influyente

influenza *n* : gripe *f,* influenza *f*

influx *n* : afluencia *f*

inform *vt* **1** : informar **2 keep me ~ed** : manténme al corriente — *vi* **~ on** : delatar, denunciar

informal *adj* **1** : informal **2** : familiar (dícese del lenguaje) — **informality** *n, pl* **-ties** : falta *f* de ceremonia — **informally** *adv* : de manera informal

information *n* : información *f* — **informative** *adj* : informativo — **informer** *n* : informante *mf*

infrared *adj* : infrarrojo

infrastructure *n* : infraestructura *f*

infrequent *adj* : infrecuente — **infrequently** *adv* : raramente

infringe *v* **-fringed; -fringing** *vt* : infringir — *vi* **~ on** : violar — **infringement** *n* : violación *f*

infuriate *vt* **-ated; -ating** : enfurecer, poner furioso — **infuriating** *adj* : exasperante

infuse *vt* **-fused; -fusing** : infundir — **infusion** *n* : infusión *f*

ingenious *adj* : ingenioso — **ingenuity** *n, pl* **-ities** : ingenio

ingenuous *adj* : ingenuo

ingest *vt* : ingerir

ingot *n* : lingote *m*

ingrained *adj* : arraigado

ingratiate *vt* **-ated; -ating ~ oneself with** : congraciarse con

ingratitude *n* : ingratitud *f*

ingredient *n* : ingrediente *m*

ingrown *adj* **~ nail** : uña *f* encarnada

inhabit *vt* : habitar — **inhabitant** *n* : habitante *mf*

inhale *v* **-haled; -haling** *vt* : inhalar, aspirar — *vi* : inspirar

inherent *adj* : inherente — **inherently** *adv* : intrínsecamente

inherit *vt* : heredar — **inheritance** *n* : herencia *f*

inhibit *vt* IMPEDE : inhibir — **inhibition** *n* : inhibición *f*

inhuman *adj* : inhumano — **inhumane** *adj* : inhumano — **inhumanity** *n, pl* **-ties** : inhumanidad *f*

initial *adj* : inicial — *n* : inicial *f* — *vt* **-tialed** *or* **-tialled; -tialing** *or* **-tialling** : poner las iniciales a

initiate *vt* **-ated; -ating 1** BEGIN : iniciar **2** ∼ **s.o. into sth** : iniciar a algn en algo — **initiation** *n* : iniciación *f* — **initiative** *n* : iniciativa *f*

inject *vt* : inyectar — **injection** *n* : inyección *f*

injure *vt* **-jured; -juring 1** : herir **2** ∼ **oneself** : hacerse daño — **injurious** *adj* : perjudicial — **injury** *n, pl* **-ries 1** : herida *f* **2** HARM : perjuicio *m*

injustice *n* : injusticia *f*

ink *n* : tinta *f* — **inkwell** *n* : tintero *m*

inland *adj* : interior — ∼ *adv* : hacia el interior, tierra adentro

in–laws *npl* : suegros *mpl*

inlet *n* : ensenada *f,* cala *f*

inmate *n* **1** PATIENT : paciente *mf* **2** PRISONER : preso *m,* -sa *f*

inn *n* : posada *f,* hostería *f*

innards *npl* : entrañas *fpl,* tripas *fpl fam*

innate *adj* : innato

inner *adj* : interior, interno — **innermost** *adj* : más íntimo, más profundo

inning *n* : entrada *f*

innocent *adj* : inocente — ∼ *n* : inocente *mf* — **innocence** *n* : inocencia *f*

innocuous *adj* : inocuo

innovate *vi* **-vated; -vating** : innovar — **innovation** *n* : innovación *f* — **innovative** *adj* : innovador — **innovator** *n* : innovador *m,* -dora *f*

innuendo *n, pl* **-dos** *or* **-does** : insinuación *f,* indirecta *f*

innumerable *adj* : innumerable

inoculate *vt* **-lated; -lating** : inocular — **inoculation** *n* : inoculación *f*

inoffensive *adj* : inofensivo

inpatient *n* : paciente *mf* hospitalizado

input *n* **1** : contribución *f* **2** : entrada *f* (de datos) — ∼ *vt* **-putted** *or* **-put; -putting** : entrar (datos, etc.)

inquire *v* **-quired; -quiring** *vt* : preguntar — *vi* **1** ∼ **about** : informarse sobre **2** ∼ **into** : investigar — **inquiry** *n, pl* **-ries 1** QUESTION : pregunta *f* **2** INVESTIGATION : investigación *f* — **inquisition** *n* : inquisición *f* —

inquisitive *adj* : curioso

insane *adj* : loco — **insanity** *n, pl* **-ties** : locura *f*

insatiable *adj* : insaciable

inscribe *vt* **-scribed; -scribing** : inscribir — **inscription** *n* : inscripción *f*

inscrutable *adj* : inescrutable

insect *n* : insecto *m* — **insecticide** *n* : insecticida *m*

insecure *adj* : inseguro, poco seguro — **insecurity** *n, pl* **-ties** : inseguridad *f*

insensitive *adj* : insensible — **insensitivity** *n, pl* **-ties** : insensibilidad *f*

inseparable *adj* : inseparable

insert *vt* : insertar (texto), introducir (una moneda, etc.)

inside *n* **1** : interior *m* **2** ∼ **out** : al revés — *adv* : dentro, adentro — ∼ *adj* : interior — ∼ *prep* **1** *or* ∼ **of** : dentro de **2** ∼ **an hour** : en menos de una hora

insidious *adj* : insidioso

insight *n* : perspicacia *f*

insignia *or* **insigne** *n, pl* **-nia** *or* **-nias** : insignia *f,* enseña *f*

insignificant *adj* : insignificante

insincere *adj* : insincero

insinuate *vt* **-ated; -ating** : insinuar — **insinuation** *n* : insinuación *f*

insipid *adj* : insípido

insist *v* : insistir — **insistent** *adj* : insistente

insofar as *conj* : en la medida en que

insole *n* : plantilla *f*

insolent *adj* : insolente — **insolence** *n* : insolencia *f*

insolvent *adj* : insolvente

insomnia *n* : insomnio *m*

inspect *vt* : inspeccionar, revisar — **inspection** *n* : inspección *f* — **inspector** *n* : inspector *m,* -tora *f*

inspire *vt* **-spired; -spiring** : inspirar — **inspiration** *n* : inspiración *f* — **inspirational** *adj* : inspirador

instability *n, pl* **-ties** : inestabilidad *f*

install *vt* **-stalled; -stalling** : instalar — **installation** *n* : instalación *f* — **installment** *n* **1** PAYMENT : plazo *m,* cuota *f* **2** : entrega *f* (de una publicación o telenovela)

instance *n* **1** : ejemplo *m* **2 for** ∼ : por ejemplo **3 in this** ∼ : en este caso

instant *n* : instante *m* — ∼ *adj* **1** IMMEDIATE : inmediato **2** ∼ **coffee** : café *m* instantáneo — **instantaneous** *adj* : instantáneo — **instantly** *adv* : al instante, instantáneamente

instead *adv* **1** : en cambio **2 I went** ∼ : fui en su lugar — **instead of** *prep* : en vez de, en lugar de

instep *n* : empeine *m*

instigate *vt* **-gated; -gating** : instigar a —

instigation n : instigación f — **instigator** n : instigador m, -dora f

instill or Brit **instil** vt **-stilled; -stilling** : inculcar, infundir

instinct n : instinto m — **instinctive** or **instinctual** adj : instintivo

institute vt **-tuted; -tuting 1** : instituir **2** INITIATE : iniciar — ∼ n : instituto m — **institution** n : institución f

instruct vt **1** : instruir **2** COMMAND : mandar — **instruction** n : instrucción f — **instructor** n : instructor m, -tora f

instrument n : instrumento m — **instrumental** adj **1** : instrumental **2 be** ∼ **in** : jugar un papel fundamental en

insubordinate adj : insubordinado — **insubordination** n : insubordinación f

insufferable adj : insoportable

insufficient adj : insuficiente

insular adj **1** : insular **2** NARROW-MINDED : estrecho de miras

insulate vt **-lated; -lating** : aislar — **insulation** n : aislamiento m

insulin n : insulina f

insult vt : insultar — ∼ n : insulto m — **insulting** adj : insultante, ofensivo

insure vt **-sured; -suring** : asegurar — **insurance** n : seguro m

insurmountable adj : insuperable

intact adj : intacto

intake n : consumo m (de alimentos), entrada f (de aire, etc.)

intangible adj : intangible

integral adj : integral

integrate v **-grated; -grating** vt : integrar — vi : integrarse

integrity n : integridad f

intellect n : intelecto m — **intellectual** adj : intelectual — ∼ n : intelectual mf — **intelligence** n : inteligencia f — **intelligent** adj : inteligente — **intelligible** adj : inteligible

intend vt **1 be** ∼**ed for** : ser para **2** ∼ **to do** : pensar hacer, tener la intención de hacer — **intended** adj : intencionado, deliberado

intense adj : intenso — **intensely** adv : sumamente, profundamente — **intensify** v **-fied; -fying** vt : intensificar — vi : intensificarse — **intensity** n, pl **-ties** : intensidad f — **intensive** adj : intensivo

intent n : intención f — ∼ adj **1** : atento, concentrado **2** ∼ **on doing** : resuelto a hacer — **intention** n : intención f — **intentional** adj : intencional, deliberado — **intently** adv : atentamente, fijamente

interact vi **1** : interactuar **2** ∼ **with** : relacionarse con — **interaction** n : interacción f — **interactive** adj : interactivo

intercede vi **-ceded; -ceding** : interceder

intercept vt : interceptar

interchange vt **-changed; -changing** : intercambiar — ∼ n **1** : intercambio m **2** JUNCTION : enlace m — **interchangeable** adj : intercambiable

intercourse n : relaciones fpl (sexuales)

interest n : interés m — ∼ vt : interesar — **interested** adj : interesado — **interesting** adj : interesante

interface n : interfaz mf (de una computadora)

interfere vi **-fered; -fering 1** ∼ **in** : entrometerse en, interferir en **2** ∼ **with** DISRUPT : afectar (una actividad, etc.) — **interference** n **1** : interferencia f **2** : intromisión f (en el radio, etc.)

interim n **1** : interín m **2 in the** ∼ : mientras tanto — ∼ adj : interino, provisional

interior adj : interior — ∼ n : interior m

interjection n : interjección f

interlock vt : engranar

interloper n : intruso m, -sa f

interlude n **1** : intervalo m **2** : interludio m (en música, etc.)

intermediate adj : intermedio — **intermediary** n, pl **-aries** : intermediario m, -ria f

interminable adj : interminable

intermission n : intervalo m, intermedio m

intermittent adj : intermitente

intern[1] vt : confinar

intern[2] vi : hacer las prácticas — ∼ n : interno m, -na f

internal adj : interno

international adj : internacional

interpret vt : interpretar — **interpretation** n : interpretación f — **interpreter** n : intérprete mf

interrogate vt **-gated; -gating** : interrogar — **interrogation** n QUESTIONING : interrogatorio m — **interrogative** adj : interrogativo

interrupt v : interrumpir — **interruption** n : interrupción f

intersect vt : cruzar (dícese de calles), cortar (dícese de líneas) — vi : cruzarse, cortarse — **intersection** n : cruce m, intersección f

intersperse vt **-spersed; -spersing** : intercalar

interstate n or ∼ **highway** : carretera f interestatal

intertwine vi **-twined; -twining** : entrelazarse

interval n : intervalo m

intervene vi **-vened; -vening 1** : intervenir **2** ELAPSE : transcurrir, pasar — **intervention** n : intervención f

interview n : entrevista f — ∼ vt : entrevistar — **interviewer** n : entrevistador m, -dora f

intestine *n* : intestino *m* — **intestinal** *adj* : intestinal

intimate¹ *vt* -mated; -mating : insinuar, dar a entender

intimate² *adj* : íntimo — **intimacy** *n, pl* -cies : intimidad *f*

intimidate *vt* -dated; -dating : intimidar — **intimidation** *n* : intimidación *f*

into *prep* **1** : en, a **2** bump ~ : darse contra **3** (*used in mathematics*) **3** ~ **12** : 12 dividido por 3

intolerable *adj* : intolerable — **intolerance** *n* : intolerancia *f* — **intolerant** *adj* : intolerante

intoxicate *vt* -cated; -cating : embriagar — **intoxicated** *adj* **1** : embriagado **2** ~ with : ebrio de

intransitive *adj* : intransitivo

intravenous *adj* : intravenoso

intrepid *adj* : intrépido

intricate *adj* : complicado, intrincado — **intricacy** *n, pl* -cies : complejidad *f*

intrigue *n* : intriga *f* — ~ *v* -trigued; -triguing : intrigar — **intriguing** *adj* : intrigante

intrinsic *adj* : intrínseco

introduce *vt* -duced; -ducing **1** : introducir **2** : presentar (a una persona) — **introduction** *n* **1** : introducción *f* **2** : presentación *f* (de una persona) — **introductory** *adj* : introductorio

introvert *n* : introvertido *m*, -da *f* — **introverted** *adj* : introvertido

intrude *vi* -truded; -truding **1** : entrometerse **2** ~ on s.o. : molestar a algn — **intruder** *n* : intruso *m*, -sa *f* — **intrusion** *n* : intrusión *f* — **intrusive** *adj* : intruso

intuition *n* : intuición *f* — **intuitive** *adj* : intuitivo

inundate *vt* -dated; -dating : inundar

invade *vt* -vaded; -vading : invadir

invalid¹ *adj* : inválido

invalid² *n* : inválido *m*, -da *f*

invaluable *adj* : inestimable, invalorable *Lat*

invariable *adj* : invariable

invasion *n* : invasión *f*

invent *vt* : inventar — **invention** *n* : invención *f* — **inventive** *adj* : inventivo — **inventor** *n* : inventor *m*, -tora *f*

inventory *n, pl* -ries : inventario *m*

invert *vt* : invertir

invertebrate *adj* : invertebrado — ~ *n* : invertebrado *m*

invest *vt* : invertir

investigate *v* -gated; -gating : investigar — **investigation** *n* : investigación *f* — **investigator** *n* : investigador *m*, -dora *f*

investment *n* : inversión *f* — **investor** *n* : inversor *m*, -sora *f*

inveterate *adj* : inveterado

invigorating *adj* : vigorizante

invincible *adj* : invencible

invisible *adj* : invisible

invitation *n* : invitación *f* — **invite** *vt* -vited; -viting **1** : invitar **2** SEEK : buscar (problemas, etc.) — **inviting** *adj* : atrayente

invoice *n* : factura *f*

invoke *vt* -voked; -voking : invocar

involuntary *adj* : involuntario

involve *vt* -volved; -volving **1** CONCERN : concernir, afectar **2** ENTAIL : suponer — **involved** *adj* **1** COMPLEX : complicado **2** CONCERNED : afectado — **involvement** *n* : participación *f*

invulnerable *adj* : invulnerable

inward *adj* INNER : interior, interno — ~ *or* **inwards** *adv* : hacia adentro, hacia el interior

iodine *n* : yodo *m*, tintura *f* de yodo

ion *n* : ion *m*

iota *n* : pizca *f*, ápice *m*

IOU *n* : pagaré *m*, vale *m*

Iranian *adj* : iraní

Iraqi *adj* : iraquí

ire *n* : ira *f* — **irate** *adj* : furioso

iris *n, pl* **irises** *or* **irides 1** : iris *m* (del ojo) **2** : lirio *m* (planta)

Irish *adj* : irlandés

irksome *adj* : irritante, fastidioso

iron *n* **1** : hierro *m*, fierro *m Lat* (metal) **2** : plancha *f* (para la ropa) — ~ *v* : planchar

ironic *or* **ironical** *adj* : irónico

ironing board *n* : tabla *f* (de planchar)

irony *n, pl* -nies : ironía *f*

irrational *adj* : irracional

irreconcilable *adj* : irreconciliable

irrefutable *adj* : irrefutable

irregular *adj* : irregular — **irregularity** *n, pl* -ties : irregularidad *f*

irrelevant *adj* : irrelevante

irreparable *adj* : irreparable

irreplaceable *adj* : irreemplazable

irresistible *adj* : irresistible

irresolute *adj* : irresoluto

irrespective of *prep* : sin tener en cuenta

irresponsible *adj* : irresponsable — **irresponsibility** *n, pl* -ties : irresponsabilidad *f*

irreverent *adj* : irreverente

irreversible *adj* : irreversible, irrevocable

irrigate *vt* -gated; -gating : irrigar, regar — **irrigation** *n* : irrigación *f*, riego *m*

irritate *vt* -tated; -tating : irritar — **irritable** *adj* : irritable — **irritably** *adv* : con irritación — **irritating** *adj* : irritante — **irritation** *n* : irritación *f*

is → be

Islam *n* : el Islam — **Islamic** *adj* : islámico

island *n* : isla *f* — **isle** *n* : isla *f*

isolate *vt* **-lated; -lating** : aislar — **isolation**
n : aislamiento *m*
Israeli *adj* : israelí
issue *n* **1** MATTER : asunto *m*, cuestión *f* **2**
: número *m* (de una revista, etc.) **3 make an**
~ of : insistir demasiado sobre **4 take ~**
with : disentir de — **~** *v* **-sued; -suing** *vi*
~ from : surgir de — *vt* **1** : emitir (sellos,
etc.), distribuir (provisiones, etc.) **2** PUB-
LISH : publicar
isthmus *n* : istmo *m*
it *pron* **1** (*as subject*) : él, ella **2** (*as indirect
object*) : le, se **3** (*as direct object*) : lo, la **4**
(*as object of a preposition*) : él, ella **5 it's
raining** : está lloviendo **6 it's 8 o'clock**
: son las ocho **7 it's hot out** : hace calor **8
~ is necessary** : es necesario **9 who is
~?** : ¿quién es? **10 it's me** : soy yo
Italian *adj* : italiano — **~** *n* : italiano *m* (idioma)
italics *n* : cursiva *f*
itch *vi* **1** : picar **2 be ~ing to** : morirse por

— **~** *n* : picazón *f* — **itchy** *adj* **itchier; -est**
: que pica
it'd (*contraction of* **it had** *or* **it would**) →
have, would
item *n* **1** : artículo *m* **2** : punto *m* (en una
agenda) **3 ~ of clothing** : prenda *f* de vestir **4 news ~** : noticia *f* — **itemize** *vt*
-ized; -izing : detallar, enumerar
itinerant *adj* : ambulante
itinerary *n, pl* **-aries** : itinerario *m*
it'll (*contraction of* **it shall** *or* **it will**) → **shall,
will**
its *adj* : su, sus
it's (*contraction of* **it is** *or* **it has**) → **be,
have**
itself *pron* **1** (*used reflexively*) : se **2** (*used
for emphasis*) : (él) mismo, (ella) misma, sí
(mismo) **3 by ~** : solo
I've (*contraction of* **I have**) → **have**
ivory *n, pl* **-ries** : marfil *m*
ivy *n, pl* **ivies** : hiedra *f*

J

j *n, pl* **j's** *or* **js** : j *f*, décima letra del alfabeto
inglés
jab *vt* **jabbed; jabbing 1** PIERCE : pinchar **2**
POKE : golpear (con la punta de algo) — **~**
n **1** PRICK : pinchazo *m* **2** POKE : golpe *m*
abrupto
jabber *vi* : farfullar
jack *n* **1** : gato *m* (mecanismo) **2** : sota *f* (de
naipes) — **~** *vt or* **~ up 1** : levantar (con
un gato) **2** INCREASE : subir
jackal *n* : chacal *m*
jackass *n* : asno *m*, burro *m*
jacket *n* **1** : chaqueta *f* **2** : sobrecubierta *f*
(de un libro), carátula *f* (de un disco)
jackhammer *n* : martillo *m* neumático
jackknife *n* : navaja *f* — **~** *vi* **-knifed; -knif-
ing** : plegarse (dícese de un camión)
jack-o'-lantern *n* : linterna *f* hecha de una
calabaza
jackpot *n* : premio *m* gordo
jaded *adj* **1** TIRED : agotado **2** BORED : has-
tiado
jagged *adj* : dentado
jail *n* : cárcel *f* — **~** *vt* : encarcelar — **jailer**
or **jailor** *n* : carcelero *m*, -ra *f*
jalapeño *n* : jalapeño *m Lat*
jam¹ *v* **jammed; jamming** *vt* **1** CRAM
: apiñar, embutir **2** BLOCK : atascar, atorar

— *vi* : atascarse, atrancarse — **~** *n* **1** *or*
traffic ~ : embotellamiento *m* (de tráfico)
2 FIX : lío *m*, aprieto *m*
jam² *n* PRESERVES : mermelada *f*
jangle *v* **-gled; -gling** *vi* : hacer un ruido
metálico — *vt* : hacer sonar — **~** *n* : ruido
m metálico
janitor *n* : portero *m*, -ra *f*; conserje *mf*
January *n* : enero *m*
Japanese *adj* : japonés — **~** *n* : japonés *m*
(idioma)
jar¹ *v* **jarred; jarring** *vi* **1** GRATE : chirriar **2**
CLASH : desentonar **3 ~ on** IRRITATE
: crispar, enervar (a algn) — *vt* JOLT
: sacudir — **~** *n* : sacudida *f*
jar² *n* : tarro *m*
jargon *n* : jerga *f*
jaundice *n* : ictericia *f*
jaunt *n* : excursión *f*
jaunty *adj* **-tier; -est** : garboso, desenvuelto
jaw *n* : mandíbula *f* (de una persona), quijada
f (de un animal) — **jawbone** *n* : mandíbula
f, quijada *f*
jay *n* : arrendajo *m*
jazz *n* : jazz *m* — **~** *vt or* **~ up** : animar,
alegrar — **jazzy** *adj* **jazzier; -est** FLASHY
: llamativo

jealous *adj* : celoso — **jealousy** *n* : celos *mpl*, envidia *f*

jeans *npl* : jeans *mpl*, vaqueros *mpl*

jeer *vt* **1** BOO : abuchear **2** MOCK : mofarse de — *vi* **at** : mofarse de — ~ *n* : mofa *f*

jell *vi* : cuajar

jelly *n, pl* **-lies** : jalea *f* — **jellyfish** *n* : medusa *f*

jeopardy *n* : peligro *m*, riesgo *m* — **jeopardize** *vt* **-dized; -dizing** : arriesgar, poner en peligro

jerk *n* **1** JOLT : sacudida *f* brusca **2** FOOL : idiota *mf* — ~ *vt* : sacudir — *vi* JOLT : dar sacudidas

jersey *n, pl* **-seys** : jersey *m*

jest *n* : broma *f* — ~ *vi* : bromear — **jester** *n* : bufón *m*

Jesus *n* : Jesús *m*

jet *n* **1** STREAM : chorro *m* **2** *or* ~ **airplane** : avión *m* a reacción, reactor *m* — **jet–propelled** *adj* : a reacción

jettison *vt* **1** : echar al mar **2** DISCARD : deshacerse de

jetty *n, pl* **-ties** : desembarcadero *m*, muelle *m*

jewel *n* **1** : joya *f* **2** GEM : piedra *f* preciosa — **jeweler** *or* **jeweller** *n* : joyero *m*, -ra *f* — **jewelry** *n* : joyas *fpl*, alhajas *fpl*

Jewish *adj* : judío

jibe *vi* **jibed; jibing** AGREE : concordar

jiffy *n, pl* **-fies** : santiamén *m*, segundo *m*

jig *n* : giga *f*

jiggle *vt* **-gled; -gling** : sacudir, zarandear — ~ *n* : sacudida *f*

jigsaw *n* **1** : sierra *f* de vaivén **2** *or* ~ **puzzle** : rompecabezas *m*

jilt *vt* : dejar plantado

jingle *v* **-gled; -gling** *vi* : tintinear — *vt* : hacer sonar — ~ *n* TINKLE : tintineo *m*

jinx *n* CURSE : maldición *f*

jitters *npl* **have the** ~ : estar nervioso — **jittery** *adj* : nervioso

job *n* **1** EMPLOYMENT : empleo *m*, trabajo *m* **2** TASK : trabajo *m*

jockey *n, pl* **-eys** : jockey *mf*

jog *v* **jogged; jogging** *vt* ~ **s.o.'s memory** : refrescar la memoria a algn — *vi* : hacer footing — **jogging** *n* : footing *m*

join *vt* **1** UNITE : unir, juntar **2** MEET : reunirse con **3** : hacerse socio de (una organización, etc.) — *vi* **1** *or* ~ **together** : unirse **2** : hacerse socio (de una organización, etc.)

joint *n* **1** : articulación *f* **2** JUNCTURE : juntura *f*, unión *f* — ~ *adj* : conjunto — **jointly** *adv* : conjuntamente

joke *n* : chiste *m*, broma *f* — ~ *vi* **joked; joking** : bromear — **joker** *n* **1** : bromista *mf* **2** : comodín *m* (en los naipes)

jolly *adj* **-lier; -est** : alegre, jovial

jolt *vt* : sacudir — ~ *n* **1** : sacudida *f* brusca **2** SHOCK : golpe *m* (emocional)

jostle *v* **-tled; -tling** *vt* : empujar, dar empujones — *vi* : empujarse

jot *vt* **jotted; jotting** *or* ~ **down** : anotar, apuntar

journal *n* **1** DIARY : diario *m* **2** PERIODICAL : revista *f* — **journalism** *n* : periodismo *m* — **journalist** *n* : periodista *mf*

journey *n, pl* **-neys** : viaje *m* — ~ *vi* **-neyed; -neying** : viajar

jovial *adj* : jovial

joy *n* : alegría *f* — **joyful** *adj* : alegre, feliz — **joyous** *adj* : jubiloso, alegre

jubilant *adj* : jubiloso — **jubilee** *n* : aniversario *m* especial

Judaism *n* : judaísmo *m*

judge *vt* **judged; judging** : juzgar — ~ *n* : juez *mf* — **judgment** *or* **judgement** *n* **1** RULING : fallo *m*, sentencia *f* **2** VIEW : juicio *m*

judicial *adj* : judicial — **judicious** *adj* : juicioso

jug *n* : jarra *f*

juggle *vi* **-gled; -gling** : hacer juegos malabares — **juggler** *n* : malabarista *mf*

jugular vein *n* : vena *f* yugular

juice *n* : jugo *m* — **juicy** *adj* **juicier; -est** : jugoso

jukebox *n* : máquina *f* de discos

July *n* : julio *m*

jumble *vt* **-bled; -bling** : mezclar — ~ *n* : revoltijo *m*

jumbo *adj* : gigante

jump *vi* **1** LEAP : saltar **2** START : sobresaltarse **3** RISE : subir de un golpe **4** ~ **at** : no dejar escapar (una oportunidad, etc.) — *vt* : saltar — ~ *n* **1** LEAP : salto *m* **2** INCREASE : aumento *m* — **jumper** *n* **1** : saltador *m*, -dora *f* (en deportes) **2** : jumper *m* (vestido) — **jumpy** *adj* **jumpier; -est** : nervioso

junction *n* **1** JOINING : unión *f* **2** : cruce *m* (de calles), empalme *m* (de un ferrocarril) — **juncture** *n* : coyuntura *f*

June *n* : junio *m*

jungle *n* : selva *f*

junior *adj* **1** YOUNGER : más joven **2** SUBORDINATE : subalterno — ~ *n* **1** : persona *f* de menor edad **2** SUBORDINATE : subalterno *m*, -na *f* **3** : estudiante *mf* de penúltimo año

junk *n* : trastos *mpl* (viejos) — ~ *vt* : echar a la basura

junta *n* : junta *f* (militar)

jurisdiction *n* : jurisdicción *f*

jury *n, pl* **-ries** : jurado *m* — **juror** *n* : jurado *mf*

just *adj* : justo — **~** *adv* **1** BARELY : apenas **2** EXACTLY : exactamente **3** ONLY : sólo, solamente **4 ~ now** : ahora mismo **5 she has ~ left** : acaba de salir **6 we were ~ leaving** : justo íbamos a salir

justice *n* **1** : justicia *f* **2** JUDGE : juez *mf*

justify *vt* **-fied; -fying** : justificar — **justification** *n* : justificación *f*

jut *vi* **jutted; jutting** *or* **~ out** : sobresalir

juvenile *adj* **1** YOUNG : juvenil **2** CHILDISH : infantil — **~** *n* : menor *mf*

juxtapose *vt* **-posed; -posing** : yuxtaponer

K

k *n, pl* **k's** *or* **ks** : k *f*, undécima letra del alfabeto inglés

kaleidoscope *n* : calidoscopio *m*

kangaroo *n, pl* **-roos** : canguro *m*

karat *n* : quilate *m*

karate *n* : karate *m*

keel *n* : quilla *f* — **~** *vi or* **~ over** : volcarse (dícese de un barco), desplomarse (dícese de una persona)

keen *adj* **1** SHARP : afilado **2** PENETRATING : cortante, penetrante **3** ENTHUSIASTIC : entusiasta **4 ~ eyesight** : visión *f* aguda

keep *v* **kept; keeping** *vt* **1** : guardar **2** : cumplir (una promesa), acudir a (una cita) **3** DETAIN : hacer quedar, detener **4** PREVENT : impedir **5 ~ up** : mantener — *vi* **1** REMAIN : mantenerse **2** LAST : conservarse **3** *or* **~ on** CONTINUE : no dejar — **~** *n* **1 earn one's ~** : ganarse el pan **2 for ~s** : para siempre — **keeper** *n* : guarda *mf* — **keeping** *n* **1** CARE : cuidado *m* **2 in ~ with** : de acuerdo con — **keepsake** *n* : recuerdo *m*

keg *n* : barril *m*

kennel *n* : caseta *f* para perros, perrera *f*

kept → **keep**

kerchief *n* : pañuelo *m*

kernel *n* **1** : almendra *f* **2** CORE : meollo *m*

kerosene *or* **kerosine** *n* : queroseno *m*

ketchup *n* : salsa *f* de tomate

kettle *n* : hervidor *m*, tetera *f* (para hervir)

key *n* **1** : llave *f* **2** : tecla *f* (de un piano o una máquina) — **~** *vt* **be keyed up** : estar nervioso — **~** *adj* : clave — **keyboard** *n* : teclado *m* — **keyhole** *n* : ojo *m* (de la cerradura) — **keynote** *n* : tónica *f* — **key ring** *n* : llavero *m*

khaki *adj* : caqui

kick *vt* **1** : dar una patada a **2 ~ out** : echar a patadas — *vi* **1** : dar patadas (dícese de una persona), cocear (dícese de un animal) **2** RECOIL : dar un culatazo — **~** *n* **1** : patada *f*, coz *f* (de un animal) **2** RECOIL : culatazo *m* **3** PLEASURE, THRILL : placer *m*

kid *n* **1** GOAT : chivo *m*, -va *f*; cabrito *m* **2** CHILD : niño *m*, -ña *f* — **~** *v* **kidded; kidding** *vi or* **~ around** : bromear — *vt* TEASE : tomar el pelo a — **kidnap** *vt* **-napped** *or* **-naped; -napping** *or* **-naping** : secuestrar, raptar

kidney *n, pl* **-neys** : riñón *m*

kidney bean *n* : frijol *m*

kill *vt* **1** : matar **2** DESTROY : acabar con **3 ~ time** : matar el tiempo — **~** *n* **1** KILLING : matanza *f* **2** PREY : presa *f* — **killer** *n* : asesino *m*, -na *f* — **killing** *n* **1** : matanza *f* **2** MURDER : asesinato *m*

kiln *n* : horno *m*

kilo *n, pl* **-los** : kilo *m* — **kilogram** *n* : kilogramo *m* — **kilometer** *n* : kilómetro *m* — **kilowatt** *n* : kilovatio *m*

kin *n* : parientes *mpl*

kind *n* : tipo *m*, clase *f* — **~** *adj* : amable

kindergarten *n* : jardín *m* infantil, jardín *m* de niños *Lat*

kindhearted *adj* : de buen corazón

kindle *vt* **-dled; -dling 1** : encender (un fuego) **2** AROUSE : despertar

kindly *adj* **-lier; -est** : bondadoso, amable — **~** *adv* **1** : amablemente **2 take ~ to** : aceptar de buena gana **3 we ~ ask you not smoke** : les rogamos que no fumen — **kindness** *n* : bondad *f* — **kind of** *adv* SOMEWHAT : un tanto, algo

kindred *adj* **1** : emparentado **2 ~ spirit** : alma *f* gemela

king *n* : rey *m* — **kingdom** *n* : reino *m*

kink *n* **1** TWIST : vuelta *f*, curva *f* **2** FLAW : problema *m*

kinship *n* : parentesco *m*

kiss *vt* : besar — *vi* : besarse — **~** *n* : beso *m*

kit *n* **1** : juego *m*, kit *m* **2 first–aid ~** : botiquín *m* **3 tool ~** : caja *f* de herramientas

kitchen *n* : cocina *f*

kite *n* : cometa *f*, papalote *m Lat*

kitten *n* : gatito *m*, -ta *f* — **kitty** *n, pl* **-ties** FUND : fondo *m* común

knack n : maña f, facilidad f
knapsack n : mochila f
knead vt **1** : amasar, sobar **2** MASSAGE : masajear
knee n : rodilla f — **kneecap** n : rótula f
kneel vi **knelt** or **kneeled; kneeling** : arrodillarse
knew → **know**
knickknack n : chuchería f
knife n, pl **knives** : cuchillo m — ~ vt **knifed; knifing** : acuchillar
knight n **1** : caballero m **2** : caballo m (en ajedrez) — **knighthood** n : título m de Sir
knit v **knit** or **knitted; knitting** v : tejer — ~ n : prenda f tejida
knob n : tirador m, botón m, perilla f Lat
knock vt **1** : golpear **2** CRITICIZE : criticar **3** ~ **down** : derribar, echar al suelo — vi **1** : dar un golpe, llamar (a la puerta) **2** COL-
LIDE : darse, chocar — ~ n : golpe m, llamada f (a la puerta)
knot n : nudo m — ~ vt **knotted; knotting** : anudar — **knotty** adj **-tier; -est 1** : nudoso **2** : enredado (dícese de un problema)
know v **knew; known; knowing** vt **1** : saber **2** : conocer (a una persona, un lugar) **3** ~ **how to** : saber — vi : saber — **knowing** adj : cómplice — **knowingly** adv **1** : de manera cómplice **2** DELIBERATELY : a sabiendas — **know–it–all** n : sabelotodo mf fam — **knowledge** n **1** : conocimiento m **2** LEARNING : conocimientos mpl, saber m — **knowledgeable** adj : informado, entendido
knuckle n : nudillo m
Koran n **the Koran** : el Corán m
Korean adj : coreano m, -na f — ~ n : coreano m (idioma)
kosher adj : aprobado por la ley judía

L

l n, pl **l's** or **ls** : l f, duodécima letra del alfabeto inglés
lab → **laboratory**
label n **1** TAG : etiqueta f **2** BRAND : marca f — ~ vt **-beled** or **-belled; -beling** or **-belling** : etiquetar
labor n **1** : trabajo m **2** WORKERS : mano f de obra **3 in** ~ : de parto — ~ vi **1** : trabajar **2** STRUGGLE : avanzar penosamente — vt BELABOR : insistir en (un punto)
laboratory n, pl **-ries** : laboratorio m
laborer n : trabajador m, -dora f
laborious adj : laborioso
lace n **1** : encaje m **2** SHOELACE : cordón m (de zapatos), agujeta f Lat — ~ vt **laced; lacing 1** TIE : atar **2 be laced with** : echar licor a (una bebida, etc.)
lacerate vt **-ated; -ating** : lacerar
lack vt : carecer de, no tener — vi **be lacking** : faltar — ~ n : falta f, carencia f
lackadaisical adj : apático, indolente
lackluster adj : sin brillo, apagado
laconic adj : lacónico
lacquer n : laca f
lacrosse n : lacrosse f
lacy adj **lacier; -est** : como de encaje
lad n : muchacho m, niño m
ladder n : escalera f
laden adj : cargado
ladle n : cucharón m — ~ vt **-dled; -dling** : servir con cucharón
lady n, pl **-dies** : señora f, dama f — **ladybug** n : mariquita f — **ladylike** adj : elegante, como señora
lag n **1** DELAY : retraso m **2** INTERVAL : intervalo m — ~ vi **lagged; lagging** : quedarse atrás, rezagarse
lager n : cerveza f rubia
lagoon n : laguna f
laid pp → **lay¹**
lain pp → **lie¹**
lair n : guarida f
lake n : lago m
lamb n : cordero m
lame adj **lamer; lamest 1** : cojo, renco **2 a** ~ **excuse** : una excusa poco convincente
lament vt **1** MOURN : llorar **2** DEPLORE : lamentar — ~ n : lamento m — **lamentable** adj : lamentable
laminate vt **-nated; -nating** : laminar
lamp n : lámpara f — **lamppost** n : farol m — **lampshade** n : pantalla f
lance n : lanza f — ~ vt **lanced; lancing** : abrir con lanceta (en medecina)
land n **1** : tierra f **2** COUNTRY : país m **3** or **plot of** ~ : terreno m — ~ vt **1** : desembarcar (pasajeros de un barco), hacer aterrizar (un avión) **2** CATCH : sacar (un pez) del agua **3** SECURE : conseguir (empleo, etc.) — vi **1** : aterrizar (dícese de un avión) **2** FALL : caer — **landing** n **1** : aterrizaje m (de aviones) **2** : desembarco m (de barcos)

3 : descanso *m* (de una escalera) — **land-lady** *n, pl* **-dies** : casera *f* — **landlord** *n* : casero *m* — **landmark** *n* **1** : punto *m* de referencia **2** MONUMENT : monumento *m* histórico — **landowner** *n* : hacendado *m*, -da *f;* terrateniente *mf* — **landscape** *n* : paisaje *m* — ~ *vt* **-scaped; -scaping** : ajardinar — **landslide** *n* **1** : desprendimiento *m* de tierras **2** *or* ~ **victory** : victoria *f* arrolladora

lane *n* **1** : carril *m* (de una carretera) **2** PATH, ROAD : camino *m*

language *n* **1** : idioma *m*, lengua *f* **2** SPEECH : lenguaje *m*

languid *adj* : lánguido — **languish** *vi* : languidecer

lanky *adj* **lankier; -est** : delgado, larguirucho *fam*

lantern *n* : linterna *f*

lap *n* **1** : regazo *m* (de una persona) **2** : vuelta *f* (en deportes) — ~ *v* **lapped; lapping** *vt or* ~ **up** : beber a lengüetadas — *vi* ~ **against** : lamer

lapel *n* : solapa *f*

lapse *n* **1** : lapsus *m*, falla *f* (de memoria, etc.) **2** INTERVAL : lapso *m*, intervalo *m* — ~ *vi* **lapsed; lapsing 1** EXPIRE : caducar **2** ELAPSE : transcurrir, pasar **3** ~ **into** : caer en

laptop *adj* : portátil

larceny *n, pl* **-nies** : robo *m*

lard *n* : manteca *f* de cerdo

large *adj* **larger; largest 1** : grande **2 at** ~ : en libertad **3 by and** ~ : por lo general — **largely** *adv* : en gran parte

lark *n* **1** : alondra *f* (pájaro) **2 for a** ~ : por divertirse

larva *n, pl* **-vae** : larva *f*

larynx *n, pl* **-rynges** *or* **-ynxes** : laringe *f* — **laryngitis** *n* : laringitis *f*

lasagna *n* : lasaña *f*

laser *n* : láser *m*

lash *vt* **1** WHIP : azotar **2** BIND : amarrar — *vi* ~ **out at** : arremeter contra — ~ *n* **1** BLOW : latigazo *m* (con un látigo) **2** EYELASH : pestaña *f*

lass *or* **lassie** *n* : muchacha *f*, chica *f*

lasso *n, pl* **-sos** *or* **-soes** : lazo *m*

last *vi* : durar — ~ *n* **1** : último *m*, -ma *f* **2 at** ~ : por fin, finalmente — ~ *adv* **1** : por última vez, en último lugar **2 arrive** ~ : llegar el último — ~ *adj* **1** : último **2** ~ **year** : el año pasado — **lastly** *adv* : por último, finalmente

latch *n* : picaporte *m*, pestillo *m*

late *adj* **later; latest 1** : tarde **2** : avanzado (dícese de la hora) **3** DECEASED : difunto **4** RECENT : reciente — ~ *adv* **later; latest** : tarde — **lately** *adv* : recientemente, últimamente — **lateness** *n* **1** : retraso *m* **2** : lo avanzado (de la hora)

latent *adj* : latente

lateral *adj* : lateral

latest *n* **at the** ~ : a más tardar

lathe *n* : torno *m*

lather *n* : espuma *f* — ~ *vt* : enjabonar — *vi* : hacer espuma

Latin–American *adj* : latinoamericano

latitude *n* : latitud *f*

latter *adj* **1** : último **2** SECOND : segundo — ~ *pron* **the** ~ : éste, ésta, éstos *pl*, éstas *pl*

lattice *n* : enrejado *m*

laugh *vi* : reír(se) — ~ *n* : risa *f* — **laughable** *adj* : risible, ridículo — **laughter** *n* : risa *f*, risas *fpl*

launch *vt* : lanzar — ~ *n* : lanzamiento *m*

launder *vt* **1** : lavar y planchar (ropa) **2** : blanquear, lavar (dinero) — **laundry** *n, pl* **-dries 1** : ropa *f* sucia **2** : lavandería *f* (servicio) **3 do the** ~ : lavar la ropa

lava *n* : lava *f*

lavatory *n, pl* **-ries** BATHROOM : baño *m*, cuarto *m* de baño

lavender *n* : lavanda *f*

lavish *adj* **1** EXTRAVAGANT : pródigo **2** ABUNDANT : abundante **3** LUXURIOUS : lujoso — ~ *vt* : prodigar

law *n* **1** : ley *f* **2** : derecho *m* (profesión, etc.) **3 practice** ~ : ejercer la abogacía — **lawful** *adj* : legal, legítimo

lawn *n* : césped *m* — **lawn mower** *n* : cortadora *f* de césped

lawsuit *n* : pleito *m*

lawyer *n* : abogado *m*, -da *f*

lax *adj* : poco estricto, relajado

laxative *n* : laxante *m*

lay[1] *vt* **laid; laying 1** PLACE, PUT : poner, colocar **2** ~ **eggs** : poner huevos **3** ~ **off** : dispedir (un empleado) **4** ~ **out** PRESENT : presentar, exponer **5** ~ **out** DESIGN : diseñar (el trazado de)

lay[2] *pp* → **lie**[1]

lay[3] *adj* **1** SECULAR : laico **2** NONPROFESSIONAL : lego, profano

layer *n* : capa *f*

layman *n, pl* **-men** : lego *m*, laico *m* (en religión)

layout *n* ARRANGEMENT : disposición *f*

lazy *adj* **-zier; -est** : perezoso — **laziness** *n* : pereza *f*

lead[1] *vt* **led; leading 1** GUIDE : conducir **2** DIRECT : dirigir **3** HEAD : encabezar, ir al frente de — *vi* : llevar, conducir (a algo) — ~ *n* **1** : delantera *f* **2 follow s.o.'s** ~ : seguir el ejemplo de algn

lead[2] *n* **1** : plomo *m* (metal) **2** GRAPHITE : mina *f* — **leaden** *adj* **1** : de plomo **2** HEAVY : pesado

leader *n* : jefe *m*, -fa *f* — **leadership** *n* : mando *m*, dirección *f*

leaf *n, pl* **leaves 1** : hoja *f* **2 turn over a new ~** : hacer borrón y cuenta nueva — **~** *vi* **~ through** : hojear (un libro, etc.) — **leaflet** *n* : folleto *m*

league *n* **1** : liga *f* **2 be in ~ with** : estar confabulado con

leak *vt* **1** : dejar escapar (un líquido o un gas) **2** : filtrar (información) — *vi* **1** : gotear, escaparse (dícese de un líquido o un gas) **2** : filtrarse (dícese de información) — **~** *n* **1** : agujero *m* (de un cubo, etc.), gotera *f* (de un techo) **2** : fuga *f*, escape *m* (de un líquido o un gas) **3** : filtración *f* (de información) — **leaky** *adj* **leakier; -est** : que hace agua

lean¹ *v* **leaned** *or Brit* **leant; leaning** *vi* **1** BEND : inclinarse **2 ~ against** : apoyarse contra — *vt* : apoyar

lean² *adj* **1** THIN : delgado **2** : sin grasa (dícese de la carne)

leaning *n* : inclinación *f*

leanness *n* : delgadez *f* (de una persona), lo magro (de la carne)

leap *vi* **leapt** *or* **leaped; leaping** : saltar, brincar — **~** *n* : salto *m*, brinco *m* — **leap year** *n* : año *m* bisiesto

learn *v* **learned; learning** : aprender — **learned** *adj* : sabio, erudito — **learner** *n* : principiante *mf*, estudiante *mf* — **learning** *n* : erudición *f*, saber *m*

lease *n* : contrato *m* de arrendamiento — **~** *vt* **leased; leasing** : arrendar

leash *n* : correa *f*

least *adj* **1** : menor **2** SLIGHTEST : más mínimo — **~** *n* **1 at ~** : por lo menos **2 the ~** : lo menos **3 to say the ~** : por no decir más — **~** *adv* : menos

leather *n* : cuero *m*

leave *v* **left; leaving** *vt* **1** : dejar **2** : salir(se) de (un lugar) **3 ~ out** : omitir — *vi* DEPART : irse — **~** *n* **1** *or* **~ of absence** : permiso *m*, licencia *f* **2 take one's ~** : despedirse

leaves → leaf

lecture *n* **1** TALK : conferencia *f* **2** REPRIMAND : sermón *m*, reprimenda *f* — **~** *v* **-tured; -turing** *vt* : sermonear — *vi* : dar clase, dar una conferencia

led *pp* **→ lead¹**

ledge *n* : antepecho *m* (de una ventana), saliente *m* (de una montaña)

leech *n* : sanguijuela *f*

leek *n* : puerro *m*

leer *vi* : lanzar una mirada lasciva — **~** *n* : mirada *f* lasciva

leery *adj* : receloso

leeway *n* : libertad *f* de acción, margen *m*

left¹ → leave

left² *adj* : izquierdo — **~** *adv* : a la izquierda — **~** *n* : izquierda *f* — **left–handed** *adj* : zurdo

leftovers *npl* : restos *mpl*, sobras *fpl*

leg *n* **1** : pierna *f* (de una persona, de ropa), pata *f* (de un animal, de muebles) **2** : etapa *f* (de un viaje)

legacy *n, pl* **-cies** : legado *m*

legal *adj* **1** LAWFUL : legítimo, legal **2** JUDICIAL : legal, jurídico — **legality** *n, pl* **-ties** : legalidad *f* — **legalize** *vt* **-ized; -izing** : legalizar

legend *n* : leyenda *f* — **legendary** *adj* : lengendario

legible *adj* : legible

legion *n* : legión *f*

legislate *vi* **-lated; -lating** : legislar — **legislation** *n* : legislación *f* — **legislative** *adj* : legislativo, legislador — **legislature** *n* : asamblea *f* legislativa

legitimate *adj* : legítimo — **legitimacy** *n* : legitimidad *f*

leisure *n* **1** : ocio *m*, tiempo *m* libre **2 at your ~** : cuando te venga bien — **leisurely** *adj & adv* : lento, sin prisas

lemon *n* : limón *m* — **lemonade** *n* : limonada *f*

lend *vt* **lent; lending** : prestar

length *n* **1** : largo *m* **2** DURATION : duración *f* **3 at ~** FINALLY : por fin **4 at ~** : EXTENSIVELY : extensamente **5 go to any ~s** : hacer todo lo posible — **lengthen** *vt* **1** : alargar **2** PROLONG : prolongar — *vi* : alargarse — **lengthways** *or* **lengthwise** *adv* : a lo largo — **lengthy** *adj* **lengthier; -est** : largo

lenient *adj* : indulgente — **leniency** *n, pl* **-cies** : indulgencia *f*

lens *n* **1** : cristalino *m* (del ojo) **2** : lente *mf* (de un instrumento) **3 → contact lens**

Lent *n* : Cuaresma *f*

lentil *n* : lenteja *f*

leopard *n* : leopardo *m*

leotard *n* : leotardo *m*, malla *f*

lesbian *n* : lesbiana *f*

less *adv* (*comparative of* **little**) : menos — **~** *adj* (*comparative of* **little**) : menos — **~** *pron* : menos — **~** *prep* MINUS : menos — **lessen** *v* : disminuir — **lesser** *adj* : menor

lesson *n* **1** CLASS : clase *f*, curso *m* **2 learn one's ~** : aprender la lección

lest *conj* **~ we forget** : para que no olvidemos

let *vt* **let; letting 1** ALLOW : dejar, permitir **2** RENT : alquilar **3 ~'s go!** : ¡vamos!, ¡vámonos! **4 ~ down** DISAPPOINT : fallar **5 ~ in** : dejar entrar **6 ~ off** FORGIVE : perdonar **7 ~ up** ABATE : amainar, disminuir

letdown *n* : chasco *m*, decepción *f*

lethal *adj* : letal

lethargic *adj* : letárgico

let's (*contraction of* **let us**) → **let**

letter *n* **1** : carta *f* **2** : letra *f* (del alfabeto)

lettuce *n* : lechuga *f*

letup *n* : pausa *f*, descanso *m*

leukemia *n* : leucemia *f*

level *n* **1** : nivel *m* **2 be on the ~** : ser honrado — **~** *vt* **-eled** *or* **-elled; -eling** *or* **-elling 1** : nivelar **2** AIM : apuntar **3** RAZE : arrasar — **~** *adj* **1** FLAT : llano, plano **2** : nivel (de altura) — **levelheaded** *adj* : sensato, equilibrado

lever *n* : palanca *f* — **leverage** *n* **1** : apalancamiento *m* (en física) **2** INFLUENCE : influencia *f*

levity *n* : ligereza *f*

levy *n, pl* **levies** : impuesto *m* — **~** *vt* **levied; levying** : imponer, exigir (un impuesto)

lewd *adj* : lascivo

lexicon *n, pl* **-ica** *or* **-icons** : léxico *m*, lexicón *m*

liable *adj* **1** : responsable **2** LIKELY : probable **3** SUSCEPTIBLE : propenso — **liability** *n, pl* **-ties 1** RESPONSIBILITY : responsabilidad *f* **2** DRAWBACK : desventaja *f* **3 liabilities** *npl* DEBTS : deudas *fpl*, pasivo *m*

liaison *n* **1** : enlace *m* **2** AFFAIR : amorío *m*

liar *n* : mentiroso *m*, -sa *f*

libel *n* : libelo *m*, difamación *f* — **~** *vt* **-beled** *or* **-belled; -beling** *or* **-belling** : difamar

liberal *adj* : liberal — **~** *n* : liberal *mf*

liberate *vt* **-ated; -ating** : liberar — **liberation** *n* : liberación *f*

liberty *n, pl* **-ties** : libertad *f*

library *n, pl* **-braries** : biblioteca *f* — **librarian** *n* : bibliotecario *m*, -ria *f*

lice → **louse**

license *or* **licence** *n* **1** PERMIT : licencia *f* **2** FREEDOM : libertad *f* **3** AUTHORIZATION : permiso *m* — **~** *vt* **licensed; licensing** : autorizar

lick *vt* **1** : lamer **2** DEFEAT : dar una paliza a *fam* — **~** *n* : lamida *f*

licorice *n* : regaliz *m*

lid *n* **1** : tapa *f* **2** EYELID : párpado *m*

lie¹ *vi* **lay; lain; lying 1** *or* **~ down** : acostarse, echarse **2** BE : estar, encontrarse

lie² *vi* **lied; lying** : mentir — **~** *n* : mentira *f*

lieutenant *n* : teniente *mf*

life *n, pl* **lives** : vida *f* — **lifeboat** *n* : bote *m* salvavidas — **lifeguard** *n* : socorrista *mf* — **lifeless** *adj* : sin vida — **lifelike** *adj* : natural, realista — **lifelong** *adj* : de toda la vida — **life preserver** *n* : salvavidas *m* — **lifestyle** *n* : estilo *m* de vida — **lifetime** *n* : vida *f*

lift *vt* **1** RAISE : levantar **2** STEAL : robar —

vi **1** CLEAR UP : despejarse **2** *or* **~ off** : despegar (dícese de un avión, etc.) — **~** *n* **1** LIFTING : levantamiento *m* **2 give s.o. a ~** : llevar en coche a algn — **liftoff** *n* : despegue *m*

light¹ *n* **1** : luz *f* **2** LAMP : lámpara *f* **3** HEADLIGHT : faro *m* **4 do you have a ~?** : ¿tienes fuego? — **~** *adj* **1** BRIGHT : bien iluminado **2** : claro (dícese de los colores), rubio (dícese del pelo) — **~** *v* **lit** *or* **lighted; lighting** *vt* **1** : encender (un fuego) **2** ILLUMINATE : iluminar — *vi or* **~ up** : iluminarse — **lightbulb** *n* : bombilla *f*, bombillo *m Lat* — **lighten** *vt* BRIGHTEN : iluminar — **lighter** *n* : encendedor *m* — **lighthouse** *n* : faro *m* — **lighting** *n* : alumbrado *m* — **lightning** *n* : relámpago *m*, rayo *m* — **light–year** *n* : año *m* luz

light² *adj* : ligero — **lighten** *vt* : aligerar — **lightly** *adv* **1** : suavemente **2 let off ~** : tratar con indulgencia — **lightness** *n* : ligereza *f* — **lightweight** *adj* : ligero

like¹ *v* **liked; liking** *vt* **1** : gustarle (a uno) **2** WANT : querer — *vi* **if you ~** : si quieres — **likes** *npl* : preferencias *fpl*, gustos *mpl* — **likable** *or* **likeable** *adj* : simpático

like² *adj* SIMILAR : parecido — **~** *prep* : como — **~** *conj* **1** AS : como **2** AS IF : como si — **likelihood** *n* : probabilidad *f* — **likely** *adj* **-lier; -est** : probable — **liken** *vt* : comparar — **likeness** *n* : semejanza *f*, parecido *m* — **likewise** *adv* **1** : lo mismo **2** ALSO : también

liking *n* : afición *f* (por una cosa), simpatía *f* (por una persona)

lilac *n* : lila *f*

lily *n, pl* **lilies** : lirio *m*, azucena *f* — **lily of the valley** *n* : lirio *m* de los valles

lima bean *n* : frijol *m* de media luna

limb *n* **1** : miembro *m* (en anatomía) **2** : rama *f* (de un árbol)

limber *vi or* **~ up** : calentarse, hacer ejercicios preliminares — **~** *adj* : ágil

limbo *n, pl* **-bos** : limbo *m*

lime *n* : lima *f*, limón *m* verde *Lat*

limelight *n* **be in the ~** : estar en el candelero

limerick *n* : poema *m* jocoso de cinco versos

limestone *n* : (piedra *f*) caliza *f*

limit *n* : límite *m* — **~** *vt* : limitar, restringir — **limitation** *n* : limitación *f*, restricción *f* — **limited** *adj* : limitado

limousine *n* : limusina *f*

limp¹ *vi* : cojear — **~** *n* : cojera *f*

limp² *adj* : flojo, fláccido

line *n* **1** : línea *f* **2** ROPE : cuerda *f* **3** ROW : fila *f* **4** QUEUE : cola *f* **5** WRINKLE : arruga *f* **6 drop a ~** : mándar unas líneas — **~** *v* **lined; lining** *vt* **1** : forrar (un vestido, etc.),

cubrir (las paredes, etc.) **2** MARK : rayar, trazar líneas en **3** BORDER : bordear — *vi* ~ **up** : ponerse en fila, hacer cola
lineage *n* : linaje *m*
linear *adj* : lineal
linen *n* : lino *m*
liner *n* **1** LINING : forro *m* **2** SHIP : buque *m*, transatlántico *m*
lineup *n* **1** *or* **police** ~ : fila *f* de sospechosos **2** : alineación *f* (en deportes)
linger *vi* **1** : quedarse, entretenerse **2** PERSIST : persistir
lingerie *n* : ropa *f* íntima femenina, lencería *f*
lingo *n, pl* **-goes** JARGON : jerga *f*
linguistics *n* : lingüística *f* — **linguist** *n* : lingüista *mf* — **linguistic** *adj* : lingüístico
lining *n* : forro *m*
link *n* **1** : eslabón *m* (de una cadena) **2** BOND : lazo *m* **3** CONNECTION : conexión *f* — ~ *vt* : enlazar, conectar — *vi* ~ **up** : unirse, conectar
linoleum *n* : linóleo *m*
lint *n* : pelusa *f*
lion *n* : león *m* — **lioness** *n* : leona *f*
lip *n* **1** : labio *m* **2** EDGE : borde *m* — **lipstick** *n* : lápiz *m* de labios
liqueur *n* : licor *m*
liquid *adj* : líquido — ~ *n* : líquido *m* — **liquidate** *vt* **-dated; -dating** : liquidar — **liquidation** *n* : liquidación *f*
liquor *n* : bebidas *fpl* alcohólicas
lisp *vi* : cecear — ~ *n* : ceceo *m*
list[1] *n* : lista *f* — ~ *vt* **1** ENUMERATE : hacer una lista de, enumerar **2** INCLUDE : incluir (en una lista)
list[2] *vi* : escorar (dícese de un barco)
listen *vi* **1** : escuchar **2** ~ **to** HEED : hacer caso de **3** ~ **to reason** : atender a razones — **listener** *n* : oyente *mf*
listless *adj* : apático
lit *pp* → **light**
litany *n, pl* **-nies** : letanía *f*
liter *n* : litro *m*
literacy *n* : alfabetismo *m*
literal *adj* : literal — **literally** *adv* : literalmente, al pie de la letra
literate *adj* : alfabetizado
literature *n* : literatura *f* — **literary** *adj* : literario
lithe *adj* : ágil y grácil
litigation *n* : litigio *m*
litre → **liter**
litter *n* **1** RUBBISH : basura *f* **2** : camada *f* (de animales) **3** *or* **kitty** ~ : arena *f* higiénica — ~ *vt* : tirar basura en, ensuciar — *vi* : tirar basura
little *adj* **littler** *or* **less** *or* **lesser; littlest** *or* **least 1** SMALL : pequeño **2 a** ~ SOME : un poco de **3 he speaks** ~ **English** : habla

poco inglés — ~ *adv* **less; least** : poco — ~ *pron* **1** : poco *m*, -ca *f* **2** ~ **by** ~ : poco a poco
liturgy *n, pl* **-gies** : liturgia *f* — **liturgical** *adj* : litúrgico
live *vi* **lived; living 1** : vivir **2** RESIDE : residir **3** ~ **on** : vivir de — *vt* : vivir, llevar (una vida) — ~ *adj* **1** : vivo **2** : con corriente (dícese de cables eléctricos) **3** : en vivo, en directo (dícese de programas de televisión, etc.) — **livelihood** *n* : sustento *m*, medio *m* de vida — **lively** *adj* **-lier; -est** : animado, alegre — **liven** *vt or* ~ **up** : animar — *vi* : animarse
liver *n* : hígado *m*
livestock *n* : ganado *m*
livid *adj* **1** : lívido **2** ENRAGED : furioso
living *adj* : vivo — ~ *n* **make a** ~ : ganarse la vida — **living room** *n* : living *m*, sala *f* (de estar)
lizard *n* : lagarto *m*
llama *n* : llama *f*
load *n* **1** CARGO : carga *f* **2** BURDEN : carga *f*, peso *m* **3** ~**s of** : un montón de — ~ *vt* : cargar
loaf[1] *n, pl* **loaves** : pan *m*, barra *f* (de pan)
loaf[2] *vi* : holgazanear — **loafer** *n* **1** : holgazán *m*, -zana *f* **2** : mocasín *m* (zapato)
loan *n* : préstamo *m* — ~ *vt* : prestar
loathe *vt* **loathed; loathing** : odiar — **loathsome** *adj* : odioso
lobby *n, pl* **-bies 1** : vestíbulo *m* **2** *or* **political** ~ : grupo *m* de presión, lobby *m* — ~ *v* **-bied; -bying** *vt* : ejercer presión sobre
lobe *n* : lóbulo *m*
lobster *n* : langosta *f*
local *adj* : local — ~ *n* **the** ~**s** : los vecinos del lugar — **locale** *n* : escenario *m* — **locality** *n, pl* **-ties** : localidad *f*
locate *vt* **-cated; -cating 1** SITUATE : situar, ubicar **2** FIND : localizar — **location** *n* : situación *f*, lugar *m*
lock[1] *n* : mechón *m* (de pelo)
lock[2] *n* **1** : cerradura *f* (de una puerta, etc.) **2** : esclusa *f* (de un canal) — ~ *vt* **1** : cerrar (con llave) **2** *or* ~ **up** CONFINE : encerrar — *vi* **1** : cerrarse con llave **2** : bloquearse (dícese de una rueda, etc.) — **locker** *n* : armario *m* — **locket** *n* : medallón *m* — **locksmith** *n* : cerrajero *m*, -ra *f*
locomotive *n* : locomotora *f*
locust *n* : langosta *f*, chapulín *m* Lat
lodge *v* **lodged; lodging** *vt* **1** HOUSE : hospedar, alojar **2** FILE : presentar — *vi* : hospedarse, alojarse — ~ *n* : pabellón *m* — **lodger** *n* : huésped *m*, -peda *f* — **lodging** *n* **1** : alojamiento *m* **2** ~**s** *npl* : habitaciones *fpl*

loft *n* **1** : desván *m* (en una casa) **2** HAYLOFT : pajar *m* — **lofty** *adj* **loftier; -est 1** : noble, elevado **2** HAUGHTY : altanero

log *n* **1** : tronco *m*, leño *m* **2** RECORD : diario *m* — ~ *vi* **logged; logging 1** : talar (árboles) **2** RECORD : registrar, anotar **3** ~ **on** : entrar (en el sistema) **4** ~ **off** : salir (del sistema) — **logger** *n* : leñador *m*, -dora *f*

logic *n* : lógica *f* — **logical** *adj* : lógico — **logistics** *ns & pl* : logística *f*

logo *n, pl* **logos** : logotipo *m*

loin *n* : lomo *m*

loiter *vi* : vagar, holgazanear

lollipop *or* **lollypop** *n* : pirulí *m*, chupete *m* *Lat*

lone *adj* : solitario — **loneliness** *n* : soledad *f* — **lonely** *adj* **-lier; -est** : solitario, solo — **loner** *n* : solitario *m*, -ria *f* — **lonesome** *adj* : solo, solitario

long¹ *adj* **longer; longest** : largo — ~ *adv* **1** : mucho tiempo **2 all day** ~ : todo el día **3 as** ~ **as** : mientras **4 no** ~**er** : ya no **5 so** ~**!** : ¡hasta luego!, ¡adiós! — ~ *n* **1 before** ~ : dentro de poco **2 the** ~ **and the short** : lo esencial

long² *vi* ~ **for** : anhelar, desear

longevity *n* : longevidad *f*

longing *n* : ansia *f*, anhelo *m*

longitude *n* : longitud *f*

look *vi* **1** : mirar **2** SEEM : parecer **3** ~ **after** : cuidar (de) **4** ~ **for** EXPECT : esperar **5** ~ **for** SEEK : buscar **6** ~ **into** : investigar **7** ~ **out** : tener cuidado **8** ~ **over** EXAMINE : revisar **9** ~ **up to** : respetar — *vt* : mirar — ~ *n* **1** : mirada *f* **2** APPEARANCE : aspecto *m*, aire *m* — **lookout** *n* **1** : puesto *m* de observación **2** WATCHMAN : vigía *mf* **3 be on the** ~ **for** : estar al acecho de

loom¹ *n* : telar *m*

loom² *vi* **1** APPEAR : aparecer, surgir **2** APPROACH : ser inminente

loop *n* : lazada *f*, lazo *m* — ~ *vt* : hacer lazadas con — **loophole** *n* : escapatoria *f*

loose *adj* **looser; -est 1** MOVABLE : flojo, suelto **2** SLACK : flojo **3** ROOMY : holgado **4** APPROXIMATE : libre, aproximado **5** FREE : suelto **6** IMMORAL : relajado — **loosely** *adv* **1** : sin apretar **2** ROUGHLY : aproximadamente — **loosen** *vt* : aflojar

loot *n* : botín *m* — ~ *vt* : saquear, robar — **looter** *n* : saqueador *m*, -dora *f* — **looting** *n* : saqueo *m*

lop *vt* **lopped; lopping** : cortar, podar

lopsided *adj* : torcido, chueco *Lat*

lord *n* **1** : señor *m*, noble *m* **2 the Lord** : el Señor

lore *n* : saber *m* popular, tradición *f*

lose *v* **lost; losing** *vt* **1** : perder **2** ~ **one's way** : perderse **3** ~ **time** : atrasarse (dícese de un reloj) — *vi* : perder — **loser** *n* : perdedor *m*, -dora *f* — **loss** *n* **1** : pérdida *f* **2** DEFEAT : derrota *f* **3 be at a** ~ **for words** : no encontrar palabras — **lost** *adj* **1** : perdido **2 get** ~ : perderse

lot *n* **1** FATE : suerte *f* **2** PLOT : solar *m* **3 a** ~ **of** *or* ~**s of** : mucho, un montón de

lotion *n* : loción *f*

lottery *n, pl* **-teries** : lotería *f*

loud *adj* **1** : alto, fuerte **2** NOISY : ruidoso **3** FLASHY : llamativo — ~ *adv* **1** : fuerte **2** out ~ : en voz alta — **loudly** *adv* : en voz alta — **loudspeaker** *n* : altavoz *m*

lounge *vi* **lounged; lounging 1** : repantigarse **2** *or* ~ **about** : holgazanear — ~ *n* : salón *m*

louse *n, pl* **lice** : piojo *m* — **lousy** *adj* **lousier; -est 1** : piojoso **2** BAD : pésimo, muy malo

love *n* **1** : amor *m* **2 fall in** ~ : enamorarse — ~ *v* **loved; loving** : querer, amar — **lovable** *adj* : adorable, amoroso *Lat* — **lovely** *adj* **-lier; -est** : lindo, precioso — **lover** *n* : amante *mf* — **loving** *adj* : cariñoso

low *adj* **lower; -est 1** : bajo **2** SCARCE : escaso **3** DEPRESSED : deprimido — ~ *adv* **1** : bajo **2 turn the lights down** ~ : bajar las luces — ~ *n* **1** : punto *m* bajo **2** *or* ~ **gear** : primera velocidad *f* — **lower** *adj* : inferior, más bajo — ~ *vt* : bajar — **lowly** *adj* **-lier; -est** : humilde

loyal *adj* : leal, fiel — **loyalty** *n, pl* **-ties** : lealtad *f*

lozenge *n* : pastilla *f*

lubricate *vt* **-cated; -cating** : lubricar — **lubricant** *n* : lubricante *m* — **lubrication** *n* : lubricación *f*

lucid *adj* : lúcido — **lucidity** *n* : lucidez *f*

luck *n* **1** : suerte *f* **2 good** ~**!** : ¡buena suerte! — **luckily** *adv* : afortunadamente — **lucky** *adj* **luckier; -est 1** : afortunado **2** ~ **charm** : amuleto *m* (de la suerte)

lucrative *adj* : lucrativo

ludicrous *adj* : ridículo, absurdo

lug *vt* **lugged; lugging** : arrastrar

luggage *n* : equipaje *m*

lukewarm *adj* : tibio

lull *vt* **1** CALM : calmar **2** ~ **to sleep** : adormecer — ~ *n* : período *m* de calma, pausa *f*

lullaby *n, pl* **-bies** : canción *f* de cuna, nana *f*

lumber *n* : madera *f* — **lumberjack** *n* : leñador *m*, -dora *f*

luminous *adj* : luminoso

lump *n* **1** CHUNK, PIECE : pedazo *m*, trozo *m* **2** SWELLING : bulto *m* **3** : grumo *m* (en un líquido) — ~ *vt* *or* ~ **together** : juntar, agrupar — **lumpy** *adj* **lumpier; -est** : grumoso (dícese de una salsa), lleno de bultos (dícese de un colchón)

lunacy *n, pl* **-cies** : locura *f*

lunar *adj* : lunar

lunatic *n* : loco *m*, -ca *f*

lunch *n* : almuerzo *m*, comida *f* — ∼ *vi* : almorzar, comer — **luncheon** *n* : comida *f*, almuerzo *m*

lung *n* : pulmón *m*

lunge *vi* **lunged; lunging 1** : lanzarse **2** ∼ **at** : arremeter contre

lurch¹ *vi* **1** STAGGER : tambalearse **2** : dar bandazos (dícese de un vehículo)

lurch² *n* **leave in a** ∼ : dejar en la estacada

lure *n* **1** BAIT : señuelo *m* **2** ATTRACTION : atractivo *m* — ∼ *vt* **lured; luring** : atraer

lurid *adj* **1** GRUESOME : espeluznante **2** SENSATIONAL : sensacionalista **3** GAUDY : chillón

lurk *vi* : estar al acecho

luscious *adj* : delicioso, exquisito

lush *adj* : exuberante, suntuoso

lust *n* **1** : lujuria *f* **2** CRAVING : ansia *f*, anhelo *m* — ∼ *vi* ∼ **after** : desear (a una persona), codiciar (riquezas, etc.)

luster *or* **lustre** *n* : lustre *m*

lusty *adj* **lustier; -est** : fuerte, vigoroso

luxurious *adj* : lujoso — **luxury** *n, pl* **-ries** : lujo *m*

lye *n* : lejía *f*

lying → **lie**

lynch *vt* : linchar

lynx *n* : lince *m*

lyric *or* **lyrical** *adj* : lírico — **lyrics** *npl* : letra *f* (de una canción)

M

m *n, pl* **m's** *or* **ms** : m *f*, decimotercera letra del alfabeto inglés

ma'am → **madam**

macabre *adj* : macabro

macaroni *n* : macarrones *mpl*

mace *n* **1** : maza *f* (arma o símbolo) **2** : macis *f* (especia)

machete *n* : machete *m*

machine *n* : máquina *f* — **machinery** *n, pl* **-eries 1** : maquinaria *f* **2** WORKS : mecanismo *m* — **machine gun** *n* : ametralladora *f*

mad *adj* **madder; maddest 1** INSANE : loco **2** FOOLISH : insensato **3** ANGRY : furioso

madam *n, pl* **mesdames** : señora *f*

madden *vt* : enfurecer

made → **make**

madly *adv* : como un loco, locamente — **madman** *n, pl* **-men** : loco *m* — **madness** *n* : locura *f*

Mafia *n* : Mafia *f*

magazine *n* **1** PERIODICAL : revista *f* **2** : recámara *f* (de un arma de fuego)

maggot *n* : gusano *m*

magic *n* : magia *f* — ∼ *or* **magical** *adj* : mágico — **magician** *n* : mago *m*, -ga *f*

magistrate *n* : magistrado *m*, -da *f*

magnanimous *adj* : magnánimo

magnate *n* : magnate *mf*

magnet *n* : imán *m* — **magnetic** *adj* : magnético — **magnetism** *n* : magnetismo *m* — **magnetize** *vt* **-tized; -tizing** : magnetizar

magnificent *adj* : magnífico — **magnificence** *n* : magnificencia *f*

magnify *vt* **-fied; -fying 1** ENLARGE : ampliar **2** EXAGGERATE : exagerar — **magnifying glass** *n* : lupa *f*

magnitude *n* : magnitud *f*

magnolia *n* : magnolia *f*

mahogany *n, pl* **-nies** : caoba *f*

maid *n* : sirvienta *f*, criada *f*, muchacha *f* — **maiden** *adj* FIRST : inaugural — **maiden name** *n* : nombre *m* de soltera

mail *n* **1** : correo *m* **2** LETTERS : correspondencia *f* — ∼ *vt* : enviar por correo — **mailbox** *n* : buzón *m* — **mailman** *n, pl* **-men** : cartero *m*

maim *vt* : mutilar

main *n* : tubería *f* principal (de agua o gas), cable *m* principal (de un circuito) — ∼ *adj* : principal — **mainframe** *n* : computadora *f* central — **mainland** *n* : continente *m* — **mainly** *adv* : principalmente — **mainstay** *n* : sostén *m* (principal) — **mainstream** *n* : corriente *f* principal — ∼ *adj* : dominante, convencional

maintain *vt* : mantener — **maintenance** *n* : mantenimiento *m*

maize *n* : maíz *m*

majestic *adj* : majestuoso — **majesty** *n, pl* **-ties** : majestad *f*

major *adj* **1** : muy importante, principal **2** : mayor (en música) — ∼ *n* **1** : mayor *mf*, comandante *mf* (en las fuerzas armadas) **2**

: especialidad *f* (universitaria) — ~ *vi* -jored; -joring : especializarse — **majority** *n, pl* -ties : mayoría *f*

make *v* **made; making** *vt* **1** : hacer **2** MANUFACTURE : fabricar **3** CONSTITUTE : constituir **4** PREPARE : preparar **5** RENDER : poner **6** COMPEL : obligar **7** ~ **a decision** : tomar una decisión **8** ~ **a living** : ganar la vida — *vi* **1** ~ **do** : arreglárselas **2** ~ **for** : dirigirse a **3** ~ **good** SUCCEED : tener éxito — ~ *n* BRAND : marca *f* — **make–believe** *n* : fantasía *f* — ~ *adj* : imaginario — **make out** *vt* **1** : hacer (un cheque, etc.) **2** DISCERN : distinguir **3** UNDERSTAND : comprender — *vi* **how did you** ~**?** : ¿qué tal te fue? — **maker** *n* MANUFACTURER : fabricante *mf* — **makeshift** *adj* : improvisado — **makeup** *n* **1** COMPOSITION : composición *f* **2** COSMETICS : maquillaje *m* — **make up** *vt* **1** PREPARE : preparar **2** INVENT : inventar **3** CONSTITUTE : formar — *vi* RECONCILE : hacer las paces

maladjusted *adj* : inadaptado

malaria *n* : malaria *f*, paludismo *m*

male *n* : macho *m* (de animales o plantas), varón *m* (de personas) — ~ *adj* **1** : macho **2** MASCULINE : masculino

malevolent *adj* : malévolo

malfunction *vi* : funcionar mal — ~ *n* : mal funcionamiento *m*

malice *n* : mala intención *f*, rencor *m* — **malicious** *adj* : malicioso

malign *adj* : maligno — ~ *vt* : calumniar

malignant *adj* : maligno

mall *n or* **shopping** ~ : centro *m* comercial

malleable *adj* : maleable

mallet *n* : mazo *m*

malnutrition *n* : desnutrición *f*

malpractice *n* : mala práctica *f*, negligencia *f*

malt *n* : malta *f*

mama *or* **mamma** *n* : mamá *f*

mammal *n* : mamífero *m*

mammogram *n* : mamografía *f*

mammoth *adj* : gigantesco

man *n, pl* **men** : hombre *m* — ~ *vt* **manned; manning** : tripular (un barco o avión), encargarse de (un servicio)

manage *v* -aged; -aging *vt* **1** HANDLE : manejar **2** DIRECT : administrar, dirigir — *vi* COPE : arreglárselas — **manageable** *adj* : manejable — **management** *n* : dirección *f* — **manager** *n* : director *m*, -tora *f*; gerente *mf* — **managerial** *adj* : administrativo

mandarin *n or* ~ **orange** : mandarina *f*

mandate *n* : mandato *m* — **mandatory** *adj* : obligatorio

mane *n* : crin *f* (de un caballo), melena *f* (de un león)

maneuver *n* : maniobra *f* — ~ *v* -vered; -vering : maniobrar

mangle *vt* -gled; -gling : destrozar

mango *n, pl* -goes : mango *m*

mangy *adj* **mangier; -est** : sarnoso

manhandle *vi* -dled; -dling : maltratar

manhole *n* : boca *f* de alcantarilla

manhood *n* **1** : madurez *f* (de un hombre) **2** VIRILITY : virilidad *f*

mania *n* : manía *f* — **maniac** *n* : maníaco *m*, -ca *f*

manicure *n* : manicura *f* — ~ *vt* -cured; -curing : hacer la manicura a

manifest *adj* : manifiesto, patente — ~ *vt* : manifestar — **manifesto** *n, pl* -tos *or* -toes : manifiesto *m*

manipulate *vt* -lated; -lating : manipular — **manipulation** *n* : manipulación *f*

mankind *n* : género *m* humano, humanidad *f*

manly *adj* -lier; -est : viril — **manliness** *n* : virilidad *f*

man–made *adj* : artificial

mannequin *n* : maniquí *m*

manner *n* **1** : manera *f* **2** KIND : clase *f* **3** ~**s** *npl* ETIQUETTE : modales *mpl*, educación *f* — **mannerism** *n* : peculiaridad *f* (de una persona)

manoeuvre *Brit* → **maneuver**

manor *n* : casa *f* solariega

manpower *n* : mano *f* de obra

mansion *n* : mansión *f*

manslaughter *n* : homicidio *m* sin premeditación

mantel *or* **mantelpiece** *n* : repisa *f* de la chimenea

manual *adj* : manual — ~ *n* : manual *m*

manufacture *n* : fabricación *f* — ~ *vt* -tured; -turing : fabricar — **manufacturer** *n* : fabricante *mf*

manure *n* : estiércol *m*

manuscript *n* : manuscrito *m*

many *adj* **more; most 1** : muchos **2 as** ~ : tantos **3 how** ~ : cuántos **4 too** ~ : demasiados — ~ *pron* : muchos *pl*, -chas *pl*

map *n* : mapa *m* — ~ *vt* **mapped; mapping 1** : trazar el mapa de **2** *or* ~ **out** : planear, proyectar

maple *n* : arce *m*

mar *vt* **marred; marring** : estropear

marathon *n* : maratón *m*

marble *n* **1** : mármol *m* **2** ~**s** *npl* : canicas *fpl* (para jugar)

march *n* : marcha *f* — ~ *vi* : marchar, desfilar

March *n* : marzo *m*

mare *n* : yegua *f*

margarine *n* : margarina *f*

margin *n* : margen *m* — **marginal** *adj* : marginal

marigold *n* : caléndula *f*

marijuana *n* : marihuana *f*

marinate *vt* **-nated; -nating** : marinar

marine *adj* : marino — $\sim$ *n* : soldado *m* de marina

marionette *n* : marioneta *f*

marital *adj* **1** : matrimonial **2** $\sim$ **status** : estado *m* civil

maritime *adj* : marítimo

mark *n* **1** : marca *f* **2** STAIN : mancha *f* **3** IMPRINT : huella *f* **4** TARGET : blanco *m* **5** GRADE : nota *f* — $\sim$ *vt* **1** : marcar **2** STAIN : manchar **3** POINT OUT : señalar **4** : calificar (un examen, etc.) **5** COMMEMORATE : conmemorar **6** CARACTERIZE : caracterizar **7** $\sim$ **off** : delimitar — **marked** *adj* : marcado, notable — **markedly** *adv* : notablemente — **marker** *n* : marcador *m*

market *n* : mercado *m* — $\sim$ *vt* : vender, comercializar — **marketable** *adj* : vendible — **marketplace** *n* : mercado *m*

marksman *n, pl* **-men** : tirador *m* — **marksmanship** *n* : puntería *f*

marmalade *n* : mermelada *f*

maroon[1] *vt* : abandonar, aislar

maroon[2] *n* : rojo *m* oscuro

marquee *n* CANOPY : marquesina *f*

marriage *n* **1** : matrimonio *m* **2** WEDDING : casamiento *m*, boda *f* — **married** *adj* **1** : casado **2 get** $\sim$: casarse

marrow *n* : médula *f*, tuétano *m*

marry *v* **-ried; -rying** *vt* **1** : casar **2** WED : casarse con — *vi* : casarse

Mars *n* : Marte *m*

marsh *n* **1** : pantano *m* **2** *or* **salt** $\sim$: marisma *f*

marshal *n* : mariscal *m* (en el ejército); jefe *m*, -fa *f* (de policía, de bomberos, etc.) — $\sim$ *vt* **-shaled** *or* **-shalled; -shaling** *or* **-shalling** : poner en orden (los pensamientos, etc.), reunir (las tropas)

marshmallow *n* : malvavisco *m*

marshy *adj* **marshier; -est** : pantanoso

mart *n* : mercado *m*

martial *adj* : marcial

martyr *n* : mártir *mf* — $\sim$ *vt* : martirizar

marvel *n* : maravilla *f* — $\sim$ *vi* **-veled** *or* **-velled; -veling** *or* **-velling** : maravillarse — **marvelous** *or* **marvellous** *adj* : maravilloso

mascara *n* : rímel *m*

mascot *n* : mascota *f*

masculine *adj* : masculino — **masculinity** *n* : masculinidad *f*

mash *vt* **1** CRUSH : aplastar, majar **2** PUREE : hacer puré de — **mashed potatoes** *npl* : puré *m* de patatas, puré *m* de papas *Lat*

mask *n* : máscara *f* — $\sim$ *vt* : enmascarar

masochism *n* : masoquismo *m* — **maso-chist** *n* : masoquista *mf* — **masochistic** *adj* : masoquista

mason *n* : albañil *mf* — **masonry** *n, pl* **-ries** : albañilería *f*

masquerade *n* : mascarada *f* — $\sim$ *vi* **-aded; -ading** $\sim$ **as** : disfrazarse de, hacerse pasar por

mass *n* **1** : masa *f* **2** MULTITUDE : cantidad *f* **3 the** $\sim$**es** : las masas

Mass *n* : misa *f*

massacre *n* : masacre *f* — $\sim$ *vt* **-cred; -cring** : masacrar

massage *n* : masaje *m* — $\sim$ *vt* **-saged; -saging** : dar masaje a, masajear — **masseur** *n* : masajista *m* — **masseuse** *n* : masajista *f*

massive *adj* **1** BULKY, SOLID : macizo **2** HUGE : enorme, masivo

mast *n* : mástil *m*

master *n* **1** : amo *m*, señor *m* (de la casa) **2** EXPERT : maestro *m*, -tra *f* **3** $\sim$**'s degree** : maestría *f* — $\sim$ *vt* : dominar — **masterful** *adj* : magistral — **masterpiece** *n* : obra *f* maestra — **mastery** *n* : maestría *f*

masturbate *v* **-bated; -bating** *vi* : masturbarse — **masturbation** *n* : masturbación *f*

mat *n* **1** DOORMAT : felpudo *m* **2** RUG : estera *f*

matador *n* : matador *m*

match *n* **1** EQUAL : igual *mf* **2** : fósforo *m*, cerilla *f* (para encender) **3** GAME : partido *m*, combate *m* (en boxeo) **4 be a good** $\sim$: hacer buena pareja — $\sim$ *vt* **1** *or* $\sim$ **up** : emparejar **2** EQUAL : igualar **3** : combinar con, hacer juego con (ropa, colores, etc.) — *vi* : concordar, coincidir

mate *n* **1** COMPANION : compañero *m*, -ra *f*; amigo *m*, -ga *f* **2** : macho *m*, hembra *f* (de animales) — $\sim$ *vi* **mated; mating** : aparearse

material *adj* **1** : material **2** IMPORTANT : importante — $\sim$ *n* **1** : material *m* **2** CLOTH : tela *f*, tejido *m* — **materialistic** *adj* : materialista — **materialize** *vi* **-ized; -izing** : aparecer

maternal *adj* : maternal — **maternity** *n, pl* **-ties** : maternidad *f* — $\sim$ *adj* **1** : de maternidad **2** $\sim$ **clothes** : ropa *f* de futura mamá

math → **mathematics**

mathematics *ns & pl* : matemáticas *fpl* — **mathematical** *adj* : matemático — **mathematician** *n* : matemático *m*, -ca *f*

matinee *or* **matinée** *n* : matiné(e) *f*, fонción *f* de tarde

matrimony *n* : matrimonio *m* — **matrimonial** *adj* : matrimonial

matrix *n, pl* **-trices** *or* **-trixes** : matriz *f*

matte *adj* : mate

matter *n* **1** SUBSTANCE : materia *f* **2** QUES-

TION : asunto *m*, cuestión *f* **3 as a ~ of fact** : en efecto, en realidad **4 for that ~** : de hecho **5 to make ~s worse** : para colmo de males **6 what's the ~?** : ¿qué pasa? — **~** *vi* : importar

mattress *n* : colchón *m*

mature *adj* **-turer; -est** : maduro — **~** *vi* **-tured; -turing** : madurar — **maturity** *n* : madurez *f*

maul *vt* : maltratar, aporrear

mauve *n* : malva *m*

maxim *n* : máxima *f*

maximum *n, pl* **-ma** *or* **-mums** : máximo *m* — **~** *adj* : máximo — **maximize** *vt* **-mized; -mizing** : llevar al máximo

may *v aux, past* **might;** *present s & pl* **may 1** : poder **2 come what ~** : pase lo que pase **3 it ~ happen** : puede pasar **4 ~ the best man win** : que gane el mejor

May *n* : mayo *m*

maybe *adv* : quizás, tal vez

mayhem *n* : alboroto *m*

mayonnaise *n* : mayonesa *f*

mayor *n* : alcalde *m*, -desa *f*

maze *n* : laberinto *m*

me *pron* **1** : me **2 for ~** : para mí **3 give it to ~!** : ¡dámelo! **4 it's ~** : soy yo **5 with ~** : conmigo

meadow *n* : prado *m*, pradera *f*

meager *or* **meagre** *adj* : escaso

meal *n* **1** : comida *f* **2** : harina *f* (de maíz, etc.) — **mealtime** *n* : hora *f* de comer

mean[1] *vt* **meant; meaning 1** SIGNIFY : querer decir **2** INTEND : querer, tener la intención de **3 be meant for** : estar destinado a **4 he didn't ~ it** : no lo dijo en serio

mean[2] *adj* **1** UNKIND : malo **2** STINGY : mezquino, tacaño **3** HUMBLE : humilde

mean[3] *adj* AVERAGE : medio — **~** *n* : promedio *m*

meander *vi* **-dered; -dering 1** WIND : serpentear **2** WANDER : vagar

meaning *n* : significado *m*, sentido *m* — **meaningful** *adj* : significativo — **meaningless** *adj* : sin sentido

meanness *n* **1** UNKINDNESS : maldad *f* **2** STINGINESS : mezquindad *f*

means *n* **1** : medio *m* **2 by all ~** : por supuesto **3 by ~ of** : por medio de **4 by no ~** : de ninguna manera

meantime *n* **1** : interín *m* **2 in the ~** : mientras tanto — **~** *adv* → **meanwhile**

meanwhile *adv* : mientras tanto — **~** *n* → **meantime**

measles *npl* : sarampión *m*

measly *adj* **-slier; -est** : miserable, mísero

measure *n* : medida *f* — **~** *v* **-sured; -suring** : medir — **measurable** *adj* : mensurable — **measurement** *n* : medida *f* — **measure up** *vi* **~ to** : estar a la altura de

meat *n* : carne *f* — **meatball** *n* : albóndiga *f* — **meaty** *adj* **meatier, -est 1** : carnoso **2** SUBSTANTIAL : sustancioso

mechanic *n* : mecánico *m*, -ca *f* — **mechanical** *adj* : mecánico — **mechanics** *ns & pl* **1** : mecánica *f* **2** WORKINGS : mecanismo *m* — **mechanism** *n* : mecanismo *m* — **mechanize** *vt* **-nized; -nizing** : mecanizar

medal *n* : medalla *f* — **medallion** *n* : medallón *m*

meddle *vi* **-dled; -dling** : entrometerse

media *or* **mass ~** *npl* : medios *mpl* de comunicación

median *adj* : medio

mediate *vi* **-ated; -ating** : mediar — **mediation** *n* : mediación *f* — **mediator** *n* : mediador *m*, -dora *f*

medical *adj* : médico — **medicated** *adj* : medicinal — **medication** *n* : medicamento *m* — **medicinal** *adj* : medicinal — **medicine** *n* **1** : medicina *f* **2** MEDICATION : medicina *f*, medicamento *m*

medieval *or* **mediaeval** *adj* : medieval

mediocre *adj* : mediocre — **mediocrity** *n, pl* **-ties** : mediocridad *f*

meditate *vi* **-tated; -tating** : meditar — **meditation** *n* : meditación *f*

medium *n, pl* **-diums** *or* **-dia 1** MEANS : medio *m* **2** MEAN : punto *m* medio, término *m* medio **3** → **media** — **~** *adj* : mediano

medley *n, pl* **-leys 1** : mezcla *f* **2** : popurrí *m* (de canciones)

meek *adj* : dócil

meet *v* **met; meeting** *vt* **1** ENCOUNTER : encontrarse con **2** SATISFY : satisfacer **3 pleased to ~ you** : encantado de conocerlo — *vi* **1** : encontrarse **2** ASSEMBLE : reunirse **3** BE INTRODUCED : conocerse — **~** *n* : encuentro *m* — **meeting** *n* : reunión *f*

megabyte *n* : megabyte *m*

megaphone *n* : megáfono *m*

melancholy *n, pl* **-cholies** : melancolía *f* — **~** *adj* : melancólico, triste

mellow *adj* **1** : suave, dulce **2** CALM : apacible **3** : maduro (dícese de frutas), añejo (dícese de vinos) — **~** *vt* : suavizar, endulzar — **~** *vi* : suavizarse

melody *n, pl* **-dies** : melodía *f*

melon *n* : melón *m*

melt *vi* : derretirse, fundirse — *vt* : derretir

member *n* : miembro *m* — **membership** *n* **1** : calidad *f* de miembro **2** MEMBERS : miembros *mpl*

membrane *n* : membrana *f*

memory *n, pl* **-ries 1** : memoria *f* **2** RECOLLECTION : recuerdo *m* — **memento** *n, pl* **-tos**

or **-toes** : recuerdo *m* — **memo** *n, pl* **memos**
or **memorandum** *n, pl* **-dums** *or* **-da** : memorándum *m* — **memoirs** *npl* : memorias *fpl*
— **memorable** *adj* : memorable — **memorial** *adj* : conmemorativo — **~** *n* : monumento *m* (conmemorativo) — **memorize** *vt*
-rized; -rizing : aprender de memoria

men → **man**

menace *n* : amenaza *f* — **~** *vt* **-aced; -acing**
: amenazar — **menacing** *adj* : amenazador

mend *vt* **1** : reparar, arreglar **2** DARN : zurcir — *vi* HEAL : curarse

menial *adj* : servil, bajo

meningitis *n, pl* **-gitides** : meningitis *f*

menopause *n* : menopausia *f*

menstruate *vi* **-ated; -ating** : menstruar — **menstruation** *n* : menstruación *f*

mental *adj* : mental — **mentality** *n, pl* **-ties**
: mentalidad *f*

mention *n* : mención *f* — **mention** *vt* **1**
: mencionar **2 don't ~ it!** : ¡de nada!, ¡no hay de qué!

menu *n* : menú *m*

meow *n* : maullido *m*, miau *m* — **~** *vi*
: maullar

mercenary *n, pl* **-naries** : mercenario *m*, -ria *f* — **~** *adj* : mercenario

merchant *n* : comerciante *mf* — **merchandise** *n* : mercancía *f*, mercadería *f*

merciful *adj* : misericordioso, compasivo — **merciless** *adj* : despiadado

mercury *n, pl* **-ries** : mercurio *m*

Mercury *n* : Mercurio *m*

mercy *n, pl* **-cies 1** : misericordia *f*, compasión *f* **2 at the ~ of** : a merced de

mere *adj, superlative* **merest** : mero, simple
— **merely** *adv* : simplemente

merge *v* **merged; merging** *vi* : unirse, fusionarse (dícese de las compañías), confluir
(dícese de los ríos, las calles, etc.) — *vt*
: unir, fusionar, combinar — **merger** *n*
: unión *f*, fusión *f*

merit *n* : mérito *m* — **~** *vt* : merecer

mermaid *n* : sirena *f*

merry *adj* **-rier; -est** : alegre — **merry–go-round** *n* : tiovivo *m*

mesa *n* : mesa *f*

mesh *n* : malla *f*

mesmerize *vt* **-ized; -izing** : hipnotizar

mess *n* **1** : desorden *m* **2** MUDDLE : lío *m* **3**
: rancho *m* (militar) — **~** *vt* **1** *or* **~ up**
SOIL : ensuciar **2 ~ up** DISARRANGE : desordenar **3 ~ up** BUNGLE : echar a perder
— *vi* **1 ~ around** PUTTER : entretenerse **2 ~ with** PROVOKE : meterse con

message *n* : mensaje *m* — **messenger** *n*
: mensajero *m*, -ra *f*

messy *adj* **messier; -est** : desordenado, sucio

met → **meet**

metabolism *n* : metabolismo *m*

metal *n* : metal *m* — **metallic** *adj* : metálico

metamorphosis *n, pl* **-phoses** : metamorfosis *f*

metaphor *n* : metáfora *f*

meteor *n* : meteoro *m* — **meteorological**
adj : meteorológico — **meteorologist** *n*
: meteorólogo *m*, -ga *f* — **meteorology** *n*
: meteorología *f*

meter *or Brit* **metre** *n* **1** : metro *m* **2** : contador *m* (de electricidad, etc.)

method *n* : método *m* — **methodical** *adj*
: metódico

meticulous *adj* : meticuloso

metric *or* **metrical** *adj* : métrico

metropolis *n* : metrópoli *f* — **metropolitan**
adj : metropolitano

Mexican *adj* : mexicano

mice → **mouse**

microbe *n* : microbio *m*

microfilm *n* : microfilm *m*

microphone *n* : micrófono *m*

microscope *n* : microscopio *m* — **microscopic** *adj* : microscópico

microwave *n or* **~ oven** : microondas *m*

mid *adj* **1 ~ morning** : a media mañana **2
in ~-August** : a mediados de agosto **3
she is in her mid thirties** : tiene alrededor
de 35 años — **midair** *n* **in ~** : en el aire —
midday *n* : mediodía *m*

middle *adj* : de en medio, del medio — **~** *n*
1 : medio *m*, centro *m* **2 in the ~ of** : en
medio de (un espacio), a mitad de (una actividad) **3 in the ~ of the month** : a mediados del mes — **middle–aged** *adj* : de
mediana edad — **Middle Ages** *npl* : Edad *f*
Media — **middle class** *n* : clase *f* media —
middleman *n, pl* **-men** : intermediario *m*,
-ria *f*

midget *n* : enano *m*, -na *f*

midnight *n* : medianoche *f*

midriff *n* : diafragma *m*

midst *n* **1 in the ~ of** : en medio de **2 in
our ~** : entre nosotros

midsummer *n* : pleno verano *m*

midway *adv* : a mitad de camino, a medio
camino

midwife *n, pl* **-wives** : comadrona *f*

midwinter *n* : pleno invierno *m*

miff *vt* : ofender

might¹ (*used to express permission or possibility or as a polite alternative to* **may**) →
may

might² *n* : fuerza *f*, poder *m* — **mighty** *adj*
mightier; -est 1 : fuerte, poderoso **2**
GREAT : enorme — **~** *adv* : muy

migraine *n* : jaqueca *f*, migraña *f*

migrate *vi* **-grated; -grating** : emigrar — **migrant** *n* : trabajador *m*, -dora *f* ambulante

mild *adj* **1** GENTLE : suave **2** LIGHT : leve **3 a ~ climate** : una clima templada

mildew *n* : moho *m*

mildly *adv* : ligeramente, suavemente — **mildness** *n* : apacibilidad *f* (de personas), suavedad *f* (de sabores, etc.)

mile *n* : milla *f* — **mileage** *n* : distancia *f* recorrida (en millas), kilometraje *m* — **milestone** *n* : hito *m*

military *adj* : militar — **~** *n* **the ~** : las fuerzas armadas — **militant** *adj* : militante — **~** *n* : militante *mf* — **militia** *n* : milicia *f*

milk *n* : leche *f* — **~** *vt* **1** : ordeñar (una vaca, etc.) **2** EXPLOIT : explotar — **milky** *adj* **milkier; -est** : lechoso — **Milky Way** *n* **the ~** : la Vía Láctea

mill *n* **1** : molino *m* **2** FACTORY : fábrica *f* **3** GRINDER : molinillo *m* — **~** *vt* : moler — *vi* **or ~ about** : arremolinarse

millennium *n, pl* **-nia** *or* **-niums** : milenio *m*

miller *n* : molinero *m*, -ra *f*

milligram *n* : miligramo *m* — **millimeter** *or Brit* **millimetre** *n* : milímetro *m*

million *n, pl* **millions** *or* **million 1** : millón *m* **2 a ~ people** : un millón de personas — **~** *adj* **a ~** : un millón de — **millionaire** *n* : millonario *m*, -ria *f* — **millionth** *adj* : millonésimo

mime *n* **1** : mimo *mf* **2** PANTOMIME : pantomima *f* — **~** *v* **mimed; miming** *vt* : imitar — *vi* : hacer la mímica — **mimic** *vt* **-icked; -icking** : imitar, remedar — **~** *n* : imitador *m*, -dora *f* — **mimicry** *n, pl* **-ries** : imitación *f*

mince *v* **minced; mincing** *vt* **1** : picar, moler **2 not to ~ one's words** : no tener pelos en la lengua

mind *n* **1** : mente *f* **2** INTELLECT : capacidad *f* intelectual **3** OPINION : opinión *f* **4** REASON : razón *f* **5 have a ~ to** : tener intención de — **~** *vt* **1** TEND : cuidar **2** OBEY : obedecer **3** WATCH : tener cuidado con **4 I don't ~ the heat** : no me molesta el calor — *vi* **1** OBEY : obedecer **2 I don't ~** : no me importa, me es igual — **mindful** *adj* : atento — **mindless** *adj* **1** SENSELESS : estúpido, sin sentido **2** DULL : aburrido

mine¹ *pron* **1** : (el) mío, (la) mía, (los) míos, (las) mías **2 a friend of ~** : un amigo mío

mine² *n* : mina *f* — **~** *vt* **mined; mining 1** : extraer (oro, etc.) **2** : minar (con artefactos explosivos) — **minefield** *n* : campo *m* de minas — **miner** *n* : minero *m*, -ra *f*

mineral *n* : mineral *m*

mingle *v* **-gled; -gling** *vt* : mezclar — *vi* **1** : mezclarse **2** : circular (a una fiesta, etc.)

miniature *n* : miniatura *f* — **~** *adj* : en miniatura

minimal *adj* : mínimo — **minimize** *vt* **-mized; -mizing** : minimizar — **minimum** *adj* : mínimo — **~** *n, pl* **-ma** *or* **-mums** : mínimo *m*

mining *n* : minería *f*

minister *n* **1** : pastor *m*, -tora *f* (de una iglesia) **2** : ministro *m*, -tra *f* (en política) — **~** *vi* **~ to** : cuidar (de), atender a — **ministerial** *adj* : ministerial — **ministry** *n, pl* **-tries** : ministerio *m*

mink *n, pl* **mink** *or* **minks** : visón *m*

minnow *n, pl* **-nows** : pececillo *m* de agua dulce

minor *adj* **1** : menor **2** INSIGNIFICANT : sin importancia — **~** *n* **1** : menor *mf* (de edad) **2** : asignatura *f* secundaria (de estudios) — **minority** *n, pl* **-ties** : minoría *f*

mint¹ *n* **1** : menta *f* (planta) **2** : pastilla *f* de menta (dulce)

mint² *n* **1 the U.S. Mint** : la casa de la moneda de los EE.UU. **2 be worth a ~** : valer un dineral — **~** *vt* : acuñar — **~** *adj* **in ~ condition** : como nuevo

minus *prep* **1** : menos **2** WITHOUT : sin — **~** *n or* **~ sign** : signo *m* de menos

minuscule *adj* : minúsculo

minute¹ *n* **1** : minuto *m* **2** MOMENT : momento *m* **3 ~s** *npl* : actas *fpl* (de una reunión)

minute² *adj* **-nuter; -est 1** TINY : diminuto, minúsculo **2** DETAILED : minucioso

miracle *n* : milagro *m* — **miraculous** *adj* : milagroso

mirage *n* : espejismo *m*

mire *n* : lodo *m*, fango *m*

mirror *n* : espejo *m* — **~** *vt* : reflejar

mirth *n* : alegría *f*, risas *fpl*

misapprehension *n* : malentendido *m*

misbehave *vi* **-haved; -having** : portarse mal — **misbehavior** *n* : mala conducta *f*

miscalculate *v* **-lated; -lating** : calcular mal

miscarriage *n* **1** : aborto *m* **2 ~ of justice** : error *m* judicial

miscellaneous *adj* : diverso, vario

mischief *n* : travesuras *fpl* — **mischievous** *adj* : travieso

misconception *n* : concepto *m* erróneo

misconduct *n* : mala conducta *f*

misdeed *n* : fechoría *f*

misdemeanor *n* : delito *m* menor

miser *n* : avaro *m*, -ra *f*; tacaño *m*, -ña *f*

miserable *adj* **1** UNHAPPY : triste **2** WRETCHED : miserable **3 ~ weather** : tiempo *m* malo

miserly *adj* : mezquino

misery *n, pl* **-eries 1** : sufrimiento *m* **2** WRETCHEDNESS : miseria *f*

misfire *vi* **-fired; -firing** : fallar
misfit *n* : inadaptado *m*, -da *f*
misfortune *n* : desgracia *f*
misgiving *n* : duda *f*
misguided *adj* : descaminado, equivocado
mishap *n* : contratiempo *m*
misinform *vt* : informar mal
misinterpret *vt* : interpretar mal
misjudge *vt* **-judged; -judging** : juzgar mal
mislay *vt* **-laid; -laying** : extraviar, perder
mislead *vt* **-led; -leading** : engañar — **misleading** *adj* : engañoso
misnomer *n* : nombre *m* inapropiado
misplace *vt* **-placed; -placing** : extraviar, perder
misprint *n* : errata *f*, error *m* de imprenta
miss *vt* **1** : errar, faltar **2** OVERLOOK : pasar por alto **3** : perder (una oportunidad, un vuelo, etc.) **4** AVOID : evitar **5** OMIT : saltarse **6 I ~ you** : te echo de menos — **~** *n* **1** : fallo *m* (de un tiro, etc.) **2** FAILURE : fracaso *m*
Miss *n* : señorita *f*
missile *n* **1** : misil *m* **2** PROJECTILE : proyectil *m*
missing *adj* : perdido, desaparecido
mission *n* : misión *f* — **missionary** *n, pl* **-aries** : misionero *m*, -ra *f*
misspell *vt* : escribir mal
mist *n* : neblina *f*, bruma *f*
mistake *vt* **mistook; mistaken; -taking 1** MISINTERPRET : entender mal **2** CONFUSE : confundir — **~** *n* **1** : error *m* **2 make a ~** : equivocarse — **mistaken** *adj* : equivocado
mister *n* : señor *m*
mistletoe *n* : muérdago *m*
mistreat *vt* : maltratar
mistress *n* **1** : dueña *f*, señora *f* (de una casa) **2** LOVER : amante *f*
mistrust *n* : desconfianza *f* — **~** *vt* : desconfiar de
misty *adj* **mistier; -est** : neblinoso, nebuloso
misunderstand *vt* **-stood; -standing** : entender mal — **misunderstanding** *n* : malentendido *m*
misuse *vt* **-used; -using 1** : emplear mal **2** MISTREAT : maltratar — **~** *n* : mal empleo *m*, abuso *m*
mitigate *vt* **-gated; -gating** : mitigar
mitt *n* : manopla *f*, guante *m* (de béisbol) — **mitten** *n* : manopla *f*, mitón *m*
mix *vt* **1** : mezclar **2 ~ up** : confundir — *vi* : mezclarse — **~** *n* : mezcla *f* — **mixture** *n* : mezcla *f* — **mix–up** *n* : confusión *f*, lío *m* *fam*
moan *n* : gemido *m* — **~** *vi* : gemir
mob *n* : muchedumbre *f* — **~** *vt* **mobbed; mobbing** : acosar
mobile *adj* : móvil — **~** *n* : móvil *m* — **mobile home** *n* : caravana *f* — **mobility** *n* : movilidad *f* — **mobilize** *vt* **-lized; -lizing** : movilizar
moccasin *n* : mocasín *m*
mock *vt* : burlarse de, mofarse de — **~** *adj* : falso — **mockery** *n, pl* **-eries** : burla *f* — **mock–up** *n* : maqueta *f*
mode *n* **1** : modo *m* **2** FASHION : moda *f*
model *n* **1** : modelo *m* **2** MOCK-UP : maqueta *f* **3** : modelo *mf* (persona) — **~** *v* **-eled** *or* **-elled; -eling** *or* **-elling** *vt* **1** SHAPE : modelar **2** WEAR : lucir — *vi* : trabajar de modelo — **~** *adj* : modelo
modem *n* : módem *m*
moderate *adj* : moderado — **~** *n* : moderado *m*, -da *f* — **~** *v* **-ated; -ating** *vt* : moderar — *vi* : moderarse — **moderation** *n* : moderación *f* — **moderator** *n* : moderador *m*, -dora *f*
modern *adj* : moderno — **modernize** *vt* **-ized; -izing** : modernizar
modest *adj* : modesto — **modesty** *n* : modestia *f*
modify *vt* **-fied; -fying** : modificar
moist *adj* : húmedo — **moisten** *vt* : humedecer — **moisture** *n* : humedad *f* — **moisturizer** *n* : crema *f* hidratante
molar *n* : muela *f*
molasses *n* : melaza *f*
mold¹ *n* FORM : molde *m* — **~** *vt* : moldear, formar
mold² *n* FUNGUS : moho *m* — **moldy** *adj* **moldier; -est** : mohoso
mole¹ *n* : lunar *m* (en la piel)
mole² *n* : topo *m* (animal)
molecule *n* : molécula *f*
molest *vt* **1** HARASS : importunar **2** : abusar (sexualmente)
molten *adj* : fundido
mom *n* : mamá *f*
moment *n* : momento *m* — **momentarily** *adv* **1** : momentáneamente **2** SOON : dentro de poco, pronto — **momentary** *adj* : momentáneo
momentous *adj* : muy importante
momentum *n, pl* **-ta** *or* **-tums 1** : momento *m* (en física) **2** IMPETUS : ímpetu *m*
monarch *n* : monarca *mf* — **monarchy** *n, pl* **-chies** : monarquía *f*
monastery *n, pl* **-teries** : monasterio *m*
Monday *n* : lunes *m*
money *n, pl* **-eys** *or* **-ies** : dinero *m* — **monetary** *adj* : monetario — **money order** *n* : giro *m* postal
mongrel *n* : perro *m* mestizo
monitor *n* : monitor *m* (de una computadora, etc.) — **~** *vt* : controlar
monk *n* : monje *m*

monkey *n, pl* **-keys** : mono *m*, -na *f* — **monkey wrench** *n* : llave *f* inglesa
monogram *n* : monograma *m*
monologue *n* : monólogo *m*
monopoly *n, pl* **-lies** : monopolio *m* — **monopolize** *vt* **-lized; -lizing** : monopolizar
monotonous *adj* : monótono — **monotony** *n* : monotonía *f*
monster *n* : monstruo *m* — **monstrosity** *n, pl* **-ties** : monstruosidad *f* — **monstrous** *adj* **1** : monstruoso **2** HUGE : gigantesco
month *n* : mes *m* — **monthly** *adv* : mensualmente — ∼ *adj* : mensual
monument *n* : monumento *m* — **monumental** *adj* : monumental
moo *vi* : mugir — ∼ *n* : mugido *m*
mood *n* : humor *m* — **moody** *adj* **moodier; -est** **1** GLOOMY : melancólico, deprimido **2** IRRITABLE : malhumorado **3** TEMPERAMENTAL : de humor variable
moon *n* : luna *f* — **moonlight** *n* : luz *f* de la luna
moor[1] *n* : brezal *m*, páramo *m*
moor[2] *vt* : amarrar — **mooring** *n* DOCK : atracadero *m*
moose *ns & pl* : alce *m*
moot *adj* : discutible
mop *n* **1** : trapeador *m Lat*, fregona *f Spain* **2** *or* ∼ **of hair** : pelambrera *f* — ∼ *vt* **mopped; mopping** : trapear *Lat*, pasar la fregona *a Spain*
mope *vi* **moped; moping** : andar deprimido
moped *n* : ciclomotor *m*
moral *adj* : moral — ∼ *n* **1** : moraleja *f* (de un cuento, etc.) **2** ∼**s** *npl* : moral *f*, moralidad *f* — **morale** *n* : moral *f* — **morality** *n, pl* **-ties** : moralidad *f*
morbid *adj* : morboso
more *adj* : más — ∼ *adv* **1** : más **2 ∼ and** ∼ : cada vez más **3 ∼ or less** : más o menos **4 once** ∼ : una vez más — ∼ *n* : más *m* — ∼ *pron* : más — **moreover** *adv* : además
morgue *n* : depósito *m* de cadáveres
morning *n* **1** : mañana *f* **2 good** ∼**!** : ¡buenos días! **3 in the** ∼ : por la mañana
moron *n* : estúpido *m*, -da *f*; imbécil *mf*
morose *adj* : malhumorado
morphine *n* : morfina *f*
morsel *n* **1** BITE : bocado *m* **2** FRAGMENT : pedazo *m*
mortal *adj* : mortal — ∼ *n* : mortal *mf* — **mortality** *n* : mortalidad *f*
mortar *n* : mortero *m*
mortgage *n* : hipoteca *f* — ∼ *vt* **-gaged; -gaging** : hipotecar
mortify *vt* **-fied; -fying** **1** : mortificar **2** HUMILIATE : avergonzar
mosaic *n* : mosaico *m*

Moslem → **Muslim**
mosque *n* : mezquita *f*
mosquito *n, pl* **-toes** : mosquito *m*, zancudo *m Lat*
moss *n* : musgo *m*
most *adj* **1** : la mayoría de, la mayor parte de **2 (the)** ∼ : más — ∼ *adv* : más — ∼ *n* : más *m*, máximo *m* — ∼ *pron* : la mayoría, la mayor parte — **mostly** *adv* **1** MAINLY : en su mayor parte, principalmente **2** USUALLY : normalmente
motel *n* : motel *m*
moth *n* : palomilla *f*, polilla *f*
mother *n* : madre *f* — ∼ *vt* **1** : cuidar de **2** SPOIL : mimar — **motherhood** *n* : maternidad *f* — **mother–in–law** *n, pl* **mothers–in–law** : suegra *f* — **motherly** *adj* : maternal — **mother–of–pearl** *n* : nácar *m*
motif *n* : motivo *m*
motion *n* **1** : movimiento *m* **2** PROPOSAL : moción *f* **3 set in** ∼ : poner en marcha — ∼ *vi* ∼ **to s.o.** : hacer una señal a algn — **motionless** *adj* : inmóvil — **motion picture** *n* : película *f*
motive *n* : motivo *m* — **motivate** *vt* **-vated; -vating** : motivar — **motivation** *n* : motivación *f*
motor *n* : motor *m* — **motorbike** *n* : motocicleta *f* (pequeña), moto *f* — **motorboat** *n* : lancha *f* motora — **motorcycle** *n* : motocicleta *f* — **motorcyclist** *n* : motociclista *mf* — **motorist** *n* : automovilista *mf*, motorista *mf Lat*
motto *n, pl* **-toes** : lema *m*
mould → **mold**
mound *n* **1** PILE : montón *m* **2** HILL : montículo *m*
mount[1] *n* **1** HORSE : montura *f* **2** SUPPORT : soporte *m* — ∼ *vt* : montar (un caballo, etc.), subir (una escalera) — *vi* INCREASE : aumentar
mount[2] *n* HILL : monte *m* — **mountain** *n* : montaña *f* — **mountainous** *adj* : montañoso
mourn *vt* : llorar (por) — *vi* : lamentarse — **mourner** *n* : doliente *mf* — **mournful** *adj* : triste — **mourning** *n* : luto *m*
mouse *n, pl* **mice** : ratón *m* — **mousetrap** *n* : ratonera *f*
moustache → **mustache**
mouth *n* : boca *f* (de una persona o un animal), desembocadura *f* (de un río) — **mouthful** *n* : bocado *m* — **mouthpiece** *n* : boquilla *f* (de un instrumento musical)
move *v* **moved; moving** *vi* **1** GO : ir **2** RELOCATE : mudarse **3** STIR : moverse **4** ACT : tomar medidas — *vt* **1** : mover **2** AFFECT : conmover **3** TRANSPORT : transportar,

traslador **4** PROPOSE : proponer — **∼** *n* **1**
MOVEMENT : movimiento *m* **2** RELOCATION
: mudanza *f* **3** STEP : medida *f* — **movable**
or **moveable** *adj* : movible, móvil —
movement *n* : movimiento *m*

movie *n* **1** : película *f* **2** **∼s** *npl* : cine *m*

mow *vt* **mowed; mowed** *or* **mown; mow-
ing** : cortar (la hierba) — **mower** → **lawn
mower**

Mr. *n, pl* **Messrs.** : señor *m*

Mrs. *n, pl* **Mesdames** : señora *f*

Ms. *n* : señora *f*, señorita *f*

much *adj* **more; most** : mucho — **∼** *adv*
more; most **1** : mucho **2 as ∼ as** : tanto
como **3 how ∼?** : ¿cuánto? **4 too ∼** : demasiado — **∼** *pron* : mucho, -cha

muck *n* **1** DIRT : mugre *f*, suciedad *f* **2** MA-
NURE : estiércol *m*

mucus *n* : mucosidad *f*

mud *n* : barro *m*, lodo *m*

muddle *v* **-dled; -dling** *vt* **1** CONFUSE : confundir **2** JUMBLE : desordenar — *vi* **∼**
through : arreglárselas — **∼** *n* : confusión
f, lío *m fam*

muddy *adj* **-dier; -est** : fangoso, lleno de
barro

muffin *n* : mollete *m*

muffle *vt* **-fled; -fling** : amortiguar (un
sonido) — **muffler** *n* **1** SCARF : bufanda *f* **2**
: silenciador *m*, mofle *m Lat* (de un automóvil)

mug *n* CUP : tazón *m* — **∼** *vt* : asaltar,
atracar — **mugger** *n* : atracador *m*, -dora *f*

muggy *adj* **-gier; -est** : bochornoso

mule *n* : mula *f*

mull *vt or* **∼ over** : reflexionar sobre

multicolored *adj* : multicolor

multimedia *adj* : multimedia

multinational *adj* : multinacional

multiple *adj* : múltiple — **∼** *n* : múltiplo *m*
— **multiplication** *n* : multiplicación *f* —
multiply *v* **-plied; -plying** *vt* : multiplicar —
vi : multiplicarse

multitude *n* : multitud *f*

mum *adj* **keep ∼** : guardar silencio

mumble *v* **-bled; -bling** *vt* : mascullar — *vi*
: hablar entre dientes

mummy *n, pl* **-mies** : momia *f*

mumps *ns & pl* : paperas *fpl*

munch *v* : mascar, masticar

mundane *adj* : rutinario, ordinario

municipal *adj* : municipal — **municipality**
n, pl **-ties** : municipio *m*

munitions *npl* : municiónes *fpl*

mural *n* : mural *m*

murder *n* : asesinato *m*, homicidio *m* — **∼**
vt : asesinar, matar — *vi* : matar — **murderer** *n* : asesino *m*, -na *f*; homicida *mf* —
murderous *adj* : asesino, homicida

murky *adj* **-kier; -est** : turbio, oscuro

murmur *n* : murmullo *m* — **murmur** *v* : mu-
murar

muscle *n* : músculo *m* — **∼** *vi* **-cled; -cling**
or **∼ in** : meterse por la fuerza en — **muscular** *adj* **1** : muscular **2** STRONG : musculoso

muse¹ *n* : musa *f*

muse² *vi* **mused; musing** : meditar

museum *n* : museo *m*

mushroom *n* **1** : hongo *m*, seta *f* **2**
: champiñón *m* (en la cocina) — **∼** *vi* GROW
: crecer rápidamente, multiplicarse

mushy *adj* **mushier; -est** **1** SOFT : blando **2**
MAWKISH : sensiblero

music *n* : música *f* — **musical** *adj* : musical
— **∼** *n* : comedia *f* musical — **musician** *n*
: músico *m*, -ca *f*

Muslim *adj* : musulmán — **∼** *n* : musulmán
m, -mana *f*

muslin *n* : muselina *f*

mussel *n* : mejillón *m*

must *v aux* **1** : deber, tener que **2 you ∼
come** : tienes que venir **3 you ∼ be tired**
: debes (de) estar cansado — **∼** *n* : necesidad *f*

mustache *n* : bigote *m*, bigotes *mpl*

mustang *n* : mustang *m*

mustard *n* : mostaza *f*

muster *vt* **1** : reunir **2** *or* **∼ up** : armarse
de, cobrar (valor, fuerzas, etc.)

musty *adj* **mustier; -est** : que huele a cerrado

mute *adj* **muter; mutest** : mudo — **∼** *n*
: mudo *m*, -da *f*

mutilate *vt* **-lated; -lating** : mutilar

mutiny *n, pl* **-nies** : motín *m* — **∼** *vi* **-nied;
-nying** : amotinarse

mutter *vi* : murmurar

mutton *n* : carne *f* de carnero

mutual *adj* **1** : mutuo **2** COMMON : común
— **mutually** *adv* : mutuamente

muzzle *n* **1** SNOUT : hocico *m* **2** : bozal *m*
(para un perro, etc.) **3** : boca *f* (de un arma
de fuego) — **∼** *vt* **-zled; -zling** : poner un
bozal a (un animal)

my *adj* : mi

myopia *n* : miopía *f* — **myopic** *adj* : miope

myself *pron* **1** (*reflexive*) : me **2** (*emphatic*)
: yo mismo **3 by ∼** : solo

mystery *n, pl* **-teries** : misterio *m* — **mysterious** *adj* : misterioso

mystic *adj or* **mystical** : místico

mystify *vt* **-fied; -fying** : dejar perplejo, confundir

mystique *n* : aura *f* de misterio

myth *n* : mito *m* — **mythical** *adj* : mítico

N

n *n*, *pl* **n's** *or* **ns** : n *f*, decimocuarta letra del alfabeto inglés

nab *vt* **nabbed; nabbing 1** ARREST : pescar *fam* **2** GRAB : agarrar

nag *v* **nagged; nagging** *vi* COMPLAIN : quejarse — *vt* **1** ANNOY : fastidiar, dar la lata a **2** SCOLD : regañar — **nagging** *adj* : persistente

nail *n* **1** : clavo *m* **2** : uña *f* (de un dedo) — ～ *vt or* ～ **down** : clavar — **nail file** *n* : lima *f* de uñas

naive *or* **naïve** *adj* **-iver; -est** : ingenuo — **naïveté** *n* : ingenuidad *f*

naked *adj* **1** : desnudo **2 the** ～ **truth** : la pura verdad **3 to the** ～ **eye** : a simple vista

name *n* **1** : nombre *m* **2** REPUTATION : fama *f* **3 what is your** ～? : ¿cómo se llama? **4** → **first name, surname** — ～ *vt* **named; naming 1** : poner nombre a **2** APPOINT : nombrar **3** ～ **a price** : fijar un precio — **nameless** *adj* : anónimo — **namely** *adv* : a saber — **namesake** *n* : tocayo *m*, -ya *f*

nap¹ *vi* **napped; napping** : echarse una siesta — ～ *n* : siesta *f*

nap² *n* : pelo *m* (de una tela)

nape *n or* ～ **of the neck** : nuca *f*

napkin *n* **1** : servilleta *f* **2** → **sanitary napkin**

narcotic *n* : narcótico *m*, estupefaciente *m*

narrate *vt* **-rated; -rating** : narrar — **narration** *n* : narración *f* — **narrative** *n* : narración *f* — **narrator** *n* : narrador *m*, -dora *f*

narrow *adj* **1** : estrecho, angosto **2** RESTRICTED : limitado — ～ *vi* : estrecharse — *vt* **1** : estrechar **2** *or* ～ **down** : limitar — **narrowly** *adv* : por poco — **narrow-minded** *adj* : de miras estrechas

nasal *adj* : nasal

nasty *adj* **-tier; -est 1** MEAN : malo, cruel **2** UNPLEASANT : desagradable **3** REPUGNANT : asqueroso — **nastiness** *n* : maldad *f*

nation *n* : nación *f* — **national** *adj* : nacional — **nationalism** *n* : nacionalismo *m* — **nationality** *n*, *pl* **-ties** : nacionalidad *f* — **nationalize** *vt* **-ized; -izing** : nacionalizar — **nationwide** *adj* : por todo el país

native *adj* **1** : natal (dícese de un país, etc.) **2** INNATE : innato **3** ～ **language** : lengua *f* materna — ～ *n* **1** : nativo *m*, -va *f* **2 be a** ～ **of** : ser natural de — **Native American** : indio *m* americano, india *f* americana — **nativity** *n*, *pl* **-ties the Nativity** : la Navidad

nature *n* **1** : naturaleza *f* **2** KIND : índole *f*,

clase *f* **3** DISPOSITION : carácter *m*, natural *m* — **natural** *adj* : natural — **naturalize** *vt* **-ized; -izing** : naturalizar — **naturally** *adv* : naturalmente

naught *n* **1** NOTHING : nada *f* **2** ZERO : cero *m*

naughty *adj* **-tier; -est 1** : travieso, pícaro **2** RISQUÉ : picante

nausea *n* : náuseas *fpl* — **nauseating** *adj* : nauseabundo — **nauseous** *adj* **1 feel** ～ : sentir náuseas **2** SICKENING : nauseabundo

nautical *adj* : náutico

naval *adj* : naval

nave *n* : nave *f* (de una iglesia)

navel *n* : ombligo *m*

navigate *v* **-gated; -gating** *vi* : navegar — *vt* **1** : gobernar (un barco), pilotar (un avión) **2** : navegar por (un río, etc.) — **navigable** *adj* : navegable — **navigation** *n* : navegación *f* — **navigator** *n* : navegante *mf*

navy *n*, *pl* **-vies 1** : marina *f* de guerra **2** *or* ～ **blue** : azul *m* marino

near *adv* : cerca — ～ *prep* : cerca de — ～ *adj* : cercano, próximo — ～ *vt* : acercarse a — **nearby** *adv* : cerca — ～ *adj* : cercano — **nearly** *adv* : casi — **nearsighted** *adj* : miope, corto de vista

neat *adj* **1** TIDY : muy arreglado **2** CLEVER : hábil, ingenioso — **neatly** *adv* **1** : ordenadamente **2** CLEVERLY : hábilmente — **neatness** *n* : pulcritud *f*, orden *m*

nebulous *adj* : nebuloso

necessary *adj* : necesario — **necessarily** *adv* : necesariamente — **necessitate** *vt* **-tated; -tating** : exigir, requerir — **necessity** *n*, *pl* **-ties 1** : necesidad *f* **2 necessities** *npl* : cosas *fpl* indispensables

neck *n* **1** : cuello *m* (de una persona o una botella), pescuezo *m* (de un animal) **2** COLLAR : cuello *m* — **necklace** *n* : collar *m* — **necktie** *n* : corbata *f*

nectar *n* : néctar *m*

nectarine *n* : nectarina *f*

need *n* **1** : necesidad *f* **2 if** ～ **be** : si hace falta — ～ *vt* **1** : necesitar, exigir **2** ～ **to** : tener que — *v aux* : tener que

needle *n* : aguja *f* — ～ *vt* **-dled; -dling** : pinchar

needless *adj* **1** : innecesario **2** ～ **to say** : de más está decir

needlework *n* : bordado *m*

needn't (*contraction of* **need not**) → **need**

needy needier; -est *adj* : necesitado

negative *adj* : negativo — ~ *n* **1** : negación *f* (en gramática) **2** : negativo *m* (en fotografía)

neglect *vt* : descuidar — ~ *n* : descuido *m*, abandono *m*

negligee *n* : negligé *m*

negligence *n* : negligencia *f*, descuido *m* — **negligent** *adj* : negligente, descuidado

negligible *adj* : insignificante

negotiate *v* **-ated; -ating** : negociar — **negotiable** *adj* : negociable — **negotiation** *n* : negociación *f* — **negotiator** *n* : negociador *m*, -dora *f*

Negro *n, pl* **-groes** *sometimes considered offensive* : negro *m*, -gra *f*

neigh *vi* : relinchar — ~ *n* : relincho *m*

neighbor *or Brit* **neighbour** *n* : vecino *m*, -na *f* — **neighborhood** *or Brit* **neighbourhood** *n* **1** : barrio *m*, vecindario *m* **2 in the ~ of** : alrededor de — **neighborly** *or Brit* **neighbourly** *adv* : amable

neither *conj* **1** ~**...nor** : ni...ni **2** ~ **am/do I** : yo tampoco — ~ *pron* : ninguno, -na — ~ *adj* : ninguno (de los dos)

neon *n* : neón *m*

nephew *n* : sobrino *m*

Neptune *n* : Neptuno *m*

nerve *n* **1** : nervio *m* **2** COURAGE : coraje *m* **3** GALL : descaro *m* **4** ~**s** *npl* JITTERS : nervios *mpl* — **nervous** *adj* : nervioso — **nervousness** *n* : nerviosismo *m* — **nervy** *adj* **nervier; -est** : descarado

nest *n* : nido *m* — ~ *vi* : anidar

nestle *vi* **-tled; -tling** : acurrucarse

net[1] *n* : red *f* — ~ *vt* **netted; netting** : pescar, atrapar (con una red)

net[2] *adj* : neto — ~ *vt* **netted; netting** YIELD : producir neto

nettle *n* : ortiga *f*

network *n* : red *f*

neurology *n* : neurología *f*

neurosis *n, pl* **-roses** : neurosis *f* — **neurotic** *adj* : neurótico

neuter *adj* : neutro — ~ *vt* : castrar

neutral *n* : punto *m* muerto (de un automóvil) — ~ *adj* **1** : neutral **2** : neutro (en electrotecnia o química) — **neutrality** *n* : neutralidad *f* — **neutralize** *vt* **-ized; -izing** : neutralizar

neutron *n* : neutrón *m*

never *adv* **1** : nunca, jamás **2** NOT : no **3** ~ **again** : nunca más **4** ~ **mind** : no importa — **nevermore** *adv* : nunca jamás — **nevertheless** *adv* : sin embargo, no obstante

new *adj* : nuevo — **newborn** *adj* : recién nacido — **newcomer** *n* : recién llegado *m*, -da *f* — **newly** *adv* : recién, recientemente — **newlywed** *n* : recién casado *m*, -da *f* — **news** *n* : noticias *fpl* — **newscast** *n* : noticiario *m*, noticiero *m* *Lat* — **newscaster** *n* : presentador *m*, -dora *f* (de un noticiario) — **newsletter** *n* : boletín *m* informativo — **newspaper** *n* : periódico *m*, diario *m* — **newsstand** *n* : puesto *m* de periódicos

newt *n* : tritón *m*

New Year's Day *n* : día *m* del Año Nuevo

next *adj* **1** : próximo **2** FOLLOWING : siguiente — ~ *adv* **1** : la próxima vez **2** AFTERWARD : después, luego **3** NOW : ahora — **next–door** *adj* : de al lado — **next to** *adv* ALMOST : casi — ~ *prep* BESIDE : al lado de

nib *n* : plumilla *f*

nibble *vt* **-bled; -bling** : mordisquear

Nicaraguan *adj* : nicaragüense

nice *adj* **nicer; nicest 1** PLEASANT : agradable, bueno **2** KIND : amable — **nicely** *adv* **1** WELL : bien **2** KINDLY : amablemente — **niceness** *n* : amabilidad *f* — **niceties** *npl* : detalles *mpl*, sutilezas *fpl*

niche *n* **1** : nicho *m* **2 find one's ~** : hacerse su hueco

nick *n* **1** : corte *m* pequeño, muesca *f* **2 in the ~ of time** : justo a tiempo — ~ *vt* : hacer una muesca en

nickel *n* **1** : níquel *m* (metal) **2** : moneda *f* de cinco centavos

nickname *n* : apodo *m*, sobrenombre *m* — ~ *vt* **-named; -naming** : apodar

nicotine *n* : nicotina *f*

niece *n* : sobrina *f*

niggling *adj* **1** PETTY : insignificante **2** PERSISTENT : constante

night *n* **1** : noche *f* **2 at ~** : de noche **3 last ~** : anoche **4 tomorrow ~** : mañana por la noche — **nightclub** *n* : club *m* nocturno — **nightfall** *n* : anochecer *m* — **nightgown** *n* : camisón *m* (de noche) — **nightly** *adj* : de todas las noches — ~ *adv* : cada noche — **nightmare** *n* : pesadilla *f* — **nighttime** *n* : noche *f*

nil *n* NOTHING : nada *f*

nimble *adj* **-bler; -blest** : ágil

nine *adj* : nueve — ~ *n* : nueve *m* — **nine hundred** *adj* : novecientos — ~ *n* : novecientos *m* — **nineteen** *adj* : diecinueve — ~ *n* : diecinueve *m* — **nineteenth** *adj* : decimonoveno, decimonono — ~ *n* **1** : decimonoveno *m*, -na *f*; decimonono *m*, -na *f* (en una serie) **2** : diecinueveavo *m* (en matemáticas) — **ninetieth** *adj* : nonagésimo — ~ *n* **1** : nonagésimo *m*, -ma *f* (en una serie) **2** : noventavo *m* (en matemáticas) — **ninety** *adj* : noventa — ~ *n, pl* **-ties** : noventa *m* — **ninth** *adj* : noveno — ~ *n* **1** : noveno *m*, -na *f* (en una serie) **2** : noveno *m* (en matemáticas)

nip *vt* **nipped; nipping 1** PINCH : pellizcar **2** BITE : mordisquear **3 ~ in the bud** : cortar de raíz — *~ n* **1** PINCH : pellizco *m* **2** NIBBLE : mordisco *m*

nipple *n* **1** : pezón *m* (de una mujer) **2** : tetilla *f* (de un hombre o un biberón)

nitrogen *n* : nitrógeno *m*

nitwit *n* : idiota *mf*

no *adv* : no — *~ adj* **1** : ninguno **2 I have ~ money** : no tengo dinero **3 it's ~ trouble** : no es ningún problema **4 ~ smoking** : prohibido fumar — *~ n, pl* **noes** *or* **nos** : no *m*

noble *adj* **-bler; -blest** : noble — *~ n* : noble *mf* — **nobility** *n* : nobleza *f*

nobody *pron* : nadie

nocturnal *adj* : nocturno

nod *v* **nodded; nodding** *vi* **1** *or* **~ yes** : asentir con la cabeza **2 ~ off** : dormirse — *vt* **~ one's head** : asentir con la cabeza — *~ n* : señal *m* con la cabeza

noes → **no**

noise *n* : ruido *m* — **noisily** *adv* : ruidosamente — **noisy** *adj* **noisier; -est** : ruidoso

nomad *n* : nómada *mf* — **nomadic** *adj* : nómada

nominal *adj* : nominal

nominate *vt* **-nated; -nating 1** : proponer, postular *Lat* **2** APPOINT : nombrar — **nomination** *n* **1** : propuesta *f*, postulación *f Lat* **2** APPOINTMENT : nombramiento *m*

nonalcoholic *adj* : no alcohólico

nonchalant *adj* : despreocupado

noncommissioned officer *n* : suboficial *mf*

noncommittal *adj* : evasivo

nondescript *adj* : anodino, soso

none *pron* **1** : ninguno, ninguna **2 there are ~ left** : no hay más — *~ adv* **1 be ~ the worse** : no sufrir daño alguno **2 ~ too happy** : nada contento **3 ~ too soon** : a buena hora

nonentity *n, pl* **-ties** : persona *f* insignificante

nonetheless *adv* : sin embargo, no obstante

nonexistent *adj* : inexistente

nonfat *adj* : sin grasa

nonfiction *n* : no ficción *f*

nonprofit *adj* : sin fines lucrativos

nonsense *n* : tonterías *fpl*, disparates *mpl* — **nonsensical** *adj* : absurdo

nonsmoker *n* : no fumador *m*, -dora *f*

nonstop *adj* : directo — *~ adv* : sin parar

noodle *n* : fideo *m*

nook *n* : rincón *m*

noon *n* : mediodía *m*

no one *pron* : nadie

noose *n* **1** : dogal *m*, soga *f* **2** LASSO : lazo *m*

nor *conj* **1 neither...~** : ni...ni **2 ~ I** : yo tampoco

norm *n* **1** : norma *f* **2 the ~** : lo normal — **normal** *adj* : normal — **normality** *n* : normalidad *f* — **normally** *adv* : normalmente

north *adv* : al norte — *~ adj* : norte, del norte — *~ n* **1** : norte *m* **2 the North** : el Norte — **North American** *adj* : norteamericano — **northeast** *adv* : hacia el nordeste — *~ adj* : nordeste, del nordeste — *~ n* : nordeste *m*, noreste *m* — **northeastern** *adj* : nordeste, del nordeste — **northerly** *adj* : del norte — **northern** *adj* : del norte, norteño — **northwest** *adv* : hacia el noroeste — *~ adj* : noroeste, del noroeste — *~ n* : noroeste *m* — **northwestern** *adj* : noroeste, del noroeste

Norwegian *adj* : noruego

nose *n* : nariz *f* (de una persona), hocico *m* (de un animal) **2 blow one's ~** : sonarse las narices — *~ vi* **nosed; nosing** *or* **~ around** : meter las narices — **nosebleed** *n* : hemorragia *f* nasal — **nosedive** *n* : descenso *m* en picada

nostalgia *n* : nostalgia *f* — **nostalgic** *adj* : nostálgico

nostril *n* : ventana *f* de la nariz

nosy *or* **nosey** *adj* **nosier; -est** : entrometido

not *adv* **1** : no **2 he's ~ tired** : no esta cansado **3 I hope ~** : espero que no **4 ~ ... anything** : no...nada

notable *adj* : notable — *~ n* : personaje *m* — **notably** *adv* : notablemente

notary public *n, pl* **notaries public** *or* **notary publics** : notario *m*, -ria *f*

notation *n* : anotación *f*

notch *n* : muesca *f*, corte *m* — *~ vt* : hacer un corte en

note *vt* **noted; noting 1** NOTICE : observar, notar **2** RECORD : anotar — *~ n* **1** : nota *f* **2 of ~** : destacado **3 take ~ of** : prestar atención a **4 take ~s** : apuntar — **notebook** *n* : libreta *f*, cuaderno *m* — **noted** *adj* : renombrado, célebre — **noteworthy** *adj* : notable

nothing *pron* **1** : nada **2 be ~ but** : no ser más que **3 for ~** FREE : gratis — *~ n* **1** ZERO : zero *m* **2** TRIFLE : nimiedad *f*

notice *n* **1** SIGN : letrero *m*, aviso *m* **2 at a moment's ~** : sin previo aviso **3 be given one's ~** : ser despedido **4 take ~ of** : prestar atención a — *~ vt* **-ticed; -ticing** : notar — **noticeable** *adj* : perceptible, evidente

notify *vt* **-fied; -fying** : notificar, avisar — **notification** *n* : notificación *f*, aviso *m*

notion *n* **1** : noción *f*, idea *f* **2 ~s** *npl* : artículos *mpl* de mercería

notorious *adj* : de mala fama — **notoriety** *n* : mala fama *f*, notoriedad *f*

notwithstanding *prep* : a pesar de, no obstante — ~ *adv* : sin embargo — ~ *conj* : a pesar de que

nougat *n* : turrón *m*

nought → **naught**

noun *n* : nombre *m*, sustantivo *m*

nourish *vt* : nutrir — **nourishing** *adj* : nutritivo — **nourishment** *n* : alimento *m*

novel *adj* : original, novedoso — ~ *n* : novela *f* — **novelist** *n* : novelista *mf* — **novelty** *n*, *pl* **-ties** : novedad *f*

November *n* : noviembre *m*

novice *n* : novato *m*, -ta *f*; principiante *mf*

now *adv* **1** : ahora **2** THEN : entonces **3 from ~ on** : de ahora en adelante **4 ~ and then** : de vez en cuando **5 right ~** : ahora mismo — ~ *conj or* **~ that** : ahora que, ya que — ~ *n* **1 a year from ~** : dentro de un año **2 by ~** : ya **3 until ~** : hasta ahora —

nowadays *adv* : hoy en día

nowhere *adv* **1** (*indicating location*) : por ninguna parte, por ningún lado **2** (*indicating motion*) : a ninguna parte, a ningún lado **3 I'm ~ near finished** : aún me falta mucho para terminar **4 it's ~ near here** : queda bastante lejos de aquí — ~ *n* : ninguna parte *f*

nozzle *n* : boca *f* (de una manguera, etc.)

nuance *n* : matiz *m*

nucleus *n*, *pl* **-clei** : núcleo *m* — **nuclear** *adj* : nuclear

nude *adj* **nuder; nudest** : desnudo — ~ *n* : desnudo *m*

nudge *vt* **nudged; nudging** : dar un codazo a — ~ *n* : toque *m* (con el codo)

nudity *n* : desnudez *f*

nugget *n* : pepita *f* (de oro, etc.)

nuisance *n* **1** ANNOYANCE : fastidio *m*, molestia *f* **2** PEST : pesado *m*, -da *f fam*

null *adj* **~ and void** : nulo y sin efecto

numb *adj* **1** : entumecido, dormido **2 ~ with fear** : paralizado de miedo — ~ *vt* : entumecer, adormecer

number *n* **1** : número *m* **2 a ~ of** : varios — ~ *vt* **1** : numerar **2** INCLUDE : contar, incluir **3** TOTAL : ascender a

numeral *n* : número *m* — **numeric** *or* **numerical** *adj* : numérico — **numerous** *adj* : numeroso

nun *n* : monja *f*

nuptial *adj* : nupcial

nurse *n* **1** : enfermero *m*, -ra *f* **2** → **nursemaid** — ~ *vt* **nursed; nursing 1** : cuidar (de), atender **2** SUCKLE : amamantar — **nursemaid** *n* : niñera *f* — **nursery** *n*, *pl* **-eries 1** : cuarto *m* de los niños **2** *or* **day ~** : guardería *f* **3** : vivero *m* (de plantas) — **nursing home** *n* : asilo *m* de ancianos

nurture *vt* **-tured; -turing 1** NOURISH : nutrir **2** EDUCATE : criar, educar **3** FOSTER : alimentar

nut *n* **1** : nuez *f* **2** LUNATIC : loco *m*, -ca *f* **3** ENTHUSIAST : fanático *m*, -ca *f* **4 ~s and bolts** : tuercas y tornillos — **nutcracker** *n* : cascanueces *m*

nutmeg *n* : nuez *f* moscada

nutrient *n* : nutriente *m*

nutrition *n* : nutrición *f* — **nutritional** *adj* : nutritivo — **nutritious** *adj* : nutritivo

nuts *adj* : loco

nutshell *n* **1** : cáscara *f* de nuez **2 in a ~** : en pocas palabras

nutty *adj* **-tier; -tiest** : loco

nuzzle *v* **-zled; -zling** *vi* **~ to** : acurrucarse — *vt* : acariciar con el hocico

nylon *n* **1** : nilón *m* **2 ~s** *npl* : medias *fpl* de nilón

nymph *n* : ninfa *f*

O

o *n*, *pl* **o's** *or* **os 1** : o *f*, decimoquinta letra del alfabeto inglés **2** ZERO : cero *m*

O → **oh**

oaf *n* : zoquete *m*

oak *n*, *pl* **oaks** *or* **oak** : roble *m*

oar *n* : remo *m*

oasis *n*, *pl* **oases** : oasis *m*

oath *n*, *pl* **oaths 1** : juramento *m* **2** SWEARWORD : palabrota *f*

oats *npl* : avena *f* — **oatmeal** *n* : harina *f* de avena

obedient *adj* : obediente — **obedience** *n* : obediencia *f*

obese *adj* : obeso — **obesity** *n* : obesidad *f*

obey *v* **obeyed; obeying** : obedecer

obituary *n*, *pl* **-aries** : obituario *m*

object *n* **1** : objeto *m* **2** AIM : objetivo *m* **3** : complemento *m* (en gramática) — ~ *vt* : objetar — *vi* **~ to** : oponerse a — **objection** *n* : objeción *f* — **objectionable** *adj* : desagradable — **objective** *adj* : objetivo — ~ *n* : objetivo *m*

oblige *vt* **obliged; obliging 1** : obligar **2 be much ~d** : estar muy agradecido **3 ~ s.o.** : hacer un favor a algn — **obligation** *n* : obligación *f* — **obligatory** *adj* : obligatorio — **obliging** *adj* : atento, servicial

oblique *adj* **1** SLANTING : oblicuo **2** INDIRECT : indirecto

obliterate *vt* **-ated; -ating 1** ERASE : borrar **2** DESTROY : arrasar

oblivion *n* : olvido *m* — **oblivious** *adj* : inconsciente

oblong *adj* : oblongo — **~** *n* : rectángulo *m*

obnoxious *adj* : odioso

oboe *n* : oboe *m*

obscene *adj* : obsceno — **obscenity** *n, pl* **-ties** : obscenidad *f*

obscurity *n, pl* **-ties** : oscuridad *f* — **obscure** *adj* : oscuro — **~** *vt* **-scured; -scuring 1** DARKEN : oscurecer **2** HIDE : ocultar

observe *v* **-served; -serving** *vt* : observar — *vi* WATCH : mirar — **observance** *n* **1** : observancia *f* **2 religious ~s** : prácticas *fpl* religiosas — **observant** *adj* : observador — **observation** *n* : observación *f* — **observatory** *n, pl* **-ries** : observatorio *m*

obsess *vt* : obsesionar — **obsession** *n* : obsesión *f* — **obsessive** *adj* : obsesivo

obsolete *adj* : obsoleto, desusado

obstacle *n* : obstáculo *m*

obstetrics *n* : obstetricia *f*

obstinate *adj* : obstinado

obstruct *vt* **1** BLOCK : obstruir **2** HINDER : obstaculizar — **obstruction** *n* : obstrucción *f*

obtain *vt* : obtener, conseguir — **obtainable** *adj* : asequible

obtrusive *adj* : entrometido (dícese de las personas), demasiado prominente (dícese de las cosas)

obtuse *adj* : obtuso

obvious *adj* : obvio, evidente — **obviously** *adv* **1** CLEARLY : obviamente **2** OF COURSE : claro, por supuesto

occasion *n* **1** : ocasión *f* **2 on ~** : de vez en cuando — **~** *vt* : ocasionar — **occasional** *adj* : poco frecuente, ocasional — **occasionally** *adv* : de vez en cuando

occult *adj* : oculto

occupy *vt* **-pied; -pying 1** : ocupar **2 ~ oneself** : entretenerse — **occupancy** *n, pl* **-cies** : ocupación *f* — **occupant** *n* : ocupante *mf* — **occupation** *n* : ocupación *f* — **occupational** *adj* : profesional

occur *vi* **occurred; occurring 1** : ocurrir **2** APPEAR : encontrarse **3 ~ to s.o.** : ocurrirse a algn — **occurrence** *n* **1** EVENT : acontecimiento *m*, suceso *m* **2** INCIDENCE : incidencia *f*

ocean *n* : océano *m*

ocher *or* **ochre** *n* : ocre *m*

o'clock *adv* **1 at 6 ~** : a las seis **2 it's one ~** : es la una **3 it's ten ~** : son las diez

octagon *n* : octágono *m* — **octagonal** *adj* : octagonal

octave *n* : octava *f*

October *n* : octubre *m*

octopus *n, pl* **-puses** *or* **-pi** : pulpo *m*

oculist *n* : oculista *mf*

odd *adj* **1** STRANGE : extraño, raro **2** : sin pareja (dícese de un calcetín, etc.) **3 forty ~ years** : cuarenta y tantos años **4 ~ jobs** : algunos trabajos *mpl* **5 ~ number** : número *m* impar — **oddity** *n, pl* **-ties** : rareza *f* — **oddly** *adv* : de manera extraña — **odds** *npl* **1** CHANCES : probabilidades *fpl* **2 at ~** : en desacuerdo **3 five to one ~** : cinco contra uno (en apuestas) — **odds and ends** *npl* : cosas *fpl* sueltas

ode *n* : oda *f*

odious *adj* : odioso

odor *or Brit* **odour** *n* : olor *m* — **odorless** *or Brit* **odourless** *adj* : inodoro

of *prep* **1** : de **2 five minutes ~ ten** : las diez menos cinco **3 the eighth ~ April** : el ocho de abril

off *adv* **1 be ~** LEAVE : irse **2 cut ~** : cortar **3 day ~** : día *m* de descanso **4 fall ~** : caerse **5 doze ~** : dormirse **6 far ~** : lejos **7 ~ and on** : de vez en cuando **8 shut ~** : apagar **9 ten miles ~** : a diez millas de aquí — **~** *prep* **1** : de **2 be ~ duty** : estar libre **3 ~ center** : descentrado — **~** *adj* **1** CANCELED : cancelado **2** OUT : apagado **3 an ~ chance** : una posibilidad remota

offend *vt* : ofender — **offender** *n* : delincuente *mf* — **offense** *or* **offence** *n* **1** AFFRONT : afrenta *f* **2** ASSAULT : ataque *m* **3** : ofensiva *f* (en deportes) **4** CRIME : delito *m* **5 take ~** : ofenderse — **offensive** *adj* : ofensivo — **~** *n* : ofensiva *f*

offer *vt* : ofrecer — **~** *n* : oferta *f* — **offering** *n* : ofrenda *f*

offhand *adv* : de improviso, en este momento — **~** *adj* : improvisado

office *n* **1** : oficina *f* **2** POSITION : cargo *m* **3 run for ~** : presentarse como candidato — **officer** *n* **1** : oficial *mf* **2** *or* **police ~** : agente *mf* (de policía) — **official** *n* : funcionario *m*, -ria *f* — **~** *adj* : oficial

offing *n* **in the ~** : en perspectiva

offset *vt* **-set; -setting** : compensar

offshore *adv* : a una distancia de la costa

offspring *ns & pl* : prole *f*, progenie *f*

often *adv* **1** : muchas veces, a menudo, con frecuencia **2 every so ~** : de vez en cuando

ogle *vt* **ogled; ogling** : comerse con los ojos

ogre *n* : ogro *m*

oh *interj* **1** : ¡oh!, ¡ah! **2 ~ no!** : ¡ay no! **3 ~ really?** : ¿de veras?

oil *n* **1** : aceite *m* **2** PETROLEUM : petróleo *m* **3** *or* **~ painting** : óleo *m* — **~** *vt* : lubricar — **oilskin** *n* : hule *m* — **oily** *adj* **oilier; -est** : aceitoso, grasiento

ointment *n* : ungüento *m*, pomada *f*

OK *or* **okay** *adv* **1** : muy bien **2 ~!** : ¡de acuerdo!, ¡bueno! — **~** *adj* **1** ALL RIGHT : bien **2 it's ~ with me** : por mí no hay problema — **~** *n* : visto *m* bueno — **~** *vt* **OK'd** *or* **okayed**; **OK'ing** *or* **okaying** : dar el visto bueno a

okra *n* : quingombó *m*

old *adj* **1** : viejo **2** FORMER : antiguo **3 any ~** : cualquier **4 be ten years ~** : tener diez años (de edad) **5 ~ age** : vejez *f* **6 ~ man** : anciano *m* **7 ~ woman** : anciana *f* — **~** *n* **the ~** : los viejos, los ancianos — **old–fashioned** *adj* : anticuado

olive *n* **1** : aceituna *f* (fruta) **2** *or* **~ green** : verde *m* oliva

Olympic *adj* : olímpico — **Olympics** *npl* **the ~** : las Olimpiadas, las Olimpíadas

omelet *or* **omelette** *n* : omelette *mf Lat*, tortilla *f* francesa *Spain*

omen *n* : agüero *m* — **ominous** *adj* : ominoso, de mal agüero

omit *vt* **omitted; omitting** : omitir — **omission** *n* : omisión *f*

omnipotent *adj* : omnipotente

on *prep* **1** : en **2** ABOUT : sobre **3 ~ foot** : a pie **4 ~ Monday** : el lunes **5 ~ the right** : a la derecha **6 ~ vacation** : de vacaciones **7 talk ~ the phone** : hablar por teléfono — **~** *adv* **1 and so ~** : etcétera **2 from that moment ~** : a partir de ese momento **3 keep ~** : seguir **4 later ~** : más tarde **5 ~ and ~** : sin parar **6 put ~** : ponerse (ropa), poner (música, etc.) **7 turn ~** : encender (una luz, etc.), abrir (una llave) — **~** *adj* **1** : encendido (dícese de luces, etc.), abierto (dícese de llaves) **2 be ~ to** : estar enterado de

once *adv* **1** : una vez **2** FORMERLY : antes — **~** *n* **1 at ~** TOGETHER : al mismo tiempo **2 at ~** IMMEDIATELY : inmediatamente — **~** *conj* : una vez que

oncoming *adj* : que viene

one *adj* **1** : un, uno **2** ONLY : único **3** *or* **~ and the same** : el mismo — **~** *n* **1** : uno *m* (número) **2 ~ by ~** : uno a uno — **~** *pron* **1** : uno, una **2 ~ another** : el uno al otro **3 ~ never knows** : nunca se sabe **4 that ~** : aquél, aquella **5 which ~?** : ¿cuál? — **oneself** *pron* **1** (*used reflexively*) : se **2** (*used after prepositions*) : sí mismo, sí misma **3** (*used emphatically*)

: uno mismo, una misma **4 by ~** : solo — **one–sided** *adj* **1** UNEQUAL : desigual **2** BIASED : parcial — **one–way** *adj* **1** : de sentido único (dícese de una calle) **2 ~ ticket** : boleto *m* de ida

ongoing *adj* : en curso, corriente

onion *n* : cebolla *f*

only *adj* **1** : único — **~** *adv* **1** : sólo, solamente **2 if ~** : ojalá, por lo menos — **~** *conj* BUT : pero

onset *n* : comienzo *m*, llegada *f*

onslaught *n* : ataque *m*, arremetida *f*

onto *prep* : sobre

onus *n* : responsabilidad *f*

onward *adv & adj* : hacia adelante

onyx *n* : ónix *m*

ooze *v* **oozed; oozing** : rezumar

opal *n* : ópalo *m*

opaque *adj* : opaco

open *adj* **1** : abierto **2** AVAILABLE : vacante, libre **3 an ~ question** : una cuestión pendiente — **~** *vt* : abrir — *vi* **1** : abrirse **2** BEGIN : comenzar — **~** *n* **in the ~ 1** OUTDOORS : al aire libre **2** KNOWN : sacado a la luz — **open–air** *adj* : al aire libre — **opener** *n* **1** : abridor *m* **2** *or* **bottle ~** : abrebotellas *m* **3** *or* **can ~** : abrelatas *m* — **opening** *n* **1** : abertura *f* **2** BEGINNING : comienzo *m*, apertura *f* **3** OPPORTUNITY : oportunidad *f* — **openly** *adv* : abiertamente

opera *n* : ópera *f*

operate *v* **-ated; -ating** *vi* **1** FUNCTION : funcionar **2 ~ on s.o.** : operar a algn — *vt* **1** : hacer funcionar (una máquina) **2** MANAGE : dirigir, manejar — **operation** *n* **1** : operación *f* **2** FUNCTIONING : funcionamiento *m* — **operational** *adj* : operacional — **operative** *adj* : en vigor — **operator** *n* **1** : operador *m*, -dora *f* **2** *or* **machine ~** : operario *m*, -ria *f*

opinion *n* : opinión *f* — **opinionated** *adj* : dogmático

opium *n* : opio *m*

opossum *n* : zarigüeya *f*, oposum *m*

opponent *n* : adversario *m*, -ria *f*; contrincante *mf* (en deportes)

opportunity *n*, *pl* **-ties** : oportunidad *f* — **opportune** *adj* : oportuno — **opportunist** *n* : oportunista *mf*

oppose *vt* **-posed; -posing** : oponerse a — **opposed** *adj* **~ to** : en contra de

opposite *adj* **1** FACING : de enfrente **2** CONTRARY : opuesto — **~** *n* **the ~** : lo contrario, lo opuesto — **~** *adv* : enfrente — **~** *prep* : enfrente de, frente a — **opposition** *n* **1** : oposición *f* **2 in ~ to** : en contra de

oppress *vt* : oprimir — **oppression** *n* : opresión *f* — **oppressive** *adj* **1** : opresivo

2 STIFLING : agobiante — **oppressor** n
: opresor m, -sora f

opt vi ~ **for** : optar por

optic or **optical** adj : óptico — **optician** n
: óptico m, -ca f

optimism n : optimismo m — **optimist** n
: optimista mf — **optimistic** adj : optimista

optimum n, pl **-ma** : lo óptimo, lo ideal

option n **1** : opción f **2 have no** ~ : no
tener más remedio — **optional** adj : facultativo, opcional

opulence n : opulencia f — **opulent** adj
: opulento

or conj **1** (indicating an alternative) : o (u
before o- or ho-) **2** (following a negative)
: ni **3** ~ **else** : si no

oracle n : oráculo m

oral adj : oral

orange n **1** : naranja f (fruta) **2** : naranja m
(color)

orator n : orador m, -dora f

orbit n : órbita f — ~ vt : girar alrededor de
— vi : orbitar

orchard n : huerto m

orchestra n : orquesta f

orchid n : orquídea f

ordain vt **1** : ordenar (un sacerdote, etc.) **2**
DECREE : decretar

ordeal n : prueba f dura

order vt **1** : ordenar **2** : pedir (mercancías,
etc.) — vi : hacer un pedido — ~ n **1**
ARRANGEMENT : orden m **2** COMMAND
: orden f **3** REQUEST : pedido m **4** : orden f
(religiosa) **5 in** ~ **that** : para que **6 in** ~
to : para **7 out of** ~ : averiado, descompuesto Lat — **orderly** adj : ordenado — ~
n, pl **-lies 1** : ordenanza m (en el ejército) **2**
: camillero m (en un hospital)

ordinary adj **1** : normal, corriente **2** MEDI-
OCRE : ordinario — **ordinarily** adv : generalmente

ore n : mena f

oregano n : orégano m

organ n : órgano m — **organic** adj
: orgánico — **organism** n : organismo m —
organist n : organista mf — **organize** vt
-nized; -nizing : organizar — **organization**
n : organización f — **organizer** n : organizador m, -dora f

orgasm n : orgasmo m

orgy n, pl **-gies** : orgía f

Orient n **the** ~ : el Oriente — **orient** vt
: orientar — **oriental** adj : del Oriente, oriental — **orientation** n : orientación f

orifice n : orificio m

origin n : origen m — **original** n : original m
— ~ adj : original — **originality** n : originalidad f — **originally** adv : originaria-
mente — **originate** v **-nated; -nating** vt

: originar — vi **1** : originarse **2** ~ **from**
: provenir de — **originator** n : creador m,
-dora f

ornament n : adorno m — ~ vt : adornar —
ornamental adj : ornamental, de adorno —
ornate adj : elaborado, adornado

ornithology n, pl **-gies** : ornitología f

orphan n : huérfano m, -na f — ~ vt : dejar
huérfano — **orphanage** n : orfelinato m, orfanato m

orthodox adj : ortodoxo — **orthodoxy** n, pl
-doxies : ortodoxia f

orthopedic adj : ortopédico

oscillation n : oscilación f — **oscillate** vi
-lated; -lating : oscilar

ostensible adj : aparente, ostensible

ostentation n : ostentación f — **ostentatious** adj : ostentoso

osteopath n : osteópata f

ostracism n : ostracismo m — **ostracize** vt
-cized; -cizing : aislar

ostrich n : avestruz m

other adj **1** : otro **2 every** ~ **day** : cada dos
días **3 on the** ~ **hand** : por otra parte, por
otro lado — ~ pron **1** : otro, otra **2 the**
~**s** : los otros, las otras, los demás, las
demás — **other than** prep : aparte de, fuera
de — **otherwise** adv **1** : eso aparte, por lo
demás **2** DIFFERENTLY : de otro modo **3** OR
ELSE : si no

otter n : nutria f

ought v aux **1** : deber **2 you** ~ **to have
done it** : deberías haberlo hecho

ounce n : onza f

our adj : nuestro — **ours** pron **1** : (el) nuestro, (la) nuestra, (los) nuestros, (las) nues-
tras **2 a friend of** ~ : un amigo nuestro —
ourselves pron **1** (used reflexively) : nos **2**
(used after prepositions) : nosotros, nosotras **3** (used for emphasis) : nosotros mismos, nosotras mismas

oust vt : desbancar

out adv **1** OUTSIDE : fuera, afuera **2 cry** ~
: gritar **3 eat** ~ : comer afuera **4 go** ~
: salir **5 look** ~ : mirar para afuera **6 run**
~ **of** : agotar **7 turn** ~ : apagar (una luz)
8 take ~ REMOVE : sacar — ~ prep → **out
of** — ~ adj **1** ABSENT : ausente **2** UN-
FASHIONABLE : fuera de moda **3** EXTIN-
GUISHED : apagado **4 the sun is** ~ : hace
sol

outboard motor n : motor m fuera de borde

outbreak n : brote m (de una enfermedad),
comienzo m (de guerra)

outburst n : arranque m, arrebato m

outcast n : paria mf

outcome n : resultado m

outcry n, pl **-cries** : protesta f

outdated adj : anticuado

285

overflow

outdo *vt* **-did; -done; -doing; -does** : superar

outdoor *adj* : al aire libre — **outdoors** *adv* : al aire libre

outer *adj* : exterior — **outer space** *n* : espacio *m* exterior

outfit *n* **1** EQUIPMENT : equipo *m* **2** CLOTHES : conjunto *m* — ~ *vt* **-fitted; -fitting** EQUIP : equipar

outgoing *adj* **1** SOCIABLE : extrovertido **2** ~ **mail** : correo *m* (para enviar) **3** ~ **president** : presidente *m*, -ta *f* saliente

outgrow *vt* **-grew; -grown; -growing** : crecer más que

outing *n* : excursión *f*

outlandish *adj* : estrafalario

outlast *vt* : durar más que

outlaw *n* : forajido *m*, -da *f* — ~ *vt* : declarar ilegal

outlay *n* : desembolso *m*

outlet *n* **1** EXIT : salida *f* **2** RELEASE : desahogo *m* **3** *or* **electrical** ~ : toma *f* de corriente **4** *or* **retail** ~ : tienda *f* al por menor

outline *n* **1** CONTOUR : contorno *m* **2** SKETCH : bosquejo *m*, boceto *m* **3** SUMMARY : esquema *m* — ~ *vt* **-lined; -lining 1** SKETCH : bosquejar **2** EXPLAIN : delinear, esbozar

outlive *vt* **-lived; -living** : sobrevivir a

outlook *n* **1** PROSPECTS : perspectivas *fpl* **2** VIEWPOINT : punto *m* de vista

outlying *adj* : alejado, distante

outmoded *adj* : pasado de moda, anticuado

outnumber *vt* : superar en número a

out of *prep* **1** FROM : de **2** THROUGH : por **3** WITHOUT : sin **4** ~ **curiosity** : por curiosidad **5** ~ **control** : fuera de control **6 one** ~ **four** : uno de cada cuatro — **out-of-date** *adj* : anticuado — **out-of-door** *or* **out-of-doors** *adj* → outdoor

outpatient *n* : paciente *m* externo

outpost *n* : puesto *m* avanzado

output *n* **1** : producción *f*, rendimiento *m* **2** : salida *f* (informática) — ~ *vt* **-putted** *or* **-put; -putting** : producir

outrage *n* **1** : atrocidad *f*, escándalo *m* **2** ANGER : ira *f*, indignación *f* — ~ *vt* **-raged; -raging** : ultrajar — **outrageous** *adj* : escandaloso

outright *adv* **1** COMPLETELY : por completo **2** INSTANTLY : en el acto — ~ *adj* : completo, absoluto

outset *n* : comienzo *m*, principio *m*

outside *n* **1** : exterior *m* **2 from the** ~ : desde fuera, desde afuera — ~ *adj* **1** : exterior, externo **2 an** ~ **chance** : una posibilidad remota — ~ *adv* : fuera, afuera — ~ *prep or* ~ **of** : fuera de — **outsider** *n* : forastero *m*, -ra *f*

outskirts *npl* : afueras *fpl*, alrededores *mpl*

outspoken *adj* : franco, directo

outstanding *adj* **1** UNPAID : pendiente **2** EXCELLENT : excepcional

outstretched *adj* : extendido

outstrip *vt* **-stripped** *or* **-stript; -stripping** : aventajar

outward *adj* **1** : hacia afuera **2** EXTERNAL : externo, external — ~ *or* **outwards** *adv* : hacia afuera — **outwardly** *adv* APPARENTLY : aparentemente

outweigh *vt* : pesar más que

outwit *vt* **-witted; -witting** : ser más listo que

oval *n* : óvalo *m* — ~ *adj* : ovalado

ovary *n*, *pl* **-ries** : ovario *m*

ovation *n* : ovación *f*

oven *n* : horno *m*

over *adv* **1** ABOVE : por encima **2** AGAIN : otra vez, de nuevo **3** MORE : más **4 all** ~ : por todas partes **5 ask** ~ : invitar **6 cross** ~ : cruzar **7 fall** ~ : caerse **8** ~ **and** ~ : una y otra vez **9** ~ **here** : aquí **10** ~ **there** : allí — ~ *prep* **1** ABOVE, UPON : encima de, sobre **2** ACROSS : por encima de, sobre **3** DURING : en, durante **4 fight** ~ : pelearse por **5** ~ **$5** : más de $5 **6** ~ **the phone** : por teléfono — ~ *adj* : terminado, acabado

overall *adv* GENERALLY : en general — ~ *adj* : total, en conjunto — **overalls** *npl* : overol *m Lat*

overbearing *adj* : dominante, imperioso

overboard *adv* **fall** ~ : caer al agua

overburden *vt* : sobrecargar

overcast *adj* : nublado

overcharge *vt* **-charged; -charging** : cobrar demasiado

overcoat *n* : abrigo *m*

overcome *v* **-came; -come; -coming** *vt* **1** CONQUER : vencer **2** OVERWHELM : agobiar — *vi* : vencer

overcook *vt* : cocer demasiado

overcrowded *adj* : abarrotado de gente

overdo *vt* **-did; -done; -doing; -does 1** : hacer demasiado **2** EXAGGERATE : exagerar **3** → overcook

overdose *n* : sobredosis *f*

overdraw *vt* **-drew; -drawn; -drawing** : girar en descubierto — **overdraft** *n* : sobregiro *m*, descubierto *m*

overdue *adj* : fuera de plazo (dícese de pagos, libros, etc.)

overeat *vi* **-ate; -eaten; -eating** : comer demasiado

overestimate *vt* **-mated; -mating** : sobreestimar

overflow *vt* : desbordar — *vi* : desbordarse — ~ *n* : desbordamiento *m* (de un río)

overgrown *adj* : cubierto (de malas hierbas, etc.)

overhand *adv* : por encima de la cabeza

overhang *v* **-hung**; **-hanging** : sobresalir

overhaul *vt* : revisar (un motor, etc.)

overhead *adv* : por encima — $\sim$ *adj* : de arriba — $\sim$ *n* : gastos *mpl* generales

overhear *vt* **-heard**; **-hearing** : oír por casualidad

overheat *vt* : calentar demasiado — *vi* : recalentarse

overjoyed *adj* : encantado

overland *adv* & *adj* : por tierra

overlap *v* **-lapped**; **-lapping** *vt* : traslapar — *vi* : traslaparse

overload *vt* : sobrecargar

overlook *vt* **1** : dar a (un jardín, el mar, etc.) **2** MISS : pasar por alto

overly *adv* : demasiado

overnight *adv* **1** : por la noche **2** SUDDENLY : de la noche a la mañana — $\sim$ *adj* **1** : de noche **2** SUDDEN : repentino

overpass *n* : paso *m* elevado

overpopulated *adj* : superpoblado

overpower *vt* **1** SUBDUE : dominar **2** OVERWHELM : agobiar, abrumar

overrated *adj* : sobreestimado

override *vt* **-rode**; **-ridden**; **-riding 1** : predominar sobre **2** : anular (una decisión, etc.)

overrule *vt* **-ruled**; **-ruling** : anular (una decisión), rechazar (una protesta)

overrun *vt* **-ran**; **-running 1** INVADE : invadir **2** EXCEED : exceder

overseas *adv* : en el extranjero — $\sim$ *adj* : extranjero, exterior

oversee *vt* **-saw**; **-seen**; **-seeing** : supervisar

overshadow *vt* : eclipsar

oversight *n* : descuido *m*

oversleep *vi* **-slept**; **-sleeping** : quedarse dormido

overstep *vt* **-stepped**; **-stepping** : sobrepasar

overt *adj* : manifiesto

overtake *vt* **-took**; **-taken**; **-taking 1** PASS : adelantar **2** SURPASS : superar

overthrow *vt* **-threw**; **-thrown**; **-throwing** : derrocar

overtime *n* **1** : horas *fpl* extras (de trabajo) **2** : prórroga *f* (en deportes)

overtone *n* SUGGESTION : tinte *m*, insinuación *f*

overture *n* : obertura *f* (en música)

overturn *vt* **1** : dar la vuelta a **2** NULLIFY : anular — *vi* : volcar

overweight *adj* : demasiado gordo

overwhelm *vt* **1** : abrumar, agobiar **2** : aplastar (a un enemigo) — **overwhelming** *adj* : abrumador, apabullante

overwork *vt* : hacer trabajar demasiado — *vi* : trabajar demasiado

overwrought *adj* : alterado, sobreexitado

owe *vt* **owed**; **owing** : deber — **owing to** *prep* : debido a

owl *n* : búho *m*

own *adj* : propio — $\sim$ *vt* : poseer, tener — *vi* $\sim$ **up** : confesar — $\sim$ *pron* **1** my (**your, his/her/their, our**) $\sim$: el mío, la mía; el tuyo, la tuya; el suyo, la suya; el nuestro, la nuestra **2 be on one's** $\sim$: estar solo **3 to each his** $\sim$: cada uno a lo suyo — **owner** *n* : propietario *m*, -ria *f* — **ownership** *n* : propiedad *f*

ox *n*, *pl* **oxen** : buey *m*

oxygen *n* : oxígeno *m*

oyster *n* : ostra *f*

ozone *n* : ozono *m*

P

p *n*, *pl* **p's** *or* **ps** : p *f*, decimosexta letra del alfabeto inglés

pace *n* **1** STEP : paso *m* **2** RATE : ritmo *m* **3 keep** $\sim$ **with** : andar al mismo paso que — $\sim$ *vi* **paced**; **pacing** *or* $\sim$ **up and down** : caminar de arriba para abajo

pacify *vt* **-fied**; **-fying** : apaciguar — **pacifier** *n* : chupete *m* — **pacifist** *n* : pacifista *mf*

pack *n* **1** BUNDLE : fardo *m* **2** BACKPACK : mochila *f* **3** PACKAGE : paquete *m* **4** : baraja *f* (de naipes) **5** : manada *f* (de lobos, etc.), jauría *f* (de perros) — $\sim$ *vt* **1**

PACKAGE : empaquetar **2** FILL : llenar **3** : hacer (una maleta) — *vi* : hacer las maletas — **package** *vt* **-aged**; **-aging** : empaquetar — $\sim$ *n* : paquete *m* — **packet** *n* : paquete *m*

pact *n* : pacto *m*, acuerdo *m*

pad *n* **1** CUSHION : almohadilla *f* **2** TABLET : bloc *m* (de papel) **3** *or* **ink** $\sim$: tampón *m* **4 launching** $\sim$: plataforma *f* (de lanzamiento) — $\sim$ *vt* **padded**; **padding** : rellenar — **padding** *n* **1** : relleno *m* **2** : paja *f* (en un discurso, etc.)

paddle *n* **1** : canalete *m* (de una canoa) **2** : pala *f*, paleta *f* (en deportes) — ~ *vt* **-dled; -dling** : hacer avanzar (una canoa) con canalete

padlock *n* : candado *m* — ~ *vt* : cerrar con candado

pagan *n* : pagano *m*, -na *f* — ~ *adj* : pagano

page¹ *vt* **paged; paging** : llamar por altavoz

page² *n* : página *f* (de un libro, etc.)

pageant *n* : espectáculo *m* — **pageantry** *n* : pompa *f*, boato *m*

paid → **pay**

pail *n* : cubo *m Spain*, cubeta *f Lat*

pain *n* **1** : dolor *m* **2** : pena *f* (mental) **3** ~**s** *npl* EFFORT : esfuerzos *mpl* — ~ *vt* : doler — **painful** *adj* : doloroso — **painkiller** *n* : analgésico *m* — **painless** *adj* : indoloro, sin dolor — **painstaking** *adj* : meticuloso, esmerado

paint *v* : pintar — ~ *n* : pintura *f* — **paintbrush** *n* : pincel *m* (de un artista), brocha *f* (para pintar casas, etc.) — **painter** *n* : pintor *m*, -tora *f* — **painting** *n* : pintura *f*

pair *n* **1** : par *m* **2** COUPLE : pareja *f* — ~ *vt* : emparejar

pajamas *npl* : pijama *m*, piyama *mf Lat*

Pakistani *adj* : paquistaní

pal *n* : amigo *m*, -ga *f*

palace *n* : palacio *m*

palate *n* : paladar *m* — **palatable** *adj* : sabroso

pale *adj* **paler; palest 1** PALLID : pálido **2** : claro (dícese de los colores, etc.) — ~ *vi* **paled; paling** : palidecer — **paleness** *n* : palidez *f*

Palestinian *adj* : palestino

palette *n* : paleta *f*

pallbearer *n* : portador *m*, -dora *f* del féretro

pallid *adj* : pálido — **pallor** *n* : palidez *f*

palm¹ *n* : palma *f* (de la mano)

palm² *or* ~ **tree** : palmera *f* — **Palm Sunday** *n* : Domingo *m* de Ramos

palpitate *vi* **-tated; -tating** : palpitar — **palpitation** *n* : palpitación *f*

paltry *adj* **-trier; -est** : mísero, mezquino

pamper *vt* : mimar

pamphlet *n* : panfleto *m*, folleto *m*

pan *n* **1** SAUCEPAN : cacerola *f* **2** FRYING PAN : sartén *mf* — ~ *vt* **panned; panning** CRITICIZE : poner por los suelos

pancake *n* : crepe *mf*, panqueque *m Lat*

panda *n* : panda *mf*

pandemonium *n* : pandemonio *m*

pander *vi* ~ **to** : complacer a

pane *n* : cristal *m*, vidrio *m*

panel *n* **1** : panel *m* **2** GROUP : jurado *m* **3** *or* **instrument** ~ : tablero *m* (de instrumentos) — ~ *vt* **-eled** *or* **-elled; -eling** *or*

-elling : adornar con paneles — **paneling** *n* : paneles *mpl*

pang *n* : punzada *f*

panic *n* : pánico *m* — ~ *v* **-icked; -icking** *vt* : llenar del pánico — *vi* : ser presa del pánico — **panicky** *adj* : presa de pánico

panorama *n* : panorama *m* — **panoramic** *adj* : panorámico

pansy *n*, *pl* **-sies** : pensamiento *m*

pant *vi* : jadear, resoplar

panther *n* : pantera *f*

panties *npl* : bragas *fpl Spain*, calzones *mpl Lat*

pantomime *n* : pantomima *f*

pantry *n*, *pl* **-tries** : despensa *f*

pants *npl* TROUSERS : pantalón *m*, pantalones *mpl*

papa *n* : papá *m fam*

papal *adj* : papal

papaya *n* : papaya *f*

paper *n* **1** : papel *m* **2** DOCUMENT : documento *m* **3** NEWSPAPER : periódico *m* — ~ *vt* WALLPAPER : empapelar — ~ *adj* : de papel — **paperback** *n* : libro *m* en rústica — **paper clip** *n* : clip *m*, sujetapapeles *m* — **paperweight** *n* : pisapapeles *m* — **paperwork** *n* : papeleo *m*

paprika *n* : pimentón *m*

par *n* **1** : par *m* (en golf) **2 below** ~ : debajo de la par **3 on a** ~ **with** : al nivel de

parable *n* : parábola *f*

parachute *n* : paracaídas *m* — ~ *vi* **-chuted; -chuting** : lanzarse en paracaídas

parade *n* **1** : desfile *m* **2** DISPLAY : alarde *m* — ~ *v* **-raded; -rading** *vi* MARCH : desfilar — *vt* DISPLAY : hacer alarde de

paradise *n* : paraíso *m*

paradox *n* : paradoja *f* — **paradoxical** *adj* : paradójico

paraffin *n* : parafina *f*

paragraph *n* : párrafo *m*

Paraguayan *adj* : paraguayo

parakeet *n* : periquito *m*

parallel *adj* : paralelo — ~ *n* **1** : paralelo *m* (en geografía) **2** SIMILARITY : paralelismo *m*, semejanza *f* — ~ *vt* : ser paralelo a

paralysis *n*, *pl* **-yses** : parálisis *f* — **paralyze** *or Brit* **paralise** *vt* **-lyzed** *or Brit* **-lised; -lyzing** *or Brit* **-lising** : paralizar

parameter *n* : parámetro *m*

paramount *adj* **of** ~ **importance** : de suma importancia

paranoia *n* : paranoia *f* — **paranoid** *adj* : paranoico

paraphernalia *ns & pl* : parafernalia *f*

paraphrase *n* : paráfrasis *f* — ~ *vt* **-phrased; -phrasing** : parafrasear

paraplegic *n* : parapléjico *m*, -ca *f*

parasite *n* : parásito *m*

paratrooper *n* : paracaidista *mf* (militar)

parcel *n* : paquete *m*

parch *vt* : resecar

parchment *n* : pergamino *m*

pardon *n* **1** : perdón *m* **2** REPRIEVE : indulto *m* **3 I beg your ~** : perdone Ud., disculpe Ud. *Lat* **— ~** *vt* **1** : perdonar **2** REPRIEVE : indultar (a un delincuente)

parent *n* **1** : madre *f*, padre *m* **2 ~s** *npl* : padres *mpl* **— parental** *adj* : de los padres

parenthesis *n, pl* **-theses** : paréntesis *m*

parish *n* **1** : parroquia *f* **— parishioner** *n* : feligrés *m*, **-gresa** *f*

parity *n, pl* **-ties** : igualdad *f*

park *n* : parque *m* **— ~** *v* : estacionar, parquear *Lat*

parka *n* : parka *f*

parking *n* : estacionamiento *m*

parliament *n* : parlamento *m* **— parliamentary** *adj* : parlamentario

parlor *or Brit* **parlour** *n* : salón *m*

parochial *adj* **1** : parroquial **2** PROVINCIAL : de miras estrechas

parody *n, pl* **-dies** : parodia *f* **— ~** *vt* **-died; -dying** : parodiar

parole *n* : libertad *f* condicional

parrot *n* : loro *m*, papagayo *m*

parry *vt* **-ried; -rying** **1** : parar (un golpe) **2** EVADE : eludir (una pregunta, etc.)

parsley *n* : perejil *m*

parsnip *n* : chirivía *f*

parson *n* : clérigo *m*

part *n* **1** : parte *f* **2** PIECE : pieza *f* **3** ROLE : papel *m* **4** : raya *f* (del pelo) **— ~** *vi* **1** *or* **~ company** : separarse **2 ~ with** : deshacerse de **— *vt* SEPARATE** : separar

partake *vi* **-took; -taken; -taking ~ in** : participar en

partial *adj* **1** : parcial **2 be ~ to** : ser aficionado a

participate *vi* **-pated; -pating** : participar **— participant** *n* : participante *mf*

participle *n* : participio *m*

particle *n* : partícula *f*

particular *adj* **1** : particular **2** FUSSY : exigente **— ~** *n* **1 in ~** : en particular, en especial **2 ~s** *npl* DETAILS : detalles *mpl* **— particularly** *adv* : especialmente

partisan *n* : partidario *m*, **-ria** *f*

partition *n* **1** DISTRIBUTION : partición *f* **2** DIVIDER : tabique *m* **— ~** *vt* : dividir

partly *adv* : en parte

partner *n* **1** : pareja *f* (en un juego, etc.) **2** *or* **business ~** : socio *m*, **-cia** *f* **— partnership** *n* : asociación *f*

party *n, pl* **-ties** **1** : partido *m* (político) **2** GATHERING : fiesta *f* **3** GROUP : grupo *m*

pass *vi* **1** : pasar **2** CEASE : pasarse **3** : aprobar (en un examen) **4** *or* **~ away** DIE : morir **5 ~ for** : pasar por **6 ~ out** FAINT : desmayarse **— *vt* 1** : pasar **2** *or* **~ in front of** : pasar por **3** OVERTAKE : adelantar **4** : aprobar (un examen, una ley, etc.) **5 ~ down** : transmitir **— ~** *n* **1** PERMIT : pase *m*, permiso *m* **2** : pase *m* (en deportes) **3** *or* **mountain ~** : paso *m* de montaña **—**

passable *adj* **1** ADEQUATE : adecuado **2** : transitable (dícese de un camino, etc.) **—**

passage *n* **1** : paso *m* **2** CORRIDOR : pasillo *m* (dentro de un edificio), pasaje *m* (entre edificios) **3** VOYAGE : travesía *f* (por el mar) **— passageway** *n* : pasillo *m*, corredor *m*

passenger *n* : pasajero *m*, **-ra** *f*

passerby *n, pl* **passersby** : transeúnte *mf*

passion *n* : pasión *f* **— passionate** *adj* : apasionado

passive *adj* : pasivo

Passover *n* : Pascua *f* (en el judaísmo)

passport *n* : pasaporte *m*

password *n* : contraseña *f*

past *adj* **1** : pasado **2** FORMER : anterior **3 the ~ few months** : los últimos meses **— ~** *prep* **1** IN FRONT OF : por delante de **2** BEYOND : más allá de **3 half ~ two** : las dos y media **— ~** *n* : pasado *m* **— ~** *adv* : por delante

pasta *n* : pasta *f*

paste *n* **1** : pasta *f* **2** GLUE : engrudo *m* **— ~** *vt* **pasted; pasting** : pegar

pastel *n* : pastel *m* **— ~** *adj* : pastel

pasteurize *vt* **-ized; -izing** : pasteurizar

pastime *n* : pasatiempo *m*

pastor *n* : pastor *m*, **-tora** *f*

pastry *n, pl* **-ries** : pasteles *mpl*

pasture *n* : pasto *m*

pasty *adj* **pastier; -est** **1** DOUGHY : pastoso **2** PALLID : pálido

pat *n* **1** : palmadita *f* **2 a ~ of butter** : una porción de mantequilla **— ~** *vt* **patted; patting** : dar palmaditas a **— ~** *adv* **have down ~** : saberse de memoria **— ~** *adj* GLIB : fácil

patch *n* **1** : parche *m*, remiendo *m* (para la ropa) **2** SPOT : mancha *f*, trozo *m* **3** PLOT : parcela *f* (de tierra) **— ~** *vt* **1** MEND : remendar **2 ~ up** : arreglar **— patchy** *adj* **patchier; -est** **1** : desigual **2** INCOMPLETE : parcial, incompleto

patent *adj* **1** *or* **patented** : patentado **2** OBVIOUS : patente, evidente **— ~** *n* : patente *f* **— ~** *vt* : patentar

paternal *adj* **1** FATHERLY : paternal **2 ~ grandmother** : abuela *f* paterna **— paternity** *n* : paternidad *f*

path *n* **1** TRACK, TRAIL : camino *m*, sendero *m* **2** COURSE : trayectoria *f*

pathetic *adj* : patético

pathology *n, pl* **-gies** : patología *f*

pathway *n* : camino *m*, sendero *m*

patience *n* : paciencia *f* — **patient** *adj* : paciente — ~ *n* : paciente *mf* — **patiently** *adv* : con paciencia

patio *n, pl* **-tios** : patio *m*

patriot *n* : patriota *mf* — **patriotic** *adj* : patriótico

patrol *n* : patrulla *f* — ~ *v* **-trolled; -trolling** : patrullar

patron *n* **1** SPONSOR : patrocinador *m*, -dora *f* **2** CUSTOMER : cliente *m*, -ta *f* — **patronage** *n* **1** SPONSORSHIP : patrocinio *m* **2** CLIENTELE : clientela *f* — **patronize** *vt* **-ized; -izing** **1** : ser cliente de (una tienda, etc.) **2** : tratar (a algn) con condescencia

patter *n* : tamborileo *m* (de la lluvia), correteo *m* (de los pies)

pattern *n* **1** MODEL : modelo *m* **2** DESIGN : diseño *m* **3** STANDARD : pauta *f*, modo *m* **4** : patrón *m* (en costura) — ~ *vt* : basar (en un modelo)

paunch *n* : panza *f*

pause *n* : pausa *f* — ~ *vi* **paused; pausing** : hacer una pausa

pave *vt* **paved; paving** : pavimentar — **pavement** *n* : pavimento *m*

pavilion *n* : pabellón *m*

paw *n* **1** : pata *f* **2** : garra *f* (de un gato) — ~ *vt* : tocar con la pata

pawn¹ *n* : peón *m* (en ajedrez)

pawn² *vt* : empeñar — **pawnbroker** *n* : prestamista *mf* — **pawnshop** *n* : casa *f* de empeños

pay *v* **paid; paying** *vt* **1** : pagar **2** ~ **attention** : prestar atención **3** ~ **back** : devolver **4** ~ **one's respects** : presentar uno sus respetos **5** ~ **a visit** : hacer una visita — *vi* **1** : pagar **2 crime doesn't** ~ : no hay crimen sin castigo — ~ *n* : paga *f* — **payable** *adj* : pagadero — **paycheck** *n* : cheque *m* del sueldo — **payment** *n* **1** : pago *m* **2** INSTALLMENT : plazo *m*, cuota *f* *Lat* — **payroll** *n* : nómina *f*

PC *n, pl* **PCs** *or* **PC's** : PC *mf*, computadora *f* personal

pea *n* : guisante *m*, arveja *f Lat*

peace *n* : paz *f* — **peaceful** *adj* **1** : pacífico **2** CALM : tranquilo

peach *n* : melocotón *m*, durazno *m Lat*

peacock *n* : pavo *m* real

peak *n* **1** SUMMIT : cumbre *f*, cima *f*, pico *m* (de una montaña) **2** APEX : nivel *m* máximo — ~ *adj* : máximo — ~ *vi* : alcanzar su nivel máximo

peal *n* **1** : repique *m* **2** ~**s of laughter** : carcajadas *fpl*

peanut *n* : cacahuete *m*, maní *m Lat*

pear *n* : pera *f*

pearl *n* : perla *f*

peasant *n* : campesino *m*, -na *f*

peat *n* : turba *f*

pebble *n* : guijarro *m*

pecan *n* : pacana *f*, nuez *f Lat*

peck *vt* : picar, picotear — ~ *n* **1** : picotazo *m* (de un pájaro) **2** KISS : besito

peculiar *adj* **1** DISTINCTIVE : peculiar, característico **2** STRANGE : extraño, raro — **peculiarity** *n, pl* **-ties 1** : peculiaridad *f* **2** ODDITY : rareza *f*

pedal *n* : pedal *m* — ~ *vi* **-aled** *or* **-alled; -aling** *or* **-alling** : pedalear

pedantic *adj* : pedante

peddle *vt* **-dled; -dling** : vender en las calles — **peddler** *n* : vendedor *m*, -dora *f* ambulante

pedestal *n* : pedestal *m*

pedestrian *n* : peatón *m*, -tona *f* — ~ *adj* ~ **crossing** : paso *m* de peatones

pediatrics *ns & pl* : pediatría *f* — **pediatrician** *n* : pediatra *mf*

pedigree *n* : pedigrí *m* (de un animal), linaje *m* (de una persona)

peek *vi* : mirar a hurtadillas — ~ *n* : miradita *f* (furtiva)

peel *vt* : pelar (fruta, etc.) — *vi* : pelarse (dícese de la piel), desconcharse (dícese de la pintura) — ~ *n* : piel *f*, cáscara *f*

peep¹ *vi* CHEEP : piar — ~ *n* : pío *m* (de un pajarito)

peep² *vi* **1** PEEK : mirar a hurtadillas **2** *or* ~ **out** : asomar — ~ *n* GLANCE : mirada *f* (furtiva)

peer¹ *n* : par *mf*

peer² *vi* : mirar (con atención)

peeve *vt* : irritar — **peevish** *adj* : malhumorado

peg *n* **1** : clavija *f* **2** HOOK : gancho *m*

pelican *n* : pelícano *m*

pellet *n* **1** : bolita *f* **2** SHOT : perdigón *m*

pelt¹ *n* : piel *f* (de un animal)

pelt² *vt* : lanzar (algo a algn)

pelvis *n, pl* **-vises** *or* **-ves** : pelvis *f* — **pelvic** *adj* : pélvico

pen¹ *vt* **penned; penning** ENCLOSE : encerrar — ~ *n* : corral *m*, redil *m*

pen² *n* **1** *or* **ballpoint** ~ : bolígrafo *m* **2** *or* **fountain** ~ : pluma *f*

penal *adj* : penal — **penalize** *vt* **-ized; -izing** : penalizar — **penalty** *n, pl* **-ties 1** : pena *f*, castigo *m* **2** : penalty *m* (en deportes)

penance *n* : penitencia *f*

pencil *n* : lápiz *m* — **pencil sharpener** *n* : sacapuntas *m*

pendant *n* : colgante *m*

pending *adj* : pendiente — ~ *prep* : en espera de

penetrate *v* **-trated; -trating** : penetrar —

penetrating *adj* : penetrante — **penetration** *n* : penetración *f*
penguin *n* : pingüino *m*
penicillin *n* : penicilina *f*
peninsula *n* : península *f*
penis *n, pl* **-nes** *or* **-nises** : pene *m*
penitentiary *n, pl* **-ries** : penitenciaría *f*
pen name *n* : seudónimo *m*
pennant *n* : banderín *m*
penny *n, pl* **-nies** *or* **pence** : centavo *m* (de los Estados Unidos), penique *m* (del Reino Unido) — **penniless** *adj* : sin un centavo
pension *n* : pensión *m*, jubilación *f*
pensive *adj* : pensativo
pentagon *n* : pentágono *m*
penthouse *n* : ático *m*
pent–up *adj* : reprimido
people *ns & pl* **1 people** *npl* : gente *f*, personas *fpl* **2 pl** ∼**s** : pueblo *m*
pep *n* : energía *f*, vigor *m* — ∼ *vt or* ∼ **up** : animar
pepper *n* **1** : pimienta *f* (condimento) **2** : pimiento *m* (fruta) — **peppermint** *n* : menta *f*
per *prep* **1** : por **2** ACCORDING TO : según **3** ∼ **day** : al día **4 miles** ∼ **hour** : millas *fpl* por hora
perceive *vt* **-ceived; -ceiving** : percibir
percent *adv* : por ciento — **percentage** *n* : porcentaje *m*
perception *n* : percepción *f* — **perceptive** *adj* : perspicaz
perch[1] *n* : percha *f* (para los pájaros) — ∼ *vi* : posarse
perch[2] *n* : perca *f* (pez)
percolate *vi* **-lated; -lating** : filtrarse — **percolator** *n* : cafetera *f* de filtro
percussion *n* : percusión *f*
perennial *adj* : perenne — ∼ *n* : planta *f* perenne
perfect *adj* : perfecto — ∼ *vt* : perfeccionar — **perfection** *n* : perfección *f* — **perfectionist** *n* : perfeccionista *mf*
perforate *vt* **-rated; -rating** : perforar
perform *vt* **1** CARRY OUT : realizar, hacer **2** : representar (una obra teatral), interpretar (una obra musical) — *vi* **1** FUNCTION : funcionar **2** ACT : actuar — **performance** *n* **1** : realización *f* **2** INTERPRETATION : interpretación *f* **3** PRESENTATION : representación *f* — **performer** *n* : actor *m*, -triz *f*; intérprete *mf* (de música)
perfume *n* : perfume *m*
perhaps *adv* : tal vez, quizá, quizás
peril *n* : peligro *m* — **perilous** *adj* : peligroso
perimeter *n* : perímetro *m*
period *n* **1** : período *m* (de tiempo) **2** : punto *m* (en puntuación) **3** ERA : época *f*

— **periodic** *adj* : periódico — **periodical** *n* : revista *f*
peripheral *adj* : periférico
perish *vi* : perecer — **perishable** *adj* : perecedero — **perishables** *npl* : productos *mpl* perecederos
perjury *n* : perjurio *m*
perk *vi* ∼ **up** : animarse, reanimarse — ∼ *n* : extra *m* — **perky** *adj* **perkier; -est** : alegre
permanence *n* : permanencia *f* — **permanent** *adj* : permanente — ∼ *n* : permanente *f*
permeate *v* **-ated; -ating** : penetrar
permission *n* : permiso *m* — **permissible** *adj* : permisible — **permissive** *adj* : permisivo — **permit** *vt* **-mitted; -mitting** : permitir — ∼ *n* : permiso *m*
peroxide *n* : peróxido *m*
perpendicular *adj* : perpendicular
perpetrate *vt* **-trated; -trating** : cometer — **perpetrator** *n* : autor *m*, -tora *f* (de un delito)
perpetual *adj* : perpetuo
perplex *vt* : dejar perplejo — **perplexing** *adj* : desconcertante — **perplexity** *n, pl* **-ties** : perplejidad *f*
persecute *vt* **-cuted; -cuting** : perseguir — **persecution** *n* : persecución *f*
persevere *vi* **-vered; -vering** : perseverar — **perseverance** *n* : perseverancia *f*
persist *vi* : persistir — **persistence** *n* : persistencia *f* — **persistent** *adj* : persistente
person *n* : persona *f* — **personal** *adj* : personal — **personality** *n, pl* **-ties** : personalidad *f* — **personally** *adv* : personalmente, en persona — **personnel** *n* : personal *m*
perspective *n* : perspectiva *f*
perspiration *n* : transpiración *f* — **perspire** *vi* **-spired; -spiring** : transpirar
persuade *vt* **-suaded; -suading** : persuadir — **persuasion** *n* : persuasión *f*
pertain *vi* ∼ **to** : estar relacionado con — **pertinent** *adj* : pertinente
perturb *vt* : perturbar
Peruvian *adj* : peruano
pervade *vt* **-vaded; -vading** : penetrar — **pervasive** *adj* : penetrante
perverse *adj* **1** CORRUPT : perverso **2** STUBBORN : obstinado — **pervert** *n* : pervertido *m*, -da *f*
peso *n, pl* **-sos** : peso *m*
pessimism *n* : pesimismo *m* — **pessimist** *n* : pesimista *mf* — **pessimistic** *adj* : pesimista
pest *n* **1** : insecto *m* nocivo, animal *m* nocivo **2** : peste *f fam* (persona)
pester *vt* **-tered; -tering** : molestar
pesticide *n* : pesticida *m*

pet *n* **1** : animal *m* doméstico **2** FAVORITE : favorito *m*, -ta *f* — ~ *vt* **petted; petting** : acariciar
petal *n* : pétalo *m*
petite *adj* : chiquita
petition *n* : petición *f* — ~ *vt* : dirigir una petición a
petrify *vt* **-fied; -fying** : petrificar
petroleum *n* : petróleo *m*
petticoat *n* : enagua *f*, fondo *m Lat*
petty *adj* **-tier; -est 1** UNIMPORTANT : insignificante, nimio **2** MEAN : mezquino — **pettiness** *n* : mezquindad *f*
petulant *adj* : irritable, de mal genio
pew *n* : banco *m* (de iglesia)
pewter *n* : peltre *m*
phallic *adj* : fálico
phantom *n* : fantasma *m*
pharmacy *n, pl* **-cies** : farmacia *f* — **pharmacist** *n* : farmacéutico *m*, -ca *f*
phase *n* : fase *f* — ~ *vt* **phased; phasing 1** ~ **in** : introducir progresivamente **2** ~ **out** : retirar progresivamente
phenomenon *n, pl* **-na** *or* **-nons** : fenómeno *m* — **phenomenal** *adj* : fenomenal
philanthropy *n, pl* **-pies** : filantropía *f* — **philanthropist** *n* : filántropo *m*, -pa *f*
philosophy *n, pl* **-phies** : filosofía *f* — **philosopher** *n* : filósofo *m*, -fa *f*
phlegm *n* : flema *f*
phobia *n* : fobia *f*
phone → **telephone**
phonetic *adj* : fonético
phony *or* **phoney** *adj* **-nier; -est** : falso — ~ *n, pl* **-nies** : farsante *mf*
phosphorus *n* : fósforo *m*
photo *n, pl* **-tos** : foto *f* — **photocopier** *n* : fotocopiadora *f* — **photocopy** *n, pl* **-copies** : fotocopia *f* — ~ *vt* **-copied; -copying** : fotocopiar — **photograph** *n* : fotografía *f*, foto *f* — ~ *vt* : fotografiar — **photographer** *n* : fotógrafo *m*, -fa *f* — **photographic** *adj* : fotográfico — **photography** *n* : fotografía *f*
phrase *n* : frase *f* — ~ *vt* **phrased; phrasing** : expresar
physical *adj* : físico — ~ *n* : reconocimiento *m* médico
physician *n* : médico *m*, -ca *f*
physics *ns & pl* : física *f* — **physicist** *n* : físico *m*, -ca *f*
physiology *n* : fisiología *f*
physique *n* : físico *m*
piano *n, pl* **-anos** : piano *m* — **pianist** *n* : pianista *mf*
pick *vt* **1** CHOOSE : escoger **2** GATHER : recoger **3** REMOVE : quitar (poco a poco) **4** ~ **a fight** : buscar camorra — *vi* **1** ~ **and choose** : ser exigente **2** ~ **on** : me-

terse con — ~ *n* **1** CHOICE : selección *f* **2** *or* **pickax** : pico *m* **3 the** ~ **of** : lo mejor de
picket *n* **1** STAKE : estaca *f* **2** *or* ~ **line** : piquete *m* — ~ *v* : piquetear
pickle *n* **1** : pepinillo *m* (encurtido) **2** JAM : lío *m fam*, apuro *m* — ~ *vt* **-led; -ling** : encurtir
pickpocket *n* : carterista *mf*
pickup *n* **1** IMPROVEMENT : mejora *f* **2** *or* ~ **truck** : camioneta *f* — **pick up** *vt* **1** LIFT : levantar **2** TIDY : arreglar, ordenar — *vi* IMPROVE : mejorar
picnic *n* : picnic *m* — ~ *vi* **-nicked; -nicking** : ir de picnic
picture *n* **1** PAINTING : cuadro *m* **2** DRAWING : dibujo *m* **3** PHOTO : fotografía *f* **4** IMAGE : imagen *f* **5** MOVIE : película *f* — ~ *vt* **-tured; -turing 1** DEPICT : representar **2** IMAGINE : imaginarse — **picturesque** *adj* : pintoresco
pie *n* : pastel *m* (con fruta o carne), empanada *f* (con carne)
piece *n* **1** : pieza *f* **2** FRAGMENT : trozo *m*, pedazo *m* **3 a** ~ **of advice** : un consejo — ~ *vt* **pieced; piecing** *or* ~ **together** : juntar, componer — **piecemeal** *adv* : poco a poco — ~ *adj* : poco sistemático
pier *n* : muelle *m*
pierce *vt* **pierced; piercing** : perforar — **piercing** *adj* : penetrante
piety *n, pl* **-eties** : piedad *f*
pig *n* : cerdo *m*, -da *f*; puerco *m*, -ca *f*
pigeon *n* : paloma *f* — **pigeonhole** *n* : casilla *f*
piggyback *adv & adj* : a cuestas
pigment *n* : pigmento *m*
pigpen *n* : pocilga *f*
pigtail *n* : coleta *f*, trenza *f*
pile¹ *n* HEAP : montón *m*, pila *f* — ~ *v* **piled; piling** *vt* : amontonar, apilar — *vi* ~ **up** : amontonarse, acumularse
pile² *n* NAP : pelo *m* (de telas)
pilfer *vt* : robar, hurtar
pilgrim *n* : peregrino *m*, -na *f* — **pilgrimage** *n* : peregrinación *f*
pill *n* : pastilla *f*, píldora *f*
pillage *n* : saqueo *m* — ~ *vt* **-laged; -laging** : saquear
pillar *n* : pilar *m*, columna *f*
pillow *n* : almohada *f* — **pillowcase** *n* : funda *f* (de almohada)
pilot *n* : piloto *mf* — ~ *vt* : pilotar, pilotear — **pilot light** *n* : piloto *m*
pimp *n* : proxeneta *m*
pimple *n* : grano *m*
pin *n* **1** : alfiler *m* **2** BROOCH : broche *m* **3** *or* **bowling** ~ : bolo *m* — ~ *vt* **pinned; pinning 1** FASTEN : prender, sujetar (con alfileres) **2** *or* ~ **down** : inmovilizar

pincers *npl* : tenazas *fpl*
pinch *vt* **1** : pellizcar **2** STEAL : robar — *vi* : apretar — **~** *n* **1** : pellizco *m* **2** BIT : pizca *f* **3 in a ~** : en caso necesario
pine¹ *n* : pino *m* (árbol)
pine² *vi* **pined; pining 1** LANGUISH : languidecer **2 ~ for** : suspirar por
pineapple *n* : piña *f*, ananás *m*
pink *n* : rosa *m*, rosado *m* — **~** *adj* : rosa, rosado
pinnacle *n* : pináculo *m*
pinpoint *vt* : localizar, precisar
pint *n* : pinta *f*
pioneer *n* : pionero *m*, -ra *f*
pious *adj* : piadoso
pipe *n* **1** : tubo *m*, caño *m* **2** : pipa *f* (para fumar) — **pipeline** *n* **1** : conducto *m*, oleoducto *m* (para petróleo)
piquant *adj* : picante
pique *n* : resentimiento *m*
pirate *n* : pirata *mf*
pistachio *n*, *pl* **-chios** : pistacho *m*
pistol *n* : pistola *f*
piston *n* : pistón *m*
pit *n* **1** HOLE : hoyo *m*, fosa *f* **2** MINE : mina *f* **3** : hueso *m* (de una fruta) **4 ~ of the stomach** : boca *f* del estómago — **~** *vt* **pitted; pitting 1** : marcar de hoyos **2** : deshuesar (una fruta) **3 ~ against** : enfrentar a
pitch *vt* **1** : armar (una tienda) **2** THROW : lanzar — *vi* **1** *or* **~ forward** : caerse **2** LURCH : cabecear (dícese de un barco o un avión) — **~** *n* **1** DEGREE, LEVEL : grado *m*, punto *m* **2** TONE : tono *m* **3** THROW : lanzamiento *m* **4** *or* **sales ~** : presentación *f* (de un vendedor)
pitcher *n* **1** JUG : jarro *m* **2** : lanzador *m*, -dora *f* (en béisbol, etc.)
pitchfork *n* : horquilla *f*, horca *f*
pitfall *n* : riesgo *m*, dificultad *f*
pith *n* **1** : médula *f* (de un hueso, etc.) **2** CORE : meollo *m* — **pithy** *adj* **pithier; -est** : conciso y sustancioso
pity *n*, *pl* **pities 1** COMPASSION : compasión *f* **2 what a ~!** : ¡qué lástima! — **~** *vt* **pitied; pitying** : compadecerse de — **pitiful** *adj* : lastimoso — **pitiless** *adj* : despiadado
pivot *n* : pivote *m* — **~** *vi* **1** : girar sobre un eje **2 ~ on** : depender de
pizza *n* : pizza *f*
placard *n* POSTER : cartel *m*, póster *m*
placate *vt* **-cated; -cating** : apaciguar
place *n* **1** : sitio *m*, lugar *m* **2** SEAT : asiento *m* **3** POSITION : puesto *m* **4** ROLE : papel *m* **5 take ~** : tener lugar **6 take the ~ of** : sustituir a — **~** *vt* **placed; placing 1** PUT, SET : poner, colocar **2** IDENTIFY : identificar, recordar **3 ~ an order** : hacer un pedido — **placement** *n* : colocación *f*
placid *adj* : plácido, tranquilo
plagiarism *n* : plagio *m* — **plagiarize** *vt* **-rized; -rizing** : plagiar
plague *n* **1** : plaga *f* (de insectos, etc.) **2** : peste *f* (en medicina)
plaid *n* : tela *f* escocesa — **~** *adj* : escocés
plain *adj* **1** SIMPLE : sencillo **2** CLEAR : claro, evidente **3** CANDID : franco **4** HOMELY : poco atractivo **5 in ~ sight** : a la vista (de todos) — **~** *n* : llanura *f*, planicie *f* — **plainly** *adv* **1** CLEARLY : claramente **2** FRANKLY : francamente **3** SIMPLY : sencillamente
plaintiff *n* : demandante *mf*
plan *n* **1** : plan *m*, proyecto *m* **2** DIAGRAM : plano *m* — *v* **planned; planning 1** : planear, proyectar **2** INTEND : tener planeado — *vi* : hacer planes
plane¹ *n* **1** LEVEL : plano *m*, nivel *m* **2** AIRPLANE : avión *m*
plane² *n* *or* **carpenter's ~** : cepillo *m*
planet *n* : planeta *f*
plank *n* : tabla *f*
planning *n* : planificación *f*
plant *vt* : plantar (flores, árboles), sembrar (semillas) — **~** *n* **1** : planta *f* **2** FACTORY : fábrica *f*
plantain *n* : plátano *m* (grande)
plantation *n* : plantación *f*
plaque *n* : placa *f*
plaster *n* : yeso *m* — **~** *vt* **1** : enyesar **2** COVER : cubrir — **plaster cast** *n* : escayola *f*
plastic *adj* **1** : de plástico **2** FLEXIBLE : plástico, flexible **3 ~ surgery** : cirugía *f* plástica — **~** *n* : plástico *m*
plate *n* **1** SHEET : placa *f* **2** DISH : plato *m* **3** ILLUSTRATION : lámina *f* — **~** *vt* **plated; plating** : chapar (en metal)
plateau *n*, *pl* **-teaus** *or* **-teaux** : meseta *f*
platform *n* **1** : plataforma *f* **2** : andén *m* (de una estación de ferrocarril) **3** *or* **political ~** : programa *m* electoral
platinum *n* : platino *m*
platitude *n* : lugar *m* común
platoon *n* : sección *f* (en el ejército)
platter *n* : fuente *f*
plausible *adj* : creíble, verosímil
play *n* **1** : juego *m* **2** DRAMA : obra *f* de teatro — **~** *vi* **1** : jugar **2 ~ in a band** : tocar en un grupo — *vt* **1** : jugar (deportes, etc.), jugar a (juegos) **2** : tocar (música o un instrumento) **3 ~ the role of** : representar el papel de — **player** *n* **1** : jugador *m*, -dora *f* **2** ACTOR : actor *m*, actriz *f* **3** MUSICIAN : músico *m*, -ca *f* — **playful** *adj* : juguetón — **playground** *n* : patio *m* de recreo — **playing card** *n* : naipe *m*, carta *f* — **play-**

mate n : compañero m, -ra f de juego — **play-off** n : desempate m — **playpen** n : corral m (para niños) — **plaything** n : juguete m — **playwright** n : dramaturgo m, -ga f

plea n **1** : acto m de declararse (en derecho) **2** APPEAL : ruego m, súplica f — **plead** v **pleaded** or **pled**; **pleading** vi **1 ~ for** : suplicar **2 ~ guilty** : declararse culpable **3 ~ not guilty** : negar la acusación — vt **1** : alegar, pretextar **2 ~ a case** : defender un caso

pleasant adj : agradable, grato — **please** v **pleased**; **pleasing** vt **1** GRATIFY : complacer **2** SATISFY : satisfacer — vi **1** : agradar **2 do as you ~** : haz lo que quieras — **~** adv : por favor — **pleased** adj : contento — **pleasing** adj : agradable — **pleasure** n : placer m, gusto m

pleat vt : plisar — **~** n : pliegue m

pledge n **1** SECURITY : prenda f **2** PROMISE : promesa f — **~** vt **pledged**; **pledging 1** PAWN : empeñar **2** PROMISE : prometer

plenty n **1** : abundancia f **2 ~ of time** : tiempo m de sobra — **plentiful** adj : abundante

pliable adj : flexible

pliers npl : alicates mpl

plight n : situación f difícil

plod vi **plodded**; **plodding 1** : caminar con paso pesado **2** DRUDGE : trabajar laboriosamente

plot n **1** LOT : parcela f **2** : argumento m (de una novela, etc.) **3** CONSPIRACY : complot m, intriga f — **~** v **plotted**; **plotting** vt : tramar (un plan), trazar (una gráfica, etc.) — vi CONSPIRE : conspirar

plow or **plough** n **1** : arado m **2 → snow-plow** — **~** v : arar

ploy n : estratagema f

pluck vt **1** : arrancar **2** : desplumar (un pollo, etc.) **3** : recoger (flores) **4 ~ one's eyebrows** : depilarse las cejas

plug n **1** STOPPER : tapón m **2** : enchufe m (eléctrico) — **~** vt **plugged**; **plugging 1** BLOCK : tapar **2** ADVERTISE : dar publicidad a **3 ~ in** : enchufar

plum n : ciruela f

plumb adj : a plomo, vertical — **plumber** n : fontanero m, -ra f; plomero m, -ra f Lat — **plumbing** n **1** : fontanería f, plomería f Lat **2** PIPES : cañerías fpl

plume n : pluma f

plummet vi : caer en picado

plump adj : rechoncho fam

plunder vi : saquear, robar — **~** n : botín m

plunge v **plunged**; **plunging** vt **1** IMMERSE : sumergir **2** THRUST : hundir — vi **1** : zambullirse (en el agua) **2** DESCEND : descender en picada — **~** n **1** DIVE : zambullida f **2** DROP : descenso m abrupto

plural adj : plural — **~** n : plural m

plus adj : positivo — **~** n **1** or **~ sign** : signo m (de) más **2** ADVANTAGE : ventaja f — **~** prep : más — **~** conj : y, además

plush n : felpa f — **~** adj **1** : de felpa **2** LUXURIOUS : lujoso

plutonium n : plutonio m

ply vt **plied**; **plying 1** : ejercer (un oficio) **2 ~ with questions** : acosar con preguntas

plywood n : contrachapado m

pneumatic adj : neumático

pneumonia n : pulmonía f

poach¹ vt : cocer a fuego lento

poach² vt or **~ game** : cazar ilegalmente — **poacher** n : cazador m furtivo, cazadora f furtiva

pocket n : bolsillo m — **~** vt : meterse en el bolsillo — **pocketbook** n : cartera f, bolsa f Lat — **pocketknife** n, pl **-knives** : navaja f

pod n : vaina f

poem n : poema m — **poet** n : poeta mf — **poetic** or **poetical** adj : poético — **poetry** n : poesía f

poignant adj : conmovedor

point n **1** : punto m **2** PURPOSE : sentido m **3** TIP : punta f **4** FEATURE : cualidad f **5 be beside the ~** : no venir al caso **6 there's no ~ ...** : no sirve de nada...— **~** vt **1** AIM : apuntar **2** or **~ out** : señalar, indicar — vi **~ at** : señalar (con el dedo) — **point-blank** adv : a quemarropa — **pointer** n **1** NEEDLE : aguja f **2** : perro m de muestra **3** TIP : consejo m — **pointless** adj : inútil — **point of view** n : perspectiva f, punto m de vista

poise n **1** : elegancia f **2** COMPOSURE : aplomo m

poison n : veneno m — **~** vt : envenenar — **poisonous** adj : venenoso (dícese de una culebra, etc.), tóxico (dícese de una sustancia)

poke vt **poked**; **poking 1** JAB : golpear (con la punta de algo), dar **2** THRUST : introducir, asomar — **~** n : golpe m abrupto (con la punta de algo)

poker¹ n : atizador m (para el fuego)

poker² n : póquer m (juego de naipes)

polar adj : polar — **polar bear** n : oso m blanco — **polarize** vt **-ized**; **-izing** : polarizar

pole¹ n : palo m, poste m

pole² n : polo m (en geografía)

police vt **-liced**; **-licing** : mantener el orden en — **~** ns & pl **the ~** : la policía — **policeman** n, pl **-men** : policía m — **police officer** n : policía mf, agente mf de policía — **policewoman** n, pl **-women** : (mujer f) policía f

policy n, pl **-cies 1** : política f **2** or **insurance ∼** : póliza f de seguros

polio or **poliomyelitis** n : polio f, poliomielitis f

polish vt **1** : pulir **2** : limpiar (zapatos), encerar (un suelo) — **∼** n **1** LUSTER : brillo m, lustre m **2** : betún m (para zapatos), cera f (para suelos y muebles), esmalte m (para las uñas)

Polish adj : polaco — **∼** n : polaco m (idioma)

polite adj **-liter; -est** : cortés — **politeness** n : cortesía f

political adj : político — **politician** n : político m, -ca f — **politics** ns & pl : política f

polka n : polka f — **polka dot** n : lunar m

poll n **1** : encuesta f, sondeo m **2 the ∼s** : las urnas — **∼** vt **1** : obtener (votos) **2** CANVASS : encuestar, sondear

pollen n : polen m

pollute vt **-luted; -luting** : contaminar — **pollution** n : contaminación f

polyester n : poliéster m

polygon n : polígono m

pomegranate n : granada f

pomp n : pompa f — **pompous** adj : pomposo

pond n : charca f (natural), estanque m (artificial)

ponder vt : considerar — vi **∼** over : reflexionar sobre

pony n, pl **-nies** : poni m — **ponytail** n : cola f de caballo

poodle n : caniche m

pool n **1** PUDDLE : charco m **2** : fondo m común (de recursos) **3** BILLIARDS : billar m **4** or **swimming ∼** : piscina f — **∼** vt : hacer un fondo común de

poor adj **1** : pobre **2** INFERIOR : malo **3 the ∼** : los pobres — **poorly** adv : mal

pop¹ v **popped; popping** vt **1** : hacer reventar **2 ∼ sth into** : meter algo en — vi **1** BURST : reventarse, estallar **2 ∼ in** : entrar (un momento) **3 ∼ out** : saltar (dícese de los ojos) **4 ∼ up** APPEAR : aparecer — **∼** n **1** : ruido m seco **2 → soda pop**

pop² n or **∼ music** : música f popular

popcorn n : palomitas fpl

pope n : papa m

poplar n : álamo m

poppy n, pl **-pies** : amapola f

popular adj : popular — **popularity** n : popularidad f — **popularize** vt **-ized; -izing** : popularizar

populate vt **-lated; -lating** : poblar — **population** n : población f

porcelain n : porcelana f

porch n : porche m

porcupine n : puerco m espín

pore¹ vi **pored; poring ∼ over** : estudiar esmeradamente

pore² n : poro m

pork n : carne f de cerdo

pornography n : pornografía f — **pornographic** adj : pornográfico

porous adj : poroso

porpoise n : marsopa f

porridge n : avena f (cocida), gachas fpl (de avena)

port¹ n HARBOR : puerto m

port² n or **∼ side** : babor m

port³ n : oporto m (vino)

portable adj : portátil

portent n : presagio m

porter n : maletero m, mozo m (de estación)

portfolio n, pl **-lios** : cartera f

porthole n : portilla f

portion n : porción f

portrait n : retrato m

portray vt **1** : representar, retratar **2** : interpretar (un personaje)

Portuguese adj : portugués — **∼** n : portugués m (idioma)

pose v **posed; posing** vt : plantear (una pregunta, etc.), representar (una amenaza) — vi **1** : posar **2 ∼ as** : hacerse pasar por — **∼** n : pose f

posh adj : elegante, de lujo

position n **1** : posición f **2** JOB : puesto m — **∼** vt : colocar, situar

positive adj **1** : positivo **2** CERTAIN : seguro

possess vt : poseer — **possession** n **1** : posesión f **2 ∼s** npl BELONGINGS : bienes mpl — **possessive** adj : posesivo

possible adj : posible — **possibility** n, pl **-ties** : posibilidad f — **possibly** adv : posiblemente

post¹ n POLE : poste m, palo m

post² n POSITION : puesto m

post³ n MAIL : cartas fpl — **∼** vt **1** : echar al correo **2 keep ∼ed** : tener al corriente — **postage** n : franqueo m — **postal** adj : postal — **postcard** n : tarjeta f postal

poster n : cartel m

posterity n : posteridad f

posthumous adj : póstumo

postman → mailman — **post office** n : oficina f de correos

postpone vt **-poned; -poning** : aplazar — **postponement** n : aplazamiento m

postscript n : posdata f

posture n : postura f

postwar adj : de (la) posguerra

pot n **1** : olla f (de cocina) **2** FLOWERPOT : maceta f **3 ∼s and pans** : cacharros mpl

potassium n : potasio m

potato n, pl **-toes** : patata f, papa f Lat

potent *adj* **1** POWERFUL : poderoso **2** EFFECTIVE : eficaz
potential *adj* : potencial — ~ *n* : potencial *m*
pothole *n* : bache *m*
potion *n* : poción *f*
pottery *n, pl* **-teries** : cerámica *f*
pouch *n* **1** BAG : bolsa *f* pequeña **2** : bolsa *f* (de un animal)
poultry *n* : aves *fpl* de corral
pounce *vi* **pounced; pouncing** : abalanzarse
pound¹ *n* : libra *f* (unidad de dinero o de peso)
pound² *n or dog* ~ : perrera *f*
pound³ *vt* **1** CRUSH : machacar **2** HIT : golpear — *vi* : palpitar (dícese del corazón)
pour *vt* : verter — *vi* **1** FLOW : fluir, salir **2** **it's** ~**ing** : está lloviendo a cántaros
pout *vi* : hacer pucheros — ~ *n* : puchero *m*
poverty *n* : pobreza *f*
powder *vt* **1** : empolvar **2** CRUSH : pulverizar — ~ *n* **1** : polvo *m* **2** *or* **face** ~ : polvos *mpl* — **powdery** *adj* : polvoriento
power *n* **1** CONTROL : poder *m* **2** ABILITY : capacidad *f* **3** STRENGTH : fuerza *f* **4** : potencia *f* (política) **5** ENERGY : energía *f* **6** ELECTRICITY : electricidad *f* — ~ *vt* : impulsar — **powerful** *adj* : poderoso — **powerless** *adj* : impotente
practical *adj* : práctico — **practically** *adv* : casi, prácticamente
practice *or* **practise** *v* **-ticed** *or* **-tised; -ticing** *or* **-tising** *vt* **1** : practicar **2** : ejercer (una profesión) — *vi* : practicar — **practice** *n* **1** : práctica *f* **2** CUSTOM : costumbre *f* **3** : ejercicio *m* (de una profesión) **4 be out of** ~ : no estar en forma — **practitioner** *n* **1** : profesional *mf* **2 general** ~ : médico *m*, -ca *f* de medicina general
pragmatic *adj* : pragmático
prairie *n* : pradera *f*
praise *vt* **praised; praising** : elogiar, alabar — ~ *n* : elogio *m*, alabanza *f* — **praiseworthy** *adj* : loable
prance *vi* **pranced; prancing** : hacer cabriolas
prank *n* : travesura *f*
prawn *n* : gamba *f*
pray *vi* **1** : rezar **2** ~ **for** : rogar — **prayer** *n* : oración *f*
preach *v* : predicar — **preacher** *n* MINISTER : pastor *m*, -tora *f*
precarious *adj* : precario
precaution *n* : precaución *f*
precede *vt* **-ceded; -ceding** : preceder a — **precedence** *n* : precedencia *f* — **precedent** *n* : precedente *m*
precinct *n* **1** DISTRICT : distrito *m* **2** ~**s** *npl* : recinto *m*

precious *adj* : precioso
precipice *n* : precipicio *m*
precipitate *vt* **-tated; -tating** : precipitar — **precipitation** *n* **1** HASTE : precipitación *f* **2** : precipitaciones *fpl* (en meteorología)
precise *adj* : preciso — **precisely** *adv* : precisamente — **precision** *n* : precisión *f*
preclude *vt* **-cluded; -cluding** **1** PREVENT : impedir **2** EXCLUDE : excluir
precocious *adj* : precoz
preconceived *adj* : preconcebido
predator *n* : depredador *m*
predecessor *n* : antecesor *m*, -sora *f;* predecesor *m*, -sora *f*
predicament *n* : apuro *m*
predict *vt* : pronosticar, predecir — **predictable** *adj* : previsible — **prediction** *n* : pronóstico *m*, predicción *f*
predispose *vt* **-posed; -posing** : predisponer
predominant *adj* : predominante
preeminent *adj* : preeminente
preempt *vt* : adelantarse a (un ataque, etc.)
preen *vt* **1** : arreglarse (las plumas) **2** ~ **oneself** : acicalarse
prefabricated *adj* : prefabricado
preface *n* : prefacio *m*, prólogo *m*
prefer *vt* **-ferred; -ferring** : preferir — **preferable** *adj* : preferible — **preference** *n* : preferencia *f* — **preferential** *adj* : preferente
prefix *n* : prefijo *m*
pregnancy *n, pl* **-cies** : embarazo *m* — **pregnant** *adj* : embarazada
prehistoric *or* **prehistorical** *adj* : prehistórico
prejudice *n* **1** BIAS : prejuicio *m* **2** HARM : perjuicio *m* — ~ *vt* **-diced; -dicing** **1** BIAS : predisponer **2** HARM : perjudicar — **prejudiced** *adj* : parcial
preliminary *adj* : preliminar
prelude *n* : preludio *m*
premarital *adj* : prematrimonial
premature *adj* : prematuro
premeditated *adj* : premeditado
premier *adj* : principal — ~ *n* PRIME MINISTER : primer ministro *m*, primera ministra *f*
premiere *n* : estreno *m*
premise *n* **1** : premisa *f* (de un argumento) **2** ~**s** *npl* : recinto *m*, local *m*
premium *n* **1** : premio *m* **2** *or* **insurance** ~ : prima *f* (de seguro)
preoccupied *adj* : preocupado
prepare *v* **-pared; -paring** *vt* : preparar — *vi* : prepararse — **preparation** *n* **1** : preparación *f* **2** ~**s** *npl* ARRANGEMENTS : preparativos *mpl* — **preparatory** *adj* : preparatorio
prepay *vt* **-paid; -paying** : pagar por adelantado

preposition n : preposición f
preposterous adj : absurdo, ridículo
prerequisite n : requisito m previo
prerogative n : prerrogativa f
prescribe vt **-scribed; -scribing 1** : prescribir **2** : recetar (en medicina) — **prescription** n : receta f
presence n : presencia f
present¹ adj **1** CURRENT : actual **2 be ~ at** : estar presente en — **~** n **1** : presente m **2 at ~** : actualmente
present² n GIFT : regalo m — **~** vt **1** INTRODUCE : presentar **2** GIVE : entregar — **presentation** n : presentación f **2** or **~ ceremony** : ceremonia f de entrega
presently adv **1** SOON : dentro de poco **2** NOW : actualmente
preserve vt **-served; -serving 1** : conservar **2** MAINTAIN : mantener — **~** n **1** JAM : confitura f **2** or **game ~** : coto m de caza — **preservation** n : preservación f, conservación f — **preservative** n : conservante m
president n : presidente m, -ta f — **presidency** n, pl **-cies** : presidencia f — **presidential** adj : presidencial
press n : prensa f — **~** vt **1** : apretar **2** IRON : planchar — vi **1** : apretar **2** URGE : presionar — **pressing** adj : urgente — **pressure** n : presión f — **~** vt **-sured; -suring** : presionar, apremiar
prestige n : prestigio m — **prestigious** adj : prestigioso
presume vt **-sumed; -suming** : presumir — **presumably** adv : es de suponer, supuestamente — **presumption** n : presunción f — **presumptuous** adj : presuntuoso
pretend vt **1** CLAIM : pretender **2** FEIGN : fingir — vi : fingir — **pretense** or **pretence** n **1** CLAIM : pretensión f **2 under false ~s** : con pretextos falsos — **pretentious** adj : pretencioso
pretext n : pretexto m
pretty adj **-tier; -est** : lindo, bonito — **~** adv FAIRLY : bastante
pretzel n : galleta f salada
prevail vi **1** TRIUMPH : prevalecer **2** PREDOMINATE : predominar **3 ~ upon** : persuadir — **prevalent** adj : extendido
prevent vt : impedir — **prevention** n : prevención f — **preventive** adj : preventivo
preview n : preestreno m
previous adj : previo, anterior — **previously** adv : anteriormente
prey n, pl **preys** : presa f — **prey on** vt **1** : alimentarse de **2 ~ on one's mind** : atormentar a algn
price n : precio m — **~** vt **priced; pricing** : poner un precio a — **priceless** adj : inestimable

prick n : pinchazo m — **~** vt **1** : pinchar **2 ~ up one's ears** : levantar las orejas — **prickly** adj : espinoso
pride n : orgullo m — **~** vt **prided; priding ~ oneself on** : enorgullecerse de
priest n : sacerdote m — **priesthood** n : sacerdocio m
prim adj **primmer; primmest** : remilgado
primary adj **1** FIRST : primario **2** PRINCIPAL : principal — **primarily** adv : principalmente
prime¹ vt **primed; priming 1** : cebar (un arma de fuego, etc.) **2** PREPARE : preparar
prime² n **the ~ of one's life** : la flor de la vida — **~** adj **1** MAIN : principal, primero **2** EXCELLENT : excelente — **prime minister** n : primero ministro m, primera ministra f
primer¹ n : base f (de pintura)
primer² n READER : cartilla f
primitive adj : primitivo
primrose n : primavera f
prince n : príncipe m — **princess** n : princesa f
principal adj : principal — **~** n : director m, -tora f (de un colegio)
principle n : principio m
print n **1** MARK : huella f **2** LETTERING : letra f **3** ENGRAVING : grabado m **4** : estampado m (de tela) **5** : copia f (en fotografía) **6 out of ~** : agotado — **~** vt : imprimir (libros, etc.) — vi : escribir con letra de molde — **printer** n **1** : impresor m, -sora f (persona) **2** : impresora f (máquina) — **printing** n **1** : impresión f **2** : imprenta f (profesión) **3** LETTERING : letras fpl de molde
prior adj **1** : previo **2 ~ to** : antes de — **priority** n, pl **-ties** : prioridad f
prison n : prisión f, cárcel f — **prisoner** n **1** : preso m, -sa f **2 ~ of war** : prisionero m, -ra f de guerra
privacy n, pl **-cies** : intimidad f — **private** adj **1** : privado **2** SECRET : secreto — **~** n : soldado m raso — **privately** adv : en privado
privilege n : privilegio m — **privileged** adj : privilegiado
prize n : premio m — **~** adj : premiado — **~** vt **prized; prizing** : valorar, apreciar — **prizefighter** n : boxeador m, -dora f profesional — **prizewinning** adj : premiado
pro n **1** → **professional 2 the ~s and cons** : los pros y los contras
probability n, pl **-ties** : probabilidad f — **probable** adj : probable — **probably** adv : probablemente
probation n **1** : período m de prueba (de un empleado, etc.) **2** : libertad f condicional (de un preso)

probe n **1** : sonda f (en medicina, etc.) **2** INVESTIGATION : investigación f — ~ vt **probed; probing 1** : sondar **2** INVESTIGATE : investigar

problem n : problema m

procedure n : procedimiento m

proceed vi **1** ACT : proceder **2** CONTINUE : continuar **3** ADVANCE : avanzar — **proceedings** npl **1** EVENTS : actos mpl **2** : proceso m (en derecho) — **proceeds** npl : ganancias fpl

process n, pl **-cesses 1** : proceso m **2 in the ~ of** : en vías de — ~ vt : procesar — **procession** n : desfile m

proclaim vt : proclamar — **proclamation** n : proclamación f

procrastinate vi **-nated; -nating** : demorar, aplazar

procure vt **-cured; -curing** : obtener

prod vt **prodded; prodding** : pinchar, aguijonear

prodigal adj : pródigo

prodigy n, pl **-gies** : prodigio m

produce vt **-duced; -ducing 1** : producir **2** CAUSE : causar **3** SHOW : presentar, mostrar **4** : poner en escena (una obra de teatro) — ~ n : productos mpl agrícolas — **producer** n : productor m, -tora f — **product** n : producto m — **productive** adj : productivo

profane adj **1** : profano **2** IRREVERENT : blasfemo — **profanity** n, pl **-ties** : blasfemia f

profess vt : profesar — **profession** n : profesión f — **professional** adj : profesional — ~ n : profesional mf — **professor** n : profesor m, -sora f

proficiency n : competencia f — **proficient** adj : competente

profile n **1** : perfil m **2 keep a low ~** : no llamar la atención

profit n : beneficio m, ganancia f — ~ vi : sacar provecho (de), beneficiarse (de) — **profitable** adj : provechoso

profound adj : profundo

profuse adj : profuso — **profusion** n : profusión f

prognosis n, pl **-noses** : pronóstico m

program n : programa m — ~ vt **-grammed** or **-gramed; -gramming** or **-graming** : programar

progress n **1** : progreso m **2** ADVANCE : avance m — ~ vi : progresar, avanzar — **progressive** adj **1** : progresista (dícese de la política, etc.) **2** INCREASING : progresiva

prohibit vt : prohibir — **prohibition** n : prohibición f

project n : proyecto m — ~ vt : proyectar — vi PROTRUDE : sobresalir — **projectile** n : proyectil m — **projection** n **1** : proyec-

ción f **2** PROTRUSION : saliente m — **projector** n : proyector m

proliferate vi **-ated; -ating** : proliferar — **proliferation** n : proliferación f — **prolific** adj : prolífico

prologue n : prólogo m

prolong vt : prolongar

prom n : baile m formal (en un colegio)

prominent adj : prominente — **prominence** n **1** : prominencia f **2** IMPORTANCE : eminencia f

promiscuous adj : promiscuo

promise n : promesa f — ~ v **-ised; -ising** : prometer — **promising** adj : prometedor

promote vt **-moted; -moting 1** : ascender (a un alumno o un empleado) **2** FURTHER : promover, fomentar **3** ADVERTISE : promocionar — **promoter** n : promotor m, -tora f; empresario m, -ria f (en deportes) — **promotion** n **1** : ascenso m (de un alumno o un empleado) **2** ADVERTISING : publicidad f, propaganda f

prompt vt **1** INCITE : provocar (una cosa), inducir (a una persona) **2** : apuntar (a un actor, etc.) — ~ adj **1** : rápido **2** PUNCTUAL : puntual

prone adj **1** : boca abajo, decúbito prono **2 be ~ to** : ser propenso a

prong n : punta f, diente m

pronoun n : pronombre m

pronounce vt **-nounced; -nouncing** : pronunciar — **pronouncement** n : declaración f — **pronunciation** n : pronunciación f

proof n : prueba f — ~ adj ~ **against** : a prueba de — **proofread** vt **-read; -reading** : corregir

prop n **1** SUPPORT : puntal m, apoyo m **2** : accesorio m (en teatro) — ~ vt **propped; propping 1 ~ against** : apoyar contra **2 ~ up** SUPPORT : apoyar

propaganda n : propaganda f

propagate v **-gated; -gating** vt : propagar — vi : propagarse

propel vt **-pelled; -pelling** : propulsar — **propeller** n : hélice f

propensity n, pl **-ties** : propensión f

proper adj **1** SUITABLE : apropiado **2** REAL : verdadero **3** CORRECT : correcto **4** GENTEEL : cortés **5 ~ name** : nombre m propio — **properly** adv : correctamente

property n, pl **-ties 1** : propiedad f **2** BUILDING : inmueble m **3** LAND, LOT : parcela f

prophet n **1** : profeta m, profetisa f — **prophecy** n, pl **-cies** : profecía f — **prophesy** v **-sied; -sying** vt : profetizar — vi : hacer profecías — **prophetic** adj : profético

proportion n **1** : proporción f **2** SHARE : parte f — **proportional** adj : proporcional — **proportionate** adj : proporcional

proposal *n* : propuesta *f*
propose *v* **-posed; -posing** *vt* **1** SUGGEST : proponer **2 ～ to do sth** : pensar hacer algo — *vi* : proponer matrimonio — **proposition** *n* : proposición *f*
proprietor *n* : propietario *m*, -ria *f*
propriety *n, pl* **-eties** : decencia *f*, decoro *m*
propulsion *n* : propulsión *f*
prose *n* : prosa *f*
prosecute *vt* **-cuted; -cuting** : procesar — **prosecution** *n* **1** : procesamiento *m* **2 the ～** : la acusación — **prosecutor** *n* : acusador *m*, -dora *f*
prospect *n* **1** : perspectiva *f* **2** POSSIBILITY : posibilidad *f* — **prospective** *adj* : futuro, posible
prosper *vi* : prosperar — **prosperity** *n* : prosperidad *f* — **prosperous** *adj* : próspero
prostitute *n* : prostituta *f* — **prostitution** *n* : prostitución *f*
prostrate *adj* : postrado
protagonist *n* : protagonista *mf*
protect *vt* : proteger — **protection** *n* : protección *f* — **protective** *adj* : protector — **protector** *n* : protector *m*, -tora *f*
protégé *n* : protegido *m*, -da *f*
protein *n* : proteína *f*
protest *n* : protesta *f* — **～** *vt* : protestar — *vi* **～ against** : protestar contra — **Protestant** *n* : protestante *mf* — **protester** *or* **protestor** *n* : manifestante *mf*
protocol *n* : protocolo *m*
prototype *n* : prototipo *m*
protract *vt* : prolongar
protrude *vi* **-truded; -truding** : sobresalir
proud *adj* : orgulloso
prove *v* **proved; proved** *or* **proven; proving** *vt* : probar — *vi* : resultar
proverb *n* : proverbio *m*, refrán *m* — **proverbial** *adj* : proverbial
provide *v* **-vided; -viding** *vt* : proveer — *vi* **～ for** SUPPORT : mantener — **provided** *or* **～ that** *conj* : con tal (de) que, siempre que — **providence** *n* : providencia *f*
province *n* **1** : provincia *f* **2** SPHERE : campo *m*, competencia *f* — **provincial** *adj* : provinciano
provision *n* **1** : provisión *f*, suministro *m* **2** STIPULATION : condición *f* **3 ～s** *npl* : víveres *mpl* — **provisional** *adj* : provisional — **proviso** *n, pl* **-sos** *or* **-soes** : condición *f*
provoke *vt* **-voked; -voking** : provocar — **provocation** *n* : provocación *f* — **provocative** *adj* : provocador, provocativo
prow *n* : proa *f*
prowess *n* **1** BRAVERY : valor *m* **2** SKILL : habilidad *f*

prowl *vi* : merodear, rondar — *vt* : merodear por — **prowler** *n* : merodeador *m*, -dora *f*
proximity *n* : proximidad *f* — **proxy** *n, pl* **proxies by ～** : por poder
prude *n* : mojigato *m*, -ta *f*
prudence *n* : prudencia *f* — **prudent** *adj* : prudente
prune¹ *n* : ciruela *f* pasa
prune² *vt* **pruned; pruning** : podar (arbustos, etc.)
pry *v* **pried; prying** *vi* **～ into** : entrometerse en — *vt or* **～ open** : abrir (a la fuerza)
psalm *n* : salmo *m*
pseudonym *n* : seudónimo *m*
psychiatry *n* : psiquiatría *f* — **psychiatric** *adj* : psiquiátrico — **psychiatrist** *n* : psiquiatra *mf*
psychic *adj* : psíquico
psychoanalysis *n, pl* **-yses** : psicoanálisis *m* — **psychoanalyst** *n* : psicoanalista *mf* — **psychoanalyze** *vt* **-lyzed; -lyzing** : psicoanalizar
psychology *n, pl* **-gies** : psicología *f* — **psychological** *adj* : psicológico — **psychologist** *n* : psicólogo *m*, -ga *f*
psychopath *n* : psicópata *mf*
psychotherapy *n, pl* **-pies** : psicoterapia *f*
psychotic *adj* : psicótico
puberty *n* : pubertad *f*
pubic *adj* : púbico
public *adj* : público — **～** *n* : público *m* — **publication** *n* : publicación *f* — **publicity** *n* : publicidad *f* — **publicize** *vt* **-cized; -cizing** : publicitar, divulgar
publish *vt* : publicar — **publisher** *n* **1** : editor *m*, -tora *f* (persona) **2** : casa *f* editorial (negocio)
pucker *vt* : fruncir, arrugar — *vi* : arrugarse
pudding *n* : budín *m*, pudín *m*
puddle *n* : charco *m*
pudgy *adj* **pudgier; -est** : rechoncho *fam*
Puerto Rican *adj* : puertorriqueño
puff *vi* **1** BLOW : soplar **2** PANT : resoplar **3 ～ up** SWELL : hincharse — *vt* **～ out** : hinchar — **～** *n* **1** : bocanada *f* (de humo) **2** : chupada *f* (a un cigarrillo) **3** *or* **cream ～** : pastelito *m* de crema **4** *or* **powder ～** : borla *f* — **puffy** *adj* **puffier; -est** : hinchado
pull *vt* **1** : tirar de **2** EXTRACT : sacar **3** TEAR : desgarrarse (un músculo, etc.) **4 ～ off** REMOVE : quitar **5 ～ oneself together** : calmarse **6 ～ up** : levantar, subir — *vi* **1** : tirar **2 ～ through** RECOVER : reponerse **3 ～ together** COOPERATE : reunir **4 ～ up** STOP : parar — **～** *n* **1** : tirón *m* **2** INFLUENCE : influencia *f* — **pulley** *n, pl* **-leys** : polea *f* — **pullover** *n* : suéter *m*

pulp n **1** : pulpa f (de frutas, etc.) **2** or **wood ~** : pasta f de papel
pulpit n : púlpito m
pulsate vi **-sated; -sating** : palpitar — **pulse** n : pulso m
pulverize vt **-ized; -izing** : pulverizar
pummel vt **-meled; -meling** : aporrear
pump¹ n : bomba f — **~** vt **1** : bombear **2 ~ up** : inflar
pump² n SHOE : zapato m de tacón
pumpernickel n : pan m negro de centeno
pumpkin n : calabaza f, zapallo m Lat
pun n : juego m de palabras — **~** vi **punned; punning** : hacer juegos de palabras
punch¹ vt **1** : dar un puñetazo a **2** PERFORATE : perforar (papeles, etc.), picar (un boleto) — **~** n **1** : golpe m, puñetazo m **2** or **paper ~** : perforadora f
punch² n : ponche m (bebida)
punctual adj : puntual — **punctuality** n : puntualidad f
punctuate vt **-ated; -ating** : puntuar — **punctuation** n : puntuación f
puncture n : pinchazo m, ponchadura f Lat — **~** vt **-tured; -turing** : pinchar, ponchar Lat
pungent adj : acre
punish vt : castigar — **punishment** n : castigo m — **punitive** adj : punitivo
puny adj **-nier; -est** : enclenque
pup n : cachorro m, -rra f (de un perro); cría f (de otros animales)
pupil¹ n : alumno m, -na f (de colegio)
pupil² n : pupila f (del ojo)
puppet n : títere m
puppy n, pl **-pies** : cachorro m, -rra f
purchase vt **-chased; -chasing** : comprar — **~** n : compra f
pure adj **purer; purest** : puro
puree n : puré m
purely adv : puramente
purgatory n, pl **-ries** : purgatorio m — **purge** vt **purged; purging** : purgar — **~** n : purga f
purify vt **-fied; -fying** : purificar — **purification** n : purificación f
puritanical adj : puritano

purity n : pureza f
purple n : morado m
purport vt **~ to be** : pretender ser
purpose n **1** : propósito m **2** RESOLUTION : determinación f **3 on ~** : a propósito — **purposeful** adj : resuelto — **purposely** adv : a propósito
purr n : ronroneo m — **~** vi : ronronear
purse n **1** or **change ~** : monedero m **2** HANDBAG : cartera f, bolso m Spain, bolsa f Lat — **~** vt **pursed; pursing** : fruncir
pursue vt **-sued; -suing 1** CHASE : perseguir **2** SEEK : buscar — **pursuer** n : perseguidor m, -dora f — **pursuit** n **1** CHASE : persecución f **2** SEARCH : búsqueda f **3** OCCUPATION : actividad f
pus n : pus m
push vt **1** SHOVE : empujar **2** PRESS : apretar **3** URGE : presionar **4 ~ around** BULLY : mangonear — vi **1** : empujar **2 ~ for** : presionar para — **~** n **1** SHOVE : empujón m **2** DRIVE : dinamismo m **3** EFFORT : esfuerzo m — **pushy** adj **pushier; -est** : mandón, prepotente
pussy n, pl **pussies** : gatito m, -ta f; minino m, -na f
put v **put; putting** vt **1** : poner **2** INSERT : meter **3** EXPRESS : decir **4 ~ one's mind to sth** : proponerse hacer algo — vi **~ up with** : aguantar — **put away** vt **1** STORE : guardar **2** or **~ aside** : dejar a un lado — **put down** vt **1** SUPPRESS : aplastar, sofocar **2** ATTRIBUTE : atribuir — **put off** vt DEFER : aplazar, posponer — **put on** vt **1** ASSUME : adoptar **2** PRESENT : presentar (una obra de teatro, etc.) **3** WEAR : ponerse — **put out** vt INCONVENIENCE : incomodar — **put up** vt **1** BUILD : construir **2** LODGE : alojar **3** PROVIDE : poner (dinero)
putrefy vi **-fied; -fying** : pudrirse
putty n, pl **-ties** : masilla f
puzzle v **-zled; -zling** vt : confundir, dejar perplejo — vi **~ over** : tratar de descifrar — **~** n **1** : rompecabezas m **2** MYSTERY : enigma m
pylon n : pilón m
pyramid n : pirámide f
python n : pitón f

Q

q *n, pl* **q's** *or* **qs** : q *f*, decimoséptima letra del alfabeto inglés

quack[1] *vi* : graznar (dícese del pato) — ~ *n* : graznido *m*

quack[2] *n* CHARLATAN : charlatán *m*, -tana *f*

quadruple *v* **-pled; -pling** *vt* : cuadruplicar — *vi* : cuadruplicarse

quagmire *n* : atolladero *m*

quail *n, pl* **quail** *or* **quails** : codorniz *f*

quaint *adj* **1** ODD : curioso **2** PICTURESQUE : pintoresco

quake *vi* **quaked; quaking** : temblar — ~ *n* → **earthquake**

qualify *v* **-fied; -fying** *vt* **1** LIMIT : matizar **2** : calificar (en gramática) **3** EQUIP : habilitar — *vi* **1** : titularse (de abogado, etc.) **2** : clasificarse (en deportes) — **qualification** *n* **1** REQUIREMENT : requisito *m* **2** ~**s** *npl* ABILITY : capacidad *f* **3 without** ~ : sin reservas — **qualified** *adj* : capacitado

quality *n, pl* **-ties 1** : calidad *f* **2** PROPERTY : cualidad *f*

qualm *n* **1** DOUBT : duda *f* **2 have no** ~**s about** : no tener ningún escrúpulo en

quandary *n, pl* **-ries** : dilema *m*

quantity *n, pl* **-ties** : cantidad *f*

quarantine *n* : cuarentena *f* — ~ *vt* **-tined; -tining** : poner en cuarentena

quarrel *n* : pelea *f*, riña *f* — ~ *vi* **-reled** *or* **-relled; -reling** *or* **-relling** : pelearse, reñir — **quarrelsome** *adj* : pendenciero

quarry[1] *n, pl* **quarries** PREY : presa *f*

quarry[2] *n, pl* **quarries** EXCAVATION : cantera *f*

quart *n* : cuarto *m* de galón

quarter *n* **1** : cuarto *m* (en matemáticas) **2** : moneda *f* de 25 centavos **3** DISTRICT : barrio *m* **4** ~ **after three** : las tres y cuarto **5** ~**s** *npl* LODGING : alojamiento *m* — ~ *vt* **1** : dividir en cuatro partes **2** : acuartelar (tropas) — **quarterly** *adv* : cada tres meses — ~ *adj* : trimestral — ~ *n, pl* **-lies** : publicación *f* trimestral

quartet *n* : cuarteto *m*

quartz *n* : cuarzo *m*

quash *vt* **1** ANNUL : anular **2** SUPPRESS : aplastar, sofocar

quaver *vi* : temblar

quay *n* : muelle *m*

queasy *adj* **-sier; -est** : mareado

queen *n* : reina *f*

queer *adj* ODD : extraño

quell *vt* SUPPRESS : sofocar, aplastar

quench *vt* **1** EXTINGUISH : apagar **2** ~ **one's thirst** : quitar la sed

query *n, pl* **-ries** : pregunta *f* — ~ *vt* **-ried; -rying 1** ASK : preguntar **2** QUESTION : cuestionar

quest *n* : búsqueda *f*

question *n* **1** QUERY : pregunta *f* **2** ISSUE : cuestión *f* **3 be out of the** ~ : ser indiscutible **4 call into** ~ : poner en duda **5 without** ~ : sin duda — ~ *vt* **1** ASK : preguntar **2** DOUBT : cuestionar **3** INTERROGATE : interrogar — *vi* : preguntar — **questionable** *adj* : discutible — **question mark** *n* : signo *m* de interrogación — **questionnaire** *n* : cuestionario *m*

queue *n* : cola *f* — ~ *vi* **queued; queuing** *or* **queueing** : hacer cola

quibble *vi* **-bled; -bling** : discutir, quejarse por nimiedades

quick *adj* **1** : rápido **2** CLEVER : agudo — ~ *n* **to the** ~ : en lo vivo — ~ *adv* : rápidamente — **quicken** *vt* : acelerar — **quickly** *adv* : rápidamente — **quicksand** *n* : arena *f* movediza — **quick–tempered** *adj* : irascible — **quick–witted** *adj* : agudo

quiet *n* **1** : silencio *m* **2** CALM : tranquilidad *f* — ~ *adj* **1** : silencioso **2** CALM : tranquilo **3** RESERVED : callado **4** : discreto (dícese de colores, etc.) — ~ *vt* **1** SILENCE : hacer callar **2** CALM : calmar — *vi* *or* ~ **down** : calmarse — **quietly** *adv* **1** : silenciosamente **2** CALMLY : tranquilamente

quilt *n* : edredón *m*

quintet *n* : quinteto *m*

quip *n* : ocurrencia *f*, salida *f* — ~ *vt* **quipped; quipping** : decir bromeando

quirk *n* : peculiaridad *f*

quit *v* **quit; quitting** *vt* **1** LEAVE : dejar, abandonar **2** ~ **doing** : dejar de hacer — *vi* **1** STOP : parar **2** RESIGN : dimitir, renunciar

quite *adv* **1** COMPLETELY : completamente **2** RATHER : bastante

quits *adj* **call it** ~ : quedar en paz

quiver *vi* : temblar

quiz *n, pl* **quizzes** TEST : prueba *f* — ~ *vt* **quizzed; quizzing** : interrogar

quota *n* : cuota *f*, cupo *m*

quotation *n* **1** : cita *f* **2** ESTIMATE : presupuesto *m* — **quotation marks** *npl* : comillas *fpl* — **quote** *vt* **quoted; quoting 1** CITE : citar **2** : cotizar (en finanzas) — ~ *n* **1** → **quotation 2** ~**s** *npl* → **quotation marks**

quotient *n* : cociente *m*

R

r *n, pl* **r's** *or* **rs** : r *f*, decimoctava letra del alfabeto inglés

rabbi *n* : rabino *m*, -na *f*

rabbit *n, pl* **-bit** *or* **-bits** : conejo *m*, -ja *f*

rabble *n* : chusma *f*, populacho *m*

rabies *ns & pl* : rabia *f* — **rabid** *adj* **1** : rabioso **2** FANATIC : fanático

raccoon *n, pl* **-coon** *or* **-coons** : mapache *m*

race¹ *n* **1** : raza *f* **2 human ~** : género *m* humano

race² *n* : carrera *f* (competitiva) — **~** *vi* **raced; racing 1** : correr (en una carrera) **2** RUSH : ir corriendo — **racehorse** *n* : caballo *m* de carreras — **racetrack** : pista *f* (de carreras)

racial *adj* : racial — **racism** *n* : racismo *m* — **racist** *n* : racista *mf*

rack *n* **1** SHELF : estante *m* **2 luggage ~** : portaequipajes *m* — **~** *vt* **1 ~ed with** : atormentado por **2 ~ one's brains** : devanarse los sesos

racket¹ *n* : raqueta *f* (en deportes)

racket² *n* **1** DIN : alboroto *m*, bulla *f* **2** SWINDLE : estafa *f*

racy *adj* **racier; -est** : subido de tono, picante

radar *n* : radar *m*

radiant *adj* : radiante — **radiance** *n* : resplandor *m* — **radiate** *v* **-ated; -ating** *vt* : irradiar — *vi* **1** : irradiar **2** *or* **~ out** : extenderse (desde un centro) — **radiation** *n* : radiación *f* — **radiator** *n* : radiador *m*

radical *adj* : radical — **~** *n* : radical *mf*

radii → **radius**

radio *n, pl* **-dios** : radio *mf* (aparato), radio *f* (medio) — **~** *vt* : transmitir por radio — **radioactive** *adj* : radioactivo, radiactivo

radish *n* : rábano *m*

radius *n, pl* **radii** : radio *m*

raffle *vt* **-fled; -fling** : rifar — **~** *n* : rifa *f*

raft *n* : balsa *f*

rafter *n* : cabrio *m*

rag *n* **1** : trapo *m* **2 ~s** *npl* TATTERS : harapos *mpl*, andrajos *mpl*

rage *n* **1** : cólera *f*, rabia *f* **2 be all the ~** : hacer furor — **~** *vi* **raged; raging 1** : estar furioso **2** : bramar (dícese del viento, etc.)

ragged *adj* **1** UNEVEN : irregular **2** TATTERED : andrajoso, harapiento

raid *n* **1** : invasión *f* (militar) **2** : asalto *m* (por delincuentes), redada *f* (por la policía) — **~** *vt* **1** INVADE : invadir **2** ROB : asaltar **3** : hacer una redada en (dícese de la policía) — **raider** *n* ATTACKER : asaltante *mf*

rail¹ *vi* **~ at s.o.** : recriminar a algn

rail² *n* **1** BAR : barra *f* **2** HANDRAIL : pasamanos *m* **3** TRACK : riel *m* **4 by ~** : por ferrocarril — **railing** *n* **1** : baranda *f* (de un balcón), pasamanos *m* (de una escalera) **2** RAILS : reja *f* — **railroad** *n* : ferrocarril *m* — **railway** → **railroad**

rain *n* : lluvia *f* — **~** *vi* : llover — **rainbow** *n* : arco *m* iris — **raincoat** *n* : impermeable *m* — **rainfall** *n* : precipitación *f* — **rainy** *adj* **rainier; -est** : lluvioso

raise *vt* **raised; raising 1** : levantar **2** COLLECT : recaudar **3** REAR : criar **4** GROW : cultivar **5** INCREASE : aumentar **6** : sacar (objeciones, etc.) — **~** *n* : aumento *m*

raisin *n* : pasa *f*

rake *n* : rastrillo *m* — **~** *vt* **raked; raking** : rastrillar

rally *v* **-lied; -lying** *vi* **1** : unirse, reunirse **2** RECOVER : recuperarse — *vt* : conseguir (apoyo), unir a (la gente) — **~** *n, pl* **-lies** : reunión *f*, mitin *m*

ram *n* : carnero *m* (animal) — **~** *vt* **rammed; ramming 1** CRAM : meter con fuerza **2** *or* **~ into** : chocar contra

RAM *n* : RAM *f*

ramble *vi* **-bled; -bling 1** WANDER : pasear **2** *or* **~ on** : divagar — **~** *n* : paseo *m*, excursión *f*

ramp *n* : rampa *f*

rampage *vi* **-paged; -paging** : andar arrasando todo — **~** *n* : frenesí *m* (de violencia)

rampant *adj* : desenfrenado

rampart *n* : muralla *f*

ramshackle *adj* : destartalado

ran → **run**

ranch *n* : hacienda *f* — **rancher** *n* : hacendado *m*, -da *f*

rancid *adj* : rancio

rancor *n* : rencor *m*

random *adj* **1** : aleatorio **2 at ~** : al azar

rang → **ring**

range *n* **1** GRASSLAND : pradera *f* **2** STOVE : cocina *f* **3** VARIETY : gama *f* **4** SCOPE : amplitud *f* **5** *or* **mountain ~** : cordillera *f* — **~** *vi* **ranged; ranging 1** EXTEND : extenderse **2** **~ from...to...** : variar entre...y... — **ranger** *n* *or* **forest ~** : guardabosque *mf*

rank¹ *adj* **1** SMELLY : fétido **2** OUTRIGHT : completo

rank² *n* **1** ROW : fila *f* **2** : rango *m* (militar) **3 ~s** *npl* : soldados *mpl* rasos **4 the ~**

and file : las bases — ~ *vt* RATE : clasificar — *vi* : clasificarse

rankle *vi* **-kled; -kling** : causar rencor, doler

ransack *vt* **1** SEARCH : registrar **2** LOOT : saquear

ransom *n* : rescate *m* — ~ *vt* : rescatar

rant *vi or* ~ **and rave** : despotricar

rap¹ *n* KNOCK : golpecito *m* — ~ *v* **rapped; rapping** : golpear

rap² *n or* ~ **music** : rap *m*

rapacious *adj* : rapaz

rape *vt* **raped; raping** : violar — ~ *n* : violación *f*

rapid *adj* : rápido — **rapids** *npl* : rápidos *mpl*

rapist *n* : violador *m*, -dora *f*

rapport *n* **have a good** ~ : entenderse bien

rapt *adj* : absorto, embelesado

rapture *n* : éxtasis *m*

rare *adj* **rarer; rarest 1** FINE : excepcional **2** UNCOMMON : raro **3** : poco cocido (dícese de la carne) — **rarely** *adv* : raramente — **rarity** *n*, *pl* **-ties** : rareza *f*

rascal *n* : pillo *m*, -lla *f*; pícaro *m*, -ra *f*

rash¹ *adj* : imprudente, precipitado

rash² *n* : sarpullido *m*, erupción *f*

rasp *vt* SCRAPE : raspar — ~ *n* : escofina *f*

raspberry *n*, *pl* **-ries** : frambuesa *f*

rat *n* : rata *f*

rate *n* **1** PACE : velocidad *f*, ritmo *m* **2** : tipo *m*, tasa *m* (de interés, etc.) **3** PRICE : tarifa *f* **4 at any** ~ : de todos modos **5 birth** ~ : índice *m* de natalidad — ~ *vt* **rated; rating 1** REGARD : considerar **2** DESERVE : merecer

rather *adv* **1** FAIRLY : bastante **2 I'd** ~... : prefiero… **3 or** ~ : o mejor dicho

ratify *vt* **-fied; -fying** : ratificar — **ratification** *n* : ratificación *f*

rating *n* **1** : clasificación *f* **2** ~**s** *npl* : índice *m* de audiencia

ratio *n*, *pl* **-tios** : proporción *f*

ration *n* **1** : ración *f* **2** ~**s** *npl* PROVISIONS : víveres *mpl* — ~ *vt* **rationed; rationing** : racionar

rational *adj* : racional — **rationale** *n* : lógica *f*, razones *fpl* — **rationalize** *vt* **-ized; -izing** : racionalizar

rattle *v* **-tled; -tling** *vi* : traquetear — *vt* **1** SHAKE : agitar **2** UPSET : desconcertar **3** ~ **off** : decir de corrido — ~ *n* **1** : traqueteo *m* **2 baby's** ~ : sonajero *m* — **rattlesnake** *n* : serpiente *f* de cascabel

raucous *adj* **1** HOARSE : ronco **2** BOISTEROUS : bullicioso

ravage *vt* **-aged; -aging** : estragar, asolar — **ravages** *npl* : estragos *mpl*

rave *vi* **raved; raving 1** : delirar **2** ~ **about** : hablar con entusiasmo sobre

raven *n* : cuervo *m*

ravenous *adj* **1** HUNGRY : hambriento **2** VORACIOUS : voraz

ravine *n* : barranco *m*

ravishing *adj* : encantador

raw *adj* **rawer; rawest 1** UNCOOKED : crudo **2** INEXPERIENCED : inexperto **3** CHAFED : en carne viva **4** : frío y húmedo (dícese del tiempo) **5** ~ **deal** : trato *m* injusto **6** ~ **materials** : materias *fpl* primas

ray *n* : rayo *m*

rayon *n* : rayón *m*

raze *vt* **razed; razing** : arrasar

razor *n* : maquinilla *f* de afeitar — **razor blade** *n* : hoja *f* de afeitar

reach *vt* **1** : alcanzar **2** *or* ~ **out** : extender **3** : llegar a (un acuerdo, un límite, etc.) **4** CONTACT : contactar — *vi* **1** : extenderse **2** ~ **for** : tratar de agarrar — ~ *n* **1** : alcance *m* **2 within** ~ : al alcance

react *vi* : reaccionar — **reaction** *n* : reacción *f* — **reactionary** *adj* : reaccionario — ~ *n*, *pl* **-ries** : reaccionario *m*, -ria *f* — **reactor** *n* : reactor *m*

read *v* **read; reading** *vt* **1** : leer **2** INTERPRET : interpretar **3** SAY : decir **4** INDICATE : marcar — *vi* **1** : leer **2 it** ~**s as follows** : dice lo siguiente — **readable** *adj* : legible — **reader** *n* : lector *m*, -tora *f*

readily *adv* **1** WILLINGLY : de buena gana **2** EASILY : fácilmente

reading *n* : lectura *f*

readjust *vt* : reajustar — *vi* : volverse a adaptar

ready *adj* **readier; -est 1** : listo, preparado **2** WILLING : dispuesto **3** AVAILABLE : disponible **4 get** ~ : prepararse — ~ *vt* **readied; readying** : preparar

real *adj* **1** : verdadero, real **2** GENUINE : auténtico — ~ *adv* VERY : muy — **real estate** *n* : propiedad *f* inmobiliaria, bienes *mpl* raíces — **realism** *n* : realismo *m* — **realist** *n* : realista *mf* — **realistic** *adj* : realista — **reality** *n*, *pl* **-ties** : realidad *f*

realize *vt* **-ized; -izing 1** : darse cuenta de **2** ACHIEVE : realizar — **realization** *n* **1** : comprensión *f* **2** FULFILLMENT : realización *f*

really *adv* : verdaderamente

realm *n* **1** KINGDOM : reino *m* **2** SPHERE : esfera *f*

ream *n* : resma *f* (de papel)

reap *v* : cosechar

reappear *vi* : reaparecer

rear¹ *vt* **1** RAISE : levantar **2** : criar (niños, etc.) — *vi or* ~ **up** : encabritarse

rear² *n* **1** BACK : parte *f* de atrás **2** BUTTOCKS : trasero *m fam* — ~ *adj* : trasero, posterior

rearrange *vt* **-ranged; -ranging** : reorganizar, cambiar

reason *n* : razón *f* — ~ *vt* THINK : pensar — *vi* : razonar — **reasonable** *adj* : razonable — **reasoning** *n* : razonamiento *m*

reassure *vt* **-sured; -suring** : tranquilizar — **reassurance** *n* : (palabras *fpl* de) consuelo *m*

rebate *n* : reembolso *m*

rebel *n* : rebelde *mf* — ~ *vi* **-belled; -belling** : rebelarse — **rebellion** *n* : rebelión *f* — **rebellious** *adj* : rebelde

rebirth *n* : renacimiento *m*

rebound *vi* : rebotar — ~ *n* : rebote *m*

rebuff *vt* : rechazar — ~ *n* : desaire *m*

rebuild *vt* **-built; -building** : reconstruir

rebuke *vt* **-buked; -buking** : reprender — ~ *n* : reprimenda *f*

rebut *vt* **-butted; -butting** : rebatir — **rebuttal** *n* : refutación *f*

recall *vt* **1** : llamar (al servicio, etc.) **2** REMEMBER : recordar **3** REVOKE : revocar — ~ *n* **1** : retirada *f* **2** MEMORY : memoria *f*

recant *vi* : retractarse

recapitulate *v* **-lated; -lating** : recapitular

recapture *vt* **-tured; -turing 1** : recobrar **2** RELIVE : revivir

recede *vi* **-ceded; -ceding** : retirarse

receipt *n* **1** : recibo *m* **2** ~**s** *npl* : ingresos *mpl*

receive *vt* **-ceived; -ceiving** : recibir — **receiver** *n* **1** : receptor *m* (de radio, etc.) **2** *or* **telephone** ~ : auricular *m*

recent *adj* : reciente — **recently** *adv* : recientemente

receptacle *n* : receptáculo *m*, recipiente *m*

reception *n* : recepción *f* — **receptionist** *n* : recepcionista *mf* — **receptive** *adj* : receptivo

recess *n* **1** ALCOVE : hueco *m* **2** : recreo *m* (escolar) **3** ADJOURNMENT : suspensión *f* de actividades *Spain*, receso *m Lat* — **recession** *n* : recesión *f*

recharge *vt* **-charged; -charging** : recargar — **rechargeable** *adj* : recargable

recipe *n* : receta *f*

recipient *n* : recipiente *mf*

reciprocal *adj* : recíproco

recite *vt* **-cited; -citing 1** : recitar (un poema, etc.) **2** LIST : enumerar — **recital** *n* : recital *m*

reckless *adj* : imprudente — **recklessness** *n* : imprudencia *f*

reckon *vt* **1** COMPUTE : calcular **2** CONSIDER : considerar — **reckoning** *n* : cálculos *mpl*

reclaim *vt* **1** : reclamar **2** RECOVER : recuperar

recline *vi* **-clined; -clining** : reclinarse — **re-**

clining *adj* : reclinable (dícese de un asiento, etc.)

recluse *n* : solitario *m*, -ria *f*

recognition *n* : reconocimiento *m* — **recognizable** *adj* : reconocible — **recognize** *vt* **-nized; -nizing** : reconocer

recoil *vi* : retroceder — ~ *n* : culatazo *m* (de un arma de fuego)

recollect *v* : recordar — **recollection** *n* : recuerdo *m*

recommend *vt* : recomendar — **recommendation** *n* : recomendación *f*

reconcile *v* **-ciled; -ciling** *vt* **1** : reconciliar (personas), conciliar (datos, etc.) **2** ~ **oneself to** : resignarse a — *vi* MAKE UP : reconciliarse — **reconciliation** *n* : reconciliación *f*

reconnaissance *n* : reconocimiento *m* (militar)

reconsider *vt* : reconsiderar

reconstruct *vt* : reconstruir

record *vt* **1** WRITE DOWN : anotar, apuntar **2** REGISTER : registrar **3** : grabar (música, etc.) — ~ *n* **1** DOCUMENT : documento *m* **2** REGISTER : registro *m* **3** HISTORY : historial *m* **4** : disco *m* (de música, etc.) **5** **criminal** ~ : antecedentes *mpl* penales **6** **world** ~ : récord *m* mundial — **recorder** *n* **1** : flauta *f* dulce **2** *or* **tape** ~ : grabadora *f* — **recording** *n* : disco *m* — **record player** *n* : tocadiscos *m*

recount¹ *vt* NARRATE : narrar, relatar

recount² *vt* : volver a contar (votos, etc.) ~ — *n* : recuento *m*

recourse *n* **1** : recurso *m* **2** **have** ~ **to** : recurrir a

recover *vt* : recobrar — *vi* RECUPERATE : recuperarse — **recovery** *n, pl* **-eries** : recuperación *f*

recreation *n* : recreo *m* — **recreational** *adj* : de recreo

recruit *vt* : reclutar — ~ *n* : recluta *mf* — **recruitment** *n* : reclutamiento *m*

rectangle *n* : rectángulo *m* — **rectangular** *adj* : rectangular

rectify *vt* **-fied; -fying** : rectificar

rector *n* **1** : párroco *m* (clérigo) **2** : rector *m*, -tora *f* (de una universidad) — **rectory** *n, pl* **-ries** : rectoría *f*

rectum *n, pl* **-tums** *or* **-ta** : recto *m*

recuperate *v* **-ated; -ating** *vt* : recuperar — *vi* : recuperarse — **recuperation** *n* : recuperación *f*

recur *vi* **-curred; -curring** : repetirse — **recurrence** *n* : repetición *f* — **recurrent** *adj* : que se repite

recycle *vt* **-cled; -cling** : reciclar

red *adj* : rojo — ~ *n* : rojo *m* — **redden** *vt*

: enrojecer — *vi* : enrojecerse — **reddish** *adj* : rojizo

redecorate *vt* **-rated; -rating** : pintar de nuevo

redeem *vt* **1** SAVE : salvar, rescatar **2** : desempeñar (de un monte de piedad) **3** : canjear (cupones, etc.) — **redemption** *n* : redención *f*

red–handed *adv or adj* : con las manos en la masa

redhead *n* : pelirrojo *m*, -ja *f*

red–hot *adj* : al rojo vivo

redness *n* : rojez *f*

redo *vt* **-did; -done; -doing** : hacer de nuevo

redouble *vt* **-bled; -bling** : redoblar

red tape *n* : papeleo *m*

reduce *v* **-duced; -ducing** *vt* : reducir — *vi* SLIM : adelgazar — **reduction** *n* : reducción *f*

redundant *adj* : redundante

reed *n* **1** : caña *f* **2** : lengüeta *f* (de un instrumento)

reef *n* : arrecife *m*

reek *vi* : apestar

reel *n* : carrete *m* (de hilo, etc.) — **~** *vt* **1** **~ in** : enrollar (un sedal), sacar (un pez) del agua **2 ~ off** : enumerar — *vi* **1** SPIN : dar vueltas **2** STAGGER : tambalearse

reestablish *vt* : restablecer

refer *v* **-ferred; -ferring** *vt* **1** DIRECT : enviar, mandar **2** SUBMIT : remitir — *vi* **~ to 1** MENTION : referirse a **2** CONSULT : consultar

referee *n* : árbitro *m*, -tra *f* — **~** *v* **-eed; -eeing** : arbitrar

reference *n* **1** : referencia *f* **2** CONSULTATION : consulta *f* **3** *or* **~ book** : libro *m* de consulta **4 in ~ to** : con referencia a

refill *vt* : rellenar — **~** *n* : recambio *m*

refine *vt* **-fined; -fining** : refinar — **refined** *adj* : refinado — **refinement** *n* : refinamiento *m* — **refinery** *n*, *pl* **-eries** : refinería *f*

reflect *vt* : reflejar — *vi* **1** : reflejarse **2 ~ badly on** : desacreditar **3 ~ upon** : reflexionar sobre — **reflection** *n* **1** : reflexión *f* **2** IMAGE : reflejo *m* — **reflector** *n* : reflector *m*

reflex *n* : reflejo *m*

reflexive *adj* : reflexivo

reform *vt* : reformar — *vi* : reformarse — **~** *n* : reforma *f* — **reformer** *n* : reformador *m*, -dora *f*

refrain¹ *vi* **~ from** : abstenerse de

refrain² *n* : estribillo *m* (en música)

refresh *vt* : refrescar — **refreshments** *npl* : refrigerio *m*

refrigerate *vt* **-ated; -ating** : refrigerar — **refrigeration** *n* : refrigeración *f* — **refrigera-**

tor *n* : nevera *f*, refrigerador *m* *Lat*, frigorífico *m* *Spain*

refuel *v* **-eled** *or* **-elled; -eling** *or* **-elling** *vt* : llenar de carburante — *vi* : repostar

refuge *n* : refugio *m* — **refugee** *n* : refugiado *m*, -da *f*

refund *vt* : reembolsar — **~** *n* : reembolso *m*

refurbish *vt* : renovar, restaurar

refuse¹ *v* **-fused; -fusing** *vt* **1** : rehusar, rechazar **2 ~ to do sth** : negarse a hacer algo — *vi* : negarse — **refusal** *n* : negativa *f*

refuse² *n* : residuos *mpl*, desperdicios *mpl*

refute *vt* **-futed; -futing** : refutar

regain *vt* : recuperar, recobrar

regal *adj* : regio, majestuoso — **regalia** *n* : ropaje *m*, insignias *fpl*

regard *n* **1** : consideración *f* **2** ESTEEM : estima *f* **3 in this ~** : en este sentido **4 ~s** *npl* : saludos *mpl* **5 with ~ to** : respecto a — **~** *vt* **1** : mirar (con recelo, etc.) **2** HEED : tener en cuenta **3** ESTEEM : estimar **4 as ~s** : en lo que se refiere a **5 ~ as** : considerar — **regarding** *prep* : respecto a — **regardless** *adv* : a pesar de todo — **regardless of** *prep* **1** : sin tener en cuenta **2** IN SPITE OF : a pesar de

regent *n* : regente *mf*

regime *n* : régimen *m* — **regimen** *n* : régimen *m*

regiment *n* : regimiento *m*

region *n* : región *f* — **regional** *adj* : regional

register *n* : registro *m* — **~** *vt* **1** : registrar (a personas), matricular (vehículos) **2** SHOW : marcar, manifestar **3** : certificar (correo) — *vi* ENROLL : inscribirse, matricularse — **registrar** *n* : registrador *m*, -dora *f* oficial — **registration** *n* **1** : inscripción *f*, matriculación *f* **2** *or* **~ number** : número *m* de matrícula — **registry** *n*, *pl* **-tries** : registro *m*

regret *vt* **-gretted; -gretting** : lamentar — **~** *n* **1** REMORSE : arrepentimiento *m* **2** SORROW : pesar *m* — **regrettable** *adj* : lamentable

regular *adj* **1** : regular **2** CUSTOMARY : habitual — **~** *n* : cliente *mf* habitual — **regularity** *n*, *pl* **-ties** : regularidad *f* — **regularly** *adv* : regularmente — **regulate** *vt* **-lated; -lating** : regular — **regulation** *n* **1** CONTROL : regulación *f* **2** RULE : regla *f*

rehabilitate *vt* **-tated; -tating** : rehabilitar — **rehabilitation** *n* : rehabilitación *f*

rehearse *v* **-hearsed; -hearsing** : ensayar — **rehearsal** *n* : ensayo *m*

reign *n* : reinado *m* — **~** *vi* : reinar

reimburse *vt* **-bursed; -bursing** : reembolsar — **reimbursement** *n* : reembolso *m*

rein *n* : rienda *f*

reincarnation *n* : reencarnación *f*

reindeer *n* : reno *m*

reinforce *vt* **-forced; -forcing** : reforzar — **reinforcement** *n* : refuerzo *m*

reinstate *vt* **-stated; -stating** **1** : restablecer **2** : restituir (a algn en su cargo)

reiterate *vt* **-ated; -ating** : reiterar

reject *vt* : rechazar — **rejection** *n* : rechazo *m*

rejoice *vi* **-joiced; -joicing** : regocijarse

rejuvenate *vt* **-nated; -nating** : rejuvenecer

rekindle *vt* **-dled; -dling** : reavivar

relapse *n* : recaída *f* — ~ *vi* **-lapsed; -lapsing** : recaer

relate *v* **-lated; -lating** *vt* **1** TELL : relatar **2** ASSOCIATE : relacionar — *vi* ~ **to 1** CONCERN : estar relacionado con **2** UNDERSTAND : identificarse con **3** : relacionarse con (socialmente) — **related** *adj* ~ **to** : emparentado con — **relation** *n* **1** CONNECTION : relación *f* **2** RELATIVE : pariente *mf* **3** **in** ~ **to** : en relación con **4** ~**s** *npl* : relaciones *fpl* — **relationship** *n* **1** : relación *f* **2** KINSHIP : parentesco *m* — **relative** *n* : pariente *mf* — ~ *adj* : relativo — **relatively** *adv* : relativamente

relax *vt* : relajar — *vi* : relajarse — **relaxation** *n* **1** : relajación *f* **2** RECREATION : esparcimiento *m*

relay *n* **1** : relevo *m* **2** *or* ~ **race** : carrera *f* de relevos — ~ *vt* **-layed; -laying** : transmitir

release *vt* **-leased; -leasing** **1** FREE : liberar, poner en libertad **2** : soltar (un freno, etc.) **3** EMIT : despedir **4** : sacar (un libro, etc.), estrenar (una película) — ~ *n* **1** : liberación *f* **2** : estreno *m* (de una película), publicación *f* (de un libro) **3** : fuga *f* (de gases)

relegate *vt* **-gated; -gating** : relegar

relent *vi* : ceder — **relentless** *adj* : implacable

relevant *adj* : pertinente — **relevance** *n* : pertinencia *f*

reliable *adj* : fiable (dícese de personas), fidedigno (dícese de información, etc.) — **reliability** *n, pl* **-ties** : fiabilidad *f* (de una cosa), responsabilidad *f* (de una persona) — **reliance** *n* **1** : dependencia *f* **2** TRUST : confianza *f* — **reliant** *adj* : dependiente

relic *n* : reliquia *f*

relief *n* **1** : alivio *m* **2** AID : ayuda *f* **3** : relieve *m* (en la escultura) **4** REPLACEMENT : relevo *m* — **relieve** *vt* **-lieved; -lieving** **1** : aliviar **2** REPLACE : relevar (a algn) **3** ~ **s.o. of** : liberar a algn de

religion *n* : religión *f* — **religious** *adj* : religioso

relinquish *vt* : renunciar a, abandonar

relish *n* **1** : salsa *f* (condimento) **2 with** ~ : con gusto — ~ *vt* : saborear

relocate *vt* **-cated; -cating** : trasladar — *vi* : trasladarse — **relocation** *n* : traslado *m*

reluctance *n* : reticencia *f*, desgana *f* — **reluctant** *adj* : reacio, reticente — **reluctantly** *adv* : a regañadientes

rely *vi* **-lied; -lying** ~ **on 1** DEPEND ON : depender de **2** TRUST : confiar (en)

remain *vi* **1** : quedar **2** STAY : quedarse **3** CONTINUE : seguir, continuar — **remainder** *n* : resto *m* — **remains** *npl* : restos *mpl*

remark *n* : comentario *m*, observación *f* — ~ *vt* : observar — *vi* ~ **on** : observar — **remarkable** *adj* : extraordinario, notable

remedy *n, pl* **-dies** : remedio *m* — ~ *vt* **-died; -dying** : remediar — **remedial** *adj* : correctivo

remember *vt* **1** : acordarse de, recordar **2** ~ **to** : acordarse de — *vi* : acordarse, recordar — **remembrance** *n* : recuerdo *m*

remind *vt* : recordar — **reminder** *n* : recordatorio *m*

reminiscence *n* : recuerdo *m*, reminiscencia *f* — **reminisce** *vi* **-nisced; -niscing** : rememorar los viejos tiempos — **reminiscent** *adj* **be** ~ **of** : recordar

remiss *adj* : negligente, remiso

remit *vt* **-mitted; -mitting** **1** PARDON : perdonar **2** : enviar (dinero) — **remission** *n* : remisión *f*

remnant *n* **1** : resto *m* **2** TRACE : vestigio *m*

remorse *n* : remordimiento *m* — **remorseful** *adj* : arrepentido

remote *adj* **-moter; -est 1** : remoto **2** ALOOF : distante **3** ~ **from** : apartado de, alejado de — **remote control** *n* : control *m* remoto — **remotely** *adv* SLIGHTLY : remotamente

remove *vt* **-moved; -moving** **1** : quitar (una tapa, etc.), quitarse (ropa) **2** EXTRACT : sacar **3** DISMISS : destituir **4** ELIMINATE : eliminar — **removable** *adj* : separable, de quita y pon — **removal** *n* **1** : eliminación *f* **2** EXTRACTION : extracción *f*

remunerate *vt* **-ated; -ating** : remunerar

render *vt* **1** : rendir (homenaje), prestar (ayuda) **2** MAKE : hacer **3** TRANSLATE : traducir

rendezvous *ns & pl* : cita *f*

rendition *n* : interpretación *f*

renegade *n* : renegado *m*, -da *f*

renew *vt* **1** : renovar **2** RESUME : reanudar — **renewal** *n* : renovación *f*

renounce *vt* **-nounced; -nouncing** : renunciar a

renovate *vt* **-vated; -vating** : renovar — **renovation** *n* : renovación *f*

renown *n* : renombre *m* — **renowned** *adj* : célebre, renombrado

rent *n* **1** : alquiler *m*, arrendamiento *m*, renta

f **2 for ~** : se alquila — **~** *vt* : alquilar —
rental *n* : alquiler *m* — **~** *adj* : de alquiler
— **renter** *n* : arrendatario *m*, -ria *f*

renunciation *n* : renuncia *f*

reopen *vt* : volver a abrir

reorganize *vt* **-nized; -nizing** : reorganizar
— **reorganization** *n* : reorganización *f*

repair *vt* : reparar, arreglar — **~** *n* **1**
: reparación *f*, arreglo *m* **2 in bad ~** : en
mal estado

repay *vt* **-paid; -paying 1** : devolver
(dinero), pagar (una deuda) **2** : corresponder a (un favor, etc.)

repeal *vt* : abrogar, revocar — **~** *n* : abro-
gación *f*, revocación *f*

repeat *vt* : repetir — **~** *n* : repetición *f* — **repeatedly** *adv* : repetidas veces

repel *vt* **-pelled; -pelling** : repeler — **repellent** *n* : repelente *m*

repent *vi* : arrepentirse — **repentance** *n* : arrepentimiento *m*

repercussion *n* : repercusión *f*

repertoire *n* : repertorio *m*

repetition *n* : repetición *f* — **repetitious** *adj*
: repetitivo — **repetitive** *adj* : repetitivo

replace *vt* **-placed; -placing 1** : reponer **2**
SUBSTITUTE : reemplazar, sustituir **3** EX-
CHANGE : cambiar — **replacement** *n* **1**
: sustitución *f* **2** : sustituto *m*, -ta *f* (persona)
3 or ~ part : repuesto *m*

replenish *vt* **1** : reponer **2** REFILL : rellenar

replete *adj* **~ with** : repleto de

replica *n* : réplica *f*

reply *vi* **-plied; -plying** : contestar, responder — **~** *n, pl* **-plies** : respuesta *f*

report *n* **1** : informe *m* **2** RUMOR : rumor *m*
3 or news ~ : reportaje *m* **4 weather ~**
: boletín *m* meteorológico — **~** *vt* **1** RE-
LATE : anunciar **2 ~ a crime** : denunciar
un delito **3 or ~ on** : informar sobre — *vi*
1 : informar **2 ~ for duty** : presentarse —
report card *n* : boletín *m* de calificaciones
— **reportedly** *adv* : según se dice — **reporter** *n* : periodista *mf*; reportero *m*, -ra *f*

repose *vi* **-posed; -posing** : reposar — **~** *n*
: reposo *m*

reprehensible *adj* : reprensible

represent *vt* **1** : representar **2** PORTRAY
: presentar — **representation** *n* : representación *f* — **representative** *adj* : representativo — **~** *n* : representante *mf*

repress *vt* : reprimir — **repression** *n*
: represión *f*

reprieve *n* : indulto *m*

reprimand *n* : reprimenda *f* — **~** *vt*
: reprender

reprint *vt* : reimprimir — **~** *n* : reedición *f*

reprisal *n* : represalia *f*

reproach *n* **1** : reproche *m* **2 beyond ~**

: irreprochable — **~** *vt* : reprochar — **re-
proachful** *adj* : de reproche

reproduce *v* **-duced; -ducing** *vt* : reproducir — *vi* : reproducirse — **reproduction** *n*
: reproducción *f* — **reproductive** *adj* : reproductor

reproof *n* : reprobación *f*

reptile *n* : reptil *m*

republic *n* : república *f* — **republican** *n* : republicano *m*, -na *f* — **~** *adj* : republicano

repudiate *vt* **-ated; -ating** : repudiar

repugnant *adj* : repugnante, asqueroso —
repugnance *n* : repugnancia *f*

repulse *vt* **-pulsed; -pulsing** : repeler, rechazar — **repulsive** *adj* : repulsivo

reputation *n* : reputación *f* — **reputable** *adj*
: de confianza, acreditado — **reputed** *adj*
: supuesto

request *n* : petición *f* — **~** *vt* : pedir

requiem *n* : réquiem *m*

require *vt* **-quired; -quiring 1** CALL FOR
: requerir **2** NEED : necesitar — **requirement** *n* **1** NEED : necesidad *f* **2** DEMAND
: requisito *m* — **requisite** *adj* : necesario

resale *n* : reventa *f*

rescind *vt* : rescindir (un contrato), revocar
(una ley, etc.)

rescue *vt* **-cued; -cuing** : rescatar, salvar —
~ *n* : rescate *m* — **rescuer** *n* : salvador *m*,
-dora *f*

research *n* : investigación *f* — **~** *vt* : investigar — **researcher** *n* : investigador *m*,
-dora *f*

resemble *vt* **-sembled; -sembling** : parecerse a — **resemblance** *n* : parecido *m*

resent *vt* : resentirse de, ofenderse por — **resentful** *adj* : resentido — **resentment** *n*
: resentimiento *m*

reserve *vt* **-served; -serving** : reservar —
~ *n* **1** : reserva *f* **2 ~s** *npl* : reservas *fpl*
(militares) — **reservation** *n* : reserva *f* —
reserved *adj* : reservado — **reservoir** *n*
: embalse *m*

reset *vt* **-set; -setting** : volver a poner (un
reloj, etc.)

residence *n* : residencia *f* — **reside** *vi*
-sided; -siding : residir — **resident** *adj*
: residente — **~** *n* : residente *mf* — **residential** *adj* : residencial

residue *n* : residuo *m*

resign *vt* **1** QUIT : dimitir **2 ~ oneself to**
: resignarse a — **resignation** *n* **1** : dimisión
f **2** ACCEPTANCE : resignación *f*

resilient *adj* **1** : resistente (dícese de personas) **2** ELASTIC : elástico — **resilience** *n*
1 : resistencia *f* **2** ELASTICITY : elasticidad *f*

resin *n* : resina *f*

resist *vt* : resistir — *vi* : resistirse — **resist-**

ance *n* : resistencia *f* — **resistant** *adj* : resistente

resolve *vt* **-solved; -solving** : resolver — ~ *n* : resolución *f* — **resolution** *n* **1** : resolución *f* **2** DECISION, INTENTION : propósito *m* — **resolute** *adj* : resuelto

resonance *n* : resonancia *f* — **resonant** *adj* : resonante

resort *n* **1** RECOURSE : recurso *m* **2** *or* **tourist** ~ : centro *m* turístico — ~ *vi* ~ **to** : recurrir a

resounding *adj* **1** RESONANT : resonante **2** ABSOLUTE : rotundo

resource *n* : recurso *m* — **resourceful** *adj* : ingenioso

respect *n* **1** ESTEEM : respeto *m* **2 in some** ~**s** : en algún sentido **3 pay one's** ~**s** : presentar uno sus respetos **4 with** ~ **to** : (con) respecto a — ~ *vt* : respetar — **respectable** *adj* : respetable — **respectful** *adj* : respetuoso — **respective** *adj* : respectivo — **respectively** *adv* : respectivamente

respiration *n* : respiración *f* — **respiratory** *adj* : respiratorio

respite *n* : respiro *m*

response *n* : respuesta *f* — **respond** *vi* : responder — **responsibility** *n, pl* **-ties** : responsabilidad *f* — **responsible** *adj* : responsable — **responsive** *adj* : sensible, receptivo

rest[1] *n* **1** : descanso *m* **2** SUPPORT : apoyo *m* **3** : silencio *m* (en música) — ~ *vi* **1** : descansar **2** LEAN : apoyarse **3** ~ **on** DEPEND ON : depender de — *vt* **1** RELAX : descansar **2** LEAN : apoyar

rest[2] *n* REMAINDER : resto *m*

restaurant *n* : restaurante *m*

restful *adj* : tranquilo, apacible

restitution *n* : restitución *f*

restless *adj* : inquieto, agitado

restore *vt* **-stored; -storing 1** RETURN : devolver **2** REESTABLISH : restablecer **3** REPAIR : restaurar — **restoration** *n* **1** : restablecimiento *m* **2** REPAIR : restauración *f*

restrain *vt* **1** : contener **2** ~ **oneself** : contenerse — **restrained** *adj* : comedido, moderado — **restraint** *n* **1** : restricción *f* **2** SELF-CONTROL : moderación *f*, control *m* de sí mismo

restriction *n* : restricción *f* — **restrict** *vt* : restringir — **restricted** *adj* : restringido — **restrictive** *adj* : restrictivo

result *vi* : resultar — ~ *n* **1** : resultado *m* **2 as a** ~ **of** : como consecuencia de

resume *v* **-sumed; -suming** *vt* : reanudar — *vi* : reanudarse

résumé *or* **resume** *or* **resumé** *n* : currículum *m* (vitae)

resumption *n* : reanudación *f*

resurgence *n* : resurgimiento *m*

resurrection *n* : resurrección *f* — **resurrect** *vt* : resucitar

resuscitate *vt* **-tated; -tating** : resucitar

retail *vt* : vender al por menor — ~ *n* : venta *f* al por menor — ~ *adj* : detallista, minorista — ~ *adv* : al detalle, al por menor — **retailer** *n* : detallista *mf*, minorista *mf*

retain *vt* : retener

retaliate *vi* **-ated; -ating** : tomar represalias — **retaliation** *n* : represalias *fpl*

retard *vt* : retardar, retrasar — **retarded** *adj* : retrasado

retention *n* : retención *f*

reticence *n* : reticencia *f* — **reticent** *adj* : reticente

retina *n, pl* **-nas** *or* **-nae** : retina *f*

retinue *n* : séquito *m*

retire *vi* **-tired; -tiring 1** WITHDRAW : retirarse **2** : jubilarse, retirarse (de un trabajo) **3** : acostarse (en la cama) — **retirement** *n* : jubilación *f* — **retiring** *adj* SHY : retraído

retort *vt* : replicar — ~ *n* : réplica *f*

retrace *vt* **-traced; -tracing** ~ **one's steps** : volver sobre sus pasos

retract *vt* **1** WITHDRAW : retirar **2** : retraer (garras, etc.) — *vi* : retractarse

retrain *vt* : reciclar

retreat *n* **1** : retirada *f* **2** REFUGE : refugio *m* — ~ *vi* : retirarse

retribution *n* : castigo *m*

retrieve *vt* **-trieved; -trieving 1** : cobrar, recuperar **2** RESCUE : salvar — **retrieval** *n* : recuperación *f* — **retriever** *n* : perro *m* cobrador

retroactive *adj* : retroactivo

retrospect *n* **in** ~ : mirando hacia atrás — **retrospective** *adj* : retrospectivo

return *vi* **1** : volver, regresar **2** REAPPEAR : reaparecer — *vt* **1** : devolver **2** YIELD : producir — ~ *n* **1** : regreso *m*, vuelta *f* **2** : devolución *f* (de algo prestado) **3** YIELD : rendimiento *m* **4 in** ~ **for** : a cambio de **5** *or* **tax** ~ : declaración *f* de impuestos — ~ *adj* : de vuelta

reunite *vt* **-nited; -niting** : reunir — **reunion** *n* : reunión *f*

revamp *vt* : renovar

reveal *vt* **1** : revelar **2** SHOW : dejar ver

revel *vi* **-eled** *or* **-elled; -eling** *or* **-elling** ~ **in** : deleitarse en

revelation *n* : revelación *f*

revelry *n, pl* **-ries** : jolgorio *m*, regocijos *mpl*

revenge *vt* **-venged; -venging** : vengar — ~ *n* **1** : venganza *f* **2 take** ~ **on** : vengarse de

revenue *n* : ingresos *mpl*

reverberate *vi* **-ated; -ating** : retumbar, resonar

reverence *n* : reverencia *f*, veneración *f* — **revere** *vt* **-vered; -vering** : venerar — **reverend** *adj* : reverendo — **reverent** *adj* : reverente

reverie *n, pl* **-eries** : ensueño *m*

reverse *adj* : inverso, contrario — ~ *v* **-versed; -versing** *vt* **1** : invertir **2** : cambiar (una política), revocar (una decisión) **3** : dar marcha atrás a (un automóvil) — *vi* : invertirse — ~ *n* **1** BACK : dorso *m*, revés *m* **2** *or* ~ **gear** : marcha *f* atrás **3 the** ~ : lo contrario — **reversible** *adj* : reversible — **reversal** *n* **1** : inversión *f* **2** CHANGE : cambio *m* total **3** SETBACK : revés *m* — **revert** *vi* : revertir

review *n* **1** : revisión *f* **2** OVERVIEW : resumen *m* **3** CRITIQUE : reseña *f*, crítica *f* **4** : repaso *m* (para un examen) — ~ *vt* **1** EXAMINE : examinar **2** : repasar (una lección) **3** CRITIQUE : reseñar — **reviewer** *n* : crítico *m*, -ca *f*

revile *vt* **-viled; -viling** : injuriar

revise *vt* **-vised; -vising** **1** : modificar (una política, etc.) **2** : revisar, corregir (una publicación) — **revision** *n* : corrección *f*, modificación *f*

revive *v* **-vived; -viving** *vt* **1** : reanimar, reactivar **2** : resucitar (a una persona) **3** RESTORE : restablecer — *vi* **1** : reanimarse, reactivarse **2** COME TO : volver en sí — **revival** *n* : reanimación *f*, reactivación *f*

revoke *vt* **-voked; -voking** : revocar

revolt *vi* : rebelarse, sublevarse — *vt* : dar asco a — ~ *n* : revuelta *f*, sublevación *f* — **revolting** *adj* : asqueroso

revolution *n* : revolución *f* — **revolutionary** *adj* : revolucionario — ~ *n, pl* **-aries** : revolucionario *m*, -ria *f* — **revolutionize** *vt* **-ized; -izing** : revolucionar

revolve *v* **-volved; -volving** *vt* : hacer girar — *vi* : girar

revolver *n* : revólver *m*

revue *n* : revista *f* (teatral)

revulsion *n* : repugnancia *f*

reward *vt* : recompensar — ~ *n* : recompensa *f*

rewrite *vt* **-wrote; -written; -writing** : volver a escribir

rhetoric *n* : retórica *f* — **rhetorical** *adj* : retórico

rheumatism *n* : reumatismo *m* — **rheumatic** *adj* : reumático

rhino *n, pl* **-no** *or* **-nos** → **rhinoceros** — **rhinoceros** *n, pl* **-noceroses** *or* **-noceros** *or* **-noceri** : rinoceronte *m*

rhubarb *n* : ruibarbo *m*

rhyme *n* **1** : rima *f* **2** VERSE : verso *m* (en rima) — ~ *vi* **rhymed; rhyming** : rimar

rhythm *n* : ritmo *m* — **rhythmic** *or* **rhythmical** *adj* : rítmico

rib *n* : costilla *f* — ~ *vt* TEASE : tomar el pelo a

ribbon *n* : cinta *f*

rice *n* : arroz *m*

rich *adj* **1** : rico **2** ~ **foods** : comidas *fpl* pesadas — **riches** *npl* : riquezas *fpl* — **richness** *n* : riqueza *f*

rickety *adj* : desvencijado, destartalado

ricochet *n* : rebote *m* — ~ *vi* **-cheted** *or* **-chetted; -cheting** *or* **-chetting** : rebotar

rid *vt* **rid; ridding** **1** : librar **2 get** ~ **of** : deshacerse de — **riddance** *n* **good** ~! : ¡adiós y buen viaje!

riddle¹ *n* : acertijo *m*, adivinanza *f*

riddle² *vt* **-dled; -dling** **1** : acribillar **2 riddled with** : lleno de

ride *v* **rode; ridden; riding** *vt* **1** : montar (a caballo, en bicicleta), ir (en autobús, etc.) **2** TRAVERSE : recorrer — *vi* **1** *or* ~ **horseback** : montar a caballo **2** : ir (en auto, etc.) — ~ *n* **1** : paseo *m*, vuelta *f* **2** : aparato *m* (en un parque de diversiones) — **rider** *n* **1** : jinete *mf* (a caballo) **2** CYCLIST : ciclista *mf*, motociclista *mf*

ridge *n* : cadena *f* (de montañas)

ridiculous *adj* : ridículo — **ridicule** *n* : burlas *fpl* — ~ *vt* **-culed; -culing** : ridiculizar

rife *adj* **1** : extendido **2 be** ~ **with** : estar plagado de

rifle¹ *vi* **-fled; -fling** ~ **through** : revolver

rifle² *n* : rifle *m*, fusil *m*

rift *n* **1** : grieta *f* **2** : ruptura *f* (entre personas)

rig¹ *vt* : amañar (una elección)

rig² *vt* **rigged; rigging** **1** : aparejar (un barco) **2** EQUIP : equipar **3** *or* ~ **out** DRESS : vestir **4** *or* ~ **up** CONSTRUCT : construir — ~ *n* **1** : aparejo *m* (de un barco) **2** *or* **oil** ~ : plataforma *f* petrolífera — **rigging** *n* : aparejo *m*

right *adj* **1** JUST : bueno, justo **2** CORRECT : correcto **3** APPROPRIATE : apropiado, adecuado **4** STRAIGHT : recto **5 be** ~ : tener razón **6** → **right–hand** — ~ *n* **1** GOOD : bien *m* **2** ENTITLEMENT : derecho *m* **3 on the** ~ : a la derecha **4** *or* ~ **side** : derecha *f* — ~ *adv* **1** WELL : bien **2** PRECISELY : justo **3** DIRECTLY : derecho **4** IMMEDIATELY : inmediatamente **5** COMPLETELY : completamente **6** *or* **to the** ~ : a la derecha — ~ *vt* **1** STRAIGHTEN : enderezar **2** ~ **a wrong** : reparar un daño — **right angle** *n* : ángulo *m* recto — **righteous** *adj* : recto, honrado — **rightful** *adj* : legítimo — **right–hand** *adj* : derecho — **right–handed** *adj* : diestro — **rightly** *adv* **1** : justamente **2** CORRECTLY : correctamente — **right–wing** *adj* : derechista

rigid *adj* : rígido

rigor *or Brit* **rigour** *n* : rigor *m* — **rigorous** *adj* : riguroso

rim *n* **1** EDGE : borde *m* **2** : llanta *f* (de una rueda) **3** : montura *f* (de anteojos)

rind *n* : corteza *f*

ring¹ *v* **rang; rung; ringing** *vi* **1** : sonar (dícese de un timbre, etc.) **2** RESOUND : resonar — *vt* : tocar (un timbre, etc.) — *~ n* **1** : toque *m* (de un timbre, etc.) **2** CALL : llamada *f* (por teléfono)

ring² *n* **1** : anillo *m*, sortija *f* **2** BAND, HOOP : aro *m* **3** CIRCLE : círculo *m* **4** *or* boxing *~* : cuadrilátero *m* **5** NETWORK : red *f* — *~ vt* : cercar, rodear — **ringleader** *n* : cabecilla *mf*

ringlet *n* : rizo *m*, bucle *m*

rink *n* : pista *f* (de patinaje)

rinse *vt* **rinsed; rinsing** : enjuagar — *~ n* : enjuague *m*

riot *n* : disturbio *m* — *~ vi* : causar disturbios — **rioter** *n* : alborotador *m*, -dora *f*

rip *v* **ripped; ripping** *vt* **1** : rasgar, desgarrar **2** *~* **off** : arrancar — *vi* : rasgarse — *~ n* : rasgón *m*, desgarrón *m*

ripe *adj* **riper; ripest** **1** : maduro **2** *~* **for** : listo por — **ripen** *v* : madurar — **ripeness** *n* : madurez *f*

rip–off *n* : timo *m fam*

ripple *v* **-pled; -pling** *vi* : rizarse (dícese de agua) — *vt* : rizar — *~ n* : onda *f*, rizo *m*

rise *vi* **rose; risen; rising** **1** GET UP : levantarse **2** : salir (dícese del sol, etc.) **3** ASCEND : subir **4** INCREASE : aumentar **5** *~* **up** REBEL : sublevarse — *~ n* **1** ASCENT : subida *f* **2** INCREASE : aumento *m* **3** SLOPE : cuesta *f* — **riser** *n* **1** early *~* : madrugador *m*, -dora *f* **2** late *~* : dormilón *m*, -lona *f*

risk *n* : riesgo *m* — *~ vt* : arriesgar — **risky** *adj* **riskier; -est** : arriesgado, riesgoso *Lat*

rite *n* : rito *m* — **ritual** *adj* : ritual — *~ n* : ritual *m*

rival *n* : rival *mf* — *~ adj* : rival — *~ vt* **-valed** *or* **-valled; -valing** *or* **-valling** : rivalizar con — **rivalry** *n, pl* **-ries** : rivalidad *f*

river *n* : río *m*

rivet *n* : remache *m* — *~ vt* **1** : remachar **2** FIX : fijar (los ojos, etc.) **3** be *~*ed by : estar fascinado con

roach → **cockroach**

road *n* **1** : carretera *f* **2** STREET : calle *f* **3** PATH : camino *m* — **roadblock** *n* : control *m* — **roadside** *n* : borde *m* de la carretera — **roadway** *n* : carretera *f*

roam *vi* : vagar — *vt* : vagar por

roar *vi* : rugir **2** *~* **with laughter** : reírse a carcajadas — *vt* : decir a gritos — *~ n* : rugido *m* (de un animal), estruendo *m* (de un avión, etc.)

roast *vt* : asar (carne, etc.), tostar (café, etc.) — *vi* : asarse — *~ n* : asado *m* — *~ adj* : asado — **roast beef** *n* : rosbif *m*

rob *v* **robbed; robbing** *vt* **1** : robar **2** *~* **of** : privar de — *vi* : robar — **robber** *n* : ladrón *m*, -drona *f* — **robbery** *n, pl* **-beries** : robo *m*

robe *n* **1** : toga *f* (de un magistrado, etc.) **2** → **bathrobe**

robin *n* : petirrojo *m*

robot *n* : robot *m*

robust *adj* : robusto

rock¹ *vt* **1** : acunar (a un niño), mecer (una cuna) **2** SHAKE : sacudir — *vi* : mecerse — *~ n or* **music** : música *f* rock

rock² *n* **1** : roca *f* (sustancia) **2** BOULDER : peña *f*, peñasco *m* **3** STONE : piedra *f*

rocket *n* : cohete *m*

rocking chair *n* : mecedora *f*

rocky *adj* **rockier; -est** **1** : rocoso **2** SHAKY : tambaleante

rod *n* **1** : varilla *f* **2** *or* **fishing** *~* : caña *f* de pescar

rode → **ride**

rodent *n* : roedor *m*

rodeo *n, pl* **-deos** : rodeo *m*

roe *n* : hueva *f*

rogue *n* : pícaro *m*, -ra *f*

role *n* : papel *m*

roll *n* **1** : rollo *m* (de película, etc.) **2** LIST : lista *f* **3** : redoble *m* (de un tambor) **4** SWAYING : balanceo *m* **5** BUN : pancito *m Lat*, panecillo *m Spain* — *~ vt* **1** : hacer rodar **2** *or* *~* **out** : estirar (masa) **3** *~* **up** : enrollar (papel, etc.), arremangar (una manga) — *vi* **1** : rodar **2** SWAY : balancearse **3** *~* **around** : revolcarse **4** *~* **over** : darse la vuelta — **roller** *n* **1** : rodillo *m* **2** CURLER : rulo *m* — **roller coaster** *n* : montaña *f* rusa — **roller–skate** *vi* **-skated; -skating** : patinar (sobre ruedas) — **roller skate** *n* : patín *m* (de ruedas)

Roman *adj* : romano — **Roman Catholic** *adj* : católico

romance *n* **1** : novela *f* romántica **2** AFFAIR : romance *m*

Romanian *adj* : rumano — *~ n* : rumano *m* (idioma)

romantic *adj* : romántico

romp *n* : retozo *m* — *~ vi* : retozar

roof *n, pl* **roofs** **1** : tejado *m*, techo *m* **2** *~* **of the mouth** : paladar *m* — **roofing** *n* : techumbre *f* — **rooftop** *n* : tejado *m*, techo *m*

rook¹ *n* : grajo *m* (ave)

rook² *n* : torre *f* (en ajedrez)

rookie *n* : novato *m*, -ta *f*

room *n* **1** : cuarto *m*, habitación *f* **2** BEDROOM : dormitorio *m* **3** SPACE : espacio *m* **4**

OPPORTUNITY : posibilidad *f* — **roommate** *n* : compañero *m*, -ra *f* de cuarto — **roomy** *adj* **roomier; -est** : espacioso

roost *n* : percha *f* — $\sim$ *vi* : posarse — **rooster** *n* : gallo *m*

root[1] *n* : raíz *f* — $\sim$ *vt* $\sim$ **out** : extirpar

root[2] *vi* $\sim$ **around in** : hurgar en

root[3] *vi* $\sim$ **for** SUPPORT : alentar

rope *n* : cuerda *f* — $\sim$ *vt* **roped; roping** **1** : atar (con cuerda) **2** $\sim$ **off** : acordonar

rosary *n, pl* **-ries** : rosario *m*

rose[1] → **rise**

rose[2] *n* : rosa *f* (flor), rosa *m* (color) — $\sim$ *adj* : rosa — **rosebush** *n* : rosal *m*

rosemary *n, pl* **-maries** : romero *m*

Rosh Hashanah *n* : el Año Nuevo judío

roster *n* : lista *f*

rostrum *n, pl* **-tra** *or* **-trums** : tribuna *f*

rosy *adj* **rosier; -est** **1** : sonrosado **2** PROMISING : halagüeño

rot *v* **rotted; rotting** *vi* : pudrirse — *vt* : pudrir — $\sim$ *n* : putrefacción *f*

rotary *adj* : rotativo — $\sim$ *n* : rotonda *f*, glorieta *f Spain*

rotate *v* **-tated; -tating** *vi* : girar — *vt* **1** : girar **2** ALTERNATE : alternar — **rotation** *n* : rotación *f*

rote *n* **by** $\sim$: de memoria

rotor *n* : rotor *m*

rotten *adj* **1** : podrido **2** BAD : malo

rouge *n* : colorete *m*

rough *adj* **1** COARSE : áspero **2** RUGGED : accidentado **3** CHOPPY : agitado **4** DIFFICULT : duro **5** FORCEFUL : brusco **6** APPROXIMATE : aproximado **7** UNREFINED : tosco **8** $\sim$ **draft** : borrador *m* — $\sim$ *vt* **1** → **roughen 2** $\sim$ **up** BEAT : dar una paliza a — **roughage** *n* : fibra *f* — **roughen** *vt* : poner áspero — *vi* : ponerse áspero — **roughly** *adv* **1** : bruscamente **2** ABOUT : aproximadamente — **roughness** *n* COARSENESS : aspereza *f*

roulette *n* : ruleta *f*

round *adj* : redondo — $\sim$ *adv* → **around** — $\sim$ *n* **1** : círculo *m* **2** : ronda *f* (de bebidas, negociaciones, etc.) **3** : asalto *m* (en boxeo), vuelta *f* (en juegos) **4** $\sim$ **of applause** : aplauso *m* **5** $\sim$**s** *npl* : visitas *fpl* (de un médico), rondas *fpl* (de un policía, etc.) — $\sim$ *vt* **1** TURN : doblar **2** $\sim$ **off** : redondear **3** $\sim$ **off** *or* $\sim$ **out** COMPLETE : rematar **4** $\sim$ **up** GATHER : reunir (personas), rodear (ganado) — $\sim$ *prep* → **around** — **roundabout** *adj* : indirecto — **round–trip** *adj* : viaje *m* de ida y vuelta — **roundup** *n* : rodeo *m* (de animales), redada *f* (de delincuentes, etc.)

rouse *vt* **roused; rousing** **1** AWAKEN : despertar **2** EXCITE : excitar

rout *n* : derrota *f* aplastante — $\sim$ *vt* : derrotar

route *n* **1** : ruta *f* **2** *or* **delivery** $\sim$: recorrido *m*

routine *n* : rutina *f* — $\sim$ *adj* : rutinario

rove *v* **roved; roving** *vi* : errar, vagar — *vt* : errar por

row[1] *vt* **1** : llevar a remo **2** $\sim$ **a boat** : remar — *vi* : remar

row[2] *n* **1** : fila *f* (de gente o asientos), hilera *f* (de casas, etc.) **2 in a** $\sim$ SUCCESSIVELY : seguido

row[3] *n* **1** RACKET : bulla *f* **2** QUARREL : pelea *f*

rowboat *n* : bote *m* de remos

rowdy *adj* **-dier; -est** : escandaloso, alborotador — $\sim$ *n, pl* **-dies** : alborotador *m*, -dora *f*

royal *adj* : real — **royalty** *n, pl* **-ties** **1** : realeza *f* **2 royalties** *npl* : derechos *mpl* de autor

rub *v* **rubbed; rubbing** *vt* **1** : frotar **2** CHAFE : rozar **3** $\sim$ **in** : aplicar frotando — *vi* **1** $\sim$ **against** : rozar **2** $\sim$ **off** : salir (al frotar) — $\sim$ *n* : frotamiento *m*

rubber *n* **1** : goma *f*, caucho *m* **2** $\sim$**s** *npl* : chanclos *mpl* — **rubber band** *n* : goma *f* (elástica) — **rubber stamp** *n* : sello *m* (de goma) — **rubbery** *adj* : gomoso

rubbish *n* **1** : basura *f* **2** NONSENSE : tonterías *fpl*

rubble *n* : escombros *mpl*

ruby *n, pl* **-bies** : rubí *m*

rudder *n* : timón *m*

ruddy *adj* **-dier; -est** : rubicundo

rude *adj* **ruder; rudest** **1** IMPOLITE : grosero, mal educado **2** ABRUPT : brusco — **rudely** *adv* : groseramente — **rudeness** *n* : mala educación *f*

rudiment *n* : rudimento *m* — **rudimentary** *adj* : rudimentario

rue *vt* **rued; ruing** : lamentar — **rueful** *adj* : triste, arrepentido

ruffle *vt* **-fled; -fling** **1** : despeinar (pelo), erizar (plumas) **2** VEX : alterar, contrariar — $\sim$ *n* : volante *m* (de un vestido, etc.)

rug *n* : alfombra *f*, tapete *m*

rugged *adj* **1** : escabroso (dícese del terreno), escarpado (dícese de montañas) **2** HARSH : duro **3** STURDY : fuerte

ruin *n* : ruina *f* — $\sim$ *vt* : arruinar

rule *n* **1** : regla *f* **2** CONTROL : dominio *m* **3 as a** $\sim$: por lo general — $\sim$ *v* **ruled; ruling** *vt* **1** GOVERN : gobernar **2** : fallar (dícese de un juez) **3** $\sim$ **out** : descartar — *vi* : gobernar, reinar — **ruler** *n* **1** : gobernante *mf*; soberano *m*, -na *f* **2** : regla *f* (para medir) — **ruling** *n* VERDICT : fallo *m*

rum *n* : ron *m*

Rumanian → **Romanian**

rumble *vi* **-bled; -bling 1** : retumbar **2** : hacer ruidos (dícese del estómago) — **~** *n* : retumbo *m*, estruendo *m*

rummage *vi* **-maged; -maging** : hurgar

rumor *n* : rumor *m* — **~** *vt* **be ~ed** : rumorearse

rump *n* **1** : grupa *f* (de un animal) **2 ~ steak** : filete *m* de cadera

rumpus *n* : lío *m*, jaleo *m fam*

run *v* **ran; run; running** *vi* **1** : correr **2** FUNCTION : funcionar **3** LAST : durar **4** : desteñir (dícese de colores) **5** EXTEND : correr, extenderse **6** : presentarse (como candidato) **7 ~ away** : huir **8 ~ into** ENCOUNTER : tropezar con **9 ~ into** HIT : chocar contra **10 ~ late** : ir retrasado **~ out of** : quedarse sin **12 ~ over** : atropellar — *vt* **1** : correr **2** OPERATE : hacer funcionar **3** : hacer correr (agua) **4** MANAGE : dirigir **5 ~ a fever** : tener fiebre — **~** *n* **1** : carrera *f* **2** TRIP : viaje *m*, paseo *m* (en coche) **3** SERIES : serie *f* **4 in the long ~** : a la larga **5 in the short ~** : a corto plazo — **runaway** *n* : fugitivo *m*, -va *f* — **~** *adj* : fugitivo — **rundown** *n* : resumen *m* — **run–down** *adj* **1** : destartalado **2** EXHAUSTED : agotado

rung¹ → ring¹

rung² *n* : peldaño *m* (de una escalera, etc.)

runner *n* **1** : corredor *m*, -dora *f* **2** : patín *m* (de un trineo), riel *m* (de un cajón, etc.) —

runner–up *n*, *pl* **runners–up** : subcampeón *m*, -peona *f* — **running** *adj* **1** FLOWING : corriente **2** CONTINUOUS : continuo **3** CONSECUTIVE : seguido

runt *n* : animal *m* más pequeño (de una camada)

runway *n* : pista *f* de aterrizaje

rupture *n* : ruptura *f* — **~** *v* **-tured; -turing** *vt* : romper — *vi* : reventar

rural *adj* : rural

ruse *n* : ardid *m*

rush¹ *n* : junco *m* (planta)

rush² *vi* : ir de prisa — *vt* **1** : apresurar, apurar **2** ATTACK : asaltar **3** : llevar rápidamente (al hospital, etc.) — **~** *n* **1** : prisa *f*, apuro *m* **2** : ráfaga *f* (de aire), torrente *m* (de agua) — **~** *adj* : urgente — **rush hour** *n* : hora *f* punta

russet *n* : color *m* rojizo

Russian *adj* : ruso — **~** *n* : ruso *m* (idioma)

rust *n* : herrumbre *f*, óxido *m* — **~** *vi* : oxidarse — *vt* : oxidar

rustic *adj* : rústico

rustle *v* **-tled; -tling** *vt* **1** : hacer susurrar **2** : robar (ganado) — *vi* : susurrar — **~** *n* : susurro *m*

rusty *adj* **rustier; -est** : oxidado

rut *n* **1** : surco *m* **2 be in a ~** : ser esclavo de la rutina

ruthless *adj* : despiadado, cruel

rye *n* : centeno *m*

S

s *n*, *pl* **s's** *or* **ss** : s *f*, decimonovena letra del alfabeto inglés

Sabbath *n* **1** : sábado *m* (día santo judío) **2** : domingo *m* (día santo cristiano)

sabotage *n* : sabotaje *m* — **~** *vt* **-taged; -taging** : sabotear

saccharin *n* : sacarina *f*

sack *n* : saco *m* — **~** *vt* **1** FIRE : despedir **2** PLUNDER : saquear

sacrament *n* : sacramento *m*

sacred *adj* : sagrado

sacrifice *n* : sacrificio *m* — **~** *vt* **-ficed; -ficing** : sacrificar

sacrilege *n* : sacrilegio *m* — **sacrilegious** *adj* : sacrílego

sad *adj* **sadder; saddest** : triste — **sadden** *vt* : entristecer

saddle *n* : silla *f* (de montar) — **~** *vt* **-dled;**

-dling 1 : ensillar (un caballo, etc.) **2 ~ s.o. with sth** : cargar a algn con algo

sadistic *adj* : sádico

sadness *n* : tristeza *f*

safari *n* : safari *m*

safe *adj* **safer; safest 1** : seguro **2** UNHARMED : ileso **3** CAREFUL : prudente **4 ~ and sound** : sano y salvo — **~** *n* : caja *f* fuerte — **safeguard** *n* : salvaguarda *f* — **~** *vt* : salvaguardar — **safely** *adv* **1** : sin peligro **2 arrive ~** : llegar sin novedad — **safety** *n*, *pl* **-ties** : seguridad *f* — **safety belt** *n* : cinturón *m* de seguridad — **safety pin** *n* : imperdible *m*

saffron *n* : azafrán *m*

sag *vi* **sagged; sagging 1** : combarse **2** GIVE : aflojarse **3** FLAG : flaquear

saga *n* : saga *f*

sage¹ n : salvia f (planta)

sage² adj **sager; -est** : sabio — ~ n : sabio m, -bia f

said → **say**

sail n **1** : vela f (de un barco) **2 go for a** ~ : salir a navegar **3 set** ~ : zarpar — ~ vi : navegar — vt : gobernar (un barco), navegar (el mar) — **sailboat** n : velero m — **sailor** n : marinero m

saint n : santo m, -ta f — **saintly** adj **saintlier; -est** : santo

sake n **1 for goodness'** ~! : ¡por Dios! **2 for the** ~ **of** : por (el bien de)

salad n : ensalada f

salamander n : salamandra f

salami n : salami m

salary n, pl **-ries** : sueldo m

sale n **1** : venta f **2 for** ~ : se vende **3 on** ~ : de rebaja — **salesman** n, pl **-men** : vendedor m, dependiente m — **saleswoman** n, pl **-women** : vendedora f, dependienta f

salient adj : saliente

saliva n : saliva f

sallow adj : amarillento, cetrino

salmon ns & pl : salmón m

salon n → **beauty salon**

saloon n : bar m

salsa n : salsa f mexicana, salsa f picante

salt n : sal f — ~ vt : salar — **saltwater** adj : de agua salada — **salty** adj **saltier; -est** : salado

salute v **-luted; -luting** vt : saludar — vi : hacer un saludo — ~ n : saludo m

salvage n : salvamento m — ~ vt **-vaged; -vaging** : salvar

salvation n : salvación f

salve n : ungüento m

same adj **1** : mismo **2 be the** ~ **(as)** : ser igual (que) **3 the** ~ **thing (as)** : la misma cosa (que) — ~ pron **1 all the** ~ : igual **2 the** ~ : lo mismo — ~ adv **the** ~ : igual

sample n : muestra f — ~ vt **-pled; -pling** : probar

sanatorium n, pl **-riums** or **-ria** : sanatorio m

sanctify vt **-fied; -fying** : santificar

sanction n : sanción f — ~ vt : sancionar

sanctity n, pl **-ties** : santidad f

sanctuary n, pl **-aries** : santuario m

sand n : arena f — ~ vt : lijar (madera)

sandal n : sandalia f

sandpaper n : papel m de lija — ~ vt : lijar

sandwich n : sandwich m, bocadillo m Spain — ~ vt ~ **between** : meter entre

sandy adj **sandier; -est** : arenoso

sane adj **saner; sanest 1** : cuerdo **2** SENSIBLE : sensato

sang → **sing**

sanitarium n, pl **-iums** or **-ia** → **sanatorium**

sanitary adj **1** : sanitario **2** HYGIENIC : higiénico — **sanitary napkin** n : compresa f (higiénica) — **sanitation** n : sanidad f

sanity n : cordura f

sank → **sink**

Santa Claus n : Papá m Noel

sap¹ n **1** : savia f (de una planta) **2** SUCKER : inocentón m, -tona f

sap² vt **sapped; sapping** : minar (la fuerza, etc.)

sapphire n : zafiro m

sarcasm n : sarcasmo m — **sarcastic** adj : sarcástico

sardine n : sardina f

sash n : faja f (de un vestido), fajín m (de un uniforme)

sat → **sit**

satanic adj : satánico

satchel n : cartera f

satellite n : satélite m

satin n : raso m

satire n : sátira f — **satiric** or **satirical** adj : satírico

satisfaction n : satisfacción f — **satisfactory** adj : satisfactorio — **satisfy** v **-fied; -fying** vt **1** : satisfacer **2** CONVINCE : convencer — **satisfying** adj : satisfactorio

saturate vt **-rated; -rating 1** : saturar **2** DRENCH : empapar — **saturation** n : saturación f

Saturday n : sábado m

Saturn n : Saturno m

sauce n : salsa f — **saucepan** n : cacerola f — **saucer** n : platillo m — **saucy** adj **saucier; -est** IMPUDENT : descarado

sauna n : sauna mf

saunter vi : pasear

sausage n : salchicha f

sauté vt **-téed** or **-téd; -téing** : saltear, sofreír

savage adj : salvaje, feroz — ~ n : salvaje mf — **savagery** n, pl **-ries** : ferocidad f

save vt **saved; saving 1** RESCUE : salvar **2** RESERVE : guardar **3** : ahorrar (dinero, tiempo, etc.) — ~ prep EXCEPT : salvo

savior n : salvador m, -dora f

savor vt : saborear — **savory** adj : sabroso

saw¹ → **see**

saw² n : sierra f — ~ vt **sawed; sawed** or **sawn; sawing** : serrar — **sawdust** n : serrín m, aserrín m

saxophone n : saxofón m

say v **said; saying; says** vt **1** : decir **2** INDICATE : marcar (dícese de relojes, etc.) — vi **1** : decir **2 that is to** ~ : es decir — ~ n, pl **says 1 have no** ~ : no tener ni voz ni voto **2 have one's** ~ : dar su opinión — **saying** n : refrán m

scab n **1** : costra f (en una herida) **2** STRIKE-BREAKER : esquirol mf

scaffold n : andamio m (en construcción)

scald vt : escaldar

scale¹ n : balanza f (para pesar)

scale² n : escama f (de un pez, etc.) — ~ vt **scaled; scaling** : escamar

scale³ vt **scaled; scaling 1** CLIMB : escalar **2** ~ **down** : reducir — ~ n : escala f (musical, salarial, etc.)

scallion n : cebolleta f

scallop n : vieira f

scalp n : cuero m cabelludo

scam n : estafa f, timo m fam

scamper vi ~ **away** : irse corriendo

scan vt **scanned; scanning 1** : escandir (versos) **2** EXAMINE : escudriñar **3** SKIM : echar un vistazo a **4** : escanear (en informática)

scandal n **1** : escándalo m **2** GOSSIP : habladurías fpl — **scandalous** adj : escandaloso

Scandinavian adj : escandinavo

scant adj : escaso

scapegoat n : chivo m expiatorio

scar n : cicatriz f — ~ v **scarred; scarring** vt : dejar una cicatriz en — vi : cicatrizar

scarce adj **scarcer; -est** : escaso — **scarcely** adv : apenas — **scarcity** n, pl **-ties** : escasez f

scare vt **scared; scaring 1** : asustar **2 be** ~**d of** : tener miedo a — ~ n **1** FRIGHT : susto m **2** ALARM : pánico m — **scarecrow** n : espantapájaros m, espantajo m

scarf n, pl **scarves** or **scarfs 1** : bufanda f **2** KERCHIEF : pañuelo m

scarlet adj : escarlata — **scarlet fever** n : escarlatina f

scary adj **scarier; -est** : que da miedo

scathing adj : mordaz

scatter vt **1** STREW : esparcir **2** DISPERSE : dispersar — vi : dispersarse

scavenger n : carroñero m, -ra f (animal)

scenario n, pl **-ios 1** : guión m (cinemático) **2 the worst-case** ~ : el peor de los casos

scene n **1** : escena f **2 behind the** ~**s** : entre bastidores **3 make a** ~ : armar un escándalo — **scenery** n, pl **-eries 1** : decorado m **2** LANDSCAPE : paisaje m — **scenic** adj : pintoresco

scent n **1** : aroma m **2** PERFUME : perfume m **3** TRAIL : rastro m — **scented** adj : perfumado

sceptic → **skeptic**

schedule n **1** : programa m **2** TIMETABLE : horario m **3** : atrasado, con retraso **4 on** ~ : según lo previsto — ~ vt **-uled; -uling** : planear, programar

scheme n **1** PLAN : plan m **2** PLOT : intriga f **3** DESIGN : esquema f — ~ vi **schemed; scheming** : intrigar

schism n : cisma m

schizophrenia n : esquizofrenia f — **schizophrenic** adj : esquizofrénico

scholar n : erudito m, -ta f — **scholarly** adj : erudito — **scholarship** n **1** : erudición f **2** GRANT : beca f

school¹ n : banco m (de peces)

school² n **1** : escuela f **2** COLLEGE : universidad f **3** DEPARTMENT : facultad f — ~ vt : instruir — **schoolboy** n : colegial m — **schoolgirl** n : colegiala f — **schoolteacher** n → **teacher**

science n : ciencia f — **scientific** adj : científico — **scientist** n : científico m, -ca f

scissors npl : tijeras fpl

scoff vi ~ **at** : burlarse de, mofarse de

scold vt : regañar

scoop n **1** : pala f **2** : noticia f exclusiva (en periodismo) — ~ vt **1** : sacar (con pala) **2** ~ **out** : ahuecar **3** ~ **up** : recoger

scoot vi : ir rápidamente — **scooter** n **1** : patinete m **2** or **motor** ~ : escúter m

scope n **1** RANGE : alcance m **2** OPPORTUNITY : posibilidades fpl

scorch vt : chamuscar

score n, pl **scores 1** : tanteo m (en deportes) **2** RATING : puntuación f **3** : partitura f (musical) **4** or pl **score** TWENTY : veintena f **5 keep** ~ : llevar la cuenta **6 on that** ~ : en ese sentido — ~ v **scored; scoring** vt **1** : marcar, anotarse Lat (un tanto) **2** : sacar (una nota) — vi : marcar (en deportes)

scorn n : desdén m — ~ vt : desdeñar — **scornful** adj : desdeñoso

scorpion n : alacrán m, escorpión m

Scot n : escocés m, -cesa f — **Scotch** adj → **Scottish** — ~ n or ~ **whiskey** : whisky m escocés — **Scottish** adj : escocés

scoundrel n : sinvergüenza mf

scour vt **1** SCRUB : fregar **2** SEARCH : registrar

scourge n : azote m

scout n : explorador m, -dora f

scowl vi : fruncir el ceño — ~ n : ceño m fruncido

scram vi **scrammed; scramming** : largarse

scramble v **-bled; -bling** vi **1** CLAMBER : trepar **2** ~ **for** : pelearse por — vt : mezclar — ~ n : rebatiña f, pelea f — **scrambled eggs** npl : huevos mpl revueltos

scrap¹ n **1** PIECE : pedazo m **2** or ~ **metal** : chatarra f **3** ~**s** npl : sobras — ~ vt **scrapped; scrapping** : desechar

scrap² n FIGHT : pelea f

scrapbook n : álbum m de recortes

scrape v **scraped; scraping** vt **1** : rascar **2** : rasparse (la rodilla, etc.) **3** or ~ **off** : raspar **4 ~ together** : reunir — *vi* **1** RUB : rozar **2 ~ by** : arreglárselas — **~** *n* **1** : rasguño *m* **2** PREDICAMENT : apuro *m*

scratch *vt* **1** CLAW : arañar **2** MARK : rayar **3** : rascarse (la cabeza, etc.) **4 ~ out** : tachar — **~** *n* **1** : arañazo *m* **2** MARK : rayón *m* **3 start from ~** : empezar desde cero

scrawl *v* : garabatear — **~** *n* : garabato *m*

scrawny *adj* **scrawnier; -est** : escuálido

scream *vi* : gritar, chillar — **~** *n* : grito *m*, chillido *m*

screech *n* **1** : chillido *m* (de personas) **2** : chirrido *m* (de frenos, etc.) — **~** *vi* **1** : chillar **2** : chirriar (dícese de los frenos, etc.)

screen *n* **1** : pantalla *f* **2** PARTITION : mampara *f* **3** *or* **window ~** : mosquitero *m* — **~** *vt* **1** SHIELD : proteger **2** HIDE : ocultar **3** : seleccionar (candidatos, etc.)

screw *n* : tornillo *m* — **~** *vt* **1** : atornillar **2 ~ up** RUIN : fastidiar — **screwdriver** *n* : destornillador *m*

scribble *v* **-bled; -bling** : garabatear — **~** *n* : garabato *m*

script *n* **1** HANDWRITING : escritura *f* **2** : guión *m* (de cine, etc.) — **scripture** *n* **1** : escritos *mpl* sagrados **2 the Scriptures** *npl* : las Escrituras *fpl*

scroll *n* : rollo *m* (de pergamino, etc.)

scrounge *v* **scrounged; scrounging** *vt* : gorrear *fam* — *vi* **~ around for sth** : andar buscando algo

scrub[1] *n* UNDERBRUSH : maleza *f*

scrub[2] *vt* **scrubbed; scrubbing** SCOUR : fregar — **~** *n* : fregado *m*

scruff *n* **by the ~ of the neck** : por el pescuezo

scruple *n* : escrúpulo *m* — **scrupulous** *adj* : escrupuloso

scrutiny *n, pl* **-nies** : análisis *m* cuidadoso — **scrutinize** *vt* **-nized; -nizing** : escudriñar

scuff *vt* : raspar, rayar

scuffle *n* : refriega *f*

sculpture *n* : escultura *f* — **sculpt** *v* : esculpir — **sculptor** *n* : escultor *m*, -tora *f*

scum *n* **1** FROTH : espuma *f* **2** : escoria *f* (dícese de personas)

scurry *vi* **-ried; -rying** : corretear

scuttle[1] *n* : cubo *m* (para carbón)

scuttle[2] *vt* **-tled; -tling** : hundir (un barco)

scuttle[3] *vi* SCAMPER : corretear

sea *n* **1** : mar *mf* **2 at ~** : en el mar — **~** *adj* : del mar — **seafarer** *n* : marinero *m* — **seafood** *n* : mariscos *mpl* — **seagull** *n* : gaviota *f*

seal[1] *n* : foca *f* (animal)

seal[2] *n* **1** STAMP : sello *m* **2** CLOSURE : cierre *m* (hermético) — **~** *vt* : sellar

seam *n* **1** : costura *f* **2** VEIN : veta *f*

seaman *n, pl* **-men** : marinero *m*

seamy *adj* **seamier; -est** : sórdido

seaplane *n* : hidroavión *m*

seaport *n* : puerto *m* marítimo

search *vt* : registrar — *vi* **~ for** : buscar — **~** *n* **1** : registro *m* **2** HUNT : búsqueda *f* — **searchlight** *n* : reflector *m*

seashell *n* : concha *f* (marina) — **seashore** *n* : orilla *f* del mar — **seasick** *adj* **1** : mareado **2 be ~** : marearse — **seasickness** *n* : mareo *m*

season *n* **1** : estación *f* (del año) **2** : temporada *f* (en deportes, etc.) — **~** *vt* **1** FLAVOR : sazonar **2** : secar (madera) — **seasonal** *adj* : estacional — **seasoned** *adj* EXPERIENCED : veterano — **seasoning** *n* : condimento *m*

seat *n* **1** : asiento *m* **2** : fondillos *mpl* (de un pantalón) **3** BUTTOCKS : trasero *m* **4** CENTER : sede *f* — **~** *vt* **1 be ~ed** : sentarse **2 the bus ~s 30** : el autobús tiene cabida para 30 — **seat belt** *n* : cinturón *m* de seguridad

seaweed *n* : alga *f* marina

secede *vi* **-ceded; -ceding** : separarse (de una nación, etc.)

secluded *adj* : aislado — **seclusion** *n* : aislamiento *m*

second *adj* : segundo — **~** *or* **secondly** *adv* : en segundo lugar — **~** *n* **1** : segundo *m*, -da *f* **2** MOMENT : segundo *m* **3 have ~s** : repetir (en una comida) — **~** *vt* : secundar — **secondary** *adj* : secundario — **secondhand** *adj* : de segunda mano — **second-rate** *adj* : mediocre

secret *adj* : secreto — **~** *n* : secreto *m* — **secrecy** *n, pl* **-cies** : secreto *m*

secretary *n, pl* **-taries 1** : secretario *m*, -ria *f* **2** : ministro *m*, -tra *f* (del gobierno)

secretion *n* : secreción *f* — **secrete** *vt* **-creted; -creting** : secretar

secretive *adj* : reservado — **secretly** *adv* : en secreto

sect *n* : secta *f*

section *n* : sección *f*, parte *f*

sector *n* : sector *m*

secular *adj* : secular

security *n, pl* **-ties 1** : seguridad *f* **2** GUARANTEE : garantía *f* **3 securities** *npl* : valores *mpl* — **secure** *adj* **-curer; -est** : seguro — **~** *vt* **-cured; -curing 1** FASTEN : asegurar **2** GET : conseguir

sedan *n* : sedán *m*

sedate *adj* : sosegado

sedative *adj* : sedante — **~** *n* : sedante *m*

sedentary *adj* : sedentario

sediment *n* : sedimento *m*

seduce *vt* **-duced; -ducing** : seducir — **se-**

duction *n* : seducción *f* — **seductive** *adj* : seductor

see *v* **saw**; **seen**; **seeing** *vt* **1** : ver **2** UNDERSTAND : entender **3** ESCORT : acompañar **4** ~ **s.o. off** : despedirse de algn **5** ~ **sth through** : llevar algo a cabo **6** ~ **you later!** : ¡hasta luego! — *vi* **1** : ver **2** UNDERSTAND : entender **3** let's ~ : vamos a ver **4** ~ **to** : ocuparse de

seed *n*, *pl* **seed** *or* **seeds** **1** : semilla *f* **2** SOURCE : germen *m* — **seedy** *adj* **seedier**; **-est** SQUALID : sórdido

seek *v* **sought**; **seeking** *vt* **1** *or* ~ **out** : buscar **2** REQUEST : pedir **3** ~ **to** : tratar de — *vi* SEARCH : buscar

seem *vi* : parecer

seep *vi* : filtrarse

seesaw *n* : balancín *m*

seethe *vi* **seethed**; **seething** : rabiar, estar furioso

segment *n* : segmento *m*

segregate *vt* **-gated**; **-gating** : segregar — **segregation** *n* : segregación *f*

seize *v* **seized**; **seizing** *vt* **1** GRASP : agarrar **2** CAPTURE : tomar **3** : aprovechar (una oportunidad) — *vi or* ~ **up** : agarrotarse — **seizure** *n* **1** CAPTURE : toma *f* **2** : ataque *m* (en medicina)

seldom *adv* : pocas veces, raramente

select *adj* : selecto — ~ *vt* : seleccionar — **selection** *n* : selección *f* — **selective** *adj* : selectivo

self *n*, *pl* **selves** **1** : ser *m* **2** **her better** ~ : su lado bueno — **self–addressed** *adj* : con la dirección del remitente — **self–assured** *adj* : seguro de sí mismo — **self–centered** *adj* : egocéntrico — **self–confidence** *n* : confianza *f* en sí mismo — **self–confident** *adj* : seguro de sí mismo — **self–conscious** *adj* : cohibido — **self–control** *n* : dominio *m* de sí mismo — **self–defense** *n* : defensa *f* propia — **self–employed** *adj* : que trabaja por cuenta propia — **self–esteem** *n* : amor *m* propio — **self–evident** *adj* : evidente — **self–help** *n* : autoayuda *f* — **self– important** *adj* : presumido — **self–interest** *n* : interés *m* personal — **selfish** *adj* : egoísta — **selfishness** *n* : egoísmo *m* — **selfless** *adj* : desinteresado — **self–pity** *n*, *pl* **-ties** : autocompasión *f* — **self–portrait** *n* : autorretrato *m* — **self– respect** *n* : amor *m* propio — **self–righteous** *adj* : santurrón — **self–service** *adj* : de autoservicio — **self–sufficient** *adj* : autosuficiente — **self–taught** *adj* : autodidacta

sell *v* **sold**; **selling** *vt* : vender — *vi* : venderse — **seller** *n* : vendedor *m*, **-dora** *f*

selves → **self**

semantics *ns & pl* : semántica *f*

semblance *n* : apariencia *f*

semester *n* : semestre *m*

semicolon *n* : punto y coma *m*

semifinal *n* : semifinal *f*

seminary *n*, *pl* **-naries** : seminario *m* — **seminar** *n* : seminario *m*

senate *n* : senado *m* — **senator** *n* : senador *m*, **-dora** *f*

send *vt* **sent**; **sending** **1** : mandar, enviar **2** ~ **away for** : pedir **3** ~ **back** : devolver (mercancías, etc.) **4** ~ **for** : mandar a buscar — **sender** *n* : remitente *mf*

senile *adj* : senil — **senility** *n* : senilidad *f*

senior *n* **1** SUPERIOR : superior *m* **2** : estudiante *mf* de último año (en educación) **3** *or* ~ **citizen** : persona *f* mayor **4** **be s.o.'s** ~ : ser mayor que algn — ~ *adj* **1** : superior (en rango) **2** ELDER : mayor — **seniority** *n* : antigüedad *f*

sensation *n* : sensación *f* — **sensational** *adj* : sensacional

sense *n* **1** : sentido *m* **2** FEELING : sensación *f* **3** COMMON SENSE : sentido *m* común **4** **make** ~ : tener sentido — ~ *vt* **sensed**; **sensing** : sentir — **senseless** *adj* **1** : sin sentido **2** UNCONSCIOUS : inconsciente — **sensible** *adj* : sensato, práctico — **sensibility** *n*, *pl* **-ties** : sensibilidad *f* — **sensitive** *adj* **1** : sensible **2** TOUCHY : susceptible — **sensitivity** *n*, *pl* **-ties** : sensibilidad *f* — **sensual** *adj* : sensual — **sensuous** *adj* : sensual

sent → **send**

sentence *n* **1** : frase *f* **2** JUDGMENT : sentencia *f* — ~ *vt* **-tenced**; **-tencing** : sentenciar

sentiment *n* **1** : sentimiento *m* **2** BELIEF : opinión *f* — **sentimental** *adj* : sentimental — **sentimentality** *n*, *pl* **-ties** : sentimentalismo *m*

sentry *n*, *pl* **-tries** : centinela *m*

separation *n* : separación *f* — **separate** *v* **-rated**; **-rating** *vt* **1** : separar **2** DISTINGUISH : distinguir — *vi* : separarse — ~ *adj* **1** : separado **2** DETACHED : aparte **3** DISTINCT : distinto — **separately** *adv* : por separado

September *n* : septiembre *m*, setiembre *m*

sequel *n* **1** : continuación *f* **2** CONSEQUENCE : secuela *f*

sequence *n* **1** ORDER : orden *m* **2** : secuencia *f* (de números o sonidos)

Serb *or* **Serbian** *adj* : serbio

serene *adj* : sereno — **serenity** *n* : serenidad *f*

sergeant *n* : sargento *mf*

serial *adj* : seriado — ~ *n* : serial *m* — **series** *n*, *pl* **series** : serie *f*

serious *adj* : serio — **seriously** *adv* **1** : seriamente **2** GRAVELY : gravemente **3** **take** ~ : tomar en serio

sermon n : sermón m

serpent n : serpiente f

servant n : criado m, -da f

serve v **served; serving** vi **1** : servir **2** : sacar (en deportes) **3 ~ as** : servir de — vt **1** : servir **2 ~ time** : cumplir una condena — **server** n **1** WAITER : camarero m, -ra f **2** : servidor m (en informática)

service n **1** : servicio m **2** CEREMONY : oficio m **3** MAINTENANCE : revisión f **4 armed ~s** : fuerzas fpl armadas — **~** vt **-viced; -vicing** : revisar (un vehículo, etc.) — **serviceman** n, pl **-men** : militar m — **service station** n : estación f de servicio — **serving** n : porción f, ración f

session n : sesión f

set n **1** : juego m (de platos, etc.) **2** : set m (en tenis, etc.) **3** or **stage ~** : decorado m **4 television ~** : aparato m de televisión — **~** v **set; setting** vt **1** or **~ down** : poner **2** : poner en hora (un reloj) **3** FIX : fijar (una fecha, etc.) **4 ~ fire to** : prender fuego a **5 ~ free** : poner en libertad **6 ~ off** : hacer sonar (una alarma), hacer estallar (una bomba) **7 ~ out to (do sth)** : proponerse (hacer algo) **8 ~ up** ASSEMBLE : montar, armar **9 ~ up** ESTABLISH : establecer — vi **1** : cuajarse (dícese de la gelatina, etc.), fraguar (dícese del cemento) **2** : ponerse (dícese del sol, etc.) **3 ~ in** BEGIN : empezar **4 ~ off** or **~ out** : salir (de viaje) — **~** adj **1** FIXED : fijo **2** READY : listo, preparado — **setback** n : revés m — **setting** n **1** : posición f (de un control) **2** MOUNTING : engaste m (de joyas) **3** SCENE : escenario m

settle v **settled; settling** vi **1** : asentarse (dícese de polvo, colonos, etc.) **2 ~ down** RELAX : calmarse **3 ~ for** : conformarse con **4 ~ in** : instalarse — vt **1** DECIDE : fijar, decidir **2** RESOLVE : resolver **3** PAY : pagar **4** CALM : calmar **5** COLONIZE : colonizar — **settlement** n **1** PAYMENT : pago m **2** COLONY : colonia f, poblado m **3** AGREEMENT : acuerdo m — **settler** n : colono m, -na f

seven adj : siete — **~** n : siete m — **seven hundred** adj : setecientos — **~** n : setecientos m — **seventeen** adj : diecisiete — **~** n : diecisiete m — **seventeenth** adj : decimoséptimo — **~** n **1** : decimoséptimo m, -ma f (en una serie) **2** : diecisieteavo m (en matemáticas) — **seventh** adj : séptimo — **~** n **1** : séptimo m, -ma f (en una serie) **2** : séptimo m (en matemáticas) — **seventieth** adj : septuagésimo — **~** n **1** : septuagésimo m, -ma f (en una serie) — **seventy** adj : setenta — **~** n, pl **-ties** : setenta m

sever vt **-ered; -ering** : cortar, romper

several adj : varios — **~** pron : varios, varias

severance n : ruptura f

severe adj **severer; -est 1** : severo **2** SERIOUS : grave — **severely** adv **1** : severamente **2** SERIOUSLY : gravemente — **severity** n **1** : severidad f **2** SERIOUSNESS : gravedad f

sew v **sewed; sewn** or **sewed; sewing** : coser

sewer n : cloaca f — **sewage** n : aguas fpl negras

sewing n : costura f

sex n **1** : sexo m **2** INTERCOURSE : relaciones fpl sexuales — **sexism** n : sexismo m — **sexist** adj : sexista — **sexual** adj : sexual — **sexuality** n : sexualidad f — **sexy** adj **sexier; -est** : sexy

shabby adj **shabbier; -est 1** WORN : gastado **2** UNFAIR : malo, injusto

shack n : choza f

shackle n : grillete m

shade n **1** : sombra f **2** : tono m (de un color) **3** NUANCE : matiz m **4** or **lampshade** : pantalla f **5** or **window ~** : persiana f — **~** vt **shaded; shading** : proteger de la luz — **shadow** n : sombra f — **shadowy** adj INDISTINCT : vago — **shady** adj **shadier; -est 1** : sombreado **2** DISREPUTABLE : sospechoso

shaft n **1** : asta f (de una flecha, etc.) **2** HANDLE : mango m **3** AXLE : eje m **4** : rayo m (de luz) **5** or **mine ~** : pozo m

shaggy adj **shaggier; -est** : peludo

shake v **shook; shaken; shaking** vt **1** : sacudir **2** MIX : agitar **3 ~ hands with s.o.** : dar la mano a algn **4 ~ one's head** : negar con la cabeza **5 ~ up** UPSET : afectar — vi : temblar — **~** n **1** : sacudida f **2** → **handshake** — **shaker** n **1 salt ~** : salero m **2 pepper ~** : pimentero m — **shaky** adj **shakier; -est 1** : tembloroso **2** UNSTABLE : poco firme

shall v aux, past **should; pres sing & pl shall 1** (expressing volition or futurity) → **will 2** (expressing possibility or obligation) → **should 3 ~ we go?** : ¿nos vamos?

shallow adj **1** : poco profundo **2** SUPERFICIAL : superficial

sham n : farsa f — **~** v **shammed; shamming** : fingir

shambles ns & pl : caos m, desorden m

shame n **1** : vergüenza f **2 what a ~!** : ¡qué lástima! — **~** vt **shamed; shaming** : avergonzar — **shameful** adj : vergonzoso — **shameless** adj : desvergonzado

shampoo vt : lavar (el pelo) — **~** n, pl **-poos** : champú m

shamrock *n* : trébol *m*

shan't (*contraction of* **shall not**) → **shall**

shape *v* **shaped; shaping** *vt* **1** : formar **2** DETERMINE : determinar **3** be ~d like : tener forma de — *vi or* ~ **up** : tomar forma — ~ *n* **1** : forma *f* **2** get in ~ : ponerse en forma — **shapeless** *adj* : informe

share *n* **1** : porción *f* **2** : acción *f* (en una compañía) — ~ *v* **shared; sharing** *vt* **1** : compartir **2** DIVIDE : dividir — *vi* : compartir — **shareholder** *n* : accionista *mf*

shark *n* : tiburón *m*

sharp *adj* **1** : afilado **2** POINTY : puntiagudo **3** ACUTE : agudo **4** HARSH : duro, severo **5** CLEAR : nítido **6** : sostenido (en música) **7** a ~ curve : una curva cerrada — ~ *adv* at two o'clock ~ : a las dos en punto — ~ *n* : sostenido (en música) — **sharpen** *vt* : afilar (un cuchillo, etc.), sacar punta a (un lápiz) — **sharpener** *n* **1** or knife ~ : afilador *m* **2** or pencil ~ : sacapuntas *m* — **sharply** *adv* : bruscamente

shatter *vt* **1** : hacer añicos **2** DEVASTATE : destrozar — *vi* : hacerse añicos

shave *v* **shaved; shaved** *or* **shaven**; **shaving** *vt* **1** : afeitar **2** SLICE : cortar — *vi* : afeitarse — ~ *n* : afeitada *f* — **shaver** *n* : máquina *f* de afeitar

shawl *n* : chal *m*

she *pron* : ella

sheaf *n*, *pl* **sheaves** **1** : gavilla *f* **2** : fajo *m* (de papeles)

shear *vt* **sheared; sheared** *or* **shorn**; **shearing** : esquilar — **shears** *npl* : tijeras *fpl* (grandes)

sheath *n*, *pl* **sheaths** : funda *f*, vaina *f*

shed[1] *v* **shed; shedding** *vt* **1** : derramar (lágrimas, etc.) **2** : mudar (de piel, etc.), quitarse (ropa) **3** ~ light on : aclarar

shed[2] *n* : cobertizo *m*

she'd (*contraction of* **she had** *or* **she would**) → **have, would**

sheen *n* : brillo *m*, lustre *m*

sheep *n*, *pl* **sheep** : oveja *f* — **sheepish** *adj* : avergonzado

sheer *adj* **1** THIN : transparente **2** PURE : puro **3** STEEP : escarpado

sheet *n* **1** : sábana *f* (de la cama) **2** : hoja *f* (de papel) **3** : capa *f* (de hielo, etc.) **4** PLATE : placa *f*, lámina *f*

shelf *n*, *pl* **shelves** : estante *m*

shell *n* **1** : concha *f* **2** : caparazón *m* (de un crustáceo, etc.) **3** : cáscara *f* (de un huevo, etc.) **4** : armazón *mf* (de un edificio, etc.) **5** POD : vaína *f* **6** MISSILE : proyectil *m* — ~ *vt* **1** : pelar (nueces, etc.) **2** BOMBARD : bombardear

she'll (*contraction of* **she shall** *or* **she will**) → **shall, will**

shellfish *n* : marisco *m*

shelter *n* **1** : refugio *m* **2** take ~ : refugiarse — ~ *vt* **1** PROTECT : proteger **2** HARBOR : albergar

shelve *vt* **shelved; shelving** DEFER : dar carpetazo a

shepherd *n* : pastor *m* — ~ *vt* GUIDE : conducir, guiar

sherbet *n* : sorbete *m*

sheriff *n* : sheriff *mf*

sherry *n*, *pl* **-ries** : jerez *m*

she's (*contraction of* **she is** *or* **she has**) → **be, have**

shield *n* : escudo *m* — ~ *vt* : proteger

shier, shiest → **shy**

shift *vt* **1** MOVE : mover **2** SWITCH : transferir — *vi* **1** CHANGE : cambiar **2** MOVE : moverse **3** *or* ~ **gears** : cambiar de velocidad — ~ *n* **1** CHANGE : cambio *m* **2** : turno *m* (de trabajo) — **shiftless** *adj* : holgazán — **shifty** *adj* **shiftier; -est** : sospechoso

shimmer *vi* : brillar, relucir

shin *n* : espinilla *f*

shine *v* **shone** *or* **shined; shining** *vi* : brillar — *vt* **1** : alumbrar (una luz) **2** POLISH : sacar brillo a — ~ *n* : brillo *m*

shingle *n* : teja *f* plana y delgada (en construcción) — ~ **-gled; -gling** : techar — **shingles** *npl* : herpes *m*

shiny *adj* **shinier; -est** : brillante

ship *n* **1** : barco *m*, buque *m* **2** → **spaceship** — ~ *vt* **shipped; shipping** : transportar, enviar (por barco) — **shipbuilding** *n* : construcción *f* naval — **shipment** *n* : envío *m* — **shipping** *n* **1** : transporte *m* **2** SHIPS : barcos *mpl* — **shipshape** *adj* : ordenado — **shipwreck** *n* : naufragio *m* — ~ *vt* be ~ed : naufragar — **shipyard** *n* : astillero *m*

shirk *vt* : esquivar

shirt *n* : camisa *f*

shiver *vi* : temblar (del frío, etc.) — ~ *n* : escalofrío *m*

shoal *n* : banco *m*

shock *n* **1** IMPACT : choque *m* **2** SURPRISE, UPSET : golpe *m* emocional **3** : shock *m* (en medicina) **4** *or* **electric** ~ : descarga *f* (eléctrica) — ~ *vt* : escandalizar — **shock absorber** *n* : amortiguador *m* — **shocking** *adj* : escandaloso

shoddy *adj* **shoddier; -est** : de mala calidad

shoe *n* : zapato *m* — ~ *vt* **shod; shoeing** : herrar (un caballo) — **shoelace** *n* : cordón *m* (de zapato) — **shoemaker** *n* : zapatero *m*, -ra *f*

shone → **shine**

shook → **shake**

shoot *v* **shot; shooting** *vt* **1** : disparar **2** : echar (una mirada) **3** PHOTOGRAPH : foto-

grafiar **4** FILM : rodar — *vi* **1** : disparar **2**
~ by : pasar como una bala — **~** *n* : brote
m, retoño *m* (de una planta) — **shooting
star** *n* : estrella *f* fugaz
shop *n* **1** : tienda *f* **2** WORKSHOP : taller *m*
— **~** *vi* **shopped; shopping 1** : hacer
compras **2 go shopping** : ir de compras —
shopkeeper *n* : tendero *m*, -ra *f* — **shoplift**
vi : hurtar mercancía (en tiendas) — **shop-
lifter** *n* : ladrón *m*, -drona *f* (que roba en
tiendas) — **shopper** *n* : comprador *m*, -dora
f
shore *n* : orilla *f*
shorn → **shear**
short *adj* **1** : corto **2** : bajo (de estatura) **3**
CURT : brusco **4 a ~ time ago** : hace poco
5 be ~ of : estar corto de — **~** *adv* **1 stop
~** : parar en seco **2 fall ~** : quedarse corto
— **shortage** *n* : escasez *f*, carencia *f* —
shortcake *n* : tarta *f* de fruta — **shortcom-
ing** *n* : defecto *m* — **shortcut** *n* : atajo *m* —
shorten *vt* : acortar — **shorthand** *n*
: taquigrafía *f* — **short–lived** *adj* : efímero
— **shortly** *adv* : dentro de poco — **shortness** *n* **1** : lo corto (de una cosa), baja estatura *f* (de una persona) **2 ~ of breath**
: falta *f* de aliento — **shorts** *npl* : shorts
mpl, pantalones *mpl* cortos — **short-
sighted** → **nearsighted**
shot *n* **1** : disparo *m*, tiro *m* **2** : tiro *m* (en
deportes) **3** ATTEMPT : intento *m* **4** PHOTO-
GRAPH : foto *f* **5** INJECTION : inyección *f* **6**
: trago *m* (de licor) — **shotgun** *n* : escopeta
f
should *past of* **shall 1 if she ~ call** : si
llama **2 I ~ have gone** : debería haber ido
3 they ~ arrive soon : deben llegar pronto
4 what ~ we do? : ¿qué hacemos?
shoulder *n* **1** : hombro *m* **2** : arcén *m* (de
una carretera) — **~** *vt* : cargar con (la responsabilidad, etc.) — **shoulder blade** *n*
: omóplato *m*
shouldn't (*contraction of* **should not**) →
should
shout *v* : gritar — **~** *n* : grito *m*
shove *v* **shoved; shoving** : empujar — **~** *n*
: empujón *m*
shovel *n* : pala *f* — **~** *vt* **-veled** *or* **-velled;
-veling** *or* **-velling 1** : mover (tierra, etc.)
con una pala **2** DIG : cavar (con una pala)
show *v* **showed; shown** *or* **showed; showing** *vt* **1** : mostrar **2** TEACH : enseñar **3**
PROVE : demostrar **4** ESCORT : acompañar
5 : proyectar (una película), dar (un programa de televisión) **6 ~ off** : hacer alarde
de — *vi* **1** : mostrarse, verse **2 ~ off** : lucirse
3 ~ up ARRIVE : aparecer — **~** *n* **1**
: demostración *f* **2** EXHIBITION : exposición
f **3** : espectáculo *m* (teatral), programa *m*

(de televisión, etc.) — **showdown** *n* : confrontación *f*
shower *n* **1** : ducha *f* **2** : chaparrón *m* (en
meteorología) **3** PARTY : fiesta *f* — **~** *vt* **1**
SPRAY : regar **2 ~ s.o. with** : colmar a algn
de — *vi* **1** : ducharse **2** RAIN : llover
showy *adj* **showier; -est** : llamativo, ostentoso
shrank → **shrink**
shrapnel *ns & pl* : metralla *f*
shred *n* **1** : tira *f* (de tela, etc.) **2** IOTA : pizca
f — **~** *vt* **shredded; shredding 1** : hacer
tiras **2** GRATE : rallar
shrewd *adj* : astuto
shriek *vi* : chillar — **~** *n* : chillido *m*, alarido *m*
shrill *adj* : agudo, estridente
shrimp *n* : camarón *m*
shrine *n* **1** TOMB : sepulcro *m* **2** SANCTU-
ARY : santuario *m*
shrink *v* **shrank; shrunk** *or* **shrunken;
shrinking** *vt* : encoger — *vi* **1** : encogerse
(dícese de ropa), reducirse (dícese de
números, etc.) **2 ~ back** : retroceder
shrivel *vi* **-veled** *or* **-velled; -veling** *or* **-vel-
ling** *or* **~ up** : arrugarse, marchitarse
shroud *n* **1** : sudario *m*, mortaja *f* **2** VEIL
: velo *m* — **~** *vt* : envolver
shrub *n* : arbusto *m*, mata *f*
shrug *vi* **shrugged; shrugging** : encogerse
de hombros
shrunk → **shrink**
shudder *vi* : estremecerse — **~** *n* : estremecimiento *m*
shuffle *v* **-fled; -fling** *vt* : barajar (naipes),
revolver (papeles, etc.) — *vi* : caminar ar-
rastrando los pies
shun *vi* **shunned; shunning** : evitar, esquivar
shut *v* **shut; shutting** *vt* **1** CLOSE : cerrar **2**
~ off → **turn off 3 ~ up** CONFINE : encer-
rar — *vi* **~ down** : cerrarse **2 ~ up!**
: ¡cállate! — **shutter** *n* **1** *or* **window ~**
: contraventana *f* **2** : obturador *m* (de una
cámara)
shuttle *n* **1** : lanzadera *f* (para tejer) **2** *or* **~
bus** : autobús *m* (de corto recorrido) **3** →
space shuttle — **~** *v* **-tled; -tling** *vt*
: transportar — *vi* : ir y venir
shy *adj* **shier** *or* **shyer; shiest** *or* **shyest**
: tímido — **~** *vi* **shied; shying** *or* **~ away**
: retroceder — **shyness** *n* : timidez *f*
sibling *n* : hermano *m*, hermana *f*
sick *adj* **1** : enfermo **2 be ~** VOMIT : vomitar **3 be ~ of** : estar harto de **4 feel ~**
: tener náuseas — **sicken** *vt* DISGUST : dar
asco a — **sickening** *adj* : nauseabundo
sickle *n* : hoz *f*
sickly *adj* **sicklier; -est 1** UNHEALTHY : en-

fermizo **2** → **sickening** — **sickness** n : enfermedad f

side n **1** : lado m **2** : costado m (de una persona), ijada f (de un animal) **3** : parte f (en una disputa, etc.) **4** ∼ **by** ∼ : uno al lado de otro **5 take** ∼**s** : tomar partido — ∼ vi ∼ **with** : ponerse de parte de — **sideboard** n : aparador m — **sideburns** npl : patillas fpl — **side effect** n : efecto m secundario — **sideline** n : línea f de banda (en deportes) — **sidestep** vt **-stepped; -stepping** : eludir, esquivar — **sidetrack** vt **get** ∼**ed** : distraerse — **sidewalk** n : acera f — **sideways** adj & adv : de lado — **siding** n : revestimiento m exterior

siege n : sitio m

sieve n : tamiz m, cedazo m

sift vt **1** : cerner, tamizar **2** or ∼ **through** : pasar por el tamiz

sigh vi : suspirar — ∼ n : suspiro m

sight n **1** : vista f **2** SPECTACLE : espectáculo m **3** : lugar m de interés (turístico) **4 catch** ∼ **of** : avistar — ∼ vt : avistar — **sight-seer** n : turista mf

sign n **1** : signo m **2** NOTICE : letrero m **3** GESTURE : seña f, señal f — ∼ vt : firmar (un cheque, etc.) — vi **1** : firmar **2** ∼ **up** ENROLL : inscribirse

signal n : señal f — ∼ v **-naled** or **-nalled; -naling** or **-nalling** vt **1** : hacer señas a **2** INDICATE : señalar — vi **1** : hacer señas **2** : señalizar (en un vehículo)

signature n : firma f

significance n **1** : significado m **2** IMPORTANCE : importancia f — **significant** adj : importante — **signify** vt **-fied; -fying** : significar

sign language n : lenguaje m gestual — **signpost** n : poste m indicador

silence n : silencio m — ∼ vt **-lenced; -lencing** : silenciar — **silent** adj **1** : silencioso **2** MUM : callado **3** : mudo (dícese de películas y letras)

silhouette n : silueta f — ∼ vt **-etted; -etting be** ∼**d against** : perfilarse contra

silicon n : silicio m

silk n : seda f — **silky** adj **silkier; -est** : sedoso

sill n : alféizar m (de una ventana), umbral m (de una puerta)

silly adj **sillier; -est** : tonto, estúpido

silt n : cieno m

silver n **1** : plata f **2** → **silverware** — ∼ adj : de plata — **silverware** n : plata f — **silvery** adj : plateado

similar adj : similar, parecido — **similarity** n, pl **-ties** : semejanza f, parecido m

simmer v : hervir a fuego lento

simple adj **simpler; -plest 1** : simple **2** EASY : sencillo — **simplicity** n : simplicidad f, sencillez f — **simplify** vt **-fied; -fying** : simplificar — **simply** adv **1** : sencillamente **2** ABSOLUTELY : realmente

simulate vt **-lated; -lating** : simular

simultaneous adj : simultáneo

sin n : pecado m — ∼ vi **sinned; sinning** : pecar

since adv **1** or ∼ **then** : desde entonces **2 long** ∼ : hace mucho — ∼ conj **1** : desde que **2** BECAUSE : ya que, como **3 it's been years** ∼**...** : hace años que... — ∼ prep : desde

sincere adj **-cerer; -est** : sincero — **sincerely** adv : sinceramente — **sincerity** n : sinceridad f

sinful adj : pecador (dícese de las personas), pecaminoso (dícese de las acciones)

sing v **sang** or **sung; sung; singing** : cantar

singe vt **singed; singeing** : chamuscar

singer n : cantante mf

single adj **1** : solo, único **2** UNMARRIED : soltero **3 every** ∼ **day** : cada día, todos los días — ∼ n **1** : soltero m, -ra f **2** or ∼ **room** : habitación f individual — ∼ vt **-gled; -gling** ∼ **out 1** SELECT : escoger **2** DISTINGUISH : señalar — **single-handed** adj : sin ayuda, solo

singular adj : singular — ∼ n : singular m

sinister adj : siniestro

sink v **sank** or **sunk; sunk; sinking** vi **1** : hundirse (en un líquido) **2** DROP : bajar, caer — vt **1** : hundir **2** ∼ **sth into** : clavar algo en — ∼ n **1** or **kitchen** ∼ : fregadero m **2** or **bathroom** ∼ : lavabo m, lavamanos m

sinner n : pecador m, -dora f

sip v **sipped; sipping** vt : sorber — vi : beber a sorbos — ∼ n : sorbo m

siphon n : sifón m — ∼ vt **1** : sacar con sifón

sir n **1** (in titles) : sir m **2** (as a form of address) : señor m **3 Dear Sir** : Estimado señor

siren n : sirena f

sirloin n : solomillo m

sissy n, pl **-sies** : mariquita mf fam

sister n : hermana f — **sister-in-law** n, pl **sisters-in-law** : cuñada f

sit v **sat; sitting** vi **1** or ∼ **down** : sentarse **2** LIE : estar (ubicado) **3** MEET : estar en sesión **4** or ∼ **up** : incorporarse — vt : sentar

site n **1** : sitio m, lugar m **2** LOT : solar m

sitting room → **living room**

sitter → **baby-sitter**

situated adj : ubicado, situado — **situation** n : situación f

six *adj* : seis — ~ *n* : seis *m* — **six hundred** *adj* : seiscientos — ~ *n* : seiscientos *m* — **sixteen** *adj* : dieciséis — ~ *n* : dieciséis *m* — **sixteenth** *adj* : decimosexto — ~ *n* **1** : decimosexto *m*, -ta *f* (en una serie) **2** : dieciseisavo *m*, dieciseisava parte *f* — **sixth** *adj* : sexto — ~ *n* **1** : sexto *m*, -ta *f* (en una serie) **2** : sexto *m* (en matemáticas) — **sixtieth** *adj* : sexagésimo — ~ *n* **1** : sexagésimo *m*, -ma *f* (en una serie) **2** : sesentavo *m* (en matemáticas) — **sixty** *adj* : sesenta — ~ *n, pl* **-ties** : sesenta *m*

size *n* **1** : tamaño *m*, talla *f* (de ropa), número *m* (de zapatos) **2** EXTENT : magnitud *f* — ~ *vt* **sized; sizing** ~ **up** : evaluar — **sizable** *or* **sizeable** *adj* : considerable

sizzle *vi* **-zled; -zling** : chisporrotear

skate¹ *n* : raya *f* (pez)

skate² *n* : patín *m* — ~ *vi* **skated; skating** : patinar — **skateboard** *n* : monopatín *m* — **skater** *n* : patinador *m*, -dora *f*

skeleton *n* : esqueleto *m*

skeptic *n* : escéptico *m*, -ca *f* — **skeptical** *adj* : escéptico — **skepticism** *n* : escepticismo *m*

sketch *n* **1** : esbozo *m*, bosquejo *m* **2** SKIT : sketch *m* — ~ *vt* : bosquejar — *vi* : hacer bosquejos — **sketchy** *adj* **sketchier; -est** : incompleto

skewer *n* : brocheta *f*, broqueta *f*

ski *n, pl* **skis** : esquí *m* — ~ *vi* **skied; skiing** : esquiar

skid *n* : derrape *m*, patinazo *m* — ~ *vi* **skidded; skidding** : derrapar, patinar

skier *n* : esquiador *m*, -dora *f*

skill *n* **1** : habilidad *f*, destreza *f* **2** TECHNIQUE : técnica *f* — **skilled** *adj* : hábil

skillet *n* : sartén *mf*

skillful *adj* : hábil, diestro

skim *vt* **skimmed; skimming** **1** : espumar (sopa, etc.), descremar (leche) **2** : pasar rozando (una superficie) **3** *or* ~ **through** : echar un vistazo a — ~ *adj* : descremado

skimp *vi* ~ **on** : escatimar — **skimpy** *adj* **skimpier; -est** **1** : exiguo, escaso **2** : brevísimo (dícese de ropa)

skin *n* : piel *f* — ~ *vt* **skinned; skinning** : despellejar — **skin diving** *n* : buceo *m*, submarinismo *m* — **skinny** *adj* **skinnier; -est** : flaco

skip *v* **skipped; skipping** *vi* : ir brincando — *vt* OMIT : saltarse — ~ *n* : brinco *m*, salto *m*

skipper *n* : capitán *m*, -tana *f*

skirmish *n* : escaramuza *f*

skirt *n* : falda *f* — ~ *vt* **1** BORDER : bordear **2** EVADE : eludir

skull *n* : cráneo *m* (de una persona viva), calavera *f* (de un esqueleto)

skunk *n* : mofeta *f*, zorrillo *m* *Lat*

sky *n, pl* **skies** : cielo *m* — **skylight** *n* : claraboya *f*, tragaluz *m* — **skyline** *n* : horizonte *m* — **skyscraper** *n* : rascacielos *m*

slab *n* : bloque *m* (de piedra, etc.)

slack *adj* **1** LOOSE : flojo **2** CARELESS : descuidado — ~ *n* **1 take up the ~** : tensar (una cuerda, etc.) **2** ~**s** *npl* : pantalones *mpl* — **slacken** *vt* : aflojar — *vi* : aflojarse

slain → **slay**

slam *n* : golpe *m*, portazo *m* (de una puerta) — ~ *v* **slammed; slamming** *vt* **1** *or* ~ **down** : tirar, plantar **2** *or* ~ **shut** : cerrar de golpe **3** ~ **the door** : dar un portazo — *vi* **1** : cerrarse de golpe **2** ~ **into** : chocar contra

slander *vt* : calumniar, difamar — ~ *n* : calumnia *f*, difamación *f*

slang *n* : argot *m*

slant *n* : inclinación *f* — ~ *vi* : inclinarse

slap *vt* **slapped; slapping** **1** : dar una bofetada a **2** ~ **s.o. on the back** : dar una palmada en la espalda a algn — ~ *n* : bofetada *f*, cachetada *f* *Lat*

slash *vt* **1** : hacer un tajo en **2** : rebajar (precios) drásticamente — ~ *n* : tajo *m*

slat *n* : tablilla *f*

slate *n* : pizarra *f*

slaughter *n* : matanza *f* — ~ *vt* **1** : matar (animales) **2** MASSACRE : masacrar — **slaughterhouse** *n* : matadero *m*

slave *n* : esclavo *m*, -va *f* — ~ *vi* **slaved; slaving** : trabajar como un burro — **slavery** *n* : esclavitud *f*

Slavic *adj* : eslavo

slay *vt* **slew; slain; slaying** : asesinar

sleazy *adj* **sleazier; -est** : sórdido

sled *n* : trineo *m*

sledgehammer *n* : almádena *f*

sleek *adj* : liso y brillante

sleep *n* **1** : sueño *m* **2 go to** ~ : dormirse — ~ *vi* **slept; sleeping** : dormir — **sleeper** *n* **be a light** ~ : tener el sueño ligero — **sleepless** *adj* **have a** ~ **night** : pasar la noche en blanco — **sleepwalker** *n* : sonámbulo *m*, -la *f* — **sleepy** *adj* **sleepier; -est** **1** : somnoliento, soñoliento **2 be** ~ : tener sueño

sleet *n* : aguanieve *f* — ~ *vi* : caer aguanieve

sleeve *n* : manga *f* — **sleeveless** *adj* : sin mangas

sleigh *n* : trineo *m*

slender *adj* : delgado

slew → **slay**

slice *vt* **sliced; slicing** : cortar — ~ *n* : trozo *m*, rebanada *f* (de pan, etc.), tajada *f* (de carne)

slick *adj* SLIPPERY : resbaladizo, resbaloso *Lat*

slide v **slid**; **sliding** vi : deslizarse — vt : deslizar — ~ n **1** : deslizamiento m **2** : tobogán m (para niños) **3** : diapositiva f (fotográfica) **4** DECLINE : descenso m

slier, sliest → **sly**

slight adj **1** : ligero, leve **2** SLENDER : delgado — ~ vt : desairar — **slightly** adv : ligeramente, un poco

slim adj **slimmer**; **slimmest 1** : delgado **2 a ~ chance** : escasas posibilidades fpl — ~ v **slimmed**; **slimming** : adelgazar

slime n **1** : baba f (de un caracol, etc.) **2** MUD : limo m — **slimy** adj **slimier**; **-est** : viscoso

sling vt **slung**; **slinging 1** THROW : lanzar **2** HANG : colgar — ~ n **1** : honda f **2** : cabestrillo m (en medicina) — **slingshot** n : tirachinas m

slink vi **slunk**; **slinking** : andar furtivamente

slip¹ v **slipped**; **slipping** vi **1** SLIDE : resbalarse **2 let sth ~** : dejar escapar algo **3 ~ away** : escabullirse **4 ~ up** : equivocarse — vt **1** : deslizar **2 ~ into** : ponerse (una prenda) **3 it slipped my mind** : se me olvidó — ~ n **1** MISTAKE : error m, desliz m **2 ~ of the tongue** : lapsus m **3** PETTICOAT : enagua f

slip² n **~ of paper** : papelito m

slipper n : zapatilla f, pantufla f

slippery adj **slipperier**; **-est** : resbaladizo, resbaloso Lat

slit n **1** OPENING : rendija f **2** CUT : corte m, raja f — ~ vt **slit**; **slitting** : cortar

slither vi : deslizarse

sliver n : astilla f

slogan n : eslogan m

slop v **slopped**; **slopping** vt : derramar — vi : derramarse

slope vi **sloped**; **sloping** : inclinarse — ~ n : pendiente f, declive m

sloppy adj **sloppier**; **-est 1** CARELESS : descuidado **2** UNKEMPT : desaliñado

slot n : ranura f

sloth n : pereza f

slouch vi : andar con los hombros caídos (en una silla)

slovenly adj : desaliñado

slow adj **1** : lento **2 be ~** : estar atrasado (dícese de un reloj) — ~ adv → **slowly** — ~ vt : retrasar, retardar — vi or ~ **down** : ir más despacio — **slowly** adv : lentamente, despacio — **slowness** n : lentitud f

sludge n SEWAGE : aguas fpl negras

slug¹ n **1** : babosa f (molusco) **2** BULLET : bala f **3** TOKEN : ficha f

slug² vt **slugged**; **slugging** : pegar un porrazo a

sluggish adj : lento

slum n : barrio m bajo

slumber vi : dormir — ~ n : sueño m

slump vi **1** DROP : bajar **2** COLLAPSE : dejarse caer **3** → **slouch** — ~ n : bajón m

slung → **sling**

slunk → **slink**

slur¹ n ASPERSION : calumnia f, difamación f

slur² vt **slurred**; **slurring** : arrastrar (las palabras)

slurp v : beber haciendo ruido — ~ n : sorbo m (ruidoso)

slush n : nieve f medio derretida

sly adj **slier**; **sliest 1** : astuto, taimado **2 on the ~** : a escondidas

smack¹ vi **~ of** : oler a

smack² vt **1** : pegar una bofetada a **2** KISS : besar **3 ~ one's lips** : relamerse — ~ n **1** SLAP : bofetada f **2** KISS : beso m — ~ adv : justo, exactamente

small adj : pequeño, chico — **smallpox** n : viruela f

smart adj **1** : listo, inteligente **2** STYLISH : elegante — ~ vi STING : escocer — **smartly** adv : elegantemente

smash n **1** BLOW : golpe m **2** COLLISION : choque m **3** BANG, CRASH : estrépito m — ~ vt **1** BREAK : romper **2** DESTROY : aplastar — vi **1** SHATTER : hacerse pedazos **2 ~ into** : estrellarse contra

smattering n : nociones fpl

smear n : mancha f — ~ vt **1** : embadurnar (de pinta, etc.), untar (de aceite, etc.) **2** SMUDGE : manchar

smell v **smelled** or **smelt**; **smelling** : oler — ~ n **1** : (sentido m del) olfato m **2** ODOR : olor m — **smelly** adj **smellier**; **-est** : maloliente

smelt vt : fundir

smile vi **smiled**; **smiling** : sonreír — ~ n : sonrisa f

smirk vi : sonreír con suficiencia — ~ n : sonrisa f satisfecha

smitten adj **be ~ with** : estar enamorado de

smith → **blacksmith**

smock n : blusón m, bata f

smog n : smog m

smoke n : humo m — ~ v **smoked**; **smoking** vi **1** : humear (dícese de fuegos, etc.) **2** : fumar (dícese de personas) — vt **1** : ahumar (carne, etc.) **2** : fumar (cigarillos) — **smoker** n : fumador m, -dora f — **smokestack** n : chimenea f — **smoky** adj **smokier**; **-est 1** : lleno de humo **2** : a humo (dícese de sabores, etc.)

smolder vi : arder (sin llama)

smooth adj **1** : liso (dícese de superficies), suave (dícese de movimientos), tranquilo (dícese del mar) **2** : sin grumos (dícese de salsas, etc.) — ~ vt : alisar — **smoothly** adv : suavemente — **smoothness** n : suavidad f

smother *vt* : asfixiar (a algn), sofocar (llamas, etc.)

smudge *v* **smudged; smudging** *vt* : emborronar — *vi* : correrse — **~** *n* : mancha *f*, borrón *m*

smug *adj* **smugger; smuggest** : suficiente

smuggle *vt* **-gled; -gling** : pasar de contrabando — **smuggler** *n* : contrabandista *mf*

snack *n* : refrigerio *m*, tentempié *m fam*

snag *n* : problema *m* — **~** *v* **snagged; snagging** *vt* : enganchar — *vi* : engancharse

snail *n* : caracol *m*

snake *n* : culebra *f*, serpiente *f*

snap *v* **snapped; snapping** *vi* **1** BREAK : romperse **2** : intentar morder (dícese de un perro, etc.) **3 ~ at** : contestar bruscamente a — *vt* **1** BREAK : romper **2 ~ one's fingers** : chasquear los dedos **3 ~ open/shut** : abrir/cerrar de golpe — **~** *n* **1** : chasquido *m* **2** FASTENER : broche *m* (de presión) **3 be a ~** : ser facilísimo — **snappy** *adj* **snappier; -est 1** FAST : rápido **2** STYLISH : elegante — **snapshot** *n* : instantánea *f*

snare *n* : trampa *f* — **~** *vt* **snared; snaring** : atrapar

snarl[1] *vi* TANGLE : enmarañar, enredar — **~** *n* : enredo *m*, maraña *f*

snarl[2] *vi* GROWL : gruñir — *n* : gruñido *m*

snatch *vt* : arrebatar

sneak *vi* : ir a hurtadillas — *vt* : hacer furtivamente — **~** *n* : soplón *m*, -plona *f fam* — **sneakers** *npl* : tenis *mpl*, zapatillas *fpl* — **sneaky** *adj* **sneakier; -est** : solapado

sneer *vi* : sonreír con desprecio — **~** *n* : sonrisa *f* de desprecio

sneeze *vi* **sneezed; sneezing** : estornudar — **~** *n* : estornudo *m*

snide *adj* : sarcástico

sniff *vi* : oler — *vt* **1** : oler **2** → **sniffle** — **~** *n* : aspiración *f* por la nariz — **sniffle** *vi* **-fled; -fling** : sorberse la nariz — **sniffles** *npl* **have the ~** : estar resfriado

snip *n* : tijeretada *f* — **~** *vt* **snipped; snipping** : cortar (con tijeras)

snivel *vi* **-veled** *or* **-velled; -veling** *or* **-velling** : lloriquear

snob *n* : esnob *mf* — **snobbish** *adj* : esnob

snoop *vi* : husmear — **~** *n* : fisgón *m*, -gona *f*

snooze *vi* **snoozed; snoozing** : dormitar — **~** *n* : siestecita *f*, siestita *f*

snore *vi* **snored; snoring** : roncar — **~** *n* : ronquido *m*

snort *vi* : bufar — **~** *n* : bufido *m*

snout *n* : hocico *m*, morro *m*

snow *n* : nieve *f* — **~** *vi* : nevar — **snowfall** *n* : nevada *f* — **snowflake** *n* : copo *m* de nieve — **snowman** *n* : muñeco *m* de nieve — **snowplow** *n* : quitanieves *m* — **snow-**

shoe *n* : raqueta *f* (para nieve) — **snowstorm** *n* : tormenta *f* de nieve — **snowy** *adj* **snowier; -est 1 a ~ day** : un día nevoso **2 ~ mountains** : montañas *fpl* nevadas

snub *vt* **snubbed; snubbing** : desairar — **~** *n* : desaire *m*

snuff *vt or* **~ out** : apagar

snug *adj* **snugger; snuggest 1** : cómodo **2** TIGHT : ajustado — **snuggle** *vi* **-gled; -gling** : acurrucarse

so *adv* **1** LIKEWISE : también **2** THUS : así **3** THEREFORE : por lo tanto **4** *or* **~ much** : tanto **5** *or* **~ very** : tan **6 and ~ on** : etcétera **7 I think ~** : creo que sí **8 I told you ~** : te lo dije — **~** *conj* **1** THEREFORE : así que **2** *or* **~ that** : para que **3 ~ what?** : ¿y qué? — **~** *adj* TRUE : cierto — **~** *pron* **or ~** : más o menos

soak *vi* : estar en remojo — *vt* **1** : poner en remojo **2 ~ up** : absorber — **~** *n* : remojo *m*

soap *n* : jabón *m* — **~** *vt or* **~ up** : enjabonar — **soapy soapier; -est** *adj* : jabonoso

soar *vi* **1** : planear **2** SKYROCKET : dispararse

sob *vi* **sobbed; sobbing** : sollozar — **~** *n* : sollozo *m*

sober *adj* **1** : sobrio **2** SERIOUS : serio — **sobriety** *n* **1** : sobriedad *f* **2** SERIOUSNESS : seriedad *f*

so-called *adj* : supuesto, presunto

soccer *n* : futbol *m*, fútbol *m*

social *adj* : social — **~** *n* : reunión *f* social — **sociable** *adj* : sociable — **socialism** *n* : socialismo *m* — **socialist** *n* : socialista *mf* — **~** *adj* : socialista — **socialize** *v* **-ized; -izing** *vt* : socializar — *vi* **~ with** : alternar con — **society** *n, pl* **-eties** : sociedad *f* — **sociology** *n* : sociología *f*

sock[1] *n, pl* **socks** *or* **sox** : calcetín *m*

sock[2] *vt* : pegar, golpear — **~** *n* PUNCH : puñetazo *m*

socket *n* **1** *or* **electric ~** : enchufe *m*, toma *f* de corriente **2** *or* **eye ~** : órbita *f*, cuenca *f* **3** : glena *f* (de una articulación)

soda *n* **1** *or* **~ pop** : refresco *m*, gaseosa *f* **2** *or* **~ water** : soda *f*

sodium *n* : sodio *m*

sofa *n* : sofá *m*

soft *adj* **1** : blando **2** SMOOTH : suave — **softball** *n* : softbol *m* — **soft drink** *n* : refresco *m* — **soften** *vt* **1** : ablandar **2** EASE, SMOOTH : suavizar — *vi* **1** : ablandarse **2** EASE : suavizarse — **softly** *adv* : suavemente — **software** *n* : software *m*

soggy *adj* **soggier; -est** : empapado

soil *vt* : ensuciar — **~** *n* DIRT : tierra *f*

solace *n* : consuelo *m*

solar *adj* : solar

sold → **sell**

solder *n* : soldadura *f* — **~** *vt* : soldar

soldier *n* : soldado *mf*

sole[1] *n* : lenguado *m* (pez)

sole[2] *n* : planta *f* (del pie), suela *f* (de un zapato)

sole[3] *adj* : único — **solely** *adv* : únicamente, sólo

solemn *adj* : solemne — **solemnity** *n, pl* **-ties** : solemnidad *f*

solicit *vt* : solicitar

solid *adj* **1** : sólido **2** UNBROKEN : continuo **3 ~ gold** : oro *m* macizo **4 two ~ hours** : dos horas seguidas — **~** *n* : sólido *m* — **solidarity** *n* : solidaridad *f* — **solidify** *v* **-fied; -fying** *vt* : solidificar — *vi* : solidificarse — **solidity** *n, pl* **-ties** : solidez *f*

solitary *adj* : solitario — **solitude** *n* : soledad *f*

solo *n, pl* **solos** : solo *m* — **soloist** *n* : solista *mf*

solution *n* : solución *f* — **soluble** *adj* : soluble — **solve** *vt* **solved; solving** : resolver — **solvent** *n* : solvente *m*

somber *adj* : sombrío

some *adj* **1** (*of unspecified identity*) : un **2** (*of an unspecified amount*) : algo de, un poco de **3** (*of an unspecified number*) : unos **4** CERTAIN : algunos **5 that was ~ game!** : ¡fue un partidazo! — **~** *pron* **1** SEVERAL : algunos, unos **2** PART : un poco, algo — **~** *adv* **~ twenty people** : unas veinte personas — **somebody** *pron* : alguien — **someday** *adv* : algún día — **somehow** *adv* **1** : de algún modo **2 ~ or other** : de alguna manera u otra — **someone** *pron* : alguien

somersault *n* : voltereta *f*, salto *m* mortal

something *pron* **1** : algo **2 ~ else** : otra cosa — **sometime** *adv* **1** : algún día, en algún momento **2 ~ next month** : (durante) el mes que viene — **sometimes** *adv* : a veces — **somewhat** *adv* : algo — **somewhere** *adv* **1** : en alguna parte, en algún lado **2 ~ around** : alrededor de **3 ~ else** → **elsewhere**

son *n* : hijo *m*

song *n* : canción *f*

son–in–law *n, pl* **sons–in– law** : yerno *m*

sonnet *n* : soneto *m*

soon *adv* **1** : pronto **2** SHORTLY : dentro de poco **3 as ~ as** : en cuanto **4 as ~ as possible** : lo más pronto posible **5 ~ after** : poco después **6 ~er or later** : tarde o temprano **7 the ~er the better** : cuanto antes mejor

soot *n* : hollín *m*

soothe *vt* **soothed; soothing 1** CALM : calmar **2** RELIEVE : aliviar

sop *vt* **sopped; sopping ~ up** : absorber

sophistication *n* : sofisticación *f* — **sophisticated** *adj* : sofisticado

sophomore *n* : estudiante *mf* de segundo año

soprano *n, pl* **-nos** : soprano *mf*

sorcerer *n* : hechicero *m*, brujo *m* — **sorcery** *n* : hechicería *f*, brujería *f*

sordid *adj* : sórdido

sore *adj* **sorer; sorest 1** : dolorido **2** ANGRY : enfadado **3 ~ throat** : dolor *m* de garganta **4 I have a ~ throat** : me duele la garganta — **~** *n* : llaga *f* — **sorely** *adv* : muchísimo — **soreness** *n* : dolor *m*

sorrow *n* : pesar *m*, pena *f* — **sorry** *adj* **sorrier; -est 1** PITIFUL : lamentable **2 feel ~ for** : compadecer **3 I'm ~** : lo siento

sort *n* **1** : tipo *m*, clase *f* **2 a ~ of** : una especie de — **~** *vt* : clasificar — **sort of** *adv* **1** SOMEWHAT : algo **2** MORE OR LESS : más o menos

SOS *n* : SOS *m*

so–so *adj & adv* : así así *fam*

soufflé *n* : suflé *m*

sought → **seek**

soul *n* : alma *f*

sound[1] *adj* **1** HEALTHY : sano **2** FIRM : sólido **3** SENSIBLE : lógico **4 a ~ sleep** : un sueño profundo **5 safe and ~** : sano y salvo

sound[2] *n* : sonido *m* — *vt* : hacer sonar, tocar (una trompeta, etc.) — *vi* **1** : sonar **2** SEEM : parecer

sound[3] *n* CHANNEL : brazo *m* de mar — **~** *vt* : sondar (en navegación) **2** *or* **~ out** : sondear

soundly *adv* **1** SOLIDLY : sólidamente **2** DEEPLY : profundamente

soundproof *adj* : insonorizado

soup *n* : sopa *f*

sour *adj* **1** : agrio **2 ~ milk** : leche *f* cortada — **~** *vt* : agriar

source *n* : fuente *f*, origen *m*

south *adv* : al sur — **~** *adj* : (del) sur — **~** *n* : sur *m* — **South African** *adj* : sudafricano — **South American** *adj* : sudamericano — **southeast** *adv* : hacia el sureste — **~** *adj* : (del) sureste — **~** *n* : sureste *m*, sudeste *m* — **southeastern** *adj* → **southeast** — **southerly** *adv & adj* : del sur — **southern** *adj* : del sur, meridional — **southwest** *adv* : hacia el suroeste — **~** *adj* : (del) suroeste — **~** *n* : suroeste *m*, sudoeste *m* — **southwestern** *adj* → **southwest**

souvenir *n* : recuerdo *m*

sovereign *n* : soberano *m*, -na *f* — **~** *adj* : soberano — **sovereignty** *n, pl* **-ties** : soberanía *f*

Soviet *adj* : soviético

sow¹ *n* : cerda *f*

sow² *vt* **sowed; sown** *or* **sowed; sowing** : sembrar

sox → **sock**

soybean *n* : soya *f*, soja *f*

spa *n* : balneario *m*

space *n* **1** : espacio *m* **2** ROOM, SPOT : sitio *m*, lugar *m* — ~ *vt* **spaced; spacing** : espaciar — **spaceship** *n* : nave *f* espacial — **space shuttle** *n* : transbordador *m* espacial — **spacious** *adj* : espacioso, amplio

spade¹ *n* SHOVEL : pala *f*

spade² *n* : pica *f* (naipe)

spaghetti *n* : espaguetis *mpl*

span *n* **1** PERIOD : espacio *m* **2** : luz *f* (entre dos soportes) — ~ *vt* **spanned; spanning** **1** : abarcar (un período) **2** CROSS : extenderse sobre

Spaniard *n* : español *m*, -ñola *f*

spaniel *n* : spaniel *m*

Spanish *adj* : español — ~ *n* : español *m* (idioma)

spank *vt* : dar palmadas a (en las nalgas)

spar *vi* **sparred; sparring** : entrenarse (en boxeo)

spare *vt* **spared; sparing 1** PARDON : perdonar **2** SAVE : ahorrar **3 can you ~ a dollar?** : ¿me das un dólar? **4 I can't ~ the time** : no tengo tiempo **5 ~ no expense** : no reparar en gastos **6 to ~** : de sobra — ~ *adj* **1** : de repuesto **2** EXCESS : de más **3** LEAN : delgado — ~ *n or* **~ part** : repuesto *m* — **spare time** *n* : tiempo *m* libre — **sparing** *adj* : parco, económico

spark *n* : chispa *f* — ~ *vi* : chispear, echar chispas — *vt* : despertar (interés), provocar (crítica) — **sparkle** *vi* **-kled; -kling** : destellar, centellear — ~ *n* : destello *m*, centelleo *m* — **spark plug** *n* : bujía *f*

sparrow *n* : gorrión *m*

sparse *adj* **sparser; -est** : escaso

spasm *n* : espasmo *m*

spat¹ → **spit**

spat² *n* QUARREL : disputa *f*, pelea *f*

spatter *vt* : salpicar

spawn *vi* : desovar — *vt* : engendrar, producir — ~ *n* : hueva *f*

speak *v* **spoke; spoken; speaking** *vi* **1** : hablar **2 ~ out against** : denunciar **3 ~ up** : hablar más alto **4 ~ up for** : defender — *vt* **1** : decir **2** : hablar (un idioma) — **speaker** *n* **1** ORATOR : orador *m*, -dora *f* **2** : hablante *mf* (de un idioma) **3** LOUDSPEAKER : altavoz *m*

spear *n* : lanza *f* — **spearhead** *n* : punta *f* de lanza — ~ *vt* : encabezar — **spearmint** *n* : menta *f* verde

special *adj* : especial — **specialist** *n* : espe-

cialista *mf* — **specialization** *n* : especialización *f* — **specialize** *vi* **-ized; -izing** : especializarse — **specially** *adv* : especialmente — **specialty** *n, pl* **-ties** : especialidad *f*

species *ns & pl* : especie *f*

specify *vt* **-fied; -fying** : especificar — **specific** *adj* : específico — **specifically** *adv* **1** : específicamente **2** EXPLICITLY : expresamente — **specification** *n* : especificación *f*

specimen *n* : espécimen *m*

speck *n* **1** SPOT : mancha *f* **2** BIT : mota *f* — **speckled** *adj* : moteado

spectacle *n* **1** : espectáculo *m* **2 ~s** *npl* GLASSES : gafas *fpl*, lentes *fpl*, anteojos *mpl* — **spectacular** *adj* : espectacular — **spectator** *n* : espectador *m*, -dora *f*

specter *or* **spectre** *n* : espectro *m*

spectrum *n, pl* **-tra** *or* **-trums 1** : espectro *m* **2** RANGE : gama *f*

speculation *n* : especulación *f*

speech *n* **1** : habla *f* **2** ADDRESS : discurso *m* — **speechless** *adj* : mudo

speed *n* **1** : rapidez *f* **2** VELOCITY : velocidad *f* — ~ *v* **sped** *or* **speeded; speeding** *vi* **1** : conducir a exceso de velocidad **2 ~ off** : irse a toda velocidad **3 ~ up** : acelerarse — *vt or* **~ up** : acelerar — **speed limit** *n* : velocidad *f* máxima — **speedometer** *n* : velocímetro *m* — **speedy** *adj* **speedier; -est** : rápido

spell¹ *vt* **1** : escribir (las letras de) **2** *or* **~ out** : deletrear **3** MEAN : significar

spell² *n* ENCHANTMENT : hechizo *m*

spell³ *n* : período *m* (de tiempo)

spellbound *adj* : embelesado

spelling *n* : ortografía *f*

spend *v* **spent; spending 1** : gastar (dinero) **2** : pasar (las vacaciones, etc.) **3 ~ time on** : dedicar tiempo a

sperm *n, pl* **sperm** *or* **sperms** : esperma *mf*

spew *vt* : vomitar, arrojar (lava, etc.)

sphere *n* : esfera *f* — **spherical** *adj* : esférico

spice *n* : especia *f* — ~ *vt* **spiced; spicing** : condimentar, sazonar — **spicy** *adj* **spicier; -est** : picante

spider *n* : araña *f*

spigot *n* : grifo *m Spain*, llave *f Lat*

spike *n* **1** : clavo *m* (grande) **2** POINT : punta *f* — **spiky** *adj* : puntiagudo

spill *vt* : derramar — *vi* : derramarse

spin *v* **spun; spinning** *vi* **1** : girar — *vt* **1** : hilar (lana, etc.) **2** TWIRL : hacer girar — ~ *n* **1** : vuelta *f*, giro *m* **2 go for a ~** : dar una vuelta (en auto)

spinach *n* : espinacas *fpl*

spinal cord *n* : médula *f* espinal

spindle *n* : huso *m* (para hilar) — **spindly** *adj* : larguirucho *fam*

spine *n* **1** : columna *f* vertebral **2** QUILL : púa *f* **3** THORN : espina *f* **4** : lomo *m* (de un libro)

spinster *n* : soltera *f*

spiral *adj* : de espiral, en espiral — ~ *n* : espiral *f* — ~ *vi* **-raled** *or* **-ralled; -raling** *or* **-ralling** : ir en espiral

spire *n* : aguja *f*

spirit *n* **1** : espíritu *m* **2 in good ~s** : animado **3 ~s** *npl* : licores *mpl* — **spirited** *adj* : animado — **spiritual** *adj* : espiritual — **spirituality** *n, pl* **-ties** : espiritualidad *f*

spit¹ *n* ROTISSERIE : asador *m*

spit² *v* **spit** *or* **spat; spitting** : escupir — *n* SALIVA : saliva *f*

spite *n* **1** : rencor *m* **2 in ~ of** : a pesar de — ~ *vt* **spited; spiting** : fastidiar — **spiteful** *adj* : rencoroso

spittle *n* : saliva *f*

splash *vt* : salpicar — *vi* **1** : salpicar **2** *or* ~ **about** : chapotear — ~ *n* **1** : salpicadura *f* **2** : mancha *f* (de color, etc.)

splatter → **spatter**

spleen *n* : bazo *m* (órgano)

splendor *n* : esplendor *m* — **splendid** *adj* : espléndido

splint *n* : tablilla *f*

splinter *n* : astilla *f* — *vi* : astillarse

split *v* **split; splitting** *vt* **1** : partir **2** BURST : reventar **3** *or* ~ **up** : dividir — *vi* **1** : partirse, rajarse **2** *or* ~ **up** : dividirse — ~ *n* **1** CRACK : rajadura *f* **2** *or* ~ **seam** : descosido *m* **3** DIVISION : división *f*

splurge *vi* **splurged; splurging** : derrochar dinero

spoil *vt* **spoiled** *or* **spoilt; spoiling 1** RUIN : estropear **2** PAMPER : consentir, mimar — **spoils** *npl* : botín *m*

spoke¹ → **speak**

spoke² *n* : rayo *m* (de una rueda)

spoken → **speak**

spokesman *n, pl* **-men** : portavoz *mf* — **spokeswoman** *n, pl* **-women** : portavoz *f*

sponge *n* : esponja *f* — ~ *vt* **sponged; sponging** : limpiar con una esponja — **spongy** *adj* **spongier; -est** : esponjoso

sponsor *n* : patrocinador *m*, **-dora** *f* — ~ *vt* : patrocinar — **sponsorship** *n* : patrocinio *m*

spontaneity *n* : espontaneidad *f* — **spontaneous** *adj* : espontáneo

spooky *adj* **spookier; -est** : espeluznante

spool *n* : carrete *m*

spoon *n* : cuchara *f* — **spoonful** *n* : cucharada *f*

sporadic *adj* : esporádico

spore *n* : espora *f*

sport *n* **1** : deporte *m* **2 be a good ~** : tener espíritu deportivo — **sportsman** *n, pl* **-men** : deportista *m* — **sportswoman** *n, pl* **-women** : deportista *f* — **sporty** *adj* **sportier; -est** : deportivo

spot *n* **1** : mancha *f* **2** DOT : punto *m* **3** PLACE : lugar *m*, sitio *m* **4 in a tight ~** : en apuros **5 on the ~** INSTANTLY : en ese mismo momento — ~ *vt* **spotted; spotting 1** STAIN : manchar **2** DETECT, NOTICE : ver, descubrir — **spotless** *adj* : impecable — **spotlight** *n* **1** : foco *m*, reflector *m* **2 be in the ~** : ser el centro de atención — **spotty** *adj* **spottier; -est** : irregular

spouse *n* : cónyuge *mf*

spout *vi* : salir a chorros — ~ *n* **1** : pico *m* (de una jarra, etc.) **2** STREAM : chorro *m*

sprain *n* : esguince *m* — ~ *vt* : sufrir un esguince en

sprawl *vi* **1** : repantigarse (en un sillón, etc.) **2** EXTEND : extenderse — ~ *n* : extensión *f*

spray¹ *n* BOUQUET : ramillete *m*

spray² *n* **1** MIST : rocío *m* **2** *or* **aerosol ~** : spray *m* **3** *or* ~ **bottle** : atomizador *m* — ~ *vt* : rociar (una superficie), pulverizar (un líquido)

spread *v* **spread; spreading** *vt* **1** : propagar (enfermedades), difundir (noticias, etc.) **2** *or* ~ **out** : extender **3** : untar (con mantequilla, etc.) — *vi* **1** : propagarse, difundirse **2** *or* ~ **out** : extenderse — ~ *n* **1** : propagación *f*, difusión *f* **2** PASTE : pasta *f* (para untar) — **spreadsheet** *n* : hoja *f* de cálculo

spree *n* **go on a ~** : ir de juerga *fam*

sprig *n* : ramito *m*

sprightly *adj* **sprightlier; -est** : vivo

spring *v* **sprang** *or* **sprung; sprung; springing** *vi* **1** : saltar **2 ~ from** : surgir de **3 ~ up** : surgir — *vt* **1** ACTIVATE : accionar **2 ~ a leak** : hacer agua **3 ~ sth on s.o.** : sorprender a algn con algo — ~ *n* **1** : manantial *m* (de aguas) **2** : primavera *f* (estación) **3** LEAP : salto *m* **4** RESILIENCE : elasticidad *f* **5** : resorte *m* (mecanismo) **6** *or* **bedspring** : muelle *m* — **springboard** *n* : trampolín *m* — **springtime** *n* : primavera *f* — **springy** *adj* **springier; -est** : mullido

sprinkle *vt* **-kled; -kling 1** : salpicar, rociar **2** DUST : espolvorear — ~ *n* : llovizna *f* — **sprinkler** *n* : aspersor *m*

sprint *vi* **1** : correr **2** : esprintar (en deportes) — ~ *n* : esprint *m* (en deportes)

sprout *vi* : brotar — ~ *n* : brote *m*

spruce¹ *vt* **spruced; sprucing ~ up** : arreglar

spruce² *n* : picea *f* (árbol)

spry *adj* **sprier** *or* **spryer; spriest** *or* **spryest** : ágil, activo

spun → **spin**

spur *n* **1** : espuela *f* **2** STIMULUS : acicate *m* **3 on the ~ of the moment** : sin pensarlo — *~ vt* **spurred; spurring** *or* **~ on** : espolear (un caballo) **2** MOTIVATE : motivar

spurn *vt* : desdeñar, rechazar

spurt¹ *vi* : salir a chorros — *~ n* : chorro *m*

spurt² *n* **1** : arranque *m* (de energía, etc.) **2 work in ~s** : trabajar por rachas

spy *v* **spied; spying** *vt* : ver, divisar — *vi ~* **on s.o.** : espiar a algn — *~ n* : espía *mf*

squabble *n* : riña *f*, pelea *f* — *~ vi* **-bled; -bling** : reñir, pelearse

squad *n* : pelotón *m* (militar), brigada *f* (de policías)

squadron *n* : escuadrón *m* (de soldados), escuadra *f* (de aviones o naves)

squalid *adj* : miserable

squall *n* : turbión *m*

squalor *n* : miseria *f*

squander *vt* : derrochar (dinero, etc.), desperdiciar (oportunidades, etc.)

square *n* **1** : cuadrado *m* **2** : plaza *f* (de una ciudad) — *~ adj* **squarer; -est** **1** : cuadrado **2** HONEST : justo **3** EVEN : en paz **4 a ~ meal** : una comida decente — *~ vt* **squared; squaring** **1** : elevar al cuadrado (un número) **2** : saldar (una cuenta) — **square root** *n* : raíz *f* cuadrada

squash¹ *vt* **1** : aplastar **2** : acallar (protestas, etc.) — *~ n* : squash *m* (deporte)

squash² *n, pl* **squashes** *or* **squash** : calabaza *f* (vegetal)

squat *vi* **squatted; squatting** **1** *or* **~ down** : ponerse en cuclillas **2** : ocupar un lugar sin derecho — *~ adj* **squatter; squattest** : achaparrado

squawk *n* : graznido *m* — *vi* : graznar

squeak *vi* **1** : chillar **2** CREAK : chirriar — *~ n* **1** : chillido *m* **2** CREAK : chirrido *m* — **squeaky** *adj* **squeakier; -est** : chirriante

squeal *vi* **1** : chillar (dícese de personas, etc.), chirriar (dícese de frenos, etc.) **2** PROTEST : quejarse — *~ n* : chillido *m* (de una persona), chirrido *m* (de frenos, etc.)

squeamish *adj* : impresionable, delicado

squeeze *vt* **squeezed; squeezing** **1** : apretar **2** : exprimir (frutas, etc.) **3** : extraer (jugo, etc.) — *~ n* : apretón *m*

squid *n, pl* **squid** *or* **squids** : calamar *m*

squint *vi* : entrecerrar los ojos — *~ n* : estrabismo *m*

squirm *vi* : retorcerse

squirrel *n* : ardilla *f*

squirt *vt* : lanzar un chorro de — *vi* : salir a chorros — *~ n* : chorrito *m*

stab *n* **1** : puñalada *f* **2 ~ of pain** : pinchazo *m* **3 take a ~ at** : intentar — *~ vt* **stabbed; stabbing** **1** KNIFE : apuñalar — STICK : clavar

stable *n* **1** : establo *m* (para ganado) **2** *or* **horse ~** : caballeriza *f* — *~ adj* **-bler; -blest** : estable — **stability** *n, pl* **-ties** : estabilidad *f* — **stabilize** *vt* **-lized; -lizing** : estabilizar

stack *n* : montón *m*, pila *f* — *~ vt* : amontonar, apilar

stadium *n, pl* **-dia** *or* **-diums** : estadio *m*

staff *n, pl* **staffs** *or* **staves** **1** : bastón *m* **2** *pl* **staffs** PERSONNEL : personal *m* **3** *pl* **staffs** : pentagrama *m* (en música) — *~ vt* : proveer de personal

stag *n, pl* **stags** *or* **stag** : ciervo *m*, venado *m* — *~ adj* : sólo para hombres — *~ adv* **go ~** : ir solo

stage *n* **1** : escenario *m* (de un teatro) **2** PHASE : etapa *f* **3 the ~** : el teatro — *~ vt* **staged; staging** **1** : poner en escena **2** ARRANGE : montar — **stagecoach** *n* : diligencia *f*

stagger *vi* : tambalearse — *vt* **1** : escalonar (turnos, etc.) **2 be ~ed by** : quedarse estupefacto por — *~ n* : tambaleo *m* — **staggering** *adj* : asombroso

stagnant *adj* : estancado — **stagnate** *vi* **-nated; -nating** : estancarse

stain *vt* **1** : manchar **2** : teñir (madera) — *~ n* **1** : mancha *f* **2** DYE : tinte *m*, tintura *f* — **stainless steel** *n* : acero *m* inoxidable

stair *n* **1** STEP : escalón *m*, peldaño *m* **2 ~s** *npl* : escalera(s) *f(pl)* — **staircase** *n* : escalera(s) *f(pl)* — **stairway** *n* : escalera(s) *f(pl)*

stake *n* **1** POST : estaca *f* **2** BET : apuesta *f* **3** INTEREST : intereses *mpl* **4 be at ~** : estar en juego — *~ vt* **staked; staking** **1** : estacar **2** BET : jugarse **3 ~ a claim to** : reclamar

stale *adj* **staler; stalest** **1** : duro (dícese del pan) **2** OLD : viejo **3** STUFFY : viciado

stalk¹ *n* : tallo *m* (de una planta)

stalk² *vt* : acechar — *vi or* **~ off** : irse con altivez

stall¹ *n* **1** : compartimiento *m* (de un establo) **2** STAND : puesto *m* — *~ vt* : parar (un motor) — *vi* : pararse

stall² *vt* DELAY : entretener — *vi* : andar con rodeos

stallion *n* : caballo *m* semental

stalwart *adj* **1** STRONG : fornido **2 ~ supporter** : partidario *m* leal

stamina *n* : resistencia *f*

stammer *vi* : tartamudear — *~ n* : tartamudeo *m*

stamp *n* **1** SEAL : sello *m* **2** DIE : cuño *m* **3** *or* **postage ~** : sello *m*, estampilla *f* *Lat*, timbre *m* *Lat* — *~ vt* **1** : franquear (una carta) **2** IMPRINT : sellar **3** MINT : acuñar **4 ~ one's foot** : dar una patada (en el suelo)

stampede *n* : estampida *f* — $\sim$ *vi* **-peded; -peding** : salir en estampida

stance *n* : postura *f*

stand *v* **stood; standing** *vi* **1** : estar de pie, estar parado *Lat* **2** BE : estar **3** CONTINUE : seguir vigente **4** LIE, REST : reposar **5** $\sim$ **aside** *or* $\sim$ **back** : apartarse **6** $\sim$ **out** : sobresalir **7** *or* $\sim$ **up** : ponerse de pie, pararse *Lat* — *vt* **1** PLACE : poner, colocar **2** ENDURE : soportar **3** $\sim$ **a chance** : tener una posibilidad — **stand by** *vt* : mantener (una promesa, etc.) **2** SUPPORT : apoyar — **stand for** *vt* **1** MEAN : significar **2** PERMIT : permitir — **stand up** *vi* **1** $\sim$ **for** : defender **2** $\sim$ **up to** : resistir a — $\sim$ *n* **1** RESISTANCE : resistencia *f* **2** STALL : puesto *m* **3** BASE : base *f* **4** POSITION : posición *f* **5** $\sim$**s** *npl* : tribuna *f*

standard *n* **1** : norma *f* **2** BANNER : estandarte *m* **3** CRITERION : criterio *m* **4** $\sim$ **of living** : nivel *m* de vida — $\sim$ *adj* : estándar — **standardize** *vt* **-ized; -izing** : estandarizar

standing *n* **1** RANK : posición *f* **2** DURATION : duración *f*

standpoint *n* : punto *m* de vista

standstill *n* **1 be at a** $\sim$: estar paralizado **2 come to a** $\sim$: pararse

stank → **stink**

stanza *n* : estrofa *f*

staple[1] *n* : producto *m* principal — $\sim$ *adj* : principal, básico

staple[2] *n* : grapa *f* (para papeles) — $\sim$ *vt* **-pled; -pling** : grapar, engrapar *Lat* — **stapler** *n* : grapadora *f*, engrapadora *f Lat*

star *n* : estrella *f* — $\sim$ *v* **starred; starring** *vt* FEATURE : estar protagonizado por — *vi* $\sim$ **in** : protagonizar

starboard *n* : estribor *m*

starch *vt* : almidonar — $\sim$ *n* **1** : almidón *m* **2** : fécula *f* (comida)

stardom *n* : estrellato *m*

stare *vi* **stared; staring** : mirar fijamente — $\sim$ *n* : mirada *f* fija

starfish *n* : estrella *f* de mar

stark *adj* **1** PLAIN : austero **2** HARSH : severo, duro **3** SHARP : marcado — $\sim$ *adv* **1** : completamente **2** $\sim$ **naked** : en cueros (vivos)

starlight *n* : luz *f* de las estrellas

starling *n* : estornino *m*

starry *adj* **starrier; -est** : estrellado

start *vi* **1** : empezar, comenzar **2** SET OUT : salir **3** JUMP : sobresaltarse **4** *or* $\sim$ **up** : arrancar — *vt* **1** : empezar, comenzar **2** CAUSE : provocar **3** *or* $\sim$ **up** ESTABLISH : montar **4** *or* $\sim$ **up** : arrancar (un motor, etc.) — $\sim$ *n* **1** : principio *m* **2 get an early** $\sim$: salir temprano **3 give s.o. a** $\sim$: asus-

tar a algn — **starter** *n* : motor *m* de arranque (de un vehículo)

startle *vt* **-tled; -tling** : asustar

starve *v* **starved; starving** *vi* : morirse de hambre — *vt* : privar de comida — **starvation** *n* : inanición *f*, hambre *f*

stash *vt* : esconder

state *n* **1** : estado *m* **2 the States** : los Estados Unidos — $\sim$ *vt* **stated; stating 1** SAY : decir **2** REPORT : exponer — **stately** *adj* **statelier; -est** : majestuoso — **statement** *n* **1** : declaración *f* **2** *or* **bank** $\sim$: estado *m* de cuenta — **statesman** *n, pl* **-men** : estadista *mf*

static *adj* : estático — $\sim$ *n* : estática *f*

station *n* **1** : estación *f* (de trenes, etc.) **2** RANK : condición *f* (social) **3** : canal *m* (de televisión), emisora *f* (de radio) **4** → **fire station, police station** — *vt* : apostar, estacionar — **stationary** *adj* : estacionario

stationery *n* : papel *m* y sobres *mpl* (para cartas)

station wagon *n* : camioneta *f* (familiar)

statistic *n* : estadística *f* — **statistical** *adj* : estadístico

statue *n* : estatua *f*

stature *n* : estatura *f*, talla *f*

status *n* **1** : situación *f* **2** *or* **social** $\sim$: estatus *m* **3 marital** $\sim$: estado *m* civil

statute *n* : estatuto *m*

staunch *adj* : leal

stave *v* **staved** *or* **stove; staving 1** $\sim$ **in** : romper **2** $\sim$ **off** : evitar

staves → **staff**

stay[1] *vi* **1** REMAIN : quedarse, permanecer **2** LODGE : alojarse **3** $\sim$ **awake** : mantenerse despierto **4** $\sim$ **in** : quedarse en casa — *vt* : suspender (una ejecución, etc.) — $\sim$ *n* **1** : estancia *f*, estadía *f Lat* **2** SUSPENSION : suspensión *f*

stay[2] *n* SUPPORT : soporte *m*

stead *n* **1 in s.o.'s** $\sim$: en lugar de algn **2 stand s.o. in good** $\sim$: ser muy útil a algn — **steadfast** *adj* **1** FIRM : firme **2** LOYAL : leal, fiel — **steadily** *adv* **1** : progresivamente **2** INCESSANTLY : sin parar **3** FIXEDLY : fijamente — **steady** *adj* **steadier; -est 1** FIRM, SURE : firme, seguro **2** FIXED : fijo **3** DEPENDABLE : responsable **4** CONSTANT : constante — $\sim$ *vt* **steadied; steadying 1** : mantener firme **2** : calmar (los nervios)

steak *n* : bistec *m*, filete *m*

steal *v* **stole; stolen; stealing** *vt* : robar — *vi* **1** : robar **2** $\sim$ **away** : escabullirse

stealth *n* : sigilo *m* — **stealthy** *adj* **stealthier; -est** : furtivo, sigiloso

steam *n* **1** : vapor *m* **2 let off** $\sim$: desahogarse — $\sim$ *vi* : echar vapor — *vt* **1** : cocer al vapor **2 ~ up** : empañar — **steam engine** *n* : motor *m* de vapor — **steamship** *n* : (barco *m* de) vapor *m* — **steamy** *adj* **steamier; -est 1** : lleno de vapor **2** PASSIONATE : tórrido

steel *n* : acero *m* — **~** *vt* **~ oneself** : armarse de valor — **~** *adj* : de acero

steep[1] *adj* **1** : empinado **2** CONSIDERABLE : considerable **3** : muy alto (dícese de precios)

steep[2] *vt* : dejar (té, etc.) en infusión

steeple *n* : aguja *f*, campanario *m*

steer[1] *n* : buey *m*

steer[2] *vt* : dirigir (un auto, etc.), pilotear (un barco) — **steering wheel** *n* : volante

stem[1] *n* : tallo *m* (de una planta), pie *m* (de una copa) — **~** *vi* **~ from** : provenir de

stem[2] *vt* **stemmed; stemming** : contener, detener

stench *n* : hedor *m*, mal olor *m*

stencil *n* : plantilla *f* (para marcar)

step *n* **1** : paso *m* **2** RUNG, STAIR : escalón *m* **3 ~ by ~** : paso por paso **4 take ~s** : tomar medidas **5 watch your ~** : mira por dónde caminas — **~** *vi* **stepped; stepping 1** : dar un paso **2 ~ back** : retroceder **3 ~ down** RESIGN : retirarse **4 ~ in** : intervenir **5 ~ out** : salir (por un momento) **6 ~ this way** : pase por aquí — **step up** *vt* INCREASE : aumentar

stepbrother *n* : hermanastro *m* — **stepdaughter** *n* : hijastra *f* — **stepfather** *n* : padrastro *m*

stepladder *n* : escalera *f* de tijera

stepmother *n* : madrastra *f* — **stepsister** *n* : hermanastra *f* — **stepson** *n* : hijastro *m*

stereo *n*, *pl* **stereos** : estéreo *m* — **~** *adj* : estéreo

stereotype *vt* **-typed; -typing** : estereotipar — **~** *n* : estereotipo *m*

sterile *adj* : estéril — **sterility** *n* : esterilidad *f* — **sterilization** *n* : esterilización *f* — **sterilize** *vt* **-ized; -izing** : esterilizar

sterling *adj* : excelente — **sterling silver** *n* : plata *f* de ley

stern[1] *adj* : severo, adusto

stern[2] *n* : popa *f*

stethoscope *n* : estetoscopio *m*

stew *n* : estofado *m*, guiso *m* — **~** *vt* : estofar, guisar — *vi* **1** : cocer **2** FRET : preocuparse

steward *n* **1** : administrador *m*, -dora *f* **2** : auxiliar *m* de vuelo (en un avión) **3** : camarero *m* (en un barco) — **stewardess** *n* **1** : auxiliar *f* de vuelo, azafata *f* (en un avión) **2** : camarera *f* (en un barco)

stick[1] *n* **1** : palo *m* **2** TWIG : ramita *f* (suelta) **3** WALKING STICK : bastón *m*

stick[2] *v* **stuck; sticking** *vt* **1** : pegar **2** STAB

: clavar **3** PUT : poner **4 ~ out** : sacar (la lengua, etc.) — *vi* **1** : pegarse **2** JAM : atascarse **3 ~ around** : quedarse **4 ~ out** PROTRUDE : sobresalir **5 ~ out** SHOW : asomar **6 ~ up** : sobresalir **7 ~ up for** : defender — **sticker** *n* : etiqueta *f* adhesiva — **stickler** *n* **be a ~ for** : insistir mucho en — **sticky** *adj* **stickier; -est** : pegajoso

stiff *adj* **1** RIGID : rígido, tieso **2** STILTED : forzado **3** STRONG : fuerte **4** DIFFICULT : difícil **5** : entumecido (dícese de músculos) — **stiffen** *vt* : fortalecer, hacer más duro — *vi* **1** HARDEN : endurecerse **2** : entumecerse (dícese de músculos) — **stiffness** *n* : rigidez *f*

stifle *vt* **-fled; -fling** : sofocar

stigmatize *vt* **-tized; -tizing** : estigmatizar

still *adj* **1** : inmóvil **2** SILENT : callado — **~** *adv* **1** : todavía, aún **2** NEVERTHELESS : de todos modos, aún así **3 sit ~!** : ¡quédate quieto! — **~** *n* : quietud *f*, calma *f* — **stillborn** *adj* : nacido muerto — **stillness** *n* : calma *f*, silencio *m*

stilt *n* : zanco *m* — **stilted** *adj* : forzado

stimulate *vt* **-lated; -lating** : estimular — **stimulant** *n* : estimulante *m* — **stimulation** *n* : estimulación *f* — **stimulus** *n*, *pl* **-li** : estímulo *m*

sting *v* **stung; stinging** : picar — **~** *n* : picadura *f* — **stinger** *n* : aguijón *m*

stingy *adj* **stingier; -est** : tacaño — **stinginess** *n* : tacañería *f*

stink *vi* **stank** *or* **stunk; stunk; stinking** : apestar, oler mal — **~** *n* : hedor *m*, peste *f* *fam*

stint *vi* **~ on** : escatimar — **~** *n* : período *m*

stipulate *vt* **-lated; -lating** : estipular

stir *v* **stirred; stirring** *vt* **1** : remover, revolver **2** MOVE : mover **3** INCITE : incitar **4** *or* **~ up** : despertar (memorias, etc.), provocar (ira, etc.) — *vi* : moverse, agitarse — **~** *n* COMMOTION : revuelo *m*

stirrup *n* : estribo *m*

stitch *n* **1** : puntada *f* **2** PAIN : punzada *f* (en el costado) — **~** *v* : coser

stock *n* **1** INVENTORY : existencias *fpl* **2** SECURITIES : acciones *fpl* **3** ANCESTRY : linaje *m*, estirpe *f* **4** BROTH : caldo *m* **5 out of ~** : agotado **6 take ~ of** : evaluar — **~** *vt* : surtir, abastecer — *vi* **~ up on** : abastecerse de — **stockbroker** *n* : corredor *m*, -dora *f* de bolsa

stocking *n* : media *f*

stock market *n* : bolsa *f* — **stockpile** *n* : reservas *fpl* — **~** *vt* **-piled; -piling** : almacenar — **stocky** *adj* **stockier; -est** : robusto, fornido

stodgy *adj* **stodgier; -est 1** DULL : pesado **2** OLD-FASHIONED : anticuado

stoic n : estoico m, -ca f — ~ or **stoical** adj : estoico — **stoicism** n : estoicismo m

stoke vt **stoked; stoking** : echar carbón o leña a

stole¹ → **steal**

stole² n : estola f

stolen → **steal**

stomach n : estómago m — ~ vt : aguantar, soportar — **stomachache** n : dolor m de estómago

stone n 1 : piedra f 2 : hueso m (de una fruta) — ~ vt **stoned; stoning** : apedrear — **stony** adj **stonier; -est** 1 : pedregoso 2 **a ~ silence** : un silencio sepulcral

stood → **stand**

stool n : taburete m

stoop vi 1 : agacharse 2 **~ to** : rebajarse a — ~ n **have a ~** : ser encorvado

stop v **stopped; stopping** vt 1 PLUG : tapar 2 PREVENT : impedir 3 HALT : parar, detener 4 CEASE : dejar de — vi 1 : detenerse, parar 2 CEASE : cesar, dejar 3 ~ **by** : visitar — ~ n 1 : parada f, alto m 2 **come to a ~** : pararse, detenerse 3 **put a ~ to** : poner fin a — **stopgap** n : arreglo m provisorio — **stoplight** n : semáforo m — **stoppage** n or **work ~** : paro m — **stopper** n : tapón m

store vt **stored; storing** : guardar (comida, etc.), almacenar (datos, mercancías, etc.) — ~ n 1 SUPPLY : reserva f 2 SHOP : tienda f — **storage** n : almacenamiento m — **storehouse** n : almacén m — **storekeeper** n : tendero m, -ra f — **storeroom** n : almacén m

stork n : cigüeña f

storm n : tormenta f, tempestad f — ~ vi 1 RAGE : ponerse furioso 2 ~ **in/out** : entrar/salir furioso — vt ATTACK : asaltar — **stormy** adj **stormier; -est** : tormentoso

story¹ n, pl **stories** 1 TALE : cuento m 2 ACCOUNT : historia f 3 RUMOR : rumor m

story² n FLOOR : piso m, planta f

stout adj 1 BRAVE : valiente 2 RESOLUTE : tenaz 3 STURDY : fuerte 4 FAT : corpulento

stove¹ n 1 : estufa f (para calentar) 2 RANGE : cocina f

stove² → **stave**

stow vt 1 : guardar 2 LOAD : cargar — vi ~ **away** : viajar de polizón — **stowaway** n : polizón m

straddle vt **-dled; -dling** : sentarse a horcajadas sobre

straggle vi **-gled; -gling** : rezagarse, quedarse atrás — **straggler** n : rezagado m, -da f

straight adj 1 : recto, derecho 2 : lacio (dícese del pelo) 3 HONEST : franco 4 TIDY : arreglado — ~ adv 1 DIRECTLY : derecho 2 EXACTLY : justo 3 CLEARLY : con claridad 4 FRANKLY : con franqueza — **straightaway** adv : inmediatamente — **straighten** vt 1 : enderezar 2 ~ **up** : arreglar — **straightforward** adj 1 FRANK : franco 2 CLEAR : claro, sencillo

strain¹ n 1 LINEAGE : linaje m 2 STREAK : veta f 3 VARIETY : variedad f 4 ~**s** npl : acordes mpl (de música)

strain² vt 1 : forzar (la vista o la voz) 2 FILTER : colar 3 : tensar (relaciones, etc.) 4 ~ **a muscle** : sufrir un esguince 5 ~ **oneself** : hacerse daño — vi : esforzarse (por) — ~ n 1 STRESS : tensión f 2 SPRAIN : esguince m — **strainer** n : colador m

strait n 1 : estrecho m 2 **in dire ~s** : en grandes apuros

strand¹ vt **be ~ed** : quedar(se) varado

strand² n 1 : hebra f 2 **a ~ of hair** : un pelo

strange adj **stranger; -est** 1 : extraño, raro 2 UNFAMILIAR : desconocido — **strangely** adv : de manera extraña — **strangeness** n 1 : rareza f 2 UNFAMILIARITY : lo desconocido — **stranger** n : desconocido m, -da f

strangle vt **-gled; -gling** : estrangular

strap n 1 : correa f 2 or **shoulder ~** : tirante m — ~ vt **strapped; strapping** : sujetar con una correa — **strapless** n : sin tirantes — **strapping** adj : robusto, fornido

strategy n, pl **-gies** : estrategia f — **strategic** adj : estratégico

straw n 1 : paja f 2 or **drinking ~** : pajita f 3 **the last ~** : el colmo

strawberry n, pl **-ries** : fresa f

stray n : animal m perdido — ~ vi 1 : perderse, extraviarse 2 : apartarse (de un grupo, etc.) 3 DEVIATE : desviarse — ~ adj : perdido

streak n 1 : raya f 2 VEIN : veta f 3 ~ **of luck** : racha f de suerte — vi ~ **by** : pasar como una flecha

stream n 1 : arroyo m, riachuelo m 2 FLOW : chorro m, corriente f — ~ vi : correr — **streamer** n 1 PENNANT : banderín m 2 : serpentina f (de papel) — **streamlined** adj 1 : aerodinámico 2 EFFICIENT : eficiente

street n : calle f — **streetcar** n : tranvía m — **streetlight** n : farol m

strength n 1 : fuerza f 2 FORTITUDE : fortaleza f 3 TOUGHNESS : resistencia f, solidez f 4 INTENSITY : intensidad f 5 ~**s and weaknesses** : virtudes y defectos — **strengthen** vt 1 : fortalecer 2 REINFORCE : reforzar 3 INTENSIFY : intensificar

strenuous adj 1 : enérgico 2 ARDUOUS : duro, riguroso

stress n 1 : tensión f 2 EMPHASIS : énfasis m 3 : acento m (en lingüística) — ~ vt 1

EMPHASIZE : enfatizar **2** *or* ～ **out** : estresar — **stressful** *adj* : estresante

stretch *vt* **1** : estirar (músculos, elástico, etc.) **2** EXTEND : extender **3** ～ **the truth** : forzar la verdad — *vi* **1** : estirarse **2** EXTEND : extenderse — ～ *n* **1** : extensión *f* **2** ELASTICITY : elasticidad *f* **3** EXPANSE : tramo *m* **4** : período *m* (de tiempo) — **stretcher** *n* : camilla *f*

strew *vt* **strewed**; **strewed** *or* **strewn**; **strewing** : esparcir (semillas, etc.), desparramar (papeles, etc.)

stricken *adj* ～ **with** : aquejado de (una enfermedad), afligido por (tristeza, etc.)

strict *adj* : estricto — **strictly** *adv* ～ **speaking** : en rigor

stride *vi* **strode**; **stridden**; **striding** : ir dando zancadas — ～ *n* **1** : zancada *f* **2** **make great** ～**s** : hacer grandes progresos

strident *adj* : estridente

strife *n* : conflictos *mpl*

strike *v* **struck**; **struck**; **striking** *vt* **1** HIT : golpear **2** *or* ～ **against** : chocar contra **3** *or* ～ **out** DELETE : tachar **4** : dar (la hora) **5** IMPRESS : impresionar **6** : descubrir (oro o petróleo) **7 it** ～**s me as…** : me parece… **8** ～ **up** START : entablar — *vi* **1** : golpear **2** ATTACK : atacar **3** : declararse en huelga **4** : sobrevenir (dícese de una enfermedad, etc.) — ～ *n* **1** BLOW : golpe *m* **2** : huelga *f*, paro *m Lat* (de trabajadores) **3** ATTACK : ataque *m* — **strikebreaker** *n* : esquirol *mf* — **striker** *n* : huelguista *mf* — **striking** *adj* : notable, llamativo

string *n* **1** : cordel *m* **2** : sarta *f* (de perlas, insultos, etc.), serie *f* (de eventos, etc.) **3** ～**s** *npl* : cuerdas *fpl* (en música) — ～ *vt* **strung**; **stringing 1** : ensartar **2** *or* ～ **up** : colgar — **string bean** *n* : habichuela *f* verde

stringent *adj* : estricto, severo

strip¹ *v* **stripped**; **stripping** *vt* **1** REMOVE : quitar **2** UNDRESS : desnudar **3** ～ **s.o. of sth** : despojar a algn de algo — *vi* UNDRESS : desnudarse

strip² *n* : tira *f*

stripe *n* : raya *f*, lista *f* — **striped** *adj* : a rayas, rayado

strive *vi* **strove**; **striven** *or* **strived**; **striving 1** ～ **for** : luchar por **2** ～ **to** : esforzarse por

strode → **stride**

stroke *vt* **stroked**; **stroking** : acariciar — ～ *n* **1** : golpe *m* **2** : derrame *m* cerebral (en medicina)

stroll *vi* : pasearse — ～ *n* : paseo *m* — **stroller** *n* : cochecito *m* (para niños)

strong *adj* : fuerte — **stronghold** *n* : bastión *m* — **strongly** *adv* **1** DEEPLY : profunda-

mente **2** WHOLEHEARTEDLY : totalmente **3** VIGOROUSLY : enérgicamente

strove → **strive**

struck → **strike**

structure *n* : estructura *f* — **structural** *adj* : estructural

struggle *vi* **-gled**; **-gling 1** : forcejear **2** STRIVE : luchar — ～ *n* : lucha *f*

strum *vt* **strummed**; **strumming** : rasguear

strung → **string**

strut *vi* **strutted**; **strutting** : pavonearse — ～ *n* : puntal *m* (en construcción)

stub *n* : colilla *f* (de un cigarillo), cabo *m* (de un lápiz, etc.), talón *m* (de un cheque) — ～ *vt* **stubbed**; **stubbing** ～ **one's toe** : darse en el dedo

stubble *n* : barba *f* de varios días

stubborn *adj* **1** : terco, obstinado **2** PERSISTENT : tenaz

stucco *n, pl* **stuccos** *or* **stuccoes** : estuco *m*

stuck → **stick** — **stuck–up** *adj* : engreído, creído *fam*

stud¹ *n* : semental *m* (animal)

stud² *n* **1** NAIL, TACK : tachuela *f*, tachón *m* **2** *or* ～ **earring** : arete *m Lat*, pendiente *m Spain* **3** : montante *m* (en construcción)

student *n* : estudiante *mf*; alumno *m*, -na *f* (de un colegio) — **studio** *n, pl* **studios** : estudio *m* — **study** *n, pl* **studies** : estudio *m* — ～ *v* **studied**; **studying** : estudiar — **studious** *adj* : estudioso

stuff *n* **1** : cosas *fpl* **2** MATTER, SUBSTANCE : cosa *f* **3 know one's** ～ : ser experto — ～ *vt* **1** FILL : rellenar **2** CRAM : meter — **stuffing** *n* : relleno *m* — **stuffy** *adj* **stuffier**; **-est 1** STODGY : pesado, aburrido **2** : tapado (dícese de la nariz) **3** ～ **rooms** : salas *fpl* mal ventiladas

stumble *vi* **-bled**; **-bling 1** : tropezar **2** ～ **across** *or* **upon** : tropezar con

stump *n* **1** : muñón *m* (de una pierna, etc.) **2** *or* **tree** ～ : tocón *m* — ～ *vt* : dejar perplejo

stun *vt* **stunned**; **stunning 1** : aturdir (con un golpe) **2** ASTONISH : dejar atónito

stung → **sting**

stunk → **stink**

stunning *adj* **1** : increíble, sensacional **2** STRIKING : imponente

stunt¹ *vt* : atrofiar

stunt² *n* : proeza *f* (acrobática)

stupendous *adj* : estupendo

stupid *adj* **1** : estúpido **2** SILLY : tonto, bobo — **stupidity** *n* : tontería *f*, estupidez *f*

sturdy *adj* **sturdier**; **-est 1** : fuerte, resistente **2** ROBUST : robusto

stutter *vi* : tartamudear — ～ *n* : tartamudeo *m*

sty *n* **1** *pl* **sties** PIGPEN : pocilga *f* **2** *pl* **sties** *or* **styes** : orzuelo *m* (en el ojo)

style *n* **1** : estilo *m* **2** FASHION : moda *f* **3 be in ~** : estar de moda — **~** *vt* **styled; styling** : peinar (pelo), diseñar (vestidos, etc.) — **stylish** *adj* : elegante, chic — **stylist** *n* : estilista *mf*

suave *adj* : refinado y afable

sub[1] *vi* **subbed; subbing** → **substitute** — **~** *n* → **substitute**

sub[2] *n* → **submarine**

subconscious *adj* : subconsciente — **~** *n* : subconsciente *m*

subdivide *vt* **-vided; -viding** : subdividir — **subdivision** *n* : subdivisión *f*

subdue *vt* **-dued; -duing 1** CONQUER : sojuzgar **2** CONTROL : dominar **3** SOFTEN : atenuar — **subdued** *adj* : apagado

subject *n* **1** : sujeto *m* **2** : súbdito *m*, -ta *f* (de un gobierno) **3** TOPIC : tema *m* — **~** *adj* **1** : sometido **2 ~ to** : sujeto a — **~** *vt* **~ to** : someter a — **subjective** *adj* : subjetivo

subjunctive *n* : subjuntivo *m* — **subjunctive** *adj* : subjuntivo

sublime *adj* : sublime

submarine *adj* : submarino — **~** *n* : submarino *m*

submerge *v* **-merged; -merging** *vt* : sumergir — *vi* : sumergirse

submit *v* **-mitted; -mitting** *vi* **1** YIELD : rendirse **2 ~ to** : someterse a — *vt* : presentar — **submission** *n* **1** : sumisión *f* **2** PRESENTATION : presentación *f* — **submissive** *adj* : sumiso

subordinate *adj* : subordinado — **~** *n* : subordinado *m*, -da *f* — **~** *vt* **-nated; -nating** : subordinar

subpoena *n* : citación *f*

subscribe *vi* **-scribed; -scribing ~ to** : suscribirse a (una revista, etc.), suscribir (una opinión, etc.) — **subscriber** *n* : suscriptor *m*, -tora *f* (de una revista, etc.); abonado *m*, -da *f* (de un servicio) — **subscription** *n* : suscripción *f*

subsequent *adj* **1** : subsiguiente **2 ~ to** : posterior a — **subsequently** *adv* : posteriormente

subservient *adj* : servil

subside *vi* **-sided; -siding 1** SINK : hundirse **2** : amainar (dícese de tormentas, pasiones, etc.), remitir (dícese de fiebres, etc.)

subsidiary *adj* : secundario — **~** *n*, *pl* **-ries** : filial *f*

subsidy *n*, *pl* **-dies** : subvención *f* — **subsidize** *vt* **-dized; -dizing** : subvencionar

subsistence *n* : subsistencia *f* — **subsist** *vi* : subsistir

substance *n* : sustancia *f*

substandard *adj* : inferior

substantial *adj* **1** CONSIDERABLE : considerable **2** STURDY : sólido **3** : sustancioso (dícese de una comida, etc.) — **substantially** *adv* : considerablemente

substitute *n* : sustituto *m*, -ta *f* (de una persona); sucedáneo *m* (de una cosa) — **~** *vt* **-tuted; -tuting** : sustituir — **substitution** *n* : sustitución *f*

subterranean *adj* : subterráneo

subtitle *n* : subtítulo *m*

subtle *adj* **-tler; -tlest** : sutil — **subtlety** *n*, *pl* **-ties** : sutileza *f*

subtraction *n* : resta *f* — **subtract** *vt* : restar

suburb *n* **1** : barrio *m* residencial, suburbio *m* **2 the ~s** : las afueras — **suburban** *adj* : de las afueras (de una ciudad)

subversion *n* : subversión *f* — **subversive** *adj* : subversivo

subway *n* : metro *m*

succeed *vt* : suceder a — *vi* : tener éxito (dícese de personas), dar resultado (dícese de planes, etc.) — **success** *n* : éxito *m* — **successful** *adj* : de éxito, exitoso *Lat* — **successfully** *adv* : con éxito

succession *n* **1** : sucesión *f* **2 in ~** : sucesivamente, seguidos — **successive** *adj* : sucesivo — **successor** *n* : sucesor *m*, -sora *f*

succinct *adj* : sucinto

succulent *adj* : suculento

succumb *vi* : sucumbir

such *adj* **1** : tal **2 ~ as** : como **3 ~ a pity!** : ¡qué lástima! — **~** *pron* **1** : tal **2 and ~** : y cosas por el estilo **3 as ~** : como tal — **~** *adv* **1** VERY : muy **2 ~ a nice man!** : ¡qué hombre tan simpático! **3 ~ that** : de tal manera que

suck *vt* **1** *or* **~ on** : chupar **2** *or* **~ up** : sorber (bebidas), aspirar (con una máquina) — **sucker** *n* **1** SHOOT : chupón *m* **2** FOOL : imbécil *mf* — **suckle** *vt* **-led; -ling** : amamantar — **suction** *n* : succión *f*

sudden *adj* **1** : repentino **2 all of a ~** : de repente — **suddenly** *adv* : de repente

suds *npl* : espuma *f* (de jabón)

sue *vt* **sued; suing** : demandar (por)

suede *n* : ante *m*, gamuza *f*

suet *n* : sebo *m*

suffer *vi* : sufrir — *vt* **1** : sufrir **2** BEAR : tolerar — **suffering** *n* : sufrimiento *m*

suffice *vi* **-ficed; -ficing** : bastar — **sufficient** *adj* : suficiente — **sufficiently** *adv* : (lo) suficientemente

suffix *n* : sufijo *m*

suffocate *v* **-cated; -cating** *vt* : asfixiar — *vi* : asfixiarse — **suffocation** *n* : asfixia *f*

suffrage *n* : sufragio *m*

sugar *n* : azúcar *mf* — **sugarcane** *n* : caña *f* de azúcar — **sugary** *adj* : azucarado

suggestion n **1** : sugerencia f **2** TRACE : indicio m — **suggest** vt **1** : sugerir **2** INDICATE : indicar

suicide n **1** : suicidio m (acto) **2** : suicida mf (persona) — **suicidal** adj : suicida

suit n **1** LAWSUIT : pleito m **2** : traje m (ropa) **3** : palo m (de naipes) — ~ vt **1** ADAPT : adaptar **2** BEFIT : ser apropiado para **3** ~ **s.o.** : convenir a algn (dícese de fechas, etc.), quedar bien a algn (dícese de ropa) — **suitable** adj : apropiado — **suitcase** n : maleta f, valija f Lat

suite n **1** : suite f (de habitaciones) **2** : juego m (de muebles)

suitor n : pretendiente m

sulfur n : azufre m

sulk vi : enfurruñarse fam — **sulky** adj **sulkier; -est** : malhumorado

sullen adj : hosco

sultry adj **sultrier; -est 1** : bochornoso **2** SENSUAL : sensual

sum n : suma f — ~ vt **summed; summing** ~ **up** : resumir — **summarize** v **-rized; -rizing** : resumir — **summary** n, pl **-ries** : resumen m

summer n : verano m

summit n : cumbre f

summon vt **1** : llamar (a algn), convocar (una reunión) **2** : citar (en derecho) — **summons** n, pl **summonses** SUBPOENA : citación f

sumptuous adj : suntuoso

sun n : sol m — **sunbathe** vi **-bathed; -bathing** : tomar el sol — **sunbeam** n : rayo m de sol — **sunburn** n : quemadura f de sol

Sunday n : domingo m

sundry adj : varios, diversos

sunflower n : girasol m

sung → **sing**

sunglasses npl : gafas fpl de sol, lentes mpl de sol

sunk → **sink** — **sunken** adj : hundido

sunlight n : (luz f del) sol m — **sunny** adj **-nier; -est** : soleado — **sunrise** n : salida f del sol — **sunset** n : puesta f del sol — **sunshine** n : sol m, luz f del sol — **suntan** n : bronceado m

super adj : súper fam

superb adj : magnífico, espléndido

superficial adj : superficial

superfluous adj : superfluo

superimpose vt **-posed; -posing** : sobreponer

superintendent n **1** : superintendente mf (de policía) **2** or **building** ~ : portero m, -ra f **3** or **school** ~ : director m, -tora f (de un colegio)

superior adj : superior — ~ n : superior m — **superiority** n, pl **-ties** : superioridad f

superlative adj **1** : superlativo (en gramática) **2** EXCELLENT : excepcional — ~ n : superlativo m

supermarket n : supermercado m

supernatural adj : sobrenatural

superpower n : superpotencia f

supersede vt **-seded; -seding** : reemplazar, suplantar

supersonic adj : supersónico

superstition n : superstición f — **superstitious** adj : supersticioso

supervisor n : supervisor m, -sora f — **supervise** vt **-vised; -vising** : supervisar — **supervision** n : supervisión f — **supervisory** adj : de supervisor

supper n : cena f, comida f

supplant vt : suplantar

supple adj **-pler; -plest** : flexible

supplement n : suplemento m — ~ vt : complementar — **supplementary** adj : suplementario

supply vt **-plied; -plying 1** : suministrar **2** ~ **with** : proveer de — ~ n, pl **-plies 1** : suministro m, provisión f **2** ~ **and demand** : oferta y demanda **3 supplies** npl PROVISIONS : provisiones fpl, víveres mpl — **supplier** n : proveedor m, -dora f

support vt **1** BACK : apoyar **2** : mantener (una familia, etc.) **3** PROP UP : sostener — ~ n **1** : apoyo m (moral), ayuda f (económica) **2** PROP : soporte m — **supporter** n : partidario m, -ria f

suppose vt **-posed; -posing 1** : suponer **2** be ~**d to (do sth)** : tener que (hacer algo) — **supposedly** adv : supuestamente

suppress vt **1** : reprimir **2** : suprimir (noticias, etc.) — **suppression** n **1** : represión f **2** : supresión f (de información)

supreme adj : supremo — **supremacy** n, pl **-cies** : supremacía f

sure adj **surer; -est 1** : seguro **2 make** ~ **that** : asegurarse de que — ~ adv **1** OF COURSE : por supuesto, claro **2 it** ~ **is hot!** : ¡qué calor! — **surely** adv : seguramente

surfing n : surf m, surfing m

surface n : superficie f — ~ v **-faced; -facing** vi : salir a la superficie — vt : revestir

surfeit n : exceso m

surfing n : surf m, surfing m

surge vi **surged; surging 1** SWELL : hincharse (dícese del mar) **2** SWARM : moverse en tropel — ~ n **1** : oleaje m (del mar), oleada f (de gente) **2** INCREASE : aumento m (súbito)

surgeon n : cirujano m, -na f — **surgery** n, pl **-geries** : cirugía f — **surgical** adj : quirúrgico

surly *adj* **surlier; -est** : hosco, arisco

surmount *vt* : superar

surname *n* : apellido *m*

surpass *vt* : superar

surplus *n* : excedente *m*

surprise *n* **1** : sorpresa *f* **2 take by ~** : sorprender — **~** *vt* **-prised; -prising** : sorprender — **surprising** *adj* : sorprendente

surrender *vt* : entregar, rendir — *vi* : rendirse — **~** *n* : rendición *m* (de una ciudad, etc.), entrega *f* (de posesiones)

surrogate *n* : sustituto *m*

surround *vt* : rodear — **surroundings** *npl* : ambiente *m*

surveillance *n* : vigilancia *f*

survey *vt* **-veyed; -veying 1** : medir (un solar) **2** INSPECT : inspeccionar **3** POLL : sondear — **~** *n, pl* **-veys 1** INSPECTION : inspección *f* **2** : medición *f* (de un solar) **3** POLL : encuesta *f*, sondeo *m* — **surveyor** *n* : agrimensor *m*, -sora *f*

survive *v* **-vived; -viving** *vi* : sobrevivir — *vt* : sobrevivir a — **survival** *n* : supervivencia *f* — **survivor** *n* : superviviente *mf*

susceptible *adj* **~ to** : propenso a — **susceptibility** *n, pl* **-ties** : propensión *f* (a enfermedades, etc.)

suspect *adj* : sospechoso — **~** *n* : sospechoso *m*, -sa *f* — **~** *vt* : sospechar (algo), sospechar de (algn)

suspend *vt* : suspender — **suspense** *n* **1** : incertidumbre *m* **2** : suspenso *m Lat*, suspense *m Spain* (en el cine, etc.) — **suspension** *n* : suspensión *f*

suspicion *n* : sospecha *f* — **suspicious** *adj* **1** QUESTIONABLE : sospechoso **2** DISTRUSTFUL : suspicaz

sustain *vt* **1** : sostener **2** SUFFER : sufrir

swagger *vi* : pavonearse

swallow¹ *v* : tragar — **~** *n* : trago *m*

swallow² *n* : golondrina *f* (pájaro)

swam → swim

swamp *n* : pantano *m*, ciénaga *f* — **~** *vt* : inundar — **swampy** *adj* **swampier; -est** : pantanoso, cenagoso

swan *n* : cisne *f*

swap *v* **swapped; swapping 1** : intercambiar **2 ~ sth for sth** : cambiar algo por algo **3 ~ sth with s.o.** : cambiar algo a algn — **~** *n* : cambio *m*

swarm *n* : enjambre *m* — **~** *vi* : enjambrar

swat *vt* **swatted; swatting** : aplastar (un insecto)

sway *n* **1** : balanceo *m* **2** INFLUENCE : influjo *m* — **~** *vi* : balancearse — *vt* : influir en

swear *v* **swore; sworn; swearing** *vi* **1** : jurar **2** CURSE : decir palabrotas — *vt* : jurar — **swearword** *n* : palabrota *f*

sweat *vi* **sweat** *or* **sweated; sweating** : sudar — **~** *n* : sudor *m* — **sweater** *n* : suéter *m* — **sweatshirt** *n* : sudadera *f* — **sweaty** *adj* **sweatier; -est** : sudado

Swedish *adj* : sueco — **~** *n* : sueco *m* (idioma)

sweep *v* **swept; sweeping** *vt* **1** : barrer **2 ~ aside** : apartar **3 ~ through** : extenderse por — *vi* : barrer — **~** *n* **1** : barrido *m* **2** : movimiento *m* circular (de la mano, etc.) **3** SCOPE : alcance *m* — **sweeping** *adj* **1** WIDE : amplio **2** EXTENSIVE : extenso — **sweepstakes** *ns & pl* : lotería *f*

sweet *adj* **1** : dulce **2** PLEASANT : agradable — **~** *n* : dulce *m* — **sweeten** *vt* : endulzar — **sweetener** *n* : endulzante *m* — **sweetheart** *n* **1** : novio *m*, -via *f* **2** (*used as a form of address*) : cariño *m* — **sweetness** *n* : dulzura *f* — **sweet potato** *n* : batata *f*, boniato *m*

swell *vi* **swelled; swelled** *or* **swollen; swelling 1** *or* **~ up** : hincharse **2** INCREASE : aumentar, crecer — **~** *n* : oleaje *m* (del mar) — **swelling** *n* : hinchazón *f*

sweltering *adj* : sofocante

swept → sweep

swerve *vi* **swerved; swerving** : virar bruscamente

swift *adj* : rápido — **swiftly** *adv* : rápidamente

swig *n* : trago *m* — **~** *vi* **swigged; swigging** : beber a tragos

swim *vi* **swam; swum; swimming 1** : nadar **2** REEL : dar vueltas — **~** *n* **1** : baño *m* **2 go for a ~** : ir a nadar — **swimmer** *n* : nadador *m*, -dora *f*

swindle *vt* **-dled; -dling** : estafar, timar — **~** *n* : estafa *f*, timo *m fam*

swine *ns & pl* : cerdo *m*, -da *f*

swing *v* **swung; swinging** *vt* **1** : balancear, hacer oscilar **2** MANAGE : arreglar — *vi* **1** : balancearse, oscilar **2** SWIVEL : girar — **~** *n* **1** : vaivén *m*, balanceo *m* **2** SHIFT : cambio *m* **3** : columpio *m* (para niños) **4 in full ~** : en pleno proceso

swipe *v* **swiped; swiping** *vt* STEAL : birlar *fam*, robar — *vi* **~ at** : intentar pegar

swirl *vi* : arremolinarse — **~** *n* **1** EDDY : remolino *m* **2** SPIRAL : espiral *f*

swish *vt* : agitar (haciendo un sonido) — *vi* **1** RUSTLE : hacer frufrú **2 ~ by** : pasar silbando

Swiss *adj* : suizo

switch *n* **1** WHIP : vara *f* **2** CHANGE : cambio *m* **3** : interruptor *m*, llave *f* (de la luz, etc.) — **~** *vt* **1** CHANGE : cambiar de **2** EXCHANGE : intercambiar **3 ~ on** : encender, prender *Lat* **4 ~ off** : apagar — *vi* **1** : sacudir (la cola, etc.) **2** CHANGE : cambiar

3 SWAP : intercambiarse — **switchboard** n : centralita f, conmutador m Lat

swivel vi **-veled** or **-velled; -veling** or **-velling** : girar (sobre un pivote)

swollen → **swell**

swoon vi : desvanecerse

swoop vi ~ **down on** : abatirse sobre — ~ n : descenso m en picada

sword n : espada f

swordfish n : pez m espada

swore, sworn → **swear**

swum → **swim**

swung → **swing**

syllable n : sílaba f

syllabus n, pl **-bi** or **-buses** : programa m (de estudios)

symbol n : símbolo m — **symbolic** adj : simbólico — **symbolism** n : simbolismo m — **symbolize** vt **-ized; -izing** : simbolizar

symmetry n, pl **-tries** : simetría f — **symmetrical** adj : simétrico

sympathy n, pl **-thies 1** COMPASSION : compasión f **2** UNDERSTANDING : comprensión f **3** CONDOLENCES : pésame m **4 sympathies** npl LOYALTY : simpatías fpl — **sympathize** vi **-thized; -thizing 1** ~ **with** PITY : compadecerse de **2** ~ **with** UNDERSTAND : comprender — **sympathetic** adj **1** COMPASSIONATE : compasivo **2** UNDERSTANDING : comprensivo

symphony n, pl **-nies** : sinfonía f

symposium n, pl **-sia** or **-siums** : simposio m

symptom n : síntoma m — **symptomatic** adj : sintomático

synagogue n : sinagoga f

synchronize vt **-nized; -nizing** : sincronizar

syndrome n : síndrome m

synonym n : sinónimo m — **synonymous** adj : sinónimo

synopsis n, pl **-opses** : sinopsis f

syntax n : sintaxis f

synthesis n, pl **-theses** : síntesis f — **synthesize** vt **-sized; -sizing** : sintetizar — **synthetic** adj : sintético

syphilis n : sífilis f

Syrian adj : sirio

syringe n : jeringa f, jeringuilla f

syrup n : jarabe m

system n **1** : sistema m **2** BODY : organismo m **3 digestive** ~ : aparato m digestivo — **systematic** adj : sistemático

T

t n, pl **t's** or **ts** : t f, vigésima letra del alfabeto inglés

tab n **1** TAG : etiqueta f **2** FLAP : lengüeta f **3** ACCOUNT : cuenta f **4 keep** ~**s on** : vigilar

table n **1** : mesa f **2** LIST : tabla f **3** ~ **of contents** : índice m de materias — **tablecloth** n : mantel m — **tablespoon** n **1** : cuchara f grande **2** : cucharada f (cantidad)

tablet n **1** PAD : bloc m **2** PILL : pastilla f **3** or **stone** ~ : lápida f

tabloid n : tabloide m

taboo adj : tabú — ~ n : tabú m

tacit adj : tácito

taciturn adj : taciturno

tack vt **1** : fijar con tachuelas **2** ~ **on** ADD : añadir — ~ n **1** : tachuela f **2 change** ~ : cambiar de rumbo

tackle n **1** GEAR : aparejo m **2** : placaje m, tacle m Lat (acción) — ~ vt **-led; -ling 1** : placar, taclear Lat **2** CONFRONT : abordar

tacky adj **tackier; -est 1** : pegajoso **2** GAUDY : de mal gusto

tact n : tacto m — **tactful** adj : diplomático, discreto

tactical adj : táctico — **tactic** n : táctica f — **tactics** ns & pl : táctica f

tactless adj : indiscreto

tadpole n : renacuajo m

tag[1] n **1** LABEL : etiqueta f — ~ v **tagged; tagging** vt : etiquetar — vi ~ **along with s.o.** : acompañar a algn

tag[2] vt : tocar (en varios juegos)

tail n **1** : cola f **2** ~**s** npl : cruz f (de una moneda) — ~ vt FOLLOW : seguir

tailor n : sastre m, -tra f — ~ vt **1** : confeccionar (ropa) **2** ADAPT : adaptar

taint vt : contaminar

take v **took; taken; taking** vt **1** : tomar **2** BRING : llevar **3** REMOVE : sacar **4** BEAR : soportar, aguantar **5** ACCEPT : aceptar **6 I** ~ **it that...** : supongo que... **7** ~ **a bath** : bañarse **8** ~ **a walk** : dar un paseo **9** ~ **back** : retirar (palabras, etc.) **10** ~ **in** ALTER : achicar **11** ~ **in** GRASP : entender **12** ~ **in** TRICK : engañar **13** ~ **off** REMOVE : quitar, quitarse (ropa) **14** ~ **on**

: asumir (una responsabilidad, etc.) **15 ~ out** : sacar **16 ~ over** : tomar el poder de **17 ~ place** : tener lugar **18 ~ up** SHORTEN : acortar **19 ~ up** OCCUPY : ocupar — *vi* **1** : prender (dícese de una vacuna, etc.) **2 ~ off** : despegar (dícese de aviones, etc.) **3 ~ over** : asumir el mando — *~ n* **1** PROCEEDS : ingresos *mpl* **2** : toma *f* (en el cine) — **takeoff** *n* : despegue *m* (de un avión, etc.) — **takeover** *n* : toma *f* (de poder, etc.), adquisición *f* (de una empresa)

talcum powder *n* : polvos *mpl* de talco

tale *n* : cuento *m*

talent *n* : talento *m* — **talented** *adj* : talentoso

talk *vi* **1** : hablar **2 ~ about** : hablar de **3 ~ to/with** : hablar con — *vt* **1** SPEAK : hablar **2 ~ over** : hablar de, discutir — *~ n* **1** CHAT : conversación *f* **2** SPEECH : charla *f* — **talkative** *adj* : hablador

tall *adj* **1** : alto **2 how ~ are you?** : ¿cuánto mides?

tally *n, pl* **-lies** : cuenta *f* — *~ v* **-lied; -lying** *vt* RECKON : calcular — *vi* MATCH : concordar, cuadrar

talon *n* : garra *f*

tambourine *n* : pandereta *f*

tame *adj* **tamer; -est 1** : domesticado **2** DOCILE : manso **3** DULL : insípido, soso — *~ vt* **tamed; taming** : domar

tamper *vi* **~ with** : forzar (una cerradura), amañar (documentos, etc.)

tampon *n* : tampón *m*

tan *v* **tanned; tanning** *vt* : curtir (cuero) — *vi* : broncearse — *~ n* **1** SUNTAN : bronceado *m* **2** : (color *m*) café *m* con leche

tang *n* : sabor *m* fuerte

tangent *n* : tangente *f*

tangerine *n* : mandarina *f*

tangible *adj* : tangible

tangle *v* **-gled; -gling** *vt* : enredar — *vi* : enredarse — *~ n* : enredo *m*

tango *n, pl* **-gos** : tango *m*

tank *n* **1** : tanque *m*, depósito *m* **2** : tanque *m* (militar) — **tanker** *n* **1** : buque *m* tanque **2** *or* **~ truck** : camión *m* cisterna

tantalizing *adj* : tentador

tantrum *n* **throw a ~** : hacer un berrinche

tap¹ *n* FAUCET : llave *f*, grifo *m* *Spain* — *~ vt* **tapped; tapping 1** : sacar (un líquido, etc.), sangrar (un árbol) **2** : intervenir (un teléfono)

tap² *vt* **tapped; tapping** STRIKE : tocar, dar un golpecito en — *~ n* : golpecito *m*, toque *m*

tape *n* : cinta *f* — *~ vt* **taped; taping 1** : pegar con cinta **2** RECORD : grabar — **tape measure** *n* : cinta *f* métrica

taper *n* : vela *f* (larga) — *~ vi* **1** NARROW : estrecharse **2** *or* **~ off** : disminuir

tapestry *n, pl* **-tries** : tapiz *m*

tar *n* : alquitrán *m* — *~ vt* **tarred; tarring** : alquitranar

tarantula *n* : tarántula *f*

target *n* **1** : blanco *m* **2** GOAL : objetivo *m*

tariff *n* : tarifa *f*, arancel *m*

tarnish *vt* **1** : deslustrar **2** : empañar (una reputación, etc.) — *vi* : deslustrarse

tart¹ *adj* SOUR : ácido, agrio

tart² *n* : pastel *m*

tartan *n* : tartán *m*

task *n* : tarea *f*

tassel *n* : borla *f*

taste *v* **tasted; tasting** *vt* TRY : probar — *vi* **1** : saber **2 ~ like** : saber a — *~ n* **1** FLAVOR : gusto *m*, sabor *m* **2 have a ~ of** : probar **3 in good/bad ~** : de buen/mal gusto — **tasteful** *adj* : de buen gusto — **tasteless** *adj* **1** : sin sabor **2** COARSE : de mal gusto — **tasty** *adj* **tastier; -est** : sabroso

tatters *npl* : harapos *mpl* — **tattered** *adj* : harapiento

tattle *vi* **-tled; -tling ~ on s.o.** : acusar a algn

tattoo *vt* : tatuar — *~ n* : tatuaje *m*

taught → **teach**

taunt *n* : pulla *f*, burla *f* — *~ vt* : mofarse de, burlarse de

taut *adj* : tirante, tenso

tavern *n* : taberna *f*

tax *vt* **1** : gravar **2** STRAIN : poner a prueba — *~ n* **1** : impuesto *m* **2** BURDEN : carga *f* — **taxable** *adj* : imponible — **taxation** *n* : impuestos *mpl* — **tax–exempt** *adj* : libre de impuestos

taxi *n, pl* **taxis** : taxi *m* — *~ vi* **taxied; taxiing** *or* **taxying; taxis** *or* **taxies** : rodar por la pista (dícese de un avión)

taxpayer *n* : contribuyente *mf*

tea *n* : té *m*

teach *v* **taught; teaching** *vt* : enseñar, dar clases de (una asignatura) — *vi* : dar clases — **teacher** *n* : profesor *m*, -sora *f*; maestro *m*, -tra *f* (de niños pequeños) — **teaching** *n* : enseñanza *f*

teacup *n* : taza *f* de té

team *n* : equipo *m* — *~ vi* *or* **~ up** : asociarse — **teammate** *n* : compañero *m*, -ra *f* de equipo — **teamwork** *n* : trabajo *m* de equipo

teapot *n* : tetera *f*

tear¹ *v* **tore; torn; tearing** *vt* **1** : romper, rasgar **2 ~ apart** : destrozar **3 ~ down** : derribar **4 ~ off** : arrancar **5 ~ up** : romper (papel, etc.) — *vi* **1** : romperse, rasgarse **2** RUSH : ir a toda velocidad — *~ n* : desgarro *m*, rasgón *m*

tear² n : lágrima f — **tearful** adj : lloroso
tease vt **teased; teasing 1** : tomar el pelo a, burlarse de **2** ANNOY : fastidiar
teaspoon n **1** : cucharita f **2** : cucharadita f (cantidad)
technical adj : técnico — **technicality** n, pl **-ties** : detalle m técnico — **technically** adv : técnicamente — **technician** n : técnico m, -ca f
technique n : técnica f
technological adj : tecnológico — **technology** n, pl **-gies** : tecnología f
teddy bear n : oso m de peluche
tedious adj : tedioso, aburrido — **tedium** n : tedio m
tee n : tee m (en deportes)
teem vi **1** POUR : llover a cántaros **2 be ~ing with** : estar repleto de
teenage or **teenaged** adj : adolescente — **teenager** n : adolescente mf — **teens** npl : adolescencia f
teepee → tepee
teeter vi : tambalearse
teeth → tooth — **teethe** vi **teethed; teething** : echar los dientes
telecommunication n : telecomunicación f
telegram n : telegrama m
telegraph n : telégrafo m — **~** v : telegrafiar
telephone n : teléfono m — **~** v **-phoned; -phoning** : llamar por teléfono
telescope n : telescopio m
televise vt **-vised; -vising** : televisar — **television** n : televisión f
tell v **told; telling** vt **1** : decir **2** RELATE : contar **3** DISTINGUISH : distinguir **4 ~ s.o. off** : regañar a algn — vi **1** : decir **2** KNOW : saber **3** SHOW : tener efecto **4 ~ on s.o.** : acusar a algn — **teller** n or **bank ~** : cajero m, -ra f
temp n : empleado m, -da f temporal
temper vt MODERATE : temperar — **~** n **1** MOOD : humor m **2 have a bad ~** : tener mal genio **3 lose one's ~** : perder los estribos — **temperament** n : temperamento m — **temperamental** adj : temperamental — **temperate** adj **1** : moderado **2 ~ zone** : zona f templada
temperature n **1** : temperatura f **2 have a ~** : tener fiebre
tempest n : tempestad f
temple n **1** : templo m **2** : sien f (en anatomía)
tempo n, pl **-pi** or **-pos 1** : tempo m **2** PACE : ritmo m
temporarily adv : temporalmente — **temporary** adj : temporal
tempt vt : tentar — **temptation** n : tentación f
ten adj : diez — **~** n : diez m

tenacity n : tenacidad f — **tenacious** adj : tenaz
tenant n : inquilino m, -na f; arrendatario m, -ria f
tend¹ vt MIND : cuidar
tend² vi **~ to** : tender a — **tendency** n, pl **-cies** : tendencia f
tender¹ adj **1** : tierno **2** PAINFUL : dolorido
tender² vt : presentar — **~** n **1** : oferta f **2** **legal ~** : moneda f de curso legal
tenderloin n : lomo f (de cerdo o vaca)
tenderness n : ternura f
tendon n : tendón m
tenet n : principio m
tennis n : tenis m
tenor n : tenor m
tense¹ n : tiempo m (de un verbo)
tense² v **tensed; tensing** vt : tensar — vi : tensarse — **~** adj **tenser; tensest** : tenso — **tension** n : tensión f
tent n : tienda f de campaña
tentacle n : tentáculo m
tentative adj **1** HESITANT : vacilante **2** PROVISIONAL : provisional
tenth adj : décimo — **~** n **1** : décimo m, -ma f (en una serie) **2** : décimo m (en matemáticas)
tenuous adj : tenue, endeble
tepid adj : tibio
term n **1** WORD : término m **2** PERIOD : período m **3 be on good ~s** : tener buenas relaciones **4 in ~s of** : con respecto a — **~** vt : calificar de
terminal adj : terminal — **~** n **1** : terminal m **2** or **bus ~** : terminal f
terminate v **-nated; -nating** vi : terminar(se) — vt : poner fin a — **termination** n : terminación f
termite n : termita f
terrace n : terraza f
terrain n : terreno m
terrestrial adj : terrestre
terrible adj : espantoso, terrible — **terribly** adv : terriblemente
terrier n : terrier mf
terrific adj **1** HUGE : tremendo **2** EXCELLENT : estupendo
terrify vt **-fied; -fying** : aterrar, aterrorizar — **terrifying** adj : aterrador
territory n, pl **-ries** : territorio m — **territorial** adj : territorial
terror n : terror m — **terrorism** n : terrorismo m — **terrorist** n : terrorista mf — **terrorize** vt **-ized; -izing** : aterrorizar
terse adj **terser; tersest** : seco, lacónico
test n **1** TRIAL : prueba f **2** EXAM : examen m, prueba f **3** : análisis m (en medicina) — **~** vt **1** TRY : probar **2** QUIZ : examinar **3**

: analizar (la sangre, etc.), examinar (los ojos, etc.)

testament *n* **1** WILL : testamento *m* **2 the Old/New Testament** : el Antiguo/Nuevo Testamento

testicle *n* : testículo *m*

testify *v* **-fied; -fying** : testificar

testimony *n, pl* **-nies** : testimonio *m*

test tube *n* : probeta *f*, tubo *m* de ensayo

tetanus *n* : tétano *m*

tether *vt* : atar

text *n* : texto *m* — **textbook** *n* : libro *m* de texto

textile *n* : textil *m*

texture *n* : textura *f*

than *conj & prep* : que, de (con cantidades)

thank *vt* **1** : agradecer, dar (las) gracias a **2 ~ you!** : ¡gracias! — **thankful** *adj* : agradecido — **thankfully** *adv* **1** : con agradecimiento **2** FORTUNATELY : gracias a Dios — **thanks** *npl* **1** : agradecimiento *m* **2 ~!** : ¡gracias!

Thanksgiving *n* : día *m* de Acción de Gracias

that *pron, pl* **those 1** : ése, ésa, eso **2** (*more distant*) : aquél, aquélla, aquello **3 is ~ you?** : ¿eres tú? **4 like ~** : así **5 ~ is...** : es decir... **6 those who...** : los que... — **~** *conj* : que — **~** *adj, pl* **those 1** : ese, esa **2** (*more distant*) : aquel, aquella **3 ~ one** : ése, ésa — **~** *adv* : tan

thatched *adj* : con techo de paja

thaw *vt* : descongelar (alimentos), derretir (hielo) — *vi* **1** : descongelarse **2** MELT : derretirse — **~** *n* : deshielo *m*

the *art* **1** : el, la, los, las **2** PER : por — **~** *adv* **1 ~ sooner ~ better** : cuanto más pronto, mejor **2 I like this one ~ best** : éste es el que más me gusta

theater *or* **theatre** *n* : teatro *m* — **theatrical** *adj* : teatral

theft *n* : robo *m*, hurto *m*

their *adj* : su, sus, de ellos, de ellas — **theirs** *pron* **1** : (el) suyo, (la) suya, (los) suyos, (las) suyas **2 some friends of ~** : unos amigos suyos, unos amigos de ellos

them *pron* **1** (*used as direct object*) : los, las **2** (*used as indirect object*) : les, se **3** (*used as object of a preposition*) : ellos, ellas

theme *n* **1** : tema *m* **2** ESSAY : trabajo *m* (escrito)

themselves *pron* **1** (*used reflexively*) : se **2** (*used emphatically*) : ellos mismos, ellas mismas **3** (*used after a preposition*) : sí (mismos), sí (mismas)

then *adv* **1** : entonces **2** NEXT : luego, después **3** BESIDES : además — **~** *adj* : entonces

thence *adv* : de ahí (en adelante)

theology *n, pl* **-gies** : teología *f* — **theological** *adj* : teológico

theorem *n* : teorema *m* — **theoretical** *adj* : teórico — **theory** *n, pl* **-ries** : teoría *f*

therapeutic *adj* : terapéutico — **therapist** *n* : terapeuta *mf* — **therapy** *n, pl* **-pies** : terapia *f*

there *adv* **1** *or* **over ~** : allí, allá **2** *or* **right ~** : ahí **3 in ~** : ahí (dentro) **4 ~, it's done!** : ¡listo! **5 up/down ~** : ahí arriba/abajo **6 who's ~?** : ¿quién es? — **~** *pron* **1 ~ is/are** : hay **2 ~ are three of us** : somos tres — **thereabouts** *or* **thereabout** *adv* **or ~** : por ahí — **thereafter** *adv* : después — **thereby** *adv* : así — **therefore** *adv* : por lo tanto

thermal *adj* : térmico

thermometer *n* : termómetro *m*

thermos *n* : termo *m*

thermostat *n* : termostato *m*

thesaurus *n, pl* **-sauri** *or* **-sauruses** : diccionario *m* de sinónimos

these → **this**

thesis *n, pl* **theses** : tesis *f*

they *pron* **1** : ellos, ellas **2 where are ~?** : ¿dónde están? **3 as ~ say** : como dicen — **they'd** (*contraction of* **they had** *or* **they would**) → **have, would** — **they'll** (*contraction of* **they shall** *or* **they will**) → **shall, will** — **they're** (*contraction of* **they are**) → **be** — **they've** (*contraction of* **they have**) → **have**

thick *adj* **1** : grueso **2** DENSE : espeso **3 a ~ accent** : un acento marcado **4 it's two inches ~** : tiene dos pulgadas de grosor — **~** *n* **in the ~ of** : en medio de — **thicken** *vt* : espesar — *vi* : espesarse — **thicket** *n* : matorral *m* — **thickness** *n* : grosor *m*, espesor *m*

thief *n, pl* **thieves** : ladrón *m*, **-drona** *f*

thigh *n* : muslo *m*

thimble *n* : dedal *m*

thin *adj* **thinner; -est 1** : delgado **2** : ralo (dícese del pelo) **3** WATERY : claro, aguado **4** FINE : fino — **~** *v* **thinned; thinning** *vt* DILUTE : diluir — *vi* : ralear (dícese del pelo)

thing *n* **1** : cosa *f* **2 for one ~** : en primer lugar **3 how are ~s?** : ¿qué tal? **4 it's a good ~ that...** : menos mal que... **5 the important ~ is...** : lo importante es...

think *v* **thought; thinking** *vt* **1** : pensar **2** BELIEVE : creer **3 ~ up** : idear — *vi* **1** : pensar **2 ~ about** *or* **~ of** CONSIDER : pensar en **3 ~ of** REMEMBER : acordarse de **4 what do you ~ of it?** : ¿qué te parece? — **thinker** *n* : pensador *m*, **-dora** *f*

third *adj* : tercero — **~** *or* **thirdly** *adv* : en tercer lugar — **~** *n* **1** : tercero *m*, **-ra** *f* (en una serie) **2** : tercero *m* (en matemáticas) — **Third World** *n* : Tercer Mundo *m*

thirst *n* : sed *f* — **thirsty** *adj* **thirstier; -est 1** : sediento **2 be ~** : tener sed

thirteen *adj* : trece — **~** *n* : trece *m* — **thirteenth** *adj* : décimo tercero — **~** *n* **1** : decimotercero *m*, **-ra** *f* (en una serie) **2** : treceavo *m* (en matemáticas)

thirty *adj* : treinta — **~** *n, pl* **thirties** : treinta *m* — **thirtieth** *adj* : trigésimo — **~** *n* **1** : trigésimo *m*, **-ma** *f* (en una serie) **2** : treintavo *m* (en matemáticas)

this *pron, pl* **these 1** : éste, ésta, esto **2 like ~** : así — **~** *adj, pl* **these 1** : este, esta **~ one** : éste, ésta **3 ~ way** : por aquí — **~** *adv* **~ big** : así de grande

thistle *n* : cardo *m*

thong *n* **1** : correa *f* **2** SANDAL : chancla *f*

thorn *n* : espina *f* — **thorny** *adj* : espinoso

thorough *adj* **1** : meticuloso **2** COMPLETE : completo — **thoroughly** *adv* **1** : a fondo **2** COMPLETELY : completamente — **thoroughbred** *adj* : de pura sangre — **thoroughfare** *n* : vía *f* pública

those → **that**

though *conj* : aunque — **~** *adv* **1** : sin embargo **2 as ~** : como si

thought → **think** — **~** *n* **1** : pensamiento *m* **2** IDEA : idea *f* — **thoughtful** *adj* **1** : pensativo **2** KIND : amable — **thoughtless** *adj* **1** CARELESS : descuidado **2** RUDE : desconsiderado

thousand *adj* : mil — **~** *n, pl* **-sands** *or* **-sand** : mil *m* — **thousandth** *adj* : milésimo — **~** *n* **1** : milésimo *m*, **-ma** *f* (en una serie) **2** : milésimo *m* (en matemáticas)

thrash *vt* : dar una paliza a — *vi or* **~ around** : agitarse, revolcarse

thread *n* **1** : hilo *m* **2** : rosca *f* (de un tornillo) — **~** *vt* : enhilar (una aguja), ensartar (cuentas) — **threadbare** *adj* : raído

threat *n* : amenaza *f* — **threaten** *v* : amenazar — **threatening** *adj* : amenazador

three *adj* : tres — **~** *n* : tres *m* — **three hundred** *adj* : trescientos — **~** *n* : trescientos *m*

threshold *n* : umbral *m*

threw → **throw**

thrift *n* : frugalidad *f* — **thrifty** *adj* **thriftier; -est** : económico, frugal

thrill *vt* : emocionar — **~** *n* : emoción *f* — **thriller** *n* : película *f* de suspense *Spain*, película *f* de suspenso *Lat* — **thrilling** *adj* : emocionante

thrive *vi* **throve** *or* **thrived; thriven 1** FLOURISH : florecer **2** PROSPER : prosperar

throat *n* : garganta *f*

throb *vi* **throbbed; throbbing 1** PULSATE : palpitar **2** VIBRATE : vibrar **3 ~ with pain** : tener un dolor punzante

throes *npl* **1** PANGS : agonía *f* **2 in the ~ of** : en medio de

throne *n* : trono *m*

throng *n* : muchedumbre *f*, multitud *f*

throttle *vt* **-tled; -tling** : estrangular — **~** *n* : válvula *f* reguladora

through *prep* **1** : por, a través de **2** BETWEEN : entre **3** BECAUSE OF : a causa de **4** DURING : durante **5** → **throughout 6 Monday ~ Friday** : de lunes a viernes — **~** *adv* **1** : de un lado a otro (en el espacio), de principio a fin (en el tiempo) **2** COMPLETELY : completamente — **~** *adj* **1 be ~** : haber terminado **2 ~ traffic** : tráfico *m* de paso — **throughout** *prep* : por todo (un lugar), a lo largo de (un período de tiempo)

throw *v* **threw; thrown; throwing** *vt* **1** : tirar, lanzar **2** : proyectar (una sombra) **3** CONFUSE : desconcertar **4 ~ a party** : dar una fiesta **5 ~ away** *or* **~ out** : tirar, botar *Lat* — *vi* **~ up** VOMIT : vomitar — **~** *n* : tiro *m*, lanzamiento *m*

thrush *n* : tordo *m*, zorzal *m*

thrust *vt* **thrust; thrusting 1** : empujar (bruscamente) **2** PLUNGE : clavar **3 ~ upon** : imponer a — **~** *n* **1** : empujón *m* **2** : estocada *f* (en esgrima)

thud *n* : ruido *m* sordo

thug *n* : matón *m*

thumb *n* : (dedo *m*) pulgar *m* — **~** *vt or* **~ through** : hojear — **thumbnail** *n* : uña *f* del pulgar — **thumbtack** *n* : tachuela *f*, chinche *f Lat*

thump *vt* : golpear — *vi* : latir con fuerza (dícese del corazón) — **~** *n* : ruido *m* sordo

thunder *n* : truenos *mpl* — **~** *vi* : tronar — *vt* SHOUT : bramar — **thunderbolt** *n* : rayo *m* — **thunderous** *adj* : atronador — **thunderstorm** *n* : tormenta *f* eléctrica

Thursday *n* : jueves *m*

thus *adv* **1** : así **2** THEREFORE : por lo tanto

thwart *vt* : frustrar

thyme *n* : tomillo *m*

thyroid *n* : tiroides *mf*

tiara *n* : diadema *f*

tic *n* : tic *m* (nervioso)

tick¹ *n* : garrapata *f* (insecto)

tick² *n* **1** : tictac *m* (sonido) **2** CHECK : marca *f* — **~** *vi* : hacer tictac — *vt* **1 or ~ off** CHECK : marcar **2 ~ off** ANNOY : fastidiar

ticket *n* **1** : pasaje *m* (de avión), billete *m Spain* (de tren, avión, etc.), boleto *m Lat* (de tren o autobús) **2** : entrada *f* (al teatro, etc.) **3** FINE : multa *f*

tickle *v* **-led; -ling** *vt* **1** : hacer cosquillas a **2** AMUSE : divertir — *vi* : picar — **~** *n* : cosquilleo *m* — **ticklish** *adj* **1** : cosquilloso **2** TRICKY : delicado

tidal wave *n* : maremoto *m*

tidbit *n* MORSEL : golosina *f*

tide *n* : marea *f* — ∼ *vt* **tided; tiding** ∼ **over** : ayudar a superar un apuro

tidy *adj* **-dier; -est** : ordenado, arreglado — ∼ *vt* **-died; -dying** *or* ∼ **up** : ordenar, arreglar

tie *n* **1** : atadura *f*, cordón *m* **2** BOND : lazo *m* **3** : empate *m* (en deportes) **4** NECKTIE : corbata *f* — ∼ *v* **tied; tying** *or* **tieing** *vt* **1** : atar, amarrar *Lat* **2** ∼ **a knot** : hacer un nudo — *vi* : empatar (en deportes)

tier *n* : nivel *m*, piso (de un pastel), grada *f* (de un estadio)

tiger *n* : tigre *m*

tight *adj* **1** : apretado **2** SNUG : ajustado, ceñido **3** TAUT : tirante **4** STINGY : agarrado **5** SCARCE : escaso **6 a** ∼ **seal** : un cierre hermético **7 a** ∼ **spot** : un aprieto — ∼ *adv* **closed** ∼ : bien cerrado — **tighten** *vt* **1** : apretar **2** TENSE : tensar **3** : hacer más estricto (reglas, etc.) — **tightly** *adv* : bien, fuerte — **tightrope** *n* : cuerda *f* floja — **tights** *npl* : leotardo *m*, mallas *fpl*

tile *n* **1** : azulejo *m*, baldosa *f* (de piso) **2** *or* **roofing** ∼ : teja *f* — ∼ *vt* **tiled; tiling 1** : revestir de azulejos, embaldosar (un piso) **2** : tejar (un techo)

till¹ *prep & conj* → **until**

till² *vt* : cultivar

till³ *n* : caja *f* (registradora)

tilt *n* **1** : inclinación *f* **2 at full** ∼ : a toda velocidad — ∼ *vt* : inclinar — *vi* : inclinarse

timber *n* **1** : madera *f* (para construcción) **2** BEAM : viga *f*

timbre *n* : timbre *m*

time *n* **1** : tiempo *m* **2** AGE : época *f* **3** : compás *m* (en música) **4 at** ∼**s** : a veces **5 at this** ∼ : en este momento **6 for the** ∼ **being** : por el momento **7 from** ∼ **to** ∼ : de vez en cuando **8 have a good** ∼ : pasarlo bien **9 many** ∼**s** : muchas veces **10 on** ∼ : a tiempo **11** ∼ **after** ∼ : una y otra vez **12 what** ∼ **is it?** : ¿qué hora es? — ∼ *vt* **timed; timing** : tomar el tiempo a (algn), cronometrar (una carrera, etc.) — **timeless** *adj* : eterno — **timely** *adj* **-lier; -est** : oportuno — **timer** *n* : temporizador *m*, avisador *m* (de cocina) — **times** *prep* **3** ∼ **4 is 12** : 3 por 4 son 12 — **timetable** *n* : horario *m*

timid *adj* : tímido

tin *n* **1** : estaño *m* **2** CAN : lata *f*, bote *m* *Spain* — **tinfoil** *n* : papel *m* (de) aluminio

tinge *vt* **tinged; tingeing** *or* **tinging** : matizar — ∼ *n* **1** TINT : matiz *m* **2** TOUCH : dejo *m*

tingle *vi* **-gled; -gling** : sentir (un) hormigueo — ∼ *n* : hormigueo *m*

tinker *vi* ∼ **with** : intentar arreglar (con pequeños ajustes)

tinkle *vi* **-kled; -kling** : tintinear — ∼ *n* : tintineo *m*

tint *n* : tinte *m* — ∼ *vt* : teñir

tiny *adj* **-nier; -est** : diminuto, minúsculo

tip¹ *v* **tipped; tipping** *vt* **1** TILT : inclinar **2** *or* ∼ **over** : volcar — *vi* : inclinarse

tip² *n* END : punta *f*

tip³ *n* ADVICE : consejo *m* — ∼ *vt* ∼ **off** : avisar

tip⁴ *vt* : dar una propina a — ∼ *n* GRATUITY : propina *f*

tipsy *adj* **-sier; -est** : achispado

tiptoe *n* **on** ∼ : de puntillas — ∼ *vi* **-toed; -toeing** : caminar de puntillas

tip–top *adj* : excelente

tire¹ *n* : neumático *m*, llanta *f Lat*

tire² *v* **tired; tiring** *vt* : cansar — *vi* : cansarse — **tired** *adj* **1** ∼ **of** : cansado de, harto de **2** ∼ **out** : agotado — **tireless** *adj* : incansable — **tiresome** *adj* : pesado

tissue *n* **1** : pañuelo *m* de papel **2** : tejido *m* (en biología)

title *n* : título *m* — ∼ *vt* **-tled; -tling** : titular

to *prep* **1** : a **2** TOWARD : hacia **3** IN ORDER TO : para **4** UP TO : hasta **5 a quarter** ∼ **seven** : las siete menos cuarto **6 be nice** ∼ **them** : trátalos bien **7 ten** ∼ **the box** : diez por caja **8 the mate** ∼ **this shoe** : el compañero de este zapato **9 two** ∼ **four years old** : entre dos y cuatro años de edad **10 want** ∼ **do** : querer hacer — ∼ *adv* **1 come** ∼ : volver en sí **2** ∼ **and fro** : de un lado a otro

toad *n* : sapo *m*

toast *vt* **1** : tostar (pan, etc.) **2** : brindar por (una persona) — ∼ *n* **1** : pan *m* tostado, tostadas *fpl* **2** DRINK : brindis *m* — **toaster** *n* : tostador *m*

tobacco *n*, *pl* **-cos** : tabaco *m*

toboggan *n* : tobogán *m*

today *adv* : hoy — ∼ *n* : hoy *m*

toddler *n* : niño *m* pequeño, niña *f* pequeña (que comienza a caminar)

toe *n* : dedo *m* (del pie) — **toenail** *n* : uña *f* (del pie)

together *adv* **1** : juntos **2** ∼ **with** : junto con

toil *n* : trabajo *m* duro — ∼ *vi* : trabajar duro

toilet *n* **1** BATHROOM : baño *m*, servicio *m* **2** : inodoro *m* (instalación) — **toilet paper** *n* : papel *m* higiénico — **toiletries** *npl* : artículos *mpl* de tocador

token *n* **1** SIGN : muestra *f* **2** MEMENTO : recuerdo *m* **3** : ficha *f* (para un tren, etc.)

told → **tell**

tolerable *adj* : tolerable — **tolerance** *n* : tolerancia *f* — **tolerant** *adj* : tolerante — **tolerate** *vt* -**ated; -ating** : tolerar

toll¹ *n* **1** : peaje *m* **2 death** ∼ : número *m* de muertos **3 take a** ∼ **on** : afectar

toll² *vi* RING : tocar, doblar — ∼ *n* : tañido *m*

tomato *n, pl* -**toes** : tomate *m*

tomb *n* : tumba *f*, sepulcro *m* — **tombstone** *n* : lápida *f*

tome *n* : tomo *m*

tomorrow *adv* : mañana — ∼ *n* : mañana *m*

ton *n* : tonelada *f*

tone *n* : tono *m* — ∼ *vt* **toned; toning** *or* ∼ **down** : atenuar

tongs *npl* : tenazas *fpl*

tongue *n* : lengua *f*

tonic *n* **1** : tónico *m* **2** *or* ∼ **water** : tónica *f*

tonight *adv* : esta noche — ∼ *n* : esta noche *f*

tonsil *n* : amígdala *f*

too *adv* **1** ALSO : también **2** EXCESSIVELY : demasiado

took → **take**

tool *n* : herramienta *f* — **toolbox** *n* : caja *f* de herramientas

toot *vt* : sonar (un claxon, etc.) — ∼ *n* **1** WHISTLE : pitido *m* **2** HONK : bocinazo *m*

tooth *n, pl* **teeth** : diente *m* — **toothache** *n* : dolor *m* de muelas — **toothbrush** *n* : cepillo *m* de dientes — **toothpaste** *n* : pasta *f* de dientes, pasta *f* dentífrica

top¹ *n* **1** : parte *f* superior **2** SUMMIT : cima *f*, cumbre *f* **3** COVER : tapa *f*, cubierta *f* **4 on** ∼ **of** : encima de — ∼ *vt* **topped; topping 1** COVER : rematar (un edificio, etc.), bañar (un pastel, etc.) **2** SURPASS : superar **3** ∼ **off** : llenar — ∼ *adj* **1** : de arriba, superior **2** BEST : mejor **3 a** ∼ **executive** : un alto ejecutivo

top² *n* : trompo *m* (juguete)

topic *n* : tema *m* — **topical** *adj* : de interés actual

topmost *adj* : más alto

topple *v* -**pled; -pling** *vi* : caerse — *vt* **1** OVERTURN : volcar **2** OVERTHROW : derrocar

torch *n* : antorcha *f*

tore → **tear¹**

torment *n* : tormento *m* — ∼ *vt* : atormentar

torn → **tear¹**

tornado *n, pl* -**does** *or* -**dos** : tornado *m*

torpedo *n, pl* -**does** : torpedo *m* — ∼ *vt* : torpedear

torrent *n* : torrente *m*

torrid *adj* : tórrido

torso *n, pl* -**sos** *or* -**si** : torso *m*

tortilla *n* : tortilla *f*

tortoise *n* : tortuga *f* (terrestre) — **tortoiseshell** *n* : carey *m*, concha *f*

tortuous *adj* : tortuoso

torture *n* : tortura *f* — ∼ *vt* -**tured; -turing** : torturar

toss *vt* **1** : tirar, lanzar **2** : mezclar (una ensalada) — *vi* ∼ **and turn** : dar vueltas — ∼ *n* : lanzamiento *m*

tot *n* : pequeño *m*, -ña *f*

total *adj* : total — ∼ *n* : total *m* — ∼ *vt* -**taled** *or* -**talled; -taling** *or* -**talling 1** : ascender a **2** *or* ∼ **up** : totalizar, sumar

totalitarian *adj* : totalitario

tote *vt* **toted; toting** : llevar

totter *vi* : tambalearse

touch *vt* **1** : tocar **2** MOVE : conmover **3** AFFECT : afectar **4** ∼ **up** : retocar — *vi* : tocarse — ∼ *n* **1** : tacto *m* (sentido) **2** HINT : toque *m* **3** BIT : pizca *f* **4 keep in** ∼ : mantenerse en contacto **5 lose one's** ∼ : perder la habilidad — **touchdown** *n* : touchdown *m* — **touchy** *adj* **touchier; -est 1** : delicado **2 be** ∼ **about** : picarse a la mención de

tough *adj* **1** : duro **2** STRONG : fuerte **3** STRICT : severo **4** DIFFICULT : difícil — **toughen** *vt or* ∼ **up** : endurecer — *vi* : endurecerse — **toughness** *n* : dureza *f*

tour *n* **1** : viaje *m* (por un país, etc.), visita *f* (a un museo, etc.) **2** : gira *f* (de un equipo, etc.) — ∼ *vi* **1** TRAVEL : viajar **2** : hacer una gira (dícese de equipos, etc.) — *vt* : viajar por, recorrer — **tourist** *n* : turista *mf*

tournament *n* : torneo *m*

tousle *vt* -**sled; -sling** : despeinar

tout *vt* : promocionar

tow *vt* : remolcar — ∼ *n* : remolque *m*

toward *or* **towards** *prep* : hacia

towel *n* : toalla *f*

tower *n* : torre *f* — ∼ *vi* ∼ **over** : descollar sobre — **towering** *adj* : altísimo

town *n* **1** VILLAGE : pueblo *m* **2** CITY : ciudad *f* — **township** *n* : municipio *m*

tow truck *n* : grúa *f*

toxic *adj* : tóxico

toy *n* : juguete *m* — ∼ *vi* ∼ **with** : juguetear con

trace *n* **1** SIGN : rastro *m*, señal *f* **2** HINT : dejo *m* — ∼ *vt* **traced; tracing 1** : calcar (un dibujo, etc.) **2** DRAW : trazar **3** FIND : localizar

track *n* **1** : pista *f* **2** PATH : sendero *m* **3** *or* **railroad** ∼ : vía *f* (férrea) **4 keep** ∼ **of** : llevar la cuenta de — ∼ *vt* TRAIL : seguir la pista de

tract¹ *n* **1** EXPANSE : extensión *f* **2** : tracto *m* (en anatomía)

tract² *n* PAMPHLET : folleto *m*

traction *n* : tracción *f*

tractor *n* **1** : tractor *m* **2** *or* ~ **-trailer** : camión *m* (con remolque)

trade *n* **1** PROFESSION : oficio *m* **2** COMMERCE : comercio *m* **3** INDUSTRY : industria *f* **4** EXCHANGE : cambio *m* — ~ *v* **traded; trading** *vi* : comerciar — *vt* ~ **sth with s.o.** : cambiar algo a algn — **trademark** *n* : marca *f* registrada

tradition *n* : tradición *f* — **traditional** *adj* : tradicional

traffic *n* : tráfico *m* — ~ *vi* **trafficked; trafficking** ~ **in** : traficar con — **traffic light** *n* : semáforo *m*

tragedy *n, pl* **-dies** : tragedia *f* — **tragic** *adj* : trágico

trail *vi* **1** DRAG : arrastrar **2** LAG : rezagarse **3** ~ **off** : apagarse — *vt* **1** DRAG : arrastrar **2** PURSUE : seguir la pista de — ~ *n* **1** : rastro *m*, huellas *fpl* **2** PATH : sendero *m* — **trailer** *n* **1** : remolque *m* **2** : caravana *f* (vivienda)

train *n* **1** : tren *m* **2** : cola *f* (de un vestido) **3** SERIES : serie *f* **4** ~ **of thought** : hilo *m* (de las ideas) — ~ *vt* **1** : adiestrar, entrenar (atletas, etc.) **2** AIM : apuntar — *vi* : prepararse, entrenarse (en deportes, etc.) — **trainer** *n* : entrenador *m*, -dora *f*

trait *n* : rasgo *m*

traitor *n* : traidor *m*, -dora *f*

tramp *vi* : caminar (pesadamente) — ~ *n* VAGRANT : vagabundo *m*, -da *f*

trample *vt* **-pled; -pling** : pisotear

trampoline *n* : trampolín *m*

trance *n* : trance *m*

tranquillity *or* **tranquility** *n* : tranquilidad *f* — **tranquil** *adj* : tranquilo — **tranquilize** *vt* **-ized; -izing** : tranquilizar — **tranquilizer** *n* : tranquilizante *m*

transaction *n* : transacción *f*

transatlantic *adj* : transatlántico

transcend *vt* **1** : ir más allá de **2** OVERCOME : superar

transcribe *vt* **-scribed; -scribing** : transcribir — **transcript** *n* : transcripción *f*

transfer *v* **-ferred; -ferring** *vt* **1** : transferir (fondos, etc.) **2** : trasladar (a un empleado, etc.) — *vi* **1** : cambiarse (de escuelas, etc.) **2** : hacer transbordo (entre trenes, etc.) — ~ *n* **1** : transferencia *f* (de fondos, etc.), traslado *m* (de una persona) **2** : boleto *m* (para hacer transbordo) **3** DECAL : calcomanía *f*

transform *vt* : transformar — **transformation** *n* : transformación *f*

transfusion *n* : transfusión *f*

transgression *n* : transgresión *f* — **transgress** *vt* : transgredir

transient *adj* : pasajero

transit *n* **1** : tránsito *m* **2** TRANSPORTATION : transporte *m* — **transition** *n* : transición *f* — **transitive** *adj* : transitivo — **transitory** *adj* : transitorio

translate *vt* **-lated; -lating** : traducir — **translation** *n* : traducción *f* — **translator** *n* : traductor *m*, -tora *f*

translucent *adj* : translúcido

transmit *vt* **-mitted; -mitting** : transmitir — **transmission** *n* : transmisión *f* — **transmitter** *n* : transmisor *m*

transparent *adj* : transparente — **transparency** *n, pl* **-cies** : transparencia *f*

transpire *vi* **-spired; -spiring** **1** TURN OUT : resultar **2** HAPPEN : suceder

transplant *vt* : trasplantar — ~ *n* : trasplante *m*

transport *vt* : transportar — ~ *n* : transporte *m* — **transportation** *n* : transporte *m*

transpose *vt* **-posed; -posing** **1** : trasponer **2** : transportar (en música)

trap *n* : trampa *f* — ~ *vt* **trapped; trapping** : atrapar — **trapdoor** *n* : trampilla *f*

trapeze *n* : trapecio *m*

trappings *npl* : adornos *mpl*, atavíos *mpl*

trash *n* : basura *f*

trauma *n* : trauma *m* — **traumatic** *adj* : traumático

travel *vi* **-eled** *or* **-elled; -eling** *or* **-elling** **1** : viajar **2** MOVE : desplazarse — ~ *n* : viajes *mpl* — **traveler** *or* **traveller** *n* : viajero *m*, -ra *f*

traverse *vt* **-versed; -versing** : atravesar

travesty *n, pl* **-ties** : parodia *f*

trawl *vi* : pescar (con red de arrastre) — **trawler** *n* : barco *m* de pesca

tray *n* : bandeja *f*

treachery *n, pl* **-eries** : traición *f* — **treacherous** *adj* **1** : traidor **2** DANGEROUS : peligroso

tread *v* **trod; trodden** *or* **trod; treading** *vt* **1** *or* ~ **on** : pisar **2** ~ **water** : flotar — *vi* **1** STEP : pisar **2** WALK : caminar — ~ *n* **1** STEP : paso *m* **2** : banda *f* de rodadura (de un neumático) — **treadmill** *n* : rueda *f* de andar

treason *n* : traición *f* (a la patria)

treasure *n* : tesoro *m* — ~ *vt* **-sured; -suring** : apreciar — **treasurer** *n* : tesorero *m*, -ra *f* — **treasury** *n, pl* **-suries** : erario *m*, tesoro *m*

treat *vt* **1** : tratar **2** CONSIDER : considerar **3** ~ **s.o. to (dinner, etc.)** : invitar a algn (a cenar, etc.) — ~ *n* **1** : gusto *m*, placer *m* **2** **it's my** ~ : invito yo

treatise *n* : tratado *m*

treatment *n* : tratamiento *m*

treaty *n, pl* **-ties** : tratado *m*

treble *adj* **1** TRIPLE : triple **2** : de tiple (en música) — ~ *vt* **-bled; -bling** : triplicar — **treble clef** : clave *f* de sol

tree *n* : árbol *m*

trek *vi* **trekked; trekking** : viajar (con dificultad) — ⁓ *n* : viaje *m* difícil

trellis *n* : enrejado *m*

tremble *vi* **-bled; -bling** : temblar

tremendous *adj* : tremendo

tremor *n* : temblor *m*

trench *n* **1** : zanja *f* **2** : trinchera *f* (militar)

trend *n* **1** : tendencia *f* **2** FASHION : moda *f* — **trendy** *adj* **trendier; -est** : de moda

trepidation *n* : inquietud *f*

trespass *vi* : entrar ilegalmente (en propiedad ajena)

trial *n* **1** : juicio *m*, proceso *m* **2** TEST : prueba *f* **3** ORDEAL : dura prueba *f* — ⁓ *adj* : de prueba

triangle *n* : triángulo *m* — **triangular** *adj* : triangular

tribe *n* : tribu *f* — **tribal** *adj* : tribal

tribulation *n* : tribulación *f*

tribunal *n* : tribunal *m*

tribute *n* : tributo *m* — **tributary** *n*, *pl* **-taries** : afluente *m*

trick *n* **1** : trampa *f* **2** PRANK : broma *f* **3** KNACK, FEAT : truco *m* **4** : baza *f* (en naipes) — ⁓ *vt* : engañar — **trickery** *n* : engaño *m*

trickle *vi* **-led; -ling** : gotear — ⁓ *n* : goteo *m*

tricky *adj* **trickier; -est 1** SLY : astuto, taimado **2** DIFFICULT : difícil

tricycle *n* : triciclo *m*

trifle *n* **1** TRIVIALITY : nimiedad *f* **2 a ⁓** : un poco — ⁓ *vi* **-fled; -fling ⁓ with** : jugar con — **trifling** *adj* : insignificante

trigger *n* : gatillo *m* — ⁓ *vt* : causar, provocar

trill *n* : trino *m* — ⁓ *vi* : trinar

trillion *n* : billón *m*

trilogy *n*, *pl* **-gies** : trilogía *f*

trim *vt* **trimmed; trimming 1** : recortar **2** ADORN : adornar — ⁓ *adj* **trimmer; trimmest 1** SLIM : esbelto **2** NEAT : arreglado — ⁓ *n* **1** : recorte *m* **2** DECORATION : adornos *mpl* **3 in ⁓** : en buena forma — **trimming** *npl* **1** : adornos *mpl* **2** GARNISH : guarnición *f*

Trinity *n* : Trinidad *f*

trinket *n* : chuchería *f*

trio *n*, *pl* **trios** : trío *m*

trip *v* **tripped; tripping** *vi* **1** : caminar (a paso ligero) **2** STUMBLE : tropezar **3 ⁓ up** : equivocarse — *vt* **1** ACTIVATE : activar **2 ⁓ s.o.** : hacer una zancadilla a algn **3 ⁓ s.o. up** : hacer equivocar a algn — ⁓ *n* **1** : viaje *m* **2** STUMBLE : traspié *m*

tripe *n* **1** : mondongo *m*, callos *mpl* **2** NONSENSE : tonterías *fpl*

triple *vt* **-pled; -pling** : triplicar — ⁓ *n* : triple *m* — ⁓ *adj* : triple — **triplet** *n* : trillizo *m*, -za *f* — **triplicate** *n* : triplicado *m*

tripod *n* : trípode *m*

trite *adj* **triter; tritest** : trillado

triumph *n* : triunfo *m* — ⁓ *vi* : triunfar — **triumphal** *adj* : triunfal — **triumphant** *adj* : triunfante

trivial *adj* : trivial — **trivia** *ns & pl* : trivialidades *fpl* — **triviality** *n*, *pl* **-ties** : trivialidad *f*

trod, trodden → **tread**

trolley *n*, *pl* **-leys** : tranvía *m*

trombone *n* : trombón *m*

troop *n* **1** : escuadrón *m* (de caballería), compañía *f* (de soldados) **2 ⁓s** *npl* : tropas *fpl* — ⁓ *vi* **in/out** : entrar/salir en tropel — **trooper** *n* **1** : soldado *m* **2 or state ⁓** : policía *mf* estatal

trophy *n*, *pl* **-phies** : trofeo *m*

tropic *n* **1** : trópico *m* **2 the ⁓s** : el trópico — ⁓ *or* **tropical** *adj* : tropical

trot *n* : trote *m* — ⁓ *vi* **trotted; trotting** : trotar

trouble *v* **-bled; -bling** *vt* **1** WORRY : preocupar **2** BOTHER : molestar — *vi* : molestarse — ⁓ *n* **1** PROBLEMS : problemas *mpl* **2** EFFORT : molestia *f* **3 be in ⁓** : estar en apuros **4 get in ⁓** : meterse en problemas **5 I had ⁓ doing it** : me costó hacerlo — **troublemaker** *n* : alborotador *m*, -dora *f* — **troublesome** *adj* : problemático

trough *n*, *pl* **troughs 1** : depresión *f* **2 or feeding ⁓** : comedero *m* **3 or drinking ⁓** : bebedero *m*

troupe *n* : compañía *f* (de teatro)

trousers *npl* : pantalón *m*, pantalones *mpl*

trout *n*, *pl* **trout** : trucha *f*

trowel *n* : paleta *f* (de albañil), desplantador *m* (de jardinero)

truant *n* : alumno *m*, -na *f* que falta a clase

truce *n* : tregua *f*

truck *vt* : transportar en camión — ⁓ *n* **1** : camión *m* **2** CART : carro *m* — **trucker** *n* : camionero *m*, -ra *f*

trudge *vi* **trudged; trudging** : caminar a paso pesado

true *adj* **truer; truest 1** : verdadero **2** LOYAL : fiel **3** GENUINE : auténtico **4 be ⁓** : ser cierto, ser verdad

truffle *n* : trufa *f*

truly *adv* : verdaderamente

trump *n* : triunfo *m* (en naipes)

trumpet *n* : trompeta *f*

trunk *n* **1** STEM, TORSO : tronco *m* **2** : trompa *f* (de un elefante) **3** : baúl *m* (equipaje) **4** : maletero *m* (de un auto) **5 ⁓s** *npl* : traje *m* de baño (de hombre)

truss *n* **1** FRAMEWORK : armazón *m* **2** : braguero *m* (en medicina)

trust n **1** CONFIDENCE : confianza f **2** HOPE : esperanza f **3** CREDIT : crédito m **4** : trust m (en finanzas) **5 in ~** : en fideicomiso — **~ vi 1** : confiar **2** HOPE : esperar — **vt 1** : confiar en, fiarse de (en frases negativas) **2 ~ s.o. with sth** : confiar algo a algn — **trustee** n : fideicomisario m, -ria f — **trustworthy** adj : digno de confianza

truth n, pl **truths** : verdad f — **truthful** adj : sincero, veraz

try v **tried; trying** vt **1** ATTEMPT : tratar (de), intentar **2** : juzgar (un caso, etc.) **3** TEST : poner a prueba **4** or **~ out** : probar **5 ~ on** : probarse (ropa) — vi : hacer un esfuerzo — **~** n, pl **tries** : intento m — **trying** adj **1** ANNOYING : irritante, pesado **2** DIFFICULT : duro — **tryout** n : prueba f

tsar → czar

T-shirt n : camiseta f

tub n **1** : cuba f, tina f **2** CONTAINER : envase m **3** BATHTUB : bañera f

tuba n : tuba f

tube n **1** : tubo m **2** or **inner ~** : cámara f **3 the ~** : la tele

tuberculosis n, pl **-loses** : tuberculosis f

tubing n : tubería f — **tubular** adj : tubular

tuck vt **1** : meter **2 ~ away** : guardar **3 ~ in** : meter por dentro (una blusa, etc.) **4 ~ s.o. in** : arropar a algn — **~** n : jareta f

Tuesday n : martes m

tuft n : mechón m (de pelo), penacho m (de plumas)

tug vt **tugged; tugging** or **~ at** : tirar de, jalar de — **~** n : tirón m, jalón m — **tugboat** n : remolcador m — **tug-of-war** n, pl **tugs-of-war** : tira y afloja m

tuition n **1** : enseñanza f **2** or **~ fees** : matrícula f

tulip n : tulipán m

tumble vi **-bled; -bling** : caerse — **~** n : caída f — **tumbler** n : vaso m (sin pie)

tummy n, pl **-mies** : barriga f, panza f

tumor n : tumor m

tumult n : tumulto m — **tumultuous** adj : tumultuoso

tuna n, pl **-na** or **-nas** : atún m

tune n **1** MELODY : melodía f **2** SONG : tonada f **3 in ~** : afinado **4 out of ~** : desafinado — **~** v **tuned; tuning** vt : afinar — vi **~ in** : sintonizar — **tuner** n **1** : afinador m, -dora f (de pianos, etc.) **2** : sintonizador m (de un receptor)

tunic n : túnica f

tunnel n : túnel m — **~** vi **-neled** or **-nelled; -neling** or **-nelling** : hacer un túnel

turban n : turbante m

turbine n : turbina f

turbulent adj : turbulento — **turbulence** n : turbulencia f

turf n **1** GRASS : césped m **2** SOD : tepe m

turgid adj : ampuloso (dícese de prosa, etc.)

turkey n, pl **-keys** : pavo m

turmoil n : confusión f

turn vt **1** : hacer girar (una rueda, etc.), volver (la cabeza, una página, etc.) **2** : dar la vuelta a (una esquina) **3** SPRAIN : torcer **4 ~ down** REFUSE : rechazar **5 ~ down** LOWER : bajar **6 ~ in** : entregar **7 ~ off** : cerrar (una llave), apagar (la luz, etc.) **8 ~ on** : abrir (una llave), encender, prender Lat (la luz, etc.) **9 ~ out** EXPEL : echar **10 ~ out** PRODUCE : producir **11 ~ out → turn off 12** or **~ over** FLIP : dar la vuelta a, voltear Lat **13 ~ over** TRANSFER : entregar **14 ~ s.o.'s stomach** : revolver el estómago a algn **15 ~ sth into sth** : convertir algo en algo **16 ~ up** RAISE : subir — vi **1** ROTATE : girar, dar vueltas **2** BECOME : ponerse **3** SOUR : agriarse **4** RESORT : recurrir **5** or **~ around** : darse la vuelta, volverse **6 ~ into** : convertirse en **7 ~ left** : doblar a la izquierda **8 ~ out** COME : acudir **9 ~ out** RESULT : resultar **10 ~ up** APPEAR : aparecer — **~** n **1** : vuelta f **2** CHANGE : cambio m **3** CURVE : curva f **4 do a good ~** : hacer un favor **5 whose ~ is it?** : ¿a quién le toca?

turnip n : nabo m

turnout n : concurrencia f — **turnover** n **1** : tartaleta f (postre) **2** : volumen m (de ventas) **3** : movimiento f (de personal) — **turnpike** n : carretera f de peaje — **turntable** n : plato m giratorio

turpentine n : trementina f

turquoise n : turquesa f

turret n **1** : torrecilla f **2** : torreta f (de un tanque, etc.)

turtle n : tortuga f (marina) — **turtleneck** n : cuello m de tortuga

tusk n : colmillo m

tussle n : pelea f — **~** vi **-sled; -sling** : pelearse

tutor n : profesor m, -sora f particular — **~** vt : dar clases particulares a

tuxedo n, pl **-dos** or **-does** : esmoquin m, smoking m

TV → television

twang n **1** : tañido m **2** : acento m nasal (de la voz)

tweak vt : pellizcar — **~** n : pellizco m

tweed n : tweed m

tweet n : gorjeo m, pío m — **~** vi : piar

tweezers npl : pinzas fpl

twelve adj : doce — **~** n : doce m — **twelfth** adj : duodécimo — **~** n **1** : duodécimo m, -ma f (en una serie) **2** : doceavo m (en matemáticas)

twenty adj : veinte — **~** n, pl **-ties** : veinte

m — **twentieth** *adj* : vigésimo — ~ *n* 1 : vigésimo *m*, -ma *f* (en una serie) 2 : veinteavo *m* (en matemáticas)

twice *adv* 1 : dos veces 2 ~ **as much/many as** : el doble de (algo), el doble que (algn)

twig *n* : ramita *f*

twilight *n* : crepúsculo *m*

twin *n* : gemelo *m*, -la *f*; mellizo *m*, -za *f* — ~ *adj* : gemelo, mellizo

twine *n* : cordel *m*, bramante *m Spain*

twinge *n* : punzada *f*

twinkle *vi* **-kled; -kling** 1 : centellear 2 : brillar (dícese de los ojos) — ~ *n* : centelleo *m*, brillo *m* (de los ojos)

twirl *vt* : girar, dar vueltas a — *vi* : girar, dar vueltas — ~ *n* : giro *m*, vuelta *f*

twist *vt* 1 : retorcer 2 TURN : girar 3 SPRAIN : torcerse 4 : tergiversar (palabras) — *vi* 1 : retorcerse 2 COIL : enrollarse 3 : serpentear (entre montañas, etc.) — ~ *n* 1 BEND : vuelta *f* 2 TURN : giro *m* 3 ~ **of lemon** : rodajita *f* de limón — **twister** → **tornado**

twitch *vi* : moverse (espasmódicamente) — ~ *n* : tic *m* nervioso

two *adj* : dos — ~ *n, pl* **twos** : dos *m* — **twofold** *adj* : doble — ~ *adv* : al doble — **two hundred** *adj* : doscientos — ~ *n* : doscientos *m*

tycoon *n* : magnate *mf*

tying → **tie**

type *n* : tipo *m* — ~ *v* **typed; typing** : escribir a máquina — **typewritten** *adj* : escrito a máquina — **typewriter** *n* : máquina *f* de escribir

typhoon *n* : tifón *m*

typical *adj* : típico, característico — **typify** *vt* **-fied; -fying** : tipificar

typist *n* : mecanógrafo *m*, -fa *f*

typography *n* : tipografía *f*

tyranny *n, pl* **-nies** : tiranía *f* — **tyrant** *n* : tirano *m*, -na *f*

tzar → **czar**

U

u *n, pl* **u's** *or* **us** : u *f*, vigésima primera letra del alfabeto inglés

udder *n* : ubre *f*

UFO (*unidentified flying object*) *n, pl* **UFO's** *or* **UFOs** : ovni *m*, OVNI *m*

ugly *adj* **uglier; -est** : feo — **ugliness** *n* : fealdad *f*

ulcer *n* : úlcera *f*

ulterior *adj* ~ **motive** : segunda intención *f*

ultimate *adj* 1 FINAL : final, último 2 UTMOST : máximo 3 FUNDAMENTAL : fundamental — **ultimately** *adv* 1 FINALLY : por último, finalmente 2 EVENTUALLY : a la larga

ultimatum *n, pl* **-tums** *or* **-ta** : ultimátum *m*

ultraviolet *adj* : ultravioleta

umbilical cord *n* : cordón *m* umbilical

umbrella *n* : paraguas *m*

umpire *n* : árbitro *m*, -tra *f* — ~ *vt* **-pired; -piring** : arbitrar

umpteenth *adj* : enésimo

unable *adj* 1 : incapaz 2 **be** ~ **to** : no poder

unabridged *adj* : íntegro

unacceptable *adj* : inaceptable

unaccountable *adj* : inexplicable

unaccustomed *adj* **be** ~ **to** : no estar acostumbrado a

unadulterated *adj* : puro

unaffected *adj* 1 : no afectado 2 NATURAL : sin afectación, natural

unafraid *adj* : sin miedo

unaided *adj* : sin ayuda

unanimous *adj* : unánime

unannounced *adj* : sin dar aviso

unarmed *adj* : desarmado

unassuming *adj* : modesto, sin pretensiones

unattached *adj* 1 : suelto 2 UNMARRIED : soltero

unattractive *adj* : poco atractivo

unauthorized *adj* : no autorizado

unavailable *adj* : no disponible

unavoidable *adj* : inevitable

unaware *adj* 1 : inconsciente 2 **be** ~ **of** : ignorar — **unawares** *adv* **catch s.o.** ~ : agarrar a algn desprevenido

unbalanced *adj* : desequilibrado

unbearable *adj* : inaguantable, insoportable

unbelievable *adj* : increíble

unbending *adj* : inflexible

unbiased *adj* : imparcial

unborn *adj* : aún no nacido

unbreakable *adj* : irrompible

unbridled *adj* : desenfrenado

unbroken *adj* 1 INTACT : intacto 2 CONTINUOUS : continuo

unbutton *vt* : desabrochar, desabotonar
uncalled–for *adj* : inapropiado, innecesario
uncanny *adj* **-nier; -est** : extraño, misterioso
unceasing *adj* : incesante
unceremonious *adj* **1** INFORMAL : poco ceremonioso **2** ABRUPT : brusco
uncertain *adj* **1** : incierto **2 in no ~ terms** : de forma vehemente — **uncertainty** *n, pl* **-ties** : incertidumbre *f*
unchanged *adj* : igual, sin alterar — **unchanging** *adj* : inmutable
uncivilized *adj* : incivilizado
uncle *n* : tío *m*
unclear *adj* : poco claro
uncomfortable *adj* **1** : incómodo **2** DISCONCERTING : inquietante, desagradable
uncommon *adj* : raro
uncompromising *adj* : intransigente
unconcerned *adj* : indiferente
unconditional *adj* : incondicional
unconscious *adj* : inconsciente
unconstitutional *adj* : inconstitucional
uncontrollable *adj* : incontrolable
unconventional *adj* : poco convencional
uncouth *adj* : grosero
uncover *vt* **1** : destapar **2** REVEAL : descubrir
undecided *adj* : indeciso
undeniable *adj* : innegable
under *adv* **1** : debajo **2** LESS : menos **3** *or* **~ anesthetic** : bajo los efectos de la anestesia — **~** *prep* **1** BELOW, BENEATH : debajo de, abajo de **2 ~ 20 minutes** : menos de 20 minutos **3 ~ the circumstances** : dadas las circunstancias
underage *adj* : menor de edad
underclothes → **underwear**
undercover *adj* : secreto
undercurrent *n* : tendencia *f* oculta
underdeveloped *adj* : subdesarrollado
underestimate *vt* **-mated; -mating** : subestimar
underfoot *adv* : bajo los pies
undergo *vt* **-went; -gone; -going** : sufrir, experimentar
undergraduate *n* : estudiante *m* universitario, estudiante *f* universitaria
underground *adv* **1** : bajo tierra **2 go ~** : pasar a la clandestinidad — **~** *adj* **1** : subterráneo **2** SECRET : secreto, clandestino — **~** *n* : movimiento *m* clandestino
undergrowth *n* : maleza *f*
underhanded *adj* SLY : solapado
underline *vt* **-lined; -lining** : subrayar
underlying *adj* : subyacente
undermine *vt* **-mined; -mining** : socavar, minar
underneath *adv* : debajo, abajo — **~** *prep* : debajo de, abajo de *Lat*

underpants *npl* : calzoncillos *mpl*, calzones *mpl Lat*
underpass *n* : paso *m* inferior
underprivileged *adj* : desfavorecido
underrate *vt* **-rated; -rating** : subestimar
undershirt *n* : camiseta *f*
understand *v* **-stood** ; **-standing** : comprender, entender — **understandable** *adj* : comprensible — **understanding** *adj* : comprensivo, compasivo — **~** *n* **1** : comprensión *f* **2** AGREEMENT : acuerdo *m*
understatement *n* **that's an ~** : decir sólo eso es quedarse corto
understudy *n, pl* **-dies** : sobresaliente *mf* (en el teatro)
undertake *vt* **-took; -taken; -taking** : emprender (una tarea), encargarse de (una responsabilidad) — **undertaker** *n* : director *m*, -tora *f* de una funeraria — **undertaking** *n* : empresa *f*, tarea *f*
undertone *n* **1** : voz *f* baja **2** SUGGESTION : matiz *m*
undertow *n* : resaca *f*
underwater *adj* : submarino — **~** *adv* : debajo (del agua)
under way *adv* **get ~** : ponerse en marcha
underwear *n* : ropa *f* interior
underwent → **undergo**
underworld *n* **the ~** CRIMINALS : la hampa, los bajos fondos
underwriter *n* : asegurador *m*, -dora *f*
undesirable *adj* : indeseable
undeveloped *adj* : sin desarrollar
undignified *adj* : indecoroso
undisputed *adj* : indiscutible
undo *vt* **-did; -done; -doing 1** UNFASTEN : deshacer, desatar **2** : reparar (daños, etc.)
undoubtedly *adv* : indudablemente
undress *vt* : desnudar — *vi* : desnudarse
undue *adj* : indebido, excesivo
undulate *vi* **-lated; -lating** : ondular
unduly *adv* : excesivamente
undying *adj* : eterno
unearth *vt* : desenterrar
unearthly *adj* **-lier; -est** : sobrenatural, de otro mundo
uneasy *adj* **-easier; -est 1** AWKWARD : incómodo **2** WORRIED : inquieto **3** RESTLESS : agitado — **uneasily** *adv* : inquietamente — **uneasiness** *n* : inquietud *f*
uneducated *adj* : inculto
unemployed *adj* : desempleado — **unemployment** *n* : desempleo *m*
unerring *adj* : infalible
unethical *adj* : poco ético
uneven *adj* **1** : desigual **2** : impar (dícese de un número)
unexpected *adj* : inesperado

unfailing *adj* **1** CONSTANT : constante **2** IN-EXHAUSTIBLE : inagotable

unfair *adj* : injusto — **unfairly** *adv* : injustamente — **unfairness** *n* : injusticia *f*

unfaithful *adj* : infiel — **unfaithfulness** *n* : infidelidad *f*

unfamiliar *adj* **1** : desconocido **2 be ~ with** : desconocer

unfasten *vt* **1** : desabrochar (ropa, etc.) **2** UNDO : desatar (una cuerda, etc.)

unfavorable *adj* : desfavorable

unfeeling *adj* : insensible

unfinished *adj* : sin terminar

unfit *adj* **1** UNSUITABLE : impropio **2** UNSUITED : no apto, incapaz

unfold *vt* **1** : desplegar, desdoblar **2** REVEAL : revelar (un plan, etc.) — *vi* **1** : extenderse, desplegarse **2** DEVELOP : desarrollarse

unforeseen *adj* : imprevisto

unforgettable *adj* : inolvidable

unforgivable *adj* : imperdonable

unfortunate *adj* **1** UNLUCKY : desgraciado, desafortunado **2** INAPPROPRIATE : inoportuno — **unfortunately** *adv* : desgraciadamente

unfounded *adj* : infundado

unfriendly *adj* **-lier; -est** : poco amistoso

unfurl *vt* : desplegar

unfurnished *adj* : desamueblado

ungainly *adj* : desgarbado

ungodly *adj* **1** : impío **2 an ~ hour** : una hora intempestiva

ungrateful *adj* : desagradecido

unhappy *adj* **-pier; -est 1** SAD : infeliz, triste **2** UNFORTUNATE : desafortunado — **unhappily** *adv* **1** SADLY : tristemente **2** UNFORTUNATELY : desgraciadamente — **unhappiness** *n* : tristeza *f*

unharmed *adj* : salvo, ileso

unhealthy *adj* **-thier; -est 1** : malsano **2** SICKLY : enfermizo

unheard–of *adj* : sin precedente, insólito

unhook *vt* : desenganchar

unhurt *adj* : ileso

unicorn *n* : unicornio *m*

unification *n* : unificación *f*

uniform *adj* : uniforme — **~** *n* : uniforme *m* — **uniformity** *n, pl* **-ties** : uniformidad *f*

unify *vt* **-fied; -fying** : unificar

unilateral *adj* : unilateral

unimaginable *adj* : inconcebible

unimportant *adj* : insignificante

uninhabited *adj* : deshabitado, despoblado

uninjured *adj* : ileso

unintentional *adj* : involuntario

union *n* **1** : unión *f* **2** *or* **labor ~** : sindicato *m*, gremio *m Lat*

unique *adj* : único — **uniquely** *adv* EXCEPTIONALLY : excepcionalmente

unison *n* **in ~** : al unísono

unit *n* **1** : unidad *f* **2** : módulo *m* (de un mobiliario)

unite *v* **united; uniting** *vt* : unir — *vi* : unirse — **unity** *n, pl* **-ties 1** : unidad *f* **2** HARMONY : acuerdo *m*

universe *n* : universo *m* — **universal** *adj* : universal

university *n, pl* **-ties** : universidad *f*

unjust *adj* : injusto — **unjustified** *adj* : injustificado

unkempt *adj* **1** : descuidado, desaseado **2** : despeinado (dícese del pelo)

unkind *adj* : poco amable, cruel — **unkindness** *n* : falta *f* de amabilidad, crueldad *f*

unknown *adj* : desconocido

unlawful *adj* : ilegal

unless *conj* : a menos que, a no ser que

unlike *adj* : diferente — **~** *prep* : a diferencia de — **unlikelihood** *n* : improbabilidad *f* — **unlikely** *adj* **-lier; -est** : improbable

unlimited *adj* : ilimitado

unload *v* : descargar

unlock *vt* : abrir (con llave)

unlucky *adj* **-luckier; -est 1** UNFORTUNATE : desgraciado **2** : de mala suerte (dícese de un número, etc.)

unmarried *adj* : soltero

unmask *vt* : desenmascarar

unmistakable *adj* : inconfundible

unnatural *adj* **1** : anormal **2** AFFECTED : afectado, forzado

unnecessary *adj* : innecesario — **unnecessarily** *adv* : innecesariamente

unnerving *adj* : desconcertante

unnoticed *adj* : inadvertido

unobtainable *adj* : inasequible

unobtrusive *adj* : discreto

unofficial *adj* : no oficial

unorthodox *adj* : poco ortodoxo

unpack *vt* **1** : desempaquetar, desempacar *Lat* (un paquete, etc.) **2** : deshacer (una maleta) — *vi* : deshacer las maletas

unparalleled *adj* : sin igual

unpleasant *adj* : desagradable

unplug *vt* **-plugged; -plugging** : desconectar, desenchufar

unpopular *adj* : poco popular

unprecedented *adj* : sin precedente

unpredictable *adj* : imprevisible

unprepared *adj* **1** : no preparado **2** UNREADY : deprevenido

unqualified *adj* **1** : no calificado, sin título **2** COMPLETE : absoluto

unquestionable *adj* : indiscutible — **unquestioning** *adj* : incondicional

unravel *v* **-eled** *or* **-elled; -eling** *or* **-elling** *vt* : desenmarañar — *vi* : deshacerse

unreal *adj* : irreal — **unrealistic** *adj* : poco realista

unreasonable *adj* **1** : irrazonable **2** EXCESSIVE : excesivo

unrecognizable *adj* : irreconocible

unrelated *adj* : no relacionado

unrelenting *adj* : implacable

unreliable *adj* : que no es de fiar

unrepentant *adj* : impenitente

unrest *n* **1** : inquietud *f*, malestar *m* **2** *or* **political** ～ : disturbios *mpl*

unripe *adj* : verde, no maduro

unrivaled *or* **unrivalled** *adj* : incomparable, sin par

unroll *vt* : desenrollar — *vi* : desenrollarse

unruly *adj* : indisciplinado

unsafe *adj* : inseguro

unsaid *adj* : sin decir

unsanitary *adj* : antihigiénico

unsatisfactory *adj* : insatisfactorio

unscathed *adj* : ileso

unscrew *vt* : destornillar

unscrupulous *adj* : sin escrúpulos

unseemly *adj* **-lier; -est** : indecoroso

unseen *adj* **1** : no visto **2** UNNOTICED : inadvertido

unselfish *adj* : desinteresado

unsettle *vt* **-tled; -tling** DISTURB : perturbar — **unsettled** *adj* **1** CHANGEABLE : inestable **2** DISTURBED : agitado, inquieto **3** : variable (dícese del tiempo)

unsightly *adj* : feo

unskilled *adj* : no calificado — **unskillful** *adj* : torpe, poco hábil

unsociable *adj* : poco sociable

unsound *adj* **1** : defectuoso, erróneo **2 of** ～ **mind** : demente

unspeakable *adj* **1** : indecible **2** TERRIBLE : atroz

unstable *adj* : inestable

unsteady *adj* **1** : inestable **2** SHAKY : tembloroso

unsuccessful *adj* **1** : fracasado **2 be** ～ : no tener éxito

unsuitable *adj* **1** : inadecuado **2** INCONVENIENT : inconveniente

unsure *adj* : inseguro

unsuspecting *adj* : confiado

unsympathetic *adj* : indiferente

unthinkable *adj* : inconcebible

untidy *adj* : desordenado (dícese de una sala, etc.), desaliñado (dícese de una persona)

untie *vt* **-tied; -tying** *or* **-tieing** : desatar

until *prep* : hasta — ～ *conj* : hasta que

untimely *adj* **1** PREMATURE : prematuro **2** INOPPORTUNE : inoportuno

untold *adj* : incalculable

untoward *adj* **1** ADVERSE : adverso **2** IMPROPER : indecoroso

untroubled *adj* **1** : tranquilo **2 be** ～ **by** : no estar afectado por

untrue *adj* : falso

unused *adj* **1** NEW : nuevo **2 be** ～ **to** : no estar acostumbrado a

unusual *adj* : poco común, insólito — **unusually** *adv* : excepcionalmente

unveil *vt* : descubrir, revelar

unwanted *adj* : superfluo (dícese de un objeto), no deseado (dícese de un niño, etc.)

unwarranted *adj* : injustificado

unwelcome *adj* : inoportuno, molesto

unwell *adj* **be** ～ : sentirse mal

unwieldy *adj* : difícil de manejar

unwilling *adj* : poco dispuesto — **unwillingly** *adv* : de mala gana

unwind *v* **-wound; -winding** *vt* : desenrollar — *vi* **1** : desenrollarse **2** RELAX : relajarse

unwise *adj* : imprudente

unworthy *adj* **be** ～ **of** : no ser digno de

unwrap *vt* **-wrapped; -wrapping** : desenvolver

up *adv* **1** ABOVE : arriba **2** UPWARDS : hacia arriba **3 ten miles farther** ～ : diez millas más adelante **4** ～ **here/there** : aquí/allí arriba **5** ～ **north** : en el norte **6** ～ **until** : hasta — ～ *adj* **1** AWAKE : levantado **2** FINISHED : terminado **3 be** ～ **against** : enfrentarse con **4 be** ～ **on** : estar al corriente de **5 it's** ～ **to you** : depende de tí **6 prices are** ～ : los precios han aumentado **7 the sun is** ～ : ha salido el sol **8 what's** ～? : ¿qué pasa? — ～ *prep* **1 go** ～ **the river** : ir río arriba **2 go** ～ **the stairs** : subir la escalera **3** ～ **the coast** : a lo largo de la costa — ～ *v* **upped; upping** *vt* : aumentar — *vi* **she** ～ **and left** : agarró y se fue

upbringing *n* : educación *f*

upcoming *adj* : próximo

update *vt* **-dated; -dating** : poner al día, actualizar — ～ *n* : puesta *f* al día

upgrade *vt* **-graded; -grading** : elevar la categoría de (un puesto, etc.), mejorar (una facilidad, etc.)

upheaval *n* : trastorno *m*

uphill *adv* : cuesta arriba — ～ *adj* **1** : en subida **2 be an** ～ **battle** : ser muy difícil

uphold *vt* **-held; -holding** : sostener, apoyar

upholstery *n, pl* **-steries** : tapicería *f*

upkeep *n* : mantenimiento *m*

upon *prep* **1** : en, sobre **2** ～ **leaving** : al salir

upper *adj* : superior — ～ *n* : parte *f* superior (del calzado, etc.)

uppercase *adj* : mayúsculo

upper class *n* : clase *f* alta

upper hand *n* : ventaja *f*, dominio *m*

uppermost *adj* : más alto

upright *adj* **1** VERTICAL : vertical **2** ERECT : derecho **3** JUST : recto, honesto — **~** *n* : montante *m*, poste *m*

uprising *n* : insurrección *f*, revuelta *f*

uproar *n* COMMOTION : alboroto *m*

uproot *vt* : desarraigar

upset *vt* **-set; -setting 1** OVERTURN : volcar **2** DISTRESS : alterar, inquietar **3** DISRUPT : trastornar — **~** *adj* **1** DISTRESSED : alterado **2 have an ~ stomach** : estar mal del estómago — **~** *n* : trastorno *m*

upshot *n* : resultado *m* final

upside down *adv* **1** : al revés **2 turn ~** : volver — **upside– down** *adj* : al revés

upstairs *adv* : arriba — **~** *adj* : de arriba — **~** *ns & pl* : piso *m* de arriba

upstart *n* : advenedizo *m*, -za *f*

upstream *adv* : río arriba

upswing *n* **be on the ~** : estar mejorándose

up–to–date *adj* **1** : corriente, al día **2** MODERN : moderno

uptown *adv* : hacia la parte alta de la ciudad, hacia el distrito residencial

upturn *n* : mejora *f*, auge *m* (económico)

upward *or* **upwards** *adv* : hacia arriba — **upward** *adj* : ascendente, hacia arriba

uranium *n* : uranio *m*

urban *adj* : urbano

urbane *adj* : urbano, cortés

urge *vt* **urged; urging 1** PRESS : instar, exhortar **2 ~ on** : animar — **~** *n* : impulso *m*, ganas *fpl* — **urgency** *n, pl* **-cies** : urgencia *f* — **urgent** *adj* **1** : urgente **2 be ~** : urgir

urine *n* : orina *f* — **urinate** *vi* **-nated; -nating** : orinar

urn *n* : urna *f*

Uruguayan *adj* : uruguayo

us *pron* **1** (*as direct or indirect object*) : nos **2** (*as object of a preposition*) : nosotros, nosotras **3 both of ~** : nosotros dos **4 it's ~!** : ¡somos nosotros!

usage *n* : uso *m*

use *v* **used; using** *vt* **1** : usar **2** CONSUME : consumir, tomar (drogas, etc.) **3 ~ up** : agotar, consumir — *vi* **1 she ~d to dance** : acostumbraba bailar **2 winters ~d to be colder** : los inviernos solían ser más fríos — **~** *n* **1** : uso *m* **2 have no ~ for** : no necesitar **3 have the ~ of** : poder usar, tener acceso a **4 it's no ~!** : ¡es inútil! — **used** *adj* **1** SECONDHAND : usado **2 be ~ to** : estar acostumbrado a — **useful** *adj* : útil, práctico — **usefulness** *n* : utilidad *f* — **useless** *adj* : inútil — **user** *n* : usuario *m*, -ria *f*

usher *vt* **1** : acompañar, conducir **2 ~ in** : hacer entrar — **~** *n* : acomodador *m*, -dora *f*

usual *adj* **1** : habitual, usual **2 as ~** : como de costumbre — **usually** *adv* : usualmente

usurp *vt* : usurpar

utensil *n* : utensilio *m*

uterus *n, pl* **uteri** : útero *m*, matriz *f*

utility *n, pl* **-ties 1** : utilidad *f* **2** *or* **public ~** : empresa *f* de servicio público

utilize *vt* **-lized; -lizing** : utilizar

utmost *adj* **1** FARTHEST : extremo **2 of the ~ importance** : de suma importancia — **~** *n* **do one's ~** : hacer todo lo posible

utopia *n* : utopía *f* — **utopian** *adj* : utópico

utter¹ *adj* : absoluto, completo

utter² *vt* : decir, pronunciar (palabras) — **utterance** *n* : declaración *f*, expresión *f*

utterly *adv* : completamente, totalmente

V

v *n, pl* **v's** *or* **vs** : v *f*, vigésima segunda letra del alfabeto inglés

vacant *adj* **1** AVAILABLE : libre **2** UNOCCUPIED : desocupado **3** : vacante (dícese de un puesto) **4** : ausente (dícese de una mirada) — **vacancy** *n, pl* **-cies 1** : (puesto *m*) vacante *f* **2** : habitación *f* libre (en un hotel, etc.)

vacate *vt* **-cated; -cating** : desalojar, desocupar

vacation *n* : vacaciones *fpl*

vaccination *n* : vacunación *f* — **vaccinate** *vt*

-nated; -nating : vacunar — **vaccine** *n* : vacuna *f*

vacuum *n, pl* **vacuums** *or* **vacua** : vacío *m* — **~** *vt* : pasar la aspiradora por — **vacuum cleaner** *n* : aspiradora *f*

vagina *n, pl* **-nae** *or* **-nas** : vagina *f*

vagrant *n* : vagabundo *m*, -da *f*

vague *adj* **vaguer; -est** : vago, indistinto

vain *adj* **1** CONCEITED : vanidoso **2 in ~** : en vano

valentine *n* : tarjeta *f* del día de San Valentín

valiant *adj* : valiente, valeroso

valid *adj* : válido — **validate** *vt* **-dated; -dating** : validar — **validity** *n* : validez *f*
valley *n, pl* **-leys** : valle *m*
valor *n* : valor *m*, valentía *f*
value *n* : valor *m* — ~ *vt* **-ued; -uing** : valorar — **valuable** *adj* : valioso — **valuables** *npl* : objetos *mpl* de valor
valve *n* : válvula *f*
vampire *n* : vampiro *m*
van *n* : furgoneta *f*, camioneta *f*
vandal *n* : vándalo *m* — **vandalism** *n* : vandalismo *m* — **vandalize** *vt* : destrozar, destruir
vane *n or* **weather** ~ : veleta *f*
vanguard *n* : vanguardia *f*
vanilla *n* : vainilla *f*
vanish *vi* : desaparecer
vanity *n, pl* **-ties** **1** : vanidad *f* **2** *or* ~ **table** : tocador *m*
vantage point *n* : posición *f* ventajosa
vapor *n* : vapor *m*
variable *adj* : variable — ~ *n* : variable *f* — **variance** *n* **at** ~ **with** : en desacuerdo con — **variant** *n* : variante *f* — **variation** *n* : variación *f* — **varied** *adj* : variado — **variegated** *adj* : abigarrado, multicolor — **variety** *n, pl* **-ties** **1** : variedad *f* **2** ASSORTMENT : surtido *m* **3** SORT : clase *f* — **various** *adj* : varios, diversos
varnish *n* : barniz *f* — ~ *vt* : barnizar
vary *v* **varied; varying** : variar
vase *n* **1** : jarrón *m* **2** *or* **flower** ~ : florero *m*
vast *adj* : vasto, enorme — **vastness** *n* : inmensidad *f*
vat *n* : cuba *f*
vault[1] *vi* LEAP : saltar — ~ *n* : salto *m*
vault[2] *n* **1** DOME : bóveda *f* **2** *or* **bank** ~ : cámara *f* acorazada, bóveda *f* de seguridad *Lat* **3** CRYPT : cripta *f*
VCR (*videocassette recorder*) *n* : video *m*
veal *n* : (carne *f* de) ternera *f*
veer *vi* : virar
vegetable *adj* : vegetal — ~ *n* **1** : vegetal *m* (planta) **2** ~**s** *npl* : verduras *fpl* — **vegetarian** *n* : vegetariano *mf* — **vegetation** *n* : vegetación *f*
vehemence *n* : vehemencia *f* — **vehement** *adj* : vehemente
vehicle *n* : vehículo *m*
veil *n* : velo *m* — ~ *vt* **1** : cubrir con un velo **2** CONCEAL : velar
vein *n* **1** : vena *f* **2** : veta *f* (de un mineral, etc.)
velocity *n, pl* **-ties** : velocidad *f*
velvet *n* : terciopelo *m* — **velvety** *adj* : aterciopelado
vending machine *vt* : máquina *f* expendedora

vendor *n* : vendedor *m*, -dora *f*
veneer *n* **1** : chapa *f* **2** FACADE : apariencia *f*
venerable *adj* : venerable — **venerate** *vt* **-ated; -ating** : venerar — **veneration** *n* : veneración *f*
venereal *adj* : venéreo
venetian blind *n* : persiana *f* veneciana
Venezuelan *adj* : venezolano
vengeance *n* **1** : venganza *f* **2 take** ~ **on** : vengarse de — **vengeful** *adj* : vengativo
venison *n* : (carne *f* de) venado *m*
venom *n* : veneno *m* — **venomous** *adj* : venenoso
vent *vt* : desahogar — ~ *n* **1** *or* **air** ~ : rejilla *f* de ventilación **2** OUTLET : desahogo *m* — **ventilate** *vt* **-lated; -lating** : ventilar — **ventilation** *n* : ventilación *f* — **ventilator** *n* : ventilador *m*
ventriloquist *n* : ventrílocuo *m*, -cua *f*
venture *v* **-tured; -turing** *vt* **1** RISK : arriesgar **2** : aventurar (una opinión, etc.) — *vi* : atreverse — ~ *n or* **business** ~ : empresa *f*
venue *n* : lugar *m*
Venus *n* : Venus *m*
veranda *or* **verandah** *n* : veranda *f*
verb *n* : verbo *m* — **verbal** *adj* : verbal — **verbatim** *adv* : palabra por palabra — ~ *adj* : literal — **verbose** *adj* : verboso
verdict *n* **1** : veredicto *m* **2** OPINION : opinión *f*
verge *n* **1** : borde *m* **2 on the** ~ **of** : a punto de (hacer algo), al borde de (algo) — ~ *vi* **verged; verging** ~ **on** : rayar en
verify *vt* **-fied; -fying** : verificar — **verification** *n* : verificación *f*
vermin *ns & pl* : alimañas *fpl*
vermouth *n* : vermut *m*
versatile *adj* : versátil — **versatility** *n* : versatilidad *f*
verse *n* **1** LINE : verso *m* **2** POETRY : poesía *f* **3** : versículo *m* (en la Biblia) — **versed** *adj* **be well** ~ **in** : ser muy versado en
version *n* : versión *f*
versus *prep* : versus
vertebra *n, pl* **-brae** *or* **-bras** : vértebra *f*
vertical *adj* : vertical — ~ *n* : vertical *f*
vertigo *n, pl* **-goes** *or* **-gos** : vértigo *m*
verve *n* : brío *m*
very *adv* **1** : muy **2 at the** ~ **least** : por lo menos **3 the** ~ **same thing** : la misma cosa **4** ~ **much** : mucho **5** ~ **well** : muy bien — ~ *adj* **verier; -est** **1** PRECISE, SAME : mismo **2** MERE : solo, mero **3 the** ~ **thing** : justo lo que hacía falta
vessel *n* **1** CONTAINER : recipiente *m* **2** SHIP : nave *f*, buque *m* **3** *or* **blood** ~ : vaso *m* sanguíneo

vest *n* **1** : chaleco *m* **2** *Brit* UNDERSHIRT : camiseta *f*

vestibule *n* : vestíbulo *m*

vestige *n* : vestigio *m*

vet *n* **1** → **veterinarian** **2** → **veteran**

veteran *n* : veterano *m*, -na *f*

veterinarian *n* : veterinario *m*, -ria *f* — **veterinary** *adj* : veterinario

veto *n, pl* **-toes** : veto *m* — ~ *vt* : vetar

vex *vt* ANNOY : irritar

via *prep* : por, vía

viable *adj* : viable

viaduct *n* : viaducto *m*

vial *n* : frasco *m*

vibrant *adj* : vibrante — **vibrate** *vi* **-brated; -brating** : vibrar — **vibration** *n* : vibración *f*

vicar *n* : vicario *m*, -ria *f*

vicarious *adj* : indirecto

vice *n* : vicio *m*

vice president *n* : vicepresidente *m*, -ta *f*

vice versa *adv* : viceversa

vicinity *n, pl* **-ties** **1** : inmediaciones *fpl* **2 in the** ~ **of** ABOUT : alrededor de

vicious *adj* **1** SAVAGE : feroz **2** MALICIOUS : malicioso

victim *n* : víctima *f*

victor *n* : vencedor *m*, -dora *f*

victory *n, pl* **-ries** : victoria *f* — **victorious** *adj* : victorioso

video *n* : video *m*, vídeo *m Spain* — ~ *adj* : de video — **videocassette** *n* : videocasete *m* — **videotape** *n* : videocinta *f* — ~ *vt* **-taped; -taping** : videograbar

vie *vi* **vied; vying** : competir

Vietnamese *adj* : vietnamita

view *n* **1** : vista *f* **2** OPINION : opinión *f* **3 come into** ~ : aparecer **4 in** ~ **of** : en vista de (que) — ~ *vt* **1** : ver **2** CONSIDER : considerar — **viewer** *n or* **television** ~ : televidente *mf* — **viewpoint** *n* : punto *m* de vista

vigil *n* : vela *f* — **vigilance** *n* : vigilancia *f* — **vigilant** *adj* : vigilante

vigor *or Brit* **vigour** *n* : vigor *m* — **vigorous** *adj* **1** : enérgico **2** ROBUST : vigoroso

Viking *n* : vikingo *m*, -ga *f*

vile *adj* **viler; vilest** **1** : vil **2** REVOLTING : asqueroso **3** TERRIBLE : horrible

villa *n* : casa *f* de campo

village *n* : pueblo *m* (grande), aldea *f* (pequeña) — **villager** *n* : vecino *m*, -na *f* (de un pueblo); aldeano *m*, -na *f* (de una aldea)

villain *n* : villano *m*, -na *f*

vindicate *vt* **-cated; -cating** **1** : vindicar **2** JUSTIFY : justificar

vindictive *adj* : vengativo

vine *n* **1** : enredadera *f* **2** GRAPEVINE : vid *f*

vinegar *n* : vinagre *m*

vineyard *n* : viña *f*, viñedo *m*

vintage *n* **1** : cosecha *f* (de vino) **2** ERA : época *f* — ~ *adj* **1** : añejo (dícese de un vino) **2** CLASSIC : de época

vinyl *n* : vinilo *m*

viola *n* : viola *f*

violate *vt* **-lated; -lating** : violar — **violation** *n* : violación *f*

violence *n* : violencia *f* — **violent** *adj* : violento

violet *n* : violeta *f* (flor), violeta *m* (color)

violin *n* : violín *m* — **violinist** *n* : violinista *mf* — **violoncello** → **cello**

VIP *n, pl* **VIPs** : VIP *mf*

viper *n* : víbora *f*

virgin *n* : virgen *mf* — ~ *adj* **1** : virgen (dícese de la lana, etc.) **2** CHASTE : virginal — **virginity** *n* : virginidad *f*

virile *adj* : viril — **virility** *n* : virilidad *f*

virtual *adj* : virtual — **virtually** *adv* : prácticamente

virtue *n* **1** : virtud *f* **2 by** ~ **of** : en virtud de

virtuoso *n, pl* **-sos** *or* **-si** : virtuoso *m*, -sa *f*

virtuous *adj* : virtuoso

virulent *adj* : virulento

virus *n* : virus *m*

visa *n* : visado *m*, visa *f Lat*

vis-à-vis *prep* : con respecto a

viscous *adj* : viscoso

vise *n* : torno *m* de banco

visible *adj* **1** : visible **2** NOTICEABLE : evidente — **visibility** *n, pl* **-ties** : visibilidad *f*

vision *n* **1** : visión *f* **2 have** ~**s of** : imaginarse — **visionary** *adj* : visionario — ~ *n, pl* **-ries** : visionario *m*, -ria *f*

visit *vt* : visitar — *vi* **1** : hacer una visita **2 be** ~**ing** : estar de visita — ~ *n* : visita *f* — **visitor** *n* **1** : visitante *mf* **2** GUEST : visita *f*

visor *n* : visera *f*

vista *n* : vista *f*

visual *adj* : visual — **visualize** *vt* **-ized; -izing** : visualizar

vital *adj* **1** : vital **2** CRUCIAL : esencial — **vitality** *n, pl* **-ties** : vitalidad *f*, energía *f*

vitamin *n* : vitamina *f*

vivacious *adj* : vivaz, animado

vivid *adj* : vivo (dícese de colores), vívido (dícese de sueños, etc.)

vocabulary *n, pl* **-laries** : vocabulario *m*

vocal *adj* **1** : vocal **2** OUTSPOKEN : vociferante — **vocal cords** *npl* : cuerdas *fpl* vocales — **vocalist** *n* : cantante *mf*, vocalista *mf*

vocation *n* : vocación *f* — **vocational** *adj* : profesional

vociferous *adj* : vociferante, ruidoso

vodka *n* : vodka *m*

vogue *n* **1** : moda *f*, boga *f* **2 be in** ~ : estar de moda, estar en boga

voice *n* : voz *f* — ~ *vt* **voiced; voicing** : expresar

void *adj* **1** INVALID : nulo **2** ~ **of** : falto de — ~ *n* : vacío *m* — ~ *vt* : anular

volatile *adj* : volátil — **volatility** *n* : volatilidad *f*

volcano *n, pl* **-noes** *or* **-nos** : volcán *m* — **volcanic** *adj* : volcánico

volition *n* **of one's own** ~ : por voluntad propia

volley *n, pl* **-leys 1** : descarga *f* (de tiros) **2** : torrente *m* (de insultos, etc.) **3** : volea *f* (en deportes) — **volleyball** *n* : voleibol *m*

volt *n* : voltio *m* — **voltage** *n* : voltaje *m*

voluble *adj* : locuaz

volume *n* : volumen *m* — **voluminous** *adj* : voluminoso

voluntary *adj* : voluntario — **volunteer** *n* : voluntario *m*, -ria *f* — ~ *vt* : ofrecer — *vi* ~ **to** : ofrecerse a

voluptuous *adj* : voluptuoso

vomit *n* : vómito *m* — ~ *v* : vomitar

voracious *adj* : voraz

vote *n* **1** : voto *m* **2** SUFFRAGE : derecho *m* al voto — ~ *vi* **voted; voting** : votar — **voter** *n* : votante *mf* — **voting** *n* : votación *f*

vouch *vi* ~ **for** : responder de (algo), responder por (algn) — **voucher** *n* : vale *m*

vow *n* : voto *m* — ~ *vt* : jurar

vowel *n* : vocal *m*

voyage *n* : viaje *m*

vulgar *adj* **1** COMMON : ordinario **2** CRUDE : grosero, vulgar — **vulgarity** *n, pl* **-ties** : vulgaridad *f*

vulnerable *adj* : vulnerable — **vulnerability** *n, pl* **-ties** : vulnerabilidad *f*

vulture *n* : buitre *m*

vying → **vie**

W

w *n, pl* **w's** *or* **ws** : w *f*, vigésima tercera letra del alfabeto inglés

wad *n* : taco *m* (de papel, etc.), fajo *m* (de billetes)

waddle *vi* **-dled; -dling** : andar como un pato

wade *v* **waded; wading** *vi* : caminar por el agua — *vt or* ~ **across** : vadear

wafer *n* : barquillo *m*

waffle *n* : gofre *m Spain,* wafle *m Lat*

waft *vt* : llevar por el aire — *vi* : flotar

wag *v* **wagged; wagging** *vt* : menear — *vi* : menearse

wage *n or* **wages** *npl* : salario *m* — ~ *vt* **waged; waging** ~ **war** : hacer la guerra

wager *n* : apuesta *f* — ~ *v* : apostar

wagon *n* **1** CART : carrito *m* **2** → **station wagon**

waif *n* : niño *m* abandonado

wail *vi* : lamentarse — ~ *n* : lamento *m*

waist *n* : cintura *f* — **waistline** *n* : cintura *f*

wait *vi* : esperar — *vt* **1** AWAIT : esperar **2** ~ **tables** : servir a la mesa — ~ *n* **1** : espera *f* **2 lie in** ~ : estar al acecho — **waiter** *n* : camarero *m*, mozo *m Lat* — **waiting room** *n* : sala *f* de espera — **waitress** *n* : camarera *f*, moza *f Lat*

waive *vt* **waived; waiving** : renunciar a — **waiver** *n* : renuncia *f*

wake¹ *v* **woke; woken** *or* **waked; waking**

vi or ~ **up** : despertarse — *vt* : despertar — ~ *n* : velatorio *m* (de un difunto)

wake² *n* **1** : estela *f* (de un barco) **2 in the** ~ **of** : tras, como consecuencia de

waken *vt* : despertar — *vi* : despertarse

walk *vi* **1** : caminar, andar **2** STROLL : pasear **3 too far to** ~ : demasiado lejos para ir a pie — *vt* **1** : caminar por **2** : sacar a pasear (a un perro) — ~ *n* **1** : paseo *m* **2** PATH : camino *m* **3** GAIT : andar *m* — **walker** *n* **1** : paseante *mf* **2** HIKER : excursionista *mf* — **walking stick** *n* : bastón *m* — **walkout** *n* STRIKE : huelga *f* — **walk out** *vi* **1** STRIKE : declararse en huelga **2** LEAVE : salir, irse **3** ~ **on** : abandonar

wall *n* : muro *m* (exterior), pared *f* (interior), muralla *f* (de una ciudad)

wallet *n* : billetera *f*, cartera *f*

wallflower *n* **be a** ~ : comer pavo

wallop *vt* : pegar fuerte — ~ *n* : golpe *m* fuerte

wallow *vi* : revolcarse

wallpaper *n* : papel *m* pintado — ~ *vt* : empapelar

walnut *n* : nuez *f*

walrus *n, pl* **-rus** *or* **-ruses** : morsa *f*

waltz *n* : vals *m* — ~ *vi* : valsar

wan *adj* **wanner; -est** : pálido

wand *n* : varita *f* (mágica)

wander *vi* **1** : vagar, pasear **2** STRAY : diva-

gar — *vt* : pasear por — **wanderer** *n*
: vagabundo *m*, -da *f* — **wanderlust** *n*
: pasión *f* por viajar
wane *vi* **waned; waning** : menguar — **~** *n*
be on the ~ : estar disminuyendo
want *vt* **1** DESIRE : querer **2** NEED : necesitar **3** LACK : carecer de — **~** *n* **1** NEED
: necesidad *f* **2** LACK : falta *f* **3** DESIRE
: deseo *m* — **wanting** *adj* **be ~** : carecer
wanton *adj* **1** LEWD : lascivo **2 ~ cruelty**
: crueldad *f* despiadada
war *n* : guerra *f*
ward *n* **1** : sala *f* (de un hospital, etc.) **2**
: distrito *m* electoral **3** : pupilo *m*, -la *f* (de
un tutor, etc.) — **~** *vt* **~ off** : protegerse
contra — **warden** *n* **1** : guardián *m*, -diana *f*
2 *or* **game ~** : guardabosque *mf* **3** *or*
prison ~ : alcaide *m*
wardrobe *n* **1** CLOSET : armario *m* **2**
CLOTHES : vestuario *m*
warehouse *n* : almacén *m*, bodega *f Lat* —
wares *npl* : mercancías *fpl*
warfare *n* : guerra *f*
warily *adv* : cautelosamente
warlike *adj* : belicoso
warm *adj* **1** : caliente **2** LUKEWARM : tibio
3 CARING : cariñoso **4 I feel ~** : tengo
calor **5 ~ clothes** : ropa *f* de abrigo — *vt or* **~ up** : calentar — *vi* **1** *or* **~ up** : calentarse **2 ~ to** : tomar simpatía a (algn),
entusiasmarse con (algo) — **warm-
blooded** *adj* : de sangre caliente — **warm-
hearted** *adj* : cariñoso — **warmly** *adv* **1**
: calurosamente **2 dress ~** : abrigarse —
warmth *n* **1** : calor *m* **2** AFFECTION : cariño
m, afecto *m*
warn *vt* : advertir, avisar— **warning** *n* : advertencia *f*, aviso *m*
warp *vt* **1** : alabear (madera, etc.) **2** DISTORT
: deformar — *vi* : alabearse
warrant *n* **1** : autorización *f* **2 arrest ~**
: orden *f* judicial — **~** *vt* : justificar — **warranty** *n, pl* **-ties** : garantía *f*
warrior *n* : guerrero *m*, -ra *f*
warship *n* : buque *m* de guerra
wart *n* : verruga *f*
wartime *n* : tiempo *m* de guerra
wary *adj* **warier; -est** : cauteloso
was → **be**
wash *vt* **1** : lavar(se) **2** CARRY : arrastrar **3**
~ away : llevarse **4 ~ over** : bañar — *vi*
: lavarse — **~** *n* **1** : lavado *m* **2** LAUNDRY
: ropa *f* sucia — **washable** *adj* : lavable —
washcloth *n* : toallita *f* (para lavarse) —
washed–out *adj* **1** : desvaído (dícese de
colores) **2** EXHAUSTED : agotado —
washer *n* **1** → **washing machine 2** : aran-
dela *f* (de una llave, etc.) — **washing machine** *n* : máquina *f* de lavar, lavadora *f* —

washroom *n* : servicios *mpl* (públicos),
baño *m*
wasn't (*contraction of* **was not**) → **be**
wasp *n* : avispa *f*
waste *v* **wasted; wasting** *vt* **1** : desperdiciar, derrochar, malgastar **2 ~ time**
: perder tiempo — *vi or* **~ away** : consumirse — **~** *adj* : de desecho — **~** *n* **1**
: derroche *m*, desperdicio *m* **2** RUBBISH
: desechos *mpl* **3 a ~ of time** : una pérdida
de tiempo — **wastebasket** *n* : papelera *f* —
wasteful *adj* : derrochador — **wasteland** *n*
: yermo *m*
watch *vi* **1** : mirar **2** *or* **keep ~** : velar **3**
~ out! : ¡ten cuidado!, ¡ojo! — *vt* **1:** mirar
2 *or* **~ over** : vigilar, cuidar **3 ~ what
you do** : ten cuidado con lo que haces — **~**
n **1** reloj *m* **2** SURVEILLANCE : vigilancia *f* **3**
LOOKOUT : guardia *mf* — **watchdog** *n*
: perro *m* guardián — **watchful** *adj* : vigilante — **watchman** *n, pl* **-men** : vigilante *m*,
guarda *m* — **watchword** *n* : santo *m* y seña
water *n* : agua *f* — **~** *vt* **1** : regar (el jardín,
etc.) **2 ~ down** DILUTE : diluir, aguar — *vi*
1 : lagrimar (dícese de los ojos) **2 my
mouth is ~ing** : se me hace agua la boca
— **watercolor** *n* : acuarela *f* — **watercress**
n : berro *m* — **waterfall** *n* : cascada *f*, salto
m de agua — **water lily** *n* : nenúfar *m* — **wa-
terlogged** *adj* : lleno de agua, empapado —
watermelon *n* : sandía *f* — **waterpower** *n*
: energía *f* hidráulica — **waterproof** *adj*
: impermeable — **watershed** *n* **1** : cuenca *f*
(de un río) **2** : momento *m* crítico — **waterskiing** *n* : esquí *m* acuático — **watertight**
adj : hermético — **waterway** *n* : vía *f* navegable — **waterworks** *npl* : central *f* de
abastecimiento de agua — **watery** *adj* **1**
: acuoso **2** DILUTED : aguado, diluido **3**
WASHED-OUT : desvaído (dícese de colores)
watt *n* : vatio *m* — **wattage** *n* : vataje *m*
wave *v* **waved; waving** *vi* **1** : saludar con la
mano **2** : flotar (dícese de una bandera) —
vt **1** SHAKE : agitar **2** CURL : ondular **3** SIG-
NAL : hacer señas a (con la mano) — **~** *n* **1**
: ola *f* (de agua) **2** CURL : onda *f* **3** : onda *f*
(en física) **4** : señal *f* (con la mano) **5**
SURGE : oleada *f* — **wavelength** *n* : longitud *f* de onda
waver *vi* : vacilar
wax¹ *vi* : crecer (dícese de la luna)
wax² *n* **1** : cera *f* (para pisos, etc.) — **~** *vt*
: encerar — **waxy** *adj* **waxier; -est** : ceroso
way *n* **1** : camino *m* **2** MEANS : manera *f*,
modo *m* **3 by the ~** : a propósito, por
cierto **4 by ~ of** : vía, pasando por **5
come a long ~** : hacer grandes progresos
6 get in the ~ : meterse en el camino **7 get
one's own ~** : salirse uno con la suya **8**

mend one's ~s : dejar las malas costumbres **9 out of the ~** REMOTE : remoto, recóndito **10 which ~ did he go? :** ¿por dónde fue?

we *pron* : nosotros, nosotras

weak *adj* **1** : débil **2** DILUTED : aguado **3 a ~ excuse** : una excusa poco convincente — **weaken** *vt* : debilitar — *vi* : debilitarse — **weakling** *n* : debilucho *m*, -cha *f* — **weakly** *adv* : débilmente — **~** *adj* **weaklier; -est** : enfermizo — **weakness** *n* **1** : debilidad *f* **2** FLAW : flaqueza *f*, punto *m* débil

wealth *n* : riqueza *f* — **wealthy** *adj* **wealthier; -est** : rico

wean *vt* : destetar

weapon *n* : arma *f*

wear *v* **wore; worn; wearing** *vt* **1** : llevar (ropa, etc.), calzar (zapatos) **2** *or* **~ away** : desgastar **3 ~ oneself out** : agotarse **4 ~ out** : gastar — *vi* **1** LAST : durar **2 ~ off** : desaparecer **3 ~ out** : gastarse — **~** *n* **1** USE : uso *m* **2** CLOTHING : ropa *f* **3 be the worse for ~** : estar deteriorado — **wear and tear** *n* : desgaste *m*

weary *adj* **-rier; -est** : cansado — **~** *v* **-ried; -rying** *vt* : cansar — *vi* : cansarse — **weariness** *n* : cansancio *m* — **wearisome** *adj* : cansado

weasel *n* : comadreja *f*

weather *n* : tiempo *m* — **~** *vt* **1** WEAR : erosionar, desgastar **2** ENDURE, OVERCOME : superar — **weather-beaten** *adj* : curtido — **weatherman** *n*, *pl* **-men** : meteorólogo *m*, -ga *f* — **weather vane** *n* : valeta *f*

weave *v* **wove** *or* **weaved; woven** *or* **weaved; weaving** *vt* **1** : tejer (tela) **2** INTERLACE : entretejer **3 ~ one's way** : abrirse camino — *vi* : tejer — **~** *n* : tejido *m* — **weaver** *n* : tejedor *m*, -dora *f*

web *n* **1** : telaraña *f* (de araña) **2** : membrana *f* interdigital (de aves) **3** NETWORK : red *f*

wed *v* **wedded; wedding** *vt* : casarse con — *vi* : casarse

we'd (*contraction of* **we had, we should,** *or* **we would**) → **have, should, would**

wedding *n* : boda *f*, casamiento *m*

wedge *n* **1** : cuña *f* **2** PIECE : porción *f*, trozo *m* — **~** *vt* **wedged; wedging 1** : apretar (con una cuña) **2** CRAM : meter

Wednesday *n* : miércoles *m*

wee *adj* **1** : pequeñito **2 in the ~ hours** : a las altas horas

weed *n* : mala hierba *f* — **~** *vt* **1** : desherbar **2 ~ out** : eliminar

week *n* : semana *f* — **weekday** *n* : día *m* laborable — **weekend** *n* : fin *m* de semana — **weekly** *adv* : semanalmente — **~** *adj* : semanal — **~** *n*, *pl* **-lies** : semanario *m*

weep *v* **wept; weeping** : llorar — **weeping willow** *n* : sauce *m* llorón — **weepy** *adj* **weepier; -est** : lloroso

weigh *vt* **1** : pesar **2** CONSIDER : sopesar **3 ~ down** : sobrecargar (con una carga), abrumar (con preocupaciones, etc.) — *vi* : pesar

weight *n* **1** : peso *m* **2 gain ~** : engordar **3 lose ~** : adelgazar — **weighty** *adj* **weightier; -est 1** HEAVY : pesado **2** IMPORTANT : importante, de peso

weird *adj* **1** : misterioso **2** STRANGE : extraño

welcome *vt* **-comed; -coming** : dar la bienvenida a, recibir — **~** *adj* **1** : bienvenido **2 you're ~** : de nada — **~** *n* : bienvenida *f*, acojida *f*

weld *v* : soldar

welfare *n* **1** WELL-BEING : bienestar *m* **2** AID : asistencia *f* social

well¹ *adv* **better; best 1** : bien **2** CONSIDERABLY : bastante **3 as ~** : también **4 as ~ as** : además de — **~** *adj* : bien — **~** *interj* **1** (*used to introduce a remark*) : bueno **2** (*used to express surprise*) : ¡vaya!

well² *n* : pozo *m* — **~** *vi* *or* **~ up** : brotar, manar

we'll (*contraction of* **we shall** *or* **we will**) → **shall, will**

well-being *n* : bienestar *m* — **well-bred** *adj* : fino, bien educado — **well-done** *adj* **1** : bien hecho **2** : bien cocido (dícese de la carne, etc.) — **well-known** *adj* : famoso, bien conocido — **well-meaning** *adj* : bienintencionado — **well-off** *adj* : acomodado — **well-rounded** *adj* : completo — **well-to-do** *adj* : próspero, adinerado

Welsh *adj* : galés — **~** *n* **1** : galés *m* (idioma) **2 the ~** : los galeses

went → **go**

wept → **weep**

were → **be**

we're (*contraction of* **we are**) → **be**

weren't (*contraction of* **were not**) → **be**

west *adv* : al oeste — **~** *adj* : oeste, del oeste — **~** *n* **1** : oeste *m* **2 the West** : el Oeste, el Occidente — **westerly** *adv* & *adj* : del oeste — **western** *adj* **1** : del oeste **2 Western** : occidental — **Westerner** *n* : habitante *mf* del oeste — **westward** *adv* & *adj* : hacia el oeste

wet *adj* **wetter; wettest 1** : mojado **2** RAINY : lluvioso **3 ~ paint** : pintura *f* fresca — **~** *vt* **wet** *or* **wetted; wetting** : mojar, humedecer

we've (*contraction of* **we have**) → **have**

whack *vt* : golpear fuertemente — **~** *n* : golpe *m* fuerte

whale *n*, *pl* **whales** *or* **whale** : ballena *f*

wharf *n*, *pl* **wharves** : muelle *m*, embarcadero *m*

what *adj* **1** (*used in questions and exclamations*) : qué **2** WHATEVER : cualquier — ~ *pron* **1** (*used in questions*) : qué **2** (*used in indirect statements*) : lo que, que **3** ~ **does it cost?** : ¿cuánto cuesta? **4** ~ **for?** : ¿por qué? **5** ~ **if** : y si — **whatever** *adj* **1** : cualquier **2 there's no chance** ~ : no hay ninguna posibilidad **3 nothing** ~ : nada en absoluto — ~ *pron* **1** ANYTHING : lo que **2** (*used in questions*) : qué **3** ~ **it may be** : sea lo que sea — **whatsoever** *adj* & *pron* → **whatever**

wheat *n* : trigo *m*

wheedle *vt* **-dled; -dling** : engatusar

wheel *n* **1** : rueda *f* **2** *or* **steering** ~ : volante *m* (de automóviles, etc.), timón *m* (de barcos) — *vt* : empujar (algo sobre ruedas) — *vi or* ~ **around** : darse la vuelta — **wheelbarrow** *n* : carretilla *f* — **wheelchair** *n* : silla *f* de ruedas

wheeze *vi* **wheezed; wheezing** : resollar — ~ *n* : resuello *m*

when *adv* : cuándo — ~ *conj* **1** : cuando **2 the days** ~ **I clean the house** : los días (en) que limpio la casa — ~ *pron* : cuándo — **whenever** *adv* : cuando sea — ~ *conj* **1** : cada vez que **2** ~ **you like** : cuando quieras

where *adv* **1** : dónde **2** ~ **are you going?** : ¿adónde vas? — ~ *conj* & *pron* : donde — **whereabouts** *adv* : (por) dónde — ~ *ns* & *pl* : paradero *m* — **wherever** *adv* **1** : en cualquier parte **2** WHERE : dónde, adónde — ~ *conj* : dondequiera que

whet *vt* **whetted; whetting 1** : afilar **2** ~ **the appetite** : estimular el apetito

whether *conj* **1** : si **2 we doubt** ~ **he'll show up** : dudamos que aparezca **3** ~ **you like it or not** : tanto si quieras como si no

which *adj* **1** : qué, cuál **2 in** ~ **case** : en cuyo caso — ~ *pron* **1** (*used in questions*) : cuál **2** (*used in relative clauses*) : que, el (la) cual — **whichever** *adj* : cualquier — ~ *pron* : el (la) que, cualquiera que

whiff *n* **1** PUFF : soplo *m* **2** SMELL : olorcillo *m*

while *n* **1** : rato *m* **2 be worth one's** ~ : valer la pena **3 in a** ~ : dentro de poco — ~ *conj* **1** : mientras **2** WHEREAS : mientras que **3** ALTHOUGH : aunque — ~ *vt* **whiled; whiling** ~ **away the time** : matar el tiempo

whim *n* : capricho *m*, antojo *m*

whimper *vi* : lloriquear — ~ *n* : quejido *m*

whimsical *adj* : caprichoso, fantasioso

whine *vi* **whined; whining 1** : gimotear **2** COMPLAIN : quejarse — ~ *n* : quejido *m*, gemido *m*

whip *v* **whipped; whipping** *vt* **1** : azotar **2** BEAT : batir (huevos, crema, etc.) **3** ~ **up** AROUSE : avivar, despertar — *vi* FLAP : agitarse — ~ *n* : látigo *m*

whir *vi* **whirred; whirring** : zumbar — ~ *n* : zumbido *m*

whirl *vi* **1** : dar vueltas, girar **2** *or* ~ **about** : arremolinarse — ~ *n* **1** : giro *m* **2** SWIRL : torbellino *m* — **whirlpool** *n* : remolino *m* — **whirlwind** *n* : torbellino *m*

whisk *vt* **1** : batir **2** ~ **away** : llevarse — ~ *n or* **egg** ~ : batidor *m* — **whisk broom** *n* : escobilla *f*

whisker *n* **1** : pelo *m* (de la barba) **2** ~**s** *npl* : bigotes *mpl* (de animales)

whiskey *or* **whisky** *n*, *pl* **-keys** *or* **-kies** : whisky *m*

whisper *vi* : cuchichear, susurrar — *vt* : susurrar — ~ *n* : susurro *m*

whistle *v* **-tled; -tling** *vi* **1** : silbar, chiflar *Lat* **2** : pitar (dícese de un tren, etc.) — *vt* : silbar — ~ *n* **1** : silbido *m*, chiflido *m* (sonido) **2** : silbato *m*, pito *m* (instrumento)

white *adj* **whiter; -est** : blanco — ~ *n* **1** : blanco *m* (color) **2** : clara *f* (de huevos) **3** *or* ~ **person** : blanco *m*, -ca *f* — **white-collar** *adj* **1** : de oficina **2** ~ **worker** : oficinista *mf* — **whiten** *vt* : blanquear — **whiteness** *n* : blancura *f* — **whitewash** *vt* **1** : enjalbegar **2** CONCEAL : encubrir (un escándalo, etc.) — ~ *n* **1** : jalbegue *m*, lechada *f* **2** COVER-UP : encubrimiento *m*

whittle *vt* **-tled; -tling 1** : tallar (madera) **2** *or* ~ **down** : reducir

whiz *or* **whizz** *vi* **whizzed; whizzing 1** BUZZ : zumbar **2** ~ **by** : pasar muy rápido — ~ *or* **whizz** *n*, *pl* **whizzes** : zumbido *m* — **whiz kid** *n* : joven *m* prometedor

who *pron* **1** (*used in direct and indirect questions*) : quién **2** (*used in relative clauses*) : que, quien — **whodunit** *n* : novela *f* policíaca — **whoever** *pron* **1** : quienquiera que, quien **2** (*used in questions*) : quién

whole *adj* **1** : entero **2** INTACT : intacto **3 a** ~ **lot** : muchísimo — ~ *n* **1** : todo *m* **2 as a** ~ : en conjunto **3 on the** ~ : en general — **wholehearted** *adj* : sincero — **wholesale** *n* : venta *f* al por mayor — ~ *adj* **1** : al por mayor **2** ~ **slaughter** : matanza *f* sistemática — ~ *adv* : al por mayor — **wholesaler** *n* : mayorista *mf* — **wholesome** *adj* : sano — **whole wheat** *adj* : de trigo integral — **wholly** *adv* : completamente

whom *pron* **1** (*used in direct questions*) : a quién **2** (*used in indirect questions*) : de quién, con quién, en quién **3** (*used in relative clauses*) : que, a quien

whooping cough *n* : tos *f* ferina

whore *n* : puta *f*

whose *adj* **1** (*used in questions*) : de quién **2** (*used in relative clauses*) : cuyo — **~** *pron* : de quién

why *adv* : por qué — **~** *n, pl* **whys** : porqué *m* — **~** *conj* : por qué — **~** *interj* (*used to express surprise*) : ¡vaya!, ¡mira!

wick *n* : mecha *f*

wicked *adj* **1** : malo, malvado **2** MISCHIEVOUS : travieso **3** TERRIBLE : terrible, horrible — **wickedness** *n* : maldad *f*

wicker *n* : mimbre *m* — **~** *adj* : de mimbre

wide *adj* **wider; widest 1** : ancho **2** VAST : amplio, extenso **3** *or* **~ of the mark** : desviado — **~** *adv* **1 ~ apart** : muy separados **2 far and ~** : por todas partes **3 ~ open** : abierto de par en par — **wide-awake** *adj* : (completamente) despierto — **widely** *adv* : extensivamente — **widespread** *adj* : extendido

widow *n* : viuda *f* — **~** *vt* : dejar viuda — **widower** *n* : viudo *m*

width *n* : ancho *m*, anchura *f*

wield *vt* **1** : usar, manejar **2** EXERT : ejercer

wiener → **frankfurter**

wife *n, pl* **wives** : esposa *f*, mujer *f*

wig *n* : peluca *f*

wiggle *v* **-gled; -gling** *vt* : menear, contonear — *vi* : menearse — **~** *n* : meneo *m*

wigwam *n* : wigwam *m*

wild *adj* **1** : salvaje **2** DESOLATE : agreste **3** UNRULY : desenfrenado **4** RANDOM : al azar **5** FRANTIC : frenético **6** OUTRAGEOUS : extravagante — **~** *adv* **1** → **wildly 2 run ~** : volver al estado silvestre (dícese de las plantas), desmandarse (dícese de los niños) — **wildcat** *n* : gato *m* montés — **wilderness** *n* : yermo *m*, desierto *m* — **wildfire** *n* **1** : fuego *m* descontrolado **2 spread like ~** : propagarse como un reguero de pólvora — **wildflower** *n* : flor *f* silvestre — **wildlife** *n* : fauna *f* — **wildly** *adv* **1** FRANTICALLY : frenéticamente **2** EXTREMELY : locamente

will¹ *v past* **would;** *pres sing & pl* **will** *vi* WISH : querer — *v aux* **1 tomorrow we ~ go shopping** : mañana iremos de compras **2 he ~ get angry over nothing** : se pone furioso por cualquier cosa **3 I ~ go despite them** : iré a pesar de ellos **4 I won't do it** : no lo haré **5 that ~ be the mailman** : eso ha de ser el cartero **6 the couch ~ hold three people** : en el sofá cabrán tres personas **7 accidents ~ happen** : los accidentes ocurrirán **8 you ~ do as I say** : harás lo que digo

will² *n* **1** : voluntad *f* **2** TESTAMENT : testamento *m* **3 free ~** : libre albedrío *m* — **willful** *or* **wilful** *adj* **1** OBSTINATE : terco **2** INTENTIONAL : intencionado — **willing** *adj*

1 : complaciente **2 be ~ to** : estar dispuesto a — **willingly** *adv* : con gusto — **willingness** *n* : buena voluntad *f*

willow *n* : sauce *m*

willpower *n* : fuerza *f* de voluntad

wilt *vi* : marchitarse

wily *adj* **wilier; -est** : artero, astuto

win *v* **won; winning** *vi* : ganar — *vt* **1** : ganar, conseguir **2 ~ over** : ganarse a — **~** *n* : triunfo *m*, victoria *f*

wince *vi* **winced; wincing** : hacer una mueca de dolor — **~** *n* : mueca *f* de dolor

winch *n* : torno *m*

wind¹ *n* **1** : viento *m* **2** BREATH : aliento *m* **3** FLATULENCE : flatulencia *f* **4 get ~ of** : enterarse de

wind² *v* **wound; winding** *vi* : serpentear — *vt* **1** COIL : enrollar **2 ~ a clock** : dar cuerda a un reloj

windfall *n* : beneficio *m* imprevisto

winding *adj* : tortuoso

wind instrument *n* : instrumento *m* de viento

windmill *n* : molino *m* de viento

window *n* : ventana *f* (de un edificio o una computadora), ventanilla *f* (de un vehículo), vitrina *f* (de una tienda) — **windowpane** *n* : vidrio *m* — **windowsill** *n* : repisa *f* de la ventana

windpipe *n* : tráquea *f*

windshield *n* **1** : parabrisas *m* **2 ~ wiper** : limpiaparabrisas *m*

window–shop *vi* **-shopped; -shopping** : mirar las vitrinas

wind up *vt* : terminar, concluir — *vi* : terminar, acabar — **windup** *n* : conclusión *f*

windy *adj* **windier; -est 1** : ventoso **2 it's ~** : hace viento

wine *n* : vino *m* — **wine cellar** *n* : bodega *f*

wing *n* **1** : ala *f* **2 under s.o.'s ~** : bajo el cargo de algn — **winged** *adj* : alado

wink *vi* : guiñar — **~** *n* **1** : guiño *m* **2 not sleep a ~** : no pegar el ojo

winner *n* : ganador *m*, -dora *f* — **winning** *adj* **1** : ganador **2** CHARMING : encantador — **winnings** *npl* : ganancias *fpl*

winter *n* : invierno *m* — **~** *adj* : invernal, de invierno — **wintergreen** *n* : gaulteria *f* — **wintertime** *n* : invierno *m* — **wintry** *adj* **wintrier; -est** : invernal, de invierno

wipe *vt* **wiped; wiping 1** : limpiar **2 ~ away** : enjugar (lágrimas), borrar (una memoria) **3 ~ out** : aniquilar, destruir — **~** *n* : pasada *f* (con un trapo, etc.)

wire *n* **1** : alambre *m* **2** : cable *m* (eléctrico o telefónico) **3** TELEGRAM : telegrama *m* — **~** *vt* **-wired; wiring 1** : instalar el cableado en (una casa, etc.) **2** BIND : atar con alambre **3** TELEGRAPH : enviar un telegrama a — **wireless** *adj* : inalámbrico

— **wiring** *n* : cableado *m* — **wiry** *adj* **wirier;
-est** **1** : hirsuto, tieso (dícese del pelo) **2**
: esbelto y musculoso (dícese del cuerpo)
wisdom *n* : sabiduría *f* — **wisdom tooth** *n*
: muela *f* de juicio
wise *adj* **wiser; wisest** **1** : sabio **2** SENSI-
BLE : prudente — **wisecrack** *n* : broma *f*,
chiste *m* — **wisely** *adv* : sabiamente
wish *vt* **1** : desear **2** ~ **s.o. well** : desear lo
mejor a algn — *vi* **1** : pedir (como deseo) **2**
as you ~ : como quieras — ~ *n* **1** : deseo
m **2 best** ~ **es** : muchos recuerdos —
wishbone *n* : espoleta *f* — **wishful** *adj* **1**
: deseoso **2** ~ **thinking** : ilusiones *fpl*
wishy-washy *adj* : insípido, soso
wisp *n* **1** : mechón *m* (de pelo) **2** : voluta *f*
(de humo)
wistful *adj* : melancólico
wit *n* **1** CLEVERNESS : ingenio *m* **2** HUMOR
: agudeza *f* **3 at one's** ~'**s end** : desesperado **4 scared out of one's** ~ **s** : muerto de
miedo
witch *n* : bruja *f* — **witchcraft** *n* : brujería *f*,
hechicería *f*
with *prep* **1** : con **2 I'm going** ~ **you** : voy
contigo **3 it varies** ~ **the season** : varía
según la estación **4 the girl** ~ **red hair** : la
muchacha de pelo rojo **5** ~ **all his work,
the business failed** : a pesar de su trabajo,
el negocio fracasó
withdraw *v* **-drew; -drawn; -drawing** *vt* : retirar — *vi* : apartarse — **withdrawal** *n* **1**
: retirada *f* **2** : abandono (de drogas, etc.) —
withdrawn *adj* : introvertido
wither *vi* : marchitarse
withhold *vt* **-held; -holding** : retener (fondos), negar (permiso, etc.)
within *adv* : dentro — ~ *prep* **1** : dentro de
2 (*in expressions of distance*) : a menos de
3 (*in expressions of time*) : dentro de, en
menos de **4** ~ **reach** : al alcance de la
mano
without *adv* **do** ~ : pasar sin algo — ~
prep : sin
withstand *vt* **-stood; -standing** **1** BEAR
: aguantar **2** RESIST : resistir
witness *n* **1** : testigo *mf* **2** EVIDENCE : testimonio *m* **3 bear** ~ : atestiguar — ~ *vt* **1**
SEE : ser testigo de **2** : atestiguar (una
firma, etc.)
witticism *n* : agudeza *f*, ocurrencia *f*
witty *adj* **-tier; -est** : ingenioso, ocurrente
wives → **wife**
wizard *n* **1** : mago *m*, brujo *m* **2 a math** ~
: un genio de matemáticas
wizened *adj* : arrugado
wobble *vi* **-bled; -bling** **1** : tambalearse **2**
: temblar (dícese de la voz, etc.) — **wobbly**
adj : cojo

woe *n* **1** : aflicción *f* **2** ~ **s** *npl* TROUBLES
: penas *fpl* — **woeful** *adj* : triste
woke, woken → **wake**
wolf *n*, *pl* **wolves** : lobo *m*, -ba *f* — ~ *vt or*
~ **down** : engullir
woman *n*, *pl* **women** : mujer *f* — **womanly**
adj : femenino
womb *n* : útero *m*, matriz *f*
won → **win**
wonder *n* **1** MARVEL : maravilla *f* **2** AMAZE-
MENT : asombro *m* — ~ *v* : preguntarse —
wonderful *adj* : maravilloso, estupendo
won't (*contraction of* **will not**) → **will**
woo *vt* **1** COURT : cortejar **2** : buscar el
apoyo de (clientes, votantes, etc.)
wood *n* **1** : madera *f* (materia) **2** FIREWOOD
: leña *f* **3** *or* ~ **s** *npl* FOREST : bosque *m* —
~ *adj* : de madera — **woodchuck** *n* : marmota *f* de América — **wooded** *adj* : arbo-
lado, boscoso — **wooden** *adj* : de madera
— **woodpecker** *n* : pájaro *m* carpintero —
woodshed *n* : leñera *f* — **woodwind** *n* : instrumento *m* de viento de madera — **wood-
work** *n* : carpintería *f*
wool *n* : lana *f* — **woolen** *or* **woollen** *adj*
: de lana — ~ *n* **1** : lana *f* (tela) **2** ~ **s** *npl*
: prendas *fpl* de lana — **woolly** *adj* **-lier;
-est** : lanudo
word *n* **1** : palabra *f* **2** NEWS : noticias *fpl* **3**
~ **s** *npl* : letra *f* (de una canción, etc.) **4**
have ~ **s with** : reñir con **5 just say the**
~ : no tienes que decirlo **6 keep one's** ~
: cumplir su palabra — ~ *vt* : expresar —
word processing *n* : procesamiento *m* de
textos — **word processor** *n* : procesador *m*
de textos — **wordy** *adj* **wordier; -est** : prolijo
wore → **wear**
work *n* **1** LABOR : trabajo *m* **2** EMPLOYMENT
: trabajo *m*, empleo *m* **3** : obra *f* (de arte,
etc.) **4** ~ **s** *npl* FACTORY : fábrica *f* **5** ~ **s**
npl MECHANISM : mecanismo *m* — ~ *v*
worked (*or* **wrought**); **working** *vt* **1** : hacer
trabajar (a una persona) **2** : manejar, operar
(una máquina, etc.) — *vi* **1** : trabajar **2**
FUNCTION : funcionar **3** : surtir efecto
(dícese de una droga), resultar (dícese de
una idea, etc.) — **worked up** *adj* : nervioso
— **worker** *n* : trabajador *m*, -dora *f;* obrero
m, -ra *f* — **working** *adj* **1** : que trabaja
(dícese de personas), de trabajo (dícese de
la ropa, etc.) **2 be in** ~ **order** : funcionar
bien — **working class** *n* : clase *f* obrera —
workingman *n*, *pl* **-men** : obrero *m* —
workman *n*, *pl* **-men** **1** : obrero *m* **2** ARTI-
SAN : artesano *m* — **workmanship** *n* : artesanía *f*, destreza *f* — **workout** *n* : ejercicios
mpl (físicos) — **work out** *vt* **1** DEVELOP
: elaborar **2** SOLVE : resolver — *vi* **1** TURN

OUT : resultar **2** SUCCEED : lograr, salir bien **3** EXERCISE : hacer ejercicio — **workshop** *n* : taller *m* — **work up** *vt* **1** EXCITE : ponerse como loco **2** GENERATE : desarrollar

world *n* : mundo *m* **2 think the ~ of s.o.** : tener a algn en alta estima — **~** *adj* : mundial, del mundo — **worldly** *adj* : mundano — **worldwide** *adv* : en todo el mundo — **~** *adj* : global, mundial

worm *n* **1** : gusano *m*, lombriz *f* **2 ~s** *npl* : lombrices *fpl* (parásitos)

worn → **wear** — **worn–out** *adj* **1** USED : gastado **2** TIRED : agotado

worry *v* **-ried; -rying** *vt* : preocupar, inquietar — *vi* : preocuparse, inquietarse — **~** *n, pl* **-ries** : preocupación *f* — **worried** *adj* : preocupado — **worrisome** *adj* : inquietante

worse *adv* (*comparative of* **bad** *or of* **ill**) : peor — **~** *adj* (*comparative of* **bad** *or of* **ill**) **1** : peor **2 from bad to ~** : de mal en peor **3 get ~** : empeorar — **~** *n* **1 the ~** : el (la) peor, lo peor **2 take a turn for the ~** : ponerse peor — **worsen** *v* : empeorar

worship *v* **-shiped** *or* **-shipped; -shiping** *or* **-shipping** *vt* : adorar — *vi* : practicar una religión — **~** *n* : adoración *f*, culto *m* — **worshiper** *or* **worshipper** *n* : adorador *m*, -dora *f*

worst *adv* (*superlative of* **ill** *or of* **bad** *or* **badly**) : peor — **~** *adj* (*superlative of* **bad** *or of* **ill**) : peor — **~** *n* **the ~** : lo peor, el (la) peor

worth *n* **1** : valor *m* (monetario) **2** MERIT : mérito *m*, valía *f* **3 ten dollars' ~ of gas** : diez dólares de gasolina — **~** *prep* **1 it's ~ $ 10** : vale $ 10 **2 it's ~ doing** : vale la pena hacerlo — **worthless** *adj* **1** : sin valor **2** USELESS : inútil — **worthwhile** *adj* : que vale la pena — **worthy** *adj* **-thier; -est** : digno

would *past of* **will 1 he ~ often take his children to the park** : solía llevar a sus hijos al parque **2 I ~ go if I had the money** : iría yo si tuviera el dinero **3 I ~ rather go alone** : preferiría ir sola **4 she ~ have won if she hadn't tripped** : habría ganado si no hubiera tropezado **5 ~ you kindly help me with this?** : ¿tendría la bondad de ayudarme con esto? — **would-be** *adj* **a ~ poet** : un aspirante a poeta — **wouldn't** (*contraction of* **would not**) → **would**

wound¹ *n* : herida *f* — **~** *vt* : herir

wound² → **wind**

wove, woven → **weave**

wrangle *vi* **-gled; -gling** : reñir — **~** *n* : riña *f*, disputa *f*

wrap *vt* **wrapped; wrapping 1** : envolver **2**

~ up FINISH : dar fin a — **~** *n* **1** : prenda *f* que envuelve (como un chal) **2** WRAPPER : envoltura *f* — **wrapper** *n* : envoltura *f*, envoltorio *m* — **wrapping** *n* : envoltura *f*, envoltorio *m*

wrath *n* : ira *f*, cólera *f* — **wrathful** *adj* : iracundo

wreath *n, pl* **wreaths** : corona *f* (de flores, etc.)

wreck *n* **1** WRECKAGE : restos *mpl* **2** RUIN : ruina *f*, desastre *m* **3 be a nervous ~** : tener los nervios destrozados — **~** *vt* : destrozar (un automóvil), naufragar (un barco) — **wreckage** *n* : restos *mpl* (de un buque naufragado, etc.), ruinas *fpl* (de un edificio)

wren *n* : chochín *m*

wrench *vt* **1** PULL : arrancar (de un tirón) **2** SPRAIN, TWIST : torcerse — **~** *n* **1** TUG : tirón *m*, jalón *m* **2** SPRAIN : torcedura *f* **3** *or* **monkey ~** : llave *f* inglesa

wrestle *vi* **-tled; -tling** : luchar — **wrestler** *n* : luchador *m*, -dora *f* — **wrestling** *n* : lucha *f*

wretch *n* : desgraciado *m*, -da *f* — **wretched** *adj* **1** : miserable **2 ~ weather** : tiempo *m* espantoso

wriggle *vi* **-gled; -gling** : retorcerse, menearse

wring *vt* **wrung; wringing 1** *or* **~ out** : escurrir (el lavado, etc.) **2** TWIST : retorcer **3** EXTRACT : arrancar (información, etc.)

wrinkle *n* : arruga *f* — **~** *v* **-kled; -kling** *vt* : arrugar — *vi* : arrugarse

wrist *n* : muñeca *f* — **wristwatch** *n* : reloj *m* de pulsera

writ *n* : orden *f* (judicial)

write *v* **wrote; written; writing** : escribir — **write down** *vt* : apuntar, anotar — **write off** *vt* CANCEL : cancelar — **writer** *n* : escritor *m*, -tora *f*

writhe *vi* **writhed; writhing** : retorcerse

writing *n* : escritura *f*

wrong *n* **1** INJUSTICE : injusticia *f*, mal *m* **2** : agravio *m* (en derecho) **3 be in the ~** : haber hecho mal — **~** *adj* **wronger; wrongest 1** : malo **2** UNSUITABLE : inadecuado, inapropiado **3** INCORRECT : incorrecto, equivocado **4 be ~** : no tener razón — **~** *adv* : mal, incorrectamente — **~** *vt* **wronged; wronging** : ofender, ser injusto con — **wrongful** *adj* **1** UNJUST : injusto **2** UNLAWFUL : ilegal — **wrongly** *adv* **1** UNJUSTLY : injustamente **2** INCORRECTLY : mal

wrote → **write**

wrought iron *n* : hierro *m* forjado

wrung → **wring**

wry *adj* **wrier; wriest** : irónico, sardónico (dícese del humor)

XYZ

x *n, pl* **x's** *or* **xs** : x *f*, vigésima cuarta letra del alfabeto inglés

xenophobia *n* : xenofobia *f*

Xmas *n* : Navidad *f*

X ray *n* **1** : rayo *m* X **2** *or* ~ **photograph** : radiografía *f* — **x-ray** *vt* : radiografiar

xylophone *n* : xilófono *m*

y *n, pl* **y's** *or* **ys** : y *f*, vigésima quinta letra del alfabeto inglés

yacht *n* : yate *m*

yam *n* **1** : ñame *m* **2** SWEET POTATO : batata *f*, boniato *m*

yank *vt* : tirar de, jalar *Lat* — ~ *n* : tirón *m*, jalón *m Lat*

Yankee *n* : yanqui *mf*

yap *vi* **yapped; yapping** : ladrar — ~ *n* : ladrido *m*

yard *n* **1** : yarda *f* (medida) **2** COURTYARD : patio *m* **3** : jardín *m* (de una casa) — **yardstick** *n* **1** : vara *f* (de medir) **2** CRITERION : criterio *m*

yarn *n* **1** : hilado *m* **2** TALE : historia *f*, cuento *m*

yawn *vi* : bostezar — ~ *n* : bostezo *m*

year *n* **1** : año *m* **2 she's ten** ~**s old** : tiene diez años **3 I haven't seen them in** ~**s** : hace siglos que no los veo — **yearbook** *n* : anuario *m* — **yearling** *n* : animal *m* menor de dos años — **yearly** *adv* **1** : anualmente **2 three times** ~ : tres veces al año — ~ *adj* : anual

yearn *vi* : anhelar — **yearning** *n* : anhelo *m*, ansia *f*

yeast *n* : levadura *f*

yell *vi* : gritar, chillar — *vt* : gritar — ~ *n* : grito *m*, chillido *m*

yellow *adj* : amarillo — ~ *n* : amarillo *m* — **yellowish** *adj* : amarillento

yelp *n* : gañido *m* — *vi* : dar un gañido

yes *adv* **1** : sí **2 say** ~ : decir que sí — ~ *n* : sí *m*

yesterday *adv* : ayer — ~ *n* **1** : ayer *m* **2 the day before** ~ : anteayer

yet *adv* **1** : aún, todavía **2 has he come** ~? : ¿ya ha venido? **3 not** ~ : todavía no **4** ~ **more problems** : más problemas aún **5** NEVERTHELESS : sin embargo — ~ *conj* : pero

yield *vt* **1** PRODUCE : producir **2** ~ **the right of way** : ceder el paso — *vi* : ceder — ~ *n* : rendimiento *m*, rédito *m* (en finanzas)

yoga *n* : yoga *m*

yogurt *n* : yogur *m*, yogurt *m*

yoke *n* : yugo *m*

yolk *n* : yema *f* (de un huevo)

you *pron* **1** (*used as subject—familiar*) : tú; vos (*in some Latin American countries*); ustedes *pl*; vosotros, vosotras *pl Spain* **2** (*used as subject—formal*) : usted, ustedes *pl* **3** (*used as indirect object—familiar*) : te, les *pl* (*se before lo, la, los, las*), os *pl Spain* **4** (*used as indirect object—formal*) : lo (*Spain sometimes* le), la; los (*Spain sometimes* les), las *pl* **5** (*used after a preposition—familiar*) : ti; vos (*in some Latin American countries*); ustedes *pl*; vosotros, vosotras *pl Spain* **6** (*used after a preposition—formal*) : usted, ustedes *pl* **7 with** ~ (*familiar*) : contigo; con ustedes *pl*; con vosotros, con vosotras *pl Spain* **8 with** ~ (*formal*) : con usted, con ustedes *pl* **9** ~ **never know** : nunca se sabe — **you'd** (*contraction of* **you had** *or* **you would**) → **have**, **would** — **you'll** (*contraction of* **you shall** *or* **you will**) → **shall, will**

young *adj* **younger; youngest 1** : joven **2 my** ~**er brother** : mi hermano menor **3 she is the** ~**est** : es la más pequeña **4 the** ~ : los jóvenes — ~ *npl* : jóvenes *mfpl* (de los humanos), crías *fpl* (de los animales) — **youngster** *n* : chico *m*, -ca *f*; joven *mf*

your *adj* **1** (*familiar singular*) : tu **2** (*familiar plural*) su, vuestro *Spain* **3** (*formal*) : su **4 on** ~ **left** : a la izquierda

you're (*contraction of* **you are**) → **be**

yours *pron* **1** (*belonging to one person—familiar*) : (el) tuyo, (la) tuya, (los) tuyos, (las) tuyas **2** (*belonging to more than one person—familiar*) : (el) suyo, (la) suya, (los) suyos, (las) suyas; (el) vuestro, (la) vuestra, (los) vuestros, (las) vuestras *Spain* **3** (*formal*) : (el) suyo, (la) suya, (los) suyos, (las) suyas

yourself *pron, pl* **yourselves 1** (*used reflexively—familiar*) : te, se *pl*, os *pl Spain* **2** (*used reflexively—formal*) : se **3** (*used for emphasis*) : tú mismo, tú misma; usted mismo, usted misma; ustedes mismos, ustedes mismas *pl*; vosotros mismos, vosotras mismas *pl Spain*

youth *n, pl* **youths 1** : juventud *f* **2** BOY : joven *m* **3 today's** ~ : los jóvenes de hoy — **youthful** *adj* **1** : juvenil, de juventud **2** YOUNG : joven

you've (*contraction of* **you have**) → **have**

yowl *vi* : aullar — ~ *n* : aullido *m*

yucca *n* : yuca *f*

Yugoslavian *adj* : yugoslavo

yule *n* CHRISTMAS : Navidad *f* — **yuletide** *n* : Navidades *fpl*

z *n, pl* **z's** *or* **zs** : z *f,* vigésima sexta letra del alfabeto inglés

zany *adj* **-nier; -est** : alocado, disparatado

zeal *n* : fervor *m,* celo *m* — **zealous** *adj* : entusiasta

zebra *n* : cebra *f*

zenith *n* **1** : cenit *m* (en astronomía) **2** PEAK : apogeo *m*

zero *n, pl* **-ros** : cero *m*

zest *n* **1** : gusto *m* **2** FLAVOR : sazón *f*

zigzag *n* : zigzag *m* — ～ *vi* **-zagged; -zagging** : zigzaguear

zinc *n* : cinc *m,* zinc *m*

zip *v* **zipped; zipping** *vt or* ～ **up** : cerrar la cremallera de, cerrar el cierre de *Lat* — *vi* SPEED : pasarse volando — **zip code** *n* : código *m* postal — **zipper** *n* : cremallera *f,* cierre *m Lat*

zodiac *n* : zodíaco *m*

zone *n* : zona *f*

zoo *n, pl* **zoos** : zoológico *m,* zoo *m* — **zoology** *n* : zoología *f*

zoom *vi* : zumbar, ir volando — ～ *n* **1** : zumbido *m* **2** *or* ～ **lens** : zoom *m*

zucchini *n, pl* **-ni** *or* **-nis** : calabacín *m,* calabacita *f Lat*

Common Spanish Abbreviations

SPANISH ABBREVIATION AND EXPANSION		ENGLISH EQUIVALENT	
abr.	abril	**Apr.**	April
A.C., a.C.	antes de Cristo	**BC**	before Christ
a. de J.C.	antes de Jesucristo	**BC**	before Christ
admon., admón.	administración	—	administration
a/f	a favor	—	in favor
ago.	agosto	**Aug.**	August
Apdo.	apartado (de correos)	—	P.O. box
aprox.	aproximadamente	**approx.**	approximately
Aptdo.	apartado (de correos)	—	P.O. box
Arq.	arquitecto	**arch.**	architect
A.T.	Antiguo Testamento	**O.T.**	Old Testament
atte.	atentamente	—	sincerely
atto., atta.	atento, atenta	—	kind, courteous
av., avda.	avenida	**ave.**	avenue
a/v.	a vista	—	on receipt
BID	Banco Interamericano de Desarrollo	**IDB**	Interamerican Development Bank
Bo	banco	—	bank
BM	Banco Mundial	—	World Bank
c/, C/	calle	**st.**	street
C	centígrado, Celsius	**C**	centigrade, Celsius
C.	compañía	**Co.**	company
CA	corriente alterna	**AC**	alternating current
cap.	capítulo	**ch., chap.**	chapter
c/c	cuenta corriente	—	current account, checking account
c.c.	centímetros cúbicos	**cu. cm**	cubic centimeters
CC	corriente continua	**DC**	direct current
c/d	con descuento	—	with discount
Cd.	ciudad	—	city
CE	Comunidad Europea	**EC**	European Community
CEE	Comunidad Económica Europea	**EEC**	European Economic Community
cf.	confróntese	**cf.**	compare
cg.	centígramo	**cg**	centigram
CGT	Confederación General de Trabajadores *o* del Trabajo	—	confederation of workers, workers' union
CI	coeficiente intelectual *o* de inteligencia	**IQ**	intelligence quotient
Cía.	compañía	**Co.**	company
cm.	centímetro	**cm**	centimeter
Cnel.	coronel	**Col.**	colonel
col.	columna	**col.**	column
Col. *Mex*	colonia	—	residential area
Com.	comandante	**Cmdr.**	commander
comp.	compárese	**comp.**	compare
Cor.	coronel	**Col.**	colonel
C.P.	código postal	—	zip code
CSF, c.s.f.	coste, seguro y flete	**c.i.f.**	cost, insurance, and freight
cta.	cuenta	**ac., acct.**	account
cte.	corriente	**cur.**	current

SPANISH ABBREVIATION AND EXPANSION		ENGLISH EQUIVALENT	
c/u	cada uno, cada una	**ea.**	each
CV	caballo de vapor	**hp**	horsepower
D.	Don	—	—
Da., D.ª	Doña	—	—
d.C.	después de Cristo	**AD**	anno Domini (in the year of our Lord)
dcha.	derecha	**—**	right
d. de J.C.	después de Jesucristo	**AD**	anno Domini (in the year of our lord)
dep.	departamento	**dept.**	department
DF, D.F.	Distrito Federal	—	Federal District
dic.	diciembre	**Dec.**	December
dir.	director, directora	**dir.**	director
dir.	dirección	—	address
Dña.	Doña	**—**	—
do.	domingo	**Sun.**	Sunday
dpto.	departamento	**dept.**	department
Dr.	doctor	**Dr.**	doctor
Dra.	doctora	**Dr.**	doctor
dto.	descuento	**—**	discount
E, E.	Este, este	**E**	East, east
Ed.	editorial	**—**	publishing house
Ed., ed.	edición	**ed.**	edition
edif.	edificio	**bldg.**	building
edo.	estado	**st.**	state
EEUU, EE.UU.	Estados Unidos	**US, U.S.**	United States
ej.	por ejemplo	**e.g.**	for example
E.M.	esclerosis multiple	**MS**	multiple sclerosis
ene.	enero	**Jan.**	January
etc.	etcétera	**etc.**	et cetera
ext.	extensión	**ext.**	extension
F	Fahrenheit	**F**	Fahrenheit
f.a.b.	franco a bordo	**f.o.b.**	free on board
FC	ferrocarril	**RR**	railroad
feb.	febrero	**Feb.**	February
FF AA, FF.AA.	Fuerzas Armadas	**—**	armed forces
FMI	Fondo Monetario Internacional	**IMF**	International Monetary Fund
g.	gramo	**g., gm, gr.**	gram
G.P.	giro postal	**M.O.**	money order
gr.	gramo	**g., gm, gr.**	gram
Gral.	general	**Gen.**	general
h.	hora	**hr.**	hour
Hnos.	hermanos	**Bros.**	brothers
I + D, I & D, I y D	investigación y desarrollo	**R & D**	research and development
i.e.	esto es, es decir	**i.e.**	that is
incl.	inclusive	**incl.**	inclusive, inclusively
Ing.	ingeniero, ingeniera	**eng.**	engineer
IPC	índice de precios al consumo	**CPI**	consumer price index
IVA	impuesto al valor agregado	**VAT**	value-added tax
izq.	izquierda	**l.**	left
juev.	jueves	**Thurs.**	Thursday
jul.	julio	**Jul.**	July

SPANISH ABBREVIATION AND EXPANSION		ENGLISH EQUIVALENT	
jun.	junio	**Jun.**	June
kg.	kilogramo	**kg**	kilogram
km.	kilómetro	**km**	kilometer
km/h	kilómetros por hora	**kph**	kilometers per hour
kv, kV	kilovatio	**kw, kW**	kilowatt
l.	litro	**l, lit.**	liter
Lic.	licenciado, licenciada	—	—
Ltda.	limitada	**Ltd.**	limited
lun.	lunes	**Mon.**	Monday
m	masculino	**m**	masculine
m	metro	**m**	meter
m	minuto	**m**	minute
mar.	marzo	**Mar.**	March
mart.	martes	**Tues.**	Tuesday
mg.	miligramo	**mg**	milligram
miérc.	miércoles	**Wed.**	Wednesday
min	minuto	**min.**	minute
mm.	milímetro	**mm**	millimeter
M-N, m/n	moneda nacional	—	national currency
Mons.	monseñor	**Msgr.**	monsignor
Mtra.	maestra	—	teacher
Mtro.	maestro	—	teacher
N, N.	Norte, norte	**N, no.**	North, north
n/o	nuestro	—	our
n.º	número	**no.**	number
N. de (la) R.	nota de (la) redacción	—	editor's note
NE	nordeste	**NE**	northeast
NN.UU.	Naciones Unidas	**UN**	United Nations
NO	noroeste	**NW**	northwest
nov.	noviembre	**Nov.**	November
N.T.	Nuevo Testamento	**N.T.**	New Testament
ntra., ntro.	nuestra, nuestro	—	our
NU	Naciones Unidas	**UN**	United Nations
núm.	número	**num.**	number
O, O.	Oeste, oeste	**W**	West, west
oct.	octubre	**Oct.**	October
OEA, O.E.A.	Organización de Estados Americanos	**OAS**	Organization of American States
OMS	Organización Mundial de la Salud	**WHO**	World Health Organization
ONG	organización no gubernamental	**NGO**	non-governmental organization
ONU	Organización de las Naciones Unidas	**UN**	United Nations
OTAN	Organización del Tratado del Atlántico Norte	**NATO**	North Atlantic Treaty Organization
p.	página	**p.**	page
P, P.	padre	**Fr.**	father
pág.	página	**pg.**	page
pat.	patente	**pat.**	patent
PCL	pantalla de cristal líquido	**LCD**	liquid crystal display
P.D.	post data	**P.S.**	postscript
p. ej.	por ejemplo	**e.g.**	for example
PNB	Producto Nacional Bruto	**GNP**	gross national product
pº	paseo	**Ave.**	avenue
p.p.	porte pagado	**ppd.**	postpaid

SPANISH ABBREVIATION AND EXPANSION		ENGLISH EQUIVALENT	
PP, p.p.	por poder, por poderes	**p.p.**	by proxy
prom.	promedio	**av., avg.**	average
ptas., pts.	pesetas	—	—
q.e.p.d.	que en paz descanse	**R.I.P.**	may he/she rest in peace
R, R/	remite	—	sender
RAE	Real Academia Española	—	—
ref., ref.ª	referencia	**ref.**	reference
rep.	república	**rep.**	republic
r.p.m.	revoluciones por minuto	**rpm.**	revolutions per minute
rte.	remite, remitente	—	sender
s.	siglo	**c., cent.**	century
s/	su, sus	—	his, her, your, their
S, S.	Sur, sur	**S, so.**	South, south
S.	san, santo	**St.**	saint
S.A.	sociedad anónima	**Inc.**	incorporated (company)
sáb.	sábado	**Sat.**	Saturday
s/c	su cuenta	—	your account
SE	sudeste, sureste	**SE**	southeast
seg.	segundo, segundos	**sec.**	second, seconds
sep., sept.	septiembre	**Sept.**	September
s.e.u.o.	salvo error u omisión	—	errors and omissions excepted
Sgto.	sargento	**Sgt.**	sergeant
S.L.	sociedad limitada	**Ltd.**	limited (corporation)
S.M.	Su Majestad	**HM**	His Majesty, Her Majesty
s/n	sin número	—	no (street) number
s.n.m.	sobre el nivel de mar	**a.s.l.**	above sea level
SO	sudoeste/suroeste	**SW**	southwest
S.R.C.	se ruega contestación	**R.S.V.P.**	please reply
ss.	siguientes	—	the following ones
SS, S.S.	Su Santidad	**H.H.**	His Holiness
Sta.	santa	**St.**	Saint
Sto.	santo	**St.**	saint
t, t.	tonelada	**t., tn**	ton
TAE	tasa anual efectiva	**APR**	annual percentage rate
tb.	también	—	also
tel., Tel.	teléfono	**tel.**	telephone
Tm.	tonelada métrica	**MT**	metric ton
Tn.	tonelada	**t., tn**	ton
trad.	traducido	**tr., trans., transl.**	translated
UE	Unión Europea	**EU**	European Union
Univ.	universidad	**Univ., U.**	university
UPC	unidad procesadora central	**CPU**	central processing unit
Urb.	urbanización	—	residential area
v	versus	**v., vs.**	versus
v	verso	**v., ver., vs.**	verse
v.	véase	**vid.**	see
Vda.	viuda	—	widow
v.g., v.gr.	verbigracia	**e.g.**	for example
vier., viern.	viernes	**Fri.**	Friday
V.M.	Vuestra Majestad	—	Your Majesty
VᵒBᵒ, V.ᵒB.ᵒ	visto bueno	—	OK, approved
vol, vol.	volumen	**vol.**	volume
vra., vro.	vuestra, vuestro	—	your

Spanish Numbers

Cardinal Numbers

1	uno	28	veintiocho
2	dos	29	veintinueve
3	tres	30	treinta
4	cuatro	31	treinta y uno
5	cinco	40	cuarenta
6	seis	50	cincuenta
7	siete	60	sesenta
8	ocho	70	setenta
9	nueve	80	ochenta
10	diez	90	noventa
11	once	100	cien
12	doce	101	ciento uno
13	trece	200	doscientos
14	catorce	300	trescientos
15	quince	400	cuatrocientos
16	dieciséis	500	quinientos
17	diecisiete	600	seiscientos
18	dieciocho	700	setecientos
19	diecinueve	800	ochocientos
20	veinte	900	novecientos
21	veintiuno	1,000	mil
22	veintidós	1,001	mil uno
23	veintitrés	2,000	dos mil
24	veinticuatro	100,000	cien mil
25	veinticinco	1,000,000	un millón
26	veintiséis	1,000,000,000	mil millones
27	veintisiete	1,000,000,000,000	un billón

Ordinal Numbers

1st	primero, -ra	17th	decimoséptimo, -ma
2nd	segundo, -da	18th	decimoctavo, -va
3rd	tercero, -ra	19th	decimonoveno, -na; *or*
4th	cuarto, -ta		decimonono, -na
5th	quinto, -ta	20th	vigésimo, -ma
6th	sexto, -ta	21st	vigésimoprimero,
7th	séptimo, -ta		vigésimaprimera
8th	octavo, -ta	30th	trigésimo, -ma
9th	noveno, -na	40th	cuadragésimo, -ma
10th	décimo, -ma	50th	quincuagésimo, -ma
11th	undécimo, -ca	60th	sexagésimo, -ma
12th	duodécimo, -ma	70th	septuagésimo, -ma
13th	decimotercero, -ra	80th	octogésimo, -ma
14th	decimocuarto, -ta	90th	nonagésimo, -ma
15th	decimoquinto, -ta	100th	centésimo, -ma
16th	decimosexto, -ta	1,000th	milésimo, -ma

English Numbers

Cardinal Numbers

1	one	20	twenty
2	two	21	twenty-one
3	three	30	thirty
4	four	40	forty
5	five	50	fifty
6	six	60	sixty
7	seven	70	seventy
8	eight	80	eighty
9	nine	90	ninety
10	ten	100	one hundred
11	eleven	101	one hundred and one
12	twelve	200	two hundred
13	thirteen	1,000	one thousand
14	fourteen	1,001	one thousand and one
15	fifteen	2,000	two thousand
16	sixteen	100,000	one hundred thousand
17	seventeen	1,000,000	one million
18	eighteen	1,000,000,000	one billion
19	nineteen	1,000,000,000,000	one trillion

Ordinal Numbers

1st	first	16th	sixteenth
2nd	second	17th	seventeenth
3rd	third	18th	eighteenth
4th	fourth	19th	nineteenth
5th	fifth	20th	twentieth
6th	sixth	21st	twenty-first
7th	seventh	30th	thirtieth
8th	eighth	40th	fortieth
9th	ninth	50th	fiftieth
10th	tenth	60th	sixtieth
11th	eleventh	70th	seventieth
12th	twelfth	80th	eightieth
13th	thirteenth	90th	ninetieth
14th	fourteenth	100th	hundredth
15th	fifteenth	1,000th	thousandth